# The Doctrine and Covenants Student Manual

(Religion 324-325)

Prepared by the Church Educational System

Published by The Church of Jesus Christ of Latter-day Saints • Salt Lake City, Utah

# Table of Contents

# Preface

## Introduction

You are about to begin a study of the Doctrine and Covenants. Think for a moment about that title and its significance to you. These revelations contain the truths necessary to save you. They reveal the doctrines of salvation, the principles that will bring men to a fulness of joy. In the earliest dispensations of the world the Lord made covenants with man whereby they could bind themselves to him. Now in the last dispensation those covenants have been revealed again. Within the 138 sections of this work you can find the doctrine and the covenants that are more important than all the treasures of the earth. As the Twelve Apostles testified in the introduction to the Doctrine and Covenants, it is a book that is truly "profitable for all men."

## How This Manual Is Organized

President Joseph Fielding Smith made this observation about how to most effectively study the Doctrine and Covenants:

"I heard a brother say he could not read the Doctrine and Covenants because it was so much like a dictionary. It is not a consecutive story—it changes the subject, and so on—well of course it does.

"Many years ago when I was a president in a quorum of seventies—and in those days we did not have any supervision so far as our study was concerned—it was decided by that quorum of seventies that they would study the Doctrine and Covenants, and I was appointed to be the class teacher. We took it up section by section. You are not going to get all there is out of it in any other way. You may take it up if you want to by topics, or doctrines, that is good; but you are not going to understand the Doctrine and Covenants, you are not going to get out of it all there is in it unless you take it up section by section; and then when you do that, you will have to study it with its setting as you get it in the history of the Church." (*Doctrines of Salvation,* 3:199.)

This manual is organized to help you study the Doctrine and Covenants in the way recommended by President Smith. Three kinds of information are given in the manual. Each section is treated individually in the order in which it appears. Because many of the revelations came forth in response to a particular situation that the Prophet Joseph Smith was in, a short historical background is given for each section, followed by notes and commentary on the revelations themselves.

Though the revelations were given independently over a period of about twenty years, you will quickly find certain major themes being emphasized again and again through many sections of the Doctrine and Covenants. Such themes are dealt with in doctrinal enrichment sections in the appendix at the end of the manual. Thus, if you wish to study what the Doctrine and Covenants teaches about a specific doctrine, such as the second coming of Christ, rather than going from section to section, you can turn to Enrichment H for a detailed treatment of this theme. The enrichment sections are cross-referenced throughout the manual.

## How to Use Your Student Manual

The basic text for your study is the Doctrine and Covenants, *not this manual.* You will find that you cannot simply read the manual and have it be very significant. Only when you use it as a supplement in your study of the Doctrine and Covenants will the quotations and information given be as helpful as they should be.

If you are studying the manual on your own, without a teacher and formal classes, you may work through the manual at your own speed, studying section by section. Enrichment sections should be studied as they are referred to in the text. If you are enrolled in a class, however, the teacher will assign you a schedule for your study. He or she may combine sections for class assignments. They may not always be in exactly the order in which they appear. It will also be the instructor's responsibility to decide when or if each enrichment section is studied.

Sources are given with shortened references throughout the manual. Complete bibliographical data is given in the Bibliography.

# MAPS

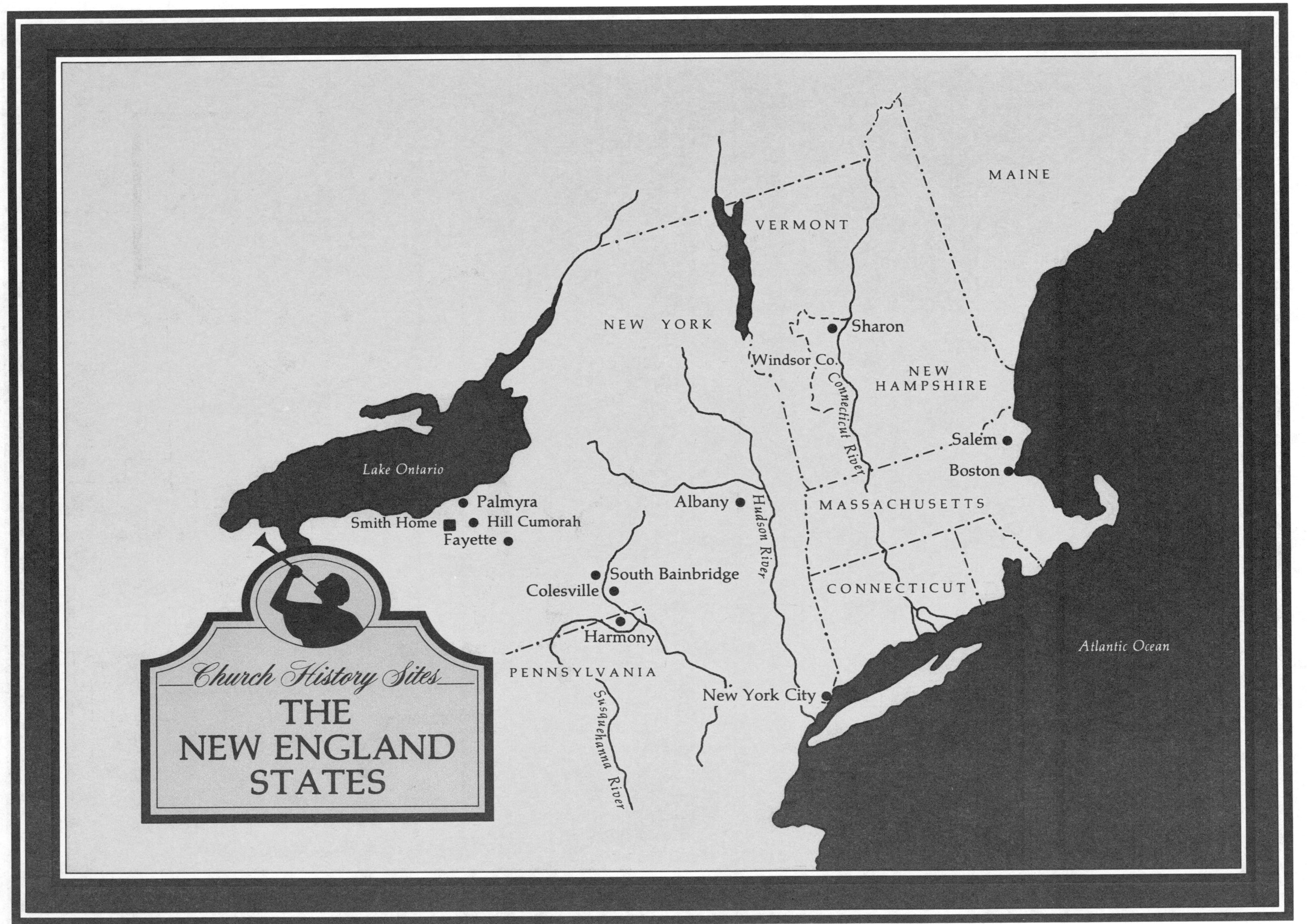
Church History Sites
THE NEW ENGLAND STATES
MAINE
VERMONT
NEW HAMPSHIRE
MASSACHUSETTS
CONNECTICUT
NEW YORK
PENNSYLVANIA
Lake Ontario
Atlantic Ocean
Sharon
Windsor Co.
Connecticut River
Salem
Boston
Albany
Hudson River
Palmyra
Smith Home
Hill Cumorah
Fayette
South Bainbridge
Colesville
Harmony
Susquehanna River
New York City

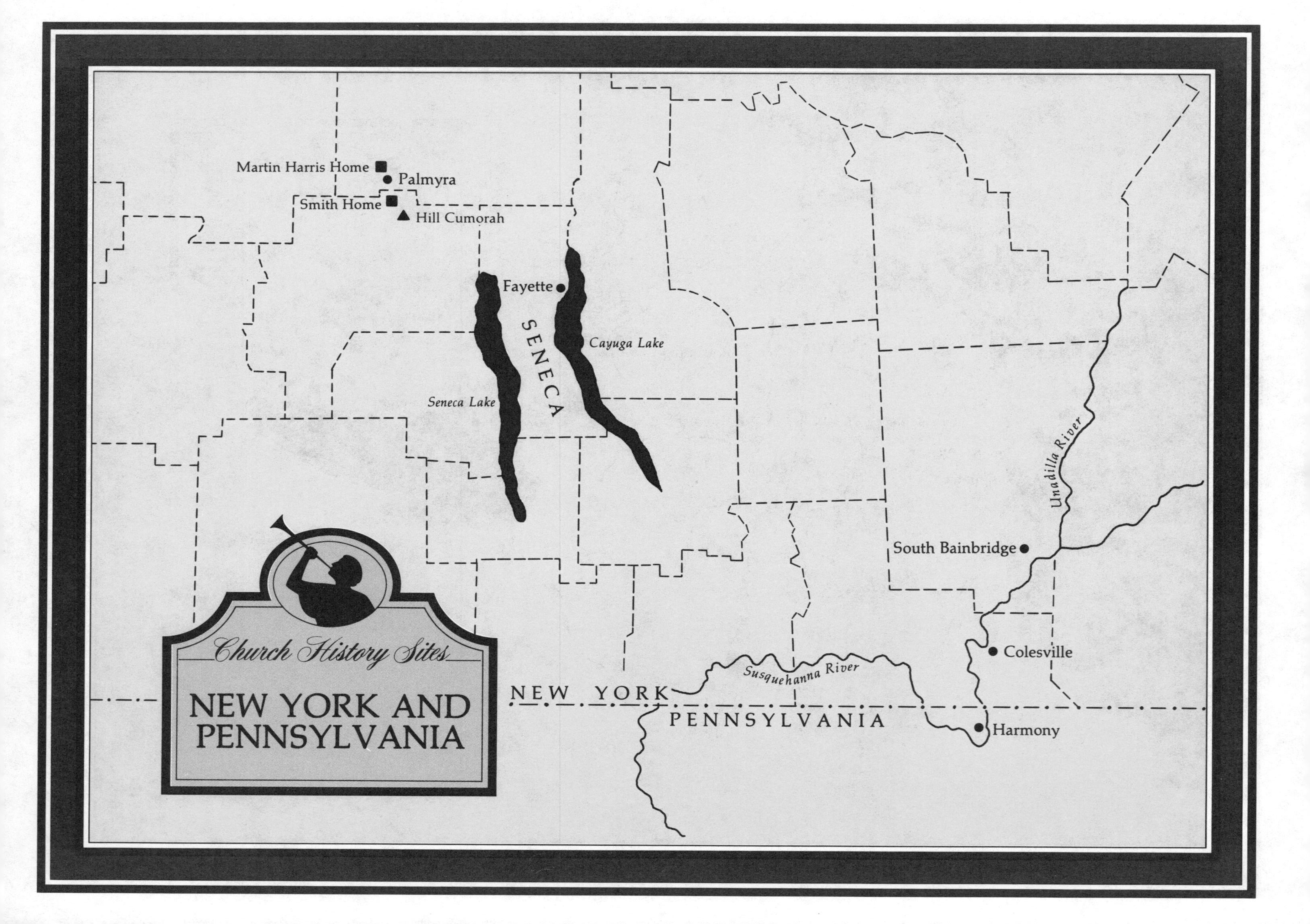
Church History Sites
NEW YORK AND PENNSYLVANIA
Martin Harris Home
Palmyra
Smith Home
Hill Cumorah
Fayette
SENECA
Cayuga Lake
Seneca Lake
Unadilla River
South Bainbridge
Colesville
Harmony
Susquehanna River
NEW YORK
PENNSYLVANIA

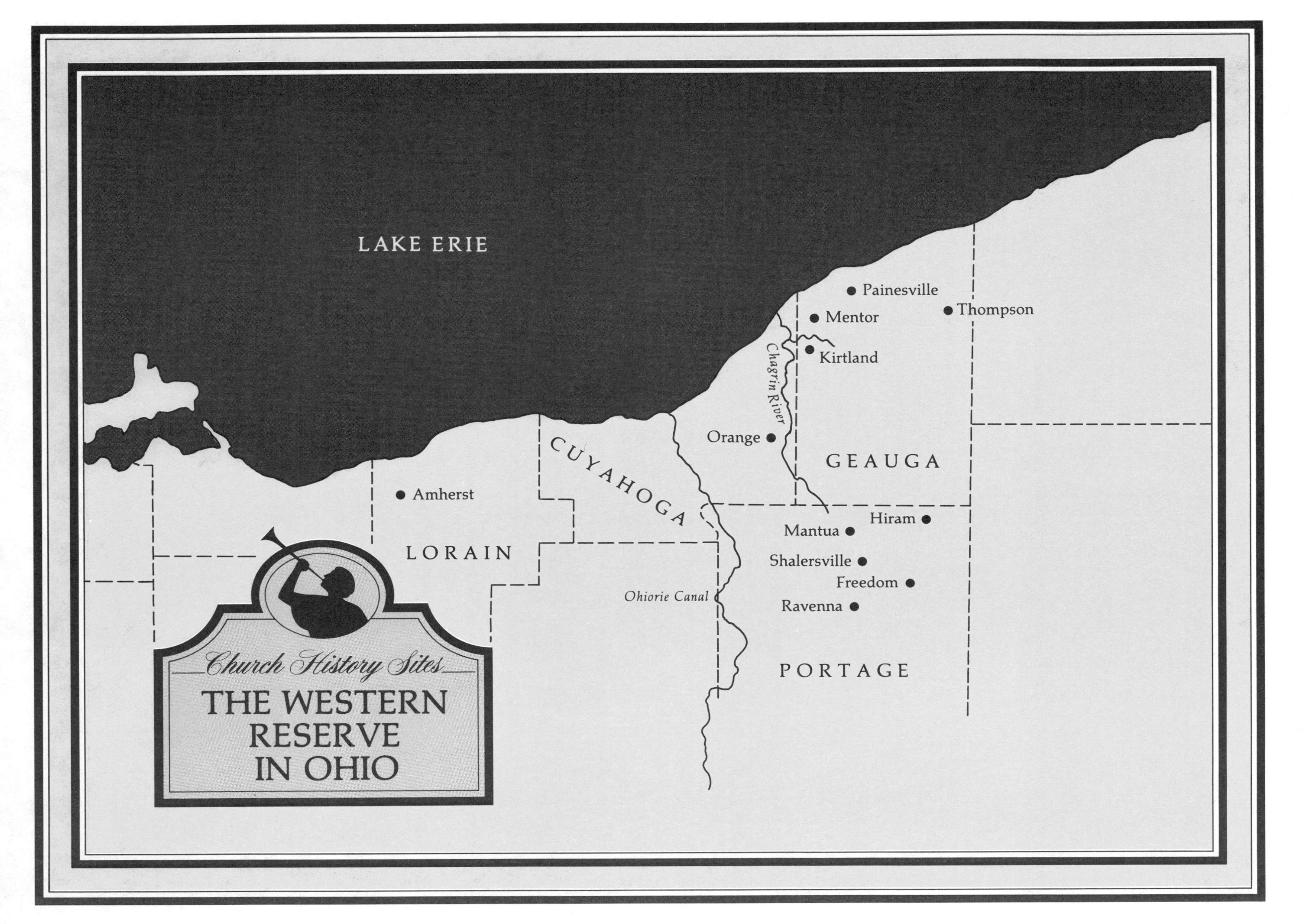
LAKE ERIE
Painesville
Thompson
Mentor
Kirtland
Chagrin River
Orange
GEAUGA
CUYAHOGA
Amherst
LORAIN
Hiram
Mantua
Shalersville
Freedom
Ohiorie Canal
Ravenna
PORTAGE
Church History Sites
THE WESTERN
RESERVE
IN OHIO

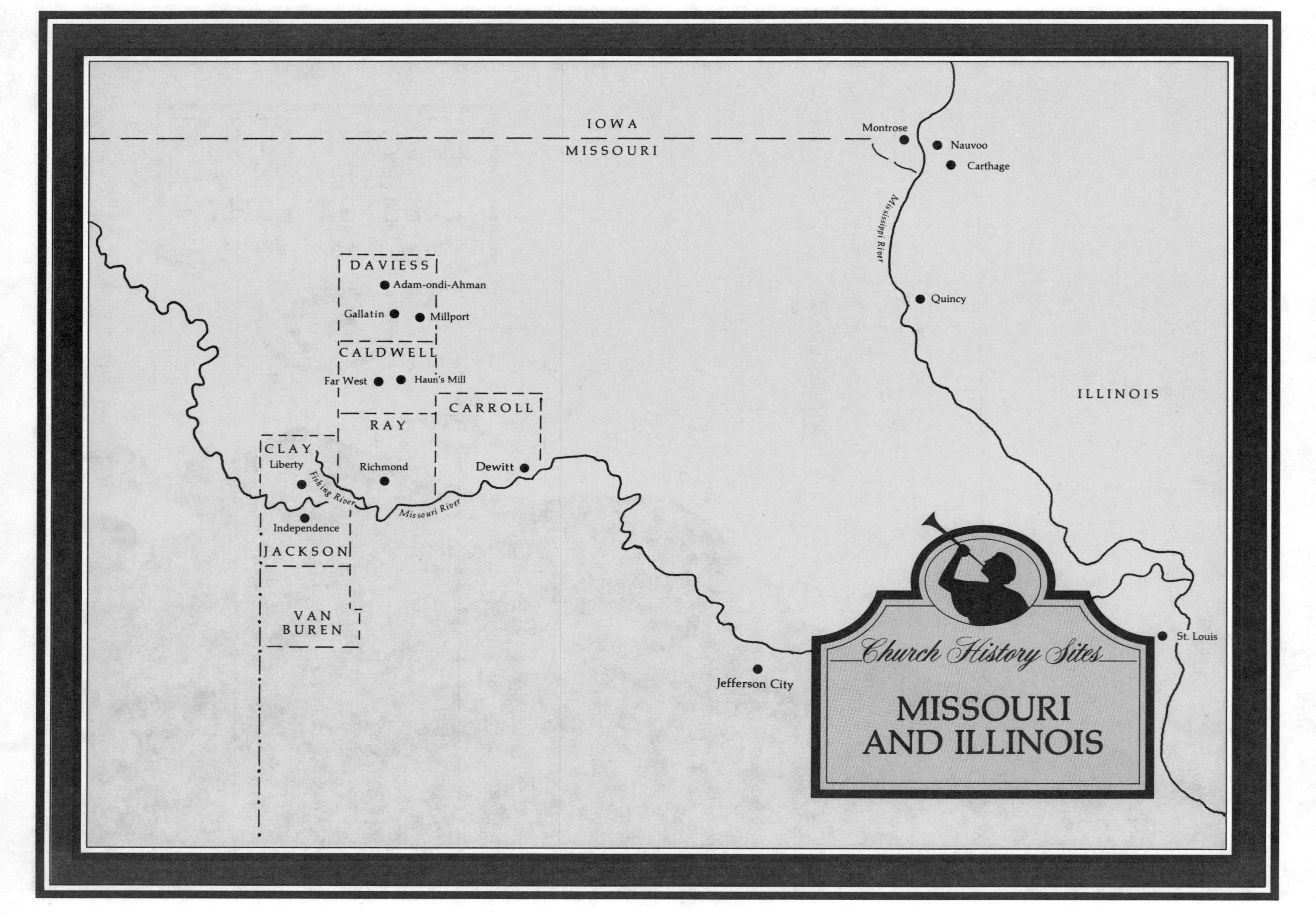
Church History Sites
MISSOURI AND ILLINOIS
IOWA
MISSOURI
ILLINOIS
Montrose
Nauvoo
Carthage
Mississippi River
Quincy
DAVIESS
Adam-ondi-Ahman
Gallatin
Millport
CALDWELL
Far West
Haun's Mill
CARROLL
RAY
CLAY
Liberty
Richmond
Dewitt
Fishing River
Missouri River
Independence
JACKSON
VAN BUREN
Jefferson City
St. Louis

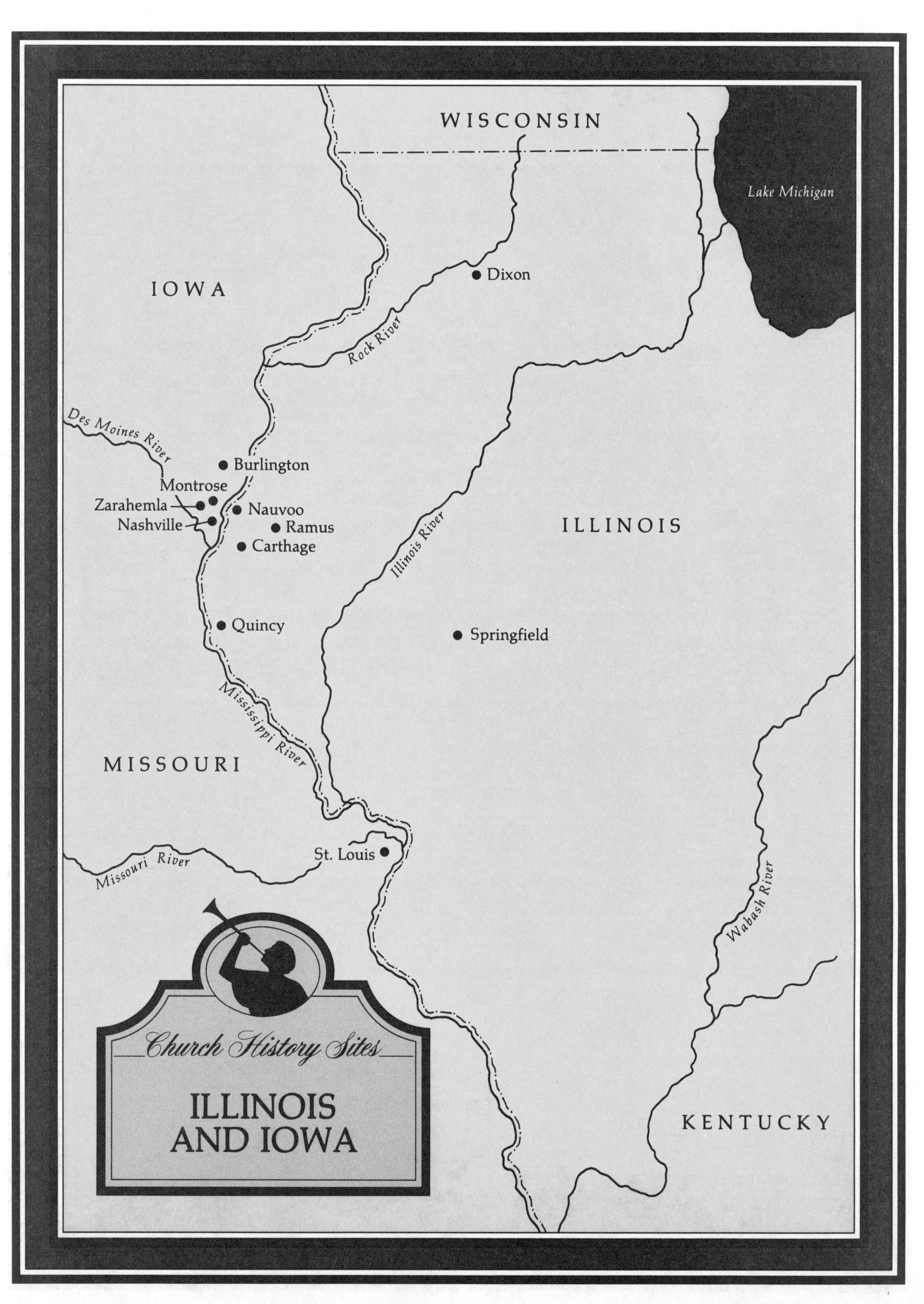
WISCONSIN
Lake Michigan
IOWA
Dixon
Rock River
Des Moines River
Burlington
Montrose
Zarahemla
Nauvoo
Nashville
Ramus
Carthage
Illinois River
ILLINOIS
Quincy
Springfield
Mississippi River
MISSOURI
St. Louis
Missouri River
Wabash River
KENTUCKY
Church History Sites
ILLINOIS
AND IOWA

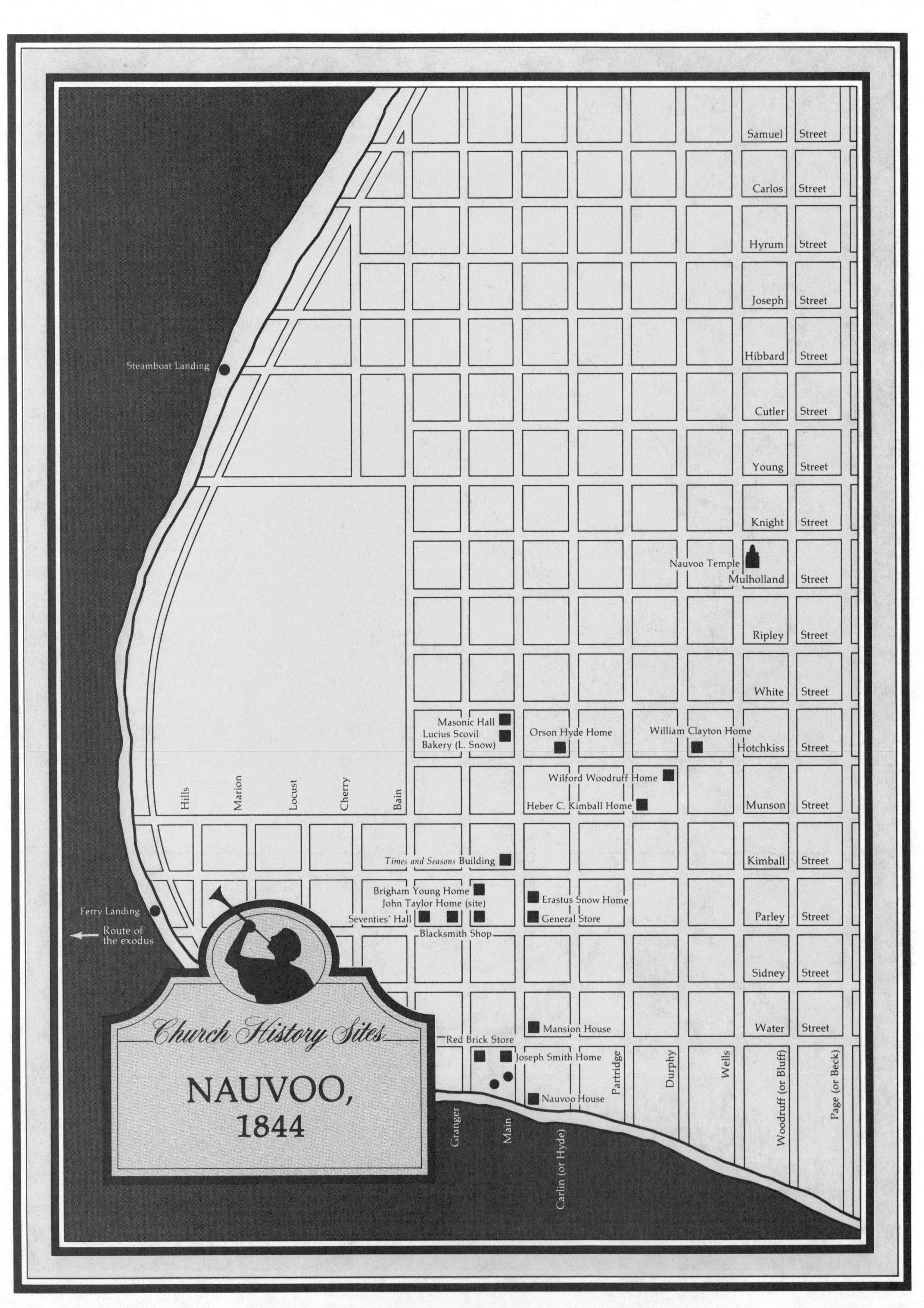

Church History Sites
NAUVOO, 1844
Samuel Street
Carlos Street
Hyrum Street
Joseph Street
Hibbard Street
Cutler Street
Young Street
Knight Street
Mulholland Street
Ripley Street
White Street
Hotchkiss Street
Munson Street
Kimball Street
Parley Street
Sidney Street
Water Street
Hills
Marion
Locust
Cherry
Bain
Granger
Main
Carlin (or Hyde)
Partridge
Durphy
Wells
Woodruff (or Bluff)
Page (or Beck)
Steamboat Landing
Ferry Landing
Route of the exodus
Nauvoo Temple
Masonic Hall
Lucius Scovil Bakery (L. Snow)
Orson Hyde Home
William Clayton Home
Wilford Woodruff Home
Heber C. Kimball Home
Times and Seasons Building
Brigham Young Home
John Taylor Home (site)
Seventies' Hall
Blacksmith Shop
Erastus Snow Home
General Store
Mansion House
Red Brick Store
Joseph Smith Home
Nauvoo House

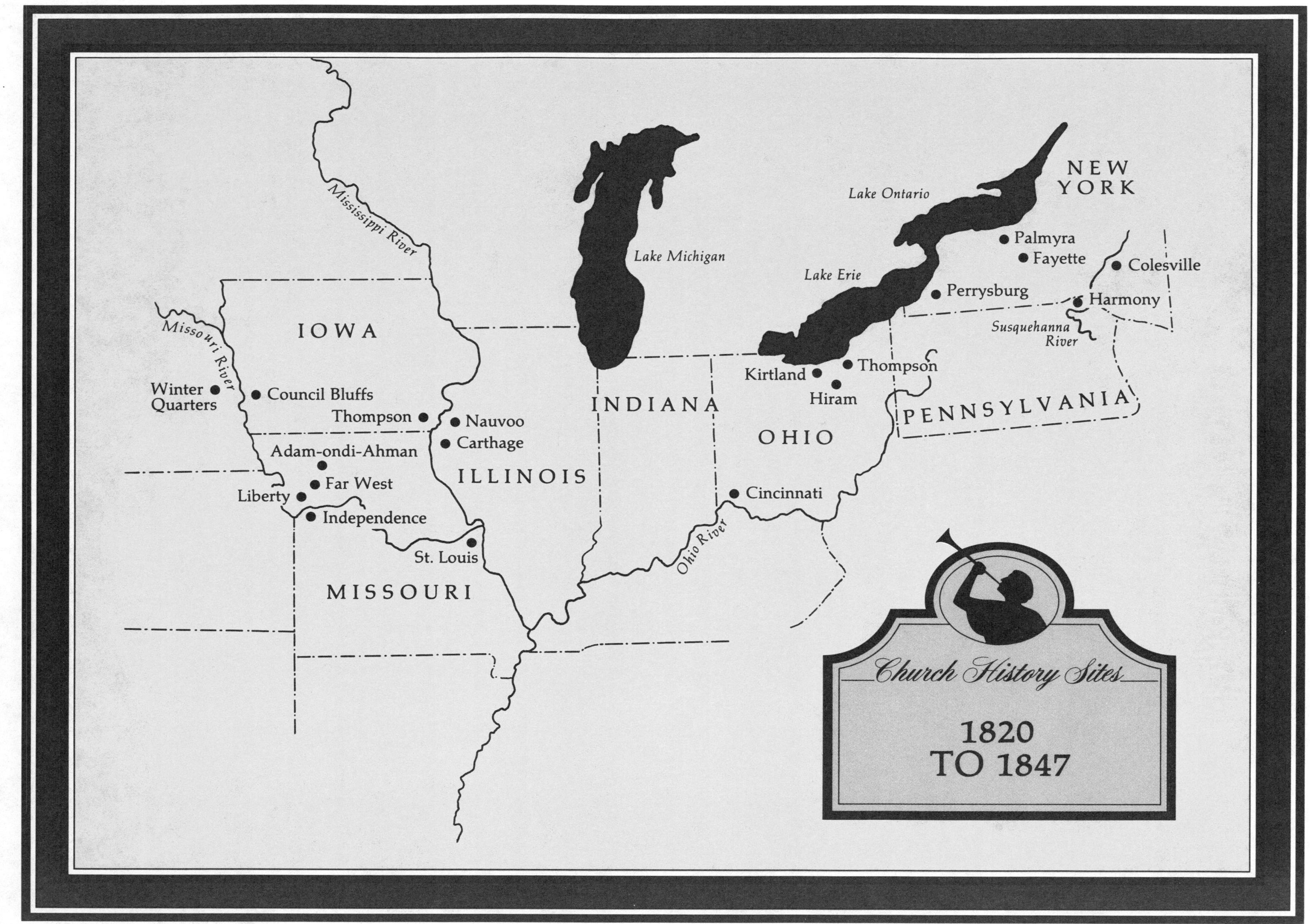
Church History Sites
1820
TO 1847
NEW YORK
Lake Ontario
Lake Michigan
Lake Erie
Palmyra
Fayette
Colesville
Perrysburg
Harmony
Susquehanna River
Thompson
Kirtland
Hiram
PENNSYLVANIA
OHIO
INDIANA
Cincinnati
Ohio River
ILLINOIS
Nauvoo
Carthage
IOWA
Mississippi River
Missouri River
Winter Quarters
Council Bluffs
Thompson
Adam-ondi-Ahman
Far West
Liberty
Independence
St. Louis
MISSOURI

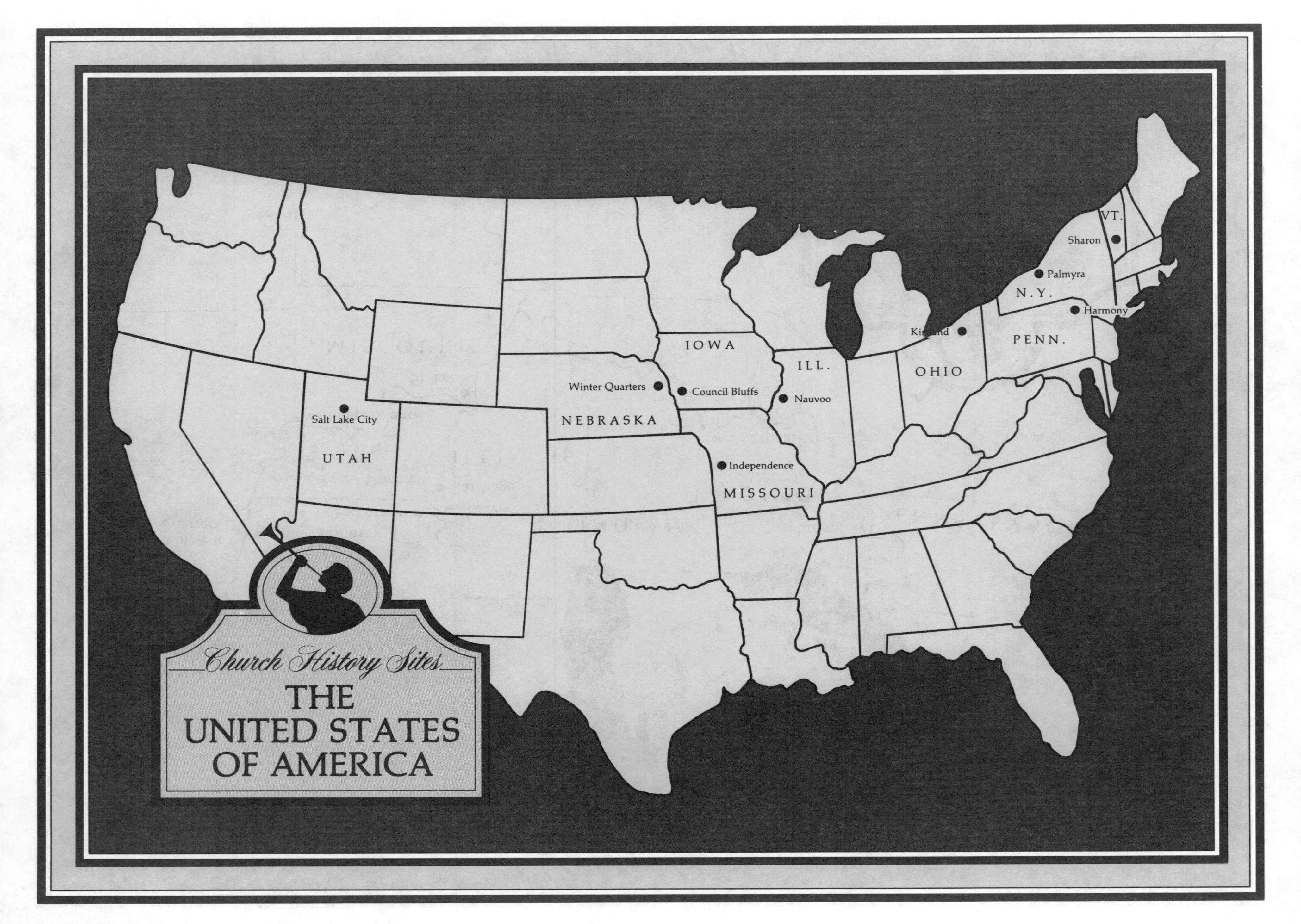
Church History Sites
THE
UNITED STATES
OF AMERICA
VT.
Sharon
Palmyra
N.Y.
Harmony
PENN.
OHIO
ILL.
Nauvoo
IOWA
Council Bluffs
Winter Quarters
NEBRASKA
Independence
MISSOURI
Salt Lake City
UTAH

# The Doctrine and Covenants: The Voice of the Lord to All Men

Introduction

**Revelation Comes Anew**

After the death of Jesus and the Apostles, the priesthood power was no longer available to the people in the Old World and the great apostasy set in. The Christian world was left with what revelations had been written and passed on to the Saints. Later these were collected and placed with writings from the ancient prophets to form the Old and New Testaments. One cannot underestimate the impact and value of the Bible in the history and development of Christianity. With no additional scriptural revelations being given to the people in general, it is not surprising that soon the Bible was the only source of God's word. One creed, for example, states that the Bible contains "the whole counsel of God," and another says, "Holy Scripture containeth all things necessary to salvation" (Backman, *American Religions,* p. 449).

From this very book, which many considered closed and complete, came the words that caused young Joseph Smith to seek God in prayer: "If any of you lack wisdom, let him ask of God, that giveth to all men liberally, and upbraideth not; and it shall be given him" (James 1:5).

It was in answer to this humble petition that a glorious vision burst forth. The heavens that had been silent for fourteen hundred years were rent, and revelation began to pour out upon the earth once again. For over a millennium there had been no living, mortal prophets on the earth. Now, God himself appeared, angels ministered, the Urim and Thummim was restored, ancient scriptures were translated, and the Church was restored. Revelation was again a reality. The Church was not yet two years old when the Prophet Joseph wrote, "In these infant days of the Church, there was a great anxiety to obtain the word of the Lord upon every subject that in any way concerned our salvation" (*History of the Church,* 1:207).

From that spring day of 1820 until the bleak afternoon of 27 June 1844, revelation upon revelation flowed through the man chosen to open the last dispensation. The Bible is loved and accepted by the Saints as the word of the Lord, but it is not the only word. The Prophet Joseph Smith wrote: "We are differently situated from any other people that ever existed upon this earth. Consequently those former revelations cannot be suited to our condition, because they were given to other people who were before us; but in these last days, God was to call a remnant, in which was to be deliverance, as well as in Jerusalem, and Zion. Now if God should give no more revelation, where will we find Zion and this remnant. He said that the time was near when desolation was to cover the earth, and then God would have a place of deliverance in his remnant, and in Zion, etc." ("Kirtland Council Minute Book," Archives of The Church of Jesus Christ of Latter-day Saints, Salt Lake City, pp. 43-44.)

Nor did revelation cease when the mobs finally succeeded in killing the Prophet. The mantle was passed on from man to man, prophet to prophet, and is still borne today by a living prophet. With the transfer of the keys to each succeeding prophet came revelation. President Spencer W. Kimball testified: "There are those who would assume that with the printing and binding of these sacred records, that would be the 'end of the prophets.' But again we testify to the world that revelation continues and that the vaults and files of the Church contain these revelations which come month to month and day to day." (In Conference Report, Apr. 1977, p. 115; or *Ensign,* May 1977, p. 78.)

**From Revelation to Publication: How the Saints Got the Doctrine and Covenants**

President Joseph Fielding Smith briefly traced the development of the Doctrine and Covenants:

"Shortly after the organization of the Church, the members were desirous of obtaining copies of the revelations given up to that time. In the summer of 1830, the Prophet, by divine commandment, commenced to copy and prepare the revelations, no doubt with the thought in mind of having them published. Some of the elders were carrying copies in their pockets, as far as the Lord would permit them, for there were some revelations at that time they were forbidden to publish to the world.

"On November 1st and 2nd, 1831, a conference of the elders was held at Hiram, Ohio, when it was decided that the revelations should be compiled and published. On the first day of the conference the Lord gave approval to this plan by giving a revelation which he called his 'preface unto the book of my commandments, which I have given them to publish unto you, O inhabitants of the earth' [D&C 1:6].

"While this was not the first revelation given to Joseph Smith, it appears as the first revelation in the Doctrine and Covenants, naturally, as it is the custom to place the preface of any book today in the beginning of the volume. Oliver Cowdery and John Whitmer were appointed to carry the revelations to Independence, Missouri, where they were to be published. The Prophet made haste in the choosing and preparation of these revelations so that the brethren could start on their journey to Missouri about the middle of November.

" . . . W. W. Phelps, one of the early members of the Church, was by trade a printer. He had gone down into Missouri. The printing press and type were brought down the Ohio River from Cincinnati where it was purchased, and across the country to Independence, and the revelations which had been selected by the Prophet were set in type, that is, most of them. But this was slow work.

We must remember that they were living in pioneer times, that Kirtland was about as far from Missouri as we are here in Salt Lake City from Winter Quarters, from which point the pioneers started on their journey to the Rocky Mountains. We do not stop to think of that, and so it took some time. By the summer of 1833 most of these revelations had been printed, but not all.

"At that time trouble arose, and a mob destroyed the press, scattered the type, and destroyed most of the copies that had been printed; however, a few were saved. This was known as the Book of Commandments. [There were sixty-five sections in the first edition.] As I have said, very few of the sheets were preserved so that there are very few copies of the book, so far as it was completed, in existence. I only know of five or six copies that are to be found today.

". . . In the year 1834, a committee was formed, consisting of the Presidency of the Church, and some others, for the purpose of again preparing the revelations and having them published. This selection of revelations went on, and in 1835 it was presented at a conference of the Church held on the 17th day of August and there was approved. [The 1835 edition had 102 sections.] When the Prophet made this selection, he made the statement that he prized these revelations beyond the wealth of this whole earth. . . .

". . . At this conference it was decided to include in this publication of the Doctrine and Covenants seven *Lectures on Faith.* These lectures had been given before the schools of the elders in Kirtland during the years 1834-1835. In accepting these seven *Lectures on Faith,* it was made very clear to that conference that they were not received on a parallel with the revelations, but were accepted as helps in the study of the doctrines of the Church, and so they were added to the Doctrine and Covenants with that understanding." (*Doctrines of Salvation,* 3:192-95.)

Two other articles, also not revelations, were added in this edition (see Historical Background for D&C 134). One article was on marriage, one on government.

After the martyrdom of the Prophet on 27 June 1844, one edition containing 111 sections was printed before the Saints were driven from Nauvoo. A new edition containing 136 sections was published in 1876. In this edition, for the first time, the sections were divided into verses and standardized by Elder Orson Pratt under the direction of President Brigham Young. Three years later footnotes were added, again by Orson Pratt. The article on marriage was not printed in this edition.

In 1921 Elder James E. Talmage of the Quorum of the Twelve was assigned to further modify the study aids and rework the format of publication. Under his direction the sections were divided into double-columned pages, brief headings were written for each section, the footnotes were expanded and revised, and an index was prepared. The seven lectures on faith were deleted from this edition since they were not considered formal revelations, and the letter renouncing plural marriage was added as an official declaration known as the Manifesto.

In general conference of April 1976 the Church canonized two revelations, sustaining President Kimball's proposal that they be made scripture and added to the four standard works. The two revelations were the Prophet Joseph Smith's vision of the celestial kingdom (received in 1836) and President Joseph F. Smith's vision of the redemption of the dead (received in 1918). These revelations were first added to the Pearl of Great Price, but when it was decided to print a new edition of the standard works with greatly expanded footnotes, cross-references, and a topical guide to the scriptures, these two revelations were added to the Doctrine and Covenants as sections 137 and 138. The new edition has 138 sections and two official declarations: the Manifesto, issued in 1890 by President Wilford Woodruff, and the declaration on priesthood, issued in 1978 by President Spencer W. Kimball.

### The Doctrine and Covenants: Scripture for the Latter Days

President Joseph Fielding Smith bore witness of the significance of the book for the latter days, saying:

"In my judgment there is no book on earth yet come to man as important as the book known as the Doctrine and Covenants, with all due respect to the Book of Mormon, and the Bible, and the Pearl of Great Price, which we say are our standards in doctrine. The book of Doctrine and Covenants to us stands in a peculiar position above them all.

"I am going to tell you why. When I say that, do not for a moment think I do not value the Book of Mormon, the Bible, and the Pearl of Great Price, just as much as any man that lives; I think I do. I do not know of anybody who has read them more, and I appreciate them; they are wonderful; they contain doctrine and revelation and commandments that we should heed; but the Bible is a history containing the doctrine and commandments given to the people anciently. That applies also to the Book of Mormon. It is the doctrine and the history and the commandments of the people who dwelt upon this continent anciently.

"But this Doctrine and Covenants contains the word of God to those who dwell here now. It is our book. It belongs to the Latter-day Saints. More precious than gold, the Prophet says we should treasure it more than the riches of the whole earth. I wonder if we do? If we value it, understand it, and know what it contains, we will value it more than wealth; it is worth more to us than the riches of the earth." (*Doctrines of Salvation,* 3:198-99.)

On another occasion President Smith made this promise to those who study the revelations in the Doctrine and Covenants: "If we will put them into practice, if we will keep the commandments of the Lord, we will know the truth and there shall be no weapon formed against us that shall prosper [see D&C 71:9-11]. There shall be no false doctrines, no teaching of men that will deceive us. There are many cults and many false faiths, there are many strange ideas in the world, but if we will search these revelations then we will be fortified against errors and we will be made strong." (In Conference Report, Oct. 1931, p. 17.)

# The Lord's Preface: "The Voice of Warning"

Section 1

## Historical Background

The heavens had been opened, revelations had been given, and the Church had seen over a year's growth since its organization when a council of elders convened in a conference in Hyrum, Ohio, on 1 November 1831. The conference was assembled to consider plans for the publication of the revelations already received. The decision was to publish them in a book to be called the Book of Commandments and to authorize ten thousand copies in the first printing. Following the first session of the conference in which this decision was made, the Prophet Joseph Smith inquired of the Lord to receive divine confirmation of their resolve. This confirmation was given in a marvelous manner, for the Lord not only approved the work but gave a revelation as his own preface to the book. This preface became section 1.

## Notes and Commentary

**D&C 1:1-4. The Doctrine and Covenants Is a Voice of Warning unto All People**

The preface of the Doctrine and Covenants introduces the message of the book. The entire book of scripture stands as a warning to the nations that God will not be mocked. Those who heed the voice of warning will find protection and peace, but those who refuse it will reap bitter fruit. President Joseph Fielding Smith said that the Doctrine and Covenants is not a book just for the Latter-day Saints; it is "more than that, it belongs to all the world, to the Catholics, to the Presbyterians, to the Methodists, to the infidel, to the non-believer. It is his book if he will accept it, if he will receive it. The Lord has given it unto the world for their salvation. If you do not believe it, you read the first section in this book, the preface, and you will find that the Lord has sent this book and the things which it contains unto the people afar off, on the islands of the sea, in foreign lands, and his voice is unto all people, that all may hear. And so I say it belongs to all the world, not only to the Latter-day Saints, and they will be judged by it, and you will be judged by it." (In Conference Report, Oct. 1919, p. 146.)

> 4. And the voice of warning shall be unto all people, by the mouths of my disciples, whom I have chosen in these last days.

*"The voice of warning . . . unto all people" (D&C 1:4)*

The Lord declared in verse 4 that the Doctrine and Covenants is to serve as "the voice of warning . . . unto all people." This theme is heard again and again throughout the Doctrine and Covenants, showing forth the judgments that are to come upon the world and the means whereby the children of the world can be saved from them. For a more complete treatment of this doctrinal theme see Enrichment A, in the Appendix.

**D&C 1:6-7. The Lord Calls This Section His Preface**

The purpose of a preface is to prepare the reader for the contents of a book. It summarizes the message of the book and the purposes of the author. Although this revelation was not the first received by Joseph Smith, it has been placed in the book as section 1 because of this identification by the Lord.

President Joseph Fielding Smith observed that "the Doctrine and Covenants is distinctively peculiar and interesting to all who believe in it that it is the only book in existence which bears the honor of a preface given by the Lord himself. . . . It was not written by Joseph Smith, but was dictated by Jesus Christ, and contains his and his Father's word to the Church and to all the world that faith in God, repentance from sin and membership in his Church might be given to all who will believe, and that once again the New and Everlasting covenant might be established." (*Church History and Modern Revelation,* 1:252.)

*Joseph Fielding Smith affirmed that the preface was dictated by Jesus Christ*

**D&C 1:8-10. What Does It Mean to Seal the "Unbelieving and Rebellious"?**

"The power to seal conferred upon the servants of the Lord in this, the last dispensation, extends to the 'unbelieving' and 'rebellious.' . . . They have power to put the seal of disapprobation upon the children of men who persist in unbelief and rebellion, and those who are thus 'sealed' and remain in that condition, will suffer the wrath of God. This sealing concerns the 'unbelievers,' those who refuse to accept the gospel message; and the 'rebellious,' i.e., those who turn against the servants of the Lord, especially those who do so after having enjoyed the privileges and blessings of membership in the Church." (Smith and Sjodahl, Commentary, p. 6.)

**D&C 1:12-13. "Prepare Ye for That Which Is to Come"**

The word *prepare* appears about ninety times in the Doctrine and Covenants. This warning is a major theme of the book. The Lord always gives the people a chance to prepare for that which is to come, and the revelations given in this dispensation will help the Saints prepare.

**D&C 1:13-14. What Is the Sword and the Arm of the Lord?**

The sword is a metaphor that symbolizes destruction and judgments that will be poured out upon the wicked, as in a day of war. The sword is raised in striking position, ready to administer the will of the Lord.

"Although the word 'arm' must have been commonly used in ancient colloquial Hebrew to designate the strength of men, it is used in the overwhelming majority of instances in the Bible for the strength of God. The most vividly anthropomorphic picture of God's arm in action is in Isa. 30:30, which depicts the lightning as the 'descending blow of his arm.' There are many references also to God's arm as 'outstretched' in a militant gesture (e.g., Exod. 6:6; Ps. 136:12; Jer. 27:5), but in most of these cases it is probable that the phrase has lost its original pictorial vividness and is merely a conventional expression for God's irresistible power, as is obviously the case in Jer. 32:17, where 'outstretched arm' is synonymous with 'great power.' " (*Interpreter's Dictionary of the Bible,* s.v. "arm.")

The imagery is not always used in the sense of negative power. For example, Doctrine and Covenants 29:1 speaks of the Lord's "arm of mercy," which has atoned for sins. This phrase suggests that the merciful plan of redemption has power to save. The Lord told Joseph Smith after the loss of the 116 pages of Book of Mormon manuscript that he would have "extended his arm" and supported him against the temptations. Here again the word *arm* denotes power, only power extended in mercy to help an individual and not just in anger.

**D&C 1:14. "They Who Will Not Hear . . . Shall Be Cut Off"**

As part of the voice of warning to all people, the Lord prophesies that the time is coming when those who will not hear his servants will be cut off. President George Q. Cannon explained the spiritual dangers of turning away from the prophets: "God has chosen His servants. He claims it as His prerogative to condemn them, if they need condemnation. He has not given it to us individually to censure and condemn them. No man, however strong he may be in the faith, however high in the Priesthood, can speak evil of the Lord's anointed and find fault with God's authority on the earth without incurring His displeasure. The Holy Spirit will withdraw itself from such a man, and he will go into darkness. This being the case, do you not see how important it is that we should be careful? However difficult it may be for us to understand the reason for any action of the authorities of the Church, we should not too hastily call their acts in question and pronounce them wrong." (*Gospel Truth,* 1:278.)

Enrichment F, in the Appendix, examines the theme of following the prophets.

**D&C 1:15-16. Existing Conditions in the World Anger the Lord**

Elder Spencer W. Kimball dispelled the notion that idolatry is a sin of the past that must involve some kind of image or figure.

"Idolatry is among the most serious of sins. There are unfortunately millions today who prostrate themselves before images of gold and silver and wood and stone and clay. But the idolatry we are most concerned with here is the conscious worshipping of still other gods. Some are of metal and plush and chrome, of wood and stone and fabrics. They are not in the image of God or of man, but are developed to give man comfort and enjoyment, to satisfy his wants, ambitions, passions and desires. Some are in no physical form at all, but are intangible.

"Many seem to 'worship' on an elemental basis—they live to eat and drink. They are like the children of Israel who, though offered the great freedoms associated with national development under God's personal guidance, could not lift their minds above the 'flesh pots of Egypt.' They cannot seem to rise above satisfying their bodily appetites. As Paul put it, their 'God is their belly.' (Phil. 3:19.)

"Modern idols or false gods can take such forms as clothes, homes, businesses, machines, automobiles, pleasure boats, and numerous other material deflectors from the path to godhood. What difference does it make that the item concerned is not shaped like an idol? Brigham Young said: 'I would as soon see a man worshipping a little god made of brass or of wood as to see him worshipping his property.'

"Intangible things make just as ready gods. Degrees and letters and titles can become idols. Many young men decide to attend college when they should be on missions first. The degree, and the wealth and the security which come through it, appear so desirable that the mission takes second place. Some neglect Church service through their college years, feeling to give preference to the secular training and ignoring the spiritual covenants they have made.

*"Where your treasure is, there will your heart be also" (Matthew 6:21)*

"Many people build and furnish a home and buy the automobile first—and then find they 'cannot afford' to pay tithing. Whom do they worship? Certainly not the Lord of heaven and earth, for we serve whom we love and give first consideration to the object of our affection and desires. Young married couples who postpone parenthood until their degrees are attained might be shocked if their expressed preference were labeled idolatry." (*Miracle of Forgiveness,* pp. 40-41.)

### D&C 1:17-18. How Was the Calling of the Prophet Joseph Smith Related to the Lord's Warning the Nations of the Earth?

The Lord called the Prophet Joseph Smith, as well as the prophets of other ages (see D&C 1:18), to cry repentance to the world and warn the world to return to follow after Christ. Elder Melvin J. Ballard explained the need for Joseph Smith and the other prophets in this way: "I understand from this that the Lord plainly knew the condition of the world, what it was in 1830, and what it would be today. . . . Knowing the calamities that were coming to his children, unless they changed their course, knowing their disposition that there would be no repentance in their hearts, and yet with a great desire to save them, he called upon his servant, Joseph Smith, to warn men, to call repentance, and others to join in this great proclamation to all men: 'Repent, for the Kingdom of God is at hand.' And not only to warn men that there was peril and danger ahead, but to offer the means of escape from the perils that would come." (In Conference Report, Oct. 1923, pp. 30-31.)

### D&C 1:19-20, 23. Why Does God Choose the "Weak Things of the World" to Do His Work?

President Joseph Fielding Smith answered this question when he said that "the Lord called Joseph Smith and others from among the weak things of the world, because he and his associates were contrite and humble. The great and mighty ones in the nations the Lord could not use because of their pride and self-righteousness. . . .

"The Lord's ways are not man's ways, and he cannot choose those who in their own judgment are too wise to be taught. Therefore he chooses those who are willing to be taught and he makes them mighty even to the breaking down of the great and mighty. . . . When we think of our missionary system, we can see how the weak have gone forth among the strong ones and have prevailed. The mighty and strong ones have been broken down by the humble elders of the Church." (*Church History and Modern Revelation,* 1:255.)

### D&C 1:19. What Is the "Arm of Flesh"

The phrase "arm of flesh" suggests the weakness, frailty, and imperfections of men. The admonition not to trust in man's power is a common one throughout the scriptures. (See D&C 3:7; 2 Nephi 28:31; Mosiah 23:14; 2 Chronicles 32:8.)

### D&C 1:30. "The Only True and Living Church upon the Face of the Whole Earth"

"There is much difference between a dead and living church. While one may have the form and shape, the ritual and dimension, the living church has life. A living prophet leads the Church today. There is a vibrant, living movement to it, a captivating spirit about it, a glory to it that lifts and builds and helps and blesses the lives of all it touches. The Church will move forward to its divine destiny." (A. Theodore Tuttle, in Conference Report, Apr. 1975, p. 135; or *Ensign,* May 1975, p. 92.)

### D&C 1:33-35. "My Spirit Shall Not Always Strive with Man"

President Joseph Fielding Smith explained what "spirit" is referred to in this verse:

"Now the Lord has withdrawn His Spirit from the world. Do not let this thought become confused in your minds. The Spirit He has withdrawn from the world is not the Holy Ghost (for they never had that!), but it is the light of truth, spoken of in our scriptures as the Spirit of Christ, which is given to every man that cometh into the world, as you find recorded in Section 84 [vs. 46] of the Doctrine and Covenants.

"Now because of the wickedness of the world, that Spirit has been withdrawn, and when the Spirit of the Lord is not striving with men, the spirit of Satan is. Therefore, we may be sure that the time has come spoken of in Section 1 of the Doctrine and Covenants. . . . Peace *has* been taken from the earth. The devil *has* power over his own dominion. The Spirit of the Lord *has* been withdrawn. Not because the Lord desires to withdraw that Spirit, but because of the wickedness of mankind, it becomes necessary that this Spirit of the Lord be withdrawn." (*The Predicted Judgments,* Brigham Young University Speeches of the Year [Provo, 21 Mar. 1967], pp. 5-6.)

### D&C 1:35. Why Isn't the Lord a Respecter of Persons?

President Joseph Fielding Smith explained what the term *respecter of persons* actually means: "It does not mean that the Lord does not respect those who obey him in all things more than he does the ungodly. Without question the Lord does respect those who love him and keep his commandments more than he does those who rebel against him. The proper interpretation of this passage is that the Lord is not partial and grants to each man, if he will repent, the same privileges and opportunities of salvation and exaltation. He is just to every man, both the righteous and the wicked. He will receive any soul who will turn from iniquity to righteousness, and will love him with a just love and bless him with all that the Father has to give; but let it not be thought that he will grant the same blessings to those who will not obey him and keep his law. If the Lord did bless the rebellious as he does the righteous, without their repentance, then he would be a respecter of persons." (*Church History and Modern Revelation,* 1:255.)

### D&C 1:36. Idumea

"*Idumea* or Edom, of which Bozrah was the principal city, was a nation to the south of the Salt Sea, through which the trade route (called the King's Highway) ran between Egypt and Arabia. The Idumeans or Edomites were a wicked non-Israelitish people; hence, traveling through their country symbolized to the prophetic mind the pilgrimage of men through a wicked world; and so, Idumea meant the world." (McConkie, *Mormon Doctrine,* p. 374.)

### D&C 1:37. The Lord Commands a Search of These Scriptures

"All members of the Church are commanded to search and obey these commandments. This is also true of all others. If we fail to do so and remain ignorant of the doctrines, covenants and commandments, the Lord has given us, we shall stand condemned before his throne in the day of judgment when the books are opened. It behooves us to search that we may know the will of the Lord and thus grow in faith, knowledge and wisdom." (Smith, *Church History and Modern Revelation,* 1:256.)

# "The Promises Made to the Fathers"

Section 2

## Historical Background

After writing an account of his glorious vision in the spring of 1820, the Prophet Joseph Smith recorded the circumstances of the heavenly manifestation wherein the angel Moroni visited him and gave him instruction (see JS—H 1:37-39). In the course of his communication, Moroni quoted scriptures to the youthful prophet, including Malachi 4:5-6; however, he quoted them differently from the way they are found in the King James Version of the Bible. Doctrine and Covenants 2:1-3 is the record of that rendering and was placed in the Doctrine and Covenants in 1876 by Elder Orson Pratt at the direction of President Brigham Young. "Elder John A. Widtsoe one time had this to say about this section:

" 'The beginning and the end of the gospel is written in section two of the Doctrine and Covenants. It is the keystone of the wonderful gospel arch; and if that center stone should weaken and fall out, the whole gospel structure would topple down in unorganized doctrinal blocks.' " (ElRay L. Christiansen, in Conference Report, Apr. 1960, p. 48.)

The message of Malachi is so important that it has been repeated in each of the standard works:

Bible—Malachi 4:5-6
Book of Mormon—3 Nephi 25:5-6
Doctrine and Covenants—2; 27:9; 128:17
Pearl of Great Price—Joseph Smith—History 1:37-39

Moroni's rendering of Malachi's message helps Latter-day Saints to understand the prophecy. For example, President Joseph Fielding Smith noted an interesting aspect of Elijah's return to the earth on 3 April 1836.

"Edersheim in his work, *The Temple,* says: 'To this day, in every Jewish home, at a certain part of the Paschal service [i.e., when they drink the "third cup"]—the door is opened to admit Elijah the prophet as forerunner of the Messiah, while appropriate passages are at the same time read which foretell the destruction of all heathen nations. It is a remarkable coincidence that, in instituting his own Supper, the Lord Jesus connected the symbol, not of judgment, but of his dying love, with his "third cup." '

"It was, I am informed, on the third day of April, 1836, that the Jews, in their homes at the Paschal feast, opened their doors for Elijah to enter. On that very day Elijah did enter—not in the home of the Jews to partake of the Passover with them—but he appeared in the house of the Lord, erected to his name and received by the Lord in Kirtland, and there bestowed his keys to bring to pass the very things for which these Jews, assembled in their homes, were seeking." (*Doctrines of Salvation,* 2:100-101.)

## Notes and Commentary

### D&C 2:1. What Priesthood Authority Was Elijah to Reveal or Restore to the Prophet Joseph Smith?

By the time Elijah appeared in the Kirtland Temple on 3 April 1836, Joseph Smith and Oliver Cowdery had already received the Melchizedek Priesthood under the hands of Peter, James, and John (June 1829); however, they yet lacked essential keys to that priesthood. President Joseph Fielding Smith explained the power and authority Elijah came to restore:

"The keys that Elijah held were the keys of the everlasting priesthood, the keys of the sealing power, which the Lord gave unto him. And that is what he . . . gave to the Prophet Joseph Smith; and that included a ministry of sealing for the living as well as the dead—and it is not confined to the living and it is not confined to the dead, but includes them both. . . .

"Elijah's mission was the sealing power. He held the keys by which the parents could be sealed together and children sealed to parents. He bestowed these keys upon the Prophet Joseph Smith. And that applies to the dead as well as the living since the coming of the Lord Jesus Christ.

"But what was the nature of his mission to the earth in these latter days? It was to restore power and authority which once was given to men on the earth and which is essential to the complete salvation and exaltation of man in the kingdom of God. In other words, Elijah came to *restore* to the earth, by conferring on mortal prophets duly commissioned of the Lord, the fulness of the power of priesthood. This priesthood holds the keys of binding and sealing on earth and in heaven of all the ordinances and principles pertaining to the salvation of man, that they may thus become valid in the celestial kingdom of God." (*Doctrines of Salvation,* 2:111-12, 117.)

### D&C 2:1. Why Was Elijah the One Chosen to Restore the Sealing Powers of the Priesthood?

According to President Joseph Fielding Smith an understanding of the central role of Elijah comes from an understanding of his role when he lived on this earth.

"It has been a mystery to many members of the Church why this important mission was reserved for Elijah and why these authorities could not have been bestowed by some other prophet, or prophets, presumably Peter, James, and John, who held the keys of authority in the days of the dispensation of the meridian of time. Without question Peter, James, and John could have bestowed this authority, if they had been commissioned; so could Adam, for he held the keys of all the dispensations. The reason why Elijah was reserved for this mission, according to the Prophet Joseph Smith, was that:

" 'Elijah was the last prophet that held the keys of the priesthood, and who will, before the last dispensation, restore the authority and deliver the keys of the priesthood, in order that all the ordinances may be attended to in righteousness. It is true the Savior had authority and power to bestow this blessing; but the sons of Levi were too prejudiced. . . . Why send Elijah? Because he holds the keys of the authority to administer in all the ordinances of the priesthood; and without the authority is given, the ordinances could not be administered in righteousness.' " (*Doctrines of Salvation,* 2:113-14.)

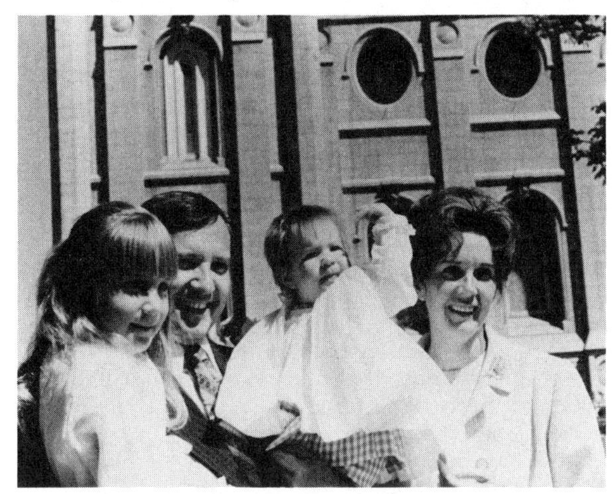

*The keys of the sealing powers were restored by Elijah*

### D&C 2:1. Elijah's Return Was to Precede the "Great and Dreadful Day of the Lord"

The coming of Elijah is "an event to take place, according to the plain prediction, shortly preceding the great and dreadful day of the Lord. The great and dreadful day of the Lord, this prophecy proclaims, is the day of the coming of our Lord in the clouds of heaven in great glory and when he shall take vengeance upon the ungodly. It is to be a day dreadful to all who are unrepentant and full of sin, but to the just it shall be a day of peace and salvation. However, before it comes there is to be some mighty work performed by the restoration of Elijah's authority, which is so potent that it will save the earth from destruction, or from being smitten with a curse." (Smith, *Doctrines of Salvation,* 2:112-13.)

### D&C 2:2. Who Are the Fathers and Who Are the Children Referred to by Malachi?

Understanding this phrase is central to understanding the whole passage in Malachi: "The fathers are our dead ancestors who died without the privilege of receiving the gospel, but who received the promise that the time would come when that privilege would be granted them. The children are those now living who are preparing genealogical data and who are performing the vicarious ordinances in the temples.

"The turning of the hearts of the children to the fathers is placing or planting in the hearts of the children that feeling and desire which will inspire them to search out the records of the dead. Moreover the planting of the desire and inspiration in their hearts is necessary. This they must have in order that they might go into the house of the Lord and perform the necessary labor for their fathers, who died without a knowledge of the gospel, or without the privilege of receiving the fulness of the gospel." (Smith, *Doctrines of Salvation,* 2:127-28.)

**D&C 2:2. What Are the Promises "Made to the Fathers"?**

Abraham and others of the fathers received promises from the Lord of an exalted reward for faithfulness to their covenants with him. It is expected that the hearts of Abraham's descendants would turn to their forefathers and desire the same blessings for themselves and their dead loved ones. Otherwise, the earth would be wasted. Elder John A. Widtsoe explained the significance of these promises and the Latter-day Saints' part in them: "In our preexistent state, in the day of the great council, we made a certain agreement with the Almighty. The Lord proposed a plan, conceived by him. We accepted it. Since the plan is intended for all men, we become parties to the salvation of every person under that plan. We agreed, right then and there, to be not only saviors for ourselves but measurably, saviors for the whole human family. We went into a partnership with the Lord. The working out of the plan became then not merely the Father's work, and the Savior's work, but also our work. The least of us, the humblest, is in partnership with the Almighty in achieving the purpose of the eternal plan of salvation." (*Utah Genealogical and Historical Magazine,* Oct. 1934, p. 189; see also *History of the Church,* 6:59-61.)

**D&C 2:3. Why Would the Earth Be Cursed and Utterly Wasted If the Sealing Powers Had Not Been Restored?**

Ratification in heaven is given to all ordinances of the gospel through the sealing powers of the priesthood. This sealing power makes possible the welding together of fathers and children, a work essential for exaltation to the living and the dead (see D&C 128:18). The curse spoken of by Malachi is clarified by Moroni, who explained that "the whole earth would be utterly wasted" at the Lord's coming if the sealing powers were not restored. President Joseph Fielding Smith explained why: "The sealing power of Elijah makes it possible for this joining of the families, generation to generation, back to the beginning. Now, if these units of authority were not here, then the work of sealing, by which the family units are preserved, could not be performed; then the binding power by which all blessings are sealed in heaven, as well as on earth, would be lacking. If this were so, the earth would be smitten with a curse, for all work which had been done, without these binding or sealing ordinances, would fall to the ground unfulfilled." (*Doctrines of Salvation,* 2:121-22.)

*"The hearts of the children shall turn to their fathers" (D&C 2:2)*

# "The Works and the Designs . . . of God Cannot Be Frustrated"

Section 3

## Historical Background

In the famous Wentworth letter, written in 1842, the Prophet Joseph Smith proclaimed the power of the restored Church: "No unhallowed hand can stop the work from progressing; persecutions may rage, mobs may combine, armies may assemble, calumny may defame, but the truth of God will go forth boldly, nobly, and independent, till it has penetrated every continent, visited every clime, swept every country, and sounded in every ear, till the purposes of God shall be accomplished, and the Great Jehovah shall say the work is done" (*History of the Church*, 4:540).

Fourteen years earlier, in the summer of 1828, God had dramatically taught Joseph Smith that very lesson. The Prophet wrote the details of the situation:

"Some time after Mr. [Martin] Harris had begun to write for me, he began to importune me to give him liberty to carry the writings home and show them; and desired of me that I would inquire of the Lord, through the Urim and Thummim, if he might not do so. I did inquire, and the answer was that he must not. However, he was not satisfied with this answer, and desired that I should inquire again. I did so, and the answer was as before. Still he could not be contented, but insisted that I should inquire once more. After much solicitation I again inquired of the Lord, and permission was granted him to have the writings on certain conditions; which were, that he show them only to his brother, Preserved Harris, his own wife, his father and his mother, and a Mrs. Cobb, a sister to his wife. In accordance with this last answer, I required of him that he should bind himself in a covenant to me in a most solemn manner that he would not do otherwise than had been directed. He did so. He bound himself as I required of him, took the writings, and went his way. Notwithstanding, however, the great restrictions which he had been laid under, and the solemnity of the covenant which he had made with me, he did show them to others, and by stratagem they got them away from him, and they never have been recovered unto this day.

"In the meantime, while Martin Harris was gone with the writings, I went to visit my father's family at Manchester." (*History of the Church*, 1:21.)

His mother, Lucy Mack Smith, wrote about Joseph's arrival at their home in Manchester and of his anguish when he learned that Martin Harris had lost the manuscript. After a long delay, Martin showed up at the house and confessed that he could not find the papers.

"Joseph who had not expressed his fears till now, sprang from the table, exclaiming, 'Martin, have you lost that manuscript? Have you broken your oath, and brought down condemnation upon my head as well as your own?'

" 'Yes; it is gone,' replied Martin, 'and I know not where.'

" 'Oh, my God!' said Joseph, clenching his hands. 'All is lost! all is lost! What shall I do? I have sinned—it is I who tempted the wrath of God. I should have been satisfied with the first answer which I received from the Lord; for he told me that it was not safe to let the writing go out of my possession.' He wept and groaned, and walked the floor continually.

"At length he told Martin to go back and search again.

" 'No'; said Martin, 'it is all in vain; for I have ripped open beds and pillows; and I know it is not there.'

" 'Then must I,' said Joseph, 'return with such a tale as this? I dare not do it. And how shall I appear before the Lord? Of what rebuke am I not worthy from the angel of the Most High?' . . .

"The next morning, he set out for home. We parted with heavy hearts, for it now appeared that all which we had so fondly anticipated, and which had been the source of so much secret gratification, had in a moment fled, and fled forever." (*History of Joseph Smith*, pp. 128-29.)

*Martin Harris lost 116 manuscript pages*

Of subsequent events the Prophet wrote: "After my return home, I was walking out a little distance, when, behold, the former heavenly messenger appeared and handed to me the Urim and Thummim again—for it had been taken from me in consequence of my having wearied the Lord in asking for the privilege of letting Martin Harris take the writings, which he lost by transgression—and I inquired of the Lord through it, and obtained [D&C 3]" (*History of the Church*, 1:21-22).

## Notes and Commentary

**D&C 3:1-2. In What Way Is God's Course "One Eternal Round"?**

"God governs by law—wholly, completely, invaryingly, and always. He has ordained that identical results always flow from the same causes. There is no respect of persons with him, and he is a Being 'with whom is no variableness, neither shadow of turning.' (Jas. 1:17; D. & C. 3:1-2.) Hence, the Lord's 'course is *one eternal round*, the same today as yesterday, and forever.' (D. & C. 35:1.)" (McConkie, *Mormon Doctrine*, pp. 545-46.)

**D&C 3:3. Why Is It That the Works neither of Man nor of Satan Can Thwart the Designs of God?**

President Joseph Fielding Smith answered this question by asserting God's omniscience: "In his infinite wisdom, our Father has provided for every problem or difficulty that may arise to stop or hinder the progress of his work. No power on earth or in hell can overthrow or defeat that which God has decreed. Every plan of the Adversary will fail, for the Lord knows the secret thoughts of men, and sees the future with a vision clear and perfect, even as though it were in the past. Jacob, son of Lehi, in his rejoicing declared: 'O how great the holiness of our God! For he knoweth all things, and there is not anything save he knows it.' (2 Nephi 9:20.) He knew that Satan would try to frustrate the coming forth of the Book of Mormon by the stealing and changing of the manuscript, and provided for it hundreds of years before the birth of Jesus Christ." (*Church History and Modern Revelation*, 1:26.)

**D&C 3:5. What Strict Commandments and What Promises Were Given to Joseph Smith?**

This verse refers in part to Joseph Smith's first interview with Moroni and the cautions and promises made to him (see JS—H 1:33-54, 59).

**D&C 3:6-8. "You Should Not Have Feared Man More Than God"**

The Prophet Joseph Smith transgressed the commandments and laws of God because he feared man more than he feared God. Joseph's fear was not that of a coward but was more probably caused by the fact that he was only a youth and was greatly inexperienced. (Joseph Smith stated that youth and inexperience were the cause of many of his mistakes; see JS—H 1:28-29). In the case of Martin Harris, Joseph was dealing with a man over twenty-three years his senior, a prominent and wealthy farmer and one of the few who believed Joseph's story and supported him with both money and labor. There would have been tremendous inner pressure for Joseph to want to show his appreciation to Martin Harris.

"His faith in God was absolutely firm, but he lacked experience in trusting his untried friend in his constant pleadings" (Smith and Sjodahl, Commentary, p. 19).

**D&C 3:12-14. In What Sense Was Martin Harris "a Wicked Man"?**

"Martin Harris was 'wicked' in persisting to ask for what God at first refused to grant. He was 'wicked' in not keeping the sacred pledge to guard the manuscript. But otherwise he was not a wicked man, as that term is generally understood. A father will sometimes call his boy 'wicked,' meaning disobedient for the time being." (Smith and Sjodahl, Commentary, p. 20.) The Lord clarified the term in verse 13. He gave four reasons why Martin Harris was "wicked." (See also D&C 10:7.)

**D&C 3:16-20. "Nevertheless, My Work Shall Go Forth"**

President Joseph Fielding Smith explained the significance of this prophecy and its fulfillment: "Joseph Smith, in his own strength, would scarcely have dared to predict to a bitterly hostile world that no power could stay this work and that it would go forth as a witness to all the world. The Lord has decreed that his work would be established. He called it a 'Marvelous work and a wonder,' even before the organization of the Church. If Joseph Smith had been guilty of practising a fraud; if he had endeavored to palm off the Book of Mormon on this hostile, unbelieving world, he never would have dared to say that it would go forth to the convincing of Jew and Gentile that Jesus is the Christ. Even if he had been foolish enough to make such a declaration, and the work being spurious, it would have come to a speedy and ridiculous end. It never would have survived the first year of its existence. It would have been so filled with flaws that the scrutinizing gaze of the world would have exposed it in all its folly. The truth remains that, after the thousands of attacks and scores of books that have been published, not one criticism or attack has survived, and thousands have borne witness that the Lord has revealed to them the truth of this marvelous work." (*Church History and Modern Revelation*, 1:28-29.)

**D&C 3:17-20. Are There Nephites, Jacobites, Josephites, and Zoramites in the Land of America Today, or Are There Only Lamanites?**

It is commonly believed that there are no more Nephites because that nation was completely destroyed by the Lamanites about A.D. 400. At the time the Savior visited the people of the Book of Mormon, however, they were all united as children of Christ, and there were no Nephites and Lamanites (see 4 Nephi 1:17). Later on, when wickedness was again rampant among them, they divided up into groups called Lamanites and

Nephites, only this time the division was not according to descent but according to righteousness—the Nephites were those that wanted to live the commandments of God, and the Lamanites were those that did not (see 4 Nephi 1:38). Thus, descendants of Nephi, Jacob, Joseph, and Zoram were found among the Lamanites of that day, and some of their descendants are among native Americans today. Others of Nephi's descendants can also be accounted for by the scripture in Mormon 6:15, which records that some of Mormon's people dissented and joined the Lamanites in the last great battle.

# "O Ye That Embark in the Service of God"

Section 4

## Historical Background

The Prophet Joseph Smith wrote:

"After I had obtained the above revelation [D&C 3], both the plates and the Urim and Thummim were taken from me again; but in a few days they were returned to me, when I inquired of the Lord, and the Lord said thus unto me: [D&C 10].

"I did not, however, go immediately to translating, but went to laboring with my hands upon a small farm which I had purchased of my wife's father, in order to provide for my family. In the month of February, 1829, my father came to visit us, at which time I received the following revelation for him: [D&C 4]." (*History of the Church,* 1:23, 28.)

Even though this revelation was given for the Prophet's father, it is addressed to all people who would serve God. Elder Joseph Fielding Smith pointed out that while only seven verses long, "it contains sufficient counsel and instruction for a lifetime of study. No one has yet mastered it. It was not intended as a personal revelation to Joseph Smith, but to be of benefit to all who desire to embark in the service of God. It is a revelation to each member of the Church, especially to all who hold the Priesthood. Perhaps there is no other revelation in all our scriptures that embodies greater instruction pertaining to the manner of qualification of members of the Church for the service of God, and in such condensed form than this revelation. It is as broad, as high and as deep as eternity. No elder of the Church is qualified to teach in the Church, or carry the message of Salvation to the world, until he has absorbed, in part at least, this heaven-sent instruction." (*Church History and Modern Revelation,* 1:35.)

*Joseph Smith, Sr., sought the will of the Lord*

## Notes and Commentary

**D&C 4:1. The Great and Marvelous Work Is Predicted**

Doctrine and Covenants 6:1; 11:1; 12:1; 14:1 were also given before the Church was organized on 6 April 1830.

If the Lord calls something great and marvelous, then it truly is. Though the latter-day work had small beginnings, it will yet penetrate the entire world of the living and the dead, until every knee will bow and every tongue confess. Elder John A. Widtsoe declared that this prophecy has literally been fulfilled: "Unknown, untaught, with no reputation, [Joseph Smith] should have been forgotten in the small hamlet, almost nameless, in the backwoods of a great state; but he dared to say that the work that he was doing, under God's instruction, was to become a marvel and a wonder in the world. We know, my brethren and sisters, that whether it be friend or enemy who speaks of us, if he is a sober-thinking, honest man, he will declare that whatever in his opinion the foundations of this work may be—we know the foundations—it is a marvelous work and a wonder, none like it in the long history of the world. The truths set loose by the Prophet Joseph Smith have touched every man of faith throughout the whole civilized world, and measurably changed their beliefs for good." (In Conference Report, Apr. 1946, pp. 21-22.)

### D&C 4:2. "Serve Him with All Your Heart, Might, Mind and Strength"

This is a way of saying that a person must be totally committed to the work and have no reservation. This commitment involves the emotional, spiritual, intellectual, and physical energy of the person. Other ways of saying the same thing are "with an eye single to the glory of God" (D&C 4:5) and "no man can serve two masters" (Matthew 6:24).

### D&C 4:3. "If Ye Have Desires to Serve God Ye Are Called"

Does this injunction apply only to full-time missionaries, or does it apply to every member of the Church? If a person desires to serve, must he be set apart as a missionary? Elder George Albert Smith, later the eighth President of the Church, showed that this scripture applies to all Latter-day Saints.

"My understanding is that the most important mission that I have in this life is: first, to keep the commandments of God, as they have been taught to me; and next, to teach them to my Father's children who do not understand them. . . .

"It is not necessary for you to be called to go into the mission field in order to proclaim the truth. Begin on the man who lives next door by inspiring confidence in him, by inspiring love in him for you because of your righteousness, and your missionary work has already begun." (In Conference Report, Oct. 1916, pp. 50-51.)

### D&C 4:4. "The Field Is White Already to Harvest"

The imagery here is of a field of wheat, no longer green, but a brilliant gold, which almost seems dazzling white in the summer sunshine. Such a sight signified that the time of the harvest was at hand. (See Matthew 9:36-38; Luke 10:1-2; D&C 33:3; 101:64-66, where the imagery the Lord used in this verse is further made clear.)

In the early days of the Restoration, thousands were prepared to receive the gospel; so many came into the Church that the enemies of the work were frightened. It was not one of a city or two of a family who joined; whole congregations united themselves with the work. Wilford Woodruff alone baptized over two thousand converts in less than a year's ministry in Great Britain. Tens of thousands joined with the Church during its first decade of existence. Nor is the time of the harvest yet over. During the years 1960 to 1973, the Church in the United States grew by 103 percent. Outside the United States the growth rate for that same period was 350 percent. (See *Church News,* 11 Aug. 1973, pp. 8-9.) At present approximately one hundred new stakes are being added to the Church each year (see *Ensign,* Apr. 1980, p. 15). Truly, the statement of the Lord given in 1829 is still being realized. The field is still white and ready for the harvest.

### D&C 4:6. Attributes to Develop for the Service of God

Peter, in his injunction to the Saints to take upon them the "divine nature" (2 Peter 1:4-8), lists nearly the same characteristics found in Doctrine and Covenants 4:6. Peter encouraged them to give all diligence in developing these godlike characteristics. President David O. McKay applied Peter's teachings to Latter-day Saints:

"[Peter] wrote on one occasion: ' . . . that we might be partakers of the divine nature.' (2 Peter 1:4.) He realized what it means to be in touch with the spiritual, to rise above the temporal, the sensual, and partake of the divine Spirit of God.

" . . . that is the purpose of making us more capable of responding to the Spirit and subduing the sensual. . . .

"That is why we like to have every young man and every young woman utilize his or her time intelligently, usefully, to bring the soul in harmony with the spirit, that we all might be partakers of God's Spirit, partakers of his divine nature." (In Conference Report, Oct. 1961, p. 90.)

# The Testimony of Three Witnesses

Section 5

## Historical Background

After humbly repenting of his foolishness in losing the manuscript, Martin Harris still seemed troubled by a desire to have direct evidence of the existence of the plates. In March 1829 the Lord gave Joseph Smith section 5 of the Doctrine and Covenants. In that revelation, it is clear that Martin still wanted a "witness" that Joseph had the plates (verse 1), and verse 24 suggests that his specific desire was to actually see the plates. The Lord told Martin through Joseph that he could receive his desires by being faithful and humble so he would be called as one of the three special witnesses who would see the plates.

## Notes and Commentary

### D&C 5:1. What Kind of Evidence Had Martin Harris Desired?

"Martin Harris was a religious minded, prosperous farmer. He appears to have been a rather wilful but honest man, who wanted to be sure of everything he undertook. It was he who took the transcript of characters from the Book of Mormon plates to Professor Anthon for verification." (Widtsoe, *Joseph Smith*, p. 53.)

"Martin Harris had already received a remarkable proof of the truth of the claims made by the Prophet Joseph regarding the Book of Mormon, when he carried a facsimile of the engravings to New York scientists. Professor Anthon had told him, as he himself states, that the 'hieroglyphics were true characters.' He had also, through the Prophet received revelations (Sec. 3:12). But he was not yet satisfied. He seems to have asked for further evidence that the Prophet Joseph actually had the plates from which the lost manuscript had been translated." (Smith and Sjodahl, Commentary, p. 25.)

**D&C 5:10. What Is Meant by "This Generation Shall Have My Word through You"?**

President Joseph Fielding Smith explained the significance of the Lord's message coming through the Prophet rather than by some miraculous manifestation: "This revelation declared that this generation shall have the word of the Lord through Joseph Smith. There may be some who think that this is unreasonable, and the Lord should use some miraculous means to convert the world. Frequently when strangers . . . hear the story of the coming forth of the Book of Mormon, they ask if the plates are in some museum where they may be seen. Some of them with some scientific training, express themselves to the effect that if the scholars could see and examine the plates and learn to read them, they would then bear witness to the truth of the Book of Mormon and the veracity of Joseph Smith, and the whole world would then be converted. When they are informed that the angel took the plates back again, they turn away in their skepticism, shaking their heads. But the Lord has said: 'For my thoughts are not your thoughts, neither are your ways my ways, saith the Lord. For as the heavens are higher than the earth, so are my ways higher than your ways, and my thoughts than your thoughts.' (Isa. 55:8-9.) We have learned that people are not converted by miracles or by examining records. If the Lord had placed the plates where the scholars could examine them, they would have scoffed at them just as much as they do today. People are converted by their hearts being penetrated by the Spirit of the Lord when they humbly hearken to the testimonies of the Lord's servants. The Jews witnessed the miracles of our Lord, but this did not prevent them from crying out against him and having him crucified." (*Church History and Modern Revelation*, 1:39-40.)

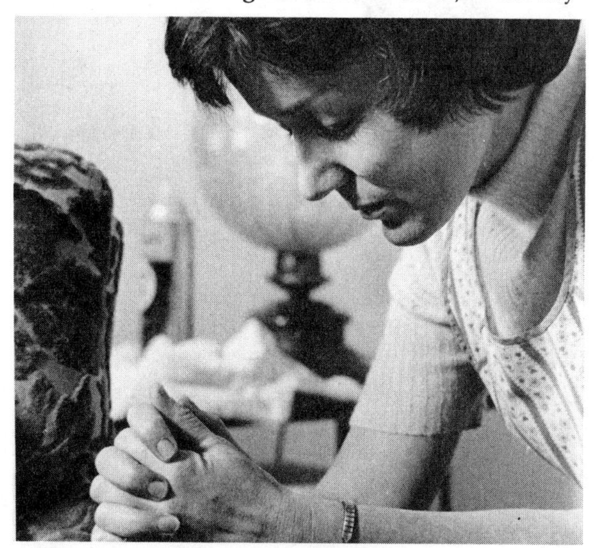

*The Spirit of the Lord is the true source of conversion*

**D&C 5:11-14. The Lord's Use of Witnesses**

Paul taught the principle that "in the mouth of two or three witnesses shall every word be established" (2 Corinthians 13:1). President Joseph Fielding Smith said of this law: "In giving the world the testimony of three witnesses in addition to Joseph Smith, the Lord fulfilled the law. We are called upon in this life to walk by faith, not by sight, not by the proclamation of heavenly messengers with the voice of thunder, but by the proclamation of accredited witnesses whom the Lord sends and by whom every word shall be established." (*Church History and Modern Revelation*, 1:40.)

**D&C 5:14. "And to None Else Will I Grant . . . This Same Testimony"**

The testimony of the Three Witnesses was unique in that they obtained a view of the plates by the hand of an angel. Eight other persons were also shown the plates, but that experience was not accompanied by the appearance of a heavenly messenger. Hence, no others received "this same testimony" (D&C 5:14; see also *History of the Church*, 1:52-58.)

**D&C 5:15-20. A Solemn Promise and Warning**

The world may take lightly the recorded testimony of the three chosen witnesses, but solemn promises are given to both those who accept and those who reject their words. Those who heed their testimony will find God's word in the Book of Mormon and will receive the Holy Ghost and be born again (see D&C 5:16). But those who reject this testimony shall come under condemnation. "The Lord always warns the people of a new dispensation through prophets raised up unto them in their own day," said Elder Marion G. Romney. "This he has done for this generation through the great prophet of the restoration, Joseph Smith, Jr. Through him the Lord repeatedly declared that the world was ripening in iniquity and that unless men repented destruction would overtake them.

"For example, in March 1829, he said: [D&C 5:19-20].

"You will note that this prediction, as were like predictions in the past, is conditional. 'If they repent not,' is the condition. For this generation as for all others, the Lord has provided the means of escape. This means is now, and has always been, the gospel of Jesus Christ." (In Conference Report, Apr. 1958, p. 128.)

**D&C 5:22. "Even If You Should Be Slain"**

This verse and Doctrine and Covenants 6:30 intimate the Lord's foreknowledge of the Prophet Joseph's death by violence for his part in the latter-day work (see also D&C 136:39; Hebrews 9:16-17).

**D&C 5:23-28. Martin Harris Was Given a Conditional Promise to Become One of the Three Witnesses**

Martin Harris was promised that he could become a witness of the plates or "these things" (D&C 5:2, 11) if he would humble himself and acknowledge the wrongs he had committed (see vss. 24, 28). Even after the lesson learned from the loss of the 116 pages, humility came hard for Martin, though he succeeded, and he finally saw the angel and the plates. (For the Prophet's record of the event, see Notes and Commentary on D&C 17:1.)

# The Arrival of Oliver Cowdery

Section 6

## Historical Background

In the winter of 1829 Oliver Cowdery taught school near the home of Joseph Smith, Sr. It was the custom of the day for teachers to board in the homes of their pupils, and since the Smiths had children in Oliver's school, he came to stay with them. While there he heard stories about the Book of Mormon plates and asked Father Smith to tell him the details. Father Smith finally consented, and Oliver Cowdery became one of the few in whom the family confided the story. Lucy Mack Smith recorded the events that followed:

"Shortly after receiving this information, he [Oliver] told Mr. Smith that he was highly delighted with what he had heard, that he had been in a deep study upon the subject all day, and that it was impressed upon his mind, that he should yet have the privilege of writing for Joseph. Furthermore, that he had determined to pay him a visit at the close of the school. . . .

"On coming in on the following day, he said, 'The subject upon which we were yesterday conversing seems working in my very bones, and I cannot, for a moment, get it out of my mind; finally, I have resolved on what I will do. Samuel [Smith], I understand, is going down to Pennsylvania to spend the spring with Joseph; I shall make my arrangements to be ready to accompany him thither, . . . for I have made it a subject of prayer, and I firmly believe that it is the will of the Lord that I should go. If there is a work for me to do in this thing, I am determined to attend to it.' " (*History of Joseph Smith,* p. 139.)

In April Samuel and Oliver went to Harmony, Pennsylvania, to visit Joseph. Lucy Mack Smith recorded the following: "Joseph had been so hurried with his secular affairs that he could not proceed with his spiritual concerns so fast as was necessary for the speedy completion of the work; there was also another disadvantage under which he labored, his wife had so much of her time taken up with the care of her house, that she could write for him but a small portion of the time. On account of these embarrassments, Joseph called upon the Lord, three days prior to the arrival of Samuel and Oliver, to send him a scribe, according to the promise of the angel; and he was informed that the same should be forthcoming in a few days. Accordingly, when Mr. Cowdery told him the business that he had come upon, Joseph was not at all surprised." (*History of Joseph Smith,* p. 141.)

The narrative is picked up at this point in the history of the Prophet: "Two days after the arrival of Mr. Cowdery (being the 7th of April) I commenced to translate the Book of Mormon, and he began to write for me, which having continued for some time, I inquired of the Lord through the Urim and Thummim, and obtained the following: [D&C 6]" (*History of the Church,* 1:32-33).

*Oliver Cowdery was a schoolteacher to the Smith children*

# Notes and Commentary

### D&C 6:1-9. Why Are There Repetitions in the Doctrine and Covenants?

Verses 1 through 9 in section 6 are identical to verses 1 through 9 of section 11. Verses 1 through 5 are identical to section 12, verses 1 through 5, and section 14, 1 through 5. The message in these verses is of universal importance to all Saints—indeed, the Lord has said, "What I say unto one I say unto all" (D&C 61:18, 36; 82:5; 92:1; 93:49). The repetition stresses that great importance.

### D&C 6:2. "Quick and Powerful, Sharper Than a Two-edged Sword"

*Quick* as used in the Bible does not mean swift but rather means something "living, alive" (Bible dictionary, s.v. "quick"). Thus, to be quickened by the Spirit means to be given spiritual life. The word of the Lord is quick and powerful because it is a source of life, energy, and real power.

Many swords of ancient times had only one cutting edge. When someone decided to make a two-edged sword, the effectiveness of the weapon was increased tremendously. Now it could cut in any direction, no matter how the blow was struck. Thus, the likening of the word of God to the two-edged sword is a vivid simile. Just as a sharp sword can cut deep enough to sever limbs and destroy life, so the word of the Lord is powerful enough that it can bring destruction of the soul (spiritual death) to those who do not give heed to it (see Hebrews 4:12; Revelations 1:16; 2:12, 16). The word of God also has power to pierce the soul as a sword and penetrate to the inmost parts of man (see 3 Nephi 11:3; D&C 85:6). It can cut through error and falsehood with double-edged efficiency.

### D&C 6:5-7, 14. The Lord Giveth Bountifully to Faithful Saints Who Ask

"There is no reason in the world why any soul should not know where to find the truth. If he will only humble himself and seek in the spirit of humility and faith, going to the Lord just as the Prophet Joseph Smith went to the Lord to find the truth, he will find it. There's no doubt about it. There is no reason in the world, if men would only hearken to the whisperings of the Spirit of the Lord and seek as he would have them seek for the knowledge and understanding of the gospel of Jesus Christ, for them not to find it—no reason, except the hardness of their hearts and their love of the world. 'Knock, and it shall be opened unto you.' This is my testimony, I know it is true." (Joseph Fielding Smith, in Conference Report, Apr. 1951, p. 59.)

### D&C 6:6. The Bringing Forth and Establishment of Zion Is the Grand Purpose of the Restoration

As early as 1829, one year before the Church was organized in this dispensation, the Lord counseled certain Saints to "seek to bring forth and establish the cause of Zion" (D&C 6:6). Regarding Zion, the Prophet Joseph Smith later declared: "The building up of Zion is a cause that has interested the people of God in every age; it is a theme upon which prophets, priests and kings have dwelt with peculiar delight; they have looked forward with joyful anticipation to the day in which we live; and fired with heavenly and joyful anticipations they have sung and written and prophesied of this our day; . . . we are the favored people that God has made choice of to bring about the Latter-day glory; it is left for us to see, participate in and help to roll forward the Latter-day glory." (*History of the Church,* 4:609-10.)

Similarly, President Joseph Fielding Smith taught that "in the early days of the Church the brethren came to the Prophet Joseph Smith asking what the Lord would have them do. The answer given to them was 'to bring forth the cause of Zion.' That is our work, to establish Zion, to build up the kingdom of God, to preach the gospel to every creature in the world, that not one soul may be overlooked where there is the possibility for us to present unto him the truth." (In Conference Report, Apr. 1951, pp. 152-53.)

Enrichment B, in the Appendix, more fully develops the theme of establishing the cause of Zion.

### D&C 6:7, 11. The Mysteries of God—Should One Seek to Know Them?

"A mystery is a truth that cannot be known except through divine revelation—a sacred secret" (Smith and Sjodahl, Commentary, p. 141; see also D&C 42:61, 65; 76:5-10; 89:18-19; 1 Nephi 10:19; Alma 12:9-11).

President Joseph Fielding Smith defined *mysteries* in a similar way: "The Lord has promised to reveal his mysteries to those who serve him in faithfulness. . . . There are no mysteries pertaining to the Gospel, only as we, in our weakness, fail to comprehend Gospel truth. . . . The 'simple' principles of the Gospel, such as baptism, the atonement, are mysteries to those who do not have the guidance of the Spirit of the Lord." (*Church History and Modern Revelation,* 1:43.)

A common expression heard in the Church is that we should stay away from the "mysteries," yet these verses speak of the mysteries in a very positive sense, promising them to the righteous who seek after them. Elder Bruce R. McConkie explained the seeming contradiction:

"There is also a restricted and limited usage of the expression *mysteries;* it is more of a colloquial than a scriptural usage, and it has reference to that body of teachings in the speculative field, those things which the Lord has not revealed in plainness in this day. It is to these things that reference is made when the elders are counseled to leave the mysteries alone.

" 'Oh, ye elders of Israel, hearken to my voice,' the Prophet said, 'and when you are sent into the world to preach, tell those things you are sent to tell; preach and cry aloud, "Repent ye, for the kingdom of heaven is at hand; repent and believe the gospel." Declare the first principles, and let mysteries alone, lest ye be overthrown. Never meddle with the visions of beasts and subjects you do not understand.' (*Teachings,* p. 292.)" (*Mormon Doctrine,* p. 524.)

**:10. What Gift Did the Lord Give Oliver ery?**

Notes and Commentary for Doctrine and enants 8:6-9.

**D&C 6:10-13. "And If Thou Wilt Inquire"**

Elder Bruce R. McConkie spoke of the Lord's promise of revelation to his Saints, pointing out that "it is the privilege and the right of every member of the Church to receive revelation and to enjoy the gifts of the Spirit. When we are confirmed members of the Church, we receive the gift of the Holy Ghost, which is the right to the constant companionship of that member of the Godhead, based on faithfulness. The actual enjoyment of this gift depends upon personal worthiness. . . .

"It is the right of members of the Church to receive revelation. Joseph Smith said: '. . . God hath not revealed anything to Joseph, but what he will make known unto the Twelve, and even the least Saint may know all things as fast as he is able to bear them. . . .' (*Teachings,* p. 149.) . . .

"Also: 'It is the privilege of every Elder to speak of the things of God; and could we all come together with one heart and one mind in perfect faith the veil might as well be rent today as next week, or any other time. . . .' (*Teachings,* p. 9.) . . .

"Religion comes from God by revelation and deals with spiritual things; and unless and until a man has received revelation, he has not received religion, and he is not on the path leading to salvation in our Father's kingdom." (In Conference Report, Apr. 1971, pp. 100-101.)

**D&C 6:13. "There Is No Gift Greater Than the Gift of Salvation"**

"*Salvation* in its true and full meaning is synonymous with *exaltation* or *eternal life* and consists in gaining an inheritance in the highest of the three heavens within the celestial kingdom. With few exceptions this is the salvation of which the scriptures speak. It is the salvation which the saints seek. It is of this which the Lord says, '*There is no gift greater than the gift of salvation.*' (D. & C. 6:13.) This full salvation is obtained in and through the continuation of the family unit in eternity, and those who obtain it are gods. (D. & C. 131:1-4; 132.)" (McConkie, *Mormon Doctrine,* p. 670.)

**D&C 6:16. How Private Are One's Thoughts?**

"Men's thoughts are secret and cannot be pried into by other men, or for that matter by devils" (McConkie, *Mormon Doctrine,* p. 777; see also 1 Kings 8:39).

**D&C 6:22-24. "I Have Told You Things Which No Man Knoweth"**

"After we had received this revelation [D&C 6], Oliver Cowdery stated to me that after he had gone to my father's to board, and after the family had communicated to him concerning my having obtained the plates, that one night after he had retired to bed he called upon the Lord to know if these things were so, and the Lord manifested to him that they were true, but he had kept the circumstance entirely secret, and had mentioned it to no one; so that after this revelation was given, he knew that the work was true, because no being living knew of the thing alluded to in the revelation, but God and himself" (*History of the Church,* 1:35).

**D&C 6:23. "Did I Not Speak Peace to Your Mind?"**

Revelation can come in many ways and in various degrees of directness. In some cases God himself may appear to a person; in other cases he may send an angel, show a vision, or speak through the whisperings of the still, small voice. Here the Lord bore witness to Oliver Cowdery of one way of giving revelation—a feeling of peace. When one is torn with despair or confusion, the sweet feeling of peace conveyed by the Comforter can instantly dispel the turmoil that reigned in the soul previously. Such a feeling is a real, definable experience, and as much a revelation as a vision, though more subtle and less direct in the way it is given.

**D&C 6:25-28. Other Records**

See Doctrine and Covenants 8:1, 11.

**D&C 6:29-31. "They Can Do No More to You Than to Me"**

The wicked people of the Savior's day had power to bring about the Crucifixion, but they could not stop the work of the Lord, nor could they destroy his soul so that he would not be exalted in the life hereafter. The Lord said here that the worst thing that could happen to Joseph Smith and Oliver Cowdery because of their work and their testimonies was death, but that their deaths would not stop the latter-day work of the Lord nor would the wicked have power to destroy their souls. Oliver Cowdery, however, lost faith and left the Church for a time, but Joseph Smith remained faithful and was eventually persecuted to the limit.

President Joseph Fielding Smith wrote the following concerning Oliver Cowdery and the martyrdom of Hyrum Smith: "Had Oliver Cowdery remained true, had he been faithful to his testimony and his calling as the 'Second Elder' and Assistant President of the Church, I am just as satisfied as I am that I am here that Oliver Cowdery would have gone to Carthage with the Prophet Joseph Smith and laid down his life instead of Hyrum Smith. That would have been his right. Maybe it sounds a little strange to speak of martyrdom as being a right, but it was a right. Oliver Cowdery lost it and Hyrum Smith received it. According to the law of witnesses—and this is a divine law—it had to be." (*Doctrines of Salvation,* 1:221-22.)

# John the Revelator

Section 7

## Historical Background

The future of the Apostle John, sometimes called the Beloved or the Revelator, is a mystery to the Christian world. Confusion comes because of the statement in John 21:20-23. Referring to John and speaking to Peter, the Savior said: "If I will that he tarry till I come, what is that to thee? follow thou me. Then went this saying abroad among the brethren, that that disciple [John] should not die: yet Jesus said not unto him, He shall not die; but, If I will that he tarry till I come, what is that to thee?"

From this statement questions naturally arise: Did John die? If not, what is his status? If he did, why did Jesus make the statement? The issue has been debated for centuries among the various Christian sects with some scholars saying that he indeed died and was buried at Ephesus, while others believe he still walks the earth. A third school of thought states that even though he was buried at Ephesus, he is not really dead but simply sleeps in the grave until the second coming of the Savior. (See Sperry, *Compendium,* pp. 66-67.)

Joseph Smith and Oliver Cowdery finally solved the issue through an appeal to the Lord. The Prophet Joseph Smith recorded: "During the month of April [1829, at Harmony, Pennsylvania] I continued to translate, and he [Oliver Cowdery] to write, with little cessation, during which time we received several revelations. A difference of opinion arising between us about the account of John the Apostle, mentioned in the New Testament, as to whether he died or continued to live, we mutually agreed to settle it by the Urim and Thummim." (*History of the Church,* 1:35-36.)

The result of their inquiry is given in the heading of section 7. It is not known whether Joseph saw the parchment referred to and was given power to translate it, or if its contents were revealed to Joseph without his seeing the original source. It makes no difference, since the material was given by revelation to the Prophet.

## Notes and Commentary

### D&C 7:1-3

See 3 Nephi 28:1-7 for a similar account of the Nephite disciples' receiving the same gift because they had the same desires as John.

### D&C 7:2. What Does It Mean to Have "Power over Death"?

This passage does not refer to the fact that a person would never die, for all must die (see 1 Corinthians 15:22). Even Christ died, though he had power over death (see John 10:17-18). To one who has power over death, death is held in abeyance according to the will of God (see Matthew 16:28; Mark 9:1; Luke 9:27; 3 Nephi 28:7-8). Such persons are called translated beings (see 3 Nephi 28:1-40; McConkie, *Mormon Doctrine,* pp. 804-8).

The Prophet Joseph Smith said that "translated bodies cannot enter into rest until they have undergone a change equivalent to death. Translated bodies are designed for future missions." (*History of the Church,* 4:425; for further discussion of translated beings see Smith, *Teachings,* pp. 170-71; Taylor, *Mediation and Atonement,* pp. 74-78.)

### D&C 7:3-6. How Has John Prophesied before Nations and Ministered to Heirs of Salvation?

Five of the books of the Bible were written by John: the Gospel of John, three epistles, and the book of Revelation. The world's most widely distributed book is the Bible, portions of which have been translated into 1,631 languages as of 1979. It has been estimated that between 1815 and 1975 some 2½ billion Bibles were printed (see McWhirter, *Guinness Book of World Records,* p. 214). Certainly John's written prophecy has gone forth among the nations.

The Apostle John ministered to the Prophet Joseph Smith and Oliver Cowdery in 1829 when he assisted Peter and James in the restoration of the Melchizedek Priesthood (see D&C 27:12).

In a conference of the Church on 3 June 1831,

*Heber C. Kimball recorded the appearance of John the Beloved in the Kirtland Temple*

the Prophet Joseph Smith taught concerning John's ministry: "John the Revelator was then among the Ten Tribes of Israel who had been led away by Shalmaneser, king of Assyria, to prepare them for their return from their long dispersion" (*History of the Church,* 1:176).

Elder Heber C. Kimball recorded an appearance of John the Revelator in the Kirtland Temple, as follows:

"When the Prophet Joseph had finished the endowments of the First Presidency, the Twelve and the Presiding Bishops, the First Presidency proceeded to lay hands upon each one of them to seal and confirm the anointing; and at the close of each blessing the whole of the quorums responded to it with a loud shout of Hosanna! Hosanna! etc.

"While these things were being attended to the beloved disciple John was seen in our midst by the Prophet Joseph, Oliver Cowdery and others." (In Whitney, *Life of Heber C. Kimball,* pp. 91-92.)

**D&C 7:7. What Are the Keys Held by Peter, James, and John?**

"The keys of the ministry which John says (Sec. 7:7) were given to Peter, James and himself, constituted the authority of Presidency of the Church in their dispensation. (See *D.H.C.,* Vol. 3:387; Matt. 17:1-9; D. and C. 81:1-2.) These keys were given at the transfiguration to these three Apostles, and they in turn gave them to Joseph Smith and Oliver Cowdery in this dispensation. (D. & C. 27:12-13; 128:20.)" (Smith, *Church History and Modern Revelation,* 1:49.)

# The Spirit of Revelation

Section 8

## Historical Background

Joseph Smith and Oliver Cowdery had received from God the gift to translate ancient records (see D&C 6:25-28). From the beginning of their work together Joseph Smith translated and Oliver Cowdery acted as scribe. Oliver Cowdery desired to have a more active role in the translating process, and so the Prophet inquired of the Lord through the Urim and Thummim and received a revelation (see Smith, *Church History and Modern Revelation,* 1:50).

The Prophet Joseph wrote: "Whilst continuing the work of translation, during the month of April, Oliver Cowdery became exceedingly anxious to have the power to translate bestowed upon him, and in relation to this desire the following revelations were obtained: [D&C 8-9]" (*History of the Church,* 1:36).

## Notes and Commentary

**D&C 8:1. Ask in Faith and Ye Shall Receive**

The Lord giveth liberally to the spiritually prepared if they will only ask in faith, nothing wavering (see James 1:5-6). This promise was reiterated to Oliver Cowdery, but it is available to all faithful Saints (cf. 3 Nephi 18:19-20). Actually, it was this promise that opened the heavens in the present dispensation (see JS—H 1:11-18).

**D&C 8:1, 11. What Was Oliver Cowdery's Gift Concerning Ancient Records?**

President Joseph Fielding Smith explained that "the Lord seemed perfectly willing that Oliver Cowdery as well as Joseph Smith should engage in this labor of translating the plates, and he gave in some detail what qualifications are necessary for the reception of knowledge by revelation and also the procedure necessary in translating ancient records. Oliver was informed that this power could not be received except by the exercise of faith with an honest heart, and by this faith, knowledge of the ancient records and their engravings should be made known. . . .

"The Lord told him that he was to continue as scribe until the translation of the Book of Mormon was completed, and that there were other ancient records to come forth, and that he might have the privilege of translating these at some future day if he would remain faithful. We learn from the Book of Mormon that there are many records and that at some time, when the people are prepared by faith to receive them, that they shall also be translated and published for the knowledge and salvation of the faithful. (II Nephi 27:7-8; III Nephi 26:6-11; Ether 3:22-28 and 4:5-7.)" (*Church History and Modern Revelation,* 1:50, 52.)

*Oliver Cowdery was a scribe to Joseph Smith*

**D&C 8:1-3. What Is the Spirit of Revelation?**

Elder George Q. Cannon taught that this spirit is "the same spirit of revelation that Moses had . . . rests upon him who holds the presidency as senior apostle in the midst of the people of God. The apostles of this Church have all the authority, they have all the keys, . . . all the spirit of revelation necessary to lead this people into the presence of the Lamb in the celestial kingdom of our God. . . .

"But it is the truth, that the same spirit of revelation that rested upon Moses, and which enabled him to lead the children of Israel through the Red Sea, rests upon the servants of God in the midst of this people, and you will find it so to your entire satisfaction if you will listen to their counsels and be guided by them." (In *Journal of Discourses,* 21:270-71.)

Enrichment C, in the Appendix, contains a more complete discussion of personal revelation and how it is received.

**D&C 8:4. A Warning Given to Oliver Cowdery that Applies to Everyone**

Oliver Cowdery was given the gift of understanding the voice of the Spirit. If he hearkened to the inspiration of the Holy Ghost, he could protect himself from those who would seek to bring about his physical death and also from those who would tempt him to sin and thus bring his soul "to destruction" (D&C 8:4).

Concerning the destruction of the soul, President Joseph Fielding Smith wrote:

"A soul cannot be destroyed.

"Every soul born into this world shall receive the resurrection and immortality and shall endure forever. Destruction does not mean, then, annihilation. When the Lord says they shall be destroyed, he means that they shall be banished from his presence, that they shall be cut off from the presence of light and truth, and shall not have the privilege of gaining this exaltation; and that is destruction." (*Doctrines of Salvation,* 2:227-28; see also Alma 12:16; Helaman 14:18.)

The Lord's response to those who neglect gifts he gives them is recorded in 2 Nephi 28:30; Matthew 25:14-29; D&C 9:1, 5, 10-11.

**D&C 8:6-9. What Was the Gift of Aaron?**

"There was another gift bestowed upon Oliver Cowdery, and that was the gift of Aaron. Like Aaron with his rod in his hand going before Moses as a spokesman, so Oliver Cowdery was to go before Joseph Smith. Whatever he should ask the Lord by power of this gift should be granted if asked in faith and in wisdom. Oliver was blessed with the great honor of holding the keys of this dispensation with Joseph Smith, and, like Aaron, did become a spokesman on numerous occasions. It was Oliver who delivered the first public discourse in this dispensation." (Smith, *Church History and Modern Revelation,* 1:52.)

"Oliver Cowdery also had the 'gift of Aaron.' Aaron was the elder brother of Moses. Being prompted by the Spirit of the Lord, he met his younger brother in the wilderness and accompanied him to Egypt. He introduced him to the children of Israel in the land of Goshen. He was his spokesman before Pharaoh, and he assisted him in opening up the dispensation which Moses was commissioned to proclaim (Exodus 4:27-31). This was the gift of Aaron. In some respects Oliver Cowdery was the Aaron of the new and last dispensation." (Smith and Sjodahl, Commentary, p. 44.)

**D&C 8:10-11. How Powerful Is Faith?**

President J. Reuben Clark, Jr., declared:

"As I think about faith, this principle of power, I am obliged to believe that it is an intelligent force. Of what kind, I do not know. But it is superior to and overrules all other forces of which we know. . . .

"You brethren, we brethren, have had this great power given unto us, this power of faith. What are we doing about it? Can you, can we, do the mighty things that the Savior did? Yes. They have been done by the members of the Church who had the faith and the righteousness so to do. Think of what is within your power if you but live the Gospel, if you but live so that you may invoke the power which is within you." (In Conference Report, Apr. 1960, p. 21.)

# "Your Bosom Shall Burn within You"

## Section 9

## Historical Background

In its infancy the Church required stalwart leaders who had been trained in the ways of the Lord. One such leader was Oliver Cowdery, a capable young man eager to do the work of God.

But Oliver was not content merely to assist in the work of translating by serving as Joseph's scribe. He wanted to translate as Joseph did. The Lord's desire, on the other hand, was for Oliver to continue to serve as scribe and then seek for greater gifts (see D&C 9:2-3). Oliver, however, became impatient and was given permission to translate on his own. Doctrine and Covenants 9 is an explanation of Oliver's failure to translate as he had wished.

President Joseph Fielding Smith pointed out that "it seems probable that Oliver Cowdery desired to translate out of curiosity, and the Lord taught him his place by showing him that translating was not the easy thing he had thought it to be. In a subsequent revelation (Sec. 9), the explanation was made that Oliver's failure came because he did not continue as he commenced, and the task being a difficult one, his faith deserted him. The lesson he learned was very necessary, for he was shown that his place was to act as scribe for Joseph Smith and that it was the latter who was called and appointed by command of the Lord to do the translating. There must have been some desire on the part of Oliver Cowdery to be equal with the Prophet and some impatience in having to sit and act as scribe, but when he failed to master the gift of translating, he was then willing to accept the will of the Lord." (*Church History and Modern Revelation,* 1:50-51.)

## Notes and Commentary

**D&C 9:1. Wherein Did Oliver Cowdery Fail?**

The Lord assigned Oliver's failure to translate to the fact that he did not translate according to that which he desired of the Lord. Oliver had to learn that translating as Joseph Smith was doing was by the gift and power of God. Evidently, Oliver had received sufficient instruction, but instead went his own way, using his own wisdom. He was therefore stopped from translating (see vs. 5).

**D&C 9:2. Are Other Records Yet to Come Forth?**

The Book of Mormon teaches that there are many records of God's dealings with his children yet to come forth (see 2 Nephi 27:7-8; 3 Nephi 26:6-11; Ether 3:22-28; 4:5-7). Several years after this revelation was given, the records from which the book of Abraham was translated fell into Joseph Smith's hands. Perhaps this was one of those other records which the Lord had in mind. It should also be remembered that a portion of the gold plates was sealed. These too shall come forth some time in the future and may have been among those referred to in this statement by the Lord.

President Joseph Fielding Smith indicated how both Oliver Cowdery and the general Church membership contributed to the failure of the Saints to have these records today: "It is possible that some of them might have been translated had the people received the Book of Mormon with full purpose of heart and had been faithful to its teachings. This was the promise the Lord made through Mormon. He said he would try the faith of the people and if they were willing to accept the lesser things (i.e., the Book of Mormon) then he would make known to them the greater things. That we have failed in this is very apparent, we have not accepted the revelations in the Book of Mormon, neither in the Doctrine and Covenants, with that faith and willingness to know the will of the Lord which would entitle us to receive this greater information. Oliver Cowdery was a party to this failure by turning away from the Church for a number of years when it needed his service. He therefore lost his privilege to translate through his own disobedience, and the people have lost the privilege of receiving the 'greater things' spoken of by the Lord to Mormon (III Nephi 26:8-11) until the day shall come when they are willing to be obedient in all things and will exercise faith such as was had by the brother of Jared. It should be remembered that such faith has rarely been seen on the earth. It appears, therefore, that we must wait until the reign of unrighteousness is at an end before the Lord will give to the people these writings, containing 'a revelation from God, from the beginning of the world to the ending thereof.' (II Nephi 27:7.)" (Smith, *Church History and Modern Revelation,* 1:52-53.)

**D&C 9:5-6. Why Did the Lord Take Away Oliver's Right to Translate?**

Without question the Lord knew in 1829 that Oliver would eventually leave the Church. Some have thought this was why the Lord said, "It is wisdom in me that I have dealt with you after this manner." (D&C 9:6.) The Lord, however, does not punish a person for sins he has not yet committed, even though He knows that he will commit them sometime in the future. Oliver had demonstrated by his present insufficient faith that it was better for him to wait for a season before he translated. Also, Joseph needed a scribe, and Oliver's impatience at being only a scribe had been satisfied since he had learned that translation was not nearly as simple a task as it first appeared. It was therefore wisdom in God to have Oliver wait.

### D&C 9:7-8. What Mistake Did Oliver Make in Attempting to Translate?

Ludlow, in his work on the Doctrine and Covenants, noted the real problem in Oliver Cowdery's attempt to translate: "Spiritual effort, as well as mental and physical effort, was required in order to translate the sacred records of the Book of Mormon. Oliver Cowdery thought that all he needed to do in order to translate was to ask the Lord, but here he is told that he must also 'study it out' in his mind as well as to ask the Lord whether or not it is right. The Lord also gives Oliver a key so that he will know when the translation is right: his bosom shall burn within him." (*Companion,* 1:94.)

*"You must study it out in your mind; then you must ask me if it be right" (D&C 9:8)*

### D&C 9:8-9. What Is Meant by "Your Bosom Shall Burn within You"?

Elder S. Dilworth Young pointed out that the promise of confirmation can be had by all Saints: "If I am to receive revelation from the Lord, I must be in harmony with him by keeping his commandments. Then as needed, according to his wisdom, his word will come into my mind through my thoughts, accompanied by a feeling in the region of my bosom. It is a feeling which cannot be described, but the nearest word we have is 'burn' or 'burning.' Accompanying this always is a feeling of peace, a further witness that what one heard is right. Once one recognizes this burning, this feeling, this peace, one need never be drawn astray in his daily life or in the guidance he may receive." ("The Still Small Voice," *Ensign,* May 1976, p. 23.)

Oliver Cowdery had apparently not received the burning confirmation spoken of. He was therefore unable to perform the work of translation.

### D&C 9:9. "You Cannot Write That Which Is Sacred Save It Be Given You from Me"

Elder John A. Widtsoe wrote that the Prophet received revelation in different ways as he matured in his calling. At first his communications with the heavens were direct—visitations from God, his Son, and angels. Then he used the Urim and Thummim as a medium. Finally, "he learned to bring his mind into such harmony with divine forces that it became, as it were, itself a Urim and Thummim to him; and God's will was revealed without the intervention of external aids" (Widtsoe, *Joseph Smith,* p. 267.)

### D&C 9:8-9. Do These Verses Apply to All Members of the Church?

Though the principle of studying something out in one's mind and seeking confirmation through the burning of the bosom or a stupor of thought was given to Oliver Cowdery to use in translating the Book of Mormon, this process of receiving revelation can be of value to all Saints. President Joseph Fielding Smith explained that "a similar privilege is given to any member of the Church who seeks knowledge in the spirit of prayer and faith. The Lord will cause the feeling of security and truth to take hold of the individual and burn within the bosom, and there will be an overwhelming feeling that the thing is right. Missionaries have felt the manifestation of this gift while laboring in the field; when searching the scriptures; when speaking before congregations on the streets and in public gatherings. When you have been listening to some inspired speaker who has presented a new thought to you, have you not felt that burning within and the satisfaction in your heart that this new thought is true? On the other hand, have you experienced the feeling of stupor, gloom, or uneasiness when some thought has been presented which was in conflict with the revealed word of the Lord, and you have felt by this manifestation of the Spirit that what was said is not true? It is a great gift, which all may receive, to have this spirit of discernment, or revelation, for it is the spirit of revelation." (*Church History and Modern Revelation,* 1:51.)

### D&C 9:10-11. "But You Feared"

Given here is an additional reason why Oliver Cowdery failed in his efforts to translate: he "feared" (D&C 9:11). Fear is the result of a lack of faith and an unwillingness to follow through. Had Oliver continued as he commenced, the gift of translation would have been his (see vs. 5). As it was, he feared and consequently lost the proffered gift.

### D&C 9:12. How Did the Lord Compensate for Oliver Cowdery's Failure?

"As indicated in this revelation, the Lord had given Oliver Cowdery the right to translate part of the record. When Oliver failed in his attempts, the Lord gave unto his 'servant Joseph sufficient strength, whereby it is made up.' Thus, the total responsibility for translation was left with Joseph." (Ludlow, *Companion,* 1:96.)

# God's Wisdom "Is Greater Than the Cunning of the Devil"

Section 10

## Historical Background

"As soon as the 116 pages of manuscript had been lost through the carelessness of Martin Harris, the Urim and Thummim was taken from the Prophet. The sacred instrument was restored after a short time, and the Revelation in Section 3, especially rebuking Martin Harris, was received. Then both the plates and the Urim and Thummim were removed for a few days. It was necessary that the young Prophet should learn the lesson that he was entirely dependent on the Lord. When they were restored, he received the Revelation in Section 10, containing instructions to himself with regard to the lost portion of the manuscript." (Smith and Sjodahl, Commentary, p. 49.)

Concerning the circumstances that surrounded the reception of this revelation, Joseph Smith wrote: "After I had obtained the above revelation [D&C 3], both the plates and the Urim and Thummim were taken from me again; but in a few days they were returned to me, when I inquired of the Lord, and the Lord said thus unto me: [D&C 10]" (*History of the Church,* 1:23).

## Notes and Commentary

### D&C 10:2. "Your Mind Became Darkened"

Lucy Mack Smith gave a vivid description of the darkness her son Joseph felt when he learned that the 116 pages were lost:

"I besought him not to mourn so, for perhaps the Lord would forgive him, after a short season of humiliation and repentance. But what could I do to comfort him, when he saw all the family in the same situation of mind as himself; for sobs and groans, and the most bitter lamentations filled the house. However, Joseph was more distressed than the rest, as he better understood the consequences of disobedience. And he continued pacing back and forth, meantime weeping and grieving, until about sunset, when, by persuasion, he took a little nourishment.

"The next morning, he set out for home. We parted with heavy hearts, for it now appeared that all which we had so fondly anticipated, and which had been the source of so much secret gratification, had in a moment fled, and fled forever." (*History of Joseph Smith,* p. 129; see also Historical Background for D&C 3.)

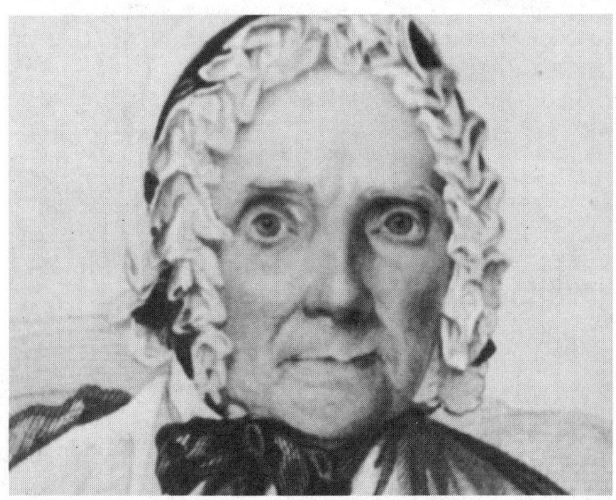

*Lucy Mack Smith, mother of the Prophet*

### D&C 10:4. Why Would the Lord Warn Joseph Not to Run Faster Than He Was Able?

Now that the Prophet Joseph Smith had again received the Urim and Thummim and the plates, perhaps he felt that he needed to make up for lost time. The Lord, however, counseled him to not "run faster or labor more" than he had strength (D&C 10:4).

The same counsel was given by King Benjamin in the Book of Mormon. After giving his people an extensive discourse on the attributes of a Saint, he said, "And see that all these things are done in wisdom and order; for it is not requisite that a man should run faster than he has strength. And again, it is expedient that he should be diligent, that thereby he might win the prize; therefore, all things must be done in order." (Mosiah 4:27.) In the Lord's counsel to the Prophet Joseph Smith and in King Benjamin's to the Nephites, the emphasis is on diligence and direction rather than on speed in climbing the path to exaltation (see also D&C 84:43). Sometimes overzealous effort without wisdom and patience leads into errors.

### D&C 10:5. How Does a Person "Pray Always"?

Sometimes prayer is thought of only as vocal petitions to God. President Joseph F. Smith said that prayer is not so much words as it is feelings: "It is not the words we use particularly that constitute prayer. Prayer does not consist of words, altogether. True, faithful, earnest prayer consists more in the feeling that rises from the heart and from the inward desire of our spirits to supplicate the Lord in humility and in faith, that we may receive his blessings." (*Gospel Doctrine,* p. 219.)

Because prayer involves one's feelings toward God, would not the command to "pray always" involve a condition of feeling that one has for God? The Apostle Paul wrote: "Pray without ceasing. In every thing give thanks." (1 Thessalonians 5:17-18.) Could not a feeling of gratitude and love for Heavenly Father and a constant yearning to live to please him be considered a way to pray always? Amulek gave similar counsel when he said, "Let your hearts be full, drawn out in prayer unto him *continually* for your welfare, and also for the welfare of those who are around you" (Alma 34:27; emphasis added).

The benefit comes from a prayerful attitude coupled with constant formal prayers. Prayer is the source of the power necessary to overcome Satan and his servants.

### D&C 10:6. How Did These Men Seek to Destroy Joseph Smith?

From the text it appears that the men who had taken the manuscript (see vss. 8-27) and who had allowed themselves to fall under the power and influence of Satan were seeking to show to their fellowmen that Joseph Smith was not a prophet but a fraud and that the Book of Mormon was false. Thus they would destroy Joseph Smith's claim to be a prophet and destroy, or bring to naught, his influence among men. Similarly, by showing that the Book of Mormon was false, they would also destroy that part of the work of the Lord in the latter days. So, in verse 6, "destroy" means to negate or to bring to naught. The same meaning is given in verses 7, 12, 19, 23, 25, 43, 52, and 54. "Destroy" in verse 27 and "destruction" in verse 22 mean to bring about spiritual death and the eventual destruction of the soul.

Because Martin Harris lost the manuscript of the forepart of the Book of Mormon, Joseph Smith was not allowed to translate for a time (see D&C 3:12-14). It appears that Martin Harris later wanted to view the plates themselves, but permission was denied by the Lord through inspiration to the Prophet Joseph Smith until Martin had humbled himself (see D&C 5:1-3). He was then permitted to see the plates as one of the Three Witnesses. Even though Martin Harris was not intentionally trying to destroy the Prophet and his work, if he had continued in the course he was pursuing, he would have been the cause of such destruction.

### D&C 10:12, 23-29, 63. Satan Is Extremely Well Organized and Has Devised a "Cunning Plan"

Section 10 gives a partial list of some of the methods Satan uses to attack the truth.

*Verse 20.* He stirs up the wicked to iniquity against the righteous.

*Verse 24.* He inspires the wicked to anger against God's work.

*Verses 25-36.* He uses deceptions, lies, and flattery. Many sections of the Doctrine and Covenants were given to help the Saints detect the deceptions of Satan (see D&C 28, 43, 45, 46, 49, 50, 52). The subject of avoiding deception is dealt with at length in Enrichment J, in the Appendix.

*Verse 63.* He encourages contention over doctrine. Jesus upbraided the Nephites for this problem (see 3 Nephi 11:28-29). The Lord warned Joseph that Satan would use this method among the members of the Church.

### D&C 10:23. "I Will Require This at Their Hands"

The Lord says he would hold accountable those who sought to destroy his work. Though Satan is behind it, men have their agency either to reject or to follow the promptings of the adversary and therefore are held accountable before the Lord. (See also D&C 93:31-32.)

### D&C 10:25. Satan Is the Father of Lies and Deception

President Joseph F. Smith explained how Lucifer functions: "By every possible means he seeks to darken the minds of men and then offers them falsehood and deception in the guise of truth. Satan is a skillful imitator, and as genuine gospel truth is given the world in ever-increasing abundance, so he spreads the counterfeit coin of false doctrine. Beware of his spurious currency, it will purchase for you nothing but disappointment, misery and spiritual death. The 'father of lies' he has been called, and such an adept has he become through the ages of practice in his nefarious work, that were it possible he would deceive the very elect." ("Witchcraft," *Juvenile Instructor,* Sept. 1902, p. 562.)

Elder Spencer W. Kimball said that Satan "will use his logic to confuse and his rationalizations to destroy. He will shade meanings, open doors an inch at a time, and lead from purest white through all the shades of gray to the darkest black." (*Faith Precedes the Miracle,* p. 152; see also Moroni 7:17.)

### D&C 10:33. What Was Satan's Purpose in Seeking Joseph's Downfall?

This verse is the Lord's warning to the Prophet Joseph Smith. Why was Satan so concerned about Joseph Smith's testimony and about the coming forth of the Book of Mormon? He, of course, has opposed the work of God in all dispensations, but in this last dispensation the forces restored by Joseph Smith (including the Book of Mormon, the priesthood powers, and the establishment of the kingdom) will roll forth until they fill the whole earth (see Daniel 2:44). Zion will be established, and Babylon (Satan's dominions) will be utterly overthrown. Satan himself will be bound and have no power for a thousand years (see Revelation 20:1-2; 1 Nephi 22:22-26). Is it any wonder that Satan sought from the beginning to destroy Joseph and to overthrow the work? The Prophet Joseph Smith's mission signaled the eventual triumph of God's kingdom over Satan's own.

### D&C 10:38-45. Foreknowledge of God

Centuries before the Prophet Joseph Smith was born, Nephi testified that God had commanded him to make two sets of plates (the large plates of Nephi and the small plates of Nephi), the purpose of which Nephi did not understand (see 1 Nephi 9:5-6). Mormon, who lived almost a thousand years after Nephi, included the small plates of Nephi with his abridgment, admitting that he did not understand why, save the Lord had commanded him to do it (see Words of Mormon 1:3-7).

The loss of the 116-page manuscript makes it apparent why the Lord commanded Nephi and Mormon to do what they did. Joseph was told to leave the portion he had already translated from the large plates and start again with Nephi's record.

Knowing that God sees the end from the beginning should give one confidence in him as one lives in the present and works toward the future.To better understand the foreknowledge of

God see Isaiah 42:9; 48:3; Jeremiah 1:4-5; Acts 2:23; 17:26; Romans 11:2; 1 Peter 1:2; 1 Nephi 20:3; Alma 13:3, 7; 40:10; Helaman 8:8; Moroni 7:22; D&C 1:17; 38:2; Moses 1:6; Abraham 2:8.

**D&C 10:55. Will *Every* Church Member Really Be Saved in the Kingdom of God?**

An important insight that every student of the scriptures should have is that the Lord uses certain terms in a special way. He has a definition and meaning different from those used every day. Obviously many baptized members of the Church are not going to inherit the "kingdom of heaven" unless they repent of their ways. So why does the Lord say "whosoever belongeth to my church need not fear"? The answer is clear. Later in this section the Lord describes those who actually constitute his Church. It is not simply those who receive baptism that become true members, but rather "whosoever repenteth and cometh unto me, the same is my church" (D&C 10:67). By this definition of *church,* indeed, all members of his church will inherit the kingdom of heaven, and all such who endure to the end "will I establish upon my rock, and the gates of hell shall not prevail against them" (D&C 10:69).

**D&C 10:57-70. Some Purposes of the Book of Mormon**

In these verses the Lord outlined the important purposes of the Book of Mormon in bearing witness of the Savior.

*Verse 60.* It shows that the Lord has other "sheep" and that they are of Israel (see John 10:16; 3 Nephi 15:21-24).

*Verse 61.* The Book of Mormon will present the marvelous works the Book of Mormon peoples did in his name.

*Verse 62.* It will bring to light true doctrine.

*Verse 63.* It will help stop the contention over doctrine that characterizes so much of Christianity.

*Verse 65.* It foretells the gathering of Israel to the true Church in the last days.

*Verse 67-68.* It helps establish the doctrine of Christ.

# "First Seek to Obtain My Word"

# Section 11

## Historical Background

Following the baptisms of Joseph Smith and Oliver Cowdery on 15 May 1829, the Prophet Joseph reported:

"Our minds begin now enlightened, we began to have the Scriptures laid open to our understandings, and the true meaning and intention of their more mysterious passages revealed unto us in a manner which we never could attain to previously, nor ever before had thought of. In the meantime we were forced to keep secret the circumstances of having received the Priesthood and our having been baptized, owing to a spirit of persecution which had already manifested itself in the neighborhood. . . .

"After a few days, however, feeling it to be our duty, we commenced to reason out of the Scriptures with our acquaintances and friends, as we happened to meet with them. About this time my brother Samuel H. Smith came to visit us. . . .

"Not many days afterwards, my brother Hyrum Smith came to us to inquire concerning these things, when at his earnest request, I inquired of the Lord through the Urim and Thummin, and received for him the following: [D&C 11]." (*History of the Church,* 1:43-45.)

## Notes and Commentary

**D&C 11:1-9**

For a discussion of these verses, see Notes and Commentary for Doctrine and Covenants 4:1-4; 6:1-9.

**D&C 11:9. What Does It Mean to "Say Nothing but Repentance unto This Generation"?**

"When the Lord calls upon his servants to cry nothing but repentance, he does not mean that they may not cry baptism, and call upon the people to obey the commandments of the Lord, but he wishes that all that they say and do be *in the spirit of bringing the people to repentance. Any missionary who fails to do this in his ministry is derelict in his duty.*" (Smith, *Church History and Modern Revelation,* 1:57; emphasis added.)

**D&C 11:10-11. What Was the Gift Hyrum Smith Was Promised?**

Like Oliver Cowdery (see D&C 8:6-9) Hyrum Smith was promised a gift from the Lord. President Joseph Fielding Smith explained what the gift was: "The Lord declared that Hyrum Smith had a gift. The great gift which he possessed was that of a tender, sympathetic heart; a merciful spirit. The Lord on a later occasion said: 'Blessed is my servant Hyrum Smith; for I, the Lord, love him because of the integrity of his heart, and because he loveth that which is right before me, saith the Lord.' (D. & C., 124:15.) This great gift was manifest in his jealous watch care over the Prophet lest some harm come to him." (*Church History and Modern Revelation,* 1:57.)

Hyrum's gift was not promised unconditionally.

It was to come only after he exercised faith in Jesus Christ. (See D&C 11:10.)

*"Blessed is my servant Hyrum Smith" (D&C 124:15)*

**D&C 11:12-14. What Is Meant by the Phrase "My Spirit . . . Shall Enlighten Your Mind"?**

President Lorenzo Snow taught of the powerful influence that following the Spirit can have on one's life: "There is a way by which persons can keep their consciences clear before God and man, and that is to preserve within them the spirit of God, which is the spirit of revelation to every man and woman. It will reveal to them, even in the simplest of matters, what they shall do, by making suggestions to them. We should try to learn the nature of this spirit, that we may understand its suggestions, and then we will always be able to do right. This is the grand privilege of every Latter-day Saint. We know that it is our right to have the manifestations of the spirit every day of our lives. . . . From the time we receive the Gospel, go down into the waters of baptism and have hands laid upon us afterwards for the gift of the Holy Ghost, we have a friend, if we do not drive it from us by doing wrong. That friend is the Holy Spirit, the Holy Ghost, which partakes of the things of God and shows them unto us. This is a grand means that the Lord has provided for us, that we may know the light, and not be groveling continually in the dark." (In Conference Report, Apr. 1899, p. 52.)

**D&C 11:15-16. How Does One Prepare to Serve the Lord?**

Ludlow outlined the important teachings given here to Hyrum Smith that are of value to anyone preparing for a mission:

"1. Desire to serve the Lord. (11:10, 17.)

"2. Live worthily to receive the Spirit of the Lord so it can 'enlighten your mind, which shall fill your soul with joy.' (11:13.)

"3. Keep the commandments of the Lord, assisting in the work of the Lord in any way that you might be asked. (11:18-20.)

"4. Seek to obtain the word of the Lord through (a) studying the word of the Lord that had already gone forth—the Bible—and (b) studying the word of the Lord that was then being translated—the Book of Mormon. (11:21-22.)

"5. Build upon the gospel, denying not either the spirit of revelation nor the spirit of prophecy. (11:24-25.)

"The Lord indicates further that these suggestions are for 'all who have good desires' to serve. (11:27.)" (*Companion*, 1:108-9.)

**D&C 11:15-17. "You Need Not Suppose That You Are Called to Preach Until You Are Called"**

The concept of having proper authority from God in order to act for him is central to the Latter-day Saint understanding of Church organization. President Joseph Fielding Smith explained that "it is quite the common thing in the world for men to assume authority and to act in the name of the Lord when he has not called them. No man is authorized to act in the name of the Lord, or to officiate in any ordinance, unless he has been properly called. For this reason the Priesthood was restored and the Church organized. When this revelation was given the Church had not been organized. Presumably some of those who sought light and the will of the Lord felt that when the Lord spoke to them, they were authorized to go forth to act in his name. Here he informs Hyrum Smith that he was to wait (v. 15), yet he was to put his trust in the Holy Spirit and to walk humbly, to judge righteously, 'and this is my Spirit.' " (*Church History and Modern Revelation*, 1:57.)

**D&C 11:18-20. "Keep My Commandments," a Prerequisite to Service in the Kingdom**

The Lord often repeated the instruction to keep the commandments (see vss. 9, 18, 20).

In Moses 1:39 the Lord says, "For behold, *this is my work* and my glory—to bring to pass the immortality and eternal life of man" (emphasis added), whereas to Hyrum the Lord says, "*This is your work*, to keep my commandments, yea, with all your might, mind and strength" (D&C 11:20; emphasis added).

Similar language was used by the Lord to respond to the question of the Pharisees about which is the great commandment in the law (see Matthew 22:36-37). Only by keeping the Lord's commandments can one show love for the Lord and accomplish his work.

**D&C 11:24. "My Rock . . . Is My Gospel"**

On several occasions the Lord used the word *rock* to refer to the gospel (see Matthew 7:24-25; 3 Nephi 11:32-39; D&C 18:4-5, 17; 12:12-13).

The word *rock* also refers to a principle of the gospel as explained by the Prophet Joseph Smith:

"Jesus in His teachings says, 'Upon this rock I will build my Church, and the gates of hell shall not prevail against it.' What rock? Revelation." (*History of the Church,* 5:258.)

Another use of the word *rock* in the scriptures applies directly to the Lord himself (see D&C 50:43-44; Deuteronomy 32:2-4).

**D&C 11:25. "Deny Not the Spirit of Revelation"**

President Joseph Fielding Smith explained that this counsel to Hyrum Smith would serve as "good counsel for all of us today. There are some members of the Church who seemingly complain because the Lord is not giving revelations to be placed in the Doctrine and Covenants, as in the beginning, and they ask why revelation has ceased in the Church. Usually it is the case that these critics are not faithfully keeping the commandments the Lord has already given and their eyes are blind to the fact that revelation and the guidance of the Lord is being meted out to the Church constantly. No one with the spirit of discernment can fail to see that the hand of the Lord has guided this people from the beginning and this guidance is manifest today as in other times to all who are humble and have a contrite spirit. (See Jacob 4:8.)" (*Church History and Modern Revelation,* 1:57.)

President Hugh B. Brown also taught the central importance of revelation in the Church: "The things of God can only be understood by the Spirit of God and the Spirit of God is a revealing spirit. The Master promised before he left the earth to send another Comforter which would lead men into all truth. [See John 15:26; 16:7.] Divine revelation had always been a characteristic of the living Church—it is absolutely essential to its continued existence in an organized state on the earth." (In Conference Report, Oct. 1961, pp. 93-94.)

Enrichment C, in the Appendix, contains a further discussion of the subject of personal revelation.

**D&C 11:26-27. "Treasure Up in Your Heart"**

See Doctrine and Covenants 84:85 for a discussion of the significance of this command and the blessings that will result from obedience to it.

**D&C 11:29-30. What Are the Implications of Receiving the Lord and Becoming the Sons of God?**

See Doctrine and Covenants 76:51-60; 84:33-38; 132:22-24; Moses 6:57-68; 1 John 3:1-10.

# Revelation to Joseph Knight, Sr.

Section 12

## Historical Background

"For fifteen years he has been faithful and true, and even-handed and exemplary, and virtuous and kind, never deviating to the right hand or to the left. Behold he is a righteous man . . . and it shall be said of him, by the sons of Zion, while there is one of them remaining, that this man was a faithful man in Israel; therefore his name shall never be forgotten." (*History of the Church,* 5:124-25.)

This tribute was written by Joseph Smith of his true and trusted friend, Joseph Knight, Sr., on 22 August 1842.

Joseph Knight, Sr., had early in the history of the Church become a close and helpful friend of the Prophet. Joseph Smith first met him in 1826 when Joseph Knight hired him to work at his farm and grist mill in Colesville, Broome County, New York. From that time forth Joseph Knight offered both material and spiritual support to Joseph Smith, including provisions that allowed the Prophet and his scribe to work on the translation of the Book of Mormon at a very crucial time of its production. Joseph Smith wrote:

"About the same time an old gentleman came to visit us of whose name I wish to make honorable

*Joseph Knight offered his means to aid Joseph Smith*

mention—Mr. Joseph Knight, Sen., of Colesville, Broome county, New York, who, having heard of the manner in which we were occupying our time, very kindly and considerately brought us a quantity of provisions, in order that we might not be interrupted in the work of translation by the want of such necessaries of life; and I would just mention here, as in duty bound, that he several times brought us supplies, a distance of at least thirty miles, which enabled us to continue the work when otherwise we must have relinquished it for a season.

"Being very anxious to know his duty as to this work, I inquired of the Lord for him, and obtained the following: [D&C 12]." (*History of the Church,* 1:47-48.)

The Prophet received the revelation sometime in May 1829 while living in Harmony, Pennsylvania.

## Notes and Commentary

### D&C 12:1-6. Repetition in the Doctrine and Covenants

Notes and Commentary on Doctrine and Covenants 6:1-9 explains why certain sections have identical verses.

### D&C 12:8. "Except He Shall Be Humble"

After briefly describing the Savior's life, Elder Spencer W. Kimball gave the following definition of humility:

"If the Lord was meek and lowly and humble, then to become humble one must do what He did in boldly denouncing evil, bravely advancing righteous works, courageously meeting every problem, becoming the master of himself and the situations about him and being near oblivious to personal credit. . . .

"Humble and meek properly suggest virtues, not weaknesses. They suggest a consistent mildness of temper and an absence of wrath and passion. Humility suggests no affectation, no bombastic actions. It is not turbid nor grandiloquent. It is not servile submissiveness. It is not cowed nor frightened. No shadow or the shaking of a leaf terrorizes it.

"How does one get humble? To me, one must constantly be reminded of his dependence. On whom dependent? On the Lord. How remind one's self? By real, constant, worshipful, grateful prayer." (*Humility,* Brigham Young University Speeches of the Year [Provo, 16 Jan. 1963], pp. 2-3.)

### D&C 12:8. "Full of Love"

Love is a motivator. When a person is full of love for God and his fellowman, he is motivated to serve both. The Prophet Joseph Smith taught that "Love is one of the chief characteristics of Deity, and ought to be manifested by those who aspire to be the sons of God. A man filled with the love of God, is not content with blessing his family alone, but ranges through the whole world, anxious to bless the whole human race." (*History of the Church,* 4:227.)

### D&C 12:9. Who Is the Light and Life of the World?

"It is our Lord who is speaking. He calls Himself the Light and the Life of the World . . . (John 1:4, 9; 3:19; 6:35; 12:35; 14:6). The Savior frequently quotes in these Revelations; or, rather, expressions familiar to the readers of John's writing meet us here again and again. John had a prominent part in the ushering in of this dispensation. On the Isle of Patmos he saw the coming, in our day, of the 'mighty angel' with the 'little book open,' and it was said to him, 'Thou must prophesy again before many peoples, and nations, and tongues, and kings' (Rev. 10:11). In fulfilment of this prediction, he and two fellow Apostles conferred the Melchizedek Priesthood upon Joseph Smith and Oliver Cowdery. No wonder if the spirit of the teachings of these Apostles, and especially that of John, the last of the first Twelve, should be discernible in these Revelations." (Smith and Sjodahl, Commentary, p. 67.)

# The Restoration of the Aaronic Priesthood

Section 13

## Historical Background

Universal apostasy followed the death of the Savior and his Apostles. Over the centuries that followed, man was no longer authorized to act for God. This condition helped to fulfill prophecy: "The earth also is defiled under the inhabitants thereof; because they have transgressed the laws, changed the ordinance, broken the everlasting covenant" (Isaiah 24:5).

The coming of John the Baptist in this dispensation, as promised by the Savior (see Matthew 17:11-13), meant that mortal man was once again divinely commissioned to act in behalf of his creator.

Joseph Smith explained the circumstances surrounding the restoration of the Aaronic Priesthood (see JS—History 1:68-72), which took place somewhere along the banks of the Susquehanna River near Harmony, Pennsylvania. Oliver Cowdery, who was with the Prophet on this occasion, was filled with awe and wonder, for it was his first experience with a heavenly messenger. He wrote:

"On a sudden, as from the midst of eternity, the voice of the Redeemer spake peace to us, while the vail was parted and the angel of God came down clothed with glory, and delivered the anxiously looked for message, and the keys of the gospel of repentance!—What joy! what wonder! what amazement! While the world was racked and distracted—while millions were groping as the blind for the wall, and while all men were resting upon uncertainty, as a general mass, our eyes beheld—our ears heard. As in the 'blaze of days;' yes, more—above the glitter of the May Sun beam, which then shed its brilliancy over the face of nature! Then his voice, though mild, pierced to the center, and his words, 'I am thy fellow-servant,' dispelled every fear. We listened—we gazed—we admired! 'Twas the voice of an angel from glory—'twas a message from the Most High! and as we heard we rejoiced, while his love enkindled upon our souls, and we were wrapt in the vision of the Almighty! Where was room for doubt? No where; uncertainty had fled, doubt had sunk, no more to rise, while fiction and deception had fled forever!

"But, dear brother think, further think for a moment, what joy filled our hearts and with what surprise we must have bowed, (for who would not have bowed the knee for such a blessing?) when we received under his hand the holy priesthood." (*Times and Seasons*, 1 Nov. 1840, p. 202.)

## Notes and Commentary

**D&C 13:1. Why Is the Lesser Priesthood Called the "Priesthood of Aaron"?**

See Doctrine and Covenants 107:13-14, and compare Doctrine and Covenants 84:26-27.

**D&C 13:1. The Ministering of Angels to Bearers of the Aaronic Priesthood**

President Wilford Woodruff recorded the following about his experience with the ministering of angels:

"I had the administration of angels while holding the office of a priest. I had visions and revelations. I traveled thousands of miles. I baptized men, though I could not confirm them because I had not the authority to do it.

"I speak of these things to show that a man should not be ashamed of any portion of the priesthood." (*Discourses of Wilford Woodruff*, p. 298.)

**D&C 13:1. "This Shall Never Be Taken Again from the Earth"**

"We may be sure that the Aaronic Priesthood will never be taken from the earth while mortality endures, for there will always be need for temporal direction and the performance of ordinances pertaining to 'the preparatory Gospel.' " (Smith, *Church History and Modern Revelation*, p. 1:62.)

**D&C 13:1. Who Are the "Sons of Levi"?**

President Joseph Fielding Smith explained that "after the children of Israel came out of Egypt and while they were sojourning in the wilderness,

*John the Baptist restored the Aaronic Priesthood*

Moses received a commandment from the Lord to take Aaron and his sons and ordain them and consecrate them as priests for the people. (Ex. 28.) At that time the males of the entire tribe of Levi were chosen to be the priests instead of the first-born of all the tribes, and Aaron and his sons were given the presidency over the Priesthood thus conferred. Since that time it has been known as the Priesthood of Aaron, including the Levitical Priesthood." (*Church History and Modern Revelation,* 1:63.)

**D&C 13:1. What Is Meant by the Sons of Levi Offering an Offering of Righteousness unto the Lord?**

The Prophet Joseph Smith commented as follows on this scripture:

"It is generally supposed that sacrifice was entirely done away when the Great Sacrifice [i.e.,] the sacrifice of the Lord Jesus was offered up, and that there will be no necessity for the ordinance of sacrifice in the future; but those who assert this are certainly not acquainted with the duties, privileges and authority of the Priesthood, or with the Prophets.

"The offering of sacrifice has ever been connected and forms a part of the duties of the Priesthood. It began with the Priesthood, and will be continued until after the coming of Christ, from generation to generation. . . .

"These sacrifices, as well as every ordinance belonging to the Priesthood, will, when the Temple of the Lord shall be built, and the sons of Levi be purified, be fully restored and attended to in all their powers, ramifications, and blessings. This ever did and ever will exist when the powers of the Melchizedek Priesthood are sufficiently manifest; else how can the restitution of all things spoken of by the Holy Prophets be brought to pass. It is not to be understood that the law of Moses will be established again with all its rites and variety of ceremonies; this has never been spoken of by the prophets; but those things which existed prior to Moses' day, namely, sacrifice, will be continued." (*Teachings,* pp. 172-73.)

President Joseph Fielding Smith further explained that "we are living in the dispensation of the fulness of times into which all things are to be gathered, and all things are to be restored since the beginning. Even this earth is to be restored to the condition which prevailed before Adam's transgression. Now in the nature of things, the law of sacrifice will have to be restored, or all things which were decreed by the Lord would not be restored. It will be necessary, therefore, for the sons of Levi, who offered the blood sacrifices anciently in Israel, to offer such a sacrifice again to round out and complete this ordinance in this dispensation. Sacrifice by the shedding of blood was instituted in the days of Adam and of necessity will have to be restored.

"The sacrifice of animals will be done to complete the restoration when the temple spoken of is built; at the beginning of the millennium, or in the restoration, blood sacrifices will be performed long enough to complete the fulness of the restoration in this dispensation. Afterwards sacrifice will be of some other character." (*Doctrines of Salvation,* 3:94.)

Notes and Commentary for Doctrine and Covenants 128:24 contains additional insights into what else might be included in the offering of the sons of Levi.

# Revelation to David Whitmer

Section 14

## Historical Background

While Joseph Smith and Oliver Cowdery worked on the translation of the Book of Mormon at the Prophet's farm in Harmony, Pennsylvania, persecution began to increase, making it more and more difficult to finish the work. At this time Oliver Cowdery wrote to David Whitmer requesting him to come to Harmony to take him and Joseph Smith to the home of David's father, Peter Whitmer, Sr., who was a resident of Fayette, New York. They desired to reside with the Whitmer family while they completed the work of translation. Earlier Joseph Smith had become acquainted with Peter Whitmer and several members of the family. Oliver Cowdery had also been corresponding with David Whitmer while the Book of Mormon was translated. Through this correspondence the whole Whitmer family became acquainted with the work of the Restoration.

The Prophet Joseph Smith recorded that "in the beginning of the month of June, his [Peter Whitmer, Sr.,] son, David Whitmer, came to the place where we were residing, and brought with him a two-horse wagon, for the purpose of having us accompany him to his father's place, and there remain until we should finish the work. It was arranged that we should have our board free of charge, and the assistance of one of his brothers to write for me, and also his own assistance when convenient. Having much need of such timely aid in an undertaking so arduous, and being informed that the people in the neighborhood of the Whitmers were anxiously awaiting the opportunity

*The Peter Whitmer home, now restored, is the place where the Book of Mormon translation was completed*

to inquire into these things, we accepted the invitation, and accompanied Mr. Whitmer to his father's house, and there resided until the translation was finished and the copyright secured. Upon our arrival, we found Mr. Whitmer's family very anxious concerning the work, and very friendly toward ourselves. They continued so, boarded and lodged us according to arrangements; and John Whitmer, in particular, assisted us very much in writing during the remainder of the work.

"In the meantime, David, John and Peter Whitmer, Jun., became our zealous friends and assistants in the work; and being anxious to know their respective duties, and having desired with much earnestness that I should inquire of the Lord concerning them, I did so, through the means of the Urim and Thummim, and obtained for them in succession the following revelations: [D&C 14-16]." (*History of the Church,* 1:48-49.)

# Notes and Commentary

### D&C 14:1-7. "A Great and Marvelous Work Is about to Come Forth"

Several key concepts were repeated in some of the first revelations given to Joseph Smith. Notes and Commentary on Doctrine and Covenants 4, 6, and 11 discusses these concepts.

### D&C 14:7. Keep the Commandments and Endure to the End

In order for David Whitmer or any of God's children to have eternal life they must endure to the end, that is, remain faithful throughout their mortal probation. The scriptures are replete with this doctrine (see Matthew 10:22; 24:13; Mark 13:13; 1 Corinthians 13:7; 1 Nephi 13:37; 2 Nephi 9:24; 31:20; 3 Nephi 15:9; 27:16-17; D&C 10:69; 53:7; Articles of Faith 1:13; see also topical guide, s.v. "endure").

### D&C 14:8. "You May Stand As a Witness"

The Lord counseled David Whitmer to ask in faith and to be believing so that he would receive the Holy Ghost and also that he might see, hear, and know the truthfulness of the Book of Mormon. David's faith was sufficient, and he became one of the three special witnesses of the Book of Mormon.

### D&C 14:9-11. Who Are the Gentiles Referred to Here?

President Wilford Woodruff pointed out that Saints use the word *Gentiles* in a special way: "Sometimes our neighbors and friends think hard of us because we call them Gentiles; but, bless your souls, we are all Gentiles. The Latter-day Saints are all Gentiles in a national capacity. The Gospel came to us among the Gentiles. We are not Jews, and the Gentile nations have got to hear the Gospel first. The whole Christian world have got to hear the Gospel, and when they reject it, the law will be bound and the testimony sealed, and it will turn to the house of Israel. Up to the present day we have been called to preach the Gospel to the Gentiles, and we have had to do it. For the last time we have been warning the world, and we have been engaged in that work for forty-five years." (In *Journal of Discourses,* 18:112.)

# Revelations to John Whitmer and Peter Whitmer, Jr.

Sections 15-16

## Historical Background

See Historical Background for Doctrine and Covenants 14.

## Notes and Commentary

### D&C 15-16. The Inclusion of Personal Revelation in the Doctrine and Covenants

Elder John A. Widtsoe gave these insights about why personal revelations for specific individuals are included in the Doctrine and Covenants:

"The Doctrine and Covenants is a compilation of the revelations received by Joseph Smith to individuals and for the guidance of the Church. From the first years of the work the Prophet kept every scrap of paper pertaining to the progress of the work. In fact this care of things that must have seemed trivial is one of the evidences of the sincerity of the man. For example, when John and Peter Whitmer asked for help, he received for each of them a revelation, substantially the same: [D&C 15-16].

"This simple revelation is directed to the individual and at first sight has no permanent value for the Church. Yet as a revelation from God it was preserved and published. An insincere man could have eliminated this and other similar revelations as of little consequence. Not so with Joseph. The Lord had spoken. The words were part of the building of the kingdom of God, and the same advice would be useful to many men then and now." (*Joseph Smith*, pp. 251-52.)

*The Book of Commandments contained early revelations to Joseph Smith*

### D&C 15:2. What Does the Phrase "Mine Arm Is over All the Earth" Mean?

A man's arm represents his strength and power. Similarly, the phrase "arm of God" denotes in scripture his power and authority. The following references illustrate different ways this phrase is used: Doctrine and Covenants 1:14; 3:8; 35:8; Isaiah 52:10; John 12:38; 3 Nephi 9:14; see also Notes and Commentary on Doctrine and Covenants 1:14.

### D&C 15:3-5. "I Will Tell You That Which No Man Knoweth"

Earlier the Lord had given Oliver Cowdery a similar revelation concerning the thoughts and intents of his heart (see Notes and Commentary on D&C 6:16).

### D&C 15:6. "The Thing Which Will Be of the Most Worth unto You"

Elder Rudger Clawson, of the Quorum of the Twelve, commented on the significance of this revelation for all: "Cast your minds back to the early days of this Church, and there stood this man John Whitmer, recently come into the Church of Christ. Various occupations in which he might engage were before him. He had the opportunity to labor upon the farm, to engage in merchandising, to follow mining, to study the profession of medicine or law, or to adopt one of the many other occupations in which men employ themselves. The question he asked himself at that time was, What would be of the most worth to him? By his industry and thrift he might acquire the wealth of a Gould or a Vanderbilt; he might obtain a beautiful home, well furnished in every detail, and most desirable for the comfort and convenience of himself and family; he might obtain worldly renown in one of the professions, and by study and reflection become a skillful practitioner in medicine or a wise and able lawyer. I say, these opportunities were before him, because the country was before him, and this country is full of opportunities, which are within the reach of all. We live in a free country, and the way is open to you and to me, as it was to this man. He stood there in this situation, not having been trained long in the Gospel of Christ, and I say to you—for it is on record here—that a voice came to that man from the eternal worlds, and that voice set at rest in him every doubt, every dubiety, every fearful anticipation. At a critical time in his life, when he must choose which way to go, that voice said unto him that that which would be of most worth unto him was to declare repentance unto the people and bring souls unto Christ. The message was of such importance that it came to him with 'sharpness and with power.' It was the voice of Jesus Christ." (In Conference Report, Apr. 1901, p. 7.)

# Revelation to the Three Witnesses

Section 17

## Historical Background

As the translation of the Book of Mormon continued, the Prophet Joseph Smith recorded, "we ascertained that three special witnesses [see D&C 5:11-15] were to be provided by the Lord, to whom He would grant that they should see the plates from which this work (the Book of Mormon) should be translated; and that these witnesses should bear record of the same [see Ether 5:2-4; 2 Nephi 11:3; 27:12] . . . . Almost immediately after we had made this discovery, it occurred to Oliver Cowdery, David Whitmer and the aforementioned Martin Harris (who had come to inquire after our progress in the work) that they would have me inquire of the Lord to know if they might not obtain of him the privilege to be these three special witnesses; and finally they became so very solicitous, and urged me so much to inquire that at length I complied; and through the Urim and Thummim, I obtained of the Lord for them the following: [D&C 17]." (*History of the Church,* 1:52-53.)

*The Three Witnesses: Oliver Cowdery, David Whitmer, and Martin Harris*

## Notes and Commentary

### D&C 17:1. Obtaining God's Promises

The Prophet Joseph Smith described how the men who sought to be the Lord's witnesses to the Book of Mormon were granted this privilege:

"Not many days after the above commandment was given, we four, viz., Martin Harris, David Whitmer, Oliver Cowdery and myself, agreed to retire into the woods, and try to obtain, by fervent and humble prayer, the fulfilment of the promises given in the above revelation—that they should have a view of the plates. We accordingly made choice of a piece of woods convenient to Mr. Whitmer's house, to which we retired, and having knelt down, we began to pray in much faith to Almighty God to bestow upon us a realization of these promises.

"According to previous arrangement, I commenced by vocal prayer to our Heavenly Father, and was followed by each of the others in succession. We did not at the first trial, however, obtain any answer or manifestation of divine favor in our behalf. We again observed the same order of prayer, each calling on and praying fervently to God in rotation, but with the same result as before.

"Upon this, our second failure, Martin Harris proposed that he should withdraw himself from us, believing, as he expressed himself, that his presence was the cause of our not obtaining what we wished for. He accordingly withdrew from us, and we knelt down again, and had not been many minutes engaged in prayer, when presently we beheld a light above us in the air, of exceeding brightness; and behold, an angel stood before us. In his hands he held the plates which we had been praying for these to have a view of. He turned over the leaves one by one, so that we could see them, and discern the engravings thereon distinctly. He then addressed himself to David Whitmer, and said, 'David, blessed is the Lord, and he that keeps His commandments;' when, immediately afterwards, we heard a voice from out of the bright light above us, saying, 'These plates have been revealed by the power of God, and they have been translated by the power of God. The translation of them which you have seen is correct, and I command you to bear record of what you now see and hear.' " (*History of the Church,* 1:54-55.)

Joseph Smith then concerned himself with Martin Harris, who had departed from them: "I now left David and Oliver, and went in pursuit of Martin Harris, whom I found at a considerable distance, fervently engaged in prayer. He soon told me, however, that he had not yet prevailed with the Lord, and earnestly requested me to join him in prayer, that he also might realize the same blessings which we had just received. We accordingly joined in prayer, and ultimately obtained our desires, for before we had yet finished, the same vision was opened to our view, at least it was again opened to me, and I once more beheld and heard the same things; whilst at the same moment, Martin Harris cried out, apparently in an ecstasy of joy, ' 'Tis enough; 'tis enough; mine eyes have beheld; mine eyes have beheld;' and jumping up, he shouted, 'Hosanna,' blessing God, and otherwise rejoiced exceedingly." (*History of the Church,* 1:55.)

### D&C 17:1. What Did the Three Witnesses See?

Refer to the following scriptures: Joseph Smith—History 1:34-35; 1 Nephi 4:8-9; 16:10, 16, 26-30; 2 Nephi 5:14; Jacob 1:10; Ether 3:23-24, 28.

### D&C 17:3. Testimony Given by the Power of God

Though the Three Witnesses were privileged to see an angel and see and feel the plates, the real power of their witness came through the Holy Ghost. President Joseph Fielding Smith explained why: "Christ is the second person in the Godhead. But Christ has himself declared that the manifestations we might have of the Spirit of Christ, or from a visitation of an angel, a tangible resurrected being, would not leave the impression and would not convince us and place within us that something which we cannot get away from which we receive through a manifestation of the Holy Ghost. Personal visitations might become dim as time goes on, but this guidance of the Holy Ghost is renewed and continued, day after day, year after year, if we live to be worthy of it." (*Doctrines of Salvation,* 1:44; see also Luke 16:27-31; D&C 5:7-10.)

**D&C 17:3-4. The Lord's Law of Witnesses**

The Three Witnesses fulfilled an important law established by the Lord. Elder Bruce R. McConkie pointed out that "whenever the Lord has established a dispensation by revealing his gospel and by conferring priesthood and keys upon men, he has acted in accordance with the *law of witnesses* which he himself ordained. This law is: 'In the mouth of two or three witnesses shall every word be established.' (2 Cor. 13:1; Deut. 17:6; 19:15; Matt. 18:15-16; John 8:12-29.)

"Never does one man stand alone in establishing a new dispensation of revealed truth, or in carrying the burden of such a message and warning to the world. In every dispensation, from Adam to the present, two or more witnesses have always joined their testimonies, thus leaving their hearers without excuse in the day of judgment should the testimony be rejected." (*Mormon Doctrine,* p. 436.)

**D&C 17:4. Joseph Smith Preserved by the Testimony of Witnesses**

Lucy Mack Smith, the Prophet's mother, gave the following account describing Joseph's feelings after he returned home from the manifestation to the Three Witnesses: "When they returned to the house it was between three and four o'clock p.m. Mrs. Whitmer, Mr. Smith and myself, were sitting in a bedroom at the time. On coming in, Joseph threw himself down beside me, and exclaimed, 'Father, mother, you do not know how happy I am: the Lord has now caused the plates to be shown to three more besides myself. They have seen an angel, who has testified to them, and they will have to bear witness to the truth of what I have said, for now they know for themselves, that I do not go about to deceive the people, and I feel as if I was relieved of a burden which was almost too heavy for me to bear, and it rejoices my soul, that I am not any longer to be entirely alone in the world.' " (*History of Joseph Smith,* p. 152.)

**D&C 17:5. "Ye Shall Testify"**

The testimony of the Three Witnesses is given in the preface to the Book of Mormon.

Oliver Cowdery, David Whitmer, and Martin Harris never faltered in bearing testimony of the truthfulness of the Book of Mormon. As history attests, however, they did falter in other Church-related areas. David Whitmer left the Church and never came back. Oliver Cowdery and Martin Harris both left the Church but were eventually rebaptized and died in full fellowship. But even while they were out of the Church, all three continued to bear solemn witness of the reality of their experience on that day. They undoubtedly felt the weight of the Lord's warning to them to keep his commandments or the gates of hell would prevail against them.

Francis W. Kirkham wrote about Oliver Cowdery's death that "in the year 1878, David Whitmer said to Elders Orson Pratt and Joseph F. Smith concerning his departure: 'Oliver died the happiest man I ever saw. After shaking hands with the family and kissing his wife and daughter, he said, "Now I lay me down for the last time; I am going to my Savior"; and he died immediately, with a smile on his face.' " (*New Witness for Christ,* 1:248.)

The *Richmond Democrat* carried the following account of David Whitmer: "On Sunday evening, at 5:30 (Jan. 22, 1888), Mr. Whitmer called his family and some friends to his bedside, and addressing himself to the attending physician, said: 'Dr. Buchanan, I want you to say whether or not I am in my right mind, before I give my dying testimony.' The doctor answered: 'Yes, you are in your right mind, for I have just had a conversation with you.' He then addressed himself to all around his bedside in these words: 'Now you must all be faithful in Christ. I want to say to you all, the Bible and the record of the Nephites (Book of Mormon) is true, so you can say that you have heard me bear my testimony on my death-bed. All be faithful in Christ, and your reward will be according to your works. God bless you all. My trust is in Christ forever, worlds without end. Amen.' " (In Jenson, *Biographical Encyclopedia,* 1:270.)

The last testimony of Martin Harris was given to Elder William Harrison Homer, who was with him at the time of his death. Elder Homer recorded:

"The next day, July 10, 1875, marked the end. It was in the evening. It was milking time, and Martin Harris, Jr., and his wife, Nancy Homer Harris, had gone out to milk and to do the evening's chores. In the house with the stricken man were left my mother, Eliza Williamson Homer, and myself, who had had so interesting a day with Martin Harris at Kirtland. I stood by the bedside holding the patient's right hand and my mother at the foot of the bed, Martin Harris had been unconscious for a number of days. When we first entered the room the old gentleman appeared to be sleeping. He soon woke up and asked for a drink of water. I put my arm under the old gentleman, raised him, and my mother held the glass to his lips. He drank freely, then he looked up at me and recognized me. He said, 'I know you. You are my friend.' He said, 'Yes, I did see the plates on which the Book of Mormon was written; I did see the angel; I did hear the voice of God; and I do know that Joseph Smith is a Prophet of God, holding the keys of the Holy Priesthood.' This was the end. Martin Harris, divinely-chosen witness of the work of God, relaxed, gave up my hand. He lay back on his pillow and just as the sun went down behind the Clarkston mountains, the soul of Martin Harris passed on. . . .

(Signed) William Harrison Homer.

"Signed in the presence of Mrs. W. H. Homer, Joseph Homer, Leah Widtsoe, John A. Widtsoe." (In *New Witness for Christ,* 1:253-54.)

**D&C 17:8. "For My Grace Is Sufficient for You"**

After a man has done all that he can for himself, it is only by the grace of the Lord (that is, by his love, mercy, and condescension) that he can gain salvation (see 2 Nephi 11:24; 25:23). These three men were promised that if they would do all that they were instructed in this revelation, the Lord's grace is sufficient to ensure their salvation (see also 2 Corinthians 12:9; Ether 12:26-27).

President Joseph Fielding Smith taught that "we are all transgressors of the law to some extent, no matter how good we have tried to be—we are therefore unable in and of ourselves to receive redemption from our sins by any act of our own.

" . . . it is by the grace of Jesus Christ that we are saved." (*Doctrines of Salvation,* 2:309.)

# The Worth of a Soul

Section 18

## Historical Background

After John the Baptist had appeared and foretold the restoration of a higher priesthood (see D&C 13), the Prophet Joseph and Oliver Cowdery "now became anxious to have that promise realized to us, which the angel that conferred upon us the Aaronic Priesthood had given us, viz., that provided we continued faithful, we should also have the Melchizedek Priesthood, which holds the authority of the laying on of hands for the gift of the Holy Ghost. We had for some time made this matter a subject of humble prayer, and at length we got together in the chamber of Mr. Whitmer's house, in order more particularly to seek of the Lord what we now so earnestly desired; and here, to our unspeakable satisfaction, did we realize the truth of the Savior's promise—'Ask, and it shall be given you; seek, and ye shall find; knock, and it shall be opened unto you'—for we had not long been engaged in solemn and fervent prayer, when the word of the Lord came unto us in the chamber, commanding us that I should ordain Oliver Cowdery to be an Elder in the Church of Jesus Christ; and that he also should ordain me to the same office; and then to ordain others, as it should be made known unto us from time to time. We were, however, commanded to defer this our ordination until such times as it should be practicable to have our brethren, who had been and who should be baptized, assembled together, when we must have their sanction to our thus proceeding to ordain each other, and have them decide by vote whether they were willing to accept us as spiritual teachers or not; when also we were commanded to bless bread and break it with them, and to take wine, bless it, and drink it with them; afterward proceed to ordain each other according to commandment; then call out such men as the Spirit should dictate, and ordain them; and then attend to the laying on of hands for the gift of the Holy Ghost, upon all those whom we had previously baptized, doing all things in the name of the Lord. The following commandment will further illustrate the nature of our calling to this Priesthood, as well as that of others who were yet to be sought after: [D&C 18]." (*History of the Church,* 1:60-62.)

## Notes and Commentary

**D&C 18:1-4. The Lord's Testimony to Oliver of the Truth of the Work**

"In this revelation, Oliver Cowdery was informed that he had received a witness by the Spirit of Truth of the work, especially of the Book of Mormon. Many times during the translating of the record, manifestations of this kind had come to him. Not only had the Spirit made this truth manifest, but he had previous to this revelation stood in the presence of a heavenly messenger and under his hands received the Holy Aaronic Priesthood. Therefore, the Lord could say to him: 'I have manifested unto you by my Spirit in many instances, that the things which you have written (i.e., as scribe) are true; wherefore you know that they are true.' " (Smith, *Church History and Modern Revelation,* 1:81.)

**D&C 18:4-5, 17. What Is the Significance of the Words "My Church, My Gospel, and My Rock"?**

When the Lord refers to "his church," he is referring to the assembled believers and disciples who have taken upon themselves his name and covenanted to be obedient to his gospel (see D&C 10:67). The Lord defined his gospel in Doctrine and Covenants 39:6. The rock spoken of here and elsewhere is explained in Notes and Commentary on Doctrine and Covenants 11:24.

**D&C 18:8. How Is the Name *Joseph* Significant?**

"Attention is called to the name, because the Scriptures predict the coming of a great deliverer in the latter days, so named. Nephi says that Joseph, the Patriarch, predicted the coming forth of the House of Israel on the American continents, of a 'righteous branch' and a Seer, whose name, he said, 'shall be called after me' (Joseph), and after the name of his father (II. Nephi 3:1-15)." (Smith and Sjodahl, Commentary, p. 83.)

In Hebrew the name *yasaph* means "may God add sons" (see Genesis 30:24n). Great sons of God have borne this name: Joseph, the mighty son of Jacob, inheritor of the birthright of Israel; Joseph, the husband of Mary, the mother of Christ; Joseph Smith, Sr., the first Patriarch to the Church in these last days; Joseph Smith, the mighty seer to these last days; Joseph F. Smith, sixth President of the Church, who beheld the mighty hosts of Israel in vision (see D&C 138:38-46); and Joseph Fielding Smith, tenth President of the Church, a mighty preacher of righteousness in these last days. Surely the Lord has added great sons to Israel through the loins of Joseph, who saw the house of Israel bow before him (see Genesis 37:3-11).

### D&C 18:9. What Does It Mean to Be Called with the Calling of Paul?

"In New Testament times, the Savior called and ordained twelve men whom he called both disciples and apostles to be special witnesses for him. Later other men, including Paul, were called and ordained as apostles. In this revelation, the Lord announces that he is going to give some men in this dispensation the same powers and authority he gave anciently to Paul. (18:9.)" (Ludlow, *Companion,* 1:133-34.)

Brigham Young taught that Joseph Smith, Oliver Cowdery, and David Whitmer were the first Apostles of this dispensation (see *Journal of Discourses,* 6:320). To these, according to Heber C. Kimball, Martin Harris was later added (see *Journal of Discourses,* 6:29). These men were instructed to find and ordain twelve others who would form the Quorum of the Twelve.

### D&C 18:10-16. "The Worth of Souls Is Great"

Elder Rudger Clawson, of the Quorum of the Twelve, asked: "And how are we to determine the value of souls? This matter has been determined for us also by revelation. The souls of men are so precious in the sight of God that He gave to the world His Only Begotten Son, that by the shedding of His blood He might draw all men unto Him. That is why the great Prophet of this dispensation, Joseph Smith, and these others, John Whitmer, Oliver Cowdery, David Whitmer, and the rest, were called to bring souls unto Christ. And if one of these men should labor all his days, and bring save it be but one soul unto Christ, and that one should be his wife, what great joy he would have with his wife in heaven. Then if he should labor all his days and bring unto Christ the souls of his wife and his children, and none else perchance, how great would be his joy in heaven with his wife and children." (In Conference Report, Apr. 1901, pp. 7-8.)

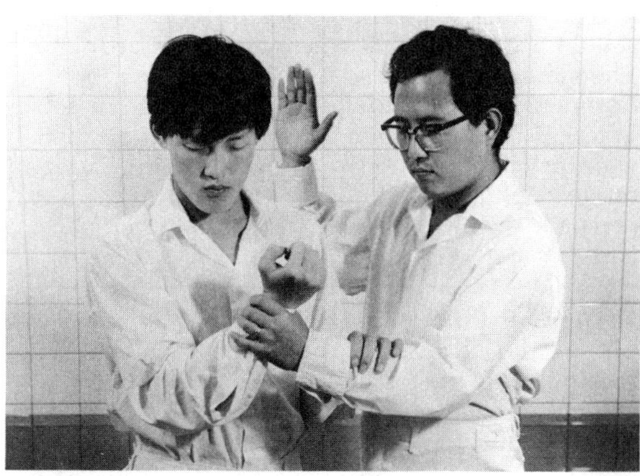

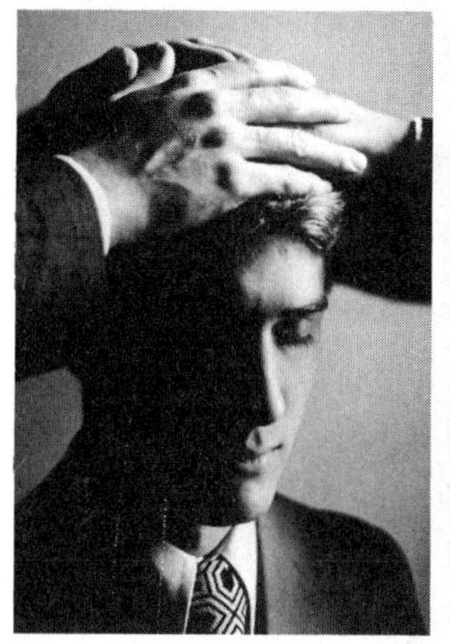

*"The worth of souls is great" (D&C 18:10)*

### D&C 18:20. What Is the "Church of the Devil"?

The use of the word *church* to describe the organization sponsored and directed by Satan has confused some people because they think of the term in the more limited sense of a specific religious organization. But if one thinks of the phrase "the church and kingdom of God," one has a better concept of what is meant by the church of the devil. It is his kingdom, the sphere of his influence, the whole of his area of power.

Elder Bruce R. McConkie explained that "the titles *church of the devil* and *great and abominable church* are used to identify all churches or organizations of whatever name or nature—whether political, philosophical, educational, economic, social, fraternal, civic, or religious—which are designed to take men on a course that leads away from God and his laws and thus from salvation in the kingdom of God" (*Mormon Doctrine,* pp. 137-38).

This definition explains why Nephi was taught that "there are save two churches only; the one is the church of the Lamb of God, the other is the church of the devil; wherefore, whoso belongeth not to the church of the Lamb of God belongeth to that great church" (1 Nephi 14:10). In the scriptures Satan's kingdom is called by various names: Babylon, the great and abominable church, the mother of harlots, the church of the devil, and the kingdom of the devil (see 1 Nephi 22:22; 2 Nephi 28:18-19; Mormon 8:28-38; D&C 10:56; 18:20).

It is, therefore, the obligation of the Saints to stand forth against evil wherever it may be found. The method of doing so is clear, according to President Joseph Fielding Smith: "All who go forth to teach should do so in wisdom and not contend with the churches or engage in profitless debates, but teach in the spirit of kindness and try to persuade people to receive the truth" (*Church History and Modern Revelation,* 1:83).

**D&C 18:20-21. Why Is It Improper to Contend?**
The word *contend* carries with it ideas of debate, striving, struggling, and even quarreling and disputing. The Savior taught that such a method of doing missionary work is contrary to gospel principles (see 3 Nephi 11:28-30). The Prophet Joseph Smith taught the same principle: "The Elders would go forth, and each must stand for himself . . . to go in all meekness, in sobriety, and preach Jesus Christ and Him crucified; not to contend with others on account of their faith, or systems of religion, but pursue a steady course. This I delivered by way of commandment; and all who observe it not will pull down persecution upon their heads, while those who do, shall always be filled with the Holy Ghost; this I pronounced as a prophecy, and sealed with hosanna and amen." (*History of the Church,* 2:431.)

**D&C 18:34-36. Hearing the Voice of the Lord**
Explaining how one hears the voice of the Lord, Elder S. Dilworth Young declared:

"In 1835 the Twelve were chosen, as you know, and on one occasion they were called together and given their instructions. Oliver Cowdery was the spokesman; and after having given them some very powerful and heartwarming instruction, so moved was he, himself, that he had to stop two or three times to weep. He finally read the revelation [now designated as section 18].

"Brigham Young was so impressed by it that he copied it in his laborious handwriting into his diary. I am impressed by it likewise. These are the words: [D&C 18:34-36].

"The thing that impresses me about this is, and I have never thought of it before, when I read a verse in the Doctrine and Covenants I am hearing the voice of the Lord as well as reading his words, if I hear by the Spirit.

"Now I have heard it said many times by men that they have often asked the Lord for a special testimony and oftentimes haven't had it. They seem to want to hear the voice of the Lord. I confess I have often wanted to hear the voice of the Lord, without knowing that all these years I have been hearing it with deaf ears. This woke me up." (In Conference Report, Apr. 1963, p. 74.)

**D&C 18:37-40. The Choosing of the Twelve Special Witnesses by the Special Witness of the Book of Mormon**
Joseph Smith was the first apostolic witness of the present dispensation. Oliver Cowdery, as noted in Doctrine and Covenants 20:3, was the second. David Whitmer and Martin Harris also became special witnesses. Thus, the original quorum of twelve special witnesses was called by the first special witnesses of the Restoration.

# The Gift of Repentance — Section 19

## Historical Background

President Joseph Fielding Smith gave the following background to this section: "This revelation was given some time in March, 1830 [in Manchester, New York]. It would seem that Martin Harris had come to Joseph Smith seeking further assurance in relation to his standing before the Lord, being sorely troubled in spirit because of his transgression. He had already been granted the privilege, on his earnest solicitation, of being one of the Three Witnesses, and that wonderful vision had been given. Perhaps out of this came much serious reflection and he sought further light. However, there is no indication in the *History of the Church* as to the reason why the revelation was given, and the exact day is unknown when it was given. It was without question a revelation of great comfort to Martin, and it is one of the great revelations given in this dispensation; there are few of greater import than this. The doctrine of the atonement of the Lord, as directly applying to the individual, and his exposition of 'Eternal Punishment,' as here set forth, give to the members of the Church light which was not previously known." (*Church History and Modern Revelation,* 1:85.)

## Notes and Commentary

**D&C 19:1. The Names of the Lord**
Smith and Sjodahl explained the significance of the names given here:

"Our Lord begins this Revelation by introducing Himself under five different names, each indicating His nature or work:

"*Alpha and Omega.* The first and the last letter of the Greek alphabet, used as symbols of the beginning and the ending. Christ is so called, because He is the Author and the Preserver of all things (Heb. 1:2, 10).

"*Christ the Lord.* 'Christ' means 'anointed.' Prophets, Priests, and Kings were anointed, and our Lord unites all these offices in Him. He is the anointed Lord. The Greek word Christ is the same as the Hebrew Messiah (Mashiac), the title used in John 1:41, and 4:25.

"*I am He.* This is equivalent to Jehovah (See notes on Sec. 18:21).

"*The Beginning and the End.* He was in the beginning and will remain throughout all eternities. He is endless (v. 4).

"*The Redeemer of the World.* Christ is our Redeemer. He delivers those who turn to Him from the bondage of sin and guilt. He has 'bought' us (I. Cor. 6:20; 7:23; II. Pet. 2:1). And the world will in due time be delivered from the power of Satan, from sin and all its consequences, such as war, poverty, ignorance, sickness, and even death." (Commentary, p. 91.)

**D&C 19:3. What Is Meant by the Phrase "End of the World"?**

Elder Bruce R. McConkie explained that this expression does not mean the end of the earth: "*The end of the world* is the end of unrighteousness or of worldliness as we know it, and this will be brought about by 'the destruction of the wicked' [JS—M 1:4]. When our world ends and the millennial era begins, there will be a new heaven and a new earth. (Isa. 65:17-25; D. & C. 101:23-24.) Lust, carnality, and sensuousness of every sort will cease, for it will be *the end of the world.*" (*Mormon Doctrine,* p. 848.)

**D&C 19:4-12. Great Additional Truths Concerning God's Punishments**

These verses provide one of the most important insights into the Judgment found anywhere in scripture. Elder James E. Talmage stated: "During this hundred years [of Church history] many other great truths not known before, have been declared to the people, and one of the greatest is that to hell there is an exit as well as an entrance. Hell is no place to which a vindictive judge sends prisoners to suffer and to be punished principally for his glory; but it is a place prepared for the teaching, the disciplining of those who failed to learn here upon the earth what they should have learned. True, we read of everlasting punishment, unending suffering, eternal damnation. That is a direful expression; but in his mercy the Lord has made plain what those words mean. 'Eternal punishment,' he says, is God's punishment, for he is eternal; and that condition or state or possibility will ever exist for the sinner who deserves and really needs such condemnation; but this does not mean that the individual sufferer or sinner is to be eternally and everlastingly made to endure and suffer. No man will be kept in hell longer than is necessary to bring him to a fitness for something better. When he reaches that stage the prison doors will open and there will be rejoicing among the hosts who welcome him into a better state. The Lord has not abated in the least what he has said in earlier dispensations concerning the operation of his law and his gospel, but he has made clear unto us his goodness and mercy through it all, for it is his glory and his work to bring about the immortality and eternal life of man." (In Conference Report, Apr. 1930, p. 97.)

**D&C 19:7. Is There a Difference between Eternal Punishment and Eternal Damnation?**

Elder Bruce R. McConkie explained the difference between these two terms:

"*Eternal damnation* is the opposite of eternal life, and all those who do not gain eternal life, or exaltation in the highest heaven within the celestial kingdom, are partakers of eternal damnation. Their *eternal condemnation* is to have limitations imposed upon them so that they cannot progress to the state of godhood and gain a fulness of all things.

"They 'remain separately and singly, without exaltation, . . . *to all eternity*; and from henceforth are not gods, but are angels of God *forever and ever.*' (D. & C. 132:17.) Their kingdom or progress has an 'end,' and they 'cannot have an increase.' (D. & C. 131:4.) Spirit children are denied to them to all eternity, and they inherit 'the deaths,' meaning an absence of posterity in the resurrection. (D. & C. 132:16-25.)

"They are never redeemed from their spiritual fall and taken back into the full presence and glory of God. Only the obedient are 'raised in immortality unto eternal life.' The disobedient, 'they that believe not,' are raised in immortality '*unto eternal damnation*; for they cannot be redeemed from their spiritual fall, because they repent not.' (D. & C. 29:42-44.)" (*Mormon Doctrine,* p. 234.)

**D&C 19:13-41. Instructions to Martin Harris**

"These verses contain special instructions to Martin Harris. Notwithstanding the many manifestations he had received concerning the Book of Mormon, he was still tormented with doubts, to such an extent that it became sinful. Skepticism has its legitimate use, in so far as it prompts one to investigate, but to doubt in the face of overwhelming evidence is perversity." (Smith and Sjodahl, Commentary, p. 96.)

**D&C 19:13-20. The Terrible Reality of Christ's Suffering**

Here, in a personal revelation of his own suffering, Jesus revealed how unbearable his pain was during the Atonement. Luke's is the only Gospel that mentions the blood during the agony of Gethsemane: "And his sweat was as it were great drops of blood" (Luke 22:44). For this reason many commentators have said Luke only used a metaphor, that it was not actually blood but only like blood. In this revelation Jesus dispelled that heresy once and for all. Suffering is the price paid for violating the laws of God. In the Garden the Savior paid that price for all the sins of the world.

Speaking of the extent of the suffering required of Christ, President Joseph Fielding Smith said:

"We cannot comprehend the great suffering that the Lord had to take upon himself to bring to pass this redemption from death and from sin. . . .

"We get into the habit of thinking, I suppose, that his great suffering was when he was nailed to the cross by his hands and his feet and was left there to suffer until he died. As excruciating as that pain was, that was not the greatest suffering that he had to undergo, for in some way which I cannot understand, but which I accept on faith, and which you must accept on faith, he carried on his back the burden of the sins of the whole world. It is hard enough for me to carry my own sins. How is it with you? And yet he had to carry the sins of the whole world, as our Savior and the Redeemer of a fallen world, and so great was his suffering before he ever went to the cross, we are informed, that blood oozed from the pores of his body." (In Conference Report, Oct. 1947, pp. 147-48.)

Similarly, Elder James E. Talmage wrote:

"Christ's agony in the garden is unfathomable by the finite mind, both as to intensity and cause. . . . He struggled and groaned under a burden such as no other being who has lived on earth might even conceive as possible. It was not physical pain, nor mental anguish alone, that caused Him to suffer such torture as to produce an extrusion of blood from every pore; but a spiritual agony of soul such as only God was capable of experiencing. No other man, however great his powers of physical or mental endurance, could have suffered so; for his human organism would have succumbed, and syncope would have produced unconsciousness and welcome oblivion. In that hour of anguish Christ met and overcame all the horrors that Satan, 'the prince of this world' could inflict. . . .

"In some manner, actual and terribly real though to man incomprehensible, the Savior took upon Himself the burden of the sins of mankind from Adam to the end of the world." (*Jesus the Christ,* p. 613.)

*"If they would not repent they must suffer even as I" (D&C 19:17)*

**D&C 19:13-21. "I Command You to Repent"**

Ludlow pointed out that "the heading of this section of the Doctrine and Covenants indicates that it is 'A Commandment of God' rather than referring to it only as a 'revelation' as is the usual format. Section 19 might thus be referred to as a revelatory commandment, for the revelation contains not only instruction but also a definite and clear commandment—to repent: 'I command you to repent' (verse 15), 'I command you again to repent' (verse 20), 'I command you that you preach naught but repentance' (verse 21).

"When the doctrine of repentance is fully understood, then it is seen that repentance is all that ever needs to be taught, for repentance means not only to stop doing those things which are wrong but also to start doing those things which are right." (*Companion,* 1:143; see also D&C 1:31-32; 58:42-43; 82:7.)

**D&C 19:24. "I Am Jesus Christ"**

Enrichment D, in the Appendix, discusses the Doctrine and Covenants as a witness for Christ.

**D&C 19:27. How Are the Lamanites a Remnant of the Jews?**

President Joseph Fielding Smith taught that "Lehi was a citizen of Jerusalem, in the kingdom of Judah. Presumably his family had lived there for several generations, and all of the inhabitants of the kingdom of Judah, no matter which tribe they had descended through, were known as Jews. . . .

"Not only in the Book of Mormon are the descendants of Lehi called Jews, but also in the Doctrine and Covenants. In section 19, verse 27, this is found: [D&C 19:27]. Again, in giving instruction to the elders who had journeyed from Kirtland to Missouri, the Lord revealed the place for the building of the temple and gave instruction for the purchase of land 'lying westward, even unto the line running directly between Jew and Gentile.' (Section 57:4.) This line westward was the dividing line between the whites and Indians." ("How Was Lehi a Descendant of the Jews?" *Improvement Era,* Oct. 1955, p. 702.)

The Mulekites in the Book of Mormon were of Judah (see Mosiah 25:2; Omni 1:14-19; Helaman 8:21), and present-day Lamanites share this heritage. Also, in the Book of Mormon *Jew* is sometimes used to mean the whole house of Israel (see, for example, 1 Nephi 15:17, 20).

**D&C 19:28, 38. The Commandment to Pray**

Elder Rudger Clawson, deeply impressed by these verses, said that "they enter into a man's life and comprehend his whole existence, at least from the years of his accountability until he passes into the grave. He must pray under all circumstances.

*It is a commandment to pray*

Prayer is not reserved for the Sabbath day or for any particular occasion. It is not only to be used at the general conferences of the Church, but the spirit of prayer must be in our hearts unceasingly. We must pray in our families; we must pray in secret; we must pray in our hearts. The spirit of prayer must be with us when we retire at night and when we arise in the morning. It must be upon us when we leave our homes for our daily employment; in the office; in the shop; in the field; in the mountains or in the valleys, or wherever we are. We are told . . . that if that spirit is upon us the Lord will bless us, and the blessings which will come in answer to prayer will be of more importance to us than treasures of earth." (In Conference Report, Apr. 1904, pp. 42-43; see also Alma 34:17-28; 3 Nephi 18:15; Matthew 26:41; D&C 10:5; 88:126.)

**D&C 19:29-32. Sharing the Gospel**

The Lord commanded Martin Harris to "declare glad tidings" of the restored gospel to all people he might be permitted to be among (D&C 19:29). All Saints are under the same obligation (see Mosiah 18:9-10). The Prophet Joseph Smith said, "After all that has been said, the greatest and most important duty is to preach the Gospel" (*Teachings,* p. 113).

For a discussion of the restoration of the gospel and the Saints' obligation to share the message through missionary work, see Enrichment A.

**D&C 19:37. What Is the Meaning of *Hosanna*?**

"*Hosanna* is a transliteration of a Hebrew (or Semitic) word that literally means 'save now' and that could be translated 'grant us salvation.' Most of the prayers said by the Jews at the Feast of Tabernacles begin with this word, and it was also used by the multitude as they greeted Jesus Christ when he came into Jerusalem during the last week of His life upon the earth. (Matt. 21:9, 15.) This term appears in five sections of the D&C—19:37; 36:3; 39:19; 109:79; 124:101." (Ludlow, *Companion,* 2:136.)

# The Articles and Covenants of the Church

Section 20

## Historical Background

This great revelation is associated with a number of firsts in Church history. In the first conference of the Church (9 June 1830) this revelation, along with what is now known as section 22, was read to the Church membership as "Articles and Covenants of the Church" and unanimously accepted by those present (see *Far West Record,* Archives of The Church of Jesus Christ of Latter-day Saints, Salt Lake City, p. 1). It thus became the first revelation given through Joseph Smith to be formally sustained by Church membership. In June 1832 "Articles and Covenants of the Church" appeared on the first page of the first issue of the *Evening and Morning Star,* the first newspaper published by the Church in this dispensation.

Section 20 is a very basic and concise treatment of doctrine, ordinances, and requirements for membership in The Church of Jesus Christ of Latter-day Saints. It reflects the use of the Book of Mormon and revelations previously given to Joseph Smith and also Oliver Cowdery's assisting Joseph Smith (see D&C 18:1-5).

Of this section the Prophet wrote: "In this manner did the Lord continue to give us instructions from time to time, concerning the duties which now devolved upon us; and among many other things of the kind, we obtained of Him the following [D&C 20], by the spirit of prophecy and revelation; which not only gave us much information, but also pointed out to us the precise day upon which, according to His will and commandment, we should proceed to organize His Church once more here upon the earth" (*History of the Church,* 1:64).

# Notes and Commentary

### D&C 20:1. Why Was the Church Organized on 6 April?

The Prophet Joseph Smith recorded that the Lord commanded them to organize the Church on 6 April 1830 (see *History of the Church,* 1:64). The importance of 6 April was explained by President Harold B. Lee: "April 6, 1973, is a particularly significant date because it commemorates not only the anniversary of the organization of The Church of Jesus Christ of Latter-day Saints in this dispensation, but also the anniversary of the birth of the Savior, our Lord and Master, Jesus Christ" (in Conference Report, Apr. 1973, p. 4; or *Ensign,* Apr. 1973, p. 2).

President Spencer W. Kimball commented that "the name Jesus Christ and what it represents has been plowed deep into the history of the world, never to be uprooted. Christ was born on the sixth of April. Being one of the sons of God and His Only Begotten, his birth is of supreme importance." (In Conference Report, Apr. 1975, pp. 3-4; or *Ensign,* May 1975, p. 4.)

The Prophet Joseph Smith, on the anniversary of the Church in 1833, recorded: "The day was spent in a very agreeable manner, in giving and receiving knowledge which appertained to this last kingdom—it being just 1800 years since the Savior laid down His life that men might have everlasting life, and only three years since the Church had come out of the wilderness, preparatory for the last dispensation" (*History of the Church,* 1:337).

*Peter Whitmer's home, place where the Church was organized*

### D&C 20:2-4. Why Was the Prophet Designated As the "First Elder" of the Church?

The propriety of having only one revelator for the Church explains why the Lord designated a "first" and a "second" elder in the early stages of the existence of the Church.

The Prophet Joseph Smith stated: "I will inform you that it is contrary to the economy of God for any member of the Church, or any one, to receive instructions for those in authority, higher than themselves; therefore you will see the impropriety of giving heed to them; but if any person have a vision or a visitation from a heavenly messenger, it must be for his own benefit and instruction; for the fundamental principles, government, and doctrine of the Church are vested in the keys of the kingdom" (*History of the Church,* 1:338).

Thus, if Joseph had not been clearly established as the head, confusion and problems could have arisen.

### D&C 20:5. What Is Meant by "Entangled Again in the Vanities of the World"?

The Prophet Joseph Smith described the time period involved and the activities referred to by the Lord: "During the space of time which intervened between the time I had the vision and the year eighteen hundred and twenty-three—having been forbidden to join any of the religious sects of the day, and being of very tender years, and persecuted by those who ought to have been my friends, and to have treated me kindly, and if they supposed me to be deluded to have endeavored in a proper and affectionate manner to have reclaimed me,—I was left to all kinds of temptations; and mingling with all kinds of society, I frequently fell into many foolish errors, and displayed the weakness of youth, and the foibles of human nature; which, I am sorry to say, led me into divers temptations, offensive in the sight of God. In making this confession, no one need suppose me guilty of any great or malignant sins. A disposition to commit such was never in my nature. But I was guilty of levity, and sometimes associated with jovial company, etc., not consistent with that character which ought to be maintained by one who was called of God as I had been. But this will not seem very strange to any one who recollects my youth, and is acquainted with my native cheery temperament." (*History of the Church,* 1:9-10.)

### D&C 20:9. Why Is the Book of Mormon Referred to As Having a "Fulness of the Gospel"?

"Our revelations say that the Book of Mormon contains the fulness of the gospel. (D. & C. 20:9; 27:5; 42:12; 135:3.) This is true in the sense that the Book of Mormon is a record of God's dealings with a people who had the fulness of the gospel, and therefore the laws and principles leading to the highest salvation are found recorded in that book." (McConkie, *Mormon Doctrine,* p. 333; see also 3 Nephi 27:13-20.)

### D&C 20:18-20. The Natural or Fallen Man

One of the basic questions that has troubled man throughout history has to do with the basic goodness or inherent evil of mankind. Is man by nature good or evil? Does he by virtue of his birth inherit some kind of original sin, or is he instinctively good? Those who argue that man is inherently wicked and his very nature sinful cite the abundant evidence of a world full of wickedness. Man has demonstrated a widespread tendency to be selfish, immoral, cruel, and greedy. Those who think man is basically good point out that if man is inherently evil by nature, then he would have had to inherit that evil from God, since he is His child. That is, of course, contradictory to all that is known of God's nature.

Even some Latter-day Saints are troubled by the controversy. They think that modern scriptures teach that man's nature is evil. King Benjamin taught that the "*natural* man is an enemy to God" (Mosiah 3:19; emphasis added), and Alma said that men had "become carnal, sensual, and devilish, by *nature*" (Alma 42:10; emphasis added). But section 20 in the Doctrine and Covenants, combined with these other scriptures, clearly teaches that the word *natural,* or *nature,* does not mean something inherent in man's eternal being, but refers to a state to which man has fallen through disobedience to God's law (see especially vs. 20; Alma 42:12).

The scriptural definition of "natural man" is fallen, disobedient man, and this "nature" (see Alma 42:10) can be overcome when a person "yields to the enticings of the Holy Spirit, and putteth off the natural man and becometh a saint through the atonement of Christ the Lord" (Mosiah 3:19).

Thus, as in so many other areas, the revelations of the Doctrine and Covenants clear up questions that trouble even the wisest of men.

### D&C 20:28. The Father, the Son, and the Holy Ghost Are One God

This passage has troubled some Latter-day Saints, since the Church teaches that there are three distinct, individual members of the Godhead. President Joseph Fielding Smith explained that both concepts are true: "It is perfectly true, as recorded in the Pearl of Great Price and in the Bible, that to us there is but one God [see Moses 1:6; Mark 12:32]. Correctly interpreted God in this sense means Godhead, for it is composed of Father, Son, and Holy Spirit. This Godhead presides over us, and to us, the inhabitants of this world, they constitute the only God, or Godhead. There is none other besides them. [See 1 Corinthians 8:5-6.] To them we are amenable, and subject to their authority, and there is no other Godhead unto whom we are subject. However, as the Prophet has shown, there can be, and are, other Gods." (*Answers to Gospel Questions,* 2:142.)

### D&C 20:30. How Does One Receive "Justification"?

Elder Bruce R. McConkie defined the law of justification as being "all covenants, contracts, bonds, obligations, oaths, vows, performances, connections, associations, or expectations (D. & C. 132:7), in which men must abide to be saved and exalted, [that] must be entered into and performed in righteousness so that the Holy Spirit can justify the candidate for salvation in what has been done. . . . *An act that is justified by the Spirit is one that is sealed by the Holy Spirit of Promise, or in other words, ratified and approved by the Holy Ghost.* This law of justification is the provision the Lord has placed in the gospel to assure that no unrighteous performance will be binding on earth and in heaven, and that no person will add to his position or glory in the hereafter by gaining an unearned blessing.

"As with all other doctrines of salvation, justification is available because of the atoning sacrifice of Christ, but it becomes operative in the life of an individual only on conditions of personal righteousness." (*Mormon Doctrine,* p. 408.)

### D&C 20:31. What Is "Sanctification"?

President Brigham Young explained what sanctification means to the Saints by declaring:

"I will put my own definition to the term sanctification, and say it consists in overcoming every sin and bringing all into subjection to the law of Christ. God has placed in us a pure spirit; when this reigns predominant, without let or hindrance, and triumphs over the flesh and rules and governs and controls as the Lord controls the heavens and the earth, this I call the blessing of sanctification. . . .

"All the Lord has called us to do is to renovate our own hearts, then our families, extending the principles to neighborhoods, to the earth we occupy, and so continue until we drive the power of Satan from the earth and Satan to his own place. That is the work Jesus is engaged in, and we will be co-workers with him. Do not suppose that we shall ever in the flesh be free from temptations to sin. Some suppose that they can in the flesh be sanctified body and spirit and become so pure that they will never again feel the effects of the power of the adversary of truth. Were it possible for a person to attain to this degree of perfection in the flesh, he could not die neither remain in a world where sin predominates. Sin has entered into the world, and death by sin. I think we shall more or less feel the effects of sin so long as we live, and finally have to pass the ordeals of death." (In *Journal of Discourses,* 10:173.)

### D&C 20:32. What Does It Mean to "Fall from Grace"?

Elder Theodore M. Burton said that this scripture, as he understood it, "means that Jesus Christ is kind and merciful to us when we serve him with our whole hearts, but not any of us can take refuge in past righteousness or service. It also means that there is a possibility that any one of us can fall out of good standing, even those who have already achieved a certain degree of righteousness. Therefore, we need to be on our constant guard, each of us, that we not allow ourselves to fall into habits of carelessness in our faith, in our prayers, or in our various Church activities or responsibilities. It is for this reason that I am resolving again to live closer to God each day and to follow his chosen prophets and apostles more diligently than I have ever done in the past." (In Conference Report, Oct. 1973, p. 153; or *Ensign,* Jan. 1974, p. 116.)

### D&C 20:37. What Does It Mean to "Come Forth with Broken Hearts and Contrite Spirits"?

President Joseph Fielding Smith defined both of these terms:

"*Contrition* is manifestation of a broken heart

with deep sorrow for sin, a realization of the nature of wrongdoing and a desire for forgiveness through the grace of God. A contrite spirit is essential to salvation." (*Religious Truths Defined*, p. 273.)

"What is a broken heart? One that is humble, one that is touched by the Spirit of the Lord, and which is willing to abide in all the covenants and the obligations which the Gospel entails." (In Conference Report, Oct. 1941, p. 93.)

**D&C 20:38. What Is Meant by "an Apostle Is an Elder"?**

"We learn at this time the Lord revealed that the designation 'Elder' is one applicable to the apostles and likewise to all others who hold the Melchizedek Priesthood. The use of this designation makes it needless to use unnecessarily sacred terms as 'Apostle,' 'Patriarch,' 'High Priest,' etc. It is proper in general usage to speak of the apostles, the seventies and all others holding the Melchizedek Priesthood as 'elders.' Of course, the term President, in speaking of the First Presidency, is the proper designation." (Smith, *Church History and Modern Revelation,* 1:95.)

**D&C 20:41. "The Baptism of Fire and the Holy Ghost"**

Elder Bruce R. McConkie outlined the importance of both kinds of baptism:

"To gain salvation every accountable person must receive two baptisms. They are the baptism of water and of the Spirit. (John 3:3-5.) The baptism of the Spirit is called the *baptism of fire and of the Holy Ghost.* (Matt. 3:11; Luke 3:16; 2 Ne. 31:13-14; 3 Ne. 11:35; 12:1-2; Morm. 7:10; D. & C. 20:41; 33:11; 39:6.) By the power of the Holy Ghost—who is the Sanctifier (3 Ne. 27:19-21)—dross, iniquity, carnality, sensuality, and every evil thing is burned out of the repentant soul as if by fire; the cleansed person becomes literally a new creature of the Holy Ghost. (Mosiah 27:24-26.) He is born again.

"The baptism of fire is not something in addition to the receipt of the Holy Ghost; rather, it is the actual enjoyment of the gift which is offered by the laying on of hands at the time of baptism. 'Remission of sins,' the Lord says, comes *'by baptism, and by fire, yea, even the Holy Ghost.'* (D. & C. 19:31; 2 Ne. 31:17.) Those who receive the baptism of fire are *'filled as if with fire.'* (Hela. 5:45.)" (*Mormon Doctrine,* p. 73.)

In addition, as Elder Harold B. Lee explained, "baptism by immersion symbolizes the death and burial of the man of sin; and the coming forth out of the water, the resurrection to a newness of spiritual life. After baptism, hands are laid upon the head of the baptized believer, and he is blessed to receive the Holy Ghost. Thus does the one baptized receive the promise or gift of the Holy Ghost or the privilege of being brought back into the presence of one of the Godhead, by obedience to whom and through his faithfulness one so blessed might receive the guidance and direction of the Holy Ghost in his daily walks and talks, even as Adam walked and talked in the Garden of Eden with God, his Heavenly Father. To receive such guidance and such direction from the Holy Ghost is to be spiritually reborn." (In Conference Report, Oct. 1947, p. 64.)

**D&C 20:57. What Is the Major Function of the Office of Deacon?**

With no specific responsibilities assigned to the office of deacon, "the duty of Deacons is to assist the Teachers. A Deacon holds the power and authority first bestowed in the Aaronic Priesthood. One who performs those duties well, thereby qualifies himself for the more advanced positions." (Smith and Sjodahl, Commentary, p. 108; see also Enrichments M and N, in the Appendix.)

**D&C 20:60. Why Didn't the Lord Make Known All Priesthood Offices When the Church Was First Organized?**

Said President Joseph Fielding Smith: "The Lord could not reveal to the Church in the beginning all the knowledge and organization which would be essential to the full and complete organization of the Church. Had this been done, it would have been like an overwhelming flood that would have brought destruction. The truth had to come piecemeal—line upon line, precept upon precept, just like knowledge comes to all of us. However, all that was revealed in this section was expedient for the government of the Church at the time of its organization." (*Church History and Modern Revelation,* 1:95.)

**D&C 20:61-62. The Purposes of Church Conferences**

President Harold B. Lee taught why conferences are so important to the Latter-day Saints: "Now, you Latter-day Saints, I think you have never attended a conference where in these three days you have heard more inspired declarations on most every subject and problem about which you have been worrying. If you want to know what the Lord would have the Saints know and to have his guidance and direction for the next six months, get a copy of the proceedings of this conference, and you will have the latest word of the Lord as far as the Saints are concerned." (In Conference Report, Oct. 1973, p. 168; or *Ensign,* Jan. 1974, p. 128.)

**D&C 20:65. The Principle of Common Consent**

See Notes and Commentary on Doctrine and Covenants 26.

**D&C 20:65. How Does One Sustain a Church Officer?**

President John Taylor explained the implications of sustaining a person to office:"What is meant by sustaining a person? Do we understand it? It is a very simple thing to me; I do not know how it is with you. For instance, if a man be a teacher, and I vote that I will sustain him in his position, when he visits me in an official capacity I will welcome him and treat him with consideration, kindness and respect and if I need counsel I will ask it at his hand, and I will do everything I can to sustain him. That would be proper and a principle of righteousness, and I would not say anything derogatory to his character. If that is not correct I have it yet to learn. And then if anybody in my presence were to whisper something about him disparaging to his reputation, I would say, Look here! are you a Saint? Yes. Did you not hold up your hand to sustain him? Yes. Then why do you not do it? Now, I would call an action of that kind sustaining him. If any man make an attack upon his reputation—for all men's reputations are of importance to them—I would defend him in some such way." (In *Journal of Discourses,* 21:207-8.)

**D&C 20:70. Why Are Little Children to Be Blessed before the Church?**

President John Taylor pointed out that in addition to this injunction's being "a direct command of Jehovah, and as such should be studiously complied with without hesitancy or objection, we think quite a number of excellent reasons can be adduced to prove that this command is attended with beneficial results to babe and to parents, who by bringing their child before the Church manifest their faith in the sight of their brethren and sisters, in God's word and in his promises, as well as their thankfulness to him for increasing their posterity and for the safe delivery of his handmaiden. The child is also benefited by the united faith and responsive prayers of the assembled Saints." (*Millennial Star,* 15 Apr. 1878, p. 235.)

**D&C 20:71. Why Aren't Infants Baptized?**

"Baptism is for the remission of sins, and no man can repent of a sin until he is accountable before God" (Smith, *Doctrines of Salvation,* 2:50; see also Moroni 8:5-26).

**D&C 20:73, 77, 79. Set Prayers**

The baptismal prayer and the two sacramental prayers are set prayers. A set prayer is one that is read or memorized and repeated word for word. That lack of flexibility gives added significance to these prayers: "These two set prayers are very dignified, spiritual, and beautiful, and merit our most careful attention and study. Notice that the emblems of our Lord's flesh and blood are to be taken in remembrance of His great sacrifice." (Sperry, *Compendium,* p. 97.)

**D&C 20:75, 79. Is Wine Acceptable for Sacramental Use?**

See Notes and Commentary for Doctrine and Covenants 27:1-4.

**D&C 20:83**

Enrichment I gives a more detailed treatment of the laws of the Church for dealing with transgressions committed by members.

# "His Word Ye Shall Receive, As If from Mine Own Mouth"

Section 21

## Historical Background

For over seventeen centuries the Church of Jesus Christ had been, as John the Revelator prophesied, in "the wilderness" because of apostasy (Revelation 12:14; see also D&C 86), and Christ's church had been corrupted by the doctrines of men.

On Tuesday, 6 April 1830, in the state of New York, a small group of people convened in the home of Peter Whitmer, Sr. No heads of nations were invited to this meeting, nor were the religious leaders of the day. No newspapers heralded the events of this meeting. But in heaven the angels rejoiced, and on earth this select group, under the direction of a modern prophet, organized the Church of Jesus Christ.

The meeting was opened by solemn prayer. Joseph Smith and Oliver Cowdery were sustained as leaders in the kingdom of God and were given unanimous approval to organize The Church of Jesus Christ of Latter-day Saints. The Prophet Joseph Smith recorded the events that ensued:

"I then laid my hands upon Oliver Cowdery, and ordained him an Elder of the 'Church of Jesus Christ of Latter-day Saints;' after which, he ordained me also to the office of an Elder of said Church. [Although they had been ordained to the Melchizedek Priesthood earlier, they were told to defer ordaining each other to the office of elder until the Church was organized (see *History of the Church,* 1:61).] We then took bread, blessed it, and brake it with them; also wine, blessed it, and drank it with them. We then laid our hands on each individual member of the Church present, that they might receive the gift of the Holy Ghost, and be confirmed members of the Church of Christ. The Holy Ghost was poured out upon us to a very great degree—some prophesied, whilst we all praised the Lord, and rejoiced exceedingly. Whilst yet together, I received the following commandment: [D&C 21]." (*History of the Church,* 1:77-78.)

## Notes and Commentary

**D&C 21:1. "There Shall Be a Record Kept among You"**

From the very day the Church was organized the Lord instructed his servants in the importance of keeping records of his revelations and in keeping a regular day-by-day history of the Church (see D&C 128:4-5; see also Notes and Commentary for D&C 47).

*An excerpt from the historical record preserved in Wilford Woodruff's journal*

### D&C 21:1. What Are the Special Spiritual Gifts of the One Called to Be the Lord's Prophet?

The following definitions may help clarify the special callings of the President of the Church:

*Seer.* Elder John A. Widtsoe defined a seer as "one who sees with spiritual eyes. He perceives the meaning of that which seems obscure to others; therefore he is an interpreter and clarifier of eternal truth. He foresees the future from the past and the present. This he does by the power of the Lord operating through him directly, or indirectly with the aid of divine instruments such as the Urim and Thummim. In short, he is one who sees, who walks in the Lord's light with open eyes. (Book of Mormon, Mosiah 8:15-17.)" (*Evidences and Reconciliations,* 1:205-6; see also Moses 6:36.)

*Translator.* The title "translator" may refer to one who has received two blessings given a prophet by the spirit of God:

1. The power to convert the written or spoken word into another language (see D&C 20:8).
2. The power to give a clearer meaning to a given language.

Through the gift of translation a prophet does not merely convey in the language of the reader the words that were recorded by the writer but by revelation preserves for the reader the thoughts or intent of the original writer.

*Prophet.* According to Elder Widtsoe, "A prophet is a teacher. That is the essential meaning of the word. He teaches the body of truth, the gospel, revealed by the Lord to man; and under inspiration explains it to the understanding of the people. He is an expounder of truth. Moreover, he shows that the way to human happiness is through obedience to God's law. He calls to repentance those who wander away from the truth. He becomes a warrior for the consummation of the Lord's purposes with respect to the human family. The purpose of his life is to uphold the Lord's plan of salvation. All this he does by close communion with the Lord, until he is 'full of power by the spirit of the Lord.' (Micah 3:8; see also D. & C. 20:26; 34:10; 43:16) . . .

"In the course of time the word 'prophet' has come to mean, perhaps chiefly, a man who receives revelations and directions from the Lord. The principal business of a prophet has mistakenly been thought to foretell coming events, to utter prophecies, which is only one of the several prophetic functions.

"In the sense that a prophet is a man who receives revelations from the Lord, the titles 'seer and revelator' merely amplify the larger and inclusive meaning of the title 'prophet.' " (*Evidences and Reconciliations,* 1:204-5.)

Scriptural insights into the role of a prophet are found in Exodus 4:15-16; 7:1-2.

*Apostle.* An Apostle is a special witness of Jesus Christ to all the world (see D&C 107:23). The Prophet Joseph Smith explained the important calling of an Apostle by asking a question and then giving the answer:

"What importance is there attached to the calling of these Twelve Apostles, different from the other callings or officers of the Church? . . .

"They are the Twelve Apostles, who are called to the office of the Traveling High Council, who are to preside over the churches of the Saints, among the Gentiles, where there is a presidency established; and they are to travel and preach among the Gentiles, until the Lord shall command them to go to the Jews. They are to hold the keys of this ministry, to unlock the door of the Kingdom of heaven unto all nations, and to preach the Gospel to every creature. This is the power, authority, and virtue of their apostleship." (*History of the Church,* 2:200.)

*Elder.* The name of an office in the Melchizedek Priesthood, *elder* is also the general title used to address one who bears this priesthood. Elder Bruce R. McConkie added that an elder is a representative of the Lord: "*What is an elder? An elder is a minister of the Lord Jesus Christ.* He holds the holy Melchizedek Priesthood. He is commissioned to stand in the place and stead of his Master—who is the Chief Elder—in ministering to his fellowmen. He is the Lord's agent. His appointment is to preach the gospel and perfect the Saints." ("Only an Elder," *Ensign,* June 1975, p. 66.)

### D&C 21:4-5. Whose Words Are the Saints to Receive As If from the Lord's "Own Mouth"?

President Joseph Fielding Smith answered that

question in this manner: "There has been much speculation in relation to the statement of the Lord to the Prophet Joseph Smith: 'For his word ye shall receive, as if from mine own mouth, in all patience and faith.' This is the word which the Lord gave to Israel in relation to Moses. It is just as true in the case of any other person who is sustained as the mouthpiece of the Almighty. Later, in speaking of his inspired servants, the Lord said: 'And whatsoever they shall speak when moved upon by the Holy Ghost shall be scripture, shall be the will of the Lord, shall be the mind of the Lord, shall be the word of the Lord, shall be the voice of the Lord, and the power of God unto salvation.' (D. & C. 68:4.) In this dispensation the same characteristics are shown by the people as were in ancient times. We are more inclined to accept as the word of the Lord something which was uttered in some former dispensation, but look with critical eye and unbelief upon that which the Lord delivers today through his chosen servants. Yet the word of the Lord is very clear on this matter. Let us not lose sight of the word of the Lord, that by hearkening to his chosen servant—and this is true whether it is Joseph Smith or some other President of the Church—'the gates of hell shall not prevail against us.' " (*Church History and Modern Revelation,* 1:107-8.)

### D&C 21:5. Why Might It Require Patience and Faith to Sustain the Lord's Prophets?

President Harold B. Lee warned of the special challenges in sustaining the prophet of the Lord:

"Now the only safety we have as members of this church is to do exactly what the Lord said to the Church in that day when the Church was organized. We must learn to give heed to the words and commandments that the Lord shall give through his prophet, 'as he receiveth them, walking in all holiness before me; . . . as if from mine own mouth, in all patience and faith.' (D&C 21:4-5.) There will be some things that take patience and faith. You may not like what comes from the authority of the Church. It may contradict your political views. It may contradict your social views. It may interfere with some of your social life.

" . . . Your safety and ours depends upon whether or not we follow the ones whom the Lord has placed to preside over his church. He knows whom he wants to preside over this church, and he will make no mistake. The Lord doesn't do things by accident. . . .

"Let's keep our eye on the President of the Church." (In Conference Report, Oct. 1970, pp. 152-53.)

### D&C 21:6. What Special Blessings Are Given to Those Who "Receive" the Lord's Servants?

In this verse three blessings are promised to those who give heed to the words of the prophet:

1. "The gates of hell shall not prevail against you." Elder Bruce R. McConkie gave the following explanation of this concept: "The gates of hell are the entrances to the benighted realms of the damned where the wicked go to await the day when they shall come forth in the resurrection of damnation. Those beckoning gates prevail against all who pass through them. But those who obey the laws and ordinances of the gospel have the promise that the gates of hell shall not prevail against them." (*Doctrinal New Testament Commentary,* 1:388-89.)

2. "God will disperse the powers of darkness from before you."

3. He will "cause the heavens to shake for your good."

### D&C 21:7. God's Prophet Leads the Cause of Zion—to Follow Him Is the Path of Safety

In verse 7 the word *him* refers to Joseph Smith, but this verse also applies to any other man who is given the keys to lead the Church. For the Saints in 1830 Joseph Smith was the prophet whom God inspired to move the cause of Zion. For the Saints in 1860, the one called "to move the cause of Zion" was Brigham Young. For the Saints in 1980, the one who had this calling was Spencer W. Kimball. The following two statements indicate why following the living prophets is the path of safety. Elder Delbert L. Stapley declared:

"I bear witness to you, my brothers and sisters, that God sustains him [the living prophet], and no one else in the world today but him, because he has the holy calling of prophet, seer, and revelator, representing the Lord upon the earth in our time. *He only has the right to revelation for the people of the Church,* and if all people would understand that, they would not be tossed about by those who would seek to divert their minds from the Church and its glorious principles. . . .

" . . . They will be fortified against false teachers and anti-Christs, and we do have them among us." (In Conference Report, Oct. 1953, p. 70; emphasis added.)

And Elder Harold B. Lee testified: "We are not dependent only upon the revelations given in the past as contained in our standard works—as wonderful as they are. . . . We have a mouthpiece to whom God does and is revealing his mind and will. God will never permit him to lead us astray. As has been said, God would remove us out of our place if we should attempt to do it. You have no concern. Let the management and government of God, then, be with the Lord. Do not try to find fault with the management and affairs that pertain to him alone and by revelation through his prophet—his living prophet, his seer, and his revelator." (*The Place of the Living Prophet* [ address delivered to seminary and institute of religion personnel], 8 July 1964, p. 16; emphasis added.)

The place of the living prophet is taught in several places in the Doctrine and Covenants. Enrichment F, in the Appendix, contains a complete treatment of this theme.

### D&C 21:7-8. He Shall Mourn for Zion No Longer

Though the sorrow Joseph Smith would experience in "moving the cause of Zion" (D&C 21:7) was not yet over—indeed, had hardly begun—the Lord had heard his pleadings for help in establishing the work. His sins were remitted, the Lord manifested his blessings on Joseph's work, and Joseph needed no longer to stand alone in carrying forth the kingdom. With the organization of the Church, the kingdom was set up. The stone cut out of the mountain without hands would now roll forth until Zion was fully established and filled the whole earth (see Daniel 2).

**D&C 21:11**

See Doctrine and Covenants 20:2-3.

# Baptism: A New and Everlasting Covenant

Section 22

## Historical Background

Some who had previously been baptized desired to become members of the Church without being rebaptized. President Joseph Fielding Smith commented on the problem of helping these new converts understand the concept of authority: "Immediately after the Church was organized, converts were made. Some of these had belonged to churches which believed in baptism by immersion. In fact, many of the early converts of the Church had previously accepted this mode, believing that it was right. The question of divine authority, however, was not firmly fixed in their minds. When they desired to come into the Church, having received the testimony that Joseph Smith had told a true story, they wondered why it was necessary for them to be baptized again when they had complied with an ordinance of baptism by immersion." (*Church History and Modern Revelation,* 1:109.)

In response to the situation, Joseph Smith inquired of the Lord and received section 22.

## Notes and Commentary

**D&C 22:1-4. How Important Is It to Have Priesthood Authority in Performing a Sacred Ordinance?**

Elder James E. Talmage explained how each dispensation must receive its own authority: "When the Lord established his Church amongst the Nephites upon this continent, he told those who were chosen and ordained, unto whom authority was given, just how to administer the ordinance of baptism. They were to say: 'Having authority given me of Jesus Christ, I baptize you in the name of the Father and of the Son, and of the Holy Ghost.' That does not give us in this age any such authority. The words that Christ spoke unto his apostles of old would be no authority unto the apostles today, nor unto any of the elders of the Church. I repeat, the words that he, the Lord, spoke unto the disciples who were chosen from among the Nephites would be no authority unto us; but in this day and age he has spoken again, and has given that same power and authority to speak in his name, and to administer the ordinances of the gospel, after the pattern that he has set; and therefore the elders and priests who take candidates, who have professed their faith, and who have repented of their sins, into the waters of baptism today, declare that they have authority given them; and, being commissioned of Jesus Christ, they baptize in the name of the Father and of the Son and of the Holy Ghost." (In Conference Report, Apr. 1924, p. 68.)

**D&C 22:1. What Is the "New and Everlasting Covenant"?**

The term *new and everlasting covenant* is used frequently throughout the Doctrine and Covenants. President Joseph Fielding Smith gave the following definition of it:

"The new and everlasting covenant is the fulness of the gospel. It is composed of 'All covenants, contracts, bonds, obligations, oaths, vows, performances, connections, associations, or expectations' that are sealed upon members of the Church by the Holy Spirit of promise, or the Holy Ghost, by the authority of the President of the Church who holds the keys. The President of the Church holds the keys of the Melchizedek Priesthood. He delegates authority to others and authorizes them to perform the sacred ordinances of the priesthood.

"Marriage for eternity is a new and everlasting covenant. Baptism is also a new and everlasting covenant, and likewise ordination to the priesthood, and every other covenant is everlasting and a part of the new and everlasting covenant which embraces all things." (*Answers to Gospel Questions,* 1:65.)

**D&C 22:4. "Enter Ye In at the Gate"**

Baptism is the gateway, or requirement, for entry into the celestial kingdom for anyone who has reached the age of accountability (see 2 Nephi 31:15-21). The ordinance of baptism, while absolutely essential, becomes valid only when it is accompanied by a corresponding change of life. To be born again suggests that one begins a new life, that he is a new person. Elder John A. Widtsoe described such a changed life: "I remember the man who baptized me into the Church, a very

*"Enter ye in at the gate" (D&C 22:4)*

common, ordinary man to begin with, a ropewalker with a jug of beer two or three times a day, a glass of whiskey a little later, and a cud of tobacco mostly all day long, living a useless, purposeless life, except for three meals a day, and the satisfaction of some of the carnal appetites. He heard the Gospel and accepted it. It was good. It was something he had been longing for. The man grew in power and stature in the Church. As I recall it, he filled five or six missions of the Church. He was the same man, with the same arms, same feet, same body, same mind, but changed because of the Spirit that comes with the acceptance of eternal truth. Have not we seen this in our own families and friends, in the little towns in which we live? Have not we felt our own strength grow mightier in love for our fellow men, in love for our daily tasks, in love for all the good things of life?" (In Conference Report, Apr. 1952, p. 34.)

**D&C 22:4. "Seek Not to Counsel Your God"**

Consider the following scriptures: Doctrine and Covenants 3:1-9; 63:55; 124:84; 136:19; Jacob 4:10; Mosiah 4:9; Isaiah 55:8-9.

# "Strengthen the Church Continually"

# Section 23

## Historical Background

In April 1830 at Manchester, New York, Oliver Cowdery, Hyrum Smith, Samuel H. Smith, Joseph Smith, Sr., and Joseph Knight, Sr., came to Joseph Smith to receive from him the mind and will of the Lord in their behalf. The Prophet consented to their request and received the revelation known as section 23. (See *History of the Church,* 1:80.)

When this revelation was first published in the Book of Commandments, it was divided into five parts comprising chapters 17 through 21. In all later editions, however, they were combined into one section.

## Notes and Commentary

**D&C 23:1-6. Early Church Leaders Received a Revelation**

President Joseph Fielding Smith wrote about each of the men mentioned in this revelation.

*Oliver Cowdery.* "First the Lord spoke to Oliver Cowdery, informing him that he was to beware of pride, lest thou shouldst enter into temptation. This was one of Oliver Cowdery's besetting sins. If he could have humbled himself in the troubled days of Kirtland he would not have lost his place and membership in the Church. That which had been bestowed upon him was exceedingly great and had he been willing to humble himself, it was his privilege to stand with the Prophet Joseph Smith through all time and eternity, holding the keys of the Dispensation of the Fulness of Times. However, at this particular time when this word was sought, he was free from condemnation. He was commanded to make known his calling to both the Church and also to the world, and while doing this his heart would be opened to teach them the truth from henceforth and forever. His great mission was to stand shoulder to shoulder with the Prophet Joseph Smith holding the keys of salvation for this dispensation. It was also his duty to bear witness to all mankind of the restoration of the Gospel." (*Church History and Modern Revelation,* 1:120-21.)

*Hyrum Smith.* "There is another thing of great significance in this brief blessing to Hyrum Smith (Sec. 23:3) which is: 'Wherefore thy duty is unto the church forever, and this because of thy family. Amen.' It is doubtful if the Prophet Joseph Smith understood the meaning of this expression when this revelation was given. In later years it was made clear. Evidently it has reference to the office of Patriarch." (Smith, *Church History and Modern Revelation,* 1:121.)

*Samuel Smith.* "To Samuel Smith the Lord said it was his duty also to strengthen the Church, although he was not yet called to preach before the world. It will be recalled that Samuel was the third person baptized in this dispensation. He was one of the first to be ordained to the office of Elder, and it was not long after this revelation when he was sent forth to teach, which he did with marked success, far beyond his own realization." (Smith, *Church History and Modern Revelation,* 1:121.)

*Joseph Smith, Sr.* "To Joseph Smith, Sr., who was so faithful and devoted to his son in the commencement of this marvelous work, the Lord said: He was not under any condemnation, and he also was called to exhort, and to strengthen the Church, and this was his duty from henceforth and forever" (Smith, *Church History and Modern Revelation,* 1:121).

*Samuel Smith was the first missionary of the last dispensation*

*Joseph Knight, Sr.* "It is quite possible that Joseph Knight, before he joined the Church, was not given to prayer to any great extent. He was a Universalist with very liberal views. This revelation was given before he had united himself with the Church. He was baptized at the time the enemies destroyed the dam in Colesville, following the first conference of the Church." (Smith, *Church History and Modern Revelation,* 1:122.)

Newell Knight, the son of Joseph Knight, also found it difficult to pray.

### D&C 23:6. What Does It Mean to Take Up the Cross?

Ludlow explained that "the term *take up your cross* is found in both ancient and modern scripture, including at least three references in the Doctrine and Covenants (23:6; 56:2; 112:14). In Matthew 16:24 the Savior says, 'If any man will come after me, let him deny himself, and take up his cross, and follow me.' The Inspired Version of the Bible provides the meaning of this term as given by Jesus Christ himself: 'And now for a man to take up his cross, is to deny himself all ungodliness, and every worldly lust, and keep my commandments.' (Matt. 16:25-26.)" (*Companion,* 2:56.)

Elder James E. Talmage wrote: "The cross to be taken up may be heavy, perhaps to be dragged because too burdensome to be borne. We are apt to assume that self-denial is the sole material of our cross; but this is true only as we regard self-denial in its broadest sense, comprising both positive and negative aspects. One man's cross may consist mostly in refraining from doings to which he is inclined, another's in doing what he would fain escape. One's besetting sin is evil indulgence; his neighbor's a lazy inattention to the activities required by the Gospel of Jesus Christ, coupled perchance with puritanical rigor in other observances." (*Vitality of Mormonism,* p. 339; see also Notes and Commentary on D&C 56:2.)

# "Declare My Gospel As with the Voice of a Trump"

Section 24

## Historical Background

During the month of April 1830, Joseph Smith spent time at the home of Joseph Knight, Sr., of Colesville, New York. The Knights were willing to hear Joseph Smith's message. While there, the Prophet cast out an evil spirit from Newel Knight, one of Joseph Knight's sons. (See *History of the Church,* 1:82-83.) Most of those who witnessed the miracle eventually sought baptism. This result increased opposition, which manifested itself in efforts to prevent baptisms and in involving the Prophet in many vexatious lawsuits based on trumped-up charges. Although he was adequately defended and acquitted of the charges, much time was lost. (See *History of the Church,* 1:88-89, 95-96.) He was faced with the responsibility of caring for his family and at the same time leading, counseling, and directing the newly organized Church.

After the Prophet returned from Colesville, New York, to his home in Harmony, Pennsylvania, the Lord gave him what is now known as section 24. Joseph did not record a specific reason for this

*The gospel is to be proclaimed "as with the voice of a trump" (D&C 24:12)*

revelation, but the courtroom experiences certainly made him aware that efforts were being made to absorb his time and prevent, if possible, progress of the great latter-day movement.

## Notes and Commentary

### D&C 24:1. "Thou Hast Been Delivered"

The mention of blessings and deliverance in the past was a reminder to the Prophet Joseph Smith as he contemplated the vastness of his call and witnessed the marshaled forces working in opposition. He must have experienced some of the feelings of Enoch (see Moses 6:31) and of Moses (see Exodus 4:1) and of many others who have been called to perform a work beyond human capacity. (See *History of the Church,* 1:86.)

### D&C 24:3-9. "And They Shall Support Thee"

In addition to his many responsibilities in the Church, Joseph Smith had a family, and he could not neglect them, although his responsibility was chiefly a spiritual one. Although not completely relieved from responsibility for his temporal needs at that time, the Prophet was told by the Lord to look to the Church for temporal support. Elder Bruce R. McConkie commented about those who are asked to give full-time service to the Church:

"All our service in God's kingdom is predicated on his eternal law which states: 'The laborer in Zion shall labor for Zion; for if they labor for money they shall perish.' (2 Ne. 26:31.)

"We know full well that the laborer is worthy of his hire, and that those who devote all their time to the building up of the kingdom must be provided with food, clothing, shelter, and the necessaries of life. We must employ teachers in our schools, architects to design our temples, contractors to build our synagogues, and managers to run our businesses. But those so employed, along with the whole membership of the Church, participate also on a freewill and voluntary basis in otherwise furthering the Lord's work. Bank presidents work on welfare projects. Architects leave their drafting boards to go on missions. Contractors lay down their tools to serve as home teachers or bishops. Lawyers put aside *Corpus Juris* and the Civil Code to act as guides on Temple Square. Teachers leave the classroom to visit the fatherless and widows in their afflictions. Musicians who make their livelihood from their artistry willingly direct church choirs and perform in church gatherings. Artists who paint for a living are pleased to volunteer their services freely." (In Conference Report, Apr. 1975, p. 77; or *Ensign,* May 1975, p. 52.)

Temporal support from the members is probably only part of what is implied in these verses, however. The members were encouraged to support and sustain the Prophet in every possible way.

### D&C 24:3-9. "In Temporal Labors Thou Shalt Not Have Strength"

"The Prophet Joseph's gifts were of a spiritual, not financial nature, but the Lord promised him that, if he would magnify his calling, he would always have what he needed. Financial ability is also a gift that can be used for the glory of God, but the Prophet was not a financier. He did not live for the accumulation of wealth. The Kingdom of God was his first and chief concern." (Smith and Sjodahl, Commentary, p. 124.)

### D&C 24:10. "Continue in Bearing My Name before the World"

All persons who are baptized as members of the Church covenant to take upon them the name of Christ and be known as Christians. They thus bear witness to all others by their words and deeds concerning the Savior and his mission (see D&C 20:69).

### D&C 24:13-14. "Require Not Miracles"

Oliver Cowdery was commanded to avoid requiring miracles outside of those associated with the preaching of the gospel unless commanded of the Lord (see Matthew 10:8; Mark 16:17-18; D&C 84:66-72). It is expected that priesthood holders acting properly will do works of the priesthood (see D&C 63:7-12).

The miracles mentioned by the Lord in verse 13

are identical to the signs mentioned in Mark 16:16-20; Mormon 9:24-25; and Doctrine and Covenants 84:64-72. They are gifts of the Spirit (Holy Ghost) bestowed upon those who believe and obey the gospel of Christ and are intended not to convert people to the truth but to bless those who are already converted. By requiring the person who is in need of having a miracle performed request that it be done, the scriptures are fulfilled, that is, the miracle is performed in behalf of one who believes and is, therefore, a sign of his faith.

**D&C 24:15. "Ye Shall Leave a Cursing"**

Cursings as well as blessings may be administered by the power and authority of the priesthood (see D&C 124:93) and include the sealing up of the unbelieving and rebellious to punishment (see D&C 1:8-9). The act of cleansing the feet as a testimony against those who reject the servants of the Lord is an ordinance of cursing and is not just a demonstration that a witness of the truth has been given and has been rejected. Through this cleansing ordinance, those who rejected the truth are on their own, and those who preached the gospel to them are no longer responsible for them before the Lord (see D&C 88:81-82). It is apparent in this and other scriptures given later in the Doctrine and Covenants that this ordinance is to be performed only when the Lord expressly commands it (see also D&C 75:20-22).

**D&C 24:19. Pruning the Vineyard**

"In this dispensation the Lord's vineyard covers the whole earth, and the laborers are going forth to gather scattered Israel before the appointed day of burning when the vineyard will be purified of corruption. (D. & C. 33:2-7; 72:2; 75:2-5; 101:44-62; 135:6.)" (McConkie, *Mormon Doctrine,* p. 452.)

The imagery in this passage is similar to that used in the allegory of the olive tree (see Jacob 5).

# "An Elect Lady"

Section 25

## Historical Background

It had been just over three years since the Prophet Joseph Smith and Emma Hale had been married in the small village of South Bainbridge, New York. Joseph was now twenty-five years of age and Emma twenty-six.

The seventh of nine children born to Isaac and Elizabeth Hale, Emma was born on 10 July 1804 in Harmony, Pennsylvania. There the Prophet met and courted her while he was working for Josiah Stowell. It is reported that Emma was a beautiful woman with an attractive personality, and she had the reputation of being a refined and dignified woman who was an excellent housekeeper and cook. Her Methodist upbringing had helped her develop a great love of music.

The first three years for the newly married couple were indeed tense and trying ones. Eight months after their marriage Joseph received the golden plates from the angel Moroni. From that moment on their lives were punctuated with persecution and trial. Emma passed through these trying experiences with her husband. She was at his side during those agonizing months when Joseph lost the gift to translate. She served as his scribe for a while. Her heart must have ached when the Prophet was arrested on trumped-up charges again and again. (See Historical Background for D&C 24.) She traveled with the Prophet on many of his missionary journeys and shared with him the joy and sorrow associated with the preaching of the gospel. Emma was a woman of great courage and strong will. Of her the Prophet's mother, Lucy Mack Smith, wrote: "I have never seen a woman in my life, who would endure every species of fatigue and hardship, from month to month, and from year to year, with that unflinching courage, zeal, and patience, which she has ever done; for I know that which she has had to endure . . . she has breasted the storms of persecution, and buffeted the rage of men and devils, which would have borne down almost any other woman." (*History of Joseph Smith,* pp. 190-91.)

Now, in July of 1830, possibly near her birthday, the Lord directed to Emma a revelation known as section 25 of the Doctrine and Covenants.

## Notes and Commentary

**D&C 25:1. "Sons and Daughters in My Kingdom"**

Jesus identified himself in this verse as "the Lord your God," which is a name-title of the Savior. In this verse he acknowledged Emma Smith as his daughter. The scriptures clearly teach the doctrine that all those who make the covenants of baptism can be born again into the kingdom of God and become sons or daughters of the Savior because they are "spiritually begotten" by him (see, for example, Mosiah 5:7; Moses 6:64-68). Such persons are distinguished from all the other children of God who live on this earth through the reception of these covenants. Those who will not enter into such covenants are called the sons and daughters of men (see Moses 8:14-15), and others who sin to the extent that Cain did are called sons of perdition (see Moses 5:24; D&C 76:31-32).

### D&C 25:3. In What Sense Was Emma "an Elect Lady"?

Emma had received a call to serve as a companion and helpmeet to Joseph Smith, the Prophet of the Restoration. In this revelation she was also called as an elect lady. Later she received an additional responsibility when the Prophet Joseph Smith organized the Relief Society on 17 March 1842. The Prophet wrote: "I assisted in commencing the organization of 'The Female Relief Society of Nauvoo' in the Lodge Room. Sister Emma Smith, President, and Sister Elizabeth Ann Whitney and Sarah M. Cleveland, Counselors. I gave much instruction, read in the New Testament, and Book of Doctrine and Covenants, concerning the Elect Lady, and showed that the elect meant to be elected to a certain work, &c., and that the revelation was then fulfilled by Sister Emma's election to the Presidency of the Society, she having previously been ordained to expound the Scriptures." (*History of the Church,* 4:552-53.)

### D&C 25:4. Why Did Emma Murmur?

This section of the Doctrine and Covenants offers some insights into the particular challenges Emma Smith faced. Verse 14 and the following passage by President Joseph Fielding Smith are significant: "Emma Smith was human, possessing many of the characteristics which are found in most of us. Being the wife of the man whom the Almighty had blessed, she felt, as most women would have felt under like circumstances, that she was entitled to some special favors. It was difficult for her to understand why she could not view the plates, the Urim and Thummim, and other sacred things, which view had been given to special witnesses. At times this human thought caused her to murmur and ask the question of the Prophet why she was denied this privilege." (*Church History and Modern Revelation,* 1:125.)

### D&C 25:7. What Is the Meaning of the Word Ordained As It Is Used in This Verse?

"The term 'ordain' was used generally in the early days of the Church in reference to both ordination and setting apart, and, too, correctly according to the meaning of the word. Men holding the Priesthood were said to have been 'ordained' to preside over branches and to perform special work. Sisters also were said to have been 'ordained' when they were called to some special duty or responsibility. In later years we developed a distinction between ordain and setting apart. Men are ordained to offices in the Priesthood and set apart to preside over stakes, wards, branches, missions, and auxiliary organizations. The sisters are set apart—not ordained—as presidents of auxiliary organizations, to missions, etc. This saying that Emma Smith was 'ordained' to expound scripture, does not mean that she had conferred upon her the Priesthood, but that she was set apart to this calling, which found its fulfillment in the Relief Society of the Church." (Smith, *Church History and Modern Revelation,* 1:126.)

### D&C 25:7. How Does Emma's Calling to Exhort the Church Relate to the Apostle Paul's Statement That Women Are Not to "Speak" in Church?

The correct meaning of the statement of the Apostle Paul that women should not speak in church (see 1 Corinthians 14:34-35) was given in the Prophet Joseph Smith's revision of the Bible. The Prophet changed this verse to say that women are not to "rule" in the Church. The evident meaning of the passage is that women are to be directed in the Church by the priesthood. This principle was stated by the Prophet Joseph Smith to the members of the first Relief Society: "You will receive instructions through the order of the Priesthood which God has established, through the medium of those appointed to lead, guide and direct the affairs of the Church in this last dispensation; and I now turn the key in your behalf in the name of the Lord, and this Society shall rejoice, and knowledge and intelligence shall flow down from this time henceforth; this is the beginning of better days to the poor and needy, who shall be made to rejoice and pour forth blessings on your heads." (*History of the Church,* 4:607.)

Emma Smith's calling to exhort the Church was in complete harmony with her future calling, under the direction of the priesthood, in the Relief Society.

### D&C 25:11. Emma Smith Was Called to Compile the First Book of Hymns

President Joseph Fielding Smith explained the

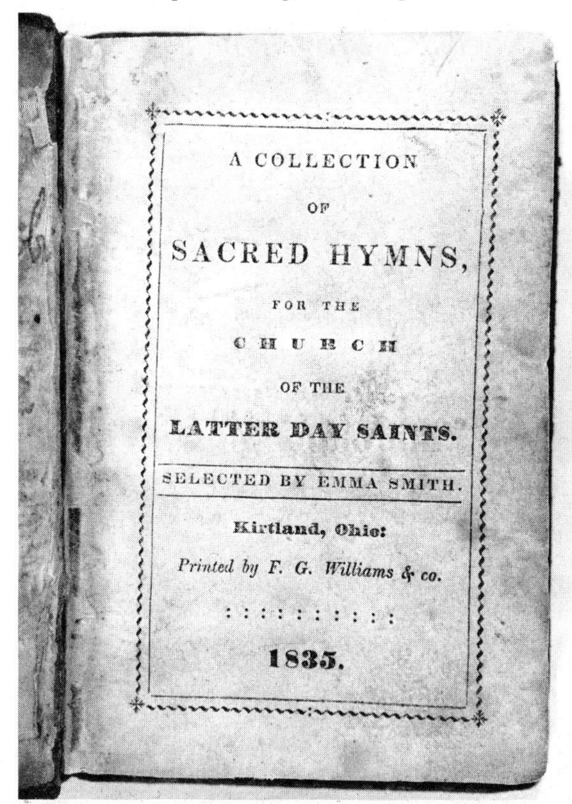
A COLLECTION

OF

SACRED HYMNS,

FOR THE

CHURCH

OF THE

LATTER DAY SAINTS.

SELECTED BY EMMA SMITH.

Kirtland, Ohio:

*Printed by F. G. Williams & co.*

1835.

*"The song of the righteous is a prayer unto me" (D&C 25:12)*

significance of this assignment given to Emma: "The necessity of having a book of hymns became apparent at the time of the organization of the Church, and while Emma Smith may have felt she had been slighted in not having the privilege of viewing the plates, yet it was a signal honor to her to be called to be an 'elect lady' and preside over the women in the Church in matters of relief, to have the privilege of divine appointment to expound scriptures in the Church, and also to be chosen to select hymns to be published for the use of the Church. Evidently she had talent for this work. That talent is shown in the selection which was made. With the help of Elder William W. Phelps she went to work, and a selection of hymns was made, but it was not published until 1835. Wisdom and discretion are shown in this compilation. The title page of the book is as follows: 'A Collection of Sacred Hymns for the Church of the Latter-day Saints. Selected by Emma Smith, Kirtland, Ohio. Printed by F. G. Williams & Co., 1835.' In this collection are found, because of lack of Latter-day Saint composers, many sectarian hymns, but it also contains a goodly number of hymns by William W. Phelps, Parley P. Pratt and Eliza R. Snow." (*Church History and Modern Revelation,* 1:126.)

This first hymnal contained 90 selections; the second, published in 1841, contained 340 hymns. The first hymn book classified the selections as mourning hymns, farewell hymns, evening hymns, hymns on baptism, sacramental hymns, and hymns for marriage. Some of the first selections made by Emma Smith are among the favorites today of Latter-day Saints. These include "The Spirit of God Like a Fire Is Burning," "I Know That My Redeemer Lives," "Redeemer of Israel," and "How Firm a Foundation." (See Doxey, *Doctrine and Covenants Speaks,* 1:152-53.)

**D&C 25:12. "The Song of the Righteous Is a Prayer"**

What is a song of the heart? In what way might feelings of the heart be associated with true worship?

Writing on the importance of music, Elder Bruce R. McConkie said:

"Music is given of God to further his purposes. Sweet melodies mellow the souls of men and help prepare them for the *gospel.* After men receive the truth, *songs of praise* to Deity help to sanctify and cleanse their souls. It follows that the best and greatest music is that in which, by both note and word, God is praised and his truths are extolled. On the other hand, music can be used for sensuous and carnal purposes. To accomplish the Lord's aims both word and melody must be edifying and lead to wholesome thoughts and emotions. There is vulgar as well as virtuous music.

"Wholesome light music designed primarily to entertain has its place. So do the heavy classical presentations that appeal to the more musically gifted. But in meetings set apart to worship the Lord, the saints should sing songs which teach the gospel and enhance faith. Beautiful melodies alone do not suffice; the word-message must also conform to true principles. Truths taught in the hymns should be as accurately presented as they are in the scriptures themselves." (*Mormon Doctrine,* p. 521; emphasis added; see also D&C 45:71; 136:28; 1 Corinthians 14:26; Ephesians 5:18-19.)

Elder Boyd K. Packer suggested that inspiring music can become a source of spiritual power in one's life:

"This is what I would teach you. Choose from among the sacred music of the Church a favorite hymn, one with words that are uplifting and music that is reverent, one that makes you feel something akin to inspiration. Remember President Lee's counsel: perhaps 'I am a Child of God' would do. Go over it in your mind carefully. Memorize it. Even though you have had no musical training, you can think through a hymn.

"Now, use this hymn as the place for your thoughts to go. Make it your emergency channel. Whenever you find these shady actors have slipped from the sidelines of your thinking onto the stage of your mind, put on this record, as it were.

"As the music begins and as the words form in your thoughts, the unworthy ones will slip shamefully away. It will change the whole mood on the stage of your mind. Because it is uplifting and clean, the baser thoughts will disappear. For while virtue, by choice, *will not* associate with filth, evil *cannot* tolerate the presence of light.

"In due time you will find yourself, on occasion, humming the music inwardly. As you retrace your thoughts, you discover some influence from the world about you encouraged an unworthy thought to move on stage in your mind, and the music almost automatically began. . . .

"There are many references in the scriptures, both ancient and modern, that attest to the influence of righteous music. The Lord, Himself, was prepared for His greatest test through its influence, for the scripture records: 'And when they had sung an hymn, they went out into the mount of Olives.' (Mark 14:26.)" (In Conference Report, Oct. 1973, pp. 24-25; or *Ensign,* Jan. 1974, p. 28.)

**D&C 25:16. "This Is My Voice unto All"**

The final admonition suggests that while the revelation was given specifically to Emma Smith, it has application to all, especially all women. Several points describe how an elect lady in any time or place functions:

1. Comfort husband in affliction (see vs. 5)
2. Expound scripture by Spirit (see vs. 7)
3. Exhort the Church by the Spirit (see vs. 7)
4. Give time to writing and learning much (see vs. 8)
5. Be supported by husband in the Church (see vs. 9)
6. Lay aside things of the world (see vs. 10)
7. Seek for things of a better world (see vs. 10)
8. Select sacred hymns (see vs. 11; see also Notes and Commentary on D&C 25:12)
9. Lift up thy heart and rejoice (see vs. 13)
10. "Cleave unto the covenants" (vs. 13)
11. "Continue in the spirit of meekness" (vs. 14)

12. "Beware of pride" (vs. 14)

13. "Let thy soul delight in thy husband and the glory which shall come upon him" (vs. 14)

14. Keep the commandments continually (see vs. 15)

Elder Neal A. Maxwell said of women and their importance in the Lord's plan:

"We know so little, brothers and sisters, about the reasons for the division of duties between womanhood and manhood as well as between motherhood and priesthood. These were divinely determined in another time and another place. We are accustomed to focusing on the men of God because theirs is the priesthood and leadership line. But paralleling that authority line is a stream of righteous influence reflecting the remarkable women of God who have existed in all ages and dispensations, including our own. Greatness is not measured by coverage in column inches, either in newspapers or in the scriptures. The story of the women of God, therefore, is, for now, an untold drama within a drama. . . .

"Just as certain men were foreordained from before the foundations of the world, so were certain women appointed to certain tasks. Divine design—not chance—brought Mary forward to be the mother of Jesus. The boy prophet, Joseph Smith, was blessed not only with a great father but also with a superb mother, Lucy Mack, who influenced a whole dispensation.

"In our modern kingdom, it is no accident that women were, through the Relief Society, assigned compassionate service. So often the service of women seems instinctive, while that of some men seems more labored. It is precisely because the daughters of Zion are so uncommon that the adversary will not leave them alone. . . .

"So often our sisters comfort others when their own needs are greater than those being comforted. That quality is like the generosity of Jesus on the cross. Empathy during agony is a portion of divinity!

"When the real history of mankind is fully disclosed, will it feature the echoes of gunfire or the shaping sound of lullabies? The great armistices made by military men or the peacemaking of women in homes and neighborhoods? Will what happened in cradles and kitchens prove to be more controlling than what happened in congresses? When the surf of the centuries has made the great pyramids so much sand, the everlasting family will still be standing, because it is a celestial institution, formed outside telestial time. The women of God know this.

*Emma Smith's instruction to "delight" in her husband is a commission to all wives (D&C 25:14)*

"No wonder the men of God support and sustain you sisters in your unique roles, for the act of deserting home in order to shape society is like thoughtlessly removing crucial fingers from an imperiled dike in order to teach people to swim. . . .

"Finally, remember: When we return to our real home, it will be with the 'mutual approbation' of those who reign in the 'royal courts on high.' There we will find beauty such as mortal 'eye hath not seen'; we will hear sounds of surpassing music which mortal 'ear hath not heard.' Could such a regal homecoming be possible without the anticipatory arrangements of a Heavenly Mother?" (In Conference Report, Apr. 1978, pp. 13-15; or *Ensign*, May 1978, pp. 10-11.)

# The Law of Common Consent

Section 26

## Historical Background

See Historical Background for Doctrine and Covenants 24. Sections 24, 25, and 26 were received about the same time.

## Notes and Commentary

### D&C 26:1. The Lord's Instruction until Conference

"Going 'to the west' meant going to Fayette, New York, a distance of about a hundred miles; and the 'next conference' was held at Fayette on September 26 and 27, 1830. 'Studying the scriptures' probably had something to do with the translation of the Bible, since the earliest manuscript entries, recorded in the summer and fall of 1830, are in the handwriting of John Whitmer and Oliver Cowdery. Apparently the 'translation' and the 'study' were being conducted at the same time; perhaps they were actually one and the same." (Matthews, *Joseph Smith's Translation of the Bible,* p. 27.)

### D&C 26:2. The Law of Common Consent

Elder Bruce R. McConkie explained that "administrative affairs of the Church are handled in accordance with the law of *common consent.* This law is that in God's earthly kingdom, the King counsels what should be done, but then he allows his subjects to accept or reject his proposals. Unless the principle of free agency is operated in righteousness men do not progress to ultimate salvation in the heavenly kingdom hereafter. Accordingly, church officers are selected by the spirit of revelation in those appointed to choose them, but before the officers may serve in their positions, they must receive a formal sustaining vote of the people over whom they are to preside. (D. & C. 20:60-67; 26:2; 28; 38:34-35; 41:9-11; 42:11; 102:9; 124:124-145.)" (*Mormon Doctrine,* pp. 149-50.)

Not only are Church officers sustained by common consent, but this same principle operates for policies, major decisions, acceptance of new scripture, and other things that affect the lives of the Saints (see D&C 26:2).

### D&C 26:2. Could a Person Hold an Office in the Church without the Consent of the People?

"No man can preside in this Church in any capacity without the consent of the people. The Lord has placed upon us the responsibility of sustaining by vote those who are called to various positions of responsibility. No man, should the people decide to the contrary, could preside over any body of Latter-day Saints in this Church, and yet it is not the right of the people to nominate, to choose, for that is the right of the priesthood." (Smith, *Doctrines of Salvation,* 3:123; see also D&C 20:65.)

### D&C 26:2. When Should a Person Cast a Negative Vote?

"I have no right to raise my hand in opposition to a man who is appointed to any position in this Church, simply because I may not like him, or because of some personal disagreement or feeling I may have, but only on the grounds that he is guilty of wrong doing, of transgression of the laws of the Church which would disqualify him for the position which he is called to hold." (Smith, *Doctrines of Salvation,* 3:124.)

### D&C 26:2. Responsibilities of Those Who Sustain Others

Elder Loren C. Dunn explained the responsibilities that accompany the sustaining process: "When we sustain officers, we are given the opportunity of sustaining those whom the Lord has already called by revelation. . . . The Lord, then, gives us the opportunity to sustain the action of a divine calling and in effect express ourselves if for any reason we may feel otherwise. To sustain is to make the action binding on ourselves to support those people whom we have sustained. When a person goes through the sacred act of raising his arm to the square, he should remember, with soberness, that which he has done and commence to act in harmony with his sustaining vote both in public and in private." (In Conference Report, Apr. 1972, p. 19; or *Ensign,* July 1972, p. 43.)

"When you vote affirmatively you make a solemn covenant with the Lord that you will sustain, that is, give your full loyalty and support, without equivocation or reservation, to the officer for whom you vote" (Harold B. Lee, in Conference Report, Apr. 1970, p. 103).

*"All things shall be done by common consent" (D&C 26:2)*

# "When Ye Partake of the Sacrament"

Section 27

## Historical Background

The Prophet Joseph Smith wrote: "Early in the month of August Newel Knight and his wife paid us a visit at my place in Harmony, Pennsylvania; and as neither his wife nor mine had been as yet confirmed, it was proposed that we should confirm them, and partake together of the Sacrament, before he and his wife should leave us. In order to prepare for this I set out to procure some wine for the occasion, but had gone only a short distance when I was met by a heavenly messenger, and received the following revelation, the first four paragraphs of which were written at this time, and the remainder in the September following: [D&C 27]." (*History of the Church,* 1:106.)

## Notes and Commentary

**D&C 27:1-4. "It Mattereth Not What Ye Shall Eat or What Ye Shall Drink When Ye Partake of the Sacrament"**

President Joseph Fielding Smith explained why this revelation was given and what it meant: "This heavenly messenger told Joseph Smith that it mattered not what should be used for the Sacrament, and he was not to purchase wine or strong drink from his enemies. The reason for this is obvious, for the Prophet had many enemies. However, this reason went farther than merely protection against his enemies, for it was a caution against evil and designing persons who would adulterate these things. (See Word of Wisdom, Sec. 89.) Joseph Smith was also told that wine should not be used for the sacrament unless it was made by the Saints and should be had new among them. While the Church did not adopt the custom of using water exclusively in the sacrament at that early time, yet it was from this time that water was used as a substitute for wine, which had been used principally because of its resemblance to blood. Today throughout the Church water is used in the Sacrament in remembrance of the blood of Jesus Christ which was shed for the remission of sins in behalf of all who repent and accept the Gospel." (*Church History and Modern Revelation,* 1:132.)

**D&C 27:5-14. The Lord Will Drink of the Fruit of the Vine**

The Savior included prophets from Old Testament, New Testament, and Book of Mormon times as being among those with whom he will partake of the sacrament in his Father's kingdom "on the earth" (D&C 27:5). It is interesting that Joseph who was sold into Egypt was included, for the Bible usually refers to the God of Abraham, Isaac, and Jacob. Joseph is mentioned prominently in both the Bible and the Book of Mormon and, of course, is the forefather of many of the peoples of the Book of Mormon.

"The Savior informed his Apostles on the night he ate the Passover that he would not drink of the 'fruit of the vine' with them again, until he should 'drink it new with them in the kingdom of God.' [See Matthew 26:29; Luke 22:18.] This was reiterated in the revelation to Joseph Smith, wherein the Lord promised to drink and eat with his prophets and saints, in his Father's kingdom which shall be built up on the earth." (Smith, *Church History and Modern Revelation,* 1:132-33.)

**D&C 27:5. The Stick of Ephraim**

President Joseph Fielding Smith defined this term and explained its application to the Church today:

"One significant expression in the prophecy of Ezekiel is that the stick of Joseph and his fellows was to be in the hand of Ephraim. Ephraim was to stand at the head of the tribes of Israel in the latter-days, according to his birthright. Joseph Smith, unto whom the record of the Nephites was delivered and who translated it, is of the tribe of Ephraim. The Lord so revealed it. So are most of those who have received the gospel in this dispensation. Therefore this stick of Joseph is in the hand of Ephraim and by him has been joined to the stick of Judah, fulfilling the prophecy of Ezekiel.

"The Book of Mormon is the record of Joseph. It contains the history of the descendants of Joseph on this land, both of Ephraim and of Manasseh. It was in the hands of Ephraim when it was given to Joseph Smith, and it is still in the hands of Ephraim when our missionaries go forth proclaiming its truths to the world, for they also are of Ephraim." (*Doctrines of Salvation,* 3:210; see also Ezekiel 37:15-19.)

**D&C 27:6-7. Who Is This Elias?**

Since *Elias* refers to more than one person, it is sometimes confusing. Elder Bruce R. McConkie explained:

"Correcting the Bible by the spirit of revelation, the Prophet restored a statement of John the Baptist which says that Christ is the Elias who was to restore all things. (*Inspired Version,* John 1:21-28.) By revelation we are also informed that the Elias who was to restore all things is the angel Gabriel who was known in mortality as Noah. (D. & C. 27:6-7; Luke 1:5-25; *Teachings,* p. 157.) From the same authentic source we also learn that the promised Elias is John the Revelator. (D. & C. 77:9, 14.) Thus there are three different revelations which name Elias as being three different persons. What are we to conclude?

"By finding answer to the question, by whom has the restoration been effected, we shall find who

Elias is and find there is no problem in harmonizing these apparently contradictory revelations. Who has restored all things? Was it one man? Certainly not. Many angelic ministrants have been sent from the courts of glory to confer keys and powers, to commit their dispensations and glories again to men on earth. At least the following have come: Moroni, John the Baptist, Peter, James, and John, Moses, Elijah, Elias, Gabriel, Raphael, and Michael. (D. & C. 13; 110; 128:19-21.) Since it is apparent that no one messenger has carried the whole burden of the restoration, but rather that each has come with a specific endowment from on high, it becomes clear that Elias is a composite personage. The expression must be understood to be a name and a title for those whose mission it was to commit keys and powers to men in this final dispensation." (*Mormon Doctrine,* p. 221; see also D&C 110:12-16.)

### D&C 27:13. The Dispensation of the Fulness of Times

Elder David W. Patten, one of the first Apostles and martyrs in this dispensation, said: "Now the thing to be known is, what the fullness of times means, or the extent or authority thereof. It means this, that the dispensation of the fullness of times is made up of all the dispensations that ever have been given since the world began, until this time. Unto Adam first was given a dispensation. It is well known that God spake to him with His own voice in the garden, and gave him the promise of the Messiah. And unto Noah also was a dispensation given; for Jesus said, 'As it was in the days of Noah, so shall it be also in the days of the Son of Man;' and as the righteous were saved then, and the wicked destroyed, so it will be now. And from Noah to Abraham, and from Abraham to Moses, and from Moses to Elias, and from Elias to John the Baptist, and from then to Jesus Christ, and from Jesus Christ to Peter, James, and John, the Apostles—all received in their time a dispensation by revelation from God, to accomplish the great scheme of restitution, spoken of by all the holy prophets since the world began; the end of which is the dispensation of the fullness of times, in the which all things shall be fulfilled that have been spoken of since the earth was made." (In *History of the Church,* 3:51.)

### D&C 27:15-18. "Take upon You My Whole Armour"

Elder Harold B. Lee explained the meaning of the symbolism of this passage:

"We have the four parts of the body that . . . [are] the most vulnerable to the powers of darkness. The loins, typifying virtue, chastity. The heart typifying our conduct. Our feet, our goals or objectives in life and finally our head, our thoughts. . . .

"We should have our loins girt about with truth. What is truth? Truth, the Lord said, was knowledge of things as they are, things as they were and things as they are to come. [D&C 93:24.] . . . 'Our loins shall be girt about with truth,' the prophet said.

"And the heart, what kind of a breastplate shall protect our conduct in life? We shall have over our hearts a breastplate of righteousness. Well, having learned truth we have a measure by which we can judge between right and wrong and so our conduct will always be gauged by that thing which we know to be true. Our breastplate to cover our conduct shall be the breastplate of righteousness.

"[By] what shall we protect our feet, or by what shall we gauge our objectives or our goals in life? . . . 'Your feet should be shod with the preparation of the gospel of peace.' (Ephesians 6:15) . . .

"How fortunate are you if in your childhood in the home of your father and mother you were taught the doctrine of repentance, faith in Christ, the son of the living God, the meaning of baptism and what you gain by the laying on of hands for the gift of the Holy Ghost. Fortunate is the child who has been taught to pray and who has been given those steps to take on through life. Feet shod with the preparation of the gospel of peace! . . .

"And then finally the helmet of salvation. . . . What is salvation? Salvation is to be saved. Saved from what? Saved from death and saved from sin. . . .

"[The Apostle Paul] had his armoured man holding in his hand a shield and in his other hand a sword, which were the weapons of those days. That shield was the shield of faith and the sword was the sword of the spirit which is the Word of God. I can't think of any more powerful weapons than faith and a knowledge of the scriptures in the which are contained the Word of God. One so armoured and one so prepared with those weapons is prepared to go out against the enemy that is more to be feared than the enemies of the light. . . . More to be feared than the enemies that come in the daylight that we can see are the enemies that strike in the darkness of the night that we can't see with our eyes." (*Feet Shod with the Preparation of the Gospel of Peace,* Brigham Young University Speeches of the Year [Provo, 9 Nov. 1954], pp. 3-7.)

# "Thou Shalt Not Command Him Who Is at Thy Head"

Section 28

## Historical Background

The Church, having been organized only a few short months, faced one of its first major problems at the time this revelation was given in September 1830: Who is entitled to receive revelation for the Church? The question arose because Hiram Page had found a stone through which he claimed to be receiving revelation.

Many of the early converts came from a congregationalist background, that is, from churches in which anyone had the right to proclaim doctrine if the rest of the congregation concurred. Thus, it seemed natural to them to respond to Hiram Page's revelation as valid. But as a result of this revelation, the Saints in New York understood that only one could receive revelation from the Lord for the whole Church. The new converts in Kirtland also had to learn this same lesson (see D&C 43).

Newel Knight, who was an eyewitness to these events, recorded this account in his diary:

"After arranging my affairs at home, I again set out for Fayette, to attend our second conference, which had been appointed to be held at Father Whitmer's where Joseph then resided. On my arrival I found Brother Joseph in great distress of mind on account of Hyrum Page, who had managed to get up some dissension of feeling among the brethren by giving revelations concerning the government of the Church and other matters, which he claimed to have received through the medium of a stone he possessed. He had quite a roll of papers full of these revelations, and many in the Church were led astray by them. Even Oliver Cowdery and the Whitmer family had given heed to them, although they were in contradiction to the New Testament and the revelations of these last days. Here was a chance for Satan to work among the little flock, and he sought by this means to accomplish what persecution failed to do. Joseph was perplexed and scarcely knew how to meet this new exigency. That night I occupied the same room that he did and the greater part of the night was spent in prayer and supplication. After much labor with these brethren they were convinced of their error, and confessed the same, renouncing the revelations as not being of God, but acknowledged that Satan had conspired to overthrow their belief in the true plan of salvation. In consequence of these things Joseph enquired of the Lord before conference commenced and received the revelation published on page 140 of the Doctrine and Covenants [section 28], wherein God explicitly states His mind and will concerning the receiving of revelations.

"Conference having assembled, the first thing done was to consider the subject of the stone in connection with Hyrum Page, and after considerable investigation and discussion, Brother Page and all the members of the Church present renounced the stone, and the revelations connected with it, much to our joy and satisfaction." (Journal History, 26 Sept. 1830.)

## Notes and Commentary

**D&C 28:1. Why Did the Lord Tell the Church to Listen to Oliver Cowdery?**

Oliver Cowdery was at this time the second elder of the Church (see D&C 20:3). Just as the Saints were to listen to the counsel of all the General Authorities, so were they admonished to heed the words of Oliver Cowdery.

**D&C 28:2-3. In What Way Did Hiram Page Violate the True Order of Divine Guidance for the Church?**

The Prophet taught that "it is contrary to the economy of God for any member of the Church, or any one, to receive instructions for those in authority, higher than themselves; therefore you will see the impropriety of giving heed to them; but if any person have a vision or a visitation from a heavenly messenger, it must be for his own benefit and instruction; for the fundamental principles, government, and doctrine of the Church are vested in the keys of the kingdom." (*History of the Church,* 1:338.)

An official statement by the First Presidency of the Church in 1913 gave additional illumination to this principle: "From the days of Hiram Page (Doc. and Cov., Sec. 28), at different periods there have been manifestations from delusive spirits to members of the Church. Sometimes these have come to the men and women who because of transgression became easy prey to the Arch-Deceiver. At other times people who pride themselves on their strict observance of the rules and ordinances and ceremonies of the Church are led astray by false spirits, who exercise an influence so imitative of that which proceeds from a Divine source that even these persons, who think they are 'the very elect,' find it difficult to discern the essential difference. Satan himself has transformed himself to be apparently 'an angel of light.'

"When visions, dreams, tongues, prophecy, impressions or any extraordinary gift or inspiration, convey something out of harmony with the accepted revelations of the Church or contrary to the decisions of its constituted authorities, Latter-day Saints may know that it is not of God, no matter how plausible it may appear. Also, they should understand that directions for the guidance of the Church will come, by revelation, through the

*The First Presidency (1911–18): Anthon H. Lund, First Counselor; Joseph F. Smith, President; Charles W. Penrose, Second Counselor*

head. All faithful members are entitled to the inspiration of the Holy Spirit for themselves, their families, and for those over whom they are appointed and ordained to preside. But anything at discord with that which comes from God through the head of the Church is not to be received as authoritative or reliable. In secular as well as spiritual affairs, Saints may receive Divine guidance and revelation affecting themselves, but this does not convey authority to direct others, and is not to be accepted when contrary to Church covenants, doctrine or discipline, or to known facts, demonstrated truths, or good common sense. . . .

"Be not led by any spirit or influence that discredits established authority and contradicts true scientific principles and discoveries, or leads away from the direct revelations of God for the government of the Church. The Holy Ghost does not contradict its own revealings. Truth is always harmonious with itself. Piety is often the cloak of error. The counsels of the Lord through the channel he has appointed will be followed with safety, therefore, O! ye Latter-day Saints, profit by these words of warning." (Joseph F. Smith, Anthon H. Lund, and Charles W. Penrose, "A Warning Voice," *Improvement Era,* Sept. 1913, pp. 1148-49.)

Oliver Cowdery was told by the Lord that he might "not write by way of commandment, but by wisdom" (D&C 28:5). In other words, the Lord was telling Oliver that while he might give counsel and advice to the Saints, he was not to establish Church doctrine or revelation. That was the office of the prophet only.

### D&C 28:5-6. "Thou Shalt Not Command Him Who Is at Thy Head"

President Joseph Fielding Smith explained that "it was very necessary that Oliver Cowdery should receive this admonition, for he was inclined to take issue with the Prophet even in regard to matters of revelation. Much good came out of this unpleasant incident, for the members were taught that there was order in the Church and only one appointed to receive commandments and revelations for their guidance, and he was the one God had called. The members at that time were largely excusable for falling into this error, because they had but recently come into the Church and had to be taught in all things pertaining to the kingdom of God and its government. They did not know that it was wrong for a man other than the Prophet to claim to be the spokesman for the Almighty, and this revelation taught them that confusion would result from such a course, and that Joseph Smith held the keys of revelation until another was appointed to succeed him." (*Church History and Modern Revelation,* 1:135-36.)

### D&C 28:8-16. Oliver Cowdery Is Called on a Mission to the Lamanites

"The Lamanite mission was a very important movement of the young but vigorous Church. Oliver Cowdery was the first-appointed member of the party. Peter Whitmer, Jr., was added by Revelation (Sec. 30); and then Parley P. Pratt and Ziba Peterson (Sec. 32). Soon after the Conference the little party set out on the perilous journey of about 1,500 miles. They started on foot, trusting in the Lord to open the way. Near Buffalo they visited the Catteraugus Indians and left the Book of Mormon with them. Then they proceeded to Kirtland, Ohio. Here they visited Sidney Rigdon, then a popular Campbellite minister. He and some of his friends joined the Church. Night and day, for some time, the missionaries were teaching the people in Kirtland and vicinity. After having ordained Rigdon, Isaac Morley, John Murdock, Lyman Wight and others, to the ministry, the missionaries left for the West. Near Sandusky they visited the Wyandot tribe and preached the gospel. In Cincinnati and St. Louis they met with very little success. At the latter place their progress was impeded by heavy snowstorms. With the opening of the New Year, 1831, they continued their journey, traveling on foot 300 miles over prairies, without shelter and fire, living on frozen corn, bread and raw pork. At length they reached Independence, Mo., on the extreme western frontier of the State. They had traveled four months and suffered untold hardships; they had preached to two Indian nations and to thousands of white people, and organized several strong branches of the Church.

"After having rested a little at Independence, three of the brethren crossed the frontier and visited the Shawnee Indians. Then they went among the Delawares. These manifested a great deal of interest in the Book of Mormon. Therefore the jealousy of ministers was aroused and these prevailed upon the Indian agents to expel the missionaries from the Indian country. They, accordingly, returned to Jackson county, where they labored for some time with encouraging success." (Smith and Sjodahl, Commentary, p. 144.)

**D&C 28:9. "It Shall Be Given Hereafter"**

Through the revelation of Moses and Enoch received by Joseph Smith, the early Saints learned that Zion was to be established again on the earth (see Moses 7:62). It was only natural that the Saints would inquire about its location.

"It is not improbable that some of the pseudo-revelations of Hiram Page related to this very subject [the location of Zion]. The Saints were full of enthusiasm, looking for the immediate fulfilment of the prophecies. The Lord now made it known that the locality of that holy city had not yet been revealed, but that it might be looked for 'on the borders by the Lamanites.' Further revelation on this subject would come later (Sec. 57:2, 3)." (Smith and Sjodahl, Commentary, p. 142.)

By "Lamanites" Joseph Smith had reference to the Indians, and to go out to the "borders by the Lamanites" meant to go to the frontier (D&C 28:9). The natural way to travel would be by the most frequently traveled roads to the most populous area. Even at that, Independence was a town that was organized only about four years before the missionaries arrived.

**D&C 28:12. Church Covenants**

The Church covenants mentioned here include the articles and covenants of the Church found in section 20 of the Doctrine and Covenants. In that revelation the Lord specified who presided over the Church (see D&C 20:2-3) and outlined the duties of all the other members and priesthood holders (see D&C 20:38-71). Hiram Page's claim that he received revelation for the whole Church was out of harmony with the teachings of that section of the Doctrine and Covenants. Linked with this teaching is the doctrine of common consent (explained in D&C 20:63-67), which principle, according to Doctrine and Covenants 28:13, had been violated by Hiram Page in preaching that the revelations he had received were to be obeyed by all the members of the Church.

# Prepare Against the Day of Tribulation

Section 29

## Historical Background

In the months previous to September 1830, Joseph Smith had been greatly persecuted in Harmony, Pennsylvania. So, Newel Knight helped move the Prophet's family to Fayette, New York, where the Smiths had been invited to live with David Whitmer's family.

The Church was less than six months old. The first conference had been held in June, and great spiritual strength had been felt from it. The Saints were looking forward to the second conference to be held on 26 September 1830. Shortly before the conference convened, Joseph inquired of the Lord concerning a stone through which Hiram Page had been claiming to receive revelations (see D&C 28). The Prophet Joseph Smith made the following record of the event: "As a conference meeting had been appointed for the 26th day of September, I thought it wisdom not to do much more than to converse with the brethren on the subject [of the stone], until the conference should meet. Finding, however, that many, especially the Whitmer family and Oliver Cowdery, were believing much in the things set forth by this stone, we thought best to inquire of the Lord concerning so important a matter; and before conference convened, we received the following: [D&C 28-29]." (*History of the Church,* 1:110.)

## Notes and Commentary

**D&C 29:1-2. "Even As a Hen Gathereth Her Chickens"**

This expression is used three times in the Doctrine and Covenants (D&C 10:65; 29:2 and 43:24). It evokes the vivid picture of a mother hen who, when danger appears to threaten her chicks, raises her wings and clucks excitedly. The chicks, although they may be scattered over the barnyard, instantly obey that call and scurry under the protection of her wings.

*"Even as a hen gathereth her chickens" (D&C 29:2)*

In this passage the Lord describes those who will come to him for protection as having three characteristics: (1) they hearken to his voice; (2) they humble themselves; and (3) they call upon him in mighty prayer. The Jewish nation and the Nephite people in America refused to heed that call and meet those conditions, and as a result they suffered great tragedy and destruction (see Matthew 23:37; 3 Nephi 10:4-6). For a further treatment of the doctrine of gathering see D&C 29:7-8; 101:17-23; Enrichment A, in the Appendix.

**D&C 29:7. Who Are the "Elect"?**

"The *elect of God* comprise a very select group, an inner circle of faithful members of The Church of Jesus Christ of Latter-day Saints. They are the portion of church members who are striving with all their hearts to keep the fulness of the gospel law in this life so that they can become inheritors of the fulness of gospel rewards in the life to come." (McConkie, *Mormon Doctrine,* p. 217.)

Concerning the means by which the elect are gathered, Elder George Q. Cannon explained: "Where people are pure and chaste in their thoughts and actions, the Spirit of God has such power with them that they readily perceive and comprehend the truth. It is by this means that the best among the children of God are being gathered out from the various nations. Truth cleaves to truth, light to light and purity to purity. The gospel gathers with its influence those who love its principles; and if any should be gathered in who cannot abide its requirements, they pass off and mingle with the elements that are congenial to the spirit they possess." ("The Sin of Adultery and Its Consequences," *Millennial Star,* 14 Mar. 1863, p. 169.)

**D&C 29:8. "They Shall Be Gathered into One Place"**

In the time of Joseph Smith, the Saints were commanded to gather in the land of Missouri to build the city of Zion (see D&C 57:1-2). The Saints today still look forward to the building of Zion in the originally designated spot (see D&C 101:17-18), but the gathering of the Saints is taking place according to instructions adapted to the needs of the time. Elder Harold B. Lee gave the following explanation of the gathering:

"The spirit of gathering has been with the Church from the days of that restoration. Those who are of the blood of Israel, have a righteous desire after they are baptized, to gather together with the body of the Saints at the designated place. . . .

". . . The Lord has placed the responsibility for directing the work of gathering in the hands of the leaders of the Church to whom he will reveal his will where and when such gatherings would take place in the future. It would be well—before the frightening events concerning the fulfilment of all God's promises and predictions are upon us, that the Saints in every land prepare themselves and look forward to the instruction that shall come to them from the First Presidency of this Church as to where they shall be gathered and not be disturbed in their feelings until such instruction is given to them as it is revealed by the Lord to the proper authority." (In Conference Report, Apr. 1948, p. 55.)

Accordingly, the Saints must look to the First Presidency and gather at whatever time and in whatever manner they prescribe.

**D&C 29:8. What Is the Purpose of the Gathering?**

The Prophet Joseph Smith answered this question when he wrote:

"The main object [of gathering] was to build unto the Lord a house whereby He could reveal unto His people the ordinances of His house and the glories of His kingdom, and teach the people the way of salvation; for there are certain ordinances and principles that, when they are taught and practiced, must be done in a place or house built for that purpose.

"It was the design of the councils of heaven before the world was, that the principles and laws of the priesthood should be predicated upon the gathering of the people in every age of the world. . . .

"It is for the same purpose that God gathers together His people in the last days, to build unto the Lord a house to prepare them for the ordinances and endowments, washings and anointings, etc." (*History of the Church,* 5:423-24.)

**D&C 29:9. The Wicked Shall Be Burned As Stubble**

Is this passage figurative, or will the wicked really burn? President Joseph Fielding Smith said: "It is not a figure of speech that is meaningless, or one not to be taken literally when the Lord speaks of the burning. All through the scriptures we have the word of the Lord that at his coming the wicked and the rebellious will be as stubble and will be consumed. Isaiah has so prophesied. . . . Surely the words of the Lord are not to be received lightly or considered meaningless." (*Church History and Modern Revelation,* 1:238.)

Christ is a glorified, celestial being, and the glory of such beings is comparable to that of the sun (see D&C 76:70). Thus, the presence of Christ when he comes in his glory will be as a consuming fire. The mountains will flow down at his presence, the elements will melt with fervent heat, and the waters will boil. Even the sun will hide its face in shame. (See Hebrews 12:29; D&C 133:40-44, 49.) The scriptures also talk about the time when "devouring fire" will be poured out upon the wicked (D&C 29:21; see also D&C 35:14; 1 Nephi 22:17, 23; Ezekiel 38:22; 39:6).

### D&C 29:9-11. "The Hour Is Nigh"

President Joseph Fielding Smith explained the eternal significance of this phrase:

"The world is rapidly coming to its end, that is, *the end of the days of wickedness. When it is fully ripe in iniquity the Lord will come* in the clouds of heaven to take vengeance on the ungodly, for his wrath is kindled against them. Do not think that he delayeth his coming. Many of the signs of his coming have been given, so we may, if we will, know that the day is even now at our doors.

"... The day of the coming of the Lord is near. I do not know when.... I sincerely believe it will come in the very day when some of us who are here today [5 April 1936] will be living upon the face of the earth. That day is close at hand. It behooves us as Latter-day Saints to set our houses in order, to keep the commandments of God, to turn from evil to righteousness, if it is necessary, and serve the Lord in humility and faith and prayer." (*Doctrines of Salvation,* 3:2-3.)

Enrichment H further discusses what the Doctrine and Covenants teaches about the Second Coming.

### D&C 29:12. The Twelve Apostles Shall Judge the Whole House of Israel

President John Taylor described the Judgment in these terms:

"We may here state that Christ is called the judge of the quick and the dead, the judge of all the earth. We further read that the Twelve Apostles who ministered in Jerusalem 'shall sit upon twelve thrones, judging the twelve tribes of Israel.' (Matthew 19:28.) Also the following: [D&C 29:12 and 1 Nephi 12:8-10].

"This exhibits a principle of adjudication or judgment in the hands, firstly, of the Great High Priest and King, Jesus of Nazareth, the Son of God; secondly, in the hands of the Twelve Apostles on the continent of Asia, bestowed by Jesus Himself; thirdly, in the Twelve Disciples on this continent, to their peoples, who it appears are under the presidency of the Twelve Apostles who ministered at Jerusalem; which presidency is also exhibited by Peter, James and John, the acknowledged presidency of the Twelve Apostles; they, holding this Priesthood first on the earth, and then in the heavens, being the legitimate custodians of the keys of the Priesthood, came and bestowed it upon Joseph Smith and Oliver Cowdery. It is also further stated that the Saints shall judge the world. Thus Christ is at the head, his apostles and disciples seem to take the next prominent part; then comes the action of the Saints, or other branches of the Priesthood, who it is stated shall judge the world. This combined Priesthood, it would appear, will hold the destiny of the human family in their hands and adjudicate in all matters pertaining to their affairs." (*Mediation and Atonement,* pp. 155-57.)

### D&C 29:17-21. "I Will Take Vengeance upon the Wicked, for They Will Not Repent"

Commenting on the grim vividness of prophecy dealing with the final judgments, Elder Bruce R. McConkie said: "Those with refined senses find it difficult to conceive of the desolation, destruction, and death that will prevail during the final great battles ushering in Christ's reign of peace. So great shall be the slaughter and mass murder, the carnage and gore, the butchery and violent death of warring men, that their decaying bodies 'shall stop the noses of the passengers,' and it shall be a task of mammoth proportions merely to dispose of them. Then shall Ezekiel's prophecy be fulfilled that every feathered fowl and every beast of the field shall assemble to 'eat the flesh of the mighty, and drink the blood of the princes of the earth.' (Ezek. 39.) And then shall the cry go forth of which John wrote: 'Come and gather yourselves together unto the *supper of the great God;* That ye may eat the flesh of kings, and the flesh of captains, and the flesh of mighty men, and the flesh of horses, and of them that sit on them, and the flesh of all men, both free and bond, both small and great.' (Rev. 19:17-18.) That all this is an actual, literal supper, an horrible but real event yet to be, has been specifically confirmed in latter-day revelation. (D. & C. 29:18-21.)" (*Mormon Doctrine,* p. 772.)

President Joseph Fielding Smith said of such grim prophecies: "I know these are unpleasant things. It is not a pleasant thing even for me to stand here and tell you that this is written in the Scriptures. If the Lord has a controversy with the nations, He will put them to the sword. Their bodies shall lie unburied like dung upon the earth. That is not nice, is it, but should we not know it? Is it not our duty to read these things and understand them? Don't you think the Lord has given us these things that we might know and we might prepare ourselves through humility, through repentance, through faith, that we might escape from these dreadful conditions that are portrayed by these ancient prophets? That is why I am reading them. I feel just as keenly as you do about the condition, and I pray for it to come to an end, but I want it to come to an end right." (*Signs of the Times,* pp. 154-55.)

The figure of a cup full of indignation (see D&C 29:17) suggests that the Lord will no longer forbear taking vengeance on the wicked who will not repent. Just as there is a limit to the amount a cup can hold, so there is a limit to the amount of patience the Lord will show towards those who perform wicked acts. To restrain himself longer would be not a virtue but a disservice to mankind for whom he has offered himself as Savior. Since the blood of his atonement will not cleanse those who do not repent, pestilence, famine, plague, and destruction are the tools he uses to reclaim those who are past feeling and will not hearken to the still, small voice (see 1 Nephi 17:45; D&C 43:20-27). These terrible judgments are the natural result of man's wickedness. God's plea is for men to turn from such wickedness and be spared these awful consequences of sin.

### D&C 29:22-25. Will This Earth Be Destroyed and a New One Created?

President Joseph Fielding Smith explained that this passage "does not mean that this earth shall pass away and another take its place, and the heaven thereof shall pass away, and another heaven take its place, but that the earth and its heaven shall, after passing away through death, be renewed again in immortality. This earth is living and must die, but since it keeps the law it shall be restored through the resurrection by which it shall become celestialized and the abode of celestial beings. The next verse of this revelation explains this as follows: [D&C 29:24-25].

"So we see that the Lord intends to save, not only the earth and the heavens, not only man who dwells upon the earth, but all things which he has created. The animals, the fishes of the sea, the fowls of the air, as well as man, are to be re-created, or renewed, through the resurrection, for they too are living souls." (In Conference Report, Oct. 1928, pp. 99-100; see also D&C 88:17-19, 25-26.)

*The earth will be resurrected*

### D&C 29:26. "Michael, Mine Archangel, Shall Sound His Trump"

"Michael, who is Adam, holds the keys of salvation for the human family, under the direction and counsel of Jesus Christ, who is the Holy One of Zion [see D&C 78:15-16]. Adam will, when the earth is cleansed and purified and becomes a celestial globe, preside over the children of men, who are of his posterity. He is Adam, 'the prince, the arch-angel.' In the eternities before this earth was formed he was the arch-angel. He became Adam when he came to this earth to be the father of the human family. (D. & C. 107:54-57.)

"The Prophet Joseph Smith said of Adam: 'Commencing with Adam, who was the first man, who is spoken of in Daniel as the "Ancient of Days," or in other words, the first and oldest of all, the great progenitor of whom it is said in another place is Michael. . . . Adam holds the keys of all the dispensations of the fulness of times, i.e. the dispensations of all times have been and will be revealed through him from the beginning.' (*Teachings of the Prophet Joseph Smith*, pp. 167-168.)" (Smith, *Church History and Modern Revelation*, 1:309.)

### D&C 29:27-29. "Depart from Me . . . into Everlasting Fire"

The wicked referred to here are cast into "everlasting fire prepared for the devil and his angels" (D&C 29:28). There is a close parallel between Doctrine and Covenants 29:28 and Doctrine and Covenants 76:36. The Lord indicated that he has never said that they should return (see D&C 29:29); rather, he has said that they cannot come where he is, and they have no power, meaning that the power of the Spirit is completely withdrawn from them (see D&C 29:30 concerning "the word of my power"). All of this additional information indicates that those spoken of here suffer the second death and are sons of perdition. (See McConkie, *Mormon Doctrine*, pp. 280–81; see also D&C 76:31–38.)

### D&C 29:30. "All My Judgments Are Not Given unto Men"

Man in his mortal condition, with very limited understanding and imperfect character, is in no position to fully understand the judgments of God, who is perfect and omniscient (see D&C 38:2). God does not reveal all of his judgments and the reasons for his actions. It is certain, however, that all God's judgments are just and right.

The Prophet Joseph Smith taught that "He [God] holds the reins of judgment in His hands; He is a wise Lawgiver, and will judge all men, not according to the narrow, contracted notions of men, but, 'according to the deeds done in the body whether they be good or evil.' . . . He will judge them, 'not according to what they have not, but according to what they have,' those who have lived without law, will be judged without law, and those who have a law, will be judged by that law. We need not doubt the wisdom and intelligence of the Great Jehovah; He will award judgment or mercy to all nations according to their several deserts, their means of obtaining intelligence, the laws by which they are governed, the facilities afforded them of obtaining correct information, and His inscrutable designs in relation to the human family; and when the designs of God shall be made manifest, and the curtain of futurity be withdrawn, we shall all of us eventually have to confess that the Judge of all the earth has done right." (*History of the Church*, 4:595-96.)

**D&C 29:31-35. "All Things unto Me Are Spiritual"**

When the Lord created the earth, he first created all things spiritually (see Moses 3:5-9). After the Fall all things became temporal (see D&C 77:6). At the end of the earth, the temporal will again become spiritual (Articles of Faith 1:10). Thus, in the beginning things were spiritual first and temporal second. In the end things will be temporal first and spiritual second (see McConkie, *Doctrinal New Testament Commentary,* 1:669). These expressions are given by the Lord only for the sake of man's understanding in mortality, however. From God's point of view there is neither beginning nor end, and all things are spiritual.

"Man makes a distinction between temporal and spiritual laws, and some are very much concerned about keeping the two separate. To the Lord everything is both spiritual and temporal, and the laws He gives are consequently spiritual, because they concern spiritual beings. When He commanded Adam to eat bread in the sweat of his brow, or Moses to strike the rock that the people might drink, or the Prophet Joseph to erect the Nauvoo House, or the Saints in Utah to build fences and roads, such laws were for their spiritual welfare, as well as physical. To obey such laws, when given, is a spiritual duty. One who performs his daily labor 'as to the Lord, and not to men' (Eph. 6:7) derives spiritual benefit from whatever his duties are." (Smith and Sjodahl, Commentary, p. 156.)

**D&C 29:34. "Adam . . . Whom I Created"**

Since this revelation came from Christ (see D&C 29:1), some may feel that this verse teaches that Adam was the offspring of Christ. In reality Adam and all the earth's inhabitants are the offspring of God the Father. In this case Christ is speaking for the Father by a principle called "divine investiture of authority," as Elder Bruce R. McConkie explained:

"Since he [Christ] is one with the Father in all of the attributes of perfection, and since he exercises the power and authority of the Father, it follows that everything he says or does is and would be exactly and precisely what the Father would say and do under the same circumstances.

"Accordingly, the Father puts his own name on the Son and authorizes him to speak in the first person as though he were the Father. . . . Thus it is that our Lord can begin a revelation by saying, 'Listen to the voice of Jesus Christ,' and shortly thereafter speak of 'mine Only Begotten' (D. & C. 29:1, 41-46), such latter expression being made by Christ, but under that divine investiture of authority which permits him to speak as though he were the Father. (D. & C. 93:3-5; Mosiah 15:1-5.)" (*Mormon Doctrine,* p. 130; see also "The Father and the Son: A Doctrinal Exposition by the First Presidency," in Talmage, *Articles of Faith,* pp. 465-73.)

**D&C 29:46-48. "Little Children Are Redeemed from the Foundation of the World"**

President Joseph Fielding Smith clarified this verse, explaining that "through the atonement of Jesus Christ all little children are redeemed, for they cannot sin, and the power is not given to Satan to tempt them. The question naturally may arise as to the meaning of the words of the Lord (verse 46) that 'little children are redeemed through the Only Begotten.' This does not mean that redemption was made for them before, or at, the foundation of the world, but at that time when the plan of salvation was received provision was made for the redemption of little children and also for those who are without the law, and this was consummated in the atonement made by Jesus Christ." (*Church History and Modern Revelation,* 1:144; see also D&C 74:7; 137:10; Moroni 8:8-24; Moses 6:54.)

The Lord gives fathers a great responsibility for the salvation of little children (see vs. 48). The Lord's charge to parents is given in Doctrine and Covenants 68:25-28 and Deuteronomy 6:5-7.

**D&C 29:50. "He That Hath No Understanding"**

Little children or individuals who do not understand the laws of God because of mental deficiencies will not be judged on the same basis as those who are able to understand them (see Moroni 8:22; 2 Nephi 9:25-27). Concerning this principle, President Joseph Fielding Smith taught: "The Church of Jesus Christ of Latter-day Saints considers all deficient children with retarded capacity to understand, just the same as little children under the age of accountability. They are redeemed without baptism and will go to the celestial kingdom of God, there, we believe, to have their faculties or other deficiencies restored according to the Father's mercy and justice." (*Answers to Gospel Questions,* 3:21.)

# "Your Mind Has Been on the Things of the Earth"

Section 30

## Historical Background

This revelation was received by the Prophet Joseph Smith at Fayette, New York, in September 1830. Originally it was published as three revelations in the Book of Commandments, but later the Prophet combined them into one section in the 1835 edition of the Doctrine and Covenants.

The Prophet Joseph Smith recorded the following about the coming forth of this section:

"At length our conference assembled. The subject of the stone previously mentioned [see Historical Background for D&C 28 and 29] was discussed, and after considerable investigation, Brother Page, as well as the whole Church who were present, renounced the said stone, and all things connected therewith, much to our mutual satisfaction and happiness. We now partook of the Sacrament, confirmed and ordained many, and attended to a great variety of Church business on the first and the two following days of the conference, during which time we had much of the power of God manifested amongst us; the Holy Ghost came upon us, and filled us with joy unspeakable; and peace, and faith, and hope, and charity abounded in our midst.

"Before we separated we received the following: [D&C 30-31]." (*History of the Church,* 1:115.)

## Notes and Commentary

### D&C 30:1-4. What Had David Whitmer Done to Deserve This Rebuke from the Lord?

"David Whitmer is mildly rebuked for listening to Hiram Page, and perhaps for using his influence over other members of the family in favor of the supposed seer-stone. He was told that he had feared man, and set his mind on earthly things, instead of taking care of the ministry and listening to the Spirit and the inspired Prophet, with the result that he had been left to inquire for himself; the Prophet could not inquire for him. He was also commanded to remain at home, until further instruction should be given, and confine his labors, for the time being, to the Church and the world in the neighborhood. Deviation from the narrow path always brings with it some consequences which remain after the sin has been pardoned." (Smith and Sjodahl, Commentary, p. 162.)

### D&C 30:1-4. "Your Mind Has Been on the Things of the Earth"

Most Latter-day Saints could substitute their own names in these verses in place of David Whitmer's and find the counsel profitable. There are few who have not at one time or another set their hearts on the things of this earth, giving them a higher priority than the things of God. Like David Whitmer, at such times they too are left to themselves to wonder what is wrong.

### D&C 30:5-8. Revelation Given to Peter Whitmer

Peter Whitmer was not rebuked, perhaps because he was innocent in the matter of the seerstone.

For more information on the Lamanite mission, see Notes and Commentary on Doctrine and Covenants 28:8-16; 32.

### D&C 30:9-11. John Whitmer Is Called to Labor among the Saints in Zion

"John Whitmer is called at this time to labor especially among the Saints. He was very active in the Church as an aid to the Prophet. He assisted in the compilation of the Revelations, and accompanied Oliver Cowdery to Jackson County to superintend the printing of them. He was one of the seven High Priests appointed to preside in the Church in Jackson County. He was Church historian and editor of important Church publications. But he did not remain faithful." (Smith and Sjodahl, Commentary, p. 163.)

*John Whitmer, called to the ministry, later became Church historian*

# "Govern Your House"

Section 31

## Historical Background

This is the last of a series of four revelations given to the Prophet Joseph Smith in September 1830 at Fayette, New York.

The Restoration had begun to attract some of God's noblest sons, among them Thomas B. Marsh, to whom this revelation is directed. Elder Marsh had just been baptized into the Church and ordained an elder by Oliver Cowdery. Here indeed was a man called to greatness by the Lord. (See *History of the Church,* 1:117.)

## Notes and Commentary

### D&C 31:1. "Blessed Are You Because of Your Faith"

"Thomas B. Marsh had embraced the gospel on the testimony of the Spirit concerning sixteen pages of the Book of Mormon, and he moved to Palmyra in order to join the Church. This was faith. Many 'inquirers' cannot be moved, though they have an entire library from which to draw information. God commends him for his faith." (Smith and Sjodahl, Commentary, p. 165.)

### D&C 31:2, 9. Family Unity Is Essential in God's Work

"The great work of every man is . . . to create and perfect an eternal family unit. . . . Salvation is a family affair." (Bruce R. McConkie, in Conference Report, Apr. 1970, pp. 26-27.)

*The family is the most important unit of strength in the Lord's kingdom*

### D&C 31:3-4. "Your Tongue Shall Be Loosed"

"As long as Thomas B. Marsh was faithful he was an eloquent speaker. At the time of the troubles in Clay County, Mo., he was elected a member of a committee to lay the grievances of the Saints before the authorities of the State. On that occasion he spoke so impressively that General Atchison, who was present, shed tears, and the meeting passed resolutions to assist the Saints in finding a new location." (Smith and Sjodahl, Commentary, p. 165.)

### D&C 31:8. "Strengthen Them . . . Against the Time When They Shall Be Gathered"

"The principle of gathering had just been revealed (Sec. 29:2-8). Marsh was to be one of the servants of the Almighty whose duty it would be to strengthen and prepare the people for gathering. It takes both strength of character and preparation to gather to Zion, and this will be still more the case, when the City of Zion is to be built up, and the laws of God must be observed. Marsh, in the autumn of 1832, led a company of Saints to Jackson Co., Mo." (Smith and Sjodahl, Commentary, p. 166.)

### D&C 31:9-13. Saving Instructions to Elder Marsh and to All

"The Lord here imparts special instructions for the guidance of His servant. Among these are:—Be patient in afflictions; revile not against those that revile; govern your house and be steadfast; pray always, lest you enter into temptation and lose your reward; and be faithful unto the end.

"The Lord knew the dangers threatening Thomas B. Marsh and warned him of them." (Smith and Sjodahl, Commentary, p. 166.)

### D&C 31:10. In What Way Was Thomas B. Marsh a Physician unto the Church?

There are many recorded instances of Thomas B. Marsh's giving his time to help members of the Church resolve their problems. Elder Marsh also participated in many Church courts as the presiding authority. Here, through the rules and laws of the Church, he offered hope to the repentant. Even though Thomas B. Marsh had acquired some skills in the use of mild herbs and was able to help people with his knowledge, his greater calling was the healing of souls.

# The First Mission among the Lamanites

Section 32

## Historical Background

"Oliver Cowdery and Peter Whitmer had been called to go on a mission to the Lamanites (Sec. 28:8; 30:5). There was great interest among the Saints in this mission, for it was hoped that the time had come for the redemption of the scattered Remnant, according to the promises in the Book of Mormon (I Nephi 15:13-18, and many other places). The Prophet laid the matter before the Lord in prayer and received this Revelation, in which Parley P. Pratt and Ziba Peterson were called to join Oliver Cowdery and Peter Whitmer, Jr., on that important mission." (Smith and Sjodahl, Commentary, p. 169.)

"The Lamanite missionaries commenced their work with the Catteraugus tribe near Buffalo, New York. Here they were fairly well received, and after leaving copies of the Book of Mormon they continued their journey west. They took a slight detour to teach the gospel to a minister friend of Parley P. Pratt and his congregation near Kirtland, Ohio. . . . What must have been thought to be a diversion from their mission turned out to be a major accomplishment. Here lived Sidney Rigdon, a Reformed Baptist preacher. Parley P. Pratt was apparently convinced that with the feelings and beliefs that Sidney Rigdon held he would respond to the gospel message. He was not disappointed.

"Not only Sidney Rigdon but many of his congregation joined the Church. In a short period of time, 130 people were baptized into the Church in that area, making it the largest single group of Latter-day Saints on the earth at the time. After introducing Sidney Rigdon and the others to the gospel, the missionaries pursued their journey west toward more populous Lamanite tribes. The missionaries now numbered five, with the addition of a convert from Kirtland, Frederick G. Williams. Their missionary labors were temporarily delayed with the arrest of Parley P. Pratt [as part of the attempt to prevent the missionaries from further successes]. . . .

"The missionaries visited the Wyandot tribe at Sandusky, Ohio. From here they commenced the most difficult part of their journey through the wilderness, to the frontier village of Independence, Missouri. . . .

"Upon arriving at Independence, two of the missionaries took work to help finance their mission while the other three continued a short distance to the Indian lands. Here it appeared they would have their greatest success among the Delaware Indians. Although the Indians were at first suspicious of the missionaries because they had been exploited by some previous Christian missionaries, this suspicion was soon alleviated by the moving address delivered by Oliver Cowdery. . . .

"Chief Anderson of the Delaware Tribe was very impressed and asked the missionaries to remain during the winter and teach them the Book of Mormon. Success appeared imminent, but it was shattered when other Christian missionaries influenced the Indian agent to evict the Mormon elders from Indian lands. Asked to leave, the disappointed missionaries made their way back to Independence. Here they stayed, with the exception of Parley P. Pratt, who was chosen to report their labors to Joseph Smith and to visit the Saints they had left behind in Kirtland." (*Doctrine and Covenants, Section 1 through 102* [Sunday School Gospel Doctrine teacher's supplement, 1978], pp. 69-70.)

Some idea of the commitment of these early brethren can be found in the formal covenants they made at the time of their call. For example, Oliver Cowdery wrote: "I, Oliver, being commanded by the Lord God, to go forth unto the Lamanites, to proclaim glad tidings of great joy unto them, by presenting unto them the fullness of the Gospel, of the only begotten Son of God; and also, to rear up a pillar as a witness where the temple of God shall be built, in the glorious New Jerusalem; and having certain brothers with me, who are called of God to assist me, whose names are Parley, and Peter and Ziba, do therefore most solemnly covenant with God that I will walk humbly before him, and do this business, and this glorious work according as he shall direct me by the Holy Ghost; ever praying for mine and their prosperity, and deliverance from bonds, from imprisonment, and whatsoever may befall us, with all patience and faith. Amen. [Signed] Oliver Cowdery." (Journal History, 17 Oct. 1830).

*Parley P. Pratt, an early missionary to the Lamanites*

## Notes and Commentary

**D&C 32. The Day of the Lamanite**

President Spencer W. Kimball spoke and wrote much of today as the day of the Lamanite.

"The Lamanite people are increasing in numbers and influence. When the Navajos returned from Fort Sumner after a shameful and devastating captivity, there were only 9,000 of them left; now there are more than 100,000. There are nearly 130 million Lamanites worldwide. Their superstitions are giving way. They are becoming active politically and responsible in their communities wherever they dwell. Their employment and standard of living are increasing.

"The Church has been established among them to a degree, and it will continue to be established on an ever-increasing scale. There are now more than 350,000 Lamanite members of the Church. They attend their meetings faithfully. They have the priesthood among them. There are branch presidents, quorum leaders, bishops, stake presidents, high councilors, mission presidents, and leaders in all phases of the work among them. They are attending the temple and receiving the ordinances necessary for exaltation. They are intelligent and faithful; they are a great people and a blessed people. . . .

"And can we not exercise our faith to expand this work even further? Enos prayed a prayer of mighty faith and secured a promise from the Lord that the Lamanite would be preserved. How glorious it would be if a million Latter-day Saint families were on their knees daily asking in faith that the work among these their brethren would be hastened, that the doors might be opened.

"The Lamanites must rise again in dignity and strength to fully join their brethren and sisters of the household of God in carrying forth his work in preparation for that day when the Lord Jesus Christ will return to lead his people, when the millennium will be ushered in, when the earth will be renewed and receive its paradisiacal glory and its lands be united and become one land. For the prophets have said, 'The remnant of the house of Joseph shall be built upon this land; and it shall be a land of their inheritance; and they shall build up a holy city unto the Lord, like unto the Jerusalem of old; and they shall no more be confounded, until the end come when the earth shall pass away.' (Eth. 13:8.)

"In this I have great faith." ("Our Paths Have Met Again," *Ensign*, Dec. 1975, pp. 5, 7.)

**D&C 32:1. "Be Meek and Lowly of Heart"**

"Parley P. Pratt was admonished to be meek and lowly of heart. In the year 1837, there were 'jarrings and discord' in the Church at Kirtland, and he was overcome with that spirit. He even tried to turn John Taylor from the Prophet by pointing out to him what he regarded as Joseph's error. Elder Taylor rebuked him as a brother, and Parley P. Pratt went to the Prophet in tears and confessed his sin, whereupon the Prophet frankly forgave him, prayed with him, and blessed him. This was meekness. It was also manliness. Only a really strong character can possess true humility." (Smith and Sjodahl, Commentary, pp. 170-71.)

# "Declare My Gospel" — Section 33

## Historical Background

"The Lord, who is ever ready to instruct such as diligently seek in faith, gave the following revelation at Fayette, New York: [D&C 33]." (*History of the Church,* 1:126.)

"Ezra Thayre and Northrop Sweet came in the Church at the time of the preaching of the Lamanite missionaries. On October, 1830, they were called by revelation to enter the ministry and hearken to the voice of the Lord, 'whose word is quick and powerful, sharper than a two-edged sword, to the dividing asunder of the joints and marrow.' It was not long after this that Northrop Sweet left the Church and, with some others, formed what they called 'The Pure Church of Christ,' an organization that soon came to its end." (Smith, *Church History and Modern Revelation,* 1:152.)

## Notes and Commentary

**D&C 33:1. The Power of the Word of the Lord**

The scriptures clearly teach that there is life and power in the word of God (see 2 Nephi 1:26-29; 32:3; Jacob 4:9; Alma 4:19; 31:5; 32:27-42; D&C 1:37-38; 21:4-6; 84:44-47, 85).

**D&C 33:2. "Declare My Gospel unto a Crooked and Perverse Generation"**

President Joseph Fielding Smith explained the special obligation the Saints have to even the wicked of the world:

"Now there are many debts which we owe to the Lord. There is the debt of preaching this gospel to a wicked and a perverse generation. . . .

"The Lord has given unto men their agency. They may act for themselves, they can choose to do good, or they can choose to do evil. The Lord said that men love darkness rather than light because their deeds are evil. Yet our mission, I say, is, so far as it is within our power, to regenerate, to bring to repentance, just as many of the children of our Father in heaven as it is possible for us to do. That is one of our debts; that is an obligation the Lord has placed upon the Church, and more particularly upon the quorums of the priesthood of the Church, and yet this obligation belongs to every soul.

"It is the duty of every member of this Church to preach the gospel by precept and by example." (*Doctrines of Salvation,* 1:307-8.)

### D&C 33:3. What Is the "Eleventh Hour"?

The phrase "the eleventh hour" seems to refer to the parable of the ten virgins (see Matthew 25:1-13). The bridegroom came at midnight, catching unaware half of those waiting. Thus, to say that it is the eleventh hour is to imply that the time of the coming of the Bridegroom is drawing near.

President Joseph Fielding Smith showed how the phrase is also related to another parable given by the Master: "The time in which we live is compared to the eleventh hour, and so it is in the Lord's reckoning, for we are in the closing scenes of the present world. Elder Orson F. Whitney referred to our dispensation as the 'Saturday night' of time. And, according to the parable of the men employed in the vineyard [Matthew 20:1-16], we who labor in this hour will be rewarded if we are faithful, with equal compensation with those who labored in the previous hours, or dispensations, in the history of mankind." (*Church History and Modern Revelation,* 1:153.)

### D&C 33:3. "The Last Time"

"By the 'last time' the Lord meant the Dispensation of the Fulness of Times" (Joseph Fielding Smith, in Conference Report, Apr. 1946, p. 155; see also D&C 43:28-30; 112:30-32).

### D&C 33:4. "All Having Corrupt Minds"

Elder Hyrum M. Smith defined the special use of the term *corrupt* in this passage, saying: "Let me explain, when I use the term 'corrupt' with reference to these ministers of the gospel, that I use it in the same sense that I believe the Lord used it when he made that declaration to Joseph Smith, the Prophet, in answer to the Prophet's prayer. He did not mean, nor do I mean, that the ministers of religion are personally unvirtuous or impure. I believe as a class they, perhaps, in personal purity, stand a little above the average order of men. When I use the term 'corrupt' I mean, as I believe the Lord meant, that they have turned away from the truth . . . and have turned to that which is false. A false doctrine is a corrupt doctrine; a false religion is a corrupt religion; a false teacher is a corrupt teacher. Any man who teaches a false doctrine, who believes in and practices and teaches a false religion is a corrupt professor, because he teaches that which is impure and not true." (In Conference Report, Oct. 1916, p. 43.)

### D&C 33:5. How Has the Church Been Called Out of the Wilderness?

This imagery is drawn from the book of Revelation where the Church of Jesus Christ, symbolized as a woman, is driven into the wilderness, or apostasy, by the great dragon who is Satan (see Revelation 12:1-17; note especially JST, Revelation 12:7; compare with D&C 86:1-3). Therefore, to call the Church from out of the wilderness refers to the restoration of the Church upon the earth after centuries of apostasy.

### D&C 33:10. How Can One Make the Paths of the Lord Straight?

"Eastern potentates, when traveling from one part of the kingdom to another, would proclaim their coming and order their subjects to prepare the way for them, by building roads where there were none, if necessary; by leveling hills and filling up depressions, and straightening out the winding paths. Semiramis is said to have had roads constructed especially for her journeys. In modern times the Turkish government built a good road from Jaffa to Jerusalem, when the German Emperor signified his intention of visiting the Holy City. To prepare the way of the Lord and make His paths straight is to acknowledge His sovereignty and to make all necessary preparations for His reception. He will not come to reign until all necessary preparations for his coming have been made. 'Hear this, O Earth! The Lord will not come to reign over the righteous, in this world, in 1843 . . . nor until everything for the Bridegroom is ready' (Joseph Smith, *History of the Church,* Vol. V., p. 291.)" (Smith and Sjodahl, Commentary, p. 174.)

### D&C 33:17-18. "Praying Always, Having Your Lamps Trimmed and Burning"

Here the Lord again drew on the imagery of New Testament parables. This phrase, too, has reference to the parable of the ten virgins (see Matthew 25:1-13). When the hour of the bridegroom's coming arrived, the virgins arose and trimmed, or prepared, their lamps. It was then that the five foolish virgins discovered they had no oil. This admonition is clearly a warning for the Saints to maintain a state of spiritual readiness as the coming of the Lord draws ever closer.

*The wise have their lamps trimmed and burning and filled with oil*

# A Revelation to Orson Pratt

Section 34

## Historical Background

The Prophet wrote in his journal that "in the fore part of November, Orson Pratt, a young man nineteen years of age, who had been baptized at the first preaching of his brother, Parley P. Pratt, September 19th (his birthday), about six weeks previous, in Canaan, New York, came to inquire of the Lord what his duty was, and received the following answer: [D&C 34]." (*History of the Church,* 1:127-28.)

Elder Orson Pratt made a journal entry about this revelation: "In October, 1830, I traveled westward over two hundred miles to see Joseph Smith the Prophet. I found him in Fayette, Seneca County, New York, residing at the home of Mr. Whitmer. I soon became intimately acquainted with this good man, and also with the witnesses of the Book of Mormon. By my request, on the 4th of November, the Prophet Joseph inquired of the Lord for me and received the revelation published in the Doctrine and Covenants, Section 34." (Journal History, Nov. 1830, p. 1.)

## Notes and Commentary

**D&C 34:1-4. "My Son . . . You Have Believed"**

The Lord's calling Orson Pratt "my son" is one example of the many times he has taught that all mankind may come unto him and become his sons and daughters (see D&C 25:1; Mosiah 5:7-8; 15:10-16; Moses 1:4-6; 6:68; Romans 8:14-18; 1 John 3:1-3).

*Lorenzo Snow taught a great doctrinal principle concerning man's relationship with God*

President Lorenzo Snow wrote a poem about the doctrine of becoming sons and daughters of God.

Hast thou not been unwisely bold,
Man's destiny to thus unfold?
To raise, promote such high desire,
Such vast ambition thus inspire?

Still 'tis no phantom that we trace
Man's ultimatum in life's race;
This royal path has long been trod
By righteous men, each now a God:

As Abra'm, Isaac, Jacob, too,
First babes, then men—to gods they grew.
As man now is, our God once was;
As now God is, so man may be,—
Which doth unfold man's destiny.

. . . . . . . . . . . . . . . .

The boy, like to his father grown,
Has but attained unto his own;
To grow to sire from state of son,
Is not 'gainst Nature's course to run.

A son of God, like God to be,
Would not be robbing Deity;
And he who has this hope within,

Will purify himself from sin.

(Lorenzo Snow, "Man's Destiny," *Improvement Era,* June 1919, pp. 660-61.)

**D&C 34:5-10. "Preach My Gospel . . . [and] Prophesy"**

Elder Orson Pratt said of his calling to prophesy: " 'Lift up your voice and prophesy, and it shall be given by the power of the Holy Ghost.' This was a particular point in the revelation that seemed to me too great for me ever to attain to, and yet there was a positive command that I should do it. I have often reflected upon this revelation, and have oftentimes inquired in my heart—'Have I fulfilled that commandment as I ought to have done? Have I sought as earnestly as I ought to obtain the gift of prophecy, so as to fulfill the requirement of heaven?' And I have felt sometimes to condemn myself because of my slothfulness, and because of the little progress that I have made in relation to this great, heavenly, and divine gift. I certainly have had no inclination to prophesy to the people unless it should be given to me by the inspiration and power of the Holy Ghost; to prophesy out of my own heart is something perfectly disagreeable to my feelings, even to think of, and hence I have oftentimes, in my public discourses, avoided, when a thing would come before my mind pretty plain, uttering or declaring it for fear that I might get something out before the people in relation to the future that was wrong." (In *Journal of Discourses,* 17:290-91.)

Though Orson Pratt felt inadequate in this calling, a study of his writings clearly shows that he did indeed fulfill the Lord's admonition to prophesy. His writings are full of prophetic insights and promises.

**D&C 34:7-12. "I Come Quickly"**

The phrase "I come quickly" refers to the nearness of the second coming of Jesus Christ and is found in at least thirteen sections of the Doctrine and Covenants. Although nearly 150 years have passed since some of these revelations were given, yet that is a relatively short period of time when compared to the nearly 6,000 years that the earth has existed in a telestial condition. The fulfillment of many of the prophecies pertaining to the Second Coming indicates that that event is indeed near.

President Joseph Fielding Smith explained the phrase and its significance:

" 'I come quickly.' This is a scriptural expression that occurs frequently, especially in the book of Revelation. This is 'speaking after the manner of the Lord.' (D. & C. 63:53.) This does not mean that immediately the Lord will make his appearance, but when he does come he will come suddenly, when he is least expected. He told his disciples that the day would come when men were unawares, as the thief in the night. For this reason we should watch and pray, 'For as a snare shall it come on all them that dwell on the face of the whole earth.' (Luke 21:34-35.) There is no excuse for any of us, then, not to be prepared, for we have been fully and frequently warned." (*Church History and Modern Revelation,* 1:157.)

Enrichment H, in the Appendix, gives a further treatment of the events associated with the Second Coming.

# "I Have . . . Prepared Thee for a Greater Work"

Section 35

## Historical Background

Sidney Rigdon was living in Mentor, Ohio, on what was called the Western Reserve when he first heard the message of the restored gospel in 1830 and was baptized. Soon after his baptism he traveled to Fayette, New York, to meet the Prophet. The Prophet Joseph Smith recorded the coming of Sidney Rigdon: "In December Sidney Rigdon came to inquire of the Lord, and with him came Edward Partridge; the latter was a pattern of piety, and one of the Lord's great men. Shortly after the arrival of these two brethren, thus spake the Lord: [D&C 35]." (*History of the Church,* 1:128.)

At the time Joseph Smith was translating the Bible. Oliver Cowdery and John Whitmer, who had been scribes for the Prophet, were called to serve as missionaries, leaving the Prophet without a scribe. In this revelation Sidney Rigdon was divinely appointed to fill the vacancy.

## Notes and Commentary

**D&C 35:1. What Is the Meaning of the Phrase "One Eternal Round"?**

"God governs by law—wholly, completely, invaryingly, and always. He has ordained that identical results always flow from the same causes. There is no respect of persons with him, and he is a Being 'with whom is no variableness, neither shadow of turning.' (Jas. 1:17; D. & C. 3:1-2.) Hence, the Lord's 'course is *one eternal round,* the same today as yesterday, and forever.' (D. & C. 35:1.)" (McConkie, *Mormon Doctrine,* pp. 545-46.)

**D&C 35:1-3. What Does It Mean to Become "One in Me"?**

President Brigham Young asked: "How is it that the Latter-day Saints feel and understand alike, are of one heart and one mind, no matter where they may be when they receive the Gospel? . . . They receive that which was promised by the Savior when he was about to leave the earth, namely, the Comforter, that holy unction from on high which recognizes one God, one faith and one baptism, whose mind is the will of God the Father, in whom there dwelleth unity of faith and action, and in whom there cannot be division or confusion; when they received thus further light, it matters not whether they have seen each other or not, they at once become brothers and sisters, having been adopted into the family of Christ through the bonds of the everlasting covenant, and all can then exclaim, in the beautiful language of Ruth, 'Thy people shall be my people, and thy God my God!' [Ruth 1:16.]" (In *Journal of Discourses,* 18:259.)

**D&C 35:2. "Even As Many As Will Believe on My Name"**

In Doctrine and Covenants 11:30, believing on the name of the Savior is equated with believing in him, or in other words, receiving him as the Savior.

Believing on his name is demonstrated by obedience to the laws and ordinances of the gospel (see 2 Nephi 25:13).

**D&C 35:3-6. "Sidney, . . . Thou Wast Sent Forth . . . to Prepare the Way"**

President Joseph Fielding Smith showed how Sidney Rigdon had been prepared long before the missionaries came to Ohio and met him: "The Lord told Sidney that he had looked upon him and his works, having reference to his ministry as a Baptist and later as one of the founders of the 'Disciples' with Alexander Campbell and Walter Scott. During those years the hand of the Lord was over him and directing him in the gathering of many earnest souls who could not accept the teachings of the sects of the day. His prayers in which he sought further light than the world was able to give, were now to be answered. The Lord informed him that he had been sent to prepare the way, and in the gathering of his colony and the building up of his congregation in and around Kirtland, the hand of the Lord was directing him, and the way for the reception of the fulness of truth was being prepared. It should be carefully noted that a great number of forceful, intelligent men who became leaders in the Church had been gathered by Sidney Rigdon, with the help of the Lord, in this part of the land. Without any question, the Spirit of the Lord had rested upon these men, as it did on Sidney Rigdon and Parley P. Pratt, to direct them to gather in Kirtland at that early day. When, therefore, Parley P. Pratt, Ziba Peterson and their companions came to Kirtland they found the way prepared for them through the preaching, very largely, of Sidney Rigdon, so that it was not a difficult matter for these missionaries to convince this group of the truth. While Sidney was preaching and baptizing by immersion without authority, which the Lord informed him in this revelation, yet it all resulted in good when the Gospel message reached them. These men were not only convinced and ready for baptism, but were in a condition by which the Priesthood could be given them, and this was done." (*Church History and Modern Revelation,* 1:160.)

*Sidney Rigdon was a spokesman for Joseph Smith*

**D&C 35:8-10. "Mine Arm Is Not Shortened"**

The phrase "arm of the Lord" suggest God's power, might, and authority (see Notes and Commentary on D&C 1:14). To say that it is not shortened means that his power is not limited in any way and that he will use his arm and make it felt, especially in these last days (see D&C 133:3).

**D&C 35:11. "Drink of the Wine of the Wrath of Her Fornication"**

"This distinctive phrase appears in three sections of the Doctrine and Covenants: 35:11; 86:3; 88:94, 105. In each instance it is used in connection with Babylon (representing the apostate world and church) or with the 'great church, the mother of abominations' (representing the apostate church of the devil). Those who 'drink of the wine of the wrath of her fornication' participate in the worldly pleasures and sins of the apostate world and church, and thus will reap the desolations and destruction that will come upon the wicked when they are judged." (Ludlow, *Companion,* 1:219.)

**D&C 35:13-14. How Will the Lord "Thrash the Nations"?**

"This expression is found in Habakkuk 3:12. Threshing, in olden times, was done by treading out the grain on a threshing-floor. The going forth of the messengers of the gospel among the nations is like trampling the wheat sheaves on the hard floor. The valuable kernels are carefully gathered up; the straw is left." (Smith and Sjodahl, Commentary, p. 186.)

**D&C 35:16. The Parable of the Fig Tree**

See Notes and Commentary for Doctrine and Covenants 45:34-38.

**D&C 35:17-19. "I Have Sent Forth the Gospel by the Hand of My Servant Joseph"**

Elder Wilford Woodruff taught clearly how the Prophet Joseph Smith fulfilled the great prophecies of the Restoration: "Here is laid the foundation of the fulfillment of that mighty flood of prophecy delivered since the days of Father Adam down to the last Prophet who breathed the breath of life. There has been more prophecy fulfilled in the last forty-three years upon the face of the earth, than in two thousand years before. These mighty prophecies . . . like a band of iron, governed and controlled Joseph Smith in his labors while he lived on the earth. He lived until he received every key, ordinance and law ever given to any man on the earth, from Father Adam down, touching this dispensation. He received powers and keys from under the hands of Moses for gathering the House of Israel in the last days; he received under the hands of Elias the keys of sealing the hearts of the fathers to the children, and the hearts of the children to the fathers; he received under the hands of Peter, James and John, the Apostleship, and everything belonging thereto; he received under the hands of Moroni all the keys and powers required of the stick of Joseph in the hands of Ephraim; he received under the hands of John the Baptist the Aaronic Priesthood, with all its keys and powers, and every other key and power belonging to this dispensation, and I am not ashamed to say that he was a Prophet of God, and he laid the foundation of the greatest work and dispensation that has ever been established on the earth." (In *Journal of Discourses,* 16:267.)

**D&C 35:20. "Thou Shalt Write for Him"**

Elder George Q. Cannon explained the commandment given here: "To Sidney He gave a special command that he should write for Joseph. The Lord made known to Sidney what Joseph already understood—that the Scriptures should be given, even as they were in God's own bosom, to the salvation of His elect. And soon after this time, Joseph began a new translation of the scriptures. While he labored, many truths, buried through scores of ages, were brought forth to his understanding, and he saw in their purity and holiness all the doings of God among His children, from the days of Adam unto the birth of our Lord and Savior." (*Life of Joseph Smith,* pp. 83-84.)

# Revelation to Edward Partridge

# Section 36

## Historical Background

During the infancy of the Church, the Lord raised up righteous men to stand beside the Prophet Joseph Smith in building the kingdom. The year 1830 saw many of these future leaders join the Church, one of whom was Edward Partridge. He was born in Massachusetts and first heard the gospel in Kirtland, Ohio, when the missionaries who had been sent to the Lamanites stopped there on the way to Missouri. Shortly thereafter he traveled with Sidney Rigdon to New York, arriving in Fayette in December 1830.

Edward Partridge had not been baptized at the time he first visited the Prophet. Lucy Mack Smith recorded the following:

"In December of the same year [1830], Joseph appointed a meeting at our house. While he was preaching, Sidney Rigdon and Edward Partridge came in and seated themselves in the congregation. When Joseph had finished his discourse, he gave all who had any remarks to make, the privilege of speaking. Upon this, Mr. Partridge arose, and stated that he had been to Manchester, with the view of obtaining further information respecting the doctrine which we preached; but, not finding us, he had made some inquiry of our neighbors concerning our characters, which they stated had been unimpeachable, until Joseph deceived us relative to the Book of Mormon. He also said that he had walked over our farm, and observed the good order and industry which it exhibited; and, having seen what we had sacrificed for the sake of our faith, and having heard that our veracity was not questioned upon any other point than that of our religion, he believed our testimony, and was ready to be baptized, 'if,' said he, 'Brother Joseph will baptize me.'

" 'You are now,' replied Joseph, 'much fatigued, brother Partridge, and you had better rest to-day, and be baptized tomorrow.'

" 'Just as Brother Joseph thinks best,' replied Mr. Partridge, 'I am ready at any time.'

"He was accordingly baptized the next day." (*History of Joseph Smith,* pp. 191-92.)

## Notes and Commentary

**D&C 36:1. Christ Is the "Mighty One of Israel"**

"In this Revelation our Lord announces Himself as 'the Mighty One of Israel.' This name also occurs in Isaiah (1:24; 30:29). It means Jehovah, the Lord of Hosts, who led His people out of Egypt, with a strong arm. While the 'mighty one' of Assyria was a winged bull, and while earthly kingdoms adopt images of eagles, lions, etc., as emblems of strength, the 'Mighty One' of the Kingdom of God is Jehovah." (Smith and Sjodahl, Commentary, p. 191.)

**D&C 36:1. Preach "As with the Voice of a Trump"**

Trumpets were used anciently to sound an alarm, to signal for battle, or to announce the coming of royalty. The sounding of trumpets, therefore, symbolizes heralding or announcing something highly significant. The sound of a trumpet is loud and clear and draws the attention of those within its range. Edward Partridge was called to preach in that manner—not quietly or timidly, but boldly, with clarity and authority.

**D&C 36:2. "I Will Lay My Hand upon You"**

Edward Partridge, who had just been baptized, was promised in this verse the gift of the Holy Ghost, which is given by the laying on of hands. He was

*Edward Partridge received the priesthood "by the hand of my servant Sidney Rigdon" (D&C 36:2)*

also called into the ministry. The spirit and authority to fill such calls is similarly given by the laying on of hands.

Elder Harold B. Lee referred to this verse as an example of how the Lord manifests his power among men through his servants to whom he has committed the keys of authority: "The Lord here is saying that when one of his authorized servants puts his hands by authority upon the head of one to be blessed, it is as though he himself was putting his hand on with them to perform that ordinance. So we begin to see how he manifests his power among men through his servants to whom He has committed the keys of authority." (*Be Secure in the Gospel of Jesus Christ,* Brigham Young University Speeches of the Year [Provo, 11 Feb. 1958], p. 6.)

### D&C 36:2. What Are the "Peaceable Things of the Kingdom"?

Shortly before he was crucified, Jesus promised his disciples the gift of peace (see John 14:27). This peace is not the peace of the world but the inner peace that comes from the knowledge that one has found the truth, has had his sins remitted, and is on the path that leads to eternal life. This knowledge and assurance comes from the Holy Ghost, who is appropriately called the Comforter (see John 14:26). Thus, all Saints may in this world of strife and turmoil receive peace from Christ by the Holy Ghost and the assurance that the course they are pursuing is correct (see D&C 6:22-23; 59:23).

### D&C 36:3. What Does the Word *Hosanna* Mean?

See Notes and Commentary on Doctrine and Covenants 19:37.

### D&C 36:6. What Is an "Untoward Generation"?

The same expression is found in Acts 2:40, referring to the people of that day. An untoward people is an unruly, rebellious people whose lives are not turned toward the Lord. President Joseph Fielding Smith, in reference to those of the latter days said, "This is an untoward generation, walking in spiritual darkness" (*Church History and Modern Revelation,* 1:163).

### D&C 36:6. What Does It Mean to "Come Forth out of the Fire, Hating Even the Garments Spotted with the Flesh"?

This part of verse 6 is an allusion to Jude 1:23. Elder Bruce R. McConkie wrote of that scripture: "To stay the spread of disease in ancient Israel, clothing spotted by contagious diseases was destroyed by burning. (Lev. 13:47-59; 15:4-17.) And so with sin in the Church, the saints are to avoid the remotest contact with it; the very garments, as it were, of the sinners are to be burned with fire, meaning that anything which has had contact with the pollutions of the wicked must be shunned. And so also with those yet in the world who are invited to join the kingdom." (*Doctrinal New Testament Commentary,* 3:428.)

### D&C 36:8. What Does the Phrase "Gird Up Your Loins" Mean?

"In Biblical language, to 'gird up the loins' is to prepare for a journey, or for work. The Hebrews wore girdles [sashes] when traveling, and when at work. On such occasions they girt their clothes about them [by tucking them under the sash] to ensure free movement of the limbs. The servants of the Lord must be prepared to do His work, and to go when He calls." (Smith and Sjodahl, Commentary, p. 201.)

Concerning the need for the Saints to gird up their loins and prepare more effectively to proclaim the gospel in this day, President Spencer W. Kimball said:

"I feel that when we have done all in our power that the Lord will find a way to open doors. . . .

"But I can see no good reason why the Lord would open doors that we are not prepared to enter. . . .

"When I ask for more missionaries, I am not asking for more testimony-barren or unworthy missionaries. I am asking that we start earlier and train our missionaries better in every branch and every ward in the world. That is another challenge—that the young people will understand that it is a great privilege to go on a mission and that they must be physically well, mentally well, spiritually well, and that 'the Lord cannot look upon sin with the least degree of allowance.'

"I am asking for missionaries who have been carefully indoctrinated and trained through the family and the organizations of the Church, and who come to the mission with a great desire." ("When the World Will Be Converted," *Ensign,* Oct. 1974, p. 7.)

# "Ye Shall Go to the Ohio"

Section 37

## Historical Background

This revelation was given eight months after the Church was officially organized. Since that eventful day on 6 April 1830, the Church had grown to approximately two hundred Saints in the state of New York. Missionary efforts had been extended westward to Kirtland, Ohio, and to the borders of Missouri. Missionaries had been particularly successful in the Kirtland area, where they baptized about 127 people during the two or three weeks they spent there on their way to Missouri (see Roberts, *Comprehensive History of the Church,* 1:231). The Church continued to grow rapidly in that area after they departed.

By the time of this revelation, such notable leaders as Parley P. Pratt, Orson Pratt, Sidney Rigdon, Edward Partridge, and Thomas B. Marsh had joined the Church. Revelations had poured down from heaven as the Prophet Joseph Smith received guidance for individual Saints, direction in revising the Bible, and the records of Moses and Enoch. But Satan's efforts were unrelenting. Persecution raged, and the Prophet was arrested a number of times on false accusations. Now, in December 1830, the voice of the Lord was heard again. But this time the Lord's will was that Joseph cease revising the Bible and move to Ohio. Section 37 is the first revelation directing the Saints to gather to a central place. In it the Lord charted a westward course for the restored Church.

*Kirtland, Ohio, as viewed from the Kirtland Temple tower (c.1900)*

## Notes and Commentary

### D&C 37:1. "Not . . . Translate Any More"

This passage refers to the Joseph Smith Translation of the Bible. The Prophet Joseph had, of course, finished the translation of the Book of Mormon. But though his work on the Bible was very important, the need to move to Ohio "because of the enemy" took priority (D&C 37:1). The work on the revision of the Bible was continued later in Ohio, mainly at the home of John Johnson.

### D&C 37:1. What Was the Design of the Lord in Gathering the Saints to Ohio?

President Joseph Fielding Smith explained why the Lord commanded the Saints to move: "The call to the Ohio was for two reasons. The opposition to the Church in and around Fayette had become bitter. There had been many converts made among the followers of Sidney Rigdon in Kirtland, and the spirit there was friendly. The trend of the Church was ever westward; as persecution arose, and it became necessary to seek protection, the Church moved farther and farther west. The Lord had a design in this. The place of the City of Zion was west and it was necessary that eventually the Church be located there, although it would not be a permanent residence until Zion is redeemed. Not only were Joseph Smith and Sidney Rigdon commanded to go to Ohio, but this came as a command to the entire Church." (*Church History and Modern Revelation,* 1:163.)

### D&C 37:3. Assemble in Ohio Against the Return of Oliver Cowdery

Oliver Cowdery had been on a mission to the Lamanites since 15 October 1830 (see D&C 30:5-6; 32:2). This mission took him and his companions on a fourteen-hundred-mile journey through New York and Ohio to Missouri. The Saints were commanded to move to Ohio in preparation for receiving further instructions concerning the establishment of Zion after Oliver Cowdery's return from "the borders by the Lamanites" (D&C 28:9).

# "If Ye Are Prepared Ye Shall Not Fear"

Section 38

## Historical Background

As the year 1831 dawned, Joseph Smith envisioned "a prospect great and glorious for the welfare of the kingdom" (*History of the Church,* 1:140). The kingdom had previously been given a divine charge that set the purpose of this dispensation. That charge was to "seek to bring forth and establish the cause of Zion" (D&C 6:6; 11:6; 12:6; 14:6). From the time this commandment was first given until his martyrdom, the Prophet labored diligently to this end. He once said, "We ought to have the building up of Zion as our greatest object" (*History of the Church,* 3:390).

During the month of December 1830, Joseph Smith received by revelation the remainder of the book of Moses. Chapters 6 and 7 dealt specifically with the establishment of Zion in Enoch's day. Two things were needed before Zion could be realized in this dispensation, however: revelation from the Lord giving his law and the revealed order of Zion, and the preparation and sanctification of the Saints. The fulfillment of the first requirement was begun on 2 January 1831. During the third conference of the Church, the Prophet received Doctrine and Covenants 38. In it the Lord said that he was "the same which had taken the Zion of Enoch into mine own bosom" (D&C 38:4). He further revealed why he had commanded the Saints to move to Ohio: "There I will give unto you my law; and there you shall be endowed with power from on high" (D&C 38:32). This revelation was the Lord's answer to those who wondered why they should move three hundred miles to the west in the dead of winter.

## Notes and Commentary

### D&C 38:1. Jesus Christ Is the Great I Am, Alpha and Omega

President Joseph Fielding Smith described the significance of the name title "I Am": "When Moses was tending the flocks of his father-in-law, Jethro, at Horeb, the mountain of God, the Lord appeared to him in a flaming bush and gave him commandment to go to Egypt and lead Israel from bondage. Moses said to the Lord: 'Behold, when I come unto the children of Israel, and shall say unto them, The God of our Fathers hath sent me unto you; and they shall say to me, What is his name? what shall I say unto them? And God said unto Moses, I am that I am; and he said, Thus shalt thou say unto the children of Israel, I Am hath sent me unto you.' . . . The name given to Moses is the same as given by Jesus Christ to the Jews, and the meaning of it is expressed in the saying that God is 'omnipotent, omnipresent, and omniscient; without beginning of days or end of life; and that in him every good gift and every good principle dwell.' (Lectures on Faith, No. 2.) Jesus declared to the Jews that which they were incapable of understanding, which is that the great I Am who appeared to Moses, was himself, and that he was God and gave commandments to Abraham." (*Church History and Modern Revelation,* 1:165-66; see also Exodus 3:14; D&C 39:1.)

*Alpha* and *omega* are the first and last letters of the Greek alphabet, which was used widely at the time of Christ. The expression "Alpha and Omega" is thus the equivalent of the English expression "from A to Z." To give Jesus the title of Alpha and Omega suggests that in him all things are encompassed. Elder Bruce R. McConkie said, "These words, the first and last letters of the Greek alphabet, are used figuratively to teach the timelessness and eternal nature of our Lord's existence, that is, that 'from eternity to eternity he is the same, and his years never fail.' (D. & C. 76:4.)" (*Mormon Doctrine,* p. 31).

### D&C 38:1. "Seraphic Hosts of Heaven"

"*Seraphs* are angels who reside in the presence of God. . . . it is clear that seraphs include the unembodied spirits of pre-existence, for our Lord 'looked upon the wide expanse of eternity, *and all the seraphic hosts of heaven, before the world was made.*' (D. & C. 38:1.) Whether the name *seraphs* also applies to perfected and resurrected angels is not clear. . . .

"In Hebrew the plural of seraph is *seraphim.*" (McConkie, *Mormon Doctrine,* pp. 702-3.)

### D&C 38:2. Omniscience of God

It is surprising that some people still question whether God is omniscient, that is, whether he has all knowledge in the ultimate. They say that he knows all things in relationship to man but that he himself is still learning and progressing in the knowledge he can acquire. This scripture and numerous others (see 2 Nephi 9:20; D&C 88:41; 130:7; Moses 1:6) clearly teach that God has all knowledge. There are no reservations or limitations in that statement.

Knowledge brings power, and to say that God is limited in his knowledge is to deny his omnipotence as well. The Prophet Joseph Smith taught this principle in *Lectures on Faith*: "Without the knowledge of all things, God would not be able to save any portion of his creatures; for it is by reason of the knowledge which he has of all things, from the beginning to the end, that enables him to give that understanding to his creatures by which they are made partakers of eternal life; and if it were not for the idea existing in the minds of men that God had all knowledge it would be impossible for them to exercise faith in him." (*Lectures on Faith* 4:43; see also Enrichment D, in the Appendix.)

**D&C 38:3. Christ the Creator**

"Under the direction of his Father, Jesus Christ created this earth. No doubt others helped him, but it was Jesus Christ, our Redeemer, who, under the direction of his Father, came down and organized matter and made this planet, so that it might be inhabited by the children of God." (Smith, *Doctrines of Salvation,* 1:74; see also 2 Nephi 9:5-6; 3 Nephi 9:15; Moses 1:33; 2:1, 27.)

**D&C 38:4. I Have "Taken the Zion of Enoch into Mine Own Bosom"**

To be "in the bosom" of someone is a Hebrew idiom derived from the fact that anciently a man's clothing consisted of large flowing robes wrapped around his person and fastened with a sash, forming a spacious repository above the waist in which things, including children, were often carried. Something so carried was kept close to the chest or bosom, so the phrase "to be in the bosom of another" implied a very close and favored relationship (see 2 Samuel 12:8; Luke 16:22; John 1:18).

"Enoch, the seventh from Adam (Jude 14) built a city called Zion, after the people of God, so named by the Lord, because they were united, righteous, and prosperous. This city of Enoch flourished for three hundred and sixty-five years and then the Lord, by some process not known to us, took it with all its inhabitants, 'to His bosom,' thus saving them from destruction in the flood that was to come. 'And from thence went forth the saying, Zion is fled' (Pearl of Great Price, Book of Moses 7:18, 19, 68, 69)." (Smith and Sjodahl, Commentary, p. 199; see also D&C 45:11-14; Enrichment B.)

The Lord promises that all who have believed in his name shall also be taken into Christ's bosom—a glorious promise indeed!

**D&C 38:5-8. Why Are the Wicked Facing Doom?**

President Joseph Fielding Smith explained the final fate of the wicked: "When Christ comes the second time it will be in the clouds of heaven, and it shall be the day of vengeance against the ungodly, when those who have loved wickedness and have been guilty of transgression and rebellion against the laws of God will be destroyed. All during the ministry of Christ wickedness ruled and seemed to prevail, but when he comes in the clouds of glory as it is declared in this message of Malachi to the world, and which was said by Moroni to be near at hand, then Christ will appear as the refiner and purifier of both man and beast and all that pertains to this earth, for the earth itself shall undergo a change and receive its former paradisiacal glory." (*Doctrines of Salvation,* 3:11; see also 2 Nephi 23:6-11; Malachi 3:2-5; 4:1.)

In that hour only the purified will be able to abide the day (see D&C 38:8).

**D&C 38:7-8. "I Am in Your Midst"**

Concerning the nearness of the Lord to his servants, President Harold B. Lee said: "I have a session with the missionary groups as they go out, in the temple, where they are permitted to ask

*The London Temple*

intimate questions that wouldn't be proper to be discussed elsewhere. They sometimes ask, Could you tell us a certain place in the temple where the Savior has been seen? My answer is, 'Keep in mind that this is the house of the Lord; this is the place that we try to keep as pure and holy and sacred as any building we have. This is the most likely place he would come when he comes on earth. Don't ask for a certain place because he has walked these halls. How do you know but what he is here in your midst?" (In Conference Report, British Area Conference 1971, pp. 135-36; or *Ensign,* Nov. 1971, pp. 12-13.)

**D&C 38:9, 15. "The Enemy Shall Not Overcome"**

President Joseph Fielding Smith wrote:

"He has given to us the kingdom. He has made us the promise that the enemy of the kingdom shall not overcome. We may have trouble. We have had trouble. We may meet with opposition, but that opposition shall fail in its endeavor to destroy the work of God.

"The gospel has been restored, and the kingdom given to his saints according to the prophecy of Daniel. It is not again to be removed, destroyed, or given to other people, and in his own way and time he is going to break down all other systems, that his kingdom may prevail and that he may come and reign as Lord of lords and King of kings upon the face of the whole earth.

"The Lord has called attention to the fact that he is going to destroy systems and organizations and combinations that are false. And how is he going to do it? By giving their members the truth, if they will receive it; by giving them the privilege of coming out of those organizations to receive the truth and have every opportunity to come into his kingdom, for his hand is outstretched ready to greet them. If they will not come; if they will not receive his message; then, of course, they must fall with their systems. Truth will prevail; truth will stand when all else is removed, and it is destined to cover the face of the earth." (*Doctrines of Salvation,* 1:241.)

**D&C 38:10-12. "Eternity Is Pained, and the Angels Are Waiting"**

The imagery of angels waiting to reap down the fields comes from the parable of the wheat and the tares (see Matthew 13:24-43; D&C 86:1-7). It is the wickedness of the world that causes pain in the eternal realms, as Elder Wilford Woodruff explained: "It certainly is time that we prepare ourselves for that which is to come. Great things await this generation—both Zion and Babylon. All these revelations concerning the fall of Babylon will have their fulfillment. Forty-five years ago, in speaking to the Church, the Lord said—[D&C 38:10-11]. This causes silence to reign, and all eternity is pained. The angels of God are waiting to fulfill the great commandment given forty-five years ago, to go forth and reap down the earth because of the wickedness of men. How do you think eternity feels to-day? Why there is more wickedness, a thousand times over, in the United States now, than when that revelation was given. The whole earth is ripe in iniquity; and these inspired men, these Elders of Israel, have been commanded of the Almighty to go forth and warn the world, that their garments may be clear of the blood of all men." (In *Journal of Discourses,* 18:128.)

Notes and Commentary on Doctrine and Covenants 86:5 discusses the time when those angels will be given the command to reap down the earth.

**D&C 38:17-20. "The Lord of Your Inheritance"**

To better understand the Lord's promise in these verses, one needs to understand that the earth was designed by the Lord as a place of habitation for his children. The earth itself reflects the level of life that is lived on it. Elder Bruce R. McConkie described four of the stages the earth has gone through and will yet go through:

"*Edenic earth.* Following its physical creation, the earth was pronounced *good.* It was a *terrestrial or paradisiacal* state. There was no death either for man or for any form of life, and 'all the vast creation of animated beings breathed naught but health, and peace, and joy.' (2 Ne. 2:22; *Voice of Warning,* pp. 89-91.)

"*Telestial earth.* When Adam fell, the earth fell also and became a mortal sphere, one upon which worldly and carnal people can live. This condition was destined to continue for a period of 6,000 years, and it was while in this state that the earth was baptized in water. (D. & C. 77:6-7, 12; *Man: His Origin and Destiny,* pp. 415-436, 460-466.)

"*Terrestrial earth.* 'We believe . . . that the earth will *renewed* and receive its *paradisiacal glory.'* (Tenth Article of Faith.) Thus, the earth is to go back to the primeval, paradisiacal, or terrestrial state that prevailed in the days of the Garden of Eden. Accompanying this transition to its millennial status the earth is to be burned, that is, receive its baptism of fire. It will then be a new heaven and a new earth, and again health, peace, and joy will prevail upon its face. (D. & C. 101:23-32; Isa. 65:17-25; Mal. 3:1-6; 4:1-6; *Man: His Origin and Destiny,* pp. 380-397.)

"*Celestial earth.* Following the millennium plus 'a little season' (D. & C. 29:22-25), the earth will die, be resurrected, and becoming like a 'sea of glass' (D. & C. 130:7), attain unto 'its sanctified, immortal, and eternal state.' (D. & C. 77:1-2.) Then the poor and the meek—that is, the godfearing and the righteous—shall inherit the earth; it will become an abiding place for the Father and the Son, and celestial beings will possess it forever and ever. (D. & C. 88:14-26, 111.)" (*Mormon Doctrine,* p. 211.)

The statement that there will be no curse on the land when the Lord comes (see D&C 38:18) refers to the terrestrial earth during the Millennium, whereas the promise that the Saints will possess it during eternity (see D&C 38:18) reflects the earth's eventual celestial state.

**D&C 38:21-22. "I Will Be Your King"**

"Christ is the *King.* (Ps. 5:2; 10:16; 44:4; 47:6-7; 89:18; Isa. 6:5; 43:15; Jer. 23:5; 46:18; 1 Tim. 1:17.) By this is meant that he is the Ruler, Lawgiver, and Sovereign in whom all power rests. As King he rules over the heavens and the earth and all things that are in them (Alma 5:50); and also, in a particular sense, he rules over the kingdom of God on earth which is the Church and over the kingdom of God in heaven which is the celestial kingdom." (McConkie, *Mormon Doctrine,* p. 414.)

Though Jesus is King by right and authority, President Joseph Fielding Smith taught, at the council of Adam-ondi-Ahman, Christ will be crowned the actual, political ruler of the world (see Notes and Commentary on D&C 116:1). President Smith further explained that the kingdom of God includes both political and ecclesiastical aspects, for "when our Savior comes to rule in the millennium, all governments will become subject unto his government, and this has been referred to as the kingdom of God, which it is; but this is the political kingdom which will embrace all people whether they are in the Church or not. Of course, when every kindred, tongue and people become subject to the rule of Jesus Christ such will be in that political kingdom. We must keep these two thoughts in mind. But the kingdom of God is the Church of Jesus Christ, and it is the kingdom that shall endure forever. When the Savior prayed, 'Thy kingdom come,' he had reference to the kingdom in heaven which is to come when the millennial reign starts.

"When Christ comes, the political kingdom will be given to the Church. The Lord is going to make an end to all nations; that means this nation as well as any other. The kingdom of God is the Church, but during the millennium, the multitudes upon the face of the earth who are not in the Church will have to be governed, and many of *their officers,* who will be elected, may not be members of the Church." (*Doctrines of Salvation,* 1:229-30.)

### D&C 38:27. "If Ye Are Not One Ye Are Not Mine"

Elder Harold B. Lee explained the fundamental need for unity in the kingdom:

"If we are not united, we are not his. Here unity is the test of divine ownership as thus expressed. If we would be united in love and fellowship and harmony, this Church would convert the world, who would see in us the shining example of these qualities which evidence that divine ownership. Likewise, if in that Latter-day Saint home the husband and wife are in disharmony, bickering, and divorce is threatened, there is an evidence that one or both are not keeping the commandments of God.

"If we, in our wards and our branches, are divided, and there are factions not in harmony, it is but an evidence that there is something wrong. If two persons are at variance, arguing on different points of doctrine, no reasonable, thinking persons would say that both were speaking their different opinions by the Spirit of the Lord. . . .

"If it is so important, then, that this people be a united people, we might well expect that upon this principle the powers of Satan would descend for their greatest attack. We might well expect, also, that if there be those of apostate mind among us, they would be inclined to ridicule and to scorn this principle of oneness and unity as being narrow-minded or as being unprogressive. We would likewise expect that those who are enemies would also seek to fight against that principle." (In Conference Report, Apr. 1950, pp. 97-98.)

### D&C 38:13, 28. "The Enemy . . . Seeketh Your Lives"

The Saints should not be surprised when the world opposes the kingdom and tries to thwart the work of God, for he himself promised that such would be the case. Elder Joseph F. Smith said that "the hatred of the wicked always has and always will follow the Priesthood and the Saints. The devil will not lose sight of the power of God vested in man—the Holy Priesthood. He fears it, he hates it, and will never cease to stir up the hearts of the debased and corrupt in anger and malice towards those who hold this power, and to persecute the Saints, until he is bound." (In *Journal of Discourses,* 19:24.)

Elder Bruce R. McConkie made this observation in general conference:

"Nor are the days of our greatest sorrows and our deepest sufferings all behind us. They too lie ahead. We shall yet face greater perils, we shall yet be tested with more severe trials, and we shall yet weep more tears of sorrow than we have ever known before. . . .

"The way ahead is dark and dreary and dreadful. There will yet be martyrs; the doors in Carthage shall again enclose the innocent. We have not been promised that the trials and evils of the world will entirely pass us by.

"If we, as a people, keep the commandments of God; if we take the side of the Church on all issues, both religious and political; if we take the Holy Spirit for our guide; if we give heed to the words of the apostles and prophets who minister among us—then, from an eternal standpoint, all things will work together for our good.

"Our view of the future shall be undimmed, and, whether in life or in death, we shall see our blessed Lord return to reign on earth. We shall see the New Jerusalem coming down from God in heaven to join with the Holy City we have built. We shall mingle with those of Enoch's city while together we worship and serve the Lord forever." (In Conference Report, Apr. 1980, pp. 98-100; or *Ensign,* May 1980, pp. 71, 73.)

### D&C 38:30. "If Ye Are Prepared Ye Shall Not Fear"

President Ezra Taft Benson used this verse as the text for one of his general conference addresses:

"What are some of the calamities for which we are to prepare? In section 29 the Lord warns us of 'a great hailstorm sent forth to destroy the crops of the earth.' (D&C 29:16.) In section 45 we read of 'an overflowing scourge; for a desolating sickness shall cover the land.' (D&C 45:31.) In section 63 the Lord declares he has 'decreed wars upon the face of the earth. . . .' (D&C 63:33.)

"In Matthew, chapter 24, we learn of 'famines, and pestilences, and earthquakes. . . .' (Matt. 24:7.) The Lord declared that these and other calamities shall occur. These particular prophecies seem not to be conditional. The Lord, with his foreknowledge, knows that they will happen. Some will come about through man's manipulations; others through the forces of nature and nature's God, but that they will come seems certain. Prophecy is but history in reverse—a divine disclosure of future events.

"Yet, through all of this, the Lord Jesus Christ has said: '. . . if ye are prepared ye shall not fear.' (D&C 38:30.)

"What, then, is the Lord's way to help us prepare for these calamities? The answer is also found in section 1 of the Doctrine and Covenants, wherein he says: [D&C 1:17-18, 37].

"Here then is the key—look to the prophets for the words of God, that will show us how to prepare for the calamities which are to come [see D&C 1:38]." (In Conference Report, Oct. 1973, p. 89; or *Ensign,* Jan. 1974, p. 68.)

### D&C 38:39. Pride and the Riches of the Earth

This scripture contains one of the clearest statements found anywhere in scripture about the proper attitude one should have toward the riches of the world.

Elder George Q. Cannon discussed the relationship between pride and wealth: "There is something in the human heart of that character that when human beings are prospering they are apt to be lifted up in pride and to forget the cause or the source of their prosperity; they are apt to forget God, who is the fountain of all their blessings, and to give glory to themselves. It requires a constant preaching of the word of God, a constant pleading with the people, a constant outpouring of the Spirit of God upon the people to bring them to a true sense of their real condition. . . . Is it right that we should be prudent, that we should take care of those gifts and blessings which God has given unto us, that we should husband our resources, that we should be economical, and not extravagant? Certainly; this is right, this is proper, we should be culpable if we were not so. But with this there is also something else required, and that is, to keep constantly in view that the management and care of these things is not the object that God had in sending us here, that is not the object of our probation. . . . I have been in reduced circumstances; been on missions when I did not know where to get a mouthful to eat; turned away by the people who dare not entertain me because of the anger that was kindled against us. I could stand by and weep, being a boy and away from all my friends. But I, nevertheless, was happy. I never enjoyed myself in my life as I did then. I know that happiness does not consist in the possession of worldly things. Still it is a great relief when people can have the means necessary for the support of themselves and families. If they possess these things and the Spirit of God with them, they are blessed." (*In Journal of Discourses,* 22:100-101.)

**D&C 38:42. "Be Ye Clean That Bear the Vessels of the Lord"**

"In ancient Israel, certain vessels (bowls, urns, vases, and other containers) and utensils were used in religious feasts and ceremonies. The vessels that were to be used in the temple had special significance and were handled only by those who were worthy and authorized and who had properly prepared themselves. In a somewhat similar manner, the Lord has indicated that his saints should come 'out from among the wicked' (38:42) and leave the worldliness of Babylon so they will be worthy to 'bear the vessels of the Lord' (see 133:5)." (Ludlow, *Companion,* 2:317.)

# Revelations to James Covill

Sections 39–40

## Historical Background

"Many are called, but few are chosen" (D&C 121:40). Such is the story of James Covill, a man called by a personal revelation through the Prophet Joseph Smith to labor in the Lord's vineyard, and a man who utterly failed to give heed to the counsel given him. Every call to serve in the latter-day building of Zion requires personal sacrifice. James Covill had been a minister for about forty years. He was now called to be baptized into the Lord's Church and to preach the gospel. To accept such a call would require him to forsake many of his former beliefs, to confess to his followers that he had now found a fulness of the truth, and to move to Ohio where people were calling upon the Lord to stay the impending judgments. It would also require that he find new employment in order to sustain himself.

Shortly after the Church conference of 2 January 1831, the Prophet Joseph Smith recorded: "There was a man came to me by the name of James Covill, who had been a Baptist minister for about forty years, and covenanted with the Lord that he would obey any command that the Lord would give to him through me, as His servant, and I received the following: [D&C 39]." (*History of the Church,* 1:143.)

Marvelous promises had been made to James Covill if he would obey the word of the Lord that had been given to him. What thoughts might have filled his mind as he contemplated leaving the ministry he had been engaged in for forty years? What sacrifices would be required of him to join the Church and move to Ohio? Possibly with these thoughts and perhaps many others, James Covill decided to reject the revelation of God. The Prophet Joseph Smith recorded simply: "As James Covill rejected the word of the Lord, and returned to his former principles and people, the Lord gave unto me and Sidney Rigdon the following revelation [D&C 40], explaining why he obeyed not the word" (*History of the Church,* 1:145).

*The Lord's vineyard is to be "pruned for the last time" (D&C 39:17)*

## Notes and Commentary

### D&C 39:5-6. James Covill Was Taught the True Gospel

Elder Bruce R. McConkie explained the significance of the word *gospel*:

"The *gospel* of Jesus Christ is the plan of salvation. . . .

"Literally, gospel means good tidings from God or God-story. Thus it is the glad tidings or good news concerning Christ, his atonement, the establishment of his earthly kingdom, and a possible future inheritance in his celestial presence. 'And this is the gospel,' the Prophet recorded by way of revelation, 'the glad tidings, which the voice out of the heavens bore record unto us—That he came into the world, even Jesus, to be crucified for the world, and to bear the sins of the world, and to sanctify the world, and to cleanse it from all unrighteousness; That through him all might be saved whom the Father had put into his power and made by him.' (D&C 76:40-42.)" (*Mormon Doctrine,* pp. 331-32.)

In Doctrine and Covenants 39:5-6, the Lord explained to James Covill that repentance, baptism, and receiving the gift of the Holy Ghost are essential if one would receive Christ. What James Covill had taught before is not known, but the Savior here taught him the true gospel.

### D&C 39:7-9. With What Problem Had James Covill Been Plagued in the Past?

Verse 9 indicates that James Covill had rejected the Lord many times because of pride and the cares of the world. Very little is known about James Covill, other than what Joseph Smith recorded. It is therefore impossible to say what things he had done that caused the Lord to give him this solemn warning. But Elder Spencer W. Kimball gave modern Saints a similar warning:

"Frequently, pride gets in our way and becomes our stumbling block. But each of us needs to ask himself the question: 'Is your pride more important than your peace?'

"All too frequently, one who has done many splendid things in life and made an excellent contribution will let pride cause him to lose the rich reward to which he would be entitled otherwise." (*Miracle of Forgiveness,* p. 297; see also D&C 121:34-40.)

### D&C 39:10-11. The "Iffy" Blessings

In these verses the use of the word *if* is an indication that the blessings James Covill was to receive were conditional. President Harold B. Lee said:

"I sat in a class in Sunday School in my own ward one day, and the teacher was the son of a patriarch. He said he used to take down the blessings of his father, and he noticed that his father gave what he called 'iffy' blessings. He would give a blessing, but it was predicated on . . . 'if you will cease doing that.' And he said, 'I watched these men to whom my father gave the "iffy" blessings, and I saw that many of them did not heed the warning that my father as a patriarch had given, and the blessings were never received because they did not comply.'

"You know, this started me thinking. I went back into the Doctrine and Covenants and began to read the 'iffy' revelations that have been given to the various brethren in the Church. If you want to have an exercise in something that will startle you, read some of the warnings that were given through the Prophet Joseph Smith to Thomas B. Marsh, Martin Harris, some of the Whitmer brothers, William E. McLellin—warnings which, had they heeded, some would not have fallen by the wayside. But because they did not heed, and they didn't clear up their lives, they fell by the wayside, and some had to be dropped from membership in the Church." (In Conference Report, Oct. 1972, p. 130; or *Ensign,* Jan. 1973, pp. 107-8.)

### D&C 39:19-24. The Second Coming of Christ Is Imminent

In this revelation given in 1831, the Lord revealed some important truths about his second coming:

1. The kingdom of heaven is at hand (see vs. 19).
2. The servants of God are to prepare the way for his coming (see vs. 20).
3. The day and hour of his coming no man knows (see vs. 21).
4. Those who receive the Holy Ghost will be looking for his coming and will know him (see vs. 23).
5. He will come quickly (see vs. 24).

Elder Bruce R. McConkie said: "We do not know when the calamities and troubles of the last days will fall upon any of us as individuals or upon bodies of the Saints. The Lord deliberately withholds from us the day and hour of his coming and of the tribulations which shall precede it—all as part of the testing and probationary experiences of mortality. He simply tells us to watch and be ready." (In Conference Report, Apr. 1979, pp. 132-33; or *Ensign,* May 1979, p. 93.)

### D&C 40:1-2. Why Did James Covill Reject the Word of the Lord?

President Joseph Fielding Smith explained that James Covill "was convinced of the truth, for it is clear that the Lord revealed to him things which he and the Lord alone knew to be the truth. However, when he withdrew from the influence of the Spirit of the Lord and had time to consider the fact that he would lose the fellowship of the world, and his place and position among his associates, he failed and rejected the promises and blessings which the Lord offered him." (*Church History and Modern Revelation,* 1:174.)

In his explanation of James Covill's rejection, the Lord used language from the parable of the soils (see Matthew 13:1-9; 20-22).

# The First Bishop Is Called

Section 41

## Historical Background

Section 41 is the first revelation in the Doctrine and Covenants given in Ohio. The Prophet Joseph Smith and his wife Emma had arrived in Kirtland a few days before this revelation was received, and they found that the Kirtland Branch had grown to nearly one hundred members. Many of the new converts had belonged to a religious society known as "Disciples." Even after joining the Church, these converts continued to practice what was called "common stock," or the holding of all property in common. But discord arose among members over the manner in which this system should operate. Some considered that what belonged to one member belonged to anyone in the branch. "Therefore," wrote John Whitmer, "they would take each other's clothes and other property and use it without leave, which brought on confusion and disappointments, for they did not understand the scripture" ("Church History," *Journal of History*, Jan. 1908, p. 50).

The Prophet Joseph Smith wrote:

"The branch of the Church in this part of the Lord's vineyard, which had increased to nearly one hundred members, were striving to do the will of God, so far as they knew it, though some strange notions and false spirits had crept in among them. With a little caution and some wisdom, I soon assisted the brethren and sisters to overcome them. The plan of 'common stock,' which had existed in what was called 'the family,' whose members generally had embraced the everlasting Gospel, was readily abandoned for the more perfect law of the Lord; and the false spirits were easily discerned and rejected by the light of revelation.

"The Lord gave unto the Church the following: [D&C 41]." (*History of the Church*, 1:146-47.)

## Notes and Commentary

### D&C 41:1. Why Were Some of the Saints in Kirtland to Be Cursed?

"Because there were those who had professed the name of the Lord and made covenant to serve him, like James Covill, for instance, and then they showed by their works that they did not act in sincerity, the Lord gave a revelation for the guidance of the members and a warning to those who had professed his name who had not obeyed him. This is one of the most solemn and pointed declarations that can be found in any scripture against the hypocrite and the person who professes in sincerity, and apparently accepts in good faith, a covenant and then departs from the covenant." (Smith, *Church History and Modern Revelation*, 1:177-78; see also Matthew 23:27-28; Isaiah 32:6.)

### D&C 41:2-6. What Law Were the Saints to Receive?

The Prophet Joseph Smith persuaded the members of the Kirtland Branch to abandon the "common stock" plan for the more perfect law of the Lord to be revealed according to the promise given at Fayette, New York (see D&C 38:32). In Doctrine and Covenants 41:2-4 the Lord directed the elders of the Church to assemble in Kirtland to receive this law. The law was given a few days later and is known as the law of consecration (see D&C 42).

### D&C 41:5. What Is a Disciple?

In this verse are given the two characteristics of disciples of the Lord: they receive his law, and they do it.

Speaking of the importance of doing, President Spencer W. Kimball said of the Saints' becoming a Zion people: "As important as it is to have this vision in mind, defining and describing Zion will not bring it about. That can only be done through consistent and concerted daily effort by every single member of the Church. No matter what the cost in toil or sacrifice, we must 'do it.' That is one of my favorite phrases: 'Do It.' " (In Conference Report, Apr. 1978, p. 122; or *Ensign*, May 1978, p. 81.)

### D&C 41:6. How Should Members of the Church Esteem the Sacred Commandments and Covenants Revealed to Them?

President Joseph Fielding Smith discussed the limitations on sharing sacred things: "The things of the kingdom are not for the unworthy, whether they are in or out of the Church. It is the duty of the members to hold in the most solemn and sacred manner every commandment, every covenant, every principle of truth which the Lord has revealed for their salvation. He has given to the members, if they will humbly receive them, covenants and obligations which are not for the world. Things that are most holy and sacred, which are revealed to those who have made covenant to be 'just and true,' and who have 'overcome by faith,' things which are imparted to them as a means of bringing to pass their exaltation, should not be lightly treated, ridiculed, or spoken of before the world. 'For it is not meet that the things which belong to the children of the kingdom should be given to them that are not worthy, or to dogs, or the pearls to be cast before swine.' Yet how often do we see the foolish, the ignorant and those who fail to comprehend the vastness of these sacred principles and covenants, treating them lightly and unworthily even before the world!" (*Church History and Modern Revelation*, 1:179-80.)

### D&C 41:6-8. What Is the Meaning of the Word *Meet* in These Verses?

"Earlier definitions of the word *meet,* which are now listed as archaic in some modern dictionaries, include the idea of being proper, fit, acceptable, permissible, right, necessary, or desirable. Thus, the statement it is 'not meet that I should command in all things' (D&C 58:26) essentially means that it is not necessary or desirable for the Lord to tell us everything we should know." (Ludlow, *Companion,* 2:175.)

### D&C 41:9-11. The Calling of Edward Partridge As the First Bishop of the Church

In the law of consecration, the bishop was the spiritual and temporal agent who directed the program, assigned inheritances, received properties, and so on (see D&C 42:33; 72:9-15). The law was to be revealed shortly, so it was appropriate that Edward Partridge should be called as the first bishop in the Church.

*Edward Partridge, the first bishop*

# The Law of the Lord

Section 42

## Historical Background

Once the Prophet moved to Kirtland, Ohio, he acted swiftly to set the Church in order. Under direction from the Lord, he appointed the first bishop of the Church, put an end to a false system of having all things in common (see D&C 41), and defined many policies and procedures. Several problems developed as other members from New York began flooding into Kirtland. This place was already an area of rapid growth for the Church, because many of the people there had been prepared by Sidney Rigdon to embrace the truth.

The Prophet had been told that the Lord would reveal his law to the Saints once they had moved to Ohio (see D&C 38:32); however, after Joseph Smith arrived in Kirtland, the Lord added one further stipulation: the elders had to agree upon the word of the Lord and were to unite in a prayer of faith. Only then would they receive the law designated to help the Saints live peaceably together (see D&C 41:2-3).

Accordingly, on 9 February 1831 twelve men were called together by Joseph Smith and united in prayer and in faith and desire to receive the law. In response the Lord revealed his law to them (see *History of the Church,* 1:148). Only verses 1 through 73 of section 42 were given at that time, however. The rest of the revelation was received two weeks later, on 23 February. This latter part, according to President Joseph Fielding Smith, was "given for the establishment of the City of Zion—New Jerusalem—which was to be built by the law of consecration and obedience to the fulness of the Gospel" (*Church History and Modern Revelation,* 1:184).

Because section 42 is comprised of two distinct, though closely related, revelations, it was originally printed in the Book of Commandments as two chapters: verses 1 through 73 were chapter 44; verses 74 through 93, though not in that order, comprised chapter 47.

Speaking of the importance of this revelation known as the law of the Lord, President George Q. Cannon said: "Altogether this was a most important revelation. It threw a flood of light upon a great variety of subjects and settled many important questions. Faithful men and women were greatly delighted at being members of a Church which the Lord acknowledged as His own, and to which He communicated His word through his inspired Prophet as he did at this time." (*Life of Joseph Smith,* p. 109.)

## Notes and Commentary

### D&C 42:2. What Is Law?

The word *law* in a gospel sense refers to the statutes, judgments, and principles of salvation revealed by the Lord to man. Christ is the law (see 3 Nephi 15:9) in that he is the embodiment and personification of law. The law of the Lord in a very real sense is a revelation of his character and attributes.

God has given laws to assist man in his quest to

become like the Father and the Son. No one can come unto the Father except through obedience to the laws which Christ has given (see D&C 132:12). The violation of these laws is what constitutes sin (see 1 John 3:4). The Lord in his infinite love and wisdom often gives laws to his children commensurate with their preparation to receive those laws. Hence, the law of Moses was to prepare the children of Israel for higher laws. The laws given in section 42 were to enable the Saints to purify their lives in preparation for the establishment of Zion. (A further discussion of what the Doctrine and Covenants teaches about law can be found in Enrichment G, in the Appendix.)

### D&C 42:12-14. Those Who Teach the Gospel Are under Serious Obligation to Do It As the Lord Has Directed

Elder Spencer W. Kimball spoke of the special teaching obligations resting on those who undertake to educate others in the gospel:

"Apparently there were in the early church those who taught for doctrines the sophistries of men. There are those today who seem to take pride in disagreeing with the orthodox teachings of the Church and who present their own opinions which are at variance with the revealed truth. Some may be partially innocent in the matter; others are feeding their own egotism; and some seem to be deliberate. Men may think as they please, but they have no right to impose upon others their unorthodox views. Such persons should realize that their own souls are in jeopardy. The Lord said to us through the Prophet Joseph: [D&C 42:12-14].

"The great objective of all our work is to build character and increase faith in the lives of those whom we serve. If one cannot accept and teach the program of the Church in an orthodox way without reservations, *he should not teach.* It would be the part of honor to resign his position. Not only would he be dishonest and deceitful, but he is also actually under condemnation, for the Savior said that it were better that a millstone were hanged about his neck and he be cast into the sea than that he should lead astray doctrinally or betray the cause or give offense, destroying the faith of one of 'these little ones' who believe in him. And remember that this means not only the small children, it includes even adults who believe and trust in God. . . .

"In our own society, the murderer who kills the body is hunted, imprisoned, and executed, but the character who kills the soul by implanting doubt and shattering faith is permitted not only to go free but also is often retained in high places. The body which is killed will rise again in the resurrection with little damage to its eternal welfare, but he whose faith has been shattered may suffer long ages before complete restoration of spiritual stature can be had, if at all." (In Conference Report, Apr. 1948, pp. 109-10; see also D&C 52:9.)

### D&C 42:14. How Does One Teach by the Spirit?

President Joseph Fielding Smith forcefully stated that "no one should be called upon to teach and no one should attempt to teach the doctrines of the Church unless he is fully converted and has an abiding testimony of their truth. This testimony can only be received through prayerful study and obedience to all the commandments of the Lord. No man or woman can teach by the Spirit what he or she does not practice. Sincerity, integrity and loyalty are essential factors, and these will be accompanied by the spirit of prayer. The Comforter, 'who knoweth all things,' we should rely on, and then our teachings shall be approved of our Father in Heaven." (*Church History and Modern Revelation,* 1:184-85.)

Verse 14 can be read either as a command or as a statement of fact, and either way the statement is true. If a person does not have the Spirit, he should not teach; and in the sense of true teaching, he cannot teach.

### D&C 42:18-29. The Lord Speaks to Members of the Church

President Joseph Fielding Smith emphasized that the Ten Commandments are part of the laws of God and that they are as binding today as they were in the days of Moses (see *Church History and Modern Revelation,* 1:185). The Lord repeats these commandments in section 42 as a part of his law and gives for each the heavy penalty for members of the Church who refuse to keep these laws or to fully repent of transgressions (see also D&C 64:12).

*Murder* (*vss. 18-19*). There is no forgiveness in this world or in the world to come, because the atonement of Christ does not cover murder committed by one who has joined the Church—a murderer must suffer for the sin himself (see Smith, *Teachings,* p. 339). Further, the law dictates that a murderer should suffer capital punishment. President Joseph Fielding Smith said that the Church "cannot destroy men in the flesh, because we do not control the lives of men and do not have power to pass sentences upon them which involve capital punishment. In the days when there was a theocracy on the earth, then this decree was enforced. What the Lord will do in lieu of this, because we cannot destroy in the flesh, I am unable to say, but it will have to be made up in some other way." (*Doctrines of Salvation,* 2:97.)

*The Ten Commandments are as binding today as they were anciently*

*Stealing* (*vs. 20*). Those who will not repent are then excommunicated.

*Lying* (*vs. 21*). Those who will not repent are then excommunicated.

*Adultery and lust* (*vss. 22-26*). Lust results in the loss of the Spirit, the loss of testimony, and excommunication if there is no repentance. Those who commit adultery may repent; but if they repeat the sin, they are excommunicated.

See Notes and Commentary on Doctrine and Covenants 59:5-12.

### D&C 42:22-23. "Marriage Presupposes Total Allegiance and Fidelity"

Only two commandments in all the scriptures require a person to love with all his heart. Each person is to love God (and, by implication, godliness) with all his heart (see Deuteronomy 6:5; Matthew 22:37), and a man is commanded to love his wife with all his heart. Elder Spencer W. Kimball explained the all-encompassing meaning of this commandment:

"When the Lord says *all* thy heart, it allows for no sharing nor dividing nor depriving. And, to the woman it is paraphrased: 'Thou shalt love thy husband with *all* thy heart and shalt cleave unto him and none else.'

"The words *none else* eliminate everyone and everything. The spouse then becomes preeminent in the life of the husband or wife, and neither social life nor occupational life nor political life nor any other interest nor person nor thing shall ever take precedence over the companion spouse. We sometimes find women who absorb and hover over the children at the expense of the husband, sometimes even estranging them from him.

"The Lord says to them: 'Thou shalt cleave unto *him* and none else.'

"Marriage presupposes total allegiance and total fidelity. Each spouse takes the partner with the understanding that he or she gives totally to the spouse all the heart, strength, loyalty, honor, and affection, with all dignity. Any divergence is sin; any sharing of the heart is transgression. As we should have 'an eye single to the glory of God,' so should we have an eye, an ear, a heart single to the marriage and the spouse and family." (*Faith Precedes the Miracle,* pp. 142-43.)

### D&C 42:27. "Thou Shalt Not Speak Evil of Thy Neighbor"

There is a distinct similarity between the Ten Commandments of the Old Testament and the law given here to the Church. The ninth commandment given to Moses forbids the bearing of false witness against one's neighbor (see Exodus 20:16). Here the law is made more inclusive, and any evil speaking of one's neighbor is forbidden. Elder Adam S. Bennion explained why such a commandment is so important to Saints today:

"*Murder, adultery,* and *stealing,* dealing respectively with *life, virtue,* and *property,* are generally considered more serious offenses before the law than the bearing of false witness. And yet, what the latter may lack in severity, it more than makes up for in prevalence. As a matter of fact, most of the readers of these lessons will likely shun—as they would a plague—the first three of these major social offenses; but consciously or unconsciously, we may all at times be tempted into the carelessness of rumor and other forms of bearing false witness. . . .

"To bear false witness is to testify to or to pass along *reports, insinuations, speculations,* or *rumors* as if they were true, to the hurt of a fellow human being. Sometimes the practice stems from a lack of correct information—sometimes from lack of understanding—sometimes from misunderstandings—sometimes from a vicious disposition to distort and misrepresent.

"Whereas murder involves the taking of human life, *bearing false witness* centers in the destruction of character or its defamation. It reaches to the ruin of reputation." ("The Ninth Commandment," *Ten Commandments Today,* pp. 134-36.)

### D&C 42:30-35. What Is the Relationship between the Building of Zion and the Law of Consecration?

"In this revelation the Law of Consecration is stated definitely as the law on which the New Jerusalem is to be built. This law is given for the benefit of the poor, for the building of Zion and the work of the ministry. . . . Through this celestial law (Consecration) the Saints are to become the covenant people of the Lord. We cannot enter into the fulness of the covenants pertaining to Zion until we have reached the point where we can live such a divine law. Those who cannot abide the law of tithing cannot partake of this law of consecration, or the higher law and they will be deprived of an inheritance when the inheritances are divided." (Smith, *Church History and Modern Revelation,* 1:185; see also Enrichment L.)

### D&C 42:39. How Have the Rich Gentiles Helped the Poor of the House of Israel?

In the Book of Mormon, the United States of America was called a gentile nation by the ancient prophets and by the Savior himself (see 1 Nephi 22:7; 3 Nephi 20:27-28). This is not to say that there would be none of the house of Israel in America but that as a nation it would not be thought of as part of the house of Israel. The Lord has blessed both the United States and Canada with great wealth and temporal abundance. From the early days of the Church, Saints in the United States and Canada have enjoyed prosperity and temporal wealth unknown to most of mankind throughout history. Through their faithfulness in paying their tithes, supporting missionaries, and giving other contributions, these Saints of the gentile nations made it possible for the work of the kingdom to go forth to the nations of the earth. Now Saints in many nations who enjoy temporal prosperity join in the work so the kingdom can more quickly fulfill its destiny.

### D&C 42:40. Many Problems Are Caused by Extravagance

Elder George Albert Smith, later to be President of the Church, offered this commentary on the contemporary application of Doctrine and Covenants 42:40:

"This [verse] doesn't refer to the time of Isaiah nor to the time of Alma, but comes right down to the day in which we live. Through His prophets He admonishes us with reference to our duties, and among the things He says are these: 'And again, thou shalt not be proud in thy heart; let all thy garments be plain, and their beauty the beauty of the work of thine own hands.' What a splendid thing to contemplate in our community. . . .

"Now, my brethren and sisters, I think that is worthy of our consideration. When discussing the high cost of living, examine your own household, and I am talking to myself while I talk to you. Am I increasing the cost of living by extravagance, or am I teaching my family to make the garments they wear? . . .

"Let us set an example; let us live within our means; let us be lenders instead of borrowers; let us not place our homes or the lands that produce our living under mortgages, in order that we may ride in fine conveyances or keep up with the pace set by our neighbors who may be able to afford it. Let us be more concerned about the adornment of our minds that are eternal, rather than adornment of our persons with things that are of no lasting benefit." (In Conference Report, Apr. 1915, p. 97.)

### D&C 42:43. The Sick Are to Do All They Can to Promote Their Recovery

Sometimes members of the Church think that all sickness should be dealt with only through priesthood administrations. This is not the official doctrine of the Church, as was stated in a *Church News* editorial:

"Every man, woman and child should care for his or her body as the temple of God which it is. Attention should be given to proper rest and exercise, and a well-balanced diet. The Lord has given us the Word of Wisdom to assist us further in better caring for our bodies.

*Wise exercise and diet are important in caring for one's body as a temple of God*

"There are times when we should pray for the sick, and through the priesthood lay hands upon the head of the ill and bless them. . . .

"But our belief in the divine power of healing should in no way preclude seeking competent medical assistance. Dr. James E. Talmage, a member of the Council of the Twelve, in 1921 said in an address:

" 'I say some have charged us with inconsistency, for they say: "If you believe in the gift of healing, what is the need of doctors, what is the need of surgeons, why build hospitals?" Because we know that "there is a law irrevocably decreed in heaven, before the world was, and when we attain any blessing it is by obedience to that law upon which it is predicated;" and the law is, in the instance under consideration, that we shall do all we can of ourselves. . . .

" 'We must do all we can, and then ask the Lord to do the rest, such as we cannot do. Hence we hold the medical and surgical profession in high regard. . . . When we have done all we can then the Divine Power will be directly applicable and operative.'

"The fact that faithful Latter-day Saints today are among some of the world's eminent physicians and surgeons affirms our continuing adherence to the statement of Dr. Talmage made 56 years ago." (*Church News,* 19 Feb. 1977, p. 16.)

### D&C 42:46. How Will the Righteous "Not Taste of Death"?

Some may think this phrase is a promise of translation, but President Joseph Fielding Smith interpreted it in this way: "To some members of the Church the saying that those who die in the Lord shall not taste of death has been a hard saying. They have seen good faithful men and women suffer days and at times for months before they were taken. But here the Lord does not say they shall not suffer pain of body, but that they shall be free from the anguish and torment of soul which will be partaken of by the wicked, and although they may suffer in body, yet death to them will be sweet in that they will realize that they are worthy before the Lord. The Savior said to Martha: 'and whosoever liveth and believe in me shall never die.' That is to say, they shall never die the second death and feel the torment of the wicked when they come face to face with eternity." (*Church History and Modern Revelation,* 1:186.)

### D&C 42:48. Is There a Time When Each Person Is to Die?

Elder Spencer W. Kimball, commenting on this phrase in the Doctrine and Covenants, said,"I am confident that there is a time to die. I am not a fatalist. I believe that many people die before 'their time' because they are careless, abuse their bodies, take unnecessary chances, or expose themselves to hazards, accidents and sickness. . . .

"God controls our lives, guides and blesses us, but gives us our agency. We may live our lives in accordance with His plan for us or we may foolishly shorten or terminate them.

"I am positive in my mind that the Lord has planned our destiny. We can shorten our lives but

I think we cannot lengthen them very much. Sometime we'll understand fully, and when we see back from the vantage point of the future we shall be satisfied with many of the happenings of this life which seemed so difficult for us to comprehend." (*Tragedy or Destiny*, pp. 9, 11.)

### D&C 42:53-73. Some Counsel to the Saints Regarding Their Stewardships

Smith and Sjodahl added some brief but important insights to these verses:

"53. *Thou*] Refers to all the Saints, as in paragraphs 42 and 45.

"54. *Thou shalt not take thy brother's garment*] Business must be coupled with humane considerations. Do not exact the 'pound of flesh.'

"*Thou shalt pay*] Avoid debt. On this point modern legislators might study the Mosaic legislation with profit.

"56. *My Scriptures shall be given*] The new English version (v. 15).

"57. *Until ye have received them in full*] Note the injunction against teaching the new version as long as it was incomplete.

"59-60. *The things which thou has received*] Refers to the Revelations given. They are the law by which the Church shall be governed. According to that law men will be saved or condemned.

"61-64. Here is a promise that, in answer to prayer, the Saints shall receive revelations and knowledge. The Spirit of Revelation is with the Saints whose hearts are opened to let the light in. The promise embraces especially a Revelation concerning the location of the New Jerusalem.

"68-69. In view of such promises it is the duty of the Saints to pray for wisdom and to rejoice before the Lord. . . .

"70-73. The law of remuneration is that those who administer in spiritual affairs must have their stewardships and labor for their living, 'even as the members.' This is wisdom. For in that position they are absolutely independent and can preach the truth without fear. Those who administer in temporal affairs and give their entire time to public business are to have a just remuneration. If they were to earn a living for themselves, they could not give all their time and energy to the community." (Commentary, pp. 233-34.)

### D&C 42:74-93. God Has Delegated the Responsibility to Take Action against Transgressors

President N. Eldon Tanner gave the following counsel on the ways those appointed to judge should deal with transgressors:

"Every mission president, stake president, and bishop is directed and instructed how to investigate and handle all cases of transgression. A person who is guilty of a serious transgression cannot progress, and he is not happy while the guilt is upon him. Until he has confessed and repented he is in bondage. The transgressor who is dealt with as he should be, with love and with proper discipline, will later express his appreciation for your concern, your interest, and your leadership. As he is properly dealt with, he is in a position to repent and come back to full activity. *But he must be dealt with.* . . .

"It has been reported to me that some bishops and even stake presidents have said that they never have excommunicated or disciplined anyone and that they do not intend to. This attitude is entirely wrong. Judges in Israel have the responsiblity to sit in righteous judgment where it becomes necessary. Let me read from the the twentieth section of the Doctrine and Covenants an important reminder to those who have the responsibility of judging: 'Any member of the Church of Christ transgressing, or being overtaken in a fault, shall be dealt with as the scriptures direct.' (D&C 20:80.)

"Brethren, study the scriptures and the handbook and do as they direct and discipline the members of the Church when necessary. Remember that it is no kindness to a transgressor for his local authority to ignore or overlook or try to cover up his iniquity.

"Let me read a quotation from President John Taylor wherein he discussed this subject: 'Furthermore, I have heard of some Bishops who have been seeking to cover up the iniquities of men: I tell them, in the name of God, they will have to bear . . . that iniquity, and if any of you want to partake of the sins of men, or uphold them, you will have to bear them. Do you hear it, you Bishops and you Presidents? God will require it at your hands. You are not placed in position to tamper with the principles of righteousness, nor to cover up the infamies and corruptions of men.' (*Conference Report*, Apr., 1880, p. 78.)

"These are very strong words, brethren, and they were spoken by a president of the Church, a prophet of God. Also, George Q. Cannon makes this significant statement: 'The Spirit of God would undoubtedly be so grieved that it would forsake not only those who are guilty of these acts, but it would withdraw itself from those who would suffer them to be done in our midst unchecked and unrebuked.' " (In Conference Report, Oct. 1974, p. 110; or *Ensign*, Nov. 1974, p. 78.)

# "The Lord Shall Utter His Voice Out of Heaven"

Section 43

## Historical Background

On 6 April 1830 the Lord instructed the Saints about the channel through which revelation would come to build Zion. He said, speaking of the President of the Church, "Him have I inspired to move the cause of Zion in mighty power" (D&C 21:7). This instruction was difficult for some of the Saints to follow. Many had come from religious backgrounds that permitted any member of the congregation to proclaim doctrine for the entire assembly. Yet, on the day the Church was organized, the Lord taught the principle that only one person has the right to receive revelation for the entire Church. Even by September 1830 the Saints had not fully learned this lesson, for many believed in the deceptions of Hiram Page.

In February 1831 it became necessary for the Lord to further instruct the Saints on this matter. The incident that led to the receiving of section 43 was the activity of a Mrs. Hubble, who "came making great pretensions of revealing commandments, laws and other curious matters" (*History of the Church,* 1:154). John Whitmer recorded the following about Mrs. Hubble: "She professed to be a prophetess of the Lord, and professed to have many revelations, and knew the Book of Mormon was true, and that she should become a teacher in the church of Christ. She appeared to be very sanctimonious and deceived some who were not able to detect her in her hypocrisy; others, however, had the spirit of discernment and her follies and abominations were manifest." (*History of the Church,* 1:154n.)

Mrs. Hubble was one of many who were influenced by false spirits and claimed revelations to guide the Church or to correct the Prophet. In a discourse in Ogden, Utah, Elder George A. Smith gave several examples of the problem in the early days of the Church and said: "There was a prevalent spirit all through the early history of this church, which prompted the Elders to suppose that they knew more than the Prophet. Elders would tell you that the Prophet was going wrong." (In *Journal of Discourses,* 11:7.) Many members became confused and bewildered by the different claims. Under these circumstances the Prophet went to the Lord for guidance and received the revelation recorded as Doctrine and Covenants 43.

## Notes and Commentary

### D&C 43:2-3. Only the Living Prophet Has the Right to Revelation for the Church

See Notes and Commentary on Doctrine and Covenants 21:7 and Enrichment F, in the Appendix.

### D&C 43:7. How Can One Avoid Being Deceived by False Prophets?

If a person takes the Holy Spirit as his guide and if he studies and follows the Lord's written word, then he will be on a course of safety. With this foundation he is prepared to discern true prophets from false prophets. In his Church the Lord has provided an additional guide to ensure that the Saints are not deceived. President Joseph F. Smith gave the following explanation:

"It is not my business nor that of any other individual to rise up as a revelator, as a prophet, as a seer, as an inspired man, to give revelation for the guidance of the Church, or to assume to dictate to the presiding authorities of the Church. . . . We can accept nothing as authoritative but that which comes directly through the appointed channel, the constituted organizations of the Priesthood, which is the channel that God has appointed through which to make known His mind and will to the world. . . .

". . . the moment that individuals look to any other source, that moment they throw themselves open to the seductive influences of Satan, and render themselves liable to become servants of the devil; they lose sight of the true order through which the blessings of the Priesthood are to be enjoyed; they step outside of the pale of the kingdom of God, and are on dangerous ground. Whenever you see a man rise up claiming to have received direct revelation from the Lord to the Church, independent of the order and channel of the Priesthood, you may set him down as an impostor." (In *Journal of Discourses,* 24:188-90.)

The topic of avoiding deception is dealt with in detail in Enrichment J.

### D&C 43:9. How Does "Binding" Oneself by Covenants Help One Become Holy?

There is tremendous value in making commitments to one another and to the Lord. By entering into covenants or making commitments with others, a person binds himself by his own integrity to act in a certain way. This arrangement becomes a fortification against the powers of opposition. In other words, covenants bring a sense of responsibility, which in turn becomes a power of reinforcement for positive action and a deterrent to slothfulness. Covenant making can help a person break away from routines or habits of the past as he clearly identifies a course to pursue and then establishes a means of accountability by making the commitment known to others. There are always positive consequences for keeping covenants and negative consequences for breaking covenants. When a person makes commitments based on a correct understanding of consequences, he then unifies the forces within him and secures the blessings of heaven. The Lord, seeing his willingness to make commitments, imparts to him of his Spirit, which gives him strength to continue in the course of action he has committed himself to follow.

### D&C 43:12-14. By Supporting Joseph Smith, the Saints Could Obtain the Glories and Mysteries of the Kingdom

The Saints were counseled that if they desired to receive the mysteries and glories of the kingdom, they should provide the temporal necessities for Joseph Smith so he could spend his time doing what only he could do—fulfilling the prophetic calling. The Prophet Joseph Smith was told that "the greatest blessings which God had to bestow should be given to those who contributed to the support of his family while he was translating the fulness of the Scriptures" (*Teachings,* p. 9).

Though the Saints were somewhat helpful to Joseph in this regard, sufficient assistance was not given him. Despite several attempts by Church leaders to get members to contribute to Joseph Smith's temporal needs so that he could work on the translation of the Bible, financial difficulty hampered the progress of the work (see *History of the Church,* 4:136-37, 164, 187, 493, 517). The process of translation was slowed, and efforts to prepare a manuscript for press were delayed because Joseph constantly had to lay aside his work on the manuscript to provide food and clothing for himself and his family. As a result the Prophet Joseph Smith was unable to finish his translation, even though the Lord had instructed that it be published (see D&C 94:10; 104:58-59; 124:89). After Joseph's death the manuscript eventually ended up in the possession of the Reorganized Church of Jesus Christ of Latter Day Saints. The neglect by the early Saints of this counsel was very costly in knowledge and spiritual blessings.

### D&C 43:15-16. The Gospel Can Be Taught Effectively Only through Power from on High

These verses contain important instructions from the Lord to those who are called to preach the gospel. Teachers in God's kingdom are not to teach from the doctrines and philosophies of the world but are to base their teachings on the revelations of the Holy Spirit.

The Lord promises an endowment of power to those who sanctify themselves. The Saints had the gift of the Holy Ghost and the priesthood, and they would soon receive the endowment that was to be given in holy temples.

### D&C 43:18. "Ye Saints Arise and Live; Ye Sinners Stay and Sleep until I Shall Call Again"

See Notes and Commentary on Doctrine and Covenants 88:95-101.

### D&C 43:17-25. How Is God's Warning Voice Being Sounded Today?

The lightnings spoken of in verse 22 do not actually speak in the sense of talking, but they will be as much a warning to the inhabitants of the earth as is the warning given by the missionaries. According to verse 25, the Lord uses all kinds of natural phenomena, along with the efforts of his Church leaders, missionaries, angels, and even his own voice, to convince the people of the earth to repent and prepare for the future.

Speaking of this method of sounding warning to the world, President Brigham Young said: "Do you think there is calamity abroad now among the people? Not much. All we have yet heard and all we have experienced is scarcely a preface to the sermon that is going to be preached. When the testimony of the elders ceases to be given, and the Lord says to them, 'Come home; I will now preach my own sermons to the nations of the earth,' all you now know can scarcely be called a preface to the sermon that will be preached with fire and sword, tempests, earthquakes, hail, rain, thunders and lightnings, and fearful destruction. . . . You will hear of magnificent cities, now idolized by the people, sinking in the earth, entombing the inhabitants. The sea will heave itself beyond its bounds, engulphing mighty cities. Famine will spread over the nations." (In *Journal of Discourses,* 8:123; see also D&C 88:88-92.)

A few weeks after the eruption of Mount Saint Helens, a volcano in the Western United States, the following editorial appeared in the *Church News:*

"A series of most unusual events happened within the past few weeks. Of course the most startling was the Mt. St. Helens eruption, with all its damage and toll of human life.

"But while it was belching forth, a series of

*Brigham Young spoke of the destruction and calamities that must come*

tornadoes swept through the middle section of the United States. More than 900 'freak' storms struck America within that month. In a single day 50 tornadoes were counted in six states. The very next day 24 more tornadoes struck Iowa and Nebraska. And during this same period earthquakes shook California. . . .

"It is important that we look for significance in these upheavals. Can it be that they are signs of the times? Can it be that the Lord is speaking to America by these frightful disasters?

"He said that in the latter days, He would declare His testimony by means of tempests, floods, earthquakes and epidemics. He didn't mention volcanoes, but surely they are within His realm as much as earthquakes. Did He force Mt. St. Helens into eruption as a warning to Americans to repent and recognize Him?

"We have a tendency to forget our pains quickly, even as does a mother when her child is born. Little is said even now about the Arizona floods, although the debris and broken bridges remain.

"Even the volcano is off the front pages. And the 50 tornadoes in one day? They got only two inches of space on the front page as part of a news summary. Not so much as a headline was given them!

"It is possible to become so hardened that we brush aside the warning voice, and even forget our sufferings. Those who lost their homes and loved ones won't easily forget, though, even if the general public does.

"Must the Lord speak in louder tones? Must He send greater disasters before we listen to His warning voice?

"How much does it take to waken us to a realization that God is real, that there is an end to His patience, and that the only true security in these troubled times is through obedience to the Most High? Why fly in the face of Providence?" (*Church News*, 21 June 1980, p. 12.)

### D&C 43:31. How Will Satan Be Bound During the Millennium?

In speaking of the millennial era, Nephi said that "because of the righteousness of his [the Lord's] people, Satan has no power; wherefore, he cannot be loosed for the space of many years; for he hath no power over the hearts of the people, for they dwell in righteousness, and the Holy One of Israel reigneth" (1 Nephi 22:26).

President Joseph Fielding Smith taught concerning the binding of Satan: "There are many among us who teach that the binding of Satan will be merely the binding which those dwelling on the earth will place upon him by their refusal to hear his enticings. This is not so. He will not have the privilege during that period of time to tempt any man. (D. and C. 101:28.)" (*Church History and Modern Revelation*, 1:192.)

These two statements at first may seem to be at variance, but in reality they are not. It is true that the result of the righteousness of the Saints is that Satan cannot exert power over them. The restrictions that will come upon Satan will be a

*George Q. Cannon explained how Satan will be bound*

result of two important actions by the Lord: (1) he will destroy telestial wickedness from the earth at his second coming; and (2) as a reward for heeding his counsels, the Lord will pour out his Spirit upon the righteous who remain to the extent that Satan's power will be overwhelmed. Thus, Satan will not have the power to tempt or negatively influence the Lord's people. Both the righteousness of the Saints and the operation of the Lord's power are necessary to bind Satan: if the Saints do not give heed to God's word, he will not impart of his Spirit; and if the Lord's influence is not brought to bear to aid the Saints, they, on their own power, cannot withstand the force of the adversary.

President George Q. Cannon showed how both the power of God and the righteousness of the Saints are necessary to bind Satan:

"We talk about Satan being bound. Satan will be bound by the power of God; but he will be bound also by the determination of the people of God not to listen to him, not to be governed by him. The Lord will not bind him and take his power from the earth while there are men and women willing to be governed by him. That is contrary to the plan of salvation. To deprive men of their agency is contrary to the purposes of our God. . . . [See Lehi's teachings in 2 Nephi 2:15-16. To preserve agency it is necessary to be *enticed* by opposing forces.]

"Satan only gains power over man through man's exercise of his own agency; and when Satan shall be bound, as the Lord says he will be for a thousand years, one of the great powers that will help bring this to pass will be man's agency. The Lord has never forced men against their will to obey Him. He never will do so. If Satan, therefore, has power with man, it is because man yields to his influence. . . .

"The time is not far distant when great judgments will be poured out upon the wicked inhabitants of the earth. Every Prophet who has looked forward to our day has seen and predicted that the wicked would be destroyed. Their destruction means the destruction of Satan's power [including the literal destruction of the wicked]. The righteous will be left, and *because of their righteousness the Lord will have mercy upon them;* they, exercising their agency in the right direction, *will bring down His blessings* upon them to such an extent that Satan will be bound." (*Gospel Truth,* 1:86-87; emphasis added. See also 2 Nephi 30:18; Ether 8:26.)

### D&C 43:32. "The Earth Shall Pass Away So As by Fire"

See Notes and Commentary on Doctrine and Covenants 29:22-25.

### D&C 43:33. "The Wicked Shall Go Away into Unquenchable Fire"

The Prophet Joseph Smith taught that "some shall rise to the damnation of their own filthiness, which is as exquisite a torment as the lake of fire and brimstone" (*Teachings,* p. 361). Elder Bruce R. McConkie explained that symbolic imagery: "The nature of burning brimstone [sulfur] is such that it perfectly symbolized to the prophetic mind the eternal torment of the damned. Accordingly we read that the wicked are 'tormented with *fire and brimstone*' (Rev. 14:9-11; 19:20; 20:10), or in other words that 'their torment is as a lake of fire and brimstone, whose flame ascendeth up forever and ever and has no end.' (2 Ne. 9:16; Alma 12:17.) This burning scene, a horrifying 'lake of fire and brimstone,' symbolizes 'endless torment' (2 Ne. 9:19, 26; 28:23; Jac. 6:10; Alma 14:14; D. & C. 76:36); those who find place therein are subject to the second death. (Jac. 3:11; D. & C. 63:17.) They suffer the vengeance of eternal fire. (D. & C. 29:28; 43:33; 76:44, 105.)" (*Mormon Doctrine,* pp. 280-81.)

### D&C 43:34. What Are the "Solemnities of Eternity"?

The word *solemnity* means something very serious or sublimely important. The Lord tells the members of the Church to let the serious things of eternity—their covenants and the great blessings that will be given the faithful—rest upon their minds. What changes could come into the lives of mortal men and women if they continually let the eternal perspective guide them!

# The Fourth General Church Conference

Section 44

## Historical Background

Since the organization of the Church, three major Church conferences had been held. The first was on 9 June 1830, the second on 26 September 1830, and the third on 2 January 1831. All of these conferences were held in Fayette, New York.

In February 1831 the Lord commanded the Prophet to call another conference. This conference convened in Kirtland on 3 June 1831, the fourth general conference of the Church and the first in Ohio. Section 44 of the Doctrine and Covenants contains the commandment and outlines some of the major purposes for gathering the Saints together in conferences.

## Notes and Commentary

### D&C 44:1. What Are Some Purposes for Conferences?

President David O. McKay explained the purposes of Church conferences:

"Reference to the Doctrine and Covenants will disclose the fact that there are four principal purposes of holding conferences of the Church:

"First, to transact current Church business [D&C 20:62],

"Second, to hear reports and general Church statistics [D&C 73:2],

"Third, to 'approve of those names which I (the Lord) have appointed, or to disapprove of them' [D&C 124:144],

*A general conference session in the Tabernacle at Salt Lake City*

"Fourth, to worship the Lord in sincerity and reverence, and to give and to receive encouragement, exhortation, and instruction [D&C 58:56; 72:7]" (in Conference Report, Oct. 1938, pp. 130-31).

Doctrine and Covenants, section 52, states that one important purpose of the fourth general conference was to select brethren to go to Missouri to learn the location of the city of Zion. The conference, then, was to prepare the Saints for events and challenges yet to come. Elder Hugh B. Brown testified, "These great conferences are called for the purpose of inspiring us to prepare for the battle" (*Church News,* July 1968, p. 10).

**D&C 44:2. What Great Promises Does the Lord Make to Those Who Assemble Together in His Name?**

While this verse refers specifically to the general conference to be held at that time, the promise given can be applied to any gathering of the Saints. What is the great blessing given to those who meet together under priesthood direction? (See Matthew 18:20.)

President Spencer W. Kimball bore this testimony at the conclusion of the April 1977 general conference: "We have all felt the outpouring of the Spirit of the Lord as we have assembled in his name to worship and be instructed by the power of the Holy Ghost. This has always been the pattern of the meetings of the saints." (In Conference Report, Apr. 1977, pp. 112-13; or *Ensign,* May 1977, p. 76.)

**D&C 44:4. Why Did the Saints Need to Organize Themselves According to the Laws of Men?**

"When the Lord restored the Gospel the spirit of gathering came with it. The Lord commanded the people to gather together, and that they should not only be organized as a Church, but that they should be organized under the laws of the land, so that they might not be helpless and dependent and without influence or power; but that by means of united effort and faith they should become a power for the accomplishment of righteousness in the earth (D. & C. Sec. 44; 4-5)." (Joseph F. Smith, in Conference Report, Apr. 1900, p. 47.)

**D&C 44:6. "Ye Must Visit the Poor and the Needy and Administer to Their Relief"**

President George Q. Cannon recorded the following insight into the character of the Prophet: "At no time during the Prophet's career did the care of the poor escape his attention or become a matter of indifference to him. He was a man of large benevolence, and his sympathies were quickly aroused by any tale of sorrow or appeal for relief. In the most busy and trying periods of his life those who went to him for counsel in their troubles, always found him willing to listen, and they were sure to receive encouragement and assistance. To extend comfort to the bruised spirit, and to help the needy and distressed appeared a constant pleasure to him. His hospitality, also, was a marked feature in his character. His house was always open to entertain the stranger. One of the most cherished recollections of many of the old members of the church is the kindness with which they were treated by 'Brother Joseph,' and the warm welcome he gave them to his house upon their arrival at Kirtland and other places where he lived." (*Life of Joseph Smith,* pp. 109-10.)

# "Looking Forth for the Great Day of the Lord"

Section 45

## Historical Background

The arrival of the Prophet Joseph Smith in Kirtland, Ohio, marked the beginning of a period of rapid growth in the membership of the Church. By early June 1831, the Church had grown to two thousand in number. Among those who joined the Church at this time were Sidney Rigdon's mother and oldest brother; Luke S. Johnson, one of the first missionaries in the Church; and Ezra Booth, who joined the Church after witnessing a miracle.

Civic leaders, priests, newspaper editors, and parishioners joined together in an effort to stop the conversion of their neighbors to the new religion. In his history the Prophet recorded, "Many false reports, lies, and foolish stories, were published in the newspapers, and circulated in every direction, to prevent people from investigating the work, or embracing the faith" (*History of the Church,* 1:158).

During these trying times of slander and abuse, the Lord blessed the Saints with revelations of comfort, peace, and assurance. One of these revelations was section 45, of which the Prophet wrote, "To the joy of the Saints who had to struggle against every thing that prejudice and wickedness could invent, I received the following: [D&C 45]" (*History of the Church,* 1:158).

## Notes and Commentary

**D&C 45:2. "In an Hour When Ye Think Not"**

President Joseph Fielding Smith noted that "one of the great failings of mankind is to ignore warnings of punishment for sin. In all ages of the world it

*"The hour and the day no man knoweth" (D&C 49:7)*

has been the peculiar belief of men that the sayings of the prophets were to be fulfilled in times still future. That is true of the people today. We have had ample warning of the nearness of the coming of the great and dreadful day of the Lord. The signs are upon us in all their power. . . . In this revelation we are given the warning that the summer is passing and if we are heedless of the warning we will find the summer past, the harvest ended and our souls not saved. While no man knows the day or the hour, yet if we are taken unawares, we will be without excuse, for the signs are ample and we now see them being fulfilled." (*Church History and Modern Revelation,* 1:195.)

### D&C 45:3-5. What Is the Significance of the Title "Advocate"?

The imagery of a judicial system is often invoked when the Last Judgment is mentioned in scriptures. Man goes before the "judgment bar" (2 Nephi 33:15), there to be "arraigned" (Alma 11:44) and face God, "the Judge of all" (Hebrews 12:23). As part of that imagery, Jesus is called the *Advocate* (*paraclaytos*). In the King James Version of the New Testament, Jesus is called the "advocate" only once (1 John 2:1). The same word (*paraclaytos*) is used for the Holy Ghost, although it is translated "Comforter" (John 14:16). Thus, Jesus is one *Paraclete,* or Comforter, and the Holy Ghost is called "another Comforter" (John 14:16). The Greek word comes from *para,* to the side of, and *kalayo,* to summon. "Hence, originally, one who is called to another's side to aid him, as an advocate in a court of justice" (Vincent, *Word Studies,* 1:486).

In the terminology of today's legal system, an advocate is a lawyer who pleads another's cause in a court of law, or in other words, an attorney for the defense. Usually, the attorney for the defense pleads the cause for his client on the basis that he is innocent; or if guilty, that extenuating circumstances should be considered and mercy extended. At the time of eternal judgment, men shall stand before the bar of God accused of being imperfect and unworthy to enter God's presence, "for all have sinned, and come short of the glory of God" (Romans 3:23). At that time all men have an Advocate with the Father. He stands beside them to plead their cause before the Great Judge; however, he does not plead their case by pointing to their lack of guilt; rather, *it is his own sinlessness to which he calls God's attention* (see D&C 45:4). His perfection and his suffering pay the price to satisfy justice for those of his "brethren that believe on my name" (vs. 5). Imagine the indescribable sorrow of standing before the judgment bar with no one to step forward, no one to speak for you. What tragic foolishness that some will not come to him in true faith and repentance so that he can take their guilt upon him and become their advocate with the Father.

### D&C 45:6. "While It Is Called Today"

Three scriptures contribute to an understanding of this phrase. Modern revelation states that the earth's temporal history spans seven thousand years, divided into periods of one thousand years each (see D&C 77:6-7). Peter and Abraham taught that time on earth, compared to the time where God dwells, is at a ratio of a thousand of earth's years to one day of God's time (see 2 Peter 3:8; Abraham 3:4). Since the earth will have a temporal existence before it is celestialized, and since it is known that the earth is now in the sixth period of a thousand years, or the sixth "day," in the Lord's terminology the present period is "today" and Christ will come "tomorrow." In a later revelation, the Lord used this very terminology, indicating that "now it is called *today* until the coming of the Son of Man," that "after *today* cometh the burning," that "*tomorrow* all the proud and they that do wickedly shall be as stubble" (D&C 64:23-24; emphasis added).

### D&C 45:14. How Would Enoch's People and All Holy Men See a Future Day of Righteousness "in Their Flesh"?

"When the Millennial reign comes, the holy men of old shall see it in their 'flesh,' for they will be resurrected and take their place among the Saints" (Smith and Sjodahl, Commentary, p. 255; see also Moses 7:61-64).

### D&C 45:16. When Did Jesus Speak These Things unto His Disciples As He "Stood before Them in Flesh"?

Most of this revelation is the Savior's retelling of one of his sermons to his disciples while he was in Jerusalem. After leaving the temple, the Savior and his disciples climbed the Mount of Olives, where they had a dramatic view of the temple and Jerusalem. Here his disciples asked, "When shall these things be . . . and what is the sign of thy coming?" (JS—M 1:4). His lengthy and detailed answer provides one of the most important revelations on the signs of the times and of the Second Coming. Known as the Olivet Discourse because it was given on the Mount of Olives, the full discourse is given in Matthew 24 and 25. Joseph Smith's inspired corrections of the Olivet Discourse are so significant that they have been included in the Pearl of Great Price (see Joseph Smith—Matthew). Mark and Luke also recorded portions of the discourse, though not as fully as did Matthew (see Mark 13:1-37; Luke 21:5-36).

The Lord's citation of the same discourse in Doctrine and Covenants 45 begins in verse 16 with the words "As ye have asked of me." The Savior interrupts the quotation after verse 33 to make an explanatory comment but continues it in verse 35 with "Be not troubled." He seems to end the account at the end of verse 59 and begins speaking directly to Joseph Smith in verse 60.

### D&C 45:16-17. Why Were the Early Apostles Anxious to Know the Signs of the Second Coming?

"One reason for their anxiety to know the signs is here stated. The separation of the spirits from the bodies is, even to those who are Christ's own, a 'bondage,' which is ended only by a glorious resurrection, and they were interested in knowing by what signs they might recognize that their day of redemption was drawing near, when spirit and body should be united. The departed saints are, we may be sure, looking for the signs of the coming of the Lord, with an intense interest as the saints still in mortality. Jesus graciously showed them 'how the day of redemption shall come, and also the restoration of scattered Israel.' The two events are inseparably connected." (Smith and Sjodahl, Commentary, p. 259.)

For a more complete treatment of the subject of the Second Coming and the signs of the times see Enrichment H, in the Appendix.

### D&C 45:19-21. Jews to Be Scattered among All Nations

Smith and Sjodahl gave a brief summary of how this prophecy was fulfilled: "In the year 66 A. D., Cestus Gallus marched into Judea and threatened Jerusalem. He might have taken the City, but he retreated and met with defeat near Beth-Horon. The Christians in the City, remembering the words of our Lord, fled to the little city of Pella, but the Jews were fired, by their temporary success, to renewed resistance. Vespasian was then sent from Rome to crush the rebellion. He took some of the strongholds of the Country and approached Jerusalem. Internal strife prevailed there, and such horrors were perpetrated that Vespasian decided to give his army a rest, while the Jews destroyed each other. Vespasian was elevated to the throne, and his son, Titus, was left to continue the conquest. The siege began in the year 70 A.D. Soon famine prevailed. Citizens who ventured outside the walls to search for roots to eat, if seized, were crucified by the Roman soldiers. Sometimes hundreds in that awful position could be seen from the walls. A trench was dug around the City, in order to make its isolation complete. Prisoners of war were cut open, while alive, to enable soldiers to search their bodies for gold which they might have swallowed. Six hundred thousand persons died within the walls, and the dead bodies, too numerous to be buried, were left in the houses. The Zealots, a fanatical sect whose members maintained that God would save them at the last moment, went about murdering and urging the people to resistance. Even Titus was sick at heart at the daily horrors he witnessed or heard of. At length the temple became a fort. Titus attacked it as such. A Roman soldier, contrary to order, set fire to it. After a while the scene was one of carnage and plunder. Six thousand Jews perished in the flames. In this awful war more than a million and a half of the Jews perished, and many were sold into slavery, and thus 'scattered among all nations.' " (Commentary, pp. 260-61.)

The Savior spoke the words of the Olivet Discourse during the last week of his life, in A.D. 33. Jerusalem fell in A.D. 70. His promise "that this generation of Jews shall not pass away until every desolation . . . shall come to pass" (D&C 45:21) was fulfilled. Some of the disciples who heard Jesus speak those words were still alive when the legions of Titus put the temple to the torch.

### D&C 45:22. Is the World Going to Come to an End at Christ's Second Coming?

Elder Bruce R. McConkie explained the special way this phrase is used in the scriptures: "*The end of the world* is the end of unrighteousness or of worldliness as we know it, and this will be brought about by 'the destruction of the wicked.' (Jos. Smith 1:4.) When our world ends and the millennial era begins, there will be a new heaven and a new earth. (Isa. 65:17-25; D. & C. 101:23-24.) Lust, carnality, and sensuousness of every sort will cease, for it will be *the end of the world.*" (*Mormon Doctrine,* p. 848.)

### D&C 45:24-30. What Are the "Times of the Gentiles" and When Are They Fulfilled?

President Joseph Fielding Smith explained that "the times of the Gentiles commenced shortly after the death of our Redeemer. The Jews soon rejected the Gospel and it was then taken to the Gentiles. The times of the Gentiles have continued from that time until now. The Lord said: 'But many that are first shall be last; and the last shall be first.' In that day the Gospel was given first to the Jews and then taken to the Gentiles. In this dispensation it was taken first to the Gentiles and afterwards it will go to the Jews." (*Church History and Modern Revelation,* 1:196.)

Thus, the times of the Gentiles began with Peter's vision and the baptism of Cornelius (see Acts 10:1-48). Paul and the other Apostles then began the great missionary work to the Gentiles, since the Jewish nation, for the most part, had rejected Jesus. As President Smith indicated, the times that the major gospel effort would be with Gentile nations continued down through the Restoration. The times of the Gentiles will be over, or fulfilled, when the major efforts of gospel teaching begin to focus on the house of Israel: the Lamanites and the Jews.

In the Olivet Discourse, the Savior gave four signs to indicate when the times of the Gentiles were over. Three are given in section 45, and one is given in Luke's account of the great discourse. These signs are the following:

1. The Jews will be gathered back to the land of Jerusalem (see D&C 45:25). In the April 1960 general conference, Elder George Q. Morris of the Quorum of the Twelve described three great signs of the last days. The third of these was the gathering of the Jews:

"A third item is God's promise that he would gather Jews to Jerusalem, and I think perhaps we may well now not continue saying the Jews are going to gather in Jerusalem. I think now we may well say they *have gathered.* The ultimate returns will come later as they develop this land and are joined by others. . . .

"This statement by a writer is very interesting:

" 'Strangely enough when the State of Israel was reborn in 1948, it was a nation of 600,000, the same number which the Bible reports that Moses led out of bondage in Egypt. It now numbers some two million, the same number which it is said populated the ancient Kingdom of Solomon, when Israel was in all its glory.'

"That is why we may now say that the Jews have returned to Palestine." (In Conference Report, Apr. 1960, pp. 100-101.)

2. It will be in a time of great social turmoil (see D&C 45:26-27). One need only follow current events as reported in the news media for a day or two to know that this is the day described by the Savior.

3. The Gentiles will for the most part reject the gospel (see D&C 45:28-30). President Joseph Fielding Smith, writing about these verses, said: " 'And when the times of the Gentiles is come in, a light shall break forth among them that sit in darkness, and it shall be the fulness of my Gospel,' the Lord said in this revelation [D&C 45:28]. The meaning is that when the time had come for the restoration of the Gospel—in the times of the Gentiles—that it would not be perceived because the hearts of the people are turned away by the precepts of men. However, in that generation this should happen, the times of the Gentiles should be fulfilled." (*Church History and Modern Revelation,* 1:196.)

4. Jerusalem will no longer be "trodden down of the Gentiles" (Luke 21:24). Again President Smith explained: "When we consider the words of the Savior to his disciples, that the Jews should be scattered and 'Jerusalem shall be trodden down of the Gentiles until the times of the Gentiles are fulfilled,' we have a fair understanding of the meaning of this . . . verse [D&C 45:30] in this revelation. Jerusalem was trodden down of the Gentiles from the day of its destruction until the close of the year 1917, when it was freed from Turkish rule by General Edmund H. Allenby of the British forces. After the war Palestine became a British mandate, and Great Britain by proclamation declared that country to be a refuge for the Jews, who were invited to return. . . . It is very significant, however, that Jerusalem is no longer trodden down by the Gentiles and the Jews are again gathering there. This is the sign given by our Lord, for the end of the times of the Gentiles. We are now in the transition period and shortly the day of the Jew will dawn and the Gospel will be taken to them and to the remnants on this land." (*Church History and Modern Revelation,* 1:196-97.)

When Joseph Fielding Smith wrote those words in 1947, Israel had not yet been made a state; they were still under the British mandate. But on 15 May 1948, Israel became an independent nation and declared Jerusalem to be her capital. In the war that followed this declaration, the Jews could maintain control of western Jerusalem only. East Jerusalem became part of the state of Jordan. In general conference in 1966, Elder Smith, now President of the Quorum of the Twelve, said: "Jesus said the Jews would be scattered among all nations and Jerusalem would be trodden down by the Gentiles until the times of the Gentiles were fulfilled. (Luke 21:24.) The prophecy in Section 45, verses 24-29, of the Doctrine and Covenants regarding the Jews was literally fulfilled. Jerusalem, which was trodden down by the Gentiles, is no longer trodden down but is made the home for the Jews. They are returning to Palestine, and *by this we may know that the times of the Gentiles are near their close.*" (In Conference Report, Apr. 1966, p. 13; emphasis added.)

Then, during the Six-Day War of 1967, Israel conquered the West Bank, including Jerusalem, and for the first time since the city fell to the legions of Titus in A.D. 70, Jerusalem came completely under the control of a Jewish government.

### D&C 45:26. Men's Hearts Shall Fail Them

President Ezra Taft Benson noted the modern fulfillment of this promise:

"We live in an age when, as the Lord foretold, men's hearts are failing them, not only physically but in spirit. (See D&C 45:26.) Many are giving up heart for the battle of life. Suicide ranks as a major cause of the deaths to college students. As the showdown between good and evil approaches with its accompanying trials and tribulations, Satan is increasingly striving to overcome the Saints with despair, discouragement, despondency, and depression.

"Yet, of all people, we as Latter-day Saints should be the most optimistic and the least pessimistic. For while we know that 'peace shall be taken from the earth, and the devil shall have power over his own dominion,' we are also assured that 'the Lord shall have power over his saints, and shall reign in their midst.' (D&C 1:35-36.)" (In Conference Report, Oct. 1974, p. 90; or *Ensign,* Nov. 1974, p. 65.)

### D&C 45:27. What Will Cause the Love of Men to Wax Cold?

"The expression is the same as that found in Matt. 24:12, where we read (translated literally), 'And because lawlessness has abounded, the love of the many [this indicates more than a few] shall wax cold.' 'Love' here means Christian unity, harmony. Where in the Christian world does that love, that oneness, prevail? There is an abundance of co-operation based on self-interest, or family connections: but where is there genuine Christian love, true, unselfish, constant? Its absence in the majority of men is one of the signs of the end." (Smith and Sjodahl, Commentary, p. 262.)

### D&C 45:30-31. Why Is the Fulfilling of the Times of the Gentiles So Significant?

The fulfilling or closing out of the times of the Gentiles is one of the great signs given by the Savior in answer to the question of the disciples, "What is the sign of thy coming?" (JS—M 1:4). Doctrine and Covenants 45:31 gives its great significance: "There shall be men standing in that generation [in which the times of the Gentiles will be fulfilled] that shall not pass." That language is almost identical with the Savior's warning to the Jews, as he recounts in verse 21, and the fulfillment will be just as sure (see Notes and Commentary for D&C 45:21).

### D&C 45:19, 31. "An Overflowing Scourge" and "Desolating Sickness"

Elder Bruce R. McConkie warned of what some of the tribulations of the last days could be:

"Be it remembered that tribulations lie ahead. There will be wars in one nation and kingdom after another until war is poured out upon all nations and two hundred million men of war mass their armaments at Armageddon.

"Peace has been taken from the earth, the angels of destruction have begun their work, and their swords shall not be sheathed until the Prince of Peace comes to destroy the wicked and usher in the great Millennium.

"There will be earthquakes and floods and famines. The waves of the sea shall heave themselves beyond their bounds, the clouds shall withhold their rain, and the crops of the earth shall wither and die.

"There will be plagues and pestilence and disease and death. An overflowing scourge shall cover the earth and a desolating sickness shall sweep the land. Flies shall take hold of the inhabitants of the earth, and maggots shall come in upon them. (See D&C 29:14-20.) 'Their flesh shall fall from off their bones, and their eyes from their sockets' (D&C 29:19).

"Bands of Gadianton robbers will infest every nation, immorality and murder and crime will increase, and it will seem as though every man's hand is against his brother.

"We need not dwell more upon these things. We are commanded to search the scriptures where they are recounted with force and fervor, and they shall surely come to pass." (In Conference Report, Apr. 1979, p. 131; or *Ensign,* May 1979, p. 93; see also D&C 5:19-20; 63:32-37; 97:22-27.)

### D&C 45:32. Stand in Holy Places

President Harold B. Lee defined these holy places and how the Saints should gather to them:

"In these days of our generation, many of you are asking: Where is safety?

"The word of the Lord is not silent. He has admonished us: 'But my disciples shall stand in holy places, and shall not be moved; but among the wicked, men shall lift up their voices and curse God and die.' (D&C 45:32.)

"The Lord has told us where these 'holy places' are: 'And it shall come to pass among the wicked, that every man that will not take his sword against his neighbor must needs flee unto Zion for safety.' (D&C 45:68.)

"Where is Zion?

"During the various periods of time or dispensations, and for specific reasons, the Lord's prophets, his 'mouthpieces,' as it were, have designated gathering places where the Saints were to gather. After designating certain such places in our dispensation, the Lord then declared: 'Until the day cometh when there is found no more room for them; and then I have other places which I will appoint unto them, and they shall be called stakes, for the curtains or the strength of Zion.' (D&C 101:21.)

"Thus, clearly the Lord has placed the responsibility of directing the work of gathering in the hands of his divinely appointed leaders. May I fervently pray that all Saints and truth-seekers everywhere will attune their listening ears to these prophet-leaders. . . .

"As one studies the Lord's commandments and attending promises upon compliance therewith, one gets some definite ideas as to how we might 'stand in holy places,' as the Lord commands—if we will be preserved with such protection as accords with his holy purposes, in order that we might be numbered among the 'pure in heart' who constitute Zion, as I have read from the Lord's own words." (In Conference Report, Oct. 1968, pp. 61-62.)

### D&C 45:34-35. "Be Not Troubled"

Elder Marion G. Romney gave the following commentary on the Lord's admonition here:

"The fact that the Lord recounted these predictions to the Prophet Joseph in 1831 surely emphasizes their importance to us. And since the disciples were troubled when they were but being told of these calamities to come far in the future, it is no wonder that we are troubled as we witness their occurrence. . . .

"It was in the light of Christ's foreknowledge . . . that he said to his disciples, "be not troubled. . . ."

"I hope we are all familiar with these words of the Lord and with his predictions concerning other coming events, such as the building of the New

Jerusalem and the redemption of the old, the return of Enoch's Zion, and Christ's millennial reign.

"Not only do I hope that we are familiar with these coming events, I hope also that we keep the vision of them continually before our minds. This I do because upon a knowledge of them, and an assurance of their reality and a witness that each of us may have part therein, rests the efficacy of Christ's admonition, 'be not troubled. . . .' " (In Conference Report, Oct. 1966, pp. 51-52.)

President Jedediah M. Grant asked:"Why is it that the Latter-day Saints are perfectly calm and serene among all the convulsions of the earth—the turmoils, strife, war, pestilence, famine and distress of nations? It is because the spirit of prophecy has made known to us that such things would actually transpire upon the earth. We understand it, and view it in its true light. We have learned it by the visions of the the Almighty." ("The Hand of God in Events on Earth," *Improvement Era,* Feb. 1915, p. 286.)

Elder Bruce R. McConkie urged the Saints to prepare so they can be calm and serene in the face of the coming tribulations:

"We do not know when the calamities and troubles of the last days will fall upon any of us as individuals or upon bodies of the Saints. The Lord deliberately withholds from us the day and hour of his coming and of the tribulations which shall precede it—all as part of the testing and probationary experiences of mortality. He simply tells us to watch and be ready.

"We can rest assured that if we have done all in our power to prepare for whatever lies ahead, he will then help us with whatever else we need. . . .

"We do not say that all of the Saints will be spared and saved from the coming day of desolation. But we do say there is no promise of safety and no promise of security except for those who love the Lord and who are seeking to do all that he commands.

"It may be, for instance, that nothing except the power of faith and the authority of the priesthood can save individuals and congregations from the atomic holocausts that surely shall be.

"And so we raise the warning voice and say: Take heed; prepare; watch and be ready. There is no security in any course except the course of obedience and conformity and righteousness." (In Conference Report, Apr. 1979, pp. 132-133; or *Ensign,* May 1979, p. 93.)

**D&C 45:34-38. The Parable of the Fig Tree**

"When Jesus spoke to his disciples in answer to their query: 'Show us when the end of the world shall come, and the time of thy coming' [Matthew 24:3], he spoke of certain signs that would indicate the time of his coming, the very signs that the world, if they only had eyes to see, could be beholding today: Said he: judge the matter even as you would judge the coming of spring. When you see the fig tree putting forth its leaf, ye know that summer is near, and so when you see these signs, you may know that the coming of the Son of man is nigh at hand." (Melvin J. Ballard, in Conference Report, Oct. 1923, p. 32.)

**D&C 45:40-42. "They Shall See Signs and Wonders"**

President Joseph Fielding Smith said of the signs mentioned here:

"One wonders if we are not now seeing some of the signs in heaven—not all, for undoubtedly some of them will be among the heavenly bodies, such as the moon and the sun, the meteors and comets, but in speaking of the heavens, reference is made to that part which surrounds the earth and which belongs to it. It is in the atmosphere where many of the signs are to be given. Do we not see airships of various kinds traveling through the heavens daily? Have we not had signs in the earth and through the earth with the radio, railroad trains, automobiles, submarines, and satellites, and in many other ways? There are yet to be great signs: the heavens are to be shaken, the sign of the Son of Man is to be given, and then shall the tribes of the earth mourn. . . .

"If the great and dreadful day of the Lord were near at hand when Elijah came 130 years ago, we are just one century nearer it today. But some will say: 'But no! Elijah, you are wrong! . . . Surely you made a mistake!' So many seem to think and say, and judging by their actions they are sure, that the world is bound to go on in its present condition for millions of years before the end will come. Talk to them; hear what they have to say—these learned men of the world. 'We have had worse times,' they say. 'You are wrong in thinking there are more calamities now than in earlier times. There are not more earthquakes, the earth has always been quaking, but now we have facilities for gathering the news which our fathers did not have. These are not signs of the times; things are not different from former times.' And so the people refuse to heed the warnings the Lord so kindly gives to them, and thus they fulfill the scriptures." (In Conference Report, Apr. 1966, pp. 13, 15.)

**D&C 45:48-53. "Then Shall the Lord Set His Foot upon This Mount"**

"This mount" refers to the Mount of Olives on which the Savior was sitting when he gave this great discourse. Parley P. Pratt, in a pamphlet published while Joseph Smith was still alive, described the great events depicted here: "Zechariah, chapter 14, has told us much concerning the great battle and overthrow of the nations who fight against Jerusalem, and he has said, in plain words, that the Lord shall come at the very time of the overthrow of that army; yes, in fact, even while they are in the act of taking Jerusalem, and have already succeeded in taking one-half the city, spoiling their houses, and ravishing their women. Then, behold, their long-expected Messiah, suddenly appearing, shall stand upon the Mount of Olives, a little east of Jerusalem, to fight against those nations and deliver the Jews. Zechariah says the Mount of Olives shall cleave in twain, from east to west, and one-half of the mountain shall remove to the north while the other half falls off to the south, suddenly forming a very great valley into which the Jews shall flee for protection from their enemies as they

*The Lord shall set his foot upon the Mount of Olives*

fled from the earthquake in the days of Uzziah, king of Judah; while the Lord cometh and all the saints with Him. Then will the Jews behold that long, long-expected Messiah, coming in power to their deliverance, as they always looked for him. He will destroy their enemies and deliver them from trouble at the very time they are in the utmost consternation, and about to be swallowed up by their enemies. But what will be their astonishment when they are about to fall at the feet of their Deliverer and acknowledge him their Messiah! They discover the wounds which were once made in his hands, feet, and side; and on inquiry, at once recognize Jesus of Nazareth, the King of the Jews, the man so long rejected. Well did the prophet say that they shall mourn and weep, every family apart, and their wives apart. But, thank heaven, there will be an end to their mourning; for he will forgive their iniquities and cleanse them from uncleanness. Jerusalem shall be a holy city from that time forth, and all the land shall be turned as a plain from Geba to Rimmon. She shall be lifted up and inhabited in her place, and men shall dwell there. There shall be no more utter destruction of Jerusalem, 'And the Lord shall be king over all the earth: in that day shall there be one Lord, and his name one.' (Zechariah 14:9.)" (*Voice of Warning*, pp. 32-33.)

**D&C 45:55. "Satan Shall Be Bound"**

See Notes and Commentary on Doctrine and Covenants 43:31.

**D&C 45:56-57. The Parable of the Ten Virgins**

Though many people think the Olivet Discourse is limited to Matthew 24, a careful reading of chapter 25 clearly shows that the three parables given there (the parable of the ten virgins, the parable of the talents, and the parable of the sheep and the goats) were part of the same discourse (note especially Matthew 25:1, 31). The Lord revealed to Joseph Smith the key to the symbolism of the parable of the ten virgins. The oil, which is the central item in the parable, represents spiritual power derived from the Holy Ghost.

Elder Spencer W. Kimball explained the significance of that parable for modern Saints:

"I believe that the Ten Virgins represent the people of the Church of Jesus Christ and not the rank and file of the world. All of the virgins, wise and foolish, had accepted the invitation to the wedding supper; they had knowledge of the program and had been warned of the important day to come. They were not the gentiles or the heathens or the pagans, nor were they necessarily corrupt and reprobate, but they were knowing people who were foolishly unprepared for the vital happenings that were to affect their eternal lives.

"They had the saving, exalting gospel, but it had not been made the center of their lives. They knew the way but gave only a small measure of loyalty and devotion. I ask you: What value is a car without an engine, a cup without water, a table without food, a lamp without oil?

"Rushing for their lamps to light their way through the blackness, half of them found them empty. They had cheated themselves. They were fools, these five unprepared virgins. Apparently, the bridegroom had tarried for reasons that were sufficient and good. Time had passed, and he had not come. They had heard of his coming for so long, so many times, that the statement seemingly became meaningless to them. Would he ever come? So long had it been since they began expecting him that they were rationalizing that he would never appear. Perhaps it was a myth.

"Hundreds of thousands of us today are in this position. Confidence has been dulled and patience worn thin. It is so hard to wait and be prepared always. But we cannot allow ourselves to slumber. The Lord has given us this parable as a special warning. . . .

"At midnight! Precisely at the darkest hour, when least expected, the bridegroom came. When the world is full of tribulation and help is needed, but it seems the time must be past and hope is vain, then Christ will come. The midnights of life are the times when heaven comes to offer its joy for man's weariness. But when the cry sounds, there is no time for preparation. The lamps then make patterns of joy on the hillside, and the procession moves on toward the house of banqueting, and those without lamps or oil are left in darkness. When they have belatedly sought to fulfill the requirements and finally reach the hall, the door is shut. In the daytime, wise and unwise seemed alike; midnight is the time of test and judgment—and of offered gladness. . . .

"The foolish asked the others to share their oil, but spiritual preparedness cannot be shared in an instant. The wise had to go, else the bridegroom would have gone unwelcomed. They needed all their oil for themselves; they could not save the foolish. The responsibility was each for himself.

"This was not selfishness or unkindness. The kind of oil that is needed to illuminate the way and light up the darkness is not shareable. How can one share obedience to the principle of tithing; a mind at peace from righteous living; an accumulation of knowledge? How can one share faith or testimony? How can one share attitudes or chastity, or the experience of a mission? How can one share temple privileges? Each must obtain that kind of oil for himself.

"The foolish virgins were not averse to buying oil. They knew they should have oil. They merely procrastinated, not knowing when the bridegroom would come.

"In the parable, oil can be purchased at the market. In our lives the oil of preparedness is accumulated drop by drop in righteous living. Attendance at sacrament meetings adds oil to our lamps, drop by drop over the years. Fasting, family prayer, home teaching, control of bodily appetites, preaching the gospel, studying the scriptures—each act of dedication and obedience is a drop added to our store. Deeds of kindness, payment of offerings and tithes, chaste thoughts and actions, marriage in the covenant for eternity—these, too, contribute importantly to the oil with which we can at midnight refuel our exhausted lamps.

"Midnight is so late for those who have procrastinated." (*Faith Precedes the Miracle,* pp. 253-56.)

### D&C 45:60-62. "Translate It, That Ye May Be Prepared"

The Lord instructed Joseph Smith to translate the New Testament and said that one of the purposes for his translating the scriptures was so that he would be prepared for the things to come. This work of translation is known as the Joseph Smith Translation.

### D&C 45:64-75. Zion: A Place of Defense and Refuge

In the scriptures four words seem closely related to the concept of Zion: *gathering, preparation, defense,* and *refuge.* The tribulations and judgments that will be poured out upon the world prior to the Second Coming will be so extensive and devastating that if the Lord did not prepare a means of preservation, his people too would perish. But he has prepared a means for his people to escape those terrible times; that means is Zion. Enoch was told that the Lord would preserve his people in the tribulations of the last days by gathering his elect unto Zion where they could gird up their loins (*prepare* themselves) and look forward to his coming (see Moses 7:61-62). In an earlier revelation in the Doctrine and Covenants, the Savior called the elders of the Church to *gather* the elect so their hearts could be *prepared* for the day of tribulation (see D&C 29:7-8). In 1838 the Lord explained that the *gathering* to Zion and her stakes was to be for *defense* and *refuge* from the coming storm that will be poured out on the earth (see D&C 115:5-6). These commands and promises are found also in section 45. The Saints are to *gather* to Zion (see D&C 45:64-65), a place of *safety, peace, and refuge* (see vs. 65). Even though the rest of the world is in a state of horrible warfare (see vs. 68), in Zion (D&C 115:5-6 implies that this includes her stakes) there will be peace and joy (see D&C 45:69-71).

The Prophet Joseph Smith understood this doctrine, for he also taught that Zion was the place of deliverance in the last days: "Without Zion, and a place of deliverance, we must fall; because the time is near when the sun will be darkened, and the moon turn to blood, and the stars fall from heaven, and the earth reel to and fro. Then, if this is the case, and if we are not sanctified and gathered to the places God has appointed, with all our former professions and our great love for the Bible, we must fall; we cannot stand; we cannot be saved; for God will gather out his Saints from the Gentiles, and then comes desolation and destruction, and none can escape except the pure in heart who are gathered." (*Teachings,* p. 71; see also Enrichment B.)

# "Seek Ye Earnestly the Best Gifts"

Section 46

## Historical Background

Challenges to the Lord's newly restored Church were many and varied. The foundation years saw Satan's power unleashed in continued efforts to thwart the kingdom of God. Evil spirits were marshaled to destroy the Prophet Joseph Smith and all who aligned themselves with Christ's church. But the heavens had been opened, and God had revealed to his prophet-leader the designs and tactics of the enemy. Speaking of Satan's efforts and the need for the Saints to possess the gifts of the Spirit, the Prophet Joseph Smith said: "A man must have the discerning of spirits before he can drag into daylight this hellish influence and unfold it unto the world in all its soul-destroying, diabolical, and horrid colors; for nothing is a greater injury to the children of men than to be under the influence of a false spirit when they think they have the Spirit of God. Thousands have felt the influence of its terrible power and baneful effects. Long pilgrimages have been undertaken, penances endured, and pain, misery and ruin have followed in their train; nations have been convulsed, kingdoms overthrown, provinces laid waste, and blood, carnage and desolation are habiliaments in which it has been clothed." (*History of the Church,* 4:573.)

On 8 March 1831 at Kirtland, Ohio, the Prophet received section 46, a revelation which would assist the Saints in dragging into daylight Satan's hellish plan by describing the true gifts of the Holy Spirit.

*The First Presidency and the Quorum of the Twelve Apostles under Brigham Young. Throughout all the ages, Saints who have followed the Lord's leaders have not been deceived*

# Notes and Commentary

**D&C 46:1-7. How are Nonmembers of the Church to Be Treated at Public Sacrament Meetings?**

"John Whitmer records in his history that 'in the beginning of the Church, while yet in her infancy, the disciples used to exclude unbelievers which caused some to marvel and converse of this matter because of the things written in the Book of Mormon. (3 Nephi 18:22-24.) Therefore, the Lord deigned to speak on this subject, that his people might come to an understanding, and he said that he had always given to his elders to conduct all meetings as they were led by the Spirit.' After the

Lord gave this revelation this practice of forbidding non-members to attend the sacrament services ceased." (Smith, *Church History and Modern Revelation,* 1:199.)

**D&C 46:7-8. Not All Supernatural Manifestations Are Gifts of the Spirit**

Elder Marion G. Romney expanded the Saints' understanding of these verses, explaining:

"By the statement in the revelation on spiritual gifts, '. . . it is given by the Holy Ghost to some to know the diversities of operations, whether they be of God, . . . and to others the discerning of spirits,' it appears that there are some apparently supernatural manifestations which are not worked by the power of the Holy Ghost. The truth is there are many which are not. The world today is full of counterfeits. It has always been so. Away back in the days of Moses, when Aaron's rod became a serpent, then Pharaoh's wise men, sorcerers and magicians '. . . cast down every man his rod, and they became serpents: . . .' (Ex. 7:11-12.) Isaiah warned against seeking '. . . unto them that have familiar spirits, and unto wizards that peep, and that mutter: . . .' (Isa. 8:19.)

"The Saints were cautioned by the Lord to walk uprightly before him, doing all things with prayer and thanksgiving, that they might '. . . not be seduced by evil spirits, or doctrines of devils, or the commandments of men; . . .' (D&C 47:7.)

"These citations not only sustain the proposition that there are counterfeits to the gifts of the Spirit, but they also suggest the origin of the counterfeits. However, we are not required to rely alone upon their implications, plain as they are, for the Lord states specifically that some of the counterfeits '. . . are of men, and others of devils.' [D&C 46:7.]

"Some of these counterfeits are crude and easily detected, but others closely simulate true manifestations of the spirit. Consequently, people are confused and deceived by them. Without a key, one cannot distinguish between the genuine and the counterfeit." (In Conference Report, Apr. 1956, pp. 70-71.)

Enrichment J, in the Appendix, contains a more detailed discussion of the principles of discernment between genuine and counterfeit revelations.

**D&C 46:11-12. "And to Every Man Is Given a Gift"**

Elder Orson Pratt taught that "whenever the Holy Ghost takes up its residence in a person, it not only cleanses, sanctifies, and purifies him, in proportion as he yields himself to its influence, but also imparts to him some gift, intended for the benefit of himself and others. No one who has been born of the Spirit, and who remains sufficiently faithful, is left destitute of a spiritual gift. A person who is without a spiritual gift has not the Spirit of God dwelling in him, in a sufficient degree, to save him; he cannot be called a Saint, or a child of God; for all Saints who constitute the Church of Christ, are baptized into the same Spirit; and each one, without any exception, is made a partaker of some spiritual gift. . . .

"Each member does not receive all these gifts; but they are distributed through the whole body [of the Church], according to the will and wisdom of the Spirit. . . . Some may have all these gifts bestowed upon them, so as to understand them all, and be prepared to detect any spurious gifts, and to preside over the whole body of the Church, that all may be benefited. These spiritual gifts are distributed among the members of the Church, according to their faithfulness, circumstances, natural abilities, duties, and callings; that the whole may be properly instructed, confirmed, perfected, and saved." (*Masterful Discourses,* pp. 539-41.)

Gifts of the Spirit are also listed in 1 Corinthians 12:1-13 and Moroni 10:8-18.

**D&C 46:13. What Is the Gift "to Know That Jesus Is the Christ"?**

"This knowledge is placed first among the special gifts, because it is obtained only by revelation. To *believe* that Jesus of Nazareth was the Anointed One, the Messiah, and that He was crucified for the sins of the world, is not to *know* it. Knowledge is a special gift." (Smith and Sjodahl, Commentary, p. 274.)

Concerning the gift to know, President Joseph Fielding Smith counseled: "When Spirit speaks to spirit, the imprint upon the soul is far more difficult to erase. Every member of the Church should have impressions that Jesus is the Son of God indelibly pictured on his soul through the witness of the Holy Ghost." ("The First Presidency and the Council of the Twelve," *Improvement Era,* Nov. 1966, p. 979.)

**D&C 46:14. The Gift to Believe on the Testimony of Others**

Some receive the gift of believing in the testimony that others have received. This gift could be manifested in the lives of people who investigate the Church because they believe in the testimony of members or missionaries while not yet possessing a personal testimony of their own. Children may receive this gift of believing in the testimony of their parents until they receive their own testimony. This gift follows the one spoken of in verse 13, perhaps because it refers to the gift that prophets and Apostles have of receiving a special witness of the Savior. The gift of the Spirit spoken of in verse 14 is for the Saints in general to believe on the testimony of God's servants.

**D&C 46:15. The Gift to Know the Differences of Administration**

"By referring to the Greek text of 1 Corinthians 12:5, where the Apostle Paul is speaking about the same thing, we may get a suitable answer. Apparently by 'differences of administration' is meant the distinctive varieties of service and ministration by which things are accomplished in the Church. The Lord seems to be saying (vs. 15) that while there are diversities of services and ministers or agents, such as Apostles, High Priests, Seventies, and the like in the Church, they all depend on the same Lord and Savior, who is the head of the whole Church. One who has the gift by the Holy Ghost to know differences of administration is one who discerns correctly the services and agencies by which the Lord works." (Sperry, *Compendium*, p. 196.)

**D&C 46:16. The Gift to Know the Diversities of Operations**

The world today is filled with false philosophies and false prophets. This gift gives one the ability to distinguish between those things that are of the devil and those that are of God. To avoid deception requires constant vigilance and acquiring the gift or following those who have received the gift; otherwise, even the elect, according to the covenant, could be deceived (see JS—M 1:22; see also Notes and Commentary on D&C 46:7-8).

**D&C 46:17. The Gift of Wisdom**

This phrase does not refer to the commandment known as the Word of Wisdom; rather, it refers to the endowment of wisdom that comes to those who "ask of God, that giveth to all men liberally" (James 1:5). This gift is frequently seen in ecclesiastical leaders, such as presidents, bishops, and those who serve as their counselors. Parents may frequently be recipients of this gift when counseling their children.

**D&C 46:18. The Gift of Knowledge**

The gift of knowledge is an endowment from God that comes by study and obedience. It is not just a storehouse of factual information but is a knowledge of the things of God obtained by revelation. Thus we read, "If thou shalt ask, thou shalt receive revelation upon revelation, knowledge upon knowledge, that thou mayest know the mysteries and peaceable things—that which bringeth joy, that which bringeth life eternal" (D&C 42:61; emphasis added).

**D&C 46:23. The Gift to Discern Spirits**

Elder Stephen L Richards explained that this gift "arises largely out of an acute sensitivity to impressions—spiritual impressions, if you will—to read under the surface as it were, to detect hidden evil, and more importantly to find the good that may be concealed. The highest type of discernment is that which perceives in others and uncovers for them their better natures, the good inherent within them. It's the gift every missionary needs when he takes the gospel to the people of the world. He must make an appraisal of every personality whom he meets. He must be able to discern the hidden spark that may be lighted for truth. The gift of discernment will save him from mistakes and embarrassment, and it will never fail to inspire confidence in the one who is rightly appraised.

**D&C 46:24-25. The Gift of Tongues**

This is one of the most misunderstood gifts, and one which is a great cause of deception in the world. The Lord may use the dramatic method of speaking in tongues for the definite conveyance of an unusual message or for understanding a strange tongue, as on the day of Pentecost (see Acts 2:4-12). Yet within the true Church it is a gift so often manifested by young missionaries who quickly grasp a foreign language that it is sometimes considered commonplace.

Because this gift is often counterfeited and used to deceive, the Prophet Joseph Smith warned: "Be not so curious about tongues, do not speak in tongues except there be an interpreter present; the ultimate design of tongues is to speak to foreigners, and if persons are very anxious to display their intelligence, let them speak to such in their own tongues. The gifts of God are all useful in their place, but when they are applied to that which God does not intend, they prove an injury, a snare and a curse instead of a blessing." (*History of the Church,* 5:31-32; see also 1 Corinthians 14:1-25.)

**D&C 46:27. The Bishop Is to Be Given the Gift of Discerning All The Gifts**

Elder Stephen L Richards said that "the gift of discernment is essential to the leadership of the Church. I never ordain a bishop or set apart a president of a stake without invoking upon him this divine blessing, that he may read the lives and hearts of his people and call forth the best within them. The gift and power of discernment in this world of contention between the forces of good and the power of evil is essential equipment for every son and daughter of God." (In Conference Report, Apr. 1950, p. 163.)

Elder Abraham O. Woodruff explained the rights of a priesthood leader in the use of this gift: "The Saints should be guided by the Spirit of God, and subject to those who preside in the meetings. If the Bishop, who is a common judge in Israel, tells a person to restrain this gift, or any other gift, it is the duty of that person to do it. The Bishop has a right to the gift of discernment, whereby he may tell whether these spirits are of God or not, and if they are not they should not have place in the congregations of the Saints. No man or woman has a right to find fault with the Bishop for restraining him or her in any of these matters. The Bishop is the responsible party, and it is his privilege to say what shall be done under his presidency." (In Conference Report, Apr. 1901, p. 12.)

**D&C 46:28-33. "He That Asketh in Spirit Shall Receive in Spirit"**

The gifts of the Spirit are available to all who will pay the price, which includes entering into a covenant relationship with the Lord, obeying the commandments, and seeking perfection with all one's heart. The gifts will be the greatest to those who seek most earnestly, but they are available to all: to the missionary who needs help in learning a foreign language, to the man whose temper frequently gets the best of him, to the couple who seek help in rearing their children. President George Q. Cannon wrote:

"How many of you . . . are seeking for these gifts that God has promised to bestow? How many of you, when you bow before your Heavenly Father in your family circle or in your secret places contend for these gifts to be bestowed upon you? How many of you ask the Father, in the name of Jesus, to manifest Himself to you through these powers and these gifts? Or do you go along day by day like a door turning on its hinges, without having any feeling upon the subject, without exercising any faith whatever; content to be baptized and be members of the Church, and to rest there, thinking that your salvation is secure because you have done this? . . .

". . . If any of us are imperfect, it is our duty to pray for the gift that will make us perfect. Have I imperfections? I am full of them. What is my duty? To pray to God to give me the gifts that will correct these imperfections. If I am an angry man, it is my duty to pray for charity, which suffereth long and is kind. Am I an envious man? It is my duty to seek for charity, which envieth not. So with all the gifts of the Gospel. They are intended for this purpose. No man ought to say, 'Oh, I cannot help this; it is my nature.' He is not justified in it, for the reason that God has promised to give strength to correct these things, and to give gifts that will eradicate them. If a man lack wisdom, it is his duty to ask God for wisdom. The same with everything else. That is the design of God concerning His Church. He wants His Saints to be perfected in the truth. For this purpose He gives these gifts, and bestows them upon those who seek after them, in order that they may be a perfect people upon the face of the earth, notwithstanding their many weaknesses, because God has promised to give the gifts that are necessary for their perfection." (In *Millennial Star,* Apr. 1894, pp. 260-61.)

The Lord has outlined the way one receives these gifts in the closing verses of section 46:

1. Read verse 28. What must one do to receive these gifts? Should a person ask for specific gifts?
2. Read verse 30. How must a person ask? (see also Helaman 10:5).
3. Read verse 31. In whose name and by what power do these gifts come?
4. Read verse 32. What must a person constantly remember to do?
5. Read verse 33. What must a person practice in his daily life?

# The Importance of Church Records

Section 47

## Historical Background

Since the beginning of time the Lord has commanded his people to keep records detailing for themselves and all their posterity "what great things the Lord hath done for their fathers" (Book of Mormon title page). Adam kept a book of remembrance written by the spirit of inspiration (see Moses 6:5). Enoch kept a history of his people according to the pattern given by God (see Moses 6:46). Lehi sent his sons back to Jerusalem to obtain a genealogy of their forefathers (see 1 Nephi 3:2-4). Nephi painstakingly kept two histories of his people, a secular record and a sacred record (see 1 Nephi 9:1-6).

Likewise, in the dispensation of the fulness of times, the Prophet Joseph Smith was commanded by the Lord to keep a regular history of the Church. Oliver Cowdery and others were called to assist in the important task. John Whitmer, who previously had served as a secretary to the Prophet in Fayette, New York, was later asked to write the history of the Church. John's reaction to the call was by his own report quite negative. He did say, however, "The will of the Lord be done, and if He desires it, I wish that He would manifest it through Joseph the Seer" (in *History of the Church,* 1:166n). Accordingly, on 8 March 1831 at Kirtland, Ohio, the Prophet inquired of the Lord and received the revelation known as section 47.

## Notes and Commentary

### D&C 47:1. What Happened to John Whitmer's History?

John Whitmer's history of the Church is a mere sketch of events that actually transpired between 1831 and 1838. His work consisted of eighty-five pages, which included many of the revelations given to the Prophet Joseph Smith. He later left the Church and took his history with him. In 1893, many years after his death, a copy of his history was obtained by the Church.

### D&C 47:1. Why Is Keeping Accurate Records So Important?

The Prophet Joseph Smith said of the value of accurate records:

"It is a fact, if I now had in my possession, every decision which had been had upon important items of doctrine and duties since the commencement of this work, I would not part with them for any sum of money; we have neglected to take minutes of such things, thinking, perhaps, that they would never benefit us afterwards; which, if we had them now, would decide almost every point of doctrine which might be agitated. But this has been neglected, and now we cannot bear record to the Church and to the world, of the great and glorious manifestations which have been made to us with that degree of power and authority we otherwise could, if we now had these things to publish abroad.

*The Lord's people have always been a record-keeping people*

"Since the Twelve are now chosen, I wish to tell them a course which they may pursue, and be benefited thereafter, in a point of light of which they are not now aware. If they will, every time they assemble, appoint a person to preside over them during the meeting, and one or more to keep a record of their proceedings, and on the decision of every question or item, be it what it may, let such decision be written, and such decision will forever remain upon record, and appear an item of covenant or doctrine. An item thus decided may appear, at the time, of little or no worth, but should it be published, and one of you lay hands on it after, you will find it of infinite worth, not only to your brethren, but it will be a feast to your own souls.

"Here is another important item. If you assemble from time to time, and proceed to discuss important questions, and pass decisions upon the same, and fail to note them down, by and by you will be driven to straits from which you will not be able to extricate yourselves, because you may be in a situation not to bring your faith to bear with sufficient perfection or power to obtain the desired information; or, perhaps, for neglecting to write these things when God has revealed them, not esteeming them of sufficient worth, the Spirit may withdraw and God may be angry; and there is, or was, a vast knowledge, of infinite importance, which is now lost." (*History of the Church,* 2:198-99; see also Alma 37:8.)

Notes and Commentary for Doctrine and Covenants 128:2-4 gives additional information on the importance of record keeping.

**D&C 47:3. What Role Did Oliver Cowdery Have in Keeping Church Records?**

President Joseph Fielding Smith explained that "the earliest records of the Church are in the handwriting of Oliver Cowdery. He acted as scribe and recorder, generally, in the early conferences of the Church. These minutes and items of doctrine are recorded in manuscript books now filed in the Historian's Office. They are invaluable. Later, in February, 1831, Oliver Cowdery was relieved of this responsibility and John Whitmer was appointed to 'write and keep a regular history and assist you, my servant Joseph Smith, in transcribing all things which shall be given you,' the Lord said, 'until he is called to further duties.' Even after this, however, Oliver Cowdery continued to keep minutes of meetings and to record historical items." (*Church History and Modern Revelation,* 1:106.)

# Ohio: A Temporary Abode

Section 48

## Historical Background

"Zion!" The very word stirred the emotions of the early Saints. But where was the city of the New Jerusalem to be built? It appears that many of the Saints in 1831 thought that the command to move to Ohio was an indication that the New Jerusalem would be there. John Whitmer spoke of this feeling when he wrote: "The time drew near for the brethren from the state of New York to arrive at Kirtland, Ohio. And some had supposed that it was the place of gathering, even the place of the New Jerusalem spoken of in the Book of Mormon, according to the visions and revelations received in the last days." ("Church History," *Journal of History,* Jan. 1908, p. 53.)

The spirit of gathering was truly upon the Saints. Yet the gathering to Ohio raised many questions. Where would the newcomers be housed? Should land be purchased for them to settle on? Should they plan to remain permanently in Ohio? In answer to these and related questions, the Lord gave to the Prophet Joseph Smith the revelation now known as section 48.

## Notes and Commentary

**D&C 48:1, 3. How Long Would the Saints Stay in Ohio?**

The Lord used the phrase "present time" three times in this section, implying that Ohio would be only a temporary Church center.

### D&C 48:4. What "City" Is Referred to in This Verse?

The city is the New Jerusalem, which is to be built through the sacrifice and consecration of the Saints. The Church had first learned about the city from Ether 13:3-8 and two previous revelations to Joseph Smith (see D&C 28:9; 42:6-9). The exact location of this city had not been revealed at this point in the history of the Church (see D&C 48:5). Three months after section 48 was given, however, the Lord indicated that Missouri was the place for the gathering (see D&C 52:2-3), but he did not reveal the specific location as being Jackson County until July 1831 (see D&C 57:1-3).

### D&C 48:5-6. Who Directs the Gathering of the Saints to the New Jerusalem?

The First Presidency of the Church holds the keys of the gathering to the New Jerusalem. President Harold B. Lee emphasized this point when he said: "The Lord has clearly placed the responsibility for directing the work of gathering in the hands of the leaders of the Church, to whom He will reveal His will where and when such gatherings would take place in the future. It would be well, before the frightening events concerning the fulfillment of all God's promises and predictions are upon us, that the Saints in every land prepare themselves and look forward to the instruction that shall come to them from the First Presidency of this church as to where they shall be gathered. They should not be disturbed in their feelings until such instruction is given to them as it is revealed by the Lord to the proper authority." (*Ye Are the Light of the World*, p. 167.)

*Harold B. Lee emphasized that the First Presidency of the Church holds the keys of gathering*

### D&C 48:6. "Every Man According to His Family"

The records of the Church do not show who had the responsibility for apportioning shares in Zion at this time, and as yet the Church had no formally organized First Presidency.

# "Preach My Gospel unto the Shakers"

Section 49

## Historical Background

Not far from Kirtland, Ohio, the new headquarters of the Church, was a religious society known as the Shaking Quakers. Formerly Quakers, they were called Shaking Quakers or Shakers for two reasons: their dress and manners resembled in certain respects those of the Society of Friends (Quakers), and their manner of worship included shaking and physical contortions. The society seems to have had its beginning in England during the latter part of the 1700s. Ann Lee, founder of the Shakers, immigrated to America with her followers just before 1800. Settling in Ohio, they were in such close proximity to the Saints that it was only a matter of time until there was some intermingling between the two groups. One of the Shakers, Leman Copley, joined the Church but retained many of his former beliefs. Still, he wished to go and teach his former friends. Concerned, the Prophet inquired of the Lord and received the reply found in section 49.

## Notes and Commentary

### D&C 49:2. "They Desire to Know the Truth . . . But Not All"

Frequently people want to accept a part of the gospel, but not all of it. Some are willing to accept Sabbath day meetings but reject tithing. Others will obey the Word of Wisdom yet condone personal immorality. When the message of the Restoration was presented to the Shakers, they accepted that which was compatible with their beliefs and rejected that which was not.

### D&C 49:4. What Are Some of the Beliefs of the Shakers That Leman Copley Was to Forsake?

In his work on the Doctrine and Covenants, Sperry gave a comprehensive summary of the Shakers' beliefs:

"The most important beliefs or doctrines of the Shakers may be listed in this way:

"1. The Deity is dual in nature. God is both male and female. The male principle of Christ came to earth as Jesus, the son of a Jewish carpenter. The female principle is represented in 'Mother Ann' [Ann Lee, founder of the Shaker sect], and in her the promise of our Lord's Second Advent was fulfilled. Incidentally, the Shakers believe that even angels and spirits are both male and female.

"2. Celibacy. This must be qualified by saying that they neither condemn nor oppose marriage, but they assert the possibility of attaining a higher or angelic order of existence to which virginity is a prime requisite.

"3. Open confession of sins.

"4. Community of possessions.

"5. Separation from the world. Ostentation, luxury, and private property are regarded as sinful and unChristian.

"6. Pacifism.

"7. Equality of the sexes.

"8. Consecrated work.

"9. Continuous revelation.

"10. External ordinances, 'especially baptism and the Lord's supper, ceased in the apostolic age.' (Burder, *History of All Religions,* p. 502.)

"11. Christ's kingdom upon the earth began with the establishment of the Shaker Church. From the days of the Apostles the Lord had sent no one to preach until the Shakers were raised up to call in the elect in a new dispensation.

"12. The doctrines of the Trinity, vicarious atonement, and resurrection of the body are untrue.

"13. Disease is a sin against God.

"14. Abstinence from meat (in some groups, at least)." (*Compendium,* pp. 204-6.)

The Shakers thrived as a church until about the turn of the century. Since then their numbers have steadily declined until today only one active community is left, at Sabbathday Lake, Maine.

### D&C 49:6. "Till He Descends on the Earth"

The Shakers did not believe Christ to be divine and therefore were not looking forward to his second coming. What they were looking for was the return of the "Christ spirit," a spirit that would infuse their leader and make him or her spiritual and not carnal. They believed four persons had been given this spirit in its fulness: Adam, Abraham, Christ, and Ann Lee.

### D&C 49:8. What Holy Men Has God Reserved unto Himself?

President Joseph Fielding Smith explained that men "who were without sin, and reserved unto the Lord, are translated persons such as John the

*Sidney Rigdon, Parley P. Pratt, and Leman Copley served a mission among the Shakers*

Revelator and the Three Nephites, who do not belong to this generation and yet are in the flesh in the earth performing a special ministry until the coming of Jesus Christ" (*Church History and Modern Revelation,* 1:209).

### D&C 49:3-10. Did the Appointed Missionaries Fulfill the Lord's Command to Go among the Shakers?

John Whitmer wrote that Sidney Rigdon, Parley P. Pratt, and Leman Copley "went and proclaimed [the Gospel] according to the revelation given them, but the Shakers hearkened not to their words and received not the Gospel at that time, for they are bound in tradition and priestcraft; and thus they are led away with foolish and vain imaginations" (in *History of the Church,* 1:169n).

Sidney Rigdon had lived in close proximity to the Shakers at North Union for many years and had become well acquainted with their leaders and their doctrine. Parley P. Pratt had many relatives who were Shakers. He had also been one of the first missionaries to approach the group at North Union.

The three missionaries arrived at North Union on a Saturday evening and were allowed to give to the group a long discussion of the gospel. They spent the night, and the next morning they spoke in the regular Sunday meeting. Sidney Rigdon read the revelation to them as a part of his comments, and it was instantly rejected by the leader of the group, Ashbel Kitchell. The rest of the group agreed with Kitchell, and the missionaries withdrew.

**D&C 49:10-14. The Importance of the First Principles and Ordinances of the Gospel**

Because the Shakers rejected baptism but believed in the gifts of the Spirit, the Lord commanded the missionaries to teach them the importance of faith in the Lord, repentance, baptism, and the gift of the Holy Ghost. According to 2 Nephi 31:17, the gift of the Holy Ghost is received only after one has entered the gate of repentance and baptism. The Prophet Joseph Smith stated that the true gifts of the Spirit are enjoyed only by those who have received the gift of the Holy Ghost: "We believe in the gift of the Holy Ghost being enjoyed now, as much as it was in the Apostles' days; we believe that it [the gift of the Holy Ghost] is necessary to make and to organize the Priesthood, that no man can be called to fill any office in the ministry without it; we also believe in prophecy, in tongues, in visions, and in revelations, in gifts, and in healings; and that these things cannot be enjoyed without the gift of the Holy Ghost." (*History of the Church,* 5:27.)

Peter taught the same doctrine on the day of Pentecost (see Acts 2:37-38).

**D&C 49:15. The Shakers Believed That the Highest Type of Christian Life Was Celibacy**

President Spencer W. Kimball bore testimony about the importance of marriage: "In magazines we frequently see articles on this antimarriage revolution. . . . Let me say again, marriage is honorable. It's a plan of God. It is not a whim, a choice, a preference only; it's a must." ("Marriage Is Honorable," in *Speeches of the Year, 1973* [Provo: Brigham Young University Press, 1974], p. 261.)

President Joseph Fielding explained why marriage was mentioned in this revelation: "This statement in relation to marriage was given to correct the false doctrine of the Shakers that marriage was impure and that a true follower of Jesus Christ must remain in the condition of celibacy to be free from sin and in full fellowship with Christ" (*Church History and Modern Revelation,* 1:209).

**D&C 49:16-17. What Is the Principal "End" or Reason for the Earth's Creation?**

The Lord created the earth as a habitation for his spirit children during their mortal probation. Marriage and bringing forth children is critical in bringing about the Lord's purposes. According to President Joseph Fielding Smith: "The people who inhabit this earth were all living in the spirit life before they came to this earth. The Lord informs us that this earth was designed, before its foundations were formed, for the abode of the spirits who kept their first estate, and all such must come here and receive their tabernacles of flesh and bones, and this is according to the number, or measure, of man according to his creation before the world was made. (Compare [Deuteronomy] 32:8-9.) It is the duty of mankind, in lawful and holy wedlock, to multiply according to the commandments given to Adam and Eve and later to Noah, until every spirit appointed to receive a body in this world has had that privilege. Those who teach celibacy and look upon marriage as sinful are in opposition to the word and commandment of the Lord. Such a doctrine is from an evil source and is intended to defeat the plan of redemption and the bringing into the world the spirits who kept their first estate. Satan, in every way that he can and with all his power, endeavors to defeat the work of the Lord. It is his purpose to destroy the souls of men and if he can prevent them from having bodies by teaching men and women that marriage is unrighteous and sinful, or that they should not after they are married bring children into the world, he thinks he will accomplish his purpose. All who hearken to these evil whisperings and practice this evil will stand condemned before the throne of God." (*Church History and Modern Revelation,* 1:209-10.)

**D&C 49:18-21. "Wo Be Unto Man That Sheddeth Blood or Wasteth Flesh and Hath No Need"**

In these verses the Lord instructed the Shakers that he had ordained certain things for the use of man and included a caution in verse 21. Speaking about the intent that men should have when hunting animals or birds, President Spencer W. Kimball said:

"Now, I also would like to add some of my feelings concerning the unnecessary shedding of blood and destruction of life. I think that every soul should be impressed by the sentiments that have been expressed here by the prophets. . . .

"President Joseph F. Smith said, . . .

" 'I do not believe any man should kill animals or birds unless he needs them for food, and then he should not kill innocent little birds that are not intended for food for man. I think it is wicked for men to thirst in their souls to kill almost everything which possesses animal life. It is wrong, and I have been surprised at prominent men whom I have seen whose very souls seemed to be athirst for the shedding of animal blood.' " (In Conference Report, Oct. 1978, p. 64; or *Ensign,* Nov. 1978, p. 45.)

**D&C 49:22-23. "The Son of Man Cometh Not in the Form of a Woman"**

The concluding verses of this section focus on the erroneous beliefs held by the Shakers about the second coming of Christ (see Notes and Commentary for D&C 49:7). Verse 22 refutes the Shaker view that the "Christ spirit" was embodied in Ann Lee, and verses 23 through 25 explain some events that must precede the Lord's future appearance. The scriptures are abundantly clear that Christ will return in great glory to his temple (see Malachi 3:1-3).

**D&C 49:24-25. What Is Prophetic about These Verses?**

Two prophecies were given in this revelation so that the Shakers might know what would occur on this continent before the Lord's second coming. These two prophecies bear witness of the prophetic keys held by the Prophet Joseph Smith.

The first prophecy states that "Jacob [meaning modern Israel] shall flourish in the wilderness, and . . . Zion shall flourish upon the hills" (D&C

49:24-25). This prophecy was fulfilled when the Saints were compelled to leave Nauvoo, Illinois, and settle in the Rocky Mountains. The second prophecy is that "the Lamanites shall blossom as the rose" (vs. 24). Today those of Lamanite descent are joining the Church in ever increasing numbers and are blossoming under the genial rays of gospel light.

# "That Which Doth Not Edify Is Not of God"

Section 50

## Historical Background

During all dispensations when the gospel has been upon the earth to bless the children of God, Satan has devised various means of counterfeiting the revelatory process. One of Satan's methods is to deceive men with experiences that are difficult to understand, a technique especially evident in the very early days of the Restoration. The Prophet Joseph Smith observed: "Soon after the Gospel was established in Kirtland, and during the absence of the authorities of the Church, many false spirits were introduced, many strange visions were seen, and wild, enthusiastic notions were entertained: men ran out of doors under the influence of this spirit, and some of them got upon the stumps of trees and shouted, and all kinds of extravagances were entered into by them; one man pursued a ball that he said he saw flying in the air, until he came to a precipice, when he jumped into the top of a tree, which saved his life; and many ridiculous things were entered into, calculated to bring disgrace upon the Church of God, to cause the Spirit of God to be withdrawn, and to uproot and destroy those glorious principles which had been developed for the salvation of the human family." (*History of the Church,* 4:580.)

John Whitmer, describing the excessive spiritual aberrations that he witnessed in that early day, wrote: "Some had visions and could not tell what they saw, some would fancy to themselves that they had the sword of Laban, and would wield it as expert as a light dragon; some would act like an Indian in the act of scalping; some would slide or scoot on the floor with the rapidity of a serpent, which they termed sailing in the boat to the Lamanites, preaching the gospel. And many other vain and foolish maneuvers that are unseeming and unprofitable to mention. Thus the devil blinded the eyes of some good and honest disciples. I write these things to show how ignorant and undiscerning children are, and how easy mankind is led astray, notwithstanding the things of God that are written concerning his kingdom." ("Church History," *Journal of History,* Jan. 1908, p. 55.)

Elder Parley P. Pratt was also a witness to these unusual operations:

"All these things were new and strange to me, and had originated in the Church during the absence, and previous to the arrival of President Joseph Smith from New York.

"Feeling our weakness and inexperience, and lest we should err in judgment concerning the spiritual phenomena, myself, John Murdock, and several other Elders, went to Joseph Smith, and asked him to inquire of the Lord concerning these spirits or manifestations." (*Autobiography of Parley P. Pratt,* pp. 61-62.)

Section 50 was the response to that inquiry.

## Notes and Commentary

### D&C 50:2-9. Satan Seeks to Deceive Mankind through False Manifestations

The Prophet Joseph Smith observed: "The devil has great power to deceive; he will so transform things as to make one gape at those who are doing the will of God" (*Teachings,* p. 227). Latter-day Saints must observe the Lord's counsel if they would escape Satan's deceptions: "Let every man beware lest he do that which is not in truth and righteousness before me" (D&C 50:9).

President Joseph Fielding Smith taught that many manifestations are from Satan: "From the time of the fall of man until now Satan and his followers who were cast out of heaven, have been deceiving men. Today, as in the beginning, Lucifer is saying, 'I am also a son of God . . . believe it or not,' and men today believe not for the same reason that they refused to believe in the beginning. 'Some commandments are of men,' so the Savior informed Joseph Smith. . . . (Sec. 46:7.) Some commandments are of devils, and these are also made manifest largly through the activities of men. . . . These false spirits make themselves manifest in various ways and in all communities. Some of the most startling and prevalent forms of false manifestations are in the false gifts of tongues, and in religious meetings particularly among some sects where the worshippers fall in fits, shout, sing and pray in disorderly fashion, sometimes frothing at the mouth and their bodies partaking of unnatural contortions." (*Church History and Modern Revelation,* 1:200.)

### D&C 50:10-12. "Let Us Reason Even As a Man"

The Lord reasons with men as men reason with each other. His purpose in reasoning with them is the same as his reason for speaking to men in their own language: he wants them to "come to understanding" (D&C 1:24; see also Isaiah 1:18).

### D&C 50:13-21. How Can One Discern and Unmask Evil Spirits?

Some of the early Saints had fallen victim to excessive spiritual displays, "receiving them to be of God" (D&C 50:15). The Lord indicated that these displays are not justified. The Prophet Joseph Smith explained how righteous men can know the difference between good and evil spiritual phenomena:

"One great evil is, that men are ignorant of the nature of spirits; their power, laws, government, intelligence, etc., and imagine that when there is anything like power, revelation, or vision manifested, that it must be of God. . . .

" . . . who can drag into daylight and develop the hidden mysteries of the false spirits that so frequently are made manifest among the Latter-day Saints? We answer that no man can do this without the Priesthood, and having a knowledge of the laws by which spirits are governed; for as 'no man knows the things of God,' but by the Spirit of God, so no man knows the spirit of the devil, and his power and influence, but by possessing intelligence which is more than human, and having unfolded through the medium of the Priesthood the mysterious operations of his devices; without knowing the angelic form, the sanctified look and gesture, and the zeal that is frequently manifested by him for the glory of God, together with the prophetic spirit, the gracious influence, the godly appearance, and the holy garb, which are so characteristic of his proceedings and his mysterious windings.

"A man must have the discerning of spirits before he can drag into daylight this hellish influence and unfold it unto the world in all its soul-destroying, diabolical, and horrid colors. . . .

" . . . the great difficulty lies in the ignorance of the nature of spirits, of the laws by which they are governed, and the signs by which they may be known; . . . it requires the Spirit of God to know the things of God; and the spirit of the devil can only be unmasked through that medium." (*History of the Church,* 4:572-74; see also Notes and Commentary for D&C 129.)

### D&C 50:22-24. What Criterion Determines "That Which Is of God" and That Which Is of Satan?

The things of God edify, that is, spiritually support and lift man toward a better life. They bring him closer to his Father in Heaven. The things of Satan do the opposite. No spiritual growth occurs, no intelligence is communicated, no edification transpires. The Prophet Joseph Smith gave instruction on this matter also:

"Others frequently possess a spirit that will cause them to lie down, and during its operation, animation is frequently entirely suspended; they consider it to be the power of God, and a glorious manifestation from God—a manifestation of what? Is there any intelligence communicated? Are the curtains of heaven withdrawn, or the purposes of God developed? Have they seen and conversed

*That which is of God is light and truth, but that which is not is darkness*

with an angel—or have the glories of futurity burst upon their view? No! but their body has been inanimate, the operation of their spirit suspended, and all the intelligence that can be obtained from them when they arise, is a shout of 'glory,' or 'hallelujah,' or some incoherent expression; but they have had 'the power.'

"The Shaker will whirl around on his heel, impelled by a supernatural agency or spirit, and think that he is governed by the Spirit of God; and the Jumper will jump and enter into all kinds of extravagances. A Primitive Methodist will shout under the influence of that spirit, until he will rend the heavens with his cries; while the Quakers (or Friends) moved as they think, by the Spirit of God, will sit still and say nothing. Is God the author of all this? If not of all of it, which does He recognize? Surely, such a heterogeneous mass of confusion never can enter into the kingdom of heaven." (*Teachings,* pp. 203-4.)

President Joseph Fielding Smith taught: "There is no saying of greater truth than 'that which doth not edify is not of God.' And that which is not of God is darkness, it matters not whether it comes in the guise of religion, ethics, philosophy or revelation. No revelation from God will fail to edify." (*Church History and Modern Revelation,* 1:201-2.)

### D&C 50:25-28. How Can Man Become "Possessor of All Things"?

Those who strive to keep the Lord's commandments are made joint heirs with Jesus Christ and inherit all that the Father has to give (see Romans 8:17; D&C 84:38). But "no man is possessor of all things except he be purified and cleansed from all sin" (D&C 50:28). Keeping all the commandments of God thus becomes the key to eternal life.

"We believe that God condescended to speak from the heavens and declare His will concerning the human family, to give them just and holy laws, to regulate their conduct, and guide them in a direct way, that in due time He might take them to Himself, and make them joint heirs with His Son. . . .

"Here then, we have this part of our subject immediately before us for consideration: God has in reserve a time, or period appointed in His own bosom, when He will bring all His subjects, who have obeyed His voice and kept His commandments, into His celestial rest. This rest is of such perfection and glory, that man has need of a preparation before he can, according to the laws of that kingdom, enter it and enjoy its blessings. This being the fact, God has given certain laws to the human family, which, if observed, are sufficient to prepare them to inherit this rest." (Smith, *Teachings*, pp. 53-54.)

### D&C 50:29-30. "It Shall Be Given You What You Shall Ask"

Those who are clean before the Lord may pray with confidence and expect to receive righteous answers to their prayers. That which they ask, if expedient in the Lord's mind, shall be given (see D&C 88:64). "But know this, it shall be given you what you shall ask" (D&C 50:30). Men should pray for that which is reasonable and according to the mind and will of the Lord. If they are righteous, they will enjoy God's spirit, and it shall be "given unto them what they should pray," because they will be "filled with desire" (3 Nephi 19:24). They will desire that which is in the Lord's will that they should have, and that will be the burden of their prayers.

### D&C 50:31-35. A Key for Discernment

These are some of the most important verses in this section. When a person finds himself confronted by an evil spirit that he cannot understand, or by someone who has great spiritual power but whose claims seem in doubt, he is directed to ask God in the name of Jesus if it is a good or an evil spirit. If prayer reveals that such a person is not of God, "power over that spirit" can come only from God. One cannot control or conquer evil on his own power, but God can give sufficient power to do so (see D&C 50:32). One must then give credit to the Lord (see vs. 34), for the Lord provides the power whereby Saints may be discerned, or evil overcome, or temptations or habits set aside. The Lord's closing comment in these verses is that "power" is available "to overcome all things not ordained" of God (vs. 35).

See Enrichment J, in the Appendix, for a full discussion of the principles of discernment and how to avoid deception.

### D&C 50:40-43. "And None of Them That My Father Hath Given Me Shall Be Lost"

Elder Marriner W. Merrill took these words of solace and comfort and applied them to the family: "If we place first and foremost our obligations to the Church then we have a good chance to remain in the Church and to retain our fellowship with each other. And when we have fellowship with each other, we have fellowship with the Spirit of the Lord, which will direct us in all our ways, and we will be preserved in the truth with our families. Some of our families perhaps are wayward. They do not do as we would like them to do. Is not this the case in many families? There are sons and daughters whose course does not give satisfaction to their fathers and mothers. What shall we do about it? Do the very best we can, but see to it that we have not been the cause of their lack of integrity in the work of the Lord. I believe through our faithfulness and our entreaties with the Lord we may be the means not only of saving ourselves, but those the Lord has entrusted to us as sons and daughters. The Lord is merciful and He will hear our prayers and grant our desires through our integrity for him and his work. And peradventure, through our faithfulness, our children who are wayward and who perhaps have strayed away, will come back to the fold bye and bye, because the Lord will hear us in their behalf." (In Conference Report, Apr. 1900, p. 29.)

### D&C 50:45. "The Day Cometh That You Shall . . . See Me"

The promise that man can see the face of God is taught here and in several other places in the Doctrine and Covenants (see for example D&C 67:10; 88:68; 93:1).

Elder Orson F. Whitney pointed out that the way the Lord chooses to manifest himself to his

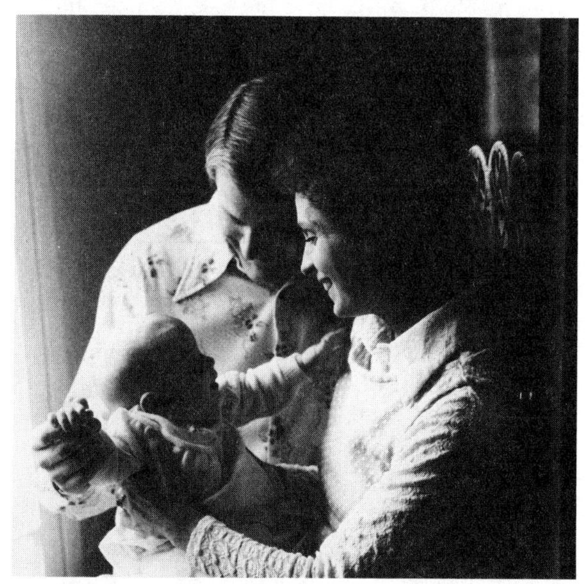

*"None of them that my Father hath given me shall be lost" (D&C 50:45)*

children depends on their personal worthiness and preparation: "It is not given to every man to look upon the face of God as did Moses [Moses 1:11], as did Joseph Smith. One must be specially prepared before he can see what Joseph saw. . . . I do not expect the Lord to manifest Himself to me in the same way that He did to Joseph the Prophet. I expect Him to communicate with me through the gifts He has endowed me with, not through those with which He has endowed my brother or sister, unless they have the right to receive for me a message from Him. When the Lord speaks to me or to you, it will be in a method and manner justified by our preparation, our gifts, our powers; for we have all been endowed in some degree." (In Conference Report, Apr. 1910, p. 60.)

# Bishop Edward Partridge and the Law of Consecration

Section 51

## Historical Background

A call for the Saints to gather in Ohio had been given in December 1830 (see D&C 37:3). In May 1831, when the Saints had begun to respond, Edward Partridge, the newly appointed bishop of the Church, felt the responsibility of caring for them when they arrived in Ohio. The basic elements of the law of consecration had been given (see D&C 42), but many situations required more detailed answers. Bishop Partridge sought help from the Prophet Joseph Smith, who inquired of the Lord and received what is now section 51 of the Doctrine and Covenants.

President Joseph Fielding Smith wrote: "The Lord endeavored to teach these members, in part, at least, and train them in the great principle of consecration as a preparatory step before they should be permitted to journey to Zion, for it was in keeping with this law upon which the City of Zion was to be built. Thus these saints from the East were to be organized according to the law of God. (Sec. 51:4-6.) This land in Ohio was in this manner to be consecrated unto them 'for a little season,' until the Lord should provide for them otherwise, and command them to go hence. (Sec. 51:15-16.)" (*Church History and Modern Revelation,* 1:204.)

The experience of Orson Pratt, who was present when Joseph Smith received this revelation at Thompson, Ohio, was reported as follows: "No great noise or physical manifestation was made; Joseph was as calm as the morning sun. But he noticed a change in his countenance that he had never noticed before, when a revelation was given to him. Joseph's face was exceedingly white, and seemed to shine. The speaker had been present many times when he was translating the New Testament, and wondered why he did not use the Urim and Thummim, as in translating the Book of Mormon. While this thought passed through the speaker's mind, Joseph, as if he read his thoughts, looked up and explained that the Lord gave him the Urim and Thummim when he was inexperienced in the Spirit of inspiration. But now he had advanced so far that he understood the operations of that Spirit, and did not need the assistance of that instrument." (*Millennial Star,* 11 Aug. 1874, pp. 498-99.)

## Notes and Commentary

### D&C 51:2. Why Does God Give Man Laws by Which They Are to Live?

In an address given at commencement services at Brigham Young University, Cecil B. DeMille, producer of the movie *The Ten Commandments,* spoke of the modern-day attitude toward law: "We are too inclined to think of law as something merely restrictive—something hemming us in. We sometimes think of law as the opposite of liberty. But that is a false conception. That is not the way that God's inspired prophets and lawgivers looked upon the law. Law has a twofold purpose. It is meant to govern. It is also meant to educate." (*Commencement Address,* Brigham Young University Speeches of the Year [Provo, 31 May 1957], p. 4.)

Elder Richard L. Evans gave further reasons for God's giving man laws to follow: "What would a loving Father want for his children? What would any father want for his children? Peace and health and happiness; learning and progress and improvement; and everlasting life, and everlasting association with those we love. What less could heaven be? What less would a Father plan or propose, for those he loves, for those whom he made 'in his own image'? (Gen. 1:27.) He has declared his work and his glory 'to bring to pass the immortality and eternal life of man.' (Pearl of Great Price, Moses 1:39). This is the ultimate objective. This is the whole purpose of the Gospel he has given." (In Conference Report, Oct. 1959, p. 127.)

### D&C 51:3. How Does the Lord Define Equality?

The law of consecration was designed to make men equal in temporal things, but as President J. Reuben Clark, Jr., pointed out, this equality is of a special kind: "One of the places in which some of the brethren are going astray is this: There is continuous reference in the revelations to equality among the brethren, but I think you will find only one place where that equality is really described, though it is referred to in other revelations. That revelation (D. & C. 51:3) affirms that every man is to be 'equal according to his family, according to his circumstances and his wants and needs.' (See also D. & C. 82:17; 78:5-6.) Obviously, this is not a case of 'dead level' equality. It is 'equality' that will vary as much as the man's circumstances, his family, his wants and needs, may vary." (In Conference Report, Oct. 1942, p. 55.)

### D&C 51:4-6. Why Did the Lord Want Inheritances in the Church to Be Secured in Writing?

President J. Reuben Clark, Jr., explained this principle as follows: "The fundamental principle of this system was the private ownership of property. Each man owned his portion, or inheritance, or stewardship, with an absolute title, which he could alienate, or hypothecate, or otherwise treat as his own. The Church did not own all of the property, and the life under the United Order was not a communal life, as the Prophet Joseph himself, said (*History of the Church,* Volume III, p. 28). The United Order is an individualistic system, not a communal system." (In Conference Report, Oct. 1942, p. 57.)

President Clark further showed that a written title or deed was issued that satisfied the requirements of civil law and secured to an individual the rights of private ownership of property. The importance of such written agreements is evident when it is remembered that people had their agency to leave the united order. A written contract between the bishop and the individual secured the terms of the agreement when the person entered the order (see D&C 51:6). So, even though a person acknowledged that all property ultimately belongs to God, for legal and practical purposes his deeded portion became his private property. It did not belong to the Church. This arrangement was true of the initial inheritance of land and buildings given to each person in the order; any surplus earned from one's stewardship was given to the Church.

*J. Reuben Clark, Jr., explained stewardships and inheritances under the law of consecration*

"If anyone transgressed and was counted unworthy of membership in the Church, he also lost his standing in the society, but in that case he was to retain the property deeded to him, but have no claim on the portion set apart for the maintenance of the poor and needy" (Smith and Sjodahl, Commentary, p. 298).

People who chose to withdraw from the order often ended up with bitter feelings against the Church. Handling the transactions through legally constituted means provided protection for both the individual and the Church. "In the community there would always be some who would wish to draw out and, perhaps, embarrass the rest by lawsuits, or otherwise. In order to prevent such designs, just and equitable provisions were to be made and secured by legal agreements." (Smith and Sjodahl, Commentary, p. 298.)

Enrichment L, in the Appendix, explains the law of consecration more fully.

### D&C 51:8. Why Did the Lord Have an "Agent" Appointed?

"The community was to be represented by an Agent, whose special duty it would be to handle the money required for food and clothing by the people. There is great wisdom manifested in the distribution of responsibilities. The Bishopric would receive the property, distribute it in 'stewardships,' and receive the earnings of each stewardship; the Agent would see to it that property was not unduly accumulated, but that the needs of all were supplied." (Smith and Sjodahl, Commentary, p. 298.)

### D&C 51:9. How Were the Saints to Be Alike?

Under the united order everyone was alike in that they were independent and had full opportunity to use their gifts and talents in building the kingdom of God. They were also alike in that all had equal opportunity to benefit from whatever talents and abilities existed in the community. The idea that everyone was alike in goods possessed or income received is an erroneous one. The order was united in love, purpose, and commitment, but unity does not mean sameness. A man with seven children has needs different from those of couples just beginning married life.

### D&C 51:10. What "Church" Is the Lord Referring To?

"The word 'church' in this paragraph stands for 'Branch,' as in Sec. 20:81; 45:64, and elsewhere. The meaning conveyed is that the property owned by the Colesville Branch could not be claimed by any other Branch." (Smith and Sjodahl, Commentary, p. 299.)

### D&C 51:11-14. The Responsibility of the Bishop

The major responsibility for implementing the united order rested with the bishop.

### D&C 51:17. Why Did the Lord Counsel the Saints to Act upon the Land "As for Years"?

People who locate in a home or apartment knowing that they will move to another in a short time may have a tendency to neglect Church attendance and other responsibilities. They rationalize, "Well, we won't be here long." The Lord wanted the Saints to live the gospel and share it in Ohio as though they were to be there for a long time.

# "Let Them Go Two by Two" Section 52

## Historical Background

A great gathering of the Church convened at Kirtland, Ohio, on 3 June 1831. So important was this conference that letters were sent to the missionaries calling them all to Kirtland (see D&C 44:1). Efforts were also made to bring the New York Saints to Ohio (see D&C 48:2-5).

During this conference a significant new office was conferred upon a number of the brethren, that of high priest in the Melchizedek Priesthood. The Prophet Joseph Smith received the spirit of prophecy and prophesied that John the Revelator was among the ten tribes preparing them to return from their long dispersion. (See *History of the Church*, 1:175-76). The Prophet recorded that "harmony prevailed" and "faith was strengthened" (*History of the Church*, 1:176). Many desired to obey the Lord's commandments but were uncertain about what specifically they could do. On the day following the conclusion of the conference the Prophet was given specific calls and instructions in what is now Doctrine and Covenants 52.

## Notes and Commentary

### D&C 52:2. How Often Were Conferences Held?

The Lord had commanded that conferences of the Church be held every three months or as often as the Saints assembled in conference decided (see D&C 20:61). Usually the leaders of the Church decided in one conference the date and place of the next. The Lord in this revelation designated Missouri as the location of the next conference.

### D&C 52:3, 7-8, 22-32. One Purpose of This Revelation

One purpose of this revelation was to call certain brethren to travel as missionaries from Ohio to Missouri. In all, twenty-eight missionaries were called in this revelation; however, thirty actually went—one of the original twenty-eight did not go, and three more were called later (see D&C 53, 55-56).

*Missionaries go forth two by two*

### D&C 52:9. The Standard by Which to Determine What Is Taught in the Church

In this revelation the Lord set a standard by which missionaries and teachers are to determine what they teach: they are to teach those things that he has revealed to his prophets and Apostles, that which is taught to them through the influence of the Holy Ghost. Many problems arise when people begin to offer their personal opinions as doctrines of the Church. In 1837 the Twelve Apostles wrote an epistle in which they warned: "Be careful that you teach not for the word of God the commandments of men, nor the doctrines of men, nor the ordinances of men, inasmuch as you are God's messengers. Study the word of God, and preach it and not your opinions, for no man's opinion is worth a straw. Advance no principle but what you can prove, for one scriptural proof is worth ten thousand opinions. We would moreover say, abide by that revelation which says 'Preach nothing but repentance to this generation,' and leave the further mysteries of the kingdom till God shall tell you to preach them, which is not now." (*History of the Church,* 3:395-96.)

Elder Bruce R. McConkie bore the following testimony: "The truth of all things is measured by the scriptures. That which harmonizes with them should be accepted; that which is contrary to their teachings, however plausible it may seem for the moment, will not endure and should be rejected." (*Mormon Doctrine,* p. 765.)

### D&C 52:14-19. The Pattern by Which One Can Avoid Deception

The dictionary defines a pattern as being, among other things, a reliable sample of traits, acts, or other observable features characterizing an individual. In these verses the Lord indicates that one observable feature of one who is inspired of God is that he or she will obey the ordinances of the gospel. (See Notes and Commentary on D&C 50:10-27; see also Enrichment J, in the Appendix.)

### D&C 52:33. "And One Man Shall Not Build upon Another's Foundation"

"Special instructions were also given to others of the elders, commanding them to go forth two by two in the proclamation of the word of God by the way, to every congregation where they could get a hearing. Though the western frontier of Missouri was their destination, they were commanded to take different routes and not build on each other's foundation or travel in each other's track." (Cannon, *Life of Joseph Smith,* p. 116.)

### D&C 52:39. Who Does the Lord Command to "Labor with Their Own Hands," and How Would Obedience to This Commandment Prevent Idolatry?

This instruction was given to those elders *not* assigned to go as missionaries to Missouri. These men were assigned to stay home and be the priesthood leaders for the Saints in Kirtland. By laboring with their own hands for their support, rather than being paid for their priesthood service, these brethren would help prevent idolatry and priestcraft from springing up in the Church (see 2 Nephi 26:29). Modern readers may wonder at the use of the word *idolatry,* since idolatry is often thought of as a practice that went out of existence centuries ago. But in the preface to the Doctrine and Covenants, the Lord warned that one of the characteristics of the last days would be that "every man walketh in his own way, and after the image of his God . . . whose substance is that of an idol" (D&C 1:16), and Paul defined covetousness as idolatry (see Ephesians 5:5; Colossians 3:5). In other words, when a man sets his heart on natural things, or prestige, or power to the point that God is no longer supreme, then that becomes as god to him. He worships, or gives his allegiance to, those things. This verse suggests that if the elders who remained in Ohio did not labor with their own hands, they might be guilty of this kind of covetousness, or idolatry.

### D&C 52:43. What City Does the Lord Refer To?

See Notes and Commentary for Doctrine and Covenants 42:35.

# A Call to Sidney Gilbert to Forsake the World

Section 53

## Historical Background

There is little information on Algernon Sidney Gilbert before he was introduced to the gospel in 1830. He was then the senior partner in the successful mercantile firm of Gilbert and Whitney in Kirtland, Ohio.

Sometime after he joined the Church, he was ordained an elder and sent to Missouri to buy land and operate a small store (see D&C 57:8). When mob violence broke loose, Sidney Gilbert closed his store upon request and helped appease the mob temporarily. On 23 July 1833 he, with others, offered himself as a ransom for the Saints. (See *History of the Church,* 1:391, 394n.) He was devoted and faithful and sacrificed all of his goods during the persecutions in Missouri. He lacked confidence in his ability to preach, however, and, according to some reports, he said he "would rather die than go forth to preach the Gospel to the Gentiles" (*History of the Church,* 2:118). Ironically, he later contracted cholera and died. Heber C. Kimball recorded in his journal that "the Lord took him at his word." Elder B. H. Roberts wrote of Brother Gilbert, "The remarks in the body of the history, and this expression from Elder Kimball's journal are liable to create a misunderstanding concerning Brother Algernon Sidney Gilbert, than whom the Lord has had few more devoted servants in this dispensation" (*History of the Church,* 2:118n).

Joseph Smith received section 53 in answer to the request of Sidney Gilbert, who desired to know what he was to do in the Church. The revelation came during a time of great excitement. A spiritual conference had ended, and many were assigned to go to Missouri and there receive further instructions from the Lord. In this revelation Algernon Sidney Gilbert was also called to go to Missouri and help with the work there as the bishop's agent over the storehouse.

## Notes and Commentary

### D&C 53:1. "I Have Heard Your Prayers"

Many people secretly request to know the Lord's divine will concerning them, but often the answer is too sacred to discuss with any mortal soul. Sidney Gilbert's request was not disregarded, for the Lord made known to him his calling and election in the Church. (See also D&C 6:22-24.)

### D&C 53:2. What Does the Phrase "Forsake the World" Mean?

The phrase "forsake the world" is the commandment given to those who have entered into a covenant relationship with the Lord. They are to forsake the standards and habits of the apostate world. Elder George Q. Cannon related this teaching to the doctrine of being born again: "We need to be born again, and have new hearts put in us. There is too much of the old leaven about us. We are not born again as we should be. Do you not believe that we ought to be born again? Do you not believe that we should become new creatures in Christ Jesus, under the influence of the Gospel? All will say, yes, who understand the Gospel. You must be born again. You must have new desires, new hearts, so to speak, in you. But what do we see? We see men following the ways of the world just as much as though they made no pretensions to being Latter-day Saints. Hundreds of people who are called Latter-day Saints you could not distinguish from the world. They have the same desires, the same feelings, the same aspirations, the same passions as the rest of the world. Is this how God wants us to be? No; He wants us to have new hearts, new desires. He wants us to be a changed people when we embrace His Gospel, and to be animated by entirely new motives, and have a faith that will lay hold of the promises of God." (In Conference Report, Oct. 1899, p. 50.)

### D&C 53:3. Ordination to the Priesthood Is a Call to Serve Others

Sidney Gilbert was directed to receive the ordination of an elder and then to use that office in preaching faith, repentance, and the remission of sins, but his feelings of inadequacy in preaching the gospel prevented him from fully responding to the call. There is, however, an account of his successful missionary labors among his friends and family in Huntington, Connecticut (see *History of the Church,* 2:119).

### D&C 53:4. What Were His Duties As an "Agent" unto the Church?

Sidney Gilbert's calling was to receive monies for the Church and to buy land. He was to assist Edward Partridge in managing the temporal affairs of the Church in Missouri (see D&C 57:6-9).

*The store owned by Sidney Gilbert from which he administered temporal affairs in the Church*

# "Stand Fast in the Office Whereunto I Have Appointed You"

Section 54

## Historical Background

The Saints in New York had been commanded to gather to Ohio (see D&C 37:3; 38:32). The Lord commanded those Saints already living in Ohio to prepare for the influx of newcomers by giving of their lands to those immigrating, or, if they did not have lands to give, to help them buy available land. In good faith the Colesville Branch arrived in Thompson, Ohio, and settled on lands offered to them by other members of the Church. Shortly thereafter the offer was withdrawn, and the Saints from Colesville were forced to seek other places to live.

Newel Knight was appointed by the Colesville Branch to ask Joseph Smith to inquire of the Lord concerning the course of action they should now pursue. B. H. Roberts recorded the following about these events: "It is difficult to determine with exactness in what the transgressions of the Saints at Thompson consisted; but it is evident that selfishness and rebellion were at the bottom of their trouble, and that Leman Copley and Ezra Thayre were immediately concerned in it. The Saints comprising the Colesville branch, when they arrived at the gathering place, in Ohio, were advised to remain together and were settled at Thompson, a place in the vicinity of Kirtland. . . . It is evident that some of the brethren already living at Thompson, had agreed to enter into the law of consecration and stewardship with the Saints from Colesville; and that afterwards they broke this covenant. Among these were Leman Copley and Ezra Thayre. 'A man by the name of Copley,' says Newel Knight in his journal, 'had a considerable tract of land there [in Thompson] which he offered to let the Saints occupy. Consequently a contract was agreed upon, and we commenced work in good faith. But in a short time Copley broke the engagement, and I went to Kirtland to see Brother Joseph,' etc. (*Scraps of Biography,* in which is published Newel Knight's journal, ch. vi.) Of this matter, John Whitmer, then the Church Historian, writes: 'At this time [the early part of June] the Church at Thompson, Ohio, was involved in difficulty because of the rebellion of Leman Copley, who would not do as he had previously agreed, which thing confused the whole Church, and finally the Lord spake through Joseph the Prophet, saying:' He then quotes the revelation to Newel Knight. . . . —(John Whitmer's *History of the Church,* chap. viii.)" (In *History of the Church,* 1:180n.)

# Notes and Commentary

### D&C 54:2. What Was the Office to Which Newel Knight Was Appointed?

Newel Knight had been appointed to lead the Colesville Saints according to the instructions given in Doctrine and Covenants 38:34-36.

### D&C 54:3. How Might One Escape His Enemies, No Matter Who They Are?

The Colesville Branch was warned of enemies from whom they were to escape. Although their enemies were not specifically identified, the method of escape was clearly defined. The Prophet Joseph

*An old building on the Copley farm in Thompson, Ohio, where the Colesville Saints temporarily settled*

Smith taught that salvation was victory over enemies: "Salvation is nothing more nor less than to triumph over all our enemies and put them under our feet. And when we have power to put all enemies under our feet in this world, and a knowledge to triumph over all evil spirits in the world to come, then we are saved, as in the case of Jesus, who was to reign until He had put all enemies under His feet, and the last enemy was death." (*Teachings,* p. 297.)

On another occasion the Prophet said: "Salvation is for a man to be saved from all his enemies; for until a man can triumph over death, he is not saved. A knowledge of the priesthood alone will do this." (*Teachings,* p. 305.)

### D&C 54:4. What Covenants Were Broken?

It is apparent that Leman Copley and Ezra Thayre had agreed to provide land for the Colesville Branch and then had gone back on their word.

### D&C 54:7-9. "Take Your Journey" and "Seek Ye a Living Like unto Men"

After their failure to obtain land in Kirtland, the Colesville Saints were directed to leave Ohio and go to Missouri; but since they would arrive in Missouri before the Lord's commandments concerning the law of consecration would be fully implemented, the Lord told them how to act until they could be properly included in the united order.

# W. W. Phelps Is Called and Chosen

Section 55

## Historical Background

William Wines Phelps was born at Hanover, Morris County, New Jersey, on 17 February 1792. He worked as editor of a newspaper called the *Western Courier* and later established anti-Masonic papers known as the *Lake Light* and the *Ontario Phoenix,* both in New York. He was nominated by his friends to run for the office of lieutenant governor of New York, and although he did not receive the nomination, he did gain much valuable experience.

On 26 March 1830 W. W. Phelps read an announcement that the Book of Mormon was about to come off the press. He later met Parley P. Pratt, who sold him a copy. After he read the Book of Mormon, he went to Kirtland, Ohio, where he met Joseph Smith. When Phelps inquired what the Lord desired of him, he was directed to be baptized and take his family to Missouri (see D&C 55, which was received shortly after W. W. Phelps and his family arrived in Kirtland in June 1831).

W. W. Phelps contributed great talent to the Church. He set up the first printing press for the Church in Missouri; he published the first Church newspaper, the *Evening and Morning Star;* he helped select, prepare, and publish the revelations in the Book of Commandments; and he wrote many hymns, including "The Spirit of God" and "Gently Raise the Sacred Strain."

*William W. Phelps, an early Church newspaper editor*

## Notes and Commentary

**D&C 55:1. What Does Having An Eye Single to the Glory of God Mean?**

"Through the natural eyes men see the light which guides them in their physical existence, through their spiritual eyes, the spiritual light which leads to eternal life. As long as the natural eyes are unimpaired, men can see and be guided by the light of day; and as long as the spiritual eyes are single to the glory of God—that is, as long as they are undimmed by sin and are focused solely on righteousness—men can view and understand the things of the Spirit. But if apostasy enters and the spiritual light turns to darkness, 'how great is that darkness!' " (McConkie, *Doctrinal New Testament Commentary,* 1:240.)

**D&C 55:4. "That Little Children Also May Receive Instruction"**

W. W. Phelps commented on the assignment he received from the Lord: "As a people we are fast approaching a desired end, which may literally be called a beginning. Thus far, we cannot be reproached with being backward in instruction. By revelation, in 1831, I was appointed to 'do the work of printing, and of selecting and writing books for schools in this church, that little children might receive instruction;' and since then I have received a further sanction. We are preparing to go out from among the people, where we can serve God in righteousness; and the first thing is, to teach our children; for they are as the Israel of old. It is our children who will take the kingdom and bear it off to all the world. The first commandment with promise to Israel was, 'Honor thy father and thy mother, that thy days may be long in the land, which the Lord thy God giveth thee.' We will instruct our children in the paths of righteousness; and we want that instruction compiled in a book." (*Times and Seasons,* 1 Nov. 1845, p. 1015.)

# The Lord Commands and the Lord Revokes

Section 56

## Historical Background

After the conference of 3 June 1831, the Lord gave a revelation to the Church (D&C 52) in which a number of brethren were called in pairs to go to Missouri, preaching the gospel as they traveled, and to hold another conference in that land. But when Ezra Thayre lost the spirit of his assignment because of problems at Thompson, Ohio, and was slow in making preparations to go on his mission, Thomas B. Marsh, his assigned companion, went to Joseph Smith seeking an answer to the dilemma. The Prophet inquired of the Lord and received what is now known as section 56 (see *History of the Church,* 1:186).

## Notes and Commentary

**D&C 56:2. "Take Up His Cross and Follow Me"**

See Notes and Commentary on Doctrine and Covenants 23:6.

**D&C 56:3-4. Under What Circumstances Does the Lord Revoke That Which He Has Commanded?**

Elder James E. Talmage noted that "only the rebellious, those who will not obey the commandments of God are to be thus dealt with, are to have their blessings revoked; only these will forfeit the blessings to which they were entitled. In another revelation given shortly after that, Section 58, the Lord takes people to task because they were in the habit of saying—and he might well take some of us to task, for we still say it—that the Lord doesn't keep his word, that he makes promises and fails to fulfil them." (In Conference Report, Apr. 1921, p. 113.)

The Lord further stated that those who are not in the Church, who hinder the Lord's work, will bear that condemnation (see D&C 124:49-50).

**D&C 56:6-8. A Change of Assignments**

In these verses the Lord changed the assignments given in Doctrine and Covenants, section 52, verses 22 and 32. Selah J. Griffin, formerly assigned to Newel Knight, was assigned to Thomas B. Marsh. Newel Knight was called to go with the Colesville Saints to Missouri, and Ezra Thayre was released from his missionary calling.

**D&C 56:8-9. How Does One Overcome Selfishness?**

"*Selfishness* consists in caring unduly or supremely for oneself; it is one of the lusts of the flesh which must be overcome by those who gain salvation. A selfish person clings to his own comfort, advantage, or position at the expense of others. Men are commanded to repent of their pride and selfishness. (D. & C. 56:8.) In practice the way to do this is to serve in the Church and make generous financial contributions to sustain its programs." (McConkie, *Mormon Doctrine,* p. 701.)

*Unselfish contributions sustain the temporal kingdom of God*

**D&C 56:16. A Proper Attitude toward the Temporal Blessings of Life**

The remainder of this revelation was directed to Ezra Thayre. Because of his selfishness, which was a direct cause of the Colesville Saints' having to leave Thompson, Ohio, the Lord gave him, and all Saints as well, counsel on the proper use of temporal things. Doctrine and Covenants 56:16 delineates the responsibility of the rich. The Lord has instructed his prophets about how the poor are to be taken care of: such principles as tithing and fast offerings assist Latter-day Saints to take care of their responsibility to the poor. (See 1 Timothy 6:9-10, 17-19; Jacob 2:17-19; Mosiah 4:26-27.)

**D&C 56:17-18. What Should Be the Attitude of the Poor?**

President George Albert Smith warned against taking what belongs to others. After quoting Doctrine and Covenants 56:17 he said:

"That is the situation of many of our own brothers and sisters in America with all the blessings that we enjoy—better wages, better homes, better opportunities for education than have ever been known before. Yet we have today men who not only will not work themselves, but they also will not permit somebody else to be employed. They are not willing to earn their living by work, but they propose to take it from the rich man. . . .

"We must not fall into the bad habits of other people. We must not get into the frame of mind that we will take what the other man has. Refer back to the ten commandments, and you will find one short paragraph, 'Thou shalt not covet.' That is what is the matter with a good many people today. They are coveting what somebody else has, when as a matter of fact, many of them have been cared for and provided with means to live by those very ones from whom they would take away property." (In Conference Report, Oct. 1949, pp. 170, 172.)

# Independence: Center Place of Zion

Section 57

## Historical Background

After the close of the June 1831 conference, a revelation was given in which several missionaries were called to go to the land of Missouri, where the Lord would reveal the center place of Zion (see D&C 52).

Joseph Smith, who was called by revelation to travel with Sidney Rigdon, recorded the following after arriving in the land of Missouri: "The meeting of our brethren [Oliver Cowdery, Peter Whitmer, Jr., Ziba Peterson, and Frederick G. Williams, all of whom had gone to Missouri as missionaries], who had long awaited our arrival, was a glorious one, and moistened with many tears. It seemed good and pleasant for brethren to meet together in unity. But our reflections were many, coming as we had from a highly cultivated state of society in the east, and standing now upon the confines or western limits of the United States, and looking into the vast wilderness of those that sat in darkness; how natural it was to observe the degradation, leanness of intellect, ferocity, and jealousy of a people that were nearly a century behind the times, and to feel for those who roamed about without the benefit of civilization, refinement, or religion; yea, and exclaim in the language of the Prophets: 'When will the wilderness blossom as the rose? When will Zion be built up in her glory, and where will Thy temple stand, unto which all nations shall come in the last days?' Our anxiety was soon relieved by receiving the following: [D&C 57]." (*History of the Church,* 1:189.)

Before this revelation was given, the members of the Church had read in the Book of Mormon about a New Jerusalem that would be located in America (see 3 Nephi 20:22; 21:23-24; Ether 13:1-12). Also, in September 1830 the Lord had explained that the holy city would be erected "on the borders by the Lamanites" (D&C 28:9). And finally, the Lord had promised he would reveal the exact location of the New Jerusalem (see D&C 42:62). It was therefore with great joy that Doctrine and Covenants 57 was received by the members of the Church.

## Notes and Commentary

**D&C 57:1-3. Independence Is the "Center Place" of Zion**

"The city of Independence is situated in one of the most attractive and healthful parts of Missouri. . . . It is an old town. It was laid out in 1827, but in 1831 it was only a village. It is now a suburb of Kansas City." (Smith and Sjodahl, Commentary, p. 331.)

In the early days of the Church, Jackson County was often referred to as the "center stake" of Zion, but this expression is not technically correct. As Smith and Sjodahl pointed out, "it might, therefore, be well to remember that no Stake was ever organized in Jackson County. Following the figure given by Isaiah Ch. 33:20 and 54:2 we cannot speak of a 'center stake of Zion.' The term 'Stake of Zion' was first used in a revelation given in November, 1831. (Sec. 68.) It is a comparison to the stakes which bind a tent. . . . Zion is the tent, and how can the tent be a stake?" (Commentary, p. 189n.) In other words, since the tent symbolizes Zion itself, and the stakes the individual units that strengthen Zion, it is more correct to speak of Zion as the "center place" rather than as the "center stake."

The accompanying map shows the original temple site in Independence (shaded area) and the present ownership of significant sites within the original parcel of more than sixty-three acres and in adjoining areas (see Cowan, *Doctrine and Covenants,* p. 93, and warranty deeds, Real Estate Department, Central File 510-8578, The Church of Jesus Christ of Latter-day Saints, Salt Lake City, Utah).

**D&C 57:4. What Is Meant by the Phrase, "the Line Running Directly between Jew and Gentile"?**

President Joseph Fielding Smith explained that this expression "has reference to the line separating the Lamanites from the settlers in Jackson County. At this time the United States Government had given to the Indians the lands west of the Missouri, only later to take them away again. The Lamanites, who

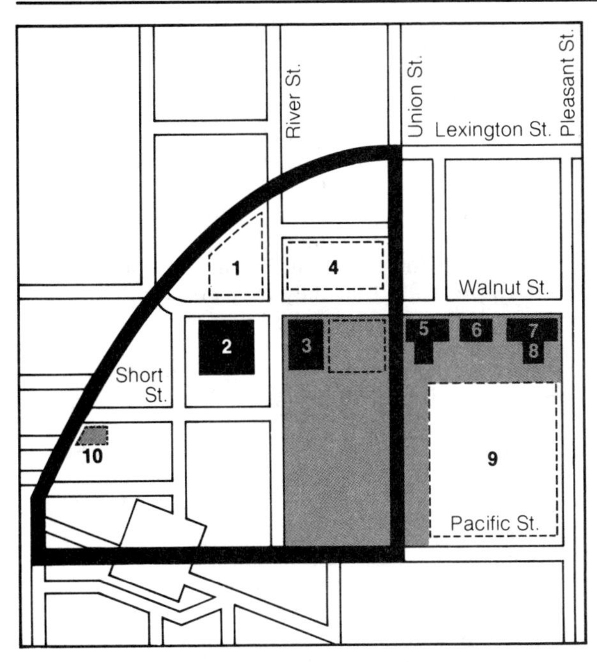


**Independence Temple Area**

**1** Church of Christ (Temple Lot)
**2** Reorganized LDS Auditorium
**3** LDS Visitors' Center
**4** Proposed RLDS temple site
**5** New Independence, Mo., Stake Center
**6** Mission Home Residence
**7** LDS Chapel (Dedicated 1914)
**8** Mission Office
**9** RLDS "The Campus" Property
**10** LDS-owned lot

 LDS Church ownership

are Israelites, were referred to as Jews, and the Gentiles were the people, many of whom were of the lawless element, living east of the river." (*Church History and Modern Revelation,* 1:206; see also the map in Notes and Commentary on D&C 28:9.)

The following references show that the Lamanites have Jewish ancestry: Omni 1:12-17; Mosiah 25:1-2; Helaman 8:21; 3 Nephi 2:15; 4 Nephi 1:17.

**D&C 57:5. Everlasting Inheritance**

See Doctrine and Covenants 38:17-20; 101:17-18.

**D&C 57:9. Obtain a License**

"Brother Gilbert is also instructed to obtain a license. This license was probably needed because of the laws of the time, in order that he might transport goods to the people by clerks or others employed in his service." (Sperry, *Compendium,* p. 234.)

**D&C 57:13. Why Was Oliver Cowdery Instructed to Assist William W. Phelps?**

"In Sec. 55:4, Phelps is appointed to assist Cowdery; here Cowdery is mentioned as the assistant. There is no discrepancy in this. It only shows that God intended them to assist each other as fellow-laborers in the same service." (Smith and Sjodahl, Commentary, p. 330.)

**D&C 57:14-15. Who Are the Families Who Are to Gather to Zion?**

"The Bishop and the agent are here instructed to make preparations for the reception of the Colesville Saints who, in obedience to the divine command (Sec. 54:7, 8), were on the road to Zion" (Smith and Sjodahl, Commentary, p. 330).

The concept of establishing Zion is discussed in Enrichment B, in the Appendix.

# The Land of Zion

Section 58

## Historical Background

The Prophet Joseph Smith gave the following explanation of the coming forth of this section:

"The first Sabbath after our arrival in Jackson county, Brother W. W. Phelps preached to a western audience over the boundary of the United States, wherein were present specimens of all the families of the earth; Shem, Ham and Japheth; several of the Lamanites or Indians—representative of Shem; quite a respectable number of negroes—descendants of Ham; and the balance was made up of citizens of the surrounding country, and fully represented themselves as pioneers of the West. At this meeting two were baptized, who had previously believed in the fulness of the Gospel.

"During this week the Colesville branch, referred to in the latter part of the last revelation [D&C 57:15], and Sidney Rigdon, Sidney Gilbert and wife and Elders Morley and Booth, arrived. I received the following: [D&C 58]." (*History of the Church,* 1:190-91).

## Notes and Commentary

**D&C 58:2-4. Why Does the Lord Allow Tribulations to Come upon His People?**

Elder George Q. Cannon suggested that "the Saints should always remember that God sees not as man sees; that he does not willingly afflict his children, and that if he requires them to endure present privation and trial, it is that they may escape greater tribulations which would otherwise inevitably overtake them. If He deprives them of any present blessing, it is that he may bestow upon them greater and more glorious ones by and by." (*Millennial Star,* 3 Oct. 1863, p. 634.)

The trials of the Saints sometimes come as a chastisement when they disregard the Lord's counsel (see D&C 101:1-8). But the Lord desires that tribulation will bring humility and repentance, and even though the Saints may be living righteously, trials also come upon them because of the unrighteousness of others. Tribulation provides the Saints with opportunities for spiritual growth and character development. Such needed attributes as humility, faith, empathy, patience, courage, and gratitude come to individuals in the refiner's fire of tribulation and persecution.

Trials give Saints the opportunity to prove themselves worthy of eternal blessings by showing their commitment to God and his kingdom, their willingness to endure privation, and their willingness to forsake the things of the world. The commitment that enables them to prove themselves worthy develops the faith necessary to obtain eternal life. The Prophet Joseph Smith taught that "a religion that does not require the sacrifice of all things never has power sufficient to produce the faith necessary unto life and salvation; for, from the first existence of man, the faith necessary unto the enjoyment of life and salvation never could be obtained without the sacrifice of all earthly things. It was through this sacrifice, and this only, that God has ordained that men should enjoy eternal life; and it is through the medium of the sacrifice of all earthly things that men do actually know that they are doing the things that are well pleasing in the sight of God. When a man has offered in sacrifice all that he has for the truth's sake, not even withholding his life, and believing before God that he has been called to make this sacrifice because he seeks to do his will, he does know, most assuredly, that God does and will accept his sacrifice and offering, and that he has not, nor will not seek his face in vain. Under these circumstances, then, he can obtain the faith necessary for him to lay hold on eternal life." (*Lectures on Faith* 6:7.)

In a general conference of the Church, Elder Bruce R. McConkie explained the testing of the Saints in mortality:

"The testing processes of mortality are for all men, saints and sinners alike. Sometimes the tests and trials of those who have received the gospel far exceed any imposed upon worldly people. Abraham was called upon to sacrifice his only son. Lehi and his family left their lands and wealth to live in a wilderness. Saints in all ages have been commanded to lay all that they have upon the altar, sometimes even their very lives.

"As to the individual trials and problems that befall any of us, all we need say is that in the wisdom of Him who knows all things, and who does all things well, all of us are given the particular and specific tests that we need in our personal situations. It is to us, His saints, that the Lord speaks when He says: 'I will prove you in all things, whether you will abide in my covenant, even unto death, that you may be found worthy.

" 'For if ye will not abide in my covenant ye are not worthy of me.' (D&C 98:14-15.) . . .

"But sometimes the Lord's people are hounded and persecuted. Sometimes He deliberately lets His faithful saints linger and suffer, in both body and spirit, to prove . . . that they may be found worthy of eternal life. If such be the lot of any of us, so be it.

"But come what may, anything that befalls us here in mortality is but for a small moment, and if we are true and faithful God will eventually exalt us on high. All our losses and sufferings will be made up to us in the resurrection." (In Conference Report, Oct. 1976, pp. 158-60; or *Ensign,* Nov. 1976, pp. 106, 108.)

President Brigham Young had a clear understanding of the necessity of trials to progression. He taught: "If the Saints could realize things as they are when they are called to pass through trials, and to suffer what they call sacrifices, they would acknowledge them to be the greatest blessings that could be bestowed upon them" (*Discourses of Brigham Young,* p. 345).

### D&C 58:3-7, 44. Were These Verses a Foreshadowing That the New Jerusalem Would Not Be Built in 1831?

Concerning God's foreknowledge in this instance, Elder Orson F. Whitney wrote:

"At all events, what occurred must have been foreseen. Divine prescience [foreknowledge] extends to all things connected with the Lord's work. When He commanded his people to build the New Jerusalem, he knew how much, or how little, they were capable of accomplishing in that direction—knew it just as well before as he did after. Such a thing as surprise or disappointment on his part is inconceivable. An all-wise, all-powerful Being who has created, peopled, redeemed and glorified 'millions of earths like this,' is not one to be astounded by anything that happens on our little planet.

"The All-knowing One knew in advance what those Zion-builders would do, or leave undone, and he shaped his plans accordingly. Evidently the time was not ripe for Zion's redemption. The Saints were not ready to build the New Jerusalem. The proof is in the trespasses committed by them against the divine laws ordained for their government." (*Saturday Night Thoughts,* p. 187.)

### D&C 58:8-11. The Supper of the Lord

Two feast symbols from ancient days apply to the Supper of the Lord: the "feast of fat things," and the "wine on the lees well refined." Both are unmistakable signs of richness, indicating that the feast mentioned here is of great importance (see also D&C 57:5-14; 65:3; Matthew 22:1-14; Revelation 19:7-9).

The "feast of fat things" refers to serving fat, full-flavored meat, available only to royalty and to the wealthy and made even richer by the addition of bone marrow (see Keil and Delitzsch, *Commentary*, bk. 7: Isaiah, "Prophecies of Isaiah," p. 439).

"Wine on the lees" is a substance described by the Hebrew word *Shmareem*, which signifies the jellies or preserves that were highly esteemed in the royal feasts of Eastern countries. These wines were prepared from lees (dregs) after the fermentation process was complete, and of grape skins, which preserved the wine and maintained remarkable color and flavor—truly a prized addition to the feast. Sometimes the rich juices of the lees were strained and served to accompany a feast; but strained or not, the preservative quality of the lees kept the juices from turning to a strong vinegar. (See Fallows, *Bible Encyclopedia*, s.v. "wine," p. 1724; Gesenius, *Hebrew and English Lexicon of the Old Testament*, pp. 1036-37; Keil and Delitzsch, *Commentary*, bk. 7: Isaiah, "Prophecies of Isaiah," p. 439; *Encyclopedia Judaica*, 6:1418.)

### D&C 58:14-16. Of What Sins Had Edward Partridge Been Guilty As the First Bishop of the Church?

During the administration of Joseph F. Smith, the First Presidency of the Church issued a statement to clarify the role played by Edward Partridge. The following is an excerpt from that statement: "On occasion of the Prophet's first visit to Independence, Missouri—Edward Partridge accompanied him—in the meetings and conferences held upon the land of Zion, Bishop Partridge several times strenuously opposed the measures of the Prophet, and was sharply reproved by the latter for his unbelief and hardness of heart. Indeed, the apostate, Ezra Booth, who was present, made the scene between the bishop and the Prophet one of the items that justified to him his apostasy. He refers to the circumstance in a letter, addressed to Bishop Partridge, which has been several times published in anti-'Mormon' literature. The Bishop, moreover, was reproved for his 'blindness of heart and unbelief,' and warned of the danger of falling from his high station, in a revelation given in August, 1831, while both he and the Prophet were still in Missouri: [D&C 58:14-15]." (In Clark, *Messages of the First Presidency*, 4:113.)

### D&C 58:16-18. What Was the Mission Appointed to Edward Partridge?

Edward Partridge was not a ward bishop, as are bishops today, for there were none in the Church at that time. He was at first the bishop of the whole Church (see D&C 41:9), which was then quite small. A short time later Newel K. Whitney was called as bishop in Kirtland, and Edward Partridge remained as bishop in Missouri (see D&C 72).

The chief responsibility of Bishop Partridge was to administer the law of consecration: he received the consecrations of the Saints and gave them their stewardships (see D&C 41:9-11; 42:30-35, 71-73; 51; 57:7, 15). He was also responsible to judge the people according to the Lord's law.

### D&C 58:19-23. What Law Were the Saints to Keep in the Land of Zion?

The Saints had entered into a covenant to keep the laws of God, which included the gospel and the law of consecration (see D&C 42:30-42, 53-55; 59:1-24). They were also expected to "be subject to the powers that be" (D&C 58:22) and live according to the laws of the land. President Joseph Fielding Smith said:

"Very strict was the command to the Saints that the law of God should be kept on the land of Zion. 'Let no man think he is ruler; but let God rule him that judgeth, according to the counsel of his own will, or, in other words, him that counseleth or sitteth upon the judgment seat.' We, today, do not realize the rigidity of this command. The Saints were to assemble in the land which had been appointed from the beginning as the site of the holy city, New Jerusalem. This land and this site were dedicated. Those who assembled there were placed under covenant that they would keep the law of God, which commandment had been repeated to them many times. Sidney Rigdon, according to appointment, stood up and asked the assembly:

" 'Do you receive this land for the land of your inheritance, with thankful hearts, from the Lord?'

" 'Do you pledge yourselves to keep the law of God on this land, which you never have kept in your own lands?'

" 'Do you pledge yourselves to see that others of your brethren who shall come hither do keep the laws of God?'

"To these questions, they each answered, 'We do,' and then the land was dedicated for their gathering and inheritance. The Lord was very jealous of these commandments. This was not to be an empty pledge. Failure to observe the covenant was to bring tribulation. . . .

"Many of the members of the Church forgot the covenant they had made to 'keep the law of God' upon the land, which was mandatory, and this brought them into trouble. Persecutions came and eventually they were driven from their inheritances. The tribulation in part, but not all, which the Lord had promised they should suffer, came upon them because of their disobedience." (*Church History and Modern Revelation*, 1:212-13.)

### D&C 58:26-29. The Lord Should Not Have to Command His People in All Things

Elder Ezra Taft Benson explained that "usually the Lord gives us the overall objectives to be accomplished and some guidelines to follow, but he expects us to work out most of the details and methods. The methods and procedures are usually developed through study and prayer and by living so that we can obtain and follow the promptings of the Spirit. Less spiritually advanced people, such as those in the days of Moses, had to be commanded in many things. Today those spiritually alert look at the objectives, check the guidelines laid down by the Lord and his prophets, and then prayerfully act—without having to be commanded 'in all things.' This attitude prepares men for godhood. . . .

"Sometimes the Lord hopefully waits on his children to act on their own, and when they do not, they lose the greater prize, and the Lord will either drop the entire matter and let them suffer the consequences or else he will have to spell it out in greater detail. Usually, I fear, the more he has to spell it out, the smaller is our reward." (In Conference Report, Apr. 1965, pp. 121-22.)

**D&C 58:30-33. To Receive the Lord's Blessings, People Must Obey His Commandments**

"The Saints sometimes fail to do their duty and to keep the commandments of God. But they expect Him to make good to them the promises He has given to the faithful. If He does not, they complain. They neglect their prayers; they absent themselves from their meetings; they break the Word of Wisdom; they withhold their tithing; but when sickness comes and falls like a dark, terrifying shadow across their path, they expect immediate Divine interference in their behalf, through the administration of the Elders. If their expectations are not realized, they say, in a rebellious spirit, 'His promises are not fulfilled.' The reply of the Lord to that is, 'Their reward lurketh beneath.' They must look 'beneath' for their reward; they have no claim on heaven." (Smith and Sjodahl, Commentary, p. 340.)

**D&C 58:42-43. The Lord Promises Complete Forgiveness to Those Who Truly Repent**

The Lord gives his word that those who truly repent of their sins are forgiven by him. This great blessing comes through the atonement of Christ who "suffered . . . for all, that they might not suffer if they would repent" (D&C 19:16). The Lord promises that he will no more remember the sins of those who repent (see Ezekiel 18:21-22).

Repentance, however, requires that a person forsake and turn completely from his sins and confess them. Elder Spencer W. Kimball taught: "No one can ever be forgiven of any transgression until there is repentance, and one has not repented until he has bared his soul and admitted his intentions and weaknesses without excuses or rationalizations. He must admit to himself that he has grievously sinned. When he has confessed to himself without the slightest minimizing of the offense, or rationalizing its seriousness, or soft-pedaling its gravity, and admits it is as big as it really is, then he is ready to begin his repentance; and any other elements of repentance are of reduced value, until the conviction is established totally, and then repentance may mature and forgiveness may eventually come." (*Love Versus Lust,* Brigham Young University Speeches of the Year [Provo, 5 Jan. 1965], p. 10.)

The Lord's forgiveness will surely come to those who truly repent. Elder Kimball also said that "those who heed the call, whether members or nonmembers of the Church, can be partakers of the miracle of forgiveness. God will wipe away from their eyes the tears of anguish, and remorse, and consternation, and fear, and guilt. Dry eyes will replace the wet ones, and smiles of satisfaction will replace the worried, anxious look.

"What relief! What comfort! What joy! Those laden with transgressions and sorrows and sin may be forgiven and cleansed and purified if they will return to their Lord, learn of him, and keep his commandments. And all of us needing to repent of day-to-day follies and weaknesses can likewise share in this miracle." (*Miracle of Forgiveness,* pp. 367-68.)

Enrichment E, in the Appendix, contains a further discussion of the laws governing forgiveness.

**D&C 58:44-48, 56. Why Were the Saints Commanded Not to All Gather Immediately to the Land of Zion?**

The time had not yet come, and would not for "many years" (D&C 58:44), for all the Saints to receive their inheritances in Zion. A great deal of work, preparation, and patience is required before Zion can be fully established. The Church had neither the strength nor the means to purchase lands sufficient for all the Saints in Zion. So, before Zion could be established, a great deal of missionary work needed to be done to strengthen the Church. The Saints were told to "push the people together from the ends of the earth" (vs. 45), that is, through missionary work they must gather together the dispersed members of the house of Israel preparatory to the establishment of Zion. The Church is still in that process.

Prophecies concerning this work are recorded in 1 Nephi 22:3-12 and 3 Nephi 21. Enrichment B contains a thorough exposition of the establishment of Zion.

**D&C 58:50-51. A Commandment to Write a Description of Zion**

The Lord commanded Sidney Rigdon to write a description of the land in Missouri and to listen to the Spirit in order to write the will of the Lord concerning the land; then he was to write a letter to the Saints in general and include a subscription to raise money for the purchase of the land. Since photographs were unobtainable, Sidney Rigdon's description could encourage the Saints in sending contributions for the purchase. Later the Lord indicated that what Sidney Rigdon had written was unacceptable (see D&C 63:55-56, a probable reference to this assignment).

The following description of Zion was included in the *History of the Church,* although whether it is a revision of Sidney Rigdon's description so that it was acceptable to the Lord or whether it was written by someone else is not clear: "The country is unlike the timbered states of the East. As far as the eye can reach the beautiful rolling prairies lie spread out like a sea of meadows; and are decorated with a growth of flowers so gorgeous and grand as to exceed description; and nothing is more fruitful, or a richer stockholder in the blooming prairie than the honey bee. Only on the water courses is timber to be found. There in strips from one to three miles in width, and following faithfully the meanderings of the streams, it grows in luxuriant forests. The forests are a mixture of oak, hickory, black walnut, elm, ash, cherry, honey locust, mulberry, coffee bean, hackberry, boxelder, and bass wood; with the addition of cottonwood, butterwood, pecan, and soft and hard maple upon the bottoms. The shrubbery is beautiful, and consists in part of plums, grapes, crab apple, and persimmons.

"The soil is rich and fertile; from three to ten feet deep, and generally composed of a rich black mould, intermingled with clay and sand. It yields in abundance, wheat, corn, sweet potatoes, cotton and many other common agricultural products. Horses, cattle and hogs, though of an inferior breed, are tolerably plentiful and seem nearly to raise themselves by grazing in the vast prairie range in summer, and feeding upon the bottoms in winter. The wild game is less plentiful of course where man has commenced the cultivation of the soil, than in the wild prairies. Buffalo, elk, deer, bear, wolves, beaver and many smaller animals here roam at pleasure. Turkeys, geese, swans, ducks, yea a variety of the feathered tribe, are among the rich abundance that grace the delightful regions of this goodly land—the heritage of the children of God.

"The season is mild and delightful nearly three quarters of the year, and as the land of Zion, situated at about equal distances from the Atlantic and Pacific oceans, as well as from the Alleghany and Rocky mountains, in the thirty-ninth degree of north latitude, and between the sixteenth and seventeenth degrees of west longitude, it bids fair—when the curse is taken from the land—to become one of the most blessed places on the globe. The winters are milder than the Atlantic states of the same parallel of latitude, and the weather is more agreeable; so that were the virtues of the inhabitants only equal to the blessings of the Lord which He permits to crown the industry of those inhabitants, there would be a measure of the good things of life for the benefit of the Saints, full, pressed down, and running over, even an hundred-fold." (*History of the Church,* 1:197-98.)

### D&C 58:52-53. Zion to Be Obtained by Purchase

The Lord commanded the Saints to purchase the area of land around Independence, Missouri, as the center place for Zion and to have clear and legal title to it. In this way any disputes over ownership could be settled by law, and violence could be avoided. Smith and Sjodahl pointed out why this commandment was given: "The Latter-day Saints are forbidden to make war in order to secure a gathering-place, and especially such a sacred place as that in which the greatest of all God's temples is to be located. They are not forbidden to defend their lives, their homes, their loved ones, their liberty and country, against murderers and thieves, but they are forbidden to be the aggressors." (Commentary, p. 379.)

Today the Church is still under the same responsibility to secure, by purchase, the land that will be the center place of Zion.

### D&C 58:57. Dedication of the Land of Zion and the Temple Lot

Sidney Rigdon was commissioned by the Lord to dedicate the land of Zion, which included the temple lot, but Joseph Smith dedicated the actual spot for the temple. Joseph recorded the following about these events:

"On the second day of August, I assisted the Colesville branch of the Church to lay the first log, for a house, as a foundation of Zion in Kaw township, twelve miles west of Independence. The log was carried and placed by twelve men, in honor of the twelve tribes of Israel. At the same time, through prayer, the land of Zion was consecrated and dedicated by Elder Sidney Rigdon for the gathering of the Saints. It was a season of joy to those present, and afforded a glimpse of the future, which time will yet unfold to the satisfaction of the faithful." (*History of the Church,* 1:196.)

"On the third day of August, I proceeded to dedicate the spot for the Temple, a little west of Independence, and there were also present Sidney Edward Partridge, W. W. Phelps, Oliver Cowdery, Martin Harris and Joseph Coe" (*History of the Church,* 1:199).

### D&C 58:64. Does the Lord Really Expect the Saints to Take the Gospel to All the World—to Every Creature?

Read Matthew 28:18-20; Mark 16:15; Luke 24:47; Acts 1:8; Revelation 14:6-7; D&C 1:2, 4; 112:1, 4, 16-17. President Spencer W. Kimball, referring to these scriptures, said:

"It seems to me that the Lord chose his words when he said 'every nation,' 'every land,' 'uttermost bounds of the earth,' 'every tongue,' 'every people,' 'every soul,' 'all the world,' 'many lands.'

"Surely there is significance in these words!

"Certainly his sheep were not limited to the thousands about him and with whom he rubbed shoulders each day. A universal family! A universal command! . . .

" . . . I feel that when we have done all in our power that the Lord will find a way to open doors. That is my faith. . . .

"With the Lord providing these miracles of communication [radio, television, cassette tape

*The Missionary Training Center: "The sound must go forth . . . into all the world" (D&C 58:64)*

players, satellites and receiving stations, and so on], and with the increased efforts and devotion of our missionaries and all of us, and all others who are 'sent,' surely the divine injunction will come to pass: [D&C 58:64]. And we must find a way. . . .

"Using all the latest inventions and equipment and paraphernalia already developed and that which will follow, can you see that perhaps the day may come when the world will be converted and covered?

"If we do all we can . . . I am sure the Lord will bring more discoveries to our use. He will bring a change of heart into kings and magistrates and emperors, or he will divert rivers or open seas or find ways to touch hearts. He will open the gates and make possible the proselyting." ("When the World Will Be Converted," *Ensign*, Oct. 1974, pp. 5, 10-11, 13.)

President Brigham Young had similar faith. He made the following statement concerning the spread of the gospel: "The kingdom will continue to increase, to grow, to spread and prosper more and more. Every time its enemies undertake to overthrow it, it will become more extensive and powerful; instead of decreasing, it will continue to increase, it will spread the more, become more wonderful and conspicuous to the nations, until it fills the whole earth." (In *Journal of Discourses*, 1:203.)

Truly the words of the Prophet Joseph Smith will be fulfilled: "No unhallowed hand can stop the work from progressing; persecutions may rage, mobs may combine, armies may assemble, calumny may defame, but the truth of God will go forth boldly, nobly, and independent, till it has penetrated every continent, visited every clime, swept every country, and sounded in every ear, till the purposes of God shall be accomplished, and the Great Jehovah shall say the work is done" (*History of the Church*, 4:540).

# "That Thou Mayest More Fully Keep Thyself Unspotted from the World"

Section 59

## Historical Background

The story of Polly Knight, mother of Newel Knight, is one of the great stories of faith in this dispensation. She was in the Colesville Branch, and although very weak because of illness, she was determined to go to the land of Zion with other members of the branch.

"Polly Knight's health had been failing for some time, according to a statement made by her son, Newel. She was very ill during her journey from Kirtland to Missouri. 'Yet,' says her son, 'she would not consent to stop traveling; her only, or her greatest desire was to set her feet upon the land of Zion, and to have her body interred in that land. I went on shore and bought lumber to make a coffin in case she should die before we arrived at our place of destination—so fast did she fail. But the Lord gave her the desire of her heart, and she lived to stand upon that land.' (*Scraps of Biography*, p. 70.)" (In *History of the Church*, 1:199n.)

Polly Knight's funeral was held on Sunday, 7 August 1831. Joseph Smith recorded: "On the 7th, I attended the funeral of Sister Polly Knight, the wife of Joseph Knight, Sen. This was the first death in the Church in this land, and I can say, a worthy member sleeps in Jesus till the resurrection.

"I also received the following: [D&C 59]." (*History of the Church*, 1:199.)

## Notes and Commentary

**D&C 59:1-4. If Righteous, Those Who Live and Those Who Die Shall Both Inherit the Earth**

Verses 1 and 2 seem to be a reference to Polly Knight, who had come up to the land with an eye single to God, although, of course, the blessings apply to all who come in a similar fashion. Thus, the Lord in these verses gave to all faithful Saints great promises.

President Joseph Fielding Smith explained how even those who die in righteousness will still inherit the land: "Today, with the earth subject to Satan's rule, it is quite generally the selfish, self-centered, proud and haughty people of the earth who apparently inherit it. This is in harmony with the spirit of unrighteousness which has prevailed on the earth since the fall of man. When Christ comes to take possession of the earth and rule in his right as King of kings, he will keep his promise and the meek shall come into their own [see Matthew 5:5]. If they die, even then their inheritance shall stand, for the earth is to be the eternal abode of those who inherit the celestial kingdom. . . . This earth eventually . . . will be prepared for the righteous, or the meek, and it is their everlasting inheritance." (*Church History and Modern Revelation*, 1:215-16.)

**D&C 59:5-6. The Two Great Commandments**

President Joseph Fielding Smith noted that "so

important is this commandment that the Latter-day Saints have had their attention called to it in a number of revelations. It is plain to be seen that on these commandments hang all the law and the prophets. If a person observes these commandments as they are given in verses 5 and 6 of this section (59) he will keep the full law of God. We cannot love our Heavenly Father, and worship him in the name of his Only Begotten Son, our Redeemer, with all our 'heart, might, mind, and strength' without keeping all other commandments. It naturally follows that we will love our neighbor as ourselves and have sympathy and love for all men who are the children of God. There would be no occasion for us to be constantly reminded that we should keep the Sabbath holy, or pay our honest tithes, or keep our bodies clean by observing the Word of Wisdom, or that we should not neglect our prayers, secret and in the family circle, we would observe all of these things and all else that we are instructed to do, IF we loved the Lord our God with all our heart, might, mind, and strength. To the extent that members of the Church observe the laws of the Lord may their love for him be measured." (*Church History and Modern Revelation,* 1:216-17.)

**D&C 59:6-13. The Ten Commandments Reiterated**

The Lord in modern times has reiterated the basic laws that define man's relationship to God and to his fellowman. A comparison of verses in Doctrine and Covenants 42 and 59 with the Ten Commandments in Exodus shows how the modern revelations clarify and amplify the earlier account. As can be seen, there is not a strict parallelism between each of the three sources, but additional insights are often given in sections 42 and 59 or both.

| Exodus 20 | D&C 42 | D&C 59 |
|---|---|---|
| "Thou shalt have no other gods before me" (vs. 3). | | "Thou shalt love the Lord thy God with all thy heart, with all thy might, mind, and strength" (vs. 5).<br>"Thou shalt offer a sacrifice unto the Lord thy God in righteousness, even that of a broken heart and a contrite spirit" (vs. 8).<br>"In the name of Jesus Christ thou shalt serve him" (vs. 5). |
| "Thou shalt not make unto thee any graven image" (vs. 4). | | |
| "Thou shalt not take the name of the Lord thy God in vain" (vs. 7). | "If thou lovest me thou shalt serve me and keep all my commandments" (vs. 29).* | |
| "Remember the sabbath day, to keep it holy" (vs. 8). | | "And that thou mayest more fully keep thyself unspotted from the world, thou shalt go to the house of prayer and offer up thy sacraments upon my holy day" (vs. 9).<br>"On this the Lord's day, thou shalt offer thine oblations and thy sacraments unto the Most High, confessing thy sins unto the brethren, and before the Lord" (vs. 12).<br>"On this day, thou shalt do none other thing, only let thy food be prepared with singleness of heart" (vs. 13). |
| "Honour thy father and thy mother" (vs. 12). | | |

| | | |
|---|---|---|
| "Thou shalt not kill" (vs. 13). | "Thou shalt not kill" (vs. 18).* | "Thou shalt not . . . kill, nor do anything like unto it" (vs. 6). |
| "Thou shalt not commit adultery" (vs. 14). | "Thou shalt not commit adultery" (vs. 24).*<br>"Thou shalt love thy wife with all thy heart, and shalt cleave unto her and none else" (vs. 22).*<br>"He that looketh upon a woman to lust after her shall deny the faith, and shall not have the spirit" (vs. 23).* | "Thou shalt not . . . commit adultery, . . . nor do anything like unto it" (vs. 6). |
| "Thou shalt not steal" (vs. 15). | "Thou shalt not steal" vs. 20).*<br>"Thou shalt not take thy brother's garment; thou shalt pay for that which thou receivest of thy brother" (vs. 54). | "Thou shalt not steal, . . . nor do anything like unto it" (vs. 6). |
| "Thou shalt not bear false witness against thy neighbour" (vs. 16). | "Thou shalt not lie" (vs. 21).*<br>"Thou shalt not speak evil of thy neighbor, nor do him any harm" (vs. 27).<br>"Thou shalt live together in love" (vs. 45). | "Thou shalt love thy neighbor as thyself" (vs. 6). |
| "Thou shalt not covet" (vs. 17). | "He that looketh upon a woman to lust after her shall deny the faith and shall not have the Spirit" (vs. 23).* | |
| | "Thou shalt not be proud in thy heart" (vs. 40). | "Thou shalt thank the Lord thy God in all things" (vs. 7).<br>"Thy vows shall be offered up in righteousness on all days and at all times" (vs. 11). |
| | "Thou shalt not be idle" (vs. 42).*<br>"Thou shalt stand in the place of thy stewardship" (vs. 53).*<br>"If thou obtainest more than that which would be for thy support, thou shalt give it into my storehouse" (vs. 55).**<br>"Thou shalt take the things which thou hast received . . . to be my law" (vs. 59).<br>"Thou shalt observe all these things, and great shall be thy reward" (vs. 65).<br>"Ye shall observe the laws which ye have received and be faithful" (vs. 66). | "God . . . hath given all these things unto man; for unto this end were they made to be used, with judgment, not to excess, neither by extortion" (vs. 20). |

*After each of these commandments, an instruction is given to the Church for dealing with violations of these laws.

**These were specific commands, or laws, applying to the law of consecration.

*Anciently, sacrifices were types of the suffering of Jesus Christ*

**D&C 59:7-8. "A Broken Heart and a Contrite Spirit"**

Before the birth of Christ on earth, the Lord commanded that sacrifices of animals or the fruits of the field be offered. These sacrifices signified both His own sacrifice and the willingness of the candidate to be obedient to God. After his resurrection, Jesus ended those sacrifices, and he commanded that the sacrifice thereafter be a broken heart and a contrite spirit (see 3 Nephi 9:15-22). Smith and Sjodahl explained the significance of the two phrases: " 'Contrite' means 'humble.' 'The sacrifices of God are a broken spirit: a broken and a contrite heart, O God, thou wilt not despise' (Psalm 51:17); a broken spirit and a contrite heart are those in which the obstinacy of pride has been replaced by the humility of repentance, frequently brought about by sorrow and affliction." (Commentary, pp. 305-6.)

**D&C 59:9-10. Pay Thy Devotion unto the Most High**

Speaking to a congregation on a Sunday morning in June 1881, President John Taylor said: "To serve the Lord, is one of the great objects of our existence; and I appreciate as a great privilege the opportunity we enjoy of worshiping God on the Sabbath day. And when we do meet to worship God, I like to see us worship him with all our hearts. I think it altogether out of place on such occasions to hear people talk about secular things; these are times, above all others perhaps, when our feelings and affections should be drawn out towards God. If we sing praises to God, let us do it in the proper spirit; if we pray, let every soul be engaged in prayer, doing it with all our hearts, that through our union our spirits may be blended in one, that our prayers and our worship may be available with God, whose Spirit permeates all things, and is always present in the assemblies of good and faithful Saints." (In *Journal of Discourses,* 22:226.)

**D&C 59:11-12. What Is an Oblation?**

Elder Bruce R. McConkie defined an oblation in the highest sense as "giving full devotion to the Lord, of offering him a broken heart and a contrite spirit. (D. & C. 59:8-12, 3 Ne. 9:19-20.) In a lesser and more temporal sense, an oblation is the offering of sacrifices, or of fast offering, or of any charitable contribution to the Church. (Ezek. 44:30.) Isaiah spoke of vain oblations meaning the ritualistic offering of sacrifices when the spirit and meaning of the ordinance and offering had been lost. (Isa. 1:13.) Ezekiel foretold that oblations would again be offered by Israel in the day of gathering. (Ezek. 20:33-44.)" (*Mormon Doctrine,* pp. 541-42.)

**D&C 59:13. "That Thy Fasting May Be Perfect"**

President Joseph F. Smith spoke of the purpose of fasting and how it is to be done more perfectly:

"Now, while the law requires the Saints in all the world to fast from 'even to even' and to abstain both from food and drink, it can easily be seen from the Scriptures, and especially from the words of Jesus, that it is more important to obtain the true spirit of love for God and man, 'purity of heart and simplicity of intention,' than it is to carry out the cold letter of the law. The Lord has instituted the fast on a reasonable and intelligent basis, and none of his works are vain or unwise. His law is perfect in this as in other things. Hence, those who can are required to comply thereto; it is a duty from which they cannot escape; but let it be remembered that the observance of the fast day by abstaining twenty-four hours from food and drink is not an absolute rule, it is no iron-clad law to us, but it is left with the people as a matter of conscience, to exercise wisdom and discretion. Many are subject to weakness, others are delicate in health, and others have nursing babies; of such it should not be required to fast. Neither should parents compel their little children to fast. I have known children to cry for something to eat on fast day. In such cases, going without food will do them no good. Instead, they dread the day to come, and in place of hailing it, dislike it; while the compulsion engenders a spirit of rebellion in them, rather than a love for the Lord and their fellows. Better teach them the principle, and let them observe it when they are old enough to choose intelligently, than to so compel them.

"But those should fast who can, and all classes among us should be taught to save the meals which they would eat, or their equivalent, for the poor. None are exempt from this; it is required of the Saints, old and young, in every part of the Church. It is no excuse that in some places there are no poor. In such cases the fast donation should be forwarded to the proper authorities for transmission to such stakes of Zion as may stand in need." (*Gospel Doctrine,* pp. 243-44.)

**D&C 59:13-14. How Can One's Fasting Be Done with Singleness of Heart?**

Fasting is sometimes thought of as going without food and drink. Here the Lord uses the terms *joy* and *rejoicing* to describe fasting. The preparation of food and fasting can go together. Smith and Sjodahl pointed out that "upon the Sabbath, even the food should be prepared 'with singleness of heart'; that is to say, in simplicity. Our hearts, our desires, on that day should not be elaborate feasts, whereby some are prevented from having a Sabbath. A simple meal should suffice. To that extent every Sabbath should be a fast day, one bringing perfect joy.

"Our Lord, on one occasion, entered the house of Martha and Mary. Martha was cumbered about much serving, desirous of giving the Master many courses, and all in grand style. Mary was anxious to listen to the Master. To Martha's rebuke of her younger sister, our Lord gently replied, 'But one thing is needful.' This might well be always remembered on our Lord's day." (Commentary, p. 352.)

### D&C 59:15. "Not with Much Laughter, for This Is Sin"

For a discussion of light-mindedness and inappropriate laughter see Notes and Commentary on Doctrine and Covenants 88:69, 121.

### D&C 59:16-20. Is There a Relationship between the Richness of the Earth and the Righteousness of the People?

One of the prominent themes of the Book of Mormon is that "as ye shall keep my commandments, ye shall prosper" (1 Nephi 2:20). "Prosper" probably implies more than an accumulation of physical wealth, but temporal prosperity is at least included in that blessing. Moses told the Israelites, "It shall come to pass, if ye hearken to these judgments, and keep, and do them, that . . . he will love thee, and bless thee, and multiply thee: he will also bless the fruit of thy womb, and the fruit of thy land, thy corn, and thy wine, and thine oil, the increase of thy kine [cattle], and the flocks of thy sheep, in the land which he sware unto thy fathers to give thee" (Deuteronomy 7:12-13). It is a promise of direct blessing upon the land as well as upon the people.

In section 59 the Lord again promises temporal blessings for spiritual obedience, including obedience to the law of the Sabbath. After a serious drought had ravaged the western United States, President Spencer W. Kimball asked if such a natural calamity might not be related to the obedience of the people, especially their observance of the Sabbath.

"The Lord uses the weather sometimes to discipline his people for the violation of his laws. He said to the children of Israel:

" 'If ye walk in my statutes, and keep my commandments, and do them;

" 'Then I will give you rain in due season, and the land shall yield her increase, and the trees of the field shall yield their fruit.

" 'And your threshing shall reach into the vintage, and the vintage shall reach unto the sowing time; and ye shall eat your bread to the full, and dwell in your land safely.

" 'And I will give peace in the land, and ye shall lie down, and none shall make you afraid: . . . neither shall the sword go through your land.' (Lev. 26:3-6.)

"With the great worry and suffering in the East and threats of drouth here in the West and elsewhere, we asked the people to join in a solemn prayer circle for moisture where needed. Quite immediately our prayers were answered, and we were grateful beyond expression. We are still in need and hope that the Lord may see fit to answer our continued prayers in this matter. . . .

"Perhaps the day has come when we should take stock of ourselves and see if we are worthy to ask or if we have been breaking the commandments, making ourselves unworthy of receiving the blessings. . . .

"But today numerous of the people of this land spend the Sabbath working, devoting the day to the beaches, to entertainment, to shows, to their weekly purchases. The Lord makes definite promises. He says:

" 'Then I will give you rain in due season, and the land shall yield her increase, and the trees of the field shall yield their fruit.' (Lev. 26:4.)

"God does what he promises, and many of us continue to defile the Sabbath day." (In Conference Report, Apr. 1977, pp. 4-5; or *Ensign*, May 1977, p. 4-5.)

### D&C 59:20. What Is Extortion?

" 'Extortion' is the act of taking something by violence, by threats, by overcharge, etc., unlawfully. It is lawful to procure, by honest labor, the means whereby the good things of the Earth may be obtained, but it is not lawful to wrest anything from another by methods contrary to this great law: 'Thou shalt love thy neighbor as thyself.' " (Smith and Sjodahl, Commentary, p. 354.)

### D&C 59:23. The Fruits of the Gospel and the Price Required for Them

Elder Marion G. Romney gave a clear and profound explanation of the blessings promised in this verse and what it takes to receive them:

"When earth life is over and things appear in their true perspective, we shall more clearly see and realize what the Lord and his prophets have repeatedly told us, that the fruits of the gospel are the only objectives worthy of life's full efforts. Their possessor obtains true wealth—wealth in the Lord's view of values. We need constantly to deepen our understandings and sharpen our realization of what the fruits of the gospel are.

"The Lord has defined them as ' . . . peace in this world, and eternal life in the world to come.' (D. & C. 59:23.) It is a bit difficult to define the 'peace in this world' referred to in the revelation. But we may be assured that it is not the ease, luxury, and freedom from struggle envisioned by the world's utopian dreamers. Jesus told his apostles that it would be found by them even in their days of tribulation. 'Peace I leave with you,' he said, 'my peace I give unto you.' And then, by way of caution, it seems to me, he added, ' . . . not as the world giveth, give I unto you.' (John 14:27.)

"The other fruit of the gospel named in the quotation—'eternal life in the world to come'—must be a glorious thing, for the Lord has said that 'he

*Marion G. Romney taught, "The fruits of the gospel are the only objectives worthy of life's full efforts" (in Conference Report, Oct. 1949, p. 39)*

that hath eternal life is rich,' (D. & C. 6:7) and that the 'gift of eternal life is the greatest of all the gifts of God.' (D. & C. 14:7.) He who obtains it will obtain an exaltation in the celestial kingdom of our Father in heaven. . . .

"This gift of eternal life in the world to come may not, of course, be fully realized during earth life. An assurance that it will be obtained in the world to come may, however, be had in this world. As a matter of fact, the blessings of the celestial kingdom are promised only to those who have such an assurance. According to the vision, a successful candidate for these blessings must qualify on three counts: First, he must have '. . . received the testimony of Jesus, and believed on his name' and been '. . . baptized after the manner of his burial'; second, he must have received 'the Holy Spirit by the laying on of the hands of him who is ordained and sealed unto this power'; and third, he must be 'sealed by the Holy Spirit of promise.' (D. & C. 76:51-53.)

"The Prophet Joseph taught that one so sealed would have within himself an assurance born of the spirit, that he would obtain eternal life in the world to come. He urgently and repeatedly admonished the Saints of his day to obtain such an assurance by making their calling and election sure. It is this assurance within a person which brings to him the peace in this world which will sustain him in every tribulation. . . .

"These fruits of the gospel—assurance that we shall obtain eternal life, peace in this world sustained by such an assurance, and finally eternal life in the world to come—are within the reach of us all. . . .

"I conceive the blessings of the gospel to be of such inestimable worth that the price for them must be very exacting, and if I correctly understand what the Lord has said on the subject, it is. The price, however, is within the reach of us all, because it is not to be paid in money nor in any of this world's goods but in righteous living. What is required is wholehearted devotion to the gospel and unreserved allegiance to the Church of Jesus Christ of Latter-day Saints. . . .

"A half-hearted performance is not enough. We cannot obtain these blessings and be like the rich young man who protested that he had kept the commandments from his youth up but who went away sorrowful when, in answer to the question, 'What lack I yet?' Jesus said unto him, 'If thou wilt be perfect, go and sell that thou hast, and give to the poor . . . and come and follow me.' (Matt. 19:21.) Evidently he could live everything but the welfare program.

"There can be no such reservation. We must be willing to sacrifice everything. Through self-discipline and devotion we must demonstrate to the Lord that we are willing to serve him under all circumstances. When we have done this, we shall receive an assurance that we shall have eternal life in the world to come. Then we shall have peace in this world. . . .

"Let us each day in solemn honesty confront ourselves with the rich man's question, 'What lack I yet?' And thus, with utter frankness, discovering our own limitations, let us conquer them one by one until we obtain peace in this world through an assurance that we shall have eternal life in the world to come." (In Conference Report, Oct. 1949, pp. 39-45.)

# "Thou Shalt Not Idle Away Thy Time nor Bury Thy Talents"

Section 60

## Historical Background

On 3 June 1831 a conference was held at Kirtland, Ohio, at which twenty-eight missionaries were called to go to the land of Missouri, preaching the gospel as they journeyed (see D&C 52). Having completed their mission, "on the 8th day of August, 1831, at the close of the first conference held in Missouri, the elders inquired what they were to do. The Prophet inquired of the Lord and received a revelation giving them direction in relation to their return journey." (Smith, *Church History and Modern Revelation,* 1:220.)

## Notes and Commentary

**D&C 60:1-3. "They Will Not Open Their Mouths, but They Hide the Talent"**

It was pleasing to the Lord that the elders had traveled to Missouri, and now they were to return speedily to Ohio. But the Lord was not pleased with some of them. President Joseph Fielding Smith noted why: "They had been commanded to preach the Gospel along the way and bear testimony among the people, but some had failed to magnify this commandment because of their fear of man. It is true that not every man is a natural missionary, and there are those who shrink from the responsibility of raising their voices in proclamation of the Gospel, and yet this is an obligation that we owe to this fallen world. The elders in the very beginning had been commanded to serve the Lord with all their 'heart, might, mind and strength,' for the field is white and ready for the harvest. A penalty was to be inflicted upon those who failed and they were not to stand blameless at the last day. The preaching of the Gospel was to be a means to them by which they were not to perish, but bring salvation to their souls. There are many who have been sent forth who have had a fear of man, yet the Lord has promised to support them in their labors if they will trust in him." (*Church History and Modern Revelation,* 1:220-21.)

*Those who have been warned are to warn their neighbors*

**D&C 60:4. "I Shall Make Up My Jewels"**

In all ages jewels have been highly esteemed by man. As these precious stones are the best and most valued that the earth can produce, so are those people who prepare themselves by obedience to the commandments, for they will be the jewels the Savior will claim when he comes in glory (see Isaiah 62:3; Zechariah 9:16; Malachi 3:17; D&C 101:3).

**D&C 60:8, 13-14. "Preach My Gospel among the Congregations of the Wicked"**

President Joseph Fielding Smith wrote that the Lord often "refers to the people scattered abroad as 'congregations of the wicked.' We have good reason to believe that wickedness prevailed among the congregations. The elders were to seek out from among the people the honest in heart and leave their warning testimony with all others, thus they would become clean from their blood." (*Church History and Modern Revelation,* 1:223.)

**D&C 60:13. "Thou Shalt Not . . . Bury Thy Talent"**

The full significance of this warning may be found in Matthew 25:14-30.

**D&C 60:15-17. "Shake Off the Dust of Thy Feet"**

The ordinance of washing the dust from one's feet was practiced in New Testament times and was reinstituted in this dispensation (see D&C 88:139-40; John 11:2; 12:3; 13:5-14.) The action of shaking or cleansing the dust from one's feet is a testimony against those who refuse to accept the gospel (see D&C 24:15; 84:92; 99:4). Because of the serious nature of this act, Church leaders have directed that it be done only at the command of the Spirit. President Joseph Fielding Smith explained the significance of the action as follows: "The cleansing of their feet, either by washing or wiping off the dust, would be recorded in heaven as a testimony against the wicked. This act, however, was not to be performed in the presence of the offenders, 'lest thou provoke them, but in secret, and wash thy feet, as a testimony against them in the day of judgment.' The missionaries of the Church who faithfully perform their duty are under the obligation of leaving their testimony with all with whom they come in contact in their work. This testimony will stand as a witness against those who reject the message, at the judgment." (*Church History and Modern Revelation,* 1:223; see also Notes and Commentary for D&C 24:15.)

# The Lord Has Blessed the Land and Cursed the Waters

Section 61

## Historical Background

This revelation was received by the Prophet Joseph Smith on the bank of the Missouri River, McIlwaine's Bend, on 12 August 1831. The Prophet wrote:

"On the 9th, in company with ten Elders, I left Independence landing for Kirtland. We started down the river in canoes, and went the first day as far as Fort Osage, where we had an excellent wild turkey for supper. Nothing very important occurred till the third day, when many of the dangers so common upon the western waters, manifested themselves; and after we had encamped upon the bank of the river, at McIlwaine's Bend, Brother Phelps, in open vision by daylight, saw the destroyer in his most horrible power, ride upon the face of the waters; others heard the noise, but saw not the vision.

"The next morning after prayer, I received the following: [D&C 61] ." (*History of the Church,* 1:202-3.)

## Notes and Commentary

### D&C 61:1-4, 6, 19. The Brethren Were to Bear Record

The Lord commanded the elders to bear record of Satan and his power upon the waters (see D&C 61:4, 19), and of the power of God for the benefit of the faithful (see vss. 1, 6). To fulfill this responsibility, it would be necessary for them to come in contact with people, hence, the Lord's reminder that while traveling by canoe they were not able to meet people who needed to hear the gospel message (see vss. 3-5, 20-22, 30-32).

### D&C 61:5-19. How Is the Water "Cursed"?

President Joseph Fielding Smith pointed out how "in the beginning the Lord blessed the waters and cursed the land, but in these last days this was reversed, the land was to be blessed and the waters to be cursed. A little reflection will bear witness to the truth of this declaration. In the early millenniums of this earth's history, men did not understand the composition of the soils, and how they needed building up when crops were taken from them. The facilities at the command of the people were primitive and limited, acreage under cultivation was limited, famines were prevalent and the luxuries which we have today were not obtainable. Someone may rise up and say that the soil in those days was just as productive as now, and this may be the case. It is not a matter of dispute, but the manner of cultivation did not lend itself to the abundant production which we are receiving today. It matters not what the causes were, in those early days of world history there could not be the production, nor the varieties of fruits coming from the earth, and the Lord can very properly speak of this as a curse, or the lack of blessing, upon the land. In those early periods we have every reason to believe that the torrents, floods, and the dangers upon the waters were not as great as they are today, and by no means as great as what the Lord has promised us. The early mariners among the ancients traversed the seas as they knew them in that day in comparative safety. . . . Today this manner of travel in such boats would be of the most dangerous and risky nature. Moreover, we have seen the dangers upon the waters increase until the hearts of men failed them and only the brave, and those who were compelled to travel the seas, ventured out upon them. In regard to the Missouri-Mississippi waters, we have seen year by year great destruction upon them, and coming from them. Millions upon millions of dollars, almost annually are lost by this great stream overflowing its banks. Many have lost their lives in these floods as they sweep over the land, and even upon this apparently tranquil or sluggish stream there can arise storms that bring destruction. Verily the word of the Lord has been, and is being, fulfilled in relation to those waters. While the Lord has spoken of the sea heaving itself beyond its bounds, and the waves roaring, yet we must include the great destruction upon the waters by means of war, and especially by submarine warfare as we have learned of it in recent years."

(*Church History and Modern Revelation,* 1:224; see also Genesis 3:17-19; Ether 7:23-25; 9:16, 28; Revelation 16:1-6; Alma 45:16; D&C 59:3; 16-19.)

**D&C 61:7. What Was the "Errand and Mission" of Sidney Gilbert and William W. Phelps?**

These men were to purchase a printing press and transport it to Missouri. William W. Phelps was to be the printer for the Church (see D&C 55:4; 57:11), and Sidney Gilbert had been appointed purchasing agent (see D&C 57:6).

**D&C 61:20-28. "I, the Lord, Was Angry with You Yesterday"**

Elder B. H. Roberts explained the reason for this statement this way: "During the three days upon the river some disagreements and ill feeling had developed among the brethren and explanations and reconciliations had become necessary; it had also been discovered that progress on their journey by the river in canoes was slow, and hence it became necessary for those who had been appointed to purchase the printing press, Sidney Gilbert and William W. Phelps; and the Prophet, Sidney Rigdon, and Oliver Cowdery, who had been commanded to hasten their return to Kirtland, found it imperative to find a more expeditious means of travel than by the canoes. The greater part of the night at McIlwaine's Bend was devoted to these matters. The brethren became reconciled to each other, and those whose affairs more especially cried haste started overland the next morning for St. Louis, and the rest of the company continued the journey via the river." (*Comprehensive History of the Church,* 1:262-63.)

**D&C 61:30-32. Why Were the Prophet and His Companions Told to Warn the Wicked at Cincinnati?**

"At the time of this revelation Cincinnati was only a village, yet it was like other western towns such as Independence, the gathering place of many who had been forced to flee from the larger cities because of the violation of the law. In all the border towns in that day wickedness to a very great extent prevailed. After fulfilling their mission in Cincinnati these two brethren [the Prophet Joseph and Sidney Rigdon] were to continue their journey back to Kirtland." (Smith, *Church History and Modern Revelation,* 1:225.)

**D&C 61:37-39. "He Cometh in an Hour You Think Not"**

No man knows the exact time of Christ's coming. The Prophet Joseph Smith said: "Jesus Christ never did reveal to any man the precise time that He would come. Go and read the Scriptures, and you cannot find anything that specifies the exact hour He would come; and all that say so are false teachers." (*History of the Church,* 6:254.)

# "Ye Are Blessed, for the Testimony Ye Have Borne"

Section 62

## Historical Background

While the Prophet and his party were on their way home from Missouri during August 1831, they met some of the elders who were going to Missouri. Joseph Smith wrote: "On the 13th [of August] I met several of the Elders on their way to the land of Zion, and after the joyful salutations with which brethren meet each other, who are actually 'contending for the faith once delivered to the Saints,' I received the following: [D&C 62]" (*History of the Church,* 1:205). The elders were not identified in the Prophet's history, but Reynolds Cahoon named them as follows: Hyrum Smith, John Murdock, Harvey Whitlock, and David Whitmer (see Journal History, 13 August 1831).

## Notes and Commentary

**D&C 62:1. The Lord Knows How to Succor Those Who Are Tempted**

"*Succor* means 'to go to the aid of one in want or distress' or 'to relieve.' Fortunately, the Savior succors those 'who are tempted' so they will not commit sin, and if they should sin, he will succor them if they repent." (Ludlow, *Companion,* 1:330.)

**D&C 62:2-3. "Your Sins Are Forgiven You"**

Effective missionary work has a redemptive effect for the missionary as well as the convert. The Apostle James wrote, "He which converteth the sinner from the error of his way shall save a soul from death, and shall hide a multitude of sins" (James 5:20). Of that teaching, Elder Bruce R. McConkie wrote: "By reclaiming an erring brother, we save both him and ourselves. Our sins are hidden (remitted) because we ministered for the salvation and blessing of another member of the kingdom. In principle this special reward for Christ's ministers applies also to those who preach the gospel and bring souls into the kingdom. The minister is rewarded with salvation and, of necessity, in the process, is freed from his own sins. (D. & C. 4:1-4.)" (*Doctrinal New Testament Commentary,* 3:279.)

**D&C 62:3. Testimony Is Recorded in Heaven**

Smith and Sjodahl noted that "in this Revelation

we are told that angels are scrutinizing the records kept of the testimonies of the Elders, and that they rejoice over the witnesses. It appears from this that the ministry on earth has its effects beyond the veil as well as on this side. An Elder who bears his faithful testimony to the truth does not know how far-reaching the result may be, though his visible audience may consist of but few." (Commentary, p. 371.)

**D&C 62:4. "Hold a Meeting"**

See Doctrine and Covenants 58:61-63.

**D&C 62:6. To What Promise Is the Lord Referring?**

See Doctrine and Covenants 35:24; 39:13; 49:25; 52:42.

**D&C 62:7-8. Why Did the Lord Refer to Riding on Horses or Mules?**

John Murdock was so ill on this occasion that he was unable to pursue his journey to Zion without some assistance. After this revelation was given, the four missionaries (John Murdock, David Whitmer, Harvey Whitlock, and Hyrum Smith) put their money together and bought a horse for John Murdock to ride, by which means they were able to continue their travels.

# "For This Is a Day of Warning, and Not a Day of Many Words"

Section 63

## Historical Background

On 27 August 1831 Joseph Smith and his party returned to Kirtland, Ohio, from their first trip to Zion, bringing news that the center place of Zion was now known. "When the report spread among the members of the Church that the Lord had revealed definitely where the city New Jerusalem was to be built, naturally there was rejoicing and many expressed the desire to know what they were to do in order to obtain inheritances. The Lord has given instruction repeatedly that all who go to Zion shall obey His law—the celestial law on which Zion was to be built. Those who were weak in the faith, or indifferent to the commandments, were warned that they would not be made welcome in that land unless they repented. 'Hearken, O ye people, and open your hearts and give ear from afar; and listen, you that call yourselves the people of the Lord, and hear the word of the Lord and his will concerning you.' These are the words by which this revelation is introduced." (Smith, *Church History and Modern Revelation,* 1:229.)

The Prophet Joseph Smith described the concern and enthusiasm of the Saints at the time: "In these infant days of the Church, there was a great anxiety to obtain the word of the Lord upon every subject that in any way concerned our salvation; and as the land of Zion was now the most important temporal object in view, I enquired of the Lord for further information upon the gathering of the Saints, and the purchase of the land, and other matters, and received the following: [D&C 63]." (*History of the Church,* 1:207.)

## Notes and Commentary

**D&C 63:1-6. "Listen, You That Call Yourselves the People of the Lord"**

The Lord in his revelations teaches the Saints that in order for them to inhabit Zion, they must be a righteous people (see D&C 58, 59, 97, 101, 103, 105). The Lord opened this revelation with a solemn reminder that his commandments are not to be taken lightly and that those who ignore them or rebel against them will be punished. The reminder was necessary, since many of the early Saints claimed to be anxious to build Zion but were not being obedient to the laws God had revealed. The Prophet Joseph Smith also tried to teach the Saints the same principle: "We know not what we shall be called to pass through before Zion is delivered and established; therefore, we have great need to live near to God, and always be in strict obedience to all His commandments, that we may have a conscience void of offense toward God and man" (*Teachings,* p. 32).

**D&C 63:7-12. How Is It That Signs Depend on Faith and the Seeking of Signs without Faith Is a Sin?**

These verses contain a very important statement on the relationship between faith and works and the miraculous powers, or signs, that accompany faith.

The process by which faith, or power, is developed is one of testing. The Lord gives certain principles, and by obedience to them, blessings and power follow. But one has no proof of that promise until one acts on the basis of trust or belief. Then comes the confirmation of the reality of the principle, but only after one acts in faith and

*Joseph Smith taught that faith is a key to the power of God*

trust. That is why James taught that "faith, if it hath not works, is dead, being alone" (James 2:17). Moroni taught the same principle when he explained that the evidence that the principles are true and will bring power cannot be known for sure at first, but can only be hoped for until one acts on the principle: "Faith is things which are hoped for and not seen; wherefore, . . . ye receive no witness [confirmation] until after the trial of your faith" (Ether 12:6).

The Lord will give confirming evidence of all gospel principles if one is willing to act on the basis of faith. Imagine a person who says, "Before I pay my tithing, I must know for sure that it is a true principle." The Lord's way is just the opposite. He says, "First act in faith and pay your tithing, then I will give you evidence it is a true principle." The Savior taught this relationship emphatically during his mortal ministry: "If any man *will do his will,* he shall *know of the doctrine*" (John 7:17; emphasis added).

When a person understands this process, he can see why sign seeking is condemned. Someone who demands outward evidence of the power of God as a condition for his believing is seeking to circumvent the process by which faith is developed. He wants proof without price. As with the adulterer, he seeks the results without accepting the responsibility. Thus it is a wicked and adulterous generation that seeks signs.

The Prophet Joseph Smith taught the following about this principle: "I will give you one of the Keys of the mysteries of the Kingdom. It is an eternal principle, that has existed with God from all eternity: That man who rises up to condemn others, finding fault with the Church, saying that they are out of the way, while he himself is righteous, then know assuredly, that that man is in the high road to apostasy; and if he does not repent, will apostatize, as God lives. The principle is as correct as the one that Jesus put forth in saying that he who seeketh a sign is an adulterous person; and that principle is eternal, undeviating, and firm as the pillars of heaven; for whenever you see a man seeking after a sign, you may set it down that he is an adulterous man." (*Teachings,* pp. 156-57.)

### D&C 63:16. "He That Looketh upon a Woman to Lust After Her"

Thought always precedes action, as President David O. McKay explained: "Let me make it simple. Many years ago a young man came to me while I was president of the European Mission and made a confession of a wrong and sinful act. He justified himself by saying that he happened to be in a bookstore at the closing hour, and when the door was locked he yielded to temptation. He rather blamed the *circumstances* for his fall.

"But I said, 'It wasn't the circumstances; it wasn't the locked door, nor the enticement. You had thought of that before you went to that bookstore. If you had never thought of that act, there would have been no circumstance strong enough to entice or to tempt you, a missionary to fall. The thought always precedes the act.' " ("Cleanliness Is Next to Godliness," *Instructor,* Mar. 1965, p. 86.)

Notes and Commentary for Doctrine and Covenants 42:23-24 contains a more extended discussion of this subject.

### D&C 63:17. What Does It Mean to Burn with Fire and Brimstone?

Elder Bruce R. McConkie defined brimstone as "sulfur, an easily melted, very inflammable mineral which burns with a blue flame and emits a suffocating odor. . . .

"The nature of burning brimstone is such that it perfectly symbolized to the prophetic mind the eternal torment of the damned. Accordingly we read that the wicked are 'tormented with *fire and brimstone*' (Rev. 14:9-11; 19:20; 20:10), or in other words that 'their torment is *as* a lake of fire and brimstone, whose flame ascendeth up forever and ever and has no end.' (2 Ne. 9:16; Alma 12:17.) This burning scene, a horrifying 'lake of fire and brimstone,' symbolizes 'endless torment' (2 Ne. 9:19, 26; 28:23; Jac. 6:10; Alma 14:14; D. & C. 76:36); those who find place therein are subject to the second death." (*Mormon Doctrine,* pp. 280-81.)

### D&C 63:20-21, 49-51. The Transfiguration of the Earth

"The earth will pass through two changes which might be called transfigurations:

"1. At the beginning of the Millennium, it will be raised from its present telestial to a terrestrial state, and only the righteous will have a place on earth at that time.

"2. After the thousand years are ended, the earth will be celestialized and the faithful who are worthy of that glory will receive their permanent inheritance thereon." (Cowan, *Doctrine and Covenants,* p. 101; see also D&C 77; 88:17-20, 25-26; 101: 24-25; 130:4-11.)

### D&C 63:24-31. How Is the Land of Zion to Be Obtained?

President Joseph Fielding Smith explained that land in Zion was to be purchased. "This fact was taught the early members. They were warned against creating antagonism among their neighbors, many of whom were extremely bitter towards the members of the Church. The Lord said the land could not be obtained by the shedding of blood. Those who had the privilege of assembling there should not go up to Zion in haste, but gradually. The reason for this advice is apparent, for haste would lead to confusion, unsatisfactory conditions and pestilence, and then, also, it creates consternation and fear in the hearts of their enemies and arouses greater opposition. Satan desired to destroy them and in his anger endeavored to stir them up to strife and contention as well as the older settlers in Missouri." (*Church History and Modern Revelation,* 1:232.)

### D&C 63:34. The Saints Also Shall Hardly Escape

The Prophet Joseph Smith "explained concerning the coming of the Son of Man; also that it is a false idea that the Saints will escape all the judgments, whilst the wicked suffer; for all flesh is subject to suffer, and 'the righteous shall hardly escape;' still many of the Saints will escape, for the just shall live by faith; yet many of the righteous shall fall a prey to disease, to pestilence, etc., by reason of the weakness of the flesh, and yet be saved in the Kingdom of God. So that it is an unhallowed principle to say that such and such have transgressed because they have been preyed upon by disease or death, for all flesh is subject to death; and the Savior has said, 'Judge not, lest ye be judged.' " (*History of the Church,* 4:11.)

### D&C 63:50-51. "Old Men Shall Die; but They Shall Not Sleep in the Dust"

These verses describe a millennial condition. See also Doctrine and Covenants 43:32; 45:57-58; 101:24-34; 3 Nephi 28:8; Isaiah 65.

### D&C 63:54. "Foolish Virgins among the Wise"

Many places in the Doctrine and Covenants use phrases or concepts from New Testament parables (see, for example, Notes and Commentary on D&C 40:2; 45:36-37, 56-57; 60:13; 86:1-7.) Here is yet another example. The phrase "foolish virgins" refers to the five virgins in the parable who did not have sufficient oil in their lamps (see Matthew 25:1-13).

### D&C 63:55-56. Sidney Rigdon's Writing Was Not Acceptable to the Lord

"Sidney Rigdon had been instructed, by revelation (Sec. 58:50), to write a description of the Land of Zion. His first effort was not acceptable to God. The reason for his failure is stated. He was too proud to receive counsel. He was, however, given another chance, and his second effort proved a success and was accepted." (Smith and Sjodahl, Commentary, p. 384.)

### D&C 63:61-64. "Let All Men Beware How They Take My Name in Their Lips"

To take the name of the Lord in vain is often thought of only as profanity. Elder James E. Talmage broadened the definition of taking the Lord's name in vain to include the following:

"1. We may take the name of God in vain by profane speech.

"2. We take it in vain when we swear falsely, not being true to our oaths and promises.

"3. We take it in vain in a blasphemous sense when we presume to speak in that name without authority.

"4. And we take his name in vain whenever we wilfully do aught that is in defiance of his commandments, since we have taken his name upon ourselves." (In Conference Report, Oct. 1931, pp. 53.)

Dealing with sacred things in an appropriate manner is discussed in Notes and Commentary for Doctrine and Covenants 88:121.

*James E. Talmage instructed all to refrain from profanity*

# "Of You It Is Required to Forgive All Men"

Section 64

## Historical Background

"Because of interference and because he needed a quiet place in which to work, the Prophet on September 12, 1831, moved to the home of John Johnson in the township of Hiram. This was in Portage County, Ohio, about thirty miles southeast of Kirtland. From the time he moved until early in October, the Prophet spent most of his spare time preparing for the continuation of the translation of the Bible. By translation is meant a revision of the Bible by inspiration or revelation as the Lord had commanded him, and which was commenced as early as June 1830. (D.H.C. 1:215.) Sidney Rigdon continued to write for the Prophet in the work of revision. The day before the Prophet moved from Kirtland he received an important revelation, Section 64, as it now appears in the Doctrine and Covenants." (Smith, *Church History and Modern Revelation,* 1:234-35.)

## Notes and Commentary

### D&C 64:1-2. "Ye Should Overcome the World"

Smith and Sjodahl noted that "John, in his First Epistle, says: 'Whatever is born of God overcometh the world,' (5:4); and, 'who is he that overcometh the world, but he that believeth that Jesus is the Son of God' (v. 5)? What he wants to say is that as long as we follow our desires to conform to the habits and customs of the world, the commandments of God are hard; but when we overcome that desire and do not conform to the spirit of the world, then His commandments are not difficult, and, if we really believe that Jesus is the Son of God, we shall not take any notice of the world, which is in rebellion against Him. In this Revelation the Lord, making use of an expression by the disciple whom He loved, tells the Elders of the Church that they should not conform to the world in their worship, in their life, in their amusements. Some had failed in this respect." (Commentary, p. 389.)

### D&C 64:7. How Does a Person Sin unto Death?

Elder Bruce R. McConkie explained that "those who turn from the light and truth of the gospel; who give themselves up to Satan; who enlist in his cause, supporting and sustaining it; and who thereby become his children—by such a course *sin unto death.* For them there is neither repentance, forgiveness, nor any hope whatever of salvation of any kind. As children of Satan, they are sons of perdition." (*Mormon Doctrine,* p. 737; see also Alma 5:41-42; Matthew 12:31-32; Hebrews 10:26-27; 1 John 5:16-17.)

### D&C 64:8. "My Disciples, in Days of Old, Sought Occasion against One Another"

President Joseph Fielding Smith described this incident as follows: "The Lord declared that when he was in his ministry his disciples sought occasion against one another and failed at times to forgive in their hearts. It was this condition which prompted Peter to ask the Lord how many times he should forgive his brother, 'till seven times?' The Lord answered him, 'I say not unto thee, until seven times, but until seventy times seven.' (Matt. 18:21-22.) As the disciples of old brought upon themselves affliction and chastening, so we, when we do not have in our hearts the spirit of forgiveness, bring upon ourselves affliction and chastening from the Lord." (*Church History and Modern Revelation,* 1:235.)

### D&C 64:9-11. "Of You It Is Required to Forgive All Men"

Elder Marion D. Hanks spoke in general conference about the importance of forgiving others:

"Someone has written: '. . . the withholding of love is the negation of the spirit of Christ, the proof that we never knew him, that for us he lived in vain. It means that he suggested nothing in all our thoughts, that we were not once near enough to him to be seized with the spell of his compassion for the world.' . . .

"What is our response when we are offended, misunderstood, unfairly or unkindly treated, or sinned against, made an offender for a word, falsely accused, passed over, hurt by those we love, our offerings rejected? Do we resent, become bitter, hold a grudge? Or do we resolve the problem if we can, forgive, and rid ourselves of the burden?

"The nature of our response to such situations may well determine the nature and quality of our lives, here and eternally. . . .

"But not only our eternal salvation depends upon our willingness and capacity to forgive wrongs committed against us. Our joy and satisfaction in this life, and our true freedom, depend upon our doing so. When Christ bade us turn the other cheek, walk the second mile, give our cloak to him who takes our coat, was it to be chiefly out of consideration for the bully, the brute, the thief? Or was it to relieve the one aggrieved of the destructive burden that resentment and anger lay upon us?

"Paul wrote to the Romans that nothing 'shall be able to separate us from the love of God, which is in Christ Jesus our Lord.' (Rom. 8:39.)

"I am sure this is true. I bear testimony that this is true. But it is also true that we can *separate ourselves* from his spirit. . . .

"In every case of sin this is true. Envy, arrogance, unrighteous dominion—these canker the soul of one who is guilty of them. It is true also if we fail to forgive. Even if it appears that another may be deserving of our resentment or hatred, none of us can afford to pay the price of resenting or hating, because of what it does to us. If we have felt the gnawing, mordant inroads of these emotions, we know the harm we suffer. . . .

"It is reported that President Brigham Young once said that he who takes offense when no offense was intended is a fool, and he who takes offense when offense *was* intended is usually a fool. It was then explained that there are two courses of action to follow when one is bitten by a rattlesnake. One may, in anger, fear, or vengefulness, pursue the creature and kill it. Or he may make full haste to get the venom out of his system. If we pursue the latter course we will likely survive, but if we attempt to follow the former, we may not be around long enough to finish it." (In Conference Report, Oct. 1973, pp. 15-16; *Ensign*, Jan. 1974, pp. 20-21.)

**D&C 64:18-21. Why Did the Lord Want "to Retain a Strong Hold in the Land of Kirtland" for Five Years?**

President Joseph Fielding Smith answered this question when he said that "it was in that land where the first temple in this dispensation was to be built. In that Temple the essential keys of restoration were to be revealed. It seems apparent that had all the people moved to Zion in Missouri at that time, the building of a temple would have been frustrated by the enemies of the people. . . . The restoration of the keys of the Priesthood held by the ancient prophets was essential to the progress of the Church. The Lord decreed that a house to his name should be reared in Kirtland where he could come and where he could send his messengers with these keys of power. The building of such a temple required time, and while the elders went to work with their might this house was not ready for dedication until March 27, 1836. It was on the third day of April 1836, that the Lord appeared in that house and where Elias, Moses and

*The Kirtland Temple, the temple of the Restoration*

Elijah appeared and conferred the keys of their dispensations and authorities. How many other messengers came at that time we do not know. We know, however, that it was necessary that every key and authority should be revealed. Some were revealed, of necessity, before there was a temple to which these messengers could come, but it was according to the divine plan that keys of this nature should be revealed in a house built to the name of the Lord. The revelation in which the Lord called upon the Saints to keep a strong hold in Kirtland, was given Sept. 11, 1831. It was in March, 1836, that the house of the Lord was dedicated and the following April when these holy keys were bestowed. After this glorious event, the members of the Church were at liberty to remove to Zion. In fact there followed a few months later an apostasy, and many turned away from the Church, but some were saved, and they were under the necessity of fleeing from the place. However, the Spirit of the Lord prevailed until his work in that place was accomplished and the appointed time had passed." (*Church History and Modern Revelation*, 1:237.)

**D&C 64:22. Why Does the Lord Require the Hearts of Men?**

Throughout the scriptures various parts of the human body are used figuratively, and this imagery is generally derived from the purpose and function of that particular organ. Thus, the eye, which is the organ that perceives light, is used as a symbol of perception of either godly or evil things (see Matthew 5:29; 6:22-23; D&C 27:2). The ear, by which one hears, becomes a symbol of hearkening or obedience (see Deuteronomy 32:1; Revelation 2:7; D&C 33:1; 43:1).

But of all the organs of the body, the heart is used as the most profound symbol. One scholar indicated that in the Bible the heart is viewed as the "innermost center" of man, and is representative of three central themes:

1. The center of bodily life and power. When the heart is strengthened, the whole man is strengthened.
2. The center of the rational and emotional nature of man. It is the seat of love and hate, the center of thought and knowledge—it understands, deliberates, reflects, estimates. It is the center of feelings and affections, experiencing joy, pain, ill will, dissatisfaction, anxiety, despair, fear, and reverence.
3. The center of moral life. Many degrees of spiritual growth are found in the heart. It is the dwelling place of either Christ or Satan; it can be hard or broken; it can be a treasure of either good or evil. "The heart is the laboratory and place of issue of all that is good and evil in thoughts, words, and deeds. . . . It is the center of the entire man, the very hearth of life's impulse." (Unger, *Bible Dictionary*, s.v. "heart," p. 462; see also topical guide, s.v. "heart.")

When one understands the profound imagery of the heart, one can better understand why the Lord requires the heart of man. In Doctrine and Covenants 34 the Lord added a willing mind to that basic requirement.

## D&C 64:23. "He That Is Tithed Shall Not Be Burned at His Coming"

Elder Rudger Clawson explained how this promise could be fulfilled: "What does that mean? Does it mean that if a man will not pay his tithing, that the Lord is going to send a ball of fire down from heaven and burn him up? No; the Lord does not do that way. The Lord works on natural principles. This is what it means, if I read correctly: a man who ignores the express command of the Lord, by failing to pay his tithing, it means that the Spirit of the Lord will withdraw from him; it means that the power of the priesthood will withdraw from that man, if he continues in the spirit of neglect to do his duty. He will drift away into darkness, gradually but surely, until finally (mark you) he will lift up his eyes among the wicked. That is where he will finally land; and then when the destruction comes and when the burning comes he will be among the wicked and will be destroyed; while those who observe the law will be found among the righteous, and they will be preserved. There is a God in heaven, and He had promised to shield and protect them. I tell you there is a day of burning, a day of destruction coming upon the wicked. And where will we be? Will we be with the wicked, or with the righteous?" (In Conference Report, Oct. 1913, p. 59.)

## D&C 64:23-25. "Behold, Now It Is Called Today"

"So near is the consummation that the intervening period is called 'today'; and, in applying this time designation in the year 1831, the Lord said: [D&C 64:23-25].

" . . . Only through watchfulness and prayer may the signs of the times be correctly interpreted and the imminence of the Lord's appearing be apprehended. To the unwatchful and the wicked the event will be as sudden and unexpected as the coming of a thief in the night. But we are not left without definite information as to precedent signs." (Talmage, *Jesus the Christ,* pp. 785-86.)

Notes and Commentary on Doctrine and Covenants 45:6 contains an explanation of why, in the Lord's terminology, from now until he comes can be called "today."

## D&C 64:34-36. "The Rebellious Are Not of the Blood of Ephraim"

It seems strange that the Lord would say that blood, a symbol for direct line descendancy, could be influenced by rebelliousness, a spiritual trait. Isn't one either a descendant of Ephraim or not a descendant of Ephraim? The answer is no, not in the eyes of the Lord who views his children in terms of their spiritual qualities. Paul taught this principle to the early Saints. The Jews took great pride in the fact that they were of the circumcision, that is, that they were the covenant people, circumcision being the token of that covenant. But Paul pointed out that if one of the circumcision violated the law, his "circumcision is made uncircumcision" (Romans 2:25). In other words, by transgression one excludes oneself from being a true Israelite. Paul concluded his reasoning with this statement: "For he is not a Jew, which is one outwardly; neither is that circumcision, which is outward in the flesh: but he is a Jew, which is one inwardly; and circumcision is that of the heart, in the spirit, and not in the letter; whose praise is not of men, but of God" (Romans 2:28-29).

Nephi also understood this principle and taught: "For behold, I say unto you that as many of the Gentiles as will repent are the covenant people of the Lord; and as many of the Jews as will not repent shall be cast off; for the Lord covenanteth with none save it be with them that repent and believe in his Son, who is the Holy One of Israel" (2 Nephi 30:2).

Ephraim received the birthright under the hands of Jacob (see Genesis 48:5-22) and was considered by the Lord to be Joseph's firstborn (see 1 Chronicles 5:1; Jeremiah 31:9). President Joseph Fielding Smith explained why:

"It is essential in this dispensation that Ephraim stand in his place at the head, exercising the birthright in Israel which was given to him by direct revelation. Therefore, Ephraim must be gathered first to prepare the way, through the gospel and the priesthood, for the rest of the tribes of Israel when the time comes for them to be gathered to Zion. The great majority of those who have come into the Church are Ephraimites. It is the exception to find one of any other tribe, unless it is of Manasseh.

"It is Ephraim, today, who holds the priesthood. It is with Ephraim that the Lord has made covenant and has revealed the fulness of the everlasting

*Priesthood is the stewardship of the house of Ephraim*

gospel. It is Ephraim who is building temples and performing the ordinances in them for both the living and for the dead. When the 'lost tribes' come—and it will be a most wonderful sight and a marvelous thing when they do come to Zion—in fulfilment of the promises made through Isaiah and Jeremiah, they will have to receive the crowning blessings from their brother Ephraim, the 'firstborn' in Israel." (*Doctrines of Salvation*, 3:252-53.)

An understanding of this mission of Ephraim helps one to understand why the Lord would say that "the rebellious are not of the blood of Ephraim" (D&C 64:36).

# "May the Kingdom of God Go Forth, That the Kingdom of Heaven May Come"

Section 65

## Historical Background

"At Hiram, several important conferences were held. There thirteen Revelations were received, including the memorable vision recorded in Section 76. There a mob, excited by the agitation of Ezra Booth, who had denied the faith and become an enemy, tried to take the life of the Prophet and Sidney Rigdon. No doubt, this Revelation came to strengthen them for the work and experiences before them." (Smith and Sjodahl, Commentary, p. 397.)

The Prophet Joseph Smith indicated that this section is a prayer. He said, "In the fore part of October, I received the following prayer [D&C 65] through revelation" (*History of the Church*, 1:218).

## Notes and Commentary

### D&C 65:1-6. Setting Up the Kingdom of God

The Prophet Joseph Smith explained his own role in the establishment of the kingdom of God:

"The ancient prophets declared that in the last days the God of heaven should set up a kingdom which should never be destroyed, nor left to other people; and the very time that was calculated on, this people were struggling to bring it out. . . .

"I calculate to be one of the instruments of setting up the kingdom of Daniel by the word of the Lord, and I intend to lay a foundation that will revolutionize the whole world. . . . It will not be by sword or gun that this kingdom will roll on: the power of truth is such that all nations will be under the necessity of obeying the Gospel." (*History of the Church*, 6:364-65.)

### D&C 65:2. What Is the Relationship between the "Kingdom of God" and the Stone Cut without Hands?

Elder Harold B. Lee discussed the relationship of the kingdom of God to the stone that Nebuchadnezzar saw in his dream (see Daniel 2:44-45).

"We might then ask, what is the kingdom of God? And again we are not left without an answer, for the Lord replied, 'The keys of the kingdom of God are committed unto man on the earth. . . .' Where there are the keys to the kingdom, there is the Church of Jesus Christ, and it is the stone which was cut out of the mountain without hands, as told in Daniel's interpretation of the dream, which was to roll forth and smite the image and break it in pieces and to roll on until it should fill the whole earth. (D. & C. 65.)

"The Prophet Joseph Smith makes this definition of the kingdom of God:

" 'Some say that the kingdom of God was not set up upon the earth until the day of Pentecost, and that John did not preach the baptism of repentance for the remission of sins, but I say to you in the name of the Lord that the kingdom of God was set up upon the earth in the days of Adam to the present time. Whenever there has been a righteous man on the earth, unto whom God revealed His word and gave power and authority to administer in His name, and where there is a priest of God . . . to administer in the ordinances of the gospel, and officiate in the priesthood of God, there is the kingdom of God. . . . Where there is a prophet, a priest, or a righteous man unto whom God gives His oracles, there is the kingdom of God; and where the oracles of God are not, there the kingdom of God is not.' (*Teachings of the Prophet Joseph Smith*, pp. 271-272).

"This is but another way of saying . . . 'Where the kingdom of God is not there is nothing.' " (In Conference Report, Oct. 1953, p. 26.)

### D&C 65:6. The Kingdom of God and the Kingdom of Heaven

Elder James E. Talmage explained the difference between these two terms:"The expression 'Kingdom of God' is used synonomously with the term 'Church of Christ'; but the Lord had made plain that He sometimes used the term 'Kingdom of Heaven' in a distinctive sense. In 1832 He called attention to that in these words, addressing Himself to the elders of the Church: [D&C 65:1-6].

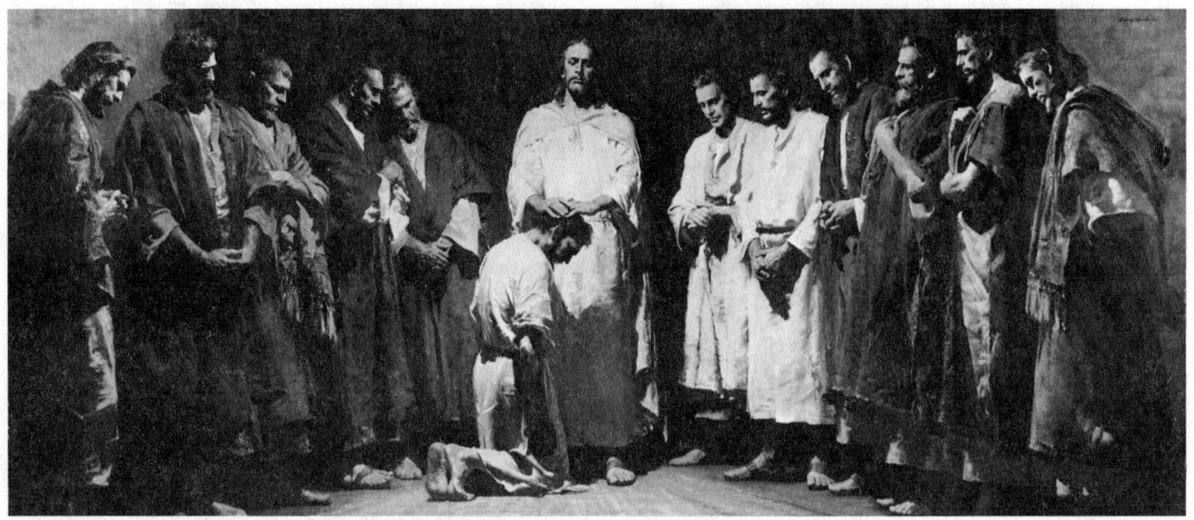

*As Christ gave power to bear off the kingdom in his day, so has he given the same power in this day*

"Such was the prayer, such is the prayer, prescribed for this people to pray, not to utter in words only, not to say only, but to pray—that the Kingdom of God may roll forth in the earth to prepare the earth for the coming of the Kingdom of Heaven. That provision in the Lord's prayer, 'Thy kingdom come, thy will be done on earth as it is in heaven' has not been abrogated. We are praying for the Kingdom of Heaven to come, and are endeavoring to prepare the earth for its coming. The Kingdom of God, already set up upon the earth, does not aspire to temporal domination among the nations. It seeks not to overthrow any existing forms of government; it does not profess to exercise control in matters that pertain to the governments of the earth, except by teaching correct principles and trying to get men to live according to the principles of true government, before the Kingdom of Heaven shall come and be established upon the earth with a King at the head. But when He comes, He shall rule and reign, for it is His right." (In Conference Report, Apr. 1916, pp. 128-29.)

# "You Are Clean, but Not All" Section 66

## Historical Background

During October 1831 a series of conferences was held in Ohio by the Prophet Joseph Smith. On the eleventh a conference was held at Hiram at the home of John Johnson where instructions were given concerning "the ancient manner of conducting meetings." On the twenty-first a conference was held at Kirtland, where a dispute had arisen that the Prophet was asked to settle. On the twenty-fifth, at Orange, a conference convened with "twelve High Priests, seventeen Elders, four Priests, three Teachers, and four Deacons," as well as a large congregation. (*History of the Church,* 1:219.) At this conference William E. M'Lellin requested to know the will of the Lord concerning him. The Prophet inquired of the Lord and received Doctrine and Covenants 66.

## Notes and Commentary

**D&C 66:1-13. What Was the Spiritual Condition of William E. M'Lellin When This Revelation Was Given?**

Though he later apostatized, at this time William E. M'Lellin was in good fellowship in the Church, though verses 3 and 10 suggest he did have some problems.

President Joseph Fielding Smith, speaking of Brother M'Lellin, said that "through his repentance and the sincere desire to do right, the Lord declared that he was clean, 'but not all.' There had come to him forgiveness, but still there lingered in some manner, evidently in his mind and thoughts, some thing from which he had not cleansed himself by full repentance. The Lord read his soul. He was commanded to go forth and preach the Gospel 'from land to land, and from city to city in the regions round about where it has not been proclaimed.' He was instructed not to go up to the land of Zion at that time, and he was to think more of the work of the Lord than of his property. In his preaching he was to have as a companion Samuel H. Smith, brother of the Prophet. This was a wonderful revelation to William E. M'Lellin and should have been a great blessing and incentive to him to remain faithful. One besetting sin, so the Lord revealed, was the temptation of sexual sin. He was not accused of committing such a sin, but the dangers, because of his failings, which lay in this direction." (*Church History and Modern Revelation,* 1:244-45.)

**D&C 66:10. How Cumbersome Is Sexual Sin?**

Speaking of the relationship of unclean thoughts and immorality, Elder Spencer W. Kimball said:

"To want, to desire, to crave—that is to lust. So when the thought is born which starts a chain reaction, a sin has already been committed. If the thought is sown, then develops into lust, it is almost certain to bring eventually the full harvest of the act of the heinous sin, adultery. . . .

" . . . adultery is not the result of a single thought. There first is a deterioration of thinking. Many sinful chain-thoughts have been coursing through the offender's mind before the physical sin is committed.

"Yes, as a man thinketh, so *does* he. If he thinks it long enough he is likely to do it, whether it be theft, moral sin, or suicide. Thus the time to protect against the calamity is when the thought begins to shape itself. Destroy the seed and the plant will never grow.

"Man alone, of all creatures of earth, can change his thought pattern and become the architect of his destiny." (*Miracle of Forgiveness,* pp. 113-14.)

*The seed is the thought; the plant is the deed*

# I Give You a Testimony of the Truth of These Commandments

Section 67

## Historical Background

In July 1831 William W. Phelps was charged with setting up a printing business in Jackson County so that Church literature could be published, and Oliver Cowdery was assigned to assist him (see D&C 57:11-14). W. W. Phelps was to go ahead, and Oliver was to raise the money for the press and join him later. Because of the danger of traveling on the western frontier alone, John Whitmer was commanded to accompany Oliver to help safeguard the money and the manuscript copies of the revelations (see D&C 69:1-2).

"When Oliver Cowdery and John Whitmer were ready to start for Jackson County, Missouri, the Prophet decided that a conference of elders should convene at the Johnson home in Hiram to consider matters of importance pertaining to the duties assigned them. Foremost on his agenda was the publication of the revelations he had been preparing and arranging for publication for over a year.

"On the first day of the conference, November 1, 1831, the Lord approved the publication of the revelations by giving what is commonly referred to as the Lord's own preface to the Book of Commandments. (D&C 1.) Its purpose was to serve as an introduction to the contents of the entire book. In this revelation the Lord proclaimed to the whole world his message of repentance and the fact that through his servant Joseph Smith, Jr., the gospel for the salvation of mankind was restored. 'Wherefore the voice of the Lord is unto the ends of the earth, that all that will hear may hear: Search these commandments, for they are true and faithful, and the prophecies and promises which are in them shall all be fulfilled.' (D&C 1:11, 37.)

"At the conference the elders decided that ten thousand copies of the sixty-five revelations should be printed under the title, 'Book of Commandments.' Oliver Cowdery read the Lord's

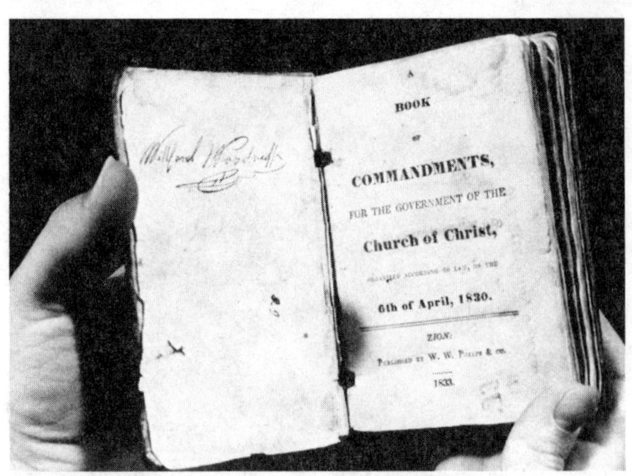


*An original copy of the Book of Commandments*

preface, and several brethren arose and bore witness to its truth and the truth of all the revelations received by the Prophet. The Prophet expressed his deep gratitude for the Lord's commandments. He entertained no doubts concerning the divine inspiration of the revelation he received for the guidance of the Church. . . .

"Not all those present at the conference fully approved the revelations. One at least, questioned the language of them: William E. McLellin. The challenge was answered in a revelation: [D&C 67:5-8].

"McLellin, who, in the words of the Prophet, had 'more learning than sense, endeavored to write a commandment like unto one of the least of the Lord's.' [*History of the Church,* 1:226.] McLellin had taught school rather successfully in five states of the Union and had acquired considerable learning. His attempt to write a revelation was a miserable failure. Joseph Smith said: '. . . It was an awful responsibility to write in the name of the Lord. The Elders and all present that witnessed this vain attempt of a man to imitate the language of Jesus Christ, renewed their faith in the fulness of the Gospel, and in the truth of the commandments and revelations which the Lord had given to the Church through my instrumentality. . . .' [*History of the Church,* 1:226]

"After the conference adjourned, Joseph arranged the revelations, and Oliver Cowdery and John Whitmer carried them to Independence for William W. Phelps to print." (Barrett, *Joseph Smith,* pp. 200-02.)

# Notes and Commentary

### D&C 67:3, 14. What Blessing Was Not Received?

Smith and Sjodahl discussed the missed blessing: "The assembled Elders, or some of them, failed to receive a blessing which they had expected. What that blessing was is not stated. It might have been a special manifestation concerning the *Book of Commandments* (v. 4); or, some miraculous manifestation after the laying on of hands by the Prophet (v. 14). But whatever it was, some had failed to receive what they expected, and the reason is here stated: they lacked faith, and were consequently, dominated by fear." (Commentary, p. 405.)

### D&C 67:5-8. Challenge from the Lord

Some of the elders at this time questioned the language of the revelations. They were looking at misspellings, errors in grammar, and other peculiarities which they thought signaled these writings to be the product of Joseph Smith. They reasoned that if these revelations were really from the Lord no such mistakes or peculiarities would be found. Thus came the challenge to them from the Lord to write a revelation. Elder Orson F. Whitney stated:

"Well, one of them, who thought himself the wisest, and who possessed some learning, took up the challenge and actually attempted to frame a revelation; but it was a flat failure. He could utter, of course, certain words, and roll out a mass of rhetoric; but the divine spirit was lacking, and he had to acknowledge himself beaten.

"It is not so easy to put the spirit of life into things. Man can make the body, but God alone can create the spirit." (In Conference Report, Apr. 1917, p. 42.)

### D&C 67:5. What Was the Book of Commandments?

The Book of Commandments was the original title for the collection of revelations that was to be published. When the press and most of the copies were destroyed by a mob in Jackson County, the Prophet decided to add additional revelations that had been received in the meantime. The expanded edition was called the Book of Doctrine and Covenants. (See the introduction to this manual.)

### D&C 67:9. What Is the Significance of the Term *Father of Lights*?

Of this expression, also found in James 1:17, Elder Bruce R. McConkie wrote:" 'God is light, and in him is no darkness at all.' (1 John 1:5.) That is, he is the embodiment, author, and source of light, or in other words the *Father of Lights.* (Jas. 1:17.)" (*Mormon Doctrine,* p. 278.)

### D&C 67:10-13. "You Shall See Me and Know That I Am"

One remarkable truth of the restored gospel is that the heavens are not sealed, that God still speaks to men and reveals his will to them. And one amazing aspect of that knowledge is that God will actually reveal himself to men who meet certain prerequisites. The scriptures record that many ancient prophets saw God, and the present dispensation was opened by a vision in which God and Christ appeared to Joseph Smith in the Sacred Grove. But several places in the Doctrine and Covenants, including section 67, clearly teach that this astounding privilege is not reserved for prophets alone but for any man willing to pay the price required in personal righteousness (see D&C 50:45-46; 88:68-69; 93:1; 130:3). The Prophet Joseph Smith taught that "after a person has faith in Christ, repents of his sins, and is baptized for the remission of his sins and receives the Holy Ghost, (by the laying on of hands), which is the first Comforter, then let him continue to humble himself before God, hungering and thirsting after righteousness, and living by every word of God, and the Lord will soon say unto him, Son, thou shalt be exalted. When the Lord has thoroughly proved him, and finds that the man is determined to serve Him at all hazards, then the man will find his calling and his election made sure, then it will be his privilege to receive the other Comforter, which the Lord hath promised the Saints, as is recorded in the testimony of St. John, in the 14th chapter, from the 12th to the 27th verses. . . .

"Now what is this other Comforter? It is no more nor less than the Lord Jesus Christ Himself; and this is the sum and substance of the whole matter; that when any man obtains this last Comforter, he will have the personage of Jesus Christ to attend him, or appear unto him from time to time, and even He will manifest the Father unto him, and they will take up their abode with him, and the visions of the heavens will be opened unto him, and the Lord will teach him face to face, and he may have a perfect knowledge of the mysteries of the Kingdom of God; and this is the state and place the ancient Saints arrived at when they had such glorious visions—Isaiah, Ezekiel, John upon the Isle of Patmos, St. Paul in the three heavens, and all the Saints who held communion with the general assembly and Church of the Firstborn." (*Teachings,* pp. 150-51.)

Such a privilege does not come easily. A high level of righteousness and commitment must be demonstrated in the life of an individual before God will appear to him, and yet step by step a person can reach that degree. The Prophet Joseph Smith taught how this growth can occur:"We consider that God has created man with a mind capable of instruction, and a faculty which may be enlarged in proportion to the heed and diligence given to the light communicated from heaven to the intellect; and that the nearer man approaches perfection, the clearer are his views, and the greater his enjoyments, till he has overcome the evils of his life and lost every desire for sin; and like the ancients, arrives at that point of faith where he is wrapped in the power and glory of his Maker and is caught up to dwell with Him. But we consider that this is a station to which no man ever arrived in a moment: he must have been instructed in the government and laws of that kingdom by proper degrees, until his mind is capable in some measure of comprehending the propriety, justice, equality, and consistency of the same." (*Teachings,* p. 51.)

### D&C 67:10, 12. What Is the Natural, or Carnal, Mind?

Ludlow explained that "a thing is natural if it is in the same essential condition as the things around it. At the present time the earth is temporarily in a telestial mortal condition, and generally speaking the people who are living on the earth are carnal, sensual, and devilish. Thus, all of these terms could be used as synonyms for *natural.* In [D&C] 29:35 we read that the commandments of God 'are not natural nor temporal, neither carnal nor sensual,' and [D&C] 67:10 indicates that man cannot see God 'with the carnal neither natural mind, but with the spiritual.' In this life, natural could be considered almost as an opposite or antonym of spiritual." (*Companion,* 2:187.)

# Scripture Is the Will, Mind, Word, Voice, and Power of God unto Salvation

Section 68

## Historical Background

President Joseph Fielding Smith explained the circumstances that brought section 68 as a revelation: "At the close of the conference of November 1-12, 1831, Elders Orson Hyde, Luke Johnson, Lyman E. Johnson and William E. M'Lellin, came to the Prophet and sought the will of the Lord concerning themselves, and their ministry. The Prophet made inquiry and received the revelation which appears as Section sixty-eight. Surely the Lord in his wisdom poured out knowledge, line upon line, precept upon precept as the members of the Church were prepared to receive it." (*Church History and Modern Revelation,* 1:257-58.)

## Notes and Commentary

### D&C 68:1. The Call of Orson Hyde Had Far-reaching Consequences

"The prophecy in this verse was literally fulfilled. Orson Hyde proclaimed the gospel 'from people to people, from land to land.' In 1832, he and Samuel H. Smith traveled in the States of New York, Massachusetts, Maine, and Rhode Island—two thousand miles—on foot. In 1835 he was ordained an Apostle, and in 1837 he went on a mission to England. In 1840 he was sent on a mission to Jerusalem. He crossed the Ocean, traveled through England and Germany, visited Constantinople, Cairo, and Alexandria, and, finally, reached the Holy City. On October 24th, 1841, he went up on the Mount of Olives and offered a prayer,

*Orson Hyde dedicated the land of Jerusalem for the return of the Jews*

dedicating Palestine for the gathering of the Jews." (Smith and Sjodahl, Commentary, p. 409.)

**D&C 68:3-5. What Is Scripture?**

Scripture is the mind and will of God revealed through his servants. Peter declared, "Prophecy came not in old time by the will of man: but holy men of God spake as they were moved by the Holy Ghost" (2 Peter 1:21). Such scripture has been written and preserved in the standard works as priceless gems of eternal truth. The standard works are not the only source of scripture, however, for, as President Joseph Fielding Smith taught, "when one of the brethren stands before a congregation of the people today, and the inspiration of the Lord is upon him, he speaks that which the Lord would have him speak. It is just as much scripture as anything you will find written in any of these records, and yet we call these the standard works of the Church. We depend, of course, upon the guidance of the brethren who are entitled to inspiration.

"There is only one man in the Church at a time who has the right to give revelation for the Church, and that is the President of the Church. But that does not bar any other member in this Church from speaking the word of the Lord, as indicated here in this revelation, section 68, but a revelation that is to be given as these revelations are given in this book, to the Church, will come through the presiding officer of the Church; yet, the word of the Lord, as spoken by other servants at the general conferences and stake conferences, or wherever they may be when they speak that which the Lord has put into their mouths, is just as much the word of the Lord as the writings and the words of other prophets in other dispensations." (*Doctrines of Salvation,* 1:186.)

Elder Harold B. Lee further defined scripture when he said: "It is not to be thought that every word spoken by the General Authorities is inspired, or that they are moved upon by the Holy Ghost in everything they read and write. Now you keep that in mind. I don't care what his position is, if he writes something or speaks something that goes beyond anything that you can find in the standard church works, unless that one be the prophet, seer, and revelator—*please note that one exception*—you may immediately say, 'Well, that is his own idea.' And if he says something that contradicts what is found in the standard church works (I think that is why we call them 'standard'—it is the standard measure of all that men teach), you may know by that same token that it is false, regardless of the position of the man who says it." (*The Place of the Living Prophet, Seer, and Revelator* [address delivered to seminary and institute of religion faculty, 8 July 1964], p. 14.)

President J. Reuben Clark, Jr., dealt with the most important question:

"How shall we know when the things they have spoken were said as they were 'moved upon by the Holy Ghost?'

"I have given some thought to this question, and the answer thereto so far as I can determine, is: We can tell when the speakers are 'moved upon by the Holy Ghost' only when we, ourselves, are 'moved upon by the Holy Ghost.'

"In a way, this completely shifts the responsibility from them to us to determine when they so speak." (*When Are the Writings or Sermons of Church Leaders Entitled to the Claim of Scripture?* [address delivered to seminary and institute of religion personnel, 7 July 1954], p. 7.)

**D&C 68:10. Signs Follow Faithful Believers**

People often desire to see a sign or hear a voice from the unseen world. This desire may be manifest in some members of the Church at some stage of their spiritual development. A few honestly believe that such an experience would greatly strengthen their testimony or convince nonbelievers of the truth of the gospel of Jesus Christ. People who possess such a notion should remember that signs are not usually given before faith is shown, for such desires and manifestations are a detriment to the development of true faith and are the symptoms of wickedness (see Matthew 12:39; Notes and Commentary on D&C 63:7-12). The truth of the matter is that signs are the natural offspring of faith and serve as the sweet confirmation of righteousness. Signs follow faith, and without faith, which links man with the source of power, no miracle can occur (see Mark 16:17; Ether 12:12). Indeed, the outward manifestation of God's power is itself an assurance that the faith and righteousness of the party involved have received divine sanction.

**D&C 68:15-21. Under What Conditions Can a Literal Descendant of Aaron Be a Bishop without Counselors?**

President Joseph Fielding Smith pointed out that this provision applied only to the office of Presiding Bishop of the Church: "It has no reference whatever to bishops of wards. Further, such a one must be designated by the First Presidency of the Church and receive his anointing and ordination under their hands. The revelation comes from the Presidency, not from the patriarch, to establish a claim to the right to preside in this office. In the absence of knowledge concerning such a descendant, any high priest, chosen by the Presidency, may hold the office of Presiding Bishop and serve with counselors." (*Doctrines of Salvation,* 3:92.)

"The office of Presiding Bishop of the Church is the same as the office which was held by Aaron. . . . It was this office which came to John the Baptist, and it was by virtue of the fact that he held the keys of this power and ministry that he was sent to Joseph Smith and Oliver Cowdery to restore that Priesthood, May 15, 1829. The person who has the legal right to this presiding office has not been discovered; perhaps is not in the Church, but should it be shown by revelation that there is one who is the 'firstborn among the sons of Aaron,' and thus entitled by birthright to this presidency, he could 'claim' his 'anointing' and the right to that office in the Church." (Smith, *Church History and Modern Revelation,* 1:259.)

### D&C 68:22-24. Are Bishops Found in Transgression to Be Tried by the First Presidency?

"In case of the transgression of the presiding bishop of the Church, he could not be tried by a high council in the stake in which he lives, but he would have to be tried by the First Presidency of the Church. The reason for this is that he . . . is not under the jurisdiction of any ward or stake in this capacity. This order given for the trial of the presiding bishop does not apply to a local bishop in a ward, who is under the jurisdiction of the presidency of the stake." (Smith, *Church History and Modern Revelation,* 1:259-60.)

### D&C 68:25-26, 31. Parents Are to Teach the Gospel to Their Children

Elder Harold B. Lee pointed out that the Lord "gave us what we might style as a five-point program by which parents could teach faith. First, he said, their children were to be baptized when they had reached the age of accountability at eight years; second, they were to be taught to pray; third, they were to be taught to walk uprightly before the Lord; fourth, they were to be taught to keep the Sabbath day holy; and fifth, they were to be schooled not to be idle, either in the Church, or in their private lives.

"All parents who have followed that formula and have so taught their children have reaped the reward of an increased faith in their family, which has stood and will yet stand the test of the difficulties into which their children would yet go." (In Conference Report, Oct. 1952, p. 17.)

In connection with the responsibility parents have in teaching their children, President N. Eldon Tanner identified an interesting by-product that benefits the parents:"Children who are taught obedience, to honor and obey the law, to have faith in God and to keep his commandments, will, as

*Parents are to teach the gospel to their children*

they grow up, honor their parents and be a credit to them; and they will be able to meet and solve their problems, find greater success and joy in life, and contribute greatly to the solution of the problems now causing the world such great concern. It is up to the parents to see to it that their children are prepared through obedience to law for the positions of leadership they will occupy in the future, where their responsibility will be to bring peace and righteousness to the world." (In Conference Report, Apr. 1970, p. 65.)

There are instances in which the righteous endeavors of parents are met with the rebelliousness of a child. There is reason for hope, however, in the case of parents who do not cease trying with their children who are unresponsive to their teaching. President Spencer W. Kimball made this observation and promise:

"I have sometimes seen children of good families rebel, resist, stray, sin, and even actually fight God. In this they bring sorrow to their parents, who have done their best to set in movement a current and to teach and live as examples. But I have repeatedly seen many of these same children, after years of wandering, mellow, realize what they have been missing, repent, and make great contribution to the spiritual life of their community. The reason I believe this can take place is that, despite all the adverse winds to which these people have been subjected, they have been influenced still more, and much more than they realized, by the current of life in the homes in which they were reared. When, in later years, they feel a longing to recreate in their own families the same atmosphere they enjoyed as children, they are likely to turn to the faith that gave meaning to their parents' lives.

"There is no guarantee, of course, that righteous

parents will succeed always in holding their children, and certainly they may lose them if they do not do all in their power. The children have their free agency.

"But if we as parents fail to influence our families and set them on the 'strait and narrow way,' then certainly the waves, the winds of temptation and evil will carry the posterity away from the path.

" 'Train up a child in the way he should go; and when he is old, he will not depart from it.' (Prov. 22:6.) What we do know is that righteous parents who strive to develop wholesome influences for their children will be held blameless at the last day, and that they will succeed in saving most of their children, if not all." (In Conference Report, Oct. 1974, p. 160; or *Ensign,* Nov. 1974, pp. 111-12.)

### D&C 68:27. Accountability of Children

See Notes and Commentary on Doctrine and Covenants 29:46-50.

### D&C 68:29. Observance of the Sabbath Day

See Notes and Commentary on Doctrine and Covenants 59:9-13.

### D&C 68:30. The Value and the Place of the Laborer

A human weakness that draws sharp rebuke from the Lord is that of an idler who lives upon the labor of others (see D&C 42:42; 56:17; 60:13; 75:29). One way in which the problem of idleness is spreading through society today is by a vast government welfare system that doles out money or products without requiring any labor in return. Elder David B. Haight warned against this evil:

"What has this monstrous thing called government welfare done to the people? Today we have second- and third-generation welfare recipients. Millions have learned how to live off the government. Children are growing up without knowing the value and the dignity of work. The government has succeeded in doing what the Church welfare program seeks to prevent. . . .

"But Church members are not immune to the perils of the government dole. There is evidence that some of our people are receiving something for nothing from the government. The fact that this condition exists in the Church highlights the need of our members to be knowledgeable about Church welfare principles. President Kimball has stated: 'No true Latter-day Saint, while physically or emotionally able, will voluntarily shift the burden of his own or his family's well-being to someone else' (*Ensign,* May 1978, p. 79)." (In Conference Report, Oct. 1978, p. 86; or *Ensign,* Nov. 1978, p. 86.)

The Lord's welfare program reenthrones the principle of work and self-respect, requiring labor according to ability.

### D&C 68:33. "Prayers . . . in the Season Thereof"

President Ezra Taft Benson spoke of the value of prayer, especially for youth, and said: "I counsel you, in the words of Jesus Christ, to 'watch and pray always lest ye enter into temptation; for Satan desireth to have you, that he may sift you as wheat.' (3 Ne. 18:18.)

"If you will earnestly seek guidance from your Heavenly Father, morning and evening, you will be given the strength to shun any temptation. President Heber J. Grant gave this timeless promise to the youth of the Church:

" 'I have little or no fear for the boy or the girl, the young man or the young woman, who *honestly and conscientiously supplicate God twice a day for the guidance of His Spirit.* I am sure that when temptation comes they will have the strength to overcome it by the inspiration that shall be given to them. Supplicating the Lord for the guidance of His Spirit places around us a safeguard, and if we earnestly and honestly seek the guidance of the Spirit of the Lord, I can assure you that we will receive it.' (*Gospel Standards,* Salt Lake City: The Improvement Era, 1969, p. 26; italics added.)" (In Conference Report, Oct. 1977, p. 46; or *Ensign,* Nov. 1977, p. 32.)

### D&C 68:33. "The Judge of My People"

"The common judge in Israel is the ward bishop. It is his duty to watch over his flock. To aid him he has the force of the Aaronic Priesthood and all of the brethren holding the Melchizedek Priesthood who are at liberty and who may be called to serve as acting teachers and priests in his ward." (Smith, *Church History and Modern Revelation,* 1:261.)

# Instructions to Preserve Historical Records

Section 69

## Historical Background

Joseph Smith received this revelation during the month of November 1831 while staying at Hiram, Ohio. According to President Joseph Fielding Smith, "following the November conference the Prophet hastened to get the revelations arranged and in readiness by the time Oliver Cowdery was to leave [for Missouri], which was to be on or before the fifteenth day of November. The Prophet writes that at this time there were many things which the elders desired to know relative to preaching the Gospel to the inhabitants of the earth, and concerning the gathering and in compliance with their wish on the 3rd of November, the day after the conference closed, he inquired of the Lord and received the revelation which was also ordered printed with the commandments, but having been considered after the conference, it was to be placed in the volume as part of an appendix. This revelation is known as Section 133. . . .

"It is an erroneous thought to believe that the Prophet selected all of the revelations he had received and placed them in the collection which was to become The Book of Commandments. Each of the revelations selected for that volume was placed there because the Prophet considered that it had some value to the Church in regard to its teachings. There are some revelations still in possession of the Church which were not included. Some of these we can readily believe were not included because the inspiration of the Prophet was that it was not necessary, or because some of them had an application which was not intended for publication and to be sent to an unbelieving world.

"The preparation for the printing was soon completed, but this took a great deal of the Prophet's time from the first of November to the twelfth, and in that time there had been held four special conferences. However, the revelations were ready for delivery to Oliver Cowdery and his companion by the fifteenth of that month." (*Church History and Modern Revelation,* 1:248-49.)

Concerning these events and the reception of this revelation, the Prophet Joseph Smith stated, "the Book of Commandments and Revelations was to be dedicated by prayer to the service of Almighty God by me; and after I had done this, I inquired of the Lord concerning these things, and received the following: [D&C 69]" (*History of the Church,* 1:234).

## Notes and Commentary

### D&C 69:1-2. Why was John Whitmer Assigned to Travel with Oliver Cowdery to Missouri?

Some enemies of the Church have tried to use this scripture as proof that Oliver was not trustworthy, but Elder B. H. Roberts explained the situation as follows: "The fact was that much of the journey between Kirtland and Independence, or Zion, was through a sparsely settled country, the western portion of it through a frontier country where there is always a gathering, more or less, of lawless people; and it was at considerable risk that a person traveled through such a country, especially when alone and carrying money with him. It was wisdom then, for the sake of Oliver Cowdery, and to insure the safety of the money and the sacred things he was to carry with him, that one should go with him that would be a true and faithful companion, hence the appointment of John Whitmer." (*Comprehensive History,* 1:268n.)

### D&C 69:3-8. John Whitmer, Church Historian

President Joseph Fielding Smith, who was the Church historian for many years, commented upon the responsibility that rested on John Whitmer: "He was to observe and make a record of all the important things which he should observe and know concerning the Church. John Whitmer was also to receive counsel from Oliver Cowdery and others. The word was also declared that the accounts of the stewards were also to be carried up to Zion, 'For,' said the Lord, 'the land of Zion shall be a seat and a place to receive and do all these things.' John Whitmer was also appointed to travel 'many times from place to place, and from church to church, that he may the more easily obtain knowledge.' " (*Church History and Modern Revelation,* 1:249.)

For further information on John Whitmer, see Doctrine and Covenants 15, 26, 30, and 47.

### D&C 69:8. Of What Benefit Are Church Records to Future Generations?

Elder Orson Pratt wrote in 1849: "If every elder had, during the last nineteen years kept a faithful record of all that he had seen, heard, and felt of the goodness, wisdom and power of God, the Church would now have been in possession of many thousand volumes, containing much important and useful information. How many thousands have been miraculously healed in this Church, and yet no one has recorded the circumstances. Is this right? Should these miraculous manifestations of the power of God be forgotten and pass into oblivion? Should the knowledge of these things slumber in the hearts of those who witnessed them? . . . We should keep a record because Jesus has commanded it. We should keep a record because the same will benefit us and the generations of our children after us. We should keep a record because it will furnish many important items for the general history of the

Church which would otherwise be lost." (*Millennial Star,* 15 May 1849, p. 152.)

When one considers the events that still lie in the future, events of great magnitude and importance, one can better see why the Saints are continually encouraged to keep personal histories and journals. The return to Jackson County, the building there of the temple, the return of the ten tribes from the north countries, the council at Adam-ondi-Ahman, the establishment of the kingdom of God, the battle of Armageddon, the return of Christ in glory—think how future generations will treasure firsthand accounts written by Saints who witness these events. President Spencer W. Kimball gave the following suggestions on how to keep a valuable journal:

"Your own private journal should record the way you face up to challenges that beset you. Do not suppose life changes so much that your experiences will not be interesting to your posterity. Experiences of work, relations with people, and an awareness of the rightness and wrongness of actions will always be relevant. . . .

*Keeping journals is a latter-day imperative*

"Your own journal, like most others, will tell of problems as old as the world and how you dealt with them.

"Your journal should contain your true self rather than a picture of you when you are 'made up' for a public performance. There is a temptation to paint one's virtues in rich color and whitewash the vices, but there is also the opposite pitfall of accentuating the negative. Personally I have little respect for anyone who delves into the ugly phases of the life he is portraying, whether it be his own or another's. The truth should be told, but we should not emphasize the negative. Even a long life full of inspiring experiences can be brought to the dust by one ugly story. Why dwell on that one ugly truth about someone whose life has been largely circumspect?

"The good biographer will not depend on passion but on good sense. He will weed out the irrelevant and seek the strong, novel, and interesting. . . .

"Your journal is your autobiography, so it should be kept carefully. You are unique, and there may be incidents in your experience that are more noble and praiseworthy in their way than those recorded in any other life. There may be a flash of illumination here and a story of faithfulness there; you should truthfully record your real self and not what other people may see in you.

"Your story should be written now while it is fresh and while the true details are available.

"A journal is the literature of superiority. Each individual can become superior in his own humble life.

"What could you do better for your children and your children's children than to record the story of your life, your triumphs over adversity, your recovery after a fall, your progress when all seemed black, your rejoicing when you had finally achieved?

"Some of what you write may be humdrum dates and places, but there will also be rich passages that will be quoted by your posterity.

"Get a notebook, my young folks, a journal that will last through all time, and maybe the angels may quote from it for eternity. Begin today and write in it your goings and comings, your deepest thoughts, your achievements and your failures, your associations and your triumphs, your impressions and your testimonies. Remember, the Savior chastised those who failed to record important events." ("The Angels May Quote from It," *New Era,* Oct. 1975, pp. 4-5.)

# The Lord's Stewards

Section 70

## Historical Background

At one of the four conferences of the Church held in Hiram, Ohio, from 1 to 12 November 1832, the brethren testified that the revelations were from God and should be published for the world. The Lord confirmed his approval of their actions by giving the preface (now D&C 1) and the appendix (now D&C 133) to the collection of revelations that were to be published, which would be called the Book of Commandments.

Efforts began toward accomplishing this objective. W. W. Phelps obtained a printing press and type, which were set up at Independence, Missouri. Oliver Cowdery and John Whitmer were commissioned to carry the manuscripts of some of the revelations from Ohio to Missouri for printing. In addition to these preparations, the Lord revealed to Joseph Smith, certain men were to have a special commission in publishing the revelations. They were to be "stewards" over the revelations, using proceeds from the sale of the Book of Commandments for their temporal needs and giving an account of their stewardship.

## Notes and Commentary

### D&C 70:3. What Does It Mean to Be a Steward?

Stewardship is not ownership. Stewardship is management with a responsibility to account to the owner or master. The basic principle was taught by the Lord when he said: "I, the Lord, stretched out the heavens, and built the earth, my very handiwork; and all things therein are mine. . . . Behold, all these properties are mine, . . . and if the properties are mine, then ye are stewards; otherwise ye are no stewards." (D&C 104:14, 55-56.)

### D&C 70:5-7. Stewardships Involve Both Spiritual and Temporal Needs

The brethren who were given the stewardship of the revelations to be published were to receive their livelihood from the proceeds. The law of consecration (see D&C 42) included temporal needs as well as spiritual needs.

Elder James E. Talmage spoke of the spiritual side of the law of consecration when he said:

"A system of unity in temporal matters has been revealed to the Church in this day; such is currently known as the Order of Enoch, or the United Order, and is founded on the law of consecration. As already stated, in the early days of the latter-day Church the people demonstrated their inability to abide this law in its fulness, and, in consequence, the lesser law of tithing was given; but the saints confidently await the day in which

*The spirit of unity is essential to the law of consecration*

they will devote not merely a tithe of their substance but all that they have and all that they are, to the service of their God; a day in which no man will speak of mine and thine, but all things shall be the Lord's and theirs.

"In this expectation they indulge no vague dream of communism, encouraging individual irresponsibility and giving the idler an excuse for hoping to live at the expense of the thrifty; but rather, a calm trust that in the promised social order, such as God can approve, every man will be a steward in the full enjoyment of liberty to do as he will with the talents committed to his care; but with the sure knowledge that an account of his stewardship shall be required at his hands." (*Articles of Faith*, pp. 439-40.)

### D&C 70:7-9. What Was the Surplus That Was to Go to the Lord's Storehouse?

President J. Reuben Clark, Jr., explained that "whatever a steward realized from the portion allotted to him over and above that which was necessary in order to keep his family under the standard provided . . . was turned over by the steward to the bishop, and this amount of surplus, plus the residues . . . , went into a bishop's storehouse (D. & C. 51:13 . . . ), and the materials of the storehouse were to be used in creating portions . . . for caring for the poor (D. & C. 78:3), the widows and orphans (D. & C. 83:6), and for the elders of the Church engaged in the ministry, who were to pay for what they received if they could, but if not, their faithful labors should answer their debt to the bishop. (D. & C. 72:11 ff).'' (In Conference Report, Oct. 1942, p. 56.)

**D&C 70:14. Temporal Equality**

The dictionary defines *equal* as being of the same quantity, size, number, value, degree, or intensity. The Lord, however, does not endorse such a definition in his gospel. President Joseph Fielding Smith explained: "To be equal did not mean that all should have the same amount of food, but each should have according to his needs. For instance, a man would receive in proportion to the number in his family, not according to the nature of his work. He was to have, 'for food and for raiment; for an inheritance; for houses and for lands, in whatsoever circumstances, I the Lord, shall place them, and whithersoever I, the Lord, shall send them [D&C 70:16].' " (*Church History and Modern Revelation,* 1:268-69.)

Notes and Commentary on Doctrine and Covenants 51:3 contains a discussion of the concept of equality.

# "If Any Man Lift His Voice against You"

Section 71

## Historical Background

At the date of this revelation, 1 December 1831, the Saints did not yet have means of publicly defending the Church when it was under attack from critics and apostates. Those who were willing to listen needed to hear viewpoints other than those of the unbelievers.

Ezra Booth, a former Methodist minister who joined the Church when he witnessed a healing, turned apostate and wrote nine letters against the Church. The letters, published in the *Ohio Star* at Ravenna, Ohio, were highly critical, and the Prophet Joseph Smith wrote that they, "by their coloring, falsity, and vain calculations to overthrow the work of the Lord, exposed his [Booth's] weakness, wickedness and folly, and left him a monument of his own shame, for the world to wonder at" (*History of the Church,* 1:217). Booth was not the first to apostatize, but he was the first Church member to write anti-Mormon literature and publish it.

While Satan was organizing the opposition, a Church conference was held 1 November 1831, during which it was decided to print and publish revelations given through Joseph Smith to strengthen and fortify the Saints against the attacks of critics and apostates. Once the arrangements were made for publishing the revelations, Joseph Smith and Sidney Rigdon resumed the work of translating the scripture. Meanwhile, the agitation caused by Ezra Booth had grown so serious that on the first day of December the Lord called Joseph and Sidney from their work of translation to proclaim the gospel to the world in power and demonstration. They left in haste for Kirtland, Ohio. As Smith and Sjodahl observed, "Sometimes it is wise to ignore the attacks of the wicked; at other times it is necessary to meet them, fearlessly and with ability" (Commentary, p. 423; see also *History of the Church,* 1:238-39).

## Notes and Commentary

**D&C 71:1. Expound the Mysteries According to the Spirit**

"The Prophet, by this time, had learned many great and glorious truths, partly by the direct Revelations he had received, and partly by close study of the Scriptures. To the world, many of these truths were 'mysteries.' The time had come to reveal them, and when they were revealed, or unveiled, they would be mysteries no longer. When the gospel of Christ was first preached by Peter, Paul, and the other Apostles of their day, the doctrine of the Incarnation was a mystery (I. Cor. 2:7; I. Tim. 3:16); the doctrine of the resurrection (I. Cor. 15:51), and the gathering of the Gentiles into the Church (Col. 1:26, 27) were mysteries. In our dispensation, the doctrines of the gathering and of the building of temples and the City of Zion are as great mysteries, until they are explained by the Holy Spirit of Promise. The Prophet Joseph and Sidney Rigdon were now to go forth and proclaim these and other truths to the Church and the world, for a season (vv. 2, 3)." (Smith and Sjodahl, Commentary, pp. 422-23.)

"A mystery is a truth that cannot be known except through divine revelation—a sacred secret. . . . In our day such great truths as those pertaining to the restoration of the priesthood, the work for the dead, and the re-establishment of the Church are 'mysteries,' because they could not have been discovered except by revelation." (Smith and Sjodahl, Commentary, p. 141.)

**D&C 71:7-11. The Place of Debate in Preaching the Gospel**

Elder Bruce R. McConkie explained the usual role of debates in the work of the Church as follows: "Except under very unusual circumstances, *debates* play no part in the approved system of presenting

Bruce R. McConkie warned against useless debate

the message of salvation to the world or of persuading members of the Church to accept a particular doctrine or view. Almost always a debate entrenches each contestant and his sympathizers more firmly in the views already held." (*Mormon Doctrine,* p. 186.)

In the commotion that followed the publication of Ezra Booth's anti-Mormon letters, the Lord commanded the elders of the Church, not to debate, but to directly refute the falsehoods and lies that had been published.

President Joseph Fielding Smith detailed the approach used by those who received this revelation: "Quite generally the Lord counsels his servants not to engage in debates and arguments, but to preach in power the fundamental principles of the Gospel. This was a condition that required some action of this kind, and the Spirit of the Lord directed these brethren to go forth and confound their enemies which they proceeded immediately to do, as their enemies were unable to substantiate their falsehoods and were surprised by this sudden challenge so boldly given. Much of the prejudice was allayed and some friends made through this action." (*Church History and Modern Revelation,* 1:269.)

### D&C 71:10. "If Any Man Lift His Voice against You"

President Harold B. Lee explained that what the Lord "is trying to have us understand is that he will take care of our enemies if we continue to keep the commandments. So, you Saints of the Most High God, when these things come, and they will come—this has been prophesied—you just say,

" 'No weapon formed against the work of the Lord will ever prosper, but all glory and majesty of this work that the Lord gave will long be remembered after those who have tried to befoul the name of the Church and those of its leaders will be forgotten, and their works will follow after them.'

"We feel sorry for them when we see these things happen." (In Conference Report, Oct. 1973, p. 167; or *Ensign,* Jan. 1974, p. 126.)

# Duties of a Bishop

Section 72

## Historical Background

Edward Partridge was called to be the first bishop of the Church in this dispensation on 4 February 1831 at Kirtland, Ohio (see D&C 41). In November 1831 the Lord revealed, "There remain hereafter, in the due time of the Lord, other bishops to be set apart unto the church, to minister even according to the first" (D&C 68:14). The Prophet Joseph Smith recorded that on 4 December 1831 "several of the Elders and members assembled together to learn their duty, and for edification, and after some time had been spent in conversing about our temporal and spiritual welfare, I received the following: [D&C 72]" (*History of the Church,* 1:239).

The first eight verses of section 72 were then received, and immediately Newel K. Whitney was ordained; then the rest of section 72 was received.

## Notes and Commentary

### D&C 72:3, 5. Elders Must Account for Their Stewardships

"At a very early day after the organization of the Church the Lord revealed the need of a bishop to look after the temporalities and stewardships in the Church. Bishop Edward Partridge was called and sent to Zion to engage in the duties of his calling. On the 4th day of December, 1831, while the Prophet and Sidney Rigdon were engaged in their ministry refuting their enemies, a meeting of the elders was called and the Lord gave them a very important revelation. The Lord declared that it was expedient that a bishop should be called to serve in the Kirtland district. One important duty of this bishop was to look after the stewardships pertaining to the inhabitants of Kirtland and other parts of Ohio, and he was 'to render an account of his stewardship, both in time and in eternity.' " (Smith, *Church History and Modern Revelation,* 1:269-70.)

### D&C 72:3-4. "He Who Is Faithful and Wise in Time"

A doctrine taught clearly in the scriptures is that the station and rewards one inherits in the life after this are determined by how firmly the individual commits himself to the gospel, seeks the power of the Atonement to overcome his sins, and takes responsibility for his stewardship over temporal blessings.

In what has for some people been a troubling parable, the Savior commented on the prudence of a steward who prepared for his future by cheating his master (see Luke 16:1-8). The Savior said, "The children of this world are in their generation wiser than the children of light. . . . If therefore ye have not been faithful in the unrighteous mammon, who will commit to your trust the true riches?" (Luke 16:8, 11). Elder James E. Talmage explained the lesson Jesus taught and its relationship to earthly stewardships:

"Our Lord's purpose was to show the contrast between the care, thoughtfulness, and devotion of men engaged in the money-making affairs of earth, and the half hearted ways of many who are professedly striving after spiritual riches. Worldly-minded men do not neglect provision for their future years, and often are sinfully eager to amass plenty; while the 'children of light,' or those who believe spiritual wealth to be above all earthly possessions, are less energetic, prudent, or wise. By 'mammon of unrighteousness' we may understand material wealth or worldly things. While far inferior to the treasures of heaven, money or that which it represents may be the means of accomplishing good, and of furthering the purposes of God. Our Lord's admonition was to utilize 'mammon' in good works, while it lasted, for some day it shall fail, and only the results achieved through its use shall endure. If the wicked steward, when cast out from his master's house because of unworthiness, might hope to be received into the homes of those whom he had favored, how much more confidently may they who are genuinely devoted to the right hope to be received into the everlasting mansions of God! Such seems to be part of the lesson.

"It was not the steward's dishonesty that was extolled; his prudence and foresight were commended. . . . The lesson may be summed up in this wise: Make such use of your wealth as shall insure you friends hereafter. Be diligent; for the day in which you can use your earthly riches will soon pass. Take a lesson from even the dishonest and the evil; if they are so prudent as to provide for the only future they think of, how much more should you, who believe in an eternal future, provide therefor! If you have not learned wisdom and prudence in the use of 'unrighteous mammon,' how can you be trusted with the more enduring riches? If you have not learned how to use properly the wealth of another, which has been committed to you as steward, how can you expect to be successful in the handling of great wealth should such be given you as your own? Emulate the unjust steward and the lovers of mammon, not in their dishonesty, cupidity, and miserly hoarding of the wealth that is at best but transitory, but in their zeal, forethought, and provision for the future." (*Jesus the Christ,* pp. 463-64.)

### D&C 72:9-23. Responsibilities of a Bishop Assigned by Revelation

In this section the responsibilities of a bishop are primarily related to the law of consecration; however, other responsibilities and duties of a bishop have been outlined to include such activities as presiding over the ward and presiding over the Aaronic Priesthood in the ward.

### D&C 72:13. What Was the Relationship between Bishop Newel K. Whitney in Kirtland and Bishop Edward Partridge in Zion?

Bishop Partridge was called as the first bishop of the Church. Later, when others were called, he became the equivalent of what today is called the Presiding Bishop. Newell K. Whitney thus was actually under the jurisdiction of Bishop Partridge. "The bishop in Kirtland was to 'hand over' to the bishop in Zion, the record of the stewardships, where the permanent records should be kept. For this responsibility Newel K. Whitney was called to

*Newel K. Whitney was called as a bishop*

act as bishop. He was to keep the Lord's storehouse in Kirtland, and to receive funds in that part of the vineyard, and to take an account of the elders as he was commanded; to administer to their wants, all those who should pay for that which they received, inasmuch as they have wherewith to pay. These funds received were to be consecrated to the good of the Church, 'to the poor and needy.' If there were any who were unable to pay, an account was to be made 'and handed over to the bishop in Zion, who shall pay the debt out of that which the Lord shall put into his hands.' " (Smith, *Church History and Modern Revelation,* 1:270.)

When Edward Partridge died in Nauvoo in May 1840, Newel K. Whitney became the Presiding Bishop.

**D&C 72:17. What Was the Value of Certificates for Members Moving from One Area to Another?**

President Joseph Fielding Smith noted that "a certificate from the judge or bishop in Kirtland was to be made and it would 'render every man acceptable and answereth all things, for an inheritance, and to be received as a wise steward, and as a faithful laborer; otherwise he shall not be accepted of the bishop in Zion.'

"From the very beginning of time the Lord has taken pains to see that proper records have been kept. This was one of the first commandments to the Church in 1830. The jealous care pertaining to the word of the Lord and other publications and documents, is shown forth in a number of revelations. . . .

"All who were to go up to Zion from other parts of the Church, were required to carry with them certificates, showing that they were in full fellowship and worthy to obtain the blessings which, in Zion, awaited the obedient." (*Church History and Modern Revelation,* 1:271.)

# Revision of the Bible

Section 73

## Historical Background

Joseph Smith and Sidney Rigdon were working on a revision of the Bible when, on 1 December 1831, the Lord called them to go on a mission for a season. The effectiveness of their efforts was recorded by the Prophet Joseph Smith: "From this time until the 8th or 10th of January, 1832, myself and Elder Rigdon continued to preach in Shalersville, Ravenna, and other places, setting forth the truth, vindicating the cause of our Redeemer; showing that the day of vengeance was coming upon this generation like a thief in the night; that prejudice, blindness and darkness filled the minds of many, and caused them to persecute the true Church, and reject the true light; by which means we did much towards allaying the excited feelings which were growing out of the scandalous letters then being published in the *Ohio Star,* at Ravenna, by the before-mentioned apostate, Ezra Booth. On the 10th of January, I received the following revelation [D&C 73] making known the will of the Lord concerning the Elders of the Church until the convening of the next conference." (*History of the Church,* 1:241.)

## Notes and Commentary

**D&C 73:1-2. Why Is Missionary Work So Important to the Church?**

President Ezra Taft Benson said: "The Church's mission is to declare the gospel of the kingdom to all the world, to redeem our kindred dead, and to perfect the Saints of the Church—a positive approach. Never in the history of the Church has there been such an expenditure of time, planning, and resources to accomplish this mission. In the final analysis, this effort is the *only* solution to the problems of the world." (In Conference Report, Apr. 1978, p. 48; or *Ensign,* May 1978, p. 33.)

**D&C 73:3. What Were Joseph and Sidney Translating?**

When the angel Moroni appeared to Joseph Smith on 21 September 1823, he quoted passages from the Bible, but he quoted them with significant differences from the King James Version (see JS—H 1:36-41.) Later, while translating the Book of Mormon, Joseph learned that many "plain and precious things" had been lost from the Bible (1 Nephi 13:25-29). And after his baptism by John the Baptist, Joseph found his mind enlightened, and the "true meaning and intention" of the scriptures was revealed to him (*History of the Church,* p. 43). So when the Prophet had finished translating the Book of Mormon, he turned his attention to the Bible.

Although the word *translation* brings to mind the use of original texts and ancient languages, Joseph's work was to restore the correctness of the scripture by the power of the Spirit, not by scholarly interpretation. In June 1830 he wrote that "line upon line of knowledge" was revealed as he received the book of Moses (*History of the Church,* p. 98), which gave a correct account of what Moses had received of the Lord, but had not survived the ages intact. As he and Sidney Rigdon were working on the New Testament, the Prophet Joseph Smith

THE

# PEARL OF GREAT PRICE

## SELECTIONS FROM THE BOOK OF MOSES

*An extract from the translation of the Bible as revealed to Joseph Smith the Prophet, June 1830—February 1831*

### CHAPTER 1
(June 1830)

*God reveals himself to Moses—Moses transfigured—Confrontation with Satan—Many inhabited worlds seen—Worlds without number created by the Son—God's work and glory to bring to pass the immortality and eternal life of man.*

THE words of God, which he [a]spake unto Moses at a time when Moses was caught up into an exceedingly high [b]mountain,

2 And he [a]saw God [b]face to face, and he [c]talked with him, and the [d]glory of God was upon Moses; therefore Moses could endure his presence.

3 And God spake unto Moses, saying: Behold, I am the Lord God [a]Almighty, and [b]Endless is my [c]name; for I am without beginning of days or end of years; and is not this endless?

4 And, behold, thou art my son; wherefore [a]look, and I will show thee the [b]workmanship of mine [c]hands; but not all, for my [d]works are without [e]end, and also my [f]words, for they never cease.

5 Wherefore, no man can behold all my [a]works, except he behold all my [b]glory; and no man can [c]behold all my [d]glory, and afterwards remain in the flesh on the earth.

6 And I have a work for thee, Moses, my son; and thou art in the [a]similitude of mine [b]Only [c]Begotten; and mine Only Begotten is and shall be the [d]Savior, for he is full of [e]grace

1 1*a* Alma 12: 30; Moses 1: 42.
*b* Ex. 19: 3; Ezek. 40: 2; Rev. 21: 10; Moses 1: 42.
2*a* Ex. 3: 6; 33: 20 (11–23); John 1: 18; Ether 3: 15; Moses 1: 11. TG God, Privilege of Seeing; Jesus Christ, Appearances, Antemortal; Vision.
*b* Num. 12: 8; Deut. 34: 10; D&C 17: 1. TG God, Manifestations of.
*c* Ex. 25: 1. TG Communication.
*d* Deut. 5: 24; Moses 1: 14 (13–14, 25). TG Glory; God, Glory of; Transfiguration.
3*a* Rev. 19: 6. TG Jesus Christ, Power of.
*b* Isa. 63: 16; D&C 19: 10 (9–12); Moses 7: 35. TG God, Eternal Nature of.
*c* Ex. 3: 15.
4*a* Moses 7: 4.
*b* Job 9: 12.
*c* Moses 7: 32 (32–37).
*d* Ps. 40: 5; 92: 5; Morm. 9: 16 (16–20); D&C 76: 114. TG God, Power of.
*e* Ps. 111: 8 (7–8); 1 Ne. 14: 7; D&C 29: 33; Moses 1: 38.
*f* Ps. 33: 11; 2 Ne. 9: 16; D&C 1: 38 (37–39).
5*a* TG God, Works of.
*b* TG Glory; Jesus Christ, Glory of.
*c* TG God, Privilege of Seeing.
*d* Ex. 24: 17; John 12: 41. TG Celestial Glory.
6*a* Gen. 1: 26; Deut. 18: 15; Acts 3: 22; 1 Ne. 22: 21; Moses 1: 16 (13–16).
*b* Moses 1: 33.
*c* Moses 6: 57.
*d* 1 Ne. 13: 40. TG Jesus Christ, Savior.
*e* John 1: 17 (14, 17); 2 Ne. 2: 6; Alma 13: 9. TG Grace.

*"One of the grandest books in sacred literature" (Smith and Sjodahl, Commentary, p. 478)*

recorded: "For while we were doing the work of translation, which the Lord had appointed unto us, we came to the twenty-ninth verse of the fifth chapter of John, which was given unto us. . . . Now this caused us to marvel, for it was *given* unto us *of the Spirit.*" (D&C 76:15, 18; emphasis added.) Joseph's work of translating the Bible was a spiritual task. Later he studied Hebrew and German, but it was not that knowledge that provided a basis to correct the scriptures.

Joseph Smith went through all of the Bible, dictating to a scribe changes, deletions, or additions, but he did not complete a revision of the entire Bible. He never considered what he had accomplished as ready for publication, and he probably would have made many more corrections had he lived longer.

# Little Children Are Holy

Section 74

## Historical Background

This revelation was given as a result of Joseph Smith's revisions in the Bible. As early as 7 March 1831 the Prophet was told to begin translating the New Testament (see D&C 45:60-61). He wrote of this period: "I recommenced the translation of the Scriptures, and labored diligently until just before the conference, which was to convene on the 25th of January. During this period, I also received the following [D&C 74], as an explanation of the First Epistle to the Corinthians, 7th chapter, 14th verse." (*History of the Church,* 1:242.)

## Notes and Commentary

### D&C 74:1-7. Little Children

*Unbelieving,* as used here, refers to those Jews who had not joined the Church of Jesus Christ. They were still living by the rituals of the Mosaic law, which included circumcision of their male children. Paul taught that little children were sanctified through the atonement of Christ and that circumcision was no longer necessary as taught by the adherents of the Mosaic law.

*Little children are holy*

### D&C 74:2. What Is Meant by the Law of Circumcision?

The word *circumcision* comes from the Latin word meaning "to cut around." It was instituted by revelation as a sign or token that one was of the covenant seed of Abraham (see JST, Genesis 17:3-7, 11). Other scriptures make it clear that it was not the act itself but rather what it stood for that gave circumcision its greatest significance (see Deuteronomy 10:16; 30:6; Jeremiah 4:4; Ezekiel 44:7; Romans 2:25-29).

### D&C 74:4-6. Why Was the Circumcision of Children a Problem in the Early Church?

Sperry described the situation in the Primitive Church that led to this problem:"When the unbelieving husband had his way, which in that day would be usual, it would too often have the effect of causing the children to give heed to the Jewish tradition which their father followed (vs. 4), the result being that they, too, would not believe the Gospel of Christ. Hence the children became 'unholy'—that is to say, they became unholy according to the false Jewish tradition which prevailed at the time, for the tradition of the Jews was that little children were unholy (vs. 6). It was for this cause, the Lord continues (vs. 5), that Paul wrote to the Corinthians giving them his own opinion, not the Lord's, that a member of the Church ('believer') should not be united in marriage to an unbeliever, unless the Law of Moses was renounced or done away by them. Then the children of a given couple would not have to be circumcised as the Law of Moses required, and the false tradition of the Jews that little children are unholy could be gradually eliminated." (*Compendium,* p. 328.)

# "Neither Be Idle but Labor with Your Might"

Section 75

## Historical Background

"On the 25th day of January 1832, a very important conference was held by the elders at Amherst, Lorain County, Ohio. The history of the Church is very brief in the report of this conference. Much business was transacted, but the most important thing was the fact that Joseph Smith was sustained and ordained, by the will of the Lord, as President of the High Priesthood." (Smith, *Church History and Modern Revelation,* 1:274.)

The Prophet Joseph Smith recorded: "A few days before the conference was to commence in Amherst, Lorain county, I started with the Elders that lived in my own vicinity, and arrived in good time. At this conference much harmony prevailed, and considerable business was done to advance the kingdom, and promulgate the Gospel to the inhabitants of the surrounding country. The Elders seemed anxious for me to inquire of the Lord that they might know His will, or learn what would be most pleasing to Him for them to do, in order to bring men to a sense of their condition; for, as it was written, all men have gone out of the way, so that none doeth good, no, not one. I inquired and received the following: [D&C 75]." (*History of the Church,* 1:242-43.)

## Notes and Commentary

### D&C 75:1. Alpha and Omega

For the significance of this title see Notes and Commentary on Doctrine and Covenants 38:1.

### D&C 75:2-5. Go Forth and Labor With Your Might

See Enrichment A, in the Appendix, for a discussion of missionary work.

### D&C 75:5. What Is the Meaning of the Sheaves and the Crowns?

A dual imagery is used in this verse to depict the rewards for the faithful. Anciently, grain was cut by hand and tied into large bundles or sheaves which were then carried to the place of threshing. To see a person or an animal "laden with many sheaves" (D&C 75:5) was proof that this person had reaped an abundant harvest and would now enjoy the fruits of his labors.

"Elders who go out to preach the gospel sometimes return and report that they know not whether they have been the means of converting anybody or not. But if they have been faithful, the harvest is sure. The seed they have sown may sprout and come to maturity years after they have been released." (Smith and Sjodahl, Commentary, p. 434.)

The promise that the faithful will have much laid in store is given to the one who understands that "the field is white already to harvest" and is willing to "thrust in his sickle with his might" (D&C 4:4).

Elder Bruce R. McConkie commented on the symbolism of being crowned: "Those who gain exaltation in the highest heaven of the celestial world shall wear *crowns.* Perhaps literal crowns may be worn on occasion—emblematic of their victory over the world and signifying that they rule and reign as kings and queens in the eternal house of Israel. But at all times they will be 'crowned with honor, and glory, and immortality, and eternal life.' (D. & C. 75:5.)" (*Mormon Doctrine,* p. 173.)

### D&C 75:6-8. I Revoke the Commission

See Doctrine and Covenants 58:32-33; 124:49-51.

### D&C 75:10-11. Calling On the Comforter and Praying Always

Smith and Sjodahl explained the importance of prayer in effective teaching of the gospel:

"They were commanded (v. 4) to preach the truth 'according to the revelations and commandments' given. They were to keep strictly to the revealed word, but even this they could not do without the aid of the Comforter, the Holy Spirit of God. Studying alone does not qualify an Elder for preaching the truth. It is the Spirit that qualifies. . . .

"Some Elders put all their faith in preaching. The Latter-day Saints generally will endorse the following, though uttered by one not a member of the Church:

" 'What is preaching without praying! Sermons are but pulpit performances, learned essays, rhetorical orations, popular lectures, or it may be political harangues, until God gives, in answer to earnest prayer, the preparation of the heart, and the answer of the tongue. It is only he who prays that can truly preach. Many a sermon that has shown no intellectual genius and has violated all homiletic rules and standards has had dynamic spiritual force. Somehow it has moved men, melted them, moulded them. The man whose lips are touched by God's living coal from off the altar may even stammer, but his hearers soon find out that he is on fire with one consuming passion to save souls' (Arthur T. Pierson, *The Fundamentals,* Vol. IX., p. 67)." (Commentary, p. 435.)

### D&C 75:19-22. Shake the Dust off Your Feet

See Notes and Commentary for Doctrine and Covenants 60:15-17.

*A preacher of righteousness must know God's will*

**D&C 75:22. Why Will It Be More Tolerable for the Heathen Than for Those Who Reject the Missionaries?**

Elder James E. Talmage noted that "man will be accounted blameless or guilty, according to his deeds as interpreted in the light of the law under which he is required to live. It is inconsistent with our conception of a just God, to believe Him capable of inflicting condemnation upon any one for noncompliance with a requirement of which the person had no knowledge. Nevertheless, the laws of the Church will not be suspended even in the case of those who have sinned in darkness and ignorance; but it is reasonable to believe that the plan of redemption will afford such benighted ones an opportunity of learning the laws of God; and surely, as fast as they so learn, will obedience be required on pain of the penalty." (*Articles of Faith,* p. 519.)

**D&C 75:24-28. The Church to Support Families of Those Called to Proclaim the Gospel**

President Joseph Fielding Smith said that "the brethren who were called to take these missionary journeys were quite generally poor men in temporal things. It was difficult for them to go out on the Lord's work and leave their families without support. Yet the call was essential, for the souls of men were at stake and there were those waiting to hear the message who would be a strength to the Church after they received the Gospel. The Lord took into account the needs of the families of these brethren, and he said, 'It is the duty of the Church to assist in supporting the families of those who are called and must needs be sent unto the world. . . . ' The commandment therefore was given that suitable places should be provided in which these families could be housed and cared for, and the members of the Church were admonished to 'open their hearts,' and assist in this undertaking. If there were brethren, however, who could support themselves and their families, this was required of them." (*Church History and Modern Revelation,* 1:276-77.)

**D&C 75:29. The Idler Shall Not Have Place in the Church**

Elder Franklin D. Richards taught: "President

McKay has said, 'Let us realize that the privilege to work is a gift, that the power to work is a blessing, that love of work is success.'

"How true this is! Yet today as in earlier times many misguided individuals embrace the philosophy of idleness, feeling that the world owes them a living. Many have a desire to destroy the establishment that has been built upon productive effort.

"In this dispensation the Lord has many times confirmed the eternal principle of work. We have been told that there is no place in the Church for the idler 'except he repent and mend his ways,' and 'he that is idle shall not eat the bread nor wear the garments of the laborer.' (D&C 75:29; 42:42.)" (In Conference Report, Oct. 1969, p. 121.)

Additional discussion of the evils of idleness and the value of work is found in Notes and Commentary for Doctrine and Covenants 68:31.

# The Vision of the Degrees of Glory

Section 76

## Historical Background

It had been over a year since the Prophet Joseph Smith began a revision of the Bible, and the months of January and February 1832 found him again involved in this assignment.

Through his diligent study of the scriptures, many questions and problems relative to the Biblical account were resolved through revelation. One such question had to do with the Christian belief in heaven. The Prophet wrote: "Upon my return from Amherst [Ohio] conference, I resumed the translation of the Scriptures. From sundry revelations which had been received, it was apparent that many important points touching the salvation of man, had been taken from the Bible, or lost before it was compiled. It appeared self-evident from what truths were left, that if God rewarded every one according to the deeds done in the body the term 'Heaven,' as intended for the Saints' eternal home must include more kingdoms than one. Accordingly, on the 16th of February, 1832, while translating St. John's Gospel, myself and Elder Rigdon saw the following vision: [D&C 76] ." (*History of the Church,* 1:245.)

Brother Philo Dibble was an eyewitness to the reception of this revelation. He wrote that "the vision which is recorded in the Book of Doctrine and Covenants was given at the house of 'Father Johnson,' in Hiram, Ohio, and during the time that Joseph and Sidney were in the spirit and saw the heavens open, there were other men in the room, perhaps twelve, among whom I was one during a part of the time—probably two-thirds of the time,—I saw the glory and felt the power, but did not see the vision.

"The events and conversation, while they were seeing what is written (and many things were seen and related that are not written,) I will relate as minutely as is necessary.

"Joseph would, at intervals, say: 'What do I see?' as one might say while looking out the window and beholding what all in the room could not see. Then he would relate what he had seen or what he was looking at. Then Sidney replied, 'I see the same.' Presently Sidney would say 'what do I see?' and would repeat what he had seen or was seeing, and Joseph would reply, 'I see the same.'

"This manner of conversation was reported at short intervals to the end of the vision, and during the whole time not a word was spoken by any other person. Not a sound nor motion made by anyone but Joseph and Sidney, and it seemed to me that they never moved a joint or limb during the time I was there, which I think was over an hour, and to the end of the vision.

"Joseph sat firmly and calmly all the time in the midst of a magnificent glory, but Sidney sat limp and pale, apparently as limber as a rag, observing which, Joseph remarked, smilingly, 'Sidney is not

*Joseph Smith and Sidney Rigdon's vision of the three degrees of glory*

used to it as I am.' " (*Juvenile Instructor,* May 1892, pp. 303-4.)

The Prophet Joseph Smith wrote: "Nothing could be more pleasing to the Saints upon the order of the kingdom of the Lord, than the light which burst upon the world through the foregoing vision. Every law, every commandment, every promise, every truth, and every point touching the destiny of man, from Genesis to Revelation, where the purity of the scriptures remains unsullied by the folly of men, go to show the perfection of the theory [of different degrees of glory in the future life] and witnesses the fact that that document is a transcript from the records of the eternal world. The sublimity of the ideas; the purity of the language; the scope for action; the continued duration for completion, in order that the heirs of salvation may confess the Lord and bow the knee; the rewards for faithfulness, and the punishments for sins, are so much beyond the narrow-mindedness of men, that every honest man is constrained to exclaim: '*It came from God.*' " (*History of the Church,* 1:252-53.)

President Wilford Woodruff said of the vision that it "gives more light, more truth, and more principle than any revelation contained in any other book we ever read. It makes plain to our understanding our present condition, where we came from, why we are here, and where we are going to. Any man may know through that revelation what his part and condition will be. For all men know what laws they keep, and the laws which men keep here will determine their position hereafter; they will be preserved by those laws and receive the blessings which belong to them." (In *Journal of Discourses,* 22:146-47.)

While it is often called "the vision," Doctrine and Covenants 76 is a series of visions combined into one grand revelation: a vision of the glory of the Son (vss. 20-24); a vision of the fall of Satan and the sufferings of those who follow him, who are sons of perdition (vss. 25-49); a vision of those who inherit the celestial glory and come forth in the resurrection of the just (vss. 50-70); a vision of those who inherit the terrestrial glory (vss. 71-80); and a vision of those who inherit the telestial glory (vss. 81-89). A comparison of the three degrees of glory is also given.

## Notes and Commentary

### D&C 76:1-4. "Beside Him There Is No Savior"

As do many sections of the Doctrine and Covenants, this vision begins with an affirmation of the power, glory, and majesty of Jesus Christ. It is fitting that the Lord would begin this revelation of the various eternal rewards with the reminder that only in him is there power to save, that none can "stay his hand" (D&C 76:3), that none can stop him from accomplishing his work, which is "to bring to pass the immortality and eternal life of man" (Moses 1:39).

### D&C 76:5-10. "I . . . Delight to Honor Those Who Serve Me in Righteousness"

These verses contain one of the most remarkable promises of revelation and blessing found in the scriptures. In plain, unmistakable language the Lord indicates that if a person fears God (that is, respects, reverences, and obeys him) and serves him to the end, God will be delighted to honor him. The honors bestowed include the following:

1. A great reward (see D&C 76:6)
2. Eternal glory (see vs. 6)
3. Revelation of all mysteries of God's kingdom, both past and present (see vs. 7; see also Notes and Commentary on D&C 6:7, 11 for the definition of *mystery*)
4. Knowledge of his will concerning all things in the kingdom (see vs. 7)
5. Knowledge of the wonders of eternity (see vs. 8)
6. Knowledge of many generations (see vs. 8)
7. Great wisdom (see vs. 9)
8. Understanding that reaches to heaven and which the world cannot equal (see vs. 9)
9. Enlightenment by the Spirit and power of God (see vs. 10)

The mention of these marvelous promises at the beginning of this revelation is significant, for Joseph Smith and Sidney Rigdon indicated that they were not allowed to write all that they were shown (see verses 113-15). Not only is it unlawful for man to reveal these things, but it is impossible for him to do so because they are so glorious that man is incapable of making them known (see vss. 115-16). The Savior clearly states, however, that those who will "purify themselves before him" through the power of the Holy Spirit shall have the "privilege of *seeing* and *knowing* [these things] for themselves" (vss. 116-17; emphasis added).

### D&C 76:15-19. "While We Meditated"

The Prophet and Sidney Rigdon were meditating when this revelation came.

Speaking of the value of pondering the words of eternal life, President Marion G. Romney said:

"As I have read the scriptures, I have been challenged by the word *ponder,* so frequently used in the Book of Mormon. The dictionary says that *ponder* means 'to weigh mentally, think deeply about, deliberate, meditate.' . . .

"*Pondering* is, in my feeling, a form of prayer. It has, at least, been an approach to the Spirit of the Lord on many occasions." (In Conference Report, Apr. 1973, p. 117; or *Ensign,* July 1973, p. 90.)

At least two other great visions came as a direct result of pondering. Nephi says that he was "pondering in mine heart" the things of his father's dream when he was "caught away in the Spirit of the Lord, yea into an exceeding high mountain" (1 Nephi 11:1). And President Joseph F. Smith said that he received his remarkable vision of the spirit world as he sat in his room "pondering over the scriptures; and reflecting" (D&C 138:1-2).

President David O. McKay taught the value of meditation: "I think we pay too little attention to the value of meditation, a principle of devotion. . . .

*Spencer W. Kimball in a moment of meditation*

"Meditation is one of the most secret, most sacred doors through which we pass into the presence of the Lord. Jesus set the example for us. As soon as he was baptized and received the Father's approval—'This is my beloved Son, in whom I am well pleased' (Matt. 3:17)—Jesus repaired to what is now known as the Mount of Temptation where, during forty days of fasting, he communed with himself and his Father and contemplated the responsibility of his own great mission. One result of this spiritual communion was such strength as enabled him to say to the tempter: 'Get thee hence, Satan: for it is written, Thou shalt worship the Lord thy God, and him only shalt thou serve.' (Matt. 4:10.)" (In Conference Report, Apr. 1967, p. 85.)

**D&C 76:20-24. The Testimony of Eyewitnesses**

This testimony of the Prophet Joseph Smith and Sidney Rigdon is yet another modern witness of the reality of the existence of the Father and the Son. Joseph and Sidney not only saw but heard, and their testimonies stand as a witness to all people. The phrase "last of all" is explained by Smith and Sjodahl as follows: "This is the last testimony to the fact that He lives, a resurrected and glorified Being; not the *final* testimony but the last up to the time of this vision" (Commentary, p. 448).

**D&C 76:24. Worlds without Number Were Created by the Lord**

Elder Bruce R. McConkie, commenting on Jesus as the Creator, said that "our Lord's jurisdiction and power extend far beyond the limits of this one small earth on which we dwell. He is, under the Father, the Creator of worlds without number. (Moses 1:33.) . . .

"Those who have ears to hear, find this doctrine taught in the following scripture: [D&C 76:20-24].

"In addition to the plain meaning of this passage, we have an explanation of it given by the Prophet Joseph Smith. He paraphrased, in poetical rhyme, the entire record of the Vision, and his words covering this portion were: . . .

'And I heard a great voice bearing record from heav'n,
*He's the Saviour and Only Begotten of God;*
*By him, of him, and through him, the worlds were all made,*
*Even all that careen in the heavens so broad.*' "
(McConkie, *Mormon Doctrine,* pp. 65-66.)

**D&C 76:26. Lucifer Was an Angel of God, a Son of the Morning**

President George Q. Cannon, commenting on Satan's title as a son of the morning, said: "Some have called him *the* son of the morning, but here it is *a* son of the morning—one among many, doubtless. This angel was a mighty personage, without doubt. The record that is given to us concerning him clearly shows that he occupied a very high position; that he was thought a great deal of, and that he was mighty in his sphere, so much so that when the matter was debated concerning the earth and the plan of salvation, he was of sufficient importance to have a plan, which he proposed as the plan by which this earth should be peopled and the inhabitants thereof redeemed. His plan, however, was not accepted; but it was so plausible and so attractive that out of the whole hosts of heaven one-third accepted his plan and were willing to cast their lot with him. [Moses 4:1-4; D&C 29:36-37.] Now, the difference between Jesus and Lucifer was this: Jesus was willing to submit to the Father." (In *Millennial Star,* 5 Sept. 1895, pp. 563-64.)

**D&C 76:26. What Do the Names *Lucifer* and *Perdition* Mean?**

Lucifer's name means "light bearer" or "shining one." The word *perdition* means "loss or destruction" (see Young, *Concordance,* s.v. "Lucifer," "Perdition"). Lucifer fell from his position as a glorious being to a position of utter loss and destruction (see Revelation 12:1-11; Moses 4:1-4). Knowing that one of Satan's names is Perdition gives added significance to the title "son of perdition."

**D&C 76:29. Who Has Satan Singled Out As His Enemies?**

This verse warns that Satan will seek to make war with the Saints (cf. Revelation 12:17). Although

Satan has great power, it is limited. The Prophet Joseph Smith stated: "There are three independent principles; the Spirit of God, the spirit of man, and the spirit of the devil. All men have power to resist the devil. They who have tabernacles, have power over those who have not." (*Teachings*, pp. 189-90.)

President George Q. Cannon testified that every man has power enough to resist Satan. "The Lord our God has sent us here to get experience in these things so that we may know the good from the evil and be able to close our hearts against the evil. . . . It is true that some have greater power of resistance than others, but everyone has the power to close his heart against doubt, against darkness, against unbelief, against depression, against anger, against hatred, against jealousy, against malice, against envy. God has given this power unto all of us, and we can gain still greater power by calling upon Him for that which we lack. If it were not so, how could we be condemned for giving way to wrong influences?

"There could be no condemnation for our doing what we could not help; but we can help yielding to wrong influences and being quarrelsome and selfish. We can help giving way to the spirit of theft, and we can resist the spirit of lust. God has given us power to resist these things, that our hearts may be kept free from them and also from doubt; and when Satan comes and assails us, it is our privilege to say, 'Get thee behind me, Satan, for I have no lot nor portion in you, and you have no part in me. I am in the service of God, and I am going to serve Him, and you can do what you please. It is no use you presenting yourself with your blandishments to me. You come and try to insinuate into my heart evil thoughts about the servants of God or about the work of God, and I will not listen to you; I will close my heart against you. . . .'

"Whenever darkness fills our minds, we may know that we are not possessed of the Spirit of God, and we must get rid of it. When we are filled with the Spirit of God, we are filled with joy, with peace and with happiness no matter what our circumstances may be; for it is a spirit of cheerfulness and of happiness." (*Gospel Truth*, 1:19-20.)

### D&C 76:31. To What Extent Must a Person Know God's Power and Be a Partaker Before He Becomes a Son of Perdition?

To become a son of perdition one must sin against the Holy Ghost; but before that is possible, one must receive the gift of the Holy Ghost. Elder Melvin J. Ballard explained that "unto the Holy Ghost has been given the right and the privilege of manifesting the truth unto men as no other power will. So that when he makes a man see and know a thing he knows it better than he shall ever know anything else; and to sin against that knowledge is to sin against the greatest light there is, and consequently commit the greatest sin there is." (*Millennial Star*, 11 Aug. 1932, pp. 499-500.)

Elder Joseph Fielding Smith further explained why sin against the Holy Ghost is so serious: "The Spirit of God speaking to the spirit of man has power to impart truth with greater effect and understanding than the truth can be imparted by personal contact even with heavenly beings. Through the Holy Ghost the truth is woven into the very fibre and sinews of the body so that it cannot be forgotten." ("The Sin against the Holy Ghost," *Instructor*, Oct. 1935, p. 431.)

The Prophet Joseph Smith asked, concerning those who become sons of perdition, "What must a man do to commit the unpardonable sin? He must receive the Holy Ghost, have the heavens opened unto him, and know God, and then sin against Him. After a man has sinned against the Holy Ghost, there is no repentance for him. He has got to say that the sun does not shine while he sees it; he has got to deny Jesus Christ when the heavens have been opened unto him, and to deny the plan of salvation with his eyes open to the truth of it; and from that time he begins to be an enemy. This is the case with many apostates of the Church of Jesus Christ of Latter-day Saints." (*Teachings*, p. 358.)

Elder Spencer W. Kimball wrote: "The sin against the Holy Ghost requires such knowledge that it is manifestly impossible for the rank and file to commit such a sin" (*Miracle of Forgiveness*, p. 123).

Of apostates who had committed the unpardonable sin, the Prophet Joseph Smith said: "When a man begins to be an enemy to this work, he hunts me, he seeks to kill me, and never ceases to thirst for my blood. He gets the spirit of the devil—the same spirit that they had who crucified the Lord of Life—the same spirit that sins against the Holy Ghost." (*Teachings*, p. 358.)

People do not come to such a state in a moment. Elder Joseph Fielding Smith described the path that some follow, which would cause them to hate God and his servants: "The change of heart does not come all at once, but is due to transgression in some form, which continues to lurk in the soul without repentance, until the Holy Ghost withdraws, and then that man is left to spiritual darkness. Sin begets sin, the darkness grows until the love of truth turns to hatred and the love of God is overcome by the wicked desire to destroy all that is just and true. In this way Christ is put to open shame, and blasphemy exalted." (*Instructor*, Oct. 1935, p. 432.)

Such people have placed themselves outside the redemptive powers of Christ (see Hebrews 6:4-9; 10:26-29; Matthew 12:31-32). They cannot partake of his mercy because they cannot incline themselves to repent, having totally lost the spirit of God. Their sin "is an offense so heinous that the sinner is unable to repent; and this is what makes his case hopeless. If he could repent, he could be forgiven; but being incapable of repentance, he cannot be reached by the pardoning power." (Orson F. Whitney, *Improvement Era*, Mar. 1920, p. 413.)

"In the realms of perdition or the kingdom of darkness, where there is no light, Satan and the unembodied spirits of the pre-existence shall dwell together with those of mortality who retrogress to the level of perdition. These have lost the power of regeneration. They have sunk so low as to have lost the inclinations and ability to repent." (Kimball, *Miracle of Forgiveness,* p. 125.)

### D&C 76:35. How Might Anyone "Crucify" the Only Begotten Son of the Father and "Put Him to an Open Shame"?

Elder Bruce R. McConkie stated that "commission of the unpardonable sin consists in crucifying unto oneself the Son of God afresh and putting him to open shame. (Heb. 6:4-8; D.&C. 76:34-35.) To commit this unpardonable crime a man must receive the gospel, gain from the Holy Ghost by revelation the absolute knowledge of the divinity of Christ, and then deny 'the new and everlasting covenant by which he was sanctified, calling it an unholy thing, and doing despite to the Spirit of grace.' (*Teachings,* p. 128.) He thereby commits murder by assenting unto the Lord's death, that is, having a perfect knowledge of the truth he comes out in open rebellion and places himself in a position wherein he would have crucified Christ knowing perfectly the while that he was the Son of God. Christ is thus crucified afresh and put to open shame. (D.& C. 132:27.)" (*Mormon Doctrine,* pp. 816-17.)

Concerning the degree to which such people become filled with the spirit of Satan, Elder Charles W. Penrose said: "Those who have followed him [Satan] so that they become imbued with his spirit, which is the spirit of destruction, in opposition to the spirit which brings life, are his. The spirit of murder enters their hearts; they are ready to put to death even the Son of God, if His existence in life comes in their way." (In Conference Report, Oct. 1911, p. 51.)

The scriptures sometimes use the phrase "shedding innocent blood" in reference to the actions of those in this condition. President Joseph Fielding Smith explained that the shedding of innocent blood is not confined to taking lives of the innocent, but is also included in seeking to destroy the word of God and putting Christ to open shame. Those who have known the truth and then fight against the authorized servants of Jesus Christ also fight against him, for they who fight against his servants also do it unto him, and thus are guilty of his blood. "Shedding innocent blood is spoken of in the scriptures as consenting to the death of Jesus Christ and putting him to open shame." (Smith, *Answers to Gospel Questions,* 1:68.)

### D&C 76:37. What Is the Second Death?

The term *second death* as used here refers to the spiritual death that will come upon those sons of perdition who have been resurrected, as Elder Bruce R. McConkie wrote: "*Spiritual death* is to be cast out of the presence of the Lord, to die as to the things of righteousness, to die as to the things of the Spirit. Spirit beings as such never die in the sense of annihilation or in the sense that their spirit bodies are disorganized; rather, they continue to live to all eternity either as spirits or as resurrected personages. . . .

"Eventually, all are redeemed from spiritual death except those who have 'sinned unto death' (D.& C. 64:7), that is, those who are destined to be sons of perdition. John teaches this by saying that after death and hell have delivered up the dead which are in them, then death and hell shall be 'cast into the lake of fire. This is the *second death.*' (Rev. 20:12-15.) And thus the Lord said in our day that the sons of perdition are 'the only ones on whom the *second death* shall have any power' (D.& C. 76:37), meaning any power *after* the resurrection." (*Mormon Doctrine,* pp. 757-58; see also Notes and Commentary on D&C 63:17; 64:7.)

### D&C 76:38-39. Will Those Born into Mortality Who Become Sons of Perdition Receive a Resurrection?

President George Q. Cannon explained this verse to correct a common misinterpretation: "A careful reading of these verses, however, and especially of the preceding paragraphs, will show that the Lord does not, in this language, exclude even the sons of perdition from the resurrection. It is plain that the intention is to refer to them explicitly as the only ones on whom the second death shall have any power: 'for *all the rest* shall be brought forth by the resurrection of the dead, through the triumph and the glory of the Lamb.' This excluded class are the only ones on whom the second death shall have any power, and 'the only ones who shall not be redeemed in the due time of the Lord, after the suffering of his wrath.'

"This is by no means to say that they are to have no resurrection. Jesus our Lord and Savior died for all, and all will be resurrected—good and bad, white and black, people of every race, whether sinners or not; and no matter how great their sins may be, the resurrection of their bodies is sure. Jesus has died for them, and they all will be redeemed from the grave through the atonement which he has made." (*Juvenile Instructor,* Feb. 1900, p. 123.)

### D&C 76:40-43. "This Is the Gospel"

The word *gospel* (Anglo-Saxon for "good story") comes from the Greek *evangelion,* which means "good tidings" or "glad tidings" (Thayer, *Greek-English Lexicon,* p. 257). In the New Testament the verb meaning "to preach or bear witness of the gospel" is *evangelidzo,* literally, "to bring good news, to announce glad tidings" (Thayer, *Greek-English Lexicon,* p. 256). Doctrine and Covenants 76 gives a summary of what the gospel, or glad tidings, consists of, namely, that all who will may be saved by the atoning power of Jesus Christ.

### D&C 76:44-49. It Is Futile to Discuss the Fate of Sons of Perdition

It appears that in the early days of the Restoration some attempted to teach the destiny of the sons of perdition. The Prophet Joseph Smith responded by writing: "Say to the brothers Hulet and to all others, that the Lord never authorized them to say that the devil, his angels, or the sons of perdition, should ever be restored; for their state of destiny was not revealed to man, is not revealed, nor ever shall be revealed, save to those who are made partakers thereof: consequently those who teach this doctrine have not received it of the Spirit of the Lord. Truly Brother Oliver declared it to be the doctrine of devils. We, therefore, command that this doctrine be taught no more in Zion. We sanction the decision of the Bishop and his council, in relation to this doctrine being a bar to communion." (*Teachings*, p. 24.)

### D&C 76:44. How Can the Sons of Perdition "Reign" in Eternity?

Smith and Sjodahl explained this peculiar but highly significant expression: "The Lord is the sovereign ruler. He reigns. Sin is said to reign, when men submit to its behests. Grace is also said to reign (Rom. 5:21). The Saints will reign with Christ. But here the sons of Perdition are said to 'reign' with the Devil and his angels in eternity, in the place where the worm dieth not and the fire is not quenched. The conflict between Lucifer and the Son has been, from the beginning, for sovereignty. Men have ranged themselves on one side or the other. The Saints are, and will be, citizens and officials in the Kingdom of God and there they will 'reign', as citizens in a free country. The sons of Perdition are, and will remain, citizens and officials in the kingdom of Lucifer. But that kingdom will, finally, be confined to *Gehenna.* There they will *'reign'*, under such laws and rules as obtain in the kingdom of the Devil, and of which we have had numerous illustrations in human history, during the dark ages of ignorance, superstition, tyranny, and iniquity. Think of a place where the evil passions of human beings and evil spirits rage, unrestrained by the influence of the gospel! Such is the kingdom of the Devil, where the sons of Perdition will reign." (Commentary, pp. 454-55.)

### D&C 76:48. Are the Sons of Perdition "Ordained" to Be Such?

"Not foreordained, in the sense of pre-elected by God, to condemnation. God has ordained that rebellion against Him shall result, if persisted in to the end, in misery, but He has not foreordained anyone to that fate. A legislature may ordain that thieves must be imprisoned and murderers killed, but that does not mean that it has foreordained any individual, or any number of individuals, to do that which ends in imprisonment, or death. The sons of Perdition pursue their course according to their own choice, and not as victims of inexorable destiny." (Smith and Sjodahl, Commentary, p. 455.)

### D&C 76:50. What Is the Resurrection of the Just?

There are two major resurrections: the resurrection of the just and the resurrection of the unjust. The resurrection of the just includes those who will receive celestial glory and terrestrial glory.

President Joseph Fielding Smith wrote about the resurrection of the just:

"In modern revelation given to the Church, the Lord has made known more in relation to this glorious event. There shall be at least two classes which shall have the privilege of the resurrection at this time: 'First, those who shall dwell in the presence of God and his Christ forever and ever'; and second, honorable men, those who belong to the terrestrial kingdom as well as those of the celestial kingdom.

*Joseph Fielding Smith spoke about the resurrection of the just*

"At the time of the coming of Christ, 'They who have slept in their graves shall come forth, for their graves shall be opened; and they also shall be caught up to meet him in the midst of the pillar of heaven. They are Christ's, the first fruits, they who shall descend with him first, and they who are first caught up to meet him; and all this by the voice of the sounding of the trump of the angel of God.' These are the just, 'whose names are written in heaven, where God and Christ are the judge of all. These are they who are just men made perfect through Jesus the mediator of the new covenant, who wrought out this perfect atonement through the shedding of his own blood.'

"Following this great event, and after the Lord and the righteous who are caught up to meet him have descended upon the earth, there will come to pass another resurrection. This may be considered as a part of the first, although it comes later. In this resurrection will come forth those of *terrestrial order,* who were not worthy to be caught up to meet him, but who are worthy to come forth to enjoy the millennial reign." (*Doctrines of Salvation,* 2:296.)

This first resurrection will extend into the Millennium and include all those worthy of the celestial kingdom who live and die during the thousand years.

### D&C 76:53. What Does It Mean to Be Sealed by the Holy Spirit of Promise?

Elder Bruce R. McConkie defined the Holy Spirit of Promise as "the Holy Spirit *promised* the saints, or in other words the Holy Ghost. This name-title is used in connection with the sealing and ratifying power of the Holy Ghost, that is, the power given him to ratify and approve the righteous acts of men so that those acts will be binding on earth and in heaven. 'All covenants, contracts, bonds, obligations, oaths, vows, performances, connections, associations, or expectations,' must be sealed by the Holy Spirit of Promise, if they are to have 'efficacy, virtue, or force in and after the resurrection from the dead; for all contracts that are not made unto this end have an end when men are dead.' (D&C 132:7.)

"To seal is to *ratify*, to *justify*, or to *approve*. Thus an act which is sealed by the Holy Spirit of Promise is one which is ratified by the Holy Ghost; it is one which is approved by the Lord; and the person who has taken the obligation upon himself is justified by the Spirit in the thing he has done. The ratifying seal of approval is put upon an act only if those entering the contract are worthy as a result of personal righteousness to receive the divine approbation. They 'are sealed by the Holy Spirit of promise, which the Father sheds forth upon all those who are *just* and *true*.' (D.& C. 76:53.) If they are not just and true and worthy the ratifying seal is withheld." (*Mormon Doctrine*, pp. 361-62; see also Notes and Commentary on D&C 132:7.)

**D&C 76:54. What Is the Church of the Firstborn?**

"Those who gain exaltation in the celestial kingdom are those who are members of the Church of the Firstborn; in other words, those who keep all the commandments of the Lord. . . .

"The Lord has made it possible for us to become members of the Church of the Firstborn, by receiving the blessings of the house of the Lord and overcoming all things. Thus we become heirs, 'priests, and kings, who have received of his fulness, and of his glory,' who shall 'dwell in the presence of God and his Christ forever and ever,' with full exaltation." (Smith, *Doctrines of Salvation*, 2:41-42.)

Certain apostates have taken this holy and sacred name upon themselves, audaciously and blasphemously claiming to have met all of these requirements, when they are in fact in a state of wickedness and rebellion.

**D&C 76:72-74. Do Those Who Receive the Gospel in the Spirit World Inherit the Terrestrial Kingdom?**

A simple answer to this question is, yes, they will receive the terrestrial kingdom if they had heard the gospel in mortality and did not accept it. If they have not had that opportunity in mortality and fully accept the gospel in the spirit world, they can inherit the celestial kingdom.

This passage must be seen in the context of the whole vision, not taken in isolation. Joseph Smith learned through another revelation that "all who have died without a knowledge of this gospel, who would have received it if they had been permitted to tarry, shall be heirs of the celestial kingdom of God" (D&C 137:7). God gives to all men the opportunity to accept the gospel of Christ, and those who are worthy of the celestial kingdom are described in the vision of the celestial kingdom (see D&C 76:50-70). Here, in the vision of the terrestrial kingdom, are shown those who were not valiant in their testimony (see vs. 79), including those who died without law but received the gospel in the spirit world. These terrestrial candidates who died without law include most of the people in the so-called heathen nations who have not known the law in this world and who would not be receptive to it later, but these qualify as honorable men (vs. 75).

Elder Melvin J. Ballard explained this distinction as follows: "Now, I wish to say to you that those who died without law, meaning the pagan nations, for lack of faithfulness, for lack of devotion, in the former life, are obtaining all that they are entitled to. I don't mean to say that all of them will be barred from entrance into the highest glory. Any one of them who repents and complies with the conditions might also obtain celestial glory, but the great bulk of them will only obtain terrestrial glory." (In Hinckley, *Sermons of Melvin J. Ballard*, p. 251.)

Though they have not led lives in conformance to law, they still inherit the terrestrial kingdom because, as President Joseph Fielding Smith stated, these are they who "are not under condemnation for a violation of the commandments of the Lord. The promise is made to them of a redemption from death in the following words: 'And then shall the heathen nations be redeemed, and they that knew no law shall have part in the first resurrection; and it shall be tolerable for them' [D&C 45:54]. These, too, shall partake of the mercies of the Lord and shall receive reuniting of spirit and body inseparably, thus becoming immortal, but not with the fulness of the glory of God." (*Doctrines of Salvation*, 2:297.)

Those "who received not the testimony of Jesus in the flesh" (D&C 76:74) are those who heard the gospel in mortality and rejected it. If they "afterwards received it" (vs. 74), that is, in the spirit world, they will go to the terrestrial kingdom. President Joseph Fielding Smith explained that "into the terrestrial kingdom will go all those who are honorable and who have lived clean virtuous lives, but who would not receive the Gospel, but in the spirit world repented and accepted it as far as it can be given unto them. Many of these have been blinded by tradition and the love of the world, and have not been able to see the beauties of the Gospel." (*Church History and Modern Revelation*, 1:287-88.)

Elder Bruce R. McConkie taught the foolishness of believing that a person can reject the gospel in this life, accept it in the next, and still inherit celestial glory. "There are those who believe that the doctrine of salvation for the dead offers men a second chance for salvation.

"I knew a man, now deceased, not a member of the Church, who was a degenerate old reprobate who found pleasure, as he supposed, in living after the manner of the world. A cigarette dangled from his lips, alcohol stenched his breath, and profane and bawdy stories defiled his lips. His moral status left much to be desired.

"His wife was a member of the Church, as faithful as she could be under the circumstances. One day she said to him, 'You know the Church is true; why won't you be baptized?' He replied, 'Of course I know the Church is true, but I have no intention of changing my habits in order to join it. I prefer to live the way I do. But that doesn't worry me in the slightest. I know that as soon as I die, you will have someone go to the temple and do the work for me and everything will come out all right in the end anyway.'

"He died and she had the work done in the temple. We do not sit in judgment and deny vicarious ordinances to people. But what will it profit him?

"There is no such thing as a second chance to gain salvation. This life is the time and day of our probation. After this day of life, which is given us to prepare for eternity, then cometh the night of darkness wherein there can be no labor performed.

"For those who do not have an opportunity to believe and obey the holy word in this life, the first chance to gain salvation will come in the spirit world. If those who hear the word for the first time in the realms ahead are the kind of people who would have accepted the gospel here, had the opportunity been afforded them, they will accept it there. Salvation for the dead is for those whose first chance to gain salvation is in the spirit world.

"There is no other promise of salvation than the one recited in that revelation [D&C 137:7-8]. Those who reject the gospel in this life and then receive it in the spirit world go not to the celestial, but to the terrestrial kingdom." ("The Seven Deadly Heresies," in *Speeches of the Year, 1980* [Provo: Brigham Young University Press, forthcoming].)

### D&C 76:79. What Does It Mean to Be Valiant in the Testimony of the Savior?

In the October 1974 general conference, Elder Bruce R. McConkie defined what it means to be valiant:

"Now what does it mean to be valiant in the testimony of Jesus?

"It is to be courageous and bold; to use all our strength, energy, and ability in the warfare with the world; to fight the good fight of faith. . . . The great cornerstone of valiance in the cause of righteousness is obedience to the whole law of the whole gospel.

"To be valiant in the testimony of Jesus is to 'come unto Christ, and be perfected in him'; it is to deny ourselves 'of all ungodliness,' and 'love God' with all our 'might, mind and strength.' (Moro. 10:32.)

"To be valiant in the testimony of Jesus is to believe in Christ and his gospel with unshakable conviction. It is to know of the verity and divinity of the Lord's work on earth.

"But this is not all. It is more than believing and knowing. We must be doers of the word and not hearers only. It is more than lip service; it is not simply confessing with the mouth the divine Sonship of the Savior. It is obedience and conformity and personal righteousness. 'Not every one that saith unto me, Lord, Lord, shall enter into the kingdom of heaven; but he that doeth the will of my Father which is in heaven.' (Matt. 7:21.)

"To be valiant in the testimony of Jesus is to 'press forward with a steadfastness in Christ, having a perfect brightness of hope, and a love of God and of all men.' It is to 'endure to the end.' (2 Ne. 31:20.) It is to live our religion, to practice what we preach, to keep the commandments. It is the manifestation of 'pure religion' in the lives of men; it is visiting 'the fatherless and widows in their affliction' and keeping ourselves 'unspotted from the world.' (James 1:27.)

"To be valiant in the testimony of Jesus is to bridle our passions, control our appetites, and rise above carnal and evil things. It is to overcome the world as did he who is our prototype and who himself was the most valiant of all our Father's children. It is to be morally clean, to pay our tithes and offerings, to honor the Sabbath day, to pray with full purpose of heart, to lay our all upon the altar if called upon to do so.

"To be valiant in the testimony of Jesus is to take the Lord's side on every issue. It is to vote as he would vote. It is to think what he thinks, to believe what he believes, to say what he would say and do what he would do in the same situation. It is to have the mind of Christ and be one with him as he is one with his Father." (In Conference Report, Oct. 1974, pp. 45-46; or *Ensign*, Nov. 1974, pp. 33-35.)

### D&C 76:81-85. Those Who Inherit the Telestial Glory Will Pass through Hell

Elder Bruce R. McConkie explained the relationship between hell and the telestial kingdom:

"That part of the spirit world inhabited by wicked spirits who are awaiting the eventual day of their resurrection is called *hell*. Between their death and resurrection, these souls of the wicked are cast out into outer darkness, into the gloomy depression of sheol, into the hades of waiting wicked spirits, into hell. There they suffer the torments of the damned; there they welter in the vengeance of eternal fire; there is found weeping and wailing and gnashing of teeth; there the fiery indignation of the wrath of God is poured out upon the wicked. (Alma 40:11-14; D. & C. 76:103-106.)

"Hell will have an end. Viewing future events, John saw that 'death and hell delivered up the dead which were in them: and they were judged every man according to their works.' (Rev. 20:13.) Jacob taught that this escape from death and hell meant the bringing of the body out of the grave and the spirit out of hell. 'And this death of which I have spoken, which is the spiritual death,' he said, 'shall deliver up its dead; which *spiritual death is hell*; wherefore, death and hell must deliver up their dead, and *hell must deliver up its captive spirits*, and the grave must deliver up its captive bodies, and the bodies and the spirits of men will be restored one to the other.' (2 Ne. 9:10-12.) It was in keeping with this principle for David to receive the promise: *'Thou wilt not leave my soul in hell.'* (Psalms 16:10; Acts 2:27.)

"After their resurrection, the great majority of those who have suffered in hell will pass into the telestial kingdom; the balance, cursed as sons of perdition, will be consigned to partake of endless wo with the devil and his angels. . . .

"Who will go to hell? This query is abundantly

answered in the scriptures. Since those going to a telestial kingdom travel to their destination through the depths of hell and as a result of obedience to telestial law, it follows that all those who live a telestial law will go to hell." (*Mormon Doctrine,* pp. 349-50.)

### D&C 76:89-106. Why Will Those Who Inherit the Telestial Kingdom Receive a Glory That "Surpasses All Understanding"?

All who receive the telestial kingdom will have paid a price for this glory. The fact that after they pay this price they inherit a telestial glory is evidence of the Father's love and mercy. Elder John A. Widtsoe explained:

"The book [Doctrine and Covenants] explains clearly that the lowest glory to which man is assigned is so glorious as to be beyond the understanding of man. It is a doctrine fundamental in Mormonism that the meanest sinner, in the final judgment, will receive a glory which is beyond human understanding, which is so great that we are unable to describe it adequately. Those who do well will receive an even more glorious place. Those who dwell in the lower may look wistfully to the higher as we do here. The hell on the other side will be felt in some such way.

"The Gospel is a gospel of tremendous love. Love is at the bottom of it. The meanest child is loved so dearly that his reward will be beyond the understanding of mortal man." (*Message of the Doctrine and Covenants,* p. 167.)

Only the sons of perdition, who deny the truth and openly defy God (see D&C 76:31), will be denied a kingdom of glory (see Notes and Commentary on D&C 76:31-49). The telestial kingdom will be glorious beyond man's present understanding, but in comparison to the higher degrees of glory it will be significantly less. It is reserved for those who in their mortal probation were the wicked of the world.

### D&C 76:107. "I Have Overcome and Have Trodden the Wine-Press Alone"

Notes and Commentary for Doctrine and Covenants 133:50 explains the meaning of treading the wine press.

### D&C 76:111. "Every Man Shall Receive According to His Own Works"

"We are not preaching the gospel with the idea of trying to save people in the terrestrial world. Ours is the salvation of exaltation. What we are trying to do with the gospel of Jesus Christ is to bring people back again, through the power of the priesthood and the ordinances of the Church, as sons and daughters of God, receiving a fulness of the Father's kingdom. That is our endeavor." (Smith, *Doctrines of Salvation,* 2:190-91.)

### D&C 76:116. They Are Only to Be Seen and Understood by the Power of the Holy Spirit

The Prophet Joseph Smith wrote: "Could we read and comprehend all that has been written from the days of Adam, on the relation of man to God and angels in a future state, we should know very little about it. Reading the experience of others, or the revelation given to *them,* can never give *us* a comprehensive view of our condition and true relation to God. Knowledge of these things can only be obtained by experience through the ordinances of God set forth for that purpose. Could you gaze into heaven five minutes, you would know more than you would by reading all that ever was written on the subject." (*History of the Church,* 6:50.)

*The fulness of temple blessings is reserved for those who overcome all things*

# Questions and Answers on the Book of Revelation

Section 77

## Historical Background

"After the return of the Prophet from Amherst, [Ohio,] he resumed his translation of the Scriptures. About the first of March, while engaged in this work, questions arose in regard to the meaning of some of the figurative and symbolical writings of John in the Book of Revelation. There are many things therein which the brethren did not understand, therefore the Prophet inquired of the Lord and received answer to his questions." (Smith, *Church History and Modern Revelation,* 1:291.)

Doctrine and Covenants 77 was given, not as a formal treatise on John's revelation or as a full commentary, but as a key to understanding and an aid to the Latter-day Saints, to whom it has great significance.

"The Book of Revelation is one of the grandest books in sacred literature, and the Lord clearly designs that the Saints should become familiar with it. Else, why this Revelation in the Doctrine and Covenants?

"But this Revelation is not a complete interpretation of the book. It is a key. A key is a very small part of the house. It unlocks the door through which an entrance may be gained, but after the key has been turned, the searcher for treasure must find it for himself. . . .

"The Lord has, in this Section, given His people a key to the book. . . . As Champollion, by the key

# THE REVELATION

## OF ST JOHN THE DIVINE

### CHAPTER 1

*Christ chooses some as kings and priests unto God—Christ shall come again—John sees the Risen Lord.*

[a]THE [b]Revelation of Jesus Christ, which God gave unto him, to shew unto his [c]servants things which must [d]shortly come to pass; and he sent and signified *it* by his [e]angel unto his servant John:

2 Who bare record of the word of God, and of the testimony of Jesus Christ, and of all things that he saw.

3 [a]Blessed *is* he that [b]readeth, and they that hear the words of this prophecy, and keep those things which are written therein: for the [c]time *is* at hand.

4 JOHN to the [a]seven churches which are in Asia: Grace *be* unto you, and peace, from him which [b]is, and which was, and which is to come; and from the seven [c]Spirits which are before his throne;

5 And from Jesus Christ, *who is* the faithful witness, *and* the [a]first begotten of the dead, and the prince of the kings of the earth. Unto him that loved us, and [b]washed us from our sins in his own [c]blood,

6 And hath made us [a]kings and [b]priests unto God and his Father; to him *be* [c]glory and [d]dominion for ever and ever. Amen.

7 Behold, he [a]cometh with clouds; and every eye shall [b]see him, and they *also* which pierced him: and all [c]kindreds of the earth shall [d]wail because of him. Even so, Amen.

8 I am [a]Alpha and Omega, the [b]beginning and the ending, saith the Lord, which is, and which was, and which is to come, the [c]Almighty.

9 I John, who also am your brother, and companion in tribulation, and

furnished in the brief test on the Rosetta stone, was able to open the secrets of Egyptian hieroglyphics, so the Bible student should be able to read the Apocalypse with a better understanding of it, by the aid of this key."(Smith and Sjodahl, Commentary, p. 478.)

# Notes and Commentary

### D&C 77:1. The Earth like a Sea of Glass

The following incident from the history of the Prophet Joseph Smith amplifies this verse: "While at dinner, I remarked to my family and friends present, that when the earth was sanctified and became like a sea of glass, it would be one great urim and thummim, and the Saints could look in it and see as they are seen" (*History of the Church,* 5:279).

President Brigham Young gave the following insight: "This Earth will become a celestial body—be like a sea of glass, or like a Urim and Thummim; and when you wish to know anything, you can look in this Earth and see all the eternities of God" (in *Journal of Discourses,* 8:200; see also D&C 88:17-20, 25-26; 130:6-9).

### D&C 77:2-3. Do the "Four Beasts" Mentioned in Revelation 4:6 Represent the Same Thing As Other Beasts Mentioned by John?

John saw four individual beasts in the presence of God giving "glory and honor and thanks" to him (Revelation 4:9). Though they were actual beasts that were saved in their sphere, they figuratively represent classes of beings (man, beasts, creeping things, fowls) that would have happiness in eternity—"enjoyment of eternal felicity" (D&C 77:3).

In a discourse during a Church conference in Nauvoo on Saturday, 8 April 1843, Joseph Smith explained John's description of the beasts he saw in heaven and compared John's references to beasts with those made by the ancient prophets. The explanation resulted from Elder Pelatiah Brown's erroneously interpreting Revelation 5:8 as saying that the four beasts represented different phases of the kingdom of God on earth. The Prophet Joseph Smith taught that the Lord would not use "the figure of a creature of the brute creation to represent that which is much more noble, glorious and important—the glories and majesty of His kingdom." God would not take "a lesser figure to represent a greater." (*Teachings,* pp. 288-89.)

Part of the confusion is that two different uses of the word *beast* are found in Revelation, and Joseph commented on both in this sermon. In places where John refers to actual creatures that are in heaven, the Greek word is *zoon* (pronounced zoh-ohn), which is translated "a living creature" (see Revelation 4:6-9; 5:6-14; 6:1-7; 7:11; 14:3; 15:7; 19:4). Where John uses *beast* as a symbol of the degenerate kingdoms of the world or the kingdom of Satan, the Greek word *therion,* translated as "a wild beast," is used (see Revelation 6:8; 11:7; 13:1-18; 14:9,11; 15:2; 16:2,10,13; 17:1-18; 19:19-20; 20:4,10). Thus, *zoon* refers to actual creatures seen in heaven; *therion* is used as a symbolic concept. The Prophet Joseph explained the significance of both:

"When God made use of the figure of a beast in visions to the prophets He did it to represent those kingdoms which had degenerated and become corrupt, savage and beast-like in their dispositions, even the degenerate kingdoms of the wicked world; but He never made use of the figure of a beast nor any of the brute kind to represent His kingdom. . . .

"There is a grand difference and distinction between the visions and figures spoken of by the ancient prophets, and those spoken of in the revelations of John. . . .

" . . . There is a grand distinction between the actual meaning of the prophets and the present translation. The prophets do not declare that they saw a beast or beasts, but that they saw the *image* or *figure* of a beast. Daniel did not see an actual bear or a lion but the images or figures of those beasts. The translation should have been rendered 'image' instead of 'beast,' in every instance where beasts are mentioned by the prophets. But John saw the actual beast in heaven, showing to John that beasts did actually exist there, and not to represent figures of things on the earth. . . .

"John saw curious looking beasts in heaven; he saw every creature that was in heaven,—all the beasts, fowls and fish in heaven,—actually there, giving glory to God. How do you prove it? (See Rev. 5:13.). . . .

"I suppose John saw beings there of a thousand forms, that had been saved from ten thousand times ten thousand earths like this,—strange beasts of which we have no conception: all might be seen in heaven. The grand secret was to show John what there was in heaven. John learned that God glorified Himself by saving all that His hands had made, whether beasts, fowls, fishes or men; and He will glorify Himself with them." (*Teachings,* pp. 289-91.)

### D&C 77:2. Are the Saints Accountable to Understand the Lord's Use of Symbolic Images of Beasts or Other Figures?

The Prophet Joseph Smith also said: "I make this broad declaration, that whenever God gives a vision of an image, or beast, or figure of any kind, He always holds Himself responsible to give a revelation or interpretation of the meaning thereof, otherwise we are not responsible or accountable for our belief in it. Don't be afraid of being damned for not knowing the meaning of a vision or figure, if God has not given a revelation or interpretation of the subject." (*Teachings,* p. 291.)

A careful study of the scriptures, however, shows that in most cases the Lord has given the key for understanding the imagery of revelation. That is why the Prophet declared that "the book of Revelation is one of the plainest books God ever caused to be written" (*Teachings,* p. 290).

### D&C 77:5. Why Was John Shown Twenty-Four Elders in the Paradise of God?

John's day was one of great persecution and martyrdom for the Saints (see Revelation 6:9-11). The Church leaders to whom John was writing were experiencing immense difficulties. In their dire circumstances they received the assurance that by faithfully enduring the trials placed upon them they would yet be exalted in the presence of God, "clothed in white raiment" with "crowns" on their heads (Revelation 4:4). How comforting it would be to them, and what a great source of strength for them, to receive this message from John.

### D&C 77:6-7. Why Was the Book Sealed That John Saw?

" 'The book which John saw' represented the real history of the world—what the eye of God has seen, what the recording angel has written; and the seven thousand years, corresponding to the seven seals of the Apocalyptic volume, are as seven great days during which Mother Earth will fulfill her mortal mission, laboring six days and resting upon the seventh, her period of sanctification. These seven days do not include the period of our planet's creation and preparation as a dwelling place for man. They are limited to Earth's 'temporal existence,' that is, to Time, considered as distinct from Eternity." (Whitney, *Saturday Night Thoughts,* p. 11)

A seal, as the term was used by John (see Revelation 5:1-2), was a bit of wax that secured a folded letter or document and bore the impression of a signet. Being thus closed, the document could not be opened without the seal's being broken. In the case of the earth's history and destiny there is only one who is worthy to open the seal and reveal the contents, and that one is Jesus Christ (see Revelation 5:2-9). Only through the atonement of Christ is the temporal existence of the earth of any value. He alone holds the key to the fulfilling of the purpose for which the earth was created. Because of him the plan of salvation will succeed; without him all would fail and come to naught, or remain sealed.

### D&C 77:8. Four Angels Sent from God with Power to Save Life and to Destroy It

President Joseph Fielding Smith explained that "these angels seem to fit the description of the angels spoken of in the parable of the wheat and the tares, (Matt. 13:24-43 and D. & C. 86:17), who plead with the Lord that they might go forth to reap down the field. They were told to let the wheat and the tares grow together to the time of the end of the harvest, which is the end of the world (Matt. 13:38-39). . . .

"These angels have been given power over the four parts [quarters] of the earth and they have the power of committing the everlasting Gospel to the peoples of the earth. The fulness of the Gospel was not restored by any one messenger sent from the presence of the Lord. All the ancient prophets who held keys and came and restored them, had a hand in this great work of restoration. There are, we learn from this revelation, four angels unto whom the power has been given, to shut up the heavens, to open them and with power unto life and also unto death and destruction. These are now at work in the earth on their sacred mission." (*Church History and Modern Revelation,* 1:300-301.)

Susa Young Gates reported an address by President Wilford Woodruff in which he declared: "Those angels have left the portals of heaven, and they stand over this people and this nation now, and are hovering over the earth waiting to pour out the judgments. And from this very day they shall be poured out." (*Young Women's Journal,* Aug. 1894, p. 512; see also Notes and Commentary for D&C 86:5.)

### D&C 77:9. What Is the Significance of the Angel from the East Sealing the Servants of God?

The four angels who are given power over the earth are kept from sending forth desolations upon the earth until God's servants are sealed in their foreheads. The Prophet Joseph Smith taught that this sealing "signifies sealing the blessing upon their heads, meaning the everlasting covenant, thereby making their calling and election sure" (*Teachings,* p. 321).

Elder Orson Pratt gave this additional explanation:

"When the Temple is built [in the New Jerusalem] the sons of the two Priesthoods [Melchizedek and Aaronic] . . . will enter into that Temple . . . and all of them who are pure in heart will behold the face of the Lord and that too before he comes in his glory in the clouds of heaven, for he will suddenly come to his Temple, and he will purify the sons of Moses and of Aaron, until they shall be prepared to offer in that Temple an offering that shall be acceptable in the sight of the Lord. In doing this, he will purify not only the minds of the Priesthood in that Temple, but he will purify their bodies until they shall be quickened, and renewed and strengthened, and they will be partially changed, not to immortality, but changed in part that they can be filled with the power of God, and they can stand in the presence of Jesus, and behold his face in the midst of that Temple.

*Temple site at Jackson County, Missouri*

"This will prepare them for further ministrations among the nations of the earth, it will prepare them to go forth in the days of tribulation and vengeance upon the nations of the wicked, when God will smite them with pestilence, plague and earthquake, such as former generations never knew. Then the servants of God will need to be armed with the power of God, they will need to have that sealing blessing pronounced upon their foreheads that they can stand forth in the midst of these desolations and plagues and not be overcome by them. When John the Revelator describes this scene he says he saw four angels sent forth, ready to hold the four winds that should blow from the four quarters of heaven. Another angel ascended from the east and cried to the four angels, and said, 'Smite not the earth now, but wait a little while.' 'How long?' 'Until the servants of our God are sealed in their foreheads.' What for? To prepare them to stand forth in the midst of these desolations and plagues, and not be overcome. When they are prepared, when they have received a renewal of their bodies in the Lord's temple, and have been filled with the Holy Ghost and purified as gold and silver in a furnace of fire, then they will be prepared to stand before the nations of the earth and preach glad tidings of salvation in the midst of judgments that are to come like a whirlwind upon the wicked." (In *Journal of Discourses,* 15:365-66.)

**D&C 77:11. Who Are the 144,000?**

"Before the Lord shall come . . . there is to be a great work among the nations. . . . The ten tribes will have to come forth and come to this land, to be crowned with glory in the midst of Zion by the hands of the servants of God, even the Children of Ephraim; and twelve thousand High Priests will be elected from each of these ten tribes, as well as from the scattered tribes, and sealed in their foreheads, and will be ordained and receive power to gather out of all nations, kindreds, tongues and people as many as will come unto the general assemblage of the Church of the first-born." (Orson Pratt, in *Journal of Discourses,* 16:325.)

**D&C 77:12. What Things Has Christ "Not Put into His Power"?**

See Doctrine and Covenants 76:31-38, 43-44.

**D&C 77:12. What Is the Purpose for the Sounding of Trumpets by Seven Angels?**

Trumpets were used anciently to herald or announce something or to draw attention to something. The seven angels who sound trumpets in Revelation 8 through 10 will signal events that will take place in the beginning of the seventh thousand years (after the seventh seal is opened; see Revelation 8:1), before the Lord comes in his glory.

**D&C 77:14. What Is the Symbolism of the Little Book Eaten by John?**

Elder Bruce R. McConkie said that "John's act of eating a book containing the word of God to him was in keeping with the custom and tradition of ancient Israel. The act signified that he was eating the bread of life, that he was partaking of the good word of God, that he was feasting upon the word of Christ—which was in his mouth sweet as honey. But it made his belly bitter; that is, the judgments and plagues promised those to whom the Lord's word was sent caused him to despair and have sorrow of soul. 'How sweet are thy words unto my taste! yea, sweeter than honey to my mouth!' (Psalm 119:103.) Such is the exulting cry of the Psalmist. And conversely, how bitter is the penalty for rebellion and disobedience. Ezekiel had a similar experience. He was commanded to eat a roll (a book), which was in his mouth as honey for sweetness, but in the writing itself there was 'lamentations, and mourning, and woe.' (Ezek. 2:6-10; 3:1-3.)" (*Doctrinal New Testament Commentary,* 3:507.)

**D&C 77:14. Are John the Revelator and the Angel Ascending from the East the Same Person?**

Verse 9 indicates that the angel from the east is Elias; in verse 14 it is seen that John is Elias; and in other scriptural passages Elias is referred to in connection with the restoration of all things. In the following passages several individuals are identified by the name Elias: Joseph Smith Translation, Matthew 17:11-14; Joseph Smith Translation, John 1:21-28; Doctrine and Covenants 77:9, 14 (see also D&C 27:6-7; Luke 1:5-25; Smith, *Teachings,* p. 157).

Elder Bruce R. McConkie explained that several individuals have been called Elias: "By finding answer to the question, by whom had the restoration been effected, we shall find who Elias is and find there is no problem in harmonizing these apparently contradictory revelations. Who has restored all things? Was it one man? Certainly not. Many angelic ministrants have been sent from the courts of glory to confer keys and powers, to commit their dispensations and glories again to men of earth. At least the following have come: Moroni, John the Baptist, Peter, James and John, Moses, Elijah, Elias, Gabriel, Raphael, and Michael. (D.& C. 13; 110; 128:19-21.) Since it is apparent that no one messenger has carried the whole burden of the restoration, but rather that each has come with a specific endowment from on high, it becomes clear that Elias is a composite personage. The expression must be understood to be a name and a title for those whose mission it was to commit keys and powers to men in this final dispensation." (*Doctrinal New Testament Commentary,* 3:492.)

In his mission to help gather the tribes of Israel, John functioned under the title "Elias." He came with Peter and James as one of the angels of the Restoration, so he must be included as part of the composite personage symbolized by the "angel ascending from the east" (D&C 77:9).

**D&C 77:15. Who Are the Two Witnesses Referred to by John?**

While the Prophet Joseph was still alive, Parley P.

Pratt wrote a tract to be used in missionary work. It was approved for publication by the Prophet. In it Elder Pratt explained the meaning of the two witnesses: "John, in the eleventh chapter of Revelation, gives us many more particulars concerning this same event [the great war in Israel after the Jews are gathered there]. He informs us that after the city and temple are rebuilt by the Jews, the Gentiles will tread it under foot forty and two months, during which time there will be two prophets continually prophesying and working mighty miracles. And it seems that the Gentile army shall be hindered from utterly destroying and overthrowing the city, while these two prophets continue. But, after a struggle of three years and a half, they will at length succeed in destroying these two prophets and then overrunning much of the city; they will send gifts to each other because of the death of the two prophets, and in the meantime will not allow their dead bodies to be put in graves, but suffer them to lie in the streets of Jerusalem three days and a half, during which time the armies of the Gentiles, consisting of many kindreds, tongues and nations, passing through the city, plundering the Jews, will see their dead bodies lying in the street. But after three days and a half, on a sudden, the spirit of life from God will enter them; they will arise and stand upon their feet, and great fear will fall upon them that see them. And then they shall hear a voice from heaven saying, 'Come up hither,' and they will ascend up to heaven in a cloud, with enemies beholding them." (*Voice of Warning,* p. 33.)

Elder Bruce R. McConkie identified the two prophets as "followers of that humble man Joseph Smith, through whom the Lord of Heaven restored the fulness of his everlasting gospel in this final dispensation of grace. No doubt they will be members of the Council of the Twelve or of the First Presidency of the Church." (*Doctrinal New Testament Commentary,* 3:509.)

The two witnesses are raised up "*to* the Jewish nation" and are not necessarily *from* the Jewish nation (see D&C 77:15-16; emphasis added.)

# Consecration: An Everlasting Covenant

Section 78

## Historical Background

"During the early part of the year 1832, the Prophet and Sidney Rigdon continued the work of the revision of the scriptures. At the time the Prophet was still residing in the house of Father John Johnson, at Hiram. It was during this time that this important revelation was given to the members of the Priesthood who were assembled imparting instructions in relation to the plan of the 'united order' or 'order of Enoch,' on which the promised Zion should be built. The Lord had revealed that it was only through obedience to his divine will, the celestial law, that Zion could be built. The members of the Church rejoiced when the Lord revealed to them the site on which the New Jerusalem, or City of Zion, should be built. Their enthusiasm, however, was not sufficient to carry them through to a conclusion in strict obedience to the divine will. In this revelation (Sec. 78) the Lord reveals his will in words of wisdom to all those holding the High Priesthood." (Smith, *Church History and Modern Revelation,* 1:304-5.)

Joseph Smith wrote of this time: "Besides the work of translating, previous to the 20th of March, I received the four following revelations: [D&C 78-81]" (*History of the Church,* 1:255).

## Notes and Commentary

### D&C 78:1-9. Why Were Substitute Names Used?

Elder Orson Pratt answered this question in this way: "The law of Enoch is so named in the Book of Doctrine and Covenants, but in other words, it is the law given by Joseph Smith, Jr. The word Enoch did not exist in the original copy; neither did some other names. The names that were incorporated when it was printed, did not exist there when the manuscript revelations were given, for I saw them myself. Some of them I copied. And when the Lord was about to have the Book of Covenants given to the world it was thought wisdom, in consequence of the persecutions of our enemies in Kirtland and some of the regions around, that some of the names should be changed, and Joseph was called Baurak Ale, which was a Hebrew word; meaning God bless you. He was also called Gazelam, being a person to whom the Lord had given the Urim and Thummim. He was also called Enoch. Sidney Rigdon was called Baneemy. And the revelation where it read so many *dollars* into the treasury was changed to *talents.* And the City of New York was changed to Cainhannoch." (In *Journal of Discourses,* 16:156.)

In the 1981 edition of the Doctrine and Covenants the substitute names were eliminated, since the need for them no longer existed.

### D&C 78:5-7. Equality in Earthly As Well As Heavenly Things

"The principle is here taught that the Latter-day Saints must be equal in things pertaining to this Earth. In celestial glory there is perfect equality (Sec. 76:95). But if they have not practiced equality here, they are not prepared to live under that law there." (Smith and Sjodahl, Commentary, p. 480.) It should be noted, however, that the Lord has a special definition of *equality* in the united order (see D&C 51:3; Notes and Commentary on D&C 51:3).

### D&C 78:11. A Bond That Cannot Be Broken

"I construe the new and everlasting covenant as I could construe, in large measure, a legal contract. I believe that our Father intended that he would obligate himself as well as obligate the beneficiaries of that contract to the performance of it. I believe that no one is entitled to the full measure of its blessings unless he subjects himself to all the conditions upon which those blessings are predicated, and I construe that covenant to be broad enough to embrace every principle of the gospel." (Stephen L Richards, in Conference Report, Oct. 1922, p. 67.)

### D&C 78:12. What Does It Mean to Be Turned Over to the Buffetings of Satan?

"To be turned over to the *buffetings of Satan* is to be given into his hands; it is to be turned over to him with all the protective power of the priesthood, of righteousness, and of godliness removed, so that Lucifer is free to torment, persecute, and afflict such a person without let or hindrance. When the bars are down, the cuffs and curses of Satan, both in this world and in the world to come, bring indescribable anguish typified by burning fire and brimstone. The damned in hell so suffer." (McConkie, *Mormon Doctrine,* p. 108.)

### D&C 78:10-12. When Is the "Day of Redemption"?

"Satan's plan is to destroy. Ever since his rebellion in the former estate he has determined to carry out his plan by exercising force and compulsion against mankind. All those who accepted the Lord's plan did so with an organized bond and covenant that was to be everlasting and not to be broken. The Lord's covenants are always intended to be everlasting or to have a bearing on everlasting life. The brethren were duly warned that if they broke this covenant evil consequences would follow. 'Satan seeketh,' said the Lord, 'to turn their hearts away from the truth, that they become blinded and understand not the things which are prepared for them.' If they failed in this everlasting covenant then they were to be turned over to the buffetings of Satan until the day of redemption. We might think that the day of redemption means that they then, after their suffering, would be reinstated and receive the blessings which were first offered them. We are not justified in this conclusion. The day of redemption is the day of the resurrection. (D. & C. 88:16.) We should remember that the Lord has said at other times that such may not come into his presence." (Smith, *Church History and Modern Revelation,* 1:308.)

### D&C 78:14. How Will the Church "Stand Independent above All Other Creatures"?

The law of consecration was withdrawn by the

*Both temporal and spiritual needs receive emphasis in the Church*

Lord because the Saints showed that they would not abide by its laws (see D&C 105:2-6, 34). In 1936, under direction of the First Presidency, the welfare program was instituted, based on the same principles that governed the Saints in the united order: love, service, self-reliance, consecration, and so on. The promise that the Church would stand independent above all other creatures (organizations, people, and so forth) will be partially fulfilled through the implementation of the welfare plan.

President Marion G. Romney said:

"I do not want to be a calamity howler. I don't know in detail what's going to happen in the future. I know what the prophets have predicted. But I tell you that the welfare program, organized to enable us to take care of our own needs, has not yet performed the function that it was set up to perform. We will see the day when we will live on what we produce.

"We're living in the latter days. We're living in the days the prophets have told about from the time of Enoch to the present day. We are living in the era just preceding the second advent of the Lord Jesus Christ. We are told to so prepare and live that we can be . . . independent of every other creature beneath the celestial kingdom. That is what we are to do.

"This welfare program was set up under inspiration in the days of President Grant. It was thoroughly analyzed and taught by his great counselor, J. Reuben Clark, Jr. It is in basic principle the same as the United Order. When we get so we can live it, we will be ready for the United Order. You brethren know that we will have to have a people ready for that order in order to receive the Savior when he comes.

"I know from my own experience and the witnesses by the thousands that I have received of the Spirit that this is the Lord's work. It is to prepare us. If you'll think of the most sacred place you ever have been, you'll remember that the final thing that we are to do is to be able and willing to consecrate all that we have to the building up of the kingdom of God, to care for our fellow men. When we do this we'll be ready for the coming of the Messiah." (In Conference Report, Apr. 1975, pp. 165-66.)

Additional material on the law of consecration is found in Enrichment L, in the Appendix.

**D&C 78:15. Adam-ondi-Ahman**

Adam-ondi-Ahman is discussed in Notes and Commentary on Doctrine and Covenants 116; 107:53-57.

**D&C 78:15-16. Michael and the Keys of Salvation**

"Adam was among the intelligences spoken of by the Lord to Abraham who were appointed to be rulers on this earth. He was Michael, a prince, and son of God chosen to come to this earth and stand at the head of his posterity, holding the 'keys of salvation under the counsel and direction of the Holy One, who is without beginning of days or end of life.' This Holy One is Jesus Christ. On the earth Michael was known as Adam. In the pre-existent state he was a spirit like the others of our Father's children." (Smith, *Answers to Gospel Questions,* 1:5-6.)

**D&C 78:20. The Son Ahman**

Elder Orson Pratt pointed out that "there is one revelation that this people are not generally acquainted with. I think it has never been published, but probably it will be in the Church History. It is given in questions and answers. The first question is, 'What is the name of God in the pure language?' The answer says, 'Ahman.' 'What is the name of the Son of God?' Answer, 'Son Ahman—the greatest of all the parts of God excepting Ahman.' " (In *Journal of Discourses,* 2:342.)

President Joseph Fielding Smith added: "We also learn from the closing verses of this revelation that Jesus Christ is also called Son Ahman. (See D&C 95:17.) Therefore his name is connected with the name of the place where Adam dwelt. For that reason Elder Orson Pratt gives it the interpretation of 'The Valley of God.' " (*Church History and Modern Revelation,* 1:310.)

**D&C 78:21. The Church of the Firstborn**

"Members of The Church of Jesus Christ of Latter-day Saints who so devote themselves to righteousness that they receive the higher ordinances of exaltation become members of the Church of the Firstborn. Baptism is the gate to the Church itself, but celestial marriage is the gate to membership in the Church of the Firstborn, the inner circle of faithful saints who are heir of exaltation and the fulness of the Father's kingdom. (D&C 76:54, 67, 71, 94, 102; 77:11; 78:21; 88:1-5; Heb. 12:23.)" (McConkie, *Mormon Doctrine,* p. 139.)

Notes and Commentary on Doctrine and Covenants 76:54 contains a further discussion of the Church of the Firstborn.

# The Lord Will Bless His Faithful Servants

Section 79

## Historical Background

This revelation was received in March 1832 at Hiram, Ohio. Whereas Joseph Smith gave no explanation or introduction about why he received it, Jared Carter explained that he had inquired of Joseph Smith regarding the will of the Lord in his behalf, and learning that he was to go on a mission to the eastern countries, he set out for Kirtland, Ohio. Jared's brother Simeon Carter joined him, and together they started east. Jared Carter recorded in his journal that he labored six months and two days in the mission field, during which time he converted seventy-nine souls. (See Journal of Jared Carter, Historical Department, The Church of Jesus Christ of Latter-day Saints, Salt Lake City, pp. 53-54, 110-12, 123-24.)

## Notes and Commentary

**D&C 79:1-4. How Important Is It to Honor the Priesthood and Accept Assignments from the Lord?**

President John Taylor taught that "it is for us to magnify our calling and honor our God in any and every position that we may be called upon to fill. . . . I would say that this Priesthood is not for the honor of man, not for his exaltation alone; but it is imparted to man in order that he may be made the medium of salvation to others. . . . Talking of the Elder, why he is a herald of salvation; he is a legate of the skies; he is commissioned of the great Jehovah to bear a message to the nations of the earth, and God has promised to sustain him. He has always sustained His faithful Elders, and He always will. And what of the Elder? He is commanded to call upon men to believe in Jesus Christ, to repent of their sins, and to be baptized for the remission of sins, promising them the gift of the Holy Ghost; and all who obey the requirements receive this divine gift. Is that true? Do you Elders not know that to be true? Does not this congregation know that it is true? And when you obeyed the Gospel, when you had hands laid upon your heads for the reception of the Holy Ghost, did you not receive it? If you were honest, you did; if you were true and sincere you did, and you are my witnesses as to the truth of these things of which I speak. What does it prove? It proves

*Priesthood gives a man the power to bless others through worthy service*

that God is with the Elders of Israel; it proves that God lives. Is not that a great witness to the Latter-day Saints, and is it not a witness to the world? Who dare come before the world with such a statement? Nobody but those that have the authority, as the Lord sanctions and acknowledges none excepting those that are authorized of Him." (In *Journal of Discourses,* 24:35-36.)

**D&C 79:3. Those Who Are Faithful**

"God has in reserve a time, or period appointed in His own bosom, when He will bring all His subjects, who have obeyed His voice and kept His commandments, into His celestial rest. This rest is of such perfection and glory, that man has need of a preparation before he can, according to the laws of that kingdom, enter it and enjoy its blessings." (*History of the Church,* 2:12.)

Notes and Commentary on Doctrine and Covenants 75:5 explains the imagery of the sheaves.

# "Declare the Things Which Ye Have Heard, and Verily Believe, and Know to Be True"

Section 80

## Historical Background

During March 1832 Joseph Smith and Sidney Rigdon were working on the translation of the Bible. The Prophet Joseph Smith recorded simply: "Besides the work of translating, previous to the 20th of March, I received the four following revelations [D&C 78-81]" (*History of the Church,* 1:255).

Section 80 was given to Stephen Burnett and Eden Smith regarding their missionary activities. At the Church conference held at Amherst, Ohio, 25 January 1832, these two brethren had been called by the Lord to serve as missionaries (see D&C 75:35-36). Now they were assigned as missionary companions and sent forth to teach the gospel.

## Notes and Commentary

**D&C 80:4. The Importance of Personal Preparation for Missionary Work**

Elder Orson Pratt made this observation about missionary work: "I have been abroad with several companies of missionaries from this place, and I have seen them lament and mourn, and have heard them tell their feelings one to another, saying—'O that I had occupied my time that I have spent as it were in folly, in treasuring up the principles of eternal life,—that I had studied the scriptures—that I had made myself acquainted more extensively with the doctrines of the Church—that I had made myself acquainted with those principles revealed from heaven for our guidance! I should then have been prepared to stand before the inhabitants of the earth and edify them with regard to our principles.' " (In *Journal of Discourses,* 7:76.)

*A sister shares the gospel at the Hill Cumorah pageant*

# The Call of Frederick G. Williams

Section 81

## Historical Background

On 15 March 1832 the Prophet Joseph Smith received a revelation calling Frederick G. Williams to be a counselor in the First Presidency of the Church. In the two manuscript copies of this revelation, however, it appears that the revelation was originally directed to Jesse Gause and not to Frederick G. Williams.

"Our earliest reference to Jesse Gause is as a member of the Shaker communities in Hancock near Pittsfield, and possibly in North Union, Ohio as well. His conversion and baptism are not found in any of the records of the Church, but one writer has suggested that he was converted by Reynolds Cahoon in late 1830. It was not until 8 March 1832, when Jesse Gause was called to be a counselor to Joseph Smith in the presidency of the high priesthood, that his name is even mentioned in surviving Church records. The notation in the Kirtland Revelation Book is as follows:

" 'March 8, 1832. Chose this day and ordained brother Jesse Gause and Broth [sic] Sidney to be my councellors [sic] of the ministry of the presidency of the high Priesthood. . . .'

"One week later, a revelation concerning Jesse Gause was received by Joseph Smith, confirming Jesse in his work and giving further direction in his office and calling. There are two manuscript copies of this revelation extant: one in the Kirtland Revelation Book, located in the Church Historical Department, and the other in the library of the Reorganized Church of Jesus Christ of Latter-day Saints. In both of these Jesse Gause's name has been crossed out and Frederick G. Williams' name written above it. Since that time, all published copies of this revelation (Section 81 of the Doctrine and Covenants) list Frederick G. Williams as the one to whom it is directed. Since this revelation contains instructions, duties, and promised blessings to the one called as counselor to the Prophet, the revelation was just as appropriate for Frederick G. Williams as it was to Jesse Gause.

"After Jesse Gause was ordained, he appeared in a leading role in the Church for only a short time. In April 1832, he accompanied Joseph Smith, Newel K. Whitney, and Peter Whitmer, Jr. on a trip to Missouri. They arrived 24 April and began holding conferences with the Saints in Zion on the 26th. In the minutes of a meeting of the Literary Firm held on Monday, 30 April, Jesse Gause was listed as a counselor to Joseph Smith. . . .

"Upon his return to Kirtland, Jesse was called to serve a mission with Zebedee Coltrin. They began their journey on 1 August 1832, and traveled until the 19th, at which time Coltrin decided to return to Kirtland because of severe pains in his head. After praying with and for each other, they parted. Jesse Gause continued east and walked right out of the history of the Church, never again to return. There appears to be no other record of the man either in or out of the Church.

"Some months after the departure of Jesse Gause, the presidency of the high priesthood was reorganized with Frederick G. Williams replacing him as counselor. This reorganization was commanded in Section 90 of the Doctrine and Covenants, and actually took place on 18 March 1833." (Robert J. Woodford, "Jesse Gause, Counselor to the Prophet," *BYU Studies,* Spring 1975, pp. 362-64.)

## Notes and Commentary

**D&C 81:1. Establishment of the First Presidency**

The Lord revealed the principles pertaining to the organization of the First Presidency in November 1831. These principles were not formally presented until 28 March 1835, when the newly formed Quorum of the Twelve requested written instructions concerning their duties. This reply, now section 107 of the Doctrine and Covenants, includes the items given and recorded earlier concerning the First Presidency (see D&C 107:56-69, 71-72, 74-75, 78-87, 89, 91-92, 99-100; see also "Kirtland Revelation Book," Archives of the Church of Jesus Christ of Latter-day Saints, Salt Lake City, pp. 84-87.)

The Prophet Joseph Smith was ordained as president of the high priesthood on 25 January 1832 (see *History of the Church,* 1:267), but he did not select his counselors until 8 March 1832 (see "Kirtland Revelation Book," p. 10). This revelation was directed to one of those counselors, Jesse Gause, but it was applied to Frederick G. Williams when he was called to the Presidency to replace Gause on 8 March 1833 (see D&C 90; *History of the Church,* 1:329-30). March 18, 1833, is the date when the organizing and ordaining of the first First Presidency in this dispensation was completed (see *History of the Church,* 1:334).

These events illustrate how the Church grew and developed as the need arose. President Anthon H. Lund explained: "When the Church was organized on the 6th day of April, 1830, . . . it was impossible to establish this perfect organization of the Priesthood. Joseph Smith and Oliver Cowdery were called and ordained Apostles; but there could not be Twelve Apostles, there could not be Seventy, for at that time the Church was too small. It took time for the work to grow; but the Lord had given revelation upon the subject, and when the proper time came the Presidency of the Church was organized, with the Prophet Joseph as President and Sidney Rigdon and Frederick G.

*The First Presidency of the Church (1833): Sidney Rigdon, Joseph Smith, and Frederick G. Williams*

Williams as his counselors. Afterwards the Twelve Apostles were chosen, and then the Seventies. But in the beginning, when there were not enough to form these different quorums, the Elders presided, because they held the Melchisedek Priesthood. The Lord, however, had a perfect organization for His Church, and He gave it unto them when they were ready to receive it." (In Conference Report, Nov. 1901, p. 75.)

### D&C 81:2. "The Keys of the Kingdom . . . Belong Always unto the Presidency"

President Joseph F. Smith explained the difference between priesthood and keys of the priesthood by noting that "the Priesthood in general is the authority given to man to act for God. Every man that has been ordained to any degree of the Priesthood, has this authority dedicated to him.

"But it is necessary that every act performed under this authority, shall be done at the proper time and place, in the proper way, and after the proper order. The power of directing these labors constitute the *keys* of the Priesthood. In their fullness, these keys are held by only one person at a time, the prophet and president of The Church. He may delegate any portion of this power to another, in which case that person holds the keys of that particular labor. Thus, the president of a temple, the president of a stake, the bishop of a ward, the president of a mission, the president of a quorum, each holds the keys of the labors performed in that particular body or locality. His Priesthood is not increased by this special appointment, for a seventy who presides over a mission has no more Priesthood than a seventy who labors under his direction; and the president of an elders' quorum, for example, has no more Priesthood than any member of that quorum. But he holds the power of directing the official labors performed in the mission or the quorum, or in other words, *the keys* of that division of that work. So it is throughout all the ramifications of the Priesthood—a distinction must be carefully made between the general authority, and the directing of the labors performed by that authority." ("Distinction between Keys of the Priesthood and Priesthood," *Improvement Era,* Jan. 1901, p. 230.)

The fact that the keys of the kingdom always belong to the First Presidency was explained by President Joseph Fielding Smith:

"These keys are the right of presidency; they are the power and authority to govern and direct all of the Lord's affairs on earth. Those who hold them have power to govern and control the manner in which all others may serve in the priesthood. All of us may hold the priesthood, but we can only use it as authorized and directed so to do by those who hold the keys.

"This priesthood and these keys were conferred upon Joseph Smith and Oliver Cowdery by Peter, James, and John, and by Moses and Elijah and others of the ancient prophets. They have been given to each man who has been set apart as a member of the Council of the Twelve. But since they are the right of presidency, they can only be exercised in full by the senior apostle of God on earth, who is the president of the Church.

"May I now say—very plainly and very emphatically—that we have the holy priesthood and that the keys of the kingdom of God are here. They are found only in The Church of Jesus Christ of Latter-day Saints.

"By revelation to Joseph Smith, the Lord said that these keys 'belong always unto the Presidency of the High Priesthood' (D&C 81:2). . . .

"Now, brethren, I think there is one thing which we should have exceedingly clear in our minds. Neither the President of the Church, nor the First Presidency, nor the united voice of the First Presidency and the Twelve will ever lead the Saints astray or send forth counsel to the world that is contrary to the mind and will of the Lord.

"An individual may fall by the wayside, or have views, or give counsel which falls short of what the Lord intends. But the voice of the First Presidency and the united voice of those others who hold with them the keys of the kingdom shall always guide the Saints and the world in those paths where the Lord wants them to be. . . .

"I testify that if we shall look to the First Presidency and follow their counsel and direction, no power on earth can stay or change our course as a church, and as individuals we shall gain peace in this life and be inheritors of eternal glory in the world to come." (In Conference Report, Apr. 1972, pp. 98-99; or *Ensign*, July 1972, pp. 87-88.)

**D&C 81:6. "If Thou Art Faithful unto the End"**

This revelation to Frederick G. Williams is similar in some respects to a patriarchal blessing, for it told him of special promises and blessings reserved for him on the condition of his faithfulness and gave him specific charges that would help him achieve these blessings. But during the apostasy in Kirtland in 1837, Frederick G. Williams became estranged from the Church. A conference of elders in Far West refused to sustain him as a member of the First Presidency, and at a conference in March 1839 he was excommunicated from the Church. Happily, about a year later he appeared during a general conference of the Church and "humbly asked forgiveness for his conduct [while in Missouri], and expressed his determination to do the will of God in the future" (*History of the Church*, 4:110). His petition was accepted, and he was rebaptized soon afterwards. He died in Nauvoo in 1842.

# "I, the Lord, Am Bound When Ye Do What I Say"

Section 82

## Historical Background

Smith and Sjodahl described the setting of this revelation:

"In the Revelation recorded in Section 78, our Savior commanded His servants of the High Priesthood to effect an organization for the temporal benefit of the people, and directed the Prophet Joseph, Newel K. Whitney, and Sidney Rigdon to go from Hiram, Ohio, to Missouri, and 'sit in council with the Saints which are in Zion,' on that matter. The Prophet commenced the journey on April 1st, 1832, accompanied by Newel K. Whitney, Peter Whitmer, and Jesse Gause, and they were joined by Sidney Rigdon at Warren, the same day. The excitement of the mob in Kirtland, owing to the falsehoods circulated by apostates, was so intense that the Prophet and his companions avoided passing through the city. Some of the mobbers followed them all the way to Cleveland, but the protecting hand of the Lord was over His servants. The captain who took them to Louisville protected them in his boat, and gave them their meals, free of charge. They arrived at Independence, Missouri, on the 24th of April, and were greeted with joy by the Saints.

"On the 26th a general council of the Church was called. The Prophet was acknowledged as the President of the High Priesthood, to which exalted position he had been ordained at the Conference at Amherst, Ohio, Jan. 25th, 1832. Bishop Partridge gave him the right hand of fellowship in behalf of the Church.

"On this occasion a misunderstanding between Sidney Rigdon and Edward Partridge was cleared up, and unity and peace prevailed. The Lord then gave this Revelation [D&C 82]." (Commentary, pp. 488-89.)

## Notes and Commentary

**D&C 82:1. Which "Servants" Are Referred to As Being Forgiven?**

This verse "refers to Sidney Rigdon and Edward Partridge. Even those who stand highest among the Church leaders have their human weaknesses. Paul may have to rebuke Peter (Gal. 2:11-13). But when they forgive each other, God forgives them. 'It is a true sentiment that great men may err; a higher finish with such is, that their greatness is enhanced by acknowledging their errors' (Orson Spencer)." (Smith and Sjodahl, Commentary, p. 489.)

**D&C 82:2. Why Did the Lord Say Many Had Sinned Exceedingly?**

Smith and Sjodahl noted that "Sidney Rigdon and Edward Partridge were not the only ones who had erred; all had sinned, some exceedingly. The Revelation does not give the particulars. But Church historians note that although the settlements in Zion increased rapidly, and were exceedingly prosperous, many of the Saints failed to obey the counsel of the authorities. Some refused to submit to the law of consecration, preferring to obtain property for themselves, and jealousy, covetousness, and general neglect of duty [resulted]. Some of the High Priests and Elders ignored the Seven Presidents appointed to have charge of the Branches in Zion, viz., Oliver Cowdery, W. W. Phelps, John Whitmer, Sidney Gilbert, Edward Partridge, Isaac Morley, and John Corrill, and took the leadership into their own hands. Hence the warning, 'Refrain from sin, lest sore judgments fall upon you.' " (Commentary, p. 489.)

**D&C 82:5. "Darkness Reigneth"**

" 'Darkness' here, as in John 1:5, means the condition of the world outside divine revelation. It refers to both spiritual and moral error. Revelation from God gives light, but when divine revelation is rejected, the adversary spreads his dominion among the children of men." (Smith and Sjodahl, Commentary, p. 490.)

**D&C 82:7. "Unto That Soul Who Sinneth Shall the Former Sins Return"**

President Brigham Young said that "it is present salvation and the present influence of the Holy Ghost that we need every day to keep us on saving ground. When an individual refuses to comply with the further requirements of Heaven, then the sins he had formerly committed return upon his head; his former righteousness departs from him, and is not accounted to him for righteousness: but if he had continued in righteousness and obedience to the requirements of heaven, he is saved all the time, through baptism, the laying on of hands, and obeying the commandments of the Lord and all that is required of him by the heavens—the living oracles. He is saved now, next week, next year, and continually, and is prepared for the celestial kingdom of God whenever the time comes for him to inherit it." (In *Journal of Discourses,* 8:124.)

**D&C 82:10. "I . . . Am Bound When Ye Do What I Say"**

This verse shows a part of God's basic nature: the way he deals with his children and the reason they can trust him. Elder James E. Talmage said:

" 'Mormonism' has taught me that God holds himself accountable to law even as he expects us to do. He has set us the example in obedience to law. I know that to say this would have been heresy a few decades ago. But we have the divine word for it: 'I, the Lord, am bound when ye do what I say; but when ye do not what I say, ye have no promise.' (Doc. and Cov. 82:10.) He operates by law and not by arbitrariness or caprice." (In Conference Report, Apr. 1930, p. 96.)

**D&C 82:11-12. Why Were These Men to Covenant with God?**

The men named were of the order of Enoch or the united order. As leaders in the Church, they were to be examples to all others, showing how the law of consecration was to be lived (see also D&C 78:9-14; 82:20-21). The "bond and covenant" (D&C 78:11) to which they were binding themselves was that of the law of consecration. They were to agree to keep the laws and rules of that order through making a solemn covenant with the Lord. The penalty for breaking that oath and covenant was very severe (see D&C 82:21; 104:8-9).

**D&C 82:13-14. How Can Zion Increase in Beauty?**

This phrase is symbolic. President Harold B. Lee explained its meaning:

"Zion, as used here, undoubtedly had reference to the Church. At that time there was but a small body of Church members just beginning to emerge as an organization, after having experienced harsh treatment from enemies outside the Church. . . .

"To be worthy of such a sacred designation as Zion, the Church must think of itself as a bride adorned for her husband, as John the Revelator recorded when he saw in vision the Holy City where the righteous dwelled, adorned as a bride for the Lamb of God as her husband. Here is portrayed the relationship the Lord desires in his people in order to be acceptable to our Lord and Master even as a wife would adorn herself in beautiful garments for her husband.

"The rule by which the people of God must live in order to be worthy of acceptance in the sight of God is indicated by the text to which I have made reference. This people must increase in beauty before the world; have an inward loveliness which may be observed by mankind as a reflection in holiness and in those inherent qualities of sanctity. The borders of Zion, where the righteous and pure in heart may dwell, must now begin to be enlarged. The stakes of Zion must be strengthened. All this so that Zion may arise and shine by becoming increasingly diligent in carrying out the plan of salvation throughout the world." (In Conference Report, Apr. 1973, pp. 4-5; or *Ensign,* July 1973, p. 3.)

**D&C 82:17-18. "You Are to Have Equal Claims on the Properties"**

Notes and Commentary on Doctrine and Covenants 51:3 contains some insights into these verses.

**D&C 82:19. Every Man Seeking the Interest of His Neighbor**

The importance of this command was explained by President Joseph Fielding Smith when he wrote:

"It is verily true that before we can enter into the celestial kingdom we will have to learn how to live in unity with the love of our fellows at heart, desiring their good as well as our own, and not preferring ourselves before them. Here the Lord gave to the Church the plan and the opportunity to prepare themselves by obedience to celestial law. They failed, and the privilege to practice this law of consecration had to be postponed because we were not able to esteem our neighbor as ourselves." (*Church History and Modern Revelation,* 1:322.)

**D&C 82:21**

Notes and Commentary on Doctrine and Covenants 78:12 explains the phrase "buffetings of Satan."

### D&C 82:22. Why Is the Church Commanded to Make Friends with the "Mammon of Unrighteousness"?

"The commandment of the Lord that the saints should make themselves 'friends with the mammon of unrighteousness,' seems to be a hard saying when not properly understood. It is not intended that in making friends of the 'mammon of unrighteousness' that the brethren were to partake with them in their sins; to receive them to their bosoms, intermarry with them and otherwise come down to their level. They were to so live that peace with their enemies might be assured. They were to treat them kindly, be friendly with them as far as correct and virtuous principles would permit, but never to swear with them or drink and carouse with them. If they could allay prejudice and show a willingness to trade with and show a kindly spirit, it might help to turn them away from their bitterness. Judgment was to be left with the Lord." (Smith, *Church History and Modern Revelation,* 1:323.)

The phrase "mammon of unrighteousness" is taken from the parable of the unjust steward (see Luke 16:11). An explanation of this parable and its significance for modern Saints is contained in Notes and Commentary on Doctrine and Covenants 72:3-4.

# The Laws of the Church Concerning Widows and Orphans

Section 83

## Historical Background

The Prophet Joseph Smith gave the following background about his receiving this revelation:

"On the 27th, we transacted considerable business for the salvation of the Saints, who were settling among a ferocious set of mobbers, like lambs among wolves. It was my endeavor to so organize the Church, that the brethren might eventually be independent of every incumbrance beneath the celestial kingdom, by bonds and covenants of mutual friendship, and mutual love.

"On the 28th and 29th, I visited the brethren above Big Blue river, in Kaw township, a few miles west of Independence, and received a welcome only known by brethren and sisters united as one in the same faith, and by the same baptism, and supported by the same Lord. The Colesville branch, in particular, rejoiced as the ancient Saints did with Paul. It is good to rejoice with the people of God. On the 30th, I returned to Independence, and again sat in council with the brethren, and received the following: [D&C 83]." (*History of the Church,* 1:269.)

## Notes and Commentary

### D&C 83:1-6. Laws of the Church Concerning Widows, Orphans, and Children

Since widows and orphans have special challenges, the Lord stated explicitly the special obligations the Church has to care for them. The edict that a widow could remain upon her inheritance and that children who came of age could lay claim upon the Lord's storehouse referred to the law of consecration (see Enrichment L, in the Appendix, for a discussion of how inheritances were given).

*A parent's stewardship is both temporal and spiritual*

While indicating the responsibility of the Church for certain Saints in unfortunate circumstances, the Lord also outlined the basic responsibility of family members to care for their own (see D&C 83:2, 4). President Spencer W. Kimball said of the principle of self-reliance:

"The Church and its members are commanded by the Lord to be self-reliant and independent. (See D&C 78:13-14.)

"The responsibility for each person's social, emotional, spiritual, physical, or economic well-being rests first upon himself, second upon his family, and third upon the Church if he is a faithful member thereof.

"No true Latter-day Saint, while physically or emotionally able will voluntarily shift the burden of his own or his family's well-being to someone else. So long as he can, under the inspiration of the Lord and with his own labors, he will supply himself and his family with the spiritual and temporal necessities of life. (See 1 Timothy 5:8.)" (In Conference Report, Oct. 1977, p. 124; or *Ensign*, Nov. 1977, pp. 77-78.)

# The Oath and Covenant of the Priesthood

Section 84

## Historical Background

The Prophet Joseph Smith, who was in Kirtland at the time, recorded the following about receiving Doctrine and Covenants 84:

"As soon as I could arrange my affairs, I recommenced the translation of the Scriptures, and thus I spent most of the summer. In July, we received the first number of *The Evening and Morning Star*, which was a joyous treat to the Saints. Delightful, indeed, was it to contemplate that the little band of brethren had become so large, and grown so strong, in so short a time as to be able to issue a paper of their own, which contained not only some of the revelations, but other information also,—which would gratify and enlighten the humble inquirer after truth. . . .

"The Elders during the month of September began to return from their missions to the Eastern States, and present the histories of their several stewardships in the Lord's vineyard; and while together in these seasons of joy, I inquired of the Lord, and received on the 22nd and 23rd of September [1832], the following revelation on Priesthood: [D&C 84]." (*History of the Church*, 1:273, 286-87.)

## Notes and Commentary

### D&C 84:2. Where Are Mount Zion and the City of New Jerusalem?

President Joseph Fielding Smith talked about the two world capitals during the Millennium:

"When Joseph Smith translated the Book of Mormon, he learned that America is the land of Zion which was given to Joseph and his children and that on this land the City Zion, or New Jerusalem, is to be built. He also learned that Jerusalem in Palestine is to be rebuilt and become a holy city. These two cities, one in the land of Zion and one in Palestine, are to become capitals for the kingdom of God during the millennium.

"In the meantime, while the work of preparation is going on and Israel is being gathered, many people are coming to the land of Zion saying: 'Come ye, and let us go up to the mountain of the Lord, to the house of the God of Jacob.' The Latter-day Saints are fulfilling this prediction, since they are being gathered from all parts of the earth and are coming to the house of the Lord in these valleys of the mountains. Here they are being taught in the ways of the Lord through the restoration of the gospel and by receiving blessings in the temples now erected. Morever, before many years have passed away, the Lord will command the building of the City Zion, and Jerusalem in Palestine will in due time be cleansed and become a holy city and the habitation of the Jews after they are cleansed and are willing to accept Jesus Christ as their Redeemer." (*Doctrines of Salvation*, 3:71.)

### D&C 84:4. "New Jerusalem Shall Be Built by the Gathering of the Saints"

In his vision of the future events of the world, Enoch saw the day just before the Millennium when great tribulations would be seen on the earth, but along with that troubling prophecy came this comforting promise: "My people will I preserve" (Moses 7:61). That preservation will be brought about by righteousness that will come down from heaven (the restoration of the gospel and the Church through angelic messengers and other revelations) and truth (the Book of Mormon) that will come out of the earth. Combined, these events will cause righteousness and truth to cover the earth (see Moses 7:62). The result of that flood of light and truth will be "to *gather out mine elect* from the four quarters of the earth, unto a place which I shall prepare . . . and it shall be called Zion, a New Jerusalem" (Moses 7:62; emphasis added).

In a later revelation the Lord indicated that the gathering of the Saints on "the land of Zion, and upon her stakes, may be for a defense, and for a refuge from the storm, and from wrath when it

*Ancient prophets saw the New Jerusalem*

shall be poured out without mixture upon the whole earth" (D&C 115:6). In yet another place, Zion is described as "a land of peace, a city of refuge, a place of safety for the saints of the Most High God" (D&C 45:66).

The scriptures clearly teach that the gathering of the Saints to Zion and her stakes will be the means by which God preserves his people during the judgments of the last days. The Prophet Joseph also taught the same concept with great clearness: "We ought to have the building up of Zion as our greatest object. When wars come, we shall have to flee to Zion. The cry is to make haste. The last revelation says, Ye shall not have time to have gone over the earth, until these things come. It will come as did the cholera, war, fires, and earthquakes; one pestilence after another, until the Ancient of Days comes, then judgment will be given to the Saints. . . . The time is soon coming, when no man will have any peace but in Zion and her stakes." (*Teachings*, pp. 160-61.)

On another occasion the Prophet Joseph Smith said: "Without Zion, and a place of deliverance, we must fall; because the time is near when the sun will be darkened, and the moon turn to blood, and the stars fall from heaven, and the earth reel to and fro. Then, if this is the case, and if we are not sanctified and gathered to the places God has appointed, with all our former professions and our great love for the Bible, we must fall; we cannot stand; we cannot be saved; for God will gather out his Saints from the Gentiles, and then comes desolation and destruction, and none can escape except the pure in heart who are gathered." (*Teachings*, p. 71.)

Zion is the antithesis of the world, or spiritual Babylon. In preparation for the Millennium, therefore, Babylon must be destroyed. The cry to all people is, "Go ye out from among the nations, even from Babylon, from the midst of wickedness, which is spiritual Babylon. . . . and he that goeth, let him not look back lest sudden destruction shall come upon him." (D&C 133:14-15.) When one *flees* Babylon, he *gathers* to Zion and her stakes.

Elder Bruce R. McConkie said,"The gathering of Israel consists of receiving the truth, gaining again a true knowledge of the Redeemer, and coming back into the true fold of the Good Shepherd" (in Conference Report, Lima Peru Area Conference 1977, p. 33; or *Ensign*, May 1977, p. 117).

### D&C 84:4. What Is the Meaning of *Generation*?

Noting that this word has been a stumbling block to some, President Joseph Fielding Smith wrote: "There have been various interpretations of the meaning of a generation. It is held by some that a generation is one hundred years; by others that it is one hundred and twenty years; by others that a generation as expressed in this and other scriptures has reference to a period of time which is indefinite. The Savior said: 'An evil and adulterous generation seeketh after a sign.' This did not have reference to a period of years, but to a period of wickedness. A generation may mean the time of this present dispensation." (*Church History and Modern Revelation*, 1:337.)

### D&C 84:4. Which Temple Is Referred to Here?

The Lord was speaking of the temple in Zion, that is, Jackson County, Missouri. The Lord later excused the Saints from building that temple because the mobs prevented it (see D&C 124:49-51) and because the Saints at that time had not kept the commandments as they should (see D&C 105:1-9).

The day will come, however, when the holy city of God will be established in Jackson County, Missouri, and the temple will be filled with the glory of God as envisioned by the prophets (see 3 Nephi 20:22; 21:23-25; Ether 13:3-4, 6-8).

### D&C 84:5. "A Cloud Shall Rest upon It"

"The Lord manifested Himself in ancient Israel in a cloud, shaped as a pillar, which became luminous at night. It guided the people on the journey to Canaan. It stood at the entrance to the Sanctuary, and in it God spoke to Moses. It rested on the Sanctuary and filled it, when that sacred tent was set up. It was the visible sign of God's guiding and protecting care over His people." (Smith and Sjodahl, Commentary, p. 497.)

### D&C 84:6-31. A Parenthetical Insertion

Smith and Sjodahl noted that in verse six is "the beginning of a sentence which is continued in . . . [verse] 31. All that intervenes is parenthetic, containing a statement regarding the lineage through which the Priesthood came to Moses and Aaron, and how it was restored in our day." (Commentary, p. 498.) Without the parenthetical insertion, the sentence would read, "And the sons

*Moses ordained Aaron*

of Moses, according to the Holy Priesthood . . . shall offer an acceptable offering and sacrifice" (D&C 84:6, 31).

The addition of numerous verses in the middle of a sentence is peculiar enough that it warrants careful attention. The following questions raise several important points that, given careful thought, will provide important insights:

1. The priesthood lineage of the sons of Moses and Aaron, "according to the Holy Priesthood" (vs. 6), is given in verses 6 through 16. The lineage begins with Adam and ends with Moses, as shown.

ADAM
ABEL
.
.
.
JETHRO
MOSES

Who would come below Moses? (see vss. 32, 34).

2. Both the sons of Moses and the sons of Aaron are mentioned in this promise. What keys do each of these have? (see vss. 19-20, 26-27).

3. Why didn't ancient Israel enjoy the privilege of seeing God and entering into his rest? (see vss. 21-24).

4. Is modern Israel in danger of losing blessings because they do not take their covenants seriously? (see vss. 47-48, 54-59).

5. John the Baptist was given power to prepare the Lord's people for Jesus' coming (see vs. 28). Is there any relationship between John's time and the present in trying to prepare a people for Christ's coming? If so, how does that relationship affect the priesthood covenants restored today?

### D&C 84:6. Who Was Jethro and How Did He Receive the Priesthood?

"The descent of this authority, or divine power, from Adam to Moses is here given in the Lord's own words to Joseph Smith. Moses received it from Jethro, a priest of the house of Midian. The Midianites were descendants of Abraham, through the children of Keturah, wife of Abraham, therefore the Midianites, who were neighbors to the Israelites in Palestine, were related to the Israelites, and were Hebrews. As descendants of Abraham they were entitled through their faithfulness to his blessings (see Abraham 2:9-11), and in the days of Moses and preceding them, in Midian the Priesthood was found." (Smith, *Church History and Modern Revelation,* 1:338.)

### D&C 84:19-22. "This Greater Priesthood . . . Holdeth the Key of the Knowledge of God"

Noting that "it is impossible for men to obtain the knowledge of the mysteries of the kingdom or the knowledge of God, without the authority of the Priesthood," President Joseph Fielding Smith observed that "secular learning, the study of the sciences, arts and history, will not reveal these vital truths to man. It is the Holy Priesthood that unlocks the door to heaven and reveals to man the mysteries of the Kingdom of God. It is this Divine Authority which makes known the knowledge of God! Is there any wonder that the world today is groping in gross darkness concerning God and the things of his kingdom? We should also remember that these great truths are not made known even to members of the Church unless they place their lives in harmony with the law on which these blessings are predicated. (D. & C. 130:20-21.)" (*Church History and Modern Revelation,* 1:338.)

### D&C 84:23-27. Was There No Melchizedek Priesthood in Ancient Israel?

Elder Bruce R. McConkie explained that "when Israel, as a people and as a whole, failed to live in harmony with the law of Christ as contained in the fulness of his everlasting gospel, the Lord 'in his wrath' withdrew the fulness of his law from them. Because 'they hardened their hearts' and would not 'enter into his rest while in the wilderness, which rest is the fulness of his glory, . . . he took Moses out of their midst, and the Holy Priesthood also' (D&C 84:19-28.) That is, he took the Melchizedek Priesthood, which administers the gospel, out of their midst in the sense that it did not continue and pass from one priesthood holder to another in the normal and usual sense of the word. The keys of the priesthood were taken away with Moses so that any future priesthood ordinations required special divine authorization. But in place of the higher priesthood the Lord gave a lesser order, and in place of the fulness of the gospel he gave a preparatory gospel—the law of carnal commandments, the law of Moses—to serve as a schoolmaster to bring them, after a long day of trial and testing, back to the law of Christ in its fulness. There is the fulness of the gospel, and there is the preparatory gospel. There is the full law of Christ, and there is a partial law of Christ. The Mosaic system was the partial law, a portion of the mind and will of Jehovah, a strict and severe testing arrangement that would qualify those who obeyed its terms and conditions to receive the eternal fulness when the Messiah came to deliver and to restore it." (*Mortal Messiah,* pp. 59-60.)

### D&C 84:28. What Authority Did John the Baptist Receive from the Angel?

Elder Bruce R. McConkie also explained the authority of John the Baptist.

"What concerns us above all else as to the coming of John, however, is that he came with power and authority. He first received his errand from the Lord. His was no ordinary message, and he was no unauthorized witness. He was called of God and sent by him, and he represented Deity in the words that he spoke and the baptisms he performed. He was a legal administrator whose words and acts were binding on earth and in heaven, and his hearers were bound, at the peril of their salvation, to believe his words and heed his counsels.

"Luke says: 'The word of God came unto John the son of Zacharias in the wilderness.' Later John is to say: 'He that sent me to baptize with water, the same said unto me,' such and such things. (John 1:33.) Who sent him we do not know. We do know that 'he was baptized while he was yet in his childhood [meaning, when he was eight years of age], and was ordained by the angel of God at the time he was eight days old unto this power [note it well, not to the Aaronic Priesthood, but] to overthrow the kingdom of the Jews, and to make straight the way of the Lord before the face of his people, to prepare them for the coming of the Lord, in whose hand is given all power.' (D&C 84:24.) We do not know when he received the Aaronic Priesthood, but obviously it came to him after his baptism, at whatever age was proper, and before he was sent by one whom he does not name to preach and baptize with water." (*Mortal Messiah,* pp. 384-85.)

### D&C 84:33-41. The Oath and Covenant of the Priesthood

President Joseph Fielding Smith gave the following definition of the oath and covenant of the priesthood:

"As all of us know, a covenant is a contract and an agreement between at least two parties. In the case of gospel covenants, the parties are the Lord in heaven and men on earth. Men agree to keep the commandments and the Lord promises to reward them accordingly. The gospel itself is the new and everlasting covenant and embraces all of the agreements, promises, and rewards which the Lord offers to his people.

"And so when we receive the Melchizedek Priesthood we do so by covenant. We solemnly promise to receive the priesthood, to magnify our callings in it, and to live by every word that proceedeth forth from the mouth of God. The Lord on his part promises us that if we keep the covenant, we shall receive all that the Father hath, which is life eternal. Can any of us conceive of a greater or more glorious agreement than this? . . .

"To swear with an oath is the most solemn and binding form of speech known to the human tongue; and it was this type of language which the Father chose to have used in the great Messianic prophecy about Christ and the priesthood. Of him it says: 'The Lord hath sworn, and will not repent, Thou art a priest for ever after the order of Melchizedek.' (Ps. 110:4.)

"In explaining this Messianic prophecy, Paul says that Jesus had 'an unchangeable priesthood,' and that through it came 'the power of an endless life.' (See Heb. 7:24, 16.) Joseph Smith said that 'all those who are ordained unto this priesthood are made like unto the Son of God, abiding a priest continually,' that is, if they are faithful and true.

"And so Christ is the great prototype where priesthood is concerned, as he is with reference to baptism and all other things. And so, even as the Father swears with an oath that his Son shall inherit all things through the priesthood, so he swears with an oath that all of us who magnify our callings in that same priesthood shall receive all that the Father hath." (In Conference Report, Oct. 1970, pp. 91-92.)

### D&C 84:33. How Does One Magnify a Calling?

"The Prophet Joseph was often asked, 'Brother Joseph, what do you mean by magnifying a calling?'

"Joseph replied: 'What does it mean to magnify a calling? It means to build it up in dignity and importance, to make it honorable and commendable in the eyes of all men, to enlarge and strengthen it, to let the light of heaven shine through it to the view of other men. And how does one magnify a calling? Simply by performing the service that pertains to it. . . . ' " (Thomas S. Monson, in Conference Report, British Area Conference 1971, p. 145.)

"In the words 'magnifying their calling,' far more seems to be implied than the mere attending of priesthood meetings, administering to the sacrament and the sick, and serving in Church work. Faithfulness to warrant the reception of the priesthood is a condition that perhaps all men do not meet. And the magnifying of their calling seems to imply a totalness which few, if any, men reach in mortality. Perfection of body and spirit seems to be included here." (*Miracle of Forgiveness,* p. 123.)

### D&C 84:34. What Does It Mean to "Become the Sons of Moses and of Aaron"?

"Who are the sons of Aaron and Levi today? They are, by virtue of the blessings of the Almighty, those who are ordained by those who hold the authority to officiate in the offices of the priesthood. It is written that those so ordained become the sons of Moses and Aaron." (Smith, *Doctrines of Salvation,* 3:93.)

" 'Sons of Moses,' and 'sons of Aaron' do not refer to their literal descendants only, for all who are faithful and obtain these Priesthoods, and magnify their calling, are sanctified by the Spirit and become the 'sons' of Moses and of Aaron, and the seed of Abraham, as well as the Church and Kingdom, and the elect of God (v. 34). Paul expresses this thought as follows, 'Know ye therefore that they which are of faith, the same are the children of Abraham' (Gal. 3:7)." (Smith and Sjodahl, Commentary, p. 504.)

**D&C 84:41. "Shall Not Have Forgiveness of Sins in This World nor in the World to Come"**

The verb *received* used here and in verse 40 may imply much more than just being ordained to the Melchizedek Priesthood.

President Marion G. Romney said of this verse: "Now, I do not think this means that all who fail to magnify their callings in the priesthood will have committed the unpardonable sin, but I do think that priesthood bearers who have entered into the covenants that we enter into—in the waters of baptism, in connection with the law of tithing, the Word of Wisdom, and the many other covenants we make—and then refuse to live up to these covenants will stand in jeopardy of losing the promise of eternal life." (In Conference Report, Apr. 1972, p. 112; or *Ensign,* July 1972, p. 99.)

**D&C 84:42. "I Have Given . . . Mine Angels Charge Concerning You"**

Smith and Sjodahl said about this promise: "How important, then, that those who bear the Holy Priesthood should live so, that they are fit companions for angels!" (Commentary, p. 508; see also Doctrine and Covenants 84:88; 109:22; Matthew 18:10; Psalm 91:11, which also refer to angels' watching over men).

**D&C 84:46. What Spirit "Enlighteneth Every Man"?**

"At the same time we have the sweet influence of the Spirit of God pleading with us to do that which is right, pleading with every human being that does not drive it from him; for every human being has a portion of the Spirit of God given unto him. We sometimes call it conscience; we call it by one name and we call it by another; but it is the Spirit of God that every man and woman possesses that is born on the earth. God has given unto all his children this Spirit. Of course it is not the gift of the Holy Ghost in its fullness; for that is only received by obedience to the commandments of God." (George Q. Cannon, in *Journal of Discourses,* 26:191.)

**D&C 84:54-57. "Repent and Remember . . . the Book of Mormon"**

The compilation and preservation of the Book of Mormon have been carefully guarded and watched over by the Savior and his prophets down through the ages. Its message is of greatest importance to the inhabitants of the earth, and to treat lightly that sacred record is a serious thing, as President Ezra Taft Benson explained:

"Some of the early missionaries, on returning home, were reproved by the Lord in section 84 of the Doctrine and Covenants because they had treated lightly the Book of Mormon. As a result, their minds had been darkened. The Lord said that this kind of treatment of the Book of Mormon brought the whole Church under condemnation, even all of the children of Zion. And then the Lord said, 'And they shall remain under this condemnation until they repent and remember the new covenant, even the Book of Mormon.' (See D&C 84:54-57.) Are we still under that condemnation? . . .

"And now grave consequences hang on our response to the Book of Mormon. 'Those who receive it,' said the Lord, 'in faith, and work righteousness, shall receive a crown of eternal life;

" 'But those who harden their hearts in unbelief, and reject it, it shall turn to their own condemnation—

" 'For the Lord God has spoken it.' (D&C 20:14-16.)

"Is the Book of Mormon true? Yes.

"Who is it for? Us.

"What is its purpose? To bring men to Christ.

"How does it do this? By testifying of Christ and revealing his enemies.

"How are we to use it? We are to get a testimony of it, we are to teach from it, we are to hold it up as a standard and 'hiss it forth.'

"Have we been doing this? Not as we should, nor as we must.

"Do eternal consequences rest upon our response to this book? Yes, either to our blessing or our condemnation.

"Every Latter-day Saint should make the study of this book a lifetime pursuit. Otherwise he is placing his soul in jeopardy and neglecting that which could give spiritual and intellectual unity to his whole life." (In Conference Report, Apr. 1975, pp. 96-97; or *Ensign,* May 1975, p. 65.)

**D&C 84:63. "Ye Are Mine Apostles"**

The Quorum of the Twelve Apostles was not organized until 1835, yet the Lord refers to these brethren as Apostles. Elder Joseph Fielding Smith gave this reasoning:

"An apostle, the dictionary states, is 'one of the twelve chosen by Christ to proclaim His gospel; also a Christian missionary who first evangelizes a certain nation; any zealous advocate of a doctrine or cause.' . . .

"The term apostle is recognized in the Church in the sense in which it is defined in the dictionary. Men have been called apostles who have been sent forth with the gospel message even when they have not been ordained to that particular office. . . .

"This revelation was given two years and four months before the first men were ordained to the special calling as apostles in the Church, but as they were commissioned to go forth proclaiming the gospel as witnesses for Christ, he designated them as his apostles." ("The Twelve Apostles," *Improvement Era*, Apr. 1935, p. 208.)

### D&C 84:64-73. "These Signs Shall Follow"

In Mark 16:17-18 the Savior made similar promises to the missionaries in New Testament times.

### D&C 84:80-85. The Lord Supports His Missionaries

"Thousands of missionaries have put this promise to the test and the Lord has kept his promise to all those who have been faithful in their calling. Surely if the Father notices when a sparrow falls, he will not forsake any who in faithful obedience to his will seek his aid. That there have been those who have gone forth and have been weary in body and mind, and who have gone hungry, there is no doubt, for there are missionaries who have not given all their heart to the Lord and they have idled away valuable time when it was needful for them to proclaim the truth." (Smith, *Church History and Modern Revelation*, 1:344.)

### D&C 84:87. How Does One "Reprove the World"?

" 'Reprove,' as stated (v. 76) is to 'convict.' God's messengers, as it were, are lawyers before the bar of God. It is their duty to 'convict' the world of sin, and to warn all men of the 'judgment which is to come.' They are not sent out to entertain the world with philosophical lectures, or ethical discourses, or flowery oratory, or amusing anecdotes. Their one duty is to secure conviction and, if possible, repentance and salvation." (Smith and Sjodahl, Commentary, p. 518.)

### D&C 84:98-102. "Sing This New Song"

"The new song which they shall sing at this great day will be concerning the redemption of Zion and the restoration of Israel. Even now there are those who have set to music these beautiful words (vs. 99-102.), but we may believe that no music has yet been produced that will compare with the music for this song when Zion is redeemed." (Smith, *Church History and Modern Revelation*, 1:345.)

### D&C 84:100. Is Time Going to Come to an End?

This phrase is also used in the book of Revelation (see Revelation 10:6). Elder Bruce R. McConkie explained that the phrase means "that there should be no more delay—not that time as such should end and eternity begin, for the Millennial Era is still ahead—but, as shown in D&C 88:110, that 'Satan shall be bound,' thus ending the 'time' (it 'shall be no longer'!) when persecution prevails" (*Doctrinal New Testament Commentary*, 3:506).

### D&C 84:114. New York, Albany, and Boston

These cities were the subject of another prophet's testimony. Elder Wilford Woodruff addressed a conference in Logan, Utah, on 22 August 1863. Speaking directly to the youth in attendance, he declared: " 'Now, my young friends, I wish you to remember these scenes you are witnessing during the visit of President Young and his brethren. Yea, my young friends, treasure up the teachings and sayings of these prophets and apostles as precious treasure while they are living men, and do not wait until they are dead. A few days and President Young and his brethren, the prophets and apostles and Brothers Benson and Maughan, will be in the spirit world. You should never forget this visitation. You are to become men and women, fathers and mothers; yea, the day will come, after your fathers, and these prophets and apostles are dead, you will have the privilege of going into the towers of a glorious Temple built unto the name of the Most High (pointing in the direction of the bench), east of us upon the Logan bench; and while you stand in the towers of the Temple and your eyes survey this glorious valley filled with cities and villages, occupied by tens of thousands of Latter-day Saints, you will then call to mind this visitation of President Young and his company. You will say: That was in the days when Presidents Benson and Maughan presided over us; that was before New York was destroyed by an earthquake; it was before Boston was swept into the sea, by the sea heaving itself beyond its bounds; it was before Albany was destroyed by fire; yea, at that time you will remember the scenes of this day. Treasure them up and forget them not.' President Young followed and said: 'What Brother Woodruff has said is revelation and will be fulfilled.' " (In Lundwall, *Temples of the Most High*, pp. 97-98.)

*Wilford Woodruff spoke of future destruction in New York, Albany, and Boston*

# Those Who Put Forth Their Hands "to Steady the Ark"

Section 85

## Historical Background

What is now known as section 85 was written as a letter by Joseph Smith to William W. Phelps on 27 November 1832. The first part of the letter read:

"I say brother, because I feel so from the heart, and although it is not long since I wrote a letter unto you, yet I feel as though you would excuse me for writing this, as I have many things which I wish to communicate. Some things which I will mention in this letter, which are lying with great weight on my mind. I am well, and my family also; God grant that you may enjoy the same, and yours, and all the brethren and sisters who remember to inquire after the commandments of the Lord, and the welfare of Zion and such a being as myself; and while I dictate this letter, I fancy to myself that you are saying or thinking something similar to these words:—'My God, great and mighty art Thou, therefore show unto Thy servant what shall become of those who are essaying to come up unto Zion, in order to keep the commandments of God, and yet receive not their inheritance by consecrations, by order of deed from the Bishop, the man that God has appointed in a legal way, agreeably to the law given to organize and regulate the Church, and all the affairs of the same.'

"Brother William, in the love of God, having the most implicit confidence in you as a man of God, having obtained this confidence by a vision of heaven, therefore I will proceed to unfold to you some of the feelings of my heart, and to answer the question." (*History of the Church,* 1:297-98.)

The body of the letter gave answers to the thoughts and questions with which William W. Phelps had been wrestling and was viewed as the word of the Lord. Now section 85, the letter was included in the 1876 edition of the Doctrine and Covenants by Elder Orson Pratt acting under the direction of President Brigham Young.

## Notes and Commentary

### D&C 85:1. Importance of Record Keeping in Missouri

President Joseph Fielding Smith noted that man will be judged out of earthly records, and "therefore they should be accurate in every detail. . . .

"To keep a record of the manner of life of these consecrated members was important because of the nature of the covenant which they were required to make when they entered into this order, or covenant. . . .

". . . The names of all faithful members were to be recorded, with an account of their stewardship, their faith and their works. What a happy people they would have been if they had hearkened with singleness of heart to these commandments, for the Lord had promised to protect them in these inheritances if they would be faithful to him. The Lord knew that there would be some among them who would falter; some who would come to Zion not willing to enroll themselves and their property to the welfare of Zion, and therefore could not be given stewardships in the covenant which the Lord had made with the saints. He, therefore, commanded that all those who came to Zion and who were not willing to receive an inheritance, and consecration agreeable to his law should not be numbered among the faithful." (*Church History and Modern Revelation,* pp. 348-49.)

### D&C 85:4, 12. Why Were Certain Genealogies Not to Be Kept?

President Joseph Fielding Smith wrote of this revelation:

"The closing verses of this revelation state that all those who are not found written in the book of remembrance, shall have no inheritance in that day. Their portion shall be with the unbelievers, where there will be wailing and gnashing of teeth. 'And they who are of the High Priesthood, whose names are not found written in the book of the law, or that are found to have apostatized, or to have been cut off from the church, as well as the lesser priesthood, or the members, in that day shall not find an inheritance among the saints of the Most High.' It is stated that with them it will be done as it was to the people in the days of Ezra after the return from Babylonian captivity. At that time the Lord said through his prophet:

" 'These sought their register among those that were reckoned by genealogy, but they were not found: therefore were they, as polluted, put from the priesthood.' (Ezra 2:62.)

"The members of the Church today should take warning from this which is written and keep themselves prepared by their faithful adherence to the principles of the Gospel, and be true to their covenants, so that when that day shall come, if they are here to share in it, they will not be found like these Jews in the days of Ezra, but will have their names written in the book of remembrance." (*Church History and Modern Revelation,* 1:352.)

### D&C 85:7-8. Who Is the "One Mighty and Strong"?

The reference to the "one mighty and strong" (D&C 85:7) who is to set in order the house of God and also the reference to one who "putteth forth his hand to steady the ark" (vs. 8) have been used by many apostates from the Church in an attempt to justify their own falling away. They claim that various Presidents of the Church have lost favor with God and are rejected, and that they, the apostates, are the "one mighty and strong" called by God to set things right. Such audacious and blasphemous claims illustrate the lengths to which some wrest the scriptures. In an official statement issued in 1905, the First Presidency (Joseph F. Smith, John R. Winder, and Anthon H. Lund) discussed the circumstances that brought this revelation forth and those to whom these two phrases referred:

"It is to be observed first of all that the subject of this whole letter, as also the part of it subsequently accepted as a revelation, relates to the affairs of the Church in Missouri, the gathering of the Saints to that land and obtaining their inheritances under the law of consecration and stewardship; and the Prophet deals especially with the matter of what is to become of those who fail to receive their inheritances by order or deed from the bishop. . . .

"It was while these conditions of rebellion, jealousy, pride, unbelief and hardness of heart prevailed among the brethren in Zion—Jackson county, Missouri—in all of which Bishop Partridge participated, that the words of the revelation taken from the letter to William W. Phelps, of the 27th of November, 1832, were written. The 'man who was called and appointed of God' to 'divide unto the Saints their inheritance'—Edward Partridge—was at that time out of order, neglecting his own duty, and putting 'forth his hand to steady the ark'; hence, he was warned of the judgment of God impending, and the prediction was made that another, 'one mighty and strong,' would be sent of God to take his place, to have his bishopric—one having the spirit and power of that high office resting upon him, by which he would have power to 'set in order the house of God, and arrange by lot the inheritance of the Saints'; in other words, one who would do the work that Bishop Edward Partridge had been appointed to do, but had failed to accomplish. . . .

"And inasmuch as through his repentance and sacrifices and suffering, Bishop Edward Partridge undoubtedly obtained a mitigation of the threatened judgment against him of falling 'by the shaft of death, like as a tree that is smitten by the vivid shaft of lightning,' so the occasion for sending another to fill his station—'one mighty and strong to set in order the house of God, and to arrange by lot the inheritances of the Saints'—may also be considered as having passed away and the whole incident of the prophecy closed." (In Clark, *Messages of the First Presidency,* 4:112, 115, 117.)

"This much, then, we have learned, *viz.*, that Edward Partridge, the Bishop of the Church, was the one 'called and appointed, to divide by lot unto the Saints their inheritances.' But was Edward Partridge the one in 1832 who was 'putting forth his hand to steady the ark,' and threatened with falling 'by the shaft of death like as a tree that is smitten by the vivid shaft of lightning'? Undoubtedly. The brethren in those days were limited in their experience. The Church had been organized but as yesterday. The order of the Priesthood was not understood then, as it is understood today. The brethren composing it had been but recently brought together. Some of them were often in rebellion against the Prophet and the order of the Church because of these conditions; and it required instruction and time and experience to enable men to understand their duties and preserve their right relationship to each other as officers of the Church.

"Bishop Partridge was one of the brethren, who—though a most worthy man, one whom the Lord loved, and whom the Prophet described as 'a pattern of piety,' and 'one of the Lord's great men'—at times arrayed himself in opposition to the Prophet in those early days, and sought to correct him in his administrations of the affairs of the Church; in other words, 'put forth his hand to steady the ark.' " (In Clark, *Messages of the First Presidency,* 4:113.)

**D&C 85:7. Why Are Individuals Still Claiming to Be the "One Mighty and Strong"?**

"Some modern people have created cults of their own, and among them are those who attempt to take refuge in section 85 of the Doctrine and Covenants.

"They endeavor to say that the Church has gone astray, that the leaders are no longer inspired, and that 'one mighty and strong' is needed to take over the affairs of the Lord. And without any evidence of modesty whatsoever on their parts, they themselves volunteer for the position." (Mark E. Petersen, in Conference Report, Apr. 1973, p. 159; or *Ensign,* July 1973, p. 110.)

Such people become guilty of the very thing this scripture warns against: they take it upon themselves to "steady the ark" (see Notes and Commentary for D&C 85:8).

**D&C 85:7. How Can a Person's Claim to Revelation for Church Leadership Be Tested?**

In answer to this critical question, Elder Bruce R. McConkie said:

"Every person properly appointed and sustained to act in an official capacity in the Church is entitled to the spirit of revelation to guide the particular organization or group over which he presides. The 'Presidency are over the Church,' the Prophet said, 'and *revelations of the mind and will of God to the Church, are to come through the Presidency.* This is the order of heaven, and the power and privilege of this priesthood. *It is also the privilege of any officer in this Church to obtain revelations, so far as relates to his particular calling and duty in the Church.*' (*Teachings,* p. 111.)

"This system of promulgating revelations through the established head of the Lord's earthly work is so unbending and inflexible that it stands as a test to establish the truth or falsity of purported revelations. *'There is none other appointed unto you to receive commandments and revelations until he be taken,'* the Lord said of the Prophet. *'And this shall be a law unto you, that ye receive not the teachings of any that shall come before you as revelations or commandments; And this I give unto you that you may not be deceived, that you may know they are not of me.'* (D. & C. 43:2-7; *Doctrines of Salvation,* vol. 1, pp. 283-89.)" (*Mormon Doctrine,* pp. 646-47.)

## D&C 85:8. What Does It Mean to "Steady the Ark of God"

This phrase refers to an event that happened during the reign of King David in ancient Israel (see 2 Samuel 6:1-11). While the ark of the covenant was being transported to its official resting place after being sent back by the Philistines who had captured it, the wagon which was carrying it passed over a rough spot, and the ark started to topple off. A man named Uzzah sought to steady it and was struck dead. At first this punishment may seem excessive, but one gains a different perspective when he remembers that the ark was the tangible object that symbolized the presence of God, his throne, his glory, his divine majesty. When first given to Israel, the ark was placed in the Holy of Holies in the tabernacle, and not even the priest was allowed to approach it. Only the high priest, a type of Christ, could approach it, and then only after going through an elaborate ritual of personal cleansing and propitiation for his sins. The holiness of God is clearly taught in scripture. No unclean thing can dwell in his presence (see Moses 6:57). His presence is like a consuming fire (see Hebrews 12:29). Those who bear the vessels of the Lord must be clean (see D&C 133:5).

However well-meaning his intentions, Uzzah approached casually what could only be approached under the strictest conditions. He had no faith in God's power. He assumed that the ark was in danger, forgetting that it was the physical symbol of the God who has all power. What man can presume to save God and his kingdom through his own efforts?

"Uzzah's offence consisted in the fact that he had touched the ark with profane feelings, although with good intentions, namely to prevent its rolling over and falling from the cart. Touching the ark, the throne of the divine glory and visible pledge of the invisible presence of the Lord, was a violation of the majesty of the holy God. 'Uzzah was therefore a type of all who with good intentions, humanly speaking, yet with unsanctified minds, interfere in the affairs of the kingdom of God, from the notion that they are in danger, and with the hope of saving them' (O.V. Gerlach)." (Keil and Delitzsch, *Commentary,* bk. 2: Joshua, Judges, Ruth, 1 and 2 Samuel, "Second Book of Samuel," p. 333.)

In modern revelation the Lord referred to this incident to teach the principle that the Lord does not need the help of men to defend his kingdom (see D&C 85:8). Yet even today there are those who fear the ark is tottering and presume to steady its course. There are those who are sure that women are not being treated fairly in the Church, those who would extend some unauthorized blessing, or those who would change the established doctrines of the Church. These are ark-steadiers. The best intentions do not justify such interference with the Lord's plan. Both President David O. McKay and President John Taylor applied this lesson to modern Saints.

"It is a little dangerous for us to go out of our own sphere and try unauthoritatively to direct the efforts of a brother. You remember the case of Uzzah who stretched forth his hand to steady the ark. (See I Chron. 13:7-10.) He seemed justified, when the oxen stumbled, in putting forth his hand to steady that symbol of the covenant. We today think his punishment was very severe. Be that as it may, the incident conveys a lesson of life. Let us look around us and see how quickly men who attempt unauthoritatively to steady the ark die spiritually. Their souls become embittered, their minds distorted, their judgments faulty, and their spirits depressed. Such is the pitiable condition of men who, neglecting their own responsibilities, spend their time in finding fault with others." (McKay, *Gospel Ideals,* p. 258.)

"We have more or less of the principles of insubordination among us. But there is a principle associated with the kingdom of God that recognizes God in all things, and that recognizes the priesthood in all things, and those who do not do it had better repent or they will come to a stand very quickly; I tell you that in the name of the Lord. Do not think you are wise and that you can manage and manipulate the priesthood, for you cannot do it. God must manage, regulate, dictate, and stand at the head, and every man in his place. The ark of God does not need steadying, especially by incompetent men without revelation and without knowledge of the kingdom of God and its laws. It is a great work that we are engaged in, and it is for us to prepare ourselves for the labor before us, and to acknowledge God, his authority, his law and his priesthood in all things." (Taylor, *Gospel Kingdom,* p. 166.)

*David O. McKay warned that unauthorized men and women who attempt to "steady the ark" die spiritually*

# The Parable of the Wheat and the Tares

Section 86

## Historical Background

The Savior often used parables to teach the people during his ministry on earth. On one occasion when he was on the shore of Galilee, the people pressed so close that he stepped into a boat and from there preached to the crowd. One of the messages he taught was in the parable of the wheat and the tares. Later, when he was alone with his Apostles, Jesus explained the parable to them (see Matthew 13:24-30).

On 6 December 1832, while Joseph Smith was working on the revision of the New Testament, he received an explanation of the parable of the wheat and the tares, "a more complete interpretation than he [Jesus] gave to his apostles as recorded by Matthew. The reason for this may be accounted for in the fact that it is to be in these last days that the harvest is gathered and the tares are to be burned." (Smith, *Church History and Modern Revelation,* 1:353.)

## Notes and Commentary

### D&C 86. What Are Parables and Why Did Jesus Use Them?

"Parables are short stories which point up and illustrate spiritual truths. Those spoken by Jesus deal with real events, or, if fictitious, are so consistent and probable that they may be viewed as the commonplace experiences of many people.

"When opposition to his message became bitter and intense, the master Teacher chose to present many of the truths of salvation in parables in order to hide his doctrine from those not prepared to receive it. It was not his purpose to cast pearls before swine." (McConkie, *Doctrinal New Testament Commentary,* 1:283.)

If a person is spiritually sensitive to gospel truths, parables teach beautiful and powerful principles. But if one is not spiritually aware, then, as Elder McConkie pointed out, "parables seldom clarify a truth; rather, they obscure and hide the doctrine involved so that none but those already enlightened and informed, on the very point presented, are able to grasp the full meaning. Nowhere is this better illustrated than in the parable of the wheat and the tares. When Jesus first gave this parable, even the disciples did not understand it. They asked for the interpretation, and he gave it, partially at least. And then with both the parable and the interpretation before the world, the Lord still had to give a special revelation in latter-days so that the full meaning of this marvelous parable might sink into the hearts of men. (D. & C. 86.)" (*Doctrinal New Testament Commentary,* 1:283-84.)

### D&C 86:1-7. The Parable of the Wheat and the Tares

When he first told the parable of the wheat and the tares (see Matthew 13:24-30, 36-43), Jesus interpreted nearly every item in the parable.

1. The man sowing seed is the Son of Man (Jesus).
2. The field is the world.
3. The good seed are the children of the kingdom (followers of Jesus).
4. The tares are children of the wicked one (those who follow the enticements of Satan).
5. The enemy is the devil.
6. The harvest is the end of the world.
7. The reapers are the angels sent to reap the field.
8. The tares bound and burned are the evil ones separated out and cast into fire (punishment) at the Judgment.
9. The wheat gathered into the barn represents the righteous who are separated out and made to shine forth in the kingdom of the Father.

The items which the Lord did not identify in Matthew 13 are as follows:

1. The wheat springing forth and starting to bear fruit
2. The men sleeping
3. The wheat and tares being allowed to grow together until the harvest
4. The wheat being uprooted in an attempt to weed out the tares

In Doctrine and Covenants 86, however, these items are explained, and more information on the first items is given:

1. The field is the world (see vs. 2).
2. The Apostles are the sowers of the seed (see vs. 2). In Matthew, Jesus identified the sower as himself. President Joseph Fielding Smith showed that there is no contradiction between these passages: "In Matthew's account the Lord declares that he is the sower of the good seed, and in the Doctrine and Covenants it is stated that the apostles were the sowers of the seed. There is no contradiction here. Christ is the author of our salvation and he it was who instructed the apostles, and under him they were sent to preach the Gospel unto all the world, or to sow the seed, and as the seed is his and it is sown under his command, he states but the fact in this revelation and also in the parable." (*Church History and Modern Revelation,* 1:353.)
3. Falling asleep implies the death of the original Apostles (see D&C 86:3).
4. The enemy is Babylon (see vs. 3), the great whore, which is elsewhere called the great and abominable church (see 1 Nephi 13:4-8). Babylon is a symbol of worldliness and evil and therefore may be said to represent the devil's power in this world.

*He will separate the wheat from the tares*

Those who remain in Babylon are those who follow the practices of the world and who do not accept the word of the Lord in their hearts. Sometimes Satan's persecution of the Church takes the form of aggressive persecution, such as killing the prophets or physically abusing the Saints; but more often the persecution consists of social pressure against the humble followers of Christ. Those in the "great and spacious building" in Lehi's dream mocked those who were pressing forward to partake of the fruit of the tree of life, and many became ashamed and fell away (see 1 Nephi 8:27-33).

5. The tares (see D&C 86:4) provide an excellent symbolic representation of evil doctrines and those who promulgate them. "Traditionally, tares have been identified with the darnel weed, a species of bearded rye-grass which closely resembles wheat in the early growth period and which is found in modern Palestine. This weed has a bitter taste; if eaten in any appreciable amount, either separately or when mixed with bread, it causes dizziness and often acts as a violent emetic." (McConkie, *Doctrinal New Testament Commentary,* 1:296.)

President Joseph Fielding Smith pointed out that "even in the Church the tares are to be found. It is the tares which are to be gathered up and burned from all over the world, but those in the Church will also be gathered out and find their place in the fire. [See D&C 112:23-26.] The Savior also bore witness of this when speaking to the Nephites he said: 'For it shall come to pass, saith the Father, that at that day whosoever will not repent and come unto my Beloved Son, them will I cut off from my people, O house of Israel.' [3 Nephi 21:20.]" (*Church History and Modern Revelation,* 1:354.)

False doctrines or individuals who present themselves as faithful members of the Church but are in reality servants of Satan are a source of temptation to the faithful and tend to choke or corrupt the word of God, or the good seed that is sown.

6. The Church being driven into the wilderness (see D&C 86:3) represents the time of the Apostasy. When the tares (the evil in the Church) grew to maturity, the result was apostasy; the wilderness represents the period of time when the Church and the priesthood were taken from the earth (see Revelation 12:12-17).

7. The tenderness of the wheat is explained in Doctrine and Covenants 86:6 as weakness, or newness, in the faith. When this revelation was given in December 1832, the Church was not yet three years old and was, therefore, still very "tender." At that time many of the tares were not yet identifiable, and attempts to systematically root out those who would eventually prove themselves to be tares would have been very destructive.

8. As in Matthew, the reapers are clearly identified as the angels of God (see D&C 86:5); but it is also clear that they were in 1832 anxiously awaiting permission to carry out their mission. (Notes and Commentary on D&C 86:5 discusses the time when that permission was given.)

9. The harvest and the burning of the tares (see vs. 7) was explained by the Prophet Joseph Smith: "The harvest and the end of the world have an allusion directly to the human family in the last days. . . . As, therefore, the tares are gathered and burned in the fire, so shall it be in the end of the world; that is, as the servants of God go forth warning the nations, both priests and people, and as they harden their hearts and reject the light of truth—these first being delivered over to the buffetings of Satan, and the law and the testimony being closed up, as it was in the case of the Jews—they are left in darkness, and delivered over unto the day of burning; thus, being bound up by their creeds, and their bands being made strong by their priests, [they] are prepared for the fulfillment of the saying of the Savior—'The Son of Man shall send forth His angels, and gather out of His Kingdom all things that offend, and them which do iniquity; and shall cast them into a furnace of fire, there shall be wailing and gnashing of teeth.' We understand that the work of gathering together of the wheat into barns, or garners, is to take place while the tares are being bound over, and [incident to] preparing for the day of burning, that after the day of burnings, the righteous shall shine forth like the sun, in the Kingdom of their Father." (*Teachings,* p. 101.)

**D&C 86:5. "The Angels Are Crying unto the Lord . . . to Be Sent Forth to Reap"**

In 1832 the Lord declared through the Prophet Joseph Smith that the angels were crying to the Lord for permission to go to the earth to separate the tares from the wheat in preparation for cleansing the earth by fire. Sixty-one years later, President Wilford Woodruff declared that the Lord had released those destroying angels, and they were now upon the earth separating the tares from the wheat in preparation for the burning that would soon take place. President Woodruff stated: "God has held the angels of destruction for many years, lest they should reap down the wheat with the tares. But I want to tell you now, that those angels have left the portals of heaven, and they stand over this people and this nation now, and are hovering over the earth waiting to pour out the judgments. *And from this very day they shall be poured out.* Calamities and troubles are increasing in the earth, and there is a meaning to these things. Remember this, and reflect upon these matters. If you do your duty, and I do my duty, we'll have protection, and shall pass through the afflictions in peace and in safety." (*Young Women's Journal,* Aug. 1894, pp. 512-13; emphasis added.)

President Joseph Fielding Smith, who was present when President Woodruff talked about these angels at the dedication of the Salt Lake Temple (see *Signs of the Times,* pp. 112-13), recorded the following:

"One day while I was sitting in the presence of my father back about 1908 or 9, somewhere in there, I called attention to these statements of President Woodruff, and I said I would like to go over the records from the time of the dedication of the Temple up until now and see what we can find in regard to calamities, destructions, plagues; and he encouraged me to do it, and so I did. So I went over the newspapers and over the magazines and jotted down year by year the destructions, the commotions among men, everything in the nature of a calamity, and to my great astonishment each year they increased, and they have been increasing ever since I quit making that record. I was greatly astonished by it; and when I called the attention of one of my neighbors to it, he almost got angry at me and he said, 'Oh, well, we have got better facilities now for discovering these things. I don't believe it.' And he is a member of the Church, too, but seemed to lack faith in these predictions. . . .

"This will be astonishing to you, I am sure, and I copied this from the [*Literary*] *Digest* of January 20, 1934.

" 'Two scientists charting the European record find that the indexed number of Wars rose from 2.678 in the twelfth to 13,735.98 in the twentieth century.

" 'Does war tend to decline as nations become more civilized? Many philosophers have said so; but now two sociologist of Harvard University have turned the cold and dispassionate eye of science upon the question, and have decided that future wars, fiercer than any ever fought before, apparently can be avoided only by a miracle. Far from declining, wars increase in number and intensity as nations progress, and the worst flareup since the dawn of history has occurred in our own century.'

" 'Now, of course, he had reference to the war from 1914 to 1918.

" 'These scientists are Professor Pitirim A. Sorokin, chairman of the Department of Sociology at Harvard, and Nicholas N. Golovin, formerly Lieutenant-General in the Imperial Russian army. They have reached their conclusions through a study of all the wars known to have taken place in Europe since Greece and the Western Roman Empire over a period of more than 2,400 years—from 500 B.C. to 1925 A.D. During this period in Greece, Rome, Central Europe, Germany, Italy, France, Great Britain, Spain, and the Netherlands and Russia, there occurred 902 wars (not battles).

" 'Each was studied from five points of view, the duration of the war, the size of the fighting force, the number of casualties, including killed and wounded, the number of countries involved, and the proportion of the combatants to the total population of the belligerent nations.

" 'From these five "variables" a total indexed number was computed for each war, in order that they might be reasonably expressed in terms of a common denominator.'

"Now, that's the quotation. Then [in 1936] I made these remarks.

"Out of this study these scientists declare that they have discovered that war has tended to increase over all Europe in the late centuries. They say they have learned that in these countries war grew from 2.678 in the twelfth century to 13,735.98 in the first twenty-five years of the twentieth century. Their tables show the growth by centuries. Up to the seventeenth century the wars were comparatively insignificant. Beginning with that century war increased during the eighteenth, with a lull in the nineteenth, yet in that century they were more than 100 times greater than in medieval times.

" 'These men conclude that "all commendable hopes that war will disappear in the near future are based on nothing more substantial than hope of a belief in miracles." '

"And then I made this prediction:

" 'If prophecy is to be fulfilled, there awaits the world a conflict more dreadful than any the world has yet seen.' (*Progress of Man,* pp. 402-404.)

"Now I want to make some comments in regard to the statement by President Woodruff and this parable.

"The Lord said that the sending forth of these angels was to be at the end of the harvest, and the harvest is the end of the world. Now, that ought to cause us some very serious reflections. And the angels have been pleading, as I have read it to you, before the Lord to be sent on their mission. Until 1893 the Lord said to them no, and then He set them loose. According to the revelation of President Woodruff, the Lord sent them out on that mission.

"What do we gather out of that? That we are at the time of the end. This is the time of the harvest. This is the time spoken of which is called the end of the world." (*Signs of the Times,* pp. 116-21.)

### D&C 86:9. What Does It Mean to Be a "Lawful Heir According to the Flesh"?

This phrase means that one's right to the priesthood is held by virtue of his being of the house of Israel. Elder Theodore M. Burton explained:

"One thing we often fail to realize is that our priesthood comes to us through the lineage of our fathers and mothers. The Lord explained it in these words: 'Therefore, thus saith the Lord unto you, with whom the priesthood hath continued through the lineage of your fathers. . . . ' (D&C 86:8.)

" 'Oh,' I can hear some of you say, 'there must be something wrong with that statement, for I am the only member of my family who has joined the Church. How could I have received the priesthood from my parents?'

"In this scripture the Lord was not talking about

your priesthood line of authority. He was talking about your inherited right to receive and use priesthood power. This readiness to listen and believe is an inherited gift which enabled you to recognize and accept the truth. Jesus explained this thought as he said: 'My sheep hear my voice, and I know them, and they follow me.' (John 10:27.)

"That spirit of acceptance is a manifestation of your inherited right to priesthood blessings. Such willingness to believe does not represent predestination, but it does represent foreordination. The Lord continues the revelation: 'For ye are lawful heirs, according to the flesh, and have been hid from the world with Christ in God.' (D&C 86:9.)

"This means we receive a right to priesthood blessings from our blood ancestry. I hope you can understand that priesthood with its accompanying blessings is dependent to a great degree on family relationship." (In Conference Report, Apr. 1975, p. 103; or *Ensign*, May 1975, p. 71.)

**D&C 86:11. How Are the Saints a Light to the Gentiles and a Savior to Israel?**

Elder Burton gave important insight into this scripture: "In this final verse the Lord reminds us of two things. First, he reminds us of our responsibility to do missionary work here on the earth. Second, he informs us that we are not only to be messengers of salvation to the living, but saviors for our ancestors who went before us and who, though now dead, have paved the way whereby we might receive our present blessings. It is through them we received our priesthood. The promise was made that even if they were born at a time and place where they could not hear the gospel preached in life, God would provide saviors for them from among their descendants. We are those saviors God promised through whom they can have every priesthood blessing." (In Conference Report, Apr. 1975, p. 105; or *Ensign*, May 1975, p. 71.)

# War in the Last Days

# Section 87

## Historical Background

The Prophet Joseph Smith wrote that the "appearances of troubles among the nations became more visible this season than they had previously been since the Church began her journey out of the wilderness. The ravages of the cholera were frightful in almost all the large cities on the globe. The plague broke out in India, while the United States, amid all her pomp and greatness, was threatened with immediate dissolution. The people of South Carolina, in convention assembled (in November), passed ordinances, declaring their state a free and independent nation; and appointed Thursday, the 31st day of January, 1833, as a day of humiliation and prayer, to implore Almighty God to vouchsafe His blessings, and restore liberty and happiness within their borders." It was the intent of South Carolina, following the day of prayer and humiliation, to sever ties with the United States on the first day of February; however, "President Jackson issued his proclamation against this rebellion, called out a force sufficient to quell it, and implored the blessings of God to assist the nation to extricate itself from the horrors of the approaching and solemn crisis.

"On Christmas day [1832]," the Prophet Joseph recorded, "I received the following revelation and prophecy on war [D&C 87]." (*History of the Church*, 1:301.)

Conflict did seem possible in the political turbulence of the early 1830s, as President Joseph Fielding Smith noted: "Scoffers have said it was nothing remarkable for Joseph Smith in 1832, to predict the outbreak of the Civil War and that others who did not claim to be inspired with prophetic vision had done the same. It has been said that Daniel Webster and William Lloyd Garrison in 1831 had predicted the dissolution of the Union. It is well known that senators and congressmen from the South had maintained that their section of the country had a right to withdraw from the Union, for it was a confederacy, and in 1832, war clouds were to be seen on the horizon. It was because of this fact that the Lord made known to Joseph Smith this revelation stating that wars would shortly come to pass, beginning with the rebellion of South Carolina, which would eventually terminate in war being poured out upon all nations and in the death and misery of many souls. It may have been an easy thing in 1832, or even 1831, for someone to predict that there would come a division of the Northern States and the Southern States, for even then there were rumblings, and South Carolina had shown the spirit of rebellion. It was not, however, within the power of man to predict in the detail which the Lord revealed to Joseph Smith, what was shortly to come to pass as an outgrowth of the Civil War and the pouring out of war upon all nations." (*Church History and Modern Revelation*, 1:358-59.)

Eleven years later, when the whole issue of nullification and secession had apparently died away, the Prophet again stated: "I prophesy, in the name of the Lord God, that the commencement of

Handwritten copy of a segment of the revelation on war

the difficulties which will cause much bloodshed previous to the coming of the Son of Man will be in South Carolina. It may probably arise through the slave question. This a voice declared to me while I was praying earnestly on the subject, December 25th, 1832." (*History of the Church*, 5:324.)

## Notes and Commentary

### D&C 87:1. Why Is It So Remarkable That Joseph Smith Predicted That the Civil War Would Start in South Carolina?

Smith and Sjodahl showed how, on the surface, it seemed unlikely in 1832 that South Carolina would be the one state that would start the war:

"At that time [1832] there was considerable commotion in the United States. The tariff question was one of great issue. The State of New York, before its acceptance of the Federal Constitution, surrounded itself with protective tariffs, and this policy was gradually approved by other Northern States. The Southern States, on the other hand, regarded free trade as best serving their interests, as their products were limited to a few articles of raw material, which they exported, while they imported practically all the manufactured commodities they needed. In 1824, Congress enacted a protective-tariff bill. A few years later, a stricter measure was adopted against Great Britain, in retaliation for efforts to exclude American trade from the British West Indies. This met with vigorous opposition in the South, especially in South Carolina. In this State, in 1832, a convention of the citizens declared that the tariff acts of 1828 and 1832 were not binding within their territory, and fixed February 1st, 1833, as the date after which they would be considered abrogated, unless Congress should, before then, remove the difficulty. Many Northerners were in favor of carrying the laws of the Union into effect by means of arms, at that time, and a bill empowering the President to use force was introduced in Congress. It was during this political agitation that the Prophet Joseph made the condition of his Country the subject of prayer and received this Revelation (See Sec. 130:12, 13).

"While all of these differences existing between the North and the South had a tendency to drive the people apart, yet it was the question of slavery, and the contention over the expansion of new territory and the creation of new states and whether or not slavery should be permitted in such new territory, that became the crux which brought upon the people the great Civil War. . . .

"South Carolina took the initiative. From a mere human point of view this appeared improbable. The probability was that the Northern States, conscious of their numerical and financial strength, would throw down the gauntlet. A bill was before Congress authorizing President Andrew Jackson to use force in defense of the Union. But, notwithstanding this, the North did not begin the war. South Carolina took the first step, by recalling her representatives in the United States Senate, November 10, 1860. This was followed by an ordinance of secession, passed by the State Legislature on the 17th of November, the same year. And on the 12th of April, 1861, the first shot of the war was fired by General Beauregard against Fort Sumter, and thus the conflict was begun by South Carolina, as foretold by the Prophet, and not by any of the Northern States." (Commentary, pp. 533-35.)

### D&C 87:1. "The Wars That Will Shortly Come to Pass . . . Will Eventually Terminate in the Death and Misery of Many Souls"

The war that started with the rebellion of South Carolina marked the beginning of the era of war that will last until the Savior returns to establish peace. In the American Civil War, "the personal valour and the enormous casualties—both in absolute numbers and in percentage of numbers engaged—have not yet ceased to astound scholars and military historians everywhere. Based on the three-year standard of enlistment, some 1,556,000 soldiers served in the Federal armies, which suffered a total of 634,703 casualties (359,528 dead and 275,175 wounded). There were probably some 800,000 men serving in the Confederate forces, which sustained approximately 483,000 casualties (about 258,000 deaths and perhaps 225,000 wounded).

"The cost in treasure was, of course, staggering for the embattled sections. Both governments, after strenuous attempts to finance the prosecution of the war by increasing taxes and floating loans, were obliged to resort to the printing press to make fiat money. While separate Confederate figures are lacking, the war finally cost the United States over $15,000,000,000. In sum, although the Union was preserved and restored, the cost in physical and moral suffering was incalculable, and some spiritual wounds caused by the holocaust still have not yet been healed." (Warren W. Hassler, Jr., in *New Encyclopaedia Britannica* [1978], s.v. "Civil War, U.S.")

### D&C 87:2. Has War Been Poured Out on All Nations?

In 1958 Elder Joseph L. Wirthlin showed how this prophecy had been fulfilled:

"The Prophet Joseph gave us this marvelous revelation in 1832. The Civil War came in 1861; the war between Denmark and Prussia in 1864; Italy and Austria in 1865 and 1866; Austria and Prussia in 1866; Russia and Turkey in 1877; China and Japan in 1894 and 1895; Spanish-American in 1898; Japan and Russia in 1904 and 1905; World War I in 1914-1918; then the next war was a comparatively small one, Ethiopia and Italy, when the people in that land of Ethiopia were taken over and controlled by Italy. I am grateful to the Lord that they now have their freedom. Then, the World War [World War II] just passed and, of course, the Korean War. [Since 1958 there have been, among numerous other wars, the Vietnam War in Southeast Asia, the war in Angola, and the Six-Day and Yom Kippur wars in the Holy Land.]

"These nations of Russia, China, Korea, Syria, Israel, Egypt, Arabia, Lebanon—all of these nations are now in an attitude of war of some kind. Just what the results are going to be, I do not know. Of course, from the revelations we can and do know that some day there will be one great war in a certain area, that area possibly may be in and around some of these countries I have mentioned, probably around Israel." (In Conference Report, Oct. 1958, p. 33.)

Elder Joseph Fielding Smith, in a lecture given in 1942, told how the Civil War was the beginning of the war that will bring about the end of the world: "We hear a great deal and we see a great deal in the prints today about this great second world war. I think in a previous talk I said I did not call it the second world war. This is the first world war. It is only a part, a continuation of the war of 1914 to 1918, and even that was not the beginning. I have been asked a great many times if I thought this present war was the great last war before the coming of Christ, and I have said yes; but I do not mean when I say this that we will not have another spell, another armistice, when they may lay down their arms for a season only to get ready to take them up again, although I hope that will not be the case. I think the great world war commenced in April, 1861. At any rate, that was the beginning of the end. . . .

"Based upon what the Lord says in this Section 87 of the Doctrine & Covenants—the Section on war which I read—I place the time of the beginning of the end at the rebellion of South Carolina. I say I place it there. I beg your pardon. The Lord places it there because it says beginning at this place these things would take place." (*Signs of the Times*, pp. 138, 140-41, 149.)

### D&C 87:3. Southern States Will Call on Great Britain

Explaining how this prophecy was fulfilled, Elder James E. Talmage said: "While no open alliance between the Southern States and the English government was effected, British influence gave indirect assistance and substantial encouragement to the South, and this in such a way as to produce serious international complications. Vessels were built and equipped at British ports in the interests of the Confederacy; and the results of this violation of the laws of neutrality cost Great Britain fifteen and a half millions of dollars, which sum was awarded the United States at the Geneva arbitration in settlement of the Alabama claims. The Confederacy appointed commissioners to Great Britain and France; these appointees were forcibly taken by United States officers from the British steamer on which they had embarked. This act, which the United States government had to admit as overt, threatened for a time to precipitate a war between this nation and Great Britain." (*Articles of Faith*, pp. 25-26.)

### D&C 87:3. Who Was to Call on Other Nations for Help?

In the phrase, "and they shall also call upon other nations," the referent for "they" is not clear. Sidney B. Sperry explained the problem: "Still another prediction is made in this verse, although probably some readers miss it because the language is somewhat involved. We have already seen that 'the Southern States will call on other nations, even ["including" as I interpret it] the nation of Great Britain, as it is called.' Immediately following these words we read: 'and *they* shall also call upon other nations, in order to defend themselves against other nations.' What is the antecedent of *they*? It cannot be the Southern States, because the Confederacy was fighting the Northern States only and was not defending itself against 'other nations.' Furthermore, the verse has already made the point that the Southern States would call (for help) on other nations. To me the antecedent of *they* is Great Britain and the other nations upon which the Confederacy would call for help, namely, France, Holland, and Belgium. The plain meaning of the words to me last quoted ('and they shall also,' etc.) is that even as the Southern States would call for help on other nations, so in turn would Great Britain, France, Holland, and Belgium eventually call for help in other conflicts to follow, in order to defend themselves. Many of us have lived to see the letter and spirit of this prophecy fulfilled in the two World Wars we have passed through. 'And then,' continues the Lord, 'war shall be poured out upon all nations.' That is to say, when Great Britain and the other nations mentioned call for help, world war would result. This has already taken place." (*Compendium*, pp. 419-20.)

President Joseph Fielding Smith noted that "following the Civil War the nations, in their great alarm because of the new methods of warfare which were being developed and their fear of other nations, entered into alliances and secret agreements in order to protect themselves from other nations. At the outbreak of the World War, these alliances had reached proportions never before known, and during the war other alliances were made until nearly every nation on the earth had taken sides with the Triple Alliance or the Triple Entente. It was during the period of the World War, 1914-1918, Great Britain made her appeal to the nations to come to the defense of the standard of Democracy. Her pleadings were heard round the world." (*Church History and Modern Revelation,* 1:361.)

### D&C 87:4-5. Who Are the "Slaves" Who Shall Rise Up against Their Masters?

This prophecy begins with reference to the Civil War, which was fought over the issue of slavery. Many have therefore assumed that the slaves mentioned in Doctrine and Covenants 87:4 were the blacks who fled north and fought in the Union armies against their former masters. Although that action partially fulfilled the prophecy, Elder Joseph L. Wirthlin suggested a further fulfillment: "In many cases I am quite sure we all think this has to do particularly with the slaves in the Southern States, but I believe, brethren and sisters, that it was intended that this referred to slaves all over the world, and I think of those, particularly in the land of Russia and other countries wherein they have been taken over by that great nation and where the people are actually the slaves of those individuals who guide and direct the affairs of Russia and China, and where the rights and the privilege to worship God and to come to a knowledge that Jesus Christ is his Son is denied them" (in Conference Report, Oct. 1958, p. 32).

### D&C 87:5. Who Are the "Remnants Who Are Left of the Land"?

In the scriptures, whenever the word *remnant* is used to refer to a people, it always refers to a segment of the house of Israel (see topical guide, s.v. "remnant"). Because the Savior made specific promises about the remnants of the Nephites and Lamanites (see 3 Nephi 20:10, 16; 21:2, 4), many have assumed that this verse refers to the Lamanite peoples who will sometime arise and "vex the Gentiles" (D&C 87:5).

President Joseph Fielding Smith saw in history a partial fulfillment of the prophecy in Doctrine and Covenants 87:5, but he cautioned against thinking of Lamanites only as the American Indians and also against thinking that the prophecy is wholly fulfilled: "The history of this American continent also gives evidence that the Lamanites have risen up in their anger and vexed the Gentiles. This warfare may not be over. It has been the fault of people in the United States to think that this prophetic saying has reference to the Indians in the United States, but we must remember that there are millions of the 'remnant' in Mexico, Central and South America. It was during our Civil War that the Indians in Mexico rose up and gained their freedom from the tyranny which Napoleon endeavored to inflict upon them contrary to the prediction of Jacob in the Book of Mormon, that there should be no kings among the Gentiles on this land. The independence of Mexico and other nations to the south has been accomplished by the uprising of the 'remnant' upon the land. However, let us not think that this prophecy has completely been fulfilled." (*Church History and Modern Revelation,* 1:363.)

In other places the word *remnant* is used generally of all Israel (see 1 Nephi 13:33), in some places it refers to the Jews (see Isaiah 37:31-32), and in some cases it refers specifically to the Latter-day Saints (see D&C 52:2.) So it is possible that the remnants mentioned in Doctrine and Covenants 87:5 could include people of the house of Israel other than the Lamanites.

### D&C 87:6. Will All Nations Be Destroyed?

"Now, I do not believe in trying to explain away the words of God that predict calamity, but are nevertheless full of assurance unto the righteous, be it a righteous man or a righteous nation. We should awaken to their dread import. The Lord is dealing with the nations of the earth, and his Spirit has departed in large measure from nations that have defied him and his commandments, and as a result, they, being left largely to themselves, war with one another, and seek all means by which they can destroy one another most expeditiously. Now, the Lord is not the author of these evil things; the nations are bringing these inflictions upon themselves, and there shall be a consummation brought about as the Lord hath decreed, which shall mean an end of all nations as such, if they will not observe the law and the commandments of the Lord their God." (James E. Talmage, in Conference Report, Oct. 1923, p. 54.)

In the judgments that precede the Millenium, all earthly kingdoms will come to an end and the kingdom of God will triumph and become the one political power during the thousand years of peace and righteousness (see Revelation 11:15).

### D&C 87:7. How Serious Is It to Shed the Blood of the Saints?

Prior to the Civil War many members of the Church lost their lives at the hand of ruthless mobs. Elder George Q. Cannon explained how serious it is to take the life of a servant of God: "There is no sin that a nation can commit, which the Lord avenges so speedily and fearfully, as he does the shedding of innocent blood, or, in other words, the killing of his anointed and authorized servants. No nation which has been guilty of this dreadful crime has ever escaped his vengeance. The thunderbolts of his wrath have been always launched forth for the destruction of the perpetrators of such wickedness. It is a rank offence against the majesty of Heaven and the authority of the Creator, which he never suffers to pass unrebuked; for such men act in his stead, and are his representatives on the earth." (*Millennial Star,* 4 June 1864, pp. 361-62; see also Notes and Commentary on D&C 101:81-95 and on D&C 136:34-36.)

**D&C 87:7. "The Lord of Sabaoth"**

" 'Sabaoth' is a Hebrew word meaning 'hosts.' It sometimes refers to the armies of Israel and other nations; sometimes to the priests officiating in the Sanctuary; sometimes to the people of God generally, and sometimes to the stars and planets in the sky. 'Lord of Hosts' is equivalent to the 'all-sovereign,' or 'omnipotent' Lord. When we pray, we should remember that He, to whom we speak, has all power in heaven and on Earth—the Lord of Hosts. The Lord has given His interpretation to this word to be: 'The Creator of the first day, the beginning and the end.' " (Smith and Sjodahl, Commentary, p. 540.)

**D&C 87:8. What Did the Lord Mean When He Said That We Should Stand in Holy Places?**

In this scripture the commission is to the disciples of Christ, and it is associated with their safety in the days of tribulation when a "desolating sickness shall cover the land" (D&C 45:32). President Harold B. Lee promised that "the true servants of God, those who are doing their duty, will be protected and preserved if they will do as the Lord has counseled: 'stand ye in holy places' " (*Stand Ye in Holy Places*, p. 87).

President Lee also wrote:

"The Lord has told us where these 'holy places' are:

" 'And it shall come to pass among the wicked, that every man that will not take his sword against his neighbor must needs flee unto Zion for safety.' (D&C 45:68.)

"Where is Zion?

"During the various periods of time or dispensations, and for specific reasons, the Lord's prophets, His 'mouthpieces,' as it were, have designated gathering places where the Saints were to gather. After designating certain such places in our dispensation, the Lord then declared:

" 'Until the day cometh when there is found no more room for them; and then I have other places which I will appoint unto them, and they shall be called stakes, for the curtains or the strength of Zion.' (D&C 101:21.) . . .

"There are several meanings of the word *Zion.*

"It may have reference to the hill named Mount Zion, or, by extension, the land of Jerusalem. . . .

"Zion was so called by Enoch in referring to the 'City of Holiness' (Moses 7:19) or the 'City of Enoch'. The land of Zion has been used to refer, in some connotations, to the Western Hemisphere.

"But there is another most significant use of the term by which the Church of God is called Zion: It comprises, according to the Lord's own definition, 'the pure in heart.' (D&C 97:21.)

"As one studies the Lord's commandments and the attending promises for compliance therewith, one gets some definite ideas as to how we might 'stand in holy places,' as the Lord commands—how we will be preserved with protection in accordance with His holy purposes, in order that we might be numbered among the 'pure in heart' who constitute Zion." (*Stand Ye in Holy Places*, pp. 22-23.)

President Lee's teachings make it clear that "holy places" have more to do with *how* one lives than *where* one lives. If a person lives worthy of the constant companionship of the Holy Ghost, a member of the Godhead, then he indeed stands in a holy place; and it is from that place that the Saints should not be moved until the day of the Lord comes.

The home is the most important institution for teaching the children of God the principles of becoming persons worthy of Zion; therefore, to parents the counsel is as follows: "Teach your families in your family home evening; teach them to keep the commandments of God, for therein is our only safety in these days. If they will do that, the powers of the Almighty will descend upon them as the dews from heaven, and the Holy Ghost will be theirs. That can be our guide, and that Spirit shall guide us and direct us to His holy home." (Lee, *Stand Ye in Holy Places*, p. 190; see also Joseph L. Wirthlin, in Conference Report, Oct. 1958, pp. 33-34.)

A holy place is any place where a man enjoys the spirit and presence of Divinity. It is the Lord's command that each member stand firmly in holy places and be not moved (falter or fall away into forbidden paths) until the Lord comes to claim his own. Each soul should ensure for himself this favored state so that he can "abide the day" (D&C 45:57).

*The home is the most important institution for teaching children the principles of Zion*

# The Olive Leaf

Section 88

## Historical Background

On 27 December 1832 a conference of ten high priests, including the Prophet, met in Kirtland to find out from the Lord his will concerning the upbuilding of Zion and the duty of the elders of the Church. Their questions seem to have stemmed from a great desire to know what the Church should do "in view of the critical times that had been predicted" (Smith and Sjodahl, Commentary, p. 540).

The conference lasted two days, during which Joseph instructed the nine other brethren on how to receive the blessings of heaven and the mind of the Lord. That the Lord was pleased with their desires is very evident from the introduction to the revelation (see D&C 88:2). In consequence his spirit was poured out upon them, and most of section 88 (vss. 1-126) was given in segments over the two days of the conference. The final part was received by Joseph Smith on 3 January 1833 and was then added to the first 126 verses for publication in the 1835 edition of the Doctrine and Covenants. (See "Kirtland Revelation Book," Historical Department, The Church of Jesus Christ of Latter-day Saints, Salt Lake City, pp. 47-48.)

In a letter written to William W. Phelps, the Prophet Joseph Smith called this revelation "the 'Olive Leaf' which we have plucked from the Tree of Paradise, the Lord's message of peace to us" (*History of the Church,* 1:316). The name is appropriate, for the olive tree is a well-known symbol of peace, and the revelation contains numerous keys for achieving spiritual peace.

*The olive tree, a symbol of peace*

## Notes and Commentary

### D&C 88:2. "The Lord of Sabaoth"

This title is explained in Notes and Commentary on Doctrine and Covenants 87:7.

### D&C 88:3-4. What Is the Other Comforter?

The promises in these four verses were given to the ten men who had assembled in conference: Joseph Smith, Sr.; Sidney Rigdon; Orson Hyde; Joseph Smith, Jr.; Hyrum Smith; Samuel H. Smith; Newel K. Whitney; Frederick G. Williams; Ezra Thayer; and John Murdock. These ten men were promised the other Comforter.

The Prophet Joseph Smith explained that "there are two Comforters spoken of. One is the Holy Ghost, the same as given on the day of Pentecost, and that all Saints receive after faith, repentance, and baptism. This first Comforter or Holy Ghost has no other effect than pure intelligence. It is more powerful in expanding the mind, enlightening the understanding, and storing the intellect with present knowledge, . . . though it may not have half as much visible effect upon the body. . . .

"The other Comforter spoken of is a subject of great interest, and perhaps understood by few of this generation. After a person has faith in Christ, repents of his sins, and is baptized for the remission of his sins and receives the Holy Ghost, (by the laying on of hands), which is the first Comforter, then let him continue to humble himself before God, hungering and thirsting after righteousness, and living by every word of God, and the Lord will soon say unto him, Son, thou shalt be exalted. When the Lord has thoroughly proved him, and finds that the man is determined to serve Him at all hazards, then the man will find his calling and his election made sure, then it will be his privilege to receive the other Comforter, which the Lord hath promised the Saints, as is recorded in the testimony of St. John, in the 14th chapter, from the 12th to the 27th verses. . . .

"Now what is this other Comforter? It is no more nor less than the Lord Jesus Christ Himself; and this is the sum and substance of the whole matter; that when any man obtains this last Comforter, he will have the personage of Jesus Christ to attend him, or appear unto him from time to time, and even He will manifest the Father unto him, and they will take up their abode with him, and the visions of the heavens will be opened unto him, and the Lord will teach him face to face, and he may have a perfect knowledge of the mysteries of the Kingdom of God; and this is the state and place the ancient Saints arrived at when they had such glorious visions—Isaiah, Ezekiel, John upon the Isle of Patmos, St. Paul in the three heavens, and all the Saints who held communion with the general assembly and Church of the Firstborn." (*Teachings*, pp. 149-51.)

The reference in this revelation to the "other Comforter" (D&C 86:3) has caused some to think that the "other Comforter" is the Second Comforter, but the context clearly defines this Comforter as the promise of eternal life (see vs. 4). Elder Bruce R. McConkie said of this passage: "In a revelation to certain selected saints in this dispensation, the Lord said that the alms of their prayers were 'recorded in the book of the names of the sanctified, even them of the celestial world' (D. & C. 88:2), which is to say that they were among those who had 'overcome by faith,' and were 'sealed by the Holy Spirit of promise, which the Father sheds forth upon all those who are just and true.' (D. & C. 76:53.) . . .

"These saints, like their Ephesian Brethren before them, had been called and chosen 'before the foundation of the world' that they 'should be holy and without blame' before the Lord, through baptism and obedience (Eph. 1:4-7), which is the sole course by which men can sanctify their souls (3 Ne. 27:19-20), thereby qualifying to have their names recorded 'in the book of the names of the sanctified.' (D. & C. 88:2.) They had then earned the right by faith and devotion to have the seal of divine acceptance placed on the conditional promises which they had theretofore made. They now had the sure 'promise . . . of eternal life' (D. & C. 88:4), which eternal life is the name of the kind of life which God our Heavenly and Eternal Father lives, and they were prepared to receive the Second Comforter." (*Doctrinal New Testament Commentary*, 3:338-39.)

The deep peace such a promise could bring alone justifies the title Olive Leaf.

**D&C 88:5. Church of the Firstborn**

See Notes and Commentary for Doctrine and Covenants 76:54.

**D&C 88:6-13. What Is the Light of Christ?**

President Joseph Fielding Smith explained that the "Light of Christ is not a personage. It has no body. I do not know what it is as far as substance is concerned; but it fills the immensity of space and emanates from God. It is the light by which the worlds are controlled, by which they are made. It is the light of the sun and all other bodies. It is the light which gives life to vegetation. It quickens the understanding of men, and has these various functions as set forth in these verses.

"It is: 'The light which is in all things, which giveth life to all things, which is the law by which all things are governed, even the power of God who sitteth upon his throne, who is in the bosom of eternity, who is in the midst of all things.'

"This is our explanation in regard to the Spirit of Christ, or Light of Truth, which every man receives and is guided by. Unless a man had the blessings that come from this Spirit, his mind would not be quickened; there would be no vegetation grown; the worlds would not stay in their orbits; because it is through this Spirit of Truth, this Light of Truth, according to this revelation, that all these things are done.

"The Lord has given to 'every man that cometh into the world,' the guidance of the Light of Truth, or Spirit of Jesus Christ, and if a man will hearken to this Spirit he will be led to the truth and will recognize it and will accept it when he hears it. We have seen this demonstrated thousands of times, where men were led to investigate and have had the desire to investigate in spite of the prejudices and traditions which they were taught in the world.

"If they refuse to come unto him, then he calls them wicked and they are under the bondage of sin. It seems to me that when a person declares that he is satisfied with his religion and therefore does not care to investigate, it is evidence that he has not hearkened to the Light of Truth which was given him; else he would not have been satisfied with the false religion which he has and would be seeking the truth." (*Doctrines of Salvation*, 1:52-53.)

**D&C 88:15. The Soul of Man**

Most people in the world think of the soul as being synonymous with the spirit of man, but, as Elder James E. Talmage wrote, "it is peculiar to the theology of the Latter-day Saints that we regard the body as an essential part of the soul. Read your dictionaries, the lexicons, and encyclopedias, and you will find that nowhere, outside of the Church of Jesus Christ, is the solemn and eternal truth taught that the soul of man is the body and the spirit combined. It is quite the rule to regard the soul as that incorporeal part of men, that immortal part which existed before the body was framed and which shall continue to exist after that body has gone to decay; nevertheless, that is not the soul; that is only a part of the soul; that is the spirit-man, the form in which every individual of us, and every individual human being, existed before called to take tabernacle in the flesh. It has been declared in the solemn word of revelation, that the spirit and the body constitute the soul of man; and, therefore, we should look upon this body as something that shall endure in the resurrected state, beyond the grave, something to be kept pure and holy." (In Conference Report, Oct. 1913, p. 117.)

**D&C 88:17-20. The Earth Must Be Sanctified**

"The entrance to celestial glory is through death and resurrection (v. 14). And the Earth itself must pass through the same process, in order to become the dwelling-place of celestial beings (vv. 18-20)," wrote Smith and Sjodahl.

"The opinion that this globe is to be annihilated

finds no support in the Word of God. Here, the important truth is revealed that our globe will be sanctified from all unrighteousness, and prepared for celestial glory, so that it will be fit for the presence of God, the Father. . . . It will not remain a dead planet, whirling about aimlessly in space; nor will it be distributed in the form of cosmic dust, throughout the universe. It will be glorified, by celestial glory, and become an abode for resurrected beings (v. 20)." (Commentary, p. 543.)

### D&C 88:21-24. Abiding the Law to Receive the Commensurate Glory

Elder James E. Talmage explained the relationship between obedience and blessings: "The Lord has said that according to the laws we obey here shall we receive from Him. We speak of rewards just as we speak of punishments. But rewards and punishments will come through the operation of law. The Lord has spoken illustrating that great truth by reference to what He had already revealed respecting the kingdoms or orders of glory, to this effect—If a man cannot or will not obey celestial laws, that is, live in accordance with the celestial requirements, he must not think that he is discriminated against when he is excluded from the celestial kingdom, because he could not abide it, he could not live there. If a man cannot or will not obey the terrestrial law he cannot rationally hope for a place in the terrestrial kingdom. If he cannot live the yet lower law—the telestial law—he cannot abide the glory of a telestial kingdom, and he will have to be assigned therefore to a kingdom without glory. I rejoice in the consistency and order of the Lord's plan and in His revelations to us." (In Conference Report, Oct. 1929, p. 69.)

### D&C 88:25-26. How Does the Earth Abide a Celestial Law?

"There are combustible elements in abundance and heat enough to consume many worlds like ours, whenever the torch is applied. Here we are told, that the Earth will abide 'the power by which it is quickened'; it will abide the fire and come out of the flames, quickened and purified, like gold out of the refiner's fire, or a beautiful vessel of potter's clay out of the fiery furnace (v. 26). In this sanctified state it will be the residence of celestial beings, resurrected and inhabiting 'the same' bodies that they had here, quickened by celestial glory (v. 28). For each individual will receive the glory by which he is quickened (vv. 29-31).

"[The earth] fills the measure of its creation, and the inference is that whatever, or whoever is true to the purpose of its, or his, or her existence lives in accordance with celestial law. To do that for which we are not created; to use our bodies or any of its organs, or faculties, for purposes for which they were not created is to break that law." (Smith and Sjodahl, Commentary, p. 545.)

### D&C 88:27. What Is the Difference between a "Spirit Body" and a "Spiritual Body"?

In a general conference, Elder Joseph Fielding Smith explained the difference:

"Modern blind teachers of the blind have a very false understanding of what is meant by a spiritual body. They have based their conclusion on the statement that Paul makes that the body is raised a spiritual body, and that flesh and blood cannot inherit the kingdom of God. They cannot conceive in their minds a body raised from the dead, being composed of flesh and bones, quickened by spirit and not by blood. When Paul spoke of the *spiritual* body he had no reference at all to the *spirit* body and there they have made their mistake. They have confused the spiritual body, or, in other words, the body quickened by the spirit, with the body of the spirit alone. . . .

"After the resurrection from the dead our bodies will be spiritual bodies, but they will be bodies that are tangible, bodies that have been purified, but they will nevertheless be bodies of flesh and bones, but they will not be blood bodies, they will no longer be quickened by blood but quickened by the spirit which is eternal and they shall become immortal and shall never die." (In Conference Report, Apr. 1917, pp. 62-63.)

### D&C 88:28. With What Bodies Will Individuals Come Forth in the Resurrection?

The Prophet Joseph Smith taught that in the Resurrection each person will receive back the very body he inhabited in mortality, that "there is no fundamental principle belonging to a human system that ever goes into another in this world or in the world to come. . . . If anyone supposes that any part of our bodies, that is, the fundamental parts thereof, ever goes into another body, he is mistaken." (*History of the Church,* 5:339; see also Alma 11:43-44; 40:23-25; 1 Corinthians 15:35-54.) The body will be resurrected to a glory equal to the level of law by which one lived. The person who keeps the commandments receives "truth and light, until he is glorified" (D&C 93:28).

### D&C 88:28. What Is a Celestial Spirit?

Elder Bruce R. McConkie defined the relationship between a celestial body and a celestial spirit: "Those who by full obedience to gospel requirements develop celestial bodies, gain at the same time *celestial spirits.* Then in the resurrection, when 'the same body which was a natural body,' (that is, the renewed body, the body sanctified by the Spirit, the celestial body) is received back again, 'they who are of a *celestial spirit'* are quickened by a celestial glory and go on to an inheritance in a celestial kingdom. (D&C 88:28.)" (*Mormon Doctrine,* p. 118.)

Elder L. Tom Perry indicated that such a celestial inclination would be observable in this life: "Surely there would be an obvious difference between one who is attempting to conduct his life as though he were a citizen of the kingdom of God, and one who is conducting his life by the standards made by man. When a person determines to live a higher law, there should be a visible difference, a marked change in his appearance, his actions, the way he treats others, and the way he serves his fellowmen and his God. The scriptures are full of dramatic changes which occurred in the lives of individuals when they were converted to living the law of the

*L. Tom Perry declared that conversion is observable in a changed life*

Lord." (In Conference Report, Apr. 1979, p. 16; or *Ensign,* May 1979, p. 12.)

**D&C 88:32-35. Who Are "They Who Remain"?**

These verses refer to those unworthy to receive a degree of glory, or the sons of perdition (see Notes and Commentary on D&C 76:26-31).

**D&C 88:37. "All Kingdoms Have a Law Given"**

"We are told here that every part of space is occupied by some 'kingdom'; that each kingdom is governed by law, and that the laws are adapted to the conditions that prevail. Some laws are universal. Such is the law of gravitation, for instance; or the great fundamental moral law, 'Thou shalt love the Lord thy God with all thy heart, and with all thy soul, and with all thy strength, and with all thy mind; and thy neighbor as thyself.' Other laws are limited; they vary as the conditions vary. By kingdoms we understand the planets and orbs that circle in space. God is capable of governing them all, because He 'comprehendeth all things, and all things are before Him' (v. 41). God visits all these kingdoms in due time." (Smith and Sjodahl, Commentary, pp. 548-49.)

**D&C 88:37-39. The Importance of Obeying Law for the Right Reason**

"We do right for various reasons," said Elder Robert L. Simpson. "Some people do right simply because they don't want to be punished for doing wrong. When we do right for fear of retribution, I think our foundation is very shaky. Another might say, 'I want to do right because I have always been taught that this is the thing to do.' Well, such reasoning is based on hearsay, on the testimony of others, and I think we need to mature beyond that point. I think we need to have our own testimonies instead of the advice of others on a perpetual basis. Others have been heard to say, 'I want to do right just to please my parents,' and although we all should have a desire to please our parents, that reason alone is not sufficient to sustain us throughout eternity. Perhaps you have heard people who have indicated that they are doing the right thing simply because they want to be obedient to God's commands; this, too, is a very high and noble purpose—provided, of course, that obedience is not blind obedience, without personal conviction. But to me the best reason of all is illustrated by the person who feels the desire to do right because he wants to add glory to his Father in heaven. Whatever stage of motivation we find ourselves in, I think we must eventually reinforce this with our own personal testimony that has been built on a foundation of gospel scholarship and understanding—a testimony which leads us to the life of unselfishness and service, one which finds its highest sanctification in the supreme thought that we are living gospel principles because we desire to glorify his great name." ("Cast Your Burden upon the Lord," *New Era,* Jan. 1977, p. 4.)

**D&C 88:40-50. God Comprehends All Things**

Charles W. Penrose, First Counselor in the First Presidency under President Joseph F. Smith, said: "It is a great puzzle to some people how it can possibly be that a person, an individual, of form and stature, occupying but one place at a time, can hear the prayers of His people or can comprehend them as David said He does: Said he: 'There is not a thought of my heart but lo! O Lord, thou knowest it altogether. If I ascend up into heaven behold thou art there. If I descend down into hell behold thou art there; and if I take the wings of the morning, and flee to the uttermost parts of the earth there will Thy hand lead me and thy right hand guide me' [Compare Psalms 139:7-10]. Of course these expressions are somewhat figurative, but there is the great fact that God can be omnipresent by the power of His universally diffused Spirit which proceeds from His presence throughout the immensity of space, and He can see and discern all things by that power, as He told Enoch, and Moses also, as you can read in The Pearl of Great Price. Moses and Enoch were each lifted up so that they could see, measurably, as Deity sees and they beheld the multiplicity of the creations of God; and when Enoch declared that if a man could count the particles of the earth or of a million earths like this, that would not be a beginning to the number of God's creations, then God told him, 'Yea, and mine eye can pierce them all' [see Moses 7:29:36]. By the power of that Spirit he sees and comprehends and understands all things, and His watchful care and His mercies are over all His works." (In Conference Report, Oct. 1915, pp. 37-38.)

Scriptures in the Book of Mormon and the

Doctrine and Covenants suggest that time as man knows it is not the same with God (see Alma 40:8; D&C 38:1; 130:4-7).

**D&C 88:51-61. What Is the Meaning of This Parable?**

Moses saw in vision that the Savior had created many worlds like this earth that were also inhabited (see Moses 1:27-29). The inhabitants of these worlds are sons and daughters of God and are precious in his sight. The Savior is responsible for these creations and visits them in their times and seasons. Elder Orson Pratt explained: "The Lord wanted to represent these kingdoms so that we could understand what he desired to impart, and he gave it as a parable, in order to assist our weak comprehensions. . . . Says the interrogator—'I do not comprehend this idea of the Lord's withdrawing from one and going to another.' In order to comprehend this let us come back to our own globe. Do we not expect that the Lord will, by and by, come and visit us and stay a little while, about a thousand years. Yes, and then we shall be made glad with the joy of the countenance of our Lord. He will be among us, and will be our King, and he will reign as a King of kings and Lord of lords. He will have a throne in Zion, and another in the Temple at Jerusalem, and he will have with him the twelve disciples who were with him during his ministry at Jerusalem; and they will eat and drink with him at his table; and all the people of this globe who are counted worthy to be called Zion, the pure in heart, will be made glad by the countenance of their Lord for a thousand years, during which the earth will rest. Then what? He withdraws. What for? To fulfill other purposes; for he has other worlds or creations and other sons and daughters, perhaps just as good as those dwelling on this planet, and they, as well as we, will be visited, and they will be made glad with the countenance of their Lord. Thus he will go, in the time and in the season thereof, from kingdom to kingdom or from world to world, causing the pure in heart, the Zion that is taken from these creations, to rejoice in his presence.

"But there is another thing I want you to understand. This will not be kept up to all eternity, it is merely a preparation for something still greater. And what is that? By and by, when each of these creations has fulfilled the measure and bounds set and the times given for its continuance in a temporal state, it and its inhabitants who are worthy will be made celestial and glorified together. Then, from that time henceforth and for ever, there will be no intervening veil between God and his people who are sanctified and glorified, and he will not be under the necessity of withdrawing from one to go and visit another, because they will all be in his presence." (In *Journal of Discourses*, 17:331-32.)

**D&C 88:63-83. A Message of Peace**

This revelation is indeed a message of peace, an "olive leaf," to the Latter-day Saints from the Savior. In these verses the Savior gives the positive principles of the gospel that man must observe in order to be acceptable to him and in order to escape the judgments of the latter days (see D&C 88:84-116). The Lord restates these positive instructions, with some additions, in verses 117 to 126.

**D&C 88:62-65. What Is Proper Prayer?**

Speaking of what constitutes true and powerful prayer, Smith and Sjodahl wrote:

"There are too many who call upon the Lord only in their expediency when they, in desperation need His help. To these he may not be near, but may be slow to hearken to their pleadings. (Doc. and Cov. 101:7-8.) . . .

"Prayer is the most wonderful institution in the kingdom of God, and none was more familiar with it than the Prophet Joseph. But there are many who have no higher conception of it than to regard it as only a means whereby to obtain gifts from God, most often of a material character. Is the gift bestowed? Then the prayer is answered. Is it withheld? Then God did not hear. 'Such theory,' as one has said, 'is obviously too simple and superficial to be true. Prayer is more subtle than this doctrine implies. It may be described as the soul speaking to God and hearing God speak to it. It is, therefore, the deepest and the most wonderful act of which a man is capable, for in it the whole universe is, as it were, concentrated.' . . .

" 'Whatsoever ye ask the Father in my name.' That is the prayer that is acceptable to God. To pray in the name of the Lord is to ask as one belonging to Him—one accepted by Him. It is to pray according to the dictation of His Spirit. Such prayers God will hear and grant, if 'expedient for you.' There is quite a difference between the mechanical petition of a street beggar and the request of one who is a friend of the son in the house. The latter is treated as the son. What is good for him he will receive. Bishop Hall well says:

" 'What God requires and looks at, is neither the arithmetic of our prayers—how many they are; not the rhetoric of our prayers—how eloquent they be; nor the geometry of our prayers—how long they be; nor the music of our prayers—how sweet our voice may be; nor the logic, nor the method, nor even the orthodoxy of our prayers.'

"God looks to our welfare, even when He does not give us that for which we ask. If we were to pray for, and receive what is not good for us, it would be for our condemnation." (Commentary, pp. 551-52.)

**D&C 88:67-68. What Great Blessing Is Promised to Those Who Sanctify Themselves?**

It is the right of every member of the house of Israel to see his King and enjoy his presence. This is a specific promise to those who will sanctify themselves. In several places in the Doctrine and Covenants the promise is given that one can see God (see D&C 50:45-46; 67:10; 93:1); however, since no unclean thing can dwell in God's presence, one must be sanctified to see him and come into his presence.

"The meaning of 'sanctification' is explained in the words that follow, 'That your minds become single to God.' Our Lord had regard only to the glory of the Father, when he undertook the salvation of man. To follow in His footsteps and to be able to say at all times, truthfully, 'Thine be the honor,' is to be sanctified; that is to be a Saint." (Smith and Sjodahl, Commentary, p. 552.)

### D&C 88:69. Is It Wrong to Laugh?

See Notes and Commentary on Doctrine and Covenants 88:121.

### D&C 88:76. How Does One Continue in Fasting and Prayer?

"These are indispensable in the preparation for the ministry. Our Lord teaches us that there are evil spirits that cannot be overcome except by those whose spiritual life and faith are made strong by self-denial and communion with God. It is, therefore, of the utmost importance that the servants of the Lord should fast and pray. Through the fasting and prayer of the servants of the Lord, the mouth of Alma was opened, and his limbs strengthened (Mos. 27:22-3). Through fasting and prayer the Nephites 'did wax stronger and stronger in their humility, and firmer and firmer in the faith of Christ' (Hel. 3:35).

"Fasting has in all ages been an outward sign of sorrow and mourning. When the heart is full of grief, the body does not crave for food as usual. When calamities sweep over a country, or when sinners are awakened to a realization of their condition abstinence from all pleasures, including those of the table, is natural to all who take things seriously. The Elders, however, are not required to fast as a sign of mourning alone, but as one of rejoicing. This is just as natural. For when the heart is filled with joy, the craving for food is forgotten for long periods, as they know who have attended meetings, lasting for many hours, where the Holy Spirit has been poured out upon the assembly. Our Lord warns His people against making a display of their fasting: 'When thou fastest, anoint thine head, and wash thy face' (Matt. 6:16-18)." (Smith and Sjodahl, Commentary, pp. 554-55.)

### D&C 88:77-80. Why Is Secular Knowledge Important?

Elder John A. Widtsoe pointed out that "theology is not the only subject in which the Elders should be interested. They should study:

"Things both in heaven—Astronomy.

"And in the earth—Everything pertaining to the cultivation of the soil.

"And under the earth—Mineralogy, geology, etc.

"Things which have been—History, in all its branches.

"Things which must shortly come to pass—Prophecies.

"Things which are at home and abroad—Domestic and foreign politics.

"Wars—perplexities—judgment—The signs of the times, by which the observer may know that the day of the Lord is at hand.

"A knowledge of countries and kingdoms—physical and political geography, languages, etc.

"These studies, the Lord considers necessary. [D&C 88:80 quoted.] God does not require all His servants to become doctors, or professors, or even profound students of these subjects, but He expects them to know enough of these things to be able to magnify their callings as His ambassadors to the world." (*Priesthood and Church Government*, pp. 55-56.)

Doctrine and Covenants 88:77-78 explains that as the Saints diligently teach one another the doctrines of the kingdom, they can be instructed more perfectly in all these other subjects.

### D&C 88:87-91. What Is the Reason for the Calamities of the Last Days?

About a year after this revelation was given, the Saints were driven from their homes in Jackson County, Missouri. The Lord told his prophet at that time that the affliction came upon them "in consequence of their transgressions" (D&C 101:2).

President Joseph Fielding Smith explained why so many severe judgments are being poured out upon the world in the last days:

"It is not the will of the Lord that there should come upon the people disaster, trouble, calamity, and depression, . . . but because man himself will violate the commandments of God and will not walk in righteousness, the Lord permits all of these evils to come upon him. . . .

"The Lord has made the declaration in our own day that it was his good pleasure to give to men the fulness of the earth, and the Lord is pleased to have them use it, and he would pour out upon them his blessings in abundance if they would only hearken and be obedient to the laws which he has given them for their guidance. But, men are rebellious; they are not willing to live in that law and profit thereby; they are not willing to receive the good things of the earth as the Lord would give to them in abundance; but in their narrow-mindedness, shortsightedness, and in their greed and selfishness, they think they know better than the Lord does. And so, they pursue another course, and the result is that the blessings of the Lord are withdrawn, and in the place thereof come calamity, destruction, plagues, and violence. Men have themselves to blame. . . .

" . . . the Lord decreed that he would withhold his spirit [the Spirit of Christ] from the inhabitants of the earth. . . . This spirit he was withdrawing from them because of their wickedness, and the withdrawal of his spirit would bring upon them these calamities." (*Doctrines of Salvation*, 3:27-29.)

### D&C 88:91. "Men's Hearts Shall Fail Them; for Fear Shall Come upon All People"

In a previous revelation the Lord said, "If ye are prepared ye shall not fear" (D&C 38:30). The people of the world will not be prepared when the Lord pours out his judgments. Sin will abound as in the days of Noah, and men will be left without excuse because the warning to repent will have been clearly sounded, yet not heeded. Knowing that the judgments are just and that they have no excuse and no escape, men and women of the world will greatly fear. The Nephites experienced

*"The sounding of the trump of the angel of God" (D&C 88:98)*

the same warnings and judgments, which are recorded in Mormon 1 through 6.

**D&C 88:92-110. What Is Meant by the Sounding of Trumps by the Lord's Angels?**

See Notes and Commentary on Doctrine and Covenants 77:12.

**D&C 88:93. The Sign of the Coming of the Son of Man**

"Immediately after the testimony of these messengers [mentioned in D&C 88:92] a great sign will appear in heaven, which, like the sun, will be seen all round the world. Our Lord calls it the 'Sign of the Son of Man' (Matt. 24:30). . . .

" . . . when the sign appears, God will make its meaning known to the Prophet, Seer and Revelator who at that time may be at the head of the Church, and through him to His people and the world in general." (Smith and Sjodahl, Commentary, p. 560.)

In a discourse during the April conference of 1843, the Prophet Joseph Smith mentioned this sign and said: "There will be wars and rumors of wars, signs in the heavens above and on the earth beneath, the sun turned into darkness and the moon to blood, earthquakes in divers places, the seas heaving beyond their bounds; *then will appear one grand sign of the Son of Man in heaven.* But what will the world do? They will say it is a planet, a comet, etc. But the Son of Man will come as the sign of the coming of the Son of Man, which will be as the light of the morning cometh out of the east." (*Teachings,* pp. 286-87.)

**D&C 88:94. Binding the "Mother of Abominations" Who Is the "Tares of the Earth"**

The first of seven angels to sound trumps after the warning to prepare for the coming of the Bridegroom will announce the binding of "that great church, the mother of abominations." This "church" is the "church of the devil," often called "the great and abominable church"—terms used to designate groups whose objective is to lead men away from Christ and his gospel and thus from salvation in his kingdom. The fall of this "church," which is the "tares of the earth," is discussed in Notes and Commentary on Doctrine and Covenants 86:1-7.

**D&C 88:95-98. "Silence in Heaven" Precedes Christ's Coming in Glory and the Celestial Resurrection**

After the angel sounds a trump "loud and long" (D&C 88:94), there will be "silence in heaven for the space of half an hour" (vs. 95). "Whether the half hour here spoken of," said Elder Orson Pratt, "is according to our reckoning—thirty minutes, or whether it be according to the reckoning of the Lord we do not know. We know that the word hour is used in some portions of the Scriptures to represent quite a lengthy period of time. For instance, we, the Latter-day Saints, are living in the eleventh hour, that is in the eleventh period of time; and for aught we know the half hour during which silence is to prevail in heavens may be quite an extensive period of time [if this measurement refers strictly to the Lord's time—one thousand of man's years to one day for the Lord—the 'half hour' would be approximately twenty-one years]. During the period of silence all things are perfectly still; no angels flying during that half hour; no trumpets sounding; no noise in the heavens above; but immediately after this great silence the curtain of heaven shall be unfolded as a scroll is unfolded. School children, who are in the habit of seeing maps hung up on the wall, know that they have rollers upon which they are rolled up, and that to expose the face of the maps they are let down. So will the curtain of heaven be unrolled so that the people may gaze upon those celestial beings who will make their appearance in the clouds. The face of the Lord will be unveiled, and those who are alive will be quickened, and they will be caught up; and the Saints who are in their graves, will come forth and be caught up, together with those who are quickened, and they will be taken into the heavens into the midst of those celestial beings who will make their appearance at that time. These are the ones who are the first fruits, that is, the first fruits at the time of his coming." (In *Journal of Discourses,* 16:328.)

At this time the resurrection of those who are celestial (see Notes and Commentary on D&C 88:28) will take place. Mortals at the time of the Lord's coming who are living celestial law will be quickened and caught up to meet him and those who are already resurrected. Those mortals will be transfigured and sanctified at that time but not immortalized. Their bodies will be prepared to dwell on earth during the Lord's millennial reign, when "the earth will be renewed and receive its paradisiacal glory" (Articles of Faith 1:10). After this event they will return to the earth and continue to live as mortals.

**D&C 88:99. What Is the "Redemption of Those Who Are Christ's at His Coming; Who Have Received Their Part in . . . Prison"?**

This passage is a reference to the resurrection of terrestrial beings. After the celestial resurrection, "after the Lord and the righteous who are caught up to meet him have descended upon the earth, there will come to pass another resurrection. This may be considered as a part of the first, although it comes later. In this resurrection will come forth those of the terrestrial order, who were not worthy to be caught up to meet him, but who are worthy to come forth to enjoy the millennial reign. . . .

"This other class, which will also have right to the first resurrection, are those who are not members of the Church of the Firstborn, but who have led honorable lives, although they refused to accept the fulness of the gospel.

"Also in this class will be numbered those who died without law and hence are not under condemnation for a violation of the commandments of the Lord." (Smith, *Doctrines of Salvation,* 2:296-97.)

**D&C 88:100-101. The Resurrection of Telestial Beings**

"All liars, and sorcerers, and adulterers and all who love and make a lie," President Joseph Fielding Smith wrote, "shall not receive the resurrection at this time, but for a thousand years shall be thrust down into hell where they shall suffer the wrath of God until they pay the price of their sinning, if it is possible, by the things which they shall suffer" (*Doctrines of Salvation,* 2:297).

After they have satisfied the demands of justice by paying for their own sins in hell, they will then be brought forth and resurrected (see D&C 76:103-6). They will not be on the earth during the Millennium, "but during that time are spending their time in torment, or anguish of soul, because of their transgressions. . . .

"This suffering will be a means of cleansing, or purifying, and through it the wicked shall be brought to a condition whereby they may, through the redemption of Jesus Christ, obtain immortality. Their spirits and bodies shall be again united, and they shall dwell in the telestial kingdom. But this resurrection will not come until the end of the world." (Smith, *Doctrines of Salvation,* 2:298.)

**D&C 88:102. Who Are Those "Who Shall Remain Filthy Still"?**

The sons of perdition, though they will be resurrected (see Alma 11:41; 2 Nephi 9:22; 1 Corinthians 15:22), will be the last to be brought forth. Like those who are telestial, they will suffer in hell before their resurrection. They will be cast back into hell after their resurrection (see D&C 76:31-39, 43-49).

**D&C 88:103-6. The Triumph of the Lord's Work**

From before the creation of the earth, Satan has made war with God and his children. Satan has sought to overthrow and destroy the plan of God so that he might usurp God's kingdom and glory (see Isaiah 14:12-13; D&C 29:36; 76:28-29; Moses 4:1-4). He will not succeed. All of God's creations, including those who choose to follow Satan, will eventually confess the supremacy of God and submit to him. The kingdom of Satan will fall, and the kingdom of God and Christ will triumph.

Notes and Commentary on Doctrine and Covenants 133:46-51 explains the phrase "the Lamb of God hath . . . trodden the wine press alone" (D&C 88:106).

**D&C 88:107. The Saints Will Be Filled with God's Glory and "Be Made Equal with Him"**

The sons and daughters of God possess the potential to become like their parents.

Elder Parley P. Pratt said, "Every man who is eventually made perfect—raised from the dead and filled, or quickened, with a fulness of celestial glory—will become like them in every respect, physically and in intellect, attributes, or powers.

"The very germs of these godlike attributes being engendered in man, the offspring of Deity, only need cultivating, improving, developing, and advancing by means of a series of progressive changes, in order to arrive at the fountain 'Head,' the standard, the climax of Divine Humanity." (*Key to the Science of Theology,* p. 20.)

**D&C 88:108-10. All Things Will Be Revealed**

These verses teach the truth that ultimately nothing can be hidden. God, who said, "all things are present with me, for I know them all" (Moses 1:6), has power to reveal all things. Those in any age of the world who have performed works of darkness, thinking their deeds could be covered and thus not be accounted to them for sin, will have their hopes blasted. When the trumps of God are sounded, each to announce the revealing of events of one-thousand-year periods of the earth's history, all things will be uncovered and made known—even the thoughts and intents of men's hearts. For some this will be dreadful. For others, who have labored and served in purity and have performed secretly acts of love, kindness, and sacrifice, this will be a time of great joy. All will know at that time that God is just. He and his servants will be vindicated, and all will acknowledge that the only desire of God and his people is for the welfare and happiness of all mankind.

**D&C 88:110. The Millennial Binding of Satan**

See Notes and Commentary on Doctrine and Covenants 43:31.

**D&C 88:111-15. The Final Conquest of Satan and His Followers**

Elder Orson Pratt said that "there will be a great division of the people" at the end of the Millennium, when the battle against Gog and

Magog commences. "The Saints then, will have become very numerous, probably more numerous than ever before; and they will be obliged to gather together in one place, as we now do from the four quarters of the earth. . . . Satan will gather his army. . . . He with his army will come against the Saints, and the beloved city, and encompass them round about. His army will be so great that it will be able to come upon the Saints on all sides: he is to encompass their camp. Because of the favorable position he is to hold, in that great last battle, and because of the vast number of his army, he doubtless believes that he will get the mastery and subdue the earth and possess it. I do not think he fully understands all about the designs of God." (In *Journal of Discourses,* 18:346.)

Those who join Satan and his host will "not rebel in ignorance or dwindle in unbelief, as the Lamanites did; but they will sin wilfully against the law of heaven, and so great will the power of Satan be over them, that he will gather them together against the Saints and against the beloved city, and fire will come down out of heaven and consume them." (Orson Pratt, in *Journal of Discourses,* 16:322.)

### D&C 88:117-41. "Therefore . . . Organize Yourselves"

The School of the Prophets founded by the Lord (see D&C 86:127) was organized in February 1833. The Prophet and the Apostles and other elders were to "teach one another words of wisdom . . . out of the best books . . . by study and also by faith" (vs. 118). Those who attended "had many manifestations of the presence of the Spirit of the Lord," including speaking in foreign tongues (Smith and Sjodahl, Commentary, p. 567).

*The School of the Prophets at Kirtland*

President Brigham Young said that "the members of that school were but few at first, and the Prophet commenced to teach them in doctrine to prepare them to go out into the world to preach the gospel unto all people, and gather the select from the four quarters of the Earth, as the prophets anciently have spoken. While this instruction prepared the Elders to administer in word and doctrine, it did not supply the teachings necessary to govern their private, or temporal, lives; it did not say whether they should be merchants, farmers, mechanics, or money-changers. The Prophet began to instruct them how to live, that they might be better prepared to perform the great work they were called to accomplish." (In Smith and Sjodahl, Commentary, p. 567.)

A "school in Zion" was organized in Independence, Missouri, in August 1833 with Parley P. Pratt as its instructor (see Notes and Commentary on D&C 97:3-5), and Brigham Young patterned a school of elders after these early schools when the Church moved to Utah.

In the later verses of Doctrine and Covenants 88, wrote Smith and Sjodahl, "rules are given for the conduct of the School of the Prophets. This school was to be established for the benefit of all who were called to the ministry of the Church (v. 127). Note the order and etiquette to be observed in everything pertaining to the school. It was to be a house of God and to be respected as such." (Commentary, p. 567.) Though the rules of order and conduct in these verses were given specifically for the School of the Prophets, many have universal application.

### D&C 88:121. "Cease From All Your Light Speeches . . . and Light-mindedness"

"Joyful *laughter* meets with divine approval, and when properly engaged in, it is wholesome and edifying. Incident to the normal experiences of mortality, there is 'A time to weep, and a time to laugh.' (Eccles. 3:4.) . . .

"Our Lord's ministers, however, are commanded: 'Cast away your idle thoughts and your *excess* of laughter far from you.' (D. & C. 88:69.) Their main concerns should be centered around 'the solemnities of eternity' (D. & C. 43:34), with laughter being reserved for occasional needed diversion. Laughter on the sabbath day is expressly curtailed (D. & C. 59:15), and while worshiping and studying in the school of the prophets, the elders were commanded to abstain 'from all laughter' (D. & C. 88:121.) This same abstinence should prevail in sacrament meetings and in all solemn assemblies." (McConkie, *Mormon Doctrine,* p. 432.)

Though laughter at the appropriate time is not sin, it must be governed. President Brigham Young said: "I like to be pleased myself; I like to be filled with joy, but if I cannot be filled with joy and gladness that is full of meat and marrow, or, in other words, full of meaning and sense, I would rather retain my gravity.

"There is but one step between life and death, between faithfulness and apostasy, between the sublime and the ridiculous. . . .

"Never give way to vain laughter." (In *Journal of Discourses,* 9:290.)

President Joseph F. Smith warned of the danger of losing the Lord's Spirit by letting small indiscretions develop into inappropriate activity. "The Lord has called upon us to be a sober-minded people, not given to much laughter, frivolity and light-mindedness, but to consider thoughtfully and thoroughly the things of his kingdom that we may be prepared in all things to understand the glorious truths of the gospel, and be prepared for blessings to come. . . .

" . . . I believe that it is necessary for the Saints to have amusement, but it must be of the proper kind. I do not believe the Lord intends and desires that we should pull a long face and look sanctimonious and hypocritical. I think he expects us to be happy and of a cheerful countenance, but he does not expect of us the indulgence in boisterous and unseemly conduct and the seeking after the vain and foolish things which amuse and entertain the world. He has commanded us to the contrary for our own good and eternal welfare." (In Conference Report, Oct. 1916, p. 70.)

Concerning the sacred calling the Saints have as the Lord's people and their need to maintain a proper perspective of eternity, the Prophet Joseph Smith said:

"The things of God are of deep import; and time, and experience, and careful and ponderous and solemn thoughts can only find them out. Thy mind, O man! if thou wilt lead a soul unto salvation, must stretch as high as the utmost heavens, and search unto and contemplate the darkest abyss, and the broad expanse of eternity—thou must commune with God. How much more dignified and noble are the thoughts of God, than the vain imaginations of the human heart! None but fools will trifle with the souls of men.

"How vain and trifling have been our spirits, our conferences, our councils, our meetings, our private as well as public conversations—too low, too mean, too vulgar, too condescending for the dignified characters of the called and chosen of God, according to the purposes of his will, from before the foundation of the world!" (*Teachings,* p. 137.)

The Prophet instructed the elders to "walk before the Lord in soberness and righteousness," and "do away with lightmindedness" (*Teachings,* p. 326).

**D&C 88:124-26. Some General Rules of Physical and Spiritual Health**

"All the instructions in this paragraph are notable. They might be included in the Word of Wisdom. Idleness is condemned: Cleanliness is inculcated. Fault-finding is classed as wrong. And this rule is laid down, 'Cease to sleep longer than is needful'; retire early; arise early; 'that your bodies and your minds may be invigorated.' This splendid rule is too often violated. Electric lights and late theaters have transformed night into day and deprived the people of some of their natural sleep, and at the same time of a portion of their physical and mental vigor.

"Note the closing injunctions, Clothe yourselves with charity 'as with a mantle;' not as a scanty piece of clothing, but as a generous covering; for charity is 'the bond of perfectness and peace.' Charity—which means brotherly affection—makes for perfection and peace. Pray always. Prayer is necessary, if we shall remain faithful till the coming of the Lord." (Smith and Sjodahl, Commentary, p. 565.)

# The Word of Wisdom — Section 89

## Historical Background

President Brigham Young spoke about the coming forth of the revelation known as the Word of Wisdom: "I think I am as well acquainted with the circumstances which led to the giving of the Word of Wisdom as any man in the Church, although I was not present at the time to witness them. The first school of the prophets was held in a small room situated over the Prophet Joseph's kitchen, in a house which belonged to Bishop Whitney. . . . The brethren came to that place for hundreds of miles to attend school in a little room probably no larger than eleven by fourteen. When they assembled together in this room after breakfast, the first they did was to light their pipes and, while smoking, talk about the great things of the kingdom and spit all over the room, and as soon as the pipe was out of their mouths a large chew of tobacco would then be taken. Often when the Prophet entered the room to give the school instructions he would find himself in a cloud of tobacco smoke. This, and the complaints of his wife at having to clean so filthy a floor, made the Prophet think upon the matter, and he inquired of the Lord relating to the conduct of the Elders in using tobacco, and the revelation known as the Word of Wisdom was the result of his inquiry. You know what it is and can read it at your leisure." (In *Journal of Discourses,* 12:158.)

## Notes and Commentary

### D&C 89:2. Is the Word of Wisdom a Commandment Today?

Although the revelation of the Word of Wisdom was received on 27 February 1833, its acceptance by the individual members of the Church was gradual. On 9 September 1851, some eighteen years after it was given, the Patriarch to the Church, John Smith, delivered a talk to the Saints on the Word of Wisdom. Following his address, President Brigham Young arose and proposed to the general conference that all Saints formally covenant to abstain from tea, coffee, tobacco, whiskey, and "all things mentioned in the Word of Wisdom" ("Minutes of the General Conference," *Millennial Star,* 1 Feb. 1852, p. 35). The motion was accepted unanimously and became binding as a commandment for all Church members thereafter.

Worthiness, a condition of individual obedience to the commandments of the Lord, is ascertained by a personal interview with a bishop and stake president for all who desire a recommend to perform sacred ordinances in the Church. Living the Word of Wisdom is an essential part of such worthiness; indeed, obedience to it is a measure of worthiness for all Latter-day Saints, and it is accepted as a commandment.

### D&C 89:2. Why Does the Lord Say "Not by Commandment or Constraint"?

"The reason undoubtedly why the Word of Wisdom was given—as not by 'commandment or restraint' was that at that time, at least, if it had been given as a commandment it would have brought every man, addicted to the use of these noxious things, under condemnation; so the Lord was merciful and gave them a chance to overcome, before He brought them under the law. Later on, it was announced from this stand, by President Brigham Young that the Word of Wisdom was a revelation and a command of the Lord [See Young, *Discourses of Brigham Young,* pp. 183–84]." (Joseph F. Smith, in Conference Report, Oct. 1913, p. 14.)

President Heber J. Grant emphasized the formalizing of the Word of Wisdom as a commandment and warned those who were not in obedience to it that "the day is gone by when the Lord will trifle with the Latter-day Saints. He has said that His Spirit shall not always strive with man." (*Gospel Standards,* pp. 55-56.) Although the Lord allowed a time of adjustment for those who were already members of the Church when the Word of Wisdom was given, today it is expected that all who wish to be known as Saints will adhere to the commandment.

### D&C 89:2. How Does the Word of Wisdom Show the Will of God in Man's Temporal Salvation?

In order for the Father to bless mankind with the spiritual endowments necessary to ensure a fulness of joy, men must strive to be clean and pure, both in mind and in body, to claim the promises of temporal salvation given by the Lord. Some of the temporal benefits resulting from obedience to the Word of Wisdom are an increase of health and vitality, strength, and endurance (see Brigham Young's promise in *Journal of Discourses,* 12:156); a greater strength to resist the temptations that lead to such physical sins as loss of virtue (see Grant, *Gospel Standards,* p. 55); a savings in money not spent on harmful substances (see Grant, *Gospel Standards,* pp. 50-52); and a greater resistance to many of the diseases that attack the body.

Nevertheless, to think that the blessings for obedience to the Word of Wisdom are only temporal or physical is neither wise nor accurate. President Joseph Fielding Smith said: "The temporal salvation of the children of men is a most important thing, but sadly neglected by many religious teachers. The truth is that the spiritual salvation is dependent upon the temporal far more than most men realize. The line of demarcation between the temporal, or physical, and the spiritual, cannot be definitely seen. The Lord has said that he has not given a temporal commandment at any time. To men some of these commandments may be temporal, but they are spiritual to the Lord because they all have a bearing on the spiritual or eternal welfare of mankind." (*Church History and Modern Revelation,* 1:383.) Obedience to the Word of Wisdom, keeping the "temple of God" undefiled (1 Corinthians 3:16), invites the Holy Ghost to strive with man in the struggle against the temptations of the world.

Every student of the gospel should clearly realize that a commandment requires obedience, that disobedience results in the loss of the Spirit, and that the loss of spiritual health carries far more serious consequences than does the loss of physical health. As President Stephen L Richards noted, "every commandment of God is spiritual in nature. There are no carnal commandments. We have learned this from modern revelation. While the commandments have effect upon the body and temporal things they are all in essence spiritual. The Word of Wisdom is spiritual. It is true that it enjoins the use of deleterious substances and makes provision for the health of the body. But the largest measure of good derived from its observance is in increased faith and the development of more spiritual power and wisdom. Likewise, the most regrettable and damaging effects of its infractions are spiritual, also. Injury to the body may be comparatively trivial to the damage to the soul in the destruction of faith and the retardation of spiritual growth. So I say, every commandment involves a spiritual growth. So I say, every commandment involves a spiritual principle." (In Conference Report, Apr. 1949, p. 141.)

### D&C 89:3. Can Every Man Live the Word of Wisdom?

The ability of the individual to live the Word of Wisdom depends on the person's desire. Anyone can live it if he will; and integral to the living of it comes the blessing of added strength, making it even easier to live.

### D&C 89:4. What Evidence Is There Today of "Evils and Designs . . . in the Hearts of Conspiring Men"?

"We, today, have before us abundant evidence of the evils and designs of wicked men. It is seen in the advertising of tobacco, tea, coffee, liquors and beers and wines. It is also seen in the advertising of prepared foods. So bad did this condition become some decades ago that the National Government had to take the matter in hand and Congress passed laws to control the evils which had arisen. These pure food laws have been very beneficial but even now there are ways by which the laws are evaded." (Smith, *Church History and Modern Revelation,* 1:384.)

In this revelation the Lord warned of the "evils and designs" of "conspiring men in the last days." President David O. McKay observed the gradual growth of these evils in his lifetime: "The purport of that [revelation] impressed me in the twenties and the thirties of this century. I just ask you . . . to recall the methods employed by certain tobacco interests to induce women to smoke cigarettes.

"You remember how insidiously they launched their plan. First, by saying that it would reduce weight. They had a slogan: 'Take a cigarette instead of a sweet.'

"Later, some of us who like the theatre, noticed that they would have a young lady light the gentleman's cigarette. Following this a woman's hand would be shown on billboards lighting or taking a cigarette. A year or two passed and soon they were brazen enough to show the lady on the screen or on the billboard smoking the cigarette. . . .

" 'Parents meekly submit to this and later deplore the fact when their children are hopeless cigarette addicts.' " (In Conference Report, Oct. 1949, pp. 185-86.)

### D&C 89:5. What Consequences Result from Taking Wine and Strong Drink?

"Over the earth, and it seems particularly in America, the demon drink is in control. Drunken with strong drink, men have lost their reason; their counsel has been destroyed; their judgment and vision are fled; they reel forward to destruction.

"Drink brings cruelty into the home; it walks arm in arm with poverty; its companions are disease and plague; it puts chastity to flight; and it knows neither honesty nor fair dealing; it is a total stranger to truth; it drowns conscience; it is the bodyguard of evil; it curses all who touch it.

"Drink has brought more woe and misery, broken more hearts, wrecked more homes, committed more crimes, filled more coffins than all the wars the world has suffered." (J. Reuben Clark, Jr., in Conference Report, Oct. 1942, p. 8; see also Kimball, *Miracle of Forgiveness,* pp. 55-57.)

### D&C 89:5-6. What Kind of Wine Was Formerly Used in the Sacrament?

The Lord told the Saints not to "purchase wine neither strong drink" for the sacrament but to "partake of none except it is made new among you" (D&C 27:3-4). Smith and Sjodahl explained this passage as follows: "The use of 'pure wine' in the Sacrament is permitted. But what is 'pure wine' if not the pure juice of the grape, before it has been adulterated by the process of fermentation? No fewer than thirteen Hebrew and Greek terms are rendered in our Bible by the word 'wine.' There is the pure grape juice, and a kind of grape syrup, the thickness of which made it necessary to mingle water with it previously to drinking (Prov. 9:2, 5). There was a wine made strong and inebriating by the addition of drugs, such as myrrh, mandragora, and opiates (Prov. 23:30; Isa. 5:22). Of the pure wine which was diluted with water, or milk, Wisdom invites her friends to drink freely (Prov. 9:2, 5). There was also 'wine on the lees,' which is supposed to have been 'preserves' or 'jellies' (Isa. 25:6). The 'pure wine' is not an intoxicating, but a harmless liquid." (Commentary, p. 572.)

Many Bible scholars support this view, suggesting that the heavier syrup, also called honey, was commonly unfermented or only mildly fermented and was called mixed wine when water was added. As mixed wine it was palatable and enjoyed as a drink. It was also the type of wine commonly used for the sacrament. (See Smith, *Dictionary of the Bible,* pp. 746-47; see also Keil and Delitzsch, *Commentary,* bk. 5, Psalms, "Psalms 75:10, 11," p. 341; bk. 6, Proverbs, Ecclesiastes, Song of Solomon, "Proverbs," p. 198, and "Proverbs of Solomon," p. 122.)

Some scholars have felt that the Hebrew word used in the description of wine refers to the fermentation process, for it is translated to mean "turbidness, or *boiling-up*"; however, this bubbling quality is "so characteristic of the appearance of the grape juice as it rushes foaming into the wine-vat" from the press, that a knowledge of ancient wine production, in which humans treading at the wine press caused bubbling juice to issue forth, indicates that this factor was more the source of the turbidness than was fermentation (Fallows, *Bible Encyclopedia,* s.v. "wine").

### D&C 89:7. Strong Drinks Are for Washing the Body

Alcohol is a valuable medicine as a cleansing agent for wounds and abrasions; therefore, when used to bathe an injured part of the body, alcohol performs a service for which it was intended.

### D&C 89:8. Tobacco Is Not for the Body

One Latter-day Saint physician noted the physiological effects of tobacco on man:

"Time and time again the medical and psychological sciences have brought forth evidence which points toward the destructive nature of the cigarette. In addition to the evidences recently found which link cigarette smoking to lung cancer, [there are] a number of interesting and arresting discoveries respecting the cigarette. E. A. Murphy and J. F. Mustard discovered that chronic smokers were less able to withstand the effects of radiation than were nonsmokers, and that smoking interfered with action of the bone marrow, the part of the body that manufactures blood. A. J. Schaffer points out that there is a higher premature birthrate among children whose mothers smoke than among nonsmokers, and that the mortality rate of these premature births was higher among offspring of smokers than of nonsmokers. There is a good deal of evidence, according to A. R. Lindesmith and A. I. Strauss, that in general, nonsmokers are more prone to be 'steady and dependable, hard workers, with stable marriages,' and that they have statistically less difficulty with marriage than do smokers.

"And so the evidence piles up. Bit by bit, piece by piece, a great mass of evidence is accumulating to substantiate from a purely scientific viewpoint the words of the Lord that 'tobacco is not for the body.' Nicotine in large quantities can take over the nervous system, causing severe convulsions. Smoking causes a man to perform at an altitude as much as 5,000 feet higher than he really is, because of the oxygen space it preempts in his blood." (W. Dean Belnap, "Tobacco and the Spirit of Man," *Instructor*, Dec. 1966, p. 464.)

As serious as the physical dangers are for using tobacco, it is the spiritual effects, especially on members of the Church who know the law, that are crucial. "In my judgment," said Elder George Albert Smith, "the use of tobacco, a little thing as it seems to some men, has been the means of destroying their spiritual life, has been the means of driving from them the companionship of the Spirit of our Father, has alienated them from the society of good men and women, and has brought upon them the disregard and reproach of the children that have been born to them, and yet the devil will say to a man, Oh, it's only a little thing!" (in Conference Report, Apr. 1918, p. 40).

### D&C 89:8. "Tobacco . . . Is an Herb for Bruises and All Sick Cattle"

Tobacco, like alcohol, also possesses certain medicinal properties for use on sick animals. When applied with skill, a tobacco poultice can be useful in healing the cuts and bruises of cattle. Alcohol and tobacco have place and purpose when used as the Lord intended.

### D&C 89:9. What Does the Phrase "Hot Drinks" Mean?

Some of the early Brethren explained what was meant by this phrase. Hyrum Smith, brother of the Prophet, wrote: "And again, 'hot drinks are not for the body, or belly;' there are many who wonder what this can mean; whether it refers to tea, or coffee, or not. I say it does refer to tea, and coffee." ("The Word of Wisdom," *Times and Seasons*, 1 June 1842, p. 800.)

And when the question was brought to the Prophet himself, Joseph Smith said: "I understand that some of the people are excusing themselves in using tea and coffee, because the Lord only said 'hot drinks' in the revelation of the Word of Wisdom. Tea and coffee are what the Lord meant when he said 'hot drinks.' " (In Widtsoe, *Word of Wisdom*, pp. 85-86.)

### D&C 89:9. Are Cola Drinks Forbidden by the Word of Wisdom?

What about soft drinks containing habit-forming drugs or caffeine, such as cola drinks? Although soft drinks are not mentioned specifically in the Word of Wisdom, an official statement by the Church's leaders reads: "With reference to cola drinks, the Church has never officially taken a position on this matter, but the leaders of the Church have advised, and we do now specifically advise, against the use of any drink containing harmful habit-forming drugs under circumstances that would result in acquiring the habit. Any beverage that contains ingredients harmful to the body should be avoided." (*Priesthood Bulletin*, Feb. 1972, p. 4.)

### D&C 89:10-11. Why Isn't the Word of Wisdom More Explicit?

The Lord has not given a revelation forbidding the use of such harmful drugs as cocaine, LSD, hashish, marijuana, and others, said President Joseph Fielding Smith, because "such revelation is unnecessary. The Word of Wisdom is a basic law. It points the way and gives us ample instruction in regard to both food and drink, good for the body and also detrimental. If we sincerely follow what is written with the aid of the Spirit of the Lord, we need no further counsel. . . .

"Thus by keeping the commandments we are promised inspiration and the guidance of the Spirit of the Lord through which we will know what is good and what is bad for the body, without the Lord presenting us with a detailed list separating the good things from the bad that we may be protected. We will learn by this faithful observance that the promises of the Lord are fulfilled." (*Improvement Era*, Feb. 1956, pp. 78-79.)

### D&C 89:10. Wholesome Herbs Are Ordained for the Use of Man

The word *herb* refers to vegetables and plants that are nourishing and healthful for man. Whereas verses 5 through 9 of Doctrine and Covenants 89 contain warnings against things not good for man, verses 10 through 17 list the things that should be used to maintain good health. These "God hath ordained for the constitution, nature, and use of man" (vs. 10).

### D&C 89:11. What Was Intended by the Phrase "in the Season Thereof"?

"Some have stumbled over the meaning of this expression and have argued that grains and fruits should only be used in the season of their growth and when they have ripened. This is not the intent, but any grain or fruit is out of season no matter what part of the year it may be, if it is unfit for use. The apple under the tree bruised and decaying is out of season while the good fruit is waiting to be plucked from the tree." (Smith, *Church History and Modern Revelation*, 1:385.)

Elder John A. Widtsoe gave this explanation: "The phrase 'in the season thereof,' referring to fruits and vegetables, has raised much speculation.

*A principle with a promise*

It indicates simply the superior value of fresh foods as demonstrated by modern science, but does not necessarily prohibit the use of fruits or vegetables out of season if preserved by proper methods." (*Evidences and Reconciliations,* 3:157.)

With the blessing of quality preservation, today it is possible to enjoy nearly every food "in the season thereof" all through the year.

**D&C 89:11. Why Are Herbs and Fruits to Be Used with "Prudence and Thanksgiving"?**

It is not necessary to be commanded in all things. With the guidelines the Lord has given in this revelation, a person should have little difficulty in determining the path of wisdom in his own eating habits, in quantity as well as in kind.

"In another revelation (Sec. 59) we are told they are not to be used 'to excess, neither by extortion.' The difficulty with most of the human family, is eating too much, and failing to heed his counsel. There would be less disease and mankind would live longer if all would also heed the counsel of the Lord concerning the use of wholesome foods." (Smith, *Church History and Modern Revelation,* 1:385.)

**D&C 89:12. Flesh Is to Be Used Sparingly**

"The Word of Wisdom is not a system of vegetarianism. Clearly, meat is permitted [see D&C 42:18]. Naturally, that includes animal products, less subject than meat to putrefactive and other disturbances, such as eggs, milk, and cheese. These products cannot be excluded simply because they are not mentioned specifically. By that token most of our foodstuffs could not be eaten." (Widtsoe, *Evidences and Reconciliations,* 3:156-57.)

**D&C 89:13. "Only in Times of Winter, or of Cold, or Famine"**

This verse has caused some to ask if meat should be eaten in the summer. Meat is a very heavy food and provides warmth and energy, both of which are less needed in summer than in winter. When the Word of Wisdom was revealed, methods for preserving meat were still primitive. Spoiled meat can be fatal if eaten, but the chance of spoilage is not as great in winter as in summer. Modern methods of refrigeration now make it possible for meat to be frozen and thereby preserved for later use in any season. The key word with respect to the use of meat is "sparingly" (D&C 89:12).

**D&C 89:14-17. "All Grain Is Ordained for the Use of Man and of Beasts"**

Grains come in many forms and varieties, the most important being the cereals wheat, rice, and corn. Others are barley, millet, sorghum, oats, and rye.

In most parts of the world grains are consumed directly by man. Grain is often used to feed livestock as well. All grain is good for the food of man and as feed for animals.

**D&C 89:18-21. Why Is Obedience to the Word of Wisdom Crucial?**

Doctrine and Covenants 89:3 states that this revelation was "given for a principle with promise." That principle is obedience: *keeping* (respecting, preserving, and cherishing) these sayings and *doing* them.

The purpose of this promise is spiritual rather than physical. The promised blessings of physical health are but the means to greater spiritual achievement (see D&C 76:5-10). Obedience to God's law is the condition upon which all blessings are predicated (see D&C 130:20-21). Only evil and conspiring men would have a person break the Word of Wisdom and suffer the loss of God's promises to the faithful.

Elder John A. Widtsoe categorized the promised

blessings as follows: "The reward for keeping the Word of Wisdom is four-fold. 1. Self-control is developed. That is implied in verse 3 of the revelation which states that the Word of Wisdom is 'adapted to the capacity of the weak and the weakest of all Saints, who are or can be called Saints.' 2. Strength of body, including resistance to contagion, is a result of wise living. 3. Clearness of mind is the gift of those whose bodies are in a healthy condition. 4. Spiritual power comes to all who conquer their appetites, live normally and look upward to God." (*Program of the Church,* pp. 39-40.)

**D&C 89:18. "Walking in Obedience to the Commandments"**

Elder Ezra T. Benson, a member of the Quorum of the Twelve under President Brigham Young, broadened the usual interpretation of the Word of Wisdom when he said: "When we first heard the revelation upon the Word of Wisdom many of us thought it consisted merely in our drinking tea and coffee, but it is not only using tea and coffee and our tobacco and whisky, but it is every other evil which is calculated to contaminate this people. The Word of Wisdom implies to cease from adultery, to cease from all manner of excesses, and from all kinds of wickedness and abomination that are common amongst this generation—it is, strictly speaking, keeping the commandments of God, and living by every word that proceedeth from His mouth." (In *Journal of Discourses,* 2:358.)

**D&C 89:19. Wisdom and Treasures of Knowledge**

Many discoveries and inventions of science are attributable to the new light and knowledge poured out upon man since the restoration of the gospel to the Prophet Joseph Smith. But there is a far more important kind of knowledge with which Latter-day Saints are also concerned. Elder LeGrand Richards asked if there is "any treasure of knowledge in this world to be sought after, more desirable than to know that God lives, that Jesus is the Christ, to know that his kingdom has been established again in the earth, to know that God has promised a reward for every commandment that he has given, to know that he has created this earth that we might prove unto him that we would do all things, not just a few of them, all things whatsoever the Lord our God hath commanded?" (in Conference Report, Apr. 1961, p. 46).

President George Albert Smith pointed out a literal fulfillment of the promise for great treasures of knowledge: "I refer you to the February, 1944, number of *The Improvement Era* wherein was published a graph showing the relative position of the states of the Union as to the number of scientists born in those states in proportion to population. Strange as it may seem, if you began at the lower corner of that graph and followed up state by state, you would come to the state of Massachusetts next to the highest on the graph, yet you would not have reached the state of Utah. You have to go twenty percent points higher up the graph to find Utah, the state that has produced more scientists born within its borders per capita than any other state in the American Union. That wasn't an accident; it was a fulfilment of the promise of God as a result of observance of the Lord's commandments." (In Conference Report, Oct. 1945, pp. 21-22.)

**D&C 89:21. "And I the Lord Give Unto Them a Promise"**

President J. Reuben Clark, Jr., explained the significance of this promise: "This does not say and this does not mean, that to keep the Word of Wisdom is to insure us against death, for death is, in the eternal plan, co-equal with birth. This is the eternal decree. [1 Cor. 15:22; 2 Nephi 9:6.] But it does mean that the destroying angel, he who comes to punish the unrighteous for their sins, as he in olden time afflicted the corrupt Egyptians in their wickedness [Ex. 12:23, 29], shall pass by the Saints, 'who are walking in obedience to the commandments,' and who 'remember to keep and do these sayings.' These promises do mean that all those who qualify themselves to enjoy them will be permitted so to live out their lives that they may gain the full experiences and get the full knowledge which they need in order to progress to the highest exaltation in eternity, all these will live until their work is finished and God calls them back to their eternal home, as a reward." (In Conference Report, Oct. 1940, pp. 17-18.)

The greatest blessing for living the Word of Wisdom is that it keeps a person a pure vessel before the Lord, who can then bestow all his glorious blessings both in this world and in the world to come.

# The Oracles of God

Section 90

## Historical Background

About a week after the Prophet Joseph Smith received the revelation known as the Word of Wisdom, the Lord again communed with him and revealed what is known as Doctrine and Covenants 90. No explanation is given about why this revelation was received. President Joseph Fielding Smith suggested that this revelation contains "information of the greatest importance and may have come through the prayers of the brethren as indicated in this divine message. It begins by saying that the sins of the Prophet are forgiven according to his petition, for 'thy prayers and the prayers of thy brethren have come up unto my ears.' " (*Church History and Modern Revelation,* 1:387.)

## Notes and Commentary

**D&C 90:1-5. What Are "the Keys of the Kingdom"?**

During his earthly ministry, Jesus bestowed on Peter, James, and John "the keys of the kingdom" (D&C 90:2-3). Those keys, he said, carried power to bind and loose on earth and in heaven (see Matthew 16:19).

Latter-day Saints make covenants with God for time and all eternity. Priesthood is the authority to seal those covenants in righteousness and have them last throughout eternity. Eternal marriage, baptism, bestowal of the Holy Ghost, temple covenants—these are all sealed by the divine authority known as priesthood (see also Notes and Commentary on D&C 81:2.)

**D&C 90:4-5. What Are the Oracles of God?**

An oracle is a revelation or the person through whom the revelation is given, and to "receive the oracles of God" means to obtain the powers of revelation and to accept the prophets who reveal the mind of the Lord. Only the President of the Church possesses the power to receive revelation, or oracles, for the entire Church. This principle was taught to Oliver Cowdery at an early date. The Lord said: "No one shall be appointed to receive commandments and revelations in this Church excepting my servant Joseph Smith, Jun., for he receiveth them even as Moses" (D&C 28:2). Those who have succeeded Joseph Smith in the prophetic office have received, each in his turn, the power to use the keys of the kingdom and lead the Church by revelation as occasion has required.

President Joseph Fielding Smith wrote: "The word of the Lord was fulfilled wherein he said that through Joseph Smith the oracles should be given to the Church, and by command of the Lord the Prophet, in Nauvoo a few months before his death, called the apostles together and said to them that the Lord had commanded him to confer upon them all the keys and authorities which he had had conferred upon him, so that the work could be 'rolled off' of his shoulders onto theirs. He thereupon conferred upon them this divine governing power, but this governing power could not be exercised by any one of the twelve while the Prophet was living. Upon his death the right to preside and set in order and to hold the keys of authority in the Priesthood and in the Church, rightfully belonged to President Brigham Young and by authority of the ordination he had received under the hands of Joseph Smith and by being sustained by his brethren and the Church, he was vested with the supreme power." (*Church History and Modern Revelation,* 1:388-89.)

*Joseph Smith holds the keys of this dispensation*

**D&C 90:6-7. In What Way Are Counselors in the First Presidency Equal with the President of the Church?**

In these verses the Lord authorized Sidney Rigdon and Frederick G. Williams to hold the keys of the priesthood jointly with Joseph Smith. The two men were set apart a short time later, as the Lord had specified. The Prophet reported: "Elder Rigdon expressed a desire that himself and Brother Frederick G. Williams should be ordained to the offices to which they had been called, viz., those of Presidents of the High Priesthood, and to be equal in holding the keys of the kingdom with Brother Joseph Smith, Jun., according to the revelation given on the 8th of March, 1833. Accordingly I laid my hands on Brothers Sidney and Frederick, and ordained them to take part with me in holding the keys of the last dispensation and to assist in the Presidency of the High Priesthood, as my Counselors." (*History of the Church,* 1:334.)

Counselors can do everything their presiding officer directs them to do, as if the president were personally acting; however, they have no power to act independent of the president. Both Sidney Rigdon and Frederick G. Williams received their ordination from the Prophet Joseph Smith, who held the keys. Since these two men received their authority from Joseph Smith, it follows that they are not equal to him in a strictly literal sense. Elder John A. Widtsoe observed that "the pre-eminence of the President of the Church was maintained. . . . The Counselors do not possess the power of the President and cannot act in Church matters without direction and consent of the President.

"All this defined clearly the position and authority of the President of the Church." (*Joseph Smith,* p. 303.)

**D&C 90:8-9. The Order for the Preaching of the Gospel in the Last Days Is unto the Gentiles First and Then unto the Jews**

"The Gospel was . . . taken first to the Jews in the Meridian Dispensation, and when the Jews rejected it, then it was taken to the Gentiles. [See Acts 11:18; 13:46.] The Lord promised that the first should be last and last first in the final dispensation. Therefore the Gospel was revealed and declared to the Gentiles in this dispensation and then it must go to the Jews." (Smith, *Church History and Modern Revelation,* 1:390.)

**D&C 90:10-11. "Every Man Shall Hear . . . the Gospel in His Own Tongue"**

Many missionaries today must learn a new language before they can be effective teachers of the gospel, for the Lord has said that every man is to hear the gospel "in his own language, through those who are ordained" to preach (D&C 90:11). It is one of the great miracles of the latter days that these missionaries, in a very short time, learn a language well enough to teach the gospel in it and be understood.

President Joseph Fielding Smith said of this remarkable phenomenon: "In order that the Gospel might be declared among the nations and kindreds

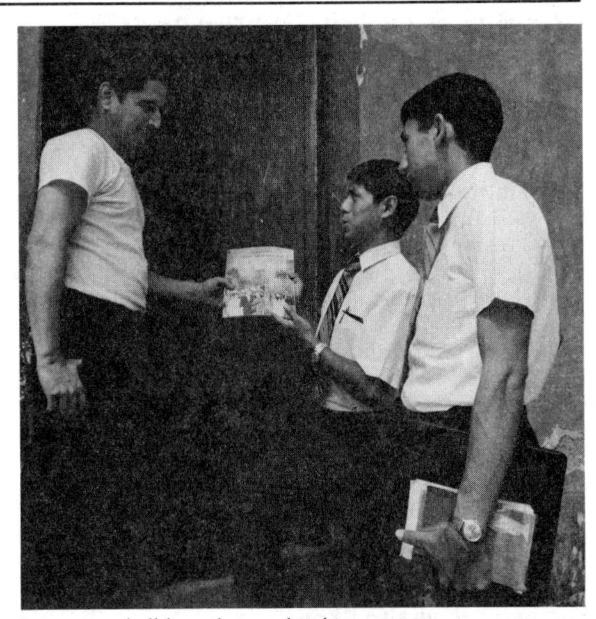

*Every man shall hear the gospel in his own tongue*

and tongues, the Lord commanded that the elders should study languages and with all good books be prepared to carry the message so that people could hear it in their own tongue. This was one great opportunity presented in the school of the prophets. It is a remarkable fact that the elders of the Church going forth to foreign lands have had the gift of tongues by which they have learned to speak these foreign tongues within very brief periods of time. Not only is this the case, but there are many instances of record where the missionaries in conversation and when preaching have been understood by others in their native language. These cases have been similar with the gift of tongues as it was made manifest on the day of Pentecost, when Peter and the apostles stood up and spoke to the assembled people from all countries who had come to Jerusalem to the celebration of Pentecost. Elders who have labored in foreign fields who have relied upon the Spirit of the Lord and have been diligent in their labors can testify from all parts of the Church that through the help of the Spirit they were able to speak the languages of the people among whom they were appointed to labor, and this beyond their natural powers." (*Church History and Modern Revelation,* 1:390.)

In recent years an even more direct fulfillment of this prophecy has begun to be seen. For generations, virtually all missionaries were sent out from the United States to teach the peoples of the world, and, although they learned the language and taught the people in their own tongue, they were not natives. Now, hundreds of missionaries from many countries are being called to labor among their own people to teach in their native languages. Because these missionaries come from the same culture and have the same traditions as the people they teach, they are more effective in teaching the gospel to every man "in his own tongue" (D&C 90:11).

### D&C 90:12-18. Counsel to the First Presidency

These verses addressed solely to the First Presidency charge the Church's presiding quorum with several important tasks:

1. Continue in the work of the ministry and presiding (see D&C 90:12).
2. Finish work on the Joseph Smith Translation (see vs. 13).
3. Preside over the School of the Prophets (see vs. 13).
4. Receive the revelations and unfold them (see vs. 14).
5. Read, study, and learn languages (see vs. 15).
6. Preside in council and set the affairs of the Church in order (see vs. 16).
7. Repent of pride and sin (see vs. 17).
8. Set their own homes in order (see vs. 18).

Leaders of the Church are expected to care for many responsibilities, not the least of which are personal and family matters.

### D&C 90:17. "Be Admonished in All Your Highmindedness and Pride"

Although this counsel is valuable to all members of the Church, it is especially significant in light of the apostasy of Sidney Rigdon and Frederick G. Williams, who, sitting in judgment upon the Prophet, left the Church through pride and highmindedness.

### D&C 90:25-27. Are the Saints to Keep Their Families "Small"?

"The Lord warns His servants, particularly the Prophet's father, to let their families be small in order that the substance provided for them by the Church be not used up by the unworthy (vs. 25), who were prone to take advantage of a situation. When the Lord advises them to let their families be small, He does not mean their immediate children; the visitors and hangers-on who had a tendency to take advantage of the brethren's open houses and open hearts are the ones meant. The brethren would not be hindered in accomplishing the Lord's work if they watched this matter." (Sperry, *Compendium*, p. 462.)

### D&C 90:28-31. Instructions to Vienna Jaques

"Vienna Jaques, a woman who had been kind to the Prophet and had cared for his wants when in need and had helped the elders, was now by revelation to be helped with means so that she could gather with the Saints in Zion" (Smith, *Church History and Modern Revelation,* 1:391).

"A conference of high priests assembled April 30, 1833, in the schoolroom in Kirtland and took steps to raise means to pay the rent for the house where their meetings had been held during the past season. John P. Green was appointed to take charge of a branch of the Church in Parkman County. It was also decided that Sister Vienna Jaques should not proceed immediately on her way to Zion, but wait until William Hobart and others were ready, as it would be a matter of safety." (Smith, *Church History and Modern Revelation,* 1:403-4.)

The word *meet* in verse 30 means fitting, proper, necessary, or desirable.

### D&C 90:32-35. Joseph Smith Is to "Preside over Zion" in the Lord's Own Due Time

"[The First Presidency] were to advise the Saints in Zion that the jurisdiction of the First Presidency extended over Jackson County and the West as well as over Kirtland and the East (v. 32). Thus the First Presidency was to be a means of preservation of the unity of the Church.

"The primitive church, after the departure of the Apostles, disintegrated and was divided into many groups, each with a head of its own, and, finally, the great division into the Roman and Greek churches occurred, the bishop of Rome and the patriarch of Constantinople, each claiming supreme authority. The Church of Jesus Christ of Latter-day Saints might have been cleft in the same way, into a Western and an Eastern division, with several smaller groups between, but for the Revelation instituting the First Presidency, which is both the symbol of the unity of the Church and the connecting link by which this unity is effected." (Smith and Sjodahl, Commentary, pp. 582-83.)

### D&C 90:34-37. Zion Warned

Smith and Sjodahl noted that section 90 "closes with a warning and a promise regarding Zion. All the brethren in Zion were not keeping the commandments of God faithfully. Some of them were jealous of the position and influence of the Prophet Joseph, and denied his authority to direct the temporal affairs of the Church. Among them were the men mentioned in Verse 35. In a letter written on behalf of the Church, by Orson Hyde and Hyrum Smith, Jan. 14th, 1833, and addressed to the Bishopric and Saints in Zion, it is pointed out that Sidney Gilbert, in a communication received from him, used 'low, dark, and blind insinuations,' which were not received 'as from the fountain of light.' In the same letter Wm. W. Phelps is kindly rebuked for a 'lightness of spirit that ill becomes a man placed in the important and responsible station that he is placed in.' Furthermore, the Saints in Zion failed to keep the laws of God concerning consecration. Hence the warning: The Lord would contend with Zion, plead with her strong ones, and chasten her 'until she overcomes and is clean before me.' That is the warning. The promise is: 'She shall not be removed out of her place.' " (Commentary, p. 583.)

### D&C 90:36-37. The Lord Will Chasten Zion until She Overcomes

Elder Melvin J. Ballard said of the Lord's promise to see that Zion overcomes and is clean: "That kind of promise entails the necessity of chastisement, when we need to be chastened and corrected and brought to a condition of repentance. I recognize that the Lord cannot fulfil his work nor accomplish his purposes without our willing obedience. He will not use this people unless we are willing to be used; but he has means of correcting, he has means of chastisement, which he will apply from time to time, and the only thing that impedes our progress today is our own lack of willingness to follow the counsel of those whom God has appointed to lead this people, because of the imagination of our hearts that we are wiser than they are." (In Conference Report, Oct. 1921, p. 100.)

# The Apocrypha

# Section 91

## Historical Background

The Prophet Joseph Smith received this revelation in Kirtland on 9 March 1833, one day after the revelation in section 90 was given. He was engaged in the revision of the Bible at the time (see D&C 90:13). The Bible from which he was making his corrections contained what is known as the Apocrypha. The Prophet inquired of the Lord whether he should also revise that part of the Bible, and the revelation known as section 91 was received (see *History of the Church,* 1:331-32).

## Notes and Commentary

**D&C 91:1. What Is the Apocrypha?**

Elder Bruce R. McConkie gave the following explanation of the apocryphal writings and why the Latter-day Saints do not accept them as scripture:

"Scholars and Biblical students have grouped certain apparently scriptural Old Testament writings, which they deem to be of doubtful authenticity or of a spurious nature, under the title of the *Apocrypha.* There has not always been agreement as to the specific writings which should be designated as apocryphal, but the following are now generally so listed: 1st and 2nd Esdras (sometimes called 3rd and 4th Esdras, because in the Douay Bible, Ezra is 1st Esdras, and Nehemiah, 2nd Esdras); Tobit; Judith; the rest of the chapters of Esther; Wisdom of Solomon; Wisdom of Jesus the Son of Sirach or Ecclesiasticus; Baruch and the Epistle of Jeremiah; additional parts of Daniel, including the Song of the Three Holy Children, the History of Susanna, and the History of the Destruction of Bel and the Dragon; Prayer of Manasses; 1st and 2nd Maccabees (called in the Douay Version, 1st and 2nd Machabees).

"These apocryphal writings were never included in the Hebrew Bible, but they were in the Greek Septuagint (the Old Testament used by the early apostles) and in the Latin Vulgate. Jerome, who translated the Vulgate, was required to include them in his translation, though he is quoted as having decided they should be read 'for example of life and instruction of manners' and should not be used 'to establish any doctrine.' Luther's German Bible grouped the apocryphal books together (omitting 1st and 2nd Esdras) at the end of the Old Testament under the heading: 'Apocrypha: these are books which are not held equal to the sacred scriptures, and yet are useful and good for reading.'

"The Apocrypha was included in the King James Version of 1611, but by 1629 some English Bibles began to appear without it, and since the early part of the 19th century it has been excluded from almost all Protestant Bibles. The American Bible Society, founded in 1816, has never printed the Apocrypha in its Bibles, and the British and Foreign Bible Society has excluded it from all but some pulpit Bibles since 1827.

"From these dates it is apparent that controversy was still raging as to the value of the Apocrypha at the time the Prophet began his ministry. Accordingly, in 1833, while engaged in revising the King James Version by the spirit of revelation, the Prophet felt impelled to inquire of the Lord as to the authenticity of the Apocrypha. From the answer it is clear that the books of the Apocrypha were inspired writings in the first instance, but that subsequent interpolations and changes had

INTRODUCTION

TO THE APOCRYPHA

THE TERM 'APOCRYPHA', a Greek word meaning 'hidden (things)', was early used in different senses. It was applied to writings which were regarded as so important and precious that they must be hidden from the general public and reserved for the initiates, the inner circle of believers. It came to be applied to writings which were hidden not because they were too good but because they were not good enough, because, that is, they were secondary or questionable or heretical. A third usage may be traced to Jerome. He was familiar with the Scriptures in their Hebrew as well as their Greek form, and for him apocryphal books were those outside the Hebrew canon.

The generally accepted modern usage is based on that of Jerome. The Apocrypha as here translated consists of fifteen books or parts of books. They are:

(1) The First Book of Esdras
(2) The Second Book of Esdras
(3) Tobit
(4) Judith
(5) The Rest of the Chapters of the Book of Esther
(6) The Wisdom of Solomon
(7) Ecclesiasticus or the Wisdom of Jesus son of Sirach
(8) Baruch
(9) A Letter of Jeremiah
(10) The Song of the Three
(11) Daniel and Susanna
(12) Daniel, Bel, and the Snake
(13) The Prayer of Manasseh
(14) The First Book of the Maccabees
(15) The Second Book of the Maccabees

*"It is not needful that the Apocrypha should be translated" (D&C 91:3)*

perverted and twisted their original contexts so as to leave them with doubtful value.

"Speaking of the Apocrypha the Lord says: 'There are many things contained therein that are true, and it is mostly translated correctly; There are many things contained therein that are not true, which are interpolations by the hands of men. Verily, I say unto you, that it is not needful that the Apocrypha should be translated. Therefore, whoso readeth it, let him understand, for the Spirit manifesteth truth; And whoso is enlightened by the Spirit shall obtain benefit therefrom; And whoso receiveth not by the Spirit, cannot be benefited. Therefore it is not needful that it should be translated.' (D. & C. 91.) . . .

"Obviously, *to gain any real value from a study of apocryphal writings, the student must first have an extended background of gospel knowledge, a comprehensive understanding of the standard works of the Church, plus the guidance of the Spirit.*" (*Mormon Doctrine,* pp. 41-42.)

# "You Shall Be a Lively Member"

Section 92

## Historical Background

"In the Revelation given on April 26th, 1832 (sec. 82), the Lord instructed the Prophet Joseph, Oliver Cowdery, Martin Harris, Sidney Rigdon, Newel K. Whitney, and a few others (v. 11) to unite their temporal interests under the rule of the Order of Enoch. In this Revelation the brethren in that organization are commanded to receive, as a member, Frederick G. Williams, whom the Lord had declared to be the equal of Joseph Smith and Sidney Rigdon in holding the keys of the kingdom (Sec. 90:6)." (Smith and Sjodahl, Commentary, pp. 586-87.)

## Notes and Commentary

**D&C 92:1. What Is the Difference between the Law of Consecration and the United Order?**

The law of consecration is the law whereby an individual consecrates his time, talents, and possessions to the Lord. The united order was the organization set up to implement the law of consecration. Elder Bruce R. McConkie explained the difference: "In order to live the law of consecration, the early saints in this dispensation set up the *United Order* as the legal organization to receive consecrations, convey stewardships back to donors, and to regulate the storehouses containing surplus properties" (*Mormon Doctrine,* p. 813).

**D&C 92:2. "You Shall be a Lively Member"**

Verse 1 of this revelation commands the members of the united order to receive Frederick G. Williams as a member. Verse 2 admonishes Williams to be "a lively member in this order" (D&C 92:2). A lively member is one who works diligently for the advancement of the goals and principles of the group or movement to which he belongs. A major purpose of the order of Enoch was to help the Church become "independent above all other creatures beneath the celestial world" (D&C 78:14).

# "Truth Is Knowledge of Things . . ."

Section 93

## Historical Background

The spring of 1833 was a time of joy but also a time of trials for the Saints. In Kirtland the Lord revealed many things concerning the knowledge and power of God in the School of the Prophets, and the Saints prepared for a stake of Zion to be established there.

In Zion, in Jackson County, Missouri, a special conference was held on 6 April to commemorate the organization of the Church. "It was an early spring, and the leaves and blossoms enlivened and gratified the soul of man like a glimpse of Paradise. The day was spent in a very agreeable manner, in giving and receiving knowledge which appertained to this last kingdom—it being just 1800 years since the Savior laid down His life that men might have everlasting life, and only three years since the Church had come out of the wilderness, preparatory for the last dispensation. The Saints had great reason to rejoice." (*History of the Church*, 1:337.)

But in April 1833 mobs gathered to persecute the Saints in Missouri. In both Kirtland and Independence members of the Church apostatized and turned against their former brethren, and Joseph contended with the possibility of a schism between the Church in Missouri and in Ohio.

On 6 May 1833 the Prophet received the revelation in Doctrine and Covenants 93, which comforted the Saints and gave instruction on several gospel themes.

## Notes and Commentary

### D&C 93:1. A Promise to Those Who Will Forsake Their Sins

All of God's faithful children will eventually realize the fulfillment of the promise to see his face, but "it shall be in his own time, and in his own way, and according to his own will" (D&C 88:68). Nevertheless, children of God need not wait to *know* that he lives until they have seen him in the flesh. They can have a witness or testimony long before they actually see God face to face.

Elder Francis M. Lyman taught that this privilege can be obtained by any faithful Saint, if he will pay the price: "Every Latter-day Saint is entitled to this witness and testimony. If we have not received [it] . . . the fault is ours, and not the Lord's; for every one is entitled to that witness through faith and repentance, forsaking all sin, baptism by immersion for the remission of sins, and the reception of the Holy Ghost through the laying on of hands. Now, if any of our brethren and sisters have lived for years without really knowing, being thoroughly satisfied and thoroughly convinced, just as positive as of anything in life, that this work is of God, if they have lacked that witness and testimony it is their fault, for it is not possible for a man to do the will of the Father and not know the doctrine." (In Conference Report, Apr. 1910, pp. 29-30.)

Elder Bruce R. McConkie wrote that the promise of seeing the face of God may be fulfilled in this life:

"*We have the power—and it is our privilege—so to live, that becoming pure in heart, we shall see the face of God while we yet dwell as mortals in a world of sin and sorrow.*

"This is the crowning blessing of mortality. It is offered by that God who is no respecter of persons to all the faithful in his kingdom." (In Conference Report, Oct. 1977, p. 52; or *Ensign*, Nov. 1977, p. 34.)

President Spencer W. Kimball bore his testimony of the promise of seeing God: "I have learned that where there is a prayerful heart, a hungering after righteousness, a forsaking of sins, and obedience to the commandments of God, the Lord pours out more and more light until there is finally power to pierce the heavenly veil and to know more than man knows. A person of such righteousness has the priceless promise that one day he shall see the Lord's face and know that he is." ("Give the Lord Your Loyalty," *Ensign*, Mar. 1980, p. 4.)

### D&C 93:2. How Is Jesus the Light of the World?

See Notes and Commentary on Doctrine and Covenants 88:6-13.

### D&C 93:6-18. What Is the "Record of John"?

Jesus was an intimate associate of two men named John: John the Baptist and John the Apostle. Both men kept records about the Son of God, but only the testimony of the Apostle is in the New Testament. The record mentioned in these verses refers to a record kept by John the Baptist, who was present when "the Holy Ghost descended upon [Jesus] in the form of a dove" (D&C 93:15; see also John 1:19, 32, 34).

Elder Orson Pratt said: "Not only the records of the ancient inhabitants of this land are to come forth, but the records of those who slept on the eastern hemisphere. The records of John, him who baptized the Lamb of God, are yet to be revealed. We are informed in the book of Doctrine and Covenants [D&C 93:18] . . . that the fullness of the record of John, is to be revealed to the Latter-day Saints." (In *Journal of Discourses*, 16:58.)

### D&C 93:9-10. This World and Many Others Were Made by the Savior under His Father's Direction

The revelation in section 93 teaches the very

important truth that this world and other worlds were not made directly by the Father but by the Lord Jesus Christ under his Father's direction. This passage is in harmony with the record of John in the New Testament: there John says, speaking of "the Word," "all things were made by him; and without him was not any thing made that was made" (John 1:3; see also verse 10). The Epistle to the Hebrews states that Christ, God's "heir of all things," is the one by whom God "made the worlds" (Hebrews 1:2). Jesus is creator of "worlds without number" (Moses 1:33)—innumerable to man, but numbered unto God.

**D&C 93:11-17. Jesus "Received Not of the Fulness at the First, but Continued from Grace to Grace"**

Commenting on the fulness of the Son of God, President Lorenzo Snow said: "When Jesus lay in the manger, a helpless infant, He knew not that He was the Son of God, and that formerly He created the earth. When the edict of Herod was issued, He knew nothing of it; He had not power to save Himself; and His father and mother had to take Him and fly into Egypt to preserve Him from the effects of that edict. Well, He grew up to manhood, and during His progress it was revealed unto Him who He was, and for what purpose He was in the world. The glory and power He possessed before He came into the world was made known unto Him." (In Conference Report, Apr. 1901, p. 3.)

Jesus grew until he had a fulness of grace and truth, a fulness of glory, and a fulness of power. John saw that Jesus "received a fulness of the glory of the Father" (D&C 93:16). Verse 17 of section 93 says that "he received all power both in heaven and on earth, and the glory of the Father was with him, for he dwelt in him." Verses 19 and 20 indicate that all men may grow to the point of receiving a fulness if they will follow the example of the Savior.

President Ezra Taft Benson discussed this truth and what it means for the Saints and for all mankind: "God the Father has given Jesus Christ a name above all others, so that eventually every knee will bow and every tongue confess that Jesus is the Christ. He is the way, the truth, and the light, and no one can come back into the presence of our Father in heaven except through him. Christ is God the Son and possesses every virtue in its perfection. Therefore, the only measure of true greatness is how close a man can become like Jesus. That man is greatest who is most like Christ, and those who love him most will be most like him." (In Conference Report, Oct. 1972, p. 53; or *Ensign*, Jan. 1973, p. 57.)

If that goal seems unachievable, one should remember the phrase "grace for grace" (D&C 93:12). Jesus did not have the fulness at first but achieved it by receiving grace for grace. The English word *grace* comes from the Greek word *charis*, which has the basic meaning of "sweetness, charm, loveliness," but which the Christians used in the special sense of "good-will, loving-kindness, favor." Thus applied to man, the grace of God was "the merciful kindness by which God, exerting his holy influence upon souls, turns them to Christ, keeps, strengthens, increases them in Christian faith, knowledge, affection, and kindles them to the exercise of Christian virtues." (Thayer, *Greek-English Lexicon*, pp. 665-66.)

In short, *grace* refers to the gifts and powers of God by which men can be brought to perfection. To say that Jesus and all other men come to a fulness by moving from grace to grace or from gift to gift means simply that through obedience more and more power is given by the Father until they receive a fulness of his power.

The Lord taught Moroni this same principle and added that his grace (his gifts and powers) are sufficient, that is, fully capable of doing what is required. "I give unto men weakness that they may be humble; and my grace is sufficient for all men that humble themselves before me; for if they humble themselves before me, and have faith in me, then will I make weak things become strong unto them" (Ether 12:27).

The condition for receiving this power, or gifts, is submission to God's will and obedience to his commandments. No man is capable of perfection through his own efforts alone. A greater endowment, or gift of power, beyond man's own capabilities is required. Through the writings of Moroni, one can see how the personal efforts of man bring the grace of God and move him step by step, from grace to grace, unto perfection (see Moroni 10:32-33).

**D&C 93:19-20. What Is Worship and How Should Man Worship the Lord?**

The word *worship* comes from two Anglo-Saxon words: *weorth*, worthy, and *scipe*, state or condition. One deserves to be worshiped because his condition is a worthy one. Elder James E. Talmage said: "The worship of which one is capable depends upon his comprehension of the worthiness characterizing the object of his reverence. Man's capacity for worship is a measure of his comprehension of God." (*Articles of Faith*, pp. 395-96.)

Man engages in worship to express his feelings about things divine. If one reverences God's fulness of truth and grace, and desires to be like God, he worships God by keeping his commandments. Elder Bruce R. McConkie explained:

"To worship the Lord is to follow after him, to seek his face, to believe his doctrine, and to think his thoughts.

"It is to walk in his paths, to be baptized as Christ was, to preach that gospel of the kingdom which fell from his lips, and to heal the sick and raise the dead as he did.

"To worship the Lord is to put first in our lives the things of his kingdom, to live by every word that proceedeth forth from the mouth of God, to center our whole hearts upon Christ and that salvation which comes because of him.

"It is to walk in the light as he is in the light, to do the things that he wants done, to do what he would do under similar circumstances, to be as he is.

"To worship the Lord is to walk in the Spirit, to

*Men may grow unto a fulness of the glory of God by following the Savior*

rise above carnal things, to bridle our passions, and to overcome the world.

"It is to pay our tithes and offerings, to act as wise stewards in caring for those things which have been entrusted to our care, and to use our talents and means for the spreading of truth and the building up of his kingdom.

"To worship the Lord is to be married in the temple, to have children, to teach them the gospel, and to bring them up in light and truth.

"It is to perfect the family unit, to honor our father and our mother; it is for a man to love his wife with all his heart and to cleave unto her and none else.

"To worship the Lord is to visit the fatherless and the widows in their affliction and to keep ourselves unspotted from the world.

"It is to work on a welfare project, to administer to the sick, to go on a mission, to go home teaching, and to hold family home evening.

"To worship the Lord is to study the gospel, to treasure up light and truth, to ponder in our hearts the things of his kingdom, and to make them part of our lives.

"It is to pray with all the energy of our souls, to preach by the power of the Spirit, to sing songs of praise and thanksgiving.

"To worship is to work, to be actively engaged in a good cause, to be about our Father's business, to love and serve our fellowmen.

"It is to feed the hungry, to clothe the naked, to comfort those that mourn, and to hold up the hands that hang down and to strengthen the feeble knees.

"To worship the Lord is to stand valiantly in the cause of truth and righteousness, to let our influence for good be felt in civic, cultural, educational, and governmental fields, and to support those laws and principles which further the Lord's interests on earth.

"To worship the Lord is to be of good cheer, to be courageous, to be valiant, to have the courage of our God-given convictions, and to keep the faith.

"It is ten thousand times ten thousand things. It is keeping the commandments of God. It is living the whole law of the whole gospel." (In Conference Report, Oct. 1971, pp. 168-69; or *Ensign,* Dec. 1971, p. 130.)

### D&C 93:23. Man Was in the Beginning with God

As explained in Doctrine and Covenants 29:30-33, the Lord used the word *beginning* only because finite mortals cannot grasp completely that all things are eternal. The word *beginning* may refer to the time when man began as the spirit offspring of God or to the time when the earth began as a temporal sphere.

The Prophet Joseph Smith taught that the intelligent part of man has always existed: "The spirit of man is not a created being; it existed from eternity, and will exist to eternity. Anything created cannot be eternal; and earth, water, etc., had their existence in an elementary state, from eternity." (*History of the Church,* 3:387.)

All mankind are born sons or daughters of God in the spirit and in that sense have a beginning. The elements of which they are made, however, are eternal. Water, earth, and other elements were in their elementary state before they were combined as they are found on earth.

"The Prophet says that anything created cannot be eternal. They become eternal, however, through the grace of God and the atonement of Jesus Christ." (Smith, *Church History and Modern Revelation,* 2:221.)

## D&C 93:24-25. Eternal Truth Is Revealed by the Spirit

Speaking of eternal truth, Elder Neal A. Maxwell said:

"For those who believe we are all going to be around forever, it is both natural and wise to concern ourselves with such questions and also with such principles which are also going to be around forever. The definition of truth given in 1833 about things 'as they are,' 'as they were,' and 'as they are to come' (D&C 93:24) is related to another scripture: ' . . . for the Spirit speaketh the truth and lieth not. Wherefore, it speaketh of things as they really are, and of things as they really will be . . . plainly, for the salvation of our souls. . . . ' (Jac. 4:13.) Note the presence of that powerful adverb *really*. The gospel of Jesus Christ and The Church of Jesus Christ of Latter-day Saints deal plainly with realities—'things as they really are,' and 'things as they really will be.' " ("Eternalism vs. Secularism," *Ensign*, Oct. 1974, p. 71.)

President Spencer W. Kimball stated: "If we live in such a way that the considerations of eternity press upon us, we will make better decisions. Perhaps this is why President Brigham Young once said that if he could do but one thing to bless the Saints, he believed it would be to give them 'eyes with which to *see things as they are*.' (*Journal of Discourses*, 3:221; italics added.) It is interesting to note how those last words reflect the words of the scripture in which truth is described as 'knowledge of things as they are, and as they were, and as they are to come.' (D&C 93:24.) Jacob reminds us also that 'the Spirit speaketh the truth . . . of things as they really are, and of things as they really will be.' (Jac. 4:13.)

"The more clearly we see eternity, the more obvious it becomes that the Lord's work in which we are engaged is one vast and grand work with striking similarities on each side of the veil." ("The Things of Eternity—Stand We in Jeopardy?" *Ensign*, Jan. 1977, p. 3.)

## D&C 93:29. How Is the Word *Intelligence* Used?

Elder John A. Widtsoe noted that "*intelligence* as used by Latter-day Saints has two chief meanings, both found in the dictionary but of secondary use. First, a man who gathers knowledge and uses it in harmony with the plan of salvation is intelligent. He has intelligence. . . . Second, the word when preceded by the article *an*, or used in the plural as *intelligences*, means a person, or persons, usually in the spiritual estate. Just as we speak of a person or persons, we speak of *an intelligence*, or *intelligences*." (*Evidences and Reconciliations*, 3:74; see also Abraham 3:22-23.)

The truth is that very little is known about the concept of intelligence. President Joseph Fielding Smith said: "Some of our writers have endeavored to explain what an intelligence is, but to do so is futile, for we have never been given any insight into this matter beyond what the Lord has fragmentarily revealed. We know, however, that there is something called intelligence which always existed. It is the real eternal part of man, which was not created or made. This intelligence combined with the spirit constitutes a spiritual identity or individual." (*Progress of Man*, p. 11.)

## D&C 93:30. Absolute Truth Is Independent and Understood Only by the Spirit

President Spencer W. Kimball talked about absolute truth and how the Spirit plays a role in our understanding of it. "The earth is spherical. If all the four billion people in the world think it flat, they are in error. That is an absolute truth, and all the arguing in the world will not change it. . . .

"We learn about these absolute truths by being taught by the Spirit. These truths are 'independent' in their spiritual sphere and are to be discovered spiritually, though they may be confirmed by experience and intellect. (See D&C 93:30.) The great prophet Jacob said that 'the Spirit speaketh the truth. . . . Wherefore, it speaketh of things as they really are, and of things as they really will be.' (Jacob 4:13.) We need to be taught in order to understand life and who we really are. . . .

"The Gods organized and gave life to man and placed him on the earth. This is absolute. It cannot be disproved. A million brilliant minds might conjecture otherwise, but it is still true. And having done all this for his Father's children, the Christ mapped out a plan of life for man—a positive and absolute program whereby man might achieve, accomplish, and overcome and perfect himself. Again, these vital truths are not matters of opinion. If they were, then your opinion would be just as good as mine, or better. But I give you these things, not as my opinion—I give them to you as divine truths which are absolute.

"Some day you will see and feel and understand and perhaps even berate yourself for the long delay and waste of time. It is not a matter of *if*. It is a matter of *when*.

"Experience in one field does not automatically create expertise in another field. Expertise in religion comes from personal righteousness and from revelation. The Lord told the Prophet Joseph Smith: 'All truth is independent in that sphere in which God has placed it.' (D&C 93:30.) A geologist who has discovered truths about the structure of the earth may be oblivious to the truths God has given us about the eternal nature of the family.

"If I can only make clear this one thing, it will give us a basis on which to build. Man cannot discover God or his ways by mere mental processes. One must be governed by the laws which control the realm into which he is delving. To become a plumber, one must study the laws which govern plumbing. He must know stresses and strains, temperatures at which pipes will freeze, laws which govern steam, hot water, expansion, contraction, and so forth. One might know much about plumbing and be a complete failure in training children or getting along with men. One might be the best of bookkeepers and yet not know anything of electricity. One might know much about buying and selling groceries and be absolutely ignorant of bridge building.

"One might be a great authority on the hydrogen bomb and yet know nothing of banking.

One might be a noted theologian and yet be wholly untrained in watchmaking. One might be the author of the law of relativity and yet know nothing of the Creator who originated every law. I repeat, these are not matters of opinion. They are absolute truths. These truths are available to every soul.

"Any intelligent man may learn what he wants to learn. He may acquire knowledge in any field, though it requires much thought and effort. It takes more than a decade to get a high school diploma; it takes an additional four years for most people to get a college degree; it takes nearly a quarter-century to become a great physician. Why, oh, why do people think they can fathom the most complex spiritual depths without the necessary experimental and laboratory work accompanied by compliance with the laws that govern it? Absurd it is, but you will frequently find popular personalities, who seem never to have lived a single law of God, discoursing in interviews on religion. How ridiculous for such persons to attempt to outline for the world a way of life!" ("Absolute Truth," *Ensign*, Sept. 1978, pp. 3-5.)

**D&C 93:33. "Man Is Spirit. The Elements Are Eternal"**

Man is a dual being comprised of both a spirit (a child of God) and a physical body (a child of man). These bodies together form the soul of man (see D&C 88:15; Notes and Commentary on D&C 88:15.) Death separates the body and the spirit temporarily, but the Resurrection connects them inseparably. The Resurrection paves the way for a "fulness of joy" (D&C 93:33).

**D&C 93:35. "The Elements Are the Tabernacle of God"**

The physical body and the life within it are gifts from God and are sacred. In this verse and elsewhere, the physical body is compared to a temple (see 1 Corinthians 3:16-17). Part of a person's judgment will be based upon his treatment of the body. The Prophet Joseph Smith explained: "We came to this earth that we might have a body and present it pure before God in the celestial kingdom. The great principle of happiness consists in having a body." (*Teachings*, p. 181.)

The devil, jealous that he cannot have a physical body, seeks to induce man to abuse it. The Lord, on the other hand, has given the Word of Wisdom and other counsel to tell man what is good and bad for the body, that is, how to care for the temple which the Lord has given him.

**D&C 93:36-37. "The Glory of God Is Intelligence"**

Elder John A. Widtsoe explained that in the scriptures the word *intelligence* is used in a way different from its customary use in the world:

"Among the many great truths revealed to the Prophet Joseph Smith, none is more beloved by the Church than 'The Glory of God is intelligence.' The word intelligence, as used in common speech, means readiness in learning, quickness of mind. Its higher Gospel meaning is more profound. The intelligent man is he who seeks knowledge and uses it in accordance with the plan of the Lord for human good. This is implied in the revelation from which the quotation is made, for the full sentence reads, 'The glory of God is intelligence, or in other words, light and truth.' When men follow the light their knowledge will always be well used.

"Intelligence, then, becomes but another name for wisdom. In the language of mathematics we may say that knowledge, plus the proper use of knowledge, equals intelligence, or wisdom. In this sense intelligence becomes the goal of the successful life. Knowledge is one of the means by which such intelligence is attained; the use of knowledge is equally as important, for it gives life and direction to knowledge. . . . Thus it often happens that a person of limited knowledge but who earnestly and prayerfully obeys the law, rises to a higher intelligence or wisdom, than one of vast Gospel learning who does not comply in his daily life with the requirements of the Gospel. Obedience to law is a mark of intelligence." (In Conference Report, Apr. 1938, p. 50.)

**D&C 93:38-39. Man Was Innocent at Spiritual Birth and Is Innocent at Physical Birth**

Elder Bruce R. McConkie explained that "there is no such thing as original sin as such is defined in the creeds of Christendom. Such a concept denies the efficacy of the atonement. Our revelation says: 'Every spirit of man was innocent in the beginning'—meaning that spirits started out in a state of purity and innocence in preexistence—'and God having redeemed man from the fall, men became again, in their infant state, innocent before God' (D&C 93:38)—meaning that all children start out their mortal probation in purity and innocence because of the atonement. Our revelations also say, 'The Son of God hath atoned for original guilt, wherein the sins of the parents cannot be answered upon the heads of the children, for they are whole from the foundation of the world.' (Moses 6:54.)" ("The Salvation of Little Children," *Ensign*, Apr. 1977, p. 4.)

**D&C 93:39-40. How May One Counter Satan's Efforts to Take Away Light and Truth?**

President Spencer W. Kimball taught that the home is the most important place to counter Satan's influence:

"In 1833 the Lord warned through his prophet, 'And that wicked one cometh and taketh away light and truth, through disobedience, from the children of men, and because of the tradition of their fathers.' (D&C 93:39.)

"And then he offered the solution, 'But I have commanded you to bring up your children in light and truth.' (D&C 93:40.)

"The spirit of the times is worldliness. Hoodlumism is common. Supposedly good youth from recognized good families express their revolt in destructive acts. Many defy and resist the law-enforcing officers. Respect for authority, secular, religious, and political, seems to be at a low ebb. Immorality, drug addiction, and general moral and spiritual deterioration seem to be increasing, and the world is in turmoil. But in our time the Lord has offered his ageless program in new dress and it gives promise to return the world to sane living, to true family life, family interdependence. It is to return the father to his rightful place at the head of the family, to bring mother home from social life and employment, the children away from unlimited fun and frolic. The home teaching program with its crowning activity, the family home evening, will neutralize the ill effects only if people will apply the remedy." ("Home: The Place to Save Society," *Ensign,* Jan. 1975, pp. 3-4.)

**D&C 93:41-50**

Frederick G. Williams, Sidney Rigdon, and the Prophet Joseph Smith had not been taking their parental responsibilities as seriously as they should have. The Lord spoke to each in turn, very personally, about the seriousness of his neglect. Even the bishop in Kirtland, Newel K. Whitney, needed to see that his family was to be "more diligent and concerned at home" (D&C 93:50).

Referring to Doctrine and Covenants 93:41-50, President Spencer W. Kimball said:

"In modern times the Lord said, 'Now, I, the Lord, am not well pleased with the inhabitants of Zion, for there are idlers among them; and their children are also growing up in wickedness.' (D&C 68:31.) We do not rear children just to please our vanity. We bring children into the world to become kings and queens, priests and priestesses for our Lord.

"To Frederick G. Williams, the Lord said, [D&C 93:41-43].

"Turning to Sidney Rigdon, the Lord charged, [D&C 93:44].

"And then the Lord said, 'What I say unto one I say unto all; pray always lest that wicked one have power in you, and remove you out of your place.' (D&C 93:49.)

"How sad if the Lord should charge any of us parents with having failed to teach our children. Truly a tremendous responsibility falls upon a couple when they bring children into the world.

*Parents have the stewardship to teach and train their children*

Not only food, clothes, and shelter are required of them, but loving, kindly disciplining, teaching, and training.

"Of course, there are a few disobedient souls regardless of training and teaching, but the great majority of children respond to such parental guidance. The scripture says, 'Train up a child in the way he should go: and when he is old, he will not depart from it.' (Prov. 22:6.) And if he departs, he will probably return if he has been brought up in the right way." ("Train Up a Child," *Ensign,* Apr. 1978, pp. 4-5.).

# Houses for the Work of the Ministry

Section 94

## Historical Background

On 23 March 1833 a council was called to appoint a committee to purchase land in Kirtland upon which to build a stake of Zion. The committee was appointed, and some large farms were purchased. Among these was the Peter French farm, so-called after its previous owner. It was purchased because it had an excellent stone quarry and facilities for making brick. (See *History of the Church,* 1:335-36, 346.) The Kirtland Temple was later built on a part of the Peter French farm.

Once the land was purchased, a city plat was surveyed, and the Saints gathered from surrounding states until the Church in Kirtland numbered about fifteen hundred souls. In this revelation, given on 6 May 1833, the same day section 93 was given, the Lord instructed the Saints "to build the city of Kirtland Stake, beginning at His house" (Smith and Sjodahl, Commentary, p. 600; see also Historical Background to Doctrine and Covenants 93).

## Notes and Commentary

### D&C 94:1-2. What Pattern Had the Lord Given for the City of the Stake of Kirtland?

"The city of the stake of Zion" at Kirtland was to be built, "beginning at my house" (D&C 94:1). The city was to be laid out with the temple as the starting point and the rest of the city being built in relation to it. Joseph Smith drafted a plan for the "Central of Zion" in the spring of 1833 as a general plan for building "cities of Zion" (Berrett, *Restored Church,* p. 92). In the copy of the plan sent to the Church in Independence, the temple was to be located in the center tier of blocks in a one-mile-square plat (see Notes and Commentary for D&C 57:1-3; see also Berrett, *Restored Church,* pp. 91-92.)

### D&C 94:3-12. Instructions for Erecting Buildings for the Work of the Kingdom

Two special buildings were to be built in Kirtland: one in which the First Presidency could meet, and the other in which Church publications could be printed. President Joseph Fielding Smith explained the functions of both buildings:

"A lot was set apart for the building of a house for the use of the First Presidency and where revelation could be given and all matters pertaining to the progress of the Church could receive proper attention. . . . It was to be dedicated unto the Lord from the foundation thereof, according to the order of the Priesthood. There is no question that the First Presidency needed a place where they could attend to the matters of Church government. This was to be a sacred house; no unclean thing was to be permitted to enter it, and if the builders would remember this the presence of the Lord should be in the building.

"The second lot south of this building was to be dedicated for the building of another house where the printing for the Church could be done and the translation of the scriptures, on which the Prophet had been working off and on for many months, could be published. . . . This house also was to be dedicated to the service of the Lord, and set apart for the printing." (*Church History and Modern Revelation,* 1:404.)

### D&C 94:8-9. How Must One Prepare to Enter the Lord's House?

In such a sacred edifice as the house of the First Presidency mentioned here, the Lord will manifest his glory for the benefit of those who enter worthily. The Spirit of the Lord is repulsed by uncleanness. Therefore, if individuals enter the Lord's house in a state of impurity, "the Spirit of the Lord is grieved" and "the heavens withdraw themselves" (D&C 121:36-37). Therefore, all who enter must purify themselves from sin. As this principle was true of the houses referred to in this revelation, so was it also true of the Kirtland Temple, which was built later, and it is certainly still true of modern temples. One purpose of the temple recommend is to ensure that those who enter the temple do so in worthiness, so that the

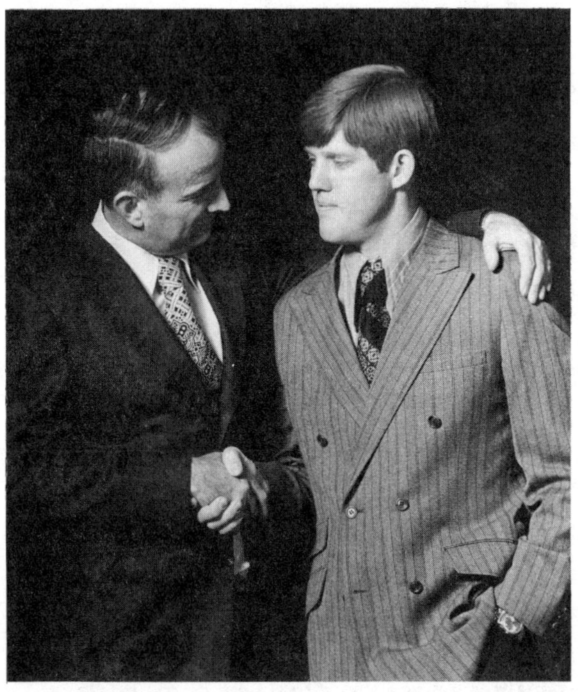

*Bishops hold the keys to judge individuals worthy to enter the temples*

Lord's house will not be defiled and the outpouring of the Lord's Spirit will not be inhibited or restrained.

**D&C 94:13-17. Work of the Building Committee Appointed by the Lord**

Hyrum Smith, Reynolds Cahoon, and Jared Carter were appointed as a committee to oversee the completion of certain buildings in Kirtland. To aid them in their assignment, the Lord gave them land adjacent to the temple lot. The Lord specified that the buildings for the First Presidency and the printing work should not be commenced "until I give unto you a commandment concerning them" (D&C 94:16). As it happened, the building of the Kirtland Temple took all the energy and finances of the Church. By the time it was completed, the faithful in Kirtland were compelled to leave for Missouri, and so the other two buildings were not completed.

# "Walking in Darkness at Noon-day"

Section 95

## Historical Background

The commandment to build a temple to the glory of God was first given in December 1832 (see D&C 88:119). As of June 1833 the Saints had not tried diligently to obey this important commandment from the Lord. The Prophet Joseph Smith reported that at the time this revelation was given "great preparations were making to commence a house of the Lord," but "the Church was poor" and the work lagged (*History of the Church,* 1:349-50.)

On 1 June 1833 the temple committee, composed of Hyrum Smith, Reynolds Cahoon, and Jared Carter, sent a circular to all the members, encouraging them to assist spiritually and temporally in building the temple. On the same day the Prophet Joseph Smith received this revelation, Doctrine and Covenants 95, in which the Lord sharply reproved the Saints for neglecting the commandment to build a temple.

## Notes and Commentary

**D&C 95:1-2. How Is Chastening a Sign of Love?**

Alma taught his son Corianton that "repentance could not come unto men except there were a punishment" (Alma 42:16). If a person loves another in the highest sense of the word *love,* he is deeply concerned for that person's eternal as well as temporal welfare. He will remember that to properly punish for transgression is the loving thing to do, for without punishment a person will not be brought to repentance. President Spencer W. Kimball, counseling priesthood leaders in the handling of transgressors, said:

"We are concerned that too many times the interviewing leader in his personal sympathies for the transgressor, and in his love perhaps for the family of the transgressor, is inclined to waive the discipline which that transgressor demands.

"Too often a transgressor is forgiven and all penalties waived when that person should have been disfellowshipped or excommunicated. Too often a sinner is disfellowshipped when he or she should have been excommunicated. . . .

"Do you remember what was said by the prophet Alma? 'Now', he said, 'repentance could not come unto men except there were a punishment.' (Al. 42:16.)

"Ponder on that for a moment. Have you realized that? There can be no forgiveness without real and total repentance, and there can be no repentance without punishment. This is as eternal as is the soul. . . .

"Please remember these things when somebody comes before you who has broken the laws of God.

"It is so easy to let our sympathies carry us out of proportion; and when a man has committed sin, he must suffer. It's an absolute requirement—not by the bishop—but it's a requirement by nature and by the very part of a man." (In Conference Report, Apr. 1975, p. 116; or *Ensign,* May 1975, p. 78.)

Sometimes chastening is the only way to bring about obedience and the inevitable happiness and joy that results. "Whom I love I also chasten," the Lord said (D&C 95:1). President Brigham Young said: "At times I may to many of the brethren appear to be severe. I sometimes chasten them; but it is because I wish them to so live that the power of God, like a flame of fire, will dwell within them and be round about them. These are my feelings and desires." (In *Journal of Discourses,* 8:62.)

**D&C 95:3. What Was the Saints' "Grievous Sin"?**

Subsequent verses of Doctrine and Covenants 95 make it clear that the Saints' neglect in building the temple was serious: it prevented the missionary work from moving ahead because the elders could not be prepared "to prune [the Lord's] vineyard" for the last time (vs. 4); and it held up the great endowment of "power from on high," which the Lord held in reserve for the faithful (vs. 8).

President Joseph Fielding Smith explained that "the Kirtland Temple was necessary before the apostles (who had not yet been called), and other elders of the Church could receive the endowment which the Lord had in store for them. The elders had been out preaching the Gospel and crying repentance ever since the Church was organized and many great men had heard and embraced the truth, nevertheless the elders could not go forth in the power and authority which the Lord intended them to possess until this Temple was built where he could restore keys and powers essential to the more complete preaching of the Gospel and the administering in its ordinances." (*Church History and Modern Revelation,* 1:406.)

The chastisement had the intended effect. "Four days after the Lord had rebuked the brethren for their neglect, without waiting for subscriptions, the brethren went to work on the Temple. Elder George A. Smith, a recent convert, hauled the first load of stone for the Temple. Hyrum Smith and Reynolds Cahoon commenced digging the trench for the walls, and they finished the same with their own hands." (Smith, *Church History and Modern Revelation,* 1:407.)

### D&C 95:4. What Does Pruning the Vineyard Mean?

"The vineyard is the harvest symbol usually used to represent the world—the earth and all of the people who live on the earth. At times the vineyard (the people of the world) has become corrupt, and it is necessary to prune it so the vine will be able to produce good fruit in abundance. The process of pruning involves the separation of one part of the plant from other parts. This could be achieved by calling out or separating the righteous from among the wicked or by the actual destruction of the wicked. It is usually in the former sense that the Lord instructs his servants (missionaries) to prune his vineyard. However, the Lord has also warned that when the pruning process is completed, the vines that continue to bring forth bad fruit will be burned. This evidently refers to the burning of the wicked, which will take place at the second coming when Jesus Christ will come in power and great glory." (Ludlow, *Companion,* 2:318.)

### D&C 95:4. What Is the Lord's "Strange Act"?

One purpose of the Kirtland Temple was to prepare the Lord's Apostles, his faithful servants, for their labor in his vineyard. This preparation was to help the Lord "bring to pass [his] strange act" of the last days (D&C 95:4). Smith and Sjodahl noted that "the expression quoted is from the Prophet Isaiah (28:21), where it refers to the fact that God would fight against His own people, because of their apostate condition. 'Shall I not, as I have done to Samaria and her idols, so do to Jerusalem and her idols' (Is. 10:11)? That was in the estimation of the Jews, who did not realize their apostate condition, 'strange.' But in this dispensation our Lord was to perform an equally strange act, in revealing His marvelous plan of salvation and making war upon an apostate church which is boasting of its intimate relations with Deity. He was now waiting for the Saints to build that house, in which His messengers were to be prepared for that strange war and endowed with power from on High (v. 8). No wonder that He

*The world is likened to a vineyard*

rebuked them for their tardiness!" (Commentary, p. 603.)

### D&C 95:5-6. Why Are Some Priesthood Holders Not Chosen or Accepted by the Lord?

It is one thing to be called to labor in the vineyard and quite another to be faithful in the performance of that work. Only those who faithfully fill their callings are chosen by the Lord for exaltation in the kingdom of God. Those who are called but not chosen "have sinned a very grievous sin, in that they are walking in darkness at noon-day" (D&C 95:6), for they do not respond to the light of the restored gospel that surrounds them (see also D&C 121:34-40).

### D&C 95:7. What Is a "Solemn Assembly"?

President Spencer W. Kimball discussed the significance of solemn assemblies, pointing out that they "have been known among the Saints since the days of Israel. They have been of various kinds but generally have been associated with the dedication of a temple or a special meeting appointed for the sustaining of a new First Presidency or a meeting for the priesthood to sustain a revelation, such as the tithing revelation to President Lorenzo Snow. . . .

"Joseph Smith and Brigham Young were first sustained by a congregation, including a fully organized priesthood. Brigham Young was sustained on March 27, 1846, and was 'unanimously elected president over the whole Camp of Israel . . . ' by the council. (B. H. Roberts, *A Comprehensive History of the Church,* vo. 3, p. 52.) Later he was sustained, and the Hosanna Shout was given.

"Each of the presidents of the Church has been sustained by the priesthood of the Church in solemn assembly down to and including President Harold B. Lee, who was sustained October 6, 1972." (In Conference Report, Apr. 1974, pp. 64-65;

or *Ensign,* May 1974, p. 45.) After President Lee's death, President Kimball was sustained as the prophet, seer, and revelator in a solemn assembly.

The Bible mentions several solemn assemblies held in ancient times (see Leviticus 23:36; Numbers 29:35; Deuteronomy 16:8; 2 Chronicles 7:9; Nehemiah 8:18; Isaiah 1:10-14; Ezekiel 45:17; 46:11). Such assemblies are sacred convocations attended by the priesthood or those who seek to separate themselves from the world by keeping God's commands.

The command to the elders to hold a solemn assembly was given in section 88, verse 70. The purpose for the assembly was to help the elders spiritually prepare to continue their missionary labors among the people of the world.

### D&C 95:8-9. What Is an Endowment "with Power from on High"?

An endowment is a gift or a bequest. Among Latter-day Saints *endowment* has the meaning of vesting an individual with special knowledge and priesthood blessings which are usually given in temples dedicated unto God. The endowment spoken of here, however, is not the same as that administered in Nauvoo and in temples today, though priesthood members did participate in a "partial endowment, the full ordinance being reserved for a future performance when a temple designed for ordinance work itself should be built [at Nauvoo]" (Bruce R. McConkie, "A New Commandment: Save Thyself and Thy Kindred!" *Ensign,* Aug. 1976, p. 10). The first complete endowment in this dispensation was given by Joseph Smith in Nauvoo on 4 May 1842.

The endowment received in Kirtland included washings and anointings, as well as the washing of feet for official priesthood brethren. The Lord also poured out his Spirit, that is, endowed them with spiritual power, and many received revelations that were also part of the promised endowment (see *History of the Church,* 2:308-10).

### D&C 95:10. Contention in the School of the Prophets

Adding to the "grievous sin" (D&C 95:10) of failing to commence the temple as commanded (see Notes and Commentary on D&C 95:3), the Lord named another serious sin: contention in the School of the Prophets. Members of that special group had been told by revelation before the school was started to "cease from all . . . [their] lustful desires, . . . pride and light-mindedness, and from all . . . wicked doings" (D&C 88:121). Having disobeyed this command, members of the school had committed a second "very grievous sin" before the Lord (D&C 95:10).

### D&C 95:11-17. "Let the House Be Built"

Commenting on the revealed purposes for the building of the Kirtland Temple, President Joseph Fielding Smith pointed out that "this building was to be erected for other and greater purposes than those made known at this time to the officers and members of the Church. The time had not come for the real purposes and the nature of the endowment to be revealed. The elders, much less the members, were not prepared in 1833 for the fulness of the revelation which the Lord declared would be bestowed upon them. The severe rebuke administered to the Church had its effect and the brethren forgot the need of other buildings and commenced to concentrate their efforts upon this house of the Lord." (*Church History and Modern Revelation,* 1:406-7.)

### D&C 95:17. What Is the Meaning of *Son Ahman, Alphus,* and *Omegus?*

The name *Ahman* is explained in Notes and Commentary on Doctrine and Covenants 78:20. *Alphus* and *Omegus* are other forms of the names *Alpha* and *Omega* (see Notes and Commentary for D&C 38:1).

# This Stake Should Be Made Strong

Section 96

## Historical Background

In the months following the purchase of land in Kirtland for the Saints, the Lord directed the preparation of a building for the Presidency, another for printing, and another to be the temple discussed in previous revelations (D&C 94-95). The Kirtland council met to consider the disposition and use of the French farm, but since they could not agree on who was to be the overseer, they decided to take the matter to the Lord (see *History of the Church,* 1:352; see also Historical Background for D&C 94).

"They also considered the matter of dividing lots according to wisdom (D. & C. 96.) and the Lord gave them counsel in relation to these matters. The Stake of Zion was to become strong. The poor were to be cared for. The bishop, Newel K. Whitney, was to take charge of the matter of assigning lots and preparing them for the building of a city and a Temple to the name of the Lord. John Johnson was to be given responsibility and admitted into the united order, so that he could assist in bringing forth the word of the Lord to the children of men." (Smith, *Church History and Modern Revelation,* 1:407.)

## Notes and Commentary

### D&C 96:1. "This Stake That I Have Set for the Strength of Zion Should Be Made Strong"

When a person pitches a tent, he drives stakes into the ground to secure it. The deeper the stakes are set, the greater the stability and strength of the tent. The revelations of the Lord liken Zion to a great tent, whose stakes are its support and therefore must be strong.

"The expression 'stake of Zion,' " wrote President Joseph Fielding Smith "is taken from the expression in Isaiah: 'Look upon Zion, the city of our solemnities; thine eyes shall see Jerusalem a quiet habitation, a tabernacle that shall not be taken down; not one of the stakes thereof shall ever be removed, neither shall any of the cords thereof be broken.' (Isa. 33:20.) Again: 'Enlarge the place of thy tent and let them stretch forth the curtains of thine habitation: spare not, lengthen thy cords, and strengthen thy stakes.' (Isa. 54:2.) Isaiah speaks of Zion as a tent, or tabernacle, having in mind the Tabernacle which was built and carried in the wilderness in the days of Moses, and the cords are the binding cables that extend from the tent, or tabernacle, to the stakes which are fastened in the ground. Now the Lord revealed that Zion was to be built and surrounding her would be the stakes helping to bind and keep her in place. This figure of speech has almost been lost through the intervening years, but it retains its significance, or beauty. To speak of Zion, the New Jerusalem, or even that section where the city will be built, as a stake of Zion, is a sad mistake. Zion is the tent, the stakes of Zion are the binding pegs that support her. Zion, therefore, cannot be a stake, it would be as improper to call a tent a stake as to apply this term to Zion." (*Church History and Modern Revelation,* 1:321-22.)

### D&C 96:4-5. "This Is the Most Expedient in Me, That My Word Should Go Forth unto the Children of Men"

The preparation of the scriptures and the location of a place in which to publish them (see D&C 94:10) continued as directed by the Lord so that his word might be sent forth (see D&C 96:5). The publication of the scriptures was an important part of preparing the people to establish Zion.

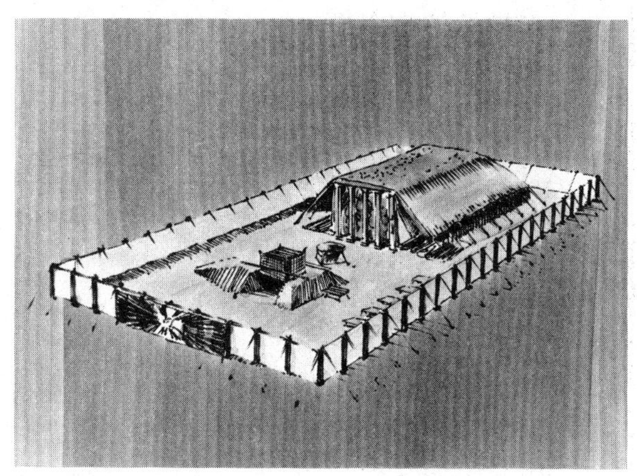

*Zion is compared to the tent of the Lord and its stakes*

"One day all the standard works will be so organized and prepared, to make them one monumental testimony that Jesus is the Christ, the Son of God, the Only Begotten of the Father. The *doctrines of salvation must be available* to all mankind, not just in their hands, but in their heads and hearts." (Boyd K. Packer, "Teach the Scriptures" [address delivered to religious educators of the Church Educational System], 14 Oct. 1977, p. 6; emphasis added.)

### D&C 96:5. "My Word Should Go Forth . . . for the Purpose of Subduing the Hearts of the Children of Men for Your Good"

Although the influence of the gospel is resisted and sometimes even fought against by the wicked, most people are tempered and influenced for good by its power and the example of those who have received it. This influence also results in the establishment of stakes of Zion, which further blesses the people of that land. That is why Elder Bruce R. McConkie counseled: "Build up Zion, but build it up in the area where God has given you birth and nationality. Build it up where he has given you citizenship, family, and friends. . . . The Saints who comprise . . . Zion are and should be a leavening influence for good in all these nations.

"And know this: *God will bless that nation which so orders its affairs as to further his work.*" ("Come: Let Israel Build Zion," *Ensign,* May 1977, p. 118; emphasis added.)

# "This Is Zion—the Pure in Heart"

Section 97

## Historical Background

On 20 July 1833 the first open violence against the Saints in Jackson County broke out. The printing press owned by William W. Phelps was destroyed, many of the Saints were turned out of their homes, and Edward Partridge and Charles Allen were tarred and feathered on the public square in Independence, Missouri. The Prophet, unaware of the problems, sent a letter to the leaders of the Church in Missouri on 6 August 1833 in response to questions concerning the School of Zion. The letter contained Doctrine and Covenants 97, given 2 August 1833, and Doctrine and Covenants 98, in which the Lord warned the inhabitants in Zion to observe his commandments or they would be visited "with sore affliction, with pestilence, with plague, with sword, with vengeance, with devouring fire" (D&C 97:26). As it turned out, the Saints did not effect a thorough reformation. The promised devastation followed early in November 1833. (See *History of the Church*, 1:390-93, 400.)

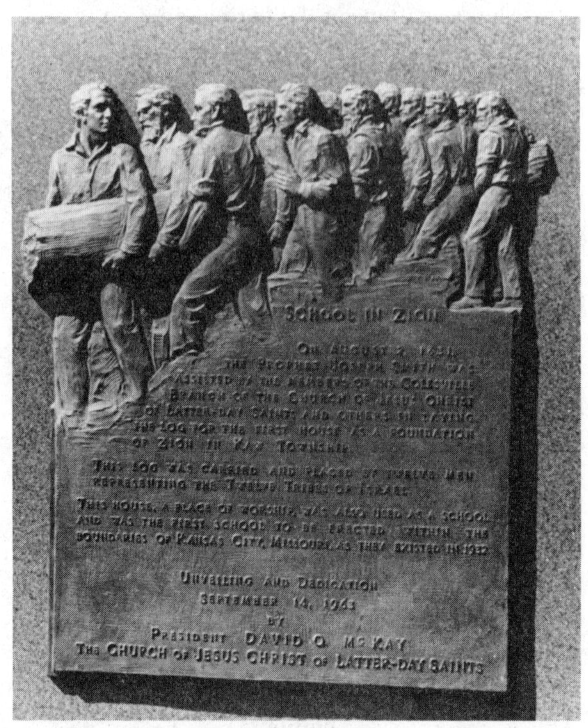


*A monument to the School of the Elders*

## Notes and Commentary

### D&C 97:1-2. The "Truly Humble" in Zion

In these verses the Lord commended those in Zion who "are truly humble and are seeking diligently to learn wisdom and to find truth" (D&C 97:1) and promised that they shall be blessed. Even though many of the Saints did not live as they were required to and were eventually driven out, the Lord indicated here that some were truly Zion people. Sometimes, unfortunately, the wickedness of some persons brings problems that affect the righteous and cause them to suffer. Such was the case many times in ancient Israel.

### D&C 97:3-5. What Was the "School in Zion" and under What Conditions Did It Meet?

In the summer of 1833, a "school of Elders" began in Zion with Parley P. Pratt as its teacher. Its major purpose was to prepare the brethren living there to go forth as missionaries during the coming winter. Elder Pratt wrote that "in the latter part of summer and in the autumn [1833], I devoted almost my entire time in ministering among the churches; holding meetings; visiting the sick; comforting the afflicted, and giving counsel. A school of Elders was also organized, over which I was called to preside. This class, to the number of about sixty, met for instruction once a week. The place of meeting was in the open air, under some tall trees, in a retired place in the wilderness, where we prayed, preached and prophesied, and exercised ourselves in the gifts of the Holy Spirit. Here great blessings were poured out, and many great and marvelous things were manifested and taught. The Lord gave me great wisdom, and enabled me to teach and edify the Elders, and comfort and encourage them in their preparations for the great work which lay before us. I was also much edified and strengthened. To attend this school I had to travel on foot, and sometimes with bare feet at that, about six miles. This I did once a week, besides visiting and preaching in five or six branches a week." (*Autobiography of Parley P. Pratt*, pp. 93-94.)

### D&C 97:6-7. "The Ax Is Laid at the Root"

In Doctrine and Covenants 97:7 the Lord says metaphorically that his people, Zion, are like the trees of a vineyard (see also Matthew 3:10). Men are like trees in that they are known by their fruits, or their works (see Matthew 7:16-20). Good fruit is brought forth by good trees, and evil fruit is brought forth by evil trees. Such evil trees are eliminated from the vineyard so that "they cumber not the ground" (Jacob 5:66). The Lord speaks of hewing down "every tree that bringeth not forth good fruit" (D&C 97:7). The phrase "the ax is laid at the root of the trees" (vs. 7) evokes a vivid image. Generally, one touches the ax to the spot chosen for the first blow before delivering that blow. Figuratively speaking, a tree which saw an ax laid at its root would be motivated to change its ways and bring forth good fruit so as not to be hewn down. Even as this revelation was given, the mobs were gathering for their initial blow in Jackson County, yet the Saints who were bringing forth unacceptable fruit, or works, still refused to repent.

### D&C 97:8-9. What Is the Principle of Sacrifice and How Is It Fulfilled?

See Notes and Commentary on Doctrine and Covenants 58:2-4.

### D&C 97:10-12. What Is a Tithe?

The dictionary defines *tithe* as a tenth part of something paid as a voluntary contribution. The Lord defined *tithe* for the Saints as "one-tenth of all their interest annually" (D&C 119:4). The revelation in Doctrine and Covenants 97, antedating as it does the Lord's official definition of the law of tithing, equates tithing with sacrifice by declaring that the sacrifice made to build a temple in Zion is "the tithing . . . which I, the Lord, require at their hands" (D&C 97:12). Such was true at that time. Today, however, tithing is a full tenth of one's annual increase, or income.

"Strictly speaking there is no such thing as a *part tithing.* Tithing is a tenth, and unless a person contributes the tenth, he has only made a contribution to the tithing funds of the Church. Somewhat inappropriately the term *part-tithepayer* is used with reference to those making such contributions." (McConkie, *Mormon Doctrine,* pp. 798-99.)

### D&C 97:13-14. The Temple Is "a Place of Instruction"

Speaking of the instructional function of the endowment, Elder John A. Widtsoe said: "Temple work, for example, gives a wonderful opportunity for keeping alive our spiritual knowledge and strength. . . . The mighty perspective of eternity is unraveled before us in the holy temples; we see time from its infinite beginning to its endless end; and the drama of eternal life is unfolded before us. Then I see more clearly my place amidst the things of the universe, my place among the purposes of God; I am better able to place myself where I belong, and I am better able to value and to weigh, to separate and to organize the common, ordinary duties of my life, so that the little things shall not oppress me or take away my vision of the greater things that God has given us." (In Conference Report, Apr. 1922, pp. 97-98.)

The Lord regards the temple as a place where the Saints "may be perfected in the understanding of their ministry, in theory, in principle and in doctrine, in all things pertaining to the kingdom of God" (D&C 97:14). For this reason the temple is truly a "place of instruction" (vs. 13).

*The Lord's house is a house of instruction*

### D&C 97:15-17. How Do the Lord's Leaders Help Maintain the Sacredness of the Temples?

A temple of God is a place of purity and holiness. Those who enter it must be worthy, so interviews for temple recommends are held yearly to determine worthiness. The Saints are under the Lord's command not to "suffer any unclean thing to come into it, that it be not defiled" (D&C 97:15). If this requirement is met, the Lord promises that he "will come into it, and all the pure in heart that shall come into it shall see God" (vs. 16).

Elder Henry D. Taylor commented on the responsibility of the President of the Church: "In general terms, and this is something that pertains to all of us, it is the Lord's plan that no unrepentant sinner enter the temple, for the Lord has declared that he will not abide in temples that have been defiled by any unclean thing. (See D&C 97:15-19.) The President of the Church, President Spencer W. Kimball, is directly responsible to the Lord to see that the sacredness of the temples and the ordinances performed therein are maintained. I can assure you that President Kimball takes that stewardship most seriously." ("I Have a Question," *Ensign,* Feb. 1976, p. 34.)

### D&C 97:18. What Is the Destiny of Zion?

Here the Lord says that Zion "shall prosper, and spread herself and become very glorious, very great, and very terrible" (D&C 97:18).

The Prophet Joseph Smith discussed the location of Zion: "You know there has been great discussion in relation to Zion—where it is, and where the gathering of the dispensation is, and which I am now going to tell you. The prophets have spoken and written upon it; but I will make a proclamation that will cover a broader ground. *The whole of America is Zion itself from north to south, and is described by the Prophets, who declare that it is the Zion where the mountain of the Lord should be, and that it should be in the center of the land.* When Elders shall take up and examine the old prophecies in the Bible, they will see it." (*History of the Church,* 6:318-19.)

President Brigham Young said: "This American continent will be Zion; for it is so spoken of by the prophets. Jerusalem will be rebuilt and will be the place of gathering, and the tribe of Judah will gather there; but this continent of America is the land of Zion." (In *Journal of Discourses,* 5:4.)

*Terrible* is used to describe Zion because the basic meaning of the word is "something that causes terror." Numerous places in the scriptures say that Zion's glory will be such that it will strike terror into the hearts of the wicked (see D&C 45:70; 105:31; see also Enrichment B, in the Appendix).

### D&C 97:21. "Verily, . . . for This Is Zion—the Pure in Heart"

Zion is not only a location but a condition as well. The Lord declares that a person worthy of Zion is one who is "pure in heart" (D&C 97:21). Hyrum Smith described Zion as "the honest and pure in heart that will harken to the everlasting covenant" (in *History of the Church,* 6:320).

### D&C 97:22-28. "Vengeance Cometh Speedily upon the Ungodly As a Whirlwind"

Great and marvelous blessings are promised for Zion, that is, for those who are pure in heart (see D&C 97:21). In this section, too, the Lord decrees punishment and devastations on the wicked for their refusal to heed his words. Even Zion will not escape unless she does the works of righteousness, for if the membership of the Church does not qualify as a Zion people, then they have no claim on the blessings promised. The Prophet Joseph taught:

"If Zion will not purify herself, so as to be approved of in all things, in His sight, He will seek another people; for His work will go on until Israel is gathered, and they who will not hear His voice, must expect to feel His wrath. Let me say unto you, seek to purify yourselves, and also the inhabitants of Zion, lest the Lord's anger be kindled to fierceness.

"Repent, repent, is the voice of God to Zion; and strange as it may appear, yet it is true, mankind will persist in self-justification until all their iniquity is exposed, and their character past being redeemed, and that which is treasured up in their hearts be exposed to the gaze of mankind. I say to you (and what I say to you I say to all), hear the warning voice of God, lest Zion fall, and the Lord swear in His wrath the inhabitants of Zion shall not enter into His rest." (*Teachings,* pp. 18-19.)

# "Renounce War and Proclaim Peace"

# Section 98

## Historical Background

On 6 August 1833, "seventeen days after the mobbing of the saints in Missouri," wrote President Joseph Fielding Smith, "the Prophet received a revelation in which the Lord said that the prayers of saints were heard in heaven, and counsel was given them to be patient in their afflictions and not seek vengeance against their enemies. Oliver Cowdery did not leave Independence on his special mission until after the 23rd of July, and if he arrived in Kirtland before the 6th of August when this revelation was received, it certainly was a miraculous journey considering the distance and the means he had of transportation. Just when he arrived we do not know, but the Prophet had learned that difficulties of a serious nature had commenced in Jackson County. Naturally the members of the Church there were extremely aroused and it was only natural that in their hearts there should be some spirit of retaliation and revenge upon their enemies. Because of this the Lord gave this revelation." (*Church History and Modern Revelation,* 1:432.)

The Prophet wrote of these days: "July, which once dawned upon the virtue and independence of the United States, now dawned upon the savage barbarity and mobocracy of Missouri" (*History of the Church,* 1:372; see also Historical Background for D&C 97).

## Notes and Commentary

### D&C 98:1-3. "In Everything Give Thanks. . . . All Things . . . Work Together for Your Good"

The first three verses of this section must have tested the faith of some of the Saints, for, in the month before this revelation was received, the Saints had seen the effects of unrestrained mobs. On 20 July 1833 a mob had gathered at the courthouse in Independence, called in the leaders of the Church in Missouri, and demanded that they prepare to leave Jackson County. The leaders asked for three months to consider their requests. When that request was denied, they asked for ten days. The mob refused and granted them only fifteen minutes. When the elders did not accept the mob's illegal and unreasonable demands, the mob determined to destroy the offices of the *Evening and Morning Star* immediately. The printing shop and the residence of W. W. Phelps were completely demolished, as was the store run by Sidney Gilbert (see D&C 57:8-9). Barrett noted that even this destruction was not sufficient to satisfy these men:

"They broke into the houses of the Saints, searching for the leading elders. Men, women, and children ran in all directions, not knowing what would befall them. They caught Bishop Partridge and Charles Allen and dragged them a half mile to the public square, where they were given two alternatives: deny the Book of Mormon or consent to leave the county. The Book of Mormon they would not deny, nor would they consent to leave the county. Bishop Partridge was granted permission to speak. . . .

"His words were drowned by the tumultuous crowd, many of whom were shouting, 'Call on your God to deliver you and your pretty Jesus you worship!' The mob stripped Partridge and Allen of their clothing, smeared their bodies with tar mixed with pearl ash, a flesh-eating acid, and emptied a pillow of feathers over them. This indignity was endured with such resignation and meekness that the mob became ashamed; their sympathies touched, they permitted the two abused men to retire in silence. . . .

"On July 23, 1833, five hundred men rushed into Independence waving a red flag and brandishing guns, dirks, whips, and clubs. With oaths and curses they searched for the leading elders of the Church, threatening to whip the ones they captured with from fifty to five hundred lashes. Negroes owned by members of the mob laid waste the crops of the Saints. Dwellings were demolished by the mob as they threatened 'We will rid Jackson county of the "Mormons," peaceably if we can, forcibly if we must. If they will not go without, we will whip and kill the men; we will destroy their children, and ravish their women.'

"To save the lives of the Saints, Edward Partridge, William Phelps, Isaac Morley, A. Sidney Gilbert, John Whitmer, and John Corrill offered themselves as a ransom for the lives of their brethren, to be scourged or put to death if need be. For this noble gesture their names will be remembered forever in the annals of the Church. But the mob, insensible to this noble manifestation of love, scoffed at the six leaders and with brutal imprecations swore they would flog every man, woman, and child until the Mormons agreed to leave the county. 'Leave the county or die' was the demand." (*Joseph Smith,* pp. 251-52, 255-56.)

It was in this setting that the Lord called on the Saints to "rejoice evermore, and in everything give thanks" (D&C 98:1) and reminded them that "all things wherewith you have been afflicted shall work together for your good" (vs. 3). This was a call to show forth tremendous faith in God. It is a relatively simple thing to pour out gratitude to God when the cup is full, the harvest plenteous, the peace secure; but it is much more challenging to have the faith to believe that even in adversity and persecution, even in times of darkness and devastation, the Lord's hand is in it for the benefit of his children. The promise that *all* things work for the good of the righteous is repeated in several other places. (See D&C 90:24; 100:15; Deuteronomy 6:24; Romans 8:28.)

"The meaning is that even the evil designs of men, in the hands of the Masterworkman, will turn out for the benefit of the people of God, and for His glory. The divine Will overrules all things for the *final* good of His children. We can see this exemplified in the history of the Latter-day Saints." (Smith and Sjodahl, Commentary, p. 616.)

In such times of trial and adversity, when "the very jaws of hell . . . gape open the mouth wide" after the Saints (D&C 122:7), the Saints can do as Job did: have faith in God no matter what happens. Upon hearing the news that his entire fortune had been wiped out and that his children had been killed in the collapse of a house—all on the same day—Job's response was, "The Lord gave, and the Lord hath taken away; blessed be the name of the Lord" (Job 1:21). When he was covered with painful boils and his wife encouraged him to curse God for the afflictions that had come upon him; he said, "Shall we receive good at the hand of God, and shall we not receive evil?" (Job 2:10). And then he said, "Though he slay me, yet will I trust in him" (Job 13:15). That is the faith and commitment that God required of his Saints in Jackson County, even in the midst of their persecutions. (See Notes and Commentary for D&C 101:4-5 and for D&C 122.)

### D&C 98:4-8. The Obligation to Uphold the Constitutional Law of the Lord

The Lord is man's lawgiver, and he commanded his Saints to befriend "that law which is the constitutional law of the land" (D&C 98:6). Freedom comes from God, and constitutional law protects that freedom. "Whatsoever is more or less than this, cometh of evil" (vs. 7). The establishment of the Constitution was an important part of the divine plan, as Elder Mark E. Petersen explained:

*Mark E. Petersen stressed the need for Church members to uphold the Constitution*

"When the Kirtland Temple was to be dedicated and the Prophet Joseph sought direction from the Lord in accomplishing this important responsibility, the Lord gave to the Prophet the dedicatory prayer for the occasion. It was revelation—the word of the Lord—and not of man. Yet in it, the Lord directed the prophet to pray: '. . . may those principles, which were so honorably and nobly defended, namely, the Constitution of our land, by our fathers, be established forever.' (D&C 109:54.) This is significant!

"Let us recall again the words of the Lord to the Nephites. Said he, in speaking of this mighty nation of the Gentiles that he said would be established on this land in latter days: 'For it is wisdom in the Father that they should be established in this land, *and be set up as a free people by the power of the Father. . . .'* (3 Nephi 21:4. Italics added.)

"Without the Constitution there would be no government such as the Lord had in mind. The Lord gave us that government by *providing the Constitution* written by the hands of wise men *whom he raised up for this very purpose.* It was an act of God. It was another step in establishing the free conditons under which the gospel could be restored and then taken by the believing Gentiles to all other nations.

"As the Lord indicated so plainly through Nephi and likewise in his own declaration to the Nephites after his resurrection as quoted above, it was a giant step in the divine plan to fulfill the promise made to Abraham, that God would recover his scattered seed by the preaching of the gospel. (See 1 Nephi 22:7-11; 3 Nephi 21:4.) His sheep would know his voice.

"This, then, is why there is a United States.

"The Prophet Joseph Smith said that 'the Constitution of the United States is a glorious standard; *it is founded in the wisdom of God. It is a heavenly banner. . . .'* (*Teachings of the Prophet Joseph Smith,* p. 147. Italics added.)

"He also said, 'I am the greatest advocate of the Constitution of the United States there is on earth.' (Ibid., p. 326.)

"The Constitution provided freedom of religion, speech, press, and assembly. Therefore, under the Constitution the Lord could restore the gospel and reestablish his church. The preparation of the Constitution was the work of his own hand. The restoration of the gospel was likewise his work. Both were part of a greater whole. Both fit into his pattern for the latter days.

"There would be no state church in America to interfere. All men in this land now were given the right to worship God according to the dictates of their own conscience, and that included Joseph Smith and his followers. It is true they were persecuted, as the people of God always have been, but the law—the Constitution—provided the very thing the Lord had in mind: freedom to reestablish his work in these last days, for he had so arranged it. . . .

"For years the Church has held that the Constitution is an inspired document. But how many know *why* it was inspired and *what* the Almighty had in mind in giving such inspiration?

"May we never forget the underlying reasons for it all: to provide a proper place for the restoration of the gospel and to allow for the worldwide preaching of that sacred word.

"Let us always remember that its formation was one of the vital steps preparatory to the second coming of the Savior." (*Great Prologue,* pp. 74-75, 78.)

### D&C 98:9-12. "Good Men and Wise Men Ye Should Observe to Uphold"

Though the Constitution was given through divine inspiration, the law is administered by mortals whose human failings can sometimes get in the way of true and righteous principles. "When the wicked rule, the people mourn" (D&C 98:9). It is therefore obligatory for citizens, wherever they have a choice, in addition to supporting constitutional law, to elect "honest and wise men" who will administer it to the best of their ability (vs. 10). The First Presidency said of this admonition:

"Laws which are enacted for the protection of society have no value except when they are administered in righteousness and justice, and they cannot be so administered if dishonest men occupy administrative offices.

"The Lord says: 'When the wicked rule, the people mourn.' Wise men, good men, patriotic men are to be found in all communities, in all political parties, among all creeds. None but such men should be chosen. . . .

"Without beneficent laws, righteously administered, the foundations of civilization crumble, anarchy reigns, decay and dissolution follow." (First Presidency, as cited by Anthony W. Ivins, in Conference Report, Oct. 1928, p. 16.)

As men seek to decide who should represent them in government, they should maintain their own honor and integrity as citizens. It is not enough to choose good and righteous men to lead governments; individuals must follow true and holy principles themselves. A righteous citizenry is the best safeguard to peace and happiness. If Zion is to be established, the Saints must forsake all evil.

### D&C 98:14. How Does a Person Learn Not to Fear His Enemies?

The real source of confidence and inner peace is the gospel, as President Joseph F. Smith noted: "We hear about living in perilous times. We are in perilous times, but I do not feel the pangs of that terror. It is not upon me. I propose to live so that it will not rest upon me. I propose to live so that I shall be immune from the perils of the world, if it be possible for me to so live, by obedience to the commandments of God and to his laws revealed for my guidance. No matter what may come to me, if I am only in the line of my duty, if I am in fellowship with God, if I am worthy of the fellowship of my brethren, if I can stand spotless before the world, without blemish, without transgression of the laws of God, what does it matter to me what may happen to me? I am always ready, if I am in this frame of understanding, mind, and conduct. It does not matter at all. Therefore, I borrow no trouble nor feel the pangs of fear." ("The Gospel a Shield from Terror," *Improvement Era*, July 1917, p. 827.)

**D&C 98:16-48. Laws by Which the Saints Are Governed in Times of Adversity**

Against the terrible and unjust actions of the mobs in Jackson County (see Notes and Commentary on D&C 98:1-3), the natural reaction of the Saints would have been a desire for revenge and retaliation. But such reactions are not in harmony with the godliness required of Saints, and here the Lord outlines the laws which must govern Christians in times of persecutions. He outlines the law of retaliation (vss. 23-32), the law of war (vss. 33-38), and the law of forgiveness (vss. 39-48). Smith and Sjodahl elaborated on these laws:

"*The Law of Retaliation.* The Lord here states what may, perhaps, be called the *lex talionis* of the gospel. . . .

"As the world is constituted at present, it is impossible to live in it without being wronged some time. What to do, when wronged, is one of the great problems of a Christian life. The world says, 'Get even!' The Master said, 'Forgive!' 'Absurd!' the world exclaims, 'What are laws and courts and jails for?' Christ bids us remember that our worst enemy is, after all, one of God's children whom Christ came to save, and that we ought to treat him as we would an erring brother. Very often Christian love in return for a wrong proves the salvation of the wrongdoer. It always has a wonderful effect upon those who practice it. It makes them strong, beautiful and God-like, whereas hatred and revenge stamp, upon the heart in which they dwell, the image of the devil. . . .

"*The Law of War.* Israel was a war-cradled nation, but the divine law placed many restrictions on their military life. All men from twenty years of age, capable of carrying arms, were liable to military service (Numbers 1:3), but all the priests and Levites, who were engaged in the Temple service were exempt (Numbers 1:47); so was also a man who had built a house and had not yet dedicated it; one who had planted a vineyard and had not yet eaten of its fruit, and one who was engaged to be married and had not yet taken his betrothed home (Deuteronomy 20:5-7). A newly-married man was exempt for one year (Deut. 24:5), and, finally, every one who was afraid, or 'faint-hearted,' was barred from the service, lest 'his brethren's heart faint as well as his heart' (Deut. 20:8). By these sweeping restrictions, the Temple service, industrial and agricultural pursuits, and domestic happiness were exalted above militarism, at a time when the military cast wielded the predominating influence in many countries.

"Israel was enjoined from going to war with any city or nation, until a peace-offer had been refused (Deut. 20:10; compare Deut. 2:26-9). When war became inevitable, the Israelites were expressly commanded not to cut down the fruit trees in the territory of the enemy (Deut. 20:19). Unnecessary vandalism was prohibited.

"Compare the instructions given to the Nephites, Alma 48:10-25." (Commentary, pp. 623-24.)

President David O. McKay gave an important insight into the circumstances under which war is justified for a godly person:

"There are, however, two conditions which may justify a truly Christian man to enter—mind you, I say *enter, not begin*—a war: (1) An attempt to dominate and to deprive another of his free agency, and (2) Loyalty to his country. Possibly there is a third, viz., Defense of a weak nation that is being unjustly crushed by a strong, ruthless one.

"Paramount among these reasons, of course, is the defense of man's freedom. An attempt to rob man of his free agency caused dissension even in heaven. . . .

"To deprive an intelligent human being of his free agency is to commit the crime of the ages. . . .

"So fundamental in man's eternal progress is his inherent right to choose, that the Lord would defend it even at the price of war. Without freedom of thought, freedom of choice, freedom of action within lawful bounds, man cannot progress. . . .

"The greatest responsibility of the state is to guard the lives, and to protect the property and rights of its citizens; and if the state is obligated to protect its citizens from lawlessness within its boundaries, it is equally obligated to protect them from lawless encroachments from without—whether the attacking criminals be individuals or nations." (In Conference Report, Apr. 1942, pp. 72-73.)

Smith and Sjodahl described the final law given in this section:

"*The Law of Forgiveness.* In [verses] 23-32 the Saints are taught to bear persecution patiently, and not to seek revenge; here they are instructed to go still farther, and forgive an enemy as often as he repents of his evil-doing, and a stated number of times, even if he does not repent (v. 43). If, however, he continues to trespass and does not repent, the case is to be brought before the Lord, in the hope that the sinner may be brought to repentance; when that object is gained, he is to be forgiven (vv. 44, 45); if there is no repentance, the matter is to be left entirely in the hands of the Lord.

"[Until seventy times seven] means, practically, an unlimited number of times. In the days of our Lord, the Rabbis taught that no one was under obligation to forgive a neighbor more than three times. Peter, asking the Master for a ruling on that question, suggested that perhaps seven times would be a liberal improvement on the rule of the Jewish teachers, but our Lord answered, 'seventy times seven.' . . .

"The gospel teaches us that if we have a grudge against any man, in our hearts, we should drive it out. It teaches us to do good to all, even to enemies, and thereby it makes us as happy as only a heart full of sunshine can be." (Commentary, pp. 625-26; see also Notes and Commentary for D&C 64:9-10.)

*Ezra Taft Benson spoke of the house of Judah's walking with the house of Ephraim*

**D&C 98:16-18. Turning the "Hearts of the Jews unto the Prophets"**

In May 1976 President Ezra Taft Benson spoke in Canada to a congregation that included many Jews. In his talk President Benson stated:

"In Jacob's blessing to Judah, he declared: 'Judah is . . . as an old lion: *who shall rouse him up?*' (Gen. 49:9; italics added.) We come as messengers bearing the legitimate authority to arouse Judah to her promises. We do not ask Judah to forsake her heritage. We are not asking her to leave father, mother, or family. We bring a message that Judah does not possess. That message constitutes 'living water' from the Fountain of living water.

"Our prophet, Joseph Smith, was given a commandment by the Lord to turn 'the hearts of the Jews unto the prophets, and the prophets unto the Jews.' (D&C 98:17.) We are presently sending our messengers to every land and people whose ideology permits us entrance. We have been gathering Joseph's descendants for 146 years. We hope you, who are of Judah, will not think it an intrusion for us to present our message to you. You are welcome to come to our meetings. We display no crosses. We collect no offerings. We honor your commitment to your unique heritage and your individuality. We approach you in a different way than any other Christian church because we represent the restored covenant to the entire house of Israel.

"Yes, we understand the Jews, as David Ben-Gurion said. We understand them because we belong to the same house of Israel. We are your brothers—Joseph. We look forward to the day of fulfillment of God's promise when 'the house of Judah shall walk with the house of Israel.' (Jer. 3:18.)" ("A Message to Judah from Joseph," *Ensign*, Dec. 1976, p. 72.)

**D&C 98:38. What Does the Word *Ensample* Mean?**

*Ensample*, a word now rarely used, means "a precedent which may be followed or imitated; a pattern or model of conduct" (*Oxford English Dictionary*, s.v. "ensample").

**D&C 98:38. "Behold This Is an Ensample to All People"**

For the past several decades, the Church has lived in relatively peaceful circumstances. The bitter persecutions of earlier generations have not been seen on a general scale. There are indications, however, that this is not to be permanent. Several scriptures speak of Satan and his forces waging war against the Saints (see, for example, Daniel 7:21-22, 25; Revelation 13:7; 1 Nephi 14:13).

President Brigham Young taught that such times of peace as are now enjoyed are only temporary respites. "If we live, we shall see the nations of the earth arrayed against this people; for that time must come, in fulfilment of prophecy. Tell about war commencing! Bitter and relentless war waged against Joseph Smith before he had received the plates of the Book of Mormon; and from that time till now the wicked have only fallen back at times to gain strength and learn how to attack the Kingdom of God." (*Discourses of Brigham Young*, p. 111.)

Elder Bruce R. McConkie bore witness that the Latter-day Saints may yet see persecution against them as a people:

"But the vision of the future is not all sweetness and light and peace. All that is yet to be shall go forward in the midst of greater evils and perils and desolations than have been known on earth at any time. . . .

"The way ahead is dark and dreary and dreadful. There will yet be martyrs; the doors in Carthage shall again enclose the innocent. We have not been promised that the trials and evils of the world will entirely pass us by." (In Conference Report, Apr. 1980, pp. 99-100; see also *Ensign*, May 1980, p. 73.)

In other words, modern Saints may yet have cause to look to the laws of retaliation, war, and forgiveness as outlined in Doctrine and Covenants 98 in order to better govern their reaction to a hostile world and to maintain their inner peace, for as the Savior himself said in another setting: "These things I have spoken unto you, that in me ye might have peace. In the world ye shall have tribulation: but be of good cheer; I have overcome the world." (John 16:33.)

# The Word of the Lord unto John Murdock



## Historical Background

The Prophet Joseph Smith received Doctrine and Covenants 99 on 24 August 1832 at Hiram, Ohio. "This is a Revelation calling Elder John Murdock to go on a mission to the Eastern States. He was one of the men who received the gospel in Kirtland when Oliver Cowdery and companions passed through that city on the first western journey to the Lamanites, and together with Sidney Rigdon, Edward Partridge, Isaac Morley, Lyman Wight, and others, he was called to the ministry at that time. He held many important positions in the Church and discharged his duties faithfully." (Smith and Sjodahl, Commentary, p. 629.)

## Notes and Commentary

### D&C 99:1-4. What Responsibility Rests upon God's Children to Accept the Testimony of His Servants?

Each individual has an obligation to accept the gospel when it is offered, or he must face the consequences of his choice. To receive the Lord's servants is to receive him; to reject the Lord's servants is to be rejected by the Lord as well. "And whoso rejecteth you shall be rejected of my Father and his house" (D&C 99:4).

"Who have rejected this gospel? The indifferent, those who would not take the trouble to investigate it, those who would not take the trouble to bow in submission before the Lord and ask his testimony concerning it, those who thought it beneath them, those who have been too proud, or too rich or too well situated or who, for some other reason, have failed to take any interest in this work; these are they who are not members of this Church and who have failed to obey this gospel when they heard it preached in its simplicity and its purity amongst the nations of the earth. . . . There will be a heavy condemnation fall upon this generation because of their inattention to these things. Judgements and calamities will be visited upon the inhabitants of the earth in consequence of neglecting the word of God written in the Scriptures, and also the word of God to his servants in these days." (George Q. Cannon, in *Journal of Discourses,* 20:248.)

### D&C 99:4. What Does the Symbolic Act of Cleansing One's Feet Mean?

See Notes and Commentary for Doctrine and Covenants 24:15 and 60:15-17.

### D&C 99:5, 8. What Responsibility Rests upon Those Who Know Truth?

The Lord's second coming in the clouds of heaven will be a time of judgment, for the sheep (the righteous) shall be separated from the goats (the unrighteous). Until then there will be foolish virgins among the wise, that is, wicked men among the righteous. But "at that hour cometh an entire separation of the righteous and the wicked" (D&C 63:54). The ungodly deeds of evil men shall then be uncovered for all to see. In the meantime, righteous men are to continue proclaiming the Lord's gospel. "Of him unto whom much is given much is required; and he who sins against the greater light shall receive the greater condemnation" (D&C 82:3).

*John Murdock filled one of the first missions to the eastern states*

"Any person who is truly converted to the gospel of Jesus Christ will naturally and anxiously want to share these truths with others. Also, the Lord has given commandments to his saints that, inasmuch as they have been warned of the impending destruction preceding the second coming of Jesus Christ, they have the responsibility to warn the others. Missionary service, then, has been one of the distinguishing characteristics of the true Church in this dispensation." (Ludlow, *Companion,* 2:183.)

**D&C 99:6-7. One's Primary Obligation Is to One's Family**

Elder John Murdock lost his wife when she gave birth to twins on 30 April 1831. That same day Emma Smith also bore twins and lost them both in death. Unable to care for his newborn children and knowing of Emma's heartache, John Murdock gave his motherless infants into the care of Joseph's wife.

But Brother Murdock had other children who were older. The Lord told him to delay his departure for his mission until his remaining children were provided for.

The word *kindly* in the nineteenth century meant more than just to perform an act with kindness. It meant "in the way suitable or appropriate . . . ; properly, fittingly." It also meant to do something "with natural affection" or "in a way that is pleasant or agreeable to the recipient or object." (*Oxford English Dictionary,* s.v. "kindly.")

# Words of Comfort to Joseph Smith and Sidney Rigdon

Section 100

## Historical Background

"While the enemies in Missouri were gathering their lawless forces for an assault upon the Church there, the Lord inspired the Prophet Joseph to go on a mission and proclaim the gospel message. He was not to mind the enemies. His calling was to testify to the world. And he went on this mission as far as Canada, as full of faith and hope as if there had been no storm clouds in the sky." (Smith and Sjodahl, Commentary, p. 630.)

On a journey full of missionary activity, teaching the receptive listener as well as the infidel, the Prophet Joseph Smith moved with the confidence so typically his when he was upon the Lord's errand. He disclosed in a journal entry dated 11 October 1833: "I feel very well in my mind. The Lord is with us, but have much anxiety about my family." (*History of the Church,* 1:419n.) On 12 October they arrived at Perrysburg, New York, where the Lord gave them the revelation now contained in Doctrine and Covenants 100.

*The warning voice is to gather the righteous*

## Notes and Commentary

**D&C 100:1. Why Is It Significant That the Lord Called Joseph and Sidney "My Friends"?**

The term *friends,* when used by the Lord, speaks peace to the souls of those for whom it is intended. It identifies the quality of the relationship between them, for the friend of the Lord knows both him and his ways. Indeed, the Lord says that he makes known to them "all things that I have heard of my Father" (John 15:15). The friend of God is the one for whom the Savior died (see John 15:13).

**D&C 100:1. "Your Families Are . . . in Mine Hands"**

Since they had left their families behind before embarking on their mission, it was only natural that Joseph Smith and Sidney Rigdon should feel some concern. In this verse the Lord assured both men that their families were in his care and that he would see to them.

Those who are on the Lord's errand need not let concern for their families deter them from their work. They may petition the Lord for the welfare of their families and then go forth in full confidence that they will be properly cared for. Elder Amasa M. Lyman said: "In going forth to do our duty in warning mankind we should not have our minds troubled and perplexed on account of our families being destitute. . . . But if a man has no cause of trouble, he can engage heart and soul in the work of the ministry and think of nothing else but the Work in which he is engaged. 'But,' says one, 'I cannot forget my wife and child that are at home.' You are not required to forget them. I could always remember my wife and child, but did I sorrow over them and fear that they were starving to death? No; . . . when absent on missions, we kneel down and pray, 'God bless the distant ones at home,' and then go on about our business." (In *Journal of Discourses,* 10:181-82.)

**D&C 100:3-5. The Church President Opened a Missionary "Door"**

Joseph and Sidney went on this mission to Canada in 1833 to save souls (see D&C 100:4). The Lord promised that if they would lift up their voices and "speak the thoughts" he put into their hearts (vs. 5) "an effectual door" to missionary labor would be opened unto them (vs. 3). And it was so. Thus began the great labor in Canada that was to result in the conversion of many souls. It was through this "door" that Parley P. Pratt walked some two years later to contact John Taylor, future President of the Church. When men place themselves in the Lord's hands, as did Joseph and Sidney, they cannot help but succeed.

**D&C 100:6-8. What Responsibility Is Associated with the Ability to Know What to Say in the Very Hour of Need?**

The Lord's agents are to speak as moved upon by the Holy Ghost (see D&C 68:4), and they are to do so "in solemnity of heart" (D&C 100:7). By his walking by the Spirit, a faithful man merits the guidance needed for safety (see 1 Nephi 4:6). But the things of God are of deep and sacred import "and must be spoken with care, and by constraint of the Spirit" (D&C 63:64). Yet men are not to hold back and fail to speak at all. Where "much is given much is required" (D&C 82:3). President Wilford Woodruff explained the importance of this responsibility: "I will say as Paul did, 'Woe be unto me if I preach not the Gospel' [1 Corinthians 9:16]. I will say the same for the Apostles, the High Priests, the Seventies, and the Elders, so far as they are called to declare the words of life and salvation to this generation; the judgments of God will rest upon us if we do not do it. You may ask why. I answer, because a dispensation of the Gospel of Jesus Christ has never been given to man in ancient days or in this age, for any other purpose than for the salvation of the human family." (In *Journal of Discourses,* 22:204.)

**D&C 100:9-11. Sidney Rigdon, a Spokesman for Joseph Smith**

Sidney Rigdon, like Aaron in an earlier time (see Exodus 4:16), was appointed a spokesman for the Prophet Joseph Smith. Blessed with great natural gifts as an orator and student of scripture, Sidney was promised "power to be mighty in testimony" (D&C 100:10). President George Q. Cannon spoke of Sidney Rigdon's effectiveness in this role: "Those who knew Sidney Rigdon, know how wonderfully God inspired him, and with what wonderful eloquence he declared the word of God to the people. He was a mighty man in the hands of God, as a spokesman, as long as the prophet lived, or up to a short time before his death. Thus you see that even this which many might look upon as a small matter, was predicted about 1,700 years before the birth of the Savior, and was quoted by Lehi 600 years before the same event, and about 2,400 years before its fulfillment [see 2 Nephi 3:18], and was translated by the power of God, through his servant Joseph, as was predicted should be the case." (In *Journal of Discourses,* 25:126.)

An important point in Doctrine and Covenants 100:11 is that while Sidney was to be a spokesman for Joseph Smith, the Prophet was to "be a revelator" unto Sidney. In this way Brother Rigdon was to "know the certainty of all things pertaining to the things of my kingdom on the earth" (vs. 11). Sidney's position as spokesman for the Prophet Joseph Smith was one of the things that caused him to claim to be guardian of the Church after Joseph's death. To lead the Church, however, was not within the scope of his calling.

**D&C 100:13-17. "Zion Shall Be Redeemed, Although She Is Chastened for a Little Season"**

Just before starting for Canada, Oliver Cowdery brought word to the Prophet that enemies of Zion were working to destroy the Church. Joseph sent Orson Hyde and John Gould from Kirtland to Jackson County, Missouri, "with advice to the Saints in their unfortunate situation" (*History of the Church,* 1:407). This journey would be very hazardous because they would be traveling near anti-Mormon mobs. The Lord assured them that he would be with them so long as they kept his commandments.

Joseph also received a promise from the Lord concerning Zion's future state: Zion would be redeemed after a chastening season. Such a season was the promised means of purifying a people who would serve the Lord in righteousness. Serving in righteousness is a prerequisite for those who will have the honor of building Zion.

# The Saints Are "Cast Out from the Land of Their Inheritance"

Section 101

## Historical Background

The Prophet Joseph Smith received this revelation at Kirtland, Ohio, on 16 December 1833. At the time the revelation was given, the Saints in Missouri had been driven from Jackson County to Clay County. Their homes destroyed and their property taken from them by the mobs in Jackson County, the Saints were suffering greatly (see *History of the Church,* 1:426-38, 458-64).

The Lord, prior to this revelation, had warned the Saints that they must keep his commandments and do his will, or they would suffer affliction, pestilence, plague, sword, vengeance, and devouring fire (see D&C 97:26). Now, in Doctrine and Covenants 101, the Lord explained why the Saints had been driven from Zion.

## Notes and Commentary

### D&C 101:1, 6. Why Was Missouri Called a Land of Inheritance for the Saints?

Anciently the Lord blessed Joseph, the son of Jacob, with the blessings of his father Abraham, which included a land of promise for his posterity. His descendants were to receive an inheritance in the land of America (see Genesis 49:1-2, 22-26; Deuteronomy 33:13-17; Richards, *Marvelous Work and a Wonder,* pp. 63-66; 3 Nephi 15:12-13; 20:10, 14.)

Commenting on the rights of heirs, President Joseph Fielding Smith taught: "Every person who embraces the gospel becomes of the house of Israel. In other words, they become members of the chosen lineage, or Abraham's children through Isaac and Jacob unto whom the promises were made. The great majority of those who become members of the Church are literal descendants of Abraham through Ephraim, son of Joseph. Those who are not literal descendants of Abraham and Israel must become such, and when they are baptized and confirmed they are grafted into the tree and are entitled to all the rights and privileges as heirs." (*Doctrines of Salvation,* 3:246.)

As descendants of Joseph, modern-day members of the Lord's church inherit the blessings promised to Joseph's posterity (see Abraham 2:9-10; D&C 86:8-9). That is why the Lord has promised those of his latter-day church an inheritance in the land promised to Joseph's posterity, with its "center place" (D&C 57:3) in Missouri (see D&C 38:17-20; 52:1-5, 42; 57:1-5).

### D&C 101:1-3. Who Are the Lord's Jewels?

See Notes and Commentary on Doctrine and Covenants 60:4.

### D&C 101:2, 6. Why Were the Saints Driven from Zion?

The Lord answered this question only in part, as the Prophet Joseph Smith recorded:

"I cannot learn from any communication by the Spirit to me, that Zion has forfeited her claim to a celestial crown, notwithstanding the Lord has caused her to be thus afflicted, except it may be some individuals, who have walked in disobedience, and forsaken the new covenant; all such will be made manifest by their works in due time. I have always expected that Zion would suffer some affliction, from what I could learn from the commandments which have been given. But I would remind you of a certain clause in one which says, that after much tribulation cometh the blessing. By this, and also others, and also one received of late, I know that Zion, in the due time of the Lord, will be redeemed; but how many will be the days of her purification, tribulation, and affliction, the Lord has kept hid from my eyes; and when I inquire concerning this subject, the voice of the Lord is: Be still, and know that I am God; all those who suffer for my name shall reign with me, and he that layeth down his life for my sake shall find it again.

"Now, there are two things of which I am ignorant; and the Lord will not show them unto me, perhaps for a wise purpose in Himself—I mean in some respects—and they are these: Why God has suffered so great a calamity to come upon Zion, and what the great moving cause of this great affliction is; and again, by what means He will return her back to her inheritance, with songs of everlasting joy upon her head. These two things, brethren, are in part kept back that they are not plainly shown unto me; but there are some things that are plainly manifest which have incurred the displeasure of the Almighty." (*Teachings,* p. 34.)

Even though the Lord did not explain all of the reasons for the expulsion of the Saints from Jackson County and the delay in building Zion, he at least explained in part some of the problems among the Saints (see D&C 105:2-4, 6).

### D&C 101:4-5. Why Does the Lord Permit His Saints to Be Chastened?

All who desire exaltation must be tested and tried to be proven in all things. President Harold B. Lee said:

"Some of us have been tried and have been tested until our very heart strings would seem to break. I have heard of persons dying with a broken heart, and I thought that was just a sort of a poetic expression, but I learned that it could be a very real experience. I came near to that thing; but when I

*Tested even as Abraham*

began to think of my own troubles, I thought of what the apostle Paul said of the Master, 'Though he were a Son, yet learned he obedience by the things which he suffered; And being made perfect, he became the author of eternal salvation unto all them that obey him.' (Hebrews 5:8, 9.)

"Don't be afraid of the testing and trials of life. Sometimes when you are going through the most severe tests, you will be nearer to God than you have any idea, for like the experience of the Master himself in the temptation on the mount, in the Garden of Gethsemane, and on the cross at Calvary, the scriptures record, 'And, behold, angels came and ministered unto him.' (Matthew 4:11.) Sometimes that may happen to you in the midst of your trials." (In Conference Report, Munich Germany Area Conference 1973, p. 114.)

The scriptures teach that the Lord chastens his children for the following reasons:

1. Chastening is a cleansing process (see D&C 90:36).
2. Chastening may lead to a forgiveness of sins (see D&C 95:1).
3. Chastening teaches them obedience (see D&C 105:6).
4. Chastening refines them as pure gold (see Job 23:10).

### D&C 101:6-8. Why Is God Sometimes Slow to Hear His Children?

One of the great problems recorded in scripture is man's indifference to God in times of prosperity. Too often man forgets his Creator, who is the giver of all good things. In times of trouble, however, men again remember their God and turn to him for mercy and help in their afflictions, but he is slow to hearken to them and to help them. That the Saints were guilty of this offense in Missouri is apparent from these verses. They had allowed the corruptions of the world to turn them from God's holy commandments and from strict observance of the covenants they had made. Therefore, the Lord did not support them in their day of affliction. He will not support any who claim his promises but fail to keep their covenants and by sin pollute their inheritance. (See D&C 84:54-59; Mosiah 11:24; 21:15; Helaman 4:11-13; 12:1-6; Judges 10:13-14; Isaiah 26:16.)

### D&C 101:9-12. What Is Meant by the Phrase "Sword of Mine Indignation"

Because a sword is a sharp-edged instrument of war, the word has come to connote power. The Lord used the word in this sense when he said that he would remember his people in mercy and let the "sword of . . . indignation," or his power, fall on those who opposed his Saints. President Joseph Fielding Smith explained why the imagery is used here: "While there was punishment in the suffering the saints had to endure and that because they were slow to hear the Lord, nevertheless the actions of their enemies were not justifiable; and therefore the Lord promised that he would let fall the sword of his indignation in behalf of his people. [D&C 101:11-12.] The sword of indignation commenced to fall upon the enemies of the saints shortly after the saints were driven from Missouri, and from time to time it has fallen, both in this land and in foreign lands." (*Church History and Modern Revelation,* 1:460.)

The phrase "without measure" (D&C 101:11) means that the Lord's wrath will not be limited or restrained but will come with great fury and intensity.

### D&C 101:10-16. How Will the Lord Help His People?

The Lord has decreed that Israel will be gathered and the New Jerusalem will be built in preparation for his second coming (see Moses 7:60-62). The tribe of Ephraim has been given this responsibility, and no unhallowed hand can stop them.

The Lord has promised the Latter-day Saints that he will assist them in the work of preparation and will defend them against their enemies. Though they may experience great difficulty and distress, they must remember that he has all power and will deliver them. He will not allow his people to be overthrown. His counsel is "be still [calm, undisturbed] and know that I am God" (D&C 101:16). Nothing can frustrate his work or defeat his purposes (see 1 Nephi 22:15-17; 2 Nephi 30:10; D&C 35:14).

### D&C 101:12, 45-47. What Is the Symbolism of Watchmen upon the Tower?

In ancient Israel walls were built around the cities, and towers were erected in key places along the walls. Men were employed to keep watch in these towers, day and night, lest the enemy come upon

*The watchmen upon the towers are the leaders of the Church*

the city and destroy it because its inhabitants were not warned. To be employed as a watchman and then be negligent in his duty could cost a guard his life, since his sloth could cost the lives of others. The Greek word most frequently used in the New Testament to convey the idea of watching "means to *keep awake,* to *watch,* and so to take heed lest through remissness and indolence some destructive calamity suddenly overtake one" (Unger, *Bible Dictionary,* s.v. "watch").

Members of the Church today stand in a position to see clearly the enemy and how he works, because they have living prophets who speak the mind of God. They are therefore called by the Savior both to warn the wicked of the destruction that awaits them if they do not repent and to secure Zion and protect her inhabitants. Thus, the Lord refers to his authorized servants today as watchmen upon the towers (see Isaiah 62:6 and Ezekiel 33:2-9).

The phrase "all mine Israel" (D&C 101:12) refers to those who have entered into the gospel covenant and by keeping it have become heirs to the promises of Abraham, Isaac, and Jacob (see Abraham 2:9-11; Romans 9:6-8).

### D&C 101:17-20. "Zion Shall Not Be Moved"

Speaking of the expulsion from Jackson County, Elder James E. Talmage said: "The saints were not permitted to enter into immediate possession of the land, which was promised them as an everlasting inheritance. Even as years elapsed between the time of the Lord's promise to Israel of old that Canaan should be their inheritance, and the time of their entering into possession thereof—years devoted to the people's toilsome and sorrowful preparation for the fulfilment—so in these latter days the divine purpose is held in abeyance, while the people are being sanctified for the great gift and for the responsibilities associated with it. In the meantime the honest in heart are gathering to the valleys of the Rocky Mountains [and, more recently, to stakes all around the world]; and here, in the tops of the mountains, exalted above the hills, Temples have been erected, and all nations are flowing unto this region. But Zion shall yet be established on the chosen site; she 'shall not be moved out of her place,' and the pure in heart shall return 'with songs of everlasting joy, to build up the waste places of Zion.' " (*Articles of Faith,* p. 353; see also Notes and Commentary on D&C 29:8.)

### D&C 101:18. What Is Meant by Building Up the "Waste Places of Zion"?

The meaning of the term *waste* is "wild and uninhabited" (*Webster's New Collegiate Dictionary,* s.v. "waste").

Of the "waste places of Zion" (D&C 101:18) Elder Orson Hyde said: "The scripture says, that in the last days His people will go forth and build up the waste places of Zion. But they must first be made desolate, before they can be called 'the waste places of Zion.' Then the hands of the Saints will be required to build them up." (In *Journal of Discourses,* 10:376.)

Elder Orson Pratt taught that the Saints would go back to Missouri and possess the properties they had once inhabited in the early days of the Church, after God's judgments have made the cities desolate: "Now that order of things will continue and will spread forth from that nucleus in Jackson county and the western counties of Missouri and the eastern counties of Kansas, where this people will be located, and it will spread abroad for hundreds and hundreds of miles on the right hand and the left, east, west, north, and south from the great central city, and all the people will be required to execute the law in all their stewardships, and then there will be a oneness and union which will continue and it will spread wider and wider, and become greater and greater, until the desolate cities of the Gentiles will be inhabited by the Saints. Then will be fulfilled the prophecy of Isaiah, in which he says, 'Thy seed shall inherit the Gentiles, and make the desolate cities to be inhabited' [Isaiah 54:3], for God will visit them in judgment, and there will be no owners left to occupy the country. Then the land will be filled up with Saints, those who will keep the celestial law; and they will receive their stewardships according to the appointment of heaven." (*Deseret Evening News,* 2 Oct. 1875, p. 265.)

Some have wondered if the promise of desolation was not fulfilled in earlier times of the history of the United States, and yet President Spencer W. Kimball noted that punishments from the Lord for wickedness still face the peoples of the world if they do not repent. Citing extensively the warnings in Leviticus 26, one of which specifically refers to making "your cities waste" (vs. 33), President Kimball added, "Those are difficult and very serious situations, but they are possible" (in Conference Report, Apr. 1977, p. 6).

### D&C 101:20-22. What Does It Mean to "Stand in Holy Places"?

Elder Harold B. Lee taught that to "stand in holy places" (D&C 101:22) is to stand in Zion, which is among the pure in heart:

"In these days of our generation, many of you are asking: Where is safety?

"The word of the Lord is not silent. He has admonished us: [D&C 45:32].

"The Lord has told us where these 'holy places' are: [D&C 45:68].

"Where is Zion?

"During the various periods of time or dispensations, and for specific reasons, the Lord's prophets, his 'mouthpieces,' as it were, have designated gathering places where the Saints were to gather. After designating certain such places in our dispensation, the Lord then declared: [D&C 101:21].

"Thus, clearly the Lord has placed the responsibility of directing the work of gathering in the hands of his divinely appointed leaders. May I fervently pray that all Saints and truth-seekers everywhere will attune their listening ears to these prophet-leaders instead of to some demagogue who seeks to make capital of social discount and gain political influence.

"There are several meanings of the word Zion. . . .

"There is . . . [a] most significant use of the term by which the Church of God is called Zion, comprising, according to the Lord's own definition, 'the pure in heart.' (D&C 97:21.)

"As one studies the Lord's commandments and attending promises upon compliance therewith, one gets some definite ideas as to how we might 'stand in holy places,' as the Lord commands: [Malachi 3:10; D&C 59:9; Isaiah 58:9, 7; D&C 89:18, 21].

"As one studies the commandments of God, it seems to be made crystal clear that the all-important thing is not where we live but whether or not our hearts are pure." (In Conference Report, Oct. 1968, pp. 61-62.)

### D&C 101:23-25. What Are Some of the Signs Attending the Second Coming of the Lord?

Three special signs are associated with the Lord's return to earth:

1. At his appearance, "all flesh shall see [him] together" (D&C 101:23). Elder Orson Pratt said that "the second advent of the Son of God is to be something . . . accompanied with great power and glory, something that will not be done in a small portion of the earth like Palestine, and seen only by a few; but it will be an event that will be seen by all—all flesh shall see the glory of the Lord; when he reveals himself the second time, every eye, not only those living at that time in the flesh, in mortality on the earth, but also the very dead themselves" (in *Journal of Discourses,* 18:170).

2. "Every corruptible thing . . . shall be consumed" (D&C 101:24). Elder Bruce R. McConkie explained: "Incident to the commencement of the millennial era, the earth (the Lord's vineyard) will be burned. Every corruptible thing will be consumed. (D. & C. 101:24); all the proud and they that do wickedly shall be burned as stubble (Mal. 4:1; D. & C. 29:9; 64:23-25; 133:63-64); the sinners will be destroyed (Isa. 13:9-14); and there will be an entire separation of the righteous and the wicked. (D. & C. 63:54.) Those only shall be able to abide that day who are worthy to live on a paradisiacal or terrestrial sphere." (*Mormon Doctrine,* p. 494.)

3. "All things shall become new" (D&C 101:25; see also D&C 29:23-24). Of this newness Elder Parley P. Pratt wrote: "A new heaven and a new earth are promised by the sacred writers. Or, in other words, the planetary systems are to be changed, purified, refined, exalted and glorified, in the similitude of the resurrection, by which means all physical evil or imperfections will be done away." (*Key to the Science of Theology,* p. 61.)

This newness of things is not the same as the ultimate "new heaven and a new earth" (Revelation 21:1) that will be the result of the celestialization of the earth at the end of the Millennium.

### D&C 101:25. How Will the Earth Be Burned by Fire?

The glory of a celestial being, of which the sun is most typical (see D&C 76:70), is so radiant that to bring that glory to the earth will cause great burning. The cleansing of the earth by fire will be caused by the coming of the Savior to earth (see D&C 5:19; McConkie, *Doctrinal New Testament Commentary,* 3:368-69; Notes and Commentary for D&C 133:40-49). Those who are not changed to withstand the presence of the Savior when he comes in his glory shall indeed perish by fire.

### D&C 101:26-34. What Will Millennial Conditions Be Like?

Five features of the Millennium, the thousand-year personal reign of Christ on earth, are as follows:

1. "The enmity of all flesh, shall cease" (D&C 101:26). Elder Orson Pratt said that "the enmity of the beasts of the field as well as that of all flesh will cease; no more one beast of prey devouring and feasting upon another that is more harmless in its nature; no more will this enmity be found in the fish of the sea, or in the birds of the air. This change will be wrought upon all flesh when Jesus comes; not a change to immortality, but a change sufficient to alter the ferocious nature of beasts, birds and fishes. . . . gentleness, will characterize all the wild and ferocious animals, as well as the venomous serpents, so much so that the little child might lead them and play with them, and nothing shall hurt or destroy in all the holy mountain of the Lord, all things becoming, in some measure, as when they were first created." (Orson Pratt, in *Journal of Discourses,* 20:18.)

2. "Whatsoever any man shall ask, it shall be given unto him" (D&C 101:27). Men sometimes pray for things they should not have. The Millennium will change that. Men will ask only for righteous things, and all requests will be honored by Heavenly Father.

3. "Satan shall not have power to tempt any man" (vs. 28). See Notes and Commentary on Doctrine and Covenants 43:31 for an explanation of how Satan's power to tempt will be limited.

4. "Death will vanish from the earth" (D&C 101:29-31). During the Millennium, death, that is, a slow decline of physical vitality and health, will cease among the righteous inhabitants of the earth. They will live to be very old, and when the time

for the change known as death arrives, they will, "be changed in the twinkling of an eye" from mortality to immortality and their "rest shall be glorious" (vs. 31). Among those that have "kept the faith" (D&C 63:50), there will not be a separation of the spirit and body where the spirit passes into the spirit world and the body is laid in the ground to await the Resurrection. Instead, at the appropriate time, there will be an instantaneous change from a mortal to a resurrected, immortal condition.

Of this change Elder Joseph Fielding Smith said: "When Christ comes the saints who are on the earth will be quickened and caught up to meet him. This does not mean that those who are living in mortality at that time will be changed and pass through the resurrection, for mortals must remain on the earth until after the thousand years are ended. A change, nevertheless, will come over all who remain on the earth; they will be quickened so that they will not be subject unto death until they are old. Men shall die when they are one hundred years of age, and the change shall be made suddenly to the immortal state. Graves will not be made during this thousand years. . . . death shall come as a peaceful transition from the mortal to the immortal state." (*Way to Perfection,* pp. 298-99, 311.)

The scriptures and the writings of the prophets indicate that during the Millennium people living a terrestrial level of righteousness will be on the earth, but eventually all will have the opportunity to receive the gospel (see Isaiah 11:9; Habakkuk 2:14; Jeremiah 31:34). Those who do not receive the gospel will be swept off the earth (see Isaiah 65:20).

Isaiah taught that during the Millennium "the sinner being an hundred years old shall be accursed" (Isaiah 65:20). Zechariah taught that at that time the heathen nations who will not come to worship in Jerusalem will be visited with the Lord's judgments and eventually destroyed from the earth (see Zechariah 14:16-19; see also Smith, *Teachings,* pp. 268-69).

The contrast between these statements and those of the Lord in Doctrine and Covenants 101:30-31 and 63:50-51 indicates a difference between the condition of the righteous and the condition of the unrighteous during the early period of the Millennium. Elder Erastus Snow said that during the Millennium "the children that shall grow up *unto the Lord* shall not taste of death; that is, they shall not sleep in the earth, but they shall be changed in a moment, in the twinkling of an eye, and they shall be caught up, and their rest shall be glorious" (in *Journal of Discourses,* 7:355-56; emphasis added).

5. "In that day . . . the Lord . . . shall reveal all things" (D&C 101:32). The Millennium is the time that the Savior will personally work with the faithful, obedient members of his church who have lived upon the earth since the days of Adam. One can only imagine the blessings that are in store for those who have been faithful. For example, the first ten chapters (about fifteen pages) in the book of Genesis cover approximately two thousand years of history. The amount of knowledge that has been lost concerning just this earth is astounding. In the Millennium all that knowledge, and more, will be restored. It is of little wonder, then, that Saints have longed for the day when Christ would be in their midst, a day in which he will make all things known.

### D&C 101:35-38. "In Patience . . . Possess Your Souls, and Ye Shall Have Eternal Life"

The Lord enjoined the Saints in these verses to place more attention on the pursuit of eternal life than on the objects and pleasures of mortal life. He indicates that those who had lost their lives in Jackson County (there were some), and those who would do so in future persecutions (six thousand lost their lives while crossing the plains to Utah) need not fear. Those who are faithful have the hope of a glorious resurrection and the blessings of eternal life with God.

President Heber C. Kimball spoke of how death does not alter man's moral nature: "Have I not told you often that the separation of body and spirit makes no difference in the moral and intellectual condition of the spirit? When a person, who has always been good and faithful to his God, lays down his body in the dust, his spirit will remain the same in the spirit world. It is not the body that has control over the spirit, as to its disposition, but it is the spirit that controls the body. When the spirit leaves the body the body becomes lifeless. The spirit has not changed one single particle of itself by leaving the body." (In *Journal of Discourses,* 3:108.)

### D&C 101:39-42. "The Salt of the Earth"

"Ye are the salt of the earth," Jesus told his followers in Palestine, "but if the salt have lost his savour, wherewith shall it [the earth] be salted?" (Matthew 5:13). Men cannot teach and testify to others of the truths of God, if they themselves do not believe and follow them.

Salt is important to the life of man. It has been used through the ages as a preservative, as a condiment, and as a religious offering (see Leviticus 2:13). Salt which has lost its savor, or its saltiness, is no longer useful. The same is true of those who embrace the gospel in faith and then lose that faith through sin or slothfulness.

Elder Carlos E. Asay explained the imagery of salt and its savor:

"When the Lord used the expression 'savor of men,' he was speaking of those who represent him. He was referring to those who have repented, who have been washed clean in the waters of baptism, and who have covenanted to take upon them his name and his cause. Moreover, he was speaking of those who would share by covenant his priesthood power. He was speaking of you and me.

"A world-renowned chemist told me that salt will not lose its savor with age. Savor is lost through mixture and contamination. Similarly, priesthood power does not dissipate with age; it, too, is lost through mixture and contamination.

"When a young man or older man mixes his thoughts with pornographic literature, he suffers a loss of savor.

"When a priesthood bearer mixes his speech

with lies or profanity, he suffers a loss of savor.

"When one of us follows the crowd and becomes involved in immoral acts and the use of drugs, tobacco, alcohol, and other injurious substances, he loses savor.

"Flavor and quality flee a man when he contaminates his mind with unclean thoughts, desecrates his mouth by speaking less than the truth, and misapplies his strength in performing evil acts. King Benjamin cautioned, 'Watch yourselves, and your thoughts, and your words, and your deeds, and observe the commandments of God' (Mosiah 4:30).

"I would offer these simple guidelines, especially to the young men, as the means to preserve one's savor: If it is not *clean,* do not think it; if it is not *true,* do not speak it; if it is not *good,* do not do it (see Marcus Aurelius, 'The Meditations of Marcus Aurelius,' in *The Harvard Classics,* Charles W. Eliot, ed., New York: P. F. Collier and Son, 1909, p. 211)." (In Conference Report, Apr. 1980, pp. 60-61; or *Ensign,* May 1980, pp. 42-43.)

### D&C 101:44-64. What Is Represented by This Parable?

Sidney B. Sperry, in his work on the Doctrine and Covenants, explained the parable in this way:

"It would seem that the parable is to be interpreted in this way: the nobleman is the Lord, whose choice land in His vineyard is Zion in Missouri. The places where the Saints live in Zion are the olive trees. The servants are the Latter-day Saint settlers, and the watchmen are their officers in the Church. While yet building in Zion, they become at variance with each other and do not build the tower or Temple whose site had been dedicated as early as August 3, 1831. Had they built it as directed, it would have been a spiritual refuge for them, for from it the Lord's watchmen could have seen by revelation the movements of the enemy from afar. This foreknowledge would have saved them and their hard work when the enemy made his assault.

"But the Saints in Missouri were slothful, lax, and asleep. The enemy came, and the Missouri persecutions were the result. The Lord's people were scattered and much of their labors wasted. The Almighty rebuked His people, as we have already seen, but He commanded one of His servants (vs. 55), Joseph Smith (103:21), to gather the 'strength of Mine house' and rescue His lands and possessions gathered against them.

"Subsequently, the Prophet and his brethren in the famous Zion's Camp did go to Missouri in 1834 in an attempt to carry out the terms of the parable. Before they went, additional revelation was received (*see* 103:21-28) concerning the redemption of Zion. The brethren were instructed to try to buy land in Missouri, not to use force; and if the enemy came against them, they were to bring a curse upon them. Zion was not redeemed at that time but we may look for it in the not-too-distant future. Verily, it will be redeemed when the Lord wills it." (*Compendium,* pp. 521-522.)

Though Joseph Smith followed the Lord's instructions to gather together the "strength of my house" (D&C 103:22) by organizing Zion's Camp to go forth to redeem Zion, the Lord's purpose in sending them and his will concerning the redemption of Zion were not fully understood by his people. The redemption of Zion did not take place at that time. When the servant in the parable asked when the land would be possessed, the Lord responded, "When I will" (D&C 101:60).

The parable further states that all things will be fulfilled "after many days" (vs. 62), which passage indicates that a long period of time will pass before Zion will be redeemed. The redemption of Zion still had not taken place even after the Saints had been expelled from Missouri and from Nauvoo. The Lord then told Brigham Young that "Zion shall be redeemed in mine own due time" (D&C 136:18). The redemption of Zion (meaning, the city of New Jerusalem in Missouri) is still future, although of course it is much closer now than it was when the Saints first sought to regain their inheritance in the land of Zion.

The time of Zion's redemption is referred to in Doctrine and Covenants 58:44; 105:15, 37. Compare the parable in Doctrine and Covenants 101 with those given in Isaiah 5:1-7 and Matthew 21:33-46.

### D&C 101:67-75. Further Instructions Concerning Zion

The Lord spoke of two important items having to do with the establishment of Zion: the gathering of the Saints to places appointed, and the purchase of land in the region of Zion. The Lord cautioned in verses 68 and 72 that the work was not to proceed with haste. Part of the difficulty experienced in the original attempt to establish Zion was caused by many Saints' coming to Zion ill-prepared. They apparently felt that the Lord would care for their needs rather than have them do it themselves. This idea was contrary to the Lord's counsel from the very beginning of Zion's founding, for he said, "And let the work of the gathering be not in haste, nor by flight" (D&C 58:56). He warned again: "And now, behold, this is the will of the Lord your God concerning his saints, that they should assemble themselves together unto the land of Zion, not in haste, lest there should be confusion, which bringeth pestilence" (D&C 63:24). The Lord's counsel was disregarded; the result is history.

Enrichment B, in the Appendix, discusses Zion.

### D&C 101:69-71. The Lord's People Are to Leave the Outcome in His Hand

See Notes and Commentary on Doctrine and Covenants 105:28-32.

### D&C 101:75. Zion Could Already Be Redeemed If the Saints Had Hearkened to the Lord's Voice

In the revelation in section 101, given in December 1833, the Lord told his people that if those who called themselves Saints would only follow his counsels, they would then have sufficient resources to redeem the land and to establish Zion, "no more to be thrown down" (D&C 101:75). In June 1834 the Lord indicated that Zion might already have been redeemed except for the transgressions of his people (see D&C 105:1-10). It is not the Lord who causes delays in bringing forth the establishment of Zion and the fulness of blessings upon the Saints. The rate at which his promises to his people are fulfilled and his blessings come to them is determined by their willingness to respond to his counsel and to do what they have been asked through his prophets.

Concerning the effect the efforts of the Saints can have on bringing about the Lord's purposes and hastening his work for the redemption of Zion, President Spencer W. Kimball said:

"It is estimated that it took 117 years, from 1830 to 1947, to attain one million members. Then it took sixteen years, from 1947 to 1963, to reach the second million members, and then nine years, 1963 to 1972, to attain the third million. It will probably take about four or five years to move up to the four million mark, and then we can guess what the future holds.

"What does this mean to us? It means that if the members of the Church do real proselyting in their home wards that the number of converts could grow to astronomical figures *and even hasten the time when the Lord will be returning to the earth in His second advent.*" (In Conference Report, Oct. 1976, p. 4; or *Ensign,* Nov. 1976, p. 4; emphasis added.)

### D&C 101:76-79. Was the Constitution of the United States Established for All Flesh?

One major purpose of government is to protect men "in their inherent and inalienable rights" (D&C 134:5), which are declared in the scriptures to be "the free exercise of conscience, the right and control of property, and the protection of life"

*"By the hands of wise men whom I raised up" (D&C 101:80)*

(D&C 134:2). The Saints in Zion were denied all these rights. The Constitution of the United States guarantees each individual the right to apply for redress when denied his God-given rights. The Lord urged the Saints in Zion "to importune for redress, and redemption" at the hands of the constituted authorities (D&C 101:76).

President Charles W. Penrose explained how this great document benefits all men: "In section 101 the Lord speaks about the constitution of this land. He says it was framed by wise men whom he raised up for that very purpose. What for? To maintain the rights and privileges *'of all flesh.'* Not alone the people of this land. The principles of that great instrument are to go forth to the nations, and the time will come when they will prevail, just as sure as the sun shines even when it appears to be in darkness and the clouds are over it." (In Conference Report, Apr. 1917, p. 20.)

### D&C 101:80. God Himself Established the United States Constitution

"To me . . . that statement of the Lord, 'I have established the Constitution of this land,' puts the Constitution of the United States in the position in which it would be if it were written in the book of Doctrine and Covenants itself. This makes the Constitution the word of the Lord to us. That it was given, not by oral utterance, but by the operation of his mind and spirit upon the minds of men, inspiring them to the working out of this great document of human government, does not alter its authority." (J. Reuben Clark, Jr., in Conference Report, Apr. 1935, p. 93.)

### D&C 101:80. "By the Hands of Wise Men Whom I Raised Up unto This Very Purpose"

President Brigham Young spoke of some of these "wise men" raised up by God:

"We believe that the Lord has been preparing that when he should bring forth his work, that, when the set time should fully come, there might be a place upon his footstool where sufficient liberty of conscience should exist, that his Saints might dwell in peace under the broad panoply of constitutional law and equal rights. In this view we consider that the men in the Revolution were inspired by the Almighty, to throw off the shackles of the mother government, with her established religion. For this cause were Adams, Jefferson, Franklin, Washington, and a host of others inspired to deeds of resistance to the acts of the King of Great Britain, who might also have been led to those aggressive acts, for aught we know, to bring to pass the purposes of God, in thus establishing a new government upon a principle of greater freedom, a basis of self-government allowing the free exercise of religious worship.

"It was the voice of the Lord inspiring all those worthy men who bore influence in those trying times, not only to go forth in battle but to exercise wisdom in council, fortitude, courage, and endurance in the tented field, as well as subsequently to form and adopt those wise and efficient measures which secured to themselves and succeeding generations, the blessings of a free and independent government." (*Discourses of Brigham Young*, pp. 359-60.)

**D&C 101:81-95. Why Was It So Important for the Saints to Appeal for Redress?**

The Lord repeated the parable in Luke 18:1-8 of the woman who so wearied a judge with her importuning that he finally granted her petition. He then likened the parable to the situation of the Saints. They were to seek redress from the judge through the governor to the president of the United States himself. If the appeals went unheeded, the Lord said that he would rise in anger and mete out justice to those who had dispossessed the Saints, for all men would "be left without excuse" (D&C 101:93). President Joseph Fielding Smith explained why:

"The saints were also to carry their grievances to the proper tribunals and seek for redress of their wrongs. This was a very necessary step, and when the Saints did this and were denied their civil and religious rights, those officials were left without excuse, and the judgments of the Almighty which later came upon them during the Civil War, were justified. . . .

"Since there is a just law of retribution, as fixed and eternal as are other laws of the Almighty [Sec. 6:33; 2 Cor. 9:6], the day must come when there shall be adjustments made before a Just Magistrate who will not be cowed by the threats of mobs." (*Church History and Modern Revelation*, 1:462, 469.)

**D&C 101:96-101. The Saints Were Not to Sell Their Lands in Jackson County**

The Saints were commanded to "hold claim" upon their Missouri lands even "though they should not be permitted to dwell thereon" (D&C 101:99). In writing to the Saints in Jackson County, the Prophet Joseph Smith said: "I would inform you that it is not the will of the Lord for you to sell your lands in Zion, if means can possibly be procured for your sustenance without. Every exertion should be made to maintain the cause you have espoused." (*Teachings*, p. 31.)

He then went on to say: "Let your sufferings be what they may, it is better in the eyes of God that you should die, than that you should give up the land of Zion, the inheritances which you have purchased with your moneys; for every man that giveth not up his inheritance, though he should die, yet, when the Lord shall come, he shall stand upon it, and with Job, in his flesh he shall see God. Therefore, this is my counsel, that you retain your lands, even unto the uttermost, and employ every lawful means to seek redress of your enemies; and pray to God, day and night, to return you in peace and in safety to the lands of your inheritance: and when the judge fail you, appeal unto the executive; and when the executive fail you, appeal unto the president; and when the president fail you, and all laws fail you, and the humanity of the people fail you, and all things else fail you but God alone, and you continue to weary Him with your importunings, as the poor woman did the unjust judge, He will not fail to execute judgment upon your enemies, and to avenge His own elect that cry unto Him day and night." (*Teachings*, pp. 35-36.)

The consecrated lands of the Saints' inheritances were polluted by the wicked mobs as they burned and pillaged, but to have the Saints consent to this pollution or contribute to it by selling their lands was, in the eyes of the Lord, "a very sore and grievous sin" (D&C 101:98).

# The Constitution of the High Council

Section 102

## Historical Background

On 17 February 1834 Joseph Smith organized the first high council of the Church in this dispensation. On the next day, 18 February, the Prophet reviewed and corrected the organizational minutes; then on 19 February the council reassembled, transacted the business, and the minutes were presented to the council (see *History of the Church*, 2:31).

The Prophet Joseph Smith spoke to the council on the necessity of prayer, "that the Spirit might be given, that the things of the Spirit might be judged thereby, because the carnal mind cannot discern the things of God. The minutes were read three times, and unanimously adopted and received for a form and constitution of the High Council of the Church of Christ hereafter; with this provision, that if the President should hereafter discover anything lacking in the same, he should be privileged to supply it." (*History of the Church*, 2:31.)

The minutes of this council meeting were included in the Doctrine and Covenants as section 102 because the order of the council had been shown to Joseph Smith in vision and was according to the order of ancient councils (see Notes and Commentary on D&C 102:4).

## Notes and Commentary

**D&C 102:2, 9-10. The Special Purpose of the First High Council**

In a special item of instruction written for

Melchizedek Priesthood holders, an important distinction was made between the first high council and present stake high councils:

"The first high council in the Church in this dispensation was organized in Kirtland, Ohio, February 17, 1834. This high council was in some particulars different from the high councils in stakes of Zion as they are constituted today. While all that is written in that revelation (D&C 102) in relation to [Church] trials still applies today, it should be remembered that the First Presidency of the Church constituted the presidency of that high council. . . . [See D&C 102:2] This council had wide jurisdiction and was not confined to the borders of a stake. It was not until high councils were organized in stakes as we find them today that stake presidencies presided in their deliberations. . . . Attention is called especially to verses 9 and 10, of section 102. . . .

"We see from this that the first high council had general jurisdiction throughout the Church. Later another high council was organized in Missouri to take care of the problems arising in that distant part of the vineyard. Later when stakes were organized as we have them today a stake presidency was appointed and a complete high council for the stake appointed." ("Melchizedek Priesthood: Further Instructions on Duties of High Councilors and Special Items," *Improvement Era,* Feb. 1955, p. 113.)

### D&C 102:4. High Councils Function "According to the Law of Heaven"

On the day of the organization of the high council, the Prophet Joseph Smith declared that the manner in which the council should function had been revealed to him, as the minutes of that meeting report:

"Bro. Joseph then said he would show the order of councils in ancient days as shown to him by vision. The law by which to govern the council in the Church of Christ. Jerusalem was the seat of the Church Council in ancient days. The apostle, Peter, was the president of the Council and held the keys of the Kingdom of God on the earth was appointed to this office by the voice of the Savior and acknowledged in it by the voice of the Church. . . . It was not the order of heaven in ancient councils to plead for and against the guilty as in our judicial Courts (so called) but that every counsellor when he arose to speak, should speak precisely according to evidence and according to the teaching of the Spirit of the Lord; that no counsellor should attempt to scorn the guilty when his guilt was manifest. That the person accused before the high council had a right to one half the members of the council to plead his cause in order that his case might be fairly presented before the President that a decision might be rendered according to truth and righteousness . . . Bro. Joseph said that this organization was an ensample to the high priests in their Councils abroad. . . . It was then voted by all present that they desired to come under the present order of things which they all considered to be the will of God. ("Kirtland High Council Minute Book," Historical Department, The Church

*A high council is organized in each stake*

of Jesus Christ of Latter-day Saints, Salt Lake City, pp. 29-32.)

On 19 February, when the corrected minutes were presented, Joseph wrote, "We all raised our hands to heaven in token of the everlasting covenant, and the Lord blessed us with His Spirit. I then declared the council organized according to the ancient order, and also according to the mind of the Lord." (*History of the Church,* 2:32-33.)

### D&C 102:6-7. Majority of Council Necessary to Conduct Business

To ensure that enough councilors are available to conduct council business, current Church policy states that permission may be granted to stake presidents by the General Authorities to appoint alternate high councilors. According to the official policy of the Church, a high council court consists of the stake presidency and twelve high councilors. Alternate high councilors may serve on the court in the absence of one of the regular councilors.

### D&C 102:12-22. Procedures Governing the Function of the High Council Court

Since conducting a high council court is an important function of a stake high council, proper order and procedure is important. In the *General Handbook of Instructions,* procedures for stake high council courts are outlined, based on the principles revealed in Doctrine and Covenants 102. Priesthood leaders should follow the guidelines and policies outlined in the handbook.

### D&C 102:18. Rights of the Accuser and the Accused

The Prophet Joseph Smith in 1840 gave instruction for high councils concerning the rights of those involved. He wrote: "The Council should try no case without both parties being present, or having had an opportunity to be present; neither should they hear one person's complaint before his case is brought up for trial; neither should they suffer the character of any one to be exposed before the High Council without the person being present and ready to defend him or herself; that the minds of the councilors be not prejudiced for or against any one whose case they may possibly have to act upon" (*History of the Church,* 4:154).

If the parties fail to appear, the court may proceed on the basis of the available evidence.

### D&C 102:19-22. The Decision Process and the Responsibilities of "Judges"

The Prophet Joseph instructed the brethren in some of the early councils of the Church concerning the strict order of ancient councils and the serious obligation placed upon all who are appointed as judges and counselors to judges:

"No man is capable of judging a matter, in council, unless his own heart is pure; and that we are frequently so filled with prejudice, or have a beam in our own eye, that we are not capable of passing right decisions.

"But to return to the subject of order; in ancient days councils were conducted with such strict propriety, that no one was allowed to whisper, be weary, leave the room, or get uneasy in the least, until the voice of the Lord, by revelation, or the voice of the council by the Spirit, was obtained, which has not been observed in this Church to the present time. It was understood in ancient days, that if one man could stay in council, another could; and if the president could spend his time, the members could also; but in our councils, generally, one will be uneasy, another asleep; one praying, another not; one's mind on the business of the council, and another thinking on something else.

"Our acts are recorded, and at a future day they will be laid before us, and if we should fail to judge right and injure our fellow-beings, they may there, perhaps, condemn us; there they are of great consequence, and to me the consequence appears to be of force, beyond anything which I am able to express. Ask yourselves, brethren, how much you have exercised yourselves in prayer since you heard of this council; and if you are now prepared to sit in council upon the soul of your brother." (*History of the Church,* 2:25-26; see also Enrichment I, in the Appendix.)

### D&C 102:26-27, 33. Record and Appeals from Church Courts

Minutes must be kept of all trials held before a high council. The original copy of the minutes of each trial is sent to the office of the First Presidency of the Church, according to this revelation.

Any person disfellowshipped or excommunicated in a Church court has the right to appeal the decision to higher courts. The decision of a bishop's court may be appealed to a high council court, and the decision of a high council court may be appealed to the First Presidency.

### D&C 102:30-32. What Is the Relationship between the Quorum of the Twelve and the Stake High Councils? Between the High Council and the Stake Presidency?

The instructions of the Prophet Joseph Smith characterize the relationship between the authority and decisions of the Quorum of the Twelve and stake high councils: "No standing High Council has authority to go into the churches abroad, and regulate the matters thereof, for this belongs to the Twelve. No standing High Council will ever be established only in Zion, or one of her stakes." (*History of the Church,* 2:220.)

Later he added: "The High Council had nothing to do with the Twelve, or the decisions of the Twelve. But if the Twelve erred they were accountable only to the General Council of the authorities of the whole Church, according to the revelations." (*History of the Church,* 2:285.)

Speaking of Zion as a stake, the Prophet Joseph declared that "the High Council has been expressly organized to administer in all her spiritual affairs" (*History of the Church,* 2:228). The supporting role of the high council is clearly one of assisting the presidency in a stake, and the high council fulfills assignments as directed by the stake presidency.

In an article on the Melchizedek Priesthood, the function of high councilors was discussed more fully:

"High councilors play a vital role in the administration of the stake. Figuratively speaking, they constitute the right arm of the stake presidency. The degree to which they are faithful, efficient, and willing to work determines their value to the stake presidency and goes far in determining the progress made by the stake and ward organizations in which they have been called to serve.

"The duties and assignments of high councilors are very extensive and varied. Such assignments absorb much time in stakes where the stake presidencies fully utilize their high councilors in carrying forward the Church program. Experience has shown that it is wisdom for stake presidencies to make very extensive use of their high councilors, because the progress of the work of the Lord within a stake and the efficiency with which it is carried forward will be determined to a large extent by the use made of high councilors by the stake presidency." ("Melchizedek Priesthood: Responsibilities of High Councilors," *Improvement Era,* Feb. 1954, p. 112.)

# The Redemption of Zion by Power

Section 103

## Historical Background

During the first week of November 1833, the Saints in Jackson County, Missouri, were driven from their homes and forced across the Missouri River into Clay County, where they were received with some degree of kindness. Elder Parley P. Pratt gave the following account of subsequent events:

"After making our escape into the county of Clay—being reduced to the lowest poverty—I made a living by day labor, jobbing, building, or wood cutting, till some time in the winter of 1834, when a general Conference was held at my house, in which it was decided that two of the Elders should be sent to Ohio, in order to counsel with President Smith and the Church at Kirtland, and take some measures for the relief or restoration of the people thus plundered and driven from their homes. The question was put to the Conference: 'Who would volunteer to perform so great a journey?'

"The poverty of all, and the inclement season of the year made all hesitate. At length Lyman Wight and myself offered our services, which were readily accepted. I was at this time entirely destitute of proper clothing for the journey; and I had neither horse, saddle, bridle, money nor provisions to take with me; or to leave with my wife, who lay sick and helpless most of the time.

"Under these circumstances I knew not what to do. Nearly all had been robbed and plundered, and all were poor. As we had to start without delay, I almost trembled at the undertaking; it seemed to be all but an impossibility; but 'to him that believeth all things are possible.'

". . . We were soon ready, and on the first of February we mounted our horses, and started in good cheer to ride one thousand or fifteen hundred miles through a wilderness country. We had not one cent of money in our pockets on starting.

"We travelled every day, whether through storm or sunshine, mud, rain or snow; except when our public duties called us to tarry. We arrived in Kirtland early in the spring, all safe and sound; we had lacked for nothing on the road, and now had plenty of funds in hand. President Joseph Smith and the Church in Kirtland received us with a hospitality and joy unknown except among the Saints; and much interest was felt there, as well as elsewhere, on the subject of our persecution." (*Autobiography of Parley P. Pratt,* pp. 107-9.)

On 24 February 1834 the high council met in Joseph Smith's home to receive the message brought from Missouri by Elders Pratt and Wight. When the council had been called to order and the opening prayer given by the Prophet Joseph Smith, the two brethren who had come from Missouri reported on the condition of their brethren and sisters in that state.

"In a previous Revelation (Section 101:55-60), it was made known to the Prophet that he would be required, at some future time, to lead 'the strength of mine house' to the land of Zion, in order to 'redeem' it. The Revelation in this Section was received four months and twelve days afterwards, directing him to begin to gather up the strength of the Church for a relief expedition. . . . The messengers from Zion told the Council that the scattered Saints had obtained food and clothing in exchange for labor, and that they were quite comfortable for the time being; but they were grief-stricken because they had been driven from their homes in Zion, and they earnestly desired to know, if possible, how and by what means Zion was to be redeemed. This Revelation [D&C 103], given before the meeting of the Council was held, is an answer to that very question. When the messengers had stated the case, the Prophet had the answer ready. He had prepared to announce that he was going to Zion and that he would call for volunteers to accompany him. The Council endorsed this, and between thirty and forty men volunteered to go, whereupon the Prophet Joseph was elected Commander-in-Chief of the expedition." (Smith and Sjodahl, Commentary, pp. 659-60.)

Four months earlier the Prophet Joseph Smith had received a revelation (D&C 101:55-60) telling him that in some future time he would be required to call the Saints to redeem Zion. Section 103 is the revelation authorizing that call.

## Notes and Commentary

**D&C 103:1-4. Why Did the Lord Permit the Devastations in Jackson County to Occur?**

The Lord gave two reasons why he allowed the Saints in Jackson County to be persecuted: (1) that the cup of iniquity of his enemies might be filled and, therefore, a just judgment brought against them (for similar cases see Alma 14:11; 60:13); and (2) that the Saints "might be chastened for a little season" (D&C 103:4) because of their failure to heed the Lord's commandments. When mob violence had first come to a head in August 1833, the Lord warned that the people of Zion would receive his protection only if they were obedient; if they were not, his judgments would come upon them as well as upon the wicked (see D&C 97:19-27). Even though the mob exhibited greater wickedness, the Saints were chastened by the Lord because "they did not hearken altogether unto the precepts and commandments" which the Lord had given to them (D&C 103:4). They had already been taught that "of him unto whom much is given much is required" (D&C 82:3).

### D&C 103:5-10. The Lord Prospers His People When They Heed His Word and Allows Them to Be Oppressed When They Do Not

Doctrine and Covenants 103:5-10 contains a promise that the Saints would prevail against their enemies from that "very hour" (vs. 5) and "never cease to prevail" (vs. 7) if they were faithful, but that they would be subdued by their enemies if they did not keep their covenants.

In a conference address, President George Q. Cannon discussed the operation of this promise: "There cannot be a doubt in any faithful man's mind concerning the truth of this promise—the promise of victory and deliverance on the one hand, the promise of punishment, disaster and trouble on the other. The Latter-day Saints have in their experience proved fully the truth of these words. They have seen them fulfilled to the very letter. When they have been faithful in keeping the commandments of God they have prospered and they have had deliverance. When they have been unfaithful they met with trouble and serious difficulty. It is necessary that the wicked should have the opportunity to exercise their agency in relation to the work of God; for they have an agency as well as we. It is their privilege to assist in building up the word of God, or they can exercise their agency in fighting the work of God. They have the privilege to do everything in their power to destroy it, and they will be permitted to do this until the cup of their iniquity is full." (In Conference Report, Oct. 1899, p. 48.)

### D&C 103:9-10. Saints Are to Be the Salt of the Earth and the "Saviors of Men"

See Notes and Commentary on Doctrine and Covenants 101:39-42.

### D&C 103:11-14. Will The Saints Actually Return to Build Zion in Jackson County?

Verses 11 through 14 state that the Lord intended to restore his people to their lands from which they were driven, and that they would "no more be thrown down" (D&C 103:13). It is also clear, however, that this restoration would not happen until after a period of "much tribulation" (vs. 12; see also D&C 58:2-4; Notes and Commentary on D&C 58:2-4). The Lord warned the Saints in Doctrine and Covenants 103 that, even though he had promised they could return to the land of Zion, if they "pollute[d] their inheritances" through sin, they would lose the Lord's support and be "thrown down" (vs. 14). Since this revelation was given, many leaders of the Church have discussed the future return to Jackson County, Missouri, including Elder Orson F. Whitney, who said: "Will our mission end here [in Utah]? Is the State of Utah the proper monument of the 'Mormon' People? No. . . . *The monument to 'Mormonism' will stand in Jackson County, Mo.* There the great City will be built: There Zion will arise and shine, 'the joy of the whole Earth,' and there the Lord will come to His temple in His own time, when His people shall have made the required preparation." (In Smith and Sjodahl, Commentary, p. 147; emphasis added.)

*The Big Blue River in Jackson County, Missouri*

President Joseph Fielding Smith taught that "the *center place* where the City New Jerusalem is to be built, is in Jackson County, Missouri. It was never the intention to substitute Utah or any other place for Jackson County." (*Doctrines of Salvation,* 3:72.)

President Brigham Young said that although there will be a return to build up Zion, all the Saints will not go there: "Are we going back to Jackson County? Yes. When? As soon as the way opens up. Are we all going? O no! of course not. The country is not large enough to hold our present numbers." (In *Journal of Discourses,* 18:355.) He also said that "a portion of the Priesthood will go and redeem and build up the centre Stake of Zion" (in *Journal of Discourses,* 11:16).

For other scriptural statements concerning the redemption of Zion, see Doctrine and Covenants 103:15-20; see also Doctrine and Covenants 100:13; 101:17-18, 43-62; 105:1-6, 9-15; 136:18; 3 Nephi 20:22; 21:22-25. Enrichment B, in the Appendix, discusses the concept of Zion as taught in the Doctrine and Covenants.

### D&C 103:15-20. The Lord's People Will Redeem Zion through His Power

Doctrine and Covenants 103:15-20 clearly teaches that Zion will not be redeemed by human strength alone. The Lord said that the redemption of modern Zion will resemble the deliverance of ancient Israel from Egypt (see vss. 18-20). The biblical account describes how the Lord attended Israel in a cloud by day and a pillar of fire by night. In 1873 Elder Orson Pratt taught that the return to Jackson County may be accompanied by similar manifestations:

"I expect that when the Lord leads forth his people to build up the city of Zion, his presence will be visible. When we speak of the presence of the Lord we speak of an exhibition of power. . . .

"We shall go back to Jackson County. Not that all this people will leave these mountains, or all be gathered together in a camp, but when we go back there will be a very large organization consisting of thousands, and tens of thousands, and they will march forward, the glory of God overshadowing their camp by day in the form of a cloud, and a pillar of flaming fire by night, the Lord's voice being uttered forth before his army. Such a period will come in the history of this people. . . . and his people will go forth and build up Zion according to celestial law.

"Will not this produce terror upon all the nations of the earth? Will not armies of this description, though they may not be as numerous as the armies of the world, cause a terror to fall upon the nations? The Lord says the banners of Zion shall be terrible. . . . But when the Lord's presence is there, when his voice is heard, and his angels go before the camp, it will be telegraphed to the uttermost parts of the earth and fear will seize upon all people, especially the wicked, and the knees of the ungodly will tremble in that day, and the high ones that are on high, and the great men of the earth." (In *Journal of Discourses,* 15:364.)

This great army of the Lord will not be like the armies of the world. They will not take possession of the land of Zion by force but will go forth under the protection and guidance of the Almighty God to take possession of that which will be rightfully theirs by purchase. (See topical guide, s.v. "purchase," and Notes and Commentary on D&C 105:28-32.) The Prophet Joseph Smith recorded that his scribe "saw, in a vision, the armies of heaven protecting the Saints in their return to Zion" (*History of the Church,* 2:381).

President Joseph F. Smith described how he saw the return to Jackson County: "When God leads the people back to Jackson County, how will he do it? Let me picture to you how some of us may be gathered and led to Jackson County. I think I see two or three hundred thousand people wending their way across the great plain enduring the nameless hardships of the journey, herding and guarding their cattle by day and by night, and defending themselves and little ones from foes on the right hand and on the left, as when they came here. They will find the journey back to Jackson County will be as real as when they came out here. Now, mark it. And though you may be led by the power of God 'with a stretched out arm,' it will not be more manifest than the leading the people out here to those that participate in it. They will think there are a great many hardships to endure in this manifestation of the power of God, and it will be left, perhaps to their children to see the glory of their deliverance, just as it is left for us to see the glory of our former deliverance, from the hands of those that sought to destroy us. This is one way to look at it. It is certainly a practical view. Some might ask, what will become of the railroads? I fear that the sifting process would be insufficient were we to travel by railroads. We are apt to overlook the manifestations of the power of God to us because we are participators in them, and regard them as commonplace events. But when it is written in history—as it will be written—it will be shown forth to future generations as one of the most marvelous, unexampled and unprecedented accomplishments that has ever been known to history." (In *Journal of Discourses,* 24:156-57.)

**D&C 103:16. Who Is the Man Who Will Lead the Saints As Moses Led Israel?**

The question of who will lead the Saints was answered by Elder John A. Widtsoe, who wrote:

"There have been many conjectures concerning this statement. There have even been misguided men who have declared themselves to be this man 'like as Moses.'

"Yet, the meaning as set forth in the scriptures, is very simple. In modern revelation the President of the Church is frequently compared to Moses. Soon after the organization of the Church, the Lord said, 'no one shall be appointed to receive commandments and revelations in this church excepting my servant Joseph Smith, Jun., for he receiveth them even as Moses' (D. & C. 28:2) In one of the great revelations upon Priesthood, this is more specifically expressed: 'the duty of the President of the office of the High Priesthood is to preside over the whole church, and to be like unto Moses' (D&C 107:91). . . .

"The man like unto Moses in the Church is the President of the Church." (*Evidences and Reconciliations,* 1:197.)

**D&C 103:19-20. Why Did the Lord Promise Modern Israel That His Angel and His Personal Presence Would Go before Them?**

The Lord sought to make ancient Israel "a kingdom of priests, and an holy nation" (Exodus 19:6). He told his prophet Moses to prepare the people so that he might "come down in the sight of all the people upon Mount Sinai" (Exodus 19:11). The people saw the power of God manifested when he presented himself before Moses on the mount, and they were fearful. They asked that the Lord not speak directly with them but rather that Moses speak with God and bring his message to them (see Exodus 10:18-21; Deuteronomy 5:22-31). Despite Moses' efforts to sanctify his people, they would not prepare themselves to see God by living the higher laws that would enable them to become a holy nation. Therefore, they were given the "law of carnal commandments" (D&C 84:27) and were led, no longer by the Lord's immediate presence, but by his angels (see D&C 84:23-26; Exodus 23:20; JST, Exodus 34:1-2).

In the final dispensation these circumstances will not exist. Latter-day Saints have been given the higher priesthood and the laws and ordinances that enable men to be brought back into the presence of God (see D&C 84:19-22; 107:18-19). There will be a pure people prepared to receive the Lord when he comes (see Moses 7:62-64; D&C 35:20-21; 100:16). Those who return to redeem Zion will live the laws of the celestial kingdom (see D&C 105:5) and thus will be prepared to be led by the presence of the Lord.

Elder Orson Pratt spoke of the need to become a sanctified people. "When we go back to Jackson County, we are to go back with power. Do you suppose that God will reveal his power among an unsanctified people, who have no regard nor respect for his laws and institutions, but who are filled with covetousness? No. When God shows forth his power among the Latter-day Saints, it will be because there is a union of feeling in regard to doctrine, and in regard to everything that God has placed in their hands; and not only a union, but a sanctification on their part, that there shall not be a spot or wrinkle as it were, but everything shall be as fair as the sun that shines in the heavens." (In *Journal of Discourses*, 15:361.)

### D&C 103:20. Zion Was Not to Be Redeemed in 1834

"In time ye shall possess the goodly land" (D&C 103:20). These words pronounced by the Lord in 1834 do not presage an immediate redemption of Zion. Rather, they seem to imply a period somewhat distant in time to that moment.

President Joseph Fielding Smith explained the implications of the phrase "in time": "It appears from this declaration that the redemption of Zion was not to come immediately, but was to be postponed to some future day. Moreover, that day would not come until the members of the Church were willing to keep their covenants and walk unitedly, for until the members of the Church learn to walk in full accord and in obedience with all of the commandments, this day cannot come. It may be necessary in order to bring this to pass for the Lord to use drastic measures and cleanse the Church from everything that offends. This he has promised to do when he is ready to redeem Zion. (See Matt. 13:41.)" (*Church History and Modern Revelation*, 1:484.)

### D&C 103:21-28, 30-35. The Call of Zion's Camp

The Lord issued a call to the young and middle-aged men of the Church to gather upon the land of Zion and "avenge me of mine enemies" (D&C 103:25). This passage sounds very much like a call to arms, for the Lord added, "Let no man be afraid to lay down his life for my sake" (vs. 27). Such were the beginnings of the army later known as Zion's Camp.

Several men were called to go on a journey to recruit men and obtain money for Zion's Camp. They were commanded to try to enlist 500 men but to recruit no fewer than 100 men. As it turned out, some 204 men (and eleven women and seven children) volunteered.

President Joseph Fielding Smith commented on the organization of Zion's Camp: "Parley P. Pratt and Lyman Wight, the messengers from the land of Zion, were commanded not to return until they had obtained companies to go up unto the land of their brethren. The companies were to be by tens, or by twenties, or by fifties, or by hundreds, until they had obtained the number of five hundred men. If they could not obtain five hundred, they were to seek diligently to get three hundred, and if they could not obtain three hundred, then they were to obtain one hundred. They were not, however, to go up to the land of Zion until they had obtained at least one hundred. The Prophet Joseph was to go up with them and preside in their midst, for, 'all victory and glory is brought to pass unto you

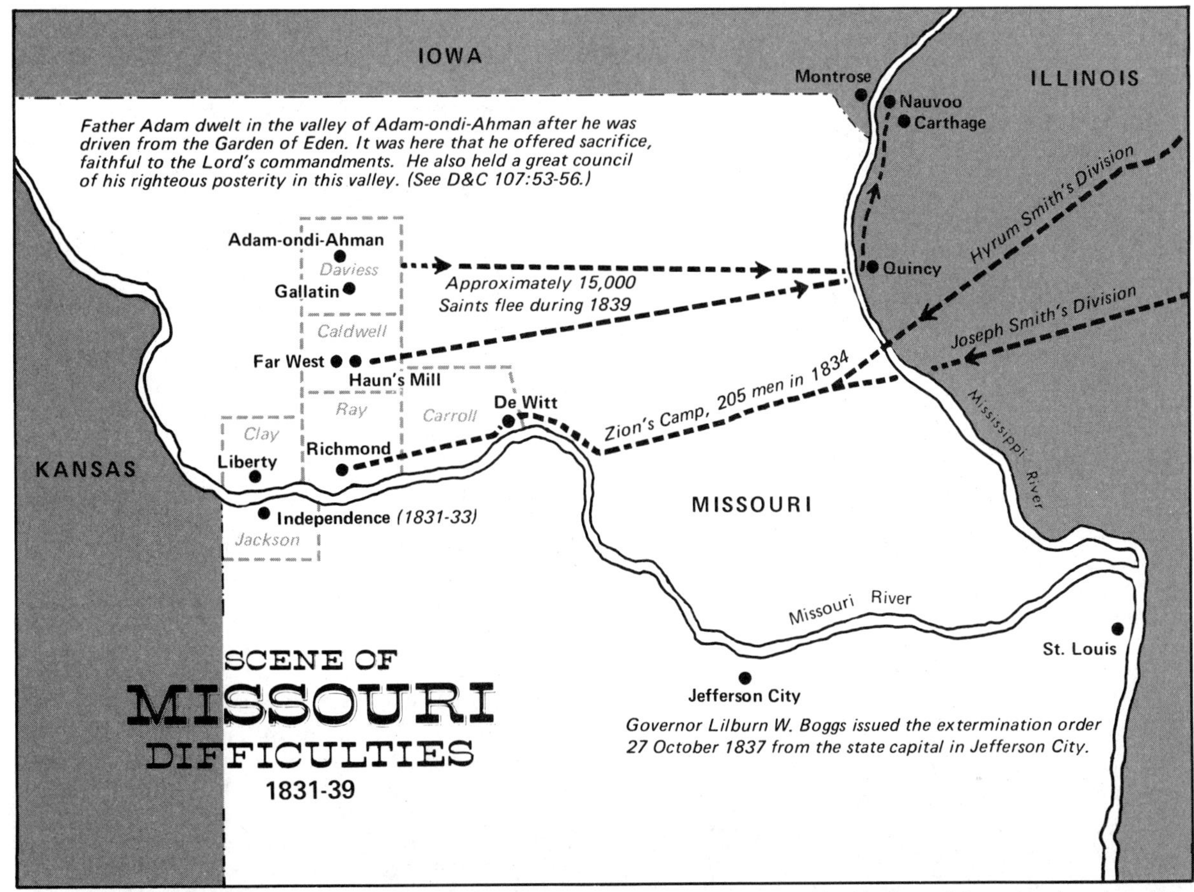


*The movements of the Saints during the Missouri difficulties (map adapted from Carter Eldredge Grant,* I Saw Another Angel Fly *[Salt Lake City: Deseret Book Co., 1959], p. 159)*

through your diligence, faithfulness and prayer of faith.' Parley P. Pratt was to go with Joseph Smith the Prophet; Lyman Wight with Sidney Rigdon; Hyrum Smith with Frederick G. Williams; Orson Hyde with Orson Pratt, on this mission to raise funds and volunteers to undertake this journey to assist their exiled brethren in the land of Zion." (*Church History and Modern Revelation,* 1:485.)

At first this situation appears to be a paradox. The Lord said that Zion must be redeemed by God's power; then he called upon the Saints to exercise their power, even to armed conflict and loss of life, if necessary, to redeem Zion. The situation, however, was not truly paradoxical, but it is characteristic of the way God works with his children. Only his power is sufficient to save, and yet his showing forth of that power depends directly on man's efforts and obedience.

**D&C 103:27-28. Why Does the Lord Require from His People a Willingness to Sacrifice All, Even Their Lives If Necessary?**

For a discussion of sacrifice see Notes and Commentary on Doctrine and Covenants 58:2-4.

**D&C 103:31. Who Is to Blame When One Does Not Get What He Desires from the Lord?**

When one does do not receive what he desires from the Lord, he has only himself to blame. The Lord says, "Ask and ye shall receive; but men do not always do my will" (D&C 103:31).

One must determine what the will of the Lord is. He expects the individual to be purified and cleansed from sin before asking (see D&C 50:28-29). Each individual needs to be sure that the thing he is asking is right before he asks (see 3 Nephi 18:20). One should resist evil and submit himself in obedience to the Lord before he can expect the Lord's blessings to be poured out (see James 4:7).

# The Order of the Church for the Benefit of the Poor

Section 104

## Historical Background

In April 1834 the men of the Church in Kirtland prepared to travel to Independence, Missouri, to redeem Zion and reestablish the Saints upon their lands there. At that time the Church was in great financial distress. Brethren had been sent out by the Prophet to collect funds to relieve the burden on Kirtland and Zion. (A strong appeal to Orson Hyde, who was in New York, is given under the date of 7 April 1834 in *History of the Church,* 2:48.)

In accordance with a revelation given in March 1832, all the Latter-day Saint communities in Ohio and Missouri were seeking to implement the united order under one administrative head (see D&C 78:3; Barrett, *Joseph Smith,* p. 198). The economic problems in Kirtland, however, made it advisable to dissolve the united order there. Accordingly, on 10 April a council of the united order was held "in which it was agreed that the Order [in Kirtland] should be dissolved, and each one have his stewardship set off to him" (*History of the Church,* 2:49).

On 23 April 1834 the Prophet Joseph Smith received Doctrine and Covenants 104, which has as its central theme the Lord's instructions concerning the temporal welfare of Zion and the order of the Church for the benefit of the poor: "Assembled in Council with Elders Sidney Rigdon, Frederick G. Williams, Newel K. Whitney, John Johnson, and Oliver Cowdery; and united in asking the Lord to give Elder Zebedee Coltrin influence over Brother Jacob Myres, to obtain the money which he has gone to borrow for us, or cause him to come to this place and bring it himself. I also received the following: [D&C 104]." (*History of the Church,* 2:54.)

## Notes and Commentary

**D&C 104:1-10. The United Order Was Established by Covenant**

The Lord explained that the united order was established for the benefit of the Church and the "salvation of men" until the second coming of Christ (D&C 104:1). All who entered into the order did so with a "promise immutable and unchangeable" (vs. 2). To enter the united order required that a man enter into a solemn covenant to accept the law of consecration, the principles of which are discussed in Enrichment L, in the Appendix. The law of consecration is the law of the celestial kingdom, and those who entered into the order were bound by a covenant, obedience to which would bring eternal exaltation and neglect of which would bring severe judgments. The Lord described the serious consequences of breaking this law in Doctrine and Covenants 78:11-12; 82:21; 101:3-10.

**D&C 104:9. What Are "the Buffetings of Satan"?**

Elder Bruce R. McConkie wrote that "to be turned over to the *buffetings of Satan* is to be given into his hands; it is to be turned over to him with all the protective power of the priesthood, of righteousness, and of godliness removed, so that Lucifer is free to torment, persecute, and afflict such a person without let or hindrance. When the bars are down, the cuffs and curses of Satan, both in this world and in the world to come, bring indescribable anguish typified by burning fire and brimstone. The damned in hell so suffer.

"Those who broke their covenants in connection with the United Order in the early days of this dispensation were to 'be delivered over to the buffetings of Satan until the day of redemption.' (D. & C. 78:12; 82:20-21; 104:9-10.) A similar fate (plus destruction in the flesh) is decreed against those who have been sealed up unto eternal life so that their callings and elections have been made sure and who thereafter turn to grievous sin. (D. & C. 131:5, 132:19-26.)" (*Mormon Doctrine,* p. 108.)

**D&C 104:13-15. The Lord Created the Earth and All Things Thereon, All of Which Are His**

As creator and provider of all things, the Lord has given man the stewardship to manage the earth and make it productive. Though arrangements are made between men for the use and transfer of the things of the earth, ultimately all things belong to the Lord. Elder Spencer W. Kimball gave the following account of a discussion with a friend about his property, which makes clear the truth concerning ownership of the earth and its resources:

"He drove to a grassy knoll. The sun was retiring behind the distant hills. He surveyed his vast domain. Pointing to the north, he asked, 'Do you see that clump of trees yonder?' I could plainly discern them in the fading day.

"He pointed to the east. 'Do you see the lake shimmering in the sunset?' It too was visible.

" 'Now, the bluff that's on the south.' We turned about to scan the distance. He identified barns, silos, the ranch house to the west. With a wide sweeping gesture, he boasted, 'From the clump of trees, to the lake, to the bluff, and to the ranch buildings and all between—all this is mine.' . . .

"And then I asked from whom he obtained it. The chain of title of his abstract went back to land grants from governments. His attorney had assured him he had an unencumbered title.

" 'From whom did the government get it?' I asked. 'What was paid for it?'

"There came into my mind the bold statement of Paul: 'For the earth is the Lord's, and the fulness thereof.' (I Cor. 10:26.) . . .

"And then I asked, 'Did title come from God, Creator of the earth and the owner thereof? Did he get paid? Was it sold or leased or given to you? If gift, from whom? If sale, with what exchange or currency? If lease, do you make proper accounting?'

"And then I asked, 'What was the price? With what treasures did you buy this farm?'

" 'Money!'

" 'Where did you get the money?'

" 'My toil, my sweat, my labor, and my strength.'

"And then I asked, 'Where did you get your strength to toil, your power to labor, your glands to sweat?'

"He spoke of food.

" 'Where did the food originate?'

" 'From sun and atmosphere and soil and water.'

" 'And who brought those elements here?'

"I quoted the psalmist: 'Thou, O God, didst send a plentiful rain, whereby thou didst confirm thine inheritance, when it was weary.' (Ps. 68:9.)

" 'If the land is not yours, then what accounting do you make to your landlord for his bounties?' . . .

"I said again: 'I seem to find no place in holy writ where God has said, "I give you title to this land unconditionally. It is now yours to give, to have, to hold, to sell, despoil, exploit as you see fit."

" 'I cannot find such scripture, but I do find this from Psalms: " . . . those that wait upon the Lord, . . . shall inherit the earth." ' (Ps. 37:9.)

" 'And I remember that our Creator covenanted in the council in heaven with us all: "We will go down, for there is space there, and we will take of these materials, and we will make an earth whereon these may dwell." (Abr. 3:24.)

" 'It seems more of a lease on which a rental is exacted than of a fee simple title.' " (In Conference Report, Apr. 1968, pp. 73-74.)

The relationship of this principle to the united order and the law of consecration was succinctly stated by President J. Reuben Clark, Jr.: "The basic principle of all the revelations on the United Order is that everything we have belongs to the Lord; therefore, the Lord may call upon us for any and all of the property which we have, because it belongs to him. This, I repeat, is the basic principle. (D. & C. 104:14-17, 54-57.)" (*Church News,* 1 Sept. 1945, p. 4.)

President Spencer W. Kimball explained the extent of an individual's personal stewardships and the purpose for which they are to be used:

"In the Church a stewardship is a sacred spiritual or temporal trust for which there is accountability. Because all things belong to the Lord, we are stewards over our bodies, minds, families, and properties. (See D&C 104:11-15.) A faithful steward is one who exercises righteous dominion, cares for his own, and looks to the poor and needy. (See D&C 104:15-18.)

"These principles govern welfare services activities. May we all learn, obey, and teach these principles. Leaders, teach them to your members; fathers, teach them to your families. Only as we apply these truths can we approach the ideal of Zion." (In Conference Report, Oct. 1977, pp. 124-25; or *Ensign,* Nov. 1977, p. 78).

**D&C 104:15-16, 18. "It Must Needs Be Done in Mine Own Way"**

President Marion G. Romney explained the relationship between the Lord's ownership of all things and man's stewardship in caring for the poor Saints in the Lord's way: "The Lord claims the earth as his, that it is not yours and mine to own and manage independently of him. No matter how many stocks and bonds or how much land and other properties we possess, they are not wholly ours. They are the Lord's. He further says that he owns and gives to us all the blessings we have and that he makes us stewards over them, responsible to him. He makes it clear that it is his purpose to provide for his Saints, but he requires that it be done in his way, which way, he explains, is for those who *have* to contribute to those who *have not.* Having made us stewards, he gives us our agency, however, and then lays down the condition that if we accept these blessings and refuse to contribute our share for the care of the poor, we shall go to— well, he tells us where we shall go." (In Conference Report, Apr. 1979, p. 136; or *Ensign,* May 1979, pp. 95-96.)

President Harold B. Lee explained how "the poor shall be exalted" and "the rich . . . made low" (D&C 104:16): "When I tell you that the poor shall be exalted, the definition we followed is, 'to be lifted up to pride and joy to success.' That is the definition we followed, and the rich being made low isn't communistic, it isn't socialistic. It means that those who have leadership, who have skills, who have means, that are willing to contribute, we put that strong man to work with the one who is in need, and we go to work on their problems." (*Church News,* 8 July 1961, p. 15.)

### D&C 104:17. "The Earth Is Full, and There Is Enough and to Spare"

President Ezra Taft Benson explained that those who question the validity of section 104, verse 17, especially as the population of the earth continues to increase, are in error:

"The precepts of men would have you believe that by limiting the population of the world, we can have peace and plenty. That is the doctrine of the devil. Small numbers do not insure peace; only righteousness does. After all, there were only a handful of men on the earth when Cain interrupted the peace of Adam's household by slaying Abel. On the other hand, the whole city of Enoch was peaceful; and it was taken into heaven because it was made up of righteous people.

"And so far as limiting the population in order to provide plenty is concerned, the Lord answered that falsehood in the Doctrine and Covenants when he said:

" 'For the earth is full, and there is enough and to spare; yea, I prepared all things, and have given unto the children of men to be agents unto themselves.' (D&C 104:17.)

"A major reason why there is famine in some parts of the world is because evil men have used the vehicle of government to abridge the freedom that men need to produce abundantly.

"True to form, many of the people who desire to frustrate God's purposes of giving mortal tabernacles to his spirit children through worldwide birth control are the very same people who support the kinds of government that perpetuate famine. They advocate an evil to cure the results of the wickedness they support." (In Conference Report, Apr. 1969, p. 12.)

### D&C 104:19-46. "And Now, . . . Concerning the Properties of the Order"

Smith and Sjodahl wrote: "Specific directions are here given for stewardships. Sidney Rigdon is given charge of the tannery (v. 20). He had, at one time, been engaged in the very useful business of a tanner and was competent in this stewardship. Martin Harris, who was a successful farmer, is given charge of a piece of land (v. 24). He was also to manage a publication business, under the direction of the Prophet (v. 26). Oliver Cowdery and Frederick G. Williams are given charge of the printing office (v. 30). John Johnson is to be a real estate agent (v. 36). Newel K. Whitney is assigned to the mercantile establishment (v. 39). Joseph Smith is given charge of the Temple lot (v. 43). He is also to take care of his father (v. 45), for the Lord recognizes the duty of children to provide for their parents, as well as the duty of parents to care for their children." (Commentary, p. 673.)

### D&C 104:47-53. Why Was the Partnership between the United Orders of Kirtland and Zion Dissolved?

President Joseph Fielding Smith explained that the "distance was too great between [Kirtland and Jackson County] for unity of purpose in all things. Each order was to be organized in the names of the brethren residing in each place, and to do business in their own names. This separation and dissolving of the former order came about also because of transgression and covetousness on the part of some. They were to understand that all the properties were the Lord's, otherwise their faith was vain, and therefore they were stewards before the Lord. All of this was to be done for the purpose of building up the Church and Kingdom of God on the earth, and to prepare the people for the time when the Lord should come to dwell upon the earth." (*Church History and Modern Revelation,* 1:489-90.)

*The four standard works are witnesses for Christ*

**D&C 104:58-59. Why Did the Lord Specify Why He Wanted the Revelations Printed?**

The Lord commanded the members of the united order to publish his revelations and then specified why. The revelations are given "for the purpose of building up my church and kingdom on the earth, and to prepare my people for the time when I shall dwell with them" (D&C 104:59). President Joseph F. Smith, after speaking of the Bible and the Book of Mormon and how they bear witness of Jesus as the Christ, added: "But is this all? No. We have here another book, the 'Doctrine and Covenants,' which contains revelations from God through the Prophet Joseph Smith, who lived contemporary with ourselves. They are Christ's words, declaring that he was the same that came to the Jews, that was lifted up on the cross, was laid in the tomb, burst the bands of death and came forth out of the grave. . . . Here, then is another testimony of this divine truth; hence we have three witnesses." (In *Journal of Discourses,* 19:262.)

**D&C 104:60-70. Why Did the Lord Prescribe That Two Treasuries Be Established?**

President J. Reuben Clark, Jr., discussed the purpose of the treasuries and how the principles are applied in the Church today:

"The Lord created two other institutions besides the storehouse: one was known as the Sacred Treasury, into which was put 'the avails of the sacred things in the treasury, for sacred and holy purposes.' While it is not clear, it would seem that into this treasury were to be put the surpluses which were derived from the publication of the revelations, the Book of Mormon, the Pearl of Great Price, and other similar things, the stewardship of which had been given to Joseph and others. (D. & C. 104:60-66)

"The Lord also provided for the creation of 'Another Treasury,' and into that other treasury went the general revenues which came to the Church, such as gifts of money and those revenues derived from the improvement of stewardships as distinguished from the residues of the original consecrations and the surpluses which came from the operation of their stewardships. (D. & C. 72:11ff) . . .

"We have in place of the two treasuries, the 'Sacred Treasury' and 'Another Treasury,' the general funds of the Church.

"Thus you will see, brethren, that in many of its great essentials, we have, as the Welfare Plan has now developed, the broad essentials of the United Order." (In Conference Report, Oct. 1942, pp. 56-58.)

**D&C 104:71-77. How Were the Sacred Funds to Be Administered?**

Money from the treasury was to be spent only with the common consent of the members of the order. There was to be no unrighteous dominion in the work of the Lord. If the Lord's properties were managed properly, it was probable that the treasury would eventually have a large amount of money in it. Such funds, used for righteous purposes, could truly bless all members of the order.

"[This fund would be] equal to the most extreme emergencies," explained President Lorenzo Snow. "Then when any misfortune befalls man, such as the burning of his property, or failure or trouble in his department of business, he could go to the treasurer and say, 'I have need of a certain amount to assist me in my stewardship. Have I not managed the affairs of my stewardship in a wise manner? Can you not have confidence in me? Have I ever misused the means put into my hands? Has it not been wisely controlled? If so, give me means to help me in my stewardship, or to build up this industry that is needed for the general interests of the whole.' Well, it is to be given to him. There is confidence reposed in him because of his past conduct, and the course which he has pursued. He has due right in exercising his talents according to the light of the spirit that is within him. He understands fully the circumstances in which he is placed, and governs himself according to the obligations that rest upon him. He is found to be a wise, economical manager; and he is assisted in his stewardship to the extent of the means that he should have." (In *Journal of Discourses,* 20:370-71.)

**D&C 104:78-80. "Humble Yourselves. . . . I Will Soften the Hearts of Those to Whom You Are in Debt"**

Very often when a person faces a great challenge in his life, he attempts to work it out through his own efforts. Such self-reliance is commendable, but there is another principle that may apply, and that is reliance on the Lord. An excellent case in point is that of Alma the Younger. The angel said to Alma the Younger, when he appeared to Alma and the four sons of Mosiah, that he had been sent because "the Lord hath heard the prayers of his people, and also the prayers of his servant, Alma, who is thy father" (Mosiah 27:14).

Alma the Elder, realizing that he had a serious problem with his rebellious son, exercised great faith and prayed with great diligence. He called on the power of God for help. The added power from God solved his problem.

In Doctrine and Covenants 104:78-80, the Lord teaches the same principle. Though the debts must have seemed almost insurmountable to them, the leaders were commanded to "obtain this blessing by your diligence and humility and the prayer of faith" (vs. 79). If they would do that, the Lord would keep his promise to "soften the hearts" of those to whom they were in debt (vs. 80).

**D&C 104:78, 83. "Pay All Your Debts. . . . You Shall Be Delivered This Once Out of Your Bondage"**

President N. Eldon Tanner provided direction to the Saints to help them avoid unnecessary debt. Most who have such difficulties do so because they do not establish proper gospel priorities for their financial stewardship.

"For most of us there are two kinds of financial debt—consumer debt and investment or business debt. Consumer debt refers to buying on credit those things we use or consume in daily living. Examples would include installment buying of clothes, appliances, furniture, etc. Consumer debt is secured by mortgaging our future earnings. This can be very dangerous. If we are laid off work, disabled, or encounter serious emergencies, we have difficulties meeting our obligations. Installment buying is the most expensive way to purchase. To the cost of the goods we buy must be added heavy interest and handling charges.

"I realize that young families find it necessary at times to purchase on credit. But we caution you not to buy more than is truly necessary and to pay off your debts as quickly as possible. When money is tight, avoid the extra burden of additional interest charges.

"Investment debt should be fully secured so as not to encumber a family's security. Don't invest in speculative ventures. The spirit of speculation can become intoxicating. Many fortunes have been wiped out by the uncontrolled appetite to accumulate more and more. Let us learn from the sorrows of the past and avoid enslaving our time, energy, and general health to a gluttonous appetite to acquire increased material goods.

"President Kimball has given this thought-provoking counsel:

" 'The Lord has blessed us as a people with a prosperity unequaled in times past. The resources

*Installment buying is attractive, but Latter-day Saints should avoid debt as they would a plague*

that have been placed in our power are good, and necessary to our work here on the earth. But I am afraid that many of us have been surfeited with flocks and herds and acres and barns and wealth and have begun to worship them as false gods, and they have power over us. Do we have more of these good things than our faith can stand? Many people spend most of their time working in the service of a self-image that includes sufficient money, stocks, bonds, investment portfolios, property, credit cards, furnishings, automobiles, and the like to *guarantee carnal* security throughout, it is hoped, a long and happy life. Forgotten is the fact that our assignment is to use these many resources in our families and quorums to build up the kingdom of God' (*Ensign*, June 1976, p. 4).

"By way of testimony, may I add this to President Kimball's statement. I know of no situation where happiness and peace of mind have increased with the amassing of property beyond the reasonable wants and needs of the family." (In Conference Report, Oct. 1979, p. 120; or *Ensign*, Nov. 1979, p. 81-82.)

Elder Franklin D. Richards taught five principles for freeing oneself from debt:

"In getting out of debt and staying out of debt, there are certain basic principles that we, as individuals and families, can apply, such as:

"1. Live within your income.

"2. Prepare and use short- and long-term budgets.

"3. Regularly save a part of your income.

"4. Use your credit wisely, if it is necessary to use it at all. For example, a reasonable debt may be justified for the acquisition of a home or education.

"5. Preserve and utilize your assets through appropriate tax and estate planning.

"I know that by following these simple, basic principles it is possible to get out of debt and stay out of debt.

"What will this mean to us as individuals and families?

"President Heber J. Grant said, 'If there is any one thing that will bring peace and contentment into the human heart, and into the family, it is to live within our means, and if there is any one thing that is grinding, and discouraging and disheartening it is to have debts and obligations that one cannot meet' (*Relief Society Magazine*, May 1932, p. 302)." (In Conference Report, Apr. 1979, p. 56; or *Ensign*, May 1979, p. 39.)

# Revelation to Zion's Camp

Section 105

## Historical Background

In October and November 1833, the Saints in Jackson County, Missouri, were driven from their homes by mobs. "A revelation was given to Joseph Smith December 16, 1833, giving the reason for the expulsion of the members of the Church from Jackson County (see D&C 101:1-9)" (Smith, *Essentials in Church History,* p. 142).

As part of that revelation the Saints were instructed, through a parable, to "gather together the strength of the Lord's house, 'My young men and they that are middle aged also among all my servants, who are the strength of mine house, save those only whom I have appointed to tarry,' said the Lord, 'and go straightway unto the land of my vineyard, and redeem my vineyard, for it is mine, I have bought it with money.' " (Smith, *Essentials in Church History,* p. 143.) The parable was explained to Joseph Smith in a revelation on 24 February 1834 (see D&C 103:21-34).

Accordingly, "Joseph Smith met with the High Council in Kirtland on February 24, 1834. The subject uppermost in the minds of everyone present was how could they relieve and rescue the Saints from the mobbers in Zion. At the meeting attended by about forty others, the group listened attentively to Parley P. Pratt and Lyman Wight, newly arrived from Zion, pleading that the Saints there be succored.

"All were quiet when the Prophet arose and stated that in response to a revelation, he intended to go to Zion to assist in redeeming it. He asked for council sanction. There was unanimous assent. He called for volunteers. Forty hands were raised. . . .

"The revelation to which the Prophet referred instructed him to do his best to recruit five hundred men. They were to be young and middle-aged. If, perchance because of poor response, he should have to accept less, he was not to start until he had a minimum of one hundred. Led by Joseph Smith and Parley P. Pratt, four pairs of elders were to seek volunteers to go to the redemption of Zion. Within two days Joseph and Parley were on their way east seeking volunteers and friends. For a month they labored diligently to obtain the required help. By that time there were 125 who had volunteered to go." (Young, *"Here Is Brigham . . . ,"* p. 89.)

When ready to start from Kirtland, the group consisted of about 150 men. This number increased to about 200 by the time the camp arrived in Missouri (see Roberts, *Comprehensive History of the Church,* 1:358).

Zion's Camp arrived at Fishing River, Missouri, on 19 June 1834. Two days later, "on Saturday, the 21st of June, Colonel Scounce and two other leading men of Ray County visited Joseph, and

*A campsite of Zion's Camp near present-day Excelsior Springs, Missouri*

begged to know his intentions, stating: 'We see that there is an Almighty Power that protects this people.' Colonel Scounce confessed that he had been leading a company of armed men to fall upon the Prophet, but had been driven back by the storm. The Prophet with all the mildness and dignity which ever sat so becomingly upon him, and which always impressed his hearers, answered that he had come to administer to the wants of his afflicted friends and did not wish to molest or injure anybody. He then made a full and fair statement of the difficulties as he understood them; and when he had closed the three ambassadors, melted into compassion, offered their hands and declared that they would use every endeavor to allay the excitement." (Cannon, *Life of Joseph Smith,* p. 180.)

"On the arrival of the camp in the vicinity of Jackson county, negotiations were opened with Governor Dunklin asking him to fulfill his promise to call out the militia in sufficient numbers to reinstate the exiled saints in their possessions. The governor admitted the justice of the demand, but expressed the fear that should he so proceed his action would excite civil war, and he dared not carry out what he admitted to be the plain duties of his office. He suggested that the delegation that waited upon him urge their brethren to sell their lands in Jackson county. This the saints could not do without repudiating the revelations that designated Jackson county as the land of their inheritance, the place for the gathering together of God's people, and the location of the city of Zion; also it meant an abandonment of their right as citizens of the United States to settle wherever they thought proper to make their homes within the confines of the Union.

"With the governor unwilling to fulfill his

engagements to the exiles by calling out the militia to reinstate them in their lands; with the inhabitants of western Missouri deeply prejudiced against them, and greatly excited by the arrival of Zion's Camp; and the brethren of the camp, and the exiled brethren, painfully conscious that the saints in the eastern branches of the church had not responded with either sufficient money or men for them to act independently of the governor, take possession of their lands, purchase other lands, and hold them despite the violence of mobs—the necessity of disbanding Zion's camp, and awaiting some future opportunity for the redemption of Zion, was apparent to the minds of its leaders. Accordingly it was disbanded from its encampment on Rush Creek, in Clay county, on the 24th of June, and word to that effect was officially sent to some of the leading citizens of Clay county." (Roberts, *Comprehensive History of the Church,* 1:359.)

Although the avowed purpose of the camp (to reinstate the Saints to their lands in Zion) was not realized, it was definitely not an exercise in futility, but rather served as the forge in which the Lord tempered the steel of many of his early leaders, including the Quorum of the Twelve Apostles.

Elder Delbert L. Stapley said: "Zion's Camp was disbanded on June 24, 1834. It had furnished the know-how and experience which made possible the subsequent exodus of more than 20,000 men, women, and children from Nauvoo to the Rocky Mountains, and prepared leaders for the great exodus. It also provided a proving ground—some 1,000 miles of it—for the future Church leaders. This is evidenced by the fact that when the Quorum of the Twelve Apostles was 'searched out' by the three witnesses to the Book of Mormon, all chosen had been members of Zion's Camp. These men had demonstrated their willingness to sacrifice everything, even life itself, when commanded by the Lord. The First Quorum of the Seventy was likewise made up of the men who followed the Prophet to Missouri in Zion's Camp." (*The Importance of Church History,* Brigham Young University Speeches of the Year [Provo, 15 Apr. 1970], p. 3.)

## Notes and Commentary

### D&C 105:1-2. Why Was Zion's Redemption Postponed?

President Lorenzo Snow taught that "the Saints in Jackson County and other localities, refused to comply with the order of consecration, consequently they were allowed to be driven from their inheritances; and should not return until they were better prepared to keep the law of God, by being more perfectly taught in reference to their duties, and learn through experience the necessity of obedience. And I think we are not justified in anticipating the privilege of returning to build up the center stake of Zion, until we shall have shown obedience to the law of consecration. One thing, however, is certain, we shall not be permitted to enter the land from whence we were expelled, till our hearts are prepared to honor this law, and we become sanctified through the practice of the truth." (In *Journal of Discourses,* 16:276; see also Notes and Commentary on D&C 101:1-8; 96:1.)

### D&C 105:4-5. Upon What Principles Is Zion to Be Built?

The Saints in Missouri were not successful in living a celestial law; therefore, they were not qualified to establish Zion. Failure to control their hearts (inward victory) cut them off from drawing on God's full power and made them unable to gain temporal freedom from their enemies (outward victory). This is the concept the Lord tried to teach them when he said, "This is Zion—THE PURE IN HEART" (D&C 97:21).

Only when the heart is pure can a man embrace and magnify celestial law. Celestial law, according to Elder Bruce R. McConkie, "is the law of the gospel, the law of Christ, and it qualifies men for admission to the celestial kingdom because in and through it men are 'sanctified by the reception of the Holy Ghost,' thus becoming clean, pure, and spotless" (*Mormon Doctrine,* p. 117). Elder McConkie also said: "If a man obeys celestial law in this life, he obtains a celestial body and spirit," thus enabling that man to live in unity with his God and his fellowmen (*Mormon Doctrine,* p. 115).

Elder Joseph F. Smith explained the importance of living a celestial law: "Those who profess to be Latter-day Saints must become acquainted with the laws of the celestial kingdom, must abide by them, must comply with the requirements of heaven and hearken to the word of the Lord, in order that Zion may be built up acceptably, and that we may partake of the benefits and blessings of this labor. For it is a labor which devolves upon those who have been called out from the midst of the world in this dispensation. We have been called, and so far as we will be faithful we are chosen to do this work. But notwithstanding we have been called, if we do not prove faithful we will be rejected. I do not speak this in reference to the whole Church, but in reference to individual members of the Church." (In Conference Report, Apr. 1880, p. 34; see also Smith, *Church History and Modern Revelation,* 2:3-4.)

### D&C 105:9-12. How Long Will the Lord Wait to Redeem Zion?

The Lord chooses to honor the agency of men, and he chooses to accomplish his work through mortals; therefore, men's wickedness or righteousness impedes or accelerates the work. In Doctrine and Covenants 105 the Lord identified preparation as essential to the establishment of Zion:

1. The leaders may be prepared (see vss. 9-10).
2. The Saints must be taught more perfectly what the Lord requires of them (see vs. 10).
3. The Saints must gain experience (see vs. 10). No one can know the things of God without doing them (see John 7:17).
4. The Saints must know their duty more perfectly (see D&C 105:10).
5. The Saints must be endowed with power from on high (see vs. 11).

6. The Saints must be faithful, enduring in humility to the end (see vs. 12).

President J. Reuben Clark, Jr., taught that the principles of the welfare system "are not too far away" from the united order, and that the Saints need to add to them "brotherly love" and "provide the things which those who are in need, must have" (*Church News*, 8 Aug. 1951, p. 15).

### D&C 105:11-12. What Is an Endowment?

An endowment is a gift given by one to another. There are many gifts given by God to his children (see Notes and Commentary on D&C 93:11-17 for the relationship between grace and gifts). The word *endowment* as it is used in Doctrine and Covenants 105:12 seems to refer to the temple ordinances, which also are called an endowment.

President Brigham Young explained what this gift or endowment of power will ultimately enable the Saints to do: "Your endowment is, to receive all those ordinances in the house of the Lord, which are necessary for you, after you have departed this life, to enable you to walk back to the presence of the Father, passing the angels who stand as sentinels, being enabled to give them the key words, the signs and tokens, pertaining to the holy Priesthood, and gain your eternal exaltation in spite of earth and hell" (*Discourses of Brigham Young*, p. 416).

Why would the brethren who were to establish Zion be required to receive an endowment in preparation for their stewardships? Because, as the Prophet Joseph Smith taught, "the endowment was to prepare the disciples for their missions unto the world" (*Teachings*, p. 274).

Elder Joseph Fielding Smith further taught:

"If we go into the temple we raise our hands and covenant that we will serve the Lord and observe his commandments and keep ourselves unspotted from the world. If we realize what we are doing then the endowment will be a protection to us all our lives—a protection which a man who does not go to the temple does not have.

"I have heard my father [Joseph F. Smith] say that in the hour of trial, in the hour of temptation, he would think of the promises, the covenants that he made in the House of the Lord, and they were a protection to him. . . . This protection is what these ceremonies are for, in part. They save us now and they exalt us hereafter, if we will honor them. I know that this protection is given for I, too, have realized it, as have thousands of others who have remembered their obligations." ("The Pearl of Great Price," *Utah Genealogical and Historical Magazine*, July 1930, p. 103.)

### D&C 105:11-12, 18, 33. Was There a Difference between the Endowment of Power Given at Kirtland and the Endowment Given Worthy Members Today?

The Kirtland temple was not meant to be a house for administering the full ordinances of endowment, which have been given in temples built since that time. Even the ordinance of baptism for the dead was not required in the Kirtland Temple. The Lord did require, however, a holy place wherein no business but the building up of his kingdom would transpire. There were keys of the priesthood yet to be restored. The direction that the first elders of the Church "should receive their endowment from on high in my house . . . in Kirtland" (D&C 105:33) referred to those keys and to the great outpouring of the Lord's Spirit and the manifestations that were to accompany the dedication of the Kirtland Temple.

The Spirit that was poured out upon the Saints at the dedication of the Kirtland Temple was the same Spirit that was poured out on the day of Pentecost upon the Apostles in New Testament times (see Acts 2). That endowment of power was promised to the latter-day elders: they would be endowed "even as my apostles at Jerusalem" (D&C 95:8). "An endowment, such as was necessary at the time, was . . . given," wrote President Joseph Fielding Smith. "This was not as complete as the endowment later revealed." (*Doctrines of Salvation*, 2:242.)

Certain initiatory ordinances were performed in the Kirtland temple, but the endowment as it is given to worthy members in temples today was not given at that period. Nevertheless, the power that the Saints were endowed with at that time ensured the ascendance of the kingdom of God over all its foes, and the keys for additional priesthood ordinances were received in the Kirtland Temple.

### D&C 105:13. How Long Was the "Little Season" to Be before Zion Would Be Established?

Most men would probably not refer to a period of more than 150 years as a "little season" (D&C 105:13), but from the Lord's perspective it is a short time. In these 150 years, the Church has been successfully meeting the conditions required by the Lord (see Notes and Commentary on D&C 105:9-12). President Spencer W. Kimball taught that the Church now has sufficient maturity to make major strides in their spiritual growth. In his closing remarks at the April 1979 General Conference he said:

"Now, my brothers and sisters, it seems clear to me, indeed, this impression weighs upon me—that the Church is at a point in its growth and maturity when we are at last ready to move forward in a major way. Some decisions have been made and others pending, which will clear the way, organizationally. But the basic decisions needed for us to move forward, as a people, must be made by the individual members of the Church. The major strides which must be made by the Church will follow upon the major strides to be made by us as individuals.

"We have paused on some plateaus long enough. Let us resume our journey forward and upward. Let us quietly put an end to our reluctance to reach out to others—whether in our own families, wards, or neighborhoods. We have been diverted, at times, from fundamentals on which we must now focus in order to move forward as a person or as a people.

"Seemingly small efforts in the life of each member could do so much to move the Church forward as never before. . . .

"Are we ready, brothers and sisters, to do these seemingly small things out of which great blessings will proceed? I think we are. I believe the Lord's church is on the verge of an upsurge in spirituality. Our individual spiritual growth is the key to major numerical growth in the kingdom. The Church is ready to accomplish these things now which it could not have done just a few years ago. So also we are ready as members. If you will accept my counsel, you will come to feel that there is a readiness in our people which must be put to work." (In Conference Report, Apr. 1979, p. 114; or *Ensign,* May 1979, p. 82.)

Such counsel from the Lord's spokesman should move every Saint into full action, doing the things he already understands how to do. The Lord does not need a people who *know* more; but, rather, he desires his people to *do* more, and to do it now.

**D&C 105:24. Is One Justified in Seeking Judgments against Evil Men?**

When a Samaritan village refused the Master hospitality, James and John requested, "Lord, wilt thou that we command fire to come down from heaven, and consume them?" (Luke 9:54). In times of unrighteous persecution or trial, it might seem natural that the righteous be given that prerogative. But as Jesus counseled James and John, so he also directed the persecuted Saints in Missouri to refrain from such "mighty works" (D&C 105:24) of judgment. The Savior repeated the injunction that everyone, member and nonmember alike, throughout the world is to remember that the Father "hath committed all judgment unto the Son" (John 5:22) and to remember that Paul said, "Avenge not yourselves, . . . for it is written, Vengeance is mine; I will repay, saith the Lord" (Romans 12:19).

**D&C 105:28-32. "It Is My Will That These Lands Be Purchased"**

During the turbulent days of persecution in Jackson County, Missouri, the Lord gave a new challenge to the Saints. President Joseph Fielding Smith explained what was asked of them and why:

"The saints were also commanded to continue to purchase lands in Jackson County and the surrounding country, for it was the will of the Lord that these lands should be purchased and consecrated unto him. If they continued to buy lands and then their enemies should come upon them the armies of Israel would be justified in taking possession of their lands and break down the towers of the enemy. Before this could be done, however, the army of the Lord should become very great that her 'banners may be terrible unto all nations.'

"The whole tenor of this commandment seems to point to the fact that the saints should have deeds to the property in Jackson County and surrounding lands, but that the time for the redemption was to wait for a long time, until the Church should become very great, and then when the time was ripe the Lord would come forth to fight their battles. Apparently it was to be when the kingdoms of this world may be constrained to acknowledge that 'the kingdom of Zion is in very deed the kingdom of our God and his Christ; therefore, let us become subject to her laws' [D&C 105:32]. From other scripture it appears that the time when the nations will acknowledge Zion as the kingdom of God is not to come until our Redeemer comes to take his place as King of kings." (*Church History and Modern Revelation,* 2:5.)

*Rush Creek, Missouri, site of a cholera outbreak in Zion's Camp*

**D&C 105:34. The Revocation of the Law of Consecration**

The law of Zion mentioned in Doctrine and Covenants 105:34 is the law of consecration and the establishment of the united order. President J. Reuben Clark, Jr., explained why the Lord revoked this law and what the phrase "after her redemption" (vs. 34) means:

"It was under these circumstances, with the Saints scattered and sometimes hunted like wild animals, with their property gone, their organization largely broken up, wounded in mind and spirit, with the condemnation of the Lord pronounced upon their heads because of their unfaithfulness, not to say wickedness, with 'Zion' to all intents and purposes destroyed, that the Lord commanded them, in the great revelation given at Fishing River,—

" 'And let those commandments which I have given concerning Zion and her law be executed and fulfilled, after her redemption.' (105:34)

"It is interesting to note that after this pronouncement, the Lord practically never referred to the United Order in his revelations to the Prophet. The people had had their opportunity and failed. He then gave them the law of tithing in a revelation given in Missouri itself, in Zion, (July 18, 1838, Sec. 119), which is still in full force and effect. . . .

"Thus the Lord directed that the law he had given regarding the setting up of the United Order in Zion was to be 'executed and fulfilled' after the redemption of Zion, that is, in the meaning in which the Lord was then using the word Zion, the 'redemption,' the reestablishment of the people in Missouri. This has not yet been accomplished." ("The United Order and Law of Consecration As Set Out in the Revelations of the Lord," *Church News*, 15 Sept. 1945, p. 9.)

# "That Ye May Be the Children of Light"

Section 106

## Historical Background

On his journey among the churches in early 1834, the Prophet Joseph Smith stopped in the village of Freedom, New York. Here he was entertained by Warren A. Cowdery, a brother of Oliver (there were eight children in the Cowdery family, of which Warren was the eldest and Oliver the youngest). The Prophet wrote that he stayed at Warren's house, where "we were blessed with a full enjoyment of temporal and spiritual blessings, even all we needed, or were worthy to receive" (*History of the Church*, 2:42).

The visit of the Prophet, as well as the influence of Oliver, who had been corresponding with his brother upon the subject of religion, resulted in the eventual conversion of Warren Cowdery to the Church. Through the efforts of the Prophet and other members of the Church, a branch was eventually established in Freedom, over which Warren Cowdery was called to preside.

That fall found the Prophet very busy, but particularly so in November. "It now being the last of the month," he wrote, "and the Elders beginning to come in, it was necessary to make preparations for the school for the Elders, wherein they might be more perfectly instructed in the great things of God, during the coming winter" (*History of the Church*, 2:169). The Prophet continued to prepare for the school, still aware of the need for spiritual leadership and training of those branches far from Kirtland. On 25 November he received the revelation contained in Doctrine and Covenants 106.

## Notes and Commentary

### D&C 106:3. "The Laborer Is Worthy of His Hire"

Warren A. Cowdery's responsibilities were not confined to the town of Freedom, but extended to "the regions round about" (D&C 106:1) and to the "adjoining counties" (vs. 2). Freedom was in Cattaraugus County, New York, and there were Saints in Perrysburg and Palmersville, also in the same county. In Chataurua County, immediately west, there were Saints in Westfield and Villanova; and in Livingston County, which was located northeast of Freedom, there were Saints in Genese, Avon, and Livonia. Livonia is about fifteen miles from Manchester, New York, where the latter-day work began, and so there were probably Saints dwelling in small towns all over the western part of New York.

Because of the size of the area that Warren Cowdery was responsible for and the time involved to carry out this responsibility, the Lord promised him all necessities, "for the laborer is worthy of his hire" (vs. 3).

### D&C 106:4-5. How Can an Event of the Magnitude of the Second Coming Come As a Surprise?

The people of the world are the ones who will be surprised at the sudden coming of the Lord. The Saints, on the other hand, should be prepared, expectant, and joyful. Paul wrote to the Saints that, in looking forward to the Second Coming, "ye, brethren, are not in darkness, that that day should overtake you as a thief. Ye are all the children of light, and the children of the day." (1 Thessalonians 5:4-5; see also 1 Peter 3:10.)

To "gird up one's loins" (D&C 106:5) is an idiom meaning to prepare oneself, as explained in Notes and Commentary on Doctrine and Covenants 36:8. To those who are prepared, or, in other words, to those who are the children of light, the coming of the Master will not be a shock, catching them unprepared.

### D&C 106:8. "If He Continue to Be a Faithful Witness"

Unfortunately, Warren A. Cowdery did not remain a faithful witness. He eventually went to Kirtland, Ohio, and was given a job in the printing office, later becoming the editor of the *Messenger and Advocate*. In the apostasy of 1837 he became associated with such dissidents in Kirtland as Warren Parrish, John F. Boynton, Leonard Rich, Luke Johnson, and Stephen Burnett. Warren Cowdery, like some others at the time, grew rebellious against the Prophet and fell away from the Church.

# The Organization of Priesthood Quorums

Section 107

## Historical Background

On 14 February 1835 the Three Witnesses to the Book of Mormon, under the direction of Joseph Smith, chose the first Quorum of Twelve Apostles in this dispensation. Shortly thereafter, during a meeting of the Twelve, Elders Orson Hyde and William E. M'Lellin, acting as clerks, recorded the following:

"This evening [12 March 1835] the Twelve assembled, and the Council was opened by President Joseph Smith, Jun., and he proposed we take our first mission through the Eastern States, to the Atlantic Ocean, and hold conferences in the vicinity of the several branches of the Church for the purpose of regulating all things necessary for their welfare.

"It was proposed that the Twelve leave Kirtland on the 4th day of May, which was unanimously agreed to. . . .

"This afternoon [28 March 1835] the Twelve met in council, and had a time of general confession. On reviewing our past course we are satisfied, and feel to confess also, that we have not realized the importance of our calling to that degree that we ought; we have been light-minded and vain, and in many things have done wrong. For all these things we have asked the forgiveness of our heavenly Father; and wherein we have grieved or wounded the feelings of the Presidency, we ask their forgiveness. The time when we are about to separate is near; and when we shall meet again, God only knows; we therefore feel to ask of him whom we have acknowledged to be our Prophet and Seer, that he inquire of God for us, and obtain a revelation, (if consistent) that we may look upon it when we are separated, that our hearts may be comforted. Our worthiness has not inspired us to make this request, but our unworthiness. We have unitedly asked God our heavenly Father to grant unto us through His Seer, a revelation of His mind and will concerning our duty [during] the coming season, even a great revelation, that will enlarge our hearts, comfort us in adversity, and brighten our hopes amidst the powers of darkness." (*History of the Church,* 2:209-10.)

The Prophet Joseph did inquire of the Lord and received on 28 March 1835 at Kirtland, Ohio, the first fifty-eight verses of this section (except for verses 53-55, which are part of a blessing Joseph Smith gave his father on 18 December 1833). The other items contained in this revelation were revealed at different times. (See *History of the Church,* 2:210n; Smith, *Teachings,* pp. 38-39.)

## Notes and Commentary

**D&C 107:1. If Joseph Smith Taught That "All Priesthood Is Melchizedek," Why Are Two Priesthoods Mentioned?**

Many people are familiar with the Prophet's statement that "all priesthood is Melchizedek" (*Teachings,* p. 180), and they wonder how that statement is to be reconciled with the opening verse of Doctrine and Covenants 107. A careful reading of the complete text of the Prophet's statements shows that there is no contradiction. His statement about all priesthood being Melchizedek Priesthood was given to answer a question about Old Testament history: "Answer to the question, Was the Priesthood of Melchizedek taken away when Moses died? All Priesthood is Melchizedek, but there are different portions or degrees of it. That portion which brought Moses to speak with God face to face was taken away; but that which brought the ministry of angels remained. All the prophets had the Melchizedek Priesthood and were ordained by God himself." (*Teachings,* pp. 180-81.)

The Prophet Joseph Smith also taught, "Although there are two Priesthoods, yet the Melchisedek Priesthood comprehends the Aaronic or Levitical Priesthood, and is the grand head, and holds the highest authority which pertains to the Priesthood, and the keys of the Kingdom of God in all ages of the world to the latest posterity on the earth, and is the channel through which all knowledge, doctrine, the plan of salvation, and every important matter is revealed from heaven" (*History of the Church,* 4:207; see also D&C 107:14).

**D&C 107:1. Are the Aaronic and Levitical Priesthoods the Same?**

Elder Bruce R. McConkie answered this question in the following way:

"When the Lord first gave the law of carnal commandments, the preparatory gospel, to school Israel for a future time when again they could enjoy the gospel fulness, of necessity a lesser order of priesthood was conferred to administer the lesser law. (Heb. 7:12; *Inspired Version,* Ex. 34:1-2.) This lesser priesthood (D. & C. 85:11) was conferred upon Aaron and his sons after him (Ex. 28; 29; 30; Lev. 1:11; 3:2; 13:2; Num. 18), as 'an everlasting priesthood throughout their generations.' (Ex. 40:15; Num. 25:10-13.) It was also conferred upon substantially the whole house of Levi who were between 30 and 50 years of age. (Num. 3; 4.) Hence it is called the *Aaronic or Levitical Priesthood;* the two names are synonymous. (D. & C. 107:1, 6, 10.)

"Aaron and his sons after him held the *keys* of the Aaronic Priesthood and acted in the full majesty and power of this Levitical order; many of their functions were comparable to those of bishops and priests in this dispensation. Though the rest of the ordained Levites held the fulness of the Aaronic Priesthood (Heb. 7:5) and participated in the offering of sacrifices, they did not hold the keys of the Aaronic ministry; many of their functions were comparable to those of teachers and deacons in this dispensation. (Num. 3; 4; 2 Chron. 29; Mal. 3:3; D. & C. 13; *Doctrines of Salvation*, vol. 3, pp. 111-114.)" (*Mormon Doctrine*, pp. 9-10.)

## D&C 107:5. The Priesthood Is Greater Than Any of Its Offices

Elder Bruce R. McConkie wrote:

"*The priesthood is greater than any of its offices. No office adds any power, dignity, or authority to the priesthood. All offices derive their rights, prerogatives, graces, and powers from the priesthood.* This principle may be diagramed by dividing a circle into segments. The priesthood is the circle; the segments of the circle are the callings or offices in the priesthood. Anyone who serves in a segment of the circle must possess the power of the whole circle. No one can hold an office in the priesthood without first holding the priesthood.

"Thus it is that priesthood is *conferred* upon worthy individuals, and they are then *ordained* to offices in the priesthood; and thus it is that all offices in the priesthood and in the Church are specifically designated as *appendages* to the priesthood; that is, they grow out of the priesthood, they are supplemental to it, they are less than the priesthood in importance. (D. & C. 84:29-30; 107:5.) It follows that it is greater and more important to hold the Melchizedek Priesthood, for instance, than it is to hold any office in that priesthood. . . .

"Further, there is no *advancement* from one office to another within the Melchizedek Priesthood. Every elder holds as much priesthood as an apostle or as the President of the Church, though these latter officers hold greater administrative assignments in the kingdom. It follows, also, that any holder of the Melchizedek Priesthood could perform any priestly function he was appointed to do by the one holding the keys of the kingdom." (*Mormon Doctrine*, pp. 595-96.)

## D&C 107:8-12. The Importance of the Presidency of the Melchizedek Priesthood

The Prophet Joseph Smith taught that it is through the presidency of the Melchizedek Priesthood (the First Presidency) that the Lord reveals his will to man: "The Melchizedek High Priesthood was no other than the Priesthood of the Son of God; . . . there are certain ordinances which belong to the Priesthood, from which flow certain results; and the Presidents or Presidency are over the Church; and revelations of the mind and will of God to the Church, are to come through the Presidency. This is the order of heaven, and the power and privilege of this Priesthood." (*History of the Church*, 2:477.)

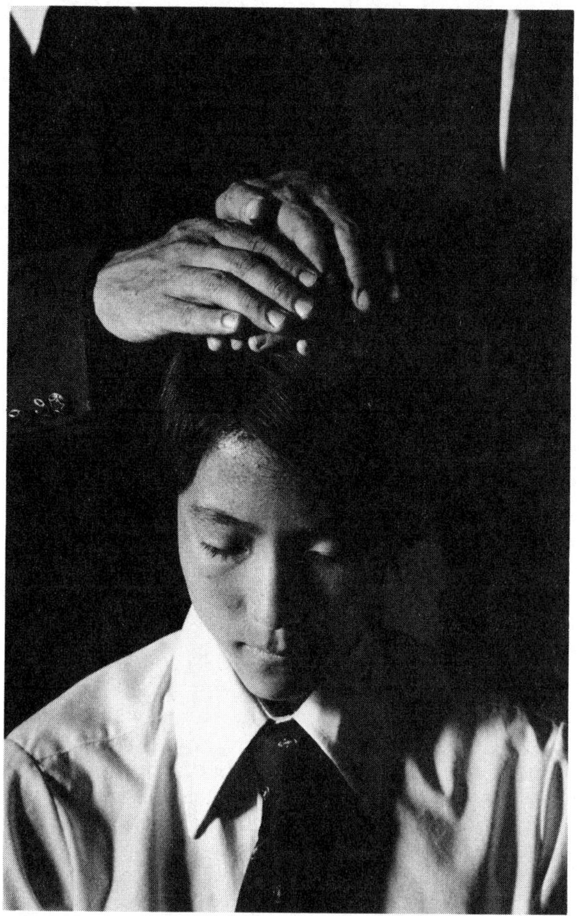

*The priesthood is conferred upon worthy males*

## D&C 107:15-17. A Literal Descendant of Aaron Has the Right to Be Presiding Bishop of the Church

Notes and Commentary on Doctrine and Covenants 68:15-21 gives an explanation of this doctrine.

## D&C 107:18. The Melchizedek Priesthood Holds the "Keys of All the Spiritual Blessings of the Church"

Through the functioning of the Melchizedek Priesthood the Lord's children may eventually obtain eternal life.

President Spencer W. Kimball made the following statement to the Church regarding the blessings of the Melchizedek Priesthood: "It is the means whereby the Lord acts through men to save souls. Without this priesthood power, men are lost. Only through this power does man 'hold the keys of all the spiritual blessings of the church,' enabling him to receive 'the mysteries of the kingdom of heaven, to have the heavens opened' unto him (see D&C 107:18-19), enabling him to enter the new and everlasting covenant of marriage and to have his wife and children bound to him in an everlasting tie, enabling him to become a patriarch to his posterity forever, and enabling him to receive a fullness of the blessings of the Lord."

("The Example of Abraham," *Ensign*, June 1975, p. 3.)

**D&C 107:18-19. What Great Blessing Can a Faithful Melchizedek Priesthood Holder Obtain?**

"The higher Priesthood after the order of the Son of God, we are told, in a modern revelation [D&C 107:18-19], . . . holds not only the power of the ministration of holy angels to be seen personally, but also the power of beholding the face of God the Father, that through the power and manifestations of the spirit of God and of his angels we may be prepared to enter into the presence of God the Father in the world to come, and enjoy continual communion with him, and be crowned with the glory of the celestial kingdom, to stand in our place and calling to all eternity, in connection with all those who hold the Priesthood in the eternal worlds." (Orson Pratt, in *Journal of Discourses*, 18:363; see also D&C 76:50-70; 84:19-22; Hebrews 12:22-24.)

**D&C 107:22. By What Body Is the President of the Church Chosen?**

President Harold B. Lee told the assembly at a general conference: "All members of the First Presidency and the Twelve are regularly sustained as 'prophets, seers, and revelators,' as you have done today. This means that any one of the apostles, so chosen and ordained, could preside over the Church if he were 'chosen by the body [which has been interpreted to mean, the entire Quorum of the Twelve], appointed and ordained to that office, and upheld by the confidence, faith, and prayer of the church,' to quote from a revelation on this subject, on one condition, and that being that he was the senior member, or the president, of that body. (See D&C 107:22.)" (In Conference Report, Apr. 1970, p. 123.)

**D&C 107:20. The Keys of the Aaronic Priesthood**

See Notes and Commentary on Doctrine and Covenants 13.

**D&C 107:22-26. Are the Quorum of the First Presidency, the Quorum of the Twelve Apostles, and the First Quorum of the Seventy Equal in Authority?**

Smith and Sjodahl explained that "there can never be two or three quorums of equal authority at the same time; therefore in the revelation where it reads that the Twelve Apostles form a quorum equal in authority with the First Presidency, and that the Seventies form a quorum equal in authority with the Twelve, it should be understood that this condition of equality could prevail only when the ranking quorum is no longer in existence, through death or otherwise. When the First Presidency becomes disorganized on the death of the President, then the Apostles become the presiding quorum, or council, of the Church with all the power to organize again the First Presidency, when they fall back again as the second ranking quorum of the Church. So with the Seventies, they would become equal only on the condition that the first two quorums ceased to exist. In regard to the Seventies, this provision, of course, concerns the first quorum of the Seventies." (Commentary, p. 700.)

**D&C 107:23. In What Way Are the Twelve Apostles Special Witnesses?**

President Joseph Fielding Smith said of the Twelve Apostles:

"These twelve men are endowed with the power and responsibility to serve as the special witnesses for Christ. They are entitled to have the inspiration and necessary guidance of the Holy Ghost to fit and qualify them for this important mission.

"All men may, by virtue of the priesthood and the gift of the Holy Ghost, become witnesses for Christ. In fact that is just what every elder in the Church should be, but there is a special calling which is given to the Twelve special witnesses that separates them from other elders of the Church in the nature of their calling as witnesses. These twelve men [as a quorum] hold the fulness of authority, keys, and priesthood, to open up the way for the preaching of the gospel to every nation, kindred, and tongue. Others who go forth go under their direction and are subject unto them. This work of proselyting is in their hands, and under the counsel of the First Presidency they are called upon to conduct all the affairs of the Church and the preaching of the gospel to every creature." (*Doctrines of Salvation*, 3:146.)

**D&C 107:27-32. The Importance of Unity**

President Lorenzo Snow described the unity in the leading councils of the Church: "Here are my counselors. We are one. We are united. . . . And here we have twelve men sitting in front with us—Twelve Apostles. There are many of these that you know. . . . We are united together. We do not quarrel with each other. We do not slander one another, but we go where counsel requires and we are heart and soul together. What for? Not to make ourselves rich, not to make ourselves wealthy, but to see what we can accomplish in the interests of the people, and we are laboring continually to see what we can do. We come together every week and we talk about what we can do for the people." (In Conference Report, Oct. 1900, p. 5.)

**D&C 107:32. How Is a Possibly Unrighteous Decision of One of the Leading Quorums Evaluated?**

If a decision of one of the leading quorums of the Church is thought to have been made in unrighteousness, the matter may be brought before "a general assembly of the several quorums" (D&C 107:32), which is the combined assembly of the First Presidency, the Quorum of the Twelve Apostles, and the First Quorum of the Seventy. These bodies are the "spiritual authorities of the church" (vs. 32), and the only appeal from a decision of one of these quorums is to this combined assembly.

**D&C 107:33-34, 38. What Is the Relationship between the Duties of the Twelve and Those of the Seventy?**

Although both the Quorum of the Twelve and the First Quorum of the Seventy are to carry the gospel to the world, their specific duties are different, as Elder Howard W. Hunter outlined:

"With the rapid growth of the Church and the heavy demands on the Twelve to provide leadership and administration and teach all nations, it becomes clear why the Lord has directed the building up of the First Quorum of the Seventy. The recent decision to do so by the First Presidency and the Quorum of the Twelve reminds us of an interesting historical parallel of an episode recorded by Luke in the Acts of the Apostles. The foreign or Hellenistic Jews in Jerusalem were complaining that their widows were being neglected and not taken care of like the widows of the native Jews. When the apostles heard of this murmuring, a significant thing happened: [Acts 6:2-4].

"In other words, the Twelve told the meeting that it was not reasonable for them to leave their important office of teaching the gospel to provide for the daily welfare of the widows and serve their tables. There were other good men who could look after these duties so the Twelve could continue to devote themselves to the charge of teaching the gospel to all persons. The result of the decision to call others to assist with the details was this: [Acts 6:7]. . . .

"In December 1978, the First Presidency and Quorum of the Twelve made a similar determination that it was no longer advisable for the Twelve to occupy their time in the details of administration of the many Church departments. They delegated seven men, designated as the presidents of the First Quorum of the Seventy, to give supervision to these details so that the Twelve could devote their full energies to the overall direction of the work, and, as directed by the Doctrine and Covenants, 'To build up the church, and regulate all the affairs of the same in all nations' [D&C 107:33].

"I fully believe that in the near future we will see some of the greatest advancements in spreading the gospel to all nations that have ever taken place in this dispensation or any previous dispensation. I am sure that we will be able to look back in retrospect—as a result of the decision recently made—and record as Luke did, 'And the word of God increased' [Acts 6:7]." ("All Are Alike unto God," in *Speeches of the Year, 1979* [Provo: Brigham Young University Press, 1980], pp. 34-35.)

**D&C 107:36-37. Standing High Councils and the High Council in Zion**

"At the time this Revelation was given, there were two standing High Councils in the Church: One in Kirtland, organized February 17th, 1834, and one in Clay County, Mo., organized July 3rd, the same year" (Smith and Sjodahl, Commentary, p. 702).

The Kirtland high council was unique, however, as President John Taylor explained: "In Kirtland, Ohio, a great many things were revealed through the Prophet. There was then a First Presidency that presided over the High Council, in Kirtland; and that High Council and another which was in Missouri, were the only High Councils in existence. As I have said, the High Council in Kirtland was presided over by Joseph Smith and his Counselors; and hence there were some things associated with this that were quite peculiar in themselves. It is stated that when they were at a loss to find out anything pertaining to any principles that might come before them in their councils, that the presidency were to inquire of the Lord and get revelation on those subjects that were difficult for them to comprehend." (In *Journal of Discourses,* 19:241.)

After the Missouri high council was organized, the Prophet said that "if I should now be taken away, I had accomplished the great work the Lord had laid before me, and that which I had desired of the Lord; and that I had done my duty in organizing the High Council, through which council the will of the Lord might be known on all important occasions, in the building up of Zion, and establishing truth in the earth" (*History of the Church,* 2:124).

"This indicates the importance attached to the organization of the High Council in Zion," wrote Smith and Sjodahl, since the government of the Church would not be in danger of being centralized, but the model of a high council in each stake of Zion had been set. "The standing High Councils in the various Stakes are presided over by the Stake presidency, and their jurisdiction is confined to the Stakes in which they are located." (Commentary, p. 703; see also Notes and Commentary on D&C 102:30-32 for an explanation of the relationship between stake high councils and the standing high council of the Church.)

Sperry said: "The Lord indicates that the High Council in Zion (Missouri) was to form a quorum equal in authority, in the affairs of the Church, to the councils of Twelve (High Councils) at the Stakes of Zion (vs. 37). And so today a High Council in any Stake of Zion is as important as that in any other Stake. The authority and power of any Stake High Council is local and confined to the boundaries of the Stake concerned." (*Compendium,* p. 565.)

**D&C 107:39. What Is an Evangelical Minister?**

The Prophet Joseph Smith said: "An Evangelist is a Patriarch, even the oldest man of the blood of Joseph or of the seed of Abraham. Wherever the Church of Christ is established in the earth, there should be a Patriarch for the benefit of the posterity of the Saints, as it was with Jacob in giving his patriarchal blessing unto his sons. [Genesis 48; 49:1-27.]" (*History of the Church,* 3:381.)

Patriarchs are ordained in each stake to give patriarchal blessings to the Saints living within the boundaries of that stake or to members who do not have a stake patriarch of their own.

**D&C 107:39-52. The Patriarchal Priesthood**

The patriarchal priesthood is passed by ordination from father to son. President Joseph Fielding Smith explained the right of lineal descent today:

"In this revelation [D&C 107] certain knowledge was revealed concerning the Patriarchal Priesthood and its descent from the beginning of time. Regarding this priesthood the Lord said: [D&C 107:39-43]. . . .

" . . . From Abraham the birthright went to Isaac and from him to Jacob, who was named Israel. From Israel it went to Joseph, the firstborn son of Rachel. . . . Therefore the birthright and the Patriarchal Priesthood continued through the seed of Joseph. Just why it was continued through Ephraim rather than through Manasseh, his older brother, we have not been informed, but we may be sure that the Lord had sufficient reason. From that time until now, this birthright has been vested in the descendants of Ephraim. [1 Chronicles 5:1-2; Jeremiah 31:9; D&C 133:30-34.]

"In the Dispensation of the Fulness of Times in which we live, the Lord revealed that this birthright of the first-born in Israel belonged to Joseph Smith, the father of the Prophet, and he was the first patriarch ordained in this dispensation. After his death the office and priesthood was conferred upon Hyrum Smith, the Prophet's oldest living brother." ("The Patriarchal Priesthood," *Improvement Era,* Nov. 1956, pp. 789, 852.)

Today the patriarchal order does not determine the organization of the Church as it did in earlier times, but in the celestial kingdom "the patriarchal order will be the order of government and rule" (McConkie, *Mormon Doctrine,* p. 559).

*John Smith, an early patriarch*

**D&C 107:53-57. The Grand Council at Adam-ondi-Ahman**

One of the greatest meetings ever held was the meeting Adam called of his righteous posterity (see D&C 107:53-57). Sometime prior to the second coming of the Savior, a similar meeting will again be held in the valley of Adam-ondi-Ahman (see D&C 78, 116).

Verses 53 through 55 of section 107 came from a blessing given by Joseph Smith, Jr., to his father on 18 December 1833 (see Smith, *Teachings,* pp. 38-39).

*Adam-ondi-Ahman*

**D&C 107:58-63. Presiding Officers Are Chosen from Quorums**

"The revealed word of God," said Elder James E. Talmage, "has provided for the establishment of presiding officers 'growing out of, or appointed of or from among those who are ordained to the several offices in these two priesthoods.' [D&C 107:21.] In accordance with the prevailing principles of order characteristic of all His work, the Lord has directed that the bearers of the Priesthood shall be organized into quorums, the better to aid them in learning and discharging the duties of their respective callings." (*Articles of Faith,* p. 209.)

**D&C 107:64-67, 91. All Others in the Kingdom Are Subject to the President of the Church**

"The President of The Church of Jesus Christ of Latter-day Saints is president of the priesthood of God on earth. . . . All others within the kingdom of God are subject to his direction. Only he has the right to receive revelation for the entire body of the Church." *When Thou Art Converted, Strengthen Thy Brethren* [Melchizedek Priesthood study guide, 1974], p. 110.)

Elder John Taylor commented on the authority of the President of the Church: "The president of the church presides over all patriarchs, presidents, and councils of the church; and this presidency does not depend so much upon genealogy as upon calling, order, and seniority" (*Times and Seasons,* 1 June 1845, p. 922; see also D&C 107:91-92).

**D&C 107:68-75. What Is the Duty of a Bishop?**

As stewards or pastors over the Lord's people, the bishops of the Church hold a high and holy calling. President Marion G. Romney discussed the duties of their office:

"As originally given, the assignments pertaining to the office [of Bishop] may be summarized in four major parts.

"First, the bishop was to receive the consecrations of the Saints and appoint unto them their inheritances (see D&C 42:31-34, 71-73; 51:13; 58:35; 72:2-6; 78; 82; 85:1).

"Second, the bishop was to be a judge unto the people, judging both their standing in the Church as well as their temporal needs if they had claim on the Church (see D&C 42:80-82; 58:17-18; 72:17; 107:72).

"Third, the bishop was to succor the poor, in both body and spirit, according to their needs (see D&C 38:35; 42:33-35, 39, 71; 70:7-8).

"Fourth, the bishop was to act as an agent for the Church doing whatever temporal business he was appointed to by the Lord through the First Presidency (see D&C 51:13-14; 84:112-13; 107:68, 71-72).

"As the Church grew and the Saints gained experience, the Lord distinguished between the responsibilities of the Presiding Bishop and local, or ward, bishops as they have come to be known. Today, in the various handbooks of the priesthood, you will find four major categories of duties appointed unto the ward bishop. Except for those duties which are unique to the Presiding Bishopric of the Church and those which were made inoperative at the time the formal law of consecration was suspended, the role of the bishop today is essentially the same as was defined in these early revelations. Bishops have been given added responsibilities for the youth and as presiding high priest of the ward. However, of all of the bishop's assignments, as important as each one is, none is more important than care for the poor." (In Conference Report, Oct. 1979, p. 137; or *Ensign*, Nov. 1979, p. 94.)

**D&C 107:72, 74. In What Way Is a Bishop a "Judge in Israel"?**

In a speech given to a group of Latter-day Saint mental health workers on the subject of the bishop's role in relation to that of professional counselors, President Spencer W. Kimball taught the following about the bishop's role as a judge:

"By virtue of his call and ordination and setting apart, he also becomes a judge in Israel and has the responsibility of making many decisions for his people which affect their progress and development and their life. He has control over their spiritual activities so that he can give them opportunities for growth and judge their accomplishments. He decides as to their worthiness and eligibility for certain blessings and privileges. He holds the key to all temples in the world and it is he who must turn that key to open the doors thereof to his members and through eternal marriage to life eternal. . . .

"It is said: 'God's ways are not man's ways.' This man, the bishop, need not be schooled in all the fields of education, for he has access to the fountain of all knowledge. There is revelation, not only for the prophet, but for every worthy and righteous man. He is entitled to divine guidance in his own jurisdiction. . . .

" . . . the bishop may draw on this limitless reservoir of knowledge and wisdom if he is in tune with his Maker." (*New Era*, Sept. 1978, pp. 16-17.)

**D&C 107:76. Who Can Try a Member of the First Presidency?**

"The bishop is a common judge in Israel, and members are amenable to his jurisdiction. In case of an accusation made against one of the First Presidency, the case would be tried before the presiding bishop and a council of high priests." (Smith, *Church History and Modern Revelation*, 2:21.)

Explaining the convening of a Presiding Bishop's court, Elder John A. Widtsoe said: "The Presiding Bishop's Court consists of the Presiding Bishop with his two counselors, and twelve High Priests especially chosen for the purpose. It is a tribunal extraordinary, from which there is no appeal, to be convened if it should be necessary to try a member of the First Presidency for crime or neglect of duty." (*Priesthood and Church Government*, p. 212.)

**D&C 107:77-84. Church Courts**

The Lord established a judicial system in the Church for the benefit of the members and to preserve the interests of his kingdom. According to Smith and Sjodahl, the following are some of its provisions: "The Latter-day Saints have been taught not to indulge in lawsuits, if not compelled to. The Church has a perfect judiciary, and the members need not suffer the expenses and inconvenience of so-called legal proceedings. The Teachers are peacemakers. They visit the Saints in their homes, as their friends, and they can generally remove, in their incipiency, all causes of trouble between members. But if they do not succeed, the matter may be taken to the Bishop's Court, where the evidence is heard and a decision may be taken to the High Council of the Stake, and the decision there given is final, unless the First Presidency, after a review of the evidence, orders a re-hearing. The Bishop's Court may, if deemed necessary, excommunicate a member who holds only the Aaronic Priesthood, and disfellowship one who holds the Melchizedek Priesthood. The High Council can excommunicate any member." (Commentary, p. 710.)

President Joseph Fielding Smith further explained: "There are several councils in the Church. The traveling high council has jurisdiction in all the world. The high councils in stakes have jurisdiction in a judicial way in the stakes. The First Presidency may sit as an appellate council, and their decision is final. The Church is so organized that no member or officer, from the President to the last member received, is 'exempted from the justice and the laws of God.' The special court, or council, presided over by the presiding bishopric has been called into existence several times. The Prophet Joseph Smith was tried before this council on charges made against him by Elder Sylvester Smith after the return of Zion's Camp. Oliver Cowdery, David Whitmer, and Frederick G. Williams were each tried by this tribunal." (*Church History and Modern Revelation,* 2:21; see also Notes and Commentary on D&C 102; Enrichment I, in the Appendix.)

**D&C 107:85-90. Duties of Quorum Presidents**

Elder David O. McKay taught that certain responsibilities rest upon presidents of priesthood quorums: "Presidents of quorums: The Lord has said to you, as you will read in the 107th section of the Doctrine and Covenants, that it is your duty to meet with your quorum. If you are the president of a deacon's quorum, you are to meet with twelve deacons, and preside over them, to sit in counsel with them, and to teach them their duties. O, deacons, throughout the world! respond to that call. Do your duty, Bishops, you who hold the presidency of the Aaronic Priesthood; guide the young men in this activity. Are they slothful? Are they inactive? If they are, some of the results of inactivity mentioned before as befalling the idle individual will afflict the quorum in your ward. Mark it, it will not fulfill its place in the councils of the Church, unless it be active as a council, as a quorum. This is true of the Teachers, of the Priests, the Elders, the Seventies, the High Priests, and all." (In Conference Report, Oct. 1909, p. 92.)

**D&C 107:91-92. The Saints Must Follow the President of the Church, the One Holding All the Gifts of God for His People**

Notes and Commentary for Doctrine and Covenants 21:4-7 and Enrichment F discuss the importance of the living prophet.

**D&C 107:93-97. The Seventy and the Ministry**

The Prophet Joseph Smith described the responsibilities given to the Seventies:

"On the 28th of February, the Church in council assembled, commenced selecting certain individuals to be Seventies, from the number of those who went up to Zion with me in the camp . . . to begin the organization of the first quorum of Seventies, according to the visions and revelations which I have received. The Seventies are to constitute traveling quorums, to go into all the earth, whithersoever the Twelve Apostles shall call them." (*History of the Church,* 2:201-2.)

"If the first Seventy are all employed, and there is a call for more laborers, it will be the duty of the seven presidents of the first Seventy to call and ordain other Seventy and send them forth to labor in the vineyard, until, if needs be, they set apart seven times seventy, and even until there are one hundred and forty-four thousand thus set apart for the ministry" (*History of the Church,* 2:221).

Although the First Quorum of the Seventy was organized by Joseph Smith, it did not continue to function as a quorum after the exodus to Utah. After the colonization of the West, quorums of seventies were organized in each stake; but on a general authority level, there was just the First Council of Seventy, or the First Seven Presidents of the Seventy.

Not until the time of President Spencer W. Kimball was the First Quorum of the Seventy organized again as an active, functioning quorum. This action was begun in the October 1975 conference, although the full quorum was not organized at that time. In that conference President Kimball said: "The First Quorum of the Seventy will be gradually organized, eventually with seventy members, the presidency of which will be made up of the seven members" (in Conference Report, Oct. 1975, p. 3; or *Ensign,* Nov. 1975, p. 4).

One year later, in the October 1976 conference, President Kimball took further action:

"Today we shall present . . . additional members of the First Quorum of the Seventy to you for your votes. . . . These changes . . . bring to thirty-nine the total number in the First Quorum of the Seventy, thus providing a quorum to do business.

"With this move, the three governing quorums of the Church defined by the revelations,—the First Presidency, the Quorum of the Twelve, and the First Quorum of the Seventy,—have been set in their places as revealed by the Lord. This will make it possible to handle efficiently the present heavy workload and to prepare for the increasing expansion and acceleration of the work, anticipating the day when the Lord will return to take direct charge of His church and kingdom." (In Conference Report, Oct. 1976, p. 10; or *Ensign,* Nov. 1976, p. 9.)

**D&C 107:98. Provisions by the Lord for General Leadership in Addition to the Three Presiding Quorums of the Church**

To meet the administrative needs of his church as it grew, the Lord in this revelation provided for general Church leaders to be called in addition to the three presiding quorums of the Church. Such leaders are the past Assistants to the Quorum of the Twelve (1941 to 1976) and the Regional Representatives of the Twelve. Those called to these positions have been given administrative duties in the Lord's kingdom under the direction of the Quorum of the Twelve Apostles. (See Harold B. Lee, in Conference Report, Oct. 1967, pp. 101, 104-5; Spencer W. Kimball, in Conference Report, Oct. 1976, p. 10.)

**D&C 107:99-100. What Is the Responsibility of All Who Accept a Call to the Priesthood?**

President Henry D. Moyle made it very clear that when brethren accept positions in the priesthood, they have the obligation to fully commit themselves to perform their duties and to live according to all of God's laws: "I am sure it would be more pleasing to our Father in heaven to have us resign our positions—and that is not a practice which we commend in the Church—but nonetheless it seems preferable to neglecting our duties in the least detail. It gives us an awesome feeling to realize that we are dedicated to the work of the Lord, and having thus committed ourselves, it is not our privilege or our prerogative to violate his commandments, even the slightest of them.

The Lord expects, and we expect it of ourselves, each one of us, to live out our lives here upon this earth in as complete conformity to the laws of God as we are capable. No means of rationalizing, no means of conjuring up excuses as to why we should do this or should not do the other, contrary to the will of our Heavenly Father, has any place in our lives." (In Conference Report, Oct. 1961, pp. 43-44.)

**D&C 107:100. What Does It Mean That the Slothful "Shall Not Be Counted Worthy to Stand"?**

Those who do not do their duty, who neglect the priesthood responsibilities they have been ordained to fulfill, will not be counted among the righteous who are worthy to stand in God's presence (see also Psalms 1:1-5; 24:3-4; Malachi 3:1-2; Luke 21:36; Alma 12:12-15; D&C 45:32).

# Obedience Brings Blessings

Section 108

## Historical Background

When the First Quorum of the Seventy was organized on 28 February 1835, many of its members were drawn from the group of men known as Zion's Camp, the body that in 1834 had gone to help the afflicted Saints in Missouri. Lyman Sherman, whose loyalty and faith had been proven in the Zion's Camp expedition, was called to be one of the Seven Presidents of the First Quorum of the Seventy.

The day after Christmas 1835, the Prophet Joseph Smith recorded in his journal that "Brother Lyman Sherman came in, and requested to have the word of the Lord through me; 'for,' said he, 'I have been wrought upon to make known to you my feelings and desires, and was promised that I should have a revelation which should make known my duty' " (*History of the Church,* 2:345).

## Notes and Commentary

**D&C 108:1. Lyman Sherman's Sins Forgiven**

Smith and Sjodahl explained why the first verse was especially significant to Lyman Sherman: "From this verse and the two following paragraphs it is evident that Lyman Sherman had passed through one of those mental struggles in which faith is tried to the utmost. It had been a question with him whether to go forward, or to turn back. It is evident, also, that he had conquered doubt and had determined to continue in the faith. At this stage of the trial, it occurred to him that he had sinned by resisting the voice of the Lord, and that perhaps he had lost his standing among the brethren. Tortured by this thought, he heard the voice of the Spirit whispering in his soul and prompting him to visit the Prophet and ask for the Word of God through His servant. The very first assurance was, 'Your sins are forgiven you.' What comfort! The Prophet knew nothing of the mental struggle through which his visitor had passed, or the condition in which it had left him. And yet he uttered the very word needed to restore peace to the troubled heart. And this word was spoken by

*Sacred vows are made in the holy temples*

one who had the authority of the Priesthood. It was no empty phrase." (Smith and Sjodahl, Commentary, p. 713.)

**D&C 108:3. The Importance of Vows**

"All that the Lord requires of us is strict obedience to the laws of life," taught President Brigham Young. "All the sacrifice that the Lord asks of his people is strict obedience to our own covenants that we have made with our God, and that is to serve him with an undivided heart." (In *Journal of Discourses,* 18:246.)

**D&C 108:4. What Is a Solemn Assembly?**

See Notes and Commentary for Doctrine and Covenants 95:7.

**D&C 108:4. What Was the "Solemn Assembly" for Which the Lord Asked Lyman Sherman to Wait?**

The Kirtland Temple was near completion when the revelation in section 108 was given. Beginning on 13 January 1836 and continuing until shortly after the dedication, meetings were held in the Kirtland Temple at which there was a great outpouring of the Spirit. Many of the Saints received revelations and saw heavenly personages. Each of these meetings could appropriately be called a solemn assembly.

The Prophet Joseph Smith recorded in his journal the proceedings of the meetings of 21 and 22 January:

"At early candle-light I met with the Presidency at the west school room, in the Temple [Kirtland], to attend to the ordinance of anointing our heads with holy oil; also the Councils of Kirtland and Zion met in the two adjoining rooms, and waited in prayer while we attended to the ordinance. . . .

"Many of my brethren who received the ordinance with me saw glorious visions also. Angels ministered unto them as well as to myself, and the power of the Highest rested upon us, the house was filled with the glory of God, and we shouted Hosanna to God and the Lamb. . . .

"Friday 22.—Attended at the school room at the usual hour, but instead of pursuing our studies, we spent the time in rehearsing to each other the glorious scenes that occurred on the preceding evening, while attending to the ordinance of holy anointing.

"In the evening we met at the same place, with the Council of the Twelve, and the Presidency of the Seventy, who were to receive this ordinance [of anointing and blessing]. The High Councils of Kirtland and Zion were present also.

"After calling to order and organizing, the Presidency proceeded to consecrate the oil. . . .

"The Twelve then proceeded to anoint and bless the Presidency of the Seventy, and seal upon their heads power and authority to anoint their brethren." (*History of the Church,* 2:379, 381-83.)

This meeting, at which Lyman Sherman and his brethren of the Presidency of the Seventy received their anointings and blessings, was one of great spiritual power and an experience similar to the Day of Pentecost. It was a great source of strength to them when they were sent forth to preach the gospel.

**D&C 108:7. Each Member of the Church Must Seek to Strengthen His Brethren through All His Doings**

The struggles of mortality and Satan's opposition to the Saints' efforts to build the Lord's kingdom will bring times of difficulty and discouragement. Many Saints will falter and faint under the load, but each one can benefit from the help and encouragement of his brethren. The counsel given to Brother Sherman to seek to lift and edify his brethren in all the ways he could applies to all of the Lord's servants (see D&C 81:5; Ecclesiastes 4:9-10).

# Prayer of Dedication for the Kirtland Temple

Section 109

## Historical Background

Smith and Sjodahl explained the significance of the dedication of the Kirtland Temple and outlined some of the important events that accompanied it:

"The dedication of the Temple in Kirtland, on the 27th of March, 1836, was an ever memorable event in the history of the Church. That structure was reared in compliance with Revelations received (See Sec. 88:119; 95:8-9), at a time when the Saints were few and poor, and when to raise the money required (between sixty and seventy thousand dollars) meant a great deal of self-sacrifice on their part. 'While the brethren labored in their departments,' says Tullidge, 'the sisters were actively engaged in boarding and clothing workmen not otherwise provided for—all living as abstemiously as possible, so that every cent might be appropriated to the grand object.' And thus they toiled on from the 23rd of July, 1833, when the corner stones were laid, until it was completed for dedication.

"In the Revelation given on the 1st of June, 1833, the Lord indicated the special object for which this house was to be built: 'I gave unto you a commandment, that you should build an house, in the which house I design to endow those whom I have chosen, with power from on high' (Sec. 95:8). It was to be a place in which the Church would receive a Pentecostal baptism in the fire of the Holy Spirit [see Acts 2]. A special house, consecrated and dedicated, was needed for that purpose, hence the commandment of God to the Saints concerning this house.

"Now the day of dedication had come. The people assembled early, full of joy and gratitude, and they were not disappointed in their expectations. The manifestations of the divine presence were such as to leave no room in the minds of the true Saints for doubt concerning the nature of the work in which they were engaged. Heber C. Kimball relates that during the ceremonies of the dedication, an angel appeared and sat near Joseph Smith, Sr., and Frederick G. Williams, so that they had a fair view of his person. He was tall, and had black eyes and white hair; wore a garment extending to near his ankles, and had sandals on his feet. 'He was sent,' President Kimball says, 'as a messenger to accept of the dedication.' (Whitney's *Life of Heber C. Kimball,* p. 103). A few days afterwards, a solemn assembly was held . . . and blessings were given. 'While these things were being attended to,' Heber C. Kimball says, 'the beloved disciple John was seen in our midst by the Prophet Joseph, Oliver

Cowdery, and others' (*Ibid.*, p. 104). On the 6th of April, a meeting was held which was prolonged into the night. On this occasion the spirit of prophecy was poured out upon the Saints, and many in the congregation saw tongues of fire upon some of those present, while to others angels appeared. 'This,' President Kimball says, 'continued several days and was attended by a marvelous spirit of prophecy. Every man's mouth was full of prophesying, and for a number of days and weeks our time was spent in visiting from house to house, administering bread and wine, and pronouncing blessings upon each other to that degree, that from the external appearances one would have supposed that the last days had truly come, in which the Spirit of the Lord was poured out upon all flesh' (*Ibid.*, p. 105; see also *Hist. of the Church,* Vol. II., p. 427). Nor were the Saints the only ones who were aware of supernatural manifestations at this time. Elder George A. Smith rose to prophesy, when a noise was heard like the sound of a rushing wind. All the congregation arose, and many began to speak in tongues and prophesy. And then people of the neighborhood came running together (hearing an unusual sound within and seeing a bright light like a pillar of fire resting upon the Temple), and were astonished at what was taking place. This continued until the meeting closed, at 11 p.m. (*History of the Church,* Vol. II., p. 428)." (Commentary, pp. 720-21.)

As the dedicatory services proceeded, Sidney Rigdon spoke to the congregation, commencing the services by reading Psalms 96 and 24. Several hymns were sung, then President Rigdon spoke on Matthew 18:18-20 and the sealing power of the priesthood. The various quorums of the priesthood were presented to the membership of the Church for their sustaining vote, then followed the dedicatory prayer by the Prophet. To the surprise of some, Joseph Smith read the dedicatory prayer, which had been written previously by revelation, instead of giving it spontaneously; thus was set the pattern for dedicatory prayers (see *History of the Church,* 2:420).

# Notes and Commentary

### D&C 109:1-5. "Thy Servants Have Done According to Thy Commandment"

President George Q. Cannon wrote that the Kirtland Temple had been built at the expense of the "utmost self-sacrifice. Nearly three years had been occupied in its construction; and during this time the Saints had given of their substance and had toiled without ceasing to make a habitation fit for the ministration of angelic visitants and of the Holy One, Himself. The consummation of this work had been very near to the Prophet's heart, especially since the tribulations in Missouri had shown that no house of the Lord could be erected speedily in the center stake of Zion." (*Life of Joseph Smith,* p. 204.)

The Lord did "accept of this house" (D&C 109:4), as is evident from the manifestations that accompanied its dedication and also the glorious vision recorded in Doctrine and Covenants 110, which took place there shortly afterwards.

### D&C 109:7-14. A House of Learning

In a revelation given to the School of the Prophets, the Lord commanded the elders to organize themselves and build a house for prayer, fasting, and learning (see D&C 88:117-20). Verses 6 through 9 quote the revelation given at that time.

Elder John A. Widtsoe explained the historical significance of the educational venture: "It is thrilling to look back over our history to the time of the Kirtland Temple. The men left their farms, fields, and shops in the evenings and climbed to the top story, the attic story of the Kirtland Temple, there, in provided classrooms, to study various subjects, languages, mathematics, history, geography, and a variety of subjects. Really our people began there what we call today adult education. It was thought that an older man could not learn; only young people could learn. Since that time the world has come to quite a different conclusion. Today a man is never too old to learn. A woman is never too old to learn. The power to assimilate knowledge remains with us to the last day. Somehow these forebears of ours in the Church understood that." (In Conference Report, Apr. 1949, p. 149.)

### D&C 109:10-60. Securing the Promises Given in Revelation

The Prophet Joseph Smith beseeched the Lord that the Saints receive the blessings promised to them in various revelations already given:

1. That God's glory would rest upon his people and upon the Kirtland Temple (see D&C 109:12-13).
2. That those who worship in the temple would be taught properly (see vs. 14).
3. That the people would "grow up" in the Lord, receiving a fulness of the Holy Ghost (vs. 15).
4. That the house of God would be all it was meant to be with no unclean thing permitted therein (see vss. 16-20, which are paraphrased from D&C 88:119-20).
5. That when the Saints transgressed, they would return quickly to the Lord (see vs. 21).
6. That his servants could go forth armed with power and protected by the angels to spread the gospel to the ends of the earth (see vss. 22-23).
7. That he would establish his people forever against all the enemies who fight against them (see vss. 24-33).
8. That their sins would be forgiven (see vs. 34).
9. That the powers of Pentecost would come upon them (see vss. 35-37).
10. That the servants of God would have the power of the covenant and bear testimony of it throughout the world (see vss. 38-44).
11. That the servants of God would be delivered from the calamity of the wicked and the judgments that are promised (see vss. 45-49).
12. That the Lord would have mercy on the nations of the earth, softening their hearts to prepare them for the gospel message (see vss. 54-58).

13. That stakes of Zion would be appointed so the gathering might roll forth (see vs. 59). (Adapted from Sperry, *Compendium*, pp. 593-96.)

**D&C 109:21. How Does One Show Reverence in the Lord's House?**

Elder Bruce R. McConkie explained that "the most decorous conduct—unmarred by loud laughter, unnecessary conversation, untoward actions of any sort, or even by evil thoughts—is essential to reverencing the Lord's sanctuary. And what is said of his temples is also true of his meetinghouses." (*Mormon Doctrine*, p. 652.)

President Joseph F. Smith also said: "Self-respect requires, among other things, that one shall behave like a true gentleman, in a house of worship. No self-respecting person will go to a house devoted to the service of God to whisper, gossip and visit; rather, it is one's duty to put on self-restraint, to give one's undivided attention to the speaker, and concentrate the mind upon his words that his thoughts may be grasped to one's benefit and profit." (*Gospel Doctrine*, p. 334.)

**D&C 109:22-23. Armed with Power and Watched Over by Angels**

"The Lord is here with us," said President Brigham Young, "not in person, but his angels are round us, and he takes cognizance of every act of the children of men, as individuals and as nations. He is here ready by his agents, the angels, and by the power of his Holy Spirit and Priesthood, which he has restored in these last days, to bring most perfect and absolute deliverance unto all who put their trust in Him, when they are ready to receive it; and, until they are ready, the work of preparation must be vigorously progressed in, while at the same time we in patience must possess our souls." (In *Journal of Discourses*, 11:14.)

**D&C 109:25-31. No Weapon Shall Prosper; No Combination of Wickedness Shall Triumph over God's People**

The Saints in the future will face opposition and persecution (see Notes and Commentary on D&C 98:38), and then this inspired dedicatory prayer will be a source of comfort, for, as the Prophet Joseph Smith taught, Satan will marshal all of his available forces to stop the kingdom, but he will not prevail: "No unhallowed hand can stop the work from progressing; persecutions may rage, mobs may combine, armies may assemble, calumny may defame, but the truth of God will go forth boldly, nobly, and independent, till it has penetrated every continent, visited every clime, swept every country, and sounded in every ear, till the purposes of God shall be accomplished, and the Great Jehovah shall say the work is done" (*History of the Church*, 4:540).

**D&C 109:30. What Is Meant by "the Hail"?**

See Doctrine and Covenants 29:16; Ezekiel 38:22; Revelation 16:21.

*Joseph Smith dedicated the Kirtland Temple*

**D&C 109:47-53. Has the Anger of the Lord Fallen upon the United States in Response to This Plea?**

As part of the dedicatory prayer, the Prophet Joseph Smith pleaded with the Lord to remember the Saints in Missouri in their afflictions. He beseeched the Lord to have mercy on the mobs so that they might repent (see D&C 109:50). But the Prophet asked the Lord to show forth his power on behalf of his people, letting his anger and indignation fall upon those guilty of causing the sufferings, if no repentance was evidenced.

On at least two other occasions the Prophet predicted that Missouri would suffer great judgments because it tolerated the mob actions against the Saints. In 1843 the Prophet, in Nauvoo, reviewed the guilt of Missouri and said, "They shall be oppressed as they have oppressed us, not by 'Mormons,' but by others in power. They shall drink a drink offering, the bitterest dregs, not from the 'Mormons', but from a mightier source than themselves. God shall curse them." (*History of the Church*, 6:95.)

And in a conversation with General Alexander Doniphan, one of the few friends of the Saints in Missouri, the Prophet said: "God's wrath hangs over Jackson county. God's people have been ruthlessly driven from it, and you will live to see the day when it will be visited by fire and sword. The Lord of Hosts will sweep it with the besom of destruction. The fields and farms and houses will be destroyed, and only the chimneys will be left to mark the desolation." (Roberts, *Comprehensive History of the Church*, 1:538.)

During the Civil War these prophecies were fulfilled in a remarkable manner, and Missouri was a scene of widespread, terrible destruction (see Roberts, *Comprehensive History of the Church*, 1:539-59, for a detailed discussion of Missouri's sufferings).

Earlier the Lord had commanded the Prophet to seek redress, even up to the president of the United States, if necessary, warning that if the government did not heed their just pleas, the Lord would "vex the nation" (D&C 101:89; see also D&C 101:85-88). Redress was sought, but no satisfaction was given. For this reason President John Taylor prophesied: "The Gospel reveals many things to us which others are unacquainted with. I knew of those terrible events which were coming upon this nation previous to the breaking out of our great fratricidal war [the Civil War], just as well as I now know that they transpired, and I have spoken of them to many. What of that? Do I not know that a nation like that in which we live, a nation which is blessed with the freest, the most enlightened and magnificent government in the world to-day, with privileges which would exalt people to heaven if lived up to—do I not know that if they do not live up to them, but violate them and trample them under their feet, and discard the sacred principles of liberty by which we ought to be governed—do I not know that their punishment will be commensurate with the enlightenment which they possess? I do. And I know—I cannot help but know—that there are a great many more afflictions yet awaiting this nation. But would I put forth my hand to help bring them on? God forbid! And you, you Latter-day Saints, would you exercise your influence to the accomplishment of an object of that kind? God forbid! But we cannot help but know these things. But our foreknowledge of these matters does not make us the agents in bringing them to pass." (In *Journal of Discourses,* 22:141-42.)

**D&C 109:54-58. The Gospel to Go Forth from America to the Nations of the Earth in the Last Days**

President George Q. Cannon stated: "God has founded this land America and the government for the express purpose that Zion might be built upon this land, and that the people of all nations might come here singing His praises and thanking him that from the darkness and the threatening evils by which they are surrounded He has provided a way of escape, a safe place, that when calamities and judgments come upon the inhabitants of the earth, they can stand in holy places and be secure by keeping the commandments of God. What a glorious theme this is for the Elders to carry to the down-trodden of the nations of the earth who groan in darkness and who see no way of deliverance! Nor will it be the down-trodden alone who will listen to these tidings. Men in high places and of commanding positions will yet listen to them, and they will take note of this extraordinary people who have done such a remarkable work and who are now traversing the globe to bring from every land all who will listen to their message; to bring them with all their traditions to this place which we call Zion, where they can, by the fusing power of the Spirit of God, be consolidated into one united people." (In Conference Report, Oct. 1900, p. 68.)

**D&C 109:60. How Are Latter-day Saints Gentiles?**

Elder Joseph Fielding Smith explained: "Let us also remember that we are of the Gentiles! By this I mean that the Latter-day Saints have come to their blessings through the Gentile nations. President Brigham Young . . . said that Joseph Smith was a pure Ephraimite. This is true; yet Joseph Smith came also of a Gentile lineage. So do most members of the Church. We may boast of our lineage, and rejoice in the fact that Patriarchs have declared us to be of Ephraim, but at the same time let us not despise the Gentiles, for we are also of them. If it were not so the scriptures would not be fulfilled. [1 Nephi 15:13-14; Ether 12:22.]" (*Way to Perfection,* p. 140.)

**D&C 109:61-67. The "Children of Judah" and the "Remnants of Jacob"**

The Prophet Joseph Smith wrote that in reading the Book of Mormon "we learn that our western tribes of Indians are descendants from that Joseph which was sold into Egypt, and that the land of America is a promised land unto them, and unto it all the tribes of Israel will come, with as many of the Gentiles as shall comply with the requisitions of the new covenant. But the tribe of Judah will return to old Jerusalem [see Doctrine and Covenants 133:8, 13, 35]. The city of Zion spoken of by David, in the one hundred and second Psalm, will be built upon the land of America, 'And the ransomed of the Lord shall return, and come to Zion with songs and everlasting joy upon their heads' (Isaiah 35:10); and then they will be delivered from the overflowing scourge that shall pass through the land. But Judah shall obtain deliverance at Jerusalem. See Joel 2:32; Isaiah 26:20 and 21; Jeremiah 31:12; Psalm 1:5; Ezekiel 34:11, 12 and 13. These are testimonies that the Good Shepherd will put forth His own sheep, and lead them out from all nations where they have been scattered in a cloudy and dark day, to Zion, and to Jerusalem; besides many more testimonies which might be brought."(*History of the Church,* 1:315.)

Notes and Commentary on Doctrine and Covenants 87:5 discusses the remnant of Jacob.

**D&C 109:72. What Is the Kingdom of God?**

See Doctrine and Covenants 65 and Daniel 2.

**D&C 109:74. When Will the Mountains Flow Down?**

"In the resurrection which now approaches," Elder Parley P. Pratt wrote, "and in connection with the glorious coming of Jesus Christ, the earth will undergo a change in its physical features, climate, soil, productions, and in its political, moral and spiritual government.

"Its mountains will be levelled, its valleys exalted, its swamps and sickly places will be drained and become healthy, while its burning deserts and its frigid polar regions will be redeemed and become temperate and fruitful." (*Key to the Science of Theology,* p. 132; see D&C 133:19-25.)

**D&C 109:75-76. When Will the Righteous Be Caught Up?**

See Notes and Commentary on Doctrine and Covenants 88:95-98.

**D&C 109:79. What are Seraphim?**

See Notes and Commentary on Doctrine and Covenants 38:1.

**D&C 109:79-80. "Help Us by the Power of Thy Spirit"**

"The rearing of a Temple of God in the world is the construction of a citadel by the followers of Prince Immanuel in the territory claimed by Diabolus. Hence his rage when the people of God build Temples. But the Temple in Kirtland served its divine purpose, as did that in Nauvoo, though both were abandoned. In it the Saints received that power from on high which enabled the Church to withstand, successfully, the attacks of all enemies. Owing to that baptism by the Holy Spirit received in the Temples, the Church, notwithstanding persecution, exile, and apostasy, has grown in spiritual power and become able to make itself felt in the world as a regenerating force. But for the Temples and the communion with God established through the Temple service, the Church might have been overwhelmed in the persecutions of Missouri and Illinois, just as the Primitive Church might have perished in the early persecutions but for the power it received on the day of Pentecost." (Smith and Sjodahl, Commentary, pp. 722-23.)

# Messengers with Keys

Section 110

## Historical Background

Excitement ran high as the Saints prepared to dedicate the Kirtland Temple in April 1836. The Lord was pleased with the sacrifices made by the Saints to complete "a house of prayer, a house of fasting, a house of faith, a house of learning, a house of glory, a house of order, a house of God" (D&C 88:119). As the house was being dedicated, the Lord's acceptance was gloriously manifested in divine endowments of "power from on high" (D&C 105:11; see also *History of the Church*, 2:427-33; Notes and Commentary on D&C 105:11-12, 18,33).

"After the dedication of the Kirtland Temple, council and spiritual meetings were held in the building almost daily. Sunday, April 3, 1836, was one of the most eventful days in the history of the Church" (Smith, *Church History and Modern Revelation*, 2:46).

The Prophet Joseph Smith wrote of his activities on Sunday, 3 April 1836, one week after the dedication of the Kirtland Temple: "Attended meeting in the Lord's House, and assisted the other Presidents of the Church [the First Presidency and quorum presidents] in seating the congregation, and then became an attentive listener to the preaching from the stand. Thomas B. Marsh and David W. Patten spoke in the forenoon to an attentive audience of about one thousand persons. In the afternoon, I assisted the other Presidents in distributing the Lord's Supper to the Church, receiving it from the Twelve, whose privilege it was to officiate at the sacred desk this day. After having performed this service to my brethren, I retired to the pulpit, the veils being dropped, and bowed myself, with Oliver Cowdery, in solemn and silent prayer. After rising from prayer, the following vision was opened to both of us." (*History of the Church*, 2:434-35.) Doctrine and Covenants 110 records the vision and visitations received on that day.

*Oliver Cowdery and Joseph Smith saw the Lord standing upon the breastwork of the pulpit*

## Notes and Commentary

**D&C 110:1-3. Why Is Simile Used in the Description of the Glorified Christ?**

An accurate, complete description of the glorified Savior is impossible; but by comparing the indescribable things of a spiritual realm to things within man's comprehension, the reader gains a feeling for the glory and appearance of the Lord. Each metaphor and simile, in its individual context, enlarges the reader's idea of the Savior's glory. The language of the Prophet's description is similar to that of the descriptions written by Daniel (see Daniel 9:4-8) and by John the Revelator (see Revelation 1:13-17).

### D&C 110:7. What Was the Relationship between the Sacrifice of the Saints in Building the Kirtland Temple and the Appearance of the Savior?

The Prophet Joseph Smith taught that "if a man would attain to the keys of the kingdom of an endless life; he must sacrifice all things" (*Teachings,* p. 322). Elder Franklin D. Richards saw a direct correlation between the sacrifices of the Saints in building the temple and the consequences: "The Saints did all the work they could on the building, and then went out and obtained work here and there, and with the money they earned they purchased those things that were necessary for its completion. It was done by sacrificing all that they had; and when we had done all that we could do, Oh! how joyous it was to know the Lord accepted the work, when He stood upon the breastwork of the Temple, conversed with the Prophet Joseph and Oliver, and revealed to them their duties, and informed them that the Gospel should go from there and be preached throughout the nations of the earth." (In Conference Report, Apr. 1898, p. 17.)

### D&C 110:7-10. What Was the "Fame" of the Kirtland Temple That Was to Spread to Foreign Lands?

The workmanship on the Kirtland Temple was the best the Saints could produce. The personal and community sacrifice of the Saints in the construction of that temple has become legend. Many of the women sacrificed by giving their china to be crushed and mixed in the outside plaster to give color and brilliance to the house of God. Nevertheless, neither the workmanship nor the sacrifice was implied by the Lord when he spoke of the "fame" of the temple (D&C 110:10), for the appearance of heavenly guests who came with unspeakable glory and restored vital saving keys and powers eclipses anything of mortal origin.

Elder Joseph Fielding Smith wrote: "That which took place [in the Kirtland Temple] on the third day of April in the year 1836 has spread forth to all lands. Thousands and tens of thousands, even hundreds of thousands have been blessed because of what took place upon that occasion. Not only the thousands in The Church of Jesus Christ of Latter-day Saints, but thousands upon thousands who are not members of the Church have partaken of the blessings which came at that time and which have spread forth throughout the earth. And while they may not know it, they have been influenced [by the Spirit of Elijah, for example], and have many of them performed a wonderful work because of the things that took place, and because of the fulfillment of this prediction [D&C 110:7-10] made by the Son of God." (In Conference Report, Apr. 1936, p. 73.)

### D&C 110:11. The Keys of Gathering Are Crucial to the Earthly Kingdom of God

Among the greatest work of all time is the gathering of Israel in the last days. In fact, the Prophet identified it as being the great task of the kingdom: "All that the prophets . . . have written, from the days of righteous Abel, down to the last man that has left any testimony on record for our consideration, in speaking of the salvation of Israel in the last days, goes directly to show that it consists in the work of the gathering" (Smith, *Teachings,* p. 83).

For this reason Moses returned with the keys of the gathering, as Elder Bruce R. McConkie explained:

"Israel's great lawgiver, the prophet whose life was in similitude of the Messiah himself, the one who delivered Israel from Egyptian bondage and led them to their land of promise, came to Joseph Smith and Oliver Cowdery on 3 April 1836, in the Kirtland Temple. He gave them: (1) 'the keys of the gathering of Israel from the four parts of the earth,' and (2) the keys of 'the leading of the ten tribes from the land of the north' (D&C 110:11).

"Since then, with increasing power and in great glory, we have gathered, from their Egyptian bondage as it were, the dispersed of Ephraim and few others, initially to the mountains of America, but now into the stakes of Zion in the various nations of the earth. The gathering of Israel is a reality. When the ten tribes return they will come at the direction of the President of The Church of Jesus Christ of Latter-day Saints, for he now holds and will then hold the keys of presidency and direction for this mighty work." ("This Final Glorious Gospel Dispensation," *Ensign,* Apr. 1980, p. 22.)

### D&C 110:11. Where Are the Ten Lost Tribes?

President Joseph Fielding Smith wrote: "Whether these tribes are in the north or not, I am not prepared to say. As I said before, they are 'lost' and until the Lord wishes it, they will not be found. All that I know about it is what the Lord has revealed, and He declares that they will come from the North. He has also made it very clear and definite that these lost people are separate and apart from the scattered Israelites now being gathered out." (*Signs of the Times,* p. 186; see also Notes and Commentary on Doctrine and Covenants 133:26-34.)

### D&C 110:12. Who Is the Elias That Committed the Dispensation of the Gospel of Abraham? What Did He Restore?

President Joseph Fielding Smith answered:

"Luke reveals the coming of the angel Gabriel to Zechariah to inform him that his wife would bear a son. He also appeared to Mary and announced the birth of our Lord and Savior.

"Gabriel then is Noah . . . [see Smith, *Teachings,* p. 157].

"Then we discover in the revelation given to the Prophet Joseph Smith in August 1830, that it was Elias who came to Zacharias and announced the birth of John the Baptist [see D&C 27:6-7]. . . .

"This is the same Elias who held the keys of the dispensation of Abraham and who came to the Prophet Joseph Smith and Oliver Cowdery, April 3, 1836, in the Kirtland Temple and restored the keys of Abraham's dispensation." (*Answers to Gospel Questions,* 3:139-40.)

After quoting Doctrine and Covenants 128:20-

21, President Smith indicated that the name-titles Gabriel and Elias pertain to the same man: "From these scriptures we learn that Noah is Gabriel and that he came to the Prophet Joseph Smith in his calling as an Elias and restored the keys of the dispensation in which the Lord made covenant with Abraham and his posterity after him to the latest generations" (*Answers to Gospel Questions,* 3:140).

Elder Bruce R. McConkie explained what Elias restored to the earth:

"Now what was the *gospel of Abraham?* Obviously it was the commission, the mission, the endowment and power, the message of salvation, given to Abraham. . . . It was a divine promise that both in the world and out of the world his seed should continue. . . .

"Thus the gospel of Abraham was one of celestial marriage; . . . it was a gospel or commission to provide a lineage for the elect portion of the pre-existent spirits, a gospel to provide a household in eternity for those who live the fulness of the celestial law. This power and commission is what Elias restored, and as a consequence, the righteous among all future generations were assured of the blessings of a continuation of the seeds forever, even as it was with Abraham of old. (D. & C. 132.)" (*Mormon Doctrine,* pp. 219-20.)

With such blessings restored again, the way was opened for teaching scattered Israel the principles of salvation. The Lord's plans, however, would all come to naught if the mighty sealing power of Elijah had not immediately followed, for Elijah's power enables Israel to have those principles here and hereafter.

**D&C 110:13-14. The Coming of Elijah**

President Joseph Fielding Smith explained the special significance of Malachi's prediction being fulfilled on 3 April 1836:

"Edersheim in his work, *The Temple,* says: 'To this day, in every Jewish home, at a certain part of the Paschal service [i.e. when they drink the "third cup"]—the door is opened to admit Elijah the prophet as forerunner of the Messiah, while appropriate passages are at the same time read which foretell the destruction of all heathen nations. It is a remarkable coincidence that, in instituting his own Supper, the Lord Jesus connected the symbol, not of judgment, but of his dying love, with his "third cup." '

"It was, I am informed, on the third day of April, 1836, that the Jews, in their homes at the Paschal feast, opened their doors for Elijah to enter. On that very day Elijah did enter—not in the home of the Jews to partake of the Passover with them—but he appeared in the house of the Lord, erected to his name and received by the Lord in Kirtland, and there bestowed his keys to bring to pass the very things for which these Jews, assembled in their homes, were seeking." (*Doctrines of Salvation,* 2:100-101.)

**D&C 110:16. What Urgent Responsibility Does Each Latter-day Saint Have Because of the Mission of Elijah?**

The Prophet Joseph Smith said: "The Bible says, 'I will send you Elijah the Prophet before the coming of the great and dreadful day of the Lord; and he shall turn the hearts of the fathers to the children, and the hearts of the children to the fathers, lest I come and smite the earth with a curse.' [Malachi 4:5-6.]

"Now, the word *turn* here should be translated *bind,* or seal. But what is the object of this important mission? or how is it to be fulfilled? The keys are to be delivered, the spirit of Elijah is to come, the Gospel to be established, the Saints of God gathered, Zion built up, and the Saints to come up as saviors on Mount Zion.

"But how are they to become saviors on Mount Zion? By building their temples, erecting their baptismal fonts, and going forth and receiving all the ordinances, baptisms, confirmations, washings, anointings, ordinations and sealing powers upon their heads, in behalf of all their progenitors who are dead, and redeem them that they may come forth in the first resurrection and be exalted to thrones of glory with them; and herein is the chain that binds the hearts of the fathers to the children, and the children to the fathers, which fulfills the mission of Elijah. And I would to God that this temple was now done, that we might go into it, and go to work and improve our time, and make use of the seals while they are on earth.

"The Saints have not too much time to save and redeem their dead, and gather together their living relatives, that they may be saved also, before the earth will be smitten, and the consumption decreed falls upon the world." (*History of the Church,* 6:183-84.)

**D&C 110:16. "By This Ye May Know"**

The Lord has revealed by direct testimony of angels that his coming is not far distant. On his first visit to Joseph Smith, Moroni quoted several prophetic promises from the Bible, saying that these were "about to be fulfilled" (JS—H 1:40; see also JS—H 1:36-45). Elijah bore direct witness that his coming not only fulfilled Malachi's prophecy but was a sign that the great and dreadful day was "at the doors" (JS—M 1:39).

President Joseph Fielding Smith spoke on the coming of Elijah in a general conference of the Church:

"If the great and dreadful day of the Lord were near at hand when Elijah came 130 years ago, we are just one century nearer it today. But some will say: 'But no! Elijah, you are wrong! Surely 130 years have passed, and are we not better off today than ever before? Look at our discoveries, our inventions, our knowledge, and our wisdom! Surely you made a mistake!' So many seem to think and say, and judging by their actions they are sure, that the world is bound to go on in its present condition for millions of years before the end will come. Talk to them; hear what they have to say—these learned men of the world. 'We have had worse times,' they say. 'You are wrong in thinking there are more calamities now than in earlier times. There are not more earthquakes, the earth has always been quaking, but now we have facilities for gathering the news which our fathers did not have. These are not signs of the times; things are not different from former times.' And so the people refuse to heed the warnings the Lord so kindly gives to them, and thus they fulfill the scriptures. Peter said such sayings would be uttered, and he warned the people. . . .

"Shall we slumber on in utter oblivion or indifference to all that the Lord has given us as warning? I say unto you, 'Watch therefore: for ye know not what hour your Lord doth come.' " (In Conference Report, Apr. 1966, p. 15.)

**D&C 110:16. What Is the Significance of the Keys Brought by Elijah?**

President Joseph Fielding Smith explained why the sealing powers restored by Elijah to the Church are so important:

"What was the nature of this restoration? It was the conferring upon men in this dispensation of the sealing power of the priesthood, by which all things are bound in heaven as well as on earth. It gave the authority to Joseph Smith to perform in the temple of God all the ordinances essential to salvation for both the living and the dead.

"Through the power of this priesthood which Elijah bestowed, husband and wife may be sealed, or married for eternity; children may be sealed to their parents for eternity; thus the family is made eternal, and death does not separate the members. This is the great principle that will save the world from utter destruction.

"Vicariously the dead may obtain the blessings of the gospel—baptism, confirmation, ordination, and the higher blessings, which are sealed upon them in the temples of the Lord, by virtue of the authority restored by Elijah. Through the restoration of these keys, the work of the Lord is fully inaugurated before the coming of Jesus Christ in glory.

"These keys of the binding, or sealing power, which were given to Peter, James, and John in their dispensation, are keys which make valid all the ordinances of the gospel. They pertain more especially to the work in the temples, both for the living and for the dead. They are the authorities which prepare men to enter the celestial kingdom and to be crowned as sons and heirs of God.

"These keys hold the power to seal husbands and wives for eternity as well as for time. They hold the power to seal children to parents, the key of adoption, by which the family organization is made intact forever. This is the power which will save the obedient from the curse in the coming of the great and dreadful day of the Lord. Through these keys the hearts of the children have turned to their fathers." (*Doctrines of Salvation,* 2:118-19.)

# The Greatest Treasure

Section 111

## Historical Background

An understanding of the history of the time when this revelation was given greatly increases one's appreciation of it. What might otherwise be considered a short and relatively insignificant revelation then becomes a profound spiritual lesson for Saints of all ages.

The Kirtland Temple had been finished and dedicated in March 1836, leaving the Saints in Kirtland and the Church itself impoverished and deeply in debt. In addition, the troubles in Zion (Missouri) had also heavily taxed the spiritual and temporal resources of the Church, which was barely six years old at this time. Joseph Smith, Sidney Rigdon, Oliver Cowdery, and Hyrum Smith left Kirtland in late July and traveled to Salem, Massachusetts. They rented a house, preached publicly, and went from house to house to teach the gospel. During their stay at Salem Doctrine and Covenants 111 was given (see *History of the Church* 2:464-65).

In *History of the Church* the Prophet did not indicate a reason for traveling to New England and Salem, but Elder Brigham H. Roberts gave the following explanation of the circumstances: "Ebenezer Robinson, for many years a faithful and prominent elder in the church, and at Nauvoo associated with Don Carlos—brother of the Prophet—in editing and publishing the *Times and Seasons,* states that the journey to Salem arose from these circumstances. There came to Kirtland a brother by the name of Burgess who stated that he had knowledge of a large amount of money secreted in the cellar of a certain house in Salem, Massachusetts, which had belonged to a widow (then deceased), and thought he was the only person who had knowledge of it, or of the location of the house. The brethren accepting the representations of Burgess as true made the journey to Salem to secure, if possible, the treasure. Burgess, according to Robinson, met the brethren in Salem, but claimed that time had wrought such changes in the town that he could not for a certainty point out the house 'and soon left.' " (*Comprehensive History of the Church,* 1:411.)

## Notes and Commentary

### D&C 111:1-6. "I . . . Am Not Displeased . . . Notwithstanding Your Follies"

Evidently the Prophet Joseph Smith's motives for following William Burgess's suggestion to search for the hidden treasure in Salem were pure, and his actions were prompted by his love for the Saints and for the Church. It appeared that in one incredible stroke of good fortune the Church could gain money enough to clear itself of its debts and care for the suffering Saints in Kirtland and Zion. The leading elders had no thought of personal gain in the trip. For this reason the Lord was not displeased with their journey, "notwithstanding [their] follies" (D&C 111:1).

Their folly lay in the fact that less than three years earlier, the Prophet Joseph Smith had received counsel from the Lord about the Church's indebtedness (see D&C 104:78-80; see also Notes and Commentary on D&C 104:78-80). At that time Church members were told that if they would humble themselves and seek through diligence and the prayer of faith to be relieved of their indebtedness, the Lord would send means for their deliverance. Now, still deeply in debt, Church leaders were trying to solve the financial difficulties of the Church through their own efforts, without seeking help from the Lord. The Lord reminded them that he could give them power to pay their debts and that he would deal mercifully with Zion (see D&C 111:5-6).

Their efforts were commendable, their motives were pure and righteous, and so they had not incurred the Lord's displeasure. But they had neglected to include him in solving the problem, and this failure was foolish indeed.

The Lord allowed the Prophet Joseph to go to Salem, for in Salem was a treasure of much greater value to the kingdom than that for which they had come. There were many souls in Salem whom the Lord knew would accept the gospel. Their conversion would greatly benefit the Lord's work because these new members of the Church would unite their efforts with those of the Saints and contribute generously to the cause of Zion.

The treasure referred to in the revelation was obtained, as is attested in part in the writings of Erastus Snow: "Until this time [6 July 1841] I had been calculating to spend the summer in the country and return home to Nauvoo late in the fall in compliance with advice given me by President Joseph Smith when I left in Nov. last—But President Hyrum Smith and [William] Law who had been east as far as Salem, Massachusetts and just returned through Philadelphia on their way home again counciled [*sic*] that I should not return to Nauvoo in the fall but that I should go immediately with Brother Winchester to Salem Mass. and try to establish the kingdom in that city. They left with us a copy of a revelation given about that people in 1836 which said the Lord had much people there whom he would gather into his kingdom in his own due time and they thought the due time of the Lord had come. Though I felt anxious to go home in the fall and thought it would involve what little property I had in the West in a difficulty to stay I felt willing to do the will of the Lord. I prayed earnestly to know his will and his spirit continually whispered to go to Salem. I also thought of the Apostles who cast lots to see which should take the place of Judas. I therefore after writing on one ballot Nauvoo and on the other Salem prayed earnestly that God would show by the ballot which way I should go and I drawed the ballot that had Salem on it twice in succession and I then resolved as soon as I had filled the appointments I had out I would go to Salem. The conference also voted that I should go and promised their prayers in my behalf that God might open an effectual door for the word." (Journal of Erastus Snow [1841-47], Historical Department, The Church of Jesus Christ of Latter-day Saints, Salt Lake City, pp. 3-5.)

Later entries in his journal reveal that Brother Snow baptized over one hundred people from the time he arrived in Salem until he returned to Nauvoo on 11 April 1843. For example, on page 27 of his journal, Elder Snow indicated that there were ninety members in the Salem Branch on 28 May 1842.

### D&C 111:4. When Will the City of Salem Be Given to the Saints That They Shall "Have Power over It"?

Sperry explained that this phrase has not yet been completely fulfilled: "In due time the Almighty will give Salem into 'your' hands (vs. 4), that the Elders shall have power over it, insomuch that 'they', probably meaning the people of the city, shall not discover 'your secret parts'. (Cf. Isa. 3:17, 'shame.') Not only that, but also the wealth of the city, its gold and silver, shall be in possession of the brethren. This verse is obviously a prophecy of some future happening, even yet future, and evidently looks forward to a day when the Lord's Kingdom will be established upon the earth, when towns, cities, and nations will be governed under his direction by brethren holding the Priesthood. When that day comes, the Elders of the Church will govern even Salem without being shamed by the people of the city. Its wealth will also be theirs. The meaning here is that it will be used, not so much for their own personal desires, as for righteous purposes." (*Compendium*, pp. 609-10.)

### D&C 111:8. God Directs His Servants through the Power of His Spirit

Righteous servants of the Lord who seek his direction in their decisions may know that their actions are agreeable to his will by the feeling of peace and confidence communicated to their souls. By being sensitive to the Spirit, the Lord's people can be continually led by him in their lives (see Alma 58:11; D&C 6:22-23; 8:2-3). This verse is also a reminder that when one follows the peaceful power of the Spirit, one knows where the Lord wants him to be.

### D&C 111:9. Who Are the Ancient Inhabitants of Salem?

Elder B. H. Roberts said that the Lord's instructions

*B. H. Roberts spoke of genealogies in Salem*

to learn about the ancient inhabitants of Salem were given, "doubtless having in view the securing of their genealogies and redemption of the past generations of men who had lived there; so that if for a moment the weakness of men was manifested in this journey, we see that fault reproved and the strength and wisdom of God made manifest by directing the attention of his servants to the real and true treasures that he would have them seek, even the salvation of men, both the living and the dead" (*Comprehensive History of the Church,* 1:412).

Verse 9 of this section was also of great importance to the Prophet because of his special association with the people of Salem. Smith and Sjodahl pointed out that "history is, perhaps, the most useful knowledge a missionary can have, next to a thorough understanding of the principles of the gospel, but 'ancient inhabitants' refers more particularly to the ancestors of the Prophet. The Revelation was given at Salem, the county seat of Essex County, Massachusetts. It was in that county that Robert Smith, the first of the Smith family in America, settled. It was the residence of many more of the pioneer immigrants to America, whose descendants joined the Church. At Salem, the county seat, the records for all the towns in the county were kept, and the Smiths' record, among others, were there. The matter of genealogy evidently entered into the inquiry concerning the 'ancient inhabitants,' for a purpose which was manifest later, of the salvation of the dead." (Commentary, p. 729.)

# The Word of the Lord unto the Twelve

Section 112

## Historical Background

Before he received this revelation, the Prophet Joseph Smith recorded in his journal that the situation in Kirtland during this period of time was one of widespread disunity, contention, and apostasy. Financial speculation had caused the Kirtland Safety Society, the financial institution of the Church, to fail. Many, even some of the leaders of the Church, blamed the Prophet for such problems. The Prophet Joseph wrote: "In this state of things, and but a few weeks before the Twelve were expecting to meet in full quorum, (some of them having been absent for some time), God revealed to me that something new must be done for the salvation of His Church. And on or about the first of June, 1837, Heber C. Kimball, one of the Twelve, was set apart by the spirit of prophecy and revelation, prayer and laying on of hands, of the First Presidency, to preside over a mission to England, to be the first foreign mission of the Church of Christ in the last days." (*History of the Church,* 2:489.)

President Joseph Fielding Smith wrote of the circumstances surrounding the receiving of Doctrine and Covenants 112: "The day that the British Missionaries preached the first sermons in England, July 23, 1837, the Lord gave a revelation to the Prophet Joseph Smith directed to Thomas B. Marsh as president of the council of the apostles. In this revelation Elder Marsh was instructed to teach the brethren in his council and point out to them their duty and responsibilities in proclaiming the Gospel. Some of the apostles had forsaken their responsibility and had turned their attention to schemes of speculation. . . . the years preceding the year 1837, were years of wild speculation throughout the United States and Elder Heber C. Kimball pointed out how this boom had struck Kirtland and some of the brethren had borrowed great sums and had gone into business, at the expense of their ministry. Then when the bauble of false prosperity broke they were left financially stranded; then they began to blame the Prophet Joseph Smith. This revelation to Thomas B. Marsh was a warning and a call to him to bring his brethren back into the line of their duty as apostles of Jesus Christ." (*Church History and Modern Revelation,* 2:71; see also *History of the Church,* 2:498-99.)

The first twelve verses of the section are directed to Thomas B. Marsh personally, giving him comfort, counsel, and admonition. The rest of the section contains the instructions he was to convey to the Twelve.

# Notes and Commentary

### D&C 112:1. Who Were Thomas B. Marsh's Brethren?

On 14 February 1835, the first Quorum of the Twelve in this dispensation was organized, its members chosen to be special witnesses of the Savior throughout the world. Because there were no precedents to act upon, the Twelve were arranged in seniority according to age. Elder Thomas B. Marsh, being the oldest, became President of the Quorum and thus responsible for the other eleven. Since that time, seniority in the Quorum has been determined by date of ordination.

### D&C 112:6. "Thy Habitation Be Known in Zion"

"In 1832, Thomas B. Marsh received an inheritance—about thirty acres—on the Big Blue river, Missouri, and there he built a comfortable log house. When the Saints were driven from Jackson County, he went to Lafayette County, while most of the exiles sought refuge in Clay County. In 1834, he, too, went to Clay County. After an extended visit to Kirtland, he returned to his home on Fishing River, Clay County. In 1836, he built a house in Far West. In June 1837, he again visited Kirtland. It was necessary, for the success of his mission, that his residence in Zion should be known, and that his house should not be moved." (Smith and Sjodahl, Commentary, p. 733.)

### D&C 112:6. Did Thomas B. Marsh Ever Publish Anything?

To publish does not just mean to have written materials produced. In the dictionary the primary meaning is "to discover or make known to mankind or to people in general what before was private or unknown, to divulge, as a private transaction; to promulgate or proclaim, as a law or edict. We *publish* a secret, by telling it to people without reserve. Laws are *published* by printing or by proclamation. Christ and his apostles *published* the glad tidings of salvation." (*American Dictionary,* s.v. "publish.")

From the meaning of the word *publish* it is apparent that President Thomas B. Marsh was to fulfill his apostolic calling by teaching as well as writing those principles that had been hidden from the world because of wickedness and indifference (see also Notes and Commentary for D&C 118:2.)

### D&C 112:7. Did Thomas B. Marsh Serve Missions to "Many Nations"?

Four days after this revelation was given, the Prophet Joseph Smith, along with Sidney Rigdon and Thomas B. Marsh, started for Canada to visit the members of the Church (see *History of the Church,* 2:502).

That the Savior had other opportunities for Thomas B. Marsh to bear witness to the nations is apparent from this verse. They were not realized, however, since Thomas B. Marsh later apostatized and left the Church. (See Notes and Commentary on D&C 112:10.)

### D&C 112:8-9. Was Thomas B. Marsh a Powerful Speaker?

President Thomas B. Marsh had the potential to be a powerful speaker. In 1836, more than a year before Doctrine and Covenants 112 was revealed, "he was a member of a committee selected to pass resolutions on behalf of the exiled Saints, at a meeting at the city of Liberty. On that occasion, he spoke of the persecution the Saints had suffered, so eloquently that General Atchinson and others wept." (Smith and Sjodahl, Commentary, p. 733.)

No incidents are known of President Thomas B. Marsh's speaking with unusual power from the time of the revelation until his apostasy a little over a year later. His is another case of a promise not being fully realized because of apostasy.

### D&C 112:10. How Important Is Humility in Church Positions?

Humility is always a prerequisite to success in any Church position, as Elder Harold B. Lee related in the following example: "I remember at a stake conference some years ago a young man was called to a high position. When we had asked him to express himself, expecting a humble testimony in his acceptance, he stood up and in a rather flamboyant, boastful way gave a dramatic performance. At the close of the service as we walked home, one of the high council whispered to me and said, calling him by name: 'When he stood up there in the pulpit this morning, he was all alone.' " (In Conference Report, Oct. 1960, p. 17.)

President Thomas B. Marsh's pride led to his eventual apostasy. His excommunication is a poignant reminder that the Lord has counseled his Saints to be humble. "Pride was the weakness of Thomas B. Marsh. If he had been humble, he would not have fallen. He began by defying the righteous decisions of the High Council and the First Presidency, in a trivial case in which his wife was interested, and he ended by becoming a traitor to the Church." (Smith and Sjodahl, Commentary, p. 733.)

The admonition to be humble should be taken to heart by every Latter-day Saint. Pride, perhaps as much as any other fault, causes a person to lose power with God; for it is only in humility that a person is willing to reach out for God and let Him lead him by the hand.

### D&C 112:11-12. A Charge to Pray for and to Admonish the Twelve

Noting the power of prayer combined with admonition, Smith and Sjodahl said:

"Our Lord instructs the President of the Council

to continue to pray for the members, and also to admonish them 'sharply.' Admonition without prayer is barren of results. He promised to feel after them, when they had passed through the tribulations awaiting them because they had yielded to temptations. And then, if they would not harden their hearts, they would be converted and healed.

"Orson Hyde, who had imbibed of the spirit of speculation, freely acknowledged his faults and asked forgiveness. Parley P. Pratt, too, at one time was overcome by the evil spirit, of strife, but, he says, 'I went to Brother Joseph Smith in tears, and with a broken heart and contrite spirit, confessed wherein I had erred. He frankly forgave me, prayed for me, blessed me.' Others did not repent. Luke S. Johnson, Lyman E. Johnson, and John F. Boynton were rejected and disfellowshiped by the Church on the 3rd of September, 1837, less than a month and a half after this Revelation was given." (Commentary, p. 734.)

### D&C 112:14. What Does It Mean to Take Up the Cross?

See Notes and Commentary for Doctrine and Covenants 23:6.

### D&C 112:15. Will Joseph Smith Always Hold the Keys?

Three important meanings are to be found in the Lord's promise to the Prophet Joseph Smith that he would always hold the keys he had been given. The first meaning is explained by President Joseph Fielding Smith: "At the time this revelation was given some of the members of the council of the apostles were in open rebellion and had displayed a very bitter spirit towards the Prophet. The Lord endeavored to impress upon them the fact that the Prophet was the one who held the keys of this dispensation and that he would hold them constantly until the Lord should come. In a former revelation (Sec. 43:4-7.) the Lord had said that the keys were in the hands of Joseph Smith and that if he should transgress and lose them they would be given to another. At that day the Prophet had not been tested and proved by tribulation and suffering, but now in July 1837, the Prophet having shown his integrity in all kinds of difficulties and tribulation the Lord declared that the keys shall never be taken from him. The Lord wished to impress upon the apostles and others in the councils of the Church that he had not forsaken his prophet and would be with him to the end." (*Church History and Modern Revelation,* 2:72-73.)

A second meaning is derived from several passages in the Doctrine and Covenants that show that when the Lord spoke of Joseph Smith, his statements pertained to Joseph's position as President and prophet of the Church. Thus the Lord's statements apply to all those who subsequently hold that office (see D&C 21:1-7). The keys of the kingdom have been given to the President of the Church, and they shall never be taken from him until the Savior comes.

Nevertheless, "Joseph Smith was called to stand at the head of the Dispensation of the Fulness of Times, preparatory to the second advent of the Son of God" (Smith, *Answers to Gospel Questions,* 4:175). So, in addition to holding the keys of the kingdom, the Prophet Joseph Smith also held the keys of this dispensation, and these keys shall never be taken from him. President Brigham Young said, "The

*A representation of the Quorum of the Twelve Apostles in 1837. Left to right: Heber C. Kimball, Brigham Young, Thomas B. Marsh, Orson Hyde, William E. McLellin, David W. Patten, Parley P. Pratt, John F. Boynton, Luke S. Johnson, William B. Smith, Lyman E. Johnson, Orson Pratt*

keys of the Priesthood were committed to Joseph, to build up the Kingdom of God on the earth, and were not to be taken from him in time or in eternity" (*Discourses of Brigham Young,* p. 138). This explanation is a third interpretation of what the Lord meant by his words to President Thomas B. Marsh.

### D&C 112:17-19. Why Were the Twelve to Go Where Joseph, Hyrum, and Sidney Could Not?

The passage in verse 17 about Joseph, Hyrum, and Sidney refers to the First Presidency as it was constituted when the revelation was given. When the First Presidency of the Church was originally organized, Jesse Gause and Sidney Rigdon were called to be counselors to the Prophet. After Jesse Gause's apostasy (see Historical Background for D&C 81), the Presidency was reorganized in 1833 with Frederick G. Williams as Second Counselor. At a conference held at Far West, Missouri, on 7 November 1837, Frederick G. Williams was replaced by Hyrum Smith (see *History of the Church,* 2:522-23).

The Twelve are to carry the work into all the world as directed by the First Presidency, since it is not possible for the presiding quorum to do all things themselves.

### D&C 112:20. In What Way Were the First Presidency Counselors to the Twelve?

President Joseph Fielding Smith explained: "The First Presidency, the Lord said, were to be counselors to the Twelve. By this is meant that the twelve should not go forth without the counsel and direction of the First Presidency." (*Church History and Modern Revelation,* 2:73.)

### D&C 112:23-24. A Day of Tribulation

"This proclamation should cause us even in this day serious reflection," wrote President Joseph Fielding Smith. "If darkness covered the earth in 1837, surely it has deepened in its blackness since that day. If that was a day of wickedness, and the Lord in several revelations testified to this fact, then it is even more so today. We are called upon to remember that the day would come when peace would be taken from the earth and the devil have power over his own dominions. (D. & C. 1:35.) Surely that day has come. We have seen days of weeping and mourning, a day of wrath and of vengeance upon the inhabitants of the earth, and yet they will not repent. We have seen this day come speedily as the whirlwind, and yet we know that we have not seen the end. There will yet be plagues, bloodshed and weeping until eventually the earth shall be cleansed of all iniquity." (*Church History and Modern Revelation,* 2:74.)

### D&C 112:24-26. "Upon My House Shall It Begin"

In the same revelation in which Zion was defined, the Lord warned the Saints that only if Zion met the Lord's qualifications would it escape the judgments that were to be poured out upon the world. If they did not qualify as a Zion people, they had no promise (see D&C 97:21-27). Severe judgments befell the Saints because they failed to build Zion and abide by its laws. Nevertheless, this prophetic statement also had reference to future members of the Church, as the following statements from the Brethren attest.

President Brigham Young warned,"If the Latter-day Saints do not desist from running after the things of this world, and begin to reform and do the work the Father has given them to do, they will be found wanting, and they, too, will be swept away and counted as unprofitable servants" (in *Journal of Discourses,* 18:262).

President Joseph Fielding Smith pointed out: "All of these things will be withheld while the nations are being punished, if the members of the Church will keep faithfully their commandments. If they will not, then we have received the warning that we, like the rest of the world, shall suffer His wrath in justice." (*Progress of Man,* p. 468.)

President Wilford Woodruff emphasized: "Zion is not going to be moved out of her place. The Lord will plead with her strong ones, and if she sins He will chastise her until she is purified before the Lord.

"I do not pretend to tell how much sorrow you or I are going to meet with before the coming of the Son of Man. That will depend upon our conduct." (In *Millennial Star,* 2 Sept. 1889, p. 547.)

### D&C 112:30-32. The Dispensation of the Fulness of Times

See Notes and Commentary on Doctrine and Covenants 128:18.

### D&C 112:33. How Can the Elders Escape the Blood of This Generation?

President John Taylor explained his understanding of the Elders' escaping "the blood of this generation" (D&C 112:33).

"I . . . wish to state to the Twelve and to the Seventies, and to the Elders, that they are not responsible for the reception or the rejection by the world of that word which God has given to them to communicate. It is proper for them to use all necessary diligence and fidelity, and to plainly and intelligently, and with prayer and faith, go forth as messengers to the nations, as the legates of the skies, clothed upon with authority from the God of Heaven, even the authority of the Holy Priesthood, which is after the order of the Son of God, which is after the order of Melchisedek, which is after the power of an endless life. He has endowed them . . . with authority to call upon men to repent of their sins, and to be baptized in the name of Jesus for the remission of sins, and then He has told them to lay hands on the people thus believing, and thus being baptized, and to confer upon them the gift of the Holy Ghost, and when they have performed their labors, and fulfilled their duties, their garments are free from the blood of this generation, and the people are then left in the hands of God their Heavenly Father. For the people, as before stated, will be held responsible to God for their rejection of the Gospel, and not to us." (In *Journal of Discourses,* 24:289.)

# Isaiah Interpreted

Section 113

## Historical Background

In January 1838 the Prophet Joseph Smith fled from Kirtland to escape the enemies who were seeking his life. He traveled to Far West, Missouri, where he arrived on 14 March 1838. The following account of events shortly after his arrival in Missouri is given in his history:

"On the 14th of March [1838], as we were about entering Far West, many of the brethren came out to meet us, who also with open arms welcomed us to their bosoms. We were immediately received under the hospitable roof of Brother George W. Harris, who treated us with all possible kindness, and we refreshed ourselves with much satisfaction, after our long and tedious journey, the brethren bringing in such things as we had need of for our comfort and convenience.

"After [our] being here two or three days, my brother Samuel arrived with his family." (*History of the Church,* 3:8-9.)

Included without explanation in the Prophet's history of this time are some answers to questions on the book of Isaiah. It is not known who asked the first questions—it may be that the Prophet asked them on his own behalf. It is known that the final questions came from Elias Higbee. The answers are directly from the Lord.

Section 113 was first published in the 1876 edition of the Doctrine and Covenants.

## Notes and Commentary

### D&C 113:1-2. Why Was Christ Referred to As the "Stem of Jesse"?

The Hebrew word which was translated into English in the King James Version of the Bible as *stem* means "the *stock* which remains in the earth after the tree is cut down" (Smith and Sjodahl, Commentary, p. 738). Rasmussen points out that Isaiah 11:1 is Hebrew poetry:

"Literally translated into common English, the poetic couplet here would be:

" 'There shall come forth a branch from the trunk of Jesse:

" 'Indeed, a shoot from his roots shall bear fruit.'

"Since the line of Jesse is the royal line of kings from David's time on, is there any question as to who this 'branch' is?" (*Introduction to the Old Testament,* 2:45.)

The branch and the stem are both Christ (see Jeremiah 23:5-6; 33:15-17); these terms refer to Christ's being of the lineage of King David, the son of Jesse (see Acts 2:30; 13:22-23; Romans 1:3; Luke 1:32).

*Some of Isaiah's writings are clarified by Doctrine and Covenants 113*

### D&C 113:3-6. Who Are the "Rod" and the "Root" Spoken of by Isaiah?

Sperry wrote concerning the "rod" and the "root":

"The writer has always assumed that the 'rod' was Joseph Smith, believing that the Prophet, out of modesty, hesitated to name himself directly. None of us would question that Joseph was destined to become a great 'servant in the hands of Christ'. Moreover, if we assume that he was the 'rod' or 'servant', observe how very well such an identification fits in with Moroni's mission of explaining to the latter-day Prophet his part in Isaiah's great vision of the future. As the 'rod' or 'servant in the hands of Christ', Joseph Smith fits naturally into Isaiah's prophecy, and it is easy to understand why Moroni quoted and explained Isaiah 11 to him. [See JS—H 1:40.]

"Despite this reasoning, we still have the uneasy feeling that better proof of Joseph Smith's being the 'rod' should be available. I believe there is better proof and that it is found in Doctrine and Covenants 113:5-6. . . .

"In order to assess this explanation intelligently, let us turn to Isaiah 11:10: [quoted].

"A closer translation of the original may be give here:

" 'And it shall come to pass in that day, that the root of Jesse, that standeth for an ensign [sign, signal] of the peoples, unto him shall the nations seek; and his resting place [refuge, residence] shall be glorious.'

"Quite obviously the 'root of Jesse' is a man, a descendant of Jesse and Joseph (as the Lord explains), who seems to have a great mission to perform in connection with gathering the remnant of Israel, as explained in Isaiah 11:11-16. I suggest that the 'rod' of verse 1 and the 'root of Jesse' of verse 10 refer to the same man, Joseph Smith. If the 'rod' in D&C 113:4 is the 'servant in the hands of Christ, who is partly a descendant of Jesse as well as of Ephraim, or of the house of Joseph', note that in verse 6 he seems to be more closely defined as a 'descendant of Jesse, as well as of Joseph, *unto whom rightly belongs the priesthood, and the keys of the kingdom, for an ensign, and for the gathering of my people in the last days.*' (Italics added.) Who better fits the description of the words in italics than Joseph Smith (see D&C 27:12-13; 86:8-11; 110:1-16; 115:18-19). He rightly holds the priesthood and its keys by lineage, and surely no one disputes the fact that the keys of the 'gathering of my people' were conferred on him by Moses in the Kirtland Temple, April 3, 1836." ("The Problem of the 'Rod' and the 'Root of Jesse' in Isaiah 11," *Improvement Era,* Oct. 1966, pp. 869, 914-15.)

In certain scriptures Christ is referred to as the "Root of David" (Revelation 5:5; 22:16). According to Elder Bruce R. McConkie, "This designation signifies that he who was the Son of David was also before David, was pre-eminent above him, and was the root or source from which the great king in Israel gained his kingdom and power" (*Mormon Doctrine,* p. 657; see also Matthew 22:44-45).

The explanation of Isaiah 11:10 given in Doctrine and Covenants 113 strongly implies that while Christ is the root of David, he is not the root of Jesse mentioned by Isaiah. There are two reasons for this conclusion. First, the Lord through the Prophet Joseph Smith in verse 2 identifies Christ as the stem of Jesse; he does not identify Christ as the root of Jesse. Second, verse 6 indicates that the root of Jesse is a servant of Christ to whom keys are given "in the last days" to gather Christ's people.

**D&C 113:9-10. The Gathering of Israel**

See Notes and Commentary on Doctrine and Covenants 45:64-75; 109:61-67; 110:11.

# Revelation to David W. Patten

# Section 114

## Historical Background

The Prophet Joseph Smith received this revelation on 17 April 1838 in behalf of David W. Patten at Far West, Missouri (see *History of the Church,* 3:23). Elder Patten was one of the original Apostles and "had for some time been located in Missouri and with Elder Thomas B. Marsh was maintaining a steady influence amidst the opposition of disaffected brethren, including the three who had been appointed to preside, David Whitmer, William W. Phelps and John Whitmer. The Lord called upon Elder Patten to settle up his business as soon as possible, make a disposition of his merchandise, and prepare to take a mission the following spring, in company with others to preach the Gospel to all the world. 'For verily thus saith the Lord, that inasmuch as there are those among you who deny my name, others shall be planted in their stead, and receive their bishopric. Amen.' Elder Patten obedient to this revelation took steps to meet this call which had come to him. Events were to develop, however, which would change the nature of his mission before the following spring could arrive." (Smith, *Church History and Modern Revelation,* 2:85.)

In October 1838 the persecutions of mobs in Missouri threatened not only the property of the Saints but also their lives. A group took three prisoners and promised to murder them, saying they would come the next morning to burn the Saints out. The Prophet Joseph Smith appointed Elder Patten to lead seventy-five volunteers against the mob of thirty or forty, hoping to rout them without bloodshed and free the three prisoners. In the confrontation Elder Patten was shot in the stomach and died that night. The Prophet said, "He was one of the Twelve Apostles, and died as he had lived, a man of God, and strong in the faith of a glorious resurrection, in a world where mobs will have no power or place" (*History of the Church,* 3:171).

Section 114 was added to the Doctrine and Covenants in 1876 by Elder Orson Pratt under the direction of President Brigham Young.

*Crooked River, Missouri, where David W. Patten sustained a fatal wound*

## Notes and Commentary

### D&C 114:1. What Mission was Assigned to the Twelve?

The Twelve were to leave Far West on 26 April 1839 for England. Before that time, however, Elder David W. Patten was killed in the battle of Crooked River on 25 October 1838 (see D&C 118; *History of the Church,* 3:170-71, 336-39).

### D&C 114:2. Several Deny the Work of the Lord

During the very month that this revelation was received, April 1838, several of the leading brethren in the Church were excommunicated. President George Q. Cannon reviewed the events of the first months of that year:

"While the Prophet had been journeying toward Missouri after escaping the Kirtland mob in January, 1838, a general assembly of the Saints in Far West was held on the 5th day of February, at which David Whitmer, John Whitmer and William W. Phelps were rejected as the local presidency; and a few days later Thomas B. Marsh and David W. Patten, of the Twelve, were selected to act as a presidency until the Prophet should arrive. Oliver Cowdery too had been suspended from his position. Persisting in unchristianlike conduct, W. W. Phelps and John Whitmer had been excommunicated by the high council in Far West, four days previous to the arrival of Joseph.

"This was the sad situation as the Prophet approached the dwelling place of the Saints in Missouri. . . .

"On the 12th of April, 1838, Oliver Cowdery was found guilty of serious wrong-doing for which he had not made repentance, and he was excommunicated by the high council at Far West. Before the same tribunal on the day following David Whitmer was charged with persistent disobedience of the word of wisdom and with unchristianlike conduct, and he was also cut off. Luke Johnson, Lyman E. Johnson and John F. Boynton were excommunicated about the same time, and less than a month later a similar fate befell William E. McLellin [all members of the Quorum of the Twelve].

"It was a sorrowful day for Joseph when he lost the companionship of these men who had been with him during many trials and who had participated with him in the glorious undertaking of heavenly things. But they were no longer anything but dead branches, harmful to the growing tree, and it was necessary for the pruner to lop them off." (*Life of Joseph Smith,* pp. 237-38.)

### D&C 114:2. What Is Meant by *Bishopric?*

The Lord said that those who were not faithful would be replaced in their bishopric. Elder Bruce R. McConkie explained the term *bishopric* as meaning "any office or position of major responsibility in the Church, any office of overseership under the supervision of which important church business is administered. . . . Thus the church affairs administered by a bishop are his bishopric. Thus, also, members of the Council of the Twelve—who hold the keys of the kingdom and are empowered to regulate all the affairs of the Church—serve in their bishopric." (*Mormon Doctrine,* p. 89.)

# "For Thus Shall My Church Be Called in the Last Days"

Section 115

## Historical Background

This revelation was received nine days after the one recorded in section 114 and is addressed to the officers and members of the Church, particularly the First Presidency and the Presiding Bishopric.

The Prophet Joseph Smith recorded that on 26 April 1838 at Far West, Missouri, he received the revelation setting forth "the will of God concerning the building up of that place, and of the Lord's House" (see *History of the Church,* 3:23).

*A scene at Far West, Missouri*

## Notes and Commentary

### D&C 115:1. The First Presidency

Notes and Commentary on Doctrine and Covenants 112:17-19 explains how this First Presidency came to be organized.

### D&C 115:1. Did Joseph Smith Have Other Counselors besides Sidney Rigdon and Hyrum Smith?

At a conference held at Kirtland, Ohio, on 3 September 1837, Oliver Cowdery, Joseph Smith, Sr., Hyrum Smith, and John Smith were sustained as assistant counselors.

At the time the revelation in Doctrine and Covenants 115 was given, however, only Joseph Smith, Sr., and John Smith were serving as assistant counselors (26 April 1838). Hyrum Smith had taken the place of Frederick G. Williams in the First Presidency, and Oliver Cowdery had lost his membership in the Church. (See *History of the Church,* 2:509; Smith, *Essentials in Church History,* p. 569.)

Later, in Nauvoo, others served as counselors to the Prophet: John C. Bennett (who served a short time because Sidney Rigdon was ill), William Law, and Amasa Lyman (see *History of the Church,* 4:255, 264, 282-86, 341).

### D&C 115:3-4. Official Name of the Church

Elder B. H. Roberts commented on the significance of the naming of the Church: "It will be observed that in verses three and four of this revelation the Lord gives to the Church its official name, 'The Church of Jesus Christ of Latter-day Saints.' Previous to this the Church had been called 'The Church of Christ,' 'The Church of Jesus Christ,' 'The Church of God,' and by a conference of Elders held at Kirtland in May, 1834, (see Church History, vol. 2, pp. 62-3), it was given the name 'The Church of the Latter-day Saints.' All these names, however, were by this revelation brushed aside, and since then the official name given in this revelation has been recognized as the true title of the Church, though often spoken of as 'The Mormon Church,' the 'Church of Christ,' etc. The appropriateness of this title is self evident, and in it there is a beautiful recognition of the relationship both of the Lord Jesus Christ and of the Saints to the organization. It is 'The Church of Jesus Christ.' It is the Lord's; He owns it, He organized it. It is the Sacred Depository of His truth. It is His instrumentality for promulgating all those spiritual truths with which He would have mankind acquainted. It is also His instrumentality for the perfecting of the Saints, as well as for the work of the ministry. It is His in all these respects; but it is an institution which also belongs to the Saints. It is their refuge from the confusion and religious doubt of the world. It is their instructor in principle, doctrine, and righteousness. It is their guide in matters of faith and morals. They have a conjoint ownership in it with Jesus Christ, which ownership is beautifully recognized in the latter part of the title. 'The Church of Jesus Christ of Latter-day Saints,' is equivalent to 'The Church of Jesus Christ,' and 'The Church of the Latter-day Saints.' " (*History of the Church,* 3:23-24n; see also 3 Nephi 27:7-8.)

### D&C 115:5. How Is the Church to Be a Standard to the Nations?

In the early years of World War II, Elder John A. Widstoe wrote:

"What is our mission to the world? I have turned to the scriptures to get the answer, and have found the answer, both in ancient and modern scriptures. It is that the Church of Christ at all times must be as a standard to the nations, a standard to which all nations, all people, all men may turn as they seek safety, peace, and happiness.

"It is our great mission . . . to be a standard to all the world, and we say without hesitation that those who obey and comply with that standard will find that which men most desire in life. It is a bold declaration, tremendously bold, that a small people in the valleys of these mountains, misunderstood, often harassed by persecution, may become the standard by which all mankind may be led to peace and happiness; but so it is. I am not saying it. It is the word of the Lord, both in ancient and modern days [see Isaiah 62:10-12]. If this standard would be accepted by the world the things we pray and hope for would soon come.

"Let me say that the Church of itself cannot be this standard. Since the Church is made up of individuals, it becomes an individual responsibility to make the Church a standard for the nations. I must be a standard in my life. I must so conduct myself that I may be a standard worthy of being followed by those who seek the greater joy in life." (In Conference Report, Apr. 1940, p. 35.)

### D&C 115:6. Wherein Is Safety?

This scripture answers the questions of many Latter-day Saints who wonder if they should leave their homes and move to Salt Lake City, Utah, or Jackson County, Missouri. They have heard that Zion will be the place of safety in times of tribulation, and they honestly wonder if members not living near the headquarters of the Church will be safe. Here the Lord specifically states that Zion *and her stakes* provide defense and refuge from the storm. Church leaders have counseled again and again that the Saints in this time are to gather to their local congregations in their own land until they can become stakes and strong places of spiritual defense. The direction for the gathering comes from the First Presidency, as Elder Harold B. Lee pointed out:

"But the designation of gathering places is qualified in another revelation by the Lord to which I would desire to call your attention. After designating certain places in that day where the Saints were to gather, the Lord said this:

" 'Until the day cometh when there is found no more room for them; and then I have other places which I will appoint unto them.' [D&C 101:21.]'

"Thus, clearly, the Lord has placed the responsibility for directing the work of gathering in the hands of the leaders of the Church to whom he will reveal his will where and when such gatherings would take place in the future. It would be well—before the frightening events concerning the fulfilment of all God's promises and predictions are upon us, that the Saints in every land prepare themselves and look forward to the instruction that shall come to them from the First Presidency of this Church as to where they shall be gathered and not be disturbed in their feelings until such instruction is given to them as it is revealed by the Lord to the proper authority." (In Conference Report, Apr. 1948, p. 55.)

The gathering to Zion is also discussed in Notes and Commentary on Doctrine and Covenants 45:64-75; 101:20-22.

**D&C 115:7-16. Why Was a Temple Never Built at Far West?**

Smith and Sjodahl explained why this commandment was not fulfilled:

"At this time there were about 150 houses at Far West, and among them were stores, hotels, and a fine school house. The City had sprung up, as by magic, in the midst of a rolling prairie. It might have been a large center of population today, into which would have been poured the wealth of continents, instead of a spot in a desert, but for the bigotry and strange madness of the neighbors.

"The corner stones of the Temple were laid on the 4th of July, 1838. The excavation, one historian says, 120 by 80 feet in area, and 5 feet in depth was completed in half a day, more than 500 men being employed in the work. Little else was done, however, for the storm of persecution broke loose in all its fury, and the Saints at that place went into exile again." (Commentary, p. 742.)

**D&C 115:17-19. Building Far West**

In earlier revelations the Lord had directed the Saints not to gather in haste (see D&C 58:56; 63:24; 101:68). Now he encouraged them to gather speedily to Far West. Smith and Sjodahl suggested a possible reason for the change: "It is quite probable that if the Saints had gathered in greater numbers and built up their Stakes and cities more rapidly, the enemies would have had less power to execute their designs. That they did not do their duty in this respect, may be inferred from Section 117:1-6." (Commentary, p. 743.)

# Grand Council

# Section 116

## Historical Background

This section, taken from an entry in the Prophet's history, was first placed in the Doctrine and Covenants in 1876 by Elder Orson Pratt under the direction of President Brigham Young. Though not a formal revelation in the same sense as other sections of the Doctrine and Covenants, nevertheless it is clearly a direct revelation from God and therefore worthy of inclusion. The entry in the Prophet Joseph Smith's history for 1838 is as follows:

"*Friday, May 18.*—I left Far West, in company with Sidney Rigdon, Thomas B. Marsh, David W. Patten, Bishop Partridge, Elias Higbee, Simeon Carter, Alanson Ripley, and many others, for the purpose of visiting the north country, and laying off a stake of Zion; making locations, and laying claim to lands to facilitate the gathering of Saints, for the benefit of the poor, in upholding the Church of God. . . .

"*Saturday, 19.*—This morning we struck our tents and formed a line of march, crossing Grand River at the mouth of Honey Creek and Nelson's Ferry. Grand River is a large, beautiful, deep and rapid stream, during the high waters of Spring, and will undoubtedly admit of navigation by steamboat and other water craft. At the mouth of Honey Creek is a good landing. We pursued our course up the river, mostly through timber, for about eighteen miles, when we arrived at Colonel Lyman Wight's home. He lives at the foot of Tower Hill (a name I gave the place in consequence of the remains of an

*Spring Hill at Adam-ondi-Ahman*

old Nephite altar or tower that stood there), where we camped for the Sabbath.

"In the afternoon I went up the river about half a mile to Wight's Ferry, accompanied by President Rigdon, and my clerk, George W. Robinson, for the purpose of selecting and laying claim to a city plat near said ferry in Daviess County, township 60, ranges 27 and 28, and sections 25, 36, 31, and 30, which the brethren called 'Spring Hill,' but by the mouth of the Lord it was named Adam-ondi-Ahman, because, said He, it is the place where Adam shall come to visit his people, or the Ancient of Days shall sit, as spoken of by Daniel the Prophet." (*History of the Church,* 3:34-35.)

On another occasion the Prophet wrote of this spot: "Adam-ondi-Ahman is located immediately on the north side of Grand River, in Daviess county, Missouri, about twenty-five miles north of Far West. It is situated on an elevated spot of ground, which renders the place as healthful as any part of the United States, and overlooking the river and the country round about, it is certainly a beautiful location." (*History of the Church,* 3:39.)

## Notes and Commentary

**D&C 116:1. What Is the Purpose of the Council at Which Adam Presides?**

Elder Joseph Fielding Smith said that the council at Adam-ondi-Ahman, as prophesied in Daniel 7:9-14, will be "of the greatest importance to this world. At that time there will be a transfer of authority from the usurper and impostor, Lucifer, to the rightful King, Jesus Christ. Judgment will be set and all who have held keys will make their reports and deliver their stewardships, as they shall be required. Adam will direct this judgment, and then he will make his report, as the one holding the keys for this earth, to his Superior Officer, Jesus Christ. Our Lord will then assume the reins of government; directions will be given to the Priesthood; and He, whose right it is to rule, will be installed officially by the voice of the Priesthood there assembled. This grand council of Priesthood will be composed, not only of those who are faithful who now dwell on this earth, but also of the prophets and apostles of old, who have had directing authority. Others may also be there, but if so they will be there by appointment, for this is to be an official council called to attend to the most momentous matters concerning the destiny of this earth.

"When this gathering is held, the world will not know of it; the members of the Church at large will not know of it, yet it shall be preparatory to the coming in the clouds of glory of our Savior Jesus Christ as the Prophet Joseph Smith has said. The world cannot know of it. The Saints cannot know of it—except those who officially shall be called into this council—for it shall precede the coming of Jesus Christ as a thief in the night, unbeknown to all the world." (*Way to Perfection,* pp. 290-91.)

# Revelation to William Marks, Newel K. Whitney, and Oliver Granger

Section 117

## Historical Background

This revelation in the Doctrine and Covenants is the first of four revelations that were all given to the Prophet Joseph Smith on 8 July 1838 at Far West, Missouri. Their order in the Doctrine and Covenants is somewhat different, however, from the order given in Joseph Smith's history.

"The Lord had commanded the Saints to gather and build up Far West speedily (See Sec. 115:17). A company of 515 souls, known as the *Kirtland Camp,* left Kirtland on the 6th of July, 1838, for Zion. On the 14th of September, it appears only 260 members were left, the others having been scattered 'to the four winds.' The camp arrived in Adam-ondi-Ahman on the 4th of October. Neither Marks, Whitney, nor Granger were members of this company. [Granger was already in Far West. He carried this revelation to Marks and Whitney in Kirtland and was instructed to return speedily to the land of Zion.] Joseph Smith at Far West had no means of knowing, at that time, who had, or who had not, left for Zion; but the Lord knew. Hence this Revelation in which He . . . calls William Marks and Newel K. Whitney to come to Zion and

*Church centers were located at Adam-ondi-Ahman and Far West, Missouri*

instructs the Saints concerning the property in Kirtland." (Smith and Sjodahl, Commentary, p. 744.)

# Notes and Commentary

### D&C 117:1-6. Property in Kirtland

"The Saints had private property in Kirtland, and there was property belonging to the Church. Many of them lingered there, reluctant to sacrifice their temporal interests. Our Lord regards this disposition as a sin (v. 4), and calls upon the people to repent and to let the property go for the liquidation of debt (v. 5). He would recompense them for any sacrifice they might make in His service." (Smith and Sjodahl, Commentary, p. 744.)

William Marks and Newel K. Whitney were mentioned by the Lord as not relinquishing their property in Kirtland and obeying the commandment to go to Missouri. Verses 4 and 5 of section 117 imply that some of this property may have been owned by the Church. Since Newel K. Whitney was a bishop in Kirtland, he may have had direct stewardship for such property. Either way, the Lord delivered a stinging rebuke to those men for forgetting the relative worth of things. President Joseph Fielding Smith commented: "It is quite evident that these two brethren had fallen under the spell of speculation and temptation so rife in Kirtland in 1837, and which was the downfall of so many of the leading brethren of the Church. However, they had not lost their faith and when the Lord gave them this call, they proceeded to obey the command." (*Church History and Modern Revelation,* 2:96.)

### D&C 117:6-7. God Has Power over the Earth and All the Affairs upon It

Those who ally themselves with the Lord will ultimately prosper. God has power over all and will cause all things to work together for the good of those who walk uprightly and follow his counsels (see D&C 90:24).

Concerning the assurance the Lord's people have of his support, Elder John Taylor said: "In relation to events that will yet take place, and the kind of trials, troubles, and sufferings which we shall have to cope with, it is to me a matter of very little moment; these things are in the hands of God, he dictates the affairs of the human family, and directs and controls our affairs; and the great thing that we, as a people, have to do is seek after and cleave unto our God, to be in close affinity with him, and to seek for his guidance, and his blessing and Holy Spirit to lead and guide us in the right path. Then it matters not what it is nor who it is that we have to contend with, God will give us strength according to our day." (In *Journal of Discourses,* 18:281.)

### D&C 117:7. Have the Latter-day Saints Seen the Solitary Places Blossom?

"This promise has been miraculously fulfilled in the history of the Latter-day Saints. Wherever they have settled, the land has been blessed, the moisture of the air has increased, and the rigor of the climate has been tempered. The so-called 'Great American Desert' exists no longer. In its place, there is an inland empire with a teeming population, centers of industry, and busy marts, and this modern wonder was performed by the location of the Church in the mountains." (Smith and Sjodahl, Commentary, p. 745.)

### D&C 117:8. Adam-ondi-Ahman—the Place Where Adam Dwelt

See Notes and Commentary on Doctrine and Covenants 116.

### D&C 117:8. What Did the Lord Mean by "Covet That Which Is but the Drop"?

Those who sought to hold on to their property in Kirtland when the Lord had commanded them to remove to join the body of Saints in Zion were most unwise. How paltry is a piece of land compared with that which the Lord has to offer his people. Moreover, can the Lord not help those who follow his will to obtain lands or whatever they need, according to his wisdom? (See Mark 10:28-30.) President Spencer W. Kimball taught:

"One man I know of was called to a position of service in the Church, but he felt that he couldn't accept because his investments required more attention and more of his time than he could spare for the Lord's work. He left the service of the Lord in search of Mammon, and he is a millionaire today.

"But I recently learned an interesting fact: If a man owns a million dollars worth of gold at today's prices, he possesses approximately one 27-billionth of all the gold that is present in the earth's thin crust alone. This is an amount so small in proportion as to be inconceivable to the mind of man. But there is more to this: The Lord who created and has power over all the earth created many other earths as well, even 'worlds without number' (Moses 1:33); and when this man received the oath and covenant of the priesthood (D&C 84:33-44), he received a promise from the Lord of 'all that my Father hath' (v. 38). To set aside all these great promises in favor of a chest of gold and a sense of carnal security is a mistake in perspective of colossal proportions. To think that he has settled for so little is a saddening and pitiful prospect indeed; the souls of men are far more precious than this." ("The False Gods We Worship," *Ensign,* June 1976, p. 5.)

### D&C 117:8. Where Is Olaha Shinehah?

"The plains of Olaha Shinehah, or the place where Adam dwelt," wrote President Joseph Fielding Smith, "must be a part of, or in the vicinity of Adam-ondi-Ahman. This name Olaha Shinehah, may be, and in all probability is, from the language of Adam. We may without great controversy believe that this is the name which Adam gave to this place, at least we may venture this as a probable guess. Shinehah, according to the Book of Abraham, is the name given to the sun. (Abraham 3:13.) It is the name applied to Kirtland when the Lord desired in a revelation to hide its identity. (Sec. 82.) Elder Janne M. Sjodahl commenting on the name, Olaha Shinehah, has said: 'Shinehah means sun, and Olaha is possibly a variant of the word Olea, which is "the moon." (Abraham 3:13.) If so the plains of Olaha Shinehah would be the Plains of the Moon and the Sun, so called, perhaps because of astronomical observations there made.' We learn from the writings of Moses that the Lord revealed to the ancients great knowledge concerning the stars, and Abraham by revelations and through the Urim and Thummim received wonderful information concerning the heavens and the governing planets, or stars. It was also revealed by the Prophet Joseph Smith that Methuselah was acquainted with the stars as were others of the antediluvian prophets including Adam. So it may be reasonable that here in this valley important information was made known anciently in relation to the stars of our universe." (*Church History and Modern Revelation,* 2:97-98.)

### D&C 117:11. What Is the Nicolaitan Band and Why Did the Lord Associate Newel K. Whitney with It?

Many scholars believe that the Nicolaitans in New Testament times were followers of Nicolas (see Acts 6:5). He was one of the seven appointed by the Church at Jerusalem to supervise the distribution of food and goods. Nicolas was believed by some of the early Church fathers to have apostatized from the true gospel and then to have established a sect of his own—the Nicolaitans (see *Interpreter's Dictionary of the Bible,* 3:548).

One Bible scholar wrote the following about the beliefs of the Nicolaitans: "They seem to have held that it was lawful to eat things sacrificed to idols, and to commit fornication, in opposition to the decree of the Church rendered in Acts 15:20, 29. . . . In a time of persecution, when the eating or not eating of things sacrificed to idols was more than ever a crucial test of faithfulness, they persuaded men more than ever that it was a thing indifferent. Rev. 2:13, 14. This was bad enough, but there was a yet worse evil. Mingling themselves in the orgies of idolatrous feasts, they brought the impurities of those feasts into the meetings of the Christian Church. And all this was done, it must be remembered, not simply as an indulgence of appetite, but as a part of a system, supported by a 'doctrine,' accompanied by the boast of a prophetic illumination." (Smith, *Dictionary of the Bible,* p. 447.)

Elder Bruce R. McConkie wrote that Nicolaitans today are "members of the Church who [are] trying to maintain their church standing while continuing to live after the manner of the world. . . . the designation has come to be used to identify those who want their names on the records of the Church, but do not want to devote themselves to the gospel cause with full purpose of heart." (*Doctrinal New Testament Commentary,* 3:446.)

As the bishop, Newel K. Whitney presided over the distribution of food and common goods in Kirtland. If Nicolas in ancient times turned from a similar sacred calling to a life of worldliness, the reference implies, then Newel K. Whitney was about to do a similar thing and was, therefore, worthy of being accused of partaking of the same spirit. His duty as bishop was to accept the consecrations of the members and give them their stewardships. If his motive in staying in Kirtland was tainted by his setting his heart on the things of the world, he was then showing a disposition similar to the Nicolaitan band of old.

### D&C 117:11. Be a Bishop "Not in Name but in Deed"

In 1951 J. Reuben Clark, Jr., was called to be Second Counselor in the First Presidency under President David O. McKay. He had previously served as First Counselor to President George Albert Smith. A lesser man could have considered this a demotion and a reason to be offended. President Clark, however, did not take such offense and at that time taught a great lesson to the Saints. He made the statement that "in the service of the Lord, it is not where you serve but how" (in Conference Report, Apr. 1951, p. 154).

Ecclesiastical position only does not guarantee exaltation. People will be judged by how they serve and not by what position they hold. It is a person's thoughts, works, words, and the desires of his heart that matter (see 2 Nephi 9:14; Mosiah 4:30; Alma 12:14; D&C 137:9).

### D&C 117:12-15. Oliver Granger Commended

"Oliver Granger was a man of faith and business ability—two qualities which form a rare combination. He characterized the Kirtland Camp as the greatest undertaking since the organization of the Church, and he firmly believed that God would bless that endeavor (*Hist. of the Church,* Vol. III., p. 96). When the Prophet fled from Kirtland, he appointed Granger his business agent, and so well did he perform this duty that he was commended by businessmen. At a conference held at Quincy, May 4th to 6th, 1839, he was appointed to return to Kirtland and take charge of the Temple and Church there. This makes the concluding verses of the Revelation perfectly clear. His name is to be held in remembrance for his faithful services as a man of business, having sanctified his talent to the service of the Lord." (Smith and Sjodahl, Commentary, p. 746.)

Though Oliver Granger is not as well known today as other early leaders of the Church, if no one but the Lord had his name in remembrance, that would be sufficient blessing.

# Revelation to the Twelve

Section 118

## Historical Background

This revelation is another of the four given to the Prophet at Far West, Missouri, on 8 July 1838. It came in response to the question, "Show unto us thy will O Lord concerning the Twelve" (*History of the Church,* 3:46).

## Notes and Commentary

### D&C 118:1. "Let a Conference Be Held Immediately"

The following is recorded in the Prophet Joseph Smith's history under the title "Minutes of a Meeting of the Twelve":

"Far West, July 9, 1838, a conference of the Twelve Apostles assembled at Far West, agreeable to the revelation, given July 8, 1838 [Section 118]. Present, Thomas B. Marsh, David W. Patten, Brigham Young, Parley P. Pratt and William Smith: T. B. Marsh, presiding.

"Resolved 1st. That the persons who are to fill the places of those who are fallen, be immediately notified to come to Far West; as also, those of the Twelve who are not present.

"Resolved 2nd. That Thomas B. Marsh notify Wilford Woodruff, that Parley P. Pratt notify Orson Pratt, and that President Rigdon notify Willard Richards, who is now in England.

"Voted that President Marsh publish the same in next number of *The Elders' Journal.*

"President Rigdon gave some counsel concerning the provisions necessary to be made for the families of the Twelve, while laboring in the cause of their Redeemer, advising them to instruct their converts to move without delay to the places of gathering, and there to strictly attend to the law of God." (*History of the Church,* 3:47.)

The minutes were signed by T. B. Marsh, president, and G. W. Robinson, clerk.

The Apostles and prophets are the foundation of the Church (see Ephesians 2:19-20), and the Lord wished to keep the Quorum of the Twelve functioning without any long delay, another evidence of the importance the Lord places on the presiding quorums.

### D&C 118:2. What Was Thomas B. Marsh to Publish?

While the rest of the Twelve were to go forth and preach the gospel (see D&C 118:3), President Thomas B. Marsh was to continue publishing the *Elders' Journal,* a responsibility he had while in Kirtland, Ohio. The *Elders' Journal* was short-lived, running from October 1837 to August 1838. (See Notes and Commentary for D&C 112:6.)

*The Twelve departed to their missions from the temple site at Far West, Missouri*

### D&C 118:4-5. Were the Twelve Able to Leave Far West on the Appointed Day?

The people of Missouri apparently knew of the Lord's injunction to meet on 26 April 1839, nearly a year later, and they were determined to impede the work of the Twelve and stop Mormonism. During the time between the revelation and the appointed day, "the whole Church was driven out of the State of Missouri, and it was as much as a man's life was worth to be found in the State if it was known that he was a Latter-day Saint; and especially was this the case with the Twelve. When the time came for the corner stone of the Temple to be laid, as directed in the revelation, the Church was in Illinois, having been expelled from Missouri by an edict from the Governor. Joseph and Hyrum Smith and Parley P. Pratt were in chains in Missouri for the testimony of Jesus. As the time drew nigh for the accomplishment of this work, the question arose. 'What is to be done?' Here is a revelation commanding the Twelve to be in Far West on the 26th day of April, to lay the cornerstone of the Temple there; it has to be fulfilled. The Missourians had sworn by all the gods of eternity that if every other revelation given through Joseph Smith were fulfilled, that should not be, for the day and date being given they declared that it would fail. The general feeling in the Church, so far as I know, was that, under the circumstances, it was impossible to accomplish the work; and the Lord would accept the will for the deed." (Wilford Woodruff, in *Journal of Discourses,* 13:159.)

But the Apostles were not to be put off their commanded duty:"On the night of April 25, 1839, the little band of apostles with a small company of faithful brethren, high priests, elders and priests, arrived at Far West. Shortly after midnight, on the morning of April 26th, they assembled on the temple lot in Far West, and there they held a conference." (Smith, *Church History and Modern Revelation,* pp. 196-97.)

Brigham Young presided; John Taylor, the clerk, wrote:

"The council then proceeded to the building spot of the Lord's House; when the following business was transacted: Part of a hymn was sung, on the mission of the twelve.

"Elder Alpheus Cutler, the master workman of the house, then recommenced laying the foundation of the Lord's House, agreeably to revelation, by rolling up a large stone near the southeast corner.

"The following of the twelve were present: Brigham Young, Heber C. Kimball, Orson Pratt, John E. Page, and John Taylor, who proceeded to ordain Wilford Woodruff and George A. Smith . . . to fill the places of those who had fallen." (*History of the Church,* 3:336-38.)

After several of the Apostles had offered prayers, the assembly sang "Adam-ondi-Ahman," and the Apostles left.

### D&C 118:6. Who Had Fallen from the Twelve by This Time?

Elders William E. M'Lellin, Luke S. Johnson, John F. Boynton, and Lyman E. Johnson had at this point fallen into disharmony with the Church and had been excommunicated. They had been in the first Quorum of the Twelve in this dispensation, which was called on 14 February 1835 (see *History of the Church,* 2:509; 3:31-32).One of the replacements, John E. Page, also eventually apostatized, but the other three remained faithful and loyal (see D&C 118:6). Two of the replacements, John Taylor and Wilford Woodruff, later became Presidents of the Church. John Taylor was ordained an Apostle at Far West on 19 December 1838. Wilford Woodruff was ordained an Apostle during the early morning meeting at Far West on 26 April 1839.

# The Law of Tithing

Section 119

## Historical Background

The Prophet Joseph Smith received the revelation on tithing on 8 July 1838 at Far West, Missouri. The revelation came in response to the following question: "O Lord! Show unto thy servant how much thou requirest of the properties of thy people for a tithing." (*History of the Church,* 3:44.)

President Joseph Fielding Smith explained: "The Lord had given to the Church the law of consecration and had called upon the members, principally the official members, to enter into a covenant that could not be broken and to be everlasting in which they were to consecrate their properties and receive stewardships, for this is the law of the celestial kingdom. Many of those who entered into this solemn covenant broke it and by so doing brought upon their heads, and the heads of their brethren and sisters, dire punishment and persecution. This celestial law of necessity was thereupon withdrawn for the time, or until the time of the redemption of Zion. While suffering intensely because of their debts and lack of means to meet their obligations Joseph Smith and Oliver Cowdery, November 29, 1834, in solemn prayer promised the Lord that they would give one tenth of all that the Lord should give unto them, as an offering to be bestowed upon the poor; they also prayed that their children, and the children's children after them should obey this law. (D.H.C., 2:174-5.) Now, however, it became necessary for the law to be given to the whole Church so the Prophet prayed for instruction. The answer they received [came] in the revelation [D&C 119]." (*Church History and Modern Revelation,* 2:90-91.)

Although tithing had been mentioned in earlier revelations, this revelation established a new and exacting law to replace the law of consecration, which had been revoked by the Lord. "The law of tithing, as understood today, had not been given to the Church previous to this revelation. The term 'tithing' in the prayer . . . and in previous revelations (64:23; 85:3; 97:11), had meant to them not just one-tenth, but all 'free-will offerings,' or 'contributions' to the Church funds." (Headnote to D&C 119 [1981 ed.]; see also Smith and Sjodahl, Commentary, p. 749.)

## Notes and Commentary

### D&C 119:1. What Was Meant by Surplus Property?

Elder Franklin D. Richards stated:

"Let us consider for a moment this word

'surplus.' What does it mean when applied to a man and his property? Surplus cannot mean that which is indispensably necessary for any given purpose, but what remains after supplying what is needed for that purpose. Is not the first and most necessary use of a man's property that he feed, clothe and provide a home for himself and family? This appears to be the great leading object for which we labor to acquire means, and as, until the time that this revelation was given, all public works and raising of all public funds had been by consecration, was not 'surplus property,' that which was over and above a comfortable and necessary subsistence? In the light of what had transpired and of subsequent events, what else could it mean? Can we take any other view of it when we consider the circumstances under which it was given in Far West in July, 1838?

"I have been unable in studying this subject to find any other definition of the term surplus, as used in this revelation, than the one I have just given. I find that it was so understood and recorded by the Bishops and people in those days, as well as by the Prophet Joseph himself, who was unquestionably the ablest and best exponent of this revelation." (In *Journal of Discourses,* 23:313.)

President Joseph Fielding Smith explained that the surplus is not required of the Saints today but that the obligation of the tenth is important: "In more recent times the Church has not called upon the members to give all their surplus property to the Church, but it has been the requirement according to the covenant, that they pay the tenth. It is remarkable how many excuses can be made and interpretations given as to what constitutes the tenth, by many members of the Church. It is written, however, that as we measure it shall be measured to us again. If we are stingy with the Lord, he may be stingy with us, or in other words, withhold his blessings. Then again, we have those among us who are hoping for the coming of the law of consecration thinking that in that day they are going to profit by the equalizing of the wealth of other members of the Church. It is definitely true, however, that all those who will not obey the law of tithing, will not be entitled to enter into the covenants of consecration, but when the day comes for the establishing of Zion and the redemption of the earth, such people will find themselves removed." (*Church History and Modern Revelation,* 2:92.)

### D&C 119:2-3. What Is the Purpose of the Law of Tithing?

The law of tithing is for now a preparatory law, as explained by Elder Orson F. Whitney: "The Law of Tithing was given to supersede, for the time being, a greater law known as the Law of Consecration [D&C 42:30-42], the object of which was and is to sanctify the Lord's people and 'prepare them for a place in the celestial world' [D&C 78:7]. To that end it was designed to do away with selfishness, greed, pride, envy, poverty, and all the ills that spring from such conditions. For none of these things can be admitted into the kingdom of heaven. It was to institute an order of equality and consequent unity, in which every man, employed at that for which he was best fitted, would be 'seeking the interest of his neighbor and doing all things with an eye single to the glory of God' [D&C 82:19]. . . . A brave attempt to practise it was made by the Latter-day Saints, soon after this Church was organized. But they lacked experience, and did not completely rise to the occasion. Selfishness within, and persecution without, prevented a perfect achievement. So the Lord withdrew the Law of Consecration [see D&C 105], and gave to his people a lesser law, one easier to live, but pointing forward, like the other, to something grand and glorious in the future. That lesser law, the Law of Tithing, is as a schoolmaster, a disciplinary agent, to bring the Saints eventually up to the practise of the higher law, and meanwhile to keep their hearts open for its reception when it returns. Those who obey the Law of Tithing will be prepared to live the Law of Consecration. Those who do not obey it will not be prepared. That is the whole thing in a nut shell." (In Conference Report, Apr. 1931, pp. 65-66.)

### D&C 119:4. What Is an Honest Tithing?

Elder John A. Widtsoe explained that *"tithing means one-tenth. Those who give less do not really pay tithing; they are lesser contributors to the Latter-day cause of the Lord.* Tithing means one-tenth of a person's income, interest, or increase. The merchant should pay tithing upon the net income of his business, the farmer upon the net income of his farming operations; the wage earner or salaried man upon the wage or salary earned by him. Out of the remaining nine-tenths he pays his current expenses, taxes, savings, etc. To deduct living costs, taxes, and similar expenses from the income and

*John A. Widtsoe taught the meaning of the word* tithe

pay tithing upon the remainder does not conform to the Lord's commandment. Under such a system most people would show nothing on which to pay tithing. There is really no place for quibbling on this point. Tithing should be given upon the basis of our full earned income. If the nature of a business requires special interpretation, the tithepayer should consult the father of his ward, the bishop." (*Evidences and Reconciliations,* 2:86; emphasis added.)

**D&C 119:5-6. Warning to Those Who Disobey the Law of Tithing**

Not only does disobedience influence one's blessings now, but it also is of great significance in determining one's future eternal inheritance. Elder Melvin J. Ballard gave this counsel: "Do we not hope and expect to have an inheritance in the celestial kingdom, even upon this earth in its redeemed and sanctified state? [D&C 88:25-26; 130:9.] What are the terms under which we may obtain that inheritance? The law of tithing is the law of inheritance. It leads to it. No man may hope or expect to have an inheritance on this celestial globe who has failed to pay his tithing. By the payment of his honest tithing he is establishing a right and a title to this inheritance, and he cannot secure it upon any other terms but by complying with this and other just requirements; and this is one of the very essential things." (In Conference Report, Oct. 1929, p. 51.)

**D&C 119:7. Tithing, an "Ensample" and Test for the Stakes of Zion**

The revelation in section 119 established the principle of tithing as an "ensample" for all the stakes of Zion (D&C 119:7; see Notes and Commentary on D&C 98:38 for a definition of the word *ensample*).

President Joseph F. Smith testified of the worth of the law of tithing as a test for the Saints: "By this principle (tithing) the loyalty of the people of this Church shall be put to the test. By this principle it shall be known who is for the kingdom of God and who is against it. By this principle it shall be seen whose hearts are set on doing the will of God and keeping His commandments, thereby sanctifying the land of Zion unto God, and who are opposed to this principle and have cut themselves off from the blessings of Zion. There is a great deal of importance connected with this principle, for by it it shall be known whether we are faithful or unfaithful." (*Gospel Doctrine,* p. 225.)

# Disposition of Church Funds

# Section 120

## Historical Background

When the Lord established the law of tithing in this dispensation (see D&C 119), he explained whose responsibility it was to handle the tithes of the Church. On 8 July 1838 the Prophet Joseph Smith received the revelation "making known the disposition of the properties tithed as named in the preceding revelation" (*History of the Church,* 3:44).

## Notes and Commentary

**D&C 120:1. How Is Tithing Administered in the Church?**

In April 1911 the First Presidency of the Church (Joseph F. Smith, Anthon H. Lund, John H. Smith) gave the following explanation of the accounting of tithes received: "The subject of Church revenues may be touched upon perhaps with profit. The Latter-day Saints believe in tithing. It is a principle of their faith. It is an ancient observance reaching back to patriarchal times, as related in the Bible. It was established in the Church in the year 1838. The manner of its payments and disbursement is revealed by Divine authority and has appeared in the Church books ever since that date. It is complied with religiously by the Church authorities themselves. It is not the property of the President. He does not claim it or collect it. Tithing is received by the local bishops in the respective wards, who are under the supervision of the local presidents of stakes. The whole income is accounted for to the presiding bishopric of the Church and is under their direction. Their office contains complete records of all the tithing paid during each year. Every tithepayer will find in that office his record. The entire receipts and disbursements are there accounted for in the most complete detail. An auditing committee, composed of men well known in the community for their independence of character and business integrity, not of the leading authorities of the Church, chosen by the general conference, thoroughly inspect and report annually upon them. The funds thus received are not the property of the President of the Church or his associates, nor of the presiding bishopric, nor of the local bishops. They belong to the Church and are used for Church purposes." (In Clark, *Messages of the First Presidency,* 4:228-29.)

President J. Reuben Clark, Jr., explained how tithing is administered:

"Under the direction of the First Presidency a budget is drawn up, as nearly as may be at the first

*Tithing money helps build chapels*

of the year, which includes all of the proposed expenditures of the tithing. This budget is the result of the careful consideration of the departments which are responsible for the expenditure of the funds.

"This budget is then taken before the Council on the Expenditure of the Tithing, composed, as the revelation provides, of the First Presidency, the Council of the Twelve, and the Presiding Bishopric. This council considers and discusses the budget so submitted, approving or disapproving, as the case may be, individual items, but finally passing the budget.

"The approved budget as it comes from that meeting is then turned over for its expenditures to a Committee on Expenditures. This committee then passes upon and authorizes the expenditures of the tithing. So that there is a complete check upon all of the tithing which is paid into the Church. None of it is expended except upon the approval and authorization of this committee." (In Conference Report, Oct. 1943, p. 12.)

Those who pay tithing do so in the faith that the funds will be properly disbursed as needed in the Lord's kingdom. Contributions to other funds in the Church are applied to specific aspects of the Lord's work known beforehand to the donor, for example, welfare, missionary, and building fund.

# Constitution of the Priesthood

Section 121

## Historical Background

On 27 October 1838 Lilburn W. Boggs, governor of Missouri, issued the infamous extermination order which read in part: "The Mormons must be treated as enemies and *must be exterminated* or driven from the state, if necessary for the public good" (*History of the Church,* 3:175). Four days later the Prophet and several leaders of the Church were betrayed into the hands of the Missourians at Far West, Missouri. For the next several weeks Joseph Smith and his associates were abused and insulted, forced to march to Independence and then to Richmond, and on 30 November 1838 incarcerated in Liberty Jail in Missouri (see *History of the Church,* 3:188-89, 215). These men had not been convicted of any crime; nevertheless, they were held in the jail for several months.

The Prophet Joseph Smith and his companions (Hyrum Smith, Lyman Wight, Caleb Baldwin, Alexander McRae and, for part of the time, Sidney Rigdon) suffered greatly while they were held in the jail awaiting trial on false charges: "Many inhumanities were heaped upon them while they were there. Insufficient and improper food was their daily fare; at times only the inspiration of the Lord saved them from the indulgence of poisoned food, which all did not escape. [Alexander McRae said, 'We could not eat it until we were driven to it by hunger' (Roberts, *Comprehensive History of the Church,* 1:521).]

"The jail had no sleeping quarters, and thus they were forced to seek rest and recuperation on beds of straw placed on hardened plank and stone floors. They were suffered very little contact with the outside world, especially during the first month or so of their confinement. And this, at a crucial time when the Latter-day Saints were at the peak of persecution in Missouri, and were desperately in need of their prophet-leader." (Dyer, *Refiner's Fire,* pp. 275-76.)

Occasionally they were permitted visits at the jail from friends and were allowed to send and receive correspondence. Between 20 March and 25 March 1839, the Prophet Joseph dictated a lengthy communication that was signed by all the prisoners (actually there were two letters, although the Prophet identified the second as a continuation of the first). President Joseph Fielding Smith wrote of this correspondence: "This is one of the greatest letters that was ever penned by the hand of man. In fact it was the result of humble inspiration. It is a prayer and a prophecy and an answer by revelation from the Lord. None other but a noble soul filled with the spirit of love of Christ could have written such a letter. Considering [their sufferings], it is no wonder that the Prophet cried out in the anguish of his soul for relief. Yet, in his earnest pleading, there breathed a spirit of tolerance and love for his fellow man." (*Church History and Modern Revelation,* 2:176.)

Sections 121, 122, and 123 were extracted from this communication and included in the 1876 edition of the Doctrine and Covenants by Elder Orson Pratt under the direction of President Brigham Young. The edition of the Doctrine and Covenants that included these three sections was sustained as scripture in the October 1880 conference of the Church. (For a full text of the letters, see *History of the Church,* 3:289-305.)

A published account of the letters in the *Times and Seasons* did not contain some parts of the original letters that are found in the Doctrine and Covenants. The Reorganized church pointed out this fact and challenged the Doctrine and Covenants account. The original letters, however, now located in the Church archives, vindicate the account as published in the Doctrine and Covenants (see *Deseret Evening News,* 27 June 1896, p. 4).

## Notes and Commentary

### D&C 121:1-5. Why Did the Prophet Use Such Words As *Pavilion* and *Hiding Place?*

"These are expressions used by the authors of the Bible. When David says, 'He made darkness his hiding-place, his pavilion round about him; darkness of waters, thick clouds of the skies' (Ps. 18:11), he considers the darkness of the thundercloud as a tent, or pavilion, in which Jehovah dwells in His majesty. The thunder-bolts, the hail, the wind, are His messengers. The Prophet Joseph, by using this grand, poetic conception, entreats the Lord to manifest Himself in His power for the salvation of the Saints from their enemies." (Smith and Sjodahl, Commentary, p. 753.)

### D&C 121:7. Is There a Place in the Divine Plan for Adversity and Affliction?

There can be a benefit from adversity in one's life, as Elder James E. Faust said: "In the pain, the agony, and the heroic endeavors of life, we pass through a refiner's fire, and the insignificant and the unimportant in our lives can melt away like dross and make our faith bright, intact, and strong. In this way the divine image can be mirrored from the soul. It is part of the purging toll exacted of some to become acquainted with God. In the agonies of life, we seem to listen better to the faint, godly whisperings of the Divine Shepherd." (In Conference Report, Apr. 1979, p. 77; or *Ensign,* May 1979, p. 53.)

Some erroneously believe that their afflictions are punishments from God, but there is a great difference between the source of tribulation and the uses of tribulation: "Unfortunately, some of our greatest tribulations are the result of our own foolishness and weakness and occur because of our own carelessness or transgression" (James E. Faust,

*James E. Faust taught about the beneficial effects of adversity*

in Conference Report, Apr. 1979, p. 78; or *Ensign,* May 1979, p. 54). Other afflictions are the result of the frailty and corruptibility of the mortal body, which is subject to disease and malfunction. Still other causes lie in the means chosen by the wicked in their misuse of agency. Finally, the judgments of God exercised upon the wicked cause famine, pestilence, earthquakes, and other tribulations.

It is not the task here to determine the cause of personal tribulation since the Saints of all ages have suffered adversity and affliction, but rather to discover what uses the Lord makes of mortal trials. Referring to the imprisonment and other terrible injustices suffered by Joseph Smith, President Brigham Young said that the Prophet progressed toward perfection more in thirty-eight years because of the severe tribulation through which he successfully passed than he would have been able to do in a thousand years without it (see *Journal of Discourses,* 2:7).

Of himself the Prophet said, "I feel like Paul, to glory in tribulation" (D&C 127:2). The Savior's life is the perfect example of enduring tribulation (see D&C 122:7-8). Here is the point of the whole concern: If one can look to the Savior or to the Prophet as models of endurance, one may find hope and strength to endure one's own afflictions.

Elder Marion G. Romney said: "All . . . who are being tried in the crucible of adversity and affliction: Take courage; revive your spirits and strengthen your faith. In these lessons so impressively taught in precept and example by our great exemplar, Jesus Christ, and his Prophet of the restoration, Joseph Smith, we have ample inspiration for comfort and for hope.

"If we can bear our afflictions with the understanding, faith, and courage, and in the spirit in which they bore theirs, we shall be strengthened and comforted in many ways. We shall be spared the torment which accompanies the mistaken idea that all suffering comes as chastisement for transgression. . . .

"We can draw assurance from the Lord's promise that 'he that is faithful in tribulation, the reward of the same is greater in the kingdom of heaven.

" 'Ye cannot behold with your natural eyes, for the present time, [he said,] the design of your God concerning those things which shall come hereafter, and the glory which shall follow much tribulation.

" 'For after much tribulation come the blessings. . . .' (D&C 58:2-4.)" (In Conference Report, Oct. 1969, p. 59.)

### D&C 121:11-25. What Is the Nature of a Member Who Falls from Activity into Apostasy?

Elder George Q. Cannon taught: "The Saints should not imagine that because they know the truth and the Work of God at the present time, that they will always know these things and therefore be able to stand. If they lose the Holy Spirit through their transgressions, from that moment their knowledge respecting the Work of God ceases to increase and becomes dead; a short time only elapses before such persons deny the faith. They may not deny that the Work was ever true, or that the Elders were ever the servants of God, but they will place a limit and say, 'Up to such a time the work was true and the Elders were all right, but, after that, they went astray',—that very period being the time at which they themselves had committed some act or acts to forfeit the Spirit of God and kill the growth of that knowledge which they had had bestowed upon them. This has been the case in numerous instances in the past. . . . It is plain that it is they who have transgressed, and thereby driven the Spirit of the Lord from them; and at the very time they say the Church of God strayed, they themselves were guilty of transgression." ("Knowledge, without the Aid of the Spirit of the Lord, Not Sufficient to Save," *Millennial Star,* 8 Aug. 1863, pp. 505-6.)

### D&C 121:15-16. Do Enemies of the Church Prosper?

Elder Heber J. Grant said: "Our enemies have never done anything that has injured this work of God, and they never will. I look around, I read, I reflect, and I ask the question, Where are the men of influence, of power and prestige, who have worked against the Latter-day Saints? Where is the reputation, for honor and courage, of the governors of Missouri and Illinois, the judges, and all others who have come here to Utah on special missions against the Latter-day Saints? Where are there people to do them honor? They can not be found. . . . Where are the men who have assailed this work? Where is their influence? They have faded away like dew before the sun. We need have no fears, we Latter-day Saints. God will continue to sustain this work; He will sustain the right. If we are loyal, if we are true, if we are worthy of this Gospel, of which God has given us a testimony, there is no danger that the world can ever injure us. We can never be injured . . . by any mortals, except ourselves." (In Conference Report, Apr. 1909, p. 110.)

### D&C 121:21. Does God Punish Later Generations for the Sins of Their Parents?

President Joseph F. Smith stated that "the infidel will impart infidelity to his children if he can. The whoremonger will not raise a pure, righteous posterity. He will impart seeds of disease and misery, if not of death and destruction, upon his offspring, which will continue upon his children and descend to his children's children to the third and fourth generation. It is perfectly natural that the children should inherit from their fathers, and if they sow the seeds of corruption, crime and loathsome disease, their children will reap the fruits thereof. Not in accordance with God's wishes for His wish is that men will not sin and therefore will not transmit the consequences of their sin to their children, but that they will keep His commandments, and be free from sin and from entailing the effects of sin upon their offspring; but inasmuch as men will not hearken unto the Lord, but will become a law unto themselves, and will commit sin they will justly reap the consequences of their own iniquity, and will naturally impart its fruits to their children to the third and fourth generation." (In Conference Report, Oct. 1912, p. 9; see also D&C 124:50.)

### D&C 121:26. In What Context Was the Prophet Speaking When He Promised the "Unspeakable Gift of the Holy Ghost"?

This section and the two following are excerpts from letters written by the Prophet Joseph Smith from Liberty Jail. The Prophet's comments that preceded this passage were not included in the Doctrine and Covenants but are of interest in setting the stage for his comments on the gifts of the Holy Ghost:

"The things of God are of deep import; and time, and experience, and careful and ponderous and solemn thoughts can only find them out. Thy mind, O man! if thou wilt lead a soul unto salvation, must stretch as high as the utmost heavens, and search into and contemplate the darkest abyss, and the broad expanse of eternity—thou must commune with God. How much more dignified and noble are the thoughts of God, than the vain imaginations of the human heart! None but fools will trifle with the souls of men.

"How vain and trifling have been our spirits, our conferences, our councils, our meetings, our private as well as public conversations—too low, too mean, too vulgar, too condescending for the dignified characters of the called and chosen of God, according to the purposes of His will, from before the foundation of the world! We are called to hold the keys of the mysteries of those things that have

*Divine light and encouragement were revealed through the Prophet Joseph Smith while he was imprisoned in Liberty Jail*

been kept hid from the foundation of the world until now. Some have tasted a little of these things, many of which are to be poured down from heaven upon the heads of babes; yea, upon the weak, obscure and despised ones of the earth. Therefore we beseech of you, brethren, that you bear with those who do not feel themselves more worthy than yourselves, while we exhort one another to a reformation with one and all, both old and young, teachers and taught, both high and low, rich and poor, bond and free, male and female; let honesty, and sobriety, and candor, and solemnity, and virtue, and pureness, and meekness, and simplicity crown our heads in every place; and in fine, become as little children, without malice, guile or hypocrisy.

"And now, brethren, after your tribulations, if you do these things, and exercise fervent prayer and faith in the sight of God always, [D&C 121:26-32]." (*History of the Church,* 3:295-96.)

**D&C 121:26-32. Do Latter-day Saints Enjoy Gifts of the Holy Ghost That Have Never Been Enjoyed Before?**

The gift of the Holy Ghost has been enjoyed by every faithful Saint since the world began. What is meant in verse 26 is that in the dispensation of the fulness of times all the keys, powers, and principles known in past dispensations individually are now enjoyed collectively. In addition, the revealed organization of the earthly kingdom is, as President Harold B. Lee said, "more perfected than in the past dispensations" (*Stand Ye in Holy Places,* p. 273; see also p. 322).

**D&C 121:28. Should One Be Concerned about the Identity of the Gods of Heaven?**

President Wilford Woodruff gave firm counsel on this question: "I want to say this to all Israel: Cease troubling yourselves about who God is; who Adam is, who Christ is, who Jehovah is. For heaven's sake, let these things alone. Why trouble yourselves about these things? God has revealed Himself, and when the 121st section of the Doctrine and Covenants is fulfilled, whether there be one God or many gods they will be revealed to the children of men, as well as thrones and dominions, principalities, and powers. Then why trouble yourselves about these things? God is God. Christ is Christ. The Holy Ghost is the Holy Ghost. That should be enough for you and me to know. If we want to know any more, wait till we get where God is in person." (In *Millennial Star,* 6 June 1895, pp. 355-56.)

**D&C 121:33. Is There Yet Knowledge to Be Poured Out upon the Heads of the Latter-day Saints?**

President Joseph Fielding Smith taught that "from the very beginning Satan through his emissaries, has endeavored to destroy this work and to stop the Church from receiving revelation. The Lord has given to the Church knowledge and guidance constantly suited to their advancement. There is much that is still held in store, many great and important truths, when we are prepared to receive them. The Lord has promised to give revelation 'and commandments not a few,' to the faithful who are diligent before the Lord. (D. & C. 59:4.)" (*Church History and Modern Revelation,* 2:177.)

President Spencer W. Kimball testified that the Church constantly receives revelations: "There are those who would assume that with the printing and binding of these sacred records, that would be the 'end of the prophets.' But again we testify to the world that revelation continues and that the vaults and files of the Church contain these revelations which come month to month and day to day." (In Conference Report, Apr. 1977, p. 115; or *Ensign,* May 1977, p. 78.)

**D&C 121:34. Who Are Those Who Are Called?**

Elder Joseph Fielding Smith explained: "I take it that every man who is ordained to an office in the priesthood has been called. The Lord is willing that any man should serve him." (In Conference Report, Oct. 1945, p. 97.)

Elder Bruce R. McConkie indicated that the call is extended to all members of the Church:

"To be called is to be a member of the Church and kingdom of God on earth; it is to be numbered with the saints; it is to accept the gospel and receive the everlasting covenant; it is to have part and lot in the earthly Zion; it is to be born again, to be a son or a daughter of the Lord Jesus Christ; to have membership in the household of faith; it is to be on the path leading to eternal life and to have the hope of eternal glory; it is to have a conditional promise of eternal life; it is to be an inheritor of all the blessings of the gospel, provided there is continued obedience to the laws and ordinances thereof.

"Within this over-all framework, there are individual calls to positions of trust and responsibility, but these are simply assignments to labor on the Lord's errand, in particular places, for a time and a season. The call itself is to the gospel cause; it is not reserved for apostles and prophets or for the great and mighty in Israel; it is for all the members of the kingdom." (*Doctrinal New Testament Commentary,* 3:326.)

### D&C 121:34-40. "Why Are They Not Chosen?"

President N. Eldon Tanner interpreted this passage as referring to those who fail to magnify their priesthood or who use it as it should not be used: "I know of many cases where a man has gradually failed to magnify his priesthood and moved away from activity in the Church. As a result, a man who has been very active loses his testimony and the Spirit of the Lord withdraws from him, and he begins to criticize those in authority, and to persecute the saints, apostatize, and fight against God." (In Conference Report, Apr. 1970, p. 52.)

President Tanner on another occasion tied the quality of dependability directly to whether or not one is chosen:

"We must not be *nearly* dependable, but *always* dependable. Let us be faithful in the little things, as well as the big ones. Can I be depended upon to fill every assignment, whether it be for a two-and-a-half minute talk, home teaching, a visit to the sick, or a call as a stake or full-time missionary?

"Remember, '. . . there are many called, but few are chosen. And why are they not chosen?

" 'Because their hearts are set so much upon the things of this world, and aspire to the honors of men, . . .' (D&C 121:34-35), and they are not dependable." ("Dependability," *Ensign,* Apr. 1974, p. 5.)

A careful analysis of Doctrine and Covenants 121:34-35 shows a cause and effect relationship between certain ways of behaving and whether or not one is chosen.

*N. Eldon Tanner explained why some are called but not chosen*

This chain reaction illustrates why some men are called but not chosen.

**When the hearts of men–**
1. Are set on the things of the world, or
2. Aspire to the honors of men,

**They will act in ways detrimental to spiritual growth, including–**
1. Covering their sins.
2. Gratifying their pride and vain ambitions.
3. Exercising unrighteous dominion over others.

**These actions cause–**
1. The heavens to withdraw themselves.
2. The Spirit of the Lord to be grieved.
3. A withdrawal of power and authority.

The chain could be stated positively to answer the question, "How does one come to be chosen?"

**When the hearts of men–**
1. Are set on the things of God, and
2. Aspire for God's approval and honors,

**They will act in ways beneficial to spiritual growth, including–**
1. Repenting of their sins.
2. Humbling themselves.
3. Seeking the kingdom of God first.
4. Exercising love and charity toward others.

**These actions cause–**
1. The heavens to draw near.
2. The Spirit of the Lord to be near.
3. An increase in power and authority.

### D&C 121:38. What Does It Mean to Kick against the Pricks?

A prick or goad is a pointed stick sometimes tipped with iron that is used to drive cattle. Elder Harold B. Lee explained the Lord's metaphorical use of this term in teaching the principle of obedience:

"These no doubt are the pricks of the gospel. I wonder, perhaps, if they are not those things . . . [President J. Reuben Clark, Jr.,] called 'restraints,' the restraints of the Word of Wisdom, the restraints imposed in keeping the Sabbath day holy, injunctions against card playing, the restraints imposed by following out the welfare program. And so we might go on. These are the restraints against which some people seem to rebel and are kicking constantly against—the 'pricks' of the gospel. . . .

"These [persons] are the ones who next begin to 'persecute the Saints' and, finally, 'to fight against God.' " (In Conference Report, Oct. 1947, pp. 65-66.)

### D&C 121:39. Why Do Most Men Have Difficulty Handling Power and Authority?

Elder Orson F. Whitney referred to misuse of power, pointing out that not all men fall into that temptation: "All men who hold position do not abuse its privileges, and the man who serves God humbly and faithfully never will, for the moment he yielded to the temptation so to do, that moment would he cease to serve the Lord; but there are many, alas! who sadly misuse the functions of their office, and prostitute every power and privilege to the gratification of self and the injury and embarrassment of their fellow men. It is dangerous to put some men into power. They swell up and become so distended with the ideas of their greatness and importance, that we are forcibly reminded of so many inflated toy balloons, which the slightest prick of a pin would burst and ruin forever. A very small office and a very little authority is sufficient to intoxicate some men and render them entirely unfit for duty." (In Rich, *Scrapbook of Mormon Literature,* 2:511-12.)

### D&C 121:41-46. A Guide to Increased Priesthood Power and Influence

The righteous application of the principles revealed here give the priesthood bearer greater power through the sanction of the Holy Ghost. The Lord also reveals here the key to the loss of these powers. When a man feels a reduction or the withdrawal of the Holy Ghost (manifested by contention, disunity, or rebellion), he may at that instant know that he has been exercising unrighteous dominion (see Smith and Sjodahl, Commentary, p. 759).

One of the crucial tests for a priesthood bearer's proper use of priesthood authority is in the intimate relationships within his own home, as President Hugh B. Brown said: "I should like to say to you fathers tonight that our conduct in our homes determines in large measure our worthiness to hold and exercise the priesthood, which is the power of God delegated to man. Almost any man can make a good showing when on parade before the public, but one's integrity is tested when 'off duty.' The real man is seen and known in the comparative solitude of the home. An office or title will not erase a fault nor guarantee a virtue." (In Conference Report, Apr. 1962, p. 88.)

### D&C 121:43. What Does the Lord Mean by "Reproving Betimes with Sharpness"?

Many people assume the word *betimes* means "occasionally" or "sometimes"; this is not its primary meaning, however. To reprove betimes means to do so "at an early time; in good time, in due time; while there is yet time, before it is too late; or in a short time, soon, speedily" (*Oxford English Dictionary,* s.v. "betimes").

### D&C 121:45. "Let Virtue Garnish Thy Thoughts Unceasingly"

To garnish means to decorate, to embellish, or to adorn. If virtue garnished all of a person's thoughts, the sins of immorality, dishonesty, greed, and so on would be eliminated. One's thoughts have a direct bearing on one's actions.

Church leaders have warned against allowing oneself to entertain impure thoughts, for the consequences of such thoughts may be very serious indeed. Recently, President Spencer W. Kimball issued a basic statement on morality, pointing out that the early Apostles and prophets had condemned various moral transgressions: "They included all sexual relations outside marriage—petting, sex perversion, masturbation, and preoccupation with sex in one's thoughts and talking. Included are every hidden and secret sin and all unholy and impure thoughts and practices."

In the final part of the statement he called on the Saints to remain clean and virtuous:

"How we pray for you every meeting we hold, every night and morning in our homes, and every night in our bedrooms; we pray for you that you will keep yourselves clean. Clean—we mean clean from beginning to end. Free from all the ugly things the world is pushing upon us—the drugs, and drinking, and smoking, the vulgarity, the pornography—all those things you don't need to participate in. You must not give yourselves to them.

"Put on the full armor of God. Attend to your personal and family prayers and family devotions; keep holy the Sabbath; live strictly the Word of Wisdom; attend to all family duties; and above all, keep your life clean and free from all unholy and impure thoughts and actions. Avoid all associations which degrade and lower the high, righteous standards set up for us. Then your life will sail smoothly and peace and joy will surround you." ("President Kimball Speaks Out on Morality," *Ensign,* Nov. 1980, pp. 95, 98.)

### D&C 121:45. "Then Shall Thy Confidence Wax Strong in the Presence of God"

Elder James E. Talmage once said that "any man may enter the highest degree of the celestial kingdom when his actions have been such that he can feel at home there" (Hugh B. Brown, *Seek to Know the Shepherd* [Brigham Young University Speeches of the Year, 9 Dec. 1959], p. 5).

President Marion G. Romney added: "I can think of no blessings to be more fervently desired than those promised to the pure and the virtuous. Jesus spoke of specific rewards for different virtues but reserved the greatest, so it seems to me, for the pure in heart, 'for they,' said he, 'shall see God' (Matt. 5:8). *And not only shall they see the Lord, but they shall feel at home in his presence.*" (In Conference Report, Apr. 1979, p. 60; or *Ensign,* 1979, p. 42; emphasis added.)

### D&C 121:45-46. What Are the Manifestations of Charity and Virtue?

The last verses of Doctrine and Covenants 121 contain sublime language and are a central message for the whole section. If understood, these phrases should lift every member of the Church to more lofty thoughts, more considerate and loving expressions, and more noble and selfless actions. The rewards for possessing charity and virtue are—

1. Increased confidence in the presence of God.
2. The doctrine of the priesthood blessing the soul as a heaven sent gift (it comes in no other way).

3. Great power and sure confidence in exercising priesthood stewardship, resulting from the mighty companionship of a member of the Godhead.

Great spiritual yearnings may spring from the heart of a righteous Saint, but no finer manifestation of God's love and trust in his worthy servants can be imagined than that promised in this closing message from the Lord. No priesthood bearer should be content until he senses the lifting fulfillment of this promise.

# "All These Things Shall Give Thee Experience"

Section 122

## Historical Background

The five months of imprisonment, abuse, malnutrition, and separation that the Prophet Joseph Smith and his friends suffered in the foul dungeon of Liberty Jail in Missouri contrast starkly with the sublime communication sent by the Prophet to the suffering Saints. The communication was recorded by the Prophet over a five-day period ending about 25 March 1839 and included Doctrine and Covenants 121, 122, and 123 (see Historical Background for D&C 121).

## Notes and Commentary

### D&C 122:1. To What Extent Is Joseph Smith's Name Had in Derision?

The Church and kingdom of God has gone forth until it is now being planted throughout the world. Wherever the Church is established, Satan tries to counteract its influence. Thousands of anti-Mormon tracts and pamphlets have been written to besmirch the name and mission of Joseph Smith, and dozens of books rail accusations against his name. He has been called a fraud, an imposter, a deluded young man, and a tool of Satan. But as President Spencer W. Kimball said, besides fulfilling prophecy, this negative attention is in one way a good sign: "We can also tell that we are making progress by the attention we get from the adversary. . . . This has been the lot of the Lord's people from the beginning, and it will be no different in our time." (In Conference Report, Apr. 1980, p. 6; or *Ensign,* May 1980, p. 6.) Indeed, the name of Joseph is had in derision, and the forces of hell rage against their recognized foe, but to no avail.

### D&C 122:3. Traitors Who Became Apostates Fought Unsuccessfully against Joseph Smith

One who truly knows a prophet, who sees him in his prophetic call, and who has witnessed the mantle fall upon him, will desire to love, support, and protect him. The testimony of a traitor is recognized by the faithful for what it really is.

"The Latter-day Saints who were acquainted with the Prophet personally, with very few exceptions, remained loyally true to him. There were some traitors in Nauvoo. One of the Prophet's counselors became his bitter enemy and sought his life. One other failed to give him loyal support. Others who had been his friends joined hands with the enemies of the Church and sought to bring him to his death, but the great majority of the people remained loyal and true.

"The influence of traitors caused him great trouble and cast him 'into bars and walls' and to his death, yet his voice speaks through his works and is more terrible and disconcerting to his enemies than the roaring of the fierce lion, and even in his death he was not forsaken by the Lord. His people remained true and the Lord has blessed them." (Smith, *Church History and Modern Revelation,* 2:181.)

### D&C 122:5-7. What Is the Purpose of Great Suffering for Joseph Smith or for the Saints Today?

Speaking of the time when Joseph Smith

*Joseph Smith: "Thou art not yet as Job" (D&C 121:10)*

languished in Liberty Jail, Elder Orson F. Whitney detailed what the Saints may learn from the example of the Prophet:

"The Prophet was lying in a dungeon [Liberty, Missouri] for the gospel's sake. He called upon God, 'who controlleth and subjecteth the devil,' and God answered telling him that his sufferings should be but 'a small moment.' 'Thou art not yet as Job,' said the Lord, 'thy friends do not contend against thee.' Job's friends, it will be remembered, tried to convince him that he must have done something wrong or those trials would not have come upon him. But Job had done no wrong; it was 'without cause' that Satan had sought to destroy him. God said to Joseph: 'If thou art called to pass through tribulation; if thou art in perils among false brethren; perils among robbers; perils by land and sea; if fierce winds become thine enemy; if the billowing surge conspire against thee, if the very jaws of hell shall gape open the mouth wide after thee, know thou, my son, that *all these things shall give thee experience and shall be for thy good.*'

"There is the reason. It is for our development, our purification, our growth, our education and advancement, that we buffet the fierce waves of sorrow and misfortune; and we shall be all the stronger and better when we have swum the flood and stand upon the farther shore." (*Improvement Era*, Nov. 1918, pp. 5-6.)

**D&C 122:8. "Art Thou Greater Than He?"**

The Prophet, both at this time and before his incarceration in Liberty Jail, had suffered greatly at the hands of his enemies. In effect, the Savior told the Prophet to be of good cheer, that he understood exactly what Joseph was going through, for He had suffered even more. No mortal could have spoken such words of solace and comfort to the great latter-day prophet. The question is one of humbling solace. No one can ever stand before the Savior and suggest that too much was asked. The Master has surpassed any possible suffering of man.

**D&C 122:9. Was There a Time Appointed for Joseph Smith to Die?**

President Joseph Fielding Smith wrote: "The Lord said that the bounds were set, his enemies could not pass. His days were known to the Lord, and notwithstanding his tribulation and persecutions and the hatred of the world, they should not be less. He was, therefore, not to fear what man can do, for through his faithfulness God would be with him for ever and ever. In this was the promise which comforted him, that suffering and the hatred of his enemies were not to shorten his life before the time appointed. There appears in this a foreshadowing of his martyrdom when his work should be finished." (*Church History and Modern Revelation*, 2:182.)

# Documenting Persecution: An Imperative Duty

Section 123

## Historical Background

Doctrine and Covenants 123 is part of Joseph Smith's epistle to the Church written in Liberty Prison, Missouri (see Historical Background for D&C 121).

## Notes and Commentary

**D&C 123:1-6. What Was the Purpose of Collecting Documents of Anti-Mormon Oppression?**

President Joseph Fielding Smith wrote: "The law of retribution is often slow, but it is sure. The Lord promised to punish his enemies and mete out to them suitable reward for all the evil they had heaped upon his servants. Punishment for sin does not always follow in this mortal life; the greater part of it quite generally is held in reserve for a future day. That records might be kept on earth as well as in heaven, the Lord commanded (Sec. 123) that there be gathered all the knowledge of all the acts, and sufferings and the abuses put upon the members of the Church by the State of Missouri. Also a record should be kept of all the property destroyed, the damages sustained, both to the character and the personal injuries and to the real property of the saints. The names of those who were engaged in this wickedness and these murders and drivings were also to be gathered and preserved. A committee was appointed to gather this evidence that it might be on file. This information would be of value when presented before the Government of the United States when the Church should seek justice at the seat of government. If redress could not be obtained there, then the evidence would stand against those who were guilty, before the Eternal Tribunal which will try all men and all things.

"This gathering of information was not to be confined to the deeds committed in Missouri, but should reach out to embrace the wickedness, falsehoods and deeds of those who fought the truth throughout all time. Magazine articles, writings in encyclopedias, all libelous histories, and other writings and 'the whole concatenation of diabolical rascality and nefarious and murderous impositions

*The* Nauvoo Expositor *building where anti-Mormon literature was printed*

that have been practiced upon this people,' were to be gathered that they might be published to the world, sent to the heads of government 'in all the dark and hellish hue, as the last effort which is enjoined on us by our Heavenly Father, before we can fully and completely claim that promise which shall call him forth from his hiding place; and also that the whole nation may be left without excuse before he can send forth the power of his mighty arm.' " (*Church History and Modern Revelation,* 2:182-83.)

## D&C 123:7-12. Purpose of Collecting Anti-Mormon Material

The Lord called it an imperative duty to collect libelous affidavits and statements because, as Smith and Sjodahl noted, he "knew that the Saints were not guilty of the crimes charged to them by enemies, and that they did not hold the doctrines credited to them, but inasmuch as they claimed to be the people of God, their vindication was, in a sense, the vindication of the Deity. If a master has a servant who is falsely accused of crime, in vindicating himself he vindicates the master, since his character reflects, to some extent, the character of his master. 'As a master, so the servant.' . . .

"The angels who are sent to administer to the Saints have a right to know whether such accusations are true or false. . . .

"Silence is sometimes more eloquent than words; but at this time it was necessary to place the accusers and persecutors in the limelight of public opinion, because wives and children had a right to know the full truth." (Commentary, pp. 764-65.)

## D&C 123:11-14. Who Would Benefit by Learning of the Injustices Done to the Saints?

Millions in the world suffer from being led and taught by strangers to truth whose labor is self-serving. When injustices are done to the Church, the need is critical to have the truth represented fairly and clearly. Many honest people in the world misrepresent the truth and propagate lies about the kingdom of God because they have received bad information; therefore, it is the imperative duty of the Saints to keep the name of the Church unsullied, by being vigilant and courageous in defending the reputation of the Church and correcting misrepresentations, in order to present to the pure in heart the truth they need.

While Church members should hate evil and do all within their stewardship to oppose those who would hinder the kingdom, the Lord has directed the Saints still to show forth love for enemies of the Church. President Spencer W. Kimball closed a conference talk with this plea: "Brothers and sisters, pray for the critics of the Church; love your enemies. Keep the faith and stay on the straight and narrow path. Use wisdom and judgment in what you say and do, so that we do not give cause to others to hold the Church or its people in disrepute. Do not be surprised or dismayed if trials and challenges come upon us. This work, which Satan seeks in vain to tear down, is that which God has placed on earth to lift mankind up!" (In Conference Report, Apr. 1980, p. 6; or *Ensign,* May 1980, p. 6.)

## D&C 123:15. Do Present Records Have Merit for Future Generations?

As the years have come and gone, and the terrible injustices of Missouri have been revealed by the records and by the patience and righteousness of the Saints of God, the tardy remorse of that state is felt in a statement President Spencer W. Kimball delivered to the membership of the Church:

"Since our last conference we have had a delightful message from Christopher S. Bond, governor of the state of Missouri, who advised us that he has rescinded the 138-year-old executive order of Governor Lilburn W. Boggs calling for the extermination or expulsion of the Mormons from the state of Missouri. Governor Bond, present Missouri governor, writes:

" 'Expressing on behalf of all Missourians our deep regret for the injustice and undue suffering which was caused by this 1838 order, I hereby rescind Executive Order No. 44 dated October 27, 1838, issued by Governor Lilburn W. Boggs.'

"To Governor Bond and the people of Missouri, we extend our deep appreciation for this reversal and for the present friendly associations between the membership of The Church of Jesus Christ of Latter-day Saints and the people of Missouri as it is now in effect.

"In Missouri now we have five stakes in fifty-one communities, with approximately 15,000 members of the Church, who, we are confident, are law-abiding citizens of the state of Missouri. Thank you, Governor Bond." (In Conference Report, Oct. 1976, p. 4-5; or *Ensign,* Nov. 1976, p. 4.)

# A Solemn Proclamation: The Priesthood Order Is Established

Section 124

## Historical Background

"Most of the Saints expelled from the State of Missouri during the winter 1838-9, found their way into Illinois and Iowa. A majority of them went to Quincy, Ill., about 200 miles from Far West, and there they were kindly and hospitably received. Governor Carlin of Illinois, legislators, and private citizens vied with each other in proffering assistance and sympathy.

"Among the prominent citizens who, at this time, extended a helping hand to the Saints were Daniel H. Wells, a native of Trenton, New York, and Dr. Isaac Galland. Daniel H. Wells was the owner of a tract of land, which he divided into lots and which the exiles were offered, practically on their own terms. Dr. Galland, also, sold his land at a reasonable price and on the most favorable terms.

"The Prophet arrived at Quincy on the 22nd of April, 1839, and two days after, a Council was convened and resolutions were passed directing some of the Saints to go to Zion [Commerce, which later became Nauvoo], and some to settle on Dr. Galland's land, near Commerce, Ill. This location soon became the central gathering place, and its name was changed to Nauvoo. In the year 1841, when this Revelation was given, this beautiful city had about 3,000 inhabitants. A charter had been granted by the Illinois Legislature, by which Nauvoo was given a liberal municipal government, with authority to form a militia and erect a university. A Temple was about to be built. The scattered Saints were gathering, and the settlements in Illinois were growing rapidly. The mission in Great Britain was highly successful. Such were the general conditions when this Revelation was given. The Church had a moment's rest. There was calm before the next storm." (Smith and Sjodahl, Commentary, p. 768.)

## Notes and Commentary

**D&C 124:1. "The Weak Things of the Earth"**

See Notes and Commentary for Doctrine and Covenants 1:19-20, 23.

**D&C 124:2-6. "Make a Solemn Proclamation . . . to All the Nations"**

The fulfillment of this directive from the Lord did not come until 1845. A number of individuals were to assist in preparing the document, but circumstances seem to have prevented it until later, when it was issued by the Twelve (see *History of the Church,* 6:80; 7:320, 558). Ezra Taft Benson, President of the Quorum of the Twelve, reaffirmed the message of the proclamation for the world:

"Today I shall speak doctrine, by way of warning and of testimony, and shall do so as one holding the holy apostleship, whose responsibility it is to proclaim the Lord's message in all the world and to all people. Each of my brethren of the Council of the Twelve has the same responsibility I have to declare these things to the world and to bear record of them before all men.

"Toward the end of his mortal ministry, the Lord commanded the Prophet Joseph Smith as follows:

" 'Make a solemn proclamation of my gospel . . . to all the kings of the world, to the four corners thereof . . . and to all nations of the earth.' (D&C 124:2-3.) He was to invite them to come to the light of truth, and use their means to build up the kingdom of God on earth.

"In the spirit of this divine direction, on the sixth day of April 1845, and shortly after the Prophet Joseph Smith and his brother Hyrum had mingled their blood with that of the other martyrs of true religion, the Council of the Twelve made such a proclamation. . . .

"It seems fitting and proper to me that we should reaffirm the great truths pronounced in this declaration and that we should proclaim them anew to the world.

"To the rulers and peoples of all nations, we solemnly declare again that the God of heaven has established his latter-day kingdom upon the earth in fulfillment of prophecies. Holy angels have again communed with men on the earth. God has again revealed himself from heaven and restored to the earth his holy priesthood with power to administer in all the sacred ordinances necessary for the exaltation of his children. His church has been reestablished among men with all the spiritual gifts enjoyed anciently. All this is done in preparation for Christ's second coming. The great and dreadful day of the Lord is near at hand. In preparation for this great event and as a means of escaping the impending judgments, inspired messengers have gone, and are now going, forth to the nations of the earth carrying this testimony and warning.

"The nations of the earth continue in their sinful and unrighteous ways. Much of the unbounded knowledge with which men have been blessed has been used to destroy mankind instead of to bless the children of men as the Lord intended. Two great world wars, with fruitless efforts at lasting peace, are solemn evidence that peace has been taken from the earth because of the wickedness of the people. Nations cannot endure in sin. They will be broken up, but the kingdom of God will endure forever.

"Therefore, as humble servants of the Lord, we call upon the leaders of nations to humble themselves before God, to seek his inspiration and guidance. We call upon rulers and people alike to repent of their evil ways. Turn unto the Lord, seek his forgiveness, and unite yourselves in humility with his kingdom. There is no other way. If you will do this, your sins will be blotted out, peace will come and remain, and you will become a part of the kingdom of God in preparation for Christ's second coming. But if you refuse to repent or to accept the testimony of his inspired messengers and unite yourselves with God's kingdom, then the terrible judgments and calamities promised the wicked will be yours. . . .

"When the voice of warning goes forth it is always attended by testimony. In the great declaration issued by the apostles of the Lord Jesus Christ in 1845, this is the testimony which was borne, and we who are the apostles today renew it as our witness:

" 'We say, then, in life or in death, in bonds or free, that the great God has spoken in this age.—*And we know it.*

" 'He has given us the Holy Priesthood and Apostleship, and the keys of the kingdom of God, to bring about the restoration of all things as promised by the holy prophets of old.—*And we know it.*

" 'He has revealed the origin and the Records of the aboriginal tribes of America, and their future destiny.—*And we know it.*

" 'He has revealed the fulness of the gospel, with its gifts, blessings, and ordinances.—*And we know it.*

" 'He has commanded us to bear witness of it, first to the Gentiles, and then to the remnants of Israel and the Jews.—*And we know it.*

" 'He has also said that, if they do not repent, and come to the knowledge of the truth, . . . and also put away all murder, lying, pride, priestcraft, whoredom, and secret abomination, they shall soon perish from the earth, and be cast down to hell.—*And we know it.*

" 'He has said, that when . . . the gospel in all its fulness [is] preached to all nations for a witness and testimony, He will come, and all Saints with him, to reign on the earth one thousand years.—*And we know it.*

" 'He has said that he will not come in his glory and destroy the wicked, till these warnings were given and these preparations were made for his reception.—*And we know it.*

" 'Heaven and earth shall pass away, but not one jot or tittle of his revealed word shall fail to be fulfilled.

" 'Therefore, again we say to all people, Repent, and be baptized in the name of Jesus Christ, for remission of sins; and you shall receive the Holy Spirit, and shall know the truth, and be numbered with the house of Israel.' (*Messages of the First Presidency,* 1:263-64.)" (In Conference Report, Oct. 1975, pp. 46-49; or *Ensign,* Nov. 1975, pp. 32-34.)

Other proclamations concerning the Church, its message and its mission, have been issued from time to time, but this early declaration best exemplifies the Lord's instruction in the revelation in the Doctrine and Covenants. (For a recent example of an official proclamation by the Quorum of the Twelve, see *Church News,* 12 Apr. 1980, pp. 3-4; see also Conference Report, Apr. 1980, pp. 75-77; or *Ensign,* May 1980, pp. 52-53.)

### D&C 124:7. All Earthly Leaders "Are As Grass"

"The servants of the Lord are encouraged to proclaim the Gospel to kings and rulers without fear, for 'they are as grass.' Their power and glory are transient. The gospel is the only permanent factor in human history. The Priesthood is eternal." (Smith and Sjodahl, Commentary, p. 769.)

### D&C 124:12-14. Robert B. Thompson to Assist in Writing the Proclamation

In May 1841 Robert B. Thompson was appointed an associate editor of the *Times and Seasons* in Nauvoo. He served in that capacity until August 1841, when he died at age thirty, never able to fulfill the divine commission. (See *History of the Church,* 4:411-12.)

### D&C 124:15. "Blessed Is My Servant Hyrum Smith"

President Heber J. Grant said: "No mortal man who ever lived in this Church desired more to do good than did Hyrum Smith, the patriarch. I have it from the lips of my own sainted mother, that of all the men she was acquainted with in her girlhood days in Nauvoo, she admired Hyrum Smith most for his absolute integrity and devotion to God, and his loyalty to the prophet of God." (In Conference Report, Oct. 1920, p. 84.)

*Hyrum Smith, a symbol of goodness*

## D&C 124:16-17. Why Was John C. Bennett Commended by the Lord When He Later Became Such an Enemy of the Church?

Smith and Sjodahl summarized John C. Bennett's introduction to the Church and his eventual apostasy to explain why the Lord commended him:

"[John C. Bennett] was well educated and possessed many gifts and accomplishments. He was a physician, a university professor, and a brigadier-general. On the 27th of July, 1840, he offered his services to the Church. The Prophet Joseph replied, inviting him to come to Commerce, if he felt so disposed, but warned him at the same time not to expect exaltation 'in this generation,' from devotion to the cause of truth and a suffering people; nor worldly riches; only the approval of God. The outcome of the correspondence was that he joined the Church and rose to prominent positions among the Saints. His fellowship with the people of God did not last long, however. On the 25th of May, 1842, he was notified that the leaders of the Church did no longer recognize him as a member, because of his impure life, and shortly afterwards the Church took action against him. Then he became one of the most bitter enemies of the Church. His slanders, his falsehoods and unscrupulous attacks, which included perjury and attempted assassination were the means of inflaming public opinion to such an extent that the tragedy at Carthage became possible.

"Why, then, did his name appear, in this Revelation, as that of a trusted assistant of Joseph? John Taylor furnishes the answer to that question. He says, 'Respecting John C. Bennett: I was well acquainted with him. At one time he was a good man, but fell into adultery, and was cut off from the Church for his iniquity' (*History of the Church,* Vol. V., p. 81). At the time of the revelation he was a good man. But he was overcome by the adversary and made the slave of his carnal desires. The Lord knew him and warned him. 'His reward shall not fail *if* he receive counsel.' 'He shall be great . . . *if* he do this,' etc. Bennett did not heed these warning 'ifs' from Him who knew what was in his heart." (Commentary, pp. 770-71.)

The Lord does not withhold present blessings because of future sinful behavior. He blessed King David as long as he was faithful and did not withhold opportunity, although he had foreknowledge of David's future transgressions with Bathsheba. As long as one obeys, the blessings come. With the perspective of history one may be tempted to ask why the Lord chose men who would eventually falter to be leaders in the Church, but one should remember that at the time of their calling they were faithful and true.

## D&C 124:22-24, 56-83, 119-21. Build a Boarding House That the Stranger Might Contemplate the Word of the Lord

"The Spirit of Revelation directs the Saints to build a fine hotel for the entertainment of strangers. There is no greater inducement for travelers to visit a place than good hotel accommodations. This Revelation proves that the Lord wanted the tourists

*A house built on the foundation of the original Nauvoo House*

of the world to visit and become acquainted with the Saints. These were not to be surrounded by a wall of isolation. They had nothing to hide from the world." (Smith and Sjodahl, Commentary, pp. 772-73.)

## D&C 124:25-27. "Build a House to My Name for the Most High to Dwell Therein"

The building of the Nauvoo Temple was the fifth attempt by the Latter-day Saints to build a house of the Lord. The first attempt was in Jackson County, Missouri; then in Kirtland, Ohio; and then in Far West and Adam-ondi-Ahman, Missouri; and finally in Nauvoo, Illinois. Only the Kirtland Temple was completed before the one in Nauvoo, and it was desecrated, as Brigham Young explained: "The Saints had to flee before mobocracy. And, by toil and daily labor, they found places in Missouri, where they laid the corner stones of Temples, in Zion and her Stakes, and then had to retreat to Illinois, to save the lives of those who could get away alive from Missouri, where fell the Apostle David W. Patten, with many like associates, and where were imprisoned in loathsome dungeons, and fed on human flesh, Joseph and Hyrum, and many others. But before all this had transpired, the Temple at Kirtland had fallen into the hands of wicked men, and by them been polluted, like the Temple at Jerusalem, and consequently it was disowned by the Father and the Son." (In *Journal of Discourses,* 2:32.)

## D&C 124:28. What Is Meant by "The Fulness of the Priesthood"?

President Joseph Fielding Smith wrote:

"Joseph Smith said . . . , 'If a man gets a fulness of the Priesthood of God, he has to get it in the same way that Jesus Christ obtained it, and that was by keeping all the commandments and obeying all the ordinances of the house of the Lord.' [*History of the Church,* 5:424.]

"I hope we understand that. If we want to receive the fullness of the Priesthood of God, then we must receive the fullness of the ordinances of the house of the Lord and keep His commandments. . . .

"Let me put this in a little different way. I do not care what office you hold in this Church, you may be an apostle, you may be patriarch, a high priest, or anything else, and you cannot receive the fullness of the Priesthood unless you go into the temple of the Lord and receive these ordinances of which the Prophet speaks. No man can get the fullness of the Priesthood outside of the temple of the Lord. There was a time when that could be done, for the Lord could give these things on the mountain tops—no doubt that is where Moses got it, that is no doubt where Elijah got it—and the Lord said that in the days of poverty, when there was no house prepared in which to receive these things, that they can be received on the mountain tops. But now you will have to go into the house of the Lord, and you cannot get the fullness of the priesthood unless you go there." (*Elijah the Prophet,* pp. 45-46.)

### D&C 124:29-36. Vicarious Baptisms for the Dead

These verses are the first mention in modern scripture of baptism for the dead. In a letter written to the Quorum of the Twelve Apostles on 19 October 1840, the Prophet Joseph Smith said:

"I presume the doctrine of 'baptism for the dead' has ere this reached your ears, and may have raised some inquiries in your minds respecting the same. I cannot in this letter give you all the information you may desire on the subject; but aside from knowledge independent of the Bible, I would say that it was certainly practiced by the ancient churches; and St. Paul endeavors to prove the doctrine of the resurrection from the same, and says, 'Else what shall they do which are baptized for the dead, if the dead rise not at all? Why are they then baptized for the dead?' [1 Cor. 15:29.]

"I first mentioned the doctrine in public when preaching the funeral sermon of Brother Seymour Brunson; and have since then given general instructions in the Church on the subject. The Saints have the privilege of being baptized for those of their relatives who are dead, whom they believe would have embraced the Gospel, if they had been privileged with hearing it, and who have received the Gospel in the spirit, through the instrumentality of those who have been commissioned to preach to them while in prison.

"Without enlarging on the subject, you will undoubtedly see its consistency and reasonableness; and it presents the Gospel of Christ in probably a more enlarged scale than some have imagined it. But as the performance of this rite is more particularly confined to this place, it will not be necessary to enter into particulars; at the same time I always feel glad to give all the information in my power, but my space will not allow me to do it." (*History of the Church,* 4:231.)

The revelation explains that the ordinance of baptism for the dead is to be done only in a place designated by the Lord. Performing the ordinance was acceptable outside the temple only under special circumstances, and before the completion of the Nauvoo Temple the Lord permitted the ordinance to be performed in the Mississippi River. In October 1841 the Prophet announced that no more baptisms for the dead would be administered until the temple's font was completed. It was finished in November, and baptisms recommenced on the twenty-first (see D&C 124:27-30).

### D&C 124:37-38. Temple Ordinances in Ancient Times

President Joseph Fielding Smith wrote: "The importance of the ordinances in the house of the Lord is shown in verses 37-39, (sec. 124), where we are informed that Moses was commanded to build a portable temple, generally called tabernacle, which could be carried with them in the wilderness. This tabernacle is the same temple where the boy Samuel heard the voice of the Lord. (1 Samuel, chapters one-three.) This sacred building was later replaced by Solomon's Temple. The question is often asked, 'What was the nature of the ordinances performed in these edifices in ancient times?' The Lord explains this in the verses above cited. It is true that in ancient Israel they did not have the fulness of ordinances as we do today, and most, if not all, of which they were privileged to receive, very likely pertained to the Aaronic Priesthood. (See D. & C. 84:21-26.) Neither did the ancients labor in their temples for the salvation of the dead. That work was reserved until after the Savior's visit to the spirit world where he unlocked the door to the prison and had the gospel carried to the spirits who had been confined." (*Church History and Modern Revelation,* 2:268.)

### D&C 124:39-40. Why Are the Lord's People Commanded to Build Temples?

The Prophet Joseph Smith taught that it is an eternal design that temples be built to provide a sacred place in which priesthood ordinances may be performed:

"What was the object of gathering the Jews, or the people of God in any age of the world. . . .

"The main object was to build unto the Lord a house whereby He could reveal unto His people the ordinances of His house and the glories of His kingdom, and teach the people the way of salvation: for there are certain ordinances and principles that, when they are taught and practiced, must be done in a place or house built for that purpose.

"It was the design of the councils of heaven before the world was, that the principles and laws of the priesthood should be predicated upon the gathering of the people in every age of the world. Jesus did everything to gather the people, and they would not be gathered, and He therefore poured out curses upon them. Ordinances instituted in the heavens before the foundation of the world, in the priesthood, for the salvation of men, are not to be altered or changed. All must be saved on the same principles.

"It is for the same purpose that God gathers together His people in the last days, to build unto the Lord a house to prepare them for the ordinances and endowments, washings and anointings, etc. One of the ordinances of the house of the Lord is baptism for the dead. God decreed before the foundation of the world that that

*The Nauvoo Temple was the first ordinance temple built in the last dispensation*

ordinance should be administered in a font prepared for that purpose in the house of the Lord." (*History of the Church,* 5:423-24.)

**D&C 124:40-44. Let a House Be Built "That I May Reveal Mine Ordinances Therein unto My People"**

After instructing the leaders of the Church in the temple ordinances, the Prophet Joseph Smith stated that only the spiritually minded would fully comprehend them and that they had to be revealed in the temple: "The communications I made to this council were of things spiritual, and to be received only by the spiritual minded: and there was nothing made known to these men but what will be made known to all the Saints of the last days, so soon as they are prepared to receive, and a proper place is prepared to communicate them, even to the weakest of the Saints; therefore let the Saints be diligent in building the Temple, and all houses which they have been, or shall hereafter be, commanded of God to build; and wait their time with patience in all meekness, faith, perseverance unto the end, knowing assuredly that all these things referred to in this council are always governed by the principle of revelation." (*History of the Church,* 5:2.)

**D&C 124:45. "If My People Will Hearken unto My Voice"**

God's revelations come through his chosen servants. Their words outline the clear path leading to eternal life. Failure to heed their words, particularly those of the living prophet, can bring about the loss of incalculable blessings, as President George Q. Cannon explained: "What can we do better than to show respect to our God by listening to His servant, by treating him with reverence, asking his counsel and seeking for his guidance? I know we pray to God for him, that he may be inspired from on high. Do you believe your prayers? Do you believe that God will and does inspire him? I hope you do; and I hope that having this feeling, you will be prompted to different action. . . . And shall we say that in some things we are willing to be guided; we think it right to be guided in matters of doctrine, etc.; but in other matters, just as important and necessary for the salvation and preservation of this people, we are not willing? Latter-day Saints, you cannot do it. You cannot get away from this authority and remain Latter-day Saints, for you sever yourselves from the Church of God, because everything you have is based on the recognition of this authority." (In Conference Report, Apr. 1900, p. 13.)

**D&C 124:46-48. If My People "Will Not Hearken to My Voice"**

"The Saints generally labored diligently and with sublime self-abnegation upon the Temple, but the spirit of apostasy possessed many of the leading men in Nauvoo, as had been the case in Jackson County and in Kirtland. They polluted the sanctuary and all pertaining thereto. They brought upon themselves and the Church wrath, indignation, and judgment (v. 48). Because of their disobedience the Church was subjected to another sifting process by which the chaff was separated from the wheat." (Smith and Sjodahl, Commentary, p. 779.)

**D&C 124:49-55. When Enemies Hinder the Work**

President Charles W. Penrose explained what happens if the Saints are prevented from fulfilling a commandment from God: "The Lord says that whenever he gives a commandment, no matter what it is about, to the children of man, and they go to with their might and endeavor to fulfil his commandment, and do that which is required of them, and they are prevented by their enemies, or by any other means, from accomplishing it, he does not require it any more at their hands. He accepts of their offering. That has applied in the past, and will apply in the future, and we should remember it. If God gives a commandment, and we do not obey it, why he revokes it, and he revokes the blessings. If he gives us a commandment to do certain things, and we find ourselves unable to do them either by restricted laws or any other obstacles in the way of physical force, the Lord requires them no more but accepts our offering, and he will visit his wrath and indignation upon those who prevent his people from accomplishing that which he required at their hands." (In Conference Report, Apr. 1924, pp. 13-14.)

**D&C 124:84. "He Aspireth to Establish His Counsel instead of the Counsel Which I Have Ordained"**

Almon Babbitt received a sharp reprimand from

the Lord for his designs to circumvent the authority of the Prophet and for his greed, which the Lord likened to setting up a golden calf. Apparently, as Smith and Sjodahl recorded, Almon Babbitt's "chief ambition was to make money, and . . . he advised the Saints to leave Nauvoo, contrary to the counsel of the Church leaders. Perhaps he was interested in the sale of land elsewhere. At all events, when the Saints left Nauvoo, he was appointed one of the real estate agents in whose hands the abandoned property was left, to be disposed of on the best terms obtainable. How he discharged this duty, we may infer from the following statement of Heber C. Kimball: 'My house was sold at 1,700, intended to be used to help to gather the Saints; but Almon W. Babbitt put it in his pocket, I suppose' (*Journal of Discourses,* Vol. VIII., p. 350)." (Commentary, p. 784.)

### D&C 124:87-90, 97-102. Did William Law Obey the Word of the Lord and Thus Reap the Promised Blessings?

"Wonderful opportunities were offered to Wm. Law, which he neglected to embrace. If he had done faithfully what God here gave him to do, he would have received the blessings promised, but when he failed to obey the Lord, even his appointment in the First Presidency could not save him from falling. When he lost the Spirit of God he became one of the most bitter enemies of the Church. Apostates and persecutors rallied around him, and he tried to form a church of his own of such material." (Smith and Sjodahl, Commentary, p. 785.)

### D&C 124:91-96. What Special Rights Were Bestowed upon Hyrum Smith?

Joseph Smith, Sr., the Prophet's father, was the first patriarch to the Church in this dispensation. He was succeeded as patriarch by his son Hyrum. In addition, Hyrum served as the second elder in the Church. Elder Joseph Fielding Smith, after citing Doctrine and Covenants 124:94, said:

"This was a special blessing given to Hyrum Smith, and in accepting it he took the place of Oliver Cowdery, upon whom these keys had previously been bestowed. It should be remembered that whenever the Lord revealed Priesthood and the keys of priesthood from the heavens, Oliver Cowdery stood with Joseph Smith in the presence of the heavenly messengers, and was a recipient, as well as Joseph Smith, of all this authority. They held it conjointly, Joseph Smith as the 'first' and Oliver Cowdery as the 'second' Elder of the Church. Thus the law pertaining to witnesses was fully established, for there were two witnesses standing with authority, keys and presidency, at the head of this the greatest of all dispensations. When through transgression Oliver Cowdery lost this wonderful and exalted blessing, Hyrum Smith was chosen by revelation of the Lord to take his place, the Lord calling him in these words: [D&C 124:95-96].

"And thus, according to promise, the Lord opened to the vision of Hyrum Smith and showed to him those things which were necessary to qualify him for this exalted position, and upon him were conferred by Joseph Smith all the keys and authorities by which he, Hyrum Smith, was able to act in concert with his younger brother as a prophet, seer and revelator, and president of the Church, 'as well as my servant Joseph.' " ("Patriarch Hyrum G. Smith," *Utah Genealogical and Historical Magazine,* Apr. 1932, pp. 51-52.)

The statement that Hyrum's name will "be had in honorable remembrance from generation to generation" has been completely fulfilled (D&C 124:96).

### D&C 124:103-10. Why Was a Warning Given to Sidney Rigdon?

Smith and Sjodahl explained some historical background of this warning:

"Sidney Rigdon, according to a generally prevailing impression, was more or less, under the influence of a spirit of apostasy. It is related that, in Liberty jail, he declared to his fellow-prisoners that the sufferings of the Lord were nothing compared with his, and while the faithful Saints were straining every nerve to complete the Nauvoo Temple, he had no word of encouragement to them. As a consequence of his disposition, he did not have good health. Like the Corinthians who partook unworthily of the Sacrament (1 Cor. 11:30), he was 'weak and sickly.' The Lord, therefore, points out to him the cause of his ailments and promises to heal him, if he will do his duty and stand by the Prophet as a true counselor.

"Sidney Rigdon had a remarkable experience some months after this Revelation was received. His daughter Eliza took sick and was pronounced dead by the physician. Some time after her departure, she rose up in the bed and said she had returned to deliver a message from the Lord. She then called the family around her. To her sister Nancy she said, It is in your heart to deny this work; and if you do, the Lord says it will be the damnation of your soul! To her sister Sarah she said, We have but once to die, and I would rather die now, than wait for another time. After having spoken for some time she fainted, but recovered again. The following evening she called her father and said to him that the Lord would make her well, if he would cease weeping for her. Sidney Rigdon related this manifestation of the power of God, in a public meeting on the 20th of August, 1842, and added a strong declaration of his allegiance to the Prophet Joseph and the Church. On the same occasion, Hyrum Smith cited Sidney Rigdon's mind back to this Revelation, in which the Lord promised that if he would move into the City and defend the truth he would be healed, and showed that Rigdon's improvement in health was a fulfilment of this Revelation (*History of the Church,* Vol. V., pp. 121-3). But, notwithstanding all, Rigdon finally lost his way. It can be said, however, that, according to his son, John Rigdon, who joined the Church, he never was an enemy of the Church." (Commentary, pp. 788-89; see also *History of the Church,* 5:121-23.)

### D&C 124:115-18. What Was Robert D. Foster's Folly and Evil?

Sperry wrote: "Unfortunately, Foster was another man who disregarded the Lord's counsel. After all the Prophet did to help him from time to time, he was one of the disloyal men who had Joseph Smith indicted on false charges, and he even conspired to bring about the Prophet's death." (*Compendium*, p. 664.)

### D&C 124:124-26. The Relationship of "Prophet" and "Patriarch"

Hyrum Smith was appointed "to be a patriarch" to the Church, whereas Joseph Smith was appointed to be the "presiding elder over all my Church." The wording of Hyrum's appointment (see D&C 124:124) has caused some to mistakenly maintain that the office of Patriarch to the Church exceeds that of the President of the Church. After the death of Joseph and Hyrum, their younger brother, William Smith, was called to the office of Patriarch. Later some people claimed that this appointment gave him supremacy over Brigham Young and the other members of the Quorum of the Twelve. John Taylor, a member of the Quorum of the Twelve, answered the claim in 1845:

"We read 'the duty of the President of the office of the high priesthood is to preside over the whole church, and to be like unto Moses' [D&C 107:91]. And from this it is evident that the president of the church, not the patriarch, is appointed by God to preside. . . .

"The president of the church presides over all patriarchs, presidents, and councils of the church; and this presidency does not depend so much upon genealogy as upon calling, order, and seniority. James and Joses were the brothers of Jesus [see Matthew 13:55], and John was his beloved disciple, yet Peter . . . [was given] the keys and presided over all the church. Brother William was in the quorum of the twelve yet he was not president of the twelve during his brother's lifetime, nor since; and if being ordained a patriarch would make him president of the church, it would have made Father Joseph Smith and Hyrum Smith presidents over the church instead of Joseph.

"Br. William understands the matter, and were it not for the folly of some men there would be no necessity for these remarks." (In *Times and Seasons*, 1 June 1845, pp. 921-22.) Even at this early date Brigham Young had been chosen of the Lord to preside over the Twelve (see D&C 124:127).

### D&C 124:127-30. The Council of the Twelve Apostles

See Doctrine and Covenants 107:33-34, 38 and Notes and Commentary on Doctrine and Covenants 107:23.

### D&C 124:130. "His Priesthood No Man Taketh from Him"

Though Elder David W. Patten was dead, his priesthood continued on, as President John Taylor stated:

"But his being dead made no difference in regard to his priesthood. He held it just the same in the heavens as on the earth. . . .

" . . . If the priesthood administers in time and in eternity, and if quorums of this kind are organized upon the earth, and this priesthood is not taken away, but continued with them in the heavens, we do not wish, I think, to break up the order of the priesthood upon the earth; and it would seem to be necessary that these principles of perpetuity or continuity should be held sacred among us." (*Gospel Kingdom*, p. 185.)

*William Smith was ordained Patriarch to the Church after the death of Joseph and Hyrum*

### D&C 124:131-32. The High Council

See Doctrine and Covenants 102 and Notes and Commentary on Doctrine and Covenants 107:36-37.

### D&C 124:133-37. "A Quorum of High Priests" and "the Quorum of Elders"

President Joseph F. Smith explained the place and function of high priests quorums and elders quorums in the stakes:

"We have in each stake of Zion an organization called the High Priests' quorum, to which all High Priests of the Church belong, including the presidency and high councilors of the stake, and also the Bishops and their counselors, all the Patriarchs and all others who have been ordained to the office of High Priest in the Church. . . . But it is the duty of these quorums of High Priests to act in their calling; not to sit idly down and be indifferent to the interests of The Church of Jesus Christ of Latter-day Saints, nor indifferent to the saving of the souls of men. It is expected that this quorum of Priesthood in the various stakes of Zion will look after all the interests of the stake; that is, that they will teach righteousness; that they will see that those who are acting in presiding authority in the stakes of Zion, are upright, honest, pure and humble men, and fit for the positions in which they are called to act. Thus this council of the Priesthood constitutes a council of power and influence in the Church. . . .

". . . A council or quorum of Elders is composed of 96 Elders. There may be a number of councils or quorums of Elders in each stake. . . . It is the duty of this body of men to be standing ministers at home; to be ready at the call of the presiding officers of the Church and the stakes, to labor in the ministry at home, and to officiate in any calling that may be required of them, whether it be to work in the temples or . . . whether it be to go out into the world, along with the Seventies, to preach the Gospel to the world." (In Conference Report, Oct. 1904, pp. 3-4; see also Enrichment M, in the Appendix.)

**D&C 124:138-42. The Seventy, the Presiding Bishopric, and the Lesser Priesthood**

The offices and quorums in the priesthood are discussed in Enrichment M and in Notes and Commentary for Doctrine and Covenants 68:13-21; 107:15-17, 68-75, 93-97.

**D&C 124:143-45. "Approve of Those Names . . . at My General Conference"**

The presentation of a new President of the Church (a reorganization of the First Presidency) follows the pattern of a solemn assembly. This pattern was first used in Kirtland, Ohio, 27 March 1836 (see *History of the Church,* 2:411, 416-418; see also Orson Pratt, in *Journal of Discourses,* 19:118). The manner of conducting solemn assemblies was given to the Church "by revelation, the order of things as it existed in former days, away back in the dispensation before the flood—the dispensation of the antediluvian Patriarchs and their order of government" (Orson Pratt, in *Journal of Discourses,* 22:36).

In the reorganization of the First Presidency after the death of President Brigham Young, President John Taylor was sustained by vote, "those votes being taken first in their quorum capacity, each quorum having voted affirmatively, then by the vote of the Presidents of the several quorums united, afterwards by the vote of the quorums and people combined, men and women." (John Taylor, in *Journal of Discourses,* 22:40; see also Roberts, *Life of John Taylor,* pp. 339-41; J. Reuben Clark, Jr., in Conference Report, Apr. 1951, p. 136).

In exercising the privilege to sustain or to refuse to sustain their officers, members of the Church are acting in accordance with the principle of common consent (see Notes and Commentary for D&C 26:2).

# The Will of God for the Saints in Iowa

# Section 125

## Historical Background

Not all of the Saints who were driven from Missouri found refuge in Illinois. Some settled across the Mississippi River from Nauvoo, in Iowa. The revelation directing such action came in response to a question about whether they should remain in Iowa or gather to the Illinois side. One of the first to suggest that the Saints locate in Iowa was Dr. Isaac Galland, the man who had sold the land on which Nauvoo was built. Elder Joseph Fielding Smith wrote that "Mr. Galland in a communication to David W. Rogers, suggested that the Saints locate in Iowa, which was a territory; for he thought they would be more likely to receive protection from mobs under the jurisdiction of the United States, than they would be in a state of the Union, 'where murder, rapine and robbery are admirable (!) traits in the character of a demagogue; and where the greatest villains often reach the highest offices.' He also wrote to Governor Robert Lucas of Iowa, who had known the 'Mormon' people in Ohio, and who spoke very highly of them as good citizens." (*Essentials in Church History,* p. 220.)

The purchase of land took place in 1839, as did the exodus from Missouri. The revelation in Doctrine and Covenants 125 was received in 1841, when many Saints were already settled in Iowa, and it is directed to them. Before the Saints arrived, there were 2,839 residents in Lee County, Iowa; by 1846 the population had swelled to 12,860—many of whom were Latter-day Saints.

## Notes and Commentary

**D&C 125:1. Asking God Opens the Door to Revelation**

This verse is one of the Prophet Joseph Smith's requests of the Lord for further light and knowledge. The pattern for revelation is that a humble seeker asks in faith; then the answer comes from the Lord in response to the proper petition. "Ask, and it shall be given unto you; seek, and ye shall find; knock, and it shall be opened unto you" (Matthew 7:7). The Lord explained that those who

*Montrose, Iowa, with Nauvoo, Illinois, across the Mississippi River*

remain in darkness do so because they either do not ask or ask amiss. As James explained, "Ye have not, because ye ask not" (James 4:2).

### D&C 125:2. Was Iowa Considered a Permanent Dwelling Place?

The Lord spoke of the Saints gathering together "unto the places which I shall appoint" in preparation "for that which is in store in a time to come" (D&C 125:2). Thus, in this revelation of March 1841 is presaged the exodus of the Latter-day Saints to the Rocky Mountains in 1846 and 1847. Iowa became a temporary gathering place for those who were driven from their homes in Illinois.

### D&C 125:3. Where Does the Term *Zarahemla* Come From? Where Was the City Located?

The precise meaning of the word *Zarahemla* is not known. The term comes from the Book of Mormon account of the people who came to America from Jerusalem at the time Zedekiah was carried captive into Babylon. They were called the people of Zarahemla after the name of their leader. They lived in a city named Zarahemla, in the land of Zarahemla (see Omni 1:12-19).

It was common in Book of Mormon times to name cities "after the name of him who first possessed them" (Alma 8:7). It became a common practice for the Latter-day Saints to name their settlements with Book of Mormon names. For example, in Utah are such cities as Nephi, Moroni, Manti, and Bountiful.

One of the first settlements named in this way by the Saints was Zarahemla, at Nashville, Lee County, Iowa. "This settlement was founded by the Saints in 1839, on the uplands about a mile west of the Mississippi River, near Montrose and opposite Nauvoo, Ill. The Church had bought an extensive tract of land here. At a conference held at Zarahemla, August 7th, 1841, seven hundred and fifty Church members were represented, of whom three hundred and twenty-six lived in Zarahemla. But when the Saints left for the Rocky Mountains, that city was lost sight of." (Smith and Sjodahl, Commentary, p. 796.)

### D&C 125:4. What Significance Was Attached to the City of Nashville?

President Joseph Fielding Smith wrote: "Across the river on the Iowa side, extensive holdings also were obtained. The village of Nashville, in Lee County, with twenty thousand acres adjoining, was purchased; also other lands opposite Nauvoo. Here the Prophet instructed the Saints that a city should be built, to be called Zarahemla. A number of members of the Church had located here when the Saints were driven from Missouri, and it appeared to be a suitable location for a permanent settlement of the people. . . . The idea seemed to be that the Latter-day Saints should spread out over considerable territory and form organizations in various parts of the country." (*Essentials in Church History*, p. 222.)

The plan was abandoned after a stake was organized in Iowa on 5 October 1839 under the direction of Elder John Smith, the Prophet's uncle. A short time later, on 6 January 1842, the stake itself was discontinued, but Brother Smith continued to preside over the Saints in Iowa, whose numbers were continually increased by immigrants, until the exodus to Utah. (See *1981 Church Almanac*, p. 140.)

# Brigham Young: Well Beloved of the Lord

Section 126

## Historical Background

"In the month of July, 1841, the Apostles began to return to Nauvoo from their missions to Europe, and their coming was a great comfort to the Prophet in his hour of affliction. At a special conference which was held at Nauvoo on the 16th of August, 1841, shortly after the return of the Twelve, Joseph stated to the people there assembled that the time had come when the Apostles must stand in their places next to the First Presidency. They had been faithful and had borne the burden and heat of the day, giving the gospel triumph in the nations of the earth, and it was right that they should now remain at home and perform duty in Zion." (Cannon, *Life of Joseph Smith,* p. 374.)

Though it was no longer required of Brigham Young to leave his family, he did fill some short-term missions: a mission through the states to refute slanderous charges by John C. Bennett and other apostates (September 1842 to 4 November 1842); a mission in the East to collect funds for the Nauvoo House and Nauvoo Temple (June 1843 to 22 October 1843); a mission to present to the citizens of the United States the name of Joseph Smith as a candidate for president of the United States (21 May 1844 to 6 August 1844) (see Whitney, *Life of Heber C. Kimball,* pp. 330-31, 334-37, 342).

In addition to being able to spend much more time with his family after this revelation than he had been able to in the previous several years, Brigham Young was also near the Prophet Joseph Smith much of the time (twenty-eight of the last thirty-six months of Joseph's life).

It seems evident that the Lord, knowing Brigham Young's future and the future of the Church, kept Brigham near Joseph so he could learn the vital lessons he would need to know in leading the Church after Joseph's death. It was fitting that the Lord speak to this obedient servant through the Prophet Joseph Smith in his own home.

*Brigham Young, successor to Joseph Smith*

## Notes and Commentary

### D&C 126:1. A Time for Learning and Preparation

The Lord called Brigham Young to remain in Nauvoo and direct the work as President of the Quorum of the Twelve. The wisdom of such a move was clearly seen in later years when Brigham Young was chosen by the Lord to succeed Joseph Smith. The Prophet Joseph was the leading inspiration of Brigham Young's life; no pain was too severe, no inconvenience too great to be where Joseph was and learn of him. Speaking of the time he spent in the Prophet's presence, Brigham Young once said: "In the days of the Prophet Joseph, such moments were more precious to me than all the wealth of the world. No matter how great my poverty—if I had to borrow meal to feed my wife and children—I never let an opportunity pass of learning what the Prophet had to impart." (In Nibley, *Brigham Young,* p. 28.)

### D&C 126:2-3. Brigham Young's Toil and Sacrifice Was Accounted to Him for Righteousness

Said President Brigham Young: "I came into this Church in the spring of 1832. Previous to my being baptized, I took a mission to Canada at my own expense; and from the time that I was baptized until the day of our sorrow and affliction, at the martyrdom of Joseph and Hyrum, no summer passed over my head but what I was traveling and preaching, and the only thing I ever received from the Church, during over twelve years, and the only means that were ever given me by the Prophet, that I now recollect, was in 1842, when brother Joseph sent me the half of a small pig that the brethren had brought to him. I did not ask him for it." (In *Journal of Discourses,* 4:34.)

Through his life as a member and as an Apostle, Brigham Young gave unselfishly with no thought of personal gain. He supported himself at home and abroad, and his family were beholden to no one. In addition he assisted in financing the work by his own toil, everywhere he went (see *Journal of Discourses,* 4:34-35).

Brigham Young was the living example of the spiritual principle taught by the Prophet Joseph Smith: "A religion that does not require the sacrifice of all things never has power sufficient to produce the faith necessary unto life and salvation" (*Lectures on Faith* 6:7).

# The Nauvoo Temple and Baptism for the Dead

Section 127

## Historical Background

As early as 10 August 1840, in a powerful address at the funeral of Seymour Brunson, the Prophet introduced the doctrine of baptism for the dead to a startled congregation of Saints. Thereafter it was frequently a topic of addresses of the Brethren, and baptisms for the dead were performed in the nearby Mississippi River (see Joseph Smith Letter Book, 6 November 1838-9 February 1843, Historical Department, The Church of Jesus Christ of Latter-day Saints, Salt Lake City, pp. 190-96; see also Notes and Commentary on D&C 124:29-36).

The minutes of the general conference of the Church held in Nauvoo on 2 October 1841, however, record that the Prophet declared it was the Lord's will that baptisms for the the dead cease until they could be performed in his house (see *History of the Church,* 4:426). The first baptisms for the dead in the uncompleted Nauvoo Temple were initiated Sunday, 21 November 1841 (see *History of the Church,* 4:454).

By the summer of 1842 persecution had escalated to the point that the Prophet Joseph Smith was forced into hiding to preserve his life. This revelation was given while he was hiding in the home of Brother Taylor, father of John Taylor. The Prophet sent instructions by letter, as did ancient prophets, to the Saints as revelation was received, clarifying the order of baptism for the dead in the house of the Lord.

Before the Prophet Joseph sent this revelation and Doctrine and Covenants 128 to the Saints, some unknown person had made a serious attempt on the life of former governor Boggs of Missouri. Blame for the deed was promptly fastened on Orrin Porter Rockwell, a Mormon, and Joseph Smith was named as his accessory. Efforts were immediately undertaken by residents of Missouri to compel the governor of Illinois, Thomas Carlin, to extradite Joseph Smith to Missouri to answer these false charges. "This was a conspiracy to get the Prophet back into the hands of the Missourian mobbers. Governor Carlin of Illinois had joined in this conspiracy contrary to every principle of correct law, as it was later shown in the trial which was held in Springfield [Illinois]. . . . From his place of concealment the Prophet wrote these two letters (Sections 127 and 128 in the Doctrine and Covenants) by revelation to the Church." (Smith, *Church History and Modern Revelation,* 2:328.)

*Orrin Porter Rockwell was blamed for the attempt on the life of Governor Boggs*

## Notes and Commentary

**D&C 127:1. Why Did Joseph Smith's Enemies Persecute Him without Cause?**

President Brigham Young asked: "Why was he hunted from neighborhood to neighborhood, from city to city, from state to state, and at last suffered death? Because he received revelations from the Father, from the Son, and was ministered to by holy angels, and published to the world the direct will of the Lord concerning his children on the earth. Again, why was he persecuted? Because he revealed to all mankind a religion so plain and so easily understood, consistent with the Bible, and so true. It is now as it was in the days of the Savior; let people believe and practise these simple, God-like truths, and it will be as it was in the old world." (In *Journal of Discourses,* 18:231.)

**D&C 127:1. Falsehoods of the "Blackest Dye"**

Throughout his life the Prophet Joseph Smith was accused of many evils—even to make a charge against him was tantamount to establishing it as truth, so unpopular was the Mormon prophet. He never broke the law (had he done so, he would not have refused to be subject to it), but men appeared in courts, perjured themselves to lie against the Prophet, and the courts accepted such testimony as evidence while refusing to hear testimony in the Prophet's favor. Upon learning the names of the Prophet's witnesses, having invited the Church to produce them, attorneys would attempt to arrest them, drive them from the country, or otherwise render them unavailable to the court (see *History of the Church,* 3:211-13). Truly Satan raged in the hearts of men as he sought to destroy the Lord's anointed.

President Brigham Young said of the legal persecutions directed against the Prophet: "Joseph, our Prophet, was hunted and driven, arrested and persecuted, and although no law was ever made in these United States that would bear against him, for he never broke a law, yet to my certain knowledge he was defendant in forty-six lawsuits, and every time Mr. Priest [a priest or a preacher] was at the head of and led the band or mob who hunted and persecuted him. And when Joseph and Hyrum were slain in Carthage jail, the mob, painted like Indians, was led by a preacher." (In *Journal of Discourses,* 14:199.)

"Joseph Smith, in forty-seven prosecutions was never proven guilty of one violation of the laws of his country. They accused him of treason, because he would not fellowship their wickedness." (Brigham Young, in *Journal of Discourses,* 10:111.)

**D&C 127:1. "I Have Left My Affairs with Agents and Clerks"**

On those occasions when the Prophet was compelled to flee for his life, it was necessary for him to turn his business affairs over to close, personal friends whom he trusted. One such friend was Oliver K. Granger, who handled the Prophet's financial concerns after Joseph fled Kirtland in January 1838 (see D&C 117:12-15; *History of the Church,* 3:164-65).

Although the agents and clerks mentioned here are not given by name, it is known that William W. Phelps, William Clayton, Willard Richards, and James Sloan were clerks in the Prophet's office at this time.

**D&C 127:2. Joseph Smith's Foreordination Implied Future Trials**

President Brigham Young said that "it was decreed in the councils of eternity, long before the foundations of the earth were laid, that he (Joseph Smith) should be the man, in the last dispensation of this world, to bring forth the word of God to the people, and receive the fulness of the keys and power of the Priesthood of the Son of God. . . . He was foreordained in eternity to preside over this last dispensation." (In *Journal of Discourses,* 7:289-90.) Because Satan's single purpose is to thwart the work of God, it was foreknown that the Prophet Joseph Smith was destined to suffer trials and persecution.

**D&C 127:4. Why Were the Saints Directed to Complete the Nauvoo Temple?**

In 1842 the Prophet and the Saints were entering a time of persecution that could have given the Saints cause to cease work on a house that might never be used—in fact, final work was done on the temple after the decision was made to evacuate Nauvoo in 1846. Yet, during all of the persecution, great blessings and endowments were given to sustain the people in the years of suffering and death that lay ahead, for it was thirty-one years before a temple of the Lord was dedicated again.

**D&C 127:6-7. Recording Work for the Dead: The Beginning of a Momentous Work**

Since the world began, no people in any era of time have received such a stewardship as have the Saints of latter days. Work for the dead had been done by the Saints of the meridian of time (see 1 Corinthians 15:29), but it falls to the Latter-day Saints to accomplish most of the work for the salvation of the dead. In these verses the Lord set forth a method of order and safety in accomplishing that work.

**D&C 127:7. "Whatsoever You Bind on Earth, May Be Bound in Heaven"**

"What is bound or sealed in the temples of the Lord," wrote President Joseph Fielding Smith, "is also sealed in heaven. This is the great authority which Elijah restored. It also covers ordinances performed for the living as well as for the dead. The Prophet said that all of the ordinances for the living are required in behalf of all the dead who are entitled to the fulness of the exaltation." (*Church History and Modern Revelation,* 2:329.)

**D&C 127:8. What Things Were Yet to Be Restored in 1842?**

During the Nauvoo period the Lord bestowed knowledge and keys for marriage for time and eternity (see D&C 132), temples to house sacred ordinances, endowments, and baptism for the dead (see D&C 124 through 128).

**D&C 127:9. What Is the Significance of Records Being Had in Order?**

The archives of the temple contain the names and ordinance dates for all persons for whom temple work has been done in the present dispensation. This important data is stored in computers for ease of retrieval. Certainly this kind of record keeping fulfills the Lord's requirement for "all the records [to] be had in order" (D&C 127:9).

# Baptism for the Dead

Section 128

## Historical Background

The circumstances surrounding the coming forth of this revelation are discussed in Historical Background for Doctrine and Covenants 127. Section 128 is the second letter written at the same instance by the Prophet Joseph Smith. The theme of work for the dead is dealt with more completely in Enrichment O, in the Appendix.

## Notes and Commentary

### D&C 128:2-4. What Happens If Ordinances Are Not Properly Recorded?

Elder Rudger Clawson explained the sacred obligation of keeping accurate temple records: "In the early days of the Church, some baptisms for the dead that were not properly witnessed and recorded, were rejected of the Lord, and the work had to be done over again. We know that great care and attention is given to this matter today in our Temples, and that efficient help must be secured to do this. . . . Truly it is a great and marvelous work, and not the least important thing about it is that these ordinances are all carefully recorded in the books and are filed away in the archives of the Temple, to be brought forth in due time. From these records the people who have gone to that house will be judged. Nothing that is done in that Temple will be accepted of the Lord, except it is properly witnessed and recorded." (In Conference Report, Apr. 1900, pp. 43-44.)

*Rudger Clawson stressed the importance of proper record keeping*

### D&C 128:6-9. In What Way Does John's Statement Deal with the Work for the Dead?

The Prophet Joseph Smith quoted John (Revelation 20:12) and set forth in Doctrine and Covenants 128:7-9 an explanation of the passage. The records of the holy work done in the temples of the Lord become witnesses in the judgment of the dead. Elder Bruce R. McConkie added that the scriptures become a standard of measurement in the Judgment and that the book of life that will be opened is figuratively "our own life, and being, the record of our acts transcribed in our souls, an account of our obedience or disobedience written in our bodies. Literally, it is the record kept in heaven of the names and righteous deeds of the faithful." (*Mormon Doctrine*, p. 97.)

The importance of records makes it greatly urgent that the Latter-day Saints honor their commitment to the dead to accomplish their work and have it properly recorded "on earth" that it may be recorded "in heaven . . . ; for out of the books shall your dead be judged" (D&C 128:8).This binding of things in heaven that are accomplished on the earth is by the power of the priesthood of God, and the sealing and binding power is, in one sense of the word, "the keys of the kingdom" (D&C 128:14). All binding actions pivot upon God's own power and authority; otherwise every effort, every ordinance performed, and every righteous intent of a person's heart is futile.

### D&C 128:12-13. How Is Baptism for the Dead a Symbolic Ordinance?

President Joseph Fielding Smith taught: "The Lord has placed the baptismal font in our temples below the foundation, or the surface of the earth. This is symbolical, since the dead are in their graves, and we are working for the dead when we are baptized for them. Moreover, baptism is also symbolical of death and the resurrection, in fact, is virtually a resurrection from the life of sin, or from spiritual death, to the life of spiritual life. (See D. & C. 29:41-45.) Therefore when the dead have had this ordinance performed in their behalf they are considered to have been brought back into the presence of God, just as this doctrine is applied to the living." (*Church History and Modern Revelation*, 2:332.)

The symbolism of the baptismal font also has

significance for the living. Paul taught that one must put the carnal (sinful) man to death, that is, put him out of existence and become a new person (see Romans 6:1-7). This "old man of sin" (Romans 6:6) is buried in the baptismal font, a similitude of the grave, and the newborn, spiritual person comes out of a total immersion in water in similitude of physical birth (see Moses 6:59-60; for a discussion of the symbolism of baptism, see Smith, *Doctrines of Salvation,* 2:323-27).

**D&C 128:14-18. Why Is Baptism for the Dead Such an Important Gospel Principle?**

The Prophet Joseph Smith expounded three essential gospel principles:

1. The salvation of an individual's dead ancestors is "essential to our salvation," that is, one's life is inextricably intertwined with his ancestors' lives, for he cannot become perfect without them nor they without him (D&C 128:15).

2. Baptism for the dead is the "most glorious of all subjects belonging to the everlasting gospel" (vs. 17). Few doctrines present more clearly the love and mercy of an all-wise Father in Heaven. Where churches of men make no provision for the salvation of those whose bodies and spirits are separated in death, the Church of Jesus Christ presents this glorious plan of God. As President Rudger Clawson said: "Oh, the beauty of the justice and mercy of God, who is no respecter of persons! And let it be remembered that what it takes to save one who is living; it takes just that much to save one who is dead." (In Conference Report, Oct. 1931, p. 79.)

3. Baptism for the dead helps to prevent the earth from being smitten with a curse. As President Joseph Fielding Smith taught, "If Elijah had not come, we are led to believe that all the work of past ages would have been of little avail, for the Lord said the whole earth, under such conditions, would be utterly wasted at his coming. Therefore his mission was of vast importance to the world. It is not the question of baptism for the dead alone, but also the sealing of parents and children to parents, so that there should be a 'whole and complete and perfect union, and welding together of dispensations, and keys, and powers, and glories,' from the beginning down to the end of time.

"If this sealing power were not on the earth, then confusion would reign and disorder would take the place of order in that day when the Lord shall come, and, of course, this could not be, for all things are governed and controlled by perfect law in the kingdom of God.

"Why would the earth be wasted? Simply because if there is not a welding link between the fathers and the children—which is the work for the dead—then we will all stand rejected; the whole work of God will fail and be utterly wasted. Such a condition, of course, shall not be." (*Doctrines of Salvation,* 2:121-22.)

**D&C 128:18. "The Dispensation of the Fulness of Times"**

Elder Charles W. Penrose explained that "in this dispensation—the grandest and greatest of all, will be gathered in one all things that are in Christ, not only His people gathered from the various nations to Zion to build it up, to prepare the place for His feet, but the hosts that have passed away, whom He will bring with Him. Not only are the people to be gathered together, but the glorious truths which have been made manifest in the ages that are past will all be brought forth in the dispensation in which we are living, and things kept hid from the foundation of the world will be made manifest; for the Lord has promised it; and His promises never fail of fulfillment. This dispensation in which we live is signalized by a great work of consummation of the purposes of the Almighty." (In Conference Report, Oct. 1911, pp. 48-49; see also D&C 27:5-13; 124:41; 128:19-24.)

**D&C 128:19-23. A Psalm of Joy**

Under the inspiration of the Spirit, the Prophet was so moved with joy that he wrote these verses poetically. Sidney B. Sperry outlined verses 19, 22, and 23 to show the psalmlike nature of this part of the Prophet's letter.

Now, what do we hear in the Gospel which we have received?
A voice of gladness!
A voice of mercy from heaven;
And a voice of truth out of the earth [cf. Ps. 85:11; Isa. 29:3-4, 11-14; 2 Nephi 27:6-29].
Glad tidings for the dead;
A voice of gladness for the living and the dead;
Glad tidings of great joy [cf. Luke 2:10].
How beautiful upon the mountains
Are the feet of those that bring glad tidings of good things,
And that say unto Zion:
Behold, thy God reigneth! [Cf. Isa. 52:7]
As the dews of Carmel,
So shall the knowledge of God descend upon them!

. . . . . . . . . . . . . . . .

Brethren, shall we not go on in so great a cause?
Go forward and not backward.
Courage, brethren; and on, on to the victory!
Let your hearts rejoice, and be exceedingly glad.
Let the earth break forth into singing.
Let the dead speak forth anthems of eternal praise
To the King Immanuel, who hath ordained, before the world was,

That which would enable us to redeem them out of their prison;
For the prisoners shall go free.

Let the mountains shout for joy,
And all ye valleys cry aloud;
And all ye seas and dry lands tell the wonders of your Eternal King!
And ye rivers, and brooks, and rills, flow down with gladness.
Let the woods and all the trees of the field praise the Lord;
And ye solid rocks weep for joy!
And let the sun, moon, and the morning stars sing together,
And let all the sons of God shout for joy! [Cf. Job 38:7.]
And let the eternal creations declare his name forever and ever!

"And again I say, how glorious is the voice we hear from heaven, proclaiming in our ears, glory, and salvation, and honor, and immortality, and eternal life; kingdoms, principalities, and powers!" (*Compendium,* pp. 681-83.)

**D&C 128:20-21. Was Joseph Smith Familiar with Leaders of Past Dispensations?**

The Prophet Joseph extolled the goodness of God in showering his blessings upon the Latter-day Saints and mentioned some of the priesthood leaders of past ages who brought the keys to those blessings to this dispensation. Elder John Taylor, discussing the reasons for these occurrences, asked, "Why was it that all these people should be associated with all these dispensations, and all could communicate with Joseph Smith? Because he stood at the head of the dispensation of the fullness of times, which comprehends all the various dispensations that have existed upon the earth, and that as the Gods in the eternal worlds and the Priesthood that officiated in time and eternity had declared that it was time for the issuing forth of all these things, they all combined together to impart to him the keys of their several missions, that he might be fully competent, through the intelligence and aid afforded him through these several parties, to introduce the Gospel in all its fullness, namely, the dispensation of the fullness of times, when says the Apostle Paul 'He might gather all things in Christ, both which are in heaven and which are in earth, even in him.' Consequently he stood in that position, and hence his familiarity with all these various dispensations and the men who administered in them. If you were to ask Joseph what sort of a looking man Adam was, he would tell you at once; he would tell you his size and appearance and all about him. You might have asked him what sort of men Peter, James, and John were, and he could have told you. Why? Because he had seen them." (In *Journal of Discourses,* 18:325-26.)

**D&C 128:22. What Urgency Is Associated with "So Great a Cause?"**

The Prophet Joseph Smith is not the only prophet whose mind has been burdened with the urgency of the work for the dead (see D&C 128:1), for President Spencer W. Kimball shared similar feelings with modern-day Saints: "As I have previously said, most members of the Church are aware of our intense interest in the missionary work in the Church and the appeals we have made in many lands for the rededication to preaching the gospel and preparing missionaries to carry the good news of the restoration to the people everywhere. I feel the same sense of urgency about temple work for the dead as I do about the missionary work for the living, since they are basically one and the same. I have told my brethren of the General Authorities that this work for the dead is constantly on my mind." (In Conference Report, Apr. 1978, p. 4; or *Ensign,* May 1978, p. 4.)

In another conference President Kimball spoke of the need to accelerate the work even more:

"With the announcement just made of the construction of seven new temples, there begins the most intensive period of temple building in the history of the Church.

"The building of these temples must be accompanied by a strong emphasis on genealogical research on the part of all members of the Church.

"We feel an urgency for this great work to be accomplished and encourage members to accept this responsibility. Members do so by writing their personal and family histories, participating in the name extraction program when called to do so, completing their four-generation research, and then continuing their family research in order to redeem their kindred dead." (In Conference Report, Apr. 1980, p. 5; or *Ensign,* May 1980, p. 5.)

*A spirit of urgency pervades genealogical activity*

### D&C 128:23. Why Was Such Exultation in the Saving Work Demonstrated by the Prophet?

Elder Orson Pratt declared:

"We are willing to go the earth over to save the living; we are willing to build temples and administer in ordinances to save the dead; we are willing to enter the eternal worlds and preach to every creature who has not placed himself beyond the reach of mercy. We are willing to labour both in this world and in the next to save men.

". . . Let all rejoice that the great day of the dispensation of the fulness of times has come. Let the living rejoice; let the dead rejoice; let the heavens and the earth rejoice; let all creations shout hosannah! glory to God in the highest! for he hath brought salvation, and glory, and honour, and immortality, and eternal life to the fallen sons of men. Amen." (In *Journal of Discourses,* 7:90-91.)

### D&C 128:24. Who Are the Sons of Levi, and What Is Their Offering in Righteousness?

Historically, the sons of Levi, including the sons of Aaron and the sons of Moses (see Exodus 6:16, 18, 20), were the custodians of the house of God and were responsible for its holy ordinances (see Exodus 25-28; Numbers 8:24-26; 10:21). Today, the sons of Levi are those called by the Lord to "build up my Church" and who are "faithful unto the obtaining these two priesthoods of which I have spoken, and the magnifying their calling, are sanctified by the Spirit unto the renewing of their bodies" (D&C 84:31-33). They are those responsible respectively for the "preparatory gospel" (D&C 84:26-27) and for the "greater priesthood" and its ordinances (temple work) wherein "the power of godliness is manifest" (D&C 84:19-21). If the present-day servants of the Lord function faithfully in this holy stewardship, they become the "sons of Moses and of Aaron and the seed of Abraham, and the church and kingdom, and the elect of God" (D&C 84:34).

As righteous Saints serve the Lord in these holy ordinances, they become saviors on Mount Zion for the living and the dead. The sacrifice they offer through their service will be part of that "offering in righteousness" which the sons of Levi, including the sons of Moses and Aaron, will present to the Lord before Christ's coming.

Never has a people had the opportunity to do so much for so many as do the Latter-day Saints; however, if they fail in the effort, they do so at the "peril of their own salvation" (Smith, *Teachings,* p. 193; see also p. 356). The dead cannot receive the ordinances that lead them to salvation unless they are performed by the living; and the living must bind themselves to their ancestral families for their own salvation. Little wonder, then, that the Prophet Joseph Smith recorded such words of exultation at the wisdom of the Lord's mighty, saving plan for the living and the dead. Every Latter-day Saint should feel the urgency of the work and wear out his life in this selfless service.

# Keys for Determining If Administrations Are from God

Section 129

## Historical Background

In the early days of the Church much curiosity centered around the subject of angels, spirits, and resurrected persons. About the time Joseph Smith recorded this revelation he had a visit from a man who claimed to have seen an angel. The Prophet related: "A man came to me in Kirtland, and told me he had seen an angel, and described his dress. I told him he had seen no angel, and that there was no such dress in heaven. He grew mad, and went into the street and commanded fire to come down out of heaven to consume me. I laughed at him, and said, You are one of Baal's prophets; your God does not hear you; jump up and cut yourself: and he commanded fire from heaven to consume my house." (*History of the Church,* 5:267-68.)

Doctrine and Covenants 129 delineates the difference between angels who have gone through mortality and have been resurrected and those who are still spirits. It also gives three keys "whereby you may know whether any administration is from God" (vs. 9).

There are indications that the Prophet Joseph Smith knew these keys for distinguishing between messengers from God and messengers from the devil long before this revelation was recorded. Earlier in the history of the Church, Michael aided the Prophet by detecting Satan, who had appeared to Joseph as an angel of light (see D&C 128:20). Nothing further is known about the incident, and whether the Prophet learned of these keys at that time is not known; however, the journal of Wilford Woodruff indicates that he learned of these keys from Joseph Smith as early as 1839 (see Journal of Wilford Woodruff, vol. 2, 27 June 1839, Historical Department, The Church of Jesus Christ of Latter-day Saints, Salt Lake City).

In an address to the Twelve on 2 July 1839, the Prophet Joseph Smith taught: "An angel of God never has wings. Some will say that they have seen a spirit; that he offered them his hand, but they did not touch it. This is a lie. First, it is contrary to the plan of God: a spirit cannot come but in glory; an angel has flesh and bones; we see not their glory. The devil may appear as an angel of light. Ask God to reveal it; if it be of the devil, he will flee from you; if of God, He will manifest Himself, or make it manifest. We may come to Jesus and ask Him; He will know all about it." (*History of the Church,* 3:392.)

## Notes and Commentary

**D&C 129:1-3. What Is the Difference between a "Spirit" and an "Angel"?**

God employs many messengers in his service. In one sense all are angels, as President George Q. Cannon explained: "In the broadest sense, any being who acts as a messenger for our Heavenly Father, is an angel, be he a God, a resurrected man, or the spirit of a just man; and the term is so used in all these senses in the ancient scriptures. In the stricter and more limited sense, an angel is, as the Prophet Joseph Smith states, a resurrected personage, having a body of flesh and bones; but it must be remembered that *none* of the angels who appeared to men before the death of the Savior could be of that class, for *none* of them was resurrected. He was the first-fruits of them that slept. He Himself appeared often to His servants before he took His mortal body; for instance, to the brother of Jared, to Abraham, to Moses, to the seventy Elders and to many others." ("Editorial Thoughts," *Juvenile Instructor,* 15 Jan. 1891, p. 53.)

As used in Doctrine and Covenants 129 the term *angel* is limited to resurrected personages having bodies of flesh and bones and translated beings

*Joseph Smith gave three grand keys for the discerning of angels or spirits*

("just men made perfect"). Spirits are children of God who have not yet entered mortality, and are thus unembodied; or spirits are those whose spirits are separated from their bodies in death, who are disembodied. In a sermon delivered in Nauvoo, Joseph Smith explained the difference between an angel and a ministering spirit: an angel is "a resurrected or translated body, with its spirit ministering to embodied spirits," and a ministering spirit is "a disembodied spirit, visiting and ministering to disembodied spirits. Jesus Christ became a ministering spirit (while His body was lying in the sepulchre) to the spirits in prison, to fulfill an important part of His mission, without which He could not have perfected His work, or enter into His rest. After His resurrection He appeared as an angel [a resurrected being] to His disciples." (*History of the Church,* 4:425; see also 1 Peter 3:18-20.)

**D&C 129:3. What Is Meant by the Phrase "Spirits of Just Men Made Perfect?"**

No mortal man lives a perfect life. Some, however, so order their lives in accordance with the gospel that they become, before their life is over, the kind of men whom the scriptures speak of as "just men." But being just is not a sufficient qualification for the spirits of the righteous departed. "Be ye therefore perfect" is the Savior's command (Matthew 5:48). Hence it is that the scriptures speak of "just men *made perfect* through Jesus the mediator of the new covenant" (D&C 76:69; emphasis added).

**D&C 129:4. Whatever Their State and Condition, Angels Are Messengers of God**

"There are angels of various appointments and stations," wrote President Charles W. Penrose. Then he went on to say:

"Angels are God's messengers, whether used in that capacity as unembodied spirits, selected according to their capacities for the work required, or as disembodied spirits, or as translated men, or as resurrected beings. They are agents of Deity of different degrees of intelligence, power and authority, under the direction of higher dignitaries, and subject to law and order in their respective spheres. Elijah, who appeared with Moses on the mount of transfiguration, was a translated man; Moses at that time was either a translated man or a spirit ministering to the Savior; both acted in the capacity of angels. (Luke 9:28-33.) Enoch's band of translated beings doubtless appeared as angels in manifestations to the patriarchs recorded in the book of Genesis [see Genesis 21:17; 22:11; 32:1].

"Angels high in authority have been clothed on special occasions with the right to represent Deity personally. They have appeared and have been recognized as God himself, just as royal ambassadors of earthly potentates have acted, as recorded in history. The Angel spoken of in Exodus 23:20-22, was one of these. So also was the Angel already spoken of who ministered to John on the isle of Patmos, and used the names and titles of the Son of God. (Rev. 1:1.)" ("Who and

What Are the Angels?" *Improvement Era,* Aug. 1912, p. 950.)

**D&C 129:4-7. What Is the Significance of Shaking Hands?**

If the messenger is a resurrected personage whose flesh one feels when shaking hands, he is, by the Prophet Joseph Smith's definition given here, an angel from God. But a spirit cannot clasp hands, since he does not possess flesh and bones with which to do it. For a spirit to pretend to an ability he does not possess would be a deceit, and one who would attempt it would not be a "just man." Therefore, he will not move when a hand is extended toward him. This is the means whereby an angel, a messenger with a resurrected body, can be distinguished from a just spirit sent from God.

**D&C 129:8-9. "The Devil As an Angel of Light"**

Just as there are righteous spirits committed to the accomplishment of God's work, so there are evil spirits committed to the destruction of his work. "These are fallen angels," President Charles W. Penrose explained, "who were cast down for transgression, as mentioned by Jude (verse 6), chief among whom on this earth is Lucifer or Satan, who has sought on many occasions to appear as an 'angel of light' to deceive and lead astray, and who tempted the Son of God, but failed in his efforts as he did with Moses and with the Prophet Joseph Smith. (See Luke 4:1-13; Visions of Moses 1:12-22; Doctrine & Covenants 128:20.) That great spiritual personage was an angel of God in his 'first estate', and yet never had a body of flesh, but 'was in authority in the presence of God' as a spirit, before he rebelled and was 'thrust down.' (Doctrine & Covenants 76:25-28.)" ("Who and What Are the Angels?" p. 951.)

Satan attempts to deceive by counterfeiting the light that accompanies the spirit of a just man made perfect, who comes in his glory as a messenger, "for that is the only way he can appear" (D&C 129:6). Righteous men must learn how to unmask the devil and his fallen angels. The Prophet Joseph Smith once said, "Wicked spirits have their bounds, limits and laws, by which they are governed . . . and, it is very evident that they possess a power that none but those who have the priesthood can control" (*History of the Church,* 4:576).

Although the reason for it is not known, the Prophet Joseph Smith taught that when the devil is offered a hand to shake, "he will offer you his hand" (D&C 129:8). The mortal will feel nothing, for the devil is an unembodied spirit. He can therefore be distinguished in this manner from a righteous spirit or an angel sent from God. The just man will not attempt to deceive (see D&C 129:7); an angel of Satan will not refrain from trying to deceive.

# Items of Instruction

Section 130

## Historical Background

"On the 2nd of April, 1843, the Prophet Joseph attended a meeting at which Orson Hyde spoke and, alluding to the coming of the Savior, said, 'When He shall appear, we shall be like Him, etc. He will appear on a white horse as a warrior, and may be we shall have some of the same spirit. Our God is a warrior. It is our privilege to have the Father and Son dwelling in our hearts.'

"At dinner time the Prophet called the attention of Orson Hyde to these statements and told him that he would offer some corrections. Orson Hyde replied that they would be thankfully received, whereupon the Prophet gave the explanations contained in these paragraphs [verses 1-17], first privately and afterwards in the meeting." (Smith and Sjodahl, Commentary, pp. 812-13.) Still later in the evening, after a meeting, the Prophet answered some questions and gave the additional instructions found in Doctrine and Covenants 130:18-23.

This section contains important items of instruction and doctrinal truths which the Prophet Joseph learned from God by revelation. No wonder that the early Saints found it a joy to be in the Prophet's company.

## Notes and Commentary

**D&C 130:1. When the Savior Returns to Earth, What Will His Appearance Be?**

This verse and others (see Acts 1:11; D&C 45:48-52; 88:95) make it clear that the Savior, when he comes, will appear just as he did at his first appearance among men: as a man. However, his body will be a resurrected, glorified one of flesh and bones (see Notes and Commentary on D&C 133:46-51).

**D&C 130:3. What Is the Proper Interpretation of John 14:23?**

The passage in question quotes Jesus as saying that he and his Father will come to man and take up their abode with him. The Prophet Joseph explained that this statement is a literal fact, not a figure of speech. It is a promise that the Father and the Son will visit a person (see *Teachings,* pp. 149-51; see also Notes and Commentary on D&C 88:3-4).

### D&C 130:4-7. The Relativity of Time

Several scriptures suggest that the way men perceive time upon the earth may not be the way time really is throughout the universe. Alma 40:8 suggests that only men measure time and that to God all time is as one day. Other scriptures suggest that all things are present before the Lord (see D&C 38:2; Moses 1:6). Verses 4 through 7 in section 130 suggest a similar concept, namely that past, present, and future are continually before the Lord and that time is relative to the planet on which one resides.

Only in the twentieth century has the field of physics begun to speak about time and space in a way that corresponds to these revelatory statements. Albert Einstein, in the early part of this century, developed what is known as the theory of relativity. Einstein postulated that what men had assumed were absolutes in the physical world—space, gravity, speed, motion, time—were not absolutes at all but were interrelated with each other. That is why the theory was called the theory of relativity. Physicists now agree that a person's time reference will vary depending on his relative position in space.

Einstein also showed that if a body moves at very fast speeds (those approaching the speed of light, which is 186,000 miles per second), that body's time slows down in relation to the time of a body that is on earth; and for the body in motion, space contracts or shrinks. In other words, time and space are not two separate things but are interrelated. Physicists refer to this phenomenon as the space-time continuum. If an astronaut were to journey out into space at speeds approaching the speed of light, though to himself all would seem perfectly normal, to someone on earth it would appear as though his clock were ticking slower, his heart were beating slower, his metabolism operating slower, and so on. He would actually age more slowly than would a person who remained on the earth. Though the finite mind tends to reject such concepts, Einstein's theory suggests that men are victims of their own limited perceptions. Reality to man is a product of his relative position in the space-time continuum.

According to this theory, if a being achieved the speed of light, to that being all space would contract to the point that it would be "here" for him, and all time would slow down until it became "now" for him. Descriptions of God use terms related to light to describe his nature. He is a being of light and glory. The theory of relativity suggests that for a being of light, *all space and all time would be present!* As incredible as such a concept is, increasingly sophisticated experiments continue to substantiate Einstein's theoretical description of the realities of the universe.

Lael Woodbury, dean of the College of Fine Arts and Communications at Brigham Young University, talked about man's perception of time and God's perception of time in an address sponsored by the Church Educational System:

"The evidence suggests that God . . . perceives time as we perceive space. That's why 'all things are before him, and all things are round about him; and he is above all things, and in all things, and is through all things, and is round about all things' [D&C 88:41]. Time, like space, is 'continually before the Lord.' . . .

" . . . Right now we perceive music in time as a blind man perceives form in space—sequentially. He explores with his fingers, noting form, texture, contours, rhythms. He holds each perception in his mind, one by one, carefully adding one to the other, until he synthesizes his concept of what that space object must be like. You and I don't do that. We perceive a space object immediately. We simply look at it, and to a certain degree we 'know' it. We do [not] go through a one-by-one, sequential, additive process. We perceive that it *is,* and we are able to distinguish it from any other object.

"I'm suggesting that God perceives time as instantaneously as we perceive space. For us, time is difficult. Lacking higher facility, we are as blind about time as a sightless man is about space. We perceive time in the same way that we perceive music—sequentially. We explore rhythm, pitch, amplitude, texture, theme, harmonies, parallels, and contrasts. And from our perceptions we synthesize our concept of the object or event—the musical artwork—that existed in its entirety before we began our examination of it.

"Equally complete now is each of our lives before the Lord. We explore them sequentially because we are time-blind. But the Lord, perceiving time as space, sees us as we are, not as we are becoming. We are, for him, beings without time. We are continually before him—the totality of our psyches, personalities, bodies, choices, and behaviors." (*Continually before the Lord,* Commissioner's Lecture Series [Provo: Brigham Young University Press, 1974], pp. 5-6.)

Einstein's theory is only a theory, although it is being substantiated again and again as a valid representation of reality. How God operates through the vastness of space and the eternity of time has not been revealed in specific detail, but what information man has been given harmonizes with what physicists are discovering about the interrelationship of space and time. While it cannot be definitely stated how God operates, modern physics suggests that since he is indeed a being of light, then past, present and future are continually before him.

### D&C 130:5. Who Are the Angels Who Minister on Earth and Where Do They Come From?

See Notes and Commentary on Doctrine and Covenants 129:1-4.

### D&C 130:6-8. Where Do the Angels of God Live? What Is It Like There?

Angels live "in the presence of God" (D&C 130:7). As messengers of the Most High, they minister among his children. The scripture states that the

*Time is relevant to mortality*

place where God and the angels live is one vast "Urim and Thummim" (vs. 8). All things necessary for the angels' glory is manifest to them there: the past, the present, and the future.

**D&C 130:9. What Is the Destiny of This Earth and Those Who Will Dwell upon It?**

President Brigham Young said, "When it [the earth] becomes celestialized, it will be like the sun, and be prepared for the habitation of the saints, and be brought back into the presence of the Father and the Son, it will not then be an opaque body as it now is, but it will be like the stars of the firmament, full of light and glory; it will be a body of light. John compared it, in its celestial state, to a sea of glass." (In *Journal of Discourses,* 7:163.)

At another time he said: "This earth, when it becomes purified and sanctified, or celestialized, will become like a sea of glass; and a person, by looking into it, can know things past, present, and to come; though none but celestialized beings can enjoy this privilege. They will look into the earth, and the things they desire to know will be exhibited to them, the same as the face is seen by looking into a mirror." (Brigham Young, in *Journal of Discourses,* 9:87.)

**D&C 130:10. What Is the Destiny of All Celestial Beings?**

Angels are in a state wherein they possess "all things for their glory" (D&C 130:7). The same is true of God and all exalted beings. Those who obtain celestial glory obtain knowledge of all inferior kingdoms, or "kingdoms of a lower order" than the one on which they live (D&C 130:9). They also receive, as verse 10 makes clear, a personal Urim and Thummim in the form of a "white stone." This stone becomes the means "whereby things pertaining to a higher order of kingdoms" are placed in their possession (vs. 10). Men are initially prepared for these great blessings by keeping God's commandments and receiving an endowment in the house of God, as President Joseph Fielding Smith explained:

"The ordinances of the temple, the endowment and sealings, pertain to exaltation in the celestial kingdom, where the sons and daughters are. The sons and daughters are not outside in some other kingdom. The sons and daughters go into the house, belong to the household, have access to the home. 'In my Father's house are many mansions' [John 14:2]. Sons and daughters have access to the home where he dwells, and you cannot receive that access until you go to the temple. Why? Because you must receive certain key words as well as make covenants by which you are able to enter. If you try to get into the house, and the door is locked, how are you going to enter, if you haven't your key? You get your key in the temple, which will admit you.

" . . . You cannot find a key on the street, for that key is never lost that will open the door that enters into our Father's mansions. You have got to go where the key is given. And each can obtain the key, if you will; but after receiving it, you may *lose* it, by having it taken away from you again unless you abide by the agreement which you entered into when you went into the house of the Lord." (*Doctrines of Salvation,* 2:40-41.)

**D&C 130:12-13. The Commencement of Difficulties in South Carolina**

Section 87 foretells a war between the Northern and Southern sections of the United States. The Prophet Joseph Smith learned of this impending war on Christmas Day 1832, and these verses written eleven years later are a second mention of the same disaster. (See Notes and Commentary on D&C 87:1.)

**D&C 130:14-17. When Will Jesus Christ Return to Earth?**

The early disciples asked Jesus the same question just before his death (see Matthew 24:3; JS—M 1:4). At that time he told them that not even the angels know the exact time (see Matthew 24:36; JS—M 1:40); however, he did reveal the signs that would precede that great event so his disciples could recognize its approach.

In latter days the Lord gave a similar answer to the Prophet Joseph, telling him the specific signs that would precede the Second Coming. The Prophet Joseph Smith wrote:

"I was once praying earnestly upon this subject [the time of the coming of the Son of Man], and a voice said unto me, 'My son, if thou livest until thou art eighty-five years of age, thou shalt see the face of the Son of Man.' I was left to draw my own conclusions concerning this; and I took the liberty to conclude that if I did live to that time, He would make His appearance. But I do not say whether He will make his appearance or I shall go where He is.

I prophesy in the name of the Lord God, and let it be written—the Son of Man will not come in the clouds of heaven till I am eighty-five years old. . . .

"Judah must return, Jerusalem must be rebuilt, and the waters of the Dead Sea be healed [see Ezekiel 47:8-12]. It will take some time to rebuild the walls of the city and the temple, &c.; and all this must be done before the Son of Man will make His appearance. There will be wars and rumors of wars, signs in the heavens above and on the earth beneath, the sun turned into darkness and the moon to blood, earth quakes in divers places, the seas heaving beyond their bounds [see D&C 29:14-20; 34:9; 45:31-42; 88:87-91]; then will appear one grand sign of the Son of Man in heaven [see D&C 88:93]. But what will the world do? They will say it is a planet, a comet, &c. But the Son of Man will come as the sign of the coming of the Son of Man, which will be as the light of the morning cometh out of the east." (*History of the Church*, 5:336-37; see also D&C 43:20-27.)

**D&C 130:18-19. "It Will Rise with Us in the Resurrection"**

"It is fair to conclude that spiritual and mental growth can be attained only by obedience to the laws on which they are predicated," wrote Elder Albert E. Bowen. "If through diligence, observance of correct principles, discipline of the mind and of the spirit, a man attains to a fine development of personality in this life, surely it is not unreasonable to suppose that that will be his imperishable possession and glory in the life he enters upon after death. On the contrary, if through lethargy or sin his self-realization in this life is dwarfed, he shall be handicapped to that extent as he enters upon the new world." (In Conference Report, Oct. 1937, p. 86.)

**D&C 130:20-21. What Is the Law on Which All Blessings from God Depend?**

Obedience is the basic law of heaven, and obedience to specific laws will result in specific blessings, culminating in the greatest blessing, as Elder Marion G. Romney explained: "The perfection upon which exaltation hangs, I repeat, is an individual matter. It is conditioned upon the observance of celestial laws as they apply to earth life. The Word of Wisdom is one of them, so also are chastity, tithing, observance of the Sabbath day, prayer, honesty, industry, love of God and fellow men, patience, kindness, charity, and all the rest of the principles and ordinances of the gospel of Jesus Christ. Each individual who observes one or more of these laws shall receive the blessings predicated thereon, and each Church member who will, with all the energy of his soul, diligently strive to live them all, shall receive the blessings predicated upon such striving. Eternal life, the greatest gift of God, is that blessing, and it will follow the living of the gospel as the night the day, regardless of statistics or averages, or of what others think or say or do." (In Conference Report, Oct. 1956, pp. 15-16; see also Enrichment G, in the Appendix.)

# Keys to Exaltation

Section 131

## Historical Background

On 16 May 1843 the Prophet Joseph Smith, in company with William Clayton and four others, left Nauvoo for Ramus, Illinois, some twenty-two miles to the southeast. The same evening found Joseph Smith and William Clayton in the home of Benjamin F. Johnson, where before retiring the Prophet gave some instructions on the priesthood to Brother and Sister Johnson. During that evening he turned to William Clayton, placed his hand upon his knee, and said, "Your life is hid with Christ in God, and so are many others. Nothing but the unpardonable sin can prevent you from inheriting eternal life for you are sealed up by the power of the Priesthood unto eternal life, having taken the step necessary for that purpose." (*History of the Church*, 5:391.)

After making other personal observations, the Prophet gave Brother Clayton the message found in Doctrine and Covenants 131:1-4.

The next morning, 17 May 1843, the Prophet Joseph Smith discoursed upon 2 Peter 1, showing that the more knowledge a person has, the more power he has. Verses 5 and 6 were given in that morning meeting (see *History of the Church*, 5:392). Four days later, in the Nauvoo Temple, the Prophet again spoke on the power of knowledge and the doctrine of making one's calling and election sure.

On the evening of 17 May the Prophet went to hear a Methodist preacher lecture. The Prophet afterwards offered some corrections to what had been said. Some of the corrections have been included in section 131, verses 7 and 8. (See *History of the Church*, 5:392-93.)

The three items of instruction given by the Prophet on 16 and 17 May 1843 were later combined into one section and added to the Doctrine and Covenants in 1876 by Elder Orson Pratt, who was acting under the direction of President Brigham Young.

## Notes and Commentary

### D&C 131:1. What Are the Three Degrees in the Celestial Kingdom?

The Lord has not revealed to the Church who will live in two of the three degrees in the celestial kingdom; therefore, any discussion on this topic is conjecture or speculation. A great deal has been revealed, however, about the highest degree of the celestial kingdom, or exaltation, because that is where the Father would have all of his children live if they keep his commandments. In Doctrine and Covenants 76:50-70 the Lord outlines the requirements and qualifications to obtain the highest degree in the celestial kingdom.

### D&C 131:2. What Is "the New and Everlasting Covenant of Marriage"?

Elder George Q. Cannon taught of the eternal nature of love and of how, through the power of the priesthood, such love can be made eternally binding: "We believe that when a man and woman are united as husband and wife, and they love each other, their hearts and feelings are one, that that love is as enduring as eternity itself, and that when death overtakes them it will neither extinguish nor cool that love, but that it will brighten and kindle it to a purer flame, and that it will endure through eternity; and that if we have offspring they will be with us and our mutual associations will be one of the chief joys of the heaven to which we are hastening. . . . God has restored the everlasting priesthood, by which ties can be formed,

*A sealing room where eternal marriages are solemnized*

consecrated and consummated, which shall be as enduring as we ourselves are enduring, that is, as our spiritual nature; and husbands and wives will be united together, and they and their children will dwell and associate together eternally, and this, as I have said, will constitute one of the chief joys of heaven; and we look forward to it with delightful anticipations." (In *Journal of Discourses,* 14:320-21; see also Notes and Commentary for D&C 22:1; 132:13-18.)

The explanatory phrase in brackets in verse 2 was inserted by Elder Orson Pratt under the direction of President Brigham Young when the section was added to the Doctrine and Covenants.

### D&C 131:4. What Is Eternal Increase?

Those who comply with the new and everlasting covenant of marriage and endure faithfully to the end gain the right to become eternal parents. The Prophet Joseph Smith, as he spoke to William Clayton the words of peace in verses 1 through 4, stated: "Except a man and his wife enter into an everlasting covenant and be married for eternity, while in this probation, by the power and authority of the Holy Priesthood, they will cease to increase when they die; that is, they will not have any children after the resurrection. But those who are married by the power and authority of the priesthood in this life, and continue without committing the sin against the Holy Ghost, will continue to increase and have children in the celestial glory." (*History of the Church,* 5:391; see also Smith, *Teachings,* pp. 300-301.)

On 30 June 1916, the First Presidency of the Church (Joseph F. Smith, Anthon H. Lund, and Charles W. Penrose) declared: "So far as the stages of eternal progression and attainment have been made known through divine revelation, we are to understand that only resurrected and glorified beings can become parents of spirit offspring. Only such exalted souls have reached maturity in the appointed course of eternal life; and the spirits born to them in the eternal worlds will pass in due sequence through the several stages or estates by which the glorified parents have attained exaltation." (In Clark, *Messages of the First Presidency,* 5:34.)

President Spencer W. Kimball taught that the right to eternal increase will depend directly on how individuals keep the marriage covenant in this life:

"One young man said that he expected to reach exaltation in the celestial kingdom as one of the Lord's messengers, without having to marry. He does not understand. No one who rejects the covenant of celestial marriage can reach exaltation in the eternal kingdom of God.

" 'In the celestial glory there are three heavens or degrees;

" 'And in order to obtain the highest, a man must enter into this order of the priesthood [meaning the new and everlasting covenant of marriage];

" 'And if he does not, he cannot obtain it.

" 'He may enter into the other, but that is the end of his kingdom; he cannot have an increase.' (D&C 131:1-4.)

"He cannot have an increase! He cannot have exaltation!

"The Lord says further in the 132nd section of the Doctrine and Covenants:

" 'No one can reject this covenant and be permitted to enter into my glory' (D&C 132:4).

"No one! It matters not how righteous they may have been, how intelligent or how well trained they are. No one will enter this highest glory unless he enters into the covenant, and this means the new and everlasting covenant of marriage." ("The Importance of Celestial Marriage," *Ensign*, Oct. 1979, pp. 5-6.)

**D&C 131:5. What Is "the More Sure Word of Prophecy"?**

Elder Bruce R. McConkie said:

"Those members of the Church who devote themselves wholly to righteousness, living by every word that proceedeth forth from the mouth of God, make their *calling and election sure.* That is, they receive the more sure word of prophecy, which means that the Lord seals their exaltation upon them while they are yet in this life. Peter summarized the course of righteousness which the saints must pursue to make their calling and election sure and then (referring to his experience on the Mount of Transfiguration with James and John) said that those three had received this more sure word of prophecy. (2 Pet. 1.) . . .

"Those so favored of the Lord are sealed up against all manner of sin and blasphemy except the blasphemy against the Holy Ghost and the shedding of innocent blood. That is, their exaltation is assured; their calling and election is made sure, because they have obeyed the fullness of God's laws and have overcome the world." (*Mormon Doctrine*, pp. 109-10; see also D&C 132:17, 26; Notes and Commentary for D&C 76:53.)

**D&C 131:6. How Important Is Knowledge?**

The Prophet Joseph Smith stated: "A man is saved no faster than he gets knowledge, for if he does not get knowledge, he will be brought into captivity by some evil power in the other world, as evil spirits will have more knowledge, and consequently more power than many men who are on the earth. Hence it needs revelation to assist us, and give us knowledge of the things of God." (*History of the Church*, 4:588.)

The statement in Doctrine and Covenants 131:6 holds true of all knowledge, but it should be remembered that it was given in connection with verse 5. In that context, the knowledge referred to is the more sure word of prophecy (vs. 5), and the implication is that no man can be saved without *that* knowledge. This is not to say that receiving the more sure word of prophecy must happen in mortality, but it is a true principle that no man can be saved (exalted) without having his calling and election made sure, or receiving the more sure word of prophecy.

**D&C 131:7. Is All Matter Eternal?**

"The materials out of which this earth was formed," said Elder Orson Pratt, "are just as eternal as the materials of the glorious personage of the Lord himself. . . . This Being, when he formed the earth, did not form it out of something that had no existence, but he formed it out of materials that had an existence from all eternity; they never had a beginning, neither will one particle of substance now in existence ever have an end. There are just as many particles now as there were at any previous period of duration, and will be while eternity lasts. Substance had no beginning; to say that laws had no beginning would be another thing; some laws might have been eternal, while others might have had a lawgiver. But the earth was formed out of eternal materials, and it was made to be inhabited and God peopled it with creatures of his own formation." (In *Journal of Discourses*, 19:286.)

Here again, as in the matter of time relativity (see Notes and Commentary on D&C 130:4-7), the revelations of the Prophet are being substantiated through modern physics. In the first half of the nineteenth century, most scientists believed that matter could be created and destroyed. Now, however, physicists agree that matter and energy are just different forms of the same thing and that while matter may be converted to energy or energy to matter, neither can be created or destroyed.

# Marriage: An Eternal Covenant

Section 132

## Historical Background

The Prophet Joseph Smith had spoken of eternal marriage to William Clayton in March 1843, two months before the revelation in Doctrine and Covenants 132 was recorded, and evidently the Prophet knew the Lord's will on plural marriage within the new and everlasting covenant as early as 1831 (see *History of the Church,* 5:xxix). He was discussing the doctrine with his brother Hyrum in the presence of William Clayton when Hyrum said, "If you will write the revelation on celestial marriage, I will take it and read it to Emma, and I believe I can convince her of its truth, and you will hereafter have peace" (*History of the Church,* 5:xxxii).

The Prophet consented and told William Clayton to get some paper to write; but to his brother's "urgent request" that the Prophet use the Urim and Thummin to recall the exact revelation, Joseph replied that he did not need that instrument, "for he knew the revelation from beginning to end" (*History of the Church,* 5:xxxii). When he had finished dictating, William Clayton read it back slowly, and Joseph said that it was exact.

Bishop Newel K. Whitney heard the revelation read and asked permission of the Prophet Joseph Smith to have it copied. With the Prophet's approval, Bishop Whitney sent Joseph C. Kingsbury the next day to copy it. Brothers Kingsbury and Clayton compared the copy line by line to the original and found it correct.

The revelation had been received prior to July 1843, when it was first recorded, but it was not made public until Elder Orson Pratt, under the direction of President Brigham Young, declared it on 29 August 1852. The revelation was finally placed in the Doctrine and Covenants in 1876.

Smith and Sjodahl pointed out that the revelation has two major sections: "The first, comprising vv. 3-33, deals mainly with the principle of celestial marriage, or marriage for time and all eternity; the second, comprising the remaining verses, deals with plural marriage. The doctrine of celestial marriage remains in force; the practice of plural marriage was abandoned by the acceptance by the Church, in Conference assembled October 6th, 1890, of the *Manifesto* of President Woodruff." (Commentary, p. 821; also see Historical Background on Official Declaration 1.)

## Notes and Commentary

### D&C 132:1-2 "Inasmuch As You Have Inquired of My Hand"

"From this introductory statement it is evident that the Prophet had made the question of marriage a subject of earnest prayer, as he did with matters concerning which he was perplexed and desired to know the truth. He did not understand how the Patriarchs, and David and Solomon could find favor with the Lord, while living in a manner contrary to certain modern moral standards, and he asked the Lord for light. Elder B. H. Roberts (*History of the Church,* Vol. V., Intr., p. 29) suggests that it was in the year 1831, when the Prophet was studying the lives of the Patriarchs in the Old Testament, in the course of his Bible revision, that he was led to offer the prayer referred to in the first verse, and received the answer contained in this Section, though it was not then committed to writing." (Smith and Sjodahl, Commentary, p. 821.)

### D&C 132:1. What Are Concubines?

*Concubine,* a word commonly used in the Old Testament, was defined by Elder Bruce R. McConkie as follows: "Anciently they were considered to be *secondary wives,* that is, wives who did not have the same standing in the caste system then prevailing as did those wives who were not called concubines. There were no concubines connected with the practice of plural marriage in this dispensation, because the caste system which caused some wives to be so designated did not exist." (*Mormon Doctrine,* pp. 154-55.)

### D&C 132:3-6. "If Ye Abide Not That Covenant, Then Are Ye Damned"

The "new and everlasting covenant" (D&C 132:4) is the covenant of celestial marriage, as President Spencer W. Kimball plainly stated: "Though relatively few people in this world understand it, the new and everlasting covenant is the marriage ordinance in the holy temple by the properly constituted leaders who hold the genuine, authoritative keys. This glorious blessing is available to men and women on this earth." ("Temples and Eternal Marriage," *Ensign,* Aug. 1974, p. 5.)

One can sense the importance of accepting this covenant by the emphasis the Lord puts in the following phrases:

"All who have this law revealed unto them must obey the same" (D&C 132:3).

"If ye abide not that covenant, then are ye damned" (vs. 4).

"No one can reject this covenant and . . . enter into my glory" (vs. 4).

"All who will have a blessing at my hands shall abide the law" (vs. 5).

"He that receiveth a fulness [of my glory] must and shall abide the law" (vs. 6).

A five-fold repetition of a concept in four verses

should indicate how strongly the Lord wishes to impress this doctrine on the minds of the Saints. President Kimball stressed forcefully how the Saints should view this commandment (see Notes and Commentary for D&C 131:4), for those who reject this covenant are truly damned, or stopped, in their eternal progression because they do not inherit the blessings of eternal increase.

**D&C 132:4. Will Those Who Do Not Have the Opportunity to Marry in This Life Be Damned?**

President Spencer W. Kimball spoke directly to those who may not have the opportunity in this life to marry:

"I am aware of some young men and women who seemingly have not been successful in total fulfillment. Some have been on missions; some have completed their education. And yet they have passed the period of their greatest opportunity for marriage. The time has passed, and while still attractive and desirable and efficient, they find themselves alone.

"To you we say this: You are making a great contribution to the world as you serve your families and the Church and the world. You must remember that the Lord loves you and the Church loves you. To you women, we can only say we have no control over the heartbeats or the affections of men, but pray that you may find fulfillment. And in the meantime, we promise you that insofar as eternity is concerned, no soul will be deprived of rich and high and eternal blessings for anything which that person could not help, that the Lord never fails in his promises, and that every righteous person will receive eventually all to which the person is entitled and which he or she has not forfeited through any fault of his or her own. We encourage both men and women to keep themselves well-groomed, well-dressed, abreast of the times, attractive mentally, spiritually, physically, and especially morally, and then they can lean heavily upon the Lord's promises for these heavenly blessings." ("The Importance of Celestial Marriage," *Ensign*, Oct. 1979, p. 5.)

*Latter-day Saints observe the new and everlasting covenant of marriage*

**D&C 132:7. What Does It Mean to Be "Sealed by the Holy Spirit of Promise"?**

In a comprehensive explanation of the role of the Holy Spirit, Elder Bruce R. McConkie commented on this verse as follows:

"The Holy Ghost is the Holy Spirit; he is the Holy Spirit promised the saints at baptism, or in other words the Holy Spirit of Promise, this exalted name-title signifying that the promised receipt of the Holy Spirit, as on the day of Pentecost, is the greatest gift man can receive in mortality.

"The gift of the Holy Ghost is the right to the constant companionship of that member of the Godhead based on faithfulness; it is bestowed with a promise that we shall receive revelation and be sanctified if we are true and faithful and so live as to qualify for the companionship of that Holy Spirit who will not dwell in an unclean temple. (1 Cor. 3:16-17; 6:19; Mosiah 2:37; Hela. 4:24.) The receipt of the promise is conditional! If after we receive the promise, we then keep the commandment, we gain the companionship of this member of the Godhead, and not otherwise.

"One of the functions assigned and delegated to the Holy Spirit is to seal, and the following expressions are identical in thought content:

"To be sealed by the Holy Spirit of Promise;

"To be justified by the Spirit;

"To be approved by the Lord; and

"To be ratified by the Holy Ghost.

"Accordingly, any act which is sealed by the Holy Spirit of Promise is one which is justified by the Spirit, one which is approved by the Lord, one which is ratified by the Holy Ghost. . . .

"As revealed to Joseph Smith, the Lord's law in this respect is: [D&C 132:7].

"By way of illustration this means that baptism, partaking of the sacrament, administering to the sick, marriage, and every covenant that man ever makes with the Lord—plus all other 'contracts, bonds, obligations, oaths, vows, perfomances, associations, or expectations'—must be performed in righteousness by and for people who are worthy to receive whatever blessing is involved, otherwise whatever is done has no binding and sealing effect in eternity.

"Since 'the Comforter knoweth all things' (D. & C. 42:17), it follows that it is not possible 'to lie to the Holy Ghost' and thereby gain an unearned or undeserved blessing, as Ananias and Sapphira found out to their sorrow. (Acts 5:1-11.) And so this provision that all things must be sealed by the Holy Spirit of Promise, if they are to have 'efficacy, virtue, or force in and after the resurrection from the dead' (D. & C. 132:7), is the Lord's system for dealing with absolute impartiality with all men, and for giving all men exactly what they merit, neither adding to nor diminishing from." (*Doctrinal New Testament Commentary,* 3:333-35; see also Notes and Commentary for D&C 76:53; 131:5.)

### D&C 132:7. Who Holds All the Keys of the Priesthood?

Elder William Critchlow, Jr., speaking in general conference, stated: "Only one mortal man at a time is privileged to hold all the priesthood keys pertaining to the kingdom of God. The President of The Church of Jesus Christ of Latter-day Saints is that man." (In Conference Report, Apr. 1963, p. 32; see also Notes and Commentary on D&C 21:4-5.) The prophet may designate these sealing powers to others, such as other General Authorities or temple workers, but the keys always reside in him, and no man can take these keys unto himself.

### D&C 132:8-14. "Everything That Is in the World . . . Shall Not Remain"

"The important truth is here taught that all institutions in this world, not founded on divine law but erected by human ingenuity, [will] cease to exist. . . . Man-made governments are obliterated, as are the sand castles children build on the tide-swept beach. Man-made religions and churches are swallowed up in death. Not a trace of them will be seen on the shores of eternity. Social customs and habits not sanctioned by God, will not continue. On the other hand, all institutions founded on the Word of God will remain throughout all eternity. The Church will remain. The family will remain. All the organizations of which God is the author are eternal." (Smith and Sjodahl, Commentary, p. 824.)

### D&C 132:13-18. "If a Man Marry . . . in the World"

After quoting Doctrine and Covenants 132:13, President Spencer W. Kimball said:

"How final! How frightening! Since we know well that mortal death does not terminate our existence, since we know that we live on and on, how devastating to realize that marriage and family life, so sweet and happy in so many homes, will end with death because we fail to follow God's instructions or because we reject his word when we understand it.

"It is clear in the Lord's announcement that righteous men and women will receive the due rewards of their deeds. They will not be damned in the commonly accepted terminology but will suffer many limitations and deprivations and fail to reach the highest kingdom, if they do not comply. They become ministering servants to those who complied with all laws and lived all commandments.

"[The Lord] then continues concerning these excellent people who lived worthily but failed to make their contracts binding:

" 'For these angels did not abide my law; therefore, they cannot be enlarged, but remain separately and singly, without exaltation, in their saved condition, to all eternity; and from henceforth are not gods, but are angels of God forever and ever.' (D&C 132:17.)

"How conclusive! How bounded! How limiting! And we come to realize again as it bears heavily upon us that this time, this life, this mortality is the time to prepare to meet God. How lonely and barren will be the so-called single blessedness throughout eternity! How sad to be separate and single and apart through countless ages when one could, by meeting requirements, have happy marriage for eternity in the temple by proper authority and continue on in ever-increasing joy and happiness, growth and development toward godhood. . . .

"Are you willing to jeopardize your eternities, your great continuing happiness, your privilege to see God and dwell in his presence? For the want of investigation and study and contemplation; because of prejudice, misunderstanding, or lack of knowledge, are you willing to forego these great blessings and privileges? Are you willing to make yourself a widow for eternity or a widower for endless ages—a single, separate individual to live alone and serve others? Are you willing to give up your children when they die or when you expire, and make them orphans? Are you willing to go through eternity alone and solitary when all of the greatest joys you have ever experienced in life could be 'added upon' and accentuated, multiplied, and eternalized? Are you willing, with the Sadducees, to ignore and reject these great truths? I sincerely pray you stop today and weigh and measure and then prayerfully proceed to make your happy marriage an eternal one. Our friends, please do not ignore this call. I beg of you, open your eyes and see; unstop your ears and hear." ("Temples and Eternal Marriage," *Ensign,* Aug. 1974, p. 6.)

### D&C 132:16. How Important Is It to Be Married by Proper Authority *Now?*

Elder James E. Talmage wrote that "in the resurrection there will be no marrying nor giving in marriage; for all questions of marital status must be settled before that time, under the authority of the Holy Priesthood, which holds the power to seal in marriage for both time and eternity" (*Jesus the Christ,* p. 548; see also Matthew 22:30; Mark 12:25).

### D&C 132:19-22. How Does an Individual Obtain a Fulness of God's Glory?

In the revelations of the Doctrine and Covenants are found all of the laws necessary for exaltation. Section 132 reveals the law of exaltation, which is celestial marriage, based on completion of the other steps necessary for eternal life: faith, repentance, baptism, priesthood, and so forth.

Achieving a celestial marriage is a covenant-making and covenant-keeping process. Covenants are contracts between two parties; they become valid only when both parties fulfill their respective parts. A covenant forms an "if . . . , then . . . " clause: *if* certain conditions are met, *then* certain promises are received. Verses 19 through 22 form such a clause.

| If a couple— | Then they will— |
|---|---|
| 1. Are married in accordance with the Lord's word and law | 1. "Inherit thrones, kingdoms, principalities, and powers, dominions, all heights and depths" (vs. 19) |
| 2. Are married by one who has the keys of the priesthood | 2. "Pass by the angels" to their exaltation (vs. 19) |
| 3. Have their marriage sealed by the Holy Spirit of Promise | 3. Be gods for all eternity (see vs. 20) |
| 4. Abide in the covenant | 4. Have a "continuation of the lives" (vs. 22) |

Some members of the Church mistakenly believe that marriage in the temple fulfills the requirements of the covenant. But marriage in the temple fulfills only the first two prerequisites of the covenant. Abiding in the covenant to the point that the Holy Spirit seals the promises of eternal marriage upon a couple requires a lifelong commitment to righteousness (see Notes and Commentary on D&C 132:7). Elder Bruce R. McConkie taught that "baptism is the gate to the celestial kingdom; celestial marriage is the gate to an exaltation in the highest heaven within the celestial world. (D. & C. 131:1-4.) To gain salvation after baptism it is necessary to keep the commandments of God and endure to the end (2 Ne. 31:17-21); to gain exaltation after celestial marriage it is necessary to continue the same devotion and righteousness. Those who have been married in the temples for eternity know that the ceremony itself expressly conditions the receipt of all promised blessings upon the subsequent faithfulness of the husband and wife.

"Making one's calling and election sure is an *addition* to celestial marriage and results from undeviating and perfect devotion to the cause of righteousness. Those married in the temple can never under any circumstances gain exaltation unless they keep the commandments of God and abide in the covenant of marriage which they have taken upon themselves." (*Mormon Doctrine,* p. 118.)

**D&C 132:19. What Is the Lamb's Book of Life?**

Elder Bruce R. McConkie explained that "in a literal sense, the *book of life,* or *Lamb's book of Life,* is the record kept in heaven which contains the names of the faithful and an account of their righteous covenants and deeds. (D. & C. 128:6-7; Ps. 69:28; Rev. 3:5; 21:27.) The book of life is the book containing the names of those who shall inherit eternal life; it is the book of eternal life. (Dan. 12:1-4; Heb. 12:23; D. & C. 76:68; 132:19.) It is 'the book of the names of the sanctified, even them of the celestial world.' (D. & C. 88:2.) Names of faithful saints are recorded in the book of life while they are yet in mortality. (Luke 10:20; Philip. 4:3; *Teachings,* p. 9.) But those names are blotted out in the event of wickedness. (Rev. 13:8; 17:8; 22:19.)" (*Mormon Doctrine,* p. 97; the phrase "innocent blood" is explained in Notes and Commentary on D&C 132:27.)

**D&C 132:22-25. What Is "the Continuation of the Lives" and the "Deaths"?**

Elder Bruce R. McConkie taught: "Those who gain eternal life (exaltation) also gain *eternal lives,* meaning that in the resurrection they have *eternal 'increase,' 'a continuation of the seeds,'* a *'continuation of the lives.'* Their spirit progeny will 'continue as innumerable as the stars; or, if ye were to count the sand upon the seashore ye could not number them.' (D. & C. 131:1-4; 132:19-25, 30, 55.)" (*Mormon Doctrine,* p. 238; see also Notes and Commentary on D&C 131:4.)

President Joseph Fielding Smith further explained that "the term 'deaths' mentioned here has reference to the cutting off of all those who reject this eternal covenant of marriage and therefore they are denied the power of exaltation and the continuation of posterity. To be denied posterity and the family organization, leads to the 'deaths,' or end of increase in the life to come." (*Church History and Modern Revelation,* 2:360; see also McConkie, *Mormon Doctrine,* p. 283.)

**D&C 132:26-27. Does Marriage in the Temple Assure One of Exaltation, No Matter How One Lives?**

A few people have sought to twist the meaning of these verses to suggest that once one is married in the temple one is assured of exaltation. Such reasoning is what Peter meant by wresting the scriptures "unto their own destruction" (2 Peter 3:16). President Harold B. Lee indicated that a temple marriage *can* be perfected and sealed for eternity, but that there is no guarantee in the ceremony itself: "Some folks have the mistaken notion that if somehow, by hook or crook, they can get into the House of the Lord and be married they are assured of exaltation regardless of what they do, and they'll quote the 132 Section, the 26th verse. But that isn't what the Lord means. The Lord does assure an exaltation to those who make mistakes, if they repent." (*Cram for Life's Final Examination,* Brigham Young University Speeches of the Year [Provo, 5 Jan. 1954] , p. 7.)

President Joseph Fielding Smith commented:

"Verse 26, in Section 132, is the most abused passage in any scripture. The Lord has never promised any soul that he may be taken into exaltation without the spirit of repentance. While repentance is not stated in this passage, yet it is, and must be, implied. It is strange to me that everyone knows about verse 26, but it seems that they have never read or heard of Matthew 12:31-32, where the Lord tells us the same thing in substance as we find in verse 26, section 132. . . .

"So we must conclude that those spoken of in verse 26 are those who, having sinned, have *fully repented* and are willing to pay the price of their sinning, else the blessings of exaltation will not follow. Repentance is absolutely necessary for the forgiveness, and the person having sinned must be cleansed." (*Doctrines of Salvation,* 2:95-96.)

*To gain eternal life, individuals must keep the covenants they make in the temple*

The key phrase is "and they are sealed by the Holy Spirit of Promise" (D&C 132:26.) This sealing is related to having one's calling and election made sure. (See Notes and Commentary for D&C 76:53; 131:5; 132:7.)

Speaking specifically of the promise in Doctrine and Covenants 132:26, Elder Bruce R. McConkie said:

"Making one's calling and election sure comes after and grows out of celestial marriage. Eternal life does not and cannot exist for a man or a woman alone, because in its very nature it consists of the continuation of the family unit in eternity. Thus the revelation on marriage speaks both of celestial marriage (in which the conditional promises of eternal life are given) and of making one's calling and election sure (in which the unconditional promises of eternal life are given) in one and the same sentence—which sentence also says that those who commit sins (except 'murder whereby to shed innocent blood') after being sealed up unto eternal life shall still gain exaltation. This is the language: 'Then'—that is, after their calling and election has been made sure—[D&C 132:19-20 cited].

"Then the revelation [D&C 132:26] speaks of that obedience out of which eternal life grows, and still speaking both of celestial marriage and of making one's calling and election sure says: 'Verily, verily, I say unto you, if a man marry a wife according to my word, and they are sealed by the Holy Spirit of promise, according to mine appointment'—that is, if they are both married and have their calling and election made sure . . . 'they shall come forth in the first resurrection and enter into their exaltation.' " (*Doctrinal New Testament Commentary*, 3:343-44.)

If one has his calling and election made sure, and has that promise sealed by the Holy Spirit of Promise, continued Elder McConkie, it does not mean that he can sin with impunity: "*What if those whose calling and election has been made sure thereafter commit grievous sins? Suppose they backslide and walk in the ways of wickedness? Or fight the truth and rebel against God—what then?*

"That all men commit sin, before and after baptism, and for that matter, before and after their calling and election is made sure, is self-evident. There has been only one Sinless One—the Lord Jesus who was God's own Son.

"Thus in the revelation announcing the setting up of the restored church in this day, the Lord says: 'There is a possibility that man may fall from grace and depart from the living God; Therefore let the church take heed and pray always, lest they fall into temptation; Yea, and even let those who are sanctified take heed also.' (D. & C. 20:32-34.)

"The prophets and apostles from Adam and Enoch down, and all men, whether cleansed and sanctified from sin or not, are yet subject to and do in fact commit sin. This is the case even after men have seen the visions of eternity and been sealed by that Holy Spirit of Promise which makes their calling and election sure. Since these chosen ones have the sure promise of eternal life, and since 'no unclean thing can enter into' the Father's 'kingdom' (3 Ne. 27:19), 'or dwell in his presence' (Moses 6:57), what of sins committed after being sealed up into eternal life?

"Obviously the laws of repentance still apply, and the more enlightened a person is, the more he seeks the gift of repentance, and the harder he strives to free himself from sin as often as he falls short of the divine will and becomes subject in any degree to the Master of Sin who is Lucifer. It follows that the sins of the godfearing and the righteous are continually remitted because they repent and seek the Lord anew every day and every hour.

"And as a matter of fact, the added blessing of having one's calling and election made sure is itself an encouragement to avoid sin and a hedge against its further commission. By that long course of obedience and trial which enabled them to gain so great a blessing the sanctified saints have charted a course and developed a pattern of living which avoids sin and encourages righteousness. Thus the Lord said: 'I give unto you Hyrum Smith to be a patriarch unto you, to hold the sealing blessings of my church, even the Holy Spirit of promise, whereby ye are sealed up unto the day of redemption, that ye may not fall notwithstanding the hour of temptation that may come upon you.' (D. & C. 124:124.)

"But suppose such persons become disaffected and the spirit of repentance leaves them—which is a seldom and an almost unheard of eventuality—still, what then? The answer is—and the revelations and teachings of the Prophet Joseph Smith so recite!—they must then pay the penalty of their own sins, for the blood of Christ will not cleanse them. Or if they commit murder or adultery, they lose their promised inheritance because these sins are exempt from the sealing promises. Or if they commit the unpardonable sin, they become sons of perdition." (*Doctrinal New Testament Commentary*, 3:342-43.)

**D&C 132:26. What are the Buffetings of Satan?**

See Notes and Commentary on Doctrine and Covenants 78:12.

**D&C 132:27. What Is the Blasphemy against the Holy Ghost?**

See Notes and Commentary on Doctrine and Covenants 76:31, 35, 37-39.

**D&C 132:27. What Is "Innocent Blood"?**

As used in the scriptures, "innocent blood" has a more specific meaning than it does in normal usage. Ultimately, as Elder Bruce R. McConkie pointed out, the only truly innocent blood is that of the Savior: "The innocent blood is that of Christ; and those who commit blasphemy against the Holy Ghost, which is the unpardonable sin (Matt. 12:31-32), thereby 'crucify to themselves the Son of God afresh, and put him to an open shame.' (Heb. 6:6.) They are, in other words, people who would have crucified Christ, having the while a perfect knowledge that he was the Son of God." (*Doctrinal New Testament Commentary*, 3:345.)

Other scriptures teach that those who martyr the Lord's servants are also shedding innocent blood (see Mosiah 17:10; D&C 135:4; see also President Joseph Fielding Smith's statement in Notes and Commentary on D&C 76:35). In other words, those who fight against the prophets are in reality fighting against him whom the prophets serve. Thus, while murder of any kind is an extremely serious sin, not all who murder are guilty of shedding "innocent blood," thereby becoming sons of perdition.

**D&C 132:29-33. "Go Ye, Therefore, and Do the Works of Abraham"**

In these verses the Lord answers the Prophet's original question about whether Abraham and the other early patriarchs were justified in having plural wives (see D&C 132:1). The Lord began by saying that Abraham has now entered his exaltation because he faithfully received the promises and commandments of the Lord. The same promises are offered to modern Saints, and the Lord commands that they too should "do the works of Abraham." This is not a commandment to engage in plural marriage (that commandment is given in verses 34 through 37) but rather a commandment for the Saints to receive the covenants and commandments of God in the same faith and righteousness as Abraham did. Since Abraham has achieved exaltation, one can look to him as a model for his own progression, as President Spencer W. Kimball said:

"Abraham was true with God in all respects. Oft cited is the instance when Abraham gave to God 'tithes of all.' Do you think it was any easier for

*Those who desire eternal life must follow the Lord in all things as did Abraham*

Abraham to be righteous than it is for you? Do you inwardly suspect that Abraham was given a little extra help by the Lord so that he could become a great and righteous man, or do you feel that we can all become as Abraham if we will learn to put God first in our lives? I testify to you that we can become as Abraham, who now, as a result of his valiance, 'hath entered into his exaltation and sitteth upon his throne.' (D&C 132:29.) Is such exaltation a blessing reserved only for General Authorities, or stake presidents, or quorum presidents, or bishops? It is not. It is a blessing reserved for all who will prepare themselves by forsaking their sins, by truly receiving the Holy Ghost into their lives, and by following the example Abraham has set.

"If members of the Church could only have such integrity, such obedience, such revelation, such faith, such service as Abraham had! If parents would seek the blessings Abraham sought, they could also receive such revelation, covenants, promises, and eternal rewards as Abraham received." ("The Example of Abraham," *Ensign,* June 1975, pp. 6-7.)

**D&C 132:34, 65. "Sarah Gave Hagar to Abraham"**

These verses are best understood after reading Genesis 16:1-3, which implies that Sarah was following a custom of the time. Because she could not bear children, she gave her handmaid to her husband that she might "obtain children by her" (vs. 2) This revelation from the Lord makes it clear, however, that God commanded Abraham to accept Sarah's recommendation that he take Hagar to wife.

**D&C 132:37. "They Have Entered into Their Exaltation"**

Elder Bruce R. McConkie added a significant insight to this verse: "What we say for Abraham, Isaac, and Jacob we say also for Sarah, Rebekah, and Rachel, the wives who stood at their sides and who with them were true and faithful in all things. Men are not saved alone, and women do not gain an eternal fullness except in and through the continuation of the family unit in eternity. Salvation is a family affair." ("Mothers in Israel and Daughters of Zion," *New Era,* May 1978, p. 37.)

**D&C 132:38-39. "And in Nothing Did They Sin Save in Those Things Which They Received Not of Me"**

In the case of David this passage is a clear reference to Bathsheba, wife of Uriah, whom David took to himself without permission from the Lord.

David's story is one of tragedy and a lesson to all of God's children, for he represents a man who went from the apex of favor with God to the abyss of wickedness. He had all that this life could offer, but through carelessness and disobedience he lost it all—even exaltation and the right to associate eternally with his Father in Heaven. Elder Bruce R. McConkie explained the special circumstances that brought about David's punishment.

"As to the fact that the sealing power cannot seal a man up unto eternal life if he thereafter commits murder and thereby sheds innocent blood (not in this case the blood of Christ, but the blood of any person slain unlawfully and with malice) the Prophet says: 'A murderer, for instance, one that sheds innocent blood, cannot have forgiveness. David sought repentance at the hand of God carefully with tears, for the murder of Uriah; but he could only get it through hell; he got a promise that his soul should not be left in hell.

" 'Although David was a king, he never did obtain the spirit and power of Elijah and the fullness of the priesthood; and the priesthood that he received, and the throne and kingdom of David is to be taken from him and given to another by the name of David in the last days, raised up out of his lineage.' (*Teachings,* p. 339.) Thus, even though a man's calling and election has been made sure, if he then commits murder, all of the promises are of no effect, and he goes to a telestial kingdom (Rev. 21:8; D. & C. 76:103), because when he was sealed up unto eternal life, it was with a reservation. The sealing was not to apply in the case of murder." (*Doctrinal New Testament Commentary,* 3:347.)

**D&C 132:41-44. Sin of Adultery**

Smith and Sjodahl wrote: "The Prophet, in his prayer on this subject, had asked the Lord for information concerning the ground on which the Patriarchs were justified in their domestic relations, and the answer was the definition of adultery here given. Plural marriage, the Revelation says, in substance, is not adultery, but to violate the marriage covenant is to commit that sin, the penalty being destruction (vv. 41, 52); but God Himself will execute that judgment (v. 54)." (Commentary, p. 833.)

**D&C 132:46. Can the Sealing of a Temple Marriage Be Broken?**

Members of the Church should clearly understand that the power to seal is also the power to unseal. This power is held by the President of the Church, as it has been in all dispensations (see Matthew 16:19). Concerning this power to seal and to cancel sealings of a temple marriage, Elder Bruce R. McConkie wrote: "Properly speaking there is no such thing as a *temple divorce;* divorces in this day are civil matters handled by the courts of the land. But following a civil divorce of persons who have been married for eternity in the temples, if the circumstances are sufficiently serious to warrant it, the President of the Church has power to *cancel the sealings* involved. He holds the keys and power both to bind and loose on earth and in heaven. (Matt. 16:19; D. & C. 132:46; *Doctrines of Salvation,* vol. 2, p. 84.)" (*Mormon Doctrine,* pp. 110-11.)

**D&C 132:46. Can the President of the Church Forgive Sins?**

Ultimately only God can forgive sins, but under inspiration, a servant of the Lord may announce that God has forgiven sins. A bishop or other priesthood leaders also have the stewardship to extend forgiveness on behalf of the Church for serious sins, but the Lord's forgiveness can only come from God through revelation. Elder Bruce R. McConkie explained this doctrine:

"Revelation from the Lord is always required to retain or remit sins. Since God is the one who must cleanse and purify a human soul, the use of his priestly powers to do so must be authorized and approved by him, and this approval comes by revelation from his Holy Spirit. In many cases in this dispensation the Lord by revelation announced that the sins of certain persons were forgiven. (D. & C. 60:7; 61:2; 62:3; 64:3.) Accordingly, if by revelation he should tell his apostles to act for him, using his power which is priesthood, and to thus retain or remit sins, they would do so, and their acts would in effect be his. See Matt. 16:13-20; 17:1-9; 18:18.

"This same apostolic power is always found in the true Church, and hence we find the Lord saying to Joseph Smith: 'I have conferred upon you the keys and power of the priesthood, . . . and whosesoever sins you remit on earth shall be remitted eternally in the heavens; and whosesoever sins you retain on earth shall be retained in heaven.' (D. & C. 132:45-46.)" (*Doctrinal New Testament Commentary,* 1:857-58.)

President Spencer W. Kimball explained how the bishop plays a role in the process of obtaining forgiveness: "The offender should seek the forgiveness of the Church through his bishop. No priest or elder is authorized to thus act for the Church. The Lord has a consistent, orderly plan. Every soul in stakes is given a bishop who, by the very order of his calling and his ordination, is a 'judge in Israel.' The bishop is our best earthly friend. He will hear the problems, judge the seriousness, then determine the degree of repentance and decide if it warrants an eventual forgiveness. He does this as the earthly representative of God—the master physician, the master psychologist, the master psychiatrist. If repentance is sufficient he may waive penalties, which is tantamount to forgiveness. The bishop claims no authority to absolve sins, but he does share the burden, waive penalties, relieve tension and strain; and he may assure a continuance of activity. He will keep the whole matter most confidential." ("President Kimball Speaks Out on Morality," *Ensign,* Nov. 1980, p. 98; or *New Era,* Nov. 1980, p. 44.)

### D&C 132:49-50. Exaltation Assured to Joseph Smith

The Prophet Joseph Smith received the promise of eternal life—he had his calling and election made sure. God will extend the same promise to all of his children if they will obey him. Verse 50 explains why the Prophet Joseph received this promise. He was willing to lay all he had upon the altar. He was hunted and persecuted, sued in courts of law, torn from family and loved ones; and all because he had testified that the heavens were not closed and that God does speak to his children. The Prophet Joseph is the great example in this dispensation of how sons and daughters of God should conduct themselves. (See Notes and Commentary on D&C 131:5.)

### D&C 132:50-56. What Was Emma Commanded Not to Partake of?

No indication is given here or elsewhere about what the Lord had commanded the Prophet Joseph to offer to his wife, but the context seems to suggest that it was a special test of faith similar to the great test of Abraham's faith when the Lord commanded him to sacrifice Isaac. Beyond that, it is useless to speculate, for the record is silent; however, Emma was given additional counsel from the Lord, including commandments to "receive all those that have been given to her husband" (D&C 132:52) to obey the voice of the Lord (see vs. 53), to "abide and cleave unto" the Prophet (vs. 54), and to forgive him of his trespasses (see vs. 56). Warnings against rejecting these commandments and promises for keeping them were also given by the Lord.

President Wilford Woodruff, who was closely associated with the Prophet Joseph Smith, spoke of Emma's later denial that Joseph had practiced plural marriage: "Emma Smith, the widow of the Prophet, is said to have maintained to her dying moments that her husband had nothing to do with the patriarchal order of marriage, but that it was Brigham Young that got that up. I bear record before God, angels and men that Joseph Smith received that revelation, and I bear record that Emma Smith gave her husband in marriage to several women while he was living, some of whom are to-day living in this city, and some may be present in this congregation, and who, if called upon, would confirm my words. But lo and behold, we hear of publication after publication now-a-days, declaring that Joseph Smith had nothing to do with these things. Joseph Smith himself organized every endowment in our Church and revealed the same to the Church, and he lived to receive every key of the Aaronic and Melchizedek priesthoods from the hands of the men who held them while in the flesh, and who hold them in eternity." (In *Journal of Discourses,* 23:131.)

### D&C 132:59. How Was Aaron Called?

Elder Bruce R. McConkie wrote: "Aaron's call to the Levitical ministry stands as the perfect example of the choosing of legal administrators to do the Lord's work; ever since that day, the legality of priestly administration has been determined by whether the professing minister was 'called of God, as was Aaron' (Heb. 5:4; D. & C. 27:8; 132:59), that is, by revelation and ordination, and with the full approval of the body of the Lord's true worshipers" (*Mormon Doctrine,* p. 9).

### D&C 132:60-64. The Law of the Priesthood

"The truth is here reiterated, that whatever is done in the name of God, according to His law and by His direction, cannot be sin. What human law regards as a crime may, or may not, from the Divine point of view, be a sin. Sometimes the Innocent dies on Calvary, because criminals have acted as judge and jury." (Smith and Sjodahl, Commentary, p. 835.)

# The Lord's Appendix to the Doctrine and Covenants

Section 133

## Historical Background

On 1 November 1831 a special conference of the Church was held at Hiram, Ohio. Many revelations had been received from the Lord prior to that time, and the compiling of these revelations for publication was one of the principal subjects passed on at the conference (see Historical Background to D&C 1). The compilation was to be entitled the *Book of Commandments;* however, all but a few copies of the Book of Commandments were destroyed by the mobs in Jackson County (see Historical Background for D&C 98). Since additional revelations were subsequently received, a new collection was published in Ohio and called the Doctrine and Covenants.

The Prophet Joseph Smith recorded the decision of the conference: "It had been decided by the conference that Elder Oliver Cowdery should carry the commandments and revelations to Independence, Missouri, for printing, and that I should arrange and get them in readiness by the time that he left, which was to be by—or, if possible, before—the 15th of the month [November]. At this time there were many things which the Elders desired to know relative to preaching the Gospel to the inhabitants of the earth, and concerning the gathering; and in order to walk by the true light, and be instructed from on high, on the 3rd of November, 1831, I inquired of the Lord and received the following important revelation, which has since been added to the book of Doctrine and Covenants, and called the Appendix: [D&C 133]." (*History of the Church,* 1:229.)

Elder John A. Widtsoe explained that "the 'Appendix' [D&C 133], supplements the introduction [D&C 1]. The two sections together encompass the contents of the book in a condensed form. An appendix is something which the writer thinks should be added to amplify that which is in the book, to emphasize it, to make it stronger or to explain the contents a little more completely." (*Message of the Doctrine and Covenants,* p. 17.)

Some of the major themes presented by the Lord in this revelation are summarized in the tenth article of faith.

## Notes and Commentary

### D&C 133. A Collection of Key Concepts

All scripture forms a great interwoven, interdependent latticework of gospel concepts. It seems that the Lord's purpose in writing the scriptures was not to collect the concepts by topic but to scatter them throughout the sacred writings, here a little and there a little. Only diligent searching and studying of the scriptures so arranged can bring a fulness of understanding. The more one immerses oneself in the scriptures, the more familiar he becomes with language and concepts that trigger a host of associations. The phrase "lengthen our stride" (see D&C 133:8, 16, 37) has become such a familiar concept to many Latter-day Saints that one need only say "lengthen," and most Saints can instantly complete the phrase.

Section 133 contains an unusual number of such key concepts that presuppose a knowledge of other scriptures. The section is written in a kind of literary shorthand. If one is not familiar with such scriptural concepts as the Lord coming to his temple (see D&C 133:2), Babylon (see vss. 4-7, 14), the parable of the ten virgins (see vs. 10), the story of Lot's wife (see vs. 15), the Lamb standing on Mount Zion (see vs. 18), or the time when Jesus will stand on the Mount of Olives (see vs. 20), one will be missing significant insights into what the Lord says in this section. Therefore, the commentary on this section will focus on the background of such key scriptures to help the reader better appreciate the concepts that lie behind them.

### D&C 133:1, 16. To Whom Does the Lord Direct This Revelation?

The revelation is directed to members of the Church (see D&C 133:1) and to the inhabitants of the earth (see vs. 16). Compare these verses with the preface given at the same conference (see D&C 1:1-4).

### D&C 133:2. Has the Lord Suddenly Come to His Temple?

The verb tense used in verse 2 indicates that the Lord's appearance was still in the future as of November 1831.

Elder Orson Pratt answered the question about the Lord's coming to his temple: "We read in the scriptures of divine truth that the Lord our God is to come to his temple in the last days. . . . It is recorded in the 3rd chapter of Malachi that 'the Lord whom ye seek shall suddenly come to his temple.' This had no reference to the first coming of the Messiah, to the day when he appeared in the flesh; but it has reference to that glorious period termed the last days, when the Lord will again have a house, or a temple reared up on the earth to his holy name." (In *Journal of Discourses,* 14:274.)

Smith and Sjodahl pointed out that the appearance promised has more than one fulfillment: "This prediction has in part been fulfilled, for the Lord appeared to Joseph Smith and Oliver Cowdery in the Kirtland Temple and there ministered to them in 1836; but this prophecy has a broader meaning, and the Lord shall come, without a doubt, to His Temple, where He will sit as 'a refiner and purifier of silver,' purging the house of Israel and ministering to His people. This appearing will be separate and distinct from the great coming in the clouds of heaven, when He will appear with power and great glory (Matt. 24:30) with a curse to judgment (v. 2) upon all the nations that forget God. This coming will be for the blessing and benefit of the most faithful of His saints, and when He comes to take final vengeance on the world, He will be preceded by a sign (Matt. 24:30; Sec. 88:93), that all peoples shall see and judgment shall be poured out upon the wicked." (Commentary, p. 840.)

### D&C 133:3. "Make Bare His Holy Arm"

The arm is a symbol of strength and power. For the Lord to make bare his arm is to reveal his strength and power before the eyes of the world. (See Exodus 15:1-18 where an example of this is given; see also Notes and Commentary on D&C 15:2; 35:8-10.)

### D&C 133:3. What Does the Phrase Mean—All Nations "Shall See the Salvation of Their God"?

"By 'see the salvation of their God' is meant that all peoples shall see the victory or deliverance which the Almighty shall bring about in favor of His people [see Isaiah 12:2; 52:10]" (Sperry, *Compendium,* p. 300).

### D&C 133:4. "Wherefore, Prepare Ye, Prepare Ye"

The scriptures and the living prophets teach that the Saints, as a people, must strive for three important things as they ready themselves for the Second Coming.

*Preparation.* Elder Harold B. Lee outlined three steps of preparation for the Second Coming.

"This preparation demands first that a people, to receive the coming of the Lord, must be taught the personality and the nature of God and his Son, Jesus Christ.

" . . . How can one meet a person whose identity is unknown? How can one be prepared to meet a person about whom he has no knowledge? How can one be prepared to meet a being whose personality he cannot comprehend? . . .

"To my thinking, another requisite of that preparation to receive the Lord at the beginning of his millennial reign demands that the people be taught to accept the divinity of the mission of Jesus as the Savior of the world [see Alma 11:37, 40]. . . .

" . . . We must accept the divine mission of the Prophet Joseph Smith as the instrumentality through which the restoration of the gospel and the organization of the Church of Jesus Christ was accomplished. Each member of the Church, to be prepared for the millennial reign, must receive a testimony, each for himself, of the divinity of the work established by Joseph Smith. . . . [As Heber C. Kimball said,] 'The time will come when no man nor woman will be able to endure on borrowed light. Each will have to be guided by the light within himself.' " (In Conference Report, Oct. 1956, pp. 61-62.)

*Sanctification.* The individual imperative in mortality is to become free of the condemnation of sin. Elder Bruce R. McConkie explained it this way:

"To be *sanctified* is to become clean, pure, and spotless; to be free from the blood and sins of the world; to become a new creature of the Holy Ghost, one whose body has been renewed by the rebirth of the Spirit. *Sanctification* is a state of saintliness, a state attained only by conformity to the laws and ordinances of the gospel. The plan of salvation is the system and means provided whereby men may sanctify their souls and thereby become worthy of a celestial inheritance.

"Sanctification is a basic doctrine of the gospel (D. & C. 20:31-34); indeed, the very reason men are commanded to believe, repent, and be baptized is so they 'may be sanctified by the reception of the Holy Ghost,' and thereby be enabled to stand spotless before the judgment bar of Christ. (2 Ne. 27:19-21.)" (*Mormon Doctrine,* p. 675.)

Since the scriptures teach that no unclean thing can dwell in his presence (see Moses 6:57), it is clear that the Saints who are caught up to meet him must be sanctified.

*Gathering.* In a sermon on 27 February 1977 in Lima, Peru, Elder Bruce R. McConkie explained the spirit of the gathering of Israel to Zion in this dispensation:

"Two things are accomplished by the gathering of Israel: First, those who have thus chosen Christ as their Shepherd; those who have taken upon themselves his name in the waters of baptism; those who are seeking to enjoy his Spirit here and now and to be inheritors of eternal life hereafter—such people need to be gathered together to strengthen each other and to help one another perfect their lives.

"And second, those who are seeking the highest rewards in eternity need to be where they can receive the blessings of the house of the Lord, both for themselves and for their ancestors in Israel who died without a knowledge of the gospel, but who would have received it with all their heart had opportunity afforded.

"Manifestly in the early days of this dispensation, this meant gathering to the mountain of the Lord's house in the tops of the mountains of North America. There alone were congregations strong enough for the Saints to strengthen each other. There alone were the temples of the Most High where the fulness of the ordinances of exaltation are performed.

"However, in the providences of Him who knoweth all things, in the providences of Him who scattered Israel and who is now gathering that favored people again, the day has now come when the fold of Christ is reaching out to the ends of the earth. We are not established in all nations, but we surely shall be before the second coming of the Son of Man.

"As the Book of Mormon says, in the last days, 'the saints of God' shall be found 'upon all the face of the earth.' Also: 'The saints of the church of the Lamb and . . . the covenant people of the Lord'—scattered as they are 'upon all the face of the earth'—shall be 'armed with righteousness and with

*"Go ye therefore, and teach all nations"* (Matthew 28:19)

the power of God in great glory.' (1 Ne. 14:12, 14.)

"We are living in a new day. The Church of Jesus Christ of Latter-day Saints is fast becoming a worldwide church. Congregations of Saints are now, or soon will be, strong enough to support and sustain their members no matter where they reside. Temples are being built wherever the need justifies." ("Come: Let Israel Build Zion," *Ensign*, May 1977, p. 117.)

**D&C 133:5, 14. Babylon**

In Old Testament days, Babylon was both the city and the country of great wickedness and worldly glory that enslaved Israel. Because of that historical fact, Babylon became a symbol of physical and spiritual enslavement, a representation of sin, wickedness, ungodliness, and evil, and the crowning symbol of the world and worldiness. The followers of Christ are commanded to come out of Babylon and flee spiritually to Zion, which is the pure in heart. (See Notes and Commentary on D&C 35:11; 86:1-7; Enrichment B, in the Appendix.)

**D&C 133:5. What Is Meant by the "Vessels of the Lord"?**

Vessels used in the temple by the ancient Israelites were handled only by authorized priesthood holders who were worthy. The phrase, "Be ye clean that bear the vessels of the Lord" (D&C 133:5), has since been used to mean the worthiness with which all priesthood bearers should function.

**D&C 133:6. What Are Solemn Assemblies?**

See Notes and Commentary on Doctrine and Covenants 95:7.

**D&C 133:8, 16, 37. What Did the Lord Mean When He Said to "Call upon All Nations"?**

President Spencer W. Kimball comments on the meaning of the phrase "to call upon all nations."

"I ask you, what did he mean when the Lord took his Twelve Apostles to the top of the Mount of Olives and said:

"'. . . And ye shall be witnesses unto me both in Jerusalem, and in all Judea, and in Samaria, and unto the *uttermost part of the earth.*' (Acts 1:8.)

"These were his last words on earth before he went to his heavenly home.

"What is the significance of the phrase 'uttermost part of the earth'? He had already covered the area known to the apostles. Was it the people in Judea? Or those in Samaria? Or the few millions in the Near East? Where were the 'uttermost parts of the earth'? Did he mean the millions in what is now America? Did he include the hundreds of thousands, or even millions, in Greece, Italy, around the Mediterranean, the inhabitants of central Europe? What did he mean? Or did he mean all the living people of all the world and those spirits assigned to this world to come in centuries ahead? Have we underestimated his language or its meaning? How can we be satisfied with 100,000 converts out of nearly four billion people in the world who need the gospel? . . .

"It seems to me that the Lord chose his words when he said 'every nation,' 'every land,' 'uttermost bounds of the earth,' 'every tongue,' 'every people,' 'every soul,' 'all the world,' 'many lands.'

"Surely there is significance in these words!

"Certainly his sheep were not limited to the thousands about him and with whom he rubbed shoulders each day. A universal family! A universal command!

"My brethren, I wonder if we are doing all we can. Are we complacent in our approach to teaching all the world? We have been proselyting now 144 years. Are we prepared to lengthen our stride? To enlarge our vision?

"Remember, our ally is our God. He is our commander. He made the plans. He gave the commandment. . . .

"Somehow, brethren, I feel that when we have done all in our power that the Lord will find a way to open doors. That is my faith. . . .

"I believe the Lord can do anything he sets his mind to do.

"But I can see no good reason why the Lord would open doors that we are not prepared to enter. Why should he break down the Iron Curtain or the Bamboo Curtain or any other curtain if we are still unprepared to enter?" ("When the World Will Be Converted," *Ensign*, Oct. 1974, pp. 4-5, 7.)

### D&C 133:8. Why Are the Jews Last When They Are the Blood of Israel?

From the twelve tribes of Israel, it was the privilege of Judah to be the host tribe when the Son of God was born into mortality. One of the saddest accounts recorded in scripture is the rejection by the majority of the Jews (who are the house of Judah) of their king. Because the Jews as a nation would not accept the King of Israel, the gospel was taken from them and given to the Gentiles; because of the love the Savior has for all of Israel, the gospel will again be taken to the tribe of Judah before the second coming of the Savior (see 1 Nephi 13:42; Ether 13:12). They who first received the Master shall receive him again, but this time they shall be the last to do so.

### D&C 133:10, 19. "The Bridegroom Cometh. . . . Prepare Yourselves"

Verse 10 of Doctrine and Covenants, section 133, refers to the parable of the ten virgins (see Matthew 25:1-13), of which Elder James E. Talmage said: "The story itself is based on oriental marriage customs, with which the Lord's attentive listeners were familiar. It was and yet is common in those lands, particularly in connection with marriage festivities among the wealthy classes, for the bridegroom to go to the home of the bride, accompanied by his friends in processional array, and later to conduct the bride to her new home with a larger body of attendants composed of groomsmen, bridesmaids, relatives and friends. As the bridal party progressed, to the accompaniment of gladsome music, it was increased by little groups who had gathered in waiting at convenient places along the route, and particularly near the end of the course where organized companies came forth to meet the advancing procession. Wedding ceremonies were appointed for the evening and night hours; and the necessary use of torches and lamps gave brilliancy and added beauty to the scene." (*Jesus the Christ*, p. 577.)

*Personal righteousness adds oil to one's lamp*

Often with such wedding processions as mentioned above, the appearance of the bridegroom came after a long wait. Bridesmaids carried a small lamp and a supply of oil that they might be prepared to help light the way when the wedding party appeared.

President Kimball taught that the oil which the wise virgins had and the foolish had not represents individual righteousness (see Notes and Commentary for D&C 45:56-57).

The following scriptures relate the parable to the Second Coming: Doctrine and Covenants 45:56-59; 63:53-54.

### D&C 133:11. When Will Christ Come to Usher in His Millennial Reign?

Elder Bruce R. McConkie asked a series of questions about Christ's second coming and its time:

"Question: Does or will anyone know when the Lord will come? Answer: As to the day and hour, No; as to the generation, Yes.

"Question: Who shall know the generation? Answer: The saints, the children of light, those who can read the signs of the times, those who treasure up the Lord's word so they will not be deceived.

"Paul told the Thessalonians that 'the coming of the Lord' would be 'as travail upon a woman with child'; that where people of the world are concerned Jesus would come 'as a thief in the night,' that is unexpectedly and without warning; but that where 'the children of light' are concerned, the Lord would not come as 'a thief in the night,' for they are aware of the 'times and seasons' connected with his return. (1 Thess. 4:13-18; 5:1-7.) Thus, though the saints do not know the day, they are aware of the season. As a woman in travail feels the pains of the approaching birth, so the saints read the signs of the times; neither knows the exact moment of the anticipated happening, but both know the approximate time." (*Doctrinal New Testament Commentary*, 1:665-66; see also Matthew 24:36, 42; D&C 45:39; 49:7; 77:6, 12; 130:14-17.)

### D&C 133:12-13. Zion and Jerusalem As Places of Gathering

"The Gentiles who obeyed the Gospel were commanded (v. 12) to gather in Zion, and those of the house of Judah were to flee to Jerusalem (v. 13). This is in harmony with the prediction of Isaiah and Micah, that out of Zion shall go forth the law, and the word of the Lord from Jerusalem. For from both these centers the Lord shall judge. Jerusalem shall be re-built and become a holy city, the capital for Judah, and Zion shall be the capital and city of our God, for Ephraim and his fellows. Both shall be seats of government in unison with each other, and the Lord shall dwell in both." (Smith and Sjodahl, Commentary, p. 841.)

### D&C 133:13. What Does the Phrase "Mountains of the Lord's House" Mean?

With reference to a similar statement in Micah 4:1, President Harold B. Lee explained: "The expression 'the mountain of the Lord's house,' as here indicated, was undoubtedly to be referred to as a place as well as a definition of a righteous people" ("The Way to Eternal Life," *Ensign,* Nov. 1971, p. 15).

Other Church leaders have also taught about "the mountain of the Lord's house." Elder Erastus Snow said: " 'The mountain of the Lord's house'—this is a peculiar phrase, and was probably used by the Prophet because it was a common mode of expression in Israel in the days of David and many of the Prophets several hundred years after him, for, in speaking of Mount Moriah, on which the Temple of Solomon was built, they spoke of it as the mountain of the Lord's house. Moriah is a hill in the city of Jerusalem, on which David located the site of the Temple, and on which his son Solomon built it, and it was called the mountain of the house of the Lord." (In *Journal of Discourses,* 16:202.)

Elder Bruce R. McConkie explained that the phrase has more than one meaning:

"The *mountain of the Lord's house* is the mountain where the temple of God is built. [Isaiah 2:2-3 quoted; see also Micah 4:1-2; 2 Nephi 12:2-3.]

"This great prophecy, as is often the case, is subject to the law of multiple fulfilment. 1. In Salt Lake City and other mountain locations temples, in the full and true sense of the word, have been erected, and representatives of all nations are flowing unto them to learn of God and his ways. . . . 2. But the day is yet future when the Lord's house is to be built on that 'Mount Zion' which is 'the city of New Jerusalem' in Jackson County, Missouri. (D. & C. 84:2-4.) Mount Zion, itself, will be the mountain of the Lord's house in the day when that glorious temple is erected. 3. When the Jews flee unto Jerusalem, it will be 'unto the mountains of the Lord's house' (D. & C. 133:13), for a holy temple is to be built there also as part of the work of the great era of restoration. (Ezek. 37:24-28.)

"The law cannot go forth from Zion and the word of the Lord from Jerusalem, in the full millennial sense that Isaiah foresaw and specified, until these two great future temples are constructed in the old and new Jerusalems." (*Mormon Doctrine,* pp. 517-18.)

### D&C 133:14-15. "He That Goeth, Let Him Not Look Back"

Lot, the nephew of Abraham, lived in Sodom and Gomorrah, another place of such gross wickedness that it has become a symbol of the world and its evil. Lot was told to take his family and flee. As they did so, Lot's wife looked back (she probably returned to Sodom and Gomorrah; see Luke 17:31-32) and was destroyed. (See Genesis 19:15-26.) In context this reference is clear. Once a person forsakes the world, he cannot turn back, or he too may get caught in the destruction that awaits Babylon.

### D&C 133:17, 36. Who Was "the Angel Crying through the Midst of Heaven"?

This passage contains another key concept. The language of this verse is similar to the language of Revelation 14:6-7. Though many commentators in the Church have tied this promise in Revelation to the angel Moroni's restoration of the Book of Mormon, Elder Bruce R. McConkie showed that although this promise includes Moroni, it is not limited to him.

"Now, as to the actual work of restoration—what angel performed this mighty deed, this work which involves the salvation of all men on earth in these latter-days? Who restored the everlasting gospel? Was it one angel or many?

"It is traditional (and true!) to reply: 'Moroni, son of Mormon, the now resurrected Nephite prophet, who holds the keys of "the stick of Ephraim" (D. & C. 27:5), the one through whose ministry the Book of Mormon was again brought to light.' The reasoning is that the Book of Mormon contains 'the fulness of the everlasting gospel' (D. & C. 135:3); that therein is God's message of salvation for all of earth's inhabitants; and that this gospel message is now being taken by the Lord's witnesses to one nation, and kindred, and tongue, and people after another. . . .

"But other angels were yet to come—Moses, Elias, Elijah, Gabriel, Raphael, and 'divers angels, . . . all declaring their dispensation, their rights, their keys, their honors, their majesty and glory, and the power of their priesthood; giving line upon line, precept upon precept; here a little, and there a little.' (D. & C. 128:21.)

"Thus the angel Moroni brought the message, that is, the word; but other angels brought the keys and priesthood, the power. And in the final analysis the fulness of the everlasting gospel consists of all of the truths and powers needed to enable men to gain a fulness of salvation in the celestial heaven." (*Doctrinal New Testament Commentary,* 3:528-30.)

### D&C 133:18. Who Are the 144,000?

See Notes and Commentary on Doctrine and Covenants 77:11.

### D&C 133:20-22. What Appearances Will the Lord Make?

Elder Charles W. Penrose explained that Christ will make several appearances, namely, to the Saints gathered to Zion, to the Jews gathered back to their homeland, and to the rest of the world:

"Among the first-mentioned of these three classes of men the Lord will make his appearance first; and that appearance will be unknown to the rest of mankind. He will come to the Temple prepared for him, and his faithful people will behold his face, hear his voice, and gaze upon his glory. From his own lips they will receive further instructions for the development and beautifying of Zion and for the extension and sure stability of his kingdom.

"His next appearance will be among the distressed and nearly vanquished sons of Judah. At the crisis of their fate, when the hostile troops of several nations are ravaging the city and all the horrors of war are overwhelming the people of Jerusalem, he will set his feet upon the Mount of Olives, which will cleave and part asunder at his touch. Attended by a host from heaven, he will overthrow and destroy the combined armies of the Gentiles, and appear to the worshipping Jews as the mighty Deliverer and Conqueror so long expected by their race; and while love, gratitude, awe, and admiration swell their bosoms, the Deliverer will show them the tokens of his crucifixion and disclose himself as Jesus of Nazareth, whom they had reviled and whom their fathers put to death. Then will unbelief part from their souls, and 'the blindness in part which has happened unto Israel' be removed. 'A fountain for sin and uncleanness shall be opened to the house of David and the inhabitants of Jerusalem,' and 'a nation will be born' unto God 'in a day.' They will be baptized for the remission of their sins, and will receive the gift of the Holy Ghost, and the government of God as established in Zion will be set up among them, no more to be thrown down for ever.

"The great and crowning advent of the Lord will be subsequent to these two appearances; but who can describe it in the language of mortals? The tongue of man falters, and the pen drops from the hand of the writer, as the mind is rapt in contemplation of the sublime and awful majesty of his coming to take vengeance on the ungodly and to reign as King of the whole earth." ("The Second Advent," *Millennial Star,* 10 Sept. 1859, pp. 582-83.)

Other revelations show that Christ will make two major appearances to the Saints in Zion. One will be to accept the temple built there; the other will be at the council held at Adam-ondi-Ahman (see Notes and Commentary for D&C 116:1).

### D&C 133:23-24. Will the Continents Be Rejoined?

Genesis indicates that in the early history of the world the land masses were united. Moses recorded that one of the great-great-grandsons of Shem was named Peleg (a Hebrew word meaning division) because "in his days was the earth divided" (Genesis 10:25). Many scholars have passed this reference off as meaning some sort of cultural or political division, but modern prophets have taught that this statement should be taken literally.

An article published early in the history of the Church under the direction of the Prophet Joseph Smith stated: "The Eternal God hath declared that the great deep shall roll back into the north countries and that the land of Zion and the land of Jerusalem shall be joined together, as they were before they were divided in the days of Peleg. No wonder the mind starts at the sound of the last days!" ("The Last Days," *Evening and Morning Star,* Feb. 1833, p. 1.)

President Joseph Fielding Smith added to the Saints' understanding of the last days: "If, however, the earth is to be restored as it was in the beginning, then all the land surface will again be in one place as it was before the days of Peleg, when this great division was accomplished. Europe, Africa, and the islands of the sea including Australia, New Zealand, and other places in the Pacific must be brought back and joined together as they were in the beginning." (*Answers to Gospel Questions,* 5:74.)

Though there had been speculation for many years in scientific circles about a time when the continents were all joined, until the late 1950s most reputable scientists looked upon these theories with great skepticism. Then an International Geophysical Year was declared. Scientists from all over the world and from many disciplines united in a major study of the earth. What followed was a revolution in scientific thinking. In an introduction to a book on continental drift published by *The Scientific American,* one scientist described this revolution:

"Formerly, most scientists regarded the earth as rigid and the continents as fixed, but now the surface of the earth is seen as slowly deformable and the continents as 'rafts' floating on a 'sea' of denser rock. The continents have repeatedly collided and joined, repeatedly broken and separated in different patterns, and, very likely, they have grown larger in the process.

"This scientific revolution, as others before it, was long in the making, but it was not until the late 1960s that it began to succeed. At a meeting of the world's geophysicists in August of 1971, it was made clear that the notion of continental drift, which had been heresy only a few years before, had become the orthodoxy of the great majority." (*Continents Adrift,* preface.)

Though the time of this division of the land is placed much earlier by scientists than by the biblical chronology, the idea of one land mass is widely accepted. This revelation in Doctrine and Covenants 133 declares that sometime in the future that geographical unity will be restored.

### D&C 133:26-34. What Do the Saints Know about the Ten Lost Tribes of Israel?

Elder Bruce R. McConkie summarized the history and destiny of the ten tribes:

"When Shalmanezer overran the *Kingdom of Israel* (about 721 B.C.), he carried the Ten Tribes comprising that kingdom captive into Assyria.

From thence they were led into the lands of the north and have been called the *Lost Tribes* because they are lost to the knowledge of other people. (1 Ne. 22:4.) 'We have no knowledge of the location or condition of that part of the Ten Tribes who went into the north country.' (*Compendium,* p. 88.)

"Esdras, an apocryphal writer, records this version of their escape from Assyria: 'Those are the ten tribes, which were carried away prisoners out of their own land in the time of Osea the king, whom Salmanasar the king of Assyria led away captive, and he carried them over the waters, and so came they into another land. *But they took this counsel among themselves, that they would leave the multitude of the heathen, and go forth into a further country, where never mankind dwelt, That they might there keep their statutes, which they never kept in their own land.* And they entered into Euphrates by the narrow passage of the river. *For the most High then shewed signs for them, and held still the flood, till they were passed over.* For through that country there was a great way to go, namely, of a year and a half: and the same region is called Arsareth. Then dwelt they there until the latter times; and now when they shall begin to come, The Highest shall stay the stream again, that they may go through.' (*Apocrypha,* 2 Esdras 13:40-47.)

"Commenting on this, Elder George Reynolds has written: . . .

" 'Is it altogether improbable that in that long journey of one and a half years, as Esdras states it, from Media the land of their captivity to the frozen north, some of the backsliding Israel rebelled, turned aside from the main body, forgot their God, by and by mingled with the Gentiles and became the leaven to leaven with the promised seed all the nations of the earth? The account given in the Book of Mormon of a single family of this same house, its waywardness, its stiffneckedness before God, its internal quarrels and family feuds are, we fear, an example on a small scale of what most probably happened in the vast bodies of Israelites who for so many months wended their tedious way northward. . . .' (*Are We of Israel,* pp. 10-11.)

"*The Lost Tribes are not lost unto the Lord.* In their northward journeyings they were led by prophets and inspired leaders. They had their Moses and their Lehi, were guided by the spirit of revelation, kept the law of Moses, and carried with them the statutes and judgments which the Lord had given them in ages past. They were still a distinct people many hundreds of years later, for the resurrected Lord visited and ministered among them following his ministry on this continent among the Nephites. (3 Ne. 16:1-4; 17:4.) Obviously he taught them in the same way and gave them the same truths which he gave his followers in Jerusalem and on the American continent; and obviously they recorded his teachings, thus creating volumes of scripture comparable to the Bible and Book of Mormon. (2 Ne. 29:12-14.)

"In due course the Lost Tribes of Israel will return and come to the children of Ephraim to receive their blessings. *This great gathering will take place under the direction of the President of The Church of Jesus Christ of Latter-day Saints,* for he holds the keys. . . . Keys are the right of presidency, the power to direct; and by this power the Lost Tribes will return, with 'their prophets' and their scriptures to 'be crowned with glory, even in Zion, by the hands of the servants of the Lord, even the children of Ephraim.' (D. & C. 133:26-35.)

"At the October, 1916, general conference of the Church, Elder James E. Talmage made this prediction: 'The tribes shall come; they are not lost unto the Lord; they shall be brought forth as hath been predicted; and I say unto you there are those now living—aye, some here present—who shall live to read the records of the Lost Tribes of Israel, which shall be made one with the record of the Jews, or the Holy Bible, and the record of the Nephites, or the Book of Mormon, even as the Lord hath predicted; and those records, which the tribes lost to man but yet to be found again shall bring, shall tell of the visit of the resurrected Christ to them, after he had manifested himself to the Nephites upon this continent.' (*Articles of Faith,* p. 513.)" (*Mormon Doctrine,* pp. 455-58.)

For a discussion of the role of John the Beloved with the ten lost tribes, see Notes and Commentary for Doctrine and Covenants 7:3-6.

### D&C 133:27. What Is the Highway That Shall Be Cast Up in the Midst of the Great Deep?

That the "great deep" means the ocean or a body of water in this verse (133:27) is attested to by the Old Testament prophet Isaiah (see Isaiah 51:10; see also Genesis 7:11).

How a highway will be cast up in the midst of the deep for the ten lost tribes to come to Zion has not been made known by the Lord; however, an interesting parallel is the story of Moses parting the Red Sea. With Pharaoh and his army at their backs and the Red Sea in front of them, Israel had come to an impasse. Then a great miracle took place: a highway was cast up in the midst of the deep, and Israel crossed over on dry ground. (See Exodus 14; Isaiah 11:15-16.)

How the Lord will bring the ten tribes to Zion is not fully clear, but that he will do it is a certainty.

### D&C 133:35. How Will the Jews Become Sanctified?

See Notes and Commentary for Doctrine and Covenants 45:48-53.

### D&C 133:46-51. Why Will the Lord Be Red in His Apparel at the Second Coming?

Verses 50 through 52 of Doctrine and Covenants 133 explain that the Lord is he who treads the winepress of judgment. Ludlow showed how this role of the Lord is related to his red apparel: "In ancient times in some parts of the world, people used to squeeze the juice out of the grapes by placing the grapes in a wine vat and then stomping on them. Naturally, the clothes of those persons who 'treadeth in the wine-vat' were soon stained with the grape juice and became the same color. When the Savior appears in the last days, his garments will be red 'like him that treadeth in the wine-vat' (D&C 133:48), and 'his voice shall be heard: I have trodden in the wine-press alone' (D&C 133:50)." (*Companion,* 1:678.)

President Joseph Fielding Smith said that "Isaiah has pictured this great day when the Lord shall come with his garments, or apparel, red and glorious, to take vengeance on the ungodly. (Isa. 64:1-6.) This will be a day of mourning to the wicked, but a day of gladness to all who have kept his commandments. Do not let anyone think that this is merely figurative language, it is literal, and as surely as we live that day of wrath will come when the cup of iniquity is full. We have received a great many warnings. The great day of the Millennium will come in; the wicked will be consumed and peace and righteousness will dwell upon all the face of the earth for one thousand years." (*Church History and Modern Revelation,* 1:191-92.)

**D&C 133:49. How Great Is the Glory of God?**

When the Lord comes the second time, he will come in the fulness of his glory. There are no other words in man's language sufficient to explain to mortal understanding what is meant by the expression "the fulness of God's glory." The scriptures, however, explain the effect of the fulness of God's glory upon the earth and upon the inhabitants thereof when the Lord returns the second time:

1. Mountains will flow down at his presence (see D&C 133:40, 44; Micah 1:4).
2. The waters upon the earth will boil (see D&C 133:41).
3. All nations will tremble at his presence (see D&C 133:42).
4. The sun will hide, the moon will withhold its light, and the stars will be hurled from their places (see D&C 133:49).
5. The wicked will be burned by the brightness or fire of the glory of the Lord (see Malachi 4:1-3; 2 Thessalonians 2:8).

*Coming in the clouds of glory*

**D&C 133:54-55. Who Was Resurrected at the Time the Savior Was?**

"Not only did Christ rise from the dead at that time, but others were seen who had risen from their graves—righteous men and women who died before Christ, and who had the privilege of rising with him. I do not believe that the resurrection then was a general one; I believe it extended to those only who, while upon earth, had proved themselves willing to do all for the kingdom of God, and to whom neither property, honor, nor life itself had been too dear to keep them from carrying out the purposes of God." (Anthon H. Lund, in Conference Report, Apr. 1904, p. 6.)

**D&C 133:56. Graves of the Saints Will Be Opened**

Elder James E. Talmage commented on this great event as follows: "It is expressly asserted that many graves shall yield up their dead at the time of Christ's advent in glory, and the just who have slept, together with many who have not died, will be caught up to meet the Lord [see 1 Thessalonians 4:14-16]." (*Articles of Faith,* p. 388.)

**D&C 133:57-60. The Gospel Is Sent through Those the World Considers Weak**

See Notes and Commentary on Doctrine and Covenants 1:17-20, 23.

**D&C 133:59. "Thrash the Nations"**

"This expression [thresh the nations] is found in Habakkuk 3:12. Threshing, in olden times, was done by treading out the grain on a threshing-floor. The going forth of the messengers of the gospel among the nations is like trampling the wheat sheaves on the hard floor. The valuable kernels are carefully gathered up; the straw is left." (Smith and Sjodahl, Commentary, p. 186.)

**D&C 133:63-74. What Is the Consequence for Those Who "Hearken Not to the Voice of the Lord"?**

The day will come when the wicked will see their folly and the judgments of God will come down upon them. Truly did Moroni say, "Fools mock, but they shall mourn" (Ether 12:26). The Lord will not suffer the unrighteous to join in the inheritance of the righteous. (See D&C 1:14; 63:54, 1 Nephi 14:7; 22:15-21; Acts 3:22-23; JS—H 1:40.)

**D&C 133:64. What Is Meant by the Expression "That It Shall Leave Them Neither Root nor Branch"?**

"This expression simply means that wicked and indifferent persons who reject the gospel of Jesus Christ will have no family inheritance or patriarchal lineage—neither root (ancestors or progenitors) nor branch (children or posterity). Such persons cannot be received into the celestial kingdom of glory of resurrected beings, but must be content with a lesser blessing." (Theodore M. Burton, in Conference Report, Oct. 1967, p. 81.)

**D&C 133:65-74**

Passages similar in content to Doctrine and Covenants 133:65-74 are found in Isaiah 8:16; 50:2-3; 2 Nephi 28:32; Doctrine and Covenants 1:8-9; 19:5; and Matthew 8:12.

**D&C 133:71. Why Are the Prophets Rejected?**

President Spencer W. Kimball discussed the various reasons why people reject the prophets:

"Various excuses have been used over the centuries to dismiss these divine messengers. There has been denial because the prophet came from an obscure place. 'Can there any good thing come out of Nazareth?' (John 1:46.) Jesus was also met with the question, 'Is not this the carpenter's son?' (Matt. 13:55.) By one means or another, the swiftest method of rejection of the holy prophets has been to find a pretext, however false or absurd, to dismiss the man so that his message could also be dismissed. Prophets who were not glib, but slow of speech, were esteemed as naught. . . .

"We wonder how often hearers first rejected the prophets because they despised them, and finally despised the prophets even more because they had rejected them. Even so, why else is the record of rejection so complete? The cares of the world are so many and so entangling, even very good people are diverted from following the truth because they care too much for the things of the world. . . .

"Sometimes people let their hearts get so set upon things and the honors of this world that they cannot learn the lessons they most need to learn. Simple truths are often rejected in favor of the much less-demanding philosophies of men, and this is another cause for the rejection of the prophets.

"But while there are various excuses for rejection, there's a certain cause for this sad record. It must not be passed over: the cares of the world, the honors of the world, and looking beyond the mark are all determined by a persuasive few who presume to speak for all. . . .

"The holy prophets have not only refused to follow erroneous human trends, but have pointed out these errors. No wonder the response to the prophets has not always been one of indifference. So often the prophets have been rejected because they first rejected the wrong ways of their own society.

"These excuses for rejection of the prophets are poor excuses. The trouble with using obscurity as a test of validity is that God has so often chosen to bring forth his work out of obscurity. He has even said it would be so. (See D&C 1:30.) Christianity did not go from Rome to Galilee; it was the other way around. In our day the routing is from Palmyra to Paris, not the reverse. Just because something is in our midst does not mean that we have been in the midst of it. We can daily drive by a museum or an art gallery but know nothing of what is inside.

"The trouble with rejection because of personal familiarity with the prophets is that the prophets are always somebody's son or somebody's neighbor. They are chosen from among the people, not transported from another planet, dramatic as that would be! . . .

"Of course, rejection of the holy prophets comes because the hearts of people are hardened, as people are shaped by their society. Yet even when the hardening is swift, it can also be subtle. Who, for instance, a scant twenty years ago would have foreseen the massive use of abortion in society today, like all the diseased doctrines of the devil. The practice is pleasing unto the carnal mind.

"Prophets have a way of jarring the carnal mind. Too often the holy prophets are wrongly perceived as harsh and as anxious to make a record in order to say, 'I told you so.' Those prophets I have known are the most loving of men. It is because of their love and integrity that they cannot modify the Lord's message merely to make people feel comfortable. They are too kind to be so cruel. I am so grateful that prophets do not crave popularity." (In Conference Report, Apr. 1978, pp. 115-16; or *Ensign*, May 1978, pp. 76-77.)

**D&C 133:73. Unrighteous Go Away into Outer Darkness**

Elder Bruce R. McConkie described outer darkness as hell: "So complete is the darkness prevailing in the minds of these spirits, so wholly has gospel light been shut out of their consciences, that they know little or nothing of the plan of salvation, and have little hope within themselves of advancement and progression through the saving grace of Christ. Hell is literally a place of outer darkness, darkness that hates light, buries truth, and revels in iniquity." (*Mormon Doctrine*, pp. 551-52.)

# Earthly Governments and Laws

# Section 134

## Historical Background

A general assembly of The Church of Jesus Christ of Latter-day Saints was held at Kirtland, Ohio, on 17 August 1835 to formally accept the collection of revelations, received through the Prophet, for printing as the first edition of the Doctrine and Covenants. After the priesthood quorums and then the congregation unanimously accepted the revelations, "Elder William W. Phelps arose and read an article prepared by Oliver Cowdery, on marriage. This was on vote ordered to be published also in the volume with the revelations. Then President Oliver Cowdery arose and read an article, 'Of Governments and Laws in General,' and this likewise was ordered by vote to be published with the book of revelations. Neither of these articles was a revelation to the Church." (Smith, *Church History and Modern Revelation,* 2:30.)

The article on government was included in that edition of the Doctrine and Covenants as a statement of belief and as a rebuttal to accusations against the Saints by their enemies. "The reason for the article on 'Government and Laws in General,' is explained in the fact that the Latter-day Saints had been accused by their bitter enemies, both in Missouri and in other places, as being opposed to law and order. They had been portrayed as setting up laws in conflict with the laws of the country." (Smith, *Church History and Modern Revelation,* 2:30-31.)

This declaration of belief has been included in editions of the Doctrine and Covenants since its proposal in 1835. When it was read and voted on, "the Prophet Joseph Smith and his second counselor, Frederick G. Williams, were in Canada on a missionary journey, and the Prophet did not return to Kirtland until Sunday, August 23rd, one week after the Assembly had been held. Since the Assembly had voted to have this article on government and one on marriage, also prepared by Oliver Cowdery, published in the Doctrine and Covenants, the Prophet accepted the decision and permitted this to be done.

"It should be noted that in the minutes, and also in the introduction to this article on government, the brethren were careful to state that this declaration was accepted as the belief, or 'opinion' of the officers of the Church, and not as a revelation, and therefore does not hold the same place in the doctrines of the Church as do the revelations." (Smith and Sjodahl, Commentary, p. 852.)

## Notes and Commentary

### D&C 134:1. "Governments Were Instituted of God for the Benefit of Man"

The principle of government was given of the Lord, but he did not institute all forms of government. Smith and Sjodahl noted that "the Lord in the very beginning revealed to Adam a perfect form of government, and this was 'instituted of God for the benefit of man;' but we do not hold that all governments, or any man-made government, was instituted of God although the Lord holds a controlling hand over them. It was not long after the Lord established His government with Adam, and had commanded him to teach correct principles to his children, that men began to rebel and turn away. [See Moses 5:12-13.]

"From that time forth the authority to rule was usurped by men and, with few exceptions ever since, the governments in the earth have been and are the governments of men, and the guiding hand of the Lord by revelation and authority vested in his servants has been ignored. The day is to come, and is near at hand, when the Lord will come in his power and make an end of all man-made governments and take His rightful place as King of kings, and Lord of lords." (Commentary, pp. 852-53.)

Though some may wonder why the Lord asks men to be in subjection to evil governments, even an evil government is better than no government at all. Speaking in the 1881 April conference, Elder Erastus Snow explained why: "Anarchy—shall I say, is the worst of all governments? No: Anarchy is the absence of all government; it is the antipodes [at opposite points] of order; it is the acme of confusion; it is the result of unbridled license, the antipodes of true liberty. The Apostle Paul says truly: 'For there is no power but of God: the powers that be are ordained of God.' At first this is a startling statement. Even the monopoly of the one-man-power as in Russia [the Czar], or the monopoly of the aristocracy as in other parts of Europe, or the imbecility and sometimes stupidity of a republic like our own, is far better than no government at all. And for this reason, says the Apostle Paul, 'The powers are ordained of God,' not that they are always the best forms of government for the people, or that they afford liberty and freedom to mankind but that any and all forms of government are better than none at all, having a tendency as they do to restrain the passions of human nature and to curb them, and to establish and maintain order to a greater or less degree. One monopoly is better than many; and the oppression of a king is tolerable, but the oppression of a mob, where every man is a law to himself and his own right arm, is his power to enforce his own will, is the worst form of government." (In *Journal of Discourses,* 22:151.)

**D&C 134:1. God Holds Men Accountable for Their Acts in Making Laws and Administering Them**

The Prophet Joseph Smith said that accountability and judgment apply to governments as well as to individuals: "We need not doubt the wisdom and intelligence of the Great Jehovah; He will award judgment or mercy to all nations according to their several deserts, their means of obtaining intelligence, the laws by which they are governed, the facilities afforded them of obtaining correct information, and His inscrutable designs in relation to the human family" (*History of the Church,* 4:596). President John Taylor added, "If for every word and secret act all men shall be brought to judgment, how much more will the public acts of public men be brought into account before God and before the holy priesthood" (in *Journal of Discourses,* 20:42-43).

**D&C 134:2. Government and the Agency of Man**

Elder John A. Widtsoe of the Quorum of the Twelve explained the importance of government's function in protecting the agency of men: "We believe that governments are instituted of God (134:1; 58:21); that individual freedom is necessary (134:2). No law should be passed that takes away from a man the right of choice. Free agency is fundamental as a law of human conduct. Men have the right to obey or disobey the law as they please, and take the consequences. That is fundamental and lies at the bottom of all Latter-day Saint thinking." (*Message of the Doctrine and Covenants,* p. 154.)

Elder David O. McKay said: "That government is best which has as its aim the administration of justice, social well-being and the promotion of prosperity among its members" (in Conference Report, Apr. 1930, p. 80).

He also said that "we must recognize that property rights are essential to human liberty," and cited former United States Supreme Court Justice George Sutherland, who came from Utah: " 'It is not the right of property which is protected, but the right *to* property. Property, per se, has no rights; but the individual—the man—has three great rights, equally sacred from arbitrary interference: the right to his life, the right to his liberty, and the right to his property. The three rights are so bound together as to be essentially *one* right. To give a man his life, but deny him his liberty, is to take from him all that makes life worth living. To give him liberty, but take from him the property which is the fruit and badge of his liberty, is to still leave him a slave.' (From George Sutherland's speech before the New York State Bar Association, January 21, 1921.)" (In Conference Report, Oct. 1962, p. 6.)

**D&C 134:3. "Such As Will Administer the Law in Equity and Justice Should Be Sought for and Upheld"**

Many leaders of the Church have spoken on the importance of members of the Church choosing righteous men to rule over them. In January 1928 the First Presidency issued a statement about the responsibilities of the Saints to choose and support righteous civic leaders. It was quoted by President Anthony W. Ivins in the October conference:

"Laws which are enacted for the protection of society have no value except when they are administered in righteousness and justice, and they cannot be so administered in righteousness and justice, if dishonest men occupy administrative offices.

"The Lord says 'When the wicked rule, the people mourn.' Wise men, good men, patriotic men are to be found in all communities, in all political parties, among all creeds. None but such men should be chosen. . . .

"Without beneficient laws, righteously administered, the foundations of civilization crumble, anarchy reigns, decay and dissolution follow.

"We call upon all members of The Church of Jesus Christ of Latter-day Saints throughout the world to honor the laws of God, and obey and uphold the law of the land; and we appeal to good men and women everywhere, regardless of creed, party affiliation, race or condition to join with us in an effort to put into operation the words of Lincoln, the great emancipator, that our country may continue to be a light to the world, a loyal, law-abiding, God-fearing nation." (In Conference Report, Oct. 1928, p. 16.)

President Ezra Taft Benson gave four excellent guidelines by which the Saints can measure the worthiness of an issue or political leader: "Not only should we seek humble, worthy, courageous leadership, but we should measure all proposals having to do with our national or local welfare by four standards:

"First, is the proposal, the policy or the idea being promoted, right as measured by the Gospel of Jesus Christ? . . .

"Second, is it right as measured by the Lord's standard of constitutional government? . . . The Lord's standard is a safe guide.

"Third, . . . is it right as measured by the counsel of the living oracles of God? . . .

"Fourth, what will be the effect upon the morale and the character of the people if this or that policy

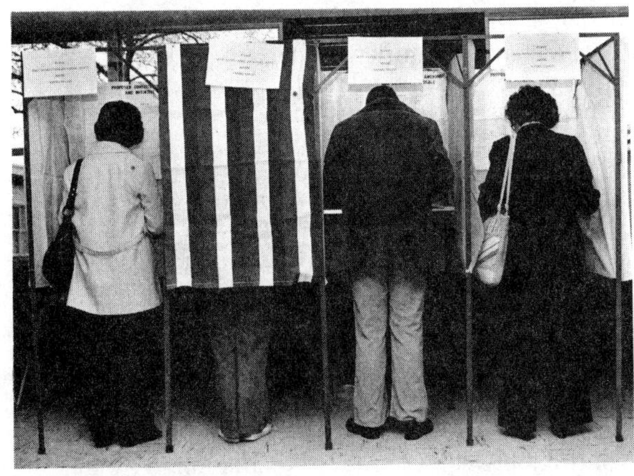

*Choose just and wise men*

is adopted?" (In *Our Prophets and Principles,* pp. 69-70.)

**D&C 134:4, 9. The Relation of Religion and Human Law**

It is a clear teaching of the Church that men are to have freedom to worship as they choose. President Heber J. Grant said:

"One of the fundamental articles of faith promulgated by the Prophet Joseph Smith was: 'We claim the privilege of worshiping Almighty God according to the dictates of our own conscience; and allow all men the same privilege, let them worship how, where, or what they may.'

"But we claim absolutely no right, no prerogative whatever, to interfere with any other people." (In Conference Report, Apr. 1921, p. 203.)

Elder John A. Widtsoe wrote that the Prophet Joseph Smith advocated that "a good government must secure for every citizen the free exercise of conscience. Matters of belief or religious practice should not be interfered with, unless they oppose laws formulated for the common good. There should be no mingling of religious influence with civil governments." (*Joseph Smith,* p. 215.)

**D&C 134:5. "Sustain and Uphold the Respective Governments in Which They Reside"**

The twelfth article of faith states, "We believe in being subject to kings, presidents, rulers, and magistrates, in obeying, honoring, and sustaining the law."

"The three significant words used in the 12th Article of Faith," commented President David O. McKay, "express the proper attitude of the membership of the Church toward law. These words are—obey, honor, and sustain. The Article does not say we believe in submission to the law. Obedience implies a higher attitude then mere submission, for obedience has its root in good intent; submission may spring from selfishness or meanness of spirit. Though obedience and submission both imply restraint on one's own will, we are obedient only from a sense of right; submissive from a sense of necessity.

"Honor expresses an act or attitude of an inferior towards a superior. When applied to things it is taken in the sense of holding in honor. Thus, in honoring the law, we look upon it as something which is above selfish desires or indulgences.

"To sustain signifies to hold up; to keep from falling. To sustain the law, therefore, is to refrain from saying or doing anything which will weaken it or make it ineffective.

"We obey law from a sense of right.

"We honor law because of its necessity and strength to society.

"We sustain law by keeping it in good repute." (In Conference Report, Apr. 1937, p. 28.)

A situation could arise in which obeying a law from God might cause one to violate a law of the land. Elder James E. Talmage said: "A question has many times been asked of the Church and of its individual members, to this effect: In the case of a conflict between the requirements made by the revealed word of God, and those imposed by the secular law, which of these authorities would the members of the Church be bound to obey? In answer, the words of Christ may be applied—it is the duty of the people to render unto Caesar the things that are Caesar's, and unto God the things that are God's [see D&C 63:26; Matthew 22:21]. At the present time the kingdom of heaven as an earthly power, with a reigning King exercising direct and personal authority in temporal matters, has not been established upon the earth. The branches of the Church as such, and the members composing the same, are subjects of the several governments within whose separate realms the Church organizations exist. In this day of comparative enlightenment and freedom there is still cause for expecting any direct interference with the rights of private worship and individual devotion; in all civilized nations the people are accorded the right to pray, and this right is assured by what may be properly called a common law of humankind. No earnest soul is cut off from communion with his God; and with such an open channel of communication, relief from burdensome laws and redress from grievances may be sought from the power that holds control of nations." (*Articles of Faith,* pp. 422-23.)

**D&C 134:5-6. "Sedition and Rebellion Are Unbecoming Every Citizen"**

President N. Eldon Tanner addressed the question of dealing with unjust laws:

"There are many who question the constitutionality of certain acts passed by their respective governments, even though such laws have been established by the highest courts in the land as being constitutional, and they feel to defy and disobey the law.

"Abraham Lincoln once observed: 'Bad laws, if they exist, should be repealed as soon as possible; still, while they continue in force, they should be religiously observed.'

"This is the attitude of the Church in regard to law observance. . . .

"There is no reason or justification for men to disregard or break the law or try to take it into their own hands.

"It is the duty of citizens of any country to remember that they have individual responsibilities, and that they must operate within the law of the country in which they have chosen to live." (In Conference Report, Oct. 1975, p. 126; or *Ensign,* Nov. 1975, p. 83.)

President Joseph Fielding Smith also taught that rebellion is not the approved way for Saints: "No member of the Church can be accepted as in good standing whose way of life is one of rebellion against the established order of decency and obedience to law. We cannot be in rebellion against the law and be in harmony with the Lord, for he has commanded us to 'be subject to the powers that be, until he reigns whose right it is to reign. . . .' (D&C 58:22.) And one of these days he is going to come." (In Conference Report, Apr. 1971, p. 48; or *Ensign,* June 1971, p. 50.)

The only exception to this principle would be when the Lord directs his people through his prophets to take an opposing stand to government. Otherwise they recognize the established authority of government.

### D&C 134:6-7. "Human Laws . . . and Divine Laws . . . Both to Be Answered by Man to His Maker"

President Brigham Young taught: "Remember that the Lord holds all of us responsible for our conduct here. He held our father Adam responsible for his conduct, but no more than He does us, in proportion to the station we hold. The kings of the earth will have to give an account to God, for their conduct in a kingly capacity. Kings are heads of nations, governors are heads of provinces; so are fathers or husbands governors of their own houses, and should act accordingly." (*History of the Church,* 4:309.)

President Wilford Woodruff added: "I will say that this nation and all nations, together with presidents, kings, emperors, judges, and all men, righteous and wicked, have got to go into the spirit world and stand before the bar of God. They have got to give an account of the deeds done in the body." (In *Millennial Star,* 24 Nov. 1890, p. 741.)

As part of that accountability to God, political rulers have an obligation to allow all men to exercise their freedoms and accountability to God. President Wilford Woodruff said further: "God will bless no king, no emperor and no president who will not give unto his subjects the rights and privileges in their relationship to God which the Father Himself has given unto them. Whenever these subjects are deprived of their rights, those who preside over them are held responsible." (*Deseret Weekly News,* 19 Apr. 1890, p. 561.)

### D&C 134:8. "All Men Should Step Forward . . . in Bringing Offenders against Good Laws to Punishment"

Said Elder James E. Talmage: "Now, the Lord has provided that those in his Church shall live according to the law, and he makes a distinction between the law pertaining to the Church and what we call the secular law, or the law of the land, but he requires obedience to each. My love for my brother in this Church does not mean that I am to . . . stand between him and righteous judgment. This Church is no organization like that of the secret combinations of old, which the Lord hath said he hates, the members of which were pledged, and bound by oath that they would cover up one another's crimes, that they would justify one another in theft and murder and in all things that were unclean. It is no such organization at all. It would not be of God if it were." (In Conference Report, Oct. 1920, p. 63.)

### D&C 134:9. Separation of Church and State

The Church upholds the principle laid down by the Constitution of the United States that religion and government should be kept separate. The First Presidency (Joseph F. Smith, John R. Winder, and Anthon H. Lund) stated the following in 1907:

"The Church of Jesus Christ of Latter-day Saints holds to the doctrine of the separation of church and state; the non-interference of church authority in political matters; and the absolute freedom and independence of the individual in the performance of his political duties. . . .

"We declare that from principle and policy, we favor:

"The absolute separation of church and state;

"No domination of the state by the church;

"No church interference with the functions of the state;

"No state interference with the functions of the church, or with the free exercise of religion;

"The absolute freedom of the individual from the domination of ecclesiastical authority in political affairs;

"The equality of all churches before the law." (In Clark, *Messages of the First Presidency,* 4:153.)

### D&C 134:10. "Religious Societies Have a Right to Deal with Their Members . . . for Fellowship and Good Standing"

Elder John A. Widtsoe wrote that "no officer in the Church has authority beyond matters pertaining to the Church" (*Priesthood and Church Government,* p. 62), and that "the Church can try offenders only for their membership in the Church. Any further punishment is in the hands of the civil courts. Members of the Church may either be disfellowshiped or excommunicated." (*Priesthood and Church Government,* p. 209.)

### D&C 134:11. "Men Are Justified in Defending Themselves"

See Notes and Commentary on Doctrine and Covenants 98:16-48.

### D&C 134:12. "Not . . . Right to Interfere with Bond Servants"

Although it is the unquestionable position of the Church that slavery is evil and counter to the fundamental rights of an individual, the Prophet Joseph Smith taught that when slavery is tolerated by a government it is not the Church's position to try to overthrow that established order: "It should be the duty of an Elder, when he enters into a house, to salute the master of that house, and if he gain his consent, then he may preach to all that are in that house; but if he gain not his consent, let him not go unto his slaves, or servants, but let the responsibility be upon the head of the master of that house, and the consequences thereof, and the guilt of that house is no longer upon his skirts. . . . But if the master of that house give consent, the Elder may preach to his family, his wife, his children and his servants, his man-servants, or his maid-servants, or his slaves." (*History of the Church,* 2:263.)

In 1834, when this statement was written, the Saints in Missouri were often accused by their enemies of seeking to overthrow slavery. Since Missouri entered the Union as a slave state, this question inflamed the Missourians. Doctrine and Covenants 134:12 was a reply to the accusations against the Saints.

# A Tribute to the Martyrs

Section 135

## Historical Background

On Tuesday, 25 June 1844, Joseph and Hyrum Smith presented themselves to the authorities in Illinois to be arrested on a charge of treason. Governor Thomas Ford that morning assembled the state militia and told them that Joseph and Hyrum Smith were "dangerous men in the community, and guilty of all that they might have alleged against them, still they were in the hands of the law" (*History of the Church*, 6:563). John Taylor and Willard Richards were allowed to stay with Joseph and Hyrum, and they joined the two brothers in jail.

On Wednesday, the twenty-sixth, Governor Ford met with Joseph Smith and said that the armed mob had not been called up by him and that he would see that the prisoners were protected (see *History of the Church*, 6:577-78).

On Thursday, the twenty-seventh, Governor Ford went to Nauvoo, where he berated the Saints in a public speech and had his troops brandish their swords. The Governor and the troops left Nauvoo about 6:30 P.M.

At the same time that the Governor and his troops were making a threatening show in Nauvoo, the Prophet and his brother Hyrum were murdered in Carthage. At about 5:00 P.M. the mob, which was composed mainly of the Carthage Greys, the militia, rushed Carthage Jail. Hyrum Smith was struck by a ball in the face, and by several other balls, and fell to the floor, saying "I am a dead man!" John Taylor was shot in several places in his body and rolled under the bed. Joseph Smith was shot in the back from inside the jail and in the chest from outside. He fell dead out the window. (See *History of the Church*, 6:602-18.)

John Taylor and Willard Richards, members of the Quorum of the Twelve, were eyewitnesses to the martyrdom of God's prophets, and each wrote an account of the events. The account contained in Doctrine and Covenants 135 "was written by Elder John Taylor who offered his life with his beloved brethren in this tragedy in Carthage, Illinois. President Taylor was severely wounded and carried the balls with which he was wounded to his grave. His devotion and willingness and that of his companion, Willard Richards, bear a strong testimony of their conviction and integrity to the truth of the mission of the Prophet Joseph Smith." (Smith and Sjodahl, Commentary, p. 855; see also *History of the Church*, 6:629-631; "Praise to the Man," *Hymns*, no. 147.)

## Notes and Commentary

**D&C 135:1. Was It Necessary That Hyrum Seal His Testimony with His Blood?**

President Joseph Fielding Smith, grandson of Hyrum Smith, explained:

"The Prophet Joseph Smith conferred upon Hyrum Smith all the keys, authority and gifts of the priesthood which he, the Prophet, held, and which were formerly held by Oliver Cowdery. The Lord also revealed to Hyrum Smith all that was necessary to make him completely and to the full degree, a witness with his brother Joseph, as a prophet, seer, revelator and president of the Church, and to stand through all time and eternity at the head of this dispensation with his brother Joseph, a witness for Jesus Christ.

"Thus, we see, Hyrum Smith became a president of the Church with Joseph Smith, which place Oliver Cowdery might have held had he not wavered and fallen from his exalted station. I am firmly of the opinion that had Oliver Cowdery remained true to his covenants and obligations as a witness with Joseph Smith, and retained his authority and place, he, and not Hyrum Smith, would have gone with Joseph Smith as a prisoner and to martyrdom at Carthage.

"The sealing of the testimony through the shedding of blood would not have been complete in the death of the Prophet Joseph Smith alone; it required the death of Hyrum Smith who jointly held the keys of this dispensation. It was needful that these martyrs seal their testimony with their

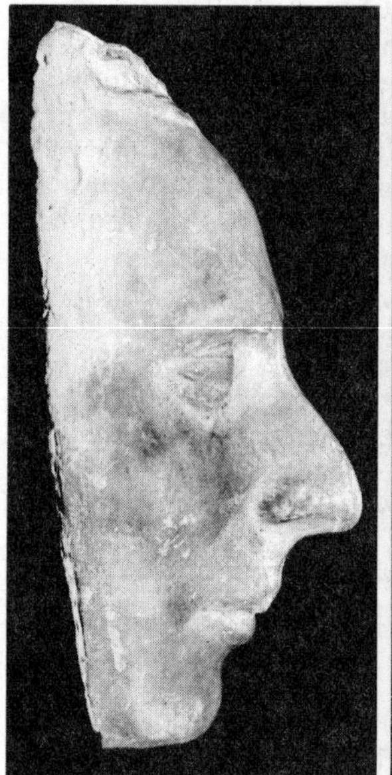

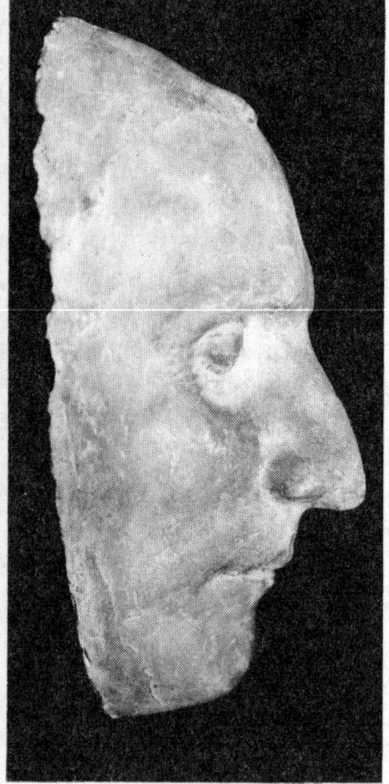

*The death masks of Joseph Smith (left) and his brother Hyrum (right)*

blood, that they 'might be honored and the wicked might be condemned.' " (*Doctrines of Salvation,* 1:218-19; see also D&C 136:39; Hebrews 9:16-17).

**D&C 135:2. Why Did Willard Richards Escape Injury?**

"Dr. Richards' escape was miraculous; he being a very large man, and in the midst of a shower of balls, yet he stood unscathed, with the exception of a ball which grazed the tip end of the lower part of his left ear. His escape fulfilled literally a prophecy which Joseph made over a year previously, that the time would come that the balls would fly around him like hail, and he should see his friends fall on the right and on the left, but that there should not be a hole in his garment." (*History of the Church,* 6:619.)

**D&C 135:3. Joseph Smith Has Done More for the Salvation of Men Than Anyone Other Than Jesus**

This bold statement has caused some critics of the Church to say that the Saints think more of Joseph Smith than they do of the Savior. Such critics ignore the fact that the Saints look to the Prophet with reverence because of what he did for their understanding of Jesus Christ and his mission.

When one thinks about such great prophets and leaders as Adam, Moses, Isaiah, Abraham, and Nephi, is it really justifiable to say that Joseph Smith did more than any of these for the salvation of men? The answer is a resounding yes. Perhaps the Prophet Joseph Smith was not greater than they were in righteousness or commitment, but only Jesus has done more for the salvation of men than did the Prophet, as is evident in the following list of some of the things he did under the direction of the Lord:

He taught correct concepts about the nature of the Father and Son.

He translated and published the Book of Mormon by the power of God.

He was the means by which the Aaronic and Melchizedek Priesthoods were restored.

He organized the Church of Jesus Christ again on the earth under the direction of the Savior.

He revealed the true meaning of Zion, its location in the last days, and the laws by which it shall be governed.

He received over a hundred revelations and published them in the Doctrine and Covenants.

He worked on a translation of the Bible, restoring lost scripture and correcting erroneous translations.

He established settlements of the Saints, teaching them principles of social order, city planning, economics, and so on, in addition to teaching them spiritual principles.

He restored the keys and knowledge of temple ordinances for both the living and the dead.

He received keys of restoration from Moses, Elias, and Elijah.

He started a missionary program that has involved tens of thousands of missionaries and resulted in millions of converts in countries all over the world.

He translated by inspiration of God papyri from Egypt, containing some of the writings of Abraham.

The Lord revealed through the Prophet Joseph Smith many principles and concepts of the gospel which had been lost or corrupted over the centuries. The Prophet Joseph Smith then—

Explained man's relationship to God.

Explained the differences between the Aaronic and Melchizedek Priesthoods.

Explained the different offices of the priesthood, the duties of each, and the manner in which they are organized.

Set forth the proper organization, name, and purpose of the Church of Jesus Christ.

Taught that man is on earth in a probation, to work out his individual salvation.

Received a revelation of the knowledge of the three degrees of glory and what one must do to prepare to live once again with God.

Explained the nature and order of the Resurrection.

Explained the saving nature of certain ordinances which may be performed vicariously for those who did not receive them on earth.

Set forth the principles pertaining to the building up of Zion, the nature of events in the Millennium, and the kingdom of God and how it will eventually be established on earth.

Added to man's knowledge of the Apostasy and why it came.

Pointed out the fulfillment of various prophecies.

Announced the coming of Elijah, and explained his mission.

Taught that marriage is intended to be eternal and that the family unit continues beyond the grave.

Exemplified the role of a living prophet.

Restored an understanding of the principle of administrations to the sick in the name of the Lord by the power of the holy priesthood.

Followed the direction of the Lord and constructed temples and taught his people temple ordinances for the living and the dead.

Brought forth the Book of Mormon, the Doctrine and Covenants, and the material contained in the Pearl of Great Price.

Set down the duties of Church members and the laws by which the Church is governed.

Taught the doctrine of common consent.

Explained the role of Satan in the gospel plan.

Gave the Saints the Lord's principles by which one can avoid being deceived in this life.

Taught the true nature of the atonement of Christ and its relationship to the principles of justice and mercy.

Explained the meaning of the covenant of the sacrament.

Explained the nature of spiritual gifts and the role of the Holy Ghost.

Clarified the role of women in the kingdom of God.

Received the revelation of the oath and covenant of the priesthood.

Emphasized the necessity of missionary work in the Lord's plan.

Received the Word of Wisdom from the Lord.
Instituted the law of tithing, the law of consecration of property and stewardship, and the law of sacrifice and obedience.

All of these accomplishments were done under the direction of Jesus Christ and, ultimately, the credit belongs to him. But Joseph Smith was his chosen instrument in bringing all these things to pass. This is why one can rightly say that the Prophet did more for the salavation of man than anyone except the Savior himself.

**D&C 135:3. In What Way Does the Book of Mormon Contain the Fulness of the Everlasting Gospel?**

See Notes and Commentary for Doctrine and Covenants 20:9.

**D&C 135:5. What Is a Testator? Why Is Death Required to Put a Testament in Force?**

A testator is one who leaves a will or testament. The will is valid only after the testator's death. While the testator lives, the will has no legal power. Gospel usage of the word *testator* denotes one who provides to man the witness of God's covenants. These covenants are his testament to mankind. The Prophet Joseph Smith's testament was that God had revealed through him the sealing power by which "all covenants, contracts, bonds, obligations, oaths, vows, performances, connections, associations," shall be in force and recognized as valid in the eternal worlds (D&C 132:7). In a special way, the death of the testator places a seal of truth upon his testament. Had Joseph and Hyrum Smith been the frauds that some have claimed, they would not have been willing to die to seal their testimony with their blood. In death, their testament is vindicated.

The Lord revealed to President Brigham Young that it was necessary for the Prophet to seal his testimony with his blood (see D&C 136:39). Elder Joseph Fielding Smith taught that this sealing would later stand as a witness: "The shedding of their blood also bound that testimony upon an unbelieving world and this testimony will stand at the judgment seat as a witness against all men who have rejected their words of eternal life" ("The Martyrs," *Improvement Era,* June 1944, p. 365).

*"In death they were not separated" (D&C 135:3)*

# Organization of the Camp of Zion

Section 136

## Historical Background

With the death of the Prophet Joseph Smith at Carthage, Illinois, the leadership of the Church fell upon the shoulders of the Quorum of the Twelve. Brigham Young, as the senior Apostle, was President of the Quorum. The opposition from enemies of the Church that led to the Martyrdom was not stilled with the death of the Prophet. Once again mobs rode against the Saints, peace was shattered, lives were threatened. President Young pressed forward with plans first initiated by the Prophet Joseph to take the Saints to the Rocky Mountains where they could find some measure of peace. In February 1846, under the direction of the Twelve, the Saints began to leave Nauvoo, Illinois, and cross the Mississippi River to Iowa. As they moved west across Iowa, they established camps for those who would follow. The winter of 1846-47 was spent at Winter Quarters (which today is Florence, Nebraska). While encamped at Winter Quarters, President Brigham Young received a revelation from the Lord.

Elder B. H. Roberts explained the circumstances of the coming forth of this revelation: "The serious business of preparing for the continuation of the

*The Saints migrated across the plains in companies*

march into the wilderness, the completion of the exodus from the United States, was not neglected. It was considered in many council meetings of the presiding authorities, it was the chief topic of conversation and of discussion wherever two or three were gathered together. Thought upon it finally so crystallized in the mind of Brigham Young that on the 14th of January, 1847, at Winter Quarters, he was prepared to announce '*The Word and Will of the Lord*' upon the march of the Camps of Israel to the west." (*Comprehensive History of the Church,* 3:154-55.)

# Notes and Commentary

### D&C 136:1-3. How Was the Camp of Israel Organized?

Smith and Sjodahl wrote: "The Saints were driven from their homes in Nauvoo under the most trying circumstances and in poverty and destitution in large measure, for they had been robbed by their enemies. Therefore it was extremely needful for a revelation from the Lord for their guidance in their journeyings to the Rocky Mountains. The Lord did not fail them in this hour of distress and gave this revelation to President Brigham Young to guide them in their journeyings and admonishing them to keep His commandments. All the members of the Church were to be organized in companies and were required to keep the commandments faithfully that they might have the guidance of His Spirit with them in all their trying circumstances. These companies were to be on the order followed by Zion's Camp in their remarkable march from Kirtland to Missouri, with captains, over hundreds, fifties and tens and all under the direction of the council of Apostles." (Commentary, p. 857.)

### D&C 136:4-11. The Saints Must Walk by Covenant

"How essential it was then in the days of tribulation for the saints to walk by covenant as they journeyed towards a new home," explained Smith and Sjodahl. "Moreover it was necessary that they provide themselves the best they could with teams, clothing and provisions, for the journey was a difficult one. Some members of necessity would be left behind until such time as they could be prepared. The officers of the companies were to decide who might go and who would better remain behind until a more suitable day. These who were to remain were to put in crops and wait until the coming harvest. Each company was to bear an equal proportion of the means for the benefit of all. Those who had substance were to share with those who were destitute, in the true spirit of charity and faith. There were among them the widows and fatherless and the wives and families of those who had gone into the 'Mormon Battalion.' If they would do this the Lord would pour out upon them his blessings. They should have flocks and herds and their fields would not fail them." (Commentary, pp. 858-59.)

### D&C 136:18-27. Zion Will Be Redeemed

Smith and Sjodahl wrote that "the members of the Church had been disappointed, if not discouraged, because Zion had not been redeemed. No doubt it was trying to the faith of some to be on the way to the unknown region of the Rocky Mountains. All that they had heard of this territory was discouraging and the redemption of Zion seemed farther away than ever from fulfillment. Now they were to take courage, for the Lord had not forgotten Zion, and it should be redeemed in the due time of the Lord. It was well, therefore, for the members to obey counsel and not seek to build themselves at the expense of others; should this be done they would lose the reward. The Lord would lead them as he led the children of Israel, and he was just as mindful of the Saints today as he was then. Every man should respect the rights and property of the rest, and all should be wise stewards." (Commentary, p. 860; see also Notes and Commentary for D&C 103:15-20.)

### D&C 136:22. Can One Compare Ancient Israel to Modern Israel?

President Anthony W. Ivins explained the similarities and differences between the exodus of the Saints to the West and the exodus of ancient Israel. He pointed out that the trek west for the Saints was a greater accomplishment for those people than was the exodus from Egypt for ancient Israel.

"Recognizing the hopelessness of reconciliation with their neighbors, determined to find a place where the Saints could worship the Lord without molestation, this modern Moses [Brigham Young] and his associates turned their faces westward, and after a journey unparalleled in the history of the world found asylum in these mountain valleys, where the body of the Church now resides.

"It is true that Moses led the Israelites out from the Egyptian captivity; the Puritans had left their homes in the old world and landed at Plymouth Rock.

"The impulse which prompted each of these great movements, which have meant so much to the world and its people, were similar, but the circumstances under which they were accomplished entirely different.

"The Israelites were going out from a grievous and humiliating bondage, and returning to their old home, in the land of their fathers. Modern

Israel were leaving their homes, the lands of their fathers, and were going into a country unknown to them, a country uninhabited by civilized man.

"The Israelites were a people of one race, influenced in the accomplishment of their purpose by the traditions and religion of their fathers. The Latter-day Saints were composed of people gathered from various nations, bringing with them different traditions, different customs and different languages.

"Ancient Israel was separated from their destination by only about two hundred and fifty miles, in a direct line, and that over a country where great armies have marched from remote times. The 'Mormon' Pioneers traveled over a road where few had gone before, a distance of more than a thousand miles.

"Ancient Israel were led by great ocular demonstrations of the power of the Lord, and their daily bread was provided by manna sent down from heaven. The 'Mormon' Pioneers walked by divine faith, and provided for their daily necessities with the labor of their own hands.

"Reaching their destination Ancient Israel found cities already built, orchards and vineyards already planted, and flocks and herds which the Lord delivered into their hands. Modern Israel found a desert waste, which could only be redeemed, and made productive by infinite toil.

"So, I feel justified in saying that this accomplishment has no parallel in the history of the world." (In Conference Report, Apr. 1922, pp. 36-37.)

**D&C 136:28. Why Did the Lord Instruct the People to Sing and Dance?**

Wrote Smith and Sjodahl: "The Lord knew that the members of the Church would be weary and discouraged as they journeyed, and therefore he gave to them a remedy by which their despondency and discouragement could be overcome. They were to 'praise the Lord with singing, and music, with dancing,' with prayer and thanksgiving. This advice was followed, and after the camp was made for the night, frequently someone with a violin furnished music for dancing and for singing the favorite hymns and melodies familiar to the group, and thus their spirits were revived." (Commentary, p. 860.)

*Music revived the weary spirits of the pioneer Saints*

**D&C 136:31. Tested and Tried in All Things**

See Notes and Commentary for Doctrine and Covenants 101:4-5; 122.

**D&C 136:34-36. Has the United States Been Vexed Because of Its Persecution of the Latter-day Saints?**

Elder B. H. Roberts saw in subsequent events a fulfillment of Doctrine and Covenants 136:34-36. After quoting 3 Nephi 16:10, the Savior's warning of what would happen if the Gentiles rejected his gospel, Elder Roberts said:

"Behold, that is what the people of the United States did when they rejected from habitation among them, the Church of Jesus Christ of Latter-day Saints, and expatriated the membership thereof, so that they were under the necessity of finding a refuge in a land, which, at the time our fathers entered it—The Salt Lake Valley—was no part of the United States of America—but was Mexican territory.

"Listen to this: it is a revelation that we do not often refer to, but it has some very choice gems in it. It is the 'Word and Will of the Lord to President Brigham Young,' given at Winter Quarters, and, among other things, this was said: [D&C 136:34-36].

"I think our country at that time did not repent of the wrongs they had done in this and other things, for this proclamation was immediately followed by the war with Mexico, in which at least those regiments that were selected from western Illinois—one of them at least, was well nigh wiped out of existence in the war with Mexico; and it was about the only disastrous engagement that we had in that war. Then followed the awful war, between 1861 and 1865, in which, as I believe, the hand of God severely punished the United States of America, in fulfilment of the wonderful prediction that was made by the Prophet Joseph Smith, in relation to the calamities that would befall the nation." (In Conference Report, Oct. 1922, pp. 17-18.)

Since the Civil War, the United States has been involved in five major wars: the Spanish-American War, World Wars I and II, and the Korean and Vietnam wars. Nor has war been the only means of vexation. Depressions, natural disasters, and other calamities have plagued the nation. The prophetic promise is that if the people of this nation do not serve the God of the land, who is Jesus Christ, they will be swept off (see Ether 2:10). As yet there has been no nationwide repentance for past and present sins, and so the Lord continues to vex the people of this nation, seeking to bring them to repentance. In verse 42 of section 136, the Lord reminds the Saints that they are under the same obligation to keep the commandments.

**D&C 136:38-40. "Many Have Marveled Because of His Death"**

Elder George Albert Smith spoke of the necessity

of the Martyrdom: "Under the Lord's direction, he [Joseph Smith] organized the Church of Christ, with apostles, prophets, pastors, teachers, evangelists, etc., as the Church should be organized, to continue thus until all should come to a unity of the faith. He ministered unto the people, he healed the sick; he loved the souls of the children of men. But, as had been the case with prophets whom the Lord had raised up before, it seemed necessary in this case that the testimony of His servant should be sealed with his life's blood. No more pathetic page will be found in the history of the world than that upon which is inscribed the last sayings of our beloved Prophet Joseph Smith. He knew that his time was near at hand; he realized that his life's mission had been fulfilled. He had given the keys for the gifts and blessings of God unto the people, and the Father had continued to bless him; finally he realized that his labor was about done." (In Conference Report, Apr. 1904, p. 63.)

# Vision of the Celestial Kingdom

# Section 137

## Historical Background

The Kirtland Temple was nearly completed in January 1836. Then, for many weeks before its dedication on 27 March 1836, the brethren held classes and meetings in it. A very important meeting was held on Thursday, 21 January 1836, in the west room of the attic, a room on the third floor that had been used as a classroom for studying Hebrew. The Prophet recorded the following account of the meeting:

"At early candle-light I met with the Presidency at the west school room, in the Temple, to attend to the ordinance of anointing our heads with holy oil; also the Councils of Kirtland and Zion met in the two adjoining rooms, and waited in prayer while we attended to the ordinance. I took the oil in my left hand, Father Smith being seated before me, and the remainder of the Presidency encircled him round about. We then stretched our right hands towards heaven, and blessed the oil, and consecrated it in the name of Jesus Christ.

"We then laid our hands upon our aged Father Smith, and invoked the blessings of heaven. I then anointed his head with the consecrated oil, and sealed many blessings upon him. The Presidency then in turn laid their hands upon his head, beginning at the oldest, until they had all laid their hands upon him, and pronounced such blessings upon his head, as the Lord put into their hearts, all blessing him to be our Patriarch, to anoint our heads, and attend to all duties that pertain to that office. The Presidency then took the seat in their turn, according to their age, beginning at the oldest, and received their anointing and blessing under the hands of Father Smith. And in my turn, my father anointed my head, and sealed upon me the blessings of Moses, to lead Israel in the latter days, even as Moses led him in days of old; also the blessings of Abraham, Isaac and Jacob. All of the Presidency laid their hands upon me, and pronounced upon my head many prophecies and blessings, many of which I shall not notice at this time. But as Paul said, so say I, let us come to visions and revelations." (*History of the Church,* 2:379-80.)

This night was one of great revelation. In addition to the vision of the celestial kingdom, the Prophet Joseph Smith also saw in vision the Savior standing in the midst of the present Twelve Apostles who were laboring in foreign lands, and he saw the Twelve Apostles and the Presidency in the celestial kingdom. Many of the other brethren saw glorious visions and received the ministration of angels. Some even saw the face of the Savior as the spirit of prophecy and revelation was poured out in mighty power. (See *History of the Church,* 2:381-82).

The vision of the celestial kingdom, which is now Doctrine and Covenants 137, was not part of the four standard works until 1976. During the April general conference of that year, the Church voted unanimously to accept this vision and the vision of the redemption of the dead (D&C 138) as canonized scripture. These revelations were originally placed in the Pearl of Great Price; however, when a new edition of the Doctrine and Covenants with study aids was commissioned, it was decided to add the two revelations as sections 137 and 138 of the Doctrine and Covenants. This decision was made by the First Presidency and the Quorum of the Twelve. (See *Church News,* 2 June 1979, p. 3.)

## Notes and Commentary

### D&C 137:1. What Did the Prophet Mean by "Whether in the Body or Out I Cannot Tell"?

The Apostle Paul made a similar statement in describing a revelation he had (see 2 Corinthians 12:3). When the Lord gives revelations to man he communicates through the power of the Holy Ghost to the spirit of man (see 1 Corinthians 2:9-14).

The Prophet Joseph Smith taught an important

principle concerning revelation: "All things whatsoever God in his infinite wisdom has seen fit and proper to reveal to us, while we are dwelling in mortality, in regard to our mortal bodies, are revealed to us in the abstract, and independent of affinity of this mortal tabernacle, but are revealed to our spirits precisely as though we had no bodies at all; and those revelations which will save our spirits will save our bodies. God reveals them to us in view of no eternal dissolution of the body, or tabernacle." (*Teachings,* p. 355.)

When the Prophet Joseph recorded his vision of the three degrees of glory, he said that "by the power of the Spirit our eyes were opened and our understandings were enlightened, so as to see and understand the things of God" (D&C 76:12). Moses, in recording his great revelations, indicated that he beheld not with his "natural, but [with his] spiritual eyes" (Moses 1:11). He said later in his account of the things he saw that he "discerned them by the spirit of God" (Moses 1:28). Enoch said concerning his vision that he saw "things which were not visible to the natural eye" (Moses 6:36).

In an account of the Prophet Joseph Smith's first vision, Elder Orson Pratt recorded: "When it [the light; see JS—H 1:16] first came upon him, it produced a peculiar sensation throughout his whole system; and, immediately, his mind was caught away from the natural objects with which he was surrounded; and he was enwrapped in a heavenly vision" (in James B. Allen, "Eight Contemporary Accounts of Joseph Smith's First Vision: What Do We Learn from Them?" *Improvement Era,* Apr. 1970, p. 10). When the Lord gives such revelations to men, they become enveloped in the spirit and filled with his glory to such an extent that they become oblivious to the things of the natural world.

### D&C 137:2-3. Why Is God's Presence Described As "Blazing" and "Like unto Circling Flames of Fire"?

The Prophet Joseph Smith taught that God's nature is one of light, fire, and glory. In his account of the First Vision he wrote that God's "brightness and glory defy all description" (JS—H 1:17). He also taught that "God Almighty Himself dwells in eternal fire; flesh and blood cannot go there, for all corruption is devoured by the fire. 'Our God is a consuming fire.' [Heb. 12:29]. . . .

". . . Immortality dwells in everlasting burnings." (*Teachings,* p. 367.) President Joseph Fielding Smith stated that a celestial body is filled with glory and power: "God is full of energy, and should we mortals stand in his presence, unless his spirit was upon us to protect us we would be consumed. That is how much energy there is in a celestial body." (*Seek Ye Earnestly,* p. 275.)

### D&C 137:5-8. The Salvation of Joseph Smith's Brother Alvin

Alvin Smith was the first son of Joseph Smith, Sr., and Lucy Mack Smith. He was born on 11

*Alvin Smith, oldest son of Joseph Smith, Sr., supported his brother Joseph*

February 1798, nearly seven years before Joseph Smith, Jr. He died on 17 November 1823, three months before his twenty-fifth birthday. His mother recorded that "Alvin manifested, if such could be the case, greater zeal and anxiety in regard to the Record that had been shown to Joseph [the Book of Mormon plates], than any of the rest of the family" (Smith, *History of Joseph Smith,* p. 89).

The Prophet Joseph Smith had great love and respect for Alvin. Upon learning of the necessity of baptism and other priesthood ordinances for exaltation, Joseph was concerned for the eternal welfare of Alvin. This revelation was a great source of joy and consolation to Joseph as he learned of God's love and mercy in providing for the salvation of all of his children. The Lord has provided the means for Alvin Smith and others who would have received the gospel with all their hearts if they had been permitted to tarry to enjoy a fulness of his blessings in the eternal worlds (see D&C 137:7).

### D&C 137:5. Salvation of Joseph Smith, Sr., and Lucy Mack Smith

The Prophet Joseph Smith saw in vision both his father and mother in the celestial kingdom. This, of course, was a vision of a future event, since they had not yet passed to the next life. The Prophet's father, in fact, was in the room with him at the time of the vision (see Historical Background for D&C 137).

### D&C 137:7-9. Upon What Basis Will All Mankind Be Judged?

The true desire of an individual's heart is the key to his future. For one who has received the laws of God, obedience to these laws demonstrates his true desires. For one who does not have these laws, the desires of his heart determine whether or not he will receive the gospel when given the opportunity, whether in this life or the next. In either case, the desires of one's heart determine how one responds to the gospel and thus are the just and right basis upon which one will be judged. All whose hearts are right will receive and live the gospel whenever they have the opportunity and will be "heirs of the celestial kingdom of God" (D&C 137:7). Vicarious ordinance work is performed in the temple for those such as Alvin Smith who did not have the opportunity to receive the ordinances of the gospel in mortality. The means of salvation is provided for all of God's children (see Alma 41:3-15).

### D&C 137:10. "All Children Who Die Before They Arrive at the Years of Accountability Are Saved in the Celestial Kingdom"

Following are some frequently asked questions concerning the status of children who die before the age of accountability.

*Are they automatically saved?* Elder Bruce R. McConkie answered: "To this question the answer is a thunderous *yes,* which echoes and re-echoes from one end of heaven to the other. Jesus taught it to his disciples. Mormon said it over and over again. Many of the prophets have spoken about it, and it is implicit in the whole plan of salvation. If it were not so the redemption would not be infinite in its application. And so, as we would expect, Joseph Smith's Vision of the Celestial Kingdom contains this statement: 'And I also beheld that all children who die before they arrive at the years of accountability are saved in the celestial kingdom of heaven.' (D&C 137:10)

"It is sometimes asked if this applies to children of all races, and of course the answer is that when the revelation says all children it means all children. There is no restriction as to race, kindred, or tongue. Little children are little children and they are all alive in Christ, and all are saved by him, through and because of the atonement. . . .

"They are saved through the atonement and because they are free from sin. They come from God in purity; no sin or taint attaches to them in this life; and they return in purity to their Maker. Accountable persons must become pure through repentance and baptism and obedience. Those who are not accountable for sins never fall spiritually and need not be redeemed from a spiritual fall which they never experienced. Hence the expression that little children are alive in Christ. . . .

"Truly it is one of the sweetest and most soul-satisfying doctrines of the gospel! It is also one of the great evidences of the divine mission of the Prophet Joseph Smith. In his day the fiery evangelists of Christendom were thundering from their pulpits that the road to hell is paved with the skulls of infants not a span long because careless

*"Little children are alive in Christ" (Moroni 8:12)*

parents had neglected to have their offspring baptized. Joseph Smith's statements, as recorded in the Book of Mormon and latter-day revelation, came as a refreshing breeze of pure truth: *little children shall be saved.* Thanks be to God for the revelations of his mind where these innocent and pure souls are concerned!" ("The Salvation of Little Children," *Ensign,* Apr. 1977, pp. 4, 7.)

*Even though little children will be saved, does that mean they will have eternal life?* Elder McConkie explained the terms *salvation* and *eternal life*: "Eternal life is life in the highest heaven of the celestial world; it is exaltation; it is the name of the kind of life God lives. It consists of a continuation of the family unity in eternity. . . . children will be saved in the celestial kingdom. Salvation means eternal life; the two terms are synonymous; they mean exactly the same thing. Joseph Smith said, 'Salvation consists in the glory, authority, majesty, power and dominion which Jehovah possesses and in nothing else.' (*Lectures on Faith,* pp. 63-67.) We have come to speak of this salvation as exaltation—which it is—but all of the scriptures in all of the standard works call it salvation. I know of only three passages in all our scriptures which use salvation to mean something other and less than exaltation." ("Salvation of Little Children," p. 5.)

President Joseph Fielding Smith gave further understanding of the same principle:

"The Lord will grant unto these children the privilege of all the sealing blessings which pertain to the exaltation.

"We were all mature spirits before we were born, and the bodies of little children will grow after the resurrection to the full stature of the spirit, and all the blessings will be theirs through their obedience, the same as if they had lived to maturity and received them on the earth.

"The Lord is just and will not deprive any person of a blessing, simply because he dies before that blessing can be received. It would be manifestly unfair to deprive a little child of the privilege of receiving all the blessings of exaltation in the world to come simply because it died in infancy. . . .

"Children who die in childhood will not be deprived of any blessing. When they grow, after the resurrection, to the full maturity of the spirit, they will be entitled to all the blessings which they would have been entitled to had they been privileged to tarry here and receive them." (*Doctrines of Salvation,* 2:54; see also Mosiah 15:25.)

*Why do some children die and others live? Are those who die better off than those who remain in mortality?* Elder McConkie answered these questions in clear and understandable words.

"We may rest assured that all things are controlled and governed by Him whose spirit children we are. He knows the end from the beginning, and he provides for each of us the testings and trials which he knows we need. President Joseph Fielding Smith once told me that we must assume that the Lord knows and arranges beforehand who shall be taken in infancy and who shall remain on earth to undergo whatever tests are needed in their cases. This accords with Joseph Smith's statement: 'The Lord takes many away, even in infancy, that they may escape the envy of man, and the sorrows and evils of this present world; they were too pure, too lovely, to live on earth.' (*Teachings,* pp. 196-97.) It is implicit in the whole scheme of things that those of us who have arrived at the years of accountability need the tests and trials to which we are subject and that our problem is to overcome the world and attain that spotless and pure state which little children already possess." ("Salvation of Little Children," p. 6.)

*Will children who die before the years of accountability ever be tested in the way that other mortals are tested?* President Joseph Fielding Smith said no: "Satan cannot tempt little children in this life, nor in the spirit world, nor after their resurrection. Little children who die before reaching the years of accountability will not be tempted." (*Doctrines of Salvation,* 2:57; see also D&C 29:47; 45:58.)

*What will be the status of children in the Resurrection?* President Joseph F. Smith explained the Latter-day Saint belief: "Joseph Smith taught the doctrine that the infant child that was laid away in death would come up in the resurrection as a child; and, pointing to the mother of a lifeless child, he said to her: 'You will have the joy, the pleasure, and satisfaction of nurturing this child, after its resurrection, until it reaches the full stature of its spirit.' There is restitution, there is growth, there is development, after the resurrection from death. I love this truth. It speaks volumes of happiness, of joy and gratitude to my soul. Thank the Lord he has revealed these principles to us." (*Gospel Doctrine,* pp. 455-56.)

# Vision of the Redemption of the Dead

Section 138

## Historical Background

President Joseph F. Smith was quite ill during the last six months of his life and spent much of his time confined to his room. His son, Elder Joseph Fielding Smith, spent many days with him taking dictation, tending to chores for him, and taking him for rides (see Smith and Stewart, *Life of Joseph Fielding Smith,* p. 200). Though he was ill, he was very much in communion with the Lord. At the October conference of 1918, six weeks before his death, he said:

"As most of you, I suppose, are aware, I have been undergoing a siege of very serious illness for the last five months. It would be impossible for me, on this occasion, to occupy sufficient time to express the desires of my heart and my feelings, as I would desire to express them to you, but I felt that it was my duty, if possible, to be present. . . .

". . . Although somewhat weakened in body, my mind is clear with reference to my duty, and with reference to the duties and responsibilities that rest upon the Latter-day Saints; and I am ever anxious for the progress of the work of the Lord, for the prosperity of the people of the Church of Jesus Christ of Latter-day Saints throughout the world. . . .

"I will not, I dare not, attempt to enter upon many things that are resting upon my mind this morning, and I shall postpone until some future time, the Lord being willing, my attempt to tell you some of the things that are in my mind, and that dwell in my heart. I have not lived alone these five months. I have dwelt in the spirit of prayer, of supplication, of faith and of determination; and I have had my communication with the Spirit of the Lord continuously." (In Conference Report, Oct. 1918, p. 2.)

Two weeks after the general conference Elder Joseph Fielding Smith wrote down the vision as his father dictated it to him (see Smith and Stewart, *Life of Joseph Fielding Smith,* p. 201). After it was endorsed by the counselors in the First Presidency and by the Quorum of the Twelve, it was published in the *Improvement Era* (Dec. 1918, pp. 166-70).

During April conference of 1976 it was accepted as scripture and approved for publication in the Pearl of Great Price. In June 1979 the First Presidency announced that it would become section 138 of the Doctrine and Covenants. (See Historical Background for D&C 137.)

## Notes and Commentary

**D&C 138:1-11. Pondering the Scriptures: Frequently a Prerequisite to Revelation**

The prophet Nephi was pondering the inspired teachings of his father Lehi when he received the great revelation recorded in 1 Nephi 11-14. Joseph Smith and Sidney Rigdon were pondering a passage from the Gospel of John when they received the transcendant vision recorded in Doctrine and Covenants 76 (see D&C 76:15-19). In his counsel to Book of Mormon readers, Moroni taught that each individual could obtain personal revelation of its truthfulness by reading it, remembering God's mercy to his children, pondering these things in their hearts, and then asking the Lord in prayer for a personal witness (see Moroni 10:3-5).

*John Wells, formerly a member of the Presiding Bishopric*

Revelations come to those who are prepared spiritually and mentally. Elder Harold B. Lee said of the need for such preparation:

"A few weeks ago, President McKay related to the Twelve an interesting experience, and I asked him yesterday if I might repeat it to you this morning. He said it is a great thing to be responsive to the whisperings of the Spirit, and we know that when these whisperings come it is a gift and our privilege to have them. They come when we are relaxed and not under pressure of appointments. (I want you to mark that.) The President then took occasion to relate an experience in the life of Bishop John Wells, former member of the Presiding Bishopric. A son of Bishop Wells was killed in Emigration Canyon on a railroad track. Brother John Wells was a great detail man and prepared many of the reports we are following up now. His boy was run over by a freight train. Sister Wells was inconsolable. She mourned during the three days prior to the funeral, received no comfort at the funeral, and was in a rather serious state of mind. One day soon after the funeral services while she was lying on her bed relaxed, still mourning, she says that her son appeared to her and said, 'Mother, do not mourn, do not cry. I am all right.' He told her that she did not understand how the accident happened and explained that he had given the signal to the engineer to move on, and then made the usual effort to catch the railing on the freight train; but as he attempted to do so his foot caught on a root and he failed to catch the hand rail, and his body fell under the train. It was clearly an accident. Now listen! He said that as soon as he realized that he was in another environment he tried to see his father, *but he couldn't reach him. His father was so busy with the duties in his office he could not respond to his call.* Therefore, he had come to his mother. He said to her, 'You tell father that all is well with me, and I want you not to mourn any more.'

"Then the President made the statement that the point he had in mind was that when we are relaxed in a private room we are more susceptible to those things; and that so far as he was concerned, his best thoughts come after he gets up in the morning and is relaxed and thinking about the duties of the day; that impressions come more clearly, as if it were to hear a voice. Those impressions are right. If we are worried about something and upset in our feelings, the inspiration does not come. If we so live that our minds are free from worry and our conscience is clear and our feelings are right toward one another, the operation of the spirit of the Lord upon our spirit is as real as when we pick up the telephone." (*Prayer* [address delivered to seminary and institute faculty], Brigham Young University [Provo, 6 July 1956], pp. 14-16.)

Studying and pondering the scriptures prepares one's mind and heart to receive the things of the Spirit. Under those conditions one can be taught from on high.

**D&C 138:7-10. The Writings of Peter**

Changes were made by the Prophet Joseph Smith in his inspired translation of 1 Peter 3:18-20 and

1 Peter 4:6 as a result of his pondering and meditation.

### D&C 138:11. What Did President Smith Mean When He Said, "The Eyes of My Understanding Were Opened"?

See Notes and Commentary for Doctrine and Covenants 137:1.

### D&C 138:12-17. Will Many People Be Saved in the Celestial Kingdom?

In his vision President Smith saw "an innumerable company" (D&C 138:12) of spirits who "had departed the mortal life, firm in the hope of a glorious resurrection" (vs. 14). These were celestial heirs who had lived on the earth from the time of Adam until Christ came. Great multitudes of people who have lived since then and those who will yet enter mortality will also become inheritors of celestial glory. Of the total number of people who come to earth, those who earn celestial glory may be a relatively small percentage, but in numbers there will be millions who inherit the glory of the sun. In addition to those who qualify for this kingdom by virtue of their faithfulness in this life or in the spirit world, there will be the millions of children who died before they reached the age of accountability. (See Notes and Commentary for D&C 137:10.)

President Spencer W. Kimball said in a general priesthood meeting about the great potential for exaltation:

"Brethren, 225,000 of you are here tonight. I suppose 225,000 of you may become gods. There seems to be plenty of space out there in the universe. And the Lord has proved that he knows how to do it. I think he could make, or probably have us help make, worlds for all of us, for every one of us 225,000.

"Just think of the possibilities, the potential. Every little boy that has just been born becomes an heir to this glorious, glorious program. When he is grown, he meets a lovely woman; they are married in the holy temple. They live all the commandments of the Lord. They keep themselves clean. And then they become sons of God, and they go forward with their great program—they go beyond the angels, beyond the angels and the gods that are waiting there. They go to their exaltation." (In Conference Report, Oct. 1975, p. 120; or *Ensign*, Nov. 1975, p. 80; see also Alma 13:10-12.)

### D&C 138:14-17. Can a Person Know Before He Dies That He Will Be Exalted?

One can have the assurance in this life of eventually obtaining eternal life, though one is not yet perfect. Elder Bruce R. McConkie said:

"All the faithful Saints, all of those who have endured to the end, depart this life with the absolute guarantee of eternal life.

"There is no equivocation, no doubt, no uncertainty in our minds. Those who have been true and faithful in this life will not fall by the wayside in the life to come. If they keep their covenants here and now and depart this life firm and true in the testimony of our blessed Lord, they shall come forth with an inheritance of eternal life.

"We do not mean to say that those who die in the Lord, and who are true and faithful in this life, must be perfect in all things when they go into the next sphere of existence. There was only one perfect man—the Lord Jesus whose Father was God.

"There have been many righteous souls who have attained relative degrees of perfection, and there have been great hosts of faithful people who have kept the faith, and lived the law, and departed this life with the full assurance of an eventual inheritance of eternal life.

"There are so many things they will do and must do, even beyond the grave, to merit the fulness of the Father's kingdom in that final glorious day when the great King shall say unto them 'Come, ye blessed of my Father, inherit the kingdom prepared for you from the foundation of the world.' (Matt. 25:34.)

"But what we are saying is that when the saints of God chart a course of righteousness, when they gain sure testimonies of the truth and divinity of the Lord's work, when they keep the commandments, when they overcome the world, when they put first in their lives the things of God's kingdom: when they do all these things, and then depart this life—though they have not yet become perfect—they shall nonetheless gain eternal life in our Father's kingdom; and eventually they shall be perfect as God their Father and Christ His Son are perfect." (In Conference Report, Oct. 1976, pp. 158-59; or *Ensign*, Nov. 1976, p. 107; see also Notes and Commentary on D&C 76:53; 131:5; 132:7.)

### D&C 138:15-19, 50. How Is the Absence of the Spirit from the Body a Bondage? Why Is Redemption from Death Necessary for a Fulness of Joy?

The Prophet Joseph Smith taught about the importance of mortal bodies:

"We came to this earth that we might have a body and present it pure before God in the celestial kingdom. The great principle of happiness consists of having a body. The devil has no body, and herein is his punishment. He is pleased when he can obtain the tabernacle of man, and when cast out by the Savior he asked to go into the herd of swine, showing that he would prefer a swine's body to having none.

"All beings who have bodies have power over those who have not." (*Teachings*, p. 181.)

Since disembodied spirits cannot obtain a fulness of joy until they are resurrected (see D&C 93:33-34), they consider their sojourn in the world of spirits, awaiting the reunion of body and spirit, a bondage. Elder Bruce R. McConkie said that "obtaining exaltation consists in gaining a fulness of joy; it is to enter into the joy of the Lord. (D. & C. 51:19.) . . . A fulness of joy is found only among resurrected exalted beings. (D. & C. 93:33.)" (*Mormon Doctrine*, p. 397.)

Those who obtain their exaltation will have the privilege of begetting spirit offspring in the eternities (see D&C 131:1-4; 132:19-20). This eternal increase is possible only through having resurrected, glorified bodies. Elder Melvin J. Ballard taught:

"Those who are denied endless increase cannot be what God is because that, in connection with other things, makes Him God. . . .

" . . . through the righteousness and faithfulness of men and women who keep the commandments of God they will come forth with celestial bodies, fitted and prepared to enter into their great, high and eternal glory in the celestial kingdom of God; and unto them, through their preparation, there will come spirit children. . . .

" . . . When the power of endless increase shall come to us, and our offspring grow and multiply through ages that shall come, they will be in due time, as we have been, provided with an earth like this wherein they too may obtain earthly bodies and pass through all the experiences through which we have passed. . . . We shall stand in our relationship to them as God our Eternal Father does to us, and thereby this is the most glorious and wonderful privilege that ever will come to any of the sons and daughters of God." (*Melvin J. Ballard,* pp. 211-12.)

Those in such a condition will certainly have a fulness of joy. Such was the anticipated reward of those who were seen by President Smith in paradise awaiting the advent of the Son of God, who would break the bands of death and provide for them resurrection and a fulness of joy in God's kingdom.

**D&C 138:27-37, 57. Missionary Work in the Spirit World**

President Wilford Woodruff said that in the work of the ministry in the spirit world "every Apostle, every Seventy, every Elder, etc., who has died in the faith, as soon as he passes to the other side of the veil, enters into the work of the ministry, and there is a thousand times more to preach to there than there is here. . . . They have work on the other side of the veil; and they want men, and they call them." (In *Journal of Discourses,* 22:334.)

In a discourse given at the funeral services of Mary A. Freeze, President Joseph F. Smith said that those "who have passed away in this dispensation . . . are preaching that same gospel that they lived and preached here, to those who are in darkness in the spirit world and who had not had the privilege before they went. The gospel must be preached to them. We are not perfect without them—they cannot be perfect without us.

"Now, among all these millions of spirits that have lived on the earth and have passed away, from generation to generation, since the beginning of the world, without knowledge of the gospel—among them you may count that at least one-half are women. Who is going to preach the gospel to the women? Who is going to carry the testimony of Jesus Christ to the hearts of the women who have passed away without a knowledge of the gospel? Well, to my mind it is a simple thing. These good sisters who have been set apart, ordained to the work, called to it, authorized by the authority of the Holy Priesthood to minister for their sex, in the House of God for the living and for the dead, will be fully authorized and empowered to preach the gospel and minister to the women while the Elders and Prophets are preaching it to the men. . . . Those who are authorized to preach the gospel here and are appointed here to do that work will not be idle after they have passed away, but will continue to exercise the rights that they obtain here under the Priesthood of the Son of God to minister for the salvation of those who have died without a knowledge of the truth." (*Gospel Doctrine,* pp. 460-61.)

**D&C 138:31. "Messengers Went Forth to Declare the Acceptable Day of the Lord and Proclaim Liberty to the Captives"**

This phrase comes from Isaiah's writings (see Isaiah 61:2) and was used by Jesus when he introduced himself as the Messiah in his home town of Nazareth. Elder Bruce R. McConkie indicated that the phrase "the acceptable year of the Lord" had reference to "the proper, designated, approved, appointed, or accepted time, in the divine order of things, for a particular work to be done," and that Isaiah's prophecy that Christ would do this work, "to proclaim liberty to the captives, and the opening of the prison to them that are bound" (Isaiah 61:1), referred "not to the freeing of mortal men from any imprisonment, but to the ministry of freedom and pardon which was prepared for the departed dead. Jesus' mission was not alone to those then living; he was also to carry the gospel, the glad tidings of salvation, to the spirits in prison. Those who had been 'gathered together, as prisoners are gathered in the pit,' those who had been 'shut up in the prison,' were, 'after many days,' to be visited by him who held the key for their release. (Isa. 24:22.)" (*Doctrinal New Testament Commentary,* 1:161.) President Smith saw that time, the acceptable year of the Lord, in his vision.

**D&C 138:32. What Is the Status of Those Who Receive the Gospel in the Spirit World?**

Notes and Commentary on Doctrine and Covenants 137:7-9 discusses the fate of those who die in their sins without a knowledge of the truth. Notes and Commentary on Doctrine and Covenants 76:72-74 discusses the fate of those who die in their sins, having rejected the prophets.

**D&C 138:33-34, 58-59. Vicarious Ordinance Work Alone Does Not Guarantee Salvation for Those in the Spirit World**

The principles of faith and repentance are taught in the spirit world. Departed spirits are also taught "all other principles of the gospel" that they need "*in order to qualify themselves*" to be judged after the manner of men in the flesh (D&C 138:34; emphasis added). They will be judged according to the heed and diligence they give to God's word. If they did not have the opportunity to receive the gospel in mortality, and if by their agency they repent and conform to God's laws when taught them in the

*A baptismal font for vicarious work for the dead*

spirit world, then they will receive benefit from the vicarious ordinances performed by mortals in their behalf. Otherwise, vicarious ordinances are of no benefit to them.

President Joseph Fielding Smith said: "If a person is in every way worthy of the blessings and was denied them while living, then any time after death the ordinances may be performed. If the person had every opportunity to receive these blessings in person and refused, or through procrastination and lack of faith did not receive them, then he is not entitled to them, and it is doubtful if the work for him will be valid if done within one week or 1,000 years. The Lord has declared that it is he who endures to the end that shall be saved, and he who rejects or neglects these blessings until death, when he has had the opportunity, is not worthy of them." (*Doctrines of Salvation,* 2:179; see also Notes and Commentary on D&C 76:72-74.)

### D&C 138:47. What Is Meant by the Phrase "Plant in the Hearts of the Children the Promises Made to Their Fathers"?

President Joseph Fielding Smith identified the "promises made to the fathers" as "the promise of the Lord made through Enoch, Isaiah, and the prophets, to the nations of the earth, that the time should come when the dead should be redeemed. And the turning of the hearts of the children is fulfilled in the performing of the vicarious temple work and in the preparation of their genealogies." (*Doctrines of Salvation,* 2:154.)

In the premortal life promises were made about the salvation of those who would not have the blessings of the gospel in mortality. President Kimball said that in the premortal existence "you and I made a solemn commitment, made an oath that we would do all things whatsoever the Lord our God shall command us" (*Church News,* 18 Jan. 1975, p. 3). Certainly the Saints have been commanded to seek after their dead and perform ordinances for them (see Smith, *Teachings,* p. 356; D&C 128:15).

### D&C 138:48. Why Will the Earth Be "Smitten with a Curse and Utterly Wasted" at Christ's Coming if the Redemption of the Dead Is Not Accomplished?

See Notes and Commentary for Doctrine and Covenants 128:14-18.

### D&C 138:51. The Lord Gave the Righteous Saints Power to Come Forth in the Resurrection

In a general conference of the Church, President Spencer W. Kimball cited President Brigham Young's teaching about the power of resurrection:

"Brigham Young, the second president of this dispensation, said: 'It is supposed by this people that we have all the ordinances in our possession for life and salvation, and exaltation, and that we are administering in those ordinances. This is not the case. We are in possession of all the ordinances that can be administered in the flesh; but there are other ordinances and administrations that must be administered beyond this world. I know you would like to ask what they are. I will mention one. We have not, neither can we receive here, the ordinance and keys of resurrection.' (*Journal of Discourses,* 15:137.)

"Do we have the keys of resurrection? Could you return to the earth as ones who would never again die—[could] your own parents, your grandparents, your ancestors? I buried my mother when I was eleven, my father when I was in my early twenties. I have missed my parents much. If I had the power of resurrection as did the Savior of the world, I would have been tempted to try to have kept them longer. I have been called to speak in numerous funerals for people whom I have known, people whom I have loved, and people whom I have served and helped in a limited way. We do not know of anyone who can resurrect the dead as did Jesus Christ when he came back to mortality.

" '[The keys] will be given to those who have passed off this stage of action and have received their bodies again. . . . They will be ordained, by those who hold the keys of the resurrection, to go forth and resurrect the Saints, just as we receive the ordinance of baptism then receive the keys of authority to baptize others for the remission of their sins. This is one of the ordinances we can not receive here [on the earth], and there are many more.' (JD, 15:137.)" (In Conference Report, Apr. 1977, p. 69; or *Ensign,* May 1977, p. 49.)

President Brigham Young also taught that "some person holding the keys of the resurrection, having previously passed through that ordeal, will be delegated to resurrect our bodies" (*Journal of Discourses,* 9:139).

### D&C 138:52. "And Continue Thenceforth Their Labor"

The Lord said, "This is my *work* and my glory—to bring to pass the immortality and eternal life of man" (Moses 1:39; emphasis added). Those who are crowned with immortality and eternal life will continue their labor in the eternal worlds. Man's goal is to become as God is, and the Lord has said *"there is no end to my works"* (Moses 1:38; emphasis added). To enter into the "rest" of the Lord means to enter into a fulness of God's glory (see D&C 84:24) where one will rest from the cares and sorrows of mortality. It does not, however, mean that one will cease to work.

**D&C 138:53-56. The Great Leaders of the Lord's Latter-day Kingdom Were Held in Reserve to Come Forth in the Final Dispensation**

The prophet Abraham was told that he was one of the noble and great spirits who was ordained in the premortal life to be a leader in God's kingdom while in mortality (see Abraham 3:23). President Joseph F. Smith was shown that many choice servants of this dispensation were also among those noble spirits. The Lord held them in the spirit world where they were taught and prepared to come forth and lay the foundations of his great latter-day work. The Prophet Joseph Smith once said that "every man who has a calling to minister to the inhabitants of the world was ordained to that very purpose in the Grand Council of heaven before this world was" (*Teachings,* p. 365).

# Manifesto

# Official Declaration 1

## Historical Background

The first legislation against the practice of plural marriage came ten years after the doctrine had been officially announced on 29 August 1852 by Elder Orson Pratt (see Historical Background for D&C 132). Stephen Harding, governor of the Territory of Utah, was able to get Justin R. Morrill of Vermont to introduce a bill into Congress. The bill was signed into law 8 July 1862 by President Abraham Lincoln. The Anti-Polygamy Act of 1862 "defined plural marriage as bigamy, and made the contracting of such a marriage punishable by a fine of five hundred dollars and imprisonment for a term of five years" (Smith, *Essentials in Church History,* p. 432). This bill was the first of a flood of anti-Mormon legislation introduced during the next twenty-five years, most of which never passed (see Roberts, *Comprehensive History of the Church,* 5:433-41, 610-11).

In 1874 the Church decided to sponsor a case to test the validity of the law of 1862. George C. Bates, the United States Attorney for Utah, and George Q. Cannon were largely responsible for this idea. The leaders of the Church strongly believed that the Supreme Court would rule the law unconstitutional since it infringed on the freedom of religion provisions of the Constitution. George Reynolds was asked by the First Presidency to serve as the test case, and he furnished the evidence necessary to convict himself. On 5 May 1879 the Supreme Court of the United States ruled against Reynolds. They concluded that although religious liberty was protected by the First Amendment, the amendment did not give one the right to commit immoral or criminal acts sanctioned by religious doctrine.

Once the constitutionality of the act of 1862 had been upheld by the highest court in the land, persecution of those who practiced plural marriage became more severe. In March 1882 Congress passed the Edmunds Bill. This law disenfranchised those who practiced plural marriage, making it illegal for them to hold any office or place of public trust (see Smith, *Essentials in Church History,* pp. 482-83). Five years later, in March 1887, Congress passed the Edmunds-Tucker Law. This law disincorporated the Church, dissolved the Perpetual Emigration Fund, gave the property of the Church to the government for the benefit of the common schools of Utah, and put a stop to female suffrage.

During these trying times President John Taylor died in hiding on 25 July 1887, at Kaysville, Utah, and the mantle of leadership for the Church fell upon Wilford Woodruff.

For at least a year prior to the issuance of the Manifesto in 1890, President Wilford Woodruff had forbidden plural marriages to be performed in the Endowment House (see Clark, *Messages of the First Presidency,* 3:193). This ban, however, was not publicized.

Not letting the enemies of the Church know that the contracting of new plural marriages had been discontinued caused some concern to many Saints, as President George Q. Cannon explained: "President Woodruff and others of us have been appealed to hundreds of times I might say. I can say for myself, that I have been appealed to many scores of times to get out something and to announce something. Some of our leading brethren have said: 'Inasmuch as we have ceased to give permission for plural marriages to be solemnized, why cannot we have the benefit of that? Why cannot we tell the world it so as to have the benefit of it? Our enemies are alleging constantly that we still practice this in secret, and that we are dishonest and guilty of evasion. Now, if we have really put a stop to granting permission to men to take more wives than one, why should not the world know it and we have the advantage of it?' These remarks have been made to us repeatedly. But at no time has the Spirit seemed to indicate that this should be done. We have waited for the Lord to move in the matter." (In *Millennial Star,* 24 Nov. 1890, p. 737.)

On 24 September 1890 President Wilford Woodruff met with the Quorum of the Twelve Apostles and his two counselors "upon an important subject." On the twenty-fifth President Woodruff recorded: "I have arrived at a point in the history of my life as the president of the Church of Jesus Christ of Latter-day Saints where I am under the necessity of acting for the temporal salvation of the church. The United States government has taken a stand and passed laws to destroy the Latter-day Saints on the subject of polygamy, or patriarchal order of marriage; and after praying to the Lord and feeling inspired, I have issued the following proclamation which is sustained by my counselors and the twelve apostles. [The Manifesto follows.]" (In Clark, *Messages of the First Presidency,* 3:192.)

General conference convened on 4 October 1890, and on the third day, 6 October, Lorenzo Snow, President of the Quorum of the Twelve, presented the Manifesto to the body of the Church. It was unanimously accepted.

Some, however, claimed that President Woodruff gave in to pressure and that the Lord had not really revealed that plural marriage was to cease. The fact that this declaration did not specifically mention revelation as the reason for stopping the practice seemed to fuel the criticism. A year later at a quarterly conference held at Brigham City, Utah, President Woodruff made it clear why he had made the decision to stop the practice of plural marriage:

"I have had some revelations of late, and very important ones to me, and I will tell you what the Lord has said to me. Let me bring your minds to

The People Accept the Manifesto!

THE VOTE UNANIMOUS

President Cannon Gives the Reasons For Its Issuance.

PRESIDENT WOODRUFF SPEAKS.

*The Manifesto ended the practice of plural marriage*

what is termed the manifesto. The Lord has told me by revelation that there are many members of the church thoughout Zion who are sorely tried in their hearts because of that manifesto, and also because of the testimony of the Presidency of this Church and the apostles before the master in chancery. Since I received that revelation I have heard of many who are tried in these things, though I had not heard of any before that particularly. Now, the Lord has commanded me to do one thing, and I fulfilled that commandment at the conference at Brigham City last Sunday, and I will do the same here today. The Lord has told me to ask the Latter-day Saints a question, and he also told me that if they would listen to what I said to them and answer the question put to them by the Spirit and power of God, they would all answer alike, and they would all believe alike with regard to this matter.

"The question is this: Which is the wisest course for the Latter-day Saints to pursue—to continue to attempt to practice plural marriage, with the laws of the nation against it and the opposition of sixty millions of people, and at the cost of the confiscation and loss of all the temples, and the stopping of all the ordinances therein, both for the living and the dead, and the imprisonment of the First Presidency and Twelve and the heads of families in the Church, and the confiscation of personal property of the people (all of which of themselves would stop the practice); or, after doing and suffering what we have through our adherence to this principle to cease the practice and submit to the law, and through doing so leave the prophets, apostles and fathers at home, so that they can instruct the people and attend to the duties of the Church, and also leave the temples in the hands of the Saints, so that they can attend to the ordinances of the gospel, both for the living and the dead?

"The Lord showed me by vision and revelation exactly what would take place if we did not stop this practice. If we had not stopped it, you would have had no use for Brother Merrill, for Brother Edlefsen, for Brother Roskelley, for Brother Leishman, or for any of the men in this temple at Logan; for all ordinances would be stopped throughout the land of Zion. Confusion would reign throughout Israel, and many men would be made prisoners. This trouble would have come upon the whole Church, and we should have been compelled to stop the practice. Now, the question is, whether it should be stopped in this manner, or in the way the Lord has manifested to us, and leave our prophets and apostles and fathers free men, and the temples in the hands of the people, so that the dead may be redeemed? . . .

"I saw exactly what would come to pass if there was not something done. I have had this spirit upon me for a long time. But I want to say this: I should have let all the temples go out of our hands; I should have gone to prison myself, and let every other man go there, had not the God of heaven commanded me to do what I did do; and when the hour came that I was commanded to do that, it was all clear to me. I went before the Lord, and I wrote what the Lord told me to write. I laid it before my brethren—such strong men as Brother George Q. Cannon, Brother Joseph F. Smith, and the Twelve Apostles. I might as well undertake to turn an army with banners out of its course as to turn them out of a course that they considered to be right. These men agreed with me, and ten thousand Latter-day Saints also agreed with me. . . . Why? Because they were moved upon by the Spirit of God and by the revelations of Jesus Christ to do it." (*Discourses of Wilford Woodruff*, pp. 214-16.)

Some in the Church continued to practice plural marriage outside the borders of the United States. Many moved to Mexico, for example, so they would not have to terminate their marriages. Some of these rationalized that new plural marriages could be performed outside of the United States. Finally, on 8 January 1900, President Lorenzo Snow, who had succeeded President Woodruff, stated: "The Church has positively abandoned the practice of polygamy, or the solemnization of plural marriages in this and every other state, and that no member or officer thereof has any authority whatever to perform a plural marriage or enter into such a relation" (in "Slanders Are Refuted by First Presidency," *Millennial Star*, 4 May 1911, p. 275).

Others who refused to follow the commandment of the Lord claimed that the Manifesto was issued only for good public relations and that in secret the Church leaders still performed marriages and supported the practice. To put down such heretical lies, President Joseph F. Smith, successor to President Lorenzo Snow, made the following official declaration in general conference:

"Now I am going to present a matter to you that is unusual and I do it because of a conviction which I feel that it is a proper thing for me to do. I have taken the liberty of having written down what I wish to present, in order that I may say to you the exact words which I would like to have conveyed to your ears, that I may not be misunderstood or misquoted. I present this to the conference for your action:

"Inasmuch as there are numerous reports in circulation that plural marriages have been entered into contrary to the official declaration of President Woodruff, of September 26, 1890, commonly called the Manifesto, which was issued by President Woodruff and adopted by the Church at its general conference, October 6, 1890, which forbade any marriages violative of the law of the land; I, Joseph F. Smith, President of the Church of Jesus Christ of Latter-day Saints, hereby affirm and declare that no such marriages have been solemnized with the sanction, consent or knowledge of the Church of Jesus Christ of Latter-day Saints, and

"I hereby announce that all such marriages are prohibited, and if any officer or member of the Church shall assume to solemnize or enter into any such marriage he will be deemed in transgression against the Church and will be liable to be dealt with, according to the rules and regulations thereof, and excommunicated therefrom." (In Conference Report, Apr. 1904, p. 75.)

*Wilford Woodruff gave the Manifesto after receiving the will of the Lord by revelation*

Seven years later, President Joseph F. Smith again emphasized the Church's stand: "And another thing, as we have announced in previous conferences—as it was announced by President Woodruff, as it was announced by President Snow, and as it was reannounced by me and my brethren, and confirmed by the Church of Jesus Christ of Latter-day Saints, plural marriages have ceased in the Church. There isn't a man today in this Church, or anywhere else, outside of it who has authority to solemnize a plural marriage—not one! There is no man or woman in the Church of Jesus Christ of Latter-day Saints who is authorized to contract a plural marriage. It is not permitted, and we have been endeavoring to the utmost of our ability to prevent men from being led by some designing person into an unfortunate condition that is forbidden by the conferences, and by the voice of the Church, a condition that has to some extent at least, brought reproach upon the people." (In Conference Report, Apr. 1911, p. 8.)

Since then every President of the Church has reiterated this stand and declared the doctrine of the Church to be against the practice of plural marriage.

# "Every Faithful, Worthy Man"

## Official Declaration 2

### Historical Background

From the dispensation of Adam until the dispensation of the fulness of times, there has been a group of people who have not been allowed to hold the priesthood of God. The scriptural basis for this policy is Abraham 1:21-27. The full reason for the denial has been kept hidden by the Lord, and one is left to assume that he will make it known in his own due time.

On 1 June 1978 the Savior revealed to President Spencer W. Kimball that the ban on this lineage pertaining to the rights of the priesthood was lifted. Elder Bruce R. McConkie described the special supplication that brought the revelation:

"On the first day of June in this year, 1978, the First Presidency and the Twelve, after full discussion of the proposition and all the premises and principles that are involved, importuned the Lord for a revelation. President Kimball was mouth, and he prayed with great faith and great fervor; this was one of those occasions when an inspired prayer was offered. You know the Doctrine and Covenants statement, that if we pray by the power of the Spirit we will receive answers to our prayers and it will be given us what we shall ask (D&C 50:30). It was given President Kimball what he should ask. He prayed by the power of the Spirit, and there was perfect unity, total and complete harmony, between the Presidency and the Twelve on the issue involved.

"And when President Kimball finished his prayer, the Lord gave a revelation by the power of the Holy Ghost. . . .

"On this occasion, because of the importuning and the faith, and because the hour and the time had arrived, the Lord in his providences poured out the Holy Ghost upon the First Presidency and the Twelve in a miraculous and marvelous manner, beyond anything that any then present had ever experienced. The revelation came to the President of the Church; it also came to each individual present. There were ten members of the Council of the Twelve and three of the First Presidency there assembled. The result was that President Kimball knew, and each one of us knew, independent of any other person, by direct and personal revelation to us, that the time had now come to extend the gospel and all its blessings and all its obligations, including the priesthood and the blessings of the house of the Lord, to those of every nation, culture, and race, including the black race. There was no question whatsoever as to what happened or as to the word and message that came.

"The revelation came to the President of the Church and, in harmony with Church government, was announced by him; the announcement was made eight days later over the signature of the First Presidency. But in this instance, in addition to the revelation coming to the man who would announce it to the Church and to the world, and who was sustained as the mouthpiece of God on earth, the revelation came to every member of the body that I have named. They all knew it in the temple.

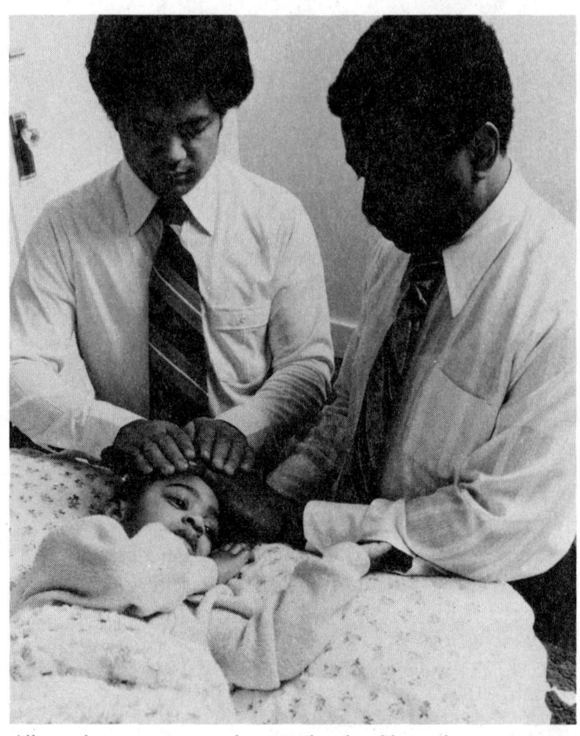

*All worthy men may use the priesthood to bless others*

"In my judgment this was done by the Lord in this way because it was a revelation of such tremendous significance and import; one which would reverse the whole direction of the Church, procedurally and administratively; one which would affect the living and the dead; one which would affect the total relationship that we have with the world; one, I say, of such significance that the Lord wanted independent witnesses who could bear record that the thing had happened." ("All Are Alike unto God," (*Symposium on the Book of Mormon,* p. 2.)

President N. Eldon Tanner, under the direction of President Kimball, presented to the Church on 30 September 1978 the official declaration of the revelation. In that conference it was unanimously supported and upheld by the members of the Church (see Conference Report, Oct. 1978, p. 22).

Elder Bruce R. McConkie explained that this revelation "affects our missionary work and all of our preaching to the world. This affects our genealogical research and all of our temple ordinances. This affects what is going on in the spirit world, because the gospel is preached in the spirit world preparatory to men's receiving vicarious ordinances which make them heirs to salvation and exaltation. This is a revelation of tremendous significance." ("All Are Alike unto God," p. 2.)

God's love for his children is indeed universal, for each is the workmanship of his hands, and he will bless and exalt all who will honor the priesthood and obey his voice.

# The Warning Voice

## Enrichment A

### (A-1) Introduction

In every era when the standard of the gospel of Jesus Christ has been raised, the authorized servants of the Lord have been called to take the message of salvation to those who do not have it and sound the warning voice: a voice of gladness in the saving principles they teach, a voice of eternal truth calling the honest in heart to the family of believers whose hope is in the Redeemer, a voice of warning of sorrow and judgments for those who reject the message. In the latter days the Lord has again called his servants to go to every nation, kindred, tongue, and people to sound the warning trump of God. The divine commission to the Church is unmistakable and when properly accomplished leaves the children of men without excuse. It is not merely the Lord's wish that the warning voice be given the world; it is his divine command.

### (A-2) What Is a Voice of Warning?

Ancient Israel grew to maturity through the adversity of Egyptian bondage and was given the breath of life by the Lord through the mighty Moses. As he led this great army of doubting disciples through forty years of wanderings, an interesting means of communicating with the people was adopted. A trumpet was sounded that could be heard throughout the entire camp (see Leviticus 25:9). This trump was very loud (see Exodus 19:16) and was the alarm that aroused Israel and called her to action both in times of war and danger (see Numbers 10:9; Ezekiel 33:3) and in times of jubilee and celebration (see Leviticus 25:9).

The Lord has used the symbol of the sounding of a trump and the raising of the warning voice to signify his call to repentance, his call to defense against evil and designing men, his call to battle in the war of righteousness against the evil foe. In short, today the warning voice gives the world a clear signal of the restoration of gospel truths. The message of the Doctrine and Covenants is one of jubilee and celebration for the righteous; but it is a terrible trump of warning to the wicked, alerting them to the immediate peril that awaits the unrepentant at the coming of the King of Glory. Indeed, for the righteous it is the voice of gladness announcing the joyous blessings that accompany gospel living and also the near advent of the Prince of Peace. But for those who will not heed, it is a voice of judgment and woe. For one last time the trump warns the camp (in this case, the world) that if they do not repent, not only will they experience spiritual misery and damnation but also the judgments of God will be unleashed on the world.

*Missionaries raise the "voice of warning" (D&C 1:4)*

Does it seem a bit audacious that we in the Church should think that the responsibility for taking the message of salvation to the world—the entire world—rests upon our shoulders?

Does the task seem a bit overwhelming? The membership of the Church in 1980 constituted only slightly more than 1/4 of one percent of the world's population (see *Ensign*, Apr. 1980, p. 15). In other words, only about one person in every thousand is a member of the Church. But you must remember that our task is not to *convert* every person in the world but to give every person in the world a chance to hear the warning voice, to listen to the message of salvation, and to choose for themselves.

Though the task may seem overwhelming at first, the Doctrine and Covenants leaves no doubt that that is exactly what the Lord expects of his Saints. Study the following scriptures and on a separate sheet of paper answer the questions.

*D&C 1:1-4.* To whom is the voice of warning in the last days? Through whom is the voice of warning to come?

The following diagram shows the relationships spoken of in this passage of scripture. What implications does this passage have for you personally?

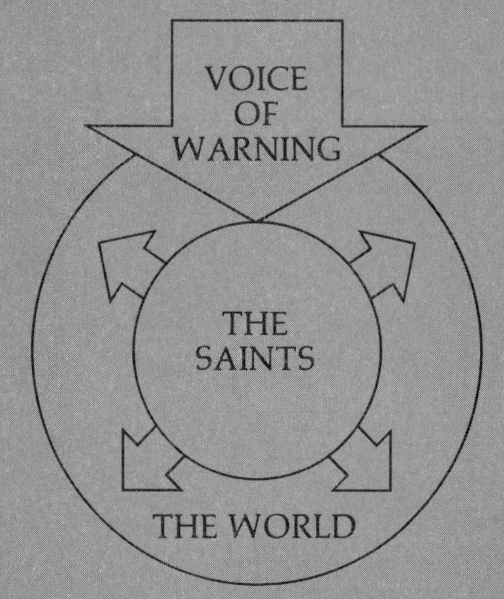


*D&C 1:11-14.* If your home caught fire and your family members were in their beds asleep, unaware of their danger, would you not feel a desperate urgency to warn them? What great spiritual disaster is coming to the inhabitants of the earth? What are your obligations in this case?

*D&C 1:17-18.* What is one of the major reasons for the Restoration? Is Joseph Smith the only person given this responsibility? Who are the "others" spoken of in verse 18?

*D&C 1:34-35.* The Lord says he is willing to make these things known to all men. What means does he use to do so? Why doesn't the Lord just appear on a mountaintop to all men and warn them directly?

*D&C 1:37.* If you seriously accept the commandment to raise the voice of warning, what should you do?

### (A-3) To Whom Is the Voice of Warning Given, and Why?

Before the Savior comes in clouds of glory to claim his own, the warning voice shall be taken to all people "by the mouths of my disciples whom I have chosen in these last days. . . . Wherefore the voice of the Lord is unto the ends of the earth, that all that will hear may hear . . . and the day cometh that they who will not hear the voice of the Lord, neither the voice of his servants, neither give heed to the words of the prophets and apostles, shall be cut off from among the people." (D&C 1:4, 11, 14.) Then the Lord added this powerful reminder:

"What I the Lord have spoken, I have spoken, and I excuse not myself; and though the heavens and the earth pass away, my word shall not pass away, but shall all be fulfilled, whether by mine own voice or by the voice of my servants, it is the same" (D&C 1:38).

The world is confused, and men of all nations run to and fro seeking they know not what while evil forces on every hand entrap and enslave the sons and daughters of God. The Lord knew the great danger to his children and sent forth the warning voice through his authorized servants. One such voice was raised by President Ezra Taft Benson, who, in general conference, charged the leaders of the nations to forsake their evil ways and humble themselves before the God of heaven. He warned that if they and their people fail to repent there will follow terrible judgments and calamities as the wicked reap the whirlwind:

"The voice of warning is to all people by the mouths of his servants. If this voice is not heeded, the angels of destruction will increasingly go forth, and the chastening hand of Almighty God will be felt upon the nations, as decreed, until a full end thereof will be the result. Wars, devastation, and untold suffering will be your lot except you turn unto the Lord in humble repentance. Destruction, even more terrible and far-reaching than attended the last great war, will come with certainty unless rulers and people alike repent and cease their evil and godless ways. God will not be mocked. He will not permit the sins of sexual immorality, secret murderous combinations, the killing of the unborn, and disregard for all his holy commandments and the messages of his servants to go unheeded without grievous punishment for such wickedness. The nations of the world cannot endure in sin. The way of escape is clear. The immutable laws of God remain steadfastly in the heavens above. When men and nations refuse to abide by them, the penalty must follow. They will be wasted away. Sin demands punishment.

"When the voice of warning goes forth it is always attended by testimony. In the declaration issued by the apostles of the Lord Jesus Christ in 1845, this is the testimony which was borne, and we who are the apostles today renew it as our witness." (In Conference Report, Oct. 1975, p. 48; or *Ensign,* Nov. 1975, p. 34.)

The world has not seen a more critical need for the saving truths of the gospel since the days of Noah, so increased numbers of laborers are being called to go to take the message of the Restoration to every people. President Spencer W. Kimball noted the present and future need for the voice of warning to be sounded in every nation: "We have established new missions covering almost all of the free world, and we are turning our attention more diligently now to one day sharing the gospel with our Father's children behind the so-called iron and bamboo curtains. We have need to prepare for that day. The urgency of that preparation weighs heavily upon us. That day may come with more swiftness than we realize." (In Conference Report, Apr. 1979, p. 3; or *Ensign,* May 1979, p. 4.)

President Kimball pointed out that God has the power to bring about what may appear to be almost impossible tasks. But President Kimball asked whether the Lord would move before his servants are ready to move with him:

"Somehow, brethren, I feel that when we have done all in our power that the Lord will find a way to open doors. That is my faith.

" 'Is any thing too hard for the Lord?' he asked, when Sarah laughed when she was told that she would have a son. . . .

"If he commands, certainly he can fulfill.

"We remember the exodus of the children of Israel crossing the uncrossable Red Sea.

"We remember Cyrus diverting a river and taking the impregnable city of Babylon.

"We remember the Lehites getting to the promised land.

"We remember the Revolutionary War and the power of God that gave us triumph.

"I believe the Lord can do anything he sets his mind to do.

"But I can see no good reason why the Lord would open doors that we are not prepared to enter. Why should he break down the Iron Curtain or the Bamboo Curtain or any other curtain if we are still unprepared to enter?

"I believe we have men who could help the apostles to open these doors—statesmen, able and trustworthy—but, when we are ready for them." ("When the World Will Be Converted," *Ensign*, Oct. 1974, p. 7.)

Can you see that you personally can make a difference in such an effort? Who knows what future use we could be put to by the Lord if we would but commit ourselves to this work and prepare ourselves for service?

### (A-4) No Unhallowed Hand Can Stop the Work

Foreseen by nearly every prophet of old, one of the most remarkable accounts of the restoration of the kingdom of God in the last days was given by Daniel. The context of the prophecy is as follows: The king of Babylon, Nebuchadnezzar, enthroned in royal splendor in one of the most renowned cities of the world, had a dream. Before him stood an image with a head of gold, breast and arms of silver, a belly of brass, legs of iron, and feet and toes part iron and part clay. He saw a stone cut from the mountain without hands that rolled forth and smote the image, breaking it to pieces. The pieces became like chaff, scattered before the wind. The stone, representing the restoration of the Church and kingdom of God, became a great mountain and filled the earth. (See Daniel 2:31-36.)

The reality of Daniel's prophecy can be seen in the pattern of growth of the Church reported by President Spencer W. Kimball: "It is estimated that it took 117 years, from 1830 to 1947, to attain one million members. Then it took sixteen years, from 1947 to 1963, to reach the second million members, and then nine years, 1963 to 1972, to attain the third million." (In Conference Report, Oct. 1976, p. 4; or *Ensign*, Nov. 1976, p. 4.) The four million mark was attained in only six years, from 1972 to 1978.

The great stone was seen to roll forth and strike the kingdoms of this world and break them into pieces. The adversary is well aware of the prophecy and the promise that his dominions will ultimately be overthrown through the power of the Restoration. Therefore he exerts every effort to thwart or frustrate the work of God (see D&C 3:3). The Doctrine and Covenants teaches that Satan inspires men of influence to marshal their forces of destruction against the kingdom of God; Nephi saw in vision the time when the kingdom of Satan would gather multitudes together to fight against the Church of the Lamb (see 1 Nephi 14:13). Nevertheless, the Lord said, "I will not suffer that they shall destroy my work; yea, I will show unto them that my wisdom is greater than the cunning of the devil" (D&C 10:43). Elder Neal A. Maxwell warned that in such a struggle the Saints "may even see a few leave the Church who cannot then leave the Church alone. Let these few departees take their brief bows in the secular spotlight; someday they will bow deeply before the throne of the Almighty, confessing that Jesus is the Christ and that this is his work. Meanwhile, be unsurprised if, as the little stone seen by Daniel rolls relentlessly forth, some seek to chip away at it (see Dan. 2)." (In Conference Report, Oct. 1980, p. 17; or *Ensign*, Nov. 1980, p. 14.)

The warning voice cannot be silenced. The Prophet Joseph Smith said, "No unhallowed hand can stop the work from progressing; persecutions may rage, mobs may combine, armies may assemble, calumny may defame, but the truth of God will go forth boldly, nobly, and independent, till it has penetrated every continent, visited every clime, swept every country, and sounded in every ear, till the purpose of God shall be accomplished, and the Great Jehovah shall say the work is done" (*History of the Church*, 4:540).

### (A-5) Who Is to Give the Voice of Warning?

The trump of God must be sounded to every nation, kindred, tongue, and people, saying, "Fear God, and give glory to him . . . for the hour of his judgment is come" (D&C 88:104). The elders of the Church have been given the responsibility to raise that warning voice (see D&C 43:15, 19-20, 28).

Since the Lord has identified the Church as the warning agent, every member is responsible to be a missionary to lift up the trump and sound the warning so that (1) the wicked will be left without excuse; (2) the member will free himself from the blood and sins of his generation; and (3) the righteous will be gathered from all nations to enjoy the blessings of salvation and escape the coming judgments.

Using the idea of a watchman on a tower, the prophet Ezekiel taught the principle of personal accountability that attends the receiving of the gospel (see Ezekiel 3:17-19). The Doctrine and Covenants teaches with equal clarity that this responsibility rests with more than just the prophets. Speaking to the elders of the Church, the

Lord said: "Behold, I sent you out to testify and warn the people, and it becometh every man who hath been warned to warn his neighbor. Therefore, they are left without excuse, and their sins are upon their own heads." (D&C 88:81-82.)

Who in the Lord's church has the responsibility for sounding the trump of warning and alarm to the world? President Spencer W. Kimball said:

"I was asked a few years ago, 'Should every young man who is a member of the Church fill a mission?' And I responded with the answer the Lord has given: 'Yes, every worthy young man should fill a mission.' The Lord expects it of him. And if he is not now worthy to fill a mission, then he should start at once to qualify himself. The Lord has instructed, 'Send forth the elders of my church unto the nations which are afar off; unto the islands of the sea; send forth unto foreign lands; call upon all nations, first upon the Gentiles, and then upon the Jews.' (D&C 133:8.)

"Thus, the elders—the young men of the Church of the age to be ordained elders—should be prepared and anxious to fill a mission for the Church throughout the world. Presently, only about one-third of the eligible young men of the Church are serving full-time missions! One-third is not 'every young man.'

"Someone might also ask, 'Should every young woman, should every father and mother, should every member of the Church serve a mission?' Again, the Lord has given the answer: Yes, every man, woman, and child—every young person and every little boy and girl—should serve a mission. . . . Each of us is responsible to bear witness of the gospel truths that we have been given. We all have relatives, neighbors, friends, and fellow workmen, and it is our responsibility to pass the truths of the gospel on to them, by example as well as by precept.

"The scriptures are abundantly clear in stating that all members of the Church are responsible to do missionary work: 'It becometh every man who hath been warned to warn his neighbor.' (D&C 88:81.) . . .

". . . Perhaps the greatest reason for missionary work is to give the world its chance to hear and accept the gospel. The scriptures are replete with *commands* and *promises* and *calls* and *rewards* for teaching the gospel. I use the word *command* advisedly, for it seems to be an insistent directive from which we, singly and collectively, cannot escape. Furthermore, the command is clear that not only must all members of His church give missionary service, but we must take the gospel to all the children of our Heavenly Father on this earth." ("It Becometh Every Man," *Ensign*, Oct. 1977, pp. 3-4.) No one can escape the charge to raise a warning voice in some way.

At baptism you made a solemn covenant with the Lord. Part of the covenant included the promise to "stand as witnesses of God at all times and in all things, and in all places that ye may be in, even until death" (Mosiah 18:9). What would the faithful completion of that covenant mean for you?

Every Sunday when you partake of the sacrament, you again solemnly affirm that you are bearing witness of something (see D&C 20:77, 79). To what are you bearing witness, and what does that witness mean for missionary work?

Christ issued the commission to go to all the world (see Matthew 28:19-20), and President Kimball has challenged us to accept that commission literally and fulfill it. Your place in its fulfillment can be of eternal and profound significance if you willingly commit yourself to the task.

**(A-6) Summary**

Mighty in power, terrible in judgment, glorious in destiny, the Church has been cut out of the mountain without hands and is rolling forth to fill the earth. Truly the kingdom of God is sounding, and every ear shall hear, every eye shall see, and every heart will be penetrated. The only question that may remain unanswered is the one that can only be answered individually by each member of the Church: Will I serve? Will I truly live by every word that proceeds from the mouth of God? (See D&C 98:11.) Therefore, now is the time to decide, if the decision has not already been made, simply to do it!

# Establishing Zion

Enrichment B

## (B-1) Introduction

The Prophet Joseph Smith placed in perspective the importance of establishing Zion when he wrote: "The building up of Zion is a cause that has interested the people of God in every age; it is a theme upon which prophets, priests and kings have dwelt with peculiar delight; they have looked forward with joyful anticipation to the day in which we live; and fired with heavenly and joyful anticipations they have sung and written and prophesied of this our day; but they died without the sight; we are the favored people that God has made choice of to bring about the Latter-day glory; it is left for us to see, participate in and help to roll forward the Latter-day glory, 'the dispensation of the fullness of times, when God will gather together all things that are in heaven, and all things that are upon the earth, even in one,' when the Saints of God will be gathered in one from every nation, and kindred, and people, and tongue, when the Jews will be gathered together into one, the wicked will also be gathered together to be destroyed, as spoken of by the prophets; the Spirit of God will also dwell with His people, and be withdrawn from the rest of the nations, and all things whether in heaven or on earth will be in one, even in Christ. The heavenly Priesthood will unite with the earthly, to bring about those great purposes; and whilst we are thus united in the one common cause, to roll forth the kingdom of God, the heavenly Priesthood are not idle spectators, the Spirit of God will be showered down from above, and it will dwell in our midst. The blessings of the Most High will rest upon our tabernacles, and our name will be handed down to future ages; our children will rise up and call us blessed; and generations yet unborn will dwell with peculiar delight upon the scenes that we have passed through, the privations that we have endured; the untiring zeal that we have manifested; the all but insurmountable difficulties that we have overcome in laying the foundation of a work that brought about the glory and blessing which they will realize; a work that God and angels have contemplated with delight for generations past; that fired the souls of the ancient patriarchs and prophets; a work that is destined to bring about the destruction of the powers of darkness, the renovation of the earth, the glory of God, and the salvation of the human family." (*History of the Church*, 4:609-10.)

A major theme of the Doctrine and Covenants is the building of Zion. Many of the revelations center on the establishment of the glorious condition described by the Prophet Joseph Smith.

## (B-2) Zion: The Pure in Heart

The Doctrine and Covenants provides the simplest and clearest definition of Zion in all scripture: "for this is Zion,—THE PURE IN HEART" (D&C 97:21).

President Stephen L Richards expanded on that basic definition:

"I know of few more salutary things for a Latter-day Saint than constantly to bear in mind the distinction between Zion and the world. Both terms are somewhat confusing because they are used with varying meanings and applications. Both have geographical application, and both have theological and moral import.

"For my purpose here today, I shall look upon Zion as being a condition and not a place, and the world likewise. '. . . verily, thus saith the Lord, let Zion rejoice, for this is Zion,—the pure in heart.' (D&C 97:21.)

"There is no fence around Zion or the world, but to one of discernment, they are separated more completely than if each were surrounded with high unscalable walls. Their underlying concepts, philosophies, and purposes are at complete variance one with the other. The philosophy of the world is self-sufficient, egotistical, materialistic, and skeptical. The philosophy of Zion is humility, not servility, but a willing recognition of the sovereignty of God and dependence on his providence." (In Conference Report, Oct. 1951, pp. 110-11.)

Elder Bruce R. McConkie summarized a similar definition of Zion: "Zion is people; Zion is the saints of God; Zion is those who have been baptized; Zion is those who have received the Holy Ghost; Zion is those who keep the commandments; Zion is the righteous; or in other words, as our revelation recites: 'This is Zion—the pure in heart. (D&C 97:21.)' " ("Come: Let Israel Build Zion," *Ensign*, May 1977, p. 117.)

The following citations from the Doctrine and Covenants provide additional insight into the principle of Zion.

*D&C 82:19.* What formula is given to aid us to achieve the goal of Zion?

*D&C 97:10-19.* What is the importance of temples in building a Zion people?

*D&C 124:54.* What is the promise to the "pure in heart"?

*D&C 97:21.* If "Zion" and the "pure in heart" are equivalent concepts, how could you paraphrase such scriptures as Matthew 5:8; Psalm 34:4; and Doctrine and Covenants 101:17-18?

## (B-3) Ancient Zion Communities Were Established

Individuals who live the principles of Zion seek always to establish a community where such principles govern the personal lives and the society of all who dwell in it. The archetype of such established Zion peoples is the city of Enoch, described by Elder Bruce R. McConkie:

"Zion has been established many times among men. From the day of Adam to the present moment—whenever the Lord has had a people of his own; whenever there have been those who have hearkened to his voice and kept his commandments; whenever his saints have served him with full purpose of heart—there has been Zion.

"Our first scriptural account relative to Zion concerns Enoch and his city. That prophet of transcendent faith and power lived while father Adam yet dwelt in mortality. It was a day of wickedness and evil, a day of darkness and rebellion, a day of war and desolation, a day leading up to the cleansing of the earth by water.

"Enoch, however, was faithful. He saw the Lord, and talked with him face to face as one man speaks with another. (Moses 7:4.) . . . Enoch made converts and assembled a congregation of true believers, all of whom became so faithful that 'the Lord came and dwelt with his people, and they dwelt in righteousness,' and were blessed from on high. 'And the Lord called his people Zion, because they were of one heart and one mind, and dwelt in righteousness; and there was no poor among them.' (Moses 7:18.) . . .

"After the Lord called his people Zion, the scripture says that Enoch 'built a city that was called the City of Holiness, even Zion'; that Zion 'was taken up into heaven where God received it up into his own bosom'; and that 'from thence went forth the saying, Zion is fled.' (Moses 7:19, 21, 69.)

"After the Lord's people were translated . . . others, being converted and desiring righteousness, looked for a city which hath foundation, whose builder and maker is God, and they too 'were caught up by the powers of heaven into Zion.' (Moses 7:27.)

"This same Zion which was taken up into heaven shall return during the Millennium, when the Lord brings again Zion; and its inhabitants shall join with the New Jerusalem which shall then be established. (See Moses 7:62-63.)" ("Come: Let Israel Build Zion," pp. 116-18.)

Other Zion communities have been set up for short periods among God's covenant people. A group established by Christ's Apostles after the Ascension "were of one heart and of one soul [mind]" and had "all things common" (Acts 4:32), just as the people of Enoch did. The Book of Mormon tells of another Zion community established as a consequence of the Savior's visit to the Nephites. This people had "all things common among them, every man dealing justly, one with another" (3 Nephi 26:19; see also 4 Nephi 1:1-2). Like the people of Enoch, these Nephites had no contention among them "because the love of God . . . did dwell in the hearts of the people" (4 Nephi 1:15).

The Doctrine and Covenants provides some interesting additional information about these early Zion peoples. Enoch "saw the Lord, and he walked with him, and was before his face continually" (D&C 107:49), and the people of Enoch were taken unto the bosom of the Savior (D&C 38:4; see also Notes and Commentary on D&C 38:4). Only in latter-day scripture does one find the startling promise that Enoch and his people will come back to the earth when the latter-day Zion is established for a thousand years (see Moses 7:63-64; D&C 45:12; 84:100).

**(B-4) Zion: The Promised Destiny of the Righteous**

The establishment of a Zion people has not been possible in every dispensation. Individuals, however, have sought to develop righteousness and purity of heart. The wickedness of men may have prevented the building of a Zion society, but it can never prevent the practice of the principles of Zion by individuals and families.

Methuselah, Enoch's son, was appointed to leave Zion and remain upon the earth to be a preacher of righteousness and the progenitor of Noah (see Moses 8:2-3). Noah, his grandson, was a "just man" (Moses 8:27; Genesis 6:9) and became an "heir of the righteousness which is by faith" (Hebrews 11:7). Melchizedek was "a man of faith who wrought righteousness" (JST, Genesis 14:26). The people of his city sought for Enoch's community of Zion and obtained it (see JST, Genesis 14:34). Abraham, a "follower of righteousness" (Abraham 1:2) was commanded to "remember the days of Enoch" (JST, Genesis 13:14) and to seek for the city "which hath foundations whose builder and maker is God" (Hebrews 11:10). The patriarchs and prophets secured the promise of the blessings of Zion through their individual righteousness (see D&C 133:52-55). This promise was reaffirmed in the days of preparation for the Second Coming.

"Wherefore, hearken ye together and let me show unto you even my wisdom—the wisdom of him whom ye say is the God of Enoch, and his brethren, who were separated from the earth, and were received unto myself—a city reserved until a day of righteousness shall come—a day which was sought for by all holy men, and they found it not because of wickedness and abominations; and confessed they were strangers and pilgrims on the earth; but obtained a promise that they should find it and see it in their flesh" (D&C 45:11-14).

*Noah was a just man*

### (B-5) Geographical Designations of Zion: Places of Safety

Ancient Jerusalem, and particularly the temple site of that city, has been referred to as Mount Zion (see 2 Samuel 5:7-9; 1 Kings 8:1; Isaiah 29:7-8), and members of The Church of Jesus Christ of Latter-day Saints have used the term *Zion* to identify their own locations (see Talmage, *Articles of Faith,* p. 347), but as used in the Doctrine and Covenants, *Zion* most often refers either to the people and their condition of purity or to the center place of Zion in the last days—namely, Jackson County, Missouri.

Though Zion is foretold in other scriptures (see 3 Nephi 21:22-25; Ether 13:2-12; Moses 7:61-64), only in the Doctrine and Covenants can be found the directives for its establishment, its laws and principles, and its location. The Prophet Joseph Smith taught that the New Jerusalem would be the first of Zion communities built in preparation for the Millennium. The New Jerusalem will be called "an 'holy city' . . . because it is a place of righteousness" (*History of the Church,* 2:254), and it will be located at Independence, Jackson County, Missouri (see D&C 45:66-67; 57:1-3). The New Jerusalem is spoken of as "the center place" (D&C 57:3), or the administrative center, or capital, for all Zion (see Dyer, *Refiner's Fire,* pp. 99-104; *History of the Church,* 5:212). It is also spoken of as "Mount Zion" (D&C 84:2) and the "mountain of the Lord" (*History of the Church,* 6:319). From the beginnings laid in the New Jerusalem, the establishment of Zion communities will go forth throughout the world. The stakes of Zion will be the means through which the Zion societies will be prepared and strengthened (see D&C 82:14, 101:21, 133:9). Zion will first grow to include all of North and South America (see *History of the Church,* 6:318-319, 321) and eventually the entire earth (see Brigham Young, in *Journal of Discourses,* 9:138).

In his vision of the future, Enoch saw that great tribulations would make necessary a means of preserving the Lord's people upon the earth in the last days. That means is to gather the elect in Zion (see Moses 7:61-62). The Doctrine and Covenants declares that in addition to the true "center place," the stakes of Zion would also be "for a defense, and for a refuge from the storm, and from wrath when it shall be poured out without mixture upon the whole earth" (D&C 115:6). The Prophet Joseph Smith taught the same principle when he said that "without Zion, and a place of deliverance, we must fall; because the time is near when the sun will be darkened, and the moon turn to blood, and the stars fall from heaven, and the earth reel to and fro. Then, if this is the case, and if we are not sanctified and gathered to the places God has appointed, with all our former professions and our great love for the Bible, we must fall; we cannot stand; we cannot be saved; for God will gather out His Saints from the Gentiles, and then comes desolation and destruction, and none can escape except the pure in heart who are gathered." (*History of the Church,* 2:52.)

On another occasion, the Prophet gave the following challenge and admonition:

"We ought to have the building up of Zion as our greatest object. When wars come, we shall have to flee to Zion. The cry is to make haste. The last revelation says, Ye shall not have time to have gone over the earth, until these things come. . . .

" . . . The time is soon coming when no man will have any peace but in Zion and her stakes.

"I saw men hunting the lives of their own sons, and brother murdering brother, women killing their own daughters, and daughters seeking the lives of their mothers. I saw armies arrayed against armies. I saw blood, desolation, fires. The Son of Man has said that the mother shall be against the daughter, and the daughter against the mother. These things are at our doors. They will follow the Saints of God from city to city. Satan will rage, and the spirit of the devil is now enraged. I know not how soon these things will take place; but with a view of them, shall I cry peace? No! I will lift up my voice and testify of them. How long you will have good crops, and the famine be kept off, I do not know; when the fig tree leaves, know then that summer is nigh at hand." (*History of the Church,* 3:390-91.)

The scriptures testify that in the days prior to the second coming of the Savior the world will be torn with war, upheaval, natural calamities, judgments, and turmoil. So great will be the turbulence of these times that men's hearts shall fail them. (See D&C 45:26.)

Have you been tempted, when you have read of the devastations to come, to wish that you will not live to see them? If so, then you understand only one aspect of the prophetic promises. Again and again the Lord has made promises that should give you faith and hope.

*1 Nephi 22:15-17, 19, 22.* Why should the righteous not have cause to fear?

*2 Nephi 30:10.* What will come to those who maintain their righteousness?

*Moses 7:61.* In the midst of the great judgments what promise does God hold out for his people?

*D&C 35:14.* Wherein lies the promise of deliverance in the last days?

*D&C 45:66.* What three phrases are used to describe Zion?

*D&C 45:67-70.* What is another promise held out for Zion?

*D&C 101:21; D&C 115:5-6.* Will Jackson County be the only place of safety in the coming trials?

As President Stephen L Richards said, Zion is primarily a condition, not a place. There are places called Zion, but they are so called only because they have been or will be gathering places for Zion people. As you have read, the Prophet Joseph Smith said, "Without Zion, and a place of deliverance, we must fall," and "We ought to have the building up of Zion as our greatest object" (*History of the Church,* 2:52).

Are you ready to gather to Zion? Do you have the building up of Zion as your greatest object? Where do you start? Where do you go? The answer is very simple if you remember the basic definition of Zion. It is a state of the heart, and that is the place you must begin. It is a matter of utmost urgency in our day, for the Lord has said, "Vengeance cometh speedily upon the ungodly as the whirlwind; and who shall escape it?" (D&C 97:22).

Isn't that what you'd like to know—who *shall* escape the day of judgment? The Lord gave the answer (see D&C 97:25-28), and it is of the utmost importance for us to understand it.

**(B-6) Laying the Foundation**

With the coming forth of the Book of Mormon in 1830, and in the part of the record of Enoch found in the book of Moses, the early Saints read the prophecies that Zion would again be established in the last days (see, for example, 3 Nephi 21:22-28; Ether 13:2-12; Moses 7:61-62). The Book of Mormon promised blessings to those who sought to bring forth Zion in the latter days (see 1 Nephi 13:37), and the early revelations to Joseph Smith specifically commanded people to "seek to bring forth and establish the cause of Zion" (D&C 6:6; 11:6; 12:6).

It is not surprising, then, that the Prophet and the people would start importuning the Lord to know of its location and gain permission to establish it. Soon the Lord answered their prayers, and they were permitted to lay the foundations of Zion. But the early Saints who gathered there did not understand fully that they would *not* build the city of Zion at that time (August 1831). The Doctrine and Covenants reveals the Lord's foreknowledge about Zion: "Ye cannot behold with your natural eyes, for the present time, the design of your God concerning those things which shall come hereafter, and the glory which shall follow after much tribulation" (D&C 58:3).

The Lord had a purpose other than starting a city when he commanded the Saints to settle in the designated part of Missouri: "For after much tribulation come the blessings. Wherefore the day cometh that ye shall be crowned with much glory; the hour is not yet, but is nigh at hand. Remember this, which I tell you before, that you may lay it to heart, and receive that which is to follow. Behold, verily I say unto you, for this cause I have sent you—that you might be obedient, and that your hearts might be prepared to bear testimony of the things which are to come; and also that you might be honored in laying the foundation, and in bearing record of the land upon which the Zion of God shall stand." (D&C 58:4-7.)

But the Saints made a serious mistake. They assumed that they could build a place of Zion without building a people who were pure in heart. They disregarded the Lord's continued warnings and were driven from the center place of Zion by the mobs.

By November 1833 the Saints had virtually completed their exodus from Jackson County. They spent the next four trying and difficult years in three other counties of Missouri, and finally they were driven from the state (see *History of the Church*, 3:175). All this, according to revelation, was in consequence of the transgressions of the people (see D&C 101:1-2; 103:3-4).

Some individuals fulfilled the personal requirements of a Zion people, but as a whole the Saints did not (see D&C 105:1-2). It was necessary that the people and the Church be prepared, under the direction of the prophets, to build Zion again. The Lord revealed the conditions required for the redemption or the establishment again of Zion. He declared that the Church was to "wait for a season" (D&C 105:9) in order that "my people may be taught more perfectly, . . . and know more perfectly concerning their duty" (D&C 105:10). They also needed to be "endowed with power from on high" (D&C 105:11) and to seek to obtain "favor in the eyes of [other] people, until the army of Israel becomes very great" (D&C 105:26). Finally, the Lord instructed that the Church, his army, "be sanctified . . . that the kingdoms of this world may be constrained to acknowledge that the kingdom of Zion is in very deed the kingdom of our God and his Christ" (D&C 105:31-32).

It has now been about a century and a half since the place of Zion was abandoned, but the Church has been striving to fulfill those requirements outlined by the Lord. The Church is preparing its people, teaching them more perfectly, and gaining experience. The Saints are being endowed with power through an increasing number of temples, as the Lord required (see D&C 105:10-11).

Elder Bruce R. McConkie outlined three developmental stages for establishing Zion:

"The gathering of Israel and the establishment of Zion in the latter days is divided into three periods or phases. The first phase is past; we are now living in the second phase; and the third lies ahead. . . .

"Phase I—From the First Vision, the setting up of the kingdom on April 6, 1830, and the coming of Moses on April 3, 1836, to the secure establishment of the Church in the United States and Canada, a period of about 125 years.

"Phase II—From the creation of stakes of Zion in overseas areas, beginning in the 1950s, to the second coming of the Son of Man, a period of unknown duration.

"Phase III—From our Lord's second coming until the kingdom is perfected and the knowledge of God covers the earth as the waters cover the sea, and from then until the end of the Millennium, a period of 1,000 years." ("Come: Let Israel Build Zion," p. 115.)

Elder McConkie further explained how the current establishment of stakes of Zion throughout the world is a vital part of the necessary preparation to build the city and land of Zion:

"As of now, the Lord has laid upon us the responsibility to lay the foundation for that which is to be. We have been commissioned to prepare a people for the second coming of the Son of Man. We have been called to preach the gospel to every nation and kindred and tongue and people. We have been commanded to lay the foundations of Zion and to get all things ready for the return of Him who shall again crown the Holy city with his presence and glory. . . .

"Stakes of Zion are . . . being organized at the ends of the earth. . . . A stake of Zion is a part of

Zion. You cannot create a stake of Zion without creating a part of Zion. Zion is the pure in heart; we gain purity of heart by baptism and by obedience. A stake has geographical boundaries. To create a stake is like founding a City of Holiness. Every stake on earth is the gathering place for the lost sheep of Israel who live in its area.

"The gathering place for Peruvians is in the stakes of Zion in Peru, or in the places which soon will become stakes. The gathering place for Chileans is in Chile; for Bolivians it is in Bolivia; for Koreans it is in Korea; and so it goes through all the length and breadth of the earth. Scattered Israel in every nation is called to gather to the fold of Christ, to the stakes of Zion, as such are established in their nations. . . .

"That is to say—Israel shall be gathered one by one, family by family, unto the stakes of Zion established in all parts of the earth so that the whole earth shall be blessed with the fruits of the gospel.

"This then is the counsel of the Brethren: Build up Zion, but build it up in the area where God has given you birth and nationality. Build it up where he has given you citizenship, family, and friends. Zion is here in South America and the Saints who comprise this part of Zion are and should be a leavening influence for good in all these nations.

"And know this: God will bless that nation which so orders its affairs as to further his work." ("Come: Let Israel Build Zion," pp. 116, 118.)

The following Doctrine and Covenants references broaden our understanding of the preparations for the Zion society going forth in the Church today:

*D&C 6:6 (11:6; 12:6).* What is the Lord's command concerning Zion?

*D&C 63:29-31.* What requirement is given for obtaining the properties of Zion?

*D&C 82:14.* Is Zion limited to one place?

*D&C 109:59; 115:6.* What are the places of Zion? What promises extend to these places?

*D&C 124:36.* What special work is to be performed in the places of Zion?

## (B-7) Building the Latter-day Zion

Preparations for building Zion continue in the programs of the Church, but individual preparation is the single most important ingredient. President Spencer W. Kimball provided a comprehensive overview of the challenge to make personal preparation to build Zion through sacrifice and consecration:

"For many years we have been taught that one important end result of our labors, hopes, and aspirations in this work is the building of a Latter-day Zion, a Zion characterized by love, harmony, and peace—a Zion in which the Lord's children are as one.

"The vision of what we are about and what should come of our labors must be kept uppermost in our minds as we learn and do our duty in the present implementation of welfare service. This applies equally to all Church activities. . . .

*The spirit of Zion is seen in unselfish service*

"This day [of power and redemption] will come; it is our destiny to help bring it about! Doesn't it motivate you to lengthen your stride and quicken your pace as you do your part in the great sanctifying work of the kingdom? It does me. It causes me to rejoice over the many opportunities for service and sacrifice afforded me and my family as we seek to do our part in establishing Zion. . . .

"The length of time required 'to accomplish all things pertaining to Zion' is strictly up to us and how we live, for creating Zion 'commences in the heart of each person.' (*Journal of Discourses,* 9:283.) That it would take some time to learn our lessons was seen by the prophets. In 1863 Brigham Young stated:

" 'If the people neglect their duty, turn away from the holy commandments which God has given us, seek their own individual wealth, and neglect the interest of the kingdom of God, we may expect to be here quite a time—perhaps a period that will be far longer than we anticipate.' (*Journal of Discourses,* 11:102.)

"Unfortunately we live in a world that largely rejects the values of Zion. Babylon has not and never will comprehend Zion. . . .

" . . . Zion can be built up only among those who are pure in heart, not a people torn by covetousness or greed, but a pure and selfless people. Not a people who are pure in appearance, rather a people who are pure in heart. Zion is to be in the world and not of the world, not dulled by a sense of carnal security, nor paralyzed by materialism. No, Zion is not things of the lower, but of the higher order, things that exalt the mind and sanctify the heart.

"Zion is 'every man seeking the interest of his neighbor, and doing all things with an eye single to the glory of God.' (D&C 82:19.) As I understand these matters, Zion can be established only by those who are pure in heart, and who labor for Zion, for 'the laborer in Zion shall labor for Zion; for if they labor for money they shall perish.' (2 Nephi 26:31.)" (In Conference Report, Apr. 1978, pp. 119, 121-22; or *Ensign,* May 1978, pp. 79-80.)

President Kimball gave concrete direction concerning specific things to be made a part of each individual's life:

"As important as it is to have this vision in mind, defining and describing Zion will not bring it about. That can only be done through consistent and concerned daily effort by every single member of the Church. No matter what the cost in toil or sacrifice, we must do it. That is one of my favorite phrases: 'Do It'. May I suggest three fundamental things we must do if we are to 'bring again Zion,' three things for which we who labor for Zion must commit ourselves.

"First, we must eliminate the individual tendency to selfishness that snares the soul, shrinks the heart, and darkens the mind. . . .

" . . . It is incumbent upon us to put away selfishness in our families, our business and professional pursuits, and our Church affairs. . . .

"Second, we must cooperate completely and work in harmony one with the other. There must be unanimity in our decisions and unity in our actions. After pleading with the Saints to 'let every man esteem his brother as himself' (D&C 38:24), the Lord concludes his instructions on cooperation to a conference of the membership in these powerful words:

" 'Behold, this I have given unto you as a parable, and it is even as I am. I say unto you, be one; and if ye are not one ye are not mine.' (D&C 38:27.) . . .

"Third, we must lay on the altar and sacrifice whatever is required by the Lord. We begin by offering a 'broken heart and a contrite spirit.' We follow this by giving our best effort in our assigned fields of labor and callings. We learn our duty and execute it fully. Finally we consecrate our time, talents, and means as called upon by our file leaders and as prompted by the whisperings of the Spirit. In the Church, as in the Welfare system also, we can give expression to every ability, every righteous desire, every thoughtful impulse. Whether a volunteer, father, home teacher, bishop, or neighbor, whether a visiting teacher, mother, homemaker, or friend—there is ample opportunity to give our all. And as we give, we find that 'sacrifice brings forth the blessings of heaven!' (Hymns, no. 147.) And in the end, we learn it was no sacrifice at all." (In Conference Report, Apr. 1978, pp. 122-24; or *Ensign,* May 1978, p. 81.)

**(B-8) Summary**

The building of Zion requires the personal prerequisite of striving to develop purity of heart. The example of ancient prophets shows that it is possible to become a Zion people and even to build a Zion society. The destiny of The Church of Jesus Christ of Latter-day Saints is to prepare a Zion people and to again build a Zion society, beginning at Jackson County, Missouri, with the New Jerusalem. The Church is working directly to assist the Saints in fulfilling this glorious destiny of establishing Zion. If, as the Prophet Joseph Smith counseled, the Saints "have the building up of Zion as [their] greatest object" (*History of the Church,* 3:390), then the Saints can see the fulfillment of Moroni's prophecy to Joseph Smith, that "the Gospel in all its fullness . . . be preached in power, unto all nations that a people might be prepared for the Millennial reign" (*History of the Church,* 4:537).

The following counsel by President Brigham Young can motivate the Saints to build Zion:

"When we conclude to make a Zion we will make it, and this work commences in the heart of each person. When the father of a family wishes to make a Zion in his own house, he must take the lead in this good work, which it is impossible for him to do unless he himself possesses the spirit of Zion. Before he can produce the work of sanctification in his family, he must sanctify himself, and by this means God can help him to sanctify his family.

"There is not one thing wanting in all the works of God's hands to make a Zion upon the earth when the people conclude to make it. We can make a Zion of God on earth at our pleasure, upon the same principle that we can raise a field of wheat, or build and inhabit. There has been no time when the material has not been here from which to produce corn, wheat, etc., and by the judicious management and arrangement of this ever-existing material a Zion of God can always be built on the earth." (*Discourses of Brigham Young,* p. 118.)

# Receiving Personal Revelation

Enrichment C

### (C-1) Introduction

A great contribution of the Doctrine and Covenants is what it adds to an understanding of the process of receiving personal revelation. Every individual senses the need of a help beyond himself to find the answers to the important questions and challenges of life. But sometimes, in one's inexperience with the process of revelation, false expectations may arise about how such assistance will come. Sincere effort and experience are required to learn to communicate with Deity. President Joseph F. Smith gave important counsel concerning revelation:

"It is a wicked and adulterous generation that seeketh after a sign. Show me Latter-day Saints who have to feed upon miracles, signs and visions in order to keep them steadfast in the Church, and I will show you members of the Church who are not in good standing before God, and who are walking in slippery paths. It is not by marvelous manifestations unto us that we shall be established in the truth, but it is by humility and faithful obedience to the commandments and laws of God. When I as a boy first started out in the ministry, I would frequently go out and ask the Lord to show me some marvelous thing, in order that I might receive a testimony. But the Lord withheld marvels from me, and showed me the truth, line upon line, precept upon precept, here a little and there a little, until he made me to know the truth from the crown of my head to the soles of my feet, and until doubt and fear had been absolutely purged from me. He did not have to send an angel from the heavens to do this, nor did he have to speak with the trump of an archangel. By the whisperings of the still small voice of the Spirit of the living God, he gave to me the testimony I possess. And by this principle and power he will give to all the children of men a knowledge of the truth that will stay with them, and it will make them to know the truth, as God knows it, and to do the will of the Father as Christ does it. And no amount of marvelous manifestations will ever accomplish this. It is obedience, humility, and submission to the requirements of heaven and to the order established in the kingdom of God upon the earth, that will establish men in the truth. Men may receive the visitation of angels; they may speak in tongues; they may heal the sick by the laying on of hands; they may have visions and dreams; but except they are faithful and pure in heart, they become an easy prey to the adversary of their souls, and he will lead them into darkness and unbelief more easily than others." (*Gospel Doctrine,* p. 7.)

It is vital to one's personal spiritual welfare to know something of the various means by which revelation comes—how to prepare for it, how to seek after it, and how to obtain its blessings in one's life.

### (C-2) What Is Revelation?

The scriptures contain a multitude of examples of the various means the Lord uses to communicate with his children. President Marion G. Romney outlined the processes of revelation:

"Just as prayer is the means by which men address the Lord, so revelation is the means by which God communicates to men. In doing so, He uses various means. The spoken word, for example, was the method He used to answer Adam's prayer. Adam and Eve '*heard* the voice of the Lord from the way toward the Garden of Eden, speaking unto them.' (Moses 5:4; italics added.)

"In addition to the spoken word, the Lord at times appears personally. . . .

"Joseph Smith the Prophet gives us this testimony of the personal appearance to him of both the Father and the Son. [JS—H 1:16-17.]

"Sometimes the Lord sends personal representatives to communicate with men. He sent Moroni, for example, to visit and instruct the Prophet Joseph Smith several times. (See Joseph Smith 2:28-59.)

"On other occasions the Lord has communicated with men by means of dreams and visions—Daniel's dream, for example, and Nephi's vision.

"Enos says, 'The voice of the Lord came into my mind again, saying: I will visit thy brethren according to their diligence in keeping my commandments.' (Enos 10.)

"I can personally testify to this form of revelation because I have experienced it.

"Now I know, . . . and bear witness to the fact that revelation from the Lord comes through the spoken word, by personal visitation, by messengers from the Lord, through dreams, and by way of visions, and by the voice of the Lord coming into one's mind.

"Most often however, revelation comes to us by means of the still, small voice." (In Conference Report, Apr. 1978, pp. 75-76; or *Ensign,* May 1978, p. 50.)

The Doctrine and Covenants describes the still, small voice as the most often used means of revelation from the Lord to his children: "Yea, behold, I will tell you in your mind and in your heart, by the Holy Ghost, which shall come upon you and which shall dwell in your heart. Now, behold, this is the spirit of revelation." (D&C 8:2-3.)

Elder Bruce R. McConkie said that "this revelation speaks of Spirit speaking to spirit—the Holy Spirit speaking to the spirit within me and in a way incomprehensible to the mind, but plain and clear to spiritual understanding—conveying knowledge, giving intelligence, giving truth, and giving sure knowledge of the things of God. Now this applies to everyone." ("How to Get Personal Revelation," *New Era,* June 1980, p. 49.)

The instrumentality of the Holy Ghost in the process of revelation was affirmed by the Prophet Joseph Smith when he said: "No man can receive the Holy Ghost without receiving revelations. The Holy Ghost is a revelator." (*History of the Church,* 6:58.)

The Doctrine and Covenants provides additional instruction pertaining to this most often used means of revelation.

*D&C 6:15, 23.* Oliver Cowdery had sought a witness of the truthfulness of the Book of Mormon plates. Here the Lord reminded him of how that communication was given. Why did the Lord communicate with him? How did the communication come? What comfort accompanied the answer?

*D&C 11:12.* The Prophet's brother Hyrum was instructed about the prompting influence of the Holy Ghost. What characteristics manifest the direction of the Spirit?

*D&C 11:13.* How would these characteristics be communicated to Hyrum? What comfort and sustenance will accompany the impressions? Many examples in the Doctrine and Covenants teach how an individual should communicate with the Lord in order to get revelation.

*D&C 19:28.* In what ways was Martin Harris "commanded" to call upon the Lord?

*D&C 20:47.* What encouragement is to be continually put before us as members of the Church?

*D&C 23:6.* What are we to do "before the world"?

*D&C 68:28.* What responsibility do parents have in assisting their children in this communication process?

The Doctrine and Covenants helps us understand the necessary preparation.

*D&C 121:36.* Upon what principles only can the "powers of heaven" be dealt with?

*D&C 121:45-46.* What prerequisites are mentioned here to prepare us to confidently communicate with the Lord?

Oliver Cowdery had sought to assist with the actual translation of the Book of Mormon and was given the power to do so (see D&C 8). He was not able to receive revelation because he did not understand his responsibility in the communication process. What lessons can you learn from his experience?

*D&C 9:6-7.* What incorrect assumption did Oliver make about the conveyance of revelation?

*D&C 9:8-9.* What part did the Lord expect the principle of agency to play? After the agency was exercised, how was the answer to come?

### (C-3) Seeking Revelation

The individual's attitude and effort are very important elements in personal revelation. President Spencer W. Kimball taught that the individual's agency is critical: "The Lord will not force himself upon people, and if they do not believe, they will receive no revelation. If they are content to depend upon their own limited calculations and interpretations, then, of course, the Lord will leave them to their chosen fate." (In Conference Report, Apr. 1977, p. 114; or *Ensign,* May 1977, p. 77.)

The Doctrine and Covenants re-echoes a familiar scriptural theme of how one requests revelation. "If thou shalt ask, thou shalt receive revelation upon revelation, knowledge upon knowledge, that thou mayest know the mysteries and peaceable things—that which bringeth joy, that which bringeth life eternal" (D&C 42:61).

"Ask the Father in my name, in faith believing that you shall receive, and you shall have the Holy Ghost, which manifesteth all things which are expedient unto the children of men" (D&C 18:18; see also D&C 88:63-65).

President Marion G. Romney explained the vital component of asking in the process of obtaining personal revelation. He discussed "the two most important mediums of communication known to man. First, prayer—the means by which men address God—and, second, about revelation—the means by which God communicates to men. . . .

"Frequently, prayers are requests for specific blessings. They may, however, and should, include expressions of thanksgiving, praise, worship, and adoration. . . .

"The importance of prayer is emphasized by the fact that the most oft-repeated command given by God to men is to pray. . . .

"The purpose of prayer, . . . is to attune oneself with the spirit or light which 'proceedeth forth from the presence of God to fill the immensity of space.' (D&C 88:12.) In that light is to be found sure answers to all our needs.

"Prayer is the key which unlocks the door and lets Christ into our lives.

" 'Behold,' said He, 'I stand at the door, and knock: if any man hear my voice, and open the door, I will come in to him, and will sup with him, and he with me.' (Rev. 3:20.)" (In Conference Report, Apr. 1978, pp. 73-75; or *Ensign,* May 1978, pp. 48-50.)

President Spencer W. Kimball provided the following instruction for the improvement of one's prayers:

"I love our hymn which, . . . reminds us that 'prayer is the soul's sincere desire' (*Hymns,* no. 220). Prayer is such a privilege—to speak to our Father in Heaven. It was a prayer, a very special prayer, which opened this whole dispensation! It began with a young man's first vocal prayer. I hope that not too many of our prayers are silent, even though when we cannot pray vocally, it is good to offer a silent prayer in our hearts and in our minds.

"Never hesitate to gather your family around you for your prayers, especially in those times when more than morning and evening family prayer is needed. Extra needs require extra prayers.

"Your little ones will learn how to talk to their Father in Heaven by listening to you as parents. They will soon see how heartfelt and honest your prayers are. If your prayers are a hurried and thoughtless ritual, they will see this too.

"Difficult as it seems, I have found when praying, other than in private and secret, that it is better to be concerned with communicating tenderly and honestly with God, rather than worrying over what the listeners may be thinking. The echoing of 'amen' by the listeners is evidence of their accord and approval. Of course, the setting of prayers needs to be taken into account. This is one reason why public prayers, or even family prayers, cannot be the whole of our praying.

"Some things are best prayed over only in private, where time and confidentiality are not considerations. If in these special moments of prayer we hold back from the Lord, it may mean that some blessing may be withheld from us. After all, we pray as petitioners before an all-wise Heavenly Father, so why should we ever think to hold back feelings or thoughts which bear upon our needs and our blessings? We hope that our people will have very bounteous prayers.

"It would not hurt us, either, if we paused at the end of our prayers to do some intense listening—even for a moment or two—always praying, as the Savior did, 'not my will, but thine, be done' (Luke 22:42)." (In Conference Report, Oct. 1979, pp. 4-5; or *Ensign*, Nov. 1979, pp. 4-5.)

### (C-4) Obtaining Revelation: Personal Preparation

To receive personal revelation, one must strengthen his spiritual awareness and make personal preparation a part of his life. Elder Boyd K. Packer outlined some important guidelines for that preparation:

"Keep the Word of Wisdom.

"Read the scriptures.

"Listen to your parents and to the leaders of the Church.

"Stay away from places and things that common sense tells you will interfere with inspiration.

"Develop your spiritual capacities.

"Learn to tune out the static and the interference.

"Avoid the substitutes and the counterfeits!

"Learn to be inspired and directed by the Holy Ghost. . . .

"There is a spiritual beam, with a constant signal. If you know how to pray and how to listen, spiritually listen, you may move through life, through clear weather, through storms, through wars, through peace, and be all right.

"Prayer can be a very public thing. We teach you often about prayer, about the asking part.

"Perhaps we have not taught you enough about the receiving part. This is a very private, a very individual thing, one that you must learn for yourself." (In Conference Report, Oct. 1979, pp. 30-31; or *Ensign*, Nov. 1979, p. 21.)

The basis of personal preparation is for the individual to become a fit vessel and a worthy recipient of the direction of the Spirit. This requirement is taught in the Doctrine and Covenants as well as in other scriptures:

"Let virtue garnish thy thoughts unceasingly" (D&C 121:45).

"Let the solemnities of eternity rest upon your minds" (D&C 43:34).

One's thoughts are a most important component

*"As he thinketh in his heart, so is he" (Proverbs 23:7)*

of the preparation process. President Marion G. Romney described their impact upon one's capacity for spiritual things:

"The great overall struggle in the world today is, as it has always been, for the souls of men. Every soul is personally engaged in the struggle, and he makes his fight with what is in his mind. In the final analysis the battleground is, for each individual, within himself. Inevitably he gravitates toward the subjects of his thoughts. Ages ago the wise man thus succinctly stated this great truth: 'As he thinketh in his heart, so is he' (Prov. 23:7).

"If we would escape the lusts of the flesh and build for ourselves and our children great and noble characters, we must keep in our minds and in their minds true and righteous principles for our thoughts and their thoughts to dwell upon. . . .

"I am persuaded, my brothers and sisters, that it is irrational to hope to escape the lusts of the world without substituting for them as the subjects of our thoughts the things of the Spirit." (In Conference Report, Apr. 1980, pp. 88-89; or *Ensign*, May 1980, pp. 66-67.)

### (C-5) Obtaining Revelation by Recognizing Spiritual Communication

The Prophet Joseph Smith emphasized the importance of the personal experience of revelation: "Reading the experience of others, or the revelation given to *them*, can never give *us* a comprehensive view of our condition and true relation to God. Knowledge of these things can only be obtained by experience through the ordinances of God set forth for that purpose." (*History of the Church*, 6:50.)

He also said, "By learning the Spirit of God and understanding it, you may grow into the principle of revelation" (*History of the Church*, 3:381).

Despite the teachings of the prophets and the scriptures that the communication or revelation comes *into the mind and heart* (see D&C 8:2), that Spirit speaks to spirit, many have not learned to recognize the process, and they look for the message to come in some natural, physical way. Elder Boyd K. Packer described how the Spirit communicates:

"I have come to know that inspiration comes more as a feeling than as a sound. . . .

"The Lord has a way of pouring pure intelligence into our minds to prompt us, to guide us, to teach us, to warn us. You can know the things you need to know *instantly*! Learn to receive inspiration." (In Conference Report, Oct. 1979, pp. 28-29; or *Ensign*, Nov. 1979, p. 20.)

On another occasion Elder Boyd K. Packer answered a question often asked by members of the Church, How can I know when I've received revelation?

"We have all been taught that revelation is available to each of us individually. The question I'm most often asked about revelation is, 'How do I know when I have received it? I've prayed about it and fasted over this problem and prayed about it and prayed about it, and I still don't quite know what to do. How can I really tell whether I'm being inspired so I won't make a mistake?'

"First, do you go to the Lord with a problem and ask Him to make your decision for you? Or do you work, read the revelations, and meditate and pray and then make a decision yourself? Measure the problem against what you know to be right and wrong, and then make the decision. Then ask Him if the decision is right or if it is wrong. Remember what He said to Oliver Cowdery about working it out in your mind.

"Listen to this sentence if you don't hear anything else: If we foolishly ask our bishop or branch president or the Lord to make a decision for us, there's precious little self-reliance in that. Think what it costs every time you have somebody else make a decision for you.

"I think I should mention one other thing, and I hope this won't be misunderstood. We often find young people who will pray with great exertion over matters that they are free to decide for themselves. Suppose, if you will, that a couple had money available to build a house. Suppose they had prayed endlessly over whether they should build an Early American style, a ranch style, modern style architecture, or perhaps a Mediterranean style. Has it ever occurred to you that perhaps the Lord just plain doesn't care? Let them build what they want to build. It's their choice. In many things we can do just what we want.

"Now, there *are* some things he cares about very much. If you're going to build that house, then be honest and pay for the material that goes into it and do a decent job of building it. When you move into it, live righteously in it. Those are the things that count.

"On occasions I've had to counsel people that the Lord would probably quite willingly approve the thing they intend to do even when they want to. It's strange when they come and almost feel guilty about doing something because they want to, even when it's righteous. The Lord is very generous with the freedom He gives us. The more we learn to follow the right, the more we are spiritually self-reliant, the more our freedom and our independence are affirmed. 'If ye continue in my word,' he said, 'then are ye my disciples indeed; And ye shall know the truth, and the truth shall make you free.' (John 8:31-32.)" ("Self-Reliance," *Ensign*, Aug. 1975, p. 89.)

President Marion G. Romney reaffirmed his experience with this divine principle of being spiritually self-reliant:

"In praying, I try to follow the teachings of these scriptures. When confronted with a problem I prayerfully weigh in my mind alternative solutions and come to a conclusion as to which of them is best. Then in prayer I submit to the Lord my problem, tell him I desire to make the right choice, what is, in my judgment, the right course. Then I ask him if I have made the right decision to give me the burning in my bosom that He promised Oliver Cowdery. When enlightenment and peace come into my mind, I know the Lord is saying yes. If I have a 'stupor of thought,' I know he is saying no, and I try again, following the same procedure.

"In conclusion, I repeat: I know when and how the Lord answers my prayers by the way I feel.

"When we learn to distinguish between the inspiration that comes from the Spirit of the Lord and that which comes from our own uninspired hopes and desires, we need make no mistakes. To this I testify." (*New Era*, Oct. 1975, p. 35.)

### (C-6) Obtaining Revelation "Line upon Line"

The Doctrine and Covenants clearly teaches that for the most part revelation comes to an individual "line upon line, precept upon precept" (D&C 98:12), that spiritual growth and development is a process rather than an event and is received "revelation upon revelation" (D&C 42:61). Often people are impatient about receiving answers to their prayers. It may seem to them as though there is no answer at all. Or they may be discontent because answers seem different from what they expected. A modern-day Apostle, Elder Boyd K. Packer, shared the following advice:

"Most people who come for counsel to the stake presidents, branch presidents, bishops, and others, and to us as General Authorities, don't come because they are confused and they are not able to see the difference between right and wrong. They come because they're tempted to do something that deep down they know is wrong, and they want that decision ratified.

"When you have a problem, work it out in your own mind first. Ponder on it and analyze it and meditate on it. Read the scriptures. Pray about it. I've come to learn that major decisions can't be forced." ("Self-Reliance," p. 88.)

On another occasion Elder Packer said:

"Sometimes you may struggle with a problem

and not get an answer. What could be wrong?

"It may be that you are not doing anything wrong. It may be that you have not done the right things long enough. Remember, you cannot force spiritual things.

"Sometimes we are confused simply because we won't take no for an answer. . . .

"Put difficult questions in the back of your minds and go about your lives. Ponder and pray quietly and persistently about them.

"The answer may not come as a lightning bolt. It may come as a little inspiration here and a little there, 'line upon line, precept upon precept' (D&C 98:12).

"Some answers will come from reading the scriptures, some from hearing speakers. And, occasionally, when it is important, some will come by very direct and powerful inspiration. The promptings will be clear and unmistakable." (In Conference Report, Oct. 1979, pp. 29-30; or *Ensign*, Nov. 1979, p. 21.)

The following questions can help us evaluate our prayers.

Do we seek answers without effort on our part?

Do we expect the communication to come through spectacular or special means?

Will the answers come if we do not follow the promptings of common sense and goodness with which we all are acquainted?

Do we pray sincerely?

Do we listen, and seek after the answers?

Have we made the proper preparations?

Are we grateful respondents to the Lord?

Do we really want answers?

President Spencer W. Kimball provided counsel to help us answer the questions. Study it carefully and consider its implications in your own efforts to receive revelation.

"Great decisions must be made by most of us. The Lord has provided a way for these answers. If the question is which school, what occupation, where to live, whom to marry, or such other vital questions, you should do all that is possible to solve it. Too often, like Oliver Cowdery, we want our answers without effort. The Lord said to him: [D&C 9:7-9].

"The Lord does answer our prayers, but sometimes we are not responsive enough to know when and how they are answered. We want the 'writing on the wall' or an angel to speak or a heavenly voice. Often our requests are so absurd that the Lord has said, 'Trifle not with these things; do not ask for that which you ought not.' (D&C 8:10.)

"There must be works with faith. How futile it would be to ask the Lord to give us knowledge, but the Lord will help us to acquire knowledge, to study constructively, to think clearly, and to retain things we have learned. How stupid to ask the Lord to protect us if we unnecessarily drive at excessive speeds, if we eat or drink destructive elements. Can we ask him to provide us material things if we give no

*The Lord stands at the door and knocks*

effort? 'Faith without works is dead.' (James 2:20.)

"You who pray sometimes, why not pray more regularly, more often, more devoutly? Is time so precious, life so short, or faith so scant? How do you pray? Like publicans or arrogant officials? . . .

"In your secret prayers do you present yourself with your soul bared, or do you dress yourself in fancy coverings and pressure God to see your virtues? Do you emphasize your goodness and cover your sins with a blanket of pretense? Or do you plead for mercy at the hands of Kind Providence?

"Do you get answers to your prayers? If not, perhaps you did not pay the price. Do you offer a few trite words and worn-out phrases, or do you talk intimately to the Lord? Do you pray occasionally when you should be praying regularly, often, constantly? Do you offer pennies to pay heavy debts when you should give dollars to erase that obligation?

"When you pray, do you just speak, or do you also listen? . . .

". . . Do you know how to listen, grasp, interpret, understand? The Lord stands knocking. He never retreats. But he will never force himself upon us. If we ever move apart, it is we who move and not the Lord. And should we ever fail to get an answer to our prayers, we must look into our lives for a reason. We have failed to do what we should, or we have done something we should not have done. We have dulled our hearing or impaired our eyesight. . . .

"... when we pierce the shell and penetrate the covering and humble ourselves with naked soul and sincere supplication and cleansed life, our prayers are answered....

"When you received your confirmation, *you* were commanded to receive the Holy Ghost. *He* was not obligated to seek you out. The Lord says, 'I will visit thy brethren according to their diligence in keeping my commandments.' (Enos 1:10.) If our lives are responsive and clean, if we are reaching and cultivating, the Holy Ghost will come, and we may retain him and have the peace his presence thus affords.

"Do you give thanks or merely ask for favors? Or are you like the lepers by the road? They begged for mercy and were healed but did not stay to thank the generous Savior." ("Prayer," *New Era,* Mar. 1978, pp. 16-17.)

**(C-7) Summary**

Receiving personal revelation is the critical need of every individual who would avoid the real failures of mortality. To know something of the means the Lord uses to communicate with his children opens the door to possible communication. Knowing how to seek properly for that revelation helps one to prepare and obtain it for himself. The importance of knowing of the things of God for oneself is vital. The Prophet Joseph Smith said: "Search the Scriptures—search the revelations which we publish, and ask your Heavenly Father, in the name of His Son Jesus Christ, to manifest the truth unto you, and if you do it with an eye single to His glory, nothing doubting, He will answer you by the power of His Holy Spirit. You will then know for yourself and not for another. You will not then be dependent on man for the knowledge of God; nor will there be any room for speculation." (*History of the Church,* 1:282.)

# Contributions of the Doctrine and Covenants to an Understanding of Jesus Christ

Enrichment D

**(D-1) Introduction**

The goal of all faithful Latter-day Saints is to obtain eternal life and live in the presence of God. Since by Adam all men have fallen and become subject to sin and corruption, all men are dependent upon the atonement of Christ and through the Savior alone are able to obtain eternal life, the greatest gift of God (see D&C 6:13; 14:7). The Doctrine and Covenants is a sustaining witness and helps in understanding the Savior. His role, his divine attributes, his mission, and his second coming in glory are all taught in a clear, concise way in this book. This sacred volume of scripture also teaches man's relationship to Christ and man's responsibility to gain eternal life.

**(D-2) The Eternal Role of Jesus the Christ**

The mighty Elohim is the Father of the spirits of all men who have ever lived or will yet live upon the earth. His spirit offspring are indeed innumerable. Among this mighty throng in the pre-earth life stood one like unto God the Eternal Father (see Abraham 3:24) who was known by the name of Jehovah, or the Great I Am (see D&C 29:1; 39:1; 109:34, 42, 56; 110:3-4; 128:9; JST, Exodus 3:13-15; Exodus 6:3; Psalm 83:18; Isaiah 12:2; 26:4; John 8:58; Abraham 2:8). It was he who would come to earth as Jesus, the Savior of mankind. The Doctrine and Covenants gives a clear understanding of the eternal role of the Savior.

Because he merited it, Jehovah was the firstborn of the spirit offspring of Elohim (see D&C 93:21), and as such, he became the legal heir to all the Father owned. Thus, the responsibility fell upon the great Jehovah to carry out the plan of salvation ordained by the Father whereby the rest of his spirit children might have the opportunity, through obedience, to become joint heirs with the Firstborn (see Hugh B. Brown, in Conference Report, Oct. 1963, p. 92).

*The Savior is the creator of all things.* The Doctrine and Covenants teaches this principle (see D&C 14:9; 29:31; 38:3; 45:1; 76:24; 93:10; 95:7).

Concerning the Savior's pre-earth role, Elder Bruce R. McConkie stated:

"We believe, and I certify that Jesus Christ is the Firstborn Spirit Child of Elohim who is God, our Heavenly Father. We believe that while he lived in the pre-existent world, by virtue of his superior intelligence, progression, and obedience, he attained unto the station of a *God.* And he then became, under the Father, the Creator of this world and all things that are in it, as also the Creator of worlds without number.

"We believe that he was the Jehovah of the Old Testament; that it was through him that God the Father dealt with all the ancient prophets, revealing his mind and his will and the plan of salvation to them.

"Christ gave the gospel to the ancients beginning

with Adam and going on down, dispensation after dispensation, until this present time. And everything that has been given in the gospel and everything that has been in any way connected with it has been designed for the express purpose of bearing record of Christ and certifying as to his divine mission." (In Conference Report, Oct. 1948, pp. 23-24.)

*The Savior is the light of the world.* In explaining this particular role of the Savior, Elder Bruce R. McConkie described "at least three ways, each intertwined with the others, in which our Lord is the Light of the World. These are:

"1. Through the Light of Christ he governs and controls the universe and gives life to all that therein is. [See D&C 88:6-10.]

"2. By this same immensity-filling light—and also, to certain faithful ones, by the power of the Holy Ghost!—he enlightens the mind and quickens the understanding. [See D&C 88:11.]

"3. By his own upright, sinless, and perfect course, in preexistence, in mortality, and in resurrected glory, he sets a perfect example and is able to say to all men: 'Follow thou me.' (2 Ne. 31:10.) [See D&C 45:4.]

"Our understanding of the Light of Christ is limited," Elder McConkie continued. "Finite powers and capacities cannot comprehend that which is infinite. But we do know certain basic principles, among which are these:

"1. That it is the light which proceeds forth from the presence and person of Deity to fill immensity, and that it is therefore everywhere present [see D&C 88:12];

"2. That it is the agency of God's power, the law by which all things are governed [see D&C 88:13];

"3. That it is the divine power which gives life to all things, and that if it were completely withdrawn life would cease [see D&C 88:13];

"4. That it enlightens the mind and quickens the understanding of every person born into the world [see D&C 84:46]; . . .

"5. That it strives with all men (the Holy Ghost testifies but does not strive) unless and until they rebel against light and truth, at which time the striving ceases, and in that sense the Spirit is withdrawn [see D&C 88:7; 93:9];

"6. That those who hearken to its voice come unto Christ, receive his gospel, are baptized, and gain the gift of the Holy Ghost. (Moro. 7:12-18; D&C 84:43-53; 88:7-13.)" (*Promised Messiah,* pp. 208-9.) In each instance, the principle used by Elder McConkie is substantiated by the Doctrine and Covenants, as indicated.

## (D-3) The Eternal Attributes of Jesus Christ

The inherent characteristics of the Savior are referred to throughout the scriptures as attributes. These divine qualities are held in fulness and perfection by the Savior because of his total obedience to the mind and will of the Father (see D&C 93:11-17; see also Notes and Commentary for those verses for an explanation of how the Savior obtained a fulness of the attributes of the Father). It is imperative that mortal man understand these attributes so that he can exercise faith in God. The Prophet Joseph Smith explained: "The real design which the God of heaven had in view in making the human family acquainted with his attributes, was, that they, through the idea of the existence of his attributes, might be enabled to exercise faith in him, and through the exercise of faith in him, might obtain eternal life; for without the idea of the existence of the attributes which belong to God, the minds of men could not have power to exercise faith in him so as to lay hold upon eternal life" (*Lectures on Faith* 4:2).

Some of the attributes of the Lord as taught by the Prophet Joseph Smith are knowledge; faith, or power; justice; judgment; mercy; and truth (see *Lectures on Faith* 4:41-43). The Doctrine and Covenants testifies of these attributes and helps to increase one's understanding of many of them.

*The omniscience of the Savior.* Some have persisted in teaching that the Savior and even God the Father are ever learning. This teaching is not consistent with the teaching of the scriptures that God *knows all things* (see D&C 38:2; 88:6, 41; 2 Nephi 2:24; 9:20; Mormon 8:17; Moroni 7:22). Speaking of the misconception that God might still be learning, Elder Bruce R. McConkie said:

"And there are even those who champion the almost unbelievable theory that God is an eternal student enrolled in the University of the Universe, where he is busily engaged in learning new truths and amassing new and strange knowledge that he never knew before.

"How belittling it is—it borders on blasphemy—to demean the Lord God Omnipotent by saying he is an idol, or an image, or an animal, or a spirit essence, or that he is ever learning but never able

*He is just and will judge the world*

to come to a knowledge of all truth (see 2 Tim. 3:7)." (In Conference Report, Oct. 1980, p. 75; or *Ensign*, Nov. 1980, pp. 50-51.)

The knowledge that God possesses includes an understanding of the past, present, and future (see D&C 130:7). The story of the loss of the 116-page manuscript by Martin Harris at the time the Prophet was translating the Book of Mormon is a great example of the foreknowledge of God (see Words of Mormon 1:3-7; D&C 3, 10).

*Christ is omnipotent.* By being perfectly obedient to the will of the Father, Jesus brought about the Atonement and, in his own words, retained "all power" unto himself (D&C 19:3; see also 49:6; 61:1). The Doctrine and Covenants, like the other standard works, bears witness that in the Godhead resides all power. There is nothing in the universe with sufficient power to "stay my hand" (D&C 38:33). The word *power* is used over two hundred times in the Doctrine and Covenants, and in most of those usages it bears witness of God's power and his use of it for the benefit of his people.

*Christ is the source of justice and judgment.* One of the most comforting things derived from faith in the Savior is the knowledge that at some time everything will be made right, that justice will be done. There is something inherent in virtually every man that cries out for the righting of wrongs, the squaring of accounts, the giving of just dues, whether those dues be blessings for obedience or punishments for disobedience. In numerous instances in the Doctrine and Covenants the Lord bears witness that he is a just God and that all men will be brought to judgment, receiving blessings for obedience and punishments for all transgressions not repented of (see, for example, D&C 3:4; 10:28; 39:16-18; 82:4; 84:102; 107:84; 109:77).

*The mercy of Christ.* Knowing of God's awesome powers and of his continual promises to bring men to judgment would be a frightening and discouraging thing if one did not know that he also has a perfection and fulness of love and mercy. In addition to many promises of mercy and forgiveness for the repentant (see, for example, D&C 3:10; 29:1; 38:14; 54:6; 61:2; 76:5; 88:40), the Doctrine and Covenants contains some of the most tender and endearing expressions of the Savior to his servants and his people:

"Be faithful and diligent . . . and I will encircle thee in the arms of my love" (D&C 6:20).

"Fear not to do good, my sons" (D&C 6:33).

"Fear not, little flock" (D&C 6:34).

"From henceforth I shall call you friends" (D&C 84:77).

"I will call you friends, for you are my friends" (D&C 93:45).

"Whom I love I also chasten . . . and I have loved you" (D&C 95:1).

*Christ is truth.* Understanding of this attribute comes primarily from the Doctrine and Covenants, where it is revealed that truth is light (see D&C 84:45; 88:6-7); truth is eternal (see D&C 88:66); truth is knowledge of things as they are, and as they were, and as they are to come (see D&C 93:24). If the Savior is the Light of the World and the Light of Christ lights every man who comes into the world, and if truth is light, then it follows that not only is the Savior the source of truth but his very nature is truth.

Elder Bruce R. McConkie explained: "Christ is the *Truth,* meaning that he is the perfect embodiment of all truth. 'I am the way, the truth, and the life' (John 14:6; Ether 4:12); 'I am the Spirit of truth.' (D&C 93:26.) He is the champion of truth, the revealer of truth, the advocate of truth. His word is truth and all his works conform thereto." (*Mormon Doctrine,* p. 810; see also D&C 93:12-13, 16-20, 28, 36.)

All scriptures bear witness and teach of the attributes of deity, and the Doctrine and Covenants joins the other standard works as a powerful voice in this testimony.

The Prophet Joseph Smith taught that one of the things necessary for faith was a "*correct* idea of [God's] character, perfections, and attributes" (*Lectures on Faith* 3:4; emphasis added). He then explained why that is the case: "An acquaintance with these attributes in the divine character, is essentially necessary, in order that the faith of any rational being can center in him for life and salvation. For if he did not, in the first instance, believe him to be God, that is, the Creator and upholder of all things, he could not *center* his faith in him for life and salvation, for fear there should be greater than he who would thwart all his plans, and he like the gods of the heathen, would be unable to fulfill his promises; but seeing he is God over all, from everlasting to everlasting, the Creator and upholder of all things, no such fear can exist in the minds of those who put their trust in him, so that in this respect their faith can be without wavering." (*Lectures on Faith* 3:19.)

The same principle holds true of all the Savior's attributes. If we did not know that God knows all things, we could conceivably wonder if we might ask him something he did not know. If we cannot believe he is longsuffering and merciful, we will quickly despair of any hope of salvation as we keenly sense our unworthiness.

At first, having this correct understanding may seem like a simple thing, and many would assume they have met the requirement of having a correct idea of God's attributes. But frequently expressions are heard, even among active, committed Latter-day Saints, that reveal some weaknesses in their understanding of God's character and attributes. Consider the following true examples, then see if you can identify which characteristic or attribute of God is being questioned.

*A.* Why did God give me a body that is fat and ugly? I'll never get a date because I'm too homely.

*B.* My bishop called me into his office after Church and asked if I would consider going on a mission. I know every young man has that obligation, but does every young woman? I'm twenty-four and not married. Won't a mission add to my chances of being an old maid? The bishop suggested I pray about it, but I'm afraid to. What if the answer is yes? I don't want to go!

*C.* Before I knew I was pregnant, my doctor had me on a strong medication for a tumor. Now my obstetrician tells me that the chances I will have a retarded baby are increased significantly by the nature of the medication. He is not LDS and is strongly encouraging me to have an abortion. Everything in me revolts at the thought, but what if I do have a baby that is retarded?

*D.* I have not partaken of the sacrament for three years. I was guilty of a moral transgression, and even though I confessed to the bishop and did all he asked of me, and even though I have sought earnestly to repent, I still feel unclean and unworthy to partake of the sacrament. I don't know if I'll ever be able to partake again.

*E.* I have a deep personal problem that I have not been able to resolve. I've prayed about this question for nearly a year now. I've pleaded with the Lord, begged him for an answer. Nothing has happened. Why won't he answer me?

Every case cited here illustrates a wavering of faith in one of the attributes of God. Though each of these persons might be surprised to think of it in that way, each is in some way doubting the nature of God. They are questioning his power to make a difference in their lives, his wisdom in allowing things to happen as they do, his love, his longsuffering, his forgiveness, his concern for them. But these people could react to their problems in other ways if they had faith in the attributes of the Savior.

*A.* I realize that I have been placed in a body that is not thought of as physically beautiful. But my study of the Savior convinces me that what really matters to him is inner beauty. If the kind of body I have to live with is important to my salvation, then he would have given me a different body. Therefore, I will try to make myself outwardly as attractive as possible, but my real desire is to become spiritually beautiful.

*B.* I can honestly say I don't want to go on a mission, and as a woman it may not be required of me to fill a full-time mission. But I have to find out what God's will for me is. I trust in him. I know that if he asks me to go on a mission, it is the best thing for me. And if the answer is not to go, then I can stay home without feeling guilty. I will pray about this matter and find out his will for me.

*C.* The will of the Lord on abortion is clear and unmistakable. I will not terminate this precious life in me. My husband and I will petition the Lord in fasting and prayer for the remainder of the pregnancy that all will be well. I'll receive a blessing from the priesthood which my husband holds. And if it is the Lord's will that this baby be born retarded, then it will be my faith that it is for the best—the best for me, the best for my family, the best for this child.

*D.* Christ suffered an infinite agony, both in the Garden of Gethsemane and on the cross so that the price of sin could be met and paid. The conditions for having that price paid for serious transgressions such as my own are demanding, but if I meet those conditions, as I have been sincerely striving to do, do I not deny the gifts offered me if I refuse to forgive myself? If Christ says that his mercy is sufficient to make me clean, how can I deny his word?

*E.* I have prayed and sought earnestly and sincerely for an answer to my problem. The fact that I have not received an answer could mean several things. I know that God has all knowledge of me and of all the circumstances involved in this problem. I know that God has all power. He can do whatever is required. I know that his love for me is perfect. Therefore, the reason nothing has happened is not because he doesn't care. It is not because he doesn't know what to do or can't do it. There must be a good reason why he hasn't answered me. Maybe I need more faith, more repentance. Or perhaps it is a way of teaching me something more important. I will not despair, but will continue to persevere, trusting in his judgment of when is the best time for my answer.

### (D-4) The Eternal Mission of Jesus Christ

Only through Christ is salvation made possible. Because he was God, even in mortality, Jesus

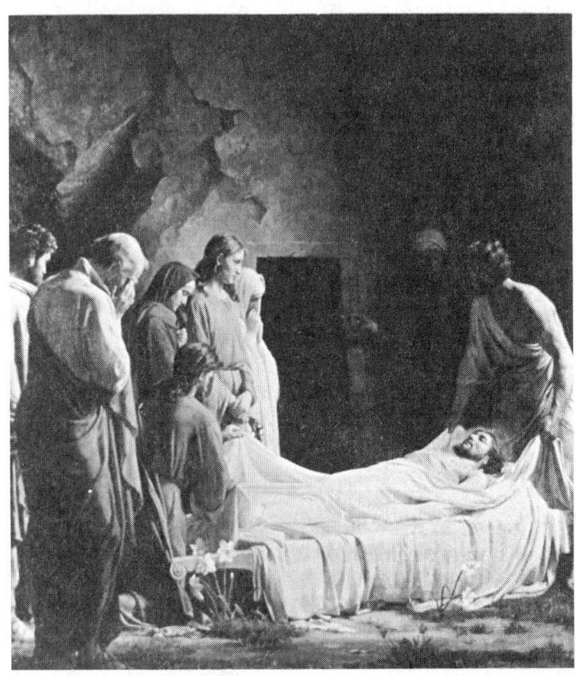

The Burial of Christ *by Carl Bloch. Original at King's Prayer Chair, Frederiksborg Castle, Denmark. Used by permission of the National Historic Museum at Frederiksborg*

Christ possessed inherent powers and abilities that no other person ever had. He was God's Only Begotten Son and thus possessed the powers and intelligence of God himself. He was perfect in nature; consequently he was able to assume the sins of all other beings, to suffer for them so that, on condition of their personal repentance, they would not have to suffer.

Not only was Jesus *able* to bear the sins of his brothers and sisters, but he was also *willing* to do so. He thereby demonstrated his great love. He accomplished this redemption by a voluntary act called the Atonement in which he took upon himself the sins of all mankind. The intense suffering of the Savior commenced in the Garden of Gethsemane and terminated at Calvary. Luke described the suffering in the Garden as being so intense that Christ's "sweat was as it were great drops of blood" (Luke 22:44.) Many scholars have tried to explain this passage as metaphorical and not literal; that is, they say that Jesus perspired heavily but did not actually bleed from his pores. The Doctrine and Covenants demolishes that rationalization, describing in some detail the incredible suffering he underwent (see D&C 19:15-19; 76:69).

Christ suffered as only a God could suffer, both in body and in spirit. Willingly he took the cup. In that solitary Garden, made sacred by his presence, he "suffered the pain of all men, that all men might repent and come unto him" (D&C 18:11). The extent of his suffering is forcefully stated by Elder Marion G. Romney in these words: "Jesus then went into the Garden of Gethsemane. There he suffered most. He suffered greatly on the cross, of course, but other men had died by crucifixion; in fact, a man hung on either side of him as he died on the cross. But no man, nor set of men, nor all men put together, ever suffered what the Redeemer suffered in the Garden." (In Conference Report, Oct. 1953, p. 35.)

Elder Romney also stated, "The suffering he undertook to endure, and which he did endure, *equaled the combined suffering of all men*" (in Conference Report, Oct. 1969, p. 57; emphasis added).

The Doctrine and Covenants testifies that Jesus, in making the atonement, descended below all things—meaning that he suffered the pains of hell for all men if they would repent (see D&C 88:6; 122:8). Because he suffered to this extent, there is no sin, no pain, no suffering that he cannot comprehend. He knows each individual's every weakness. He understands each person better than that person understands himself, and thus the Savior knows "how to succor them who are tempted" (D&C 62:1).

## (D-5) Man's Relationship to Christ

Through the atonement of Christ, salvation is extended to every son and daughter of God. The responsibility rests upon each individual to repent, to believe in Christ, and then to endure faithfully to the end (see D&C 20:29). The Savior's atonement, combined with a willing obedience to his gospel, qualifies one to become his son or daughter (see D&C 39:4-6; 11:30; 25:1).

Thus, by keeping all commandments pertaining to his gospel, one may receive the power and attributes of Christ in himself and become his son or daughter. Eventually, through the grace of God, one may receive the fulness of godly power and attributes, "*made perfect* through Jesus . . . who wrought out this perfect atonement through the shedding of his own blood" (D&C 76:69; emphasis added).

The Doctrine and Covenants commands all men to take upon themselves his name, for in his name only is there salvation: "Take upon you the name of Christ, and speak the truth in soberness. And as many as repent and are baptized in my name, which is Jesus Christ, and endure to the end, the same shall be saved. Behold, Jesus Christ is the name which is given of the Father, and there is none other name given whereby men can be saved; . . . Wherefore, if they know not the name by which they are called, they cannot have place in the kingdom of my Father." (D&C 18:21-25.) Those who believe in his name and keep his commandments shall find rest (see D&C 38:4), which is everlasting life in his presence (see D&C 45:3-5).

## (D-6) Christ's Coming in Glory

On 3 April 1836 Elijah appeared in the Kirtland Temple to Joseph Smith and Oliver Cowdery in fulfillment of the prophecy made by Malachi (see Malachi 4:5-6; D&C 110:13-16). The prophet Elijah testified that he had come so that members of the Church might "know that the great and dreadful day of the Lord is near, even at the doors" (D&C 110:16). The coming of Christ in glory (see D&C 34:7-8) to reign with the righteous for a thousand years (see D&C 29:11, 17) is an event longed for by all Saints in all dispensations. This dispensation has the privilege to make final preparation for his coming and to see that the kingdom of God is prepared to meet him (see D&C 65:6). Prior to his coming, however, there will be some who are members of his Church who will say that Christ delays his coming, and as a result, they will not be prepared (see D&C 45:26). It behooves all to live as though the Savior will come tomorrow (see D&C 64:23), for those who are prepared need not fear.

The Doctrine and Covenants is a handbook on the Second Coming. It is replete with prophecies, promises, clarifications, and new revelations on the judgments that precede this coming in glory, on the Second Coming itself, and on the conditions that will prevail during the Savior's millennial reign. Enrichment H discusses this subject in detail.

## (D-7) Summary

The Doctrine and Covenants bears testimony of Christ. Just as the Book of Mormon is called a second witness for Christ, so, and with equal validity, could the Doctrine and Covenants be described as a witness for the Savior. It affirms that he was the Firstborn of Heavenly Father; that by him the worlds were created; that he came to earth as God's Only Begotten Son in the flesh; that he suffered temptations, wrought miracles, proclaimed his gospel, and invited all men to come to him, repent, and receive the saving ordinances of the gospel. In the Doctrine and Covenants the Savior witnesses that he suffered the pains of all men and accomplished the perfect atonement; that he was crucified, buried, and went into the world of spirits where he declared his everlasting gospel and the doctrine of resurrection to an innumerable company of righteous spirits; and appointed and commissioned messengers to go to the wicked and disobedient spirits and teach them.

In the Doctrine and Covenants the Lord says that on the third day after his death he rose again and appeared to many, including the Nephites on the American continent and the ten tribes, that he ascended into heaven where he sits in glory on the right hand of his Father, and that he has promised to come to earth again to reign with the righteous Saints for one thousand years.

The Doctrine and Covenants is a source of great strength in increasing one's knowledge of the Savior in every aspect. It contributes many new insights to an understanding of the Holy One of Israel. It is a book of scripture that must be read and studied diligently by the Latter-day Saints.

# Overcoming Sin and Obtaining Forgiveness

Enrichment E

### (E-1) Introduction

As it pertains to the consequences of personal sin, the blessings and benefits of the Atonement are forgiveness of sin through repentance, sanctification through obedience to the laws and commandments of God, and the hope of eternal life in the presence of God.

The purpose of this enrichment section is to build an understanding of what the Doctrine and Covenants has to say about repentance, forgiveness, and sanctification. Only by understanding these three principles and then applying them in one's life can one obtain eternal life and live in the presence of God.

### (E-2) Repentance and Atonement for Sins

The Doctrine and Covenants states that God "cannot look upon sin with the least degree of allowance" (D&C 1:31). Yet to those who are humble and submissive to the Lord there is a way to overcome sin and its tragic effects and thus be countenanced by the Lord. The process by which sin is overcome is repentance, the second principle of the gospel of Jesus Christ. President David O. McKay said that "every principle and ordinance of the gospel of Jesus Christ is significant and important in contributing to the progress, happiness, and eternal life of man, but there is none more essential to the salvation of the human family than the divine and eternally operative principle, repentance. Without it, no one can be saved. Without it, no one can even progress." (*Gospel Ideals,* p. 13.)

Repentance would have no validity or power were it not for the Atonement. Through his suffering, the Savior paid for the sins of all mankind, "that they might not suffer if they would repent" (D&C 19:16). It is not repentance itself that pays the price for sin. No effort to reform one's life, no matter how sincere, no matter how profound, would be sufficient to save a person had there been no atoning sacrifice. No one, save Jesus only, has ever lived a life which by itself could earn him the right to return to the presence of God, because, as the Prophet noted in the dedicatory prayer on the Kirtland Temple, "all men sin" (D&C 109:34). That is why all men come short of the glory of God (see Romans 3:23). Since God cannot look upon sin with the least degree of allowance, that is, since he cannot overlook it or excuse it in the slightest way, there had to be some way for the sins to be made right. A price had to be paid. Part of that price was his suffering of such intensity that it caused Jesus, "the greatest of all, to tremble because of pain, and to bleed at every pore" (D&C 19:18). No mortal could ever have paid that price, for as Amulek taught, it was necessary that it be "an infinite and eternal sacrifice" (Alma 34:10).

The Doctrine and Covenants adds its voice to that of other scriptures in making this distinction: It is not repentance per se that saves man. It is the blood of Jesus Christ that saves him. Repentance, however, *is the condition required* so that the atonement can be applied in his behalf. If one could save himself by a sincere and honest change of behavior, then it could be said that he saves himself by his own works, and the scriptures clearly teach that such is not the case. As Nephi wrote, "We know that it is by grace that we are saved, after all we can do" (2 Nephi 25:23). Using the imagery of the courtroom, Jesus describes himself as an advocate, or one who pleads the cause of another (see D&C 45:3). Usually when one pleads another's case, he does so on the basis that the client is not guilty of the charges. No such plea is entered in this case. All are guilty of sin, all have transgressed. (See Romans 3:23.) Who could plead for any soul on the basis of absence of guilt? The Advocate does not call the attention of the Judge to man's perfection, *but to his own.* He notes the blood shed in the atoning sacrifice and then pleads that the repentant person be spared, for he has met Christ's conditions and become his brother (see D&C 45:3-5).

While repentance is one of the most important steps forward we can make, we should recognize that it is still only a returning step. If we consider the starting point as the place where we were before we repented, then repentance is definitely a forward progression. It could be diagrammed like this:

**Sin** Repentance **Righteousness** →

But in another sense, we could say that repentance is merely a return to the original point of departure. This progress could be diagrammed like this:

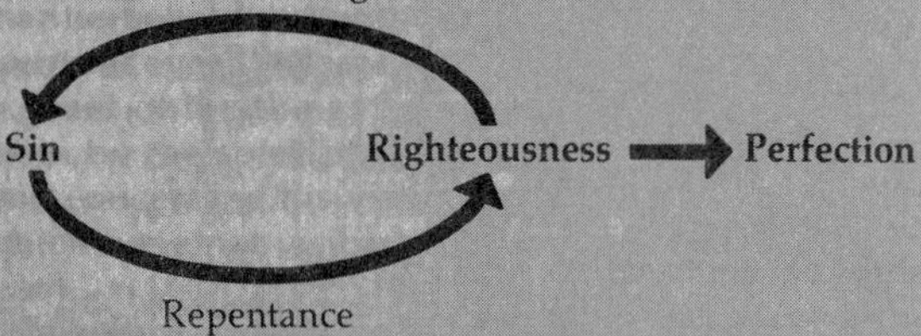


Progression toward exaltation cannot take place until we have returned to righteousness, and it is therefore absolutely critical for all of us to repent. *True repentance only brings us back to doing what we should have been doing all along.* The effects of the atonement of Christ in one's life is conditional upon one's repentance (see D&C 18:12). Those who do not repent and keep the commandments will suffer (see D&C 19:4). The Doctrine and Covenants teaches that this vital principle, forgiveness of sin upon the condition of repentance, is also being taught in the world of spirits (see D&C 138:19). Each individual then has a responsibility to forsake sin and keep the commandments of the Lord. Elder Spencer W. Kimball stated: "When we think of the great sacrifice of our Lord Jesus Christ and the sufferings he endured for us, we would be ingrates if we did not appreciate it so far as our power made it possible. He suffered and died for us, yet if we do not repent, all his anguish and pain on our account are futile." (*Miracle of Forgiveness,* p. 145.)

### (E-3) Forgive to Be Forgiven

During his mortal ministry, the Savior taught by precept and example that forgiveness of others is a condition for obtaining forgiveness for oneself (see Matthew 5:23-24; 6:12, 14-15; 18:21-35; John 8:1-11). One of the great contributions of the Doctrine and Covenants is its emphasis on and clarification of this important principle. In ringing, unmistakable words, the Savior said that an unwillingess to forgive others was an "evil" (D&C 64:8) and that "he that forgiveth not his brother his trespasses *standeth condemned before the Lord;* for there remaineth in him *the greater sin*" (D&C 64:9; emphasis added). And then, lest any should say that such a principle was good for certain sins but could not apply when someone had done

*Marion D. Hanks said that forgiveness is the ultimate form of love*

something really serious, the Lord summarized the extent of the law: "I, the Lord, will forgive whom I will forgive, *but of you it is required to forgive all men*" (D&C 64:10; emphasis added).

In the midst of the terrible persecutions in Jackson County, the Lord revealed the laws of retaliation and forgiveness (see D&C 98; Notes and Commentary on D&C 98).

The principle of repentance is so important to your obtaining personal forgiveness that you ought to take stock of where you are now. Do you hold bitterness and hostility for someone who has wronged you? It doesn't matter how deserved those feelings may be; if you cannot forgive the trespasser, according to the Lord, you have a greater sin than he who wronged you. "The ultimate form of love for God and men is forgiveness," said Elder Marion D. Hanks.

"What is our response when we are offended, misunderstood, unfairly or unkindly treated, or sinned against, made an offender for a word, falsely accused, passed over, hurt by those we love, our offerings rejected? Do we resent, become bitter, hold a grudge? Or do we resolve the problem if we can, forgive, and rid ourselves of the burden?

"The nature of our response to such situations may well determine the nature and quality of our lives, here and eternally. A courageous friend, her faith refined by many afflictions, said to me only hours ago 'Humiliation must come before exaltation' [see D&C 29:2; 61:2; 136:33].

"It is required of us to forgive. Our salvation depends upon it. . . .

"It is reported that President Brigham Young

once said that he who takes offense when no offense is intended is a fool, and he who takes offense when offense is intended is usually a fool. It was then explained that there are two courses of action to follow when one is bitten by a rattlesnake. One may in anger, fear, or vengefulness pursue the creature and kill it. Or he may make full haste to get the venom out of his system. If we pursue the latter course we will likely survive, but if we attempt to follow the former, we may not be around long enough to finish it. ("Even as Christ Forgave," *New Era*, June 1974, pp. 4-5.)

The following story from the life of President George Albert Smith illustrates the effects of forgiveness in the life of the offender and the offended:

"When George Albert Smith was a young man, he joined the Utah National Guard. Being a good rider and having an excellent mount, he made quite a dashing figure in the practice charges up Arsenal Hill. Some of his friends urged him to run for an office in the Guard, and he consented. During the next few weeks, however, a man whom he had supposed to be his friend circulated false charges to the effect that Smith was seeking to win by unfair means.

"Partly because of these rumors, Sergeant Smith failed to win the votes of his fellow guardsmen. So he did not win the promotion to which he felt he had been entitled. His heart was filled with bitterness and hate for the onetime friend who had treated him so unfairly.

"He went to Church and tried to forget about the unpleasant affair, but his heart was still full of resentment. He could not feel right about taking the sacrament. After meditating and praying, Brother George Albert Smith concluded that he, too, was in the wrong for continuing to nurse a grievance.

"He decided to relieve himself of the burden of hate that seemed to be doing him more harm than it was doing his enemy. He crossed the street and walked directly into the office of the man who had spread the rumors. As he entered the door, the man put up his arm as if in self-defense. No doubt he expected a fight. He knew in his heart that he had gravely wronged a friend. But George Albert Smith had not come to fight. On the contrary, his voice was soft and forgiving.

" 'My brother,' he said, 'I want you to forgive me for hating you the way I have for the last few weeks.'

"The man of rumors was immediately melted into contrition. 'Brother Smith,' he said, 'you have no need for forgiveness. It is I who need forgiveness from you.' Because of George Albert Smith's courage and spiritual strength, the man who had made himself an enemy was completely subdued. He repented of his evil conduct and thereafter he and Brother Smith were once more good friends." (Merlo J. Pusey, "The Inner Strength of a Leader," *Instructor*, June 1965, p. 232.)

### (E-4) Being Cleansed from One's Sins

It is an eternal law that no unclean thing can dwell in the presence of God (see Moses 6:57; 1 Nephi 10:21; Alma 7:21). It was for this reason that Paul said, "All have sinned, and come short of the glory of God" (Romans 3:23). Nevertheless, upon conditions of repentance and forgiveness of others, one can have his own sins forgiven and paid for by the Redeemer. The scriptures and the prophets bear witness again and again that through the atoning blood of Christ not only can one be forgiven of his sins but he can be cleansed from all effects of transgression and become holy and spotless, able then to enter back into the presence of God. The process by which this cleansing is done is called sanctification.

The Doctrine and Covenants, together with other scriptures, teaches the need for the blessings of sanctification: "Sanctify yourselves before me," said the Lord (D&C 43:11). "Sanctify yourselves, and ye shall be endowed with power" (D&C 43:16). "Wherefore, prepare ye, prepare ye, O my people; sanctify yourselves" (D&C 133:4). This latter-day work of scripture teaches that for any individual to be able to enjoy celestial glory and live in the presence of God he must be sanctified (see D&C 76:21; 88:2; 88:21). The following questions might then be asked: What is sanctification? What is the process by which one becomes sanctified?

Sanctification is purification from sin. Elder Bruce R. McConkie explained: "To be *sanctified* is to become clean, pure, and spotless; to be free from the blood and sins of the world; to become a new creature of the Holy Ghost, one whose body has been renewed by the rebirth of the Spirit. *Sanctification* is a state of saintliness, a state attained only by conformity to the laws and ordinances of the gospel. The plan of salvation is the system and means provided whereby men may sanctify their souls and thereby become worthy of a celestial inheritance." (*Mormon Doctrine*, p. 675.)

One of the greatest aspirations of any true Latter-day Saint is to become clean enough to see the Savior and eventually to know that he will live in the presence of God the Father. The process of sanctification, whereby one becomes clean enough to obtain such great blessings, is taught in the Doctrine and Covenants. First, an individual must be willing to repent and accept the fulness of the gospel of Jesus Christ (see D&C 39:18; 133:62). He then must be willing to "live by every word that proceedeth forth from the mouth of God" (D&C 84:44). There needs to be a willingness on the part of all who hold the priesthood to serve their fellowman and magnify their callings in the priesthood (see D&C 84:33). Also, a humble, submissive spirit is required as the Lord chastens his children unto righteousness (see D&C 101:5) and purges the iniquity from among them (see D&C 43:11). As a person complies with these steps he is purged from sin by the power of the Holy Ghost, for, according to the Doctrine and Covenants, the Holy Ghost is the Sanctifier (see D&C 19:31; 55:1; 84:33).

*The sheep of his fold are washed in the blood of the Lamb of God*

Once one has been sanctified, the burden of guilt for sins is taken away. He can know for himself that he is forgiven and made clean. President Daniel H. Wells, a counselor to President Brigham Young, said that "no man can get a greater testimony of the forgiveness of his sins by the Lord, than a knowledge within himself that he has turned away from his evil deeds. He knows it then, for God has promised to forgive every one who will comply with the requirements of the Gospel and turn from evil; and the man who forsakes evil knows it, and if he has no other testimony of his forgiveness, this is as great a one as he can possess." (In *Journal of Discourses,* 15:89.)

President Harold B. Lee also taught concerning all those who truly repent of their sins: "When you have done all within your power to overcome your mistakes, and have determined in your heart that you will never repeat them again, then too, you can come to that peace of conscience by which you will know that your sins have been forgiven" (*Church News,* 2 Sept. 1972, p. 7).

To those who despair in their present state, who wander in the wilderness of sin and wonder if they can ever return to the light and love of their Savior, the Doctrine and Covenants bears solemn witness that there is a way back. To those who will repent, it promises the blessings of forgiveness and sanctification through the atoning blood of the Master. The Doctrine and Covenants, in one of the simplest and yet most profound summaries in scripture, promises two rewards for those who do the works of righteousness: "peace in this world and eternal life in the world to come" (D&C 59:23).

Only when one has been cleansed from sin can he find true peace in this life. The role of the Comforter is to bring that peace to all who will come to Christ and sanctify or cleanse themselves in his blood. Elder Spencer W. Kimball wrote of the hope this promise should give to everyone:

"In the book of Revelation it is written that *he that overcometh* shall 'eat of the tree of life,' receive 'a crown of life,' not be hurt of the second death. He shall receive of the 'hidden manna,' a 'white stone,' and a 'new name,' shall have 'power over the nations.' He shall be clothed in 'white raiments,' and his name will 'not be blotted out.' '*To him that overcometh* will I grant to sit with me in my throne, even as I also overcame, and am set down with my Father in his throne.' (Rev. 3:21. Italics added.) How glorious and rich are the promises to those who overcome!

" 'What are these which are arrayed in white robes?' asked one of the elders in John's vision, and the answer was: ' . . . These are they which came out of great tribulation, and have washed their robes, and made them white in the blood of the Lamb. Therefore are they before the throne of God, and serve him day and night in his temple . . . ' (Rev. 7:14-15.)

"It would seem that these people had not always been perfect. They had had soiled robes and many weaknesses, but had now overcome and had washed the soiled raiment in the blood of the Lamb. They were now clean and purified, as is indicated in the blessings promised." (*Miracle of Forgiveness,* p. 354.)

The promise is clearly stated by the Lord: "And unto him that repenteth and sanctifieth himself before the Lord shall be given eternal life" (D&C 133:62).

# "As If from Mine Own Mouth": The Role of Prophets in the Church

Enrichment F

## (F-1) Introduction

"A prophet needs to be more than a priest or a minister or an elder. His voice becomes the voice of God," said President Spencer W. Kimball. (In Conference Report, Apr. 1970, p. 120.)

Heavenly Father did not intend that his children should grapple alone with the problems of mortality. Nor did he intend that they be exposed to Satan's influence without divine assistance and direction. Therefore, before the world was created, God appointed his most faithful and spiritually talented sons as prophets and revelators. He assigned each of these prophets to come to earth at a particular time and in circumstances where, in the foreknowledge of God, his talents would be most beneficial to the kingdom of God and to mankind in general.

From the very beginning, prophets have had a solemn duty to raise the warning voice, to foresee future times, and to reveal the mind and will of God. Hence, those men appointed by God are called prophets (forewarners), seers (see-ers into any period of time as it affects God's children), and revelators (revealers of God's will).

Often, prophets are not well received by the people they preach to (see Matthew 13:57). Popular reaction to Enoch was that "there is a strange thing in the land; a wild man hath come among us" (Moses 6:38). The Jews challenged Jesus' credentials as a prophet with the cynical query, "Is not this the carpenter's son?" (Matthew 13:55). So presumptuous to the worldly-minded is the claim that God has communicated to man that they reject the message immediately upon learning it. Elder Neal A. Maxwell said, "Imagine how television's six o'clock news would have portrayed Noah as he worked on his ark day by day" (in Conference Report, Oct. 1980, p. 17; or *Ensign,* Nov. 1980, p. 14). But just because a prophet's message is not popular with the people who hear it does not mean that it is not true.

The Lord spoke often in the Doctrine and Covenants about the need for living prophets and about their place in the Church of Jesus Christ. With the great apostasy, prophets were no longer sent to labor among men, and in the resulting Dark Ages the Christian world lost its understanding of the role of prophets in the Lord's plan. That knowledge was restored with the calling of the Prophet Joseph Smith. The Doctrine and Covenants reestablishes the Lord's will concerning prophets, giving the righteous of all nations the knowledge of prophets and of their obligations to them.

## (F-2) The Lord's Endorsement of His Prophets

The Doctrine and Covenants reveals many

*"For his word ye shall receive, as if from mine own mouth" (D&C 21:5)*

important aspects of having a living prophet and of his place in the Church. Of these aspects none is more important than the Lord's own view of the prophets, which is taught plainly and forcefully in the Doctrine and Covenants. A prophet's role is to speak the mind and will of the Lord to the people. When he does so, the Lord clearly teaches, it is as if the Lord himself had spoken. In the preface to the Doctrine and Covenants, for example, the Lord warned that all who refuse to heed the Apostles and prophets would be cut off (see D&C 1:14). He then promised a fulfillment of all his words, adding that it did not matter whether those words came directly from him or through his servants, for either way, *"it is the same"* (D&C 1:38; emphasis added). On the day the Church was organized, the Lord commanded the Church to give heed to the words of the prophet, saying, "For his words ye shall receive *as if from mine own mouth"* (D&C 21:5; emphasis added).

What an endorsement from the Lord. When his servants speak for him, in his eyes it is as though he were there in person. There is no difference, according to the Lord himself, in the validity of the message.

The following passages of scripture indicate the Savior's esteem and regard for his prophets. Mark these scriptures in your own standard works, and answer the accompanying questions on a separate sheet of paper.

*D&C 1:11-14.* How will the world receive the voice of the Lord? What is the prophesied result if they reject it?

*D&C 1:38.* How does the Lord view what his authorized servants say?

*D&C 18:30-36.* Whose words do we read in

the revelations given through the prophets?

*D&C 21:4-6.* What blessings are promised when the Church listens to the words of the prophet as if they were from the Lord's mouth?

*D&C 50:36; 108:1.* What is another blessing that comes from "hearing" the prophet's words?

*D&C 52:9.* How important to us are the teachings of the Apostles and prophets?

*D&C 56:14.* What may cause us to lose standing and favor with God?

*D&C 58:8.* What witness does the Lord bear about his prophets?

*D&C 84:36.* Whom do we accept when we accept the prophets?

*D&C 90:5.* How is this warning related to Doctrine and Covenants 21:6?

*D&C 124:45-46.* What could cause the Saints to be "moved out of their place"?

*D&C 133:70-71.* What will be the result if the world rejects the words of the prophets?

## (F-3) The Living Oracle: God's Spokesman in All Things

Once the central importance of the role of the prophets in God's plan for his children is understood, it is not surprising that lessening the stature and authority of these servants is one of Satan's primary goals. Even within the Church there are those who believe the prophet should give direction only on spiritual matters. All Latter-day Saints should understand clearly that the earth and the fulness thereof belong to the Lord and that his prophet, who is President of the Savior's church on the earth, is to speak on any topic the Lord directs him to speak on.

Elder John A. Widtsoe wrote: "Whenever moved upon by the Spirit of the Lord, the man called to the prophet's office assumes the prophetic mantle and speaks as a mouthpiece of the Lord. He may then interpret the word of God, apply it to the conditions of the day, governmental, social, or economic, warn against impending evil. . . . Such inspired deliverances are binding upon all who believe that the latter-day work came and is directed by revelation." (*Evidences and Reconciliations,* 1:182.)

Elder Ezra Taft Benson said, "If we are living the gospel, we will feel in our hearts that the First Presidency of the Church not only have the right, but are also duty bound under heaven to give counsel on any subject which affects the temporal or spiritual welfare of the Latter-day Saints" (in Conference Report, Oct. 1950, p. 148).

This inspired counsel comes to members of the Church in at least two ways. First, every six months a general conference is held during which inspired counsel is given by the Lord's servants. The Lord warns those who do not heed this instruction that they "shall be cut off from among the people" (D&C 1:14). Second, the Saints should read what the prophets have written (see D&C 52:9, 36), including not only the scriptures but such things as conference talks, the message of the First

*The prophet will never lead the people astray*

Presidency in the *Ensign,* and special bulletins which are mailed to priesthood leaders to be read to the Saints in the stakes of the Church.

Those who criticize the prophet for speaking on matters that do not concern him, or who accuse him of not reflecting the will of the Lord, should consider the Lord's solemn warning carefully (see D&C 121:16-22).

Whether that rejection comes through open opposition to the prophet, through flippant disregard of his counsel, or through apathetic carelessness, the penalties for turning away from the Lord's servants are serious. "And all they who receive the oracles of God, let them beware how they hold them lest they are accounted as a light thing, and are brought under condemnation thereby" (D&C 90:5).

In response to the question, If one differs with a prophet's view, is it considered apostasy? Elder George Q. Cannon stated: "A friend . . . wished to know whether . . . we considered an honest difference of opinion between a member of the Church and the authorities of the Church apostasy. . . . We replied that we had not stated that an honest difference of opinion between a member of the Church and the authorities constituted apostasy; for we could conceive of a man honestly differing in opinion from the authorities of the Church and yet not be an apostate; but *we could not conceive of a man publishing those differences of opinion,* and seeking by arguments, sophistry and special pleading to enforce them upon the people to produce division and strife, and to place the acts and counsels of the authorities of the Church, if possible, in a wrong light, and not be an apostate, *for such conduct was apostasy* as we understood the term. We further said that while a man might honestly differ in opinion from the authorities through a want of understanding, *he had to be exceedingly careful* how he acted in relation to such differences, or the adversary would take advantage of him and *he would soon become imbued with the spirit of apostasy, and be found fighting against God and the authority which He had placed here to govern His Church.*" (*Deseret News Weekly,* 3 Nov. 1869, p. 457; emphasis added.)

The Lord teaches in these early revelations that

he has such confidence in his servants that he considers their inspired words as his own. This principle, called divine investiture of authority, is represented by the Lord's words to Moses, "They shall obey thy command *as if thou wert God*" (Moses 1:25; emphasis added).

### (F-4) Some Commonly Asked Questions about Prophets

No claim is put forth by the prophets of God to suggest that they are infallible, that everything they say and do is what the Lord would say and do. Only when they act in harmony with the will of the Lord do they become the Lord's mouthpiece. Each President of the Church has been quick to point out that he has weaknesses and imperfections. These facts, together with the Lord's endorsement of his servants, raise questions about how one should respond to the counsel of the prophets. Following are some of the more common questions:

*Is every word of a prophet inspired?* The Prophet Joseph was once asked this question, and he answered, "A prophet was a prophet only when he was acting as such" (*History of the Church,* 5:265).

Elder John A. Widtsoe commented on the Prophet Joseph's words: "That statement makes a clear distinction between official and unofficial actions and utterances of officers of the Church. In this recorded statement the Prophet Joseph Smith recognizes his special right and duty, as the President and Prophet of the Church, under the inspiration of the Lord, to speak authoritatively and officially for the enlightenment and guidance of the Church. But he claims also the right, as other men, to labor and rest, to work and play, to visit and discuss, to present his opinions and hear the opinions of others, to counsel and bless as a member of the Church." (*Evidences and Reconciliations,* 1:182.)

Elder Widstoe went on to say, however, that the "unofficial expressions [of a prophet] carry greater weight than the opinions of other men of equal or greater gifts and experience but without the power of the prophetic office. . . .

" . . . The unofficial views and expressions of such a man with respect to any vital subject, should command respectful attention." (*Evidences and Reconciliations,* 1:183-84.)

*Will the prophet ever lead the Church astray?* The Savior will never allow the President of his church to lead the people into sin or apostasy.

President Joseph Fielding Smith said: "I think there is one thing which we should have exceedingly clear in our minds. Neither the President of the Church, nor the First Presidency, nor the united voice of the First Presidency and the Twelve will ever lead the Saints astray or send forth counsel to the world that is contrary to the mind and will of the Lord." ("Eternal Keys and the Right to Preside," *Ensign,* July 1972, p. 88.)

President J. Reuben Clark, Jr., counseled, "You will never make a mistake by following the instructions and the counsel of him who stands at the head as God's mouthpiece on earth" (in Conference Report, Oct. 1945, p. 166).

Elder Ezra Taft Benson added his voice to others' testimonies: "Keep your eye on the Prophet, for the Lord will never permit his Prophet to lead this Church astray. Let us live close to the Spirit, so we can test all counsel." (In Conference Report, Oct. 1966, p. 123.)

Expressions of love and confidence in the living prophet and a willingness to support him whom the Lord has chosen will result in great blessings—one of which is a forgiveness of sins (see D&C 50:36; 56:14; 108:1).

*When are the words of the prophets to be considered scripture?* The Lord said: "And this is the ensample unto them, that they shall speak as they are moved upon by the Holy Ghost. And whatsoever they shall speak when moved upon by the Holy Ghost shall be scripture, shall be the will of the Lord, shall be the mind of the Lord, shall be the word of the Lord, shall be the voice of the Lord, and the power of God unto salvation." (D&C 68:3-4.)

Although the First Presidency and the Quorum of the Twelve Apostles are sustained as prophets, seers, and revelators, "only the President of the Church," spoke President J. Reuben Clark, Jr., "the Presiding High Priest, is sustained as Prophet, Seer, and Revelator for the Church, and he alone has the right to receive revelations for the Church, either new or amendatory, or to give authoritative interpretations of scriptures that shall be binding on the Church, or change in any way the existing doctrines of the Church. He is God's sole mouthpiece on earth for the Church of Jesus Christ of Latter-day Saints, the only true Church. He alone may declare the mind and will of God to his people. No officer of any other Church in the world has this high right and lofty prerogative." (*Church News,* 31 July 1954, p. 10.)

President Clark further explained how one can tell if a prophet has been inspired of the Holy Ghost: "We can tell when the speakers are 'moved upon by the Holy Ghost' only when we, ourselves, are 'moved upon by the Holy Ghost.'

"In a way, this completely shifts the responsibility from them to us to determine when they so speak." (*Church News,* 31 July 1954, p. 9.)

*Doesn't a prophet have to preface his comments with "Thus saith the Lord" when he is speaking as a prophet?* The answer to this question is no. President J. Reuben Clark, Jr., said: "There are those who insist that unless the Prophet of the Lord declares, 'Thus saith the Lord,' the message may not be taken as a revelation. *This is a false testing standard.* For while many of our modern revelations as contained in the Doctrine and Covenants do contain these words, there are many that do not." (*Church News,* 31 July 1954, p. 10; emphasis added.)

*Isn't following a prophet's counsel surrendering one's agency?* Elder Marion G. Romney answered this question as follows:

"In response to a contention that to follow such a course [following the First Presidency] is tantamount to surrendering one's 'moral agency,' suppose a person were in a forest with his vision limited by the denseness of the growth about him. Would he be surrendering his agency in following the directions of one who stands on a lookout tower, commanding an unobstructed view? To me, our leaders are true watchmen on the towers of Zion, and those who follow their counsel are exercising their agency just as freely as would be the man in the forest. For I accept as a fact, without any reservation, that this Church is headed by the Lord Jesus Christ, and that He, through the men whom He chooses and appoints to lead His people, gives it active direction. I believe that he communicates to them His will, and that they, enjoying His spirit, counsel us. . . .

"That we may all have the vision and the courage to be loyal to the truth and loyal to the men whom God has chosen to lead in the cause of truth." (In Conference Report, Apr. 1942, p. 20.)

**(F-5) Summary**

A prophet is a revealer of God's will, a teacher of truth, a revealer of new truth. The place of the Saints in Zion will depend, to a great extent, upon their willingness to heed his counsel. Their only safety for perilous times is described by President Harold B. Lee:

"We have some tight places to go before the Lord is through with this church and the world in this dispensation, which is the last dispensation, which shall usher in the coming of the Lord. The gospel was restored to prepare a people ready to receive him. The power of Satan will increase; we see it in evidence on every hand. There will be inroads within the Church. There will be, as President Tanner has said, 'Hypocrites, those professing, but secretly are full of dead men's bones.' We will see those who profess membership but secretly are plotting and trying to lead people not to follow the leadership that the Lord has set up to preside in this church.

"Now the only safety we have as members of this church is to do exactly what the Lord said to the Church in that day when the Church was organized. We must learn to give heed to the words and commandments that the Lord shall give through his prophet, 'as he receiveth them, walking in all holiness before me; . . . as if from mine own mouth, in all patience and faith.' (D&C 21:4-5.) There will be some things that take patience and faith. You may not like what comes from the authority of the Church. It may contradict your political views. It may contradict your social views. It may interfere with some of your social life. But if you listen to these things, as if from the mouth of the Lord himself, with patience and faith, the promise is that 'the gates of hell shall not prevail against you; yea, and the Lord God will disperse the powers of darkness from before you, and cause the heavens to shake for your good, and his name's glory.' (D&C 21:6.)" (In Conference Report, Oct. 1970, p. 152.)

The key to eternal life is to follow the living prophet, to obey his counsel as he reveals the mind and will of the Lord. Elder Bruce R. McConkie stated: "Let us, then—and let all men who desire righteousness—accept the Lord and his prophets, hearken to their teachings, and strive to be like them, for it is written: 'He that receiveth a prophet in the name of a prophet shall receive a prophet's reward.' (Matt. 10:41.) And a prophet's reward is eternal life in the kingdom of God." (*Promised Messiah,* p. 41.)

You may find the following story helpful in better understanding what it means to say "I know he is a prophet."

I listened to the young girl bear an eloquent testimony near the close of fast and testimony meeting. She spoke with great sincerity, her eyes filled with tears as she fervently said, "I know with all my heart that President Spencer W. Kimball is a true prophet of God." As she sat down, I wondered.

I knew this girl and her family well—well enough to know that for the previous year she had been in open conflict with her parents over her dating. She was not yet sixteen, but she boasted openly to her friends that she and this boy were "going steady" and had done so for some time, though she flatly denied this to her parents. She told her friends, one of whom was my daughter, that she was constantly deceiving her parents. She would tell them she was going over to a girlfriend's house, or that she was working when she was not, and then would meet her boyfriend instead.

President Spencer W. Kimball said: "In order to avoid difficulty and possible temptation, I suggest again the following standard. Any dating or pairing off in social contacts should be postponed until at least the age of 16 or older, and even then there should still be much judgment used in selections and in the seriousness. Young people should still limit the close contacts for several years, since the boy will be going on his mission when he is 19 years old." ("President Kimball Speaks Out on Morality," *Ensign,* Nov. 1980, p. 96.)

This girl said, "I know President Kimball is a prophet," and I wondered.

President Kimball said: "Liars and cheaters are both dishonest and alien to our culture. Dishonesty of all kinds is most reprehensible." (In Conference Report, Apr. 1975, p. 6.)

This girl said, "I know President Kimball is a prophet," and I wondered.

I thought of the Savior's words, "Why call ye me, Lord, Lord, and do not the things which I say?" (Luke 6:46), which have often been quoted by President Kimball in conference. (See, for example, Conference Reports, Oct. 1975, p. 8; Oct. 1978, p. 5.) Couldn't the prophets paraphrase that scripture and ask, "Why do you call me a prophet of God and do not the things which I counsel you to do?"

I listened to her testimony that morning, and I wondered.

# The Nature and Purpose of Law



### (G-1) Introduction

A significant aspect of this earthly existence is that all things are governed by law. Law gives order and purpose to the universe. Law provides the way for the Saints to grow, progress, and obtain happiness. That being the case, they need to understand the nature of law; the source of law; the means by which they can know true laws; the results of the application of laws, or what one may obtain by following the laws of God; and how the Lord has counseled his children to act in relationship to laws so that they may obtain the greatest benefits.

The Doctrine and Covenants, perhaps more clearly than any other scripture, helps the Saints to understand the nature, purpose, and effects of law.

### (G-2) The Eternal Nature of Law

The Doctrine and Covenants teaches that "all kingdoms have a law given; and . . . there is no space in the which there is no kingdom" (D&C 88:36-37). Thus, it is clear that all things in the vast immensity of space are under the influence of law. All things are controlled, governed, and upheld by law—"nothing is exempt." Nothing is arbitrary or left to chance. The "same invarying result always flows from the same cause." The principles of eternal law "are immutable, eternal, everlasting." (McConkie, *Mormon Doctrine,* p. 433.)

The truth of this teaching is substantiated both by the revelations of God and by the scientific observations of man. As mankind progresses in scientific knowledge, it becomes more and more apparent that there is order in the universe, and that all things are governed by consistent and harmonious laws. From the atomic realm to the vast immensity of space there is universal order and consistency.

President Brigham Young taught that "there is no being in all the eternities but what is governed by law" (*Discourses of Brigham Young,* p. 1). Elder Bruce R. McConkie stated, similarly, that Christ "governs and is governed by law" (*Mormon Doctrine,* p. 432.) God has said, for example, that he is bound when his children do what he says (see D&C 82:10). He is bound to fulfill his promises, for he is a being of complete integrity who conforms totally to the laws of righteousness. He is a celestial being and abides by celestial law, for any being "who is not able to abide the law of a celestial kingdom cannot abide a celestial glory" (D&C 88:22).

President John Taylor said: "God is unchangeable, so are also his laws, in all their forms, and in all their applications, and *being Himself the essence of law, the giver of law, the sustainer of law,* all of those laws are eternal in all their operations, in all bodies and matter, and throughout all space. *It would be impossible for Him to violate law,* because in so doing He would strike at

*"All things are numbered unto me, for they are mine and I know them" (Moses 1:35)*

His own dignity, power, principles, glory, exaltation and existence." (*Mediation and Atonement,* p. 168; emphasis added.)

*D&C 88:36-39.* What is the extent and the influence of God's laws? What do you have to do to be justified?

*D&C 88:34.* God has all power because he is in perfect harmony with all law. What, then, is the need for us to develop the ability to conform totally to his laws? What would be the benefit of doing so?

*D&C 59:4.* The Lord promises that he will bless those who stand in Zion with "commandments not a few." Do you think of the commandments of God as blessings or as restrictions?

How do these scriptures help you understand that laws and commandments are blessings?

### (G-3) Christ Is the Lawgiver

Christ, as the Firstborn, was preeminent among the members of the Father's family. He created this earth under the direction of the Father (see Moses 1:27-32) and was given authority to be God over it. Acting through the power and authority given him by his Father, the Savior controls, directs, and governs the affairs of this earth. As God over this earth, Christ ordained laws, according to the will of the Father, for the benefit and progression of the whole human family. He is man's lawgiver (see D&C 38:22; 64:13). Christ taught the Nephites, saying, "I am the law" (3 Nephi 15:9), meaning that he is the embodiment and the source of all law to mankind. He is not only the source of law and commandments given to men, but he provides the law, or organizing power, for the whole universe. This doctrine is taught more clearly in the Doctrine and Covenants than in any of the other standard works. He declared to his disciples that he was "the way, the truth, and the life" (John 14:6). Most scholars assume that by "the life" is meant the Resurrection, but the Doctrine and Covenants clearly teaches that the Resurrection is only part of what the title means. Jesus is "the life" in a much more profound and all-inclusive way. A careful study of Doctrine and Covenants 88:6-13 yields the following insights about Christ as the source of law and light and life:

Christ is the source of an infinite, radiant stream of energy called "the light of Christ" (vs. 7) which comes "from the presence of God to fill the immensity of space" (vs. 12).

Christ is the light and power that fills the sun, moon, stars, and earth (see vss. 7-10).

This light of Christ is not only in all things, but is the source of life for all things (see vs. 13).

Somehow, this energy source which emanates from God and is named after Jesus Christ is also "the law by which *all things* are governed" (vs. 13; emphasis added).

In other words, if somehow the light of Christ were to be extinguished, there would be no law, no order, no organization, and no life in the universe. Everything would collapse into universal chaos. Paul may have had that result in mind when he said that Christ is "upholding all things by the word of his power" (Hebrews 1:3). For this reason man looks to him for guidance: he is not only the source of law, *he is the law.*

The Prophet Joseph Smith taught the same thing when he said, "God himself, finding he was in the midst of spirits and glory, because he was more intelligent, saw proper to institute laws whereby the rest could have a privilege to advance like himself" (*Teachings,* p. 354).

## (G-4) God's Purpose in Giving Laws to Mankind

This earth is a place where man is given the opportunity to learn, to prove himself, and to develop the characteristics of Heavenly Father. In the premortal life, the children of Father in Heaven saw his greatness, his perfection, and his joy in an exalted status, and desired to be like him. He also wanted his children to become as he is.

Although God's laws are exact and immovable, they are revealed and given to mankind for one specific purpose—to bring to pass their ultimate joy. The Prophet Joseph Smith taught that "the Great Parent of the universe looks upon the whole of the human family with a fatherly care and paternal regard" (*Teachings,* p. 218), and that he "never will institute an ordinance or give a commandment to His people that is not calculated in its nature to promote that happiness which He has designed, and which will not end in the greatest amount of good and glory to those who become the recipients of his law and ordinances" (*Teachings,* pp. 256-57). The Prophet also said, "Whatever God requires is right, no matter what it is, although we may not see the reason thereof till long after the events transpire" (*Teachings,* p. 256).

God gives laws and commandments to his children to provide the only possible means whereby they may become like him. The Prophet Joseph Smith taught:

"God condescended to speak from the heavens and declare His will concerning the human family, to give them just and holy laws, to regulate their conduct, and guide them in a direct way, that in due time He might take them to Himself, and make them joint heirs with His Son. . . .

". . . God has given certain laws to the human family, which, if observed, are sufficient to prepare them to inherit this rest. This, then, we conclude, was the purpose of God in giving His laws to us." (*Teachings,* pp. 53-54.)

## (G-5) Certainty of the Promises and Consequences of Law

The Doctrine and Covenants teaches that all blessings are predicated upon laws and that if one desires a particular blessing, one must abide by the law that guarantees the blessing. If one does not conform to the bounds and conditions of a law, he is not justified in receiving the blessings associated with it. This theme is repeated again and again in the Doctrine and Covenants (see D&C 82:10; 88:38-39; 130:20-21; 132:5).

God has said that no one can come unto him except by his laws. If one receives and obeys his

*"I am the law" (3 Nephi 15:9)*

laws, then he will come to know God and become like him, thus having eternal life. (See D&C 132:11-12, 21-25, 32; John 17:3). It is only by obedience to law that one can become sanctified. Those who, by their agency, submit to law and are governed by God's laws are preserved, protected, and sanctified through the operation of those laws. Those who do not live the laws of God cannot be sanctified by the Savior through those laws; therefore, they must inherit a kingdom other than the celestial. Each individual must be able to abide by the law of the kingdom he inherits (see D&C 88:21-24; 34-35).

President Wilford Woodruff said about the principles of progression and inheritance according to law: "The God of heaven, who created this earth and placed His children upon it, gave unto them a law whereby they might be exalted and saved in a kingdom of glory. For there is a law given unto all kingdoms, and all things are governed by law throughout the whole universe. Whatever law anyone keeps he is preserved by that law, and he receives whatever reward that law guarantees unto him. It is the will of God that all His children should obey the highest law, that they may receive the highest glory that is ordained for all immortal beings. But God has given all His children an agency, to choose what law they will keep." (*Millennial Star,* 20 Dec. 1886, p. 801.)

The following diagram illustrates the progressive consequences of our choice to obey or to reject the laws given to us by God:

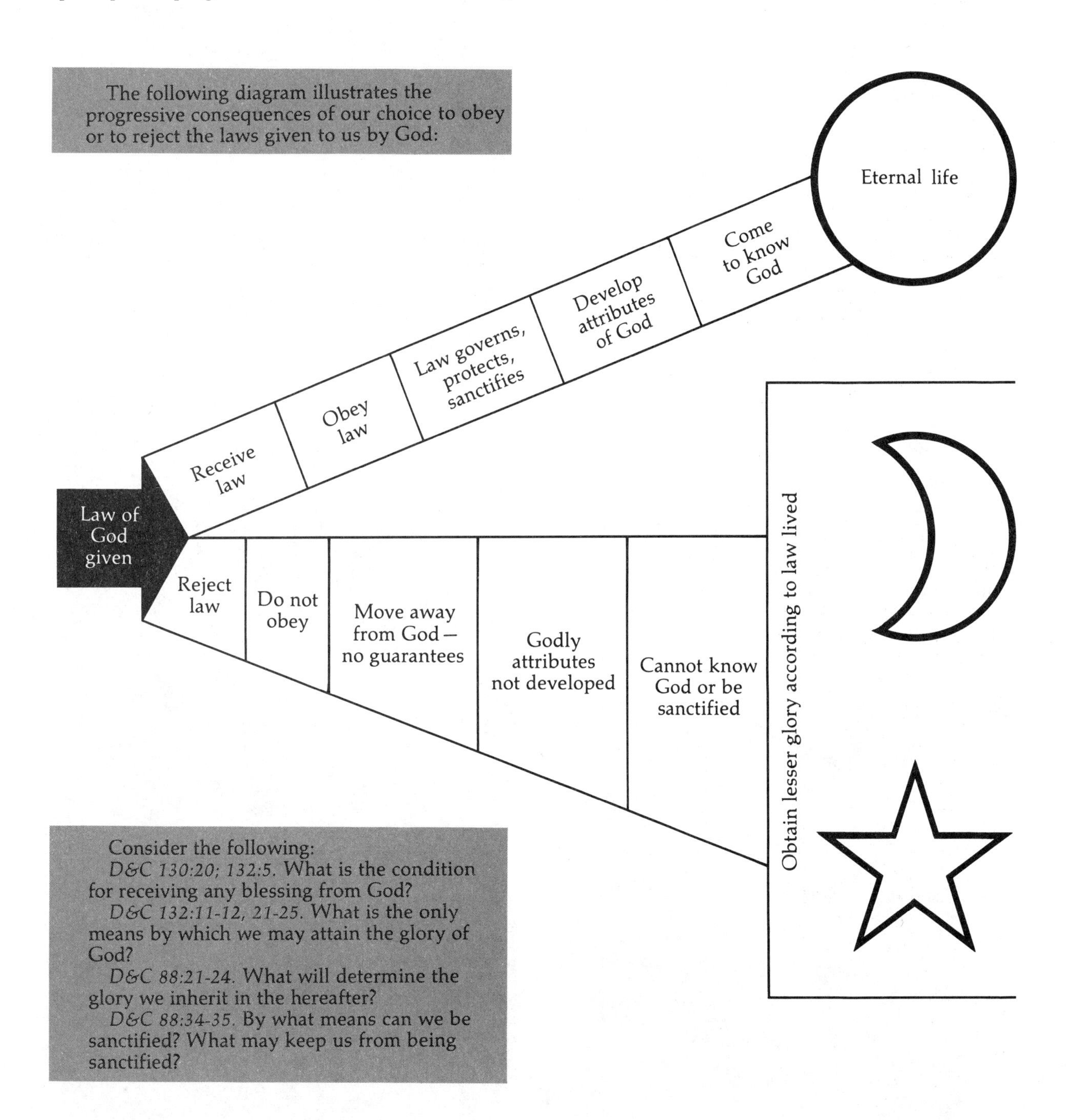


Consider the following:

*D&C 130:20; 132:5.* What is the condition for receiving any blessing from God?

*D&C 132:11-12, 21-25.* What is the only means by which we may attain the glory of God?

*D&C 88:21-24.* What will determine the glory we inherit in the hereafter?

*D&C 88:34-35.* By what means can we be sanctified? What may keep us from being sanctified?

### (G-6) How Should One Respond to Law?

The Lord has often instructed his people to learn his laws and teach them to others so that all may be edified and obtain the blessings that obedience to his laws generates (see D&C 42:12-13; 93:53; 107:99-100). Those who are his disciples will receive his laws and obey them (see D&C 41:5; 42:2). They will also obey the laws of the land in which they live (see D&C 58:21-22; 98:4-7; 134:5-6).

The Prophet Joseph Smith taught that "happiness is the object and design of our existence; and will be the end thereof, if we pursue the path that leads to it; and this path is virtue, uprightness, faithfulness, holiness, and keeping all the commandments of God" (*Teachings,* pp. 255-56). President Brigham Young reaffirmed this teaching when he said, "Great peace have they who love the law of the Lord and abide in his commandments" (*Discourses of Brigham Young,* p. 223).

The Doctrine and Covenants teaches that the Latter-day Saints have a particular responsibility to live their lives according to the principles of righteousness, for they live in the dispensation of the fulness of times in which God has restored and brought together the keys, power, and knowledge of all dispensations (see D&C 27:12-13; 128:18). "Every key, power, and authority ever dispensed from heaven to men on earth, which is necessary for their eternal salvation, has already been restored in this dispensation" (McConkie, *Mormon Doctrine,* p. 200). The Latter-day Saints are the recipients of those great blessings, and the Lord has said that where "much is given much is required" (D&C 82:3).

Elder George Albert Smith explained the nature of the responsibility that falls upon the Latter-day Saints as a result of what they have been given: "We will not be judged as our brothers and sisters of the world are judged, but according to the greater opportunities placed in our keeping. We will be among those who have received the word of the Lord, who have heard His sayings, and if we do them it will be to us eternal life, but if we fail condemnation will result." (In Conference Report, Oct. 1906, p. 47.)

The psalmist wrote, "O how love I thy law!" (Psalm 119:97). Is that a feeling you share, or do you sometimes feel resentful toward the laws of God? One of Satan's most successful lies is that the commandments of God are fettering, restrictive, and limiting. "If you would really be free," he urges, "cut yourself loose from such restraints. Be free! Be independent!" The deception lies in denying the eternal principle that only obedience to law secures the blessings guaranteed by law (see D&C 130:20-21). Disobedience to law necessitates penalties, which are ordained by a loving Father to purge the souls of his children of what hinders their progression. When a person is so purged, he can obtain as much happiness as he is willing to live for, according to the law he becomes capable of living (see D&C 88:21-24).

God's word is law, and, like the rod of iron in Lehi's dream (1 Nephi 8:4-35; 11:25), it is an anchor in a world of darkness. By clinging to it we are saved from misery and woe and can obtain all good things, the greatest of which is eternal life. Jesus taught, "If ye continue in my word, then are ye my disciples indeed; and ye shall know the truth, and the truth shall make you free" (John 8:31-32).

Of the freedom that comes from obedience, Elder Boyd K. Packer said: "*Obedience—that which God will never take by force—he will accept when freely given. And he will then return to you freedom that you can hardly dream of*—the freedom to feel and to know, the freedom to do, and the freedom to *be,* at least a thousandfold more than we offer him. . . .

"Obedience is a key to agency, . . . obedience is the doorway to freedom." (*Obedience,* Brigham Young University Speeches of the Year [Provo, 7 Dec. 1971], pp. 4, 6; emphasis added.)

The Savior taught the relationship between obedience and true freedom (see John 8:31-32). That process could be diagrammed as follows:

**If we continue in his word (obedience)**
↓
**we become disciples**
↓
**who are given the truth**
↓
**which makes us free**

Truth is the key to freedom, discipleship is the key to truth, and obedience is the key to discipleship.

Elder Spencer W. Kimball said of those who scoff at this truth, saying that what is required is blind obedience:

"To obey! To hearken! What a difficult requirement! Often we hear: 'Nobody can tell me what clothes to wear, what I shall eat or drink. No one can outline my Sabbaths, appropriate my earnings, nor in any way limit my personal freedoms! I do as I please! I give no *blind obedience!*'

"Blind obedience! How little they understand! . . .

"When men speak of *all faith* and *all obedience* as blind, are they not covering their own weaknesses? Are they not seeking an alibi to justify their own failure to hearken?

"A man obeys strictly the income tax law and pays fully and before due date his property taxes but justifies himself in disregarding the law of the Sabbath or the payment of tithes on time, if at all. In the one case he may suffer only deprivation of freedom or resources or lose his home or personal property, but in the other he opens doors to the loss of a soul. The spiritual as truly brings penalties as the temporal, the principal difference is the swiftness of punishment, the Lord being so long-suffering.

"One would hardly call the first blind

obedience, yet he sometimes regards the spiritual commands as such.

"Is it blind obedience when the student pays his tuition, reads his text assignments, attends classes, and thus qualifies for his eventual degrees? Perhaps he himself might set different and easier standards for graduation, but he obeys every requirement of the catalog whether or not he understands its total implication.

"Is it blind obedience when one regards the sign 'High Voltage—Keep Away' or is it the obedience of faith in the judgment of experts who know the hazard?

"Is it blind obedience when the air traveler fastens his seat belt as that sign flashes or is it confidence in the experience and wisdom of those who know more of hazards and dangers?

"Is it blind obedience when the little child gleefully jumps from the table into the strong arms of its smiling father, or is this implicit trust in a loving parent who feels sure of his catch and who loves the child better than life itself?

"Is it blind obedience when an afflicted one takes vile-tasting medicine prescribed by his physician or yields his own precious body to the scalpel of the surgeon or is this the obedience of faith in one in whom confidence may safely be imposed? . . .

"Is it then blind obedience when we, with our limited vision, elementary knowledge, selfish desires, ulterior motives, and carnal urges, accept and follow the guidance and obey the commands of our loving Father who begot us, created a world for us, loves us, and has planned a constructive program for us, wholly without ulterior motive, whose greatest joy and glory is to 'bring to pass the immortality and eternal life' of all his children?" (In Conference Report, Oct. 1954, pp. 51-53.)

### (G-7) Summary

All scriptures teach the value of law and the blessings that derive from obedience to it, but especially in the Doctrine and Covenants are the Saints taught the nature, purpose, and source of law. Knowing that in the last days law would come under severe attack from the world, the Lord revealed the benefits of law. He taught that through obedience to his laws his children are freed from sin, weakness, darkness, and despair; they obtain power over all their enemies and gain power to lay hold of every righteous desire of their hearts. They become free of every encumbrance that holds them back or binds them down. Thus, having become free and independent, and having the ability to live in accordance to all of God's laws, the obedient children of God have the powers of the universe at their disposal to use in obtaining a fulness of joy, which will endure forever and ever.

# The Last Days

## Enrichment H

### (H-1) Introduction

Approximately three thousand years before the birth of Christ, the Lord showed to the great prophet Enoch, in vision, the destiny of the world and its inhabitants. Enoch saw the coming of the Son of Man in the meridian of time, his crucifixion and resurrection in glory, and "all things, even unto the end of the world" (Moses 7:67; see also Moses 7:20-67). Enoch saw in vision great wickedness upon the face of the earth, and he pleaded with the Lord, "When shall the earth rest?" and "Wilt thou not come again upon the earth?" (Moses 7:58-59). The Lord answered him, "As I live, even so will I come in the last days. . . . And the day shall come that the earth shall rest." (Moses 7:60-61.)

The Saints are now living in the "last days" (D&C 86:4). This is a period of wickedness and tribulations, of calamity and great distress (see Moses 7:60-61; D&C 1:17; Luke 21:25), but it is also a period of restoration, in which the Lord is bringing to pass a restitution of the powers and blessings of all former times (see D&C 121:27-31; D&C 128:18; Moses 7:62; Acts 3:21). In this day and age, the Lord's work will triumph, and it will eventually fill the whole earth (see D&C 84:97-102; Daniel 2:28-44; Moses 7:62-65).

This generation stands at the end of the sixth "day" of the earth's history (see D&C 77:6-7, 12; Abraham 3:4; 2 Peter 3:8). Now is the "Saturday evening" of time preceding the great millennial sabbath of the earth (see McConkie, *Doctrinal New Testament Commentary* 3:485-86; Smith, *Teachings,* p. 13). It is for this generation to prepare the way for the second coming of the Lord. Modern Saints must obey the principles of the gospel and know the signs of the times, so that they may endure the trials and difficulties of this dispensation, recognize the signs of his coming, and be prepared to receive him as his own people when he comes. The Doctrine and Covenants clarifies prophecies of the past concerning the last days, and it gives many additional prophecies by which the Saints can recognize the time of the Lord's coming, that it might not "overtake [them] as a thief" (1 Thessalonians 5:4). It not only teaches how to recognize the imminence of the Lord's coming, but it also makes very clear what one must do to be prepared to receive the Lord when he comes.

*The scriptures are a handbook for the last days*

## (H-2) The Scriptures Give Authoritative Information about the Last Days

Anyone who undertakes a study of the last days should use the scriptures as his primary source. To one who seeks in righteousness with a humble heart, the scriptures will speak clearly of the events of the last days and of the path one should follow in these days. President Harold B. Lee warned the Church in general conference of possible dangers in giving other sources priority over the scriptures:

"There are among us many loose writings predicting the calamities which are about to overtake us. Some of these have been publicized as though they were necessary to wake up the world to the horrors about to overtake us. Many of these are from sources upon which there cannot be unquestioned reliance.

" . . . We need no such publications to be forewarned, if we were only conversant with what the scriptures have already spoken to us in plainness." (In Conference Report, Oct. 1972, p. 128; or *Ensign*, Jan. 1973, p. 106.)

President Lee further counseled the Saints, giving "the sure word of prophecy on which you should rely for your guide. . . .

"Read the 24th chapter of Matthew—particularly that inspired version as contained in the Pearl of Great Price. (Joseph Smith 1.)

"Then read the 45th section of the Doctrine and Covenants where the Lord, not man, has documented the signs of the times.

"Now turn to section 101 and section 133 of the Doctrine and Covenants and hear the step-by-step recounting of the events leading up to the coming of the Savior.

"Finally, turn to the promises the Lord makes to those who keep the commandments when these judgments descend upon the wicked, as set forth in the Doctrine and Covenants, section 38.

" . . . these are some of the writings with which you should concern yourselves, rather than commentaries that may come from those whose information may not be the most reliable and whose motives may be subject to question." (In Conference Report, Oct. 1972, p. 128; or *Ensign*, p. 106.)

The Doctrine and Covenants gives a great deal of information and prophecy about the last days. By following its teachings and those of the other scriptures, Latter-day Saints can be amply informed and prepared for the events of the future.

## (H-3) Signs to Precede the Lord's Second Coming

In the scriptures the Lord has given knowledge of many signs that will be shown forth to the inhabitants of the earth so that those who watch might be prepared for the great events of the last days, including his return to the earth in power and glory. Those who know the signs and who follow the counsel given through the Lord's prophets will be prepared to deal with the challenges of this momentous time and will be "looking forth for the great day of the Lord to come" (D&C 45:39; see also Moses 7:62). They will not be taken by surprise but will be anxiously awaiting the Lord's coming.

The signs of the Lord's coming may be classified into two main categories: (1) Signs which are part of the restoration of the gospel and its eventual expansion throughout the world; and (2) signs which are part of the increase of evils and the calamities and judgments to come upon the world. These two movements are taking place simultaneously in the last days. President Spencer W. Kimball said that "the progress of the church will be paralleled by a growing wickedness among mankind" and, citing Brigham Young, "in proportion to the spread of the gospel among the nations of the earth so would the power of Satan rise" (in *Church News*, 30 June 1979, p. 5).

The Saints, having the opportunity to be enlightened by the teachings of the Doctrine and Covenants as well as other scriptures, should learn the signs of the times and watch them closely to recognize the time of the Lord's return (see D&C 68:11). Although no man knows the day nor the hour, nor will anyone until the Lord comes (see D&C 49:7), yet in watching for the signs and giving heed to the Lord's prophets one may stay in constant readiness to receive the Lord.

President Joseph Fielding Smith said: "Many things have taken place during the past one hundred and thirty-six years to impress faithful members of the Church with the fact that the coming of the Lord is near. The gospel has been restored. The Church has been fully organized. The priesthood has been conferred upon man. The various dispensations from the beginning have been revealed and their keys and authorities given to the Church. Israel has been and is being gathered to the land of Zion. The Jews are returning to Jerusalem. The gospel is being preached in all the world as a witness to every nation. Temples are being built, and ordinance work for the dead, as well as for the living, is performed in them. The hearts of the children have turned to their fathers, and the children are seeking after their dead. The covenants which the Lord promised to make with Israel in the latter days have been revealed, and thousands of gathered Israel have entered into them. Thus the work of the Lord is advancing, and all these things are signs of the near approach of our Lord." (In Conference Report, Apr. 1966, pp. 12-13).

Why has the Lord not revealed the exact time of his return?

*D&C 45:24-25, 28, 30.* The Lord said that the Jews would remain scattered until the times of the Gentiles were fulfilled. What sign did the Lord give to show when they would begin to be gathered again?

*D&C 45:36-38.* What did the Lord mean by the parable of the fig tree?

*D&C 1:4, 11-12; 43:20.* What can you do to help prepare the world for the Lord's return?

If all of the Church went forth with their might in doing missionary work, what effect could that have on the coming of the Lord? President Spencer W. Kimball said, "If the people of the Church do real proselyting in their home wards . . . the number of converts could grow to astronomical figures and ever hasten the time when the Lord will be returning to the earth in his second advent" (in Conference Report, Oct. 1976, p. 4).

## (H-4) Two Great Categories of Signs

The Doctrine and Covenants contains a great deal of information on both categories of signs of the Second Coming: the restoration of the kingdom and the calamities to come.

*Restoration and promulgation of the gospel.* This dispensation is the time when the Lord is restoring and gathering together all of the "keys, and powers, and glories . . . revealed from the days of Adam even to the present time" (D&C 128:18). The Restoration was identified anciently as one of the signs to precede the Lord's return (see Acts 3:19-21; Ephesians 1:10; Revelations 14:6-7). As part of the restoration before the end of the world, the Lord said that the gospel would be "preached in all the world for a witness to all nations" (Matthew 24:14). The Lord indicated in 1833 that he had sent his angel to commit the gospel to man so that it might be preached to all the world before his coming in glory (see D&C 133:36-40).

Elder Bruce R. McConkie wrote of this period of restoration: "That period of time just preceding the millennium is named the *last days.* It is the specified time, period, or age in which the necessary prerequisites to the Second Coming will occur. The last days are the days of the dispensation of the fulness of times, the days when the signs of the Second Coming are shown forth, the days of 'restitution of all things, which God hath spoken by the mouth of all his holy prophets since the world began.' (Acts 3:21.) We are now living in that period of time, and the great restitution (or restoration) is in process." (*Mormon Doctrine,* p. 431.)

When divine messengers committed vital priesthood keys to the Prophet Joseph Smith in the Kirtland Temple, they told him that it was a sign by which he "may know that the great and dreadful day of the Lord is near, even at the doors" (D&C 110:16). The restoration of those keys made possible the fulfilling of the work necessary to prepare for the return of the Son of God.

The Lord indicated that he would, in this dispensation, call laborers into his vineyard for the last time, for it is the "eleventh hour" (D&C 33:3; see also D&C 43:28-29) before his coming "at midnight" (Matthew 25:6) to usher in the sabbath of the earth. During this final hour the voice of warning shall go to all people through the Lord's servants, who will call upon the world to repent and prepare for his imminent return (see D&C 1:1-5, 11-12). The gospel has now been restored as the kingdom of God. It will roll forth with power until it fills the whole earth and Christ returns to reign over the kingdom of heaven to be established on the earth in its renewed paradisiacal condition (see D&C 65:1-6; Articles of Faith 1:10).

As part of that preparatory work, the Doctrine and Covenants indicates, the Lord will gather the dispersed house of Israel (see D&C 110:11). Before the Lord's coming, the lost ten tribes will return (see D&C 110:11, 133:26-34); the Jews will be gathered to their homeland (see D&C 45:16-25, 43-44); and the Lamanites will be gathered into the fold of God and "blossom as a rose" (D&C 49:24; see also D&C 3:18-20; 2 Nephi 30:4-5). As the gospel spreads, Israel will be gathered, and "Zion shall flourish" (D&C 49:25). The city of New Jerusalem will be built in America as "a land of peace, a city of refuge, a place of safety for the saints of the Most High God" (D&C 45:66; see also Articles of Faith 1:10), and the righteous from all nations will gather with rejoicing to Zion (see D&C 45:66-71). To endow his people with a fulness of blessings, the Lord will cause a great temple to be built unto him in the city of the New Jerusalem, to which he shall return, and which shall be filled with his glory (see D&C 36:8; 42:35-36; 84:4-5).

*Increase of evils and the calamities and judgments to come upon the world.* Many ancient prophets saw this day and prophesied of conditions of great wickedness and commotion (see 1 Nephi 14:7-17; 2 Nephi 28:3-14, 20-23; Mormon 8:26-41). In his preface to the Doctrine and Covenants, the Lord spoke of the wickedness of the world in this time (see D&C 1:13-16). The fact that the world is rejecting his teachings is causing an increase of wickedness, wars, and commotions on the earth. The Lord has said that because of the wickedness of the inhabitants of the world he will come down upon them with judgments (see D&C 1:13, 15-16, 35-36; 29:14-21; 45:26, 31; 63:33; 84:96-97; 112:23-26).

Knowing the calamity that would inevitably come upon the inhabitants of the earth because of their iniquities, the Lord called the Prophet Joseph Smith and gave him the keys, powers, and blessings of the gospel, so that through its restoration many would be turned from the world and preserved from the judgments (see also D&C 1:17-23). Those who will heed the gospel message will be preserved, but those who reject it will meet with great distress and sorrow. All of these events are part of the signs prophesied of to signal the nearness of the Lord's second advent (see JS—M 1:22-23, 27-36, 41-43).

### (H-5) Promised Results of Wickedness

The following events are taking place among those of the world who reject the gospel warning:

*The loss of the Spirit of the Lord.* (See D&C 63:32-34.) President Joseph Fielding Smith said:

"Now the Lord has withdrawn His Spirit from the world. Do not let this thought become confused in your minds. The Spirit He has withdrawn from the world is not the Holy Ghost (for they never had that!), but it is the light of truth, spoken of in our scriptures as the Spirit of Christ, which is given to every man that cometh into the world, as you find recorded in Section 84 of the Doctrine and Covenants.

"Now because of the wickedness of the world, that Spirit has been withdrawn and when the Spirit of the Lord is not striving with men the spirit of Satan is. . . .

"The devil *has* power over his own dominion. The Spirit of the Lord *has* been withdrawn. Not because the Lord desires to withdraw that Spirit, but because of the wickedness of mankind, it becomes necessary that this Spirit of the Lord be withdrawn." (*The Predicted Judgments,* Brigham Young University Speeches of the Year [Provo, 21 Mar. 1967], pp. 5-6.)

*Peace taken from the earth.* (See D&C 1:35.) As the Lord withdraws his spirit because men reject him, the spirit of Satan and his influence increases, and peace is taken from the earth. That is the condition of the world today. President Joseph Fielding Smith said, "Peace *has* been taken from the earth" (*Predicted Judgments,* p. 6). The Prophet Joseph Smith prophesied of a time when no man would have peace except in Zion and her stakes: "I saw men hunting the lives of their own sons, and brother murdering brother, women killing their own daughters, and daughters seeking the lives of their mother. I saw armies arrayed against armies. I saw blood, desolation, fires. The Son of Man has said that the mother shall be against the daughter, and the daughter against the mother. These things are at our doors. They will follow the Saints of God from city to city. Satan will rage, and the spirit of the devil is now enraged. I know not how soon these things will take place." (*History of the Church,* 3:391.)

*The Lord calls the earth to repentance through natural calamities.* When John the Revelator saw the events of the sixth seal (the sixth period of a thousand years; see D&C 77:6-7), great natural disasters were among the things shown to him (see Revelation 6:12-13). In the Doctrine and Covenants, the Lord revealed specifically that in addition to preaching his word to the world through his servants, he himself would call upon the wicked through the

*His sheep will be gathered on his right hand*

"voice of thunderings, and by the voice of tempests, and by the voice of earth quakes and great hailstorms, and by the voice of famines and pestilences of every kind" (D&C 43:25; see vss. 20-27). He warned that the testimony of these natural calamities would follow after the testimony of his servants (see D&C 88:88-91; Notes and Commentary on D&C 43:17-25; 88:87-91).

Elder Melvin J. Ballard said he wanted "to call the attention of the Latter-day Saints, and indeed if I had the power, the attention of all the world to the fact that God is speaking through the elements. The earthquakes, the sea heaving itself beyond its bounds, bringing such dire destruction as we have seen are the voice of God crying repentance to this generation, a generation that only in part has heeded the warning voice of the servants of the Lord." (In Conference Report, Oct. 1923, p. 31.)

President Brigham Young, speaking of the revelations of natural calamities, said: "Do you think there is calamity abroad now among the people? Not much. All we have yet heard and all we have experienced is scarcely a preface to the sermon that is going to be preached. When the testimony of the Elders ceases to be given, and the Lord says to them, 'Come home; I will now preach my own sermons to the nations of the earth,' all you now know can scarcely be called a preface to the sermon that will be preached with fire and sword, tempests, earthquakes, hail, rain, thunders and lightnings, and fearful destruction. What matters the destruction of a few railway cars? You will hear of magnificent cities, now idolized by the people, sinking in the earth, entombing the inhabitants. The sea will heave itself beyond its bounds, engulfing mighty cities. Famine will spread over the nations, and nation will rise up against nation, kingdom against kingdom, and states against states, in our own country and in foreign lands." (In *Journal of Discourses,* 8:123.)

Time after time the Lord has warned the inhabitants of the earth that if they continue to ripen in iniquity, the fulness of the Lord's wrath shall be unleashed upon the world (see 1 Nephi 22:16-17; Ether 2:8-10; D&C 1:13; 97:22-24; 133:51).

The Doctrine and Covenants is a rich resource for learning about the last days and the preparations that are to precede the coming of Christ. Read the following references and answer the questions given:

*D&C 1:35-36.* Over whom will the devil have power in the last days?

*D&C 29:17, 19, 21; 133:63-74.* Why will the Lord send severe judgments upon the wicked?

*D&C 101;10-11; 103:1-3.* When does the Lord send judgments and wrath upon the wicked?

*D&C 86:4-7.* Why, when the Church was in its infancy, was it a blessing to the Saints for the Lord to hold back his judgments upon the world in spite of opposition from the world to the progress of his kingdom?

*D&C 87:6.* How will the powerful nations of the earth be subdued in order for the gospel to reign upon the earth?

*D&C 112:23-26.* Where will the Lord's judgments begin?

*D&C 35:13-14.* How will the humble servants of God be able to withstand the force brought against them by the wicked individuals and groups that will permeate the world?

*D&C 86:4-7; 88:94.* In the parable of the wheat and the tares, what did the Lord mean when he said he would gather the wheat from the tares, bind the tares in bundles, and then burn the field?

*D&C 115:6.* Where will the Saints find a place of defense and refuge amidst the judgments of the last days?

*D&C 45:66-71.* What conditions will exist in the city of New Jerusalem to preserve and protect the Saints there?

In explaining the parable of the ten virgins (see Matthew 25:1-13), Elder Spencer W. Kimball said: "At midnight! Precisely at the darkest hour, when least expected, the bridegroom came. When the world is full of tribulation and help is needed, but it seems the time must be past and hope is vain, then Christ will come." (*Faith Precedes the Miracle,* p. 255). What implications does that circumstance have for your need to exercise faith in God in the coming times of tribulation? Read 3 Nephi 1:4-21 with this idea in mind.

### (H-6) The Lord Will Preserve His People

Although the Lord's church in the last days will continue to be built up in time of severe opposition and dire calamities and judgments, the Lord has promised that he will preserve his people. It is part of the Lord's testing of his children in mortality to allow them to remain in the midst of difficulty to see if they will be true to him in times both of prosperity and of distress. Elder Bruce R. McConkie explained one of the reasons for the difficulties that the Lord's people often experience:

"The testing processes of mortality are for all men, saints and sinners alike. Sometimes the tests and trials of those who have received the gospel far exceed any imposed upon worldly people. Abraham was called upon to sacrifice his only son. Lehi and his family left their lands and wealth to live in a wilderness. Saints in all ages have been commanded to lay all they have upon the altar, sometimes even their very lives. . . .

"Sometimes the Lord's people are hounded and persecuted. Sometimes He deliberately lets His faithful saints linger and suffer, in both body and spirit, to prove them in all things, and to see if they will abide in His covenant, even unto death, that they may be found worthy of eternal life. If such be the lot of any of us, so be it.

"But come what may, anything that befalls us here in mortality is but for a small moment, and if we are true and faithful God will eventually exalt us on high. All our losses and sufferings will be made up to us in the resurrection." (In Conference Report, Oct. 1976, pp. 158-60; or *Ensign,* Nov. 1976, pp. 106, 108.)

The Prophet Joseph Smith taught that the Saints should not expect to escape all of the latter-day judgments while the wicked suffer. Many of the righteous will experience difficulty and suffering because of weaknesses of the flesh and still be saved in the kingdom of God (see *History of the Church,* 4:11). Though they will "hardly escape" (D&C 63:34), the Lord has promised that he will preserve his people in the midst of the judgments that will eventually destroy the wicked (see D&C 35:13-14; 63:33-37; 1 Nephi 22:13-17, 22-23). While in the midst of tribulations, the Saints must remember that the Lord's counsel is to be patient and have faith that they will receive his reward when he comes (see D&C 54:10). He will soon pour out his wrath and indignation upon the wicked nations of the earth to save his people Israel. Until that time, he counsels the Saints to be calm and confident in the knowledge that he is God and all flesh is in his hands and under his control (see D&C 101:10-16). He will "rend" the kingdoms of the world and "exert the powers of heaven" to preserve the Saints (D&C 84:118-19).

### (H-7) How to Escape the Calamities and God's Judgments

The Lord has promised that he will preserve his people in the last days. The question each member of the Church should be able to answer is, How can I be numbered among those whom the Lord will protect? That question is answered very clearly in the Doctrine and Covenants: It is a matter of individual worthiness. The Lord has said, "If ye are prepared ye shall not fear" (D&C 38:30). The preparation needed is to repent, to receive the gospel, and to become sanctified through following its precepts (see D&C 39:17-18). In the early days of this dispensation, the Saints were persecuted because of their lack of faithfulness (see D&C 101:6-8). The Lord has said that those who are "not purified shall not abide that day" of his coming (D&C 38:8). The Saints have been warned not to entangle themselves in sin (see D&C 88:86).

After suffering much distress at the hands of mobs in Missouri, the Saints were promised that they would prevail against their enemies from that "very hour" and never cease if they would "observe *all* the words" which the Lord spoke to them (D&C 103:5-7; emphasis added).

The same is true today. Although there may be

individual exceptions, in general the faithful Saints shall be preserved from their enemies and from the judgments which God will pour out on the world (see D&C 97:21-26; 133:4-7, 14). These same principles were taught in the October 1940 General Conference by Elder Joseph Fielding Smith:

"We have the means of escape through obedience to the Gospel of Jesus Christ. Will we escape? When I see, even among the Latter-day Saints the violation of the laws of the Lord, I fear and I tremble. I have been crying repentance among the Stakes of Zion for thirty years, calling upon the people to turn to the Lord, keep His commandments, observe the Sabbath Day, pay their honest tithing, do everything the Lord has commanded them to do, to live by every word that proceedeth forth from the mouth of God.

"By doing this we shall escape the calamities.

"I am going to repeat what I have said before, for which I have been severely criticized from certain quarters, that even in this country we have no grounds by which we may escape, no sure foundation upon which we can stand, and by which we may escape from the calamities and destruction and the plagues and the pestilences, and even the devouring fire by sword and by war, unless we repent and keep the commandments of the Lord, for it is written here in these revelations.

"So I cry repentance to the Latter-day Saints, and I cry repentance to the people of the United States, as well as to the people of all the earth. May we turn to live in accordance with divine law, and keep the commandments the Lord has given." (In Conference Report, Oct. 1940, p. 117.)

Just over one year later Pearl Harbor was attacked, and the United States entered World War II.

President Wilford Woodruff said that those who honor the priesthood would be the only ones to have the right to the Lord's protection: "Can you tell me where the people are who will be shielded and protected from these great calamities and judgments which are even now at our doors? I'll tell you. The priesthood of God who honor their priesthood, and who are worthy of their blessings are the only ones who shall have this safety and protection. They are the only mortal beings. No other people have a right to be shielded from these judgments. They are at our very doors; not even this people will escape them entirely. They will come down like the judgments of Sodom and Gomorrah. And none but the priesthood will be safe from their fury." (*Young Women's Journal,* Aug. 1894, p. 512.)

Shortly before his death, Jesus was asked by his disciples, "What is the sign of thy coming, and of the end of the world, or the destruction of the wicked, which is the end of the world?" (JS—M 1:4). In answer to that question, the Lord gave what is known as the Olivet Discourse, so named because he gave it on the Mount of Olives.

The first part of this discourse is found in Matthew 24 and also in the Pearl of Great Price, in Joseph Smith's inspired translation of Matthew 24 (see JS—M). Many do not note that Matthew 25, which contains three parables, is also part of that discourse. These are the parable of the ten virgins (see Matthew 25:1-13), the parable of the talents (see Matthew 25:14-30), and the parable of the sheep and the goats (see Matthew 25:31-46). In other words, these parables were part of the Lord's answer to the disciples' question about the end of the world. For this reason they have been called the parables of preparation.

Would you like to know how to prepare yourself so that you need not fear about the future? Then turn to Matthew 25 and study those parables carefully as you answer the following questions:

*The parable of the ten virgins.* (See Matthew 25:1-13.)

To what time does "then" (vs. 1) refer? (See Matthew 24:42; D&C 45:56.)

Who is the Bridegroom, and what does the wedding supper symbolize? (See Revelation 19:7-9; D&C 33:17; 63:3; 88:92.)

At what time did the Bridegroom come? Does this point add significance to Doctrine and Covenants 33:3?

Virgins are symbolic of purity, faithfulness, and worthiness (see, for example, Revelation 14:4). Who then do the virgins represent? Are the people of the world waiting for the Bridegroom?

Obviously oil is the critical factor in the parable. What does the oil symbolize? In other words, what did the five wise virgins have that the five foolish ones did not? (See D&C 45:56-57.)

How does one "purchase" extra oil? (See Notes and Commentary on Doctrine and Covenants 45:56-57.)

*The parable of the talents.* (See Matthew 25:14-30.) Who do you suppose is represented by the man traveling into a far country? Who are the servants?

Often this parable is used to teach that we ought to develop our talents; in the parable, however, talents are not abilities but sums of money that did not belong to the servants but were entrusted to them. In other words, the lesson of the parable really has to do with an important gospel principle. What is it? (See D&C 104:17-18, 54-57, 70.)

Compare the praise and promise of the Master for the servant who had been given five talents with the one who had been given only two. What can you conclude? (See Matthew 25:21, 23.)

At what point did the Master call the servant with one talent "wicked"? Suppose he had increased it by one talent? What can we conclude would have been his reward? (See Matthew 25:26.)

What does verse 29 imply in terms of preparing yourself for the Second Coming? (Cf. D&C 82:3-4; 107:99-100.)

*The parable of the sheep and the goats.* (See Matthew 25:31-46.) "One of the most familiar and beautiful sights of the East is that of the shepherd leading his sheep to the pasture. . . .

He depends upon the sheep to follow, and they in turn expect him never to leave them." (Mackie, *Bible Manners and Customs,* p. 33.) Goats, on the other hand, are aggressive rather than docile, independent rather than submissive, and do not depend on the protective care of the shepherd as do the sheep.

How does this information add to your understanding of the symbolism of this parable?

What is the relationship between what is taught in verse 40 and what is taught in Mosiah 2:17 and Doctrine and Covenants 1:10?

Now apply the message of these parables to your preparing yourself for Christ's coming. Three great qualities are stressed by the Savior: spiritual power, stewardship, and Christian service. The Lord's promise is, "If ye are prepared ye shall not fear" (D&C 38:30). In what better way could you prepare to be one of the wise virgins (see Matthew 25:1-13), a "good and faithful servant" (Matthew 25:23), and a sheep to whom the Lord says, "Come, ye blessed of my Father, inherit the kingdom prepared for you from the foundation of the world" (Matthew 25:34).

### (H-8) The Church Must Stand Independent

The Lord has said that amid the tribulations in the last days the Church is "to stand independent above all other creatures beneath the celestial world" (D&C 78:14). In order to do that, Elder Bruce R. McConkie explained, "the Church, which administers the gospel, and the Saints who have received the gospel, must be independent of all the powers of earth, as they work out their salvation—temporally and spiritually—with fear and trembling before the Lord!

"Be it remembered that tribulations lie ahead.

"Peace has been taken from the earth, the angels of destruction have begun their work, and their swords shall not be sheathed until the prince of Peace comes to destroy the wicked and usher in the great Millennium. . . .

"We must maintain our own health, sow our own gardens, store our own food, educate and train ourselves to handle the daily affairs of life. No one else can work out our salvation for us, either temporally or spiritually.

"We are here on earth to care for the needs of our family members. Wives have claim on their husbands for their support, children upon their parents, parents upon their children, brothers upon each other, and relatives upon their kin.

"It is the aim of the Church to help the Saints to care for themselves and, where need be, to make food and clothing and other necessities available, lest the Saints turn to the doles and evils of Babylon. To help care for the poor among them the Church must operate farms, grow vineyards, run dairies, manage factories, and ten thousand other things—all in such a way as to be independent of the powers of evil in the world.

*The battle of Armageddon will be centered upon Jerusalem*

"We do not know when the calamities and troubles of the last days will fall upon any of us as individuals or upon bodies of the Saints. The Lord deliberately withholds from us the day and hour of his coming and of the tribulations which shall precede it—all as part of the testing and probationary experiences of mortality. He simply tells us to watch and be ready.

"We can rest assured that if we have done all in our power to prepare for whatever lies ahead, he will then help us with whatever else we need. . . .

"We do not say that all of the Saints will be spared and saved from the coming day of desolation. But we do say there is no promise of safety and no promise of security except for those who love the Lord and who are seeking to do all that he commands." (In Conference Report, Apr. 1979, pp. 131-33; or *Ensign,* May 1979, p. 92-93.)

### (H-9) Conditions at the Time of Christ's Coming

As the Lord spoke with his disciples on the Mount of Olives, three days before his crucifixion, he answered their questions about the time of his second coming and of the end of the world. He said that day would be "as it was in the days of Noah" (JS—M 1:41), a time when the earth was corrupt and filled with violence and the thoughts and intents of men were evil continually as they pursued their selfish interests with no thought of their dependence on God (see Moses 8:21-22, 28-30). As the world continues to degenerate, the Saints of God will continue to build Zion and separate themselves from the world and its corruptions (see D&C 63:54; 1 Nephi 14:7). Elder Bruce R. McConkie declared it to be one of the "sad heresies" of modern times "that the Millennium will be ushered in because men will learn to live in peace . . . or that the predicted plagues and promised desolations of latter-days can in some way be avoided" (in Conference Report, Apr. 1979, pp. 131-32; or *Ensign,* May 1979, p. 93).

Instead, the Lord will usher in the Millennium by coming in vengeance and destruction upon the wicked, bringing redemption and deliverance to his Saints (see D&C 133:51-52).

### (H-10) Christ's Appearance to Mankind

When the Lord returns he will make some appearances to specific groups and then culminate his return by his appearance in great power, majesty, and glory, in such a manner that all the world will see him (see D&C 133:17-22 and 101:22-23). Four appearances of the Lord have had particular mention by the prophets: two of these appearances will be to the Saints; one appearance will be to the Jews; and the fourth will be his final coming to the world.

*The appearance at the city of New Jerusalem.* The Lord "shall suddenly come to his temple" (D&C 133:2), a temple yet to be built in Jackson County, Missouri (see D&C 84:1-5; 97:10, 15-16). Elder Charles W. Penrose said that the Lord would make his appearance first among the Saints and "that appearance will be unknown to the rest of mankind. He will come to the Temple prepared for him, and his faithful people will behold his face, hear his voice, and gaze upon his glory. From his own lips they will receive futher instructions for the development and beautifying of Zion and for the extension and sure stability of his Kingdom." (*Millennial Star,* 10 Sept. 1859, pp. 582-83.)

*The appearance at Adam-ondi-Ahman.* The Lord will appear to the Saints in a solemn assembly of priesthood to be held at Adam-ondi-Ahman in Daviess County, Missouri, attended only by those who have held the keys of the priesthood during all the gospel dispensations and by others living who are specially invited. The Prophet Joseph Smith said that "Daniel in his seventh chapter speaks of the Ancient of Days; he means the oldest man, our father Adam, Michael, he will call his children together and hold a council with them to prepare them for the coming of the Son of Man. He (Adam) is the father of the human family and presides over the spirits of all men, and all that have had the keys must stand before him in this grand council." (*History of the Church,* 3:386-87; see also D&C 116.)

Elder Joseph Fielding Smith wrote:

"Not many years hence there shall be another gathering of high priests and righteous souls in this same valley of Adam-ondi-Ahman. At this gathering Adam, the Ancient of Days, will again be present. At this time the vision which Daniel saw will be enacted. The Ancient of Days will sit. There will stand before him those who have held the keys of all dispensations, who shall render up their stewardship to the first patriarch of the race, who holds the keys of salvation. This shall be a day of judgment and preparation.

"In this council Christ will take over the reins of government, officially, on the earth, and the kingdom and dominions, and the greatness of the kingdom under the whole heaven, shall be given to the saints of the Most High . . .

"Until this grand council is held, Satan shall hold rule in the nations of the earth; but at that time thrones are to be cast down and man's rule shall come to an end . . . Then shall he give the government to the saints of the Most High. . . .

"[This council] shall precede the coming of Jesus Christ as a thief in the night, unbeknown to all the world." (*Way to Perfection,* pp. 289-91.)

President Lorenzo Snow, speaking of those who will be living in Jackson County at that time, said: "If you will not have seen the Lord Jesus at that time you may expect Him very soon, to see him, to eat and drink with Him, to shake hands with Him and to invite him to your houses as He was invited when He was here before" (*Deseret News,* 15 June 1901, p. 1).

*The appearance at the Mount of Olives.* The Savior's appearance to the Jews will occur when Jerusalem and its environs are besieged by many nations. At the close of a long and costly war, known as the battle of Armageddon, the Jews will flee for safety to the Mount of Olives. There the Savior will make his appearance. (See D&C 45:48-53; 77;15; 133:35; Revelation 11:1-13; Zechariah 14:1-9).

Elder Parley P. Pratt summarized the events associated with that appearance: "Zechariah, chapter 14, has told us much concerning the great battle and overthrow of the nations that fight against Jerusalem, and he has said, in plain words, that the Lord shall come at the very time of the overthrow of that army; yes, in fact, even while they are in the act of taking Jerusalem, and have already succeeded in taking one-half the city, spoiling their houses, and ravishing their women. Then, behold, their long-expected Messiah, suddenly appearing, shall stand upon the Mount of Olives, a little east of Jerusalem, to fight against those nations and deliver the Jews. Zechariah says the Mount of Olives shall cleave in twain, from east to west, and one-half of the mountain shall remove to the north while the other half falls off to the south, suddenly forming a very great valley into which the Jews shall flee for protection from their enemies as they fled from the earthquake in the days of Uzziah, king of Judah; while the Lord cometh and all the saints with Him. Then will the Jews behold that long, long-expected Messiah, coming in power to their deliverance, as they always looked for him. He will destroy their enemies, and deliver them from trouble at the very time they are in the utmost consternation, and about to be swallowed up by their enemies. But what will be their astonishment when they are about to fall at the feet of their Deliverer and acknowledge him their Messiah! They discover the wounds which were once made in his hands, feet, and side; and on inquiry, at once recognize Jesus of Nazareth, the King of the Jews, the man so long rejected.Well did the prophet say, they shall mourn and weep, every family apart, and their wives apart. But, thank heaven, there will be an end to their mourning; for he will forgive their iniquities and cleanse them from uncleanness. Jerusalem shall be a holy city from that time forth." (*Voice of Warning,* pp. 32-33.)

*The Second Coming: the appearance to the whole world.* As the Lord's second coming approaches, signs will mark this epochal event. One of the last of these signs is the sign of the Son of Man (see D&C 88:93; JS—M 1:36). The Prophet Joseph Smith said, "Then will appear one grand sign of the Son of Man in heaven. But what will the world do? They will say it is a planet, a comet, etc. But the Son of man will come as the sign of the coming of the Son of Man, which will be as the light of the morning cometh out of the east." (*Teachings*, p. 287.)

Following the sign there will be "silence in heaven for the space of half an hour, and immediately after shall the curtain of heaven be unfolded" and the Lord will make his glorious appearance (D&C 88:95). So great will be the glory and power of his coming that the earth will tremble, the sun shall hide his face in shame, the mountains will melt and flow down, and the waters of the seas will boil (see D&C 133:40-42, 49; 101:25). All that is corruptible shall be consumed and destroyed by the brightness of his glorious presence (see D&C 5:19; 101:24-25). The Lord will wear red apparel, signifying his great atoning sacrifice and also his judgments upon the wicked (see D&C 133:48-51).

At this long-awaited day the Lord's people will receive the reward for their faithfulness and endurance (see D&C 54:10; 133:52-53). Both the righteous living and the celestial dead will be caught up to meet the Lord in the air to be rewarded according to their deeds while the wicked are destroyed and cast into outer darkness (see D&C 88:96-97; 101:89-91). This will be the "great and dreadful day of the Lord" (D&C 110:14, 16).

**(H-11) Summary**

Throughout history the Lord has counseled his people to prepare for the time of his coming and to warn the world to do the same. The same preparations that are needed to endure the tribulations of the last days will be needed to endure the presence of the Lord when he comes. At the time of the Lord's coming the parable of the ten virgins will be fulfilled and those who "have taken the Holy Spirit for their guide . . . shall abide the day" (D&C 45:57).

President Hugh B. Brown, speaking in a general priesthood meeting in 1967, referred to this age as a time when youth must be prepared for an era fraught with trouble, yet an era in which the forces of God would eventually prevail and bring destined glory to the Lord's kingdom. His counsel to the young men of the priesthood is a fitting conclusion for this study:

"It seems to me that of all the signs of the times (and they are ominous and on every side) this is one of the significant signs of the times—that the Church of Jesus Christ, the kingdom of God, is massing its forces, getting ready for that which is to follow. . . .

"I say this is in a sense one of the signs of the times. I see thousands listening; and I would like to say to you young men that those of us who are growing older will pass on. We must pass the torch to you. You must have the faith to hold it high. . . .

"I hope that every young man under the sound of my voice will resolve tonight, 'I am going to keep myself clean. I am going to serve the Lord. I am going to prepare every way I can for future service, because I want to be prepared when the final battle shall come.'

"And some of you young men are going to engage in that battle. Some of you are going to engage in the final testing time, which is coming and which is closer to us than we know. . . .

"I want to say to you, brethren, that in the midst of all the troubles, the uncertainties, the tumult and chaos through which the world is passing, almost unnoticed by the majority of the people of the world, there has been set up a kingdom, a kingdom over which God the Father presides, and Jesus the Christ is the King. That kingdom is rolling forward, as I say, partly unnoticed, but it is rolling forward with a power and a force that will stop the enemy in its tracks while some of you live. . . .

" . . . I urge all of us to set our houses in order, to set our lives in order, to be prepared for that which lies ahead; and God will bless and sustain us in our efforts." (In Conference Report, Oct. 1967, pp. 115-16.)

# Judges in Israel: Watching over the Church

Enrichment I

### (I-1) Introduction

The Lord chooses stewards from among the members of his church and charges them to provide for others in the kingdom opportunities that will assist them in their eternal progression. The Lord also gives these stewards the responsibility of administering judgments by which the Church is cleansed from iniquity and erring souls are brought back into paths of righteousness. The specific responsibilities of these leaders to be judges and the value of their work will be discussed in this section. The Doctrine and Covenants outlines the gifts and keys given to these judges in Israel to help them perform their duties, and it explains the manner in which the Lord has instructed them to fulfill their calling. The Lord's laws of justice will be discussed and also the operation and importance of the Church's judicial system. The Doctrine and Covenants is vital in determining the manner in which this aspect of the Lord's work is to be carried out, for it gives the instructions necessary for applying eternal principles to the specific needs and conditions of the Saints of this dispensation.

### (I-2) Who Are Judges in God's Kingdom?

The Lord assigned the responsibilities for judging his people to both local and general priesthood leaders (see D&C 68:22; 102:2, 9-12, 28-32; 107:33-34, 91-92). Elder Spencer W. Kimball wrote of the reponsibility the Lord has given his chosen leaders: "The affairs of the Church of Jesus Christ are administered by the Presidency of the Church and the Twelve Apostles, with numerous other General Authorities assisting, and also through the stake and mission presidents and the bishops. These men are the shepherds of the flock. The Lord has placed these men to lead his kingdom on earth, and upon them he has placed authority and responsibility, each in his particular sphere. He has given these men the Melchizedek Priesthood, which is his own power and authority delegated to men. He recognizes and ratifies the acts of these chosen and anointed servants." (*Miracle of Forgiveness,* p. 325.)

With reference to the judicial proceedings of the Lord's kingdom, Elder Kimball wrote: "The bishop in his ordination to that office is made a 'judge in Israel' to those of his own ward, but to none who are not so placed under his jurisdiction. The stake president, by his setting apart, is made a judge over the people of the stake over which he is to preside. Likewise, a branch president and mission president have somewhat similar responsibilities. The General Authorities, of course, have general jurisdiction, and have the duty to make judgments in certain instances." (*Miracle of Forgiveness,* pp. 267-68.)

The Doctrine and Covenants indicates that to sit

*The bishop is the Lord's judge in Israel*

as a judge among the Lord's people is one of the foremost responsibilities of a bishop (see D&C 58:17-18; 64:40; 107:68, 72, 74-75). Others besides bishops are given this responsibility within the bounds of their stewardships (see D&C 46:27; Kimball, *Miracle of Forgiveness,* p. 327).

God is the judge over all, and he rules and directs those whom he has chosen to sit "upon the judgment seat" (D&C 58:20).

### (I-3) The Gifts and Keys Associated with Judgeship

The Lord said that "unto the bishop of the church, and unto such as God shall appoint and ordain to watch over the church" (D&C 46:27) is given a special gift by the Spirit of God to assist them in the solemn responsibility of sitting as judges of his people. It is given to them to discern all other gifts of the Spirit to determine whether they are of God. They may call upon God and receive guidance through revelation in order to properly fulfill their stewardships.

When John the Baptist came to Joseph Smith and Oliver Cowdery and conferred upon them the Aaronic Priesthood, he told them that this priesthood held "the keys . . . of the gospel of repentance" (D&C 13:1). Since the bishop is the president of the Aaronic Priesthood in his ward (see D&C 107:13-15), he holds the keys to repentance for the people of the ward. Those who desire to repent of sins they have committed can obtain great help from their bishop, whom the Lord has chosen and designated to be his representative in such matters. Not only is it helpful to go to one's bishop when seeking to repent, but it is necessary in the case of serious sins, for which a person cannot obtain forgiveness without confession to the appropriate priesthood leader. The bishop is the priesthood leader through whom the keys of repentance most often function. Others, however, whom the Lord has designated, may also act in that capacity. Elder Spencer W. Kimball taught that "not every person nor every holder of the priesthood is authorized to receive the transgressor's sacred confessions of guilt. The Lord has organized an orderly and consistent program. Every member in the Church is answerable to an ecclesiastical authority. In the ward, it is the bishop; in the branch, a president; in the stake or in the mission, a president; and in the higher Church echelon of authority, the General Authorities with the First Presidency and the Twelve Apostles at the head." (*Miracle of Forgiveness,* p. 327.) The process whereby individuals in the Church may obtain forgiveness for sins is discussed below.

As has been indicated, each judge in the Lord's kingdom has authority only over those within the boundaries of his ecclesiastical jurisdiction. Within those boundaries their responsibility to act as judges falls into two main categories:
(1) Determining worthiness for certain blessings and opportunities in the Lord's church, and
(2) Determining appropriate consequences for sin. A closer examination of each of those areas of responsibility may be helpful in gaining a better understanding of the stewardships of a judge in Israel.

### (I-4) Determining Worthiness for Blessings

The Doctrine and Covenants says that anyone who desires to unite with the Lord's church may do so by coming forth in humility and witnessing "before the Church" that he has met the appropriate standards (D&C 20:37). It is the responsibility of the Lord's judges to determine if a person has met those conditions and may be baptized. Thus, the Lord has given to judges in his Church the authority to extend to all people the great blessings of the gospel, the only means by which they may return to the presence of God (see D&C 18:22; 84:74; John 3:5).

It is also within the responsibility of the Lord's judges to determine the worthiness of individuals to receive other ordinances as members of the Lord's kingdom. In the early days of this dispensation, anyone who traveled from one area of the Church to another was required to obtain a certificate from his bishop to show that he was worthy to be "received . . . as a faithful laborer" (D&C 72:17-18, 25-26).

It is necessary for individuals to have an interview with their bishop to determine if they are living according to Church standards before they are given opportunities to function in positions of responsibility in the Church. In cases where people are being called as presidents of organizations or to positions that are supervised by bishop or stake president, the bishop or stake president must perform the interview and extend the opportunity for service.

One of the greatest privileges of this life, which is obtained only after recommendation from the bishop, is that of entering and receiving the blessings of the temple. The Lord warned the Prophet that the leaders of the Church had an obligation to keep unworthy persons from entering the temple. He said, "Do not suffer any unclean thing to come into it" (D&C 97:15).

"When the bishop is ordained he becomes judge of his people. He holds the keys to the temples and none of his ward members may enter one without the turning of the key by the bishop." (Kimball, *Miracle of Forgiveness,* p. 326.)

The privilege of performing priesthood ordinances is also under the control of those who hold the appropriate keys of the priesthood. The bishop holds those keys in his ward, the stake president in his stake, and, similarly, branch presidents, mission presidents, and so forth. For an individual to perform an ordinance or to receive a temple recommend requires authorization from those holding keys.

Thus, the blessings and opportunities of the Lord's kingdom are under the stewardship of the Lord's appointed judges. Any who would receive these blessings may do so only with the approval of the "judge[s] in Israel" (D&C 107:72).

### (I-5) Determining Appropriate Consequences for Sin

Elder Spencer W. Kimball gave instructions about those whose sins cause them to be in need of repentance and forgiveness and their relationship to the Lord's judges:

"Where the sin is of major proportions, there are two forgivenesses which the unrepentant one should obtain—the forgiveness of the Lord, and the forgiveness of the Lord's Church through its proper authorities. . . .

"The Lord will forgive the truly repentant. But before the Lord can forgive, the sinner must open his heart to him in full contrition and humility, unburdening himself, for the Lord sees into our very souls. Likewise, to have the forgiveness of the Church there must be an unburdening of the sin to those properly appointed within the Church.

"The function of proper Church leaders in the matter of forgiveness is two-fold: (1) to exact proper penalty—for example, to initiate official action in regard to the sinner in cases which warrant either disfellowshipment or excommunication; (2) to waive penalties and extend the hand of fellowship to the one in transgression. Whichever of the two steps is taken, either forgiveness or Church disciplinary action, it must be done in the light of all the facts and the inspiration which can come to those making the decision. Hence the importance of the repentant transgressor making full confession to the appropriate authority." (*Miracle of Forgiveness,* pp. 324-26; see also D&C 58:42-43; 61:2.)

The Doctrine and Covenants teaches that a bishop as a "judge in Israel" is to "sit in judgment upon transgressors" (D&C 107:72). Elder Spencer W. Kimball further taught that in rendering his judgments a bishop "will determine by the facts, and through the power of discernment which is his, whether the nature of the sin and the degree of repentance manifested warrant forgiveness. He may deem the sin of sufficient gravity, the degree of repentance sufficiently questionable, and the publicity and harm done of such considerable proportions as to necessitate handling the case by a Church court under the procedure outlined by the Lord. All this responsibility rests on the bishop's shoulders. Seminary teachers, institute directors and auxiliary and other Church workers can wield a powerful influence on people in distress by imparting wise counsel and sympathetic understanding, but they are without ecclesiastical authority and jurisdiction and will not attempt to waive penalties but will send the sinner to his bishop who should determine the degree of public confession and discipline that is necessary." (*Miracle of Forgiveness,* pp. 327-28.)

Bishops may remove penalties, but they may not remit sins. That is the Lord's prerogative. Elder Kimball clarified this concept:

"Although there are many ecclesiastical officers in the Church whose positions entitle and require them to be judges, the authority of those positions does not necessarily qualify them to forgive or remit sins. . . .

"The bishop, and others in comparable positions, can forgive in the sense of waiving the penalties. In our loose connotation we sometimes call this forgiveness, but it is not forgiveness in the sense of 'wiping out' or absolution. The waiver means, however, that the individual will not need to be tried again for the same error, and that he may become active and have fellowship with the people of the Church. In receiving the confession and waiving the penalties the bishop is representing the Lord. He helps to carry the burden, relieves the transgressor's strain and tension, and assures to him a continuation of Church activity.

"It is the Lord, however, who forgives sin." (*Miracle of Forgiveness,* p. 332.)

### (I-6) Consequences of Violating the Lord's Laws

Many in the Lord's kingdom are given stewardship over the Lord's laws and their application, but none is above his law (see D&C 20:80; 107:84). All members are subject to the requirements of that law, and all receive the guaranteed blessings when they abide by it. President Wilford Woodruff made this principle clear: "If there is any man in this church that does wrong, that breaks the law of God, it mattereth not what his standing may be, whether among the Twelve, the High Priests, Seventies, or Elders, or in any other standing, there is a tribunal that will reach their case in process of time, there is authority before whom they can be tried. Therefore let no one turn against the cause of God, and stop in the road to destruction, on the plea that somebody has done wrong: it is no excuse for you or I to do wrong because another does: the soul that sins, alone must bear it. Should I step aside from the path of duty it would not destroy the gospel of Jesus Christ, or even one principle of eternal truth, they would remain the same. Neither would it be any excuse for you to commit sin! but I should have to bear my own sins, and not the sins of others—so with all men." (*Millennial Star,* Dec. 1844, p. 111.)

A person who chooses to act contrary to the laws of God is left with one major choice: to repent and consequently allow the atonement of Christ to satisfy the demands of justice, or not to repent and consequently satisfy justice through his own suffering and denial of blessings. The first choice leads to eternal life; the latter leads to banishment from God's presence in the eternities (see Enrichment E).

If a person who has sinned repents fully and completely, the atonement of Christ enables the law of mercy to take effect, and he will be freed from all penalties demanded by the law of justice. Repentance is not without some pain, however. A person can never choose to sin and avoid pain. If there were no punishment, repentance would not be possible (see Alma 42:16). Even so, by repenting, a person can be forgiven and freed from past sins (see D&C 58:42-43; 61:2; 64:7).

Elder Spencer W. Kimball discussed the penalties for unrepented sins:

"Every departure from the right way is serious. One who breaks one law is guilty of them all, says the scripture. (Jas. 2:10.) Yet there are the lesser offenses which, while neither the Lord, his leaders, nor the Church can wink at them, are not punished severely. Then there are serious sins which cannot be tolerated without judgment, which must be considered by the appropriate leader, and which place the sinner's Church standing in jeopardy.

"Church penalties for sin involve deprivations—the withholding of temple privileges, priesthood advancements, Church positions and other opportunities for service and growth. Such deprivations result from errors which are not always punishable by serious measures but which render the perpetrator unworthy to give leadership and receive high honors and blessings in God's kingdom. These are all retardations in our eternal progress which a person brings on himself. . . .

" . . . If he [the priesthood leader] considers someone unworthy to receive . . . temple privileges, he may punish by withholding the privilege. Many other blessings are withheld to give the individual some time to bring his life up to the standard required. Deprivation, then, is the usual method of disciplining in the Church. In extreme cases, . . . the transgressor is deprived of Church activity and participation by disfellowshipment or is totally severed from the Church by excommunication." (*Miracle of Forgiveness,* p. 326.)

Church leaders have the right and responsibility to deal with members in transgression according to the laws of God's kingdom, and, in the absence of repentance, to withdraw fellowship or privileges; but they have no "authority to try men on the right of property or life, to take from them this world's goods, or to put them in jeopardy of either life or limb, or to inflict any physical punishment upon them" (D&C 134:10).

Many questions are asked about the handling of transgressors of God's laws. The following are some of the most common, together with their answers:

*Why is confession a necessary part of repentance*

*and forgiveness?* The Lord requires it (see D&C 19:20; 58:42-43; 61:2; Mosiah 26:29; 1 John 1:9; Proverbs 28:13). By confession the candidate demonstrates his willingness to submit to the Lord's will.

Also by confession the candidate demonstrates his humility and sincere desire to receive forgiveness. "Knowing the hearts of men, and their intents, and their abilities to repent and regenerate themselves, the Lord waits to forgive until the repentance has matured. The transgressor must have a 'broken heart and a contrite spirit' and be willing to humble himself and do all that is required." (Kimball, *Miracle of Forgiveness,* p. 179.)

The person to whom confession is made stands by the transgressor as a witness that repentance has taken place (D&C 6:28; 2 Corinthians 13:1).

By confession the transgressor demonstrates that he is not trying to cover his sins and live a lie (see D&C 121:37).

The person to whom confession is made can help the transgressor in his fight to resist temptation related to his transgression and can help him to complete all the necessary steps he must take to be completely forgiven. Bishop Robert L. Simpson said:

"It would be so much easier to talk about serious transgression to someone you have never seen before and would likely never see again; or better still, to talk in total seclusion to an unseen ear and receive your forgiveness then and there from unseen lips. But in such a process, who would then be at your side in the struggling months ahead, as you attempt with great effort to make your repentance complete, as you strive to prevent a tragic recurrence?

"Few, if any, men have the strength to walk that hill alone, and please be assured, it is uphill all the way. There needs to be help—someone who really loves you, someone who has been divinely commissioned to assist you confidentially, quietly, assuredly—and may I reemphasize the word *confidentially,* for here again, Satan has spread the false rumor that confidences are rarely kept." (In Conference Report, Apr. 1972, p. 33; or *Ensign,* July, 1972, p. 49.)

*To whom should confession be made?* President Stephen L Richards said that confession should be made "to the Lord, of course, whose law has been violated. To the aggrieved person or persons, as an essential in making due retribution if that is necessary. And then certainly to the Lord's representative, his appointed judge in Israel, under whose ecclesiastical jurisdiction the offender lives and holds membership in the Kingdom.

" . . . it is the order of the Church for confession to be made to the Bishop." (In Conference Report, Apr. 1954, pp. 11-12.)

Elder Spencer W. Kimball wrote: "Many offenders in their shame and pride have satisfied their consciences, temporarily at least, with a few silent prayers to the Lord and rationalized that this was sufficient confession of their sins. 'But I have confessed my sin to my Heavenly Father,' they will insist, 'and that is all that is necessary.' This is not true where a major sin is involved. Then two sets of forgiveness are required to bring peace to the transgressor—one from the proper authorities of the Lord's Church, and one from the Lord himself." (*Miracle of Forgiveness,* p. 179.)

*What sins must be confessed?* Elder Bruce R. McConkie wrote:

"To gain forgiveness all sins must be confessed to the Lord. The sinner must open his heart to the Almighty and with godly sorrow admit the error of his ways and plead for grace. [D&C 64:7.]

"Further, those sins which involve moral turpitude—meaning serious sins for which the court procedures of the Church could be instituted so that a person's fellowship or membership might be called in question—such sins must be confessed to the proper church officer." (*Mormon Doctrine,* pp. 292-93.)

All confessions and the revealing of personal information are held strictly confidential.

*What if a person sins grievously and is not willing to confess?* Read Doctrine and Covenants 41:5; 42:28, 75-77; 50:8; 64:12; Mosiah 27:35-36; Moroni 6:7.

*What is the value of Church courts?* Church courts are held to promote the eternal spiritual welfare of individual members and to maintain a high level of purity in the Church (see D&C 64:12-13). They provide the sinner with a way back from sin into good standing before the Lord and his Church. Those who conduct the courts are concerned with the spiritual well-being of the member being tried. Church courts are courts of love.

Elder Robert L. Simpson tells us: "Eventually, the member finds new security in his new-found freedom, in his ability to put that problem behind him. Another burden has been unloaded; another barrier to exaltation has been removed. New peace of mind can now replace a troubled heart, and that old feeling of hypocrisy is replaced by a clear conscience. Where serious transgression requires a court hearing, may I promise you, my dear young friends, that the procedure is kind, and it is gentle. The Church court system is just. As has been stated on many occasions, these are courts of love with the singular objective of helping Church members to get back on a proper course. There is no plan in Heavenly Father's realm to put his children down. Everything is designed to aid our progress, not to impede it." ("Cast Your Burden upon the Lord," in *Speeches of the Year, 1974* [Provo, Brigham Young University Press, 1975], pp. 57-58.)

*For what might a Church court be convened?* When any of the following actions have taken place, a Church court may be convened to

*Robert L. Simpson taught that Church courts are courts of love*

consider the matter:

1. Un-Christianlike conduct,
2. Deliberate violation of Church rules and regulations or open opposition to the Church,
3. Association with apostate cults, or
4. Serious infractions of the moral code. (This category includes fornication, adultery, abortion, homosexuality, incest, and child molesting. It also includes cruelty to family members, stealing, misuse or embezzlement of Church funds or funds of others, and other sins involving morality.)

In some cases the convening of a court is mandatory. Such cases include the following:

1. Murder
2. Posing a serious threat to other Church members
3. Serious transgressions that are widely known
4. Serious sins committed when the transgressor holds a prominent position of responsibility in the Church
5. Patterns of repeated serious wrongdoing
6. Other situations when the Lord's Spirit so directs

It is not necessary to convene a court when members are totally inactive in the Church (unless they are influencing others toward apostasy, or they submit a written request for excommunication). Unless an apostate cult is involved, a court should not be convened for a member who attends another church. (See *Relief Society Courses of Study, 1978-79,* p. 41.)

*What tribunals are there in the Church and what is the jurisdiction of each?* There are three standing courts in the Church:

1. The bishop's court (see D&C 107:68-72)
2. The stake high council court (see D&C 102:1-23)
3. The council, or court, of the First Presidency (D&C 107:78-81; 68:22-24)

A bishop's court, which consists of the bishop and his two counselors, has original jurisdiction over all members of the ward. The stake high council court, consisting of the stake presidency and the high council, may assume original jurisdiction over all members of the stake. The First Presidency and Quorum of the Twelve Apostles make up the First Presidency court and may take original jurisdiction over any member of the Church. An appeal may be made from the bishop's court to the high council court and then to the First Presidency court (see D&C 102:27; 107:78). All of these courts have power to disfellowship or excommunicate; however, a bishop's court may only excommunicate those who do not hold the Melchizedek Priesthood. (See *Relief Society Courses of Study, 1978-79,* p. 42.)

*What are the possible results of Church court action?* There are four possible results of Church court action: exoneration, probation, disfellowshipment, or excommunication.

*Exoneration* means that a court may conclude that the person is innocent of the charges and no action need be taken.

*Probation* means that the bishop or other judge will determine goals and a course of action to be followed by the individual to demonstrate true repentance. If the conditions are met, nothing else need be required. If, however, the individual does not show true repentance, a Church court may be convened and further action taken.

*Disfellowshipment* means that a person who is disfellowshipped loses the blessing of Church activity and participation. He may attend meetings (except priesthood and meetings of Church officers) but may not speak or offer prayer publicly. He may not partake of the sacrament, hold a temple recommend, hold a Church position, or exercise the priesthood in any way. He is, however, allowed to pay tithes and offerings and, if endowed, to continue to wear temple garments.

*Excommunication* is the action taken against members that the Doctrine and Covenants speaks of as "cast out" (D&C 41:5; 42:21, 23, 26, 28, 37, 75), being "cut off" (D&C 1:14; 50:8; 56:10; 85:11; 104:9; 133:63) or being "blotted out" (see D&C 20:83). Each of these terms means excommunicated. Concerning excommunication, Elder Spencer W. Kimball said:

"This dread action means the total severance of the individual from the Church. The person who is excommunicated loses his membership in the Church and all attendant blessings. As an excommunicant, he is in a worse situation than he was before he joined the Church. He has lost the Holy Ghost, his priesthood, his endowments, his sealings, his privileges and his claim upon eternal life. This is about the saddest thing which could happen to an individual. Better that he suffer poverty, persecution, sickness, and even death. A true Latter-day Saint would far prefer to see a loved one in his bier than excommunicated from the Church. If the one cut off did not have this feeling of desolateness and barrenness and extreme loss, it would be evidence that he did not understand the meaning of excommunication.

"An excommunicant has no Church privileges. He may not attend priesthood meetings (since he has no priesthood); he may not partake of the sacrament, serve in Church positions, offer public prayers, or speak in meetings; he may not pay tithing except under certain conditions as determined by the bishop. He is 'cut off,' 'cast out,' and turned over to his Lord for the final judgment. 'It is a fearful thing to fall into the hands of the living God' (Heb. 10:31)." (*Miracle of Forgiveness,* p. 329.)

*What if a disfellowshipped or excommunicated person repents?* Elder Kimball taught that when a person is disfellowshipped, it remains for him to "continue in his efforts to be faithful and prove himself worthy to do all that he would normally be permitted to do. When this is done sufficiently, to the satisfaction of the Church court which imposed the penalty, generally the hand of fellowship may be restored and full activity and participation be permitted the erring one." (*Miracle of Forgiveness,* p. 328.)

Elder Kimball went on to say that "there is a possibility of an excommunicant returning to the blessings of the Church with full membership, and this can be done only through baptism following satisfactory repentance. The way is hard and rough and, without the help of the Holy Ghost to whisper and plead and warn and encourage, one's climb is infinitely harder than if he were to repent before he lost the Holy Ghost, his membership, and the fellowship of the saints. The time is usually long, very long, as those who have fought their way back will attest. Any who have been finally restored would give the same advice: Repent first—do not permit yourself to be excommunicated if there is a possible way to save yourself from that dire calamity." (*Miracle of Forgiveness,* pp. 329-30.)

*Should members appeal to civil or ecclesiastical authorities for redress of grievances among themselves?* "Members of the Church should attempt to settle their own difficulties, instead of bringing them before the Church. The Priesthood ward teachers [home teachers] should secure, if possible, friendly reconciliations among contending members. It is only when these, the best means, fail, that disputes should be brought before the officers of the Church for examination and judgment." (Widtsoe, *Priesthood and Church Government,* pp. 206-7.)

"A Church court would never undertake to reverse a decision of the courts of law, neither would it take notice of matters for which the civil law makes provisions, except in cases where wickedness and depravity are evidently manifest. In such instances a person might be condemned in both courts." (Widtsoe, *Priesthood and Church Government,* p. 206.)

Read Doctrine and Covenants 42:78-93; 1 Corinthians 6:1-8.

# Keys for Avoiding Deception

## Enrichment J

### (J-1) Introduction

Since the councils in the premortal world Lucifer has "sought . . . the misery of all mankind" (2 Nephi 2:18). He "sought to destroy the agency of man" (Moses 4:3), "to deceive and to blind men, and to lead them captive . . . even as many as would not hearken unto [the Lord's] voice" (Moses 4:4). President Joseph F. Smith warned the Saints of the continuation of Satan's workings: "Let it not be forgotten that the evil one has great power in the earth, and that by every possible means he seeks to darken the minds of men and then offers them falsehood and deception in the guise of truth. Satan is a skillful imitator, and as genuine gospel truth is given the world in ever increasing abundance, so he spreads the counterfeit coin of false doctrine. Beware of his spurious currency, it will purchase for you nothing but disappointment, misery and spiritual death. The 'father of lies' he has been called, and such an adept has he become through the ages of practice in his nefarious work, that were it possible he would deceive the very elect." (*Juvenile Instructor,* Sept. 1902, p. 562.)

In order to be able to discern the deceptions, imitations, and counterfeits, one must be able to recognize manifestations that are real, legitimate, and true. The Savior warned that in the last days "there shall also arise false Christs, and false prophets, and shall show great signs and wonders, insomuch, that, if possible, they shall deceive the very elect, who are the elect according to the covenant" (JS—M 1:22). It is important to understand the principles that will enable one to avoid the deceptions of Satan.

### (J-2) The Gifts and Fruits of the Spirit in the Church of Christ

In December 1839 the Prophet Joseph Smith, who had gone to Washington, D.C., to seek redress for the complaints of Saints, met with the president of the United States. The Prophet was asked during the interview "wherein we differed in our religion from the religions of the day." The reply was "that all other considerations were contained in the gift of the Holy Ghost." (*History of the Church*, 4:42.)

The Doctrine and Covenants provides the most complete scriptural directory of the gifts of the Spirit (see D&C 46:13-25; cf. 1 Corinthians 12:7-10 and Moroni 10:8-17).

List the various gifts of the Spirit named in Doctrine and Covenants 46:13-25.

1. Verse 13 ____________
2. Verse 14 ____________
3. Verse 15 ____________
4. Verse 16 ____________
5. Verse 17 ____________
6. Verse 18 ____________
7. Verse 19 ____________
8. Verse 20 ____________
9. Verse 21 ____________
10. Verse 22 ____________
11. Verse 23 ____________
12. Verse 24 ____________
13. Verse 25 ____________

The importance of knowing the gifts and workings of the Spirit is demonstrated in the warning the Lord gave before listing them: "Beware lest ye are deceived; and that ye may not be deceived seek ye earnestly the best gifts, always remembering for what they are given" (D&C 46:8).

The Prophet Joseph Smith instructed that the manifestation of these gifts was not for public display but rather to benefit those who were already believers and who were striving to build the work of God (see *History of the Church*, 5:27-29). The nature of the gifts of the Spirit is that their effects are not readily visible when they are received. The Prophet said: "There are several gifts mentioned here, yet which of them all could be known by an observer at the imposition of hands? The word of wisdom, and the word of knowledge, are as much gifts as any other, yet if a person possessed both of these gifts, or received them by the imposition of hands, who would know it? Another might receive the gift of faith, and they would be as ignorant of it. Or suppose a man had the gift of healing or power to work miracles, that would not then be known; it would require time and circumstances to call these gifts into operation." (*History of the Church*, 5:29-30.)

The Lord told the Saints how to prepare themselves to receive these gifts as there was need (see D&C 46:9).

*D&C 46:7, 31-33.* What, according to this revelation, must we do to obtain these gifts?

*D&C 46:8-10, 12.* What is to be our motive in asking for these gifts?

*D&C 11:12-14.* Why does this section, whose subject is deception, talk about the gifts of the Spirit?

Elder Joseph Fielding Smith contrasted those who qualify for the blessings of the Holy Spirit with those who will not: "The nearer we approach God, the better we endeavor to keep His commandments, the more we will search to know His will as it has been revealed, the less likely it will be for us to be led astray by every wind of doctrine, by these false spirits that lie in wait to deceive, and by the spirits of men, as the Lord has stated in the revelations which I have read to you. We will be protected, and we will have the power to understand, to segregate truth from error, we will walk in the light and we will not be deceived. Now the man who is dilatory, the man who is unfaithful, the man who is not willing to keep the commandments of the Lord in all things lays himself open to deception because the Spirit of the Lord is not with him to lead and direct him and to show him the way of truth and righteousness, and therefore some error comes along and he absorbs it because he cannot understand and realize the difference between truth and error. I want to tell you there is much error in this world that is passed off as truth, and it behooves every man of us to seek God, and, as stated by the prophet, draw near unto Him, and the nearer we draw unto Him, and the more we seek to do His will the more light we shall receive and the less shall be the danger of our deception." (In Conference Report, Apr. 1940, pp. 98-99.)

### (J-3) Some Manifestations Are Not of the Spirit

Using the Doctrine and Covenants as a guide, Elder Marion G. Romney provided the following rules to aid in discerning the differences of manifestations:

"By the statement in the revelation on spiritual gifts, '. . . it is given by the Holy Ghost to some to know the diversities of operations, whether they be of God, . . . and to others the discerning of spirits' [D&C 46:16, 23], it appears that there are some apparently supernatural manifestations which are not worked by the power of the Holy Ghost. The truth is there are many which are not. The world today is full of counterfeits. It has always been so. . . .

"The Saints were cautioned by the Lord to walk uprightly before him, doing all things with prayer and thanksgiving, that they might '. . . not be seduced by evil spirits, or doctrines of devils, or the commandments of men.' [D&C 46:7.] . . .

"These citations not only sustain the proposition that there are counterfeits to the gifts of the spirit, but they also suggest the origin of the counterfeits. However, we are not required to rely alone upon their implications, plain as they are, for the Lord states specifically that some of the counterfeits '. . . are of men, and others of devils.' [D&C 46:7.]

"Some of these counterfeits are crude and easily detected, but others closely simulate true manifestations of the spirit. Consequently, people are confused and deceived by them. Without a key, one cannot distinguish between the genuine and the counterfeit." (In Conference Report, Apr. 1956, p. 70.)

### (J-4) Distinguishing between the Manifestations of the Spirit and the Counterfeits

The Prophet Joseph Smith emphasized the importance of being able to discern or distinguish between manifestations of the Spirit and counterfeits, between the genuine and the false. "A man must have the discerning of spirits before he can drag into daylight this hellish influence and unfold it unto the world in all its soul-destroying, diabolical, and horrid colors; for nothing is a greater injury to the children of men than to be under the influence of a false spirit when they think they have the Spirit of God. Thousands have felt the influence of its terrible power and baneful effects. Long pilgrimages have been undertaken, penances endured, and pain, misery and ruin have followed in their train; nations have been convulsed, kingdoms overthrown, provinces laid waste, and blood, carnage and desolation are habiliaments in which it has been clothed." (*History of the Church,* 4:573.)

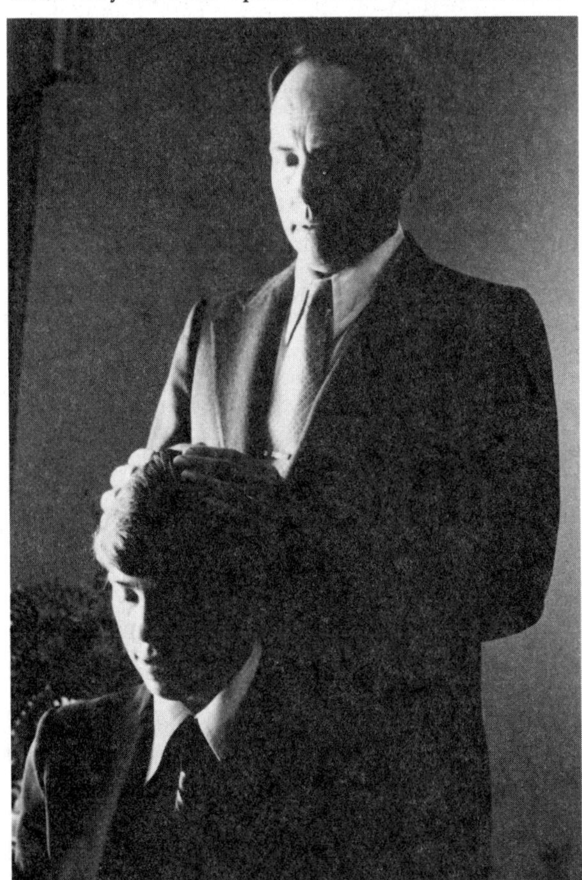

*The priesthood holds the keys to the blessings of heaven*

The Doctrine and Covenants expounds the following simple, powerful principle: "And that which doth not edify is not of God, and is darkness. That which is of God is light; and he that receiveth light, and continueth in God, receiveth more light; and that light groweth brighter and brighter until the perfect day. . . . And I say it that you may know the truth, that you may chase darkness from among you." (D&C 50:23-25.)

The manifestation of spiritual gifts is for the edification of the people of God; but there are manifestations of supernatural power outside the Church, and claims of spiritual powers by men of the world. Elder Marion G. Romney, in giving instruction about the principle of spiritual gifts, said:

"This is a key test . . . the gifts of the spirit are given by the power of the Holy Ghost. Without the gift of the Holy Ghost, the manifestations of his gifts may not be enjoyed. . . .

"Thus one who has never received the gift of the Holy Ghost cannot possibly work miracles by his power.

"Now, we know that there is but one way to obtain the gift of the Holy Ghost. That way is through the prescribed ordinances of baptism by immersion for the remission of sins and the laying on of hands for the gift of the Holy Ghost." (In Conference Report, Apr. 1956, p. 72.)

### (J-5) Those Who Pervert the Ways of the Lord

In the early Christian church, the members were warned about "wolves" among the flocks who pervert the gospel of Christ (Acts 20:29). President Harold B. Lee warned that admonitions have application today:

"There are some as wolves among us. By that, I mean some who profess membership in this church who are not sparing the flock. And among our own membership, men are arising speaking perverse things. Now *perverse* means diverting from the right or correct, and being obstinate in the wrong, willfully, in order to draw the weak and unwary members of the Church away after them.

"And as the apostle Paul said, it is likewise a marvel to us today, as it was in that day, that some members are soon removed from those who taught them the gospel and are removed from the true teachings of the gospel of Christ to be led astray into something that corrupts the true doctrines of the gospel of Christ into vicious and wicked practices and performances." (In Conference Report, Oct. 1972, p. 125; or *Ensign,* Jan. 1973, p. 105; see also Galatians 1:6-12.)

President Joseph F. Smith described those who are chiefly responsible for presenting false ideas and claims to members of the Church:

"Among the Latter-day Saints, the preaching of

false doctrines disguised as truths of the Gospel, may be expected from people of two classes, and practically from these only, they are:

"First—the hopelessly ignorant, whose lack of intelligence is due to their indolence and sloth, who make but feeble effort, if indeed any at all, to better themselves by reading and study; those who are afflicted with a dread disease that may develop into an incurable malady—laziness.

"Second—the proud and self-vaunting ones, who read by the lamp of their own conceit; who interpret by rules of their own contriving; who have become a law unto themselves, and so pose as the sole judges of their own doings. More dangerously ignorant than the first." (*Juvenile Instructor*, Mar. 1906, p. 178.)

### (J-6) Keys for Discerning the True and the False

With such forces at work in the Church, one must learn to combat these workings of Satan. Elder Marion G. Romney listed the following guidelines to assist one to distinguish between divine truth and its counterfeits:

"Anything purporting to pertain to the Gospel of Jesus Christ may be put to the following four simple tests:

"1. *Does it purport to originate in the wisdom of men, or was it revealed from heaven?* If it originated in the wisdom of men, it is not of God. . . .

"2. *Does the teaching bear the proper label?* . . . If any teaching purporting to be from Christ comes under any label other than that of Jesus Christ, we can know it is not of God. . . .

"3. . . . *The teaching must not only come under the proper label, but it must also conform to the other teaching of the Gospel of Jesus Christ.*

"4. . . . *Does it come through the proper Church channel?*" (In Conference Report, Oct. 1960, pp. 76-77.)

A closer examination of Elder Romney's four tests will be helpful to any who seek to avoid deception.

*Is it of God or of man?* The following counsel is found in the Doctrine and Covenants: "But ye are commanded in all things to ask of God, who giveth liberally; and that which the Spirit testifies unto you even so I would that ye should do in all holiness of heart, walking uprightly before me, considering the end of your salvation, doing all things with prayer and thanksgiving, that ye may not be seduced by evil spirits, or doctrines of devils, or the commandments of men; for some are of men, and others of devils" (D&C 46:7).

Elder Romney pointed out that many are "acquainted with Paul's great doctrine that the things of God are understood by the power of God, and that the things of men are understood by the wisdom of men. 'But the natural man receiveth not the things of the Spirit of God; for they are foolishness unto him: neither can he know them, because they are spiritually discerned.' (I Corinthians 2:14)

"We never need to be deceived by the learning of the world. We can always with safety reject those doctrines which are founded in the wisdom of men." (In Conference Report, Oct. 1960, p. 77.)

*The Lord's standard for truth*

*Does the claim or teaching bear the proper label?* Even though some may claim to represent Christ, their claims usually have some special, exceptional, or secret element: "Again, I say unto you, that it shall not be given to any one to go forth to preach my gospel, or to build up my church, except he be ordained by some one who has authority, and it is known to the church that he has authority and has been regularly ordained by the heads of the church" (D&C 42:11).

Elder Romney asked: "How can any man accept the doctrine of authority from some secret source unknown to the Church? The Lord could not have made it any plainer that one's authority must come through the established order of the Church, and the President of the Church stands at the head of that order." (In Conference Report, Oct. 1960, p. 77.)

President Harold B. Lee cautioned that some people may not follow the line of authority in the Church:

"We call upon you holders of the priesthood to stamp out any such [false doctrines] and to set to flight all such things as are creeping in, people rising up here and there who have had some 'marvelous' kind of a manifestation, as they claim, and who try to lead the people in a course that has not been dictated from the heads of the Church.

"As I say, it never ceases to amaze me how gullible some of our Church members are in broadcasting these sensational stories, or dreams, or visions, some alleged to have been given to Church leaders, past or present, supposedly from one person's private diary, without first verifying the report with proper Church authorities.

"If our people want to be safely guided during these troublous times of deceit and false rumors, they must follow their leaders and seek for the guidance of the Spirit of the Lord in order to avoid falling prey to clever manipulators who, with cunning sophistry, seek to draw attention and gain a following to serve their own notions and sometimes sinister motives." (In Conference Report, Oct. 1972, p. 126; or *Ensign*, Jan. 1973, p. 105.)

Sometimes a person of renowned reputation in some academic field may have his views about religion listened to with great respect because of his status in his field. Elder Boyd K. Packer warned of this kind of claimant who is a critic of the works of the kingdom:

"Many an academic giant is at once a spiritual pygmy and, if so, he is usually a moral weakling as well. Such a man may easily become a self-appointed member of a wrecking crew determined to destroy the works of God.

"Beware of the testimony of one who is intemperate, or irreverent, or immoral, who tears down and has nothing to put in its place." (In Conference Report, Apr. 1974, p. 138; or *Ensign,* May 1974, p. 95.)

*Does the claim or teaching conform to the gospel of Christ?* Even if a person claims that his message is of God or is approved by the Church, if it does not conform to established doctrine, one can safely put it down as being false. The standard works and the direction of the living prophets are the measuring rod by which the teachings of the gospel are to be evaluated. President Joseph Fielding Smith stressed the importance of using the scriptures as a standard by which to judge: "It makes no difference what is written or what anyone has said, if what has been said is in conflict with what the Lord has revealed, we can set it aside. My words, and the teachings of any other member of the Church, high or low, if they do not square with the revelations, we need not accept them. Let us have this matter clear. We have accepted the four standard works as the measuring yardsticks, or balances, by which we measure every man's doctrine." (*Doctrines of Salvation,* 3:203.)

An example of scriptural guidance for doctrinal problems is found in Doctrine and Covenants 49:15-22. A sect claiming to be true teachers of Christ's gospel taught false doctrines. After reading this revelation, list the five erroneous doctrines or principles that are discussed:

1. ____________________

2. ____________________

3. ____________________

4. ____________________

5. ____________________

*Does the claim or teaching come through the divinely established order?* At the time of the organization of the Church in the latter days, the Lord taught the Saints about the importance of the prophet and President of the Church: "Wherefore, meaning the church, thou shalt give heed unto all his words and commandments which he shall give unto you as he receiveth them, walking in all holiness before me; for his word ye shall receive, as if from mine own mouth, in all patience and faith. For by doing these things the gates of hell shall not prevail against you; yea, and the Lord God will disperse the powers of darkness from before you, and cause the heavens to shake for your good, and his name's glory." (D&C 21:4-6.)

Those who have special claims to new doctrines do so outside the established order of the Lord's kingdom. The Prophet Joseph Smith warned the Saints early in this dispensation about those who would attempt to function outside the bounds of the stewardship the Lord had given them: "I will inform you that it is contrary to the economy of God for any member of the Church, or any one, to receive instructions for those in authority, higher than themselves; therefore you will see the impropriety of giving heed to them; but if any person have a vision or a visitation from a heavenly messenger, it must be for his own benefit and instruction; for the fundamental principles, government, and doctrine of the Church are vested in the keys of the kingdom" (*History of the Church,* 1:338).

President Joseph F. Smith gave the following instruction about those who violate the divinely established principle of order: "The moment that individuals look to any other source, that moment they throw themselves open to the seductive influences of Satan, and render themselves liable to become servants of the devil; they lose sight of the true order through which the blessings of the Priesthood are to be enjoyed; they step outside of the pale of the kingdom of God, and are on dangerous ground. Whenever you see a man rise up claiming to have received direct revelation from the Lord to the Church, independent of the order and channel of the Priesthood, you may set him down as an imposter." (In *Journal of Discourses,* 24:189-90.)

Within months after the organization of the Church, there were those claiming revelation beyond their stewardship—claiming revelation for the Church, above the authority of Joseph Smith. The Lord reminded the Church of the proper order of things:

*D&C 28:2, 4-7.* Who only was appointed to receive commandments and revelations?

*D&C 43:3-6.* Even if another were to replace the currently serving President, who would make that appointment?

The Doctrine and Covenants provides many keys to avoiding deception. The following passages provide a summary of the principles discussed.

*D&C 45:56-57.* Who will "abide the day of the Lord"? What will keep them from deception?

*D&C 52:14-19.* What is the pattern given here "that ye may not be deceived"? (Cf. D&C 46:8-27.)

*D&C 52:15.* What two elements are revealed here?

*D&C 52:17.* What are the humble and faithful expected to produce?

## (J-7) Summary

The following two statements summarize the keys for avoiding deception.

First, the Prophet Joseph Smith wrote: "The

great difficulty lies in the ignorance of the nature of spirits, of the laws by which they are governed, and the signs by which they may be known; if it requires the Spirit of God to know the things of God; and the spirit of the devil can only be unmasked through that medium, then it follows as a natural consequence that unless some person or persons have a communication, or revelation from God, unfolding to them the operation of the spirit, they must eternally remain ignorant of these principles. . . . Whatever we may think of revelation, . . . without it we can neither know nor understand anything of God, or the devil." (*History of the Church,* 4:573-74.)

Second, the First Presidency (Joseph F. Smith, Anthon H. Lund, and Charles W. Penrose) wrote in 1913 about those who make false claims or declare erroneous doctrines:

"When visions, dreams, tongues, prophecy, impressions or any extraordinary gift or inspiration conveys something out of harmony with the accepted revelations of the Church or contrary to the decisions of its constituted authorities, Latter-day Saints may know that it is not of God, no matter how plausible it may appear. Also they should understand that directions for the guidance of the Church will come, by revelation, through the head. All faithful members are entitled to the inspiration of the Holy Spirit for themselves, their families, and for those over whom they are appointed and ordained to preside. But anything at discord with that which comes from God through the head of the Church is not to be received as authoritative or reliable. In secular as well as spiritual affairs, Saints may receive Divine guidance and revelation affecting themselves, but this does not convey authority to direct others, and is not to be accepted when contrary to Church covenants, doctrine or discipline, or to known facts, proven truths, or good common sense. No person has the right to induce his fellow members of the Church to engage in speculations or take stock in ventures of any kind on the specious claim of Divine revelation or vision or dream, especially when it is in opposition to the voice of recognized authority, local or general. The Lord's Church 'is a house of order.' It is not governed by individual gifts or manifestations, but by the order and power of the Holy Priesthood as sustained by the voice and vote of the Church in its appointed conferences.

"The history of the Church records many pretended revelations claimed by imposters or zealots who believed in the manifestations they sought to lead other persons to accept, and in every instance, disappointment, sorrow and disaster have resulted therefrom. Financial loss and sometimes utter ruin have followed. . . .

"Be not led by any spirit or influence that discredits established authority, contradicts true scientific principles and discoveries, or leads away from the direct revelations of God for the government of the Church. The Holy Ghost does not contradict its own revealings. Truth is always harmonious with itself. Piety is often the cloak of error. The counsels of the Lord through the channel he has appointed will be followed with safety. Therefore, O! ye Latter-day Saints, profit by these words of warning." (In Clark, *Messages of the First Presidency,* 4:285-86.)

# "Seek Learning, Even by Study and Also by Faith"

## Enrichment K

### (K-1) Introduction

The Prophet Joseph Smith taught that "in the resurrection, some are raised to be angels, others are raised to become Gods" (*Teachings,* p. 312). All who receive the gospel should have as their greatest desire to rise to the high and holy status of godhood—to become as God is. That is the great and grand objective of mortality. Without question, the attainment of that goal requires the most diligent efforts, both in mortality and after the Resurrection. One of the great elements of that effort is obtaining a knowledge of the saving principles of the gospel and learning that their proper application is crucial to exaltation in the kigdom of God. "In knowledge there is power," said the Prophet Joseph Smith. "God has more power than all other beings, because he has greater knowledge; and hence he knows how to subject all other beings to him. He has power over all." (*History of the Church,* 5:340.)

*The certain knowledge of the Resurrection gives confidence and hope to life*

In dozens of statements in the Doctrine and Covenants the Lord tells his Saints to seek knowledge, understanding, and wisdom, and speaks of those attributes in himself. The Lord knows how vital it is that his children obtain a knowledge of the truth, for they cannot apply the principles of righteousness that will enable them to become like God until they learn them.

### (K-2) All Should Diligently Seek Learning

The Doctrine and Covenants makes it very clear that the Lord intends for his people to be well educated: "Seek not for riches but for wisdom" (D&C 6:7; 11:7). "Teach one another the doctrine of the kingdom" (D&C 88:77). "Teach one another words of wisdom; yea, seek ye out of the best books words of wisdom; seek learning, even by study and also by faith" (D&C 88:118). "Study and learn and become acquainted with all good books, and with languages, tongues and people" (D&C 90:15). "Obtain a knowledge of history, and of countries, and of kingdoms, of laws of God and man" (D&C 93:53). "Let every man learn his duty" (D&C 107:99). "Let him that is ignorant learn wisdom" (D&C 136:32).

Church leaders have always taught the importance of obtaining knowledge and the great effect it has on one's progression. President Brigham Young said that "the religion embraced by the Latter-day Saints, if only slightly understood, prompts them to search diligently after knowledge. There is no other people in existence more eager to see, hear, learn, and understand truth." (*Discourses of Brigham Young,* p. 247.) He also said: "It is the duty of the Latter-day Saints according to the revelations, to give their children the best education that can be procured, both from the books of the world and the revelations of the Lord" (in *Journal of Discourses,* 17:45).

The gospel places no limits on the acquiring of truth through proper education. President Hugh B. Brown counseled Church members to "cultivate an unquenchable appetite for learning" (in Conference Report, Apr. 1968, p. 100).

Of the boundless realm in which one may grow in knowledge, President David O. McKay said: "The Church stands for education. The very purpose of its organization is to promulgate truth among men. Members of the Church are admonished to acquire learning by study, and also by faith and prayer; to seek after every thing that is virtuous, lovely, of good report, or praiseworthy. In this seeking after, they are not confined to narrow limits of dogma or creed, but are free to launch into the realm of the infinite." (In Conference Report, Apr. 1968, p. 93.)

Not only does the Church teach the importance of education but the Church has become a very effective vehicle to assist members in growing in their knowledge of the truth. Early in this dispensation the Lord commanded the Saints to teach one another and organize schools and classes for their benefit (see D&C 55:4; 88:78-79, 118-19, 127). The Nauvoo city charter provided for an educational system which included all grades from elementary to university level (see Berrett, *Restored Church,* p. 159). When the pioneers settled in the western area of what later became the United States, local settlements established schools for children and adults in religious and secular subjects. With the influx of non-Mormons into the area and the rise of secular public schools, the Church established seminaries and institutes of religion while strongly supporting secular institutions. The Church now has a worldwide education system that fosters education of Church members, yet it is careful not to usurp the prerogatives of public education sponsored by states and governments.

### (K-3) Knowledge Is a Necessary Prerequisite to Progression and Salvation

The Prophet Joseph Smith taught that "God himself, finding he was in the midst of spirits and glory, because he was more intelligent, saw proper to institute laws whereby the rest could have privilege to advance like himself. The relationship we have with God places us in a situation to advance in knowledge. He has power to institute laws to instruct the weaker intelligences, that they may be exalted with himself, so that they might have one glory upon another, and all that knowledge, power, glory, and intelligence, which is requisite in order to save them in the world of spirits." (*Teachings,* p. 354.)

Knowledge is necessary to obtain salvation; in fact, a man is saved no faster than he gets knowledge of the things of God (see Smith, *Teachings,* p. 217). The Doctrine and Covenants teaches that "it is impossible to be saved in ignorance" (D&C 131:6), but one must have the right priorities in seeking knowledge. Elder Spencer W. Kimball said:

"In proper sequence comes first the knowledge of God and his program, which is the way to eternal life, and secondly comes the knowledge of the secular things, also very important. The Creator himself gives the proper sequence and defines the order. . . .

". . . The ignorance the Lord speaks of when he says 'One cannot be saved in ignorance' is the lack of knowledge of the really first things—the kingdom of God and his righteousness." (In *Life's Directions,* pp. 175, 180.)

Individuals may progress in knowledge of the things of the kingdom of God until they arrive at a point where, if they have sufficiently applied those principles and shown their complete dedication to God, they may obtain the knowledge that they are sealed up to eternal life (see D&C 131:5). The Prophet Joseph Smith taught that "if you wish to go where God is, you must be like God, or possess the principles which God possesses, for if we are not drawing towards God in principle, we are going from Him and drawing towards the devil. . . . As far as we degenerate from God, we descend to the devil and lose knowledge, and without knowledge we cannot be saved." (*Teachings,* pp. 216-17.)

One reason that knowledge is so crucial to salvation is that salvation consists in becoming like God, and God has all knowledge (see D&C 38:2;

93:36-37; 2 Nephi 9:20; and *Lectures on Faith* 7:16). As great a task as it may seem to progress until one has the knowledge that God has, yet it is possible (see D&C 50:24; 76:55-56; 3 Nephi 27:27; Matthew 5:48).

One of the attributes of Jesus Christ is truth (see Enrichment D). The Father said of Christ that he is "full of grace and truth" (Moses 6:52). The Savior said of himself, "I am the Spirit of truth" (D&C 93:26). If we are to be like him and receive of his fulness (D&C 93:20), then we must also eventually receive the truth in its fulness. In other words, to be like God, we too must have all knowledge.

Does that seem like a hopeless task, so infinitely large as to be impossible to accomplish? If you find the thought discouraging, remember that this like all other kinds of spiritual progress, is a step-by-step process. Concerning our potential and the means by which we may attain it, the Prophet Joseph Smith taught: "When you climb up a ladder, you must begin at the bottom, and ascend step by step, until you arrive at the top; and so it is with the principles of the Gospel—you must begin with the first, and go on until you learn all the principles of exaltation. But it will be a great while after you have passed through the veil before you will have learned them. It is not all to be comprehended in this world; it will be a great work to learn our salvation and exaltation even beyond the grave." (*Teachings*, p. 348.)

The following scriptures from the Doctrine and Covenants relate to our coming to a fulness of knowledge.

*D&C 93:12-14, 19-20.* How did Christ receive his fulness? What implications does that process have for us?

*D&C 98:12.* How does a fulness of knowledge come?

*D&C 50:40.* Do you find any comfort in this statement about our natures?

*D&C 130:18-19.* Though we cannot learn all knowledge in this life, what advantage is there to diligently gain knowledge while in mortality?

To help you understand how much knowledge we can gain in this life, consider the following statement by the Prophet: "God has created man with a mind capable of instruction, and a faculty which may be enlarged in proportion to the heed and diligence given to the light communicated from heaven to the intellect; and that the nearer man approaches perfection, the clearer are his views, and the greater his enjoyments, till he has overcome the evils of his life and lost every desire for sin; and like the ancients, arrives at that point of faith where he is wrapped in the power and glory of his Maker and is caught up to dwell with Him. But we consider that this is a station to which no man ever arrived in a moment; he must have been instructed in the government and laws of that kingdom by proper degrees, until his mind is capable in some measure of comprehending the propriety, justice, equality, and consistency of the same." (*Teachings*, p. 51.)

### (K-4) The Knowledge That Saves Involves Both Principles and Applications

The statement of the Prophet Joseph Smith shows that not only must a person obtain knowledge as part of his progression, but he must also develop the capacity to live according to the principles he learns. He must develop faith, capabilities, and skills. He must be able to put his knowledge to its proper use. President David O. McKay taught that "gaining knowledge is one thing, and applying it [is] quite another. Wisdom is the right application of knowledge, and true education—the education for which the Church stands—is the application of knowledge to the development of a noble and Godlike character." (In Conference Report, Apr. 1968, p. 93.)

It is one thing to gather information in one's mind and another to develop the skills to use that knowledge effectively. Both are necessary. Cognitive knowledge without application is insufficient, yet it is a prerequisite to developing capacities and skills, both in temporal and spiritual pursuits. *Eternal life* is a term that refers to the type of life God has. When one has developed the capacity to live *and* act as He does, then he, too, will have eternal life.

The Doctrine and Covenants teaches that "the glory of God is intelligence" (D&C 93:36). President Joseph F. Smith, speaking of the difference between knowledge and intelligence, said: "There is a difference between knowledge and pure intelligence. Satan possesses knowledge, far more than we have, but he has not intelligence or he would render obedience to the principles of truth and right. I know men who have knowledge, who understand the principles of the gospel, perhaps as well as you do, who are brilliant, but who lack the essential qualification of pure intelligence. They will not accept and render obedience thereto. Pure intelligence comprises not only knowledge, but the power to properly apply that knowledge." (*Gospel Doctrine*, p. 58.)

President David O. McKay expressed the fact that, although a man may have great knowledge, "if he has not, with this knowledge, that nobility of soul which prompts him to deal justly with his fellow men, to practice virtue and honesty in personal life, he is not a truly educated man" (*Instructor*, Aug. 1961, p. 253).

True education gives a person great capacity to serve, to edify, and to move the Lord's work forward. Those who have such an education can be of great value in the Lord's kingdom. The Doctrine and Covenants indicates that the Lord instructed his people early in this dispensation to obtain knowledge "for the salvation of Zion" (D&C 93:53) and to learn their duty in order "to act in the office in which [they are] appointed in all diligence" (D&C 107:99). The Lord, through his prophet, taught that the Saints should exert righteous influence by "kindness and pure knowledge" (D&C 121:42). Blessed is the person who gains great knowledge and uses that knowledge to serve the Lord and his children.

### (K-5) Knowledge Is Power and Can Be of Great Benefit in Resisting the Adversary

By indicating the consequences of lack of knowledge, the Prophet Joseph Smith illustrated the value knowledge can have in triumphing over evil: "A man is saved no faster than he gets knowledge, for if he does not get knowledge, he will be brought into captivity by some evil power in the other world, as evil spirits will have more knowledge, and consequently more power than many men who are on the earth. Hence it needs revelation to assist us, and give us knowledge of the things of God." (*Teachings*, p. 217.)

The Savior taught that a knowledge of the truth would make men free (John 8:31-32). This freedom, in the words of Elder Bruce R. McConkie, consists of being "free from the damning power of false doctrine; free from the bondage of appetite and lust; free from the shackles of sin; free from every evil and corrupt influence and from every restraining and curtailing power; free to go on to the unlimited freedom enjoyed in its fulness only by exalted beings" (*Doctrinal New Testament Commentary*, 1:456-457).

*D&C 50:25.* As indicated by the Lord, what is one of the great benefits of knowing the truth?

*D&C 50:35.* How can we obtain power to overcome all things that are not ordained of God?

*D&C 88:77-78.* Doctrine and Covenants 93:12-14, 19-20, shows that we can come to a fulness by moving from grace to grace. What is one way that we can have the grace of God attend us?

### (K-6) What Knowledge Are the Saints Commanded to Obtain?

A man cannot be saved in ignorance of the principles of exaltation in the kingdom of God. It is also true, however, that though the things of God's kingdom and establishing his righteous principles should take top priority, the Saints should study and advance their knowledge in many areas (see D&C 88:78-79). Elder Spencer W. Kimball said of this concept:

"Secular knowledge, important as it may be, can never save a soul nor open the celestial kingdom nor create a world nor make a man a god, but it can be most helpful to that man who, placing first things first, has found the way to eternal life and who can now bring into play all knowledge to be his tool and servant. . . .

" . . . Can you see why we must let spiritual training take first place? . . . Can you see that the spiritual knowledge may be complemented with the secular in this life and on for eternities but that the secular without the foundation of the spiritual

*Study of secular things must be balanced by a study of spiritual things*

is but like the foam upon the milk, the fleeting shadow?

"Do not be deceived! One need not choose between the two but only as to the sequence, for there is opportunity for one to get both simultaneously; but can you see that the seminary courses should be given even preferential attention over the high school subjects; the institute over the college course; the study of the scriptures ahead of the study of man-written texts." (In *Life's Directions*, pp. 184, 190.)

President Brigham Young said about priorities in education: "There are a great many branches of education: some go to college to learn languages, some to study law, some to study physics, and some to study astronomy, and various other branches of science. . . . But our favorite study is that branch which particularly belongs to the Elders of Israel—namely, theology. Every Elder should become a profound theologian—should understand this branch better than all the world." (*Discourses of Brigham Young*, p. 258.)

The Lord instructed the early Saints of this dispensation to study a great variety of subjects so that they might have power to effectively carry forth his work and provide for their own needs (see D&C 88:78-79; 90:15; 93:53).

The Prophet Joseph Smith said, "Truth is 'Mormonism' " (*Teachings*, p. 139). His statement was later amplified by President Joseph F. Smith, who said: "We believe in all truth, no matter to what subject it may refer. No sect or religious denomination in the world possesses a single principle of truth that we do not accept or that we will reject. We are willing to receive all truth, from whatever source it may come; for truth will stand, truth will endure." (In Conference Report, Apr. 1909, p. 7.)

The gospel does not encourage the Saints to limit their study only to religion. Though religious truth is most important, they should feel no limit in seeking all useful knowledge. President Brigham Young gave the following counsel to the Saints: "See that your children are properly educated in the rudiments of their mother tongue, and then let them proceed to higher branches of learning; let them become more informed in every department of true and useful learning than their fathers are. When they have become well acquainted with their language, let them study other languages, and make themselves fully acquainted with the manners, customs, laws, governments, and literature of other nations, peoples, and tongues. Let them also learn all the truth pertaining to the arts and sciences and how to apply the same to their temporal wants. Let them study things that are upon the earth, that are in the earth, and that are in the heavens." (In *Journal of Discourses,* 8:9.)

If a person keeps his priorities correct, the Lord will give him power to obtain knowledge of all he desires that is for his good: "Seek first the kingdom of God and His righteousness, and all else that is desirable, including the knowledge for which you yearn, shall be given unto you" (Joseph F. Smith, *Juvenile Instructor,* Oct. 1903, p. 627).

The scriptures and quotations from the Brethren cited above make it plain that every member of the Church is encouraged to continue the quest for knowledge and truth—in all fields—throughout his life. This quest may take one to colleges and universities or to vocational schools or apprenticeship training. Education that better prepares a person to gain meaningful employment and to care for his family is especially important and should be given high priority in a person's life.

But sometimes members feel that spiritual education must be set aside for a time because of the demands of secular education. Some institute students will drop their religion classes, saying they cannot keep up with their other studies. Some graduate students find that scripture reading and sometimes even Church attendance are neglected because of the press of their other studies.

Such decisions are short-sighted and suggest that one does not fully understand the process of gaining truth. Jesus Christ is the Spirit of Truth and the source of all light and knowledge (see D&C 88:11; 93:26). If one deliberately chooses to ignore the source of truth in setting his priorities, he will to that extent be walking in darkness, no matter how much intellectual knowledge he may acquire. Gaining secular knowledge while ignoring spiritual knowledge often causes a person to have more confidence in himself or in the teachings of men than in revelation. The prophet Jacob warned of that condition when he said it was good for people to be learned "if they hearken unto the counsels of God" (2 Nephi 9:28-29). He also pointed out that those who are "puffed up because of their learning" are among those whom the Lord "despiseth" (2 Nephi 9:42). That is strong language, and such as to cause a person to have sober thoughts as he sets his priorities in education. Unless a person is willing to recognize his need for God's knowledge and his inability to get that on his own—Jacob called this recognition considering oneself a fool before God—God "will not open unto them," and, Jacob added, "the things of the wise and the prudent shall be hid from them forever" (2 Nephi 9:42-43).

The Doctrine and Covenants supports this concept. The commandments there suggest a balance: "Seek learning, even by study, and also by faith" (D&C 88:118). And when the Saints teach one another the doctrine of the kingdom with diligence, they gain access to the grace of God and then are "instructed more perfectly" in the disciplines of the world (D&C 88:78).

As President Kimball said, one is not being asked to choose between secular and spiritual learning, only that they be kept in the right perspective and priority.

### (K-7) The Process by Which One Gains Knowledge and Intelligence

As with the acquisition of all character traits and skills, obtaining knowledge is a process of growth by small increments. One learns best by a process of "line upon line, precept upon precept" (D&C 98:12; 128:21; 2 Nephi 28:30; Isaiah 28:10). One grows from small to great, from simple to more difficult, from milk to meat (see D&C 19:22; 50:40; 1 Corinthians 3:2; Hebrews 5:12-14). The Prophet Joseph Smith said: "The Lord deals with this people as a tender parent with a child, communicating light and intelligence and the knowledge of his ways as they can bear it" (*Teachings,* p. 305).

The Lord counseled that those who have understanding instruct those who do not (see D&C 88:77-79, 118; 43:8). He has also told his people to obtain knowledge by their own diligent study (see D&C 90:15; 131:18-19), and to obtain a knowledge of the truth of his teachings by applying them (see John 7:17). In the Doctrine and Covenants they are commanded to "seek learning, even by study and also by faith" (D&C 88:118).

The case of Oliver Cowdery is helpful in understanding what the Lord meant when he said to seek learning by study and faith. During the translation of the Book of Mormon, Oliver sought to translate and was granted the privilege by the Lord. His attempt failed, however. The Lord then taught him an important principle. To understand the characters on the plates he was attempting to translate, Oliver should have studied them in his mind, drawn conclusions, and then asked the Lord for confirmation. If his heart was right, he would recognize by inward feelings the confirmation of either the rightness or wrongness of his decision. Through this same process all may learn by study and by faith. Such learning comes when diligent effort to study a principle is followed by revelation that confirms truth, expands knowledge, and teaches relationships and applications, or else indicates that the decision is not the correct one.

The Prophet Joseph Smith taught that "God is the source of all wisdom and understanding" and that "the best way to obtain truth and wisdom is not to ask it from books, but to go to God in prayer, and obtain divine teaching" (*Teachings*, pp. 55; 191; see also Notes and Commentary on D&C 88:117-41). The Lord has often indicated that those who humble themselves and hearken to his word will be given great knowledge (see D&C 1:28; 76:5-10; 89:18-19; 93:28; 136:32). Those who are obedient to the Lord are able to receive and understand communications from the Spirit and in that way obtain knowledge. It is the "light of Christ" that enlightens their eyes and quickens their understanding (see D&C 88:11). The Lord said to Hyrum Smith, "I will impart unto you of my Spirit, which shall enlighten your mind" (D&C 11:13). This enlightenment comes not without great effort from the learner, however. The scriptures say that one receives intelligence through "diligence and obedience" (D&C 130:19). "Light and truth forsake that evil one" (D&C 93:37). So must the seeker of light and truth, for "intelligence cleaveth unto intelligence; wisdom receiveth wisdom; truth embraceth truth; virtue loveth virtue; light cleaveth unto light" (D&C 88:40).

**(K-8) Summary**

Nothing can hinder the Lord from "pouring down knowledge from heaven" upon righteous seekers of truth (D&C 121:33). The Lord has promised his people that if they will ask in worthiness (see D&C 50:29-30), they will receive "revelation upon revelation, knowledge upon knowledge" (D&C 42:61). He told the elders of his church that they were to be "taught from on high" (D&C 43:16). The Lord truly will teach and lead by revelation those who hearken to his words. He will not, however, teach by revelation that which one can obtain by his own efforts. Revelation will supplement and enhance one's diligent efforts (see D&C 9:7-9; 130:19-21). The Doctrine and Covenants bears witness to all that God commands his children to gain knowledge, to educate themselves, and to progress in their acquisition of truth, but it also teaches the right way for doing that most profitably.

# The Law of Consecration and Stewardship

## Enrichment L

**(L-1) Introduction**

The law of consecration and stewardship is the highest manifestation of gospel living. Many view this law as only a temporal economic program, but it is a spiritual command as well (see D&C 29:35). The personal requirements for celestial living are also the foundation for the successful practice of this holy and ancient order of gospel life. It is the basis upon which Zion, the New Jerusalem, is to be built and the preparations completed for the glorious Messianic reign (see Enrichment B).

President George Q. Cannon prophetically declared the need and circumstances that would bring the reimplementation of the law of consecration: "The time must come when we must obey that which has been revealed to us as the Order of Enoch, when there shall be no rich and no poor among the Latter-day Saints; when wealth will not be a temptation; when every man will love his neighbor as he does himself; when every man and woman will labor for the good of all as much as for self. That day must come, and we may as well prepare our hearts for it, brethren, for as wealth increases I see more and more a necessity for the institution of such an order. As wealth increases, luxury and extravagance have more power over us. The necessity for such an order is very great, and God, undoubtedly, in his own time and way, will inspire his servant [the prophet] to introduce it among the people." (In *Journal of Discourses*, 15:207.)

**(L-2) Consecration: A Celestial Law**

According to the Doctrine and Covenants, early attempts to build Zion in this dispensation failed because of transgression and because the Saints were "not united according to the union required by the law of the celestial kingdom; and Zion cannot be built up unless it is by the principles of the law of the celestial kingdom" (D&C 105:4-5). These principles are a part of the law of Christ to prepare the sanctified for celestial glory (see D&C 88:20-21). The development of personal righteousness is how the blessings of Zion are obtained, and, in due time, the celestial world. "For this is Zion—THE PURE IN HEART" (D&C 97:21).

The scriptures further describe some of the characteristics of those who strive to live the principles of Zion. Unity is of primary importance: "If ye are not one ye are not mine," said the Lord (D&C 38:27). Zion requires that all be of "one heart and . . . one mind" (D&C 45:65).

President Spencer W. Kimball reaffirmed the importance of developing unity today (see Enrichment B; see also Conference Report, Apr. 1978, p. 123; or *Ensign*, May 1978, pp. 79-81).

Another characteristic of the Zion society is that the people "had all things common among them" (3 Nephi 26:19; 4 Nephi 1:3). The expression is descriptive of the administration of the law of consecration. (See Reading L-5.)

Sacrifice is the principle through which the individual is able to practice the law of consecration. Elder Bruce R. McConkie explained the relationship of sacrifice and consecration and the covenant obligation to practice them: "Accordingly, I shall now set forth some of the principles of sacrifice and consecration to which the true saints must conform if they are ever to go where God and Christ are and have an inheritance with the faithful saints of ages past.

" . . . The law of sacrifice is a celestial law; so is the law of consecration. . . .

"Sacrifice and consecration are inseparably intertwined. The law of consecration is that we consecrate our time, our talents, and our money and property to the cause of the Church; such are to be available to the extent they are needed to further the Lord's interests on earth.

"The law of sacrifice is that we are willing to sacrifice all that we have for the truth's sake—our character and reputation; our honor and applause; our good name among men; our houses, lands, and families; all things, even our very lives if need be.

"Joseph Smith said, 'A religion that does not require the sacrifice of all things never has power sufficient to produce the faith necessary [to lead] unto life and salvation.' (*Lectures on Faith,* p. 58.)

"We are not always called upon to live the whole law of consecration and give all of our time, talents, and means to the building up of the Lord's earthly kingdom. Few of us are called upon to sacrifice much of what we possess, and at the moment there is only an occasional martyr in the cause of revealed religion.

"But what the scriptural account means is that to gain celestial salvation we must be *able* to live these laws to the full if we are called upon to do so. Implicit in this is the reality that we must in fact live them to the extent we are called upon so to do. . . .

"Now I think it is perfectly clear that the Lord expects far more of us than we sometimes render in response. We are not as other men. We are the saints of God and have the revelations of heaven. Where much is given much is expected. We are to put first in our lives the things of his kingdom." (In Conference Report, Apr. 1975, pp. 74-76; or *Ensign,* May 1975, pp. 50-51.)

What you have just read should give you cause for serious reflection and self-examination. We know from the scriptures that Zion must be established again before the Savior comes. And we know from scripture that the law of consecration is the law upon which Zion will operate. You have just read about what attitudes provide the foundation for the law of consecration. Carefully ask yourself the following questions related to the statements of the Brethren cited above.

1. Are you contributing toward or against a spirit of unity in your home? In your ward or branch? In the Church as a whole?
2. Is your life in harmony with the Spirit of the Holy Ghost so that you will contribute to a unity of thought and action in the kingdom?
3. Do you truly have an attitude of consecration? Is your primary concern in life to consecrate everything you have or with which you will be blessed to the building up of Zion and the Church on the earth?
4. Do you have enough confidence in your commitment to truly say, "I am willing to sacrifice anything and everything for God"?

Such questions are thought-provoking, especially in light of the experience of the early Saints. They were eager to build Zion. They thought they were worthy, and yet they failed.

Read Doctrine and Covenants 101:1-8 and Doctrine and Covenants 105:1-6. From these scriptures list the reasons why the Saints failed to build Zion.

1. ______________________ (101:2)
2. ______________________ (101:6)
3. ______________________ (101:6)
4. ______________________ (101:6)
5. ______________________ (101:6)
6. ______________________ (101:6)
7. ______________________ (101:7)
8. ______________________ (101:8)
9. ______________________ (105:3)
10. ______________________ (105:3)
11. ______________________ (105:3)
12. ______________________ (105:4)

Do any of these problems exist among the Saints today? Or, more to the point, do you have any of these problems in your own life? If so, they might hamper your ability to live the law of consecration. If Zion is the pure in heart, where is the best place for you to begin to build Zion?

### (L-3) The Fundamentals of Consecration

President Marion G. Romney introduced the fundamentals of consecration when he said: "The basic principle and the justification for the law of consecration 'is that everything we have belongs to the Lord; therefore, the Lord may call upon us for any and all of the property which we have, because it belongs to Him. . . . (D&C 104:14-17, 54-57)' (J. Reuben Clark, Jr., in Conference Report, Oct. 1942, p. 55)." ("Living the Principles of the Law of Consecration," *Ensign,* Feb. 1979, p. 3.)

This important principle is emphasized throughout the revelations of the Doctrine and Covenants: "And I have made the earth rich, and behold it is my footstool, wherefore, again I will stand upon it" (D&C 38:17). "It must needs be that the riches of the earth are mine to give; but beware of pride, lest ye become as the Nephites of old" (D&C 38:39). "And let not any among you say that

*"The earth is the Lord's, and the fulness thereof" (Psalm 24:1)*

it is his own; for it shall not be called his, nor any part of it" (D&C 104:70).

The unrighteous distribution of possessions causes much difficulty. The Lord has said, "It is not given that one man should possess that which is above another, wherefore the world lieth in sin" (D&C 49:20).

President Marion G. Romney demonstrated the relationship between these basic principles and the law revealed to administer consecration to the Saints:

"In this revelation [D&C 42], which the Prophet designated the 'law of the Church,' the Lord revealed the essentials of the united order, which was His program for eliminating the inequalities among men. It is based upon the underlying concept that the earth and all things therein belong to the Lord, and that men hold earthly possessions as stewards accountable to Him. . . .

" . . . 'It must needs be done in mine own way.' (D&C 104:14-16.)

"In *His way,* there are two cardinal principles: (1) consecration, and (2) stewardship.

"To enter the united order, one consecrated all his possessions to the Church by a 'covenant and a deed which [could not] be broken.' That is, he completely divested himself of all his property by conveying it to the Church." (In Conference Report, Apr. 1977, p. 118; or *Ensign,* May 1977, p. 93.)

Recognition of the Lord as the rightful owner of all things is the standard of righteous living by which one governs his temporal concerns and assists with the needs of the kingdom.

## (L-4) The Fundamentals of Stewardship

*Receiving a stewardship.* Once consecration of all things was made to the Church, the individual was ready to receive a stewardship and accept complete accountability for it. President Romney described this process: "The consecrator received from the Church a stewardship by a [deed]. This stewardship could be more or less than the original consecration, the object being to make 'every man equal according to his family, according to his circumstances and his wants and needs.' (D&C 51:3.)" (In Conference Report, Apr. 1977, p. 119; or *Ensign,* May 1977, p. 93.)

A later revelation restated this principle with the reminder that righteousness is to be the basis of receiving a stewardship. The Lord said it was to be administered to "every man according to his wants and his needs, inasmuch as his wants are just" (D&C 82:17).

In the early management of this program by the Saints in Missouri, the question arose of who should determine the amount of property to be returned by the Church to the consecrator. The Prophet Joseph Smith provided the following guidelines:

"Concerning the consecration of property:—First, it is not right to condescend to very great particulars in taking inventories. The fact is this, a man is bound by the law of the Church, to consecrate to the Bishop, before he can be considered a legal heir to the kingdom of Zion; and this, too, without constraint; and unless he does this, he cannot be acknowledged before the Lord on the Church Book therefore, to condescend to particulars, I will tell you that every man must be his own judge how much he should receive and how much he should suffer to remain in the hands of the Bishop. I speak of those who consecrate more than they need for the support of themselves and their families.

"The matter of consecration must be done by the mutual consent of both parties; for to give the Bishop power to say how much every man shall have, and he be obliged to comply with the Bishop's judgment, is giving to the Bishop more power than a king has; and upon the other hand, to let every man say how much he needs, and the Bishop be obliged to comply with his judgment, is to throw Zion into confusion, and make a slave of the Bishop. The fact is, there must be a balance or equilibrium of power, between the Bishop and the people, and thus harmony and good will may be preserved among you.

"Therefore, those persons consecrating property to the Bishop in Zion, and then receiving an inheritance back, must reasonably show to the Bishop that they need as much as they claim. But in case the two parties cannot come to a mutual agreement, the Bishop is to have nothing to do about receiving such consecrations; and the case must be laid before a council of twelve High Priests, the Bishop not being one of the council, but he is to lay the case before them." (*History of the Church,* 1:364-65.)

The expressions in the revelations describing the portion or stewardship as "equal" (D&C 51:3; see also D&C 70:14) does not mean equality in the sense that all are exactly the same. President J. Reuben Clark, Jr. explained: "One of the places in which some of the brethren are going astray is this: There is continuous reference in the revelations to equality among the brethren, but I think you will find only one place where that equality is really described, though it is referred to in other revelations. That revelation (D. & C. 51:3) affirms that every man is to be 'equal according to his family, according to his circumstances and his wants and needs.' (See also D. & C. 82:17; 78:5-6.) Obviously, this is not a case of 'dead level' equality. It is 'equality' that will vary as much as the man's circumstances, his family, his wants and needs may vary." (In Conference Report, Oct. 1942, p. 55.)

Review the directions given in the Doctrine and Covenants for determining the individual's stewardship.

*D&C 42:32-33.* Note particularly the expressions "sufficient for himself and family" and "every man who has need may be amply supplied . . . according to his wants." Would a righteous individual be concerned about not having enough to care for his family?

*D&C 48:6.* Does the Lord allow for differences in family size and age of family members?

The Doctrine and Covenants extensively treats the principle of stewardship.

*D&C 42:32.* Of whom does the Lord require accountability? Is the individual to consider the portion received as the Lord's or as his own?

*D&C 82:17.* To whom is given total managerial responsibility?

*D&C 104:11.* How many Saints are expected to receive stewardships?

*The stewardship is private, not communal, property.* The consecrator, or steward, was to be given a "writing," or deed, that would "secure unto him his portion [stewardship]" (D&C 51:4). Although it has been acknowledged that all things belong to the Lord, a stewardship represents a sacred entrustment of a portion from God to the individual. The stewardship is given with a deed of ownership so that the individual, through his agency, is fully responsible and accountable for that which is entrusted to him. The deed protects the individual if he is disqualified from participation as a steward (see D&C 51:4). For all legal intents and purposes, the stewardship was private property, even though the steward himself understood that it ultimately belonged to God. President Marion G. Romney affirmed the importance of this tenet of consecration:

"This procedure [of providing deeds] preserved in every man the right of private ownership and management of his property. Indeed, the fundamental principle of the system was the private ownership of property. Each man owned his portion, or inheritance, or stewardship, with an absolute title, which, at his option, he could alienate, keep and operate, or otherwise treat as his own. The Church did not own all of the property, and life under the united order was not, and never will be, a communal life, as the Prophet Joseph himself said.

"The intent was, however, for him to so operate his property as to produce a living for himself and his dependents." (In Conference Report, Apr. 1977, p. 119; or *Ensign,* May 1977, p. 93.)

*Accountability for stewardships.* "It is required of the Lord, at the hand of every steward, to render an account of his stewardship, both in time and in eternity. For he who is faithful and wise in time is accounted worthy to inherit the mansions prepared for him of my Father." (D&C 72:3-4.)

President Spencer W. Kimball defined the meaning and extent of stewardships: "In the Church a stewardship is a sacred spiritual or temporal trust for which there is accountability. Because all things belong to the Lord, we are stewards over our bodies, minds, families, and properties. (See D&C 104:11-15.) A faithful steward is one who exercises righteous dominion, cares for his own, and looks to the poor and needy. (See D&C 104:15-18.)" (In Conference Report, Oct. 1977, pp. 124-25; or *Ensign,* Nov. 1977, p. 78.)

### (L-5) Administration of the Law: The United Order

The Lord commanded that there "must needs be that there be an organization of my people, in regulating and establishing the affairs of the storehouse" (D&C 78:3), and that this organization was to be accompanied by all who were "joined together in this order" (D&C 78:8). The word *order* is used to describe the covenant society and organization established to administer the law of consecration and stewardship to the Saints. The territorial and jurisdictional limits were set up to coincide with those of a stake (see D&C 104:47-49). The phrase "united order" suggests that those Saints, after being organized into a covenant order or society (a stake), united in the practice of the law of consecration as the temporal and economic system under which they should live.

*Residues and surplus: storehouses and treasuries.* President J. Reuben Clark, Jr., explained the different kinds of residues and surpluses consecrated under the law. He also used the Doctrine and Covenants to illustrate the purpose for which they were to be used and the system established to administer and care for them.

"That part of a man's property which was not turned back to him, if he had more than was needed . . . became the common property of the Church, and that common property was used for the support of the poor of the Church. It is spoken of in the revelations as the 'residue' of property. (D. & C. 42:34-36)

" . . . Whatever a steward realized from the portion allotted to him over and above that which was necessary in order to keep his family under the standard provided, as already stated above, was turned over by the steward to the bishop, and amount of surplus, plus the residues to which I have already referred, went into a bishop's storehouse (D. & C. 51:13 . . . ), and the materials of the storehouse were to be used in creating portions, as above indicated, for caring for the poor (D. & C. 78:3), the widows and orphans (D. & C. 83:6), and for the elders of the Church engaged in the ministry, who were to pay for what they received if they could, but if not, their faithful labors should answer their debt to the bishop. (D. & C. 72:11ff)

". . . As . . . the system developed, the Lord created two other institutions besides the storehouse: one was known as the Sacred Treasury, into which was put 'the avails of the sacred things in the treasury, for sacred and holy purposes.' While it is not clear, it would seem that into this treasury were to be put the surpluses which were derived from the publication of the revelations, the Book of Mormon, the Pearl of Great Price, and other similar things, the stewardship of which had been given to Joseph and others. (D. & C. 104:60-66)

"The Lord also provided for the creation of 'Another Treasury,' and into that other treasury went the general revenues which came to the Church, such as gifts of money and those revenues derived from the improvement of stewardships as distinguished from the residues of the original consecrations and the surpluses which came from the operation of their stewardships. (D. & C. 72:11ff)." (In Conference Report, Oct. 1942, pp. 56-57.)

*"They had all things common."* The scriptural phrase "they had all things common" (Acts 4:32; see also Acts 2:44; 3 Nephi 26:19; 4 Nephi 1:3) is used to characterize those who lived the law of consecration in ancient times. Some have speculated that the term *common* suggests a type of communalism or "Christian Communism." This interpretation is in error. The Prophet Joseph Smith taught clearly the true nature of having all things common: "I preached on the stand about one hour on the 2nd chapter of Acts, designing to show the folly of common stock [holding property in common]. In Nauvoo every one is steward over his own [property]." (*History of the Church,* 6:37-38.)

Each stewardship is considered private property (see Reading L-4), and the residues and surpluses consecrated for the storehouse became the "common property of the whole church" (D&C 82:18). It is referred to as the "common property" because every covenant member of the order had access to it, according to his just "wants" and "needs," including the need to improve his stewardship (see D&C 82:17-18).

The word *equal* is frequently used in the revelations in the Doctrine and Covenants: "In . . . temporal things you shall be equal" (D&C 70:14); "for if ye are not equal in earthly things ye cannot be equal in obtaining heavenly things" (D&C 78:6); "appoint unto this people their portions, every man equal according to his family, according to his circumstances and his wants and needs" (D&C 51:3). The Lord gave his definition of the term *equal*: "And you are to be equal, or in other words, you are to have equal claims on the properties, for the benefit of managing the concerns of your stewardships, every man according to his wants and his needs, inasmuch as his wants are just" (D&C 82:17).

Equal claims by all members in the covenant were upon the common property or resources for the administering of stewardships. Through these mutually shared rights or claims all became "alike" (D&C 51:9) or, in other words, had equal standing. The procedure for determining whose claim should be satisfied was established through the approval and consent of all who participated in the order (see D&C 104:70-71).

*The bishop as the administrator of the order.* The bishop is the supervisor and administrator of the law of consecration and stewardship. The initial consecration and arrangement of stewardship is made to him (see D&C 42:31-33; 51:3-5; 58:33, 55). In the Zion community, the bishop appoints the inheritance (see D&C 48:6; 57:15; 85:1; 124:21). He also has the responsibility for the management of the storehouse (see D&C 42:34; 51:13; 72:9-10). One of the bishop's most important duties is to administer to the needs of the poor (see D&C 42:33-35, 39; 78:3; 84:112), the fatherless, the widows, and the orphans (see D&C 83:6). As a judge in Israel (see D&C 107:74), the bishop also receives the account of the stewardship of each covenant member of the order—a regular settlement and accounting (see D&C 72:5-7).

## (L-6) The Lord's Way Versus the World's Way

Some have suggested that the practice of the law of consecration and the system of the united order are only a religious kind of socialism or communism. Others assert that it was a development either from the economic philosophies of Joseph Smith's day or from communal experiments within the new religion. Such assumptions are false. The Prophet Joseph Smith attended a presentation on socialism in September 1843 at Nauvoo. His response was to declare that he *"did not believe the doctrine"* (*History of the Church,* 6:33). In more recent times Elder Marion G. Romney outlined the differences between the revealed system of the united order and the socialistic programs:

"(1) The cornerstone of the United Order is belief in God and acceptance of him as Lord of the earth and the author of the United Order.

"Socialism, wholly materialistic, is founded in the wisdom of men and not of God. Although all socialists may not be atheists, none of them in theory or practice seek the Lord to establish his righteousness.

"(2) The United Order is implemented by the voluntary free-will actions of men, evidenced by a consecration of all their property to the Church of God.

". . . Socialism is implemented by external force, the power of the state.

"(3) . . . The United Order is operated upon the principle of private ownership and individual management.

"Thus in both implementation and ownership and management of property, the United Order preserves to men their God-given agency, while socialism deprives them of it.

"(4) The United Order is non-political.

"Socialism is political, both in theory and practice. It is thus exposed to, and riddled by, the corruption that plagues and finally destroys all political governments that undertake to abridge man's agency.

"(5) A righteous people is a prerequisite to the United Order.

"Socialism argues that it as a system will eliminate the evils of the profit motive.

"The United Order exalts the poor and humbles the rich. In the process both are sanctified. The poor, released from the bondage and humiliating limitations of poverty, are enabled as free men to rise to their full potential, both temporally and spiritually. The rich, by consecration and by imparting of their surplus for the benefit of the poor, not by constraint but willingly as an act of free will, evidence that charity for their fellowmen characterized by Mormon as 'the pure love of Christ.' (Moro. 7:47.)" (In Conference Report, Apr. 1966, p. 97.)

President J. Reuben Clark, Jr., with equal clearness stated the position of the Church concerning these opposing systems: "The United Order has not been generally understood, . . . the United Order was not a communal system. . . . The United Order and communism [socialism] are not synonymous. Communism is Satan's counterfeit for the United Order. There is no mistake about this and those who go about telling us otherwise either do not know or have failed to understand or are wilfully misrepresenting." (In Conference Report, Oct. 1943, p. 11.)

President Marion G. Romney warned about the continuing imitations of the adversary: "In this modern world plagued with counterfeits for the Lord's plan, we must not be misled into supposing that we can discharge our obligations to the poor and the needy by shifting the responsibility to some governmental or other public agency. Only by voluntarily giving out of an abundant love for our neighbors can we develop that charity characterized by Mormon as 'the pure love of Christ.' (Moro. 7:47.)" (In Conference Report, Oct. 1972, p. 115; or *Ensign*, Jan. 1973, p. 98.)

Submitting to such counterfeits has serious repercussions for the agency and independence of the individual and the administrative system. President Romney instructed the Saints on this matter as follows:

"I suggest we consider what has happened to our agency with respect to contributing to the means used by the bureaucracy in administering government welfare services. . . .

"The difference between having the means with which to administer welfare assistance taken from us and voluntarily contributing it out of our love of God and fellowman is the difference between freedom and slavery. . . .

"When we love the Lord our God with all our hearts, might, mind, and strength, we will love our brothers as ourselves, and we will voluntarily, in the exercise of our free agency, impart of our substance for their support." (In Conference Report, Apr. 1976, pp. 164-65; or *Ensign*, May 1976, pp. 120-21.)

President Romney then turned to the wise instructions of President J. Reuben Clark, Jr., who gave this counsel concerning worldly substitutes:

"The dispensing of these great quantities of gratuities has produced in the minds of hundreds of thousands—if not millions— . . . a love for idleness, a feeling that the world owes them a living. It has made a breeding ground for some of the most destructive political doctrines that have ever found any hold . . . and I think it may lead us into serious political trouble. . . .

" . . . Society owes to no man a life of idleness, no matter what his age. I have never seen one line in Holy Writ that calls for, or even sanctions this. In the past no free society has been able to support great groups in idleness and live free. (CR, Apr. 1938, pp. 106-7.)" (In Conference Report, Apr. 1976, pp. 165-66; or *Ensign*, May 1976, p. 121.)

President Marion G. Romney placed in perspective the destiny of the two systems:

"Both history and prophecy—and I may add, common sense—bear witness to the fact that no civilization can long endure which follows the course charted by bemused manipulators and now being implemented as government welfare programs all around the world.

"Babylon shall be destroyed, and great shall be the fall thereof. (See D&C 1:16.)

"But do not be discouraged. Zion will not go down with her, because Zion shall be built on the principles of love of God and fellowman, work, and earnest labor, as God has directed." (In Conference Report, Apr. 1976, p. 169; or *Ensign*, May 1976, p. 123.)

**(L-7) The History of Consecration**

"Whenever the Lord has had a people who would accept and live the gospel, He has established the united order. He established it among the people of Enoch, of whom the record says:

" 'The Lord blessed the land, and they were blessed upon the mountains, and upon the high places, and did flourish.

" 'And the Lord called his people ZION, because they were of one heart and one mind, and dwelt in righteousness; and there was no poor among them.' (Moses 7:17-18.)" (Marion G. Romney, in Conference Report, Apr. 1977, p. 118; or *Ensign*, May 1977, p. 92.)

The scriptures record the successful practice of the law of consecration among a number of other groups since the days of Enoch. Melchizedek was, "after the order of the covenant which God made with Enoch" (JST, Genesis 14:27), "the keeper of the storehouse of God" (JST, Genesis 14:37). In New Testament times, the order of consecration was established among the members after the ascension of the Savior. They were "of one heart and of one soul," and "they had all things common" (Acts 4:32). The record provides additional testimony of the practice of the law in which "distribution was made unto every man according as he had need" (Acts 4:35). A third group is identified in the Book of Mormon after the appearance of the resurrected Savior: "They had all things common among them, every man dealing justly, one with another" (3 Nephi 26:19; see also 4 Nephi 1:3).

The law of consecration was restored in the last dispensation on 9 February 1831 in a revelation known as "the law" (see D&C 42:2). Many additional instructions concerning its principles, practices, and organization were revealed during its implementation. The Lord revealed from the beginning of its establishment that time and circumstances would not permit its successful operation for the Saints in that day, but that their endeavors would lay the foundations for the future culmination of the work (see D&C 58:4-7). President J. Reuben Clark, Jr., summarized the stumbling blocks that prevented its early success: "The United Order lasted, in theory, for some three and a quarter years, and then it was discontinued, withdrawn by the Lord, because the of greed and selfishness of men" ("Testimony of Divine Origin of Welfare Plan," *Church News,* 8 Aug. 1951, p. 3).

After the Saints moved west, they established programs in the 1850s and 1870s, many of which bore the name *united order.* President Brigham Young encouraged the many kinds of temporal programs that were established upon most of the basic principles of consecration. The First Presidency instructed the Saints in 1882 that while there was much benefit from the existing programs, the full implementation of the law of consecration was yet in the future. After talking about the principles of the law of consecration President John Taylor and his counselors wrote: "This is a simple outline of how things will exist with regard to some of these matters, when the law of God shall be fully carried out. Our relations with the world, and our own imperfections prevent the establishment of this system at the present time, and therefore, as was stated by Joseph in an early day, it can not yet be carried out." (In Clark, *Messages of the First Presidency,* 2:339.)

## (L-8) Preparing for Consecration

The united order and its attendant laws will not be fully realized until the redemption of Zion (the New Jerusalem). So there would not be any misunderstanding, President J. Reuben Clark, Jr., defined the phrase "redemption of Zion" as follows: "In the meaning in which the Lord was using the term Zion, the 'redemption' [means] the restablishment of the people in Missouri. This has not yet been accomplished." ("The United Order and the Law of Consecration As Set Out in the Revelations of the Lord," *Church News,* 15 Sept. 1945, p. 9.)

The work of the kingdom today is to prepare for that great event. The current Church temporal programs of welfare and preparation foreshadow the practice of consecration. President Marion G. Romney explained the use of the principles of consecration as a kind of schoolmaster:

"Almost from the beginning of my services in Church welfare I have had the conviction that *what we are doing in this welfare work is preliminary to the reestablishment of the law of consecration and stewardship as required under the united order.* If we could always remember the goal toward which we are working, we would never lose our bearings in this great work. What we are about is not new. It is as old as the gospel itself. . . .

"Full implementation of the united order must, according to the revelation, await the redemption of Zion. (See D&C 105:34.) In the meantime—while we are being more perfectly taught and are gaining experience—we should be strictly living the principles of the united order insofar as they are embodied in present Church requirements, such as tithing, fast offerings, welfare projects, storehouses, and other principles and practices. Through these programs we should, as individuals, implement in our own lives the bases of the united order.

"The law of tithing, for example, gives us a great opportunity to implement the principle of consecration and stewardship. When it was instituted, four years after the united order experiment was suspended, the Lord required the people to put 'all their surplus property . . . into the hands of the bishop'; thereafter they were to 'pay one-tenth of all their interest annually.' (D&C 119:1, 4.) This law, still in force, implements to a degree at least the united order principle of stewardship. It leaves in the hands of each person the ownership and management of the property from which he produces the needs of himself and family. To use . . . the words of President Clark:

" 'In lieu of residues and surpluses which were accumulated and built up under the United Order, we, today, have our fast offerings, our Welfare donations, and our tithing, all of which may be devoted to the care of the poor, as well as the

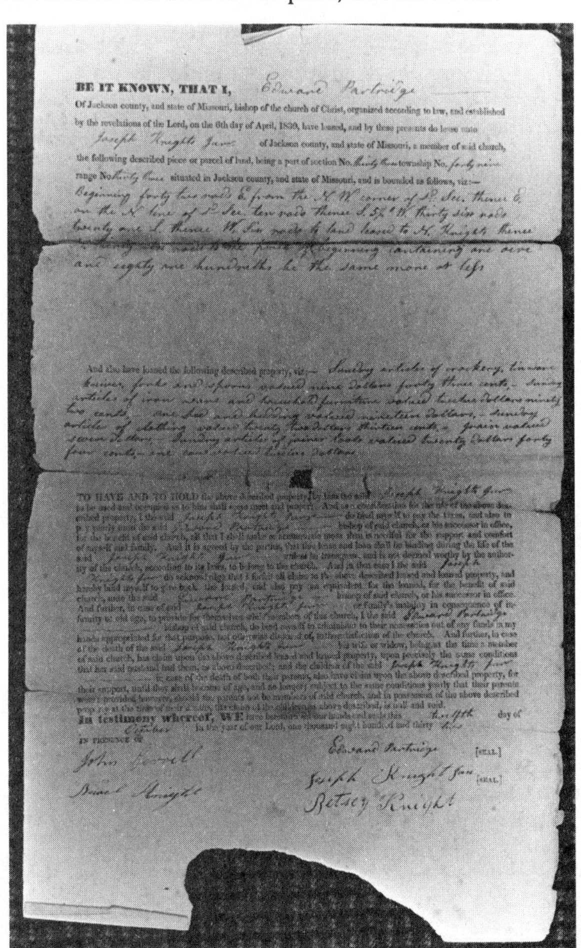

BE IT KNOWN, THAT I, Edward Partridge

Of Jackson county, and state of Missouri, bishop of the church of Christ, organized according to law, and established by the revelations of the Lord, on the 6th day of April, 1830, have leased, and by these presents do lease unto Joseph Knight Junr of Jackson county, and state of Missouri, a member of said church, the following described piece or parcel of land, being a part of section No. thirty three township No. forty nine range No. thirty three situated in Jackson county, and state of Missouri, and is bounded as follows, viz:— Beginning forty two rods E. from the N. W. corner of sd. Sec. thence E. on the N. line of sd. Sec. ten rods thence S. 5½° W. thirty six rods twenty one L. thence W. ten rods to land leased to N. Knight thence [illegible] to the place of beginning containing one acre and eighty one hundredths be the same more or less

And also have leased the following described property, viz:— Sundry articles of crockery, tinware knives, forks and spoons valued nine Dollars forty three cents,— Sundry articles of iron ware and household furniture valued twelve Dollars ninety two cents,— one bed and bedding valued nineteen Dollars,— Sundry articles of clothing valued twenty two Dollars thirteen cents,— grain valued seven Dollars,— Sundry articles of joiner tools valued twenty Dollars forty four cents,— one [illegible] valued twelve Dollars

TO HAVE AND TO HOLD the above described property, by him the said Joseph Knight Junr to be used and occupied as to him shall seem meet and proper. And as a consideration for the use of the above described property, I the said Joseph Knight Junr do bind myself to pay the taxes, and also to pay yearly unto the said Edward Partridge bishop of said church, or his successor in office, for the benefit of said church, all that I shall make or accumulate more than is needful for the support and comfort of myself and family. And it is agreed by the parties, that this lease and loan shall be binding during the life of the said Joseph Knight Junr unless he transgress, and is not deemed worthy by the authority of the church, according to its laws, to belong to the church. And in that case I the said Joseph Knight Junr do acknowledge that I forfeit all claim to the above described leased and loaned property, and hereby bind myself to give back the leased, and also pay an equivalent for the loaned, for the benefit of said church, unto the said Edward Partridge bishop of said church, or his successor in office. And further, in case of said Joseph Knight Junr or family's inability in consequence of infirmity or old age, to provide for themselves while members of this church, I the said Edward Partridge bishop of said church, do bind myself to administer to their necessities out of any funds in my hands appropriated for that purpose, not otherwise disposed of, to the satisfaction of the church. And further, in case of the death of the said Joseph Knight Junr his wife or widow, being at the time a member of said church, has claim upon the above described leased and loaned property, upon precisely the same conditions that her said husband had them, as above described; and the children of the said Joseph Knight Junr in case of the death of both their parents, also have claim upon the above described property, for their support, until they shall become of age, and no longer; subject to the same conditions yearly that their parents were: provided, however, should the parents not be members of said church, and in possession of the above described property at the time of their deaths, the claim of the children as above described, is null and void.

In testimony whereof, WE have hereunto set our hands and seals this [illegible] day of October in the year of our Lord, one thousand eight hundred and thirty [illegible]

IN PRESENCE OF

John Corrill

[illegible] Knight

Edward Partridge [SEAL.]

Joseph Knight Junr [SEAL.]

Betsey Knight

*Legal deeds to properties were issued under the law of consecration* carrying on of the activities and business of the Church. . . .

" 'Furthermore, we had under the United Order a bishop's storehouse in which were collected the materials from which to supply the needs and the wants of the poor. We have a bishop's storehouse under the Welfare Plan, used for the same purpose. . . .

" 'We have now under the Welfare Plan all over the church, . . . projects . . . farmed [or managed] for the benefit of the poor. . . .

" 'Thus . . . in many of its great essentials, we have, [in] the Welfare Plan . . . the broad essentials of the United Order.' (*Conference Report,* Oct. 1942, pp. 57-58.)

"It is thus apparent that when the principles of tithing and the fast are properly observed and the welfare plan gets fully developed and wholly into operation, 'we shall not be so very far from carrying out the great fundamentals of the United Order.' (Ibid., p. 57.) The only limitation on you and me is within ourselves." (In Conference Report, Apr. 1977, pp. 118, 120-21; or *Ensign,* May 1977, pp. 92, 94-95.)

As this program is followed, the Saints will continue to develop those characteristics which will enable them again to build Zion all over the world. Elder Bruce R. McConkie showed how these principles will move the Church toward the redemption of Zion:

"As the Saints of the Most High we shall strive to 'stand independent above all other creatures beneath the celestial world' (D&C 78:14). Our only hope is to free ourselves from the bondage of sin, to rid ourselves from the chains of darkness, to rise above the world, to live godly and upright lives.

"Relying always on the Lord, we must become independent of the world. We must be self-reliant. Using the agency God has given us, we must work out our own economic and temporal problems. . . .

"We must maintain our own health, sow our own gardens, store our own food, educate and train ourselves to handle the daily affairs of life. No one else can work out our salvation for us, either temporally or spiritually.

"We are here on earth to care for the needs of our family members. Wives have claim on their husbands for their support, children upon their parents, parents upon their children, brothers upon each other, and relatives upon their kin.

"It is the aim of the Church to help the Saints to care for themselves and, where need be, to make food and clothing and other necessities available, lest the Saints turn to the doles and evils of Babylon. To help care for the poor among them the Church must operate farms, grow vineyards, run dairies, manage factories, and ten thousand other things—all in such a way as to be independent of the powers of evil in the world." (In Conference Report, Apr. 1979, p. 132; or *Ensign,* May 1979, p. 93.)

### (L-9) The Need for Spiritual Preparation

While the Church program is the instrument of preparation for the future Zion, its success directly depends upon the personal preparation and accomplishment of the individual participant. President Spencer W. Kimball outlined what the individual must do to be ready to practice the law:

"So as to better visualize this process and firmly fix the specific principles that undergird this work, may I rehearse to you what I believe are its foundational truths.

"First is *love.* The measure of our love for our fellowman and, in a large sense, the measure of our love for the Lord, is what we do for one another and for the poor and the distressed.

" 'A new commandment I give unto you, That ye love one another; as I have loved you, that ye also love one another.

" 'By this shall all men know that ye are my disciples, if ye have love one to another.' (John 13:34-35; see Moro. 7:44-48 and Luke 10:25-37, 14:12-14.)

"Second is *service.* To serve is to abase oneself, to succor those in need of succor, and to impart of one's 'substance to the poor and the needy, feeding the hungry, and suffering all manner of afflictions, for Christ's sake.' (Al. 4:13.)

" 'Pure religion and undefiled before God and the Father is this, To visit the fatherless and widows in their affliction, and to keep himself unspotted from the world.' (James 1:27.)

"Third is *work.* Work brings happiness, self-esteem, and prosperity. It is the means of all accomplishment; it is the opposite of idleness. We are commanded to work. (See Gen. 3:19.) Attempts to obtain our temporal, social, emotional, or spiritual well-being by means of a dole violate the divine mandate that we should work for what we receive. Work should be the ruling principle in the lives of our Church membership. (See D&C 42:42; 75:29; 68:30-32; 56:17.)

"Fourth is *self-reliance.* The Church and its members are commanded by the Lord to be self-reliant and independent. (See D&C 78:13-14.)

"The responsibility for each person's social, emotional, spiritual, physical, or economic well-being rests first upon himself, second upon his family, and third upon the Church if he is a faithful member thereof.

"No true Latter-day Saint, while physically or emotionally able will voluntarily shift the burden of his own or his family's well-being to someone else. So long as he can, under the inspiration of the Lord and with his own labors, he will supply himself and his family with the spiritual and temporal necessities of life. (See 1 Timothy 5:8.)

"Fifth is *consecration,* which encompasses sacrifice. Consecration is the giving of one's time, talents, and means to care for those in need—whether spiritually or temporally—and in building the Lord's kingdom. In Welfare Services, members consecrate as they labor on production projects, donate materials to Deseret Industries, share their professional talents, give a generous fast offering, and respond to ward and quorum service projects. They consecrate their time in their home or visiting teaching. We consecrate when we give of ourselves. (See *Ensign,* June 1976, pp. 3-6.)

"Sixth is *stewardship.* In the Church a stewardship is a sacred spiritual or temporal trust for which there is accountability. Because all things belong to the Lord, we are stewards over our bodies, minds, families, and properties. (See D&C 104:11-15.) A faithful steward is one who exercises righteous dominion, cares for his own, and looks to the poor and needy. (See D&C 104:15-18.)

"These principles govern welfare services activities. May we all learn, obey, and teach these principles. Leaders, teach them to your members; fathers, teach them to your families. Only as we apply these truths can we approach the ideal of Zion.

"*Zion* is a name given by the Lord to his covenant people, who are characterized by purity of heart and faithfulness in caring for the poor, the needy, and the distressed. (See D&C 97:21.)

" 'And the Lord called his people Zion, because they were of one heart and one mind, and dwelt in righteousness; and there was no poor among them.' (Moses 7:18.)

"This highest order of priesthood society is founded on the doctrines of love, service, work, self-reliance, and stewardship, all of which are circumscribed by the covenant of consecration." (In Conference Report, Oct. 1977, pp. 123-25; or *Ensign*, Nov. 1977, pp. 77-78.)

Some procrastinate, thinking that only when the Saints go to Missouri will it be necessary to live a life of consecration. Others argue that since we do not at present have the New Jerusalem, the law of consecration cannot be lived even in principle. President Lorenzo Snow counseled that the only obstacle is the individual: "Now, here is one of the first principles of the United Order, and it was made and ordained a law by every person, and every one was required to observe it, who should be privileged to go to the land of Missouri to receive an inheritance. But this, I think, will apply, not only to those who should go to the land of Missouri, but to the people of God in every land. *Wherever there is a people of God, the principles of the United Order are applicable, if they would receive and obey them.* Some have thought that the United Order was to be kept only by the people who should go up to the land of Missouri. Now this, I believe, is incorrect. It would seem very singular that the Latter-day Saints, when they receive the Gospel, should not have the privilege of uniting themselves, according to the principles of the celestial law, and that Jackson County should be the only place where this law might be observed." (In *Journal of Discourses*, 19:343; emphasis added.)

In a somewhat humorous but sadly true commentary on the problems individuals face in living the law of consecration, President Brigham Young recounted his early experiences in attempting to get people to live the law of consecration:

"When the revelation . . . was given in 1838, I was present, and recollect the feelings of the brethren. . . . The brethren wished me to go among the Churches, and find out what surplus property the people had, with which to forward the building of the Temple we were commencing at Far West. I accordingly went from place to place through the country. Before I started, I asked brother Joseph, 'Who shall be the judge of what is surplus property?' Said he, 'Let them be the judges themselves. . . .'

"Then I replied, 'I will go and ask them for their surplus property;' and I did so; I found the people said they were willing to do about as they were counselled, but, upon asking them about their surplus property, most of the men who owned land and cattle would say, 'I have got so many hundred acres of land, and I have got so many boys, and I want each one of them to have eighty acres, therefore this is not surplus property.' Again, 'I have got so many girls, and I do not believe I shall be able to give them more than forty acres each.' 'Well, you have got two or three hundred acres left.' 'Yes, but I have a brother-in-law coming on, and he will depend on me for a living; my wife's nephew is also coming on, he is poor, and I shall have to furnish him a farm after he arrives here.' I would go on to the next one, and he would have more land and cattle than he could make use of to advantage. It is a laughable idea, but is nevertheless true, men would tell me they were young and beginning [in] the world, and would say, 'We have no children, but our prospects are good, and we think we shall have a family of children, and if we do, we want to give them eighty acres of land each; we have no surplus property.' 'How many cattle have you?' 'So many.' 'How many horses, &c?' 'So many, but I have made provisions for all these, and I have use for every thing I have got.'

"Some were disposed to do right with their surplus property, and once in a while you would find a man who had a cow which he considered surplus, but generally she was of the class that would kick a person's hat off, or eyes out. . . . You would once in a while find a man who had a horse that he considered surplus, but at the same time he had the ringbone, was broken-winded, spavined in both legs, and had the pole evil at one end of the neck and a fistula at the other, and both knees sprung." (In *Journal of Discourses*, 2:306-7.)

This is a time for sober self-evaluation. Are we of the kind who are willing to give and do whatever the Lord asks of us, or would we too begin rationalizing about why we could not fully participate?

### (L-10) Summary

President Lorenzo Snow emphasized the importance of individual agency in moving forward the work of consecration: "In things that pertain to celestial glory there can be no forced operations. We must do according as the Spirit of the Lord operates upon our understandings and feelings.

We cannot be crowded into matters, however great might be the blessing attending such procedure. We cannot be forced into living a celestial law; we must do this ourselves, of our own free will. And whatever we do in regard to the principles of the United Order, we must do it because we desire to do it. Some of us are practising in the spirit of the United Order, doing more than the law of tithing requires." (In *Journal of Discourses,* 19:346.)

President Spencer W. Kimball's admonition should be the watchword for all who desire to live in a united order and practice the law of consecration and stewardship: "We live in a world that largely rejects the values of Zion. Babylon has not and never will comprehend Zion." (In Conference Report, Apr. 1978, p. 122; or *Ensign,* May 1978, p. 81.)

"When we practice the precepts, doctrines, and programs of welfare services, the fruit of our labors is the building of Zion" (Spencer W. Kimball, in Conference Report, Oct. 1978, p. 114; or *Ensign,* Nov. 1978, p. 75).

And President Marion G. Romney summed up the matter in this way: "We're living in the latter days. We're living in the days the prophets have told about from the time of Enoch to the present day. We are living in the era just preceding the second advent of the Lord Jesus Christ. We are told to so prepare and live that we can be . . . independent of every other creature beneath the celestial kingdom [see D&C 78:14]. That is what we are to do. . . .

" . . . The final thing that we are to do is to be able and willing to consecrate all that we have to the building up of the kingdom of God, to care for our fellow men. When we do this we'll be ready for the coming of the Messiah." (In Conference Report, Apr. 1975, pp. 165-66).

# Priesthood and Church Government, Part 1

Enrichment M

### (M-1) Introduction

The most powerful force known to man in time or in eternity is the holy priesthood (see N. Eldon Tanner, in Conference Report, Oct. 1979, p. 61; or *Ensign,* Nov. 1979, p. 42). By it the earth was created and the planets are held in their cosmic orbits, but even more impressive to the mind of man is the knowledge that to have "the power of the Melchizedek Priesthood is to have the power of 'endless lives' " (*History of the Church,* 5:554). By the authority of the Melchizedek Priesthood, the entire Church and kingdom of God on earth functions, is administered, and rolls triumphantly to its foreordained destiny.

What is the meaning and purpose of the priesthood? How is the Church organized and administered through the priesthood? By what means is the Lord's will made known to the membership of the Church through the priesthood? The Doctrine and Covenants not only answers these questions but in a sense could be viewed as a divinely revealed handbook on the priesthood. In this section and Enrichment N, the doctrines and the covenants of the priesthood will be examined, particularly in three major areas: the meaning of the priesthood, priesthood organization, and Church government and administration (which is discussed in Enrichment N).

### (M-2) What Is the Priesthood?

Out of respect for the name of deity and to avoid making the Lord's name too common by overuse, the name of the priesthood was changed from the Holy Priesthood after the Order of the Son of God to the Melchizedek Priesthood "because Melchizedek was such a great high priest" (D&C 107:2; see also vss. 1-4).

What is the priesthood? The Melchizedek Priesthood is God's own power, vested in his authorized servants, that enables them to speak and act in his behalf in performing and administering every covenant, contract, vow, ordinance, or expectation that he has in store for the efficacy, virtue, and blessing of his faithful children, all being ratified by the sealing of the Holy Spirit upon the heads of the Saints in this world and in the world to come (see D&C 132:6-7).

Every prayer for salvation would be in vain without the holy ordinances being performed by those who have been anointed and appointed to the power of the priesthood. Every hope would be dashed upon the rocks of futility without the voice of authorized servants whose function it is to speak for the Lord in guiding his children in the paths that lead to exaltation and bestowing the binding blessings of eternity (see D&C 130:20-21). In short, the priesthood is the divine power needed by every son and daughter of God to lift them from a life of corruption, through the merits of the Redeemer, to a spotless life of splendor in the perfect presence of their eternal Father.

### (M-3) The Powers and Keys Associated with the Priesthood

It is a mighty responsibility to receive the Melchizedek Priesthood. President Joseph Fielding Smith said: "This matter of holding the priesthood is not a light or a small thing. We are dealing with the Lord's power and authority, which he has given to us by the opening of the heavens in this day so that every blessing might again be available to us,

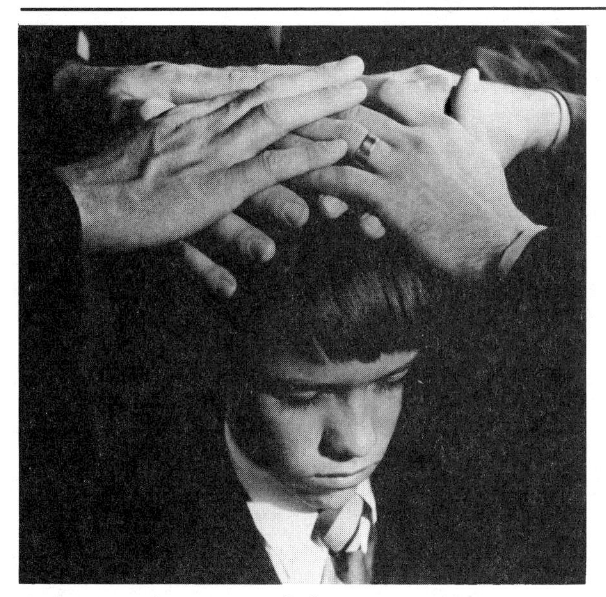

*Ordination is the transfer of God's power*

as they were when man was first placed upon the earth." (In Conference Report, Oct. 1971, p. 108; or *Ensign*, Dec. 1971, p. 98.)

Not only does one receive the power and authority to act in God's name when he has the priesthood conferred upon him, but he receives our endowment, or gift, of spiritual blessings. When Edward Partridge was called of the Lord to receive the Melchizedek Priesthood, he was told by the Lord: "I will lay my hand upon you by the hand of my servant Sidney Rigdon, and you shall receive my Spirit, the Holy Ghost, even the Comforter, which shall teach you the peaceable things of the kingdom" (D&C 36:2). Commenting on that scripture, Elder Harold B. Lee said: "Do you get the significance of that? When one is ordained by authority it is as though the Lord Himself were laying also his hand upon that person by the hand of His authorized servant, for them to receive the gifts and endowments of the spirit which come under his jurisdiction and administration." (*Church News*, 8 July 1961, p. 5.)

As you think about what it means to be a worthy holder of the priesthood, do you realize that in being given the priesthood a man receives a rich endowment of the Spirit to enable him to administer the affairs of his own life and the lives of his family in power. Think of it! When a priesthood bearer, clothed in the robes of righteousness, places his hands upon another and pronounces a blessing of guidance in an ordinance or for a calling or for his health, there is a rich outpouring of the Spirit of the Lord that both sanctifies the action and reveals the nature of the blessing.

If you traveled the world over, could you discover a more prized and peculiar possession? You will remember that Simon, a sorcerer, recognized its value and offered Peter money for its purchase, saying "Give me also this power, that on whomsoever I lay hands, he may receive the Holy Ghost" (Acts 8:19).

The purchase of the sacred power of the holy priesthood can only be realized through faithful obedience to the laws and ordinances of the gospel, and the moment a man might think to use it selfishly or unrighteously, the "Spirit of the Lord [the endowment of the Spirit associated with worthy ordination] is grieved; and when it is withdrawn, Amen to the Priesthood or the authority of that man" (D&C 121:37). No one can counterfeit the priesthood; for although man may be deceived, the Spirit never is (see D&C 45:47). Therefore the priesthood only operates "upon the principle of righteousness" (D&C 121:36).

Inherent in the priesthood is the principle of representation. Priesthood is the delegated authority of God, and so far-reaching are its powers that when those holding them are in harmony with their duties and have the spirit of their calling their official acts and utterances are as valid and as binding as if God himself were personally present doing and saying what his authorized servants do and say for him.

A distinction needs to be made between the rights of the priesthood in general and the keys of the priesthood. When the priesthood is bestowed upon a worthy man, he receives an endowment of power; however, the range or realm of the stewardship over which he may preside with that power is determined by the keys he has received. President Joseph F. Smith explained:

"The Priesthood in general is the authority given to man to act for God. Every man that has been ordained to any degree of the Priesthood, has this authority dedicated to him.

"But it is necessary that every act performed under this authority, shall be done at the proper time and place, in the proper way, and after the proper order. The power of directing these labors constitutes the *keys* of the Priesthood. In their fullness, these keys are held by only one person at a time, the prophet and president of The Church. He may delegate any portion of this power to another, in which case that person holds the keys of that particular labor. Thus, the president of a temple, the president of a stake, the bishop of a ward, the president of a mission, the president of a quorum, each holds the keys of the labors performed in that particular body or locality. His Priesthood is not increased by this special appointment, for a seventy who presides over a mission has no more Priesthood than a seventy who labors under his direction; and the president of an elders' quorum, for example, has no more Priesthood than any member of that quorum. But he holds the power of directing the official labors performed in the mission or the quorum, or in other words, *the keys* of that division of that work. So it is throughout all the ramifications of the Priesthood—a distinction must be carefully made between the general authority, and the directing of the labors performed by that authority." (*Improvement Era*, Jan. 1901, p. 230.)

The keys to administer the kingdom are not obtained automatically. When the priesthood was restored to Joseph Smith and Oliver Cowdery by the hand of John the Baptist, and then Peter, James, and John, not all of the rights to function in all of the ordinances of the gospel of salvation were restored at the same time. It was required that Elijah, Moses, Elias, and others come to bestow the keys which they held, in order to release the power of the priesthood already held by the Prophet for the work of the ministry. Without the restoration of these keys, the work of the Lord would have been frustrated and the earth would have been utterly wasted at the coming of the Lord (see D&C 2:1; 128:17).

Though keys of the priesthood always involve the *right* to use the priesthood powers bestowed upon a man, some keys are inherent in the priesthood and are held by each priesthood holder to exercise in his family or whenever the need arises, while other keys must be given in connection with special callings or assignments. Generally, when keys of the priesthood are spoken of, it is the specific, delegated keys for offices and callings that are meant, since the first are perceived as part of the general priesthood power, even though this idea is not technically true.

The right of presidency is germane to the Melchizedek Priesthood: it is part of it. Any Melchizedek Priesthood bearer may preside in righteousness over his family. But to preside in other capacities in the kingdom, specific, delegated keys are given for the period of service for which a man is called to an office in the priesthood. President Joseph Fielding Smith clarified this concept in his last conference address to the priesthood:

"Now I shall say a few words to you about the priesthood and those keys which the Lord has conferred upon us in this final gospel dispensation.

"We hold the holy Melchizedek Priesthood, which is the power and authority of God delegated to man on earth to act in all things for the salvation of men.

"We also hold the keys of the kingdom of God on earth, which kingdom is The Church of Jesus Christ of Latter-day Saints.

"These keys are the right of presidency; they are the power and authority to govern and direct all of the Lord's affairs on earth. Those who hold them have power to govern and control the manner in which all others may serve in the priesthood. All of us may hold the priesthood, but we can only use it as authorized and directed so to do by those who hold the keys." (In Conference Report, Apr. 1972, p. 98; or *Ensign*, July 1972, p. 87.)

These keys particularly "belong" to the office of the First Presidency. Stressing the need for Church members to keep their eye on those who held these keys, President Smith continued:

"May I now say—very plainly and very emphatically—that we have the holy priesthood and that the keys of the kingdom of God are here. They are found only in The Church of Jesus Christ of Latter-day Saints.

"By revelation to Joseph Smith, the Lord said that these keys 'belong always unto the Presidency of the High Priesthood' (D&C 81:2), and also, 'Whosoever receiveth my word receiveth me, and whosoever receiveth me, receiveth those, the First Presidency, whom I have sent' (D&C 112:20)." (In Conference Report, Apr. 1972, p. 99; or *Ensign*, July 1972, pp. 87-88.)

In other words, all men who hold priesthood keys, both general and specific, do so under the direction of the living prophet. He can restrict or withdraw those keys any time.

It is important for every priesthood holder to understand the keys he holds. By virtue of having the Melchizedek Priesthood conferred upon him, a man holds the keys to exercise his priesthood for the good and blessing of himself and his family. He also has the keys to function in the presidency of his home. He may exercise the priesthood to bless and comfort those in need, such as the sick, when he receives the request to do so. The bishop, however, holds the keys of presidency in a ward, and so even though a man may have the office of an elder, he can only baptize and confirm members of the Church under the direction of the bishop or branch president who presides over him. The presiding authority extends the keys to him to perform such priesthood duties. It should be clear that the keys of the priesthood are necessary for a man to preside in any capacity: whether in the Church, in the quorum, or in the home. Some keys, however, such as the keys to the power of resurrection, are not yet held by any mortal man.

### (M-4) The Doctrine of the Priesthood: Principles for Controlling the Powers of the Priesthood

No matter which keys have been given, the major message of the Doctrine and Covenants about priesthood power is that it can only be handled and controlled on the basis of righteous principles (see D&C 121:36). This fundamental doctrine of the priesthood is one of the most important contributions of latter-day revelation, for the history of the world is replete with examples of individuals who have claimed to have authority from God and to act for him, but who have operated on principles of unrighteousness.

After rehearsing certain principles of righteousness requisite to proper exercise of the priesthood, the Prophet revealed the divine promise to those who faithfully abide them: "The doctrine of the priesthood shall distil upon thy soul as the dews from heaven" (D&C 121:45).

To understand the doctrine of the priesthood requires a full appreciation of the principles upon which the promise is predicated. The Prophet revealed the principles that constitute this doctrine:

1. "There are many called, but few are chosen" (D&C 121:34). Sometimes it helps to see what disqualifies a man from being chosen in order to understand the circumstances that qualify him to be chosen. In Doctrine and Covenants 121:34-40 the Lord outlines why it is that so few are chosen. A man disqualifies

himself by having an unsatisfactory attitude of the heart. If a man's heart is set upon the things of the world and he aspires to worldly honors, then he will behave in ways that grieve the Spirit and cause a loss in his priesthood powers. Without priesthood power a man cannot be chosen by the Lord.

As ordained priesthood bearers we determine by our thoughts and by our conduct whether or not we will be chosen for eternal life. We choose whether we will be among the chosen. It is the consequence of our own disobedience if we are rejected.

2. Disobedience grieves the Spirit and causes the heavens to withdraw from an unrighteous man (see D&C 121:37). Is there a relationship between the Spirit and the priesthood? Yes! The priesthood, you will remember from reading Doctrine and Covenants 36:2, is accompanied by an endowment of the Spirit and operates only upon righteous principles. Therefore, if a man exercises unrighteous dominion or compulsion upon the souls of men, it is an offense to the Spirit and that individual loses the power of the priesthood (see D&C 121:37-40).

3. One of the keys to priesthood power is whether a man's heart is set upon the things of this world.

To determine whether one's heart is set on the things of the world, consider the following questions. Do you know anyone whose life is consumed by their desire to acquire wealth? Do you know students or professors who are so committed to their educational pursuits that they set aside their Church activity? Do you know priesthood bearers who are so wrapped up in civic and community work that they neglect their quorum and home responsibilities? Do you know of cases where athletics or hobbies have become someone's obsession and they no longer have time for the work of the Lord?

This subject has been set into poetic perspective.

---

Manacled in despair he stood,
A prisoner to passion—
Acquiring the honors prized of men;
His goal, his life's ambition.
*That* prize he won. His sons he lost,
The lesson learned, belated:
That the powers of heaven are given to man
Through righteousness unabated.

---

4. "No power or influence can or ought to be maintained by virtue of the priesthood" (D&C 121:41), except on conditions of persuasion, long-suffering, gentleness and meekness, love unfeigned, kindness, pure knowledge, having charity toward all men, and having his thoughts garnished by virtue unceasingly (see D&C 121:41-45).

An intimate relationship with the Lord is at the root of perfection. You must be able to actually feel the love of God in his heart through the gift and power of the Holy Ghost. This charity, the "pure love of Christ" (Moroni 7:47), is a gift of God and, therefore, is not a natural possession because of mortal birth. It is obtained only through being a true follower of the Master and by praying "unto the Father with all the energy of heart, that [you] may be filled with *this* love" (Moroni 7:48; emphisis added). Through properly seeking such an endowment of the Spirit in your life, you may, in Peter's words, be "a partaker of the divine nature" (2 Peter 1:4). To put it another way, through faithful, constant, yearning prayers and through righteous living, you may come to reflect these elements of godliness in your life by the grace of God (see D&C 84:33-38).

5. When a person is righteous, he may have the doctrine of the priesthood distill upon his soul. The process we speak of involves more than just understanding the priesthood principles of service. It involves the actual assimilation of the divine nature as we become like our eternal Father.

The Lord promises in Doctrine and Covenants 121:45-46 that if love abounds in you toward all men and virtuous thoughts pervade your soul, then your confidence will become strong in the knowledge that you are doing his will. The doctrine of the priesthood will then distill upon your soul, and your every care will be for the good and blessing of others. You will use your priesthood "all the day long to do unto all men as you would wish them to do unto you" (John Taylor, in *Journal of Discourses,* 10:57). The Holy Ghost will become your constant guide and companion. You will be able with his help to lay claim upon the promise of the Lord that you will have a realm, or kingdom, over which to preside eternally. Through righteousness and truth the kingdom or dominion will flow unto you without force or compulsion forever.

Can you visualize a more worthy goal or a more glorious reward? To summarize:

"It is the doctrine that those who hold this power and authority will be chosen for an inheritance of eternal life if they exercise their priesthood upon principles of righteousness; if they walk in the light; if they keep the commandments; if they put first in their lives the things of God's kingdom and let temporal concerns take a secondary place; if they serve in the kingdom with an eye single to the glory of God.

"It is the doctrine that even though men have the rights of the priesthood conferred upon them, they shall not reap its eternal blessings if they use it for unrighteous purposes; if they commit sin; if the things of this world take pre-eminence in their lives over the things of the Spirit. . . . *Behold, many are called to the priesthood, and few are chosen for eternal life.*" ("What Is the Doctrine of the Priesthood?" *Improvement Era,* Feb. 1961, p.115.)

**(M-5) Divisions of the Priesthood**

The powers of the holy priesthood flow from "two divisions or grand heads—one is the Melchizedek Priesthood and the other is the Aaronic . . . Priesthood" (D&C 107:6).

The Aaronic Priesthood, organized on a local level, includes (1) a deacon's quorum, made up of twelve members who are presided over by one of their number who has been called as the president of the quorum; (2) a teacher's quorum, which is made up of twenty-four members, led by a president called from among their number; and (3) a priest's quorum comprised of forty-eight members. There is a difference in the leadership of the priest's quorum, however, in that the bishop is the president of the quorum and is also the president of the Aaronic Priesthood in the local Church unit. Even though the office of bishop is considered the highest office of the Aaronic Priesthood, it is an appendage to the high priesthood (see D&C 84:29) and requires a worthy high priest who is recommended by the stake presidency and high council and approved by the First Presidency of the Church. (See Smith, *Teachings,* p. 112; see also Widtsoe, *Priesthood and Church Government,* p. 240.)

These quorums of the lesser priesthood are to give service to the Church and to teach their members the principles of priesthood service to prepare them for the responsibilities and blessings of the Melchizedek Priesthood.

Although the Saints speak of the Melchizedek and Aaronic Priesthoods, it is important to understand that all priesthood is Melchizedek and that the Aaronic Priesthood is an appendage thereto: "Therefore, in viewing the Church as a whole, we may strictly denominate it one Priesthood" (Smith, *Teachings,* p. 112). In general, the functions and powers of the Aaronic Priesthood are as follows: (1) to possess the keys of the ministering of angels, which include communion with them (see D&C 13); (2) to hold the keys of the preparatory gospel of repentance, baptism, and the law of carnal commandments given by Moses to a faithless Israel (see D&C 84:26-27); and (3) to fellowship its members and prepare them in all things pertaining to priesthood service so that they may be ready to receive the oath and covenant of the Melchizedek Priesthood (see Joseph Fielding Smith, in Conference Report, Oct. 1970, p. 92).

Additional perspective is added to this last statement by President Marion G. Romney: "As a general rule, great and noble men have been noble boys who built their foundations for greatness while in their Aaronic Priesthood years" (in Conference Report, Apr. 1978, p. 59; or *Ensign,* May 1978, p. 40).

Elder Orson Pratt summarized the function of the Aaronic Priesthood: "The Priesthood of Aaron, being an appendage to the higher Priesthood, has power to administer in temporal ordinances, such as that of baptism for remission of sins, the administration of the Lord's Supper, and in attending to temporal things for the benefit of the people of God. Among the privileges that are granted to this lesser Priesthood is to hold communion with holy angels that may be sent down from heaven." (In *Journal of Discourses,* 18:363-64.)

The Melchizedek Priesthood is the mighty power by which the God of heaven controls the universe and administers to man's every need. Within its broad arms is embraced every other power, office, ordinance, and principle pertaining to the salvation and exaltation of man. The greater priesthood has been termed variously the Holy Priesthood after the Order of the Son of God, the Holy Priesthood, the Melchizedek Priesthood, and the higher priesthood (see D&C 107:1-9). Its organization among men has varied, according to their needs, through the history of God's dealings with his children. In the early periods of Old Testament history, it is clearly evident that the patriarchal order of the priesthood was the type of administrative government of the Church (see D&C 107:53-56). Yet today, a different organization administers the same priesthood power.

The presence of the holy priesthood is essential in every dispensation of time and without it no manifestation of heavenly gifts and powers can be bestowed. The kingdom of God functions through, rests upon, and is administered by the priesthood.

The Prophet Joseph Smith said: "Some say the kingdom of God was not set up on the earth until the day of Pentecost, and that John did not preach the baptism of repentance for the remission of sins; but I say, in the name of the Lord, that the kingdom of God was set up on the earth from the days of Adam to the present time. Whenever there has been a righteous man on earth unto whom God revealed His word and gave power and authority to administer in His name, and where there is a priest of God—a minister who has power and authority from God to administer in the ordinances of the gospel and officiate in the priesthood of God, there is the kingdom of God." (*History of the Church,* 5:256.)

It is a divine imperative, therefore, that if a man holds all of the keys, powers, and administrations pertaining to the Melchizedek Priesthood, he holds the keys of the kingdom and is the president of the high priesthood and, therefore, is President of the Church (see Harold B. Lee, *Priesthood* [address delivered to seminary and institute of religion personnel], 17 July 1958). Indeed, true to definition, the keys of presiding are vested in the Melchizedek Priesthood. Without that power of God, the progress of the kingdom would be frustrated by the powers of the adversary.

**(M-6) Quorums in the Priesthood**

Though reference is made throughout the scriptures to various priesthood offices, only in the

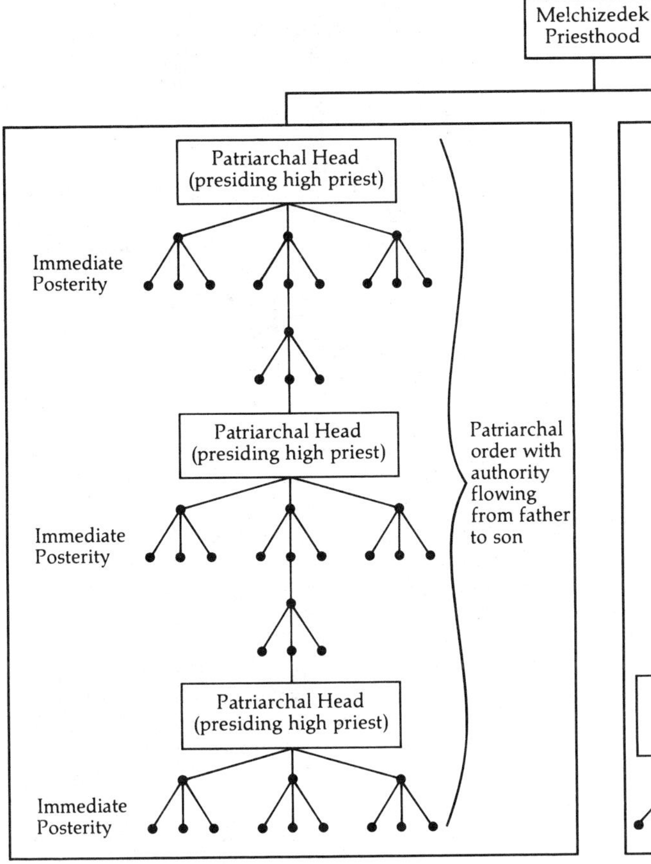


Ancient Priesthood Government



Latter-day Priesthood Government

Doctrine and Covenants is there a clear outline of priesthood quorums and their functions. Elder John A. Widtsoe defined a quorum as "a specified group of men, holding the same office in the Priesthood, organized for the more efficient advancement of the work for which the Priesthood in the Church is responsible" (*Priesthood and Church Government,* p. 134).

The bishop governs the affairs of the Aaronic Priesthood quorums on a local level, guiding them in their work of training of each individual member, and taking the lead in all temporal affairs of the members of the ward.

The stake president is the local presiding officer of the Melchizedek Priesthood and directs the work of the Lord in all the spiritual needs of the stake.

The purpose for the organization of the quorums of the Church is at least two-fold. One purpose is to organize the body of the priesthood into effective work forces to accomplish the work of building and disseminating the work of the Lord through the earth. The second purpose is to form a brotherhood strong enough to secure the spiritual freedom and rights of its members in a climate of confidence where each man may learn his duty, apply his knowledge in worthy service to his fellowman, and overcome the world. If this spirit of brotherhood is properly cultivated, wisely and persistently applied, "no other organization will become more attractive to the man who holds the Priesthood" (Widtsoe, *Priesthood and Church Government,* p. 135).

Elder Harold B. Lee quoted Rudger Clawson, who said: "Those ordained to the priesthood, both Aaronic and Melchizedek, are organized into quorums in order that both old and young may be taught and become familiar with the order of the priesthood which they hold, its keys and authorities: *the field of endeavors occupied by each quorum,* and its limitations. The method of conducting quorum meetings should always have this purpose in mind." (*Church News,* 8 July 1961, p. 11.)

In short, "the Priesthood quorums must look after their needy brethren as a continuing problem, until not only their temporal needs are met but their spiritual ones also" (Marion G. Romney, in Conference Report, Oct. 1977, p. 116; or *Ensign,* Nov. 1977, p. 80).

President David O. McKay also taught how quorums should function to help others: "It is the duty of leaders in Priesthood quorums to watch over their members, to teach them their duty. They can do that independently of the Ward bishopric. They do it because it is their responsibility; it is their duty to have their members fit to be called into ward activity, stake activity [and] missionary activity." (In Conference Report, Apr. 1960, p. 22.)

## (M-7) The Offices of the Priesthood

The office of an elder is an appendage to the

higher priesthood (see D&C 84:29). An elders quorum is organized on a ward level with ninety-six members. When a man is ordained to that office, he first has conferred upon him the Melchizedek Priesthood, and then he is ordained to the office of elder in that priesthood. The Melchizedek Priesthood is conferred only once upon a man, for when it has been done that man holds all the power of the priesthood. After that ordination, when a man is called to an office in the higher priesthood, no further priesthood is conferred, but he is given the necessary keys that pertain to the new calling.

The office of seventy is also an office of the higher priesthood. Its quorum is organized on a stake level, each ward having a part of that quorum that is organized as a group, with a maximum of seventy members. Its presidency is composed of seven presidents, one of them being designated the senior president. These presidents are called and set apart by the stake president. The stewardship of the seventy is to correlate the missionary activity of all priesthood quorums and to be active in disseminating the gospel to world. In addition, as is true with every quorum of the higher priesthood, the seventies quorum is to see that *every* program of the priesthood is fostered in the homes of its members.

High priests hold the keys of presiding over the affairs of the kingdom, and thus General Authorities, stake presidencies, bishoprics, and patriarchs are ordained as high priests. The quorum of high priests consists of all high priests in a stake, with no maximum number. The stake presidency form the presidency of the high priests quorum, though generally each local ward or branch has group leaders who assist in administering the affairs of the quorum.

Patriarchs hold a special office in the Melchizedek Priesthood. A patriarch is called to give patriarchal blessings to the members of the Church and to seal special blessings upon them. The scriptural term for patriarch is *evangelist* (see Smith, *Teachings,* p. 151). There is no quorum of patriarchs; they serve under the direction of the General Authorities through the stake president.

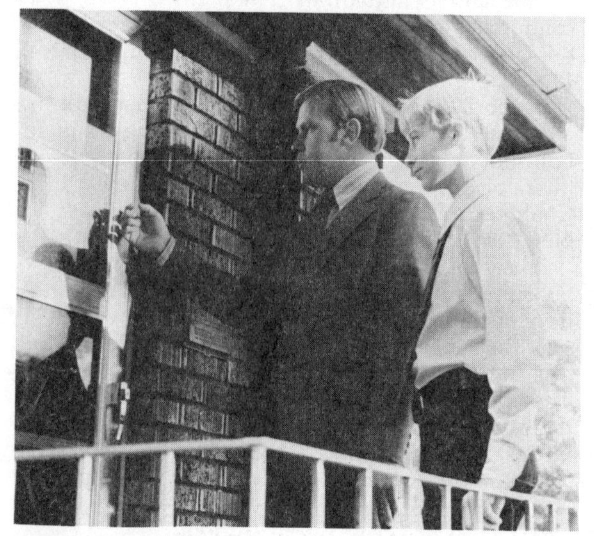

*Magnify your calling*

On the General Authority level of priesthood organization, there are three quorums: the First Quorum of the Seventy, the Quorum of the Twelve Apostles, and the Quorum of the First Presidency.

The First Quorum of the Seventy is a council of General Authorities, and though it is organized in the same general manner as local quorums, its function is different. These seventy men are called to travel throughout the world and to preside in the work of promulgating the gospel to every people (see D&C 124:138-40). This work is done under the direction of the Twelve Apostles (see D&C 107:34; see also *History of the Church,* 2:431-32).

To receive the office of Apostle is to receive the sacred call of being a "special witness of the name of Christ in all the world" (D&C 107:23), which makes this office different from all other offices of the priesthood. The quorum which they comprise is "equal in authority and power" to the Quorum of the First Presidency of the Church (see D&C 107:24; Notes and Commentary on D&C 107:22-26). The Quorum of the Twelve comprehends all lower offices in the Church, and as a quorum the Twelve hold in common every key and authority of the higher priesthood. By their common voice the living prophet is ordained and set apart as the Lord's mouthpiece to declare the doctrine of the kingdom. The Quorum of the Twelve joins the Quorum of the First Presidency in serving as the policy-making body for the Church. It should be noted that other Apostles may be called, in addition to the Quorum of the Twelve, as the prophet deems necessary for the advancement of the kingdom; however, they are not members of the quorum. (See Widtsoe, *Priesthood and Church Government,* pp. 260-63; N. Eldon Tanner, in Conference Report, Oct. 1979, pp. 64-65).

The Presiding High Priest, or the President of the Church, is the highest office of the priesthood held by mortal man. He speaks for and represents the Lord Jesus Christ in the affairs of men—all men—throughout the earth. He calls counselors to serve with him, and together they form the Quorum of the First Presidency of the Church (see D&C 107:22). This quorum presides over all Church affairs.

**(M-8) Summary**

In the Doctrine and Covenants are the revelations that give Latter-day Saints a clearer idea of priesthood and its functions than any other people on earth. From its sections one learns the name of the priesthood, its divisions, its keys, its operating principles, its doctrine, its organization, and its powers. Since priesthood is the power of God and the power by which men come to him, these revelations are one of the greatest blessings of the Restoration.

At the close of the great revelation on priesthood (D&C 107), the Lord gave this solemn charge: "Wherefore, now let every man learn his duty, and to act in the office in which he is appointed, in all diligence. He that is slothful shall not be counted worthy to stand, and he that learns not his duty and shows himself not approved shall not be counted worthy to stand. Even so. Amen." (D&C 107:99-100.)

It is this individual commitment to duty that keeps the Church moving forward toward its great destiny. When we fail in our duty, we, to that degree, slow its progress and add to the risk of losing individual souls. This fact is true of all Church members—men and women alike. We call the various organizations of the Church, such as the Primary, the Relief Society, the Sunday School, and Mutual, the auxiliaries. Auxiliary to what? The answer is, of course, they are auxiliaries to the priesthood. Thus, the charge to learn our duty and stand in our office is as true of a Primary teacher as of a priesthood holder. Elder Marion D. Hanks told a marvelous story that illustrates the importance of every soul's taking the callings of the priesthood seriously:

"Let's use the name Donna to designate another sweet young lady who left her home for a nearby bigger city for employment. She had a great desire to attend a Church university and needed funds to help her achieve her ambition. She failed to find work in the big city, and as time went by she became more and more discouraged. Then through a series of incidents, she came into the influence of an unscrupulous and designing person who took advantage of Donna's loneliness and youthfulness and the discouragement of her inability to find work and led her into an immoral experience.

"The experience was horrifying to Donna, and she returned home with a broken heart to tell her mother, and after a time her bishop, of the tragedy.

"There was counsel and compassion, admonition and direction, prayer and blessing. Donna went back home to make her adjustments and to begin to learn the sorrow of remorse of conscience and the blessing of gratitude for the graciousness and goodness and mercy of God. Then one day she had to counsel again with the bishop, to report to him that through this one fragmentary, tragic experience it was now apparent that she was with child. Now a different situation existed, and there was additional counsel and an effort to meet this new situation. There was consideration of the Relief Society Social Service program which provides for such situations, and other possibilities were considered; but the decision was finally made by Donna that she would remain at home in her small town to wait her time. Some efforts were made at dissuasion in view of the problems this course involved, but Donna decided that, under the special circumstances of her widowed mother's illness and otherwise, she would remain there.

"Donna stood up in the next fast and testimony meeting and explained her condition. She acknowledged her fault and asked forgiveness of her people. She said to them, 'I would like to walk the streets of this town knowing that you know and that you have compassion on me and forgive me. But if you cannot forgive me,' she said, 'please don't blame my mother—the Lord knows she taught me anything but this—and please don't hold it against the baby. It isn't the baby's fault.' She bore testimony of appreciation for her bitterly won but dearly treasured personal knowledge of the importance of the saving mission of Jesus Christ. Then she sat down.

"The man who told me the story reported the reaction of the congregation to this experience. There were many tearful eyes and many humble hearts. 'There were no stone throwers there,' he said. 'We were full of compassion and love, and I found myself wishing that the bishop would close the meeting and let us leave with this sense of appreciation and concern and gratitude to God.'

"The bishop did rise, but he didn't close the meeting. Instead he said, 'Brothers and Sisters, Donna's story has saddened and touched us all. She has courageously and humbly accepted full responsibility for her sorrowful situation. She has, in effect put a list of sinners on the wall of the chapel with only her name on the list. I cannot in honesty leave it there alone. At least one other name must be written—the name of one who is in part responsible for this misfortune, though he was far away when the incident occurred. The name is a familiar one to you. It is the name of your bishop. You see,' he said, 'had I fully performed the duties of my calling and accepted the opportunities of my leadership, perhaps I could have prevented this tragedy.'

"The bishop then told of his conversation with Donna and her mother before her departure for the big city. He said that he had talked with some of his associates. He had talked with his wife, expressing concern for Donna's well-being. He worried about her lack of experience and her loneliness. He had talked, he said, with the Lord about these things also.

" 'But then,' he said, 'I did nothing, I didn't write a note to the bishop or to the brethren in Salt Lake City, I didn't pick up the telephone. I didn't drive a few miles to the big city. I just hoped and prayed that Donna would be all right down there all alone. I don't know what I might have done, but I have the feeling that had I been the kind of bishop I might have been, this might have been prevented.

" 'My brothers and sisters,' he said, 'I don't know how long I am going to be bishop of this ward. But as long as I am, if there is anything I can do about it, this won't happen again to one of mine.'

"The bishop sat down in tears. His counselor stood up and said, 'I love the bishop.

He is one of the best and most conscientious human beings I have ever known. I cannot leave his name there on the list without adding my own. You see, the bishop did talk with his associates. He talked with me about this matter. I think that he thought that because I travel occasionally in my business through the big city, I might find a way to check on Donna. I might have done, but I was hurrying to this meeting or that assignment and I didn't take the time. I too talked with others. I mentioned my concern to my wife. I am almost ashamed to tell you I talked to the Lord and asked him to help Donna. And then I did nothing. I don't know what might have happened had I done what I thought to do, but I have the feeling that I might have prevented this misfortune.

" 'Brothers and sisters,' he said, 'I don't know how long I will be serving in this bishopric, but I want to tell you that as long as I am, if there is anything I can do about it, this will not happen again to one of mine.'

"The president of the YWMIA stood up and told a similar story. The bishop's counselor in charge of this auxiliary organization had talked with her. She had had some moments of thought and concern but had done nothing. She added her name to the list.

"The last witness was an older man who stood and added two names to the list—his own and that of his companion ward teacher. He noted that they were assigned to the home in which Donna and her mother lived and that they had failed in some visits and made no effective effort to be the kind of teachers that the revelations of God had contemplated.

" 'I don't know how long I will be a ward teacher,' he said, 'but as long as I am, I will not miss another home another month, and I will try to be the kind of teacher that the Lord seemed to have in mind.'

"The meeting ended, and the wonderful man who shared this great experience with me said, 'Brother Hanks, I think we could not have more clearly understood the importance of the offices and officers and organizations in the Church if the Lord himself had come down to teach us. I think that if Paul had come to repeat his instruction to the Corinthians that "the eye cannot say unto the hand, I have no need of thee: nor again the head to the feet, I have no need of you. Nay . . . the members should have the same care one for another. And whether one member suffer, all the members suffer with it; or one member be honoured, all the members rejoice with it" (1 Cor. 12:21-22, 25-26)—I think we could not have understood the point more clearly.'

"A number of years ago Brother Joseph Anderson and I had the privilege of driving with President J. Reuben Clark, Jr., to a solemn assembly in St. George. On the way I related to him this story, it having recently happened then. He thought a long time and had a tear in his eye as he said, 'Brother Hanks, that is the most significant story I ever heard to illustrate the great importance of filling our individual obligations in the Church. When you have thought about it long enough, pass it on to others.'

"I have thought about it long and often. I believe it illustrates powerfully and humblingly the purposes of the Lord in establishing his kingdom and permitting us the blessing of individual service therein. I now share it with you and pray God to bless us all to understand its implications and to act on them, in the name of Jesus Christ. Amen." (In Conference Report, Apr. 1966, pp. 151-53.)

# Priesthood and Church Government, Part 2

Enrichment N

## (N-1) Introduction

The government of the Church is to provide for the temporal and spiritual welfare of its members to the extent possible under the laws of the land where the Church may be found. The government of the Church has no purpose but to bless the lives of its members by organizing their individual efforts into a beautiful, harmonious society. Unlike the governments of men, the government of God exists to give the individual more power and to assist him in securing his exaltation. The kind of government that operates in the kingdom of God is explained in Enrichment M, which examines the meaning of the priesthood and priesthood organization. This enrichment section examines how the priesthood functions in administering the affairs of the kingdom.

## (N-2) The Government of God: A Theocratic Order of Priesthood

The Church of Jesus Christ of Latter-day Saints is a theocracy. It is ruled by the God of heaven through direct revelation. Although all members may receive revelation for their personal lives, the revelations necessary for the administration of the government of the earthly kingdom is given only to the Lord's authorized servants. These men and women are "called of God, by prophecy, and by the laying on of hands, by those who are in authority to preach the gospel and administer in the ordinances thereof" (Articles of Faith 1:5). The moving power of the Church governmental organization is revelation; the organization itself is the priesthood, or government, of God.

The Church is frequently referred to as a kingdom. The king is the Savior Jesus Christ. But, in a temporal sense, he will not claim the right to rule until the ushering in of his millennial reign.

Is the Church a democracy? This question is distinctly different from asking whether or not it is democratic. A democracy is a system of government in which the majority rules, especially "a government in which the supreme power is vested in the people" (*Webster's New Collegiate Dictionary*, s.v. "democratic"). In other words, an organization can be said to be democratic if the will and the rights of the people or the membership are always the primary concern and if force is never exercised. By such criteria The Church of Jesus Christ of Latter-day Saints is ideally democratic, though not a democracy, for a fundamental element of the government of the Church is the exercise of the law of common consent. This law allows Church members the privilege of voting to sustain or to refuse to sustain any person called to preside over them (see D&C 20:65; 28:13).

This democratic law of common consent and the way it operates in a theocracy was explained by Elder Orson F. Whitney:

*The voice of the people is fundamental to Church government*

"Man's free agency, his right to worship as his conscience dictates, and to act in all things willingly and without compulsion—a principle handed down from the eternal past, where Lucifer was overthrown for seeking to destroy it—is an integral part of Liberty's Perfect Law. As such it found expression, a concrete illustration, and that by direct, divine command, when this Church was organized, one hundred years ago. . . .

"Speaking of the word of the Lord that came to him and his co-laborer in the farmhouse of Peter Whitmer, Sr., at Fayette, Seneca County, N. Y., a word directing them to ordain each other to the office of Elder, the Prophet says:

" 'We were, however, commanded to defer this our ordination until such time as it should be practicable to have our brethren, who had been and who should be baptized, assembled together, when *we must have their sanction* to our thus proceeding to ordain each other, and have them *decide by vote* whether they were willing to accept us as spiritual teachers, or not.' . . .

"What!—exclaims one. After these men had communed with heavenly beings and received from them commandments for their guidance; after receiving divine authority to preach the Gospel, administer its ordinances, and establish once more on earth the long absent Church of Christ! After all this must they go before the people and ask their consent to organize them and preside over them as a religious body? Yes, that was precisely the situation. Notwithstanding all those glorious manifestations, they were not yet fully qualified to hold the high positions unto which they had been divinely called. One element was lacking—the consent of the people. Until that consent was given, there could be no church with these people as its members and those men as its presiding authorities. The Great Ruler of all never did and never will foist upon any of his people, in branch, ward, stake or Church capacity, a presiding officer whom they are not willing to accept and uphold.

"Happily for all concerned, the brethren associated with Joseph and Oliver on the memorable sixth of April of the year 1830, did sanction their ordination, did 'decide by vote' to accept them as their 'spiritual teachers.'

"But suppose it had been otherwise. Suppose the brethren in question had not been willing to accept the men whom the Lord had chosen, but had lifted their hands against instead of for them. What would have been the result? Would such action have taken from Joseph and Oliver their Priesthood or their gifts and powers as seers, prophets and revelators of the Most High? No. Any more than it would have blotted out the fact that Joseph had seen God, and that he and Oliver had communed with angels sent from Heaven to ordain them. Their brethren had not given them the Priesthood, had not made them prophets and seers, and they would have remained such regardless of any adverse action on the part of their associates. The Gospel, the Priesthood, the keys of the Kingdom of Heaven are not within the gift of the membership of the Church. They are bestowed by the Head of the Church, Jesus Christ, in person or by proxy, and without his consent no power on earth or under the earth could take them away.

"But if the vote had been unfavorable, this would have resulted: The brethren and sisters who were waiting to be admitted into the Church would have closed the door in their own faces, would have cut themselves off from a most precious privilege, would have deprived themselves of the inestimable benefits flowing from the exercise of the gifts and powers possessed by the men divinely commissioned to inaugurate this great Latter-day Work." (In Conference Report, Oct. 1930, pp. 44-46; see also Orson Pratt, in *Journal of Discourses,* 19:118-19.)

Therefore, in principle and in practice the Church is democratic, yet in truth it is not a democracy but a theocracy. Elder Harold B. Lee observed: "We sometimes hear people who talk about the Church as a democracy. Well, it isn't any such thing. Democracy means a government where the sole authority is vested in the people—the right to nominate, the right to release, to change. The Church is not a democracy. It is more like a kingdom than a democracy—and yet it is not wholly like a kingdom, except that we accept the Lord as the king, who has under his direction an earthly head who operates and becomes his mouthpiece. It is an organization that is defined more accurately as a theocracy, which means that it is something like a kingdom as the world would define it, and yet something like a democracy." (*The Place of the Living Prophet, Seer, and Revelator* [address delivered to seminary and institute of religion faculty], 8 July 1964, pp. 2-3.)

### (N-3) Membership in the Kingdom

The governing of the Church includes the setting of policy that specifies the requirements of membership in the kingdom. Some criticize the Church for taking court action against its members, saying that it is not fair that the Church have that power. But every organization in a free society has the right to determine what requirements and rules it may expect its members to follow, as long as those rules and requirements are in harmony with the laws of the land. By direct revelation the Lord has made it known that certain offenses may put a member's right to participate in the kingdom in jeopardy (see, for example, D&C 42:78-93; 85:11). To tolerate members who violate such laws without taking action suggests to the world that the Church teaches one standard and allows its members to live by another.

The Lord also revealed the requirements for entry into the Church (see D&C 20:37). Without direct revelation to change the requirements for entry and maintenance of membership, no one in the Church has the right to set or change requirements. God's house is a house of order, and since he is the ruling head of the kingdom, only he has the right to determine who shall enter and dwell therein.

### (N-4) Conference Meetings

Conferences are important means of governing the Church. In these meetings, officers, policies, and procedural changes are presented to the membership for a sustaining vote. Through the sustaining vote, each member is involved in a type of democratic process unique to the Church. The Lord commanded that these conferences be held often for the progress and unity of the kingdom (see D&C 20:61-62). In such conferences the presiding officers instruct and give direction to the membership of the Church. The Lord administers his will in these latter days, even as in the days of old.

### (N-5) The Earthly Kingdom Is a Type of the Heavenly Kingdom

The source of all joy is living the laws of God which were designed and given for that express purpose. Since these laws are transmitted to the Saints by and through the government of God, the servants of the Lord play a crucial role as custodians of the happiness and welfare of the Saints. It is instructive to remember that as a servant in the Church one blesses the lives of others through selfless service and that in so doing he finds that he receives an increased measure of love and joy in return.

An analogy is appropriate. Since the earthly kingdom of God is a type of the heavenly kingdom, the joy experienced through Church service in mortality is but a foreshadowing of that enjoyed in exalted realms. Further, the earthly kingdom is not merely the type of the heavenly one; it is actually an extension of it. On earth the servants of the Lord experience the loftiest joy when they are engaged in his service. In other words, if a fulness of joy is available only to exalted beings whose existence is glorified by the presence of God, then the greatest joy available to mortals is to serve in the earthly extension of his kingdom.

The direct relationship between the earthly and heavenly kingdoms was mentioned in Jesus' prayer: "Thy kingdom come. Thy will be done in earth, as it is in heaven." (Matthew 6:10.) To carry the analogy further, the member of the Church who looks to his Church leader for guidance is symbolically looking to his God. The government of the Church is the means the Lord provides by which a person, through obedience to the laws of the Church, qualifies as a son or daughter of Christ, a fit candidate for a place in his kingdom where perfect order is manifest through a perfect government inspired by the perfect love of the Savior of mankind.

In his wisdom the Lord set various offices in the priesthood and in the Church to help administer his laws and the day-to-day functioning of the kingdom. Each office in the priesthood is important in the overall function of the organization, but central to all is the role of the living prophet.

**(N-6) The Prophet and the Presidency of the Church**

The role of the mouthpiece of the Lord is interwoven with that of the priesthood. All the various keys and functions of the priesthood come from the Lord and are measured against his standard of performance. The prophet is the only one authorized to speak for the Lord and to give commandments to the Church (see D&C 107:8-9).

The Presidency of the Church are "chosen by the body, appointed and ordained to that office, and upheld by the confidence, faith, and prayer of the church" and "form a quorum of the Presidency of the Church" (D&C 107:22).

The prophet, seer, and revelator of the Church, then, is the President of the Church and is the "living oracle of God to whom the Lord reveals whatever is necessary for the conduct of the Church" (Widtsoe, *Priesthood and Church Government,* p. 131). He possesses all the keys of the kingdom, including the keys to bind on earth and in heaven, and it is from him that the keys are delegated to other officers of the Church according to their needs or stewardships. All the sealing powers, including those of the new and everlasting covenant of marriage (see D&C 131:2), depend upon the keys given by the Lord to the prophet, seer, and revelator.

The one key that the Presidency alone holds, and which cannot be delegated to others, is to declare the mind and will of the Lord by way of commandment and doctrine to the Church. Once it is declared, however, the members of the Quorum of the Twelve and other general authorities sustain it and promulgate it to the members of the Church. (See Enrichment F for a discussion of the role of a prophet.)

Though the wicked may scorn and the world scoff in doubt, the Lord speaks peace to the hearts of the righteous and causes their bosoms to burn at the sound of the voice of the Lord's anointed. Little wonder the army of Saints in latter days sings, "We thank thee, O God, for a prophet."

**(N-7) Priesthood Councils**

In April 1979 the announcement of the organization of priesthood councils at every level in the Church signaled a dramatic step forward in bringing all the affairs of the kingdom under the direction of the priesthood (see Ezra Taft Benson, in Conference Report, Apr. 1979, pp. 120-25; or *Ensign,* May 1979, pp. 86-88 ). It portended a fulfillment of a prophecy of President Joseph F. Smith when he said: "We expect to see the day, if we live long enough (and if some of us do not live long enough to see it, there are others who will), when every council of the Priesthood in the Church of Jesus Christ of Latter-day Saints will understand its duty; will assume its own responsibility, will magnify its calling, and fill its place in the Church, to the uttermost, according to the intelligence and ability possessed by it. When that day shall come, there will not be so much necessity for work that is now being done by the auxiliary organizations, because it will be done by the regular quorums of the Priesthood." (*Gospel Doctrine,* p. 159.)

Priesthood councils stand unique in the world; they stand apart from the halls of pomp and ceremony; they stand in opposition to the pride and power of men; they stand as a beacon on a hill guiding the Saints of God through troubled waters, so they can safely avoid the adversary's rocks of destruction. These councils operate upon the principle of inspired unity described by Elder Ronald E. Poelman: "The priesthood council is a form of management unique to the divine Church. It assembles to receive the Lord's law by the prayer of faith, to agree upon his word, and to learn how to govern the Church and have all things right before the Lord (see D&C 41:2-3). The council's strength and effectiveness derive from coordinating individual skills and abilities united with a shared purpose." (In Conference Report, Apr. 1980, p. 126; or *Ensign,* May 1980, p. 91.)

**(N-8) Priesthood Council Organization**

The government of the Church is administered through councils for the Church, area, multiregion, region, stake, ward, and family. This organization of councils fills the needs of the Church from the highest authority to the newest member. Stephen L Richards, a counselor to David O. McKay in the First Presidency of the Church, said:

"As I conceive it, the genius of our Church government is government through *councils.* The Council of the Presidency, the Council of the Twelve, the Council of the Stake Presidency, . . . the Council of the Bishopric. . . . I have had enough experience to know the value of councils. . . . I see the wisdom, God's wisdom, in creating councils: to govern his Kingdom. In the spirit under which we labor, men can get together with seemingly divergent views and far different backgrounds, and under the operation of that spirit, by counseling together, they can arrive at an accord." (In Conference Report, Oct. 1953, p. 86.)

The undergirding purpose of councils has not changed from the days of the Prophet Joseph Smith: they are to "facilitate communication and unity at various Church levels and help move the kingdom forward" (Benson, in Conference Report, Apr. 1979, p. 120; or *Ensign*, May 1979, p. 86).

The council stewardship at each level needs to be "*comprehensive* in representing *all* Church programs so that there will be a *correlating, coordinating, planning,* and *resolving* body" for all ecclesiastical and temporal affairs (Benson, in Conference Report, Apr. 1979, p. 121; or Ensign, May 1979, p. 87). In other words, the Church is to continue to work, through its officers, toward the "perfecting of the Saints, for the work of the ministry, for the edifying of the body of Christ, till we all come in the unity of the Faith, and of the knowledge of the Son of God, unto a perfect man, unto the measure of the stature of the fulness of Christ" (Ephesians 4:11-14.)

This charge and stewardship of the Church is fulfilled through the use of Church councils. The decisions of these councils are to be unanimous, in order that the spirit of unity pervade the working of Church government (see D&C 107:27). Such unity, manifest in the Lord's earthly kingdom, is a type of the pattern of heaven. Elder Ronald E. Poelman described how this unity is achieved: "Unity in temporal matters, as in spiritual matters, is essential to our success. At each step, consensus of the council members must be obtained, through prayer and discussion, to achieve that unity which is prerequisite to the Lord's help. To be effective, decisions must be reached by divine consensus, not by compromise. Participants are not competing advocates, representing special interests, but rather contributing members of a unified body." (In Conference Report, Apr. 1980, p. 126; or *Ensign*, May 1980, p. 91.)

### (N-9) The Church Coordinating Council

The Church Coordinating Council is comprised of the First Presidency, the Quorum of the Twelve, and the Presiding Bishopric. The Presidents of the First Quorum of the Seventy are invited to attend the meetings that pertain to their stewardships.

This council sets Church policy, authorizes exceptions to policy, authorizes implementation of the policy, and resolves any difficulties that exist at the area council level. (See Benson, in Conference Report, Apr. 1979, pp. 121-22; or *Ensign*, May 1979, p. 87.)

### (N-10) The Area Council

The area council is headed by a member of the First Quorum of the Seventy and is comprised of the Regional Representatives who are line officers between the General Authorities of the Church and stake officers. Mission presidents are invited to meetings, as they are needed, as are the Welfare Services area director, a Church-service Public Communications area director, the Church Educational System area director, and others as deemed necessary. (See Benson, in Conference Report, Apr. 1979, p. 122; or *Ensign*, May 1979, p. 87.)

The area council develops plans for the operational guidelines of the stakes. Stake presidents are invited to attend the meetings that pertain to their needs and stewardships.

### (N-11) The Multiregion Council

The multiregion council is administered by a General Authority, and its function is patterned after the area council. Its membership also includes the Welfare Services area director when needed, the "Regional Representatives of the regions involved, and the multiregion Welfare Service director. A stake bishops' council chairman and a stake Relief Society president from one of the region councils, . . . serve as members when welfare services matters are discussed." (Benson, in Conference Report, Apr. 1979, p. 123; or *Ensign*, May 1979, p. 88.)

### (N-12) The Region Council

The region council consists of the Regional Representative and the stake presidents of the region. A stake bishops' council chairman and a stake Relief Society president, as designated by the Regional Representative, could be invited when welfare matters are discussed. (See Benson, in Conference Report, Apr. 1979, p. 124; or *Ensign*, May 1979, p. 88.)

### (N-13) The Stake Councils

On the stake level there are two groups that meet and are part of the system of councils—the stake welfare committee and the stake correlation council.

The stake welfare committee is administered by the stake president, assisted by the other members of the stake presidency, and the high council and the stake Relief Society presidency are members of the committee.

The membership of the stake correlation council is identical to that of the stake welfare committee with the addition of the senior president of the seventies quorum and also the stake auxiliary presidents or leaders.

### (N-14) The Ward Councils

The ward councils are similar to the stake councils: they are comprised of a ward welfare committee and a ward correlation council.

### (N-15) The Family Council

"The family is the basic unit of the kingdom of God on earth" (Spencer W. Kimball, in Conference Report, Apr. 1978, p. 67; or *Ensign*, May 1978, p. 45). Since the family is the most important organization in eternity, the family council is the most fundamental government in eternity. It was just such a family council in which the plan of salvation was revealed to all the sons and daughters of God.

The family council is led by the father, or by the mother if no father is present in the home. Its purpose is to maintain and develop family unity and solidarity. It is convened as often as necessary, and its impact has eternal consequences. Parents should remember that the "most important work that they would ever do would be done within the walls of their own homes" (Lee, *Ye Are the Light of the World*, p. 80). Family unity and solidarity must not be just the goal of the family council but the

*The family is the most important unit in time and in eternity*

living reality of it. Failure in that stewardship is not acceptable, for some of the sharpest rebukes given by the Lord were precipitated by such failure (see D&C 93:41-44, 47-49).

The councils of the Church are to correlate priesthood activity on every level, assuring that the programs of the Church effectively support the home. Without such correlation the reverse could well be true.

### (N-16) Priesthood Administration on an Individual Level

Never is the miracle of the Melchizedek Priesthood witnessed more dramatically than when a righteous, worthy man is exercising it with all the energy of his soul to save himself and his family. It is a remarkable proof of divine grace that this marvelous gift is given to individuals. Priesthood is not some impersonal power that lies like a blanket over the Church; it is the very authority of the God of heaven extended individually to his worthy sons. Such a trust is not to be taken lightly, for, though God is a loving Father, he is also a God of justice and will not be mocked (see D&C 104:6; 63:58). Elder George Q. Cannon spoke of the responsibility that accompanies receiving the priesthood: "We must honor the Priesthood we hold or that Priesthood, instead of exalting us, will be the means of damning us; instead of exalting us at the right hand of God, for which it was given, it will drag us down to a depth of misery and woe such as we never would have reached if we had not received it and failed to honor it. It is a fearful thing to receive the Priesthood of God and not magnify it, and the man who receives it should not do so to gratify some feeling he may have that he would like to hold authority that would give him some dignity or place him in a position above others of his brethren and sisters but with the consciousness that if he does not bear off the responsibilities which are involved in receiving it, it will lead him down to the depths of misery and anguish." (*Gospel Truth,* 1:229.)

### (N-17) What Does It Mean to Magnify a Calling in the Priesthood?

Every priesthood holder who wishes to be approved of the Lord must be "faithful unto the obtaining these two priesthoods of which I have spoken, and the magnifying their calling" (D&C 84:33). Of course, if a man has been ordained, he has obtained the priesthood, but he must then magnify his calling in it. The Prophet Joseph Smith taught that to magnify a calling means "to build it up in dignity and importance, to make it honorable and commendable in the eyes of all men, to enlarge and strengthen it, to let the light of heaven shine through it to the view of other men. And how does one magnify a calling? Simply by performing the service that pertains to it." (In Thomas S. Monson, in Conference Report, British Area Conference 1971, p. 145.)

President Joseph Fielding Smith took the concept another step further when he said:

"Priesthood offices or callings are ministerial assignments to perform specially assigned service in the priesthood. And the way to magnify these callings is to do the work designed to be performed by those who hold the particular office involved.

"It does not matter what office we hold as long as we are true and faithful to our obligations. One office is not greater than another, although for administrative reasons one priesthood holder may be called to preside over and direct the labors of another." (In Conference Report, Oct. 1970, p. 91.)

An analogy may be helpful. A magnifying glass has two capabilities. It can take rays of light and magnify them so an object appears to be larger. It can also focus and concentrate the rays of light so they have greater power. When a person magnifies his callings in the priesthood, he does the same. He enlarges the calling, expands it, makes it more full and useful. He also focuses the light and power he has on specific problems so they may be solved in the Lord's way. This process is true for women's callings, too, for while they do not have callings *in* the priesthood, they have callings *of* the priesthood. As a person magnifies his calling, the Lord in turn magnifies the person, making him stronger, more capable, and wiser in the use of the gifts and powers he gains through the priesthood. And so the process begins again. The more a person does through the priesthood of God, the more he is capable of doing because of the blessings of the Lord.

The process of magnifying one's callings is the foundation for the oath and covenant of the priesthood. When the priesthood is given, it is given with an oath and received by covenant (see the Notes and Commentary on D&C 84:33-41). If a man covenants to magnify his callings in the priesthood (see D&C 84:33) and pledges to "live by every word that proceedeth forth from the mouth of God" (D&C 84:44), then the Lord swears with an oath that he will give to that faithful priesthood holder everything that he himself has (see D&C 84:38).

If you have understood the above discussion, you will sense that one who has received the priesthood is under solemn vow to live by every word of God.

As you contemplate the seriousness of such a covenant, read thoughtfully a revelation from the Lord given to President John Taylor:

"For my priesthood [those called and ordained], whom I have called and whom I have sustained and honored, shall honor me and obey my laws, and the laws of my holy priesthood, or they shall not be considered worthy to hold my priesthood, saith the Lord. And let my priesthood humble themselves before me, and seek not their own will but my will; for if my priesthood, whom I have chosen, and called, and endowed with the spirit and gifts of their several callings, and with the powers thereof, do not acknowledge me I will not acknowledge them, saith the Lord; for I will be honored and obeyed by my priesthood.

"And, then, I call upon my priesthood, and upon all of my people, to repent of all their sins and short-comings, of their covetousness and pride and self-will, and of all their iniquities wherein they sin against me; and to seek with all humility to fulfill my law, as my priesthood, my saints and my people; and I call upon the heads of families to put their houses in order according to the law of God, and attend to the various duties and responsibilities associated therewith, and to purify themselves before me, and to purge out iniquity from their households. And I will bless and be with you, saith the Lord, and ye shall gather together in your holy places wherein ye assemble to call upon me, and ye shall ask for such things as are right, and I will hear your prayers, and my Spirit and power shall be with you, and my blessing shall rest upon you, upon your families, your dwellings and your households, upon your flocks and herds and fields, your orchards and vineyards, and upon all that pertains to you; and you shall be my people and I will be your God; and your enemies shall not have dominion over you; for I will preserve you and confound them, saith the Lord, and they shall not have power nor dominion over you, for my word shall go forth, and my work shall be accomplished, and my Zion shall be established, and my rule and my power and my dominion shall prevail among my people, and all nations shall yet acknowledge me. Even so, Amen." (In Roberts, *Life of John Taylor*, pp. 350-51.)

**(N-18) Summary**

A major theme of the Doctrine and Covenants is that the Lord will bless and preserve his Saints: "What power shall stay the heavens? As well might man stretch forth his puny arm to stop the Missouri river in its decreed course, or to turn it up stream, as to hinder the Almighty from pouring down knowledge from heaven upon the heads of the Latter-day Saints." (D&C 121:33.)

President Brigham Young said: "An individual who holds a share in the Priesthood, and continues faithful to his calling, who delights himself continually in doing the things God requires at his hands, and continues through life in the performance of every duty, will secure to himself not only the privilege of receiving, but the knowledge how to receive the things of God, that he may know the mind of God continually; and he will be enabled to discern between right and wrong, between the things of God and the things that are not of God. And the Priesthood—the Spirit that is within him, will continue to increase until it becomes like a fountain of living water; until it is like the tree of life; until it is one continued source of intelligence and instruction to that individual." (In *Journal of Discourses*, 3:192.)

In such a favored state, a person is prepared to "live by every word that proceedeth forth from the mouth of God" (D&C 84:44) and, therefore, the Lord's promise of eternal life and God's glory becomes the personal possession of the faithful steward. That is the realization of what it means to make one's calling and election sure and to have peace in this world and eternal life in the world to come (see Marion G. Romney, in Conference Report, Apr. 1974, p. 115; or *Ensign*, May 1974, pp. 79-80).

# Salvation for the Dead

Enrichment O

### (O-1) Introduction

"The greatest responsibility in this world that God has laid upon us is to seek after our dead" (*History of the Church,* 6:313).

The Apostle Paul wrote that there are some doctrinal matters that are only "spiritually discerned" (1 Corinthians 2:14). The subject of salvation for the dead is one of those subjects. Latter-day Saints' knowledge of this vital doctrine is almost entirely dependent upon the Doctrine and Covenants. It is a subject comprehended only by the spiritually minded, yet its scope is so great as to include all of Heavenly Father's children, both living and dead.

### (O-2) The World of Spirits

To understand the doctrine of salvation for the dead, one should understand where departed loved ones reside. President Brigham Young taught that when individuals die they "all pass through the veil from this state and go into the world of spirits; and there they dwell waiting for their final destiny" (*Discourses of Brigham Young,* p. 376). This world of spirits, as taught by President Young, is very close:

"It is not beyond the sun, but is *on this earth* that was organized for the people that have lived and that do and will live upon it. . . .

"Where is the spirit world? It is right here. Do the good and evil spirits go together? Yes, they do. Do they both inhabit one kingdom? Yes, they do. Do they go to the sun? No. Do they go beyond the boundaries of the organized earth? No, they do not." (*Discourses of Brigham Young,* p. 376; emphasis added.)

President Young continued this theme, clarifying the condition of association that exists in the spirit world between the wicked and the righteous:

"It no doubt appears a singular idea to you that both Saint and sinner go to the same place and dwell together in the same world. You can see the same variety in this world. You see the Latter-day Saints, who have come into these valleys,—they are by themselves as a community, yet they are in the same world with other communities. . . .

"When they are in the world of spirits, there is the Prophet and the Patriarch; all righteous men are there, and all wicked men also are there." (In *Journal of Discourses,* 6:294.)

It should be clear that the wicked and the righteous live together in the spirit world much the same as they do in mortality, not that the righteous do the things of wickedness, nor that the wicked enjoy the blessings bestowed upon the righteous, but that the righteous may preach the gospel to the wicked, and upon their honest reception of these saving truths they too may lay claim upon the blessings of the Lord through the Atonement. Elder Bruce R. McConkie wrote:

"Thus, although there are two spheres within the one spirit world, there is now some intermingling of the righteous and the wicked who inhabit those spheres; and when the wicked spirits repent, they leave their prison-hell and join the righteous in paradise. Hence, we find Joseph Smith saying: 'Hades, sheol, paradise, spirits in prison, are all one: it is a world of spirits. The righteous and the wicked all go to the same world of spirits until the resurrection.' (*Teachings,* p. 310.)" (*Mormon Doctrine,* p. 762.)

The state of wicked spirits is described in Alma 40:13-14 and Mosiah 2:38. The Prophet Joseph Smith said, "The great misery of departed spirits in the world of spirits, where they go after death, is to know that they come short of the glory that others enjoy and that they might have enjoyed themselves, and they are their own accusers" (*History of the Church,* 5:425).

The Doctrine and Covenants is the primary source of knowledge concerning what took place when the Savior entered the world of spirits. During the three days that his body lay in the tomb, Jesus visited the spirits in paradise. He appeared only to the righteous dead, to whom he taught the fulness of his gospel. From among this vast throng he organized and commissioned missionaries to proclaim the gospel to those in spirit prison (see D&C 138:18-20, 29-31).

The message of those who labor in the spirit world is the same as the message of those who labor in the flesh. With the restoration of the gospel, the Lord told his servants that they should open their mouths and call upon people to repent, for the kingdom of heaven was at hand. The people were to be commanded to repent and be baptized of water and fire so that "the gates of hell shall not prevail against you" (D&C 33:13). That is exactly the message that is being preached by those in the spirit world, and in that realm the promise has particular piognancy. If "hell" refers to suffering the natural consequences of sin in the spirit prison, the promise is that through accepting the gospel and having their work done (vicarious baptisms, endowments, and so forth) on earth, the gates of hell shall not prevail against them, that is, spirit prison shall not have power to hold those who accept the gospel in the world of spirits.

Those who never heard the gospel while in mortality are given that opportunity so that if they fully accept the gospel they might be heirs to the celestial kingdom (see D&C 137:7-9). Those who had an opportunity to hear the gospel while in the flesh but rejected it, because of social pressures or any other reason, are again taught the gospel so that they might be redeemed from their misery, anguish, and captivity and come forth in the terrestrial kingdom. Otherwise they would inherit a telestial kingdom. (For an explanation of why people who have heard and rejected the gospel in mortality can only inherit the terrestial kingdom, see Notes and Commentary for D&C 76:72-74.)

Righteous spirits, those who have been converted to the gospel in the spirit prison, are still held in the spirit prison until the ordinance work is done (see Smith, *Doctrines of Salvation,* 2:230). These loyal believers are not able to fully progress because, while they can have faith and repent in their spiritual state, such ordinances as baptism and confirmation must be done in mortality, if not by themselves, then by proxies. They too await a day of deliverance. Speaking on this delay President Spencer W. Kimball said: "Some of us have had occasion to wait for someone or something for a minute, an hour, a day, a week, or even a year. Can you imagine how our progenitors must feel, some of whom have perhaps been waiting for decades and even centuries for the temple work to be done for them?" ("The Things of Eternity—Stand We in Jeopardy?" *Ensign,* Jan. 1977, p. 7.)

If you have been a member of the Church for very long you are probably familiar with the phrase "saviors on Mount Zion," which is often used in connection with genealogy and temple work. This is not just a phrase, but a very real description of the saving power of ordinance work for the dead.

Can you imagine the frustration you would feel if you had fully embraced the gospel in the spirit world but could not enter paradise because you had to wait until some of your descendants were motivated to do the ordinance work?

Imagine your own great-grandfather and great-grandmother who desire to unite their family but are helpless to do so because the saving ordinances have not been performed and they lack the power of priesthood. Thus they are unable to inspire, bless, and teach their family members. They are kept in spirit prison, which, as we have seen, is also called "hell."

Do you sense now what the Doctrine and Covenants and the prophets are saying? You can actually save people from hell by performing their ordinance work for them. You cannot, of course, determine whether they will accept the gospel in the spirit world. But if they do, they become dependent upon us in mortality to save them. We are the key to their salvation.

President Wilford Woodruff taught that we have the keys for their redemption and that neglect of that work will bring sorrow in the hereafter: "Every father and mother has a great responsibility resting upon them, to redeem their dead. Do not neglect it. You will have sorrow if you do. Any man will who neglects the redemption of his dead that he has power to officiate for here. When you get to the other side of the veil, if you have entered into these Temples and redeemed your progenitors by the ordinances of the House of God, you will hold the keys of their redemption from eternity to eternity. Do not neglect this!" (In Conference Report, Apr. 1898, p. 90.)

### (O-3) The Mission of Elijah the Prophet

The earliest recorded revelation in the Doctrine and Covenants occurred about seven years before the restoration of the Church. That revelation is the key to properly understanding the purpose of the dispensation of the fulness of times (see D&C 2). The following promises were revealed by Moroni:

1. The priesthood was to be revealed by Elijah.
2. Elijah would plant in the hearts of the children the promises made to their fathers.
3. The whole earth would be utterly wasted at the Second Coming if the hearts of the children and the hearts of the fathers were not turned to each other (see D&C 27:9; 128:17).

The Prophet Joseph Smith explained that Elijah would be sent "because he holds the keys of the authority to administer in all the ordinances of the Priesthood" (*Teachings,* p. 172). To this statement President Joseph Fielding Smith added: "In order that the binding power should come which is recognized in the heavens, and by which we pass by the angels and the Gods to exaltation, it had to come from Elijah, who held that power upon the face of the earth, for the Lord had given it to him" (*Elijah the Prophet,* p. 36).

President Joseph Fielding Smith also said: "The sealing power of Elijah makes it possible for this joining of the families, generation to generation, back to the beginning. Now, if these units of

*A sealing room in a temple*

authority were not here, then the work of sealing, by which the family units are preserved, could not be performed; then the binding power by which all blessings are sealed in heaven, as well as on earth, would be lacking. If this were so, the earth would be smitten with a curse." (*Doctrines of Salvation,* 2:121.)

Elder Joseph Fielding Smith said that the promises made to the fathers were made to those who died without a knowledge of the gospel and without the opportunity of receiving the sealing ordinances of the Priesthood in matters pertaining to their exaltation. According to these promises, the children in the latter days are to perform all such ordinances in behalf of the dead. ("The Promises Made to the Fathers," *Improvement Era,* July 1922, p. 829.)

The earth would be wasted at the Second Coming "simply because," said President Joseph Fielding Smith, "if there is not a welding link between the fathers and the children—which is the work for the dead—then we will all stand rejected; the whole work of God will fail and be utterly wasted. Such a condition, of course, shall not be." (*Doctrines of Salvation,* 2:122.)

Before Elijah could come, however, a temple had to be erected. During a three-year period from 1833 to 1836, the Saints labored at great sacrifice to construct a temple acceptable to the Lord. On 3 April 1836 Elijah came in fulfillment of Malachi's prophecy (see Malachi 4:5-6; D&C 110:14-16).

### (O-4) How the Dead May Receive Ordinances of Salvation

When the Savior appeared in the world of spirits, he organized those who had been faithful and commissioned them to proclaim his gospel. They were to teach faith in Christ, repentance, *vicarious* baptism for a remission of sins, the Holy Ghost, and "all other principles of the gospel that were necessary for them to know in order to qualify themselves" as heirs of salvation (D&C 138:34).

One of the most significant revelations given to the Prophet Joseph Smith pertained to the ordinance of vicarious baptism for the dead. At Nauvoo, Illinois, in September 1842, one of the epistles the Prophet wrote to the Saints (D&C 128) detailed the glorious doctrine and how it was to be accomplished.

Thus, the Doctrine and Covenants clearly teaches that it is the responsibility of mortal men to vicariously perform the ordinances of salvation for those who are dead. According to the Prophet Joseph Smith, this work is absolutely critical, not only for the benefit of the dead but for the living Saints as well. He taught that the Saints must go forth "building their temples, erecting their baptismal fonts, and going forth and receiving all the ordinances, baptisms, confirmations, washings, anointings, ordinations and sealing powers upon their heads, in behalf of all their progenitors who are dead, and redeem them that they may come forth in the first resurrection and be exalted to thrones of glory with them; and herein is the chain that binds the hearts of the fathers to the children, and the children to the fathers, which fulfills the mission of Elijah. . . .

"The Saints have not too much time to save and redeem their dead, and gather together their living relatives, that they may be saved also, before the earth will be smitten, and the consumption decreed falls upon the world.

"I would advise all the Saints to go with their might and gather together all their living relatives to this place, that they may be sealed and saved, that they may be prepared against the day that the destroying angel goes forth." (*Teachings,* p. 330.)

The Prophet further stated: "It is not only necessary that you should be baptized for your dead, but you will have to go through *all* the ordinances for them, the same as you have gone through to save yourselves" (*History of the Church,* 6:365; emphasis added). *All* ordinances include baptism, priesthood ordinations, endowments, and sealings. Elijah's mission included (but was more than) vicarious baptism for the dead.

Once the revelation on baptism for the dead was received, the Saints knew that the work of their progenitors must be done. "At first they made no distinction as to who would be baptized for whom, and males were baptized for females and vice versa. That was . . . corrected later." (Packer, *Holy Temple,* p. 217.)

The Saints also knew that families needed to be united by sealings. Because they did not understand the principle, some of the Saints were sealed to the prophets, a practice changed by a revelation to President Wilford Woodruff. This excerpt from President Woodruff's address announcing the revelation captures the essence of this change in policy: "When I went before the Lord to know who I should be adopted to (We were being adopted [or sealed] to prophets and apostles), the Spirit of God said to me, 'Have you not a father, who begot you?' 'Yes, I have.' 'Then why not honor him? Why not be adopted to him?' 'Yes,' says I, 'that is right.' I was adopted to my father, and should have had my father sealed to his father, and so on back; and the duty that I want every man who presides over a Temple to see performed from this day henceforth and forever, unless the Lord Almighty commands otherwise, is, let every man be adopted to his father." ("The Law of Adoption," *Deseret Weekly,* 21 Apr. 1894, p. 543.)

This revelation clearly establishes that each person is to be sealed to his own progenitors. By so doing his heart will be turned to them, and their hearts will be turned to him.

### (O-5) How One's Heart May Be Turned to His Fathers

The salvation of the living depends to a large extent upon the interest they show in their dead ancestors. The Doctrine and Covenants records that "they without us cannot be made perfect—neither can we without our dead be made perfect" (D&C 128:15).

The ordinances in behalf of the dead can only be done when the dead are properly identified. This identification is a major purpose of genealogical research in the Church. Research is but a means to an end; the end is to submit names to the temple in order that ordinance work may be completed. Some important elements of the identification of names submitted for temple work are: (1) *Name* of each person, in full; (2) *Dates* of birth, marriage, and death; (3) *Places* of birth, marriage, and death; and (4) *Relationships* to parents, brothers, sisters, spouse, and children.

One begins by recording information about himself; second, his parents; third, grandparents; and fourth, his great-grandparents. One does this by obtaining information from living parents and grandparents and then from other sources. To help the Saints gather that necessary information, The Church of Jesus Christ of Latter-day Saints maintains the largest genealogical library in the world, with branch libraries in many states and mail order service available almost worldwide. In 1978 a name extraction program was inaugurated to extract every name from civil records to be put in the name file for temple work to be done.

Every family in the Church has been asked to submit family group sheets on the first four generations of their ancestry. This assignment is given not just as a recommendation but as a priesthood obligation. Completion of this assignment does not complete one's obligation to his ancestors, however. President Wilford Woodruff said: "We want the Latter day Saints from this time to trace their genealogies as far as they can, and to be sealed to their fathers and mothers. Have children sealed to their parents, and run this chain through as far as you can get it." ("The Law of Adoption," p. 543.)

More recently, Elder Mark E. Petersen instructed the General Authorities: "We must trace our own genealogy as far as we can. The four generations are not enough. We have the extraction program and it will help, but it does not relieve us of our own personal responsibility. Our own research will tie in with the extraction program and that is good, but it will augment our efforts only; it will not replace our effort." (General Authority Board Meeting, 7 Oct. 1980.)

Elder Boyd K. Packer wrote: "Name extraction becomes an important part of genealogical work. However, this does not relieve each member from the responsibility to seek after his own kindred dead. We are all responsible, individually, to link our families in proper order." (*Holy Temple*, p. 228.)

*Architect's rendering of the Genealogical Library in Salt Lake City*

### (O-6) Two Forces at Work

Elijah's mission was to bind the hearts of living children to those of their fathers and the hearts of living fathers to those of their living children. Great evidence of this binding can be seen as families are united by the sealing ordinances of the temple, as families do genealogy research for their departed loved ones, and as families live together in love, cooperation, and unity. The mission of Elijah commences with living fathers turning to their own children so that they are not lost to the adversary's influence.

But there are also other forces at work. Speaking of these times, Jesus prophesied: "The father shall be divided against the son, and the son against the father; the mother against the daughter, and the daughter against the mother; the mother in law against her daughter in law, and the daughter in law against her mother in law" (Luke 12:53). "And a man's foes shall be they of his own household" (Matthew 10:36). Evidence of this opposing influence is seen in families that are split apart by contention, separations, and divorce. So serious is this problem that President Spencer W. Kimball warned: "Many of the social restraints which in the past have helped to reinforce and to shore up the family are dissolving and disappearing. The time will come when only those who believe deeply and actively in the family will be able to preserve their families in the midst of the gathering evil around us." ("Families Can Be Eternal," *Ensign*, Nov. 1980, p. 4.)

The early brethren of this dispensation taught that in the spirit world, as on earth, the righteous live in family units (see Heber C. Kimball, in *Journal of Discourses*, 4:135-36). Some families, however, may not dwell together because the ordinance work is not done for them. Many of the hearts of those fathers yearn over their living posterity because they have yet to rise up and complete the sacred trust committed to them to see that their progenitors' ordinance work is done. Those fathers remain powerless to unite their families.

By an individual's neglect or by his diligence, he contributes to the dissolution or uniting of his own family unit. "Somebody," said President Wilford Woodruff, "has got to administer for them by proxy here in the flesh, that they may be judged according to men in the flesh and have part in the first resurrection" (*Discourses of Wilford Woodruff*, p. 149).

### (O-7) Summary

Vicarious ordinance work done by living proxies enables them to be saviors to the dead. It is no wonder that the Prophet Joseph Smith exclaimed: "Shall we not go on in so great a cause? Go forward and not backward. Courage, brethren; and on, on to the victory! Let your hearts rejoice, and be exceedingly glad. Let the earth break forth into singing. Let the dead speak forth anthems of eternal praise to the King Immanuel, who hath ordained, before the world was, that which would enable us to redeem them out of their prison; for the prisoners shall go free.

"... Let us, therefore, as a church and a people, and as Latter-day Saints, offer unto the Lord an offering in righteousness; and let us present in his holy temple, when it is finished, a book containing the records of our dead, which shall be worthy of all acceptation." (D&C 128:22, 24.)

If the work to be done here is of such urgency to those who have gone before, one would expect that these departed spirits would take a great interest in their posterity's efforts to do genealogy work and perhaps even assist in certain cases where all efforts have been in vain. Elder Orson Pratt bore witness to the fact that such help may be forthcoming: "Do you inquire how we are to obtain the genealogies of our fathers, so as to do this work for them which they, when living, had not the opportunity of doing, and which they, as spirits in prison, cannot do? We answer, that it is the duty of all Saints among all nations to search out, as far as possible, their family records, and their genealogies, and their kindred, both the living and the dead; and when you have been diligent and procured all the information within your reach, and have gone into the holy Temple of the Most High, and done what is required of the living for the dead. Then God will show you, by his Prophets and Seers, and by holy messengers and angels, the genealogies of your fathers, back from generation to generation unto the beginning, or unto the time when the powers, and keys, and ordinances of the priesthood were upon the earth." ("Celestial Marriage," *The Seer,* Sept. 1853, p. 141.)

Elder Melvin J. Ballard told of such an experience happening in his own family.

"I recall an incident in my own father's experience. How we looked forward to the completion of the Logan Temple! It was about to be dedicated. My father had labored on that house from its very beginning, and my earliest recollection was carrying his dinner each day as he brought the rock down from the quarry. How we looked forward to that great event! I remember how in the meantime Father made every effort to obtain all the data and information he could concerning his relatives. It was the theme of his prayer night and morning that the Lord would open the way whereby he could get information concerning his dead.

"The day before the dedication while writing recommends to the members of his ward who were to be present at the first service, two elderly gentlemen walked down the streets of Logan, approached my two younger sisters, and, coming to the elder one of the two placed in her hands a newspaper and said:

" 'Take this to your father. Give it to no one else. Go quickly with it. Don't lose it.'

"The child responded and when she met her mother, her mother wanted the paper. The child said, 'No, I must give it to Father and no one else.'

"She was admitted into the room and told her story. We looked in vain for these travelers. They were not to be seen. No one else saw them. Then we turned to the paper. The newspaper, *The Newbury Weekly News,* was printed in my father's old English home, Thursday, May 15th, 1884, and reached our hands May 18th, 1884, three days after its publication. We were astonished, for by no earthly means could it have reached us, so that our curiosity increased as we examined it. Then we discovered one page devoted to the writings of a reporter of the paper, who had gone on his vacation, and among other places had visited an old cemetery. The curious inscriptions led him to write what he found on the tombstones, including the verses. He also added the names, date of birth, death, etc., filling nearly an entire page.

"It was the old cemetery where the Ballard family had been buried for generations, and very many of my father's immediate relatives and other intimate friends were mentioned.

"When the matter was presented to President Merrill of the Logan Temple, he said, 'You are authorized to do the work for those because you received it through messengers of the Lord.'

"There is no doubt that the dead who had received the gospel in the spirit world had put it into the heart of that reporter to write these things, and thus the way was prepared for my father to obtain the information he sought, and so with you who are earnest in this work, the way shall be opened and you will be able to gather data far beyond your expectations. I will tell you what will happen. When you have gone as far as you can go, the names of your righteous dead who have embraced the gospel in the spirit world will be given you through the instrumentality of your dead kindred. But only the names of those who have received the gospel will be revealed." (In Hinckley, *Melvin Joseph Ballard,* pp. 249-51.)

# Bibliography

Backman, Milton V. *American Religions and the Rise of Mormonism.* Salt Lake City: Deseret Book Co., 1965.

Ballard, Melvin R. *Melvin J. Ballard, Crusader for Righteousness.* Salt Lake City: Bookcraft, 1966.

Barrett, Ivan J. *Joseph Smith and the Restoration: A History of the Church to 1846.* Provo: BYU Press, Young House, 1973.

Berrett, William E. *The Restored Church.* Salt Lake City: Deseret Book Co., 1961.

Bowen, Albert E. *The Church Welfare Plan* [Sunday School Gospel Doctrine Course, 1946]. Salt Lake City: Deseret Sunday School Union, 1946.

Bowen, Walter Dean. "The Versatile W. W. Phelps—Mormon Writer, Educator, and Pioneer." Master's thesis, Brigham Young University, 1958.

Cannon, George Q. *Gospel Truth.* 2 vols. Compiled by Jerreld L. Newquist. Salt Lake City: Deseret Book Co., 1957-74.

———. *Life of Joseph Smith the Prophet.* Salt Lake City: Deseret Book Co., 1958.

Clark, James R. *Messages of the First Presidency of The Church of Jesus Christ of Latter-day Saints.* 6 vols. Salt Lake City: Bookcraft, 1965-75.

———. *The Story of the Pearl of Great Price.* 2d ed. Salt Lake City: Bookcraft, 1955.

*The Compact Edition of the Oxford English Dictionary.* 2 vols. London: Oxford University Press, 1971.

*Continents Adrift.* San Francisco: W. H. Freeman and Co., 1970.

Cowan, Richard O. *Doctrine and Covenants: Our Modern Scripture.* Rev. ed. Provo: Brigham Young University Press, 1969.

Doxey, Roy W. *Doctrine and Covenants Speaks.* 2 vols. Salt Lake City: Deseret Book Co., 1969-70.

———. *Latter-day Prophets and the Doctrine and Covenants.* 4 vols. Salt Lake City: Deseret Book Co., 1978.

Dyer, Alvin R. *The Refiner's Fire.* 2d ed. Salt Lake City: Deseret Book Co., 1968.

Fallows, Samuel. *The Popular and Critical Bible Encyclopedia and Scriptural Dictionary.* 3 vols. Chicago: Howard-Severance Co., 1911.

Gesenius, William. *A Hebrew and English Lexicon of the Old Testament.* Corrected ed. Translated by Edward Robinson. Oxford: Clarendon Press, 1953.

Grant, Heber J. *Gospel Standards.* Compiled by G. Homer Durham. Salt Lake City: Deseret Book Co., 1969.

Hinckley, Bryant S. *The Faith of Our Pioneer Fathers.* Salt Lake City: Bookcraft, 1956.

———. *Sermons and Missionary Services of Melvin Joseph Ballard.* Salt Lake City: Deseret Book Co., 1949.

*The Interpreter's Dictionary of the Bible.* 4 vols. New York: Abingdon Press, 1962.

Jenson, Andrew. *Latter-day Saint Biographical Encyclopedia.* 4 vols. Salt Lake City: Andrew Jenson History Co., 1901-36.

Journal History of the Church. Salt Lake City: The Church of Jesus Christ of Latter-day Saints, Historical Department, 1830-1972.

*Journal of Discourses.* 26 vols. London: Latter-day Saints' Book Depot, 1854-86.

Keil, C. F., and Delitzsch, F. *Commentary on the Old Testament.* 10 bks. Grand Rapids: William B. Eerdmans Publishing Co., n.d.

Kimball, Spencer W. *Faith Precedes the Miracle.* Salt Lake City: Deseret Book Co., 1972.

———. *The Miracle of Forgiveness.* Salt Lake City: Bookcraft, 1969.

———. *Tragedy or Destiny.* Provo: Brigham Young University Extension Publication, 1961. Reprint. Salt Lake City: Deseret Book Co., 1977.

Kirkham, Francis W. *A New Witness for Christ in America.* 4th ed. Provo: Brigham Young University, 1960.

Lee, Harold B. *Stand Ye in Holy Places.* Salt Lake City: Deseret Book Co., 1974.

———. *Ye Are the Light of the World.* Salt Lake City: Deseret Book Co., 1974.

*Life's Directions.* Salt Lake City: Deseret Book Co., 1962.

Ludlow, Daniel H. *A Companion to Your Study of the Doctrine and Covenants.* 2 vols. Salt Lake City: Deseret Book Co., 1978.

Lundwall, N. B., comp. *Temples of the Most High.* Rev. ed. Salt Lake City: Bookcraft, 1968.

Mackie, George M. *Bible Manners and Customs.* N.p.: Fleming H. Revell Co., n.d.

Madsen, Truman G. *Joseph Smith among the Prophets.* Salt Lake City: Deseret Book Co., 1965.

Matthews, Robert J. *"A Plainer Translation": Joseph Smith's Translation of the Bible, a History and Commentary.* Provo: Brigham Young University Press, 1975.

McKay, David O. *Gospel Ideals.* Salt Lake City: Improvement Era, 1954.

McConkie, Bruce R. "All Are Alike unto God." In *A Symposium on the Book of Mormon.* Salt Lake City: Church Educational System, 1979.

———. *Doctrinal New Testament Commentary.* 3 vols. Salt Lake City: Bookcraft, 1965-73.

———. *Mormon Doctrine.* 2d ed. Salt Lake City: Bookcraft, 1966.

———. *The Mortal Messiah: Book 1.* Salt Lake City: Deseret Book Co., 1979.

———. *The Promised Messiah.* Salt Lake City: Deseret Book Co., 1978.

McWhirter, Norris. *Guinness Book of World Records.* 17th ed. New York: Bantam Books, 1979.

Nibley, Preston. *Brigham Young, the Man and His Work.* Salt Lake City: Deseret Book Co., 1936.

*Our Prophets and Principles.* Salt Lake City: Instructor, 1956.

Packer, Boyd K. *The Holy Temple.* Salt Lake City: Bookcraft, 1980.

Parkin, Max. "Conflict at Kirtland." Master's thesis, Brigham Young University, 1966.

Petersen, Mark E. *The Great Prologue.* Salt Lake City: Deseret Book Co., 1975.

Pratt, Orson. *Masterful Discourses and Writings of Orson Pratt.* Compiled by N. B. Lundwall. Salt Lake City: N. B. Lundwall, n.d.

Pratt, Parley P. *Autobiography of Parley P. Pratt.* 3d ed. Edited by Parley P. Pratt [son]. Salt Lake City: Deseret Book Co., 1938.

———. *Key to the Science of Theology; A Voice of Warning.* Classics in Mormon Literature. Salt Lake City: Deseret Book Co., 1978.

Rasmussen, Ellis T. *An Introduction to the Old Testament and Its Teachings.* 2d ed. 2 vols. Provo: Brigham Young University Publications, 1972-74.

Rich, Ben E., comp. *Scrapbook of Mormon Literature.* Chicago: Henry C. Etten and Co., n.d.

Richards, LeGrand. *A Marvelous Work and a Wonder.* Rev. ed. Salt Lake City: Deseret Book Co., 1966.

Riegel, Robert E. *America Moves West.* New York: Henry Holt and Co., 1930.

Roberts, B. H. *A Comprehensive History of The Church of Jesus Christ of Latter-day Saints, Century 1.* 6 vols. Provo: The Church of Jesus Christ of Latter-day Saints, 1930.

———. *The Life of John Taylor.* Salt Lake City: Bookcraft, 1963.

Romney, George J., comp. *Look to God and Live.* Salt Lake City: Deseret Book Co., 1971.

Smith, Hyrum M., and Sjodahl, Janne M. Introduction to and commentary on *The Doctrine and Covenants.* Rev. ed. Salt Lake City: Deseret Book Co., 1972.

Smith, Joseph. *History of The Church of Jesus Christ of Latter-day Saints.* 7 vols. 2d. ed. rev. Edited by B. H. Roberts. Salt Lake City: The Church of Jesus Christ of Latter-day Saints, 1932-51.

———. *Lectures on Faith.* Compiled by N. B. Lundwall. Salt Lake City: N. B. Lundwall, n.d.

———. *Teachings of the Prophet Joseph Smith.* Selected by Joseph Fielding Smith. Salt Lake City: Deseret Book Co., 1938.

Smith, Joseph F. *Gospel Doctrine.* 5th ed. Salt Lake City: Deseret Book Co., 1939.

Smith, Joseph Fielding. *Answers to Gospel Questions.* 5 vols. Compiled by Joseph Fielding Smith, Jr. Salt Lake City: Deseret Book Co., 1957-66.

———. *Church History and Modern Revelation.* 2 vols. Salt Lake City: The Council of the Twelve Apostles, 1953.

———. *Doctrines of Salvation.* 3 vols. Compiled by Bruce R. McConkie. Salt Lake City: Bookcraft, 1954-56.

———. *Elijah the Prophet and His Mission.* Salt Lake City: Deseret Book Co., 1957.

———. *Essentials in Church History.* Classics in Mormon Literature. Salt Lake City: Deseret Book Co., 1979.

———. *The Progress of Man.* Salt Lake City: The Genealogical Society of Utah, 1952.

———. *Religious Truths Defined.* Salt Lake City: Bookcraft, 1959.

———. *Seek Ye Earnestly.* Salt Lake City: Deseret Book Co., 1970.

———. *The Signs of the Times.* Salt Lake City: Deseret Book Co., 1963.

———. *The Way to Perfection.* Salt Lake City: Deseret Book Co., 1931.

———, comp. *Life of Joseph F. Smith.* Salt Lake City: Deseret Book Co., 1969.

Smith, Joseph Fielding, Jr., and John J Stewart. *The Life of Joseph Fielding Smith.* Salt Lake City: Deseret Book Co., 1972.

Smith, Lucy Mack. *History of Joseph Smith.* Edited by Preston Nibley. Salt Lake City: Bookcraft, 1958.

Smith, William. *A Dictionary of the Bible.* Rev. ed. Grand Rapids: Zondervan Publishing House, 1948.

Sperry, Sidney B. *Doctrine and Covenants Compendium.* Salt Lake City: Bookcraft, 1960.

Talmage, James E. *The Articles of Faith.* 12th ed. Salt Lake City: The Church of Jesus Christ of Latter-day Saints, 1924.

———. *Jesus the Christ.* 3d ed. Salt Lake City: The Church of Jesus Christ of Latter-day Saints, 1916.

———. *The Vitality of Mormonism.* Salt Lake City: Deseret Book Co., 1919.

Taylor, John. *The Gospel Kingdom.* Selected by G. Homer Durham. Salt Lake City: Bookcraft, 1964.

———. *The Mediation and Atonement.* 1882. Reprint. Salt Lake City: Deseret News Company, 1964.

*The Ten Commandments Today: A Study of the Decalog.* Salt Lake City: Deseret Book Company, 1955.

Thayer, Joseph Henry. *Greek-English Lexicon of the New Testament.* Rev. and enl. ed. Grand Rapids: Zondervan Publishing House, 1975.

Unger, Merrill F. *Unger's Bible Dictionary.* Chicago: Moody Press, 1966.

Vincent, M. R. *Word Studies in the New Testament.* 2 vols. McDill Air Force Base, Florida: MacDonald Publishing Co., n.d.

Whitney, Orson F. *Life of Heber C. Kimball,* 3d ed. Salt Lake City: Bookcraft, 1945.

———. *Saturday Night Thoughts.* Rev. ed. Salt Lake City: Deseret Book Co., 1921.

Widtsoe, John A. *Evidences and Reconciliations.* 3 vols. 2d ed. Salt Lake City: Bookcraft, 1951.

———. *Joseph Smith: Seeker after Truth, Prophet of God.* Salt Lake City: Bookcraft, 1951.

———. *The Message of the Doctrine and Covenants.* Edited by G. Homer Durham. Salt Lake City: Bookcraft, 1969.

———, comp. *Priesthood and Church Government.* Rev. ed. Salt Lake City: Deseret Book Co., 1954.

———, and Leah D. Widtsoe. *The Word of Wisdom.* Salt Lake City: Deseret Book Co., 1937.

Woodruff, Wilford. *The Discourses of Wilford Woodruff.* Selected by G. Homer Durham, Salt Lake City: Bookcraft, 1946.

Young, Brigham. *Discourses of Brigham Young.* Selected by John A. Widtsoe. Salt Lake City: Deseret Book Co., 1941.

Young, Robert. *Analytical Concordance to the Bible.* 22d ed. rev. Grand Rapids: William B. Eerdmans Publishing Co., 1970.

Young, S. Dilworth. "*Here Is Brigham. . . .*" Salt Lake City: Bookcraft, 1964.

# Author Index

# Scripture Index

## Explanatory Notes

The first column designates the scripture reference; the second column identifies the reading block where this reference is found.

Example:
Doctrine and Covenants 57:2-3q 28:9

a—analysis. The scripture referred to is the subject of a whole section or chapter.

c—commentary. A short, explanatory comment is made about the scripture.

m—meaning. The meaning of a word or phrase in the scripture is discussed.

q—quotation. The scripture is quoted partially or in full.

r—reference. The scripture is merely referred to.

JST—The Joseph Smith Translation is used.

HB—Historical Background. The scripture reference is in the Historical Background section of the designated lesson.

| | | | | | |
|---|---|---|---|---|---|
| 18:9a | 18:9 | 20:31-34r | 133:4 | 24:1a | 24:1 |
| 18:10-16a | 18:10-16 | 20:32a, m | 20:32 | 24:3-9a | 24:3-9 |
| 18:11q | D-4 | 20:32-34q | 132:26-27 | 24:10a | 24:10 |
| 18:12r | E-2 | 20:37a, m | 20:37 | 24:13-14a | 24:13-14 |
| 18:18q | C-3 | 20:37q | I-4 | 24:15a | 24:15 |
| 18:20a, m | 18:20 | 20:37r | N-3 | 24:15r | 60:15-17 |
| 18:20-21a, m | 18:20-21 | 20:38a, m | 20:38 | 24:19a | 24:19 |
| 18:21-25q | D-5 | 20:38-71r | 28:12 | 25:1a | 25:1 |
| 18:22r | I-4 | 20:41a, m | 20:41 | 25:1r | 34:1-4 |
| 18:30-36c | F-2 | 20:41r | 20:41 | 25:1r | D-5 |
| 18:34-36a, r | 18:34-36 | 20:47c | C-2 | 25:3a, m | 25:3 |
| 18:37-40a | 18:37-40 | 20:57a | 20:57 | 25:4a | 25:4 |
| 19:1a, m | 19:1 | 20:60a | 20:60 | 25:5r | 25:16 |
| 19:3a, m | 19:3 | 20:61r | 52:2 | 25:7a, m | 25:7 |
| 19:3q | D-3 | 20:61-62a | 20:61-62 | 25:7r | 25:16 |
| 19:4r | 19:1 | 20:62r | 44:1 | 25:8r | 25:16 |
| 19:4r | E-2 | 20:63-67r | 28:12 | 25:9r | 25:16 |
| 19:4-12a | 19:4-12 | 20:65a, m | 20:65 | 25:10r | 25:16 |
| 19:5r | 133:65-74 | 20:65 | 26:2 | 25:11a | 25:11 |
| 19:7a, m | 19:7 | 20:65r | N-2 | 25:11r | 25:16 |
| 19:13-20a | 19:13-20 | 20:60-67r | 26:2 | 25:12a | 25:12 |
| 19:13-21a | 19:13-21 | 20:61-62r | N-4 | 25:13r | 25:16 |
| 19:13-41a | 19:13-41 | 20:69r | 24:3-9 | 25:14r | 25:16 |
| 19:15q | 19:13-21 | 20:70a | 20:70 | 25:15r | 25:16 |
| 19:15-19r | D-4 | 20:71a | 20:71 | 25:16a | 25:16 |
| 19:16q | 58:42-43 | 20:73, 77, 79a | 20:73, 77, 79 | 26r | 69:3-8 |
| 19:16q | E-2 | 20:77, 79r | A-5 | 26:1a | 26:1 |
| 19:18q | E-2 | 20:80 | 42:74-93 | 26:2a | 26:2 |
| 19:20q | 19:13-21 | 20:80r | I-6 | 27:1-4a | 27:1-4 |
| 19:20r | I-6 | 20:81r | 51:10 | 27:2r | 64:22 |
| 19:21q | 19:13-21 | 20:83r | 20:83 | 27:3-4q, m | 89:5-6 |
| 19:22r | K-7 | 20:83q | I-6 | 27:5r | 20:9 |
| 19:24r | 19:24 | 21:1a, m | 21:1 | 27:5a, m | 27:5 |
| 19:27a, q | 19:27 | 21:1-7r | 112:15 | 27:5q | 27:5-14 |
| 19:28c | C-2 | 21:4-5a | 21:4-5 | 27:5q | 133:17, 36 |
| 19:28, 38a | 19:28, 38 | 21:4-5q | 21:5 | 27:5-13r | 128:18 |
| 19:29-32a | 19:29-32 | 21:4-5q | F-5 | 27:5-14a | 27:5-14 |
| 19:37a, m | 19:37 | 21:4-6r | 33:1 | 27:6-7a, m, r | 27:6-7 |
| 19:31q | 20:41 | 21:4-6c | F-2 | 27:6-7r | 77:14 |
| 19:31r | E-4 | 21:4-6q | J-6 | 27:6-7r | 110:12 |
| 20r | 20 HB | 21:5a | 21:5 | 27:8r | 132:59 |
| 20:1a | 20:1 | 21:5q | F-2 | 27:9r | 2 HB |
| 20:2-3r | 28:12 | 21:6a | 21:6 | 27:9r | O-3 |
| 20:2-4a | 20:2-4 | 21:6q | F-5 | 27:12r | 7:3-6 |
| 20:3r | 18:37-40 | 21:7a | 21:7 | 27:12-13r | 7:7 |
| 20:3r | 28:1 | 21:7q | 43 HB | 27:12-13r | 113:3-6 |
| 20:5a, m | 20:5 | 21:7-8a | 21:7-8 | 27:12-13r | G-6 |
| 20:8 | 21:1 | 22r | 20 HB | 27:13a, m | 27:13 |
| 20:9a, r | 20:9 | 22:1a, m | 22:1 | 27:15-18a, m | 27:15-18 |
| 20:14-16q | 84:54-57 | 22:1-4a | 22:1-4 | 28r | 26:2 |
| 20:18-20a | 20:18-20 | 22:4a | 22:4 | 28r | 10:12, 23-29, 63 |
| 20:26r | 21:1 | 23:1-6a | 23:1-6 | | |
| 20:28a | 20:28 | 23:3r | 23:1-6 | 28:1a | 28:1 |
| 20:29r | D-5 | 23:6a, m | 23:6 | 28:2q | 90:4-5 |
| 20:30a, m | 20:30 | 23:6r | 56:2 | 28:2q | 103:16 |
| 20:31a, m | 20:31 | 23:6c | C-2 | 28:2-3a | 28:2-3 |

| | |
|---|---|
| 50:15q | 50:13-21 |
| 50:22-24a | 50:22-24 |
| 50:23-25q | J-4 |
| 50:24r | K-3 |
| 50:25c | K-5 |
| 50:25-28a | 50:25-28 |
| 50:28q | 50:25-28 |
| 50:28-29r | 103:31 |
| 50:29-30a | 50:29-30 |
| 50:29-30r | K-8 |
| 50:30r | OD 2 HB |
| 50:31-35a | 50:31-35 |
| 50:32r | 50:31-35 |
| 50:34c | 50:31-35 |
| 50:35c | 50:31-35 |
| 50:35c | K-5 |
| 50:36c | F-2 |
| 50:36r | F-4 |
| 50:40r | K-7 |
| 50:40-43a | 50:40-43 |
| 50:43-44r, m | 11:24 |
| 50:45a | 50:45 |
| 50:45-46r | 67:10-13 |
| 50:45-46r | 88:67-68 |
| 51:2a | 51:2 |
| 51:3a, m, r | 51:3 |
| 51:3 | 78:5-7 |
| 51:3q | L-4 |
| 51:3q, m | L-5 |
| 51:3-5r | L-5 |
| 51:4q | L-4 |
| 51:4-6r | 51 HB |
| 51:4-6a | 51:4-6 |
| 51:6r | 51:4-6 |
| 51:8a | 51:8 |
| 51:9a | 51:9 |
| 51:9q | L-5 |
| 51:10a, m | 51:10 |
| 51:11-14c | 51:11-14 |
| 51:13r | 70:7-9 |
| 51:13r | 107:68-75 |
| 51:13r | L-5 |
| 51:13-14r | 107:68-75 |
| 51:15-16r | 51 HB |
| 51:17a | 51:17 |
| 51:17q | 59:7-8 |
| 51:19q | 138:15-19, 50 |
| 52r | 10:12, 23-29, 63 |
| 52r, c | 44:1 |
| 52r | 56 HB |
| 52r | 57 HB |
| 52r | 60 HB |
| 52:1-5, 42r | 101:1, 6 |
| 52:2a | 52:2 |
| 52:2 | 87:5 |
| 52:2-3r | 48:4 |
| 52:3, 7-8, 22-23a | 52:3, 7-8, 22-23 |
| 52:9r | 42:12-14 |
| 52:9a | 52:9 |
| 52:9c | F-2 |
| 52:9, 36q | F-3 |
| 52:14-19a, m | 52:14-19 |
| 52:14-19c | J-6 |
| 52:15c | J-6 |
| 52:17c | J-6 |
| 52:33a | 52:33 |
| 52:39a | 52:39 |
| 53:r | 52:3, 7-8, 22, 23 |
| 53:1a | 53:1 |
| 53:2a, m | 53:2 |
| 53:3a | 53:3 |
| 53:4a | 53:4 |
| 53:7r | 14:7 |
| 53-55r | 58:19-23 |
| 54:2c | 54:2 |
| 54:3a | 54:3 |
| 54:4c | 54:4 |
| 54:6r | D-3 |
| 54:7-8r | 57:14-15 |
| 54:7-9a | 54:7-9 |
| 54:10r | H-6 |
| 54:10r | H-10 |
| 55r | 55 HB |
| 55-56r | 52:3, 7-8, 22-23 |
| 55:1a, m | 55:1 |
| 55:1r | E-4 |
| 55:4a | 55:4 |
| 55:4r | 57:13 |
| 55:4r | 61:7 |
| 55:4r | K-2 |
| 56:2r | 23:6 |
| 56:3-4a | 56:3-4 |
| 56:6-8a, m | 56:6-8 |
| 56:8r | 56:8-9 |
| 56:10q | I-6 |
| 56:14c | F-2 |
| 56:14r | F-4 |
| 56:16a | 56:16 |
| 56:17q | 56:17-18 |
| 56:17r | 68:30 |
| 56:17r | L-9 |
| 56:17-18a | 56:17-18 |
| 57r | 57 HB |
| 57:1-2r | 29:8 |
| 57:1-3r | 48:4 |
| 57:1-3a | 57:1-3 |
| 57:1-3r | B-5 |
| 57:1-5r | 101:1, 6 |
| 57:2-3q | 28:9 |
| 57:3q | 101:1, 6 |
| 57:3q | B-5 |
| 57:4q | 19:27 |
| 57:4a | 57:4 |
| 57:5-14r | 57:5-14 |
| 57:6r | 61:7 |
| 57:6-9r | 53:4 |
| 57:7, 15r | 58:16-18 |
| 57:8r | 53 HB |
| 57:8-9r | 98:1-3 |
| 57:9a | 57:9 |
| 57:11r | 61:7 |
| 57:11-14r | 67 HB |
| 57:13a | 57:13 |
| 57:14-15a | 57:14-15 |
| 57:15r | 58 HB |
| 57:15r | L-5 |
| 58r | 56:3-4 |
| 58r | 58 HB |
| 58r | 63:1-6 |
| 58:2-4a | 58:2-4 |
| 58:2-4r | 103:11-14 |
| 58:2-4q | 121:7 |
| 58:3q | B-6 |
| 58:3-7, 44a | 58:3-7, 44 |
| 58:4-7q | B-6 |
| 58:4-7r | L-7 |
| 58:8c | F-2 |
| 58:8-11a, m | 58:8-11 |
| 58:14-15r | 58:14-16 |
| 58:14-16a | 58:14-16 |
| 58:16-18a | 58:16-18 |
| 58:17-18r | 107:68-75 |
| 58:17-18r | I-2 |
| 58:19-23a | 58:19-23 |
| 58:20q | I-2 |
| 58:21q | 134:2 |
| 58:21-22r | G-6 |
| 58:22r | 58:19-23 |
| 58:22q | 134:5-6 |
| 58:26q | 41:6-8 |
| 58:26-29a | 58:26-29 |
| 58:30-33a | 58:30-33 |
| 58:33, 55r | L-5 |
| 58:35r | 107:68-75 |
| 58:42-43r | 19:13-21 |
| 58:42-43a | 58:42-43 |
| 58:42-43r | I-5 |
| 58:44q | 58:44-48, 56 |
| 58:44r | 101:44-64 |
| 58:44-48, 56a | 58:44-48, 56 |
| 58:45q | 58:44-48, 56 |

| | |
|---|---|
| 87:1a | 87:1 |
| 87:2a | 87:2 |
| 87:3a | 87:3 |
| 87:4-5a | 87:4-5 |
| 87:5a, m, q | 87:5 |
| 87:6a | 87:6 |
| 87:6c | H-5 |
| 87:7a, m | 87:7 |
| 87:8a | 87:8 |
| 88:1-5r | 78:21 |
| 88:2c | 88 HB |
| 88:2q | 88:3-4 |
| 88:2q | 132:19-22 |
| 88:2r, m | E-4 |
| 88:3-4a, m | 88:3-4 |
| 88:6r | D-4 |
| 88:6-7r | D-3 |
| 88:6-13a, m | 88:6-13 |
| 88:6-13r | G-3 |
| 88:6-10r | D-2 |
| 88:6, 41r | D-3 |
| 88:7r | D-2 |
| 88:7-13r | D-2 |
| 88:11r | D-2 |
| 88:11r | K-6 |
| 88:11r | K-7 |
| 88:12q | C-3 |
| 88:12r | D-2 |
| 88:13r | D-2 |
| 88:14r | 88:17-20 |
| 88:14-26, 111r | 38:17-20 |
| 88:15a | 88:15 |
| 88:15r | 93:33 |
| 88:16r | 78:12 |
| 88:17-19, 25-26r | 29:22-25 |
| 88:17-20r | 63:20-21, 49-51 |
| 88:17-20r | 77:1 |
| 88:17-20a | 88:17-20 |
| 88:20-21r | L-2 |
| 88:21r, m | E-4 |
| 88:21-24a | 88:21-24 |
| 88:21-24c | G-5 |
| 88:21-24r | G-6 |
| 88:21-24, 34-35r | G-5 |
| 88:22q | G-2 |
| 88:25-26r | 63:20-21, 49-51 |
| 88:25-26r | 77:1 |
| 88:25-26a | 88:25-26 |
| 88:25-26r | 119:5-6 |
| 88:27a | 88:27 |
| 88:28a | 88:28 |
| 88:28-31r | 88:25-26 |
| 88:34c | G-2 |
| 88:34-35c | G-5 |
| 88:36-37q | G-2 |
| 88:36-39c | G-2 |
| 88:37a | 88:37 |
| 88:37-39a | 88:37-39 |
| 88:38-39r | G-5 |
| 88:40r | D-3 |
| 88:40q | K-7 |
| 88:40-50a | 88:40-50 |
| 88:41r | 38:2 |
| 88:41q | 88:37 |
| 88:41q | 130:4-7 |
| 88:51-61a | 88:51-61 |
| 88:62-65a | 88:62-65 |
| 88:63-65r | C-3 |
| 88:63-83a | 88:63-83 |
| 88:64r | 50:29-30 |
| 88:66r | D-3 |
| 88:67-68a | 88:67-68 |
| 88:68r | 50:45 |
| 88:68q | 93:1 |
| 88:68-69r | 67:10-13 |
| 88:69q | 88:121 |
| 88:70r | 95:7 |
| 88:76a | 88:76 |
| 88:77q | K-2 |
| 88:77-78c | K-5 |
| 88:77-79, 118r | K-7 |
| 88:78q | K-6 |
| 88:78-79r | K-6 |
| 88:78-79, 118-19, 127r | K-2 |
| 88:81q | A-5 |
| 88:81-82r | 24:15 |
| 88:81-82q | A-5 |
| 88:84-116r | 88:63-83 |
| 88:86r | H-7 |
| 88:87-91r | 130:14-17 |
| 88:88-91r | H-5 |
| 88:88-92r | 43:17-25 |
| 88:91a | 88:91 |
| 88:92r | 88:93 |
| 88:92r | H-7 |
| 88:93a | 88:93 |
| 88:93r | 130:14-17 |
| 88:93r | 133:2 |
| 88:93r | H-10 |
| 88:94a | 88:94 |
| 88:94q | 88:95-98 |
| 88:94c | H-5 |
| 88:94, 105r | 35:11 |
| 88:95r | 130:1 |
| 88:95q | H-10 |
| 88:95-98 | 88:95-98 |
| 88:96-97r | H-10 |
| 88:99a | 88:99 |
| 88:100-101a | 88:100-101 |
| 88:102a | 88:102 |
| 88:103-6a | 88:103-6 |
| 88:104q | A-5 |
| 88:107a | 88:107 |
| 88:108-10a | 88:108-10 |
| 88:110q | 84:100 |
| 88:111-15a | 88:111-15 |
| 88:117-20r | 109:7-14 |
| 88:117-41a | 88:117-41 |
| 88:118q | K-2 |
| 88:118q | K-6 |
| 88:118q | K-7 |
| 88:119r | 95 HB |
| 88:119r | 109 HB |
| 88:119q | 110 HB |
| 88:121a | 88:121 |
| 88:121q | 95:10 |
| 88:124-26a | 88:124-26 |
| 88:126r | 19:28, 38 |
| 88:139-40r | 60:15-17 |
| 89r | 27:1-4 |
| 89:2a, m | 89:2 |
| 89:3a | 89:3 |
| 89:3q | 89:18-21 |
| 89:4a | 89:4 |
| 89:5a | 89:5 |
| 89:5-6a | 89:5-6 |
| 89:7a | 89:7 |
| 89:8a | 89:8 |
| 89:9a, m | 89:9 |
| 89:10a, m | 89:10 |
| 89:10-11a | 89:10-11 |
| 89:11a | 89:11 |
| 89:12a | 89:12 |
| 89:12q | 89:13 |
| 89:13a | 89:13 |
| 89:14-17a | 89:14-17 |
| 89:18a | 89:18 |
| 89:18-19r | 6:7, 11 |
| 89:18-19r | K-7 |
| 89:18-21a | 89:18-21 |
| 89:18, 21q | 101:20-21 |
| 89:19a | 89:19 |
| 89:21a | 89:21 |
| 90:1-5a | 90:1-5 |
| 90:4-5a | 90:4-5 |
| 90:5c | F-2 |
| 90:6r | 92 HB |
| 90:6-7a | 90:6-7 |
| 90:8-9a | 90:8-9 |
| 90:10-11a, q | 90:10-11 |
| 90:12-18a | 90:12-18 |
| 90:13r | 91 HB |
| 90:15q | F-3 |
| 90:15q | K-2 |
| 90:15r | K-6 |
| 90:15r | K-7 |

| | | | | | |
|---|---|---|---|---|---|
| 101:17-18r | B-2 | 103:11-14a | 103:11-14 | 105:4-5a | 105:4-5 |
| 101:17-18, 43-62r | 103:11-14 | 103:15-20r | 103:11-14 | 105:4-5q | L-2 |
| 101:17-20a | 101:17-20 | 103:15-20a | 103:15-20 | 105:6r | 101:4-5 |
| 101:17-23r | 29:1-2 | 103:16a | 103:16 | 105:9q | B-6 |
| 101:18a, m | 101:18 | 103:19-20a | 103:19-20 | 105:9-12a | 105:9-12 |
| 101:20-22a | 101:20-22 | 103:20a | 103:20 | 105:10q | B-6 |
| 101:21q | 45:32 | 103:21r | 101:44-64 | 105:10-11r | B-6 |
| 101:21q | 87:8 | 103:21-28r | 101:44-64 | 105:11q | 110 HB |
| 101:21q | 115:5 | 103:21-28, 30-35a | 103:21-28, | 105:11q | B-6 |
| 101:21r, c | B-5 | | 30-35 | 105:11-12a, m | 105:11-12 |
| 101:22-23r | H-10 | 103:21-34r | 105 HB | 105:11-12, 18, 33a | 105:11-12, 18, 33 |
| 101:23-24r | 19:3 | 103:22q | 101:44-64 | 105:13a | 105:13 |
| 101:23-24r | 45:22 | 103:31a | 103:31 | 105:15, 37r | 101:44-64 |
| 101:23-25a | 101:23-25 | 104:1-10a | 104:1-10 | 105:24a | 105:24 |
| 101:23-32r | 38:17-20 | 104:6r | N-16 | 105:26q | B-6 |
| 101:24-25r | 63:20-21, | 104:8-9r | 82:11-12 | 105:28-32a | 105:28-32 |
| | 49-51 | 104:9a, m | 104:9 | 105:31-32q | B-6 |
| 101:24-34r | 63:50-51 | 104:9q | I-6 | 105:34a | 105:34 |
| 101:25a | 101:25 | 104:11c | L-4 | 105:34r | L-8 |
| 101:25r | H-10 | 104:11-15r | L-4 | 106:1q | 106:3 |
| 101:26-34a | 101:26-34 | 104:11-15r | L-9 | 106:2q | 106:3 |
| 101:28r | 43:31 | 104:13-15a | 104:13-15 | 106:3a | 106:3 |
| 101:35-38a | 101:35-38 | 104:14, 55-56q | 70:3 | 106:4-5a | 106:4-5 |
| 101:39-42a | 101:39-42 | 104:14-16q | L-3 | 106:8a | 106:8 |
| 101:44-62r | 24:19 | 104:14-17, 54-57q | L-3 | 107r | 81:1 |
| 101:44-64a | 101:44-64 | 104:15-16, 18a | 104:15-16, 18 | 107:1a | 107:1 |
| 101:55-60c | 103 HB | 104:15-18 | 104:13-15 | 107:1, 6, 10 | 107:1 |
| 101:64-66r | 4:4 | 104:15-18r | L-4 | 107:1-4r | M-2 |
| 101:67-75a | 101:67-75 | 104:15-18r | L-9 | 107:1-9r | M-5 |
| 101:68r | 115:17-19 | 104:17a | 104:17 | 107:2q | M-2 |
| 101:75a | 101:75 | 104:17-18, 54-57, | | 107:5a | 107:5 |
| 101:76-79a | 101:76-79 | 70r | H-7 | 107:6q | M-5 |
| 101:80a | 101:80 | 104:19-46a | 104:19-46 | 107:8-9r | N-6 |
| 101:81-95a | 101:81-95 | 104:47-53a | 104:47-53 | 107:8-12a | 107:8-12 |
| 101:89q | 109:47-53 | 104:47-49r | L-5 | 107:9q | 124:124-26 |
| 101:85-88r | 109:47-53 | 104:54-57 | 104:13-15 | 107:13-14r | 13:1 |
| 101:89-91r | H-10 | 104:58-59r | 43:12-14 | 107:13-15r | I-3 |
| 101:96-101a | 101:96-101 | 104:58-59a | 104:58-59 | 107:18a | 107:18 |
| 102:1-23r | I-6 | 104:60-66q | L-5 | 107:18-19a | 107:18-19 |
| 102:2, 9-10a | 102:2, 9-10 | 104:60-70a | 104:60-70 | 107:18-19r | 103:19-20 |
| 102:2, 9-12, 28-32r | I-2 | 104:70q | L-3 | 107:21r | 107:58-63 |
| 102:4a | 102:4 | 104:70-71r | L-5 | 107:22a | 107:22 |
| 102:6-7a | 102:6-7 | 104:71-77a | 104:71-77 | 107:22r | M-7 |
| 102:9r | 26:2 | 104:78-80a | 104:78-80 | 107:22q | N-6 |
| 102:12-22a | 102:12-22 | 104:78-80r | 111:1-6 | 107:22-26a | 107:22-26 |
| 102:18a | 102:18 | 104:78, 83a | 104:78, 83 | 107:23r | 21:1 |
| 102:19-22a | 102:19-22 | 105r | 63:1-6 | 107:23a | 107:23 |
| 102:26-27, 33a | 102:26-27, 33 | 105r | 119:2-3 | 107:23q | M-7 |
| 102:27r | I-6 | 105:1-2a | 105:1-2 | 107:24r | M-7 |
| 102:30-32a | 102:30-32 | 105:1-2r | B-6 | 107:27r | N-8 |
| 103r | 63:1-6 | 105:1-6 | L-2 | 107:27-32a | 107:27-32 |
| 103:1-3c | H-5 | 105:1-6, 9-15r | 103:11-14 | 107:32a | 107:32 |
| 103:1-4a | 103:1-4 | 105:1-9r | 84:4 | 107:33-34, 38a | 107:33-34, 38 |
| 103:3-4r | B-6 | 105:1-10r | 101:75 | 107:33-34, 91-92r | I-2 |
| 103:5-7q | H-7 | 105:2-4, 6 | 101:2, 6 | 107:36-37a | 107:36-37 |
| 103:5-10a | 103:5-10 | 105:2-6, 34r | 78:14 | 107:39a, m | 107:39 |

| | |
|---|---|
| 121:37q | M-3 |
| 121:37r | M-4 |
| 121:37-40r | M-4 |
| 121:38a, m | 121:38 |
| 121:39a | 121:39 |
| 121:40q | 39-40 HB |
| 121:41q | M-4 |
| 121:41-45r | M-4 |
| 121:41-46a | 121:41-46 |
| 121:42q | K-4 |
| 121:43a | 121:43 |
| 121:45a, m | 121:45 |
| 121:45q | C-4 |
| 121:45q | M-4 |
| 121:45-46a | 121:45-46 |
| 121:45-46 | C-2 |
| 121:45-46c | M-4 |
| 122:1a | 122:1 |
| 122:3a | 122:3 |
| 122:5-7a | 122:5-7 |
| 122:7q | 93:1-3 |
| 122:7-8r | 121:7 |
| 122:8a | 122:8 |
| 122:8r | D-4 |
| 122:9a | 122:9 |
| 123:1-6a | 123:1-6 |
| 123:7-12a | 123:7-12 |
| 123:11-14a | 123:11-14 |
| 123:15a | 123:15 |
| 124:2-6a | 124:2-6 |
| 124:7a | 124:7 |
| 124:12-14a | 124:12-14 |
| 124:15q | 11:10-11 |
| 124:15a | 124:15 |
| 124:16-17a | 124:16-17 |
| 124:21r | L-5 |
| 124:22-24, 56-83, 119-21a | 124:22-24, 56-83, 119-21 |
| 124:25-27a | 124:25-27 |
| 124:28a | 124:28 |
| 124:29-36a | 124:29-36 |
| 124:36c | B-6 |
| 124:37-38a | 124:37-38 |
| 124:39-40a | 124:39-40 |
| 124:40-44a | 124:40-44 |
| 124:41r | 128:18 |
| 124:45a | 124:45 |
| 124:45-46c | F-2 |
| 124:46-48a | 124:46-48 |
| 124:49-50r | 56:3-4 |
| 124:49-51 | 84:4 |
| 124:49-55a | 124:49-55 |
| 124:50r | 121:21 |
| 124:54c | B-2 |
| 124:84r | 22:4 |
| 124:84a | 124:84 |
| 124:87-90, 97-102a | 124:87-90, 97-102 |
| 124:89r | 43:12-14 |
| 124:91-96a | 124:91-96 |
| 124:93r | 24:15 |
| 124:101r | 19:37 |
| 124:103-10a | 124:103-10 |
| 124:115-18a | 124:115-18 |
| 124:124-45r | 26:2 |
| 124:124q | 132:26-27 |
| 124:124-26a, m | 124:124-26 |
| 124-28r | 127:8 |
| 124:130a | 124:130 |
| 124:133-37a | 124:133-37 |
| 124:138-40r | M-7 |
| 124:143-45a | 124:143-45 |
| 124:144q | 44:1 |
| 125:1a | 125:1 |
| 125:2a | 125:2 |
| 125:3a | 125:3 |
| 125:4a | 125:4 |
| 126:1a | 126:1 |
| 126:2-3a | 126:2-3 |
| 127:1a | 127:1 |
| 127:2a | 127:2 |
| 127:2q | 127:7 |
| 127:4a | 127:4 |
| 127:6-7a | 127:6-7 |
| 127:7a | 127:7 |
| 127:8a | 127:8 |
| 127:9a | 127:9 |
| 128:1r | 128:22 |
| 128:2-4a | 128:2-4 |
| 128:4-5r | 21:1 |
| 128:6-7r | 132:19 |
| 128:6-9a | 128:6-9 |
| 128:9r | D-2 |
| 128:12-13a | 128:12-13 |
| 128:14q | 128:6-9 |
| 128:14-18a | 128:14-18 |
| 128:15r | 138:47 |
| 128:15q | O-5 |
| 128:17r | 2 HB |
| 128:17r | M-3 |
| 128:17r | O-3 |
| 128:18r | 2:3 |
| 128:18a | 128:18 |
| 128:18r | G-6 |
| 128:18r | H-1 |
| 128:18 | H-4 |
| 128:19-21r | 27:6-7 |
| 128:19-21r | 77:14 |
| 128:19-23a | 128:19-23 |
| 128:19-24r | 128:18 |
| 128:20r | 7:7 |
| 128:20r | 129 HB |
| 128:20r | 129:8-9 |
| 128:20-21a | 128:20-21 |
| 128:21q | 133:17, 36 |
| 128:21q | K-7 |
| 128:22a | 128:22 |
| 128:22, 24q | O-7 |
| 128:23a | 128:23 |
| 128:24a | 128:24 |
| 129:1-3a, m | 129:1-3 |
| 129:3a | 129:3 |
| 129:4a | 129:4 |
| 129:4-7a | 129:4-7 |
| 129:6q | 129:8-9 |
| 129:7r | 129:8-9 |
| 129:8-9a | 129:8-9 |
| 129:9q | 129 HB |
| 130:1a | 130:1 |
| 130:3r | 67:10-13 |
| 130:3a | 130:3 |
| 130:4-7r | 88:40-50 |
| 130:4-7a | 130:4-7 |
| 130:4-11r | 63:20-21, 49-51 |
| 130:6-8a | 130:6-8 |
| 130:6-9r | 77:1 |
| 130:7r | 38:2 |
| 130:7q | 38:17-20 |
| 130:7q | 130:10 |
| 130:7r | D-3 |
| 130:9r | 119:5-6 |
| 130:9a | 130:9 |
| 130:9q | 130:10 |
| 130:10a | 130:10 |
| 130:12-13 | 130:12-13 |
| 130:14-17a | 130:14-17 |
| 130:14-17r | 133:11 |
| 130:18-19a | 130:18-19 |
| 130:18-19c | K-3 |
| 130:19q | K-7 |
| 130:19-21r | K-8 |
| 130:20c | G-5 |
| 130:20-21r | 84:19-22 |
| 130:20-21r | 89:18-21 |
| 130:20-21a | 130:20-21 |
| 130:20-21r | G-5 |
| 130:20-21r | G-6 |
| 130:20-21r | M-2 |
| 131:1a | 131:1 |
| 131:2a | 131:2 |
| 131:2r | N-6 |
| 131:1-4r | 6:13 |
| 131:1-4r | 132:19-22 |
| 131:14-q | 132:22-25 |

# Subject Index